IRB WORLD RUGBY YEARBOOK 2009

EDITED BY PAUL MORGAN AND JOHN GRIFFITHS

2 Coombe Gardens,
London, SW20 0QU
www.visionsp.co.uk

Published by Vision Sports Publishing in 2008

ISBN 13: 978-1-905326-41-9

Cover image: Getty Images
All other pictures by Getty Images unless otherwise stated
Illustrations by www.cakebreadillustrations.com

Typeset by Palimpsest Book Production Ltd, Grangemouth, Stirlingshire

Printed and bound in the UK by Cromwell Press Ltd, Trowbridge, Wiltshire

International Rugby Board
Huguenot House
35-38 St Stephen's Green
Dublin 2
Ireland

t +353-1-240-9200
f +353-1-240-9201
e irb@irb.com

www.irb.com

INTRODUCTION

FROM THE JOINT EDITOR – PAUL MORGAN

Welcome to the 2009 edition of the IRB World Rugby Yearbook, the third since it was relaunched by Vision Sports Publishing and the International Rugby Board.

Another momentous year in our great game will culminate in a set of internationals in November, that will decide the new world order in rugby, 12 months after the breathtaking Rugby World Cup, in France.

Shane Williams adorns our cover this year, in the northern hemisphere, reflecting Wales' Grand Slam in 2008, and the incredible start Warren Gatland has made in his career as an international rugby coach.

When it comes to the Yearbook I am of course just the swan, floating serenely on top of the water, while the frantic paddling to put 632 pages into this book occurs out of sight.

A huge team were involved in the paddling this year and I need to take this chance to tip my hat to them.

Without the statistics the Yearbook would of course be almost useless and they are supplied – as they have been for decades – by the incomparable John Griffiths, his world records on page 159 being particularly fascinating.

For the last two years we have tried to bring you up to date with statistics from every one of the 20 World Cup qualifiers and that means Hugh Copping's SportStat company have come into their own, with Thomas Coggle performing a starring role this season, along with Chris Rhys, who looks after the Major Tours section.

My thanks to our sponsors Emirates, who let us get on with the job, and at our typesetters, Palimpsest a herogram is reserved for Julie Garvock, who, with her team, has once again done a magnificent job turning the prose and statistics into pages that I hope you will all enjoy.

To Iain Spragg, the principal writer I offer my gratitude, as I do to proofreader Howard Evans, all those writers from Frankie Deges in Argentina through to Jeremy Duxbury in Fiji, and to Jim Drewett and Toby Trotman at Vision Sports Publishing, who had the foresight to bring this book back into the rugby world. And last, but certainly not least my appreciation goes to Dominic Rumbles at the IRB, the true champion of the his project, and one of the key people in bringing it to life. Joining Dom at the IRB I am of course delighted to have the support of Alison Hughes, Greg Thomas, Karen Bond and Chris Thau.

No statistical based book of 632 pages can be published without the fear of one or two mistakes creeping in along the way, so I would be grateful if you email me if you spot any . . . and I would also be grateful for any general comments from readers.

You can reach me at Rugby World Magazine, where I am editor. Email me there at paul_morgan@ipcmedia.com

CONTENTS

RUGBY WORLD CUP

INTERNATIONAL TOURNAMENTS

THE COUNTRIES

CROSS-BORDER TOURNAMENTS

INTRODUCTION

OLYMPIC GAMES KEY TO FUTURE GROWTH

FROM BERNARD LAPASSET, CHAIRMAN OF THE INTERNATIONAL RUGBY BOARD

In August 2008 the International Rugby Board attended the Beijing Olympic Games as an IOC recognised International Sport Federation. The primary aims of being in Beijing were to continue our proactive campaign to have rugby re-admitted into the Olympic Games, learn event lessons for Rugby World Cup and to promote rugby in China.

Rugby's re-admission into the Olympic Games is one of the key goals in the IRB's strategic plan for rugby. Why? Development. The Olympic Games can provide the stimulus for the continued global growth of the game and its development in new and major economic markets.

Rugby is presently on a shortlist for possible re-admission to the 2016 Olympic Games along with baseball and softball (which have lost their place on the London 2012 Games sports programme), golf, karate, squash and roller sports. Rugby, along with these last four sports, was a candidate for possible inclusion in the 2012 Games but in 2005 the IOC voted to have just 26 sports at the London Games. However, the IOC is now committed to once again having 28 sports for 2016.

The IOC will make a decision on which two sports will be included in the 2016 Games in October 2009.

The Olympic Games run for 16 days, so the IRB is promoting Rugby Sevens, for men and women, as the rugby discipline for inclusion.

Rugby Sevens has a proven successful formula in multi-sport events such as the Commonwealth Games, Asian Games and World Games and has a hugely successful Sevens Rugby World Cup tournament and an annual IRB Sevens World Series. The development contribution of Rugby Sevens cannot be under estimated. Over a quarter of the 600 players at Rugby World Cup 2007 had played for their national Rugby Sevens team.

The IRB firmly believes that Rugby's re-admission would be good for the sport and for the Olympic Games:

- It would reinforce the ideals of Olympism, thanks to rugby's long-standing ethos of fair play and friendship.
- It would assist the IOC in reaching a new and young audience that is attracted by Rugby Sevens.
- A Rugby Sevens tournament would fill the Olympic Stadium in the first week of competition adding an additional vibrant and youthful tone for the Games.
- It would extend the number of potential medal-winning nations in what would be a true world championship – Fiji are the current World Sevens champions.
- It would increase funds to grow the Olympic movement by attracting new commercial partners and spectators.

Furthermore, participation would be good for rugby as it would unlock new funding worldwide and access to facilities and infrastructure (many Governments only fund Olympic sports), further establish Rugby Sevens as a global pathway to all forms of rugby and draw new fans, sponsors and broadcasters to the sport.

The campaign has been already been successful in that Rugby Sevens will be a part of the Pan American Games in 2011 and the African Games in 2012. I am also happy to report that the IRB met with over 80 IOC members in Beijing, including President Jacques Rogge.

In November 2008 we presented our case to the Olympic Programme Commission and in June 2009 we will present to the IOC Executive Board. Of course the Rugby World Cup Sevens in Dubai in March 2009 will be a major showcase for Rugby Sevens' Olympic drive. There is no doubt that competition for a place at the 2016 Olympics is going to be tough and the IRB needs the global rugby family to continue its support of the campaign.

The IRB's focus on its core business also continued strongly in 2008 including the continued roll out of global development initiatives across Africa, Asia, Europe, the Americas and Oceania. The game has already started to see the results of the unprecedented £30 million Strategic Investment programme (2006–2008) through the excellent form of the developing countries at Rugby World Cup 2007. The continued commercial success of the tournament in France has added further impetus to this essential high performance programme with the Executive Committee announcing in 2008 a further £48 million boost for the programme.

This second cycle of strategic investment for 2009–2012 represents a 20% increase in funding on the previous cycle. Notably £18.7 million of this investment is set aside for high performance initiatives in Tier 2 and 3 Unions. Add this commitment to specific tournament expenditure for these unions of £12.9 million then the combined expenditure of £31.6 million represents 66% of the overall expenditure.

Furthermore, annual grants to our Member Unions have continued to increase and when you add the £48 million strategic investment to the annual commitment to Member Unions in the form of development grants and regional tournament delivery the IRB will, over the next four years (2009–2012), invest over £150 million on the game worldwide.

The IRB announced in March the start of a global trial of its Experimental Law Variations. In March 2009 the review process will begin and include Member Union feedback. The Rugby Committee will then make a recommendation to Council in May 2009 when the decision to accept any or all of the ELVs will be made. Progress has also been made updating many Regulations of the Game, including Regulation 9 governing player release.

Planning for RWC 2011 in New Zealand is progressing well. Qualification kicked-off in 2008 with matches in the West Indies, South America, Africa and Europe, and tournament organisers RNZ 2011 announced the venues for the knockout stages.

Finally, in an historic move the IRB Council announced that it will allocate the next two tournaments – Rugby World Cup 2015 and 2019 – at the same time, in July 2009.

INTRODUCTION

FROM GARY CHAPMAN – PRESIDENT GROUP SERVICES & DNATA, EMIRATES GROUP

Emirates' affinity with the game of rugby was taken to a higher level in 2008 when the airline became the first organisation to sign up as a Worldwide Partner of IRB Rugby World Cup 2011. The tournament may well be three years away but the signing demonstrated Emirates' commitment to the IRB, to the success of Rugby World Cup, and to the host country of New Zealand.

It is, however, only a matter of months until Rugby World Cup Sevens 2009 takes place in Emirates' home city of Dubai. Emirates is proud to be the Principal Partner of this event which will be played at 'The Sevens', a unique sporting venue, which Emirates has built with the support of the Government of Dubai. It is our ambition that 'The Sevens' will encourage greater participation in rugby and other sports by Arab nationals and that the venue will serve not only the local community, but also help foster the development of sport regionally.

Emirates is a committed title sponsor of four tournaments in the IRB World Series Sevens which begins every year with our very own home grown event, the Emirates Airline Dubai Rugby Sevens.

But our commitment to rugby extends even further and includes the shirt sponsorship of the England and Samoan sevens squads, in addition to our sponsorship of the Emirates Western Force Super 14 team in Australia.

Turning to another very special rugby event, during 2008, Emirates was the Official Airline of the historic Melrose Sevens. What a glorious setting where the game of sevens began 125 years ago! With Emirates being synonymous with the game we felt that we had to be involved in this important milestone.

And, finally, further cementing our strong partnership in rugby in 2008 we announced a new four-year deal to continue as the official sponsor of the IRB's international referees, the IRB Awards, and the IRB Yearbook.

Of course Emirates has an extensive portfolio of top-class sports sponsorships around the world so, in addition to Rugby World Cup 2011, we are supporters in two other major world cups, namely the FIFA World Cup™ and the ICC Cricket World Cup. We are also a leading sponsor of wide range of other sports including golf, horse racing, tennis and sailing.

I hope that you enjoy this latest edition of the IRB Yearbook as much as Emirates enjoys its association with this fascinating sport.

THE 2009 RUGBY YEAR

CRYSTAL BALL GAZING

By Paul Morgan

David Rogers/Getty Images

Will the 2009 Lions coach, Ian McGeechan, be celebrating again, like he did in 1997 with Jeremy Guscott?

When the first International Rugby Yearbook of this series was published in 1972 it was barely conceivable that rugby union would see more than one million spectators attend games in the Six Nations Championship, 82,000 people would cram into Twickenham to witness a match to decide the champions of England and more than 30,000 fans would travel to the watch the Lions. But that is only a tiny part of what we have in store in 2009, a year that promises to bring some of the most sensational rugby that the game has ever seen.

It is almost 15 years since the game turned professional, the then chairman of the International Rugby Board, Vernon Pugh declaring the game 'open', after consulting the representatives of the major rugby unions, and there is no question that today our great game is in rude health.

Of course there are changes that need to be made and improvements will always be sought, but those critics of the way rugby union is run must remember we have only been a professional sport for 15 years and the progress that has been made in that time is staggering.

More than two million people watched games at the Rugby World Cup and another million will pack into grounds all over Europe this spring to watch the 126th running of the RBS 6 Nations. And it is not just a numbers game. No one could dispute that in our fan base we definitely have quality as well as quantity. Walk to any ground staging professional rugby with the supporters and you will see families, dads with lads, mums with daughters and it brings a great feeling to my heart when I see it. Segregation? Are you joking? Why on earth would you need such a thing in rugby union? Rival supporters not only mix well in the ground, but they do so in the pubs before, after and in some cases during games.

The next year will see another staggering season with the aforementioned RBS 6 Nations captivating six rugby nations. But in Europe we are also privileged to have a thriving domestic scene. The Guinness Premiership is one of the biggest successes of the professional era anywhere in the world, and I am delighted to say that the Magners League is now coming on leaps and bounds. Like in England a progressive and supportive sponsor is driving the game on in the Celtic nations.

Added to this domestic bliss, in Europe, we have the fabulous Heineken Cup, where weekends often rival those of a Six Nations game. The Heineken Cup is a big rival to the Super 14, which obviously stole something of a march in the mid-1990s.

But all the big global events in 2009 will be placed in the shade by a momentous British and Irish Lions tour to South Africa, where they will face the world champions, as they did back in 1997 over three 100mph Test matches. Talk to previous Lions and they still see a place in the Test team as the rugby's gold medal. And as players like Lawrence Dallaglio explain the Lions tours also give a player the chance to enjoy himself in a foreign land, in direct contrast to the wham bam thank you mam short tours so many of our countries go on in the current era.

How wrong were the doom-mongers, like Will Carling, back in the mid-1990s when they forecast the demise of the Lions, because of professionalism. They have gone from strength to strength and this trip promises to be the biggest yet. I hope the South Africans are aware of what is coming. As the great Times writer John Hopkins so memorably described the Lions: 'It is a cross between the prep school outing and the Crusades'. I for one know the 2009 will be like the Crusades, but I hope Ian McGeechan and manager Gerald Davies keep something of the prep school outing about the tour!

Having been lucky enough to travel to South Africa in 1997 I know how that country treasures the Lions. My only regret is that Percy Montgomery's retirement will mean that no Springboks will be left from 1997.

We must remember though that this great game of ours is not just about the top ten sides in the world it is about every nation that players rugby union across the world. And that is why I am delighted this Yearbook gives great prominence to magnificent competitions like the IRB Pacific Nations Cup, that stand proud in the pantheon of tournaments in 2009.

The publishers of this Yearbook have asked me to don a Mystic Meg shawl and look into my crystal ball, perhaps just to test my powers of prediction and to have a laugh in their offices when I don't get any correct. Someone once said only a fool tries to predict a sports match, but anyway here goes:

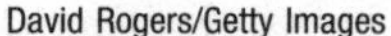

David Rogers/Getty Images

London Wasps are without Lawrence Dallaglio in 2009, but can they retain their Guinness Premiership title?

PREDICTIONS

RBS Six Nations – England

Rationale: Martin Johnson is starting to bring the best out an England team that has been in the wilderness for a few years. The trip to Croke Park will decide their tournament, and if they are hammered like they were in 2007, their dreams of tournament glory will end.

Lions v South Africa – Lions to win 2–1

Coach Ian McGeechan is one of the best identifiers of talent in the rugby world and that is the crucial skill that a successful Lions coach needs. Geech can spot in a player what many have missed and has the ability to blend four nations together.

Super 14 – The Crusaders

The side from Canterbury just keep getting better and better and Richie McCaw's men will power to another crown.

Heineken Cup – Toulouse

The French artisans should have won it in 2008 and with their victory in the French Championship they are looking far too powerful for the rest in 2009.

Guinness Premiership – Leicester Tigers

The biggest club in England are developing a side that went to Gloucester on the opening weekend and won. Toby Flood is a crucial acquisition and Heyneke Meyer a crafty enough coach to take them into the play-offs and on to Twickenham.

EDF Challenge Cup – Sale Sharks

Definitely good enough to pick up a trophy this season. Let's hope they avoid Toulon in the knockout stages so we could get the best Challenge Cup final in its history.

Magners League – The Ospreys

The star-studded south Walians are on the verge of something big. The Heineken may be two or three seasons away but if they pick their best side through the Magners campaign they will have enough to finish on top of the pile.

RUGBY WORLD CUP

THE ROAD TO AUCKLAND

By Iain Spragg

Dave Rogers/Getty Images

The journey to the 2011 World Cup finals started in the Cayman Islands in April, with the hosts taking on Trinidad & Tobago.

The old proverb that 'time and tide wait for no man' could not have been more apt in 2008 as barely six months after South Africa's victory in the World Cup in Paris, qualifying for the next tournament in New Zealand in 2011 began in earnest.

The dust had barely settled on the Springboks' famous triumph over England in the Stade de France as the sun-kissed island of Grand Cayman played proud host to the 2008 NAWIRA Caribbean Championship, and in the process signalled the official start of the battle to reach the IRB's seventh instalment of the World Cup in 2011.

The Championship began with the Cayman Islands facing Trinidad & Tobago at the National Stadium, rebuilt after being destroyed by Hurricane Ivan in 2004, and also featured sides from the Bahamas, Barbados, Jamaica, Guyana, Mexico and Bermuda.

There was, however, no home victory in the symbolic opening clash as Trinidad & Tobago emerged 39-12 winners and after comprehensively dispatching Guyana 56-0 in their second game, T&T found themselves in the final against Guyana and one tentative step closer to realising their dream of making it all the way to New Zealand.

Captained by number eight Adam Fredericks, Trinidad &Tobago were the overwhelming favourites in the final in George Town but it was Guyana who drew first blood when centre Kevin McKenzie raced over for the first try of the match after a charge down but T&T's class eventually told and a second-half hat-trick from Fredericks laid the foundations for what was eventually a comfortable 40-24 triumph.

The result sent Trinidad & Tobago through to the next round of qualifying, where they were scheduled to face Brazil, the winners of the CONSUR B tournament, in a two-legged play-off in October. The victor would then progress through to the CONSUR A competition in May 2009 to face Chile and Uruguay.

The Brazilians earned the right to play T&T after overcoming Colombia (34-6) and Venezuela (56-8) to reach the CONSUR B final in Asuncion in late June, where they faced Paraguay. Brazil had not beaten their South American rivals for 15 years but produced a gutsy display in front of 3,000 fans to stay in qualification contention.

The two sides exchanged early penalties before a clean break from centre Moises Rodrígues – one of three brothers in the Brazilian starting XV - set up a try for hooker Daniel Danielewicz. After the break, Paraguay hit back with a second penalty from full-back Rodrigo Llamosas but a quickly-taken tap penalty by Mateus Rodrígues resulted in a try for wing Erick Monfrinatti in the corner on 67 minutes to effectively settle the contest and the Brazilians were 15-6 winners.

"Our defence was one of the keys," said Brazil captain Ramiro Mina. "This is my finest moment as a rugby player. The team had a very special meeting in Peru last year after winning this same championship for a second time. We all spoke from the heart and said we had to have a new goal, to qualify for the World Cup. We've taken the first step."

Elsewhere, the battle to represent Africa in New Zealand in 2011 began in May and by the end of August, Uganda, Tunisia, Namibia and the Ivory Coast had all beaten off the competition to reach the semi-final qualifiers, to be played in 2009.

Drawn in Pool A, Namibia began their campaign with a narrow 13-10 victory over Senegal in Dakar but looked far more convincing in their second game against the Zimbabweans in at the Hage Geingob Stadium in Windhoek and ran out 35-21 winners.

In Pool B, the Ivory Coast produced a notable shock by eliminating the much-fancied Moroccans. The Ivorians beat Zambia 32-9 in Abidjan in July but were not expected to trouble Morocco a month later in Casablanca but produced a sensational performance to win 21-9 and take a step closer to a second World Cup appearance after their tournament bow in South Africa in 1995.

Tunisia, however, salvaged a degree of North African pride in topping Pool C and reaching the semi-finals. They beat Cameroon away from home in their opener and showed their class with an assured 44-15 victory over Kenya in Tunis.

In Pool D, Uganda had little trouble disposing of Botswana in their first game in June and then held their nerve in a tense second game against Madagascar in Kampala. Wing Felix Lubega raced over for Uganda's first try of the match and made it two just 40 seconds after the second-half restart and although Madagascar rallied, a late score from substitute Steven Ogwete put the result beyond doubt and the Cranes claimed a 32-22 win.

"It was tough and they exposed us in the first half, where they dominated." conceded Uganda coach Yayiro Kasasa after the match in the first half. "Our defence is still leaking and our kicks for touch fell short."

In Asia, Thailand beat Malaysia 30-7 in the HSBC Asian Five Nations Division Two final in June to earn promotion to the full Asian Five Nations in 2009, which will also serve as round two of the continent's World Cup qualifying campaign.

Leading 13-7 at half-time, Thailand scored 17 points after the break, including two tries in the first 11 minutes of the restart, in front of their own fans at the Army Stadium in Bangkok and eventually cantered to an easy victory.

Meanwhile, in the tournament's third place play-off, India routed Pakistan 92-0, a match in which Indian captain and number eight Nasser Hussain set an inaugural competition record with a haul of five tries.

"The IRB is very pleased with what the Asian Five Nations has accomplished this year," said IRB Chief Executive Officer Mike Miller, who was at the tournament to witness the rude health of the game on the Continent. "For the first time Asian rugby is being seen and talked about around the world. Asia is the future for rugby and great concepts like the Asian Five Nations can make it happen."

Dave Rogers/Getty Images

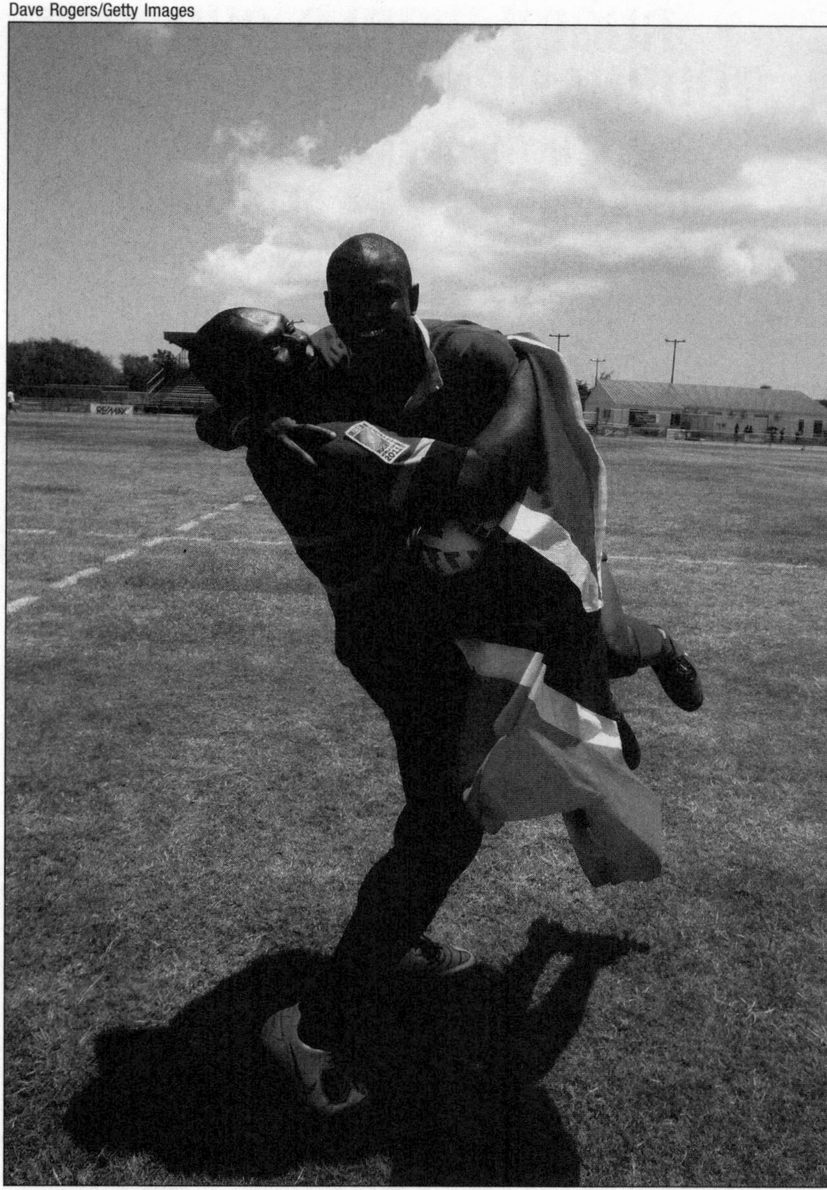

Trinidad and Tobago are ecstatic after winning the opening qualifying match of the 2011 Rugby World Cup, against Cayman Islands

RUGBY WORLD CUP TOURNAMENTS 1987-2003

SIXTH TOURNAMENT: 2007 IN FRANCE, WALES & SCOTLAND

POOL A

England	28	**United States**	10
South Africa	59	**Samoa**	7
United States	15	**Tonga**	25
England	0	**South Africa**	36
Samoa	15	**Tonga**	19
South Africa	30	**Tonga**	25
England	44	**Samoa**	22
Samoa	25	**United States**	21
England	36	**Tonga**	20
South Africa	64	**United States**	15

	P	W	D	L	F	A	Pts
South Africa	4	4	0	0	189	47	19
England	4	3	0	1	108	88	14
Tonga	4	2	0	2	89	96	9
Samoa	4	1	0	3	69	143	5
United States	4	0	0	4	61	142	1

POOL B

Australia	91	**Japan**	3
Wales	42	**Canada**	17
Japan	31	**Fiji**	35
Wales	20	**Australia**	32
Fiji	29	**Canada**	16
Wales	72	**Japan**	18
Australia	55	**Fiji**	12
Canada	12	**Japan**	12
Australia	37	**Canada**	6
Wales	34	**Fiji**	38

	P	W	D	L	F	A	Pts
Australia	4	4	0	0	215	41	20
Fiji	4	3	0	1	114	136	15
Wales	4	2	0	2	168	105	12
Japan	4	0	1	3	64	210	3
Canada	4	0	1	3	51	120	2

QUARTER-FINALS

Australia	10	**England**	12
New Zealand	18	**France**	20
South Africa	37	**Fiji**	20
Argentina	19	**Scotland**	13

POOL C

New Zealand	76	**Italy**	14
Scotland	56	**Portugal**	10
Italy	24	**Romania**	18
New Zealand	108	**Portugal**	13
Scotland	42	**Romania**	0
Italy	31	**Portugal**	5
Scotland	0	**New Zealand**	40
Romania	14	**Portugal**	10
New Zealand	85	**Romania**	8
Scotland	18	**Italy**	16

	P	W	D	L	F	A	Pts
New Zealand	4	4	0	0	309	35	20
Scotland	4	3	0	1	116	66	14
Italy	4	2	0	2	85	117	9
Romania	4	1	0	3	40	161	5
Portugal	4	0	0	4	38	209	1

POOL D

France	12	**Argentina**	17
Ireland	32	**Namibia**	17
Argentina	33	**Georgia**	3
Ireland	14	**Georgia**	10
France	87	**Namibia**	10
France	25	**Ireland**	3
Argentina	63	**Namibia**	3
Georgia	30	**Namibia**	0
France	64	**Georgia**	7
Ireland	15	**Argentina**	30

	P	W	D	L	F	A	Pts
Argentina	4	4	0	0	143	33	18
France	4	3	0	1	188	37	15
Ireland	4	2	0	2	64	82	9
Georgia	4	1	0	3	50	111	5
Namibia	4	0	0	4	30	212	0

SEMI-FINALS

France	9	**England**	14
South Africa	37	**Argentina**	13

BRONZE MEDAL MATCH

France	10	**Argentina**	34

Sixth World Cup Final, Stade de France, Paris, 20 October 2007

SOUTH AFRICA 15 (5PG) ENGLAND 6 (2PG)

SOUTH AFRICA: P C Montgomery; J-P R Pietersen, J Fourie, F P L Steyn, B G Habana; A D James, P F du Preez; J P du Randt, J W Smit (*captain*), C J van der Linde, J P Botha, V Matfield, J H Smith, D J Rossouw, S W P Burger *Substitutions:* J L van Heerden for Rossouw (72 mins); B W du Plessis for Smit (temp 71 to76 mins)

SCORERS *Penalty Goals*: Montgomery (4), Steyn

ENGLAND: J T Robinson; P H Sackey, M Tait, M J Catt, M J Cueto; J P Wilkinson, A C T Gomarsall; A J Sheridan, M P Regan, P J Vickery (*captain*), S D Shaw, B J Kay, M E Corry, N Easter, L W Moody *Substitutions:* M J H Stevens for Vickery (40 mins); D Hipkiss for Robinson (46 mins); T Flood for Catt (50 mins); G S Chuter for Regan (62 mins); J P R Worsley for Moody (62 mins); L B N Dallaglio for Easter (64 mins); P C Richards for Worsley (70 mins)

SCORER *Penalty Goals*: Wilkinson (2)

REFEREE A C Rolland (Ireland)

Julian Finney/Getty Images

The victorious coach, Jake White, gets his hands on the Webb Ellis Trophy.

FIFTH TOURNAMENT: 2003 IN AUSTRALIA

POOL A

Australia	24	Argentina	8
Ireland	45	Romania	17
Argentina	67	Namibia	14
Australia	90	Romania	8
Ireland	64	Namibia	7
Argentina	50	Romania	3
Australia	142	Namibia	0
Ireland	16	Argentina	15
Romania	37	Namibia	7
Australia	17	Ireland	16

	P	W	D	L	F	A	Pts
Australia	4	4	0	0	273	32	18
Ireland	4	3	0	1	141	56	14
Argentina	4	2	0	2	140	57	11
Romania	4	1	0	3	65	192	5
Namibia	4	0	0	4	28	310	0

POOL B

France	61	Fiji	18
Scotland	32	Japan	11
Fiji	19	United States	18
France	51	Japan	29
Scotland	39	United States	15
Fiji	41	Japan	13
France	51	Scotland	9
United States	39	Japan	26
France	41	United States	14
Scotland	22	Fiji	20

	P	W	D	L	F	A	Pts
France	4	4	0	0	204	70	20
Scotland	4	3	0	1	102	97	14
Fiji	4	2	0	2	98	114	9
United States	4	1	0	3	86	125	6
Japan	4	0	0	4	79	163	0

POOL C

South Africa	72	Uruguay	6
England	84	Georgia	6
Samoa	60	Uruguay	13
England	25	South Africa	6
Samoa	46	Georgia	9
South Africa	46	Georgia	19
England	35	Samoa	22
Uruguay	24	Georgia	12
South Africa	60	Samoa	10
England	111	Uruguay	13

	P	W	D	L	F	A	Pts
England	4	4	0	0	255	47	19
South Africa	4	3	0	1	184	60	15
Samoa	4	2	0	2	138	117	10
Uruguay	4	1	0	3	56	255	4
Georgia	4	0	0	4	46	200	0

POOL D

New Zealand	70	Italy	7
Wales	41	Canada	10
Italy	36	Tonga	12
New Zealand	68	Canada	6
Wales	27	Tonga	20
Italy	19	Canada	14
New Zealand	91	Tonga	7
Wales	27	Italy	15
Canada	24	Tonga	7
New Zealand	53	Wales	37

	P	W	D	L	F	A	Pts
New Zealand	4	4	0	0	282	57	20
Wales	4	3	0	1	132	98	14
Italy	4	2	0	2	77	123	8
Canada	4	1	0	3	54	135	5
Tonga	4	0	0	4	46	178	1

QUARTER-FINALS

New Zealand	29	South Africa	9
Australia	33	Scotland	16
France	43	Ireland	21
England	28	Wales	17

SEMI-FINALS

Australia	22	New Zealand	10
England	24	France	7

THIRD PLACE MATCH

New Zealand	40	France	13

Fifth World Cup Final, Telstra Stadium, Sydney,
22 November 2003

ENGLAND 20 (4PG 1DG 1T)
AUSTRALIA 17 (4PG 1T) *

ENGLAND: J Robinson; O J Lewsey, W J H Greenwood, M J Tindall, B C Cohen; J P Wilkinson, M J S Dawson; T J Woodman, S Thompson, P J Vickery, M O Johnson (captain), B J Kay, R A Hill, L B N Dallaglio, N A Back Substitutions: M J Catt for Tindall (78 mins); J Leonard for Vickery (80 mins); I R Balshaw for Lewsey (85 mins); L W Moody for Hill (93 mins)

SCORERS TRY: Robinson Penalty Goals: Wilkinson (4) Dropped Goal: Wilkinson

AUSTRALIA: M S Rogers; W J Sailor, S A Mortlock, E J Flatley, L Tuqiri; S J Larkham, G M Gregan (captain); W K Young, B J Cannon, A K E Baxter, J B Harrison, N C Sharpe, G B Smith, D J Lyons, P R Waugh Substitutions: D T Giffin for Sharpe (48 mins); J A Paul for Cannon (56 mins); M J Cockbain for Lyons (56 mins); J W Roff for Sailor (70 mins); M J Dunning for Young (92 mins); M J Giteau for Larkham (temp 18 to 30 mins; 55 to 63 mins; 85 to 93 mins)

SCORERS TRY: Tuqiri Penalty Goals: Flatley (4)

REFEREE A J Watson (South Africa)

* after extra time : 14-14 after normal time

Getty Images

England captain Martin Johnson (middle) leads the celebrations at the final whistle.

FOURTH TOURNAMENT: 1999 IN BRITAIN, IRELAND & FRANCE

POOL A

Spain	15	Uruguay	27
South Africa	46	Scotland	29
Scotland	43	Uruguay	12
South Africa	47	Spain	3
South Africa	39	Uruguay	3
Scotland	48	Spain	0

	P	W	D	L	F	A	Pts
South Africa	3	3	0	0	132	35	9
Scotland	3	2	0	1	120	58	7
Uruguay	3	1	0	2	42	97	5
Spain	3	0	0	3	18	122	3

POOL B

England	67	**Italy**	7
New Zealand	45	**Tonga**	9
England	16	**New Zealand**	30
Italy	25	**Tonga**	28
New Zealand	101	**Italy**	3
England	101	**Tonga**	10

	P	W	D	L	F	A	Pts
New Zealand	3	3	0	0	176	28	9
England	3	2	0	1	184	47	7
Tonga	3	1	0	2	47	171	5
Italy	3	0	0	3	35	196	3

POOL C

Fiji	67	**Namibia**	18
France	33	**Canada**	20
France	47	**Namibia**	13
Fiji	38	**Canada**	22
Canada	72	**Namibia**	11
France	28	**Fiji**	19

	P	W	D	L	F	A	Pts
France	3	3	0	0	108	52	9
Fiji	3	2	0	1	124	68	7
Canada	3	1	0	2	114	82	5
Namibia	3	0	0	3	42	186	3

POOL D

Wales	23	**Argentina**	18
Samoa	43	**Japan**	9
Wales	64	**Japan**	15
Argentina	32	**Samoa**	16
Wales	31	**Samoa**	38
Argentina	33	**Japan**	12

	P	W	D	L	F	A	Pts
Wales	3	2	0	1	118	71	7
Samoa	3	2	0	1	97	72	7
Argentina	3	2	0	1	83	51	7
Japan	3	0	0	3	36	140	3

POOL E

Ireland	53	**United States**	8
Australia	57	**Romania**	9
United States	25	**Romania**	27
Ireland	3	**Australia**	23
Australia	55	**United States**	19
Ireland	44	**Romania**	14

	P	W	D	L	F	A	Pts
Australia	3	3	0	0	135	31	9
Ireland	3	2	0	1	100	45	7
Romania	3	1	0	2	50	126	5
United States	3	0	0	3	52	135	3

PLAY-OFFS FOR QUARTER-FINAL PLACES

England	45	**Fiji**	24
Scotland	35	**Samoa**	20
Ireland	24	**Argentina**	28

QUARTER-FINALS

Wales	9	**Australia**	24
South Africa	44	**England**	21
France	47	**Argentina**	26
Scotland	18	**New Zealand**	30

SEMI-FINALS

South Africa	21	**Australia**	27
New Zealand	31	**France**	43

THIRD PLACE MATCH

South Africa	22	**New Zealand**	18

Fourth World Cup Final, Millennium Stadium, Cardiff Arms Park, 6 November 1999

AUSTRALIA 35 (2G 7PG) FRANCE 12 (4PG)

AUSTRALIA : M Burke; B N Tune, D J Herbert, T J Horan, J W Roff; S J Larkham, G M Gregan; R L L Harry, M A Foley, A T Blades, D T Giffin, J A Eales (captain), M J Cockbain, R S T Kefu, D J Wilson Substitutions J S Little for Herbert (46 mins); O D A Finegan for Cockbain (52 mins); M R Connors for Wilson (73 mins); D J Crowley for Harry (75 mins); J A Paul for Foley (85 mins); C J Whitaker for Gregan (86 mins); N P Grey for Horan (86 mins)

SCORERS TRIES : Tune, Finegan Conversions : Burke (2) Penalty Goals : Burke (7)

FRANCE : X Garbajosa; P Bernat Salles, R Dourthe, E Ntamack, C Dominici; C Lamaison, F Galthié; C Soulette, R Ibañez (captain), F Tournaire, A Benazzi, F Pelous, M Lièvremont, C Juillet, O Magne Substitutions O Brouzet for Juillet (HT); P de Villiers for Soulette (47 mins); A Costes for Magne (temp 19 to 22 mins) and for Lièvremont (67 mins); U Mola for Garbajosa (67 mins); S Glas for Dourthe (temp 49 to 55 mins and from 74 mins); S Castaignède for Galthié (76 mins); M Dal Maso for Ibañez (79 mins)

SCORER PENALTY GOALS : Lamaison (4)

REFEREE A J Watson (South Africa)

Getty Images

Wallabies wing Joe Roff drinks from the trophy after Australia won the final, in Cardiff.

THIRD TOURNAMENT: 1995 IN SOUTH AFRICA

POOL A

South Africa	27	Australia	18
Canada	34	Romania	3
South Africa	21	Romania	8
Australia	27	Canada	11
Australia	42	Romania	3
South Africa	20	Canada	0

	P	W	D	L	F	A	Pts
South Africa	3	3	0	0	68	26	9
Australia	3	2	0	1	87	41	7
Canada	3	1	0	2	45	50	5
Romania	3	0	0	3	14	97	3

POOL B

Western Samoa	42	Italy	18
England	24	Argentina	18
Western Samoa	32	Argentina	26
England	27	Italy	20
Italy	31	Argentina	25
England	44	Western Samoa	22

	P	W	D	L	F	A	Pts
England	3	3	0	0	95	60	9
Western Samoa	3	2	0	1	96	88	7
Italy	3	1	0	2	69	94	5
Argentina	3	0	0	3	69	87	3

POOL C

Wales	57	Japan	10
New Zealand	43	Ireland	19
Ireland	50	Japan	28
New Zealand	34	Wales	9
New Zealand	145	Japan	17
Ireland	24	Wales	23

	P	W	D	L	F	A	Pts
New Zealand	3	3	0	0	222	45	9
Ireland	3	2	0	1	93	94	7
Wales	3	1	0	2	89	68	5
Japan	3	0	0	3	55	252	3

POOL D

Scotland	89	Ivory Coast	0
France	38	Tonga	10
France	54	Ivory Coast	18
Scotland	41	Tonga	5
Tonga	29	Ivory Coast	11
France	22	Scotland	19

	P	W	D	L	F	A	Pts
France	3	3	0	0	114	47	9
Scotland	3	2	0	1	149	27	7
Tonga	3	1	0	2	44	90	5
Ivory Coast	3	0	0	3	29	172	3

QUARTER-FINALS

France	36	Ireland	12
South Africa	42	Western Samoa	14
England	25	Australia	22
New Zealand	48	Scotland	30

SEMI-FINALS

South Africa	19	France	15
New Zealand	45	England	29

THIRD PLACE MATCH

France	19	England	9

Third World Cup Final, Ellis Park, Johannesburg, 24 June 1995

SOUTH AFRICA 15 (3PG 2DG)
NEW ZEALAND 12 (3PG 1DG) *

SOUTH AFRICA: A J Joubert; J T Small, J C Mulder, H P Le Roux, C M Williams; J T Stransky, J H van der Westhuizen; J P du Randt, C L C Rossouw, I S Swart, J J Wiese, J J Strydom, J F Pienaar (captain), M G Andrews, R J Kruger Substitutions: G L Pagel for Swart (68 mins); R A W Straeuli for Andrews (90 mins); B Venter for Small (97 mins)

SCORER PENALTY GOALS: Stransky (3) Drop Goals: Stransky (2)

NEW ZEALAND: G M Osborne; J W Wilson, F E Bunce, W K Little, J T Lomu; A P Mehrtens, G T M Bachop; C W Dowd, S B T Fitzpatrick (captain), O M Brown, I D Jones, R M Brooke, M R Brewer, Z V Brooke, J A Kronfeld Substitutions: J W Joseph for Brewer (40 mins); M C G Ellis for Wilson (55 mins); R W Loe for Dowd (83 mins); A D Strachan for Bachop (temp 66 to 71 mins)

SCORER PENALTY GOALS: Mehrtens (3) Drop Goal: Mehrtens

REFEREE E F Morrison (England)

* after extra time : 9-9 after normal time

Getty Images

Captain Francois Pienaar (middle, with cup) leads the celebrations after South Africa's victory

SECOND TOURNAMENT: 1991 IN BRITAIN, IRELAND & FRANCE

POOL 1

New Zealand	18	England	12
Italy	30	USA	9
New Zealand	46	USA	6
England	36	Italy	6
England	37	USA	9
New Zealand	31	Italy	21

	P	W	D	L	F	A	Pts
New Zealand	3	3	0	0	95	39	9
England	3	2	0	1	85	33	7
Italy	3	1	0	2	57	76	5
USA	3	0	0	3	24	113	3

POOL 2

Scotland	47	Japan	9
Ireland	55	Zimbabwe	11
Ireland	32	Japan	16
Scotland	51	Zimbabwe	12
Scotland	24	Ireland	15
Japan	52	Zimbabwe	8

	P	W	D	L	F	A	Pts
Scotland	3	3	0	0	122	36	9
Ireland	3	2	0	1	102	51	7
Japan	3	1	0	2	77	87	5
Zimbabwe	3	0	0	3	31	158	3

POOL 3

Australia	32	Argentina	19
Western Samoa	16	Wales	13
Australia	9	Western Samoa	3
Wales	16	Argentina	7
Australia	38	Wales	3
Western Samoa	35	Argentina	12

	P	W	D	L	F	A	Pts
Australia	3	3	0	0	79	25	9
Western Samoa	3	2	0	1	54	34	7
Wales	3	1	0	2	32	61	5
Argentina	3	0	0	3	38	83	3

POOL 4

France	30	Romania	3
Canada	13	Fiji	3
France	33	Fiji	9
Canada	19	Romania	11
Romania	17	Fiji	15
France	19	Canada	13

	P	W	D	L	F	A	Pts
France	3	3	0	0	82	25	9
Canada	3	2	0	1	45	33	7
Romania	3	1	0	2	31	64	5
Fiji	3	0	0	3	27	63	3

QUARTER-FINALS

England	19	France	10
Scotland	28	Western Samoa	6
Australia	19	Ireland	18
New Zealand	29	Canada	13

SEMI-FINALS

England	9	Scotland	6
Australia	16	New Zealand	6

THIRD PLACE MATCH

New Zealand	13	Scotland	6

Second World Cup Final, Twickenham, 2 November 1991

AUSTRALIA 12 (1G 2PG)
ENGLAND 6 (2PG)

AUSTRALIA: M C Roebuck; D I Campese, J S Little, T J Horan, R H Egerton; M P Lynagh, N C Farr-Jones (captain); A J Daly, P N Kearns, E J A McKenzie, R J McCall, J A Eales, S P Poidevin, T Coker, V Ofahengaue

SCORERS TRY : Daly Conversion : Lynagh Penalty Goals : Lynagh (2)

ENGLAND: J M Webb; S J Halliday, W D C Carling (captain), J C Guscott, R Underwood; C R Andrew, R J Hill; J Leonard, B C Moore, J A Probyn, P J Ackford, W A Dooley, M G Skinner, M C Teague, P J Winterbottom

SCORER PENALTY GOALS : Webb (2)

REFEREE W D Bevan (Wales)

Getty Images

The Wallabies celebrate in the bath after the final.

FIRST TOURNAMENT: 1987 IN AUSTRALIA & NEW ZEALAND

POOL 1

Australia	19	**England**	6
USA	21	**Japan**	18
England	60	**Japan**	7
Australia	47	**USA**	12
England	34	**USA**	6
Australia	42	**Japan**	23

	P	W	D	L	F	A	Pts
Australia	3	3	0	0	108	41	6
England	3	2	0	1	100	32	4
USA	3	1	0	2	39	99	2
Japan	3	0	0	3	48	123	0

POOL 2

Canada	37	**Tonga**	4
Wales	13	**Ireland**	6
Wales	29	**Tonga**	16
Ireland	46	**Canada**	19
Wales	40	**Canada**	9
Ireland	32	**Tonga**	9

	P	W	D	L	F	A	Pts
Wales	3	3	0	0	82	31	6
Ireland	3	2	0	1	84	41	4
Canada	3	1	0	2	65	90	2
Tonga	3	0	0	3	29	98	0

POOL 3

New Zealand	70	**Italy**	6
Fiji	28	**Argentina**	9
New Zealand	74	**Fiji**	13
Argentina	25	**Italy**	16
Italy	18	**Fiji**	15
New Zealand	46	**Argentina**	15

	P	W	D	L	F	A	Pts
New Zealand	3	3	0	0	190	34	6
Fiji	3	1	0	2	56	101	2
Argentina	3	1	0	2	49	90	2
Italy	3	1	0	2	40	110	2

POOL 4

Romania	21	**Zimbabwe**	20
France	20	**Scotland**	20
France	55	**Romania**	12
Scotland	60	**Zimbabwe**	21
France	70	**Zimbabwe**	12
Scotland	55	**Romania**	28

	P	W	D	L	F	A	Pts
France	3	2	1	0	145	44	5
Scotland	3	2	1	0	135	69	5
Romania	3	1	0	2	61	130	2
Zimbabwe	3	0	0	3	53	151	0

QUARTER-FINALS

New Zealand	30	**Scotland**	3
France	31	**Fiji**	16
Australia	33	**Ireland**	15
Wales	16	**England**	3

SEMI-FINALS

France	30	**Australia**	24
New Zealand	49	**Wales**	6

THIRD PLACE MATCH

Wales	22	**Australia**	21

First World Cup Final, Eden Park, Auckland, 20 June 1987

NEW ZEALAND 29 (1G 4PG 1DG 2T)
FRANCE 9 (1G 1PG)

NEW ZEALAND: J A Gallagher; J J Kirwan, J T Stanley, W T Taylor, C I Green; G J Fox, D E Kirk (captain); S C McDowell, S B T Fitzpatrick, J A Drake, M J Pierce, G W Whetton, A J Whetton, W T Shelford, M N Jones

SCORERS TRIES : Jones, Kirk, Kirwan Conversion : Fox Penalty Goals : Fox (4) Drop Goal : Fox

FRANCE: S Blanco; D Camberabero, P Sella, D Charvet, P Lagisquet; F Mesnel, P Berbizier; P Ondarts, D Dubroca (captain), J-P Garuet, A Lorieux, J Condom, E Champ, L Rodriguez, D Erbani

SCORERS TRY : Berbizier Conversion : Camberabero Penalty Goal : Camberabero

REFEREE K V J Fitzgerald (Australia)

Getty Images

New Zealand captain David Kirk kisses the Webb Ellis Cup, and delights a nation.

RUGBY WORLD CUP RECORDS 1987–2007

(FINAL STAGES ONLY)

OVERALL RECORDS

MOST MATCHES WON IN FINAL STAGES

30	New Zealand
28	Australia
26	France
25	England

MOST OVERALL POINTS IN FINAL STAGES

249	J P Wilkinson	England	1999–2007
227	A G Hastings	Scotland	1987–95
195	M P Lynagh	Australia	1987–95
170	G J Fox	New Zealand	1987–91
163	A P Mehrtens	New Zealand	1995–99

MOST OVERALL TRIES IN FINAL STAGES

15	J T Lomu	New Zealand	1995–99
13	D C Howlett	New Zealand	2003–07
11	R Underwood	England	1987–95
11	J T Rokocoko	New Zealand	2003–07
11	C E Latham	Australia	1999–2007

MOST OVERALL CONVERSIONS IN FINAL STAGES

39	A G Hastings	Scotland	1987–95
37	G J Fox	New Zealand	1987–91
36	M P Lynagh	Australia	1987–95
29	D W Carter	New Zealand	2003–07
27	P J Grayson	England	1999–2003

MOST OVERALL PENALTIES IN FINAL STAGES

53	J P Wilkinson	England	1999–2007
36	A G Hastings	Scotland	1987–95
35	G Quesada	Argentina	1999–2003
33	M P Lynagh	Australia	1987–95
33	A P Mehrtens	New Zealand	1995–99

MOST OVERALL DROPPED GOALS IN FINAL STAGES

13	J P Wilkinson	England	1999–2007
6	J H de Beer	South Africa	1999
5	C R Andrew	England	1987–1995
5	G L Rees	Canada	1987–1999
4	J M Hernández	Argentina	2003–07

MOST MATCH APPEARANCES IN FINAL STAGES

22	J Leonard	England	1991–2003
20	G M Gregan	Australia	1995–2007
19	M J Catt	England	1995–2007
18	M O Johnson	England	1995–2003
18	B P Lima	Samoa	1991–2007
18	R Ibañez	France	1999–2007

MOST POINTS IN ONE COMPETITION

126	G J Fox	New Zealand	1987
113	J P Wilkinson	England	2003
112	T Lacroix	France	1995
105	P C Montgomery	South Africa	2007
104	A G Hastings	Scotland	1995
103	F Michalak	France	2003
102	G Quesada	Argentina	1999
101	M Burke	Australia	1999

MOST PENALTY GOALS IN ONE COMPETITION

31	G Quesada	Argentina	1999
26	T Lacroix	France	1995
23	J P Wilkinson	England	2003
21	G J Fox	New Zealand	1987
21	E J Flatley	Australia	2003
20	C R Andrew	England	1995

MOST TRIES IN ONE COMPETITION

8	J T Lomu	New Zealand	1999
8	B G Habana	South Africa	2007
7	M C G Ellis	New Zealand	1995
7	J T Lomu	New Zealand	1995
7	D C Howlett	New Zealand	2003
7	J M Muliaina	New Zealand	2003
7	D A Mitchell	Australia	2007

MOST DROPPED GOALS IN ONE COMPETITION

8	J P Wilkinson	England	2003
6	J H de Beer	South Africa	1999
5	J P Wilkinson	England	2007
4	J M Hernández	Argentina	2007

MOST CONVERSIONS IN ONE COMPETITION

30	G J Fox	New Zealand	1987
22	P C Montgomery	South Africa	2007
20	S D Culhane	New Zealand	1995
20	M P Lynagh	Australia	1987
20	L R MacDonald	New Zealand	2003
20	N J Evans	New Zealand	2007

MATCH RECORDS

MOST POINTS IN A MATCH

BY THE TEAM

145	New Zealand v Japan	1995
142	Australia v Namibia	2003
111	England v Uruguay	2003
108	New Zealand v Portugal	2007
101	New Zealand v Italy	1999
101	England v Tonga	1999

BY A PLAYER

45	S D Culhane	New Zealand v Japan	1995
44	A G Hastings	Scotland v Ivory Coast	1995
42	M S Rogers	Australia v Namibia	2003
36	T E Brown	New Zealand v Italy	1999
36	P J Grayson	England v Tonga	1999
34	J H de Beer	South Africa v England	1999
33	N J Evans	New Zealand v Portugal	2007
32	J P Wilkinson	England v Italy	1999

MOST TRIES IN A MATCH

BY THE TEAM

22	Australia v Namibia	2003
21	New Zealand v Japan	1995
17	England v Uruguay	2003
16	New Zealand v Portugal	2007
14	New Zealand v Italy	1999

BY A PLAYER

6	M C G Ellis	New Zealand v Japan	1995
5	C E Latham	Australia v Namibia	2003
5	O J Lewsey	England v Uruguay	2003
4	I C Evans	Wales v Canada	1987
4	C I Green	New Zealand v Fiji	1987
4	J A Gallagher	New Zealand v Fiji	1987
4	B F Robinson	Ireland v Zimbabwe	1991
4	A G Hastings	Scotland v Ivory Coast	1995
4	C M Williams	South Africa v Western Samoa	1995
4	J T Lomu	New Zealand v England	1995
4	K G M Wood	Ireland v United States	1999
4	J M Muliaina	New Zealand v Canada	2003
4	B G Habana	South Africa v Samoa	2007

MOST CONVERSIONS IN A MATCH

BY THE TEAM

20	New Zealand v Japan	1995
16	Australia v Namibia	2003
14	New Zealand v Portugal	2007
13	New Zealand v Tonga	2003
13	England v Uruguay	2003

BY A PLAYER

20	S D Culhane	New Zealand v Japan	1995
16	M S Rogers	Australia v Namibia	2003
14	N J Evans	New Zealand v Portugal	2007
12	P J Grayson	England v Tonga	1999
12	L R MacDonald	New Zealand v Tonga	2003

MOST PENALTY GOALS IN A MATCH

BY THE TEAM

8	Australia v South Africa	1999
8	Argentina v Samoa	1999
8	Scotland v Tonga	1995
8	France v Ireland	1995

BY A PLAYER

8	M Burke	Australia v South Africa	1999
8	G Quesada	Argentina v Samoa	1999
8	A G Hastings	Scotland v Tonga	1995
8	T Lacroix	France v Ireland	1995

MOST DROPPED GOALS IN A MATCH

BY THE TEAM

5	South Africa v England	1999
3	Fiji v Romania	1991
3	England v France	2003
3	Argentina v Ireland	2007

BY A PLAYER

5	J H de Beer	South Africa v England	1999
3	J P Wilkinson	England v France	2003
3	J M Hernández	Argentina v Ireland	2007

IRB PLAYERS OF THE YEAR

By Iain Spragg

The most coveted prize at the IRB Awards is the Player of the Year. Five players – Mike Blair, Dan Carter, Ryan Jones, Sergio Parisse and Shane Williams – have been shortlisted for the 2008 award. Here is our look at the quintet.

MIKE BLAIR (SCOTLAND)

Getty Images

Mike Blair had a vintage year, taking over the Scotland captaincy.

Although 2008 will not go down as a vintage year for Scottish rugby, it was certainly a great one for Mike Blair who produced the form of his career, took over the Scotland captaincy and then led the side to two morale-boosting victories over England and Argentina.

First capped against Canada in the summer of 2002, the Edinburgh scrum-half was handed the captain's armband by coach Frank Hadden for the Six Nations clash with Ireland at Croke Park in February following an injury to Jason White and although Scotland lost the match, a famous victory was just around the corner.

England were the next opposition in the Championship and Blair was an inspiration at Murrayfield as Scotland produced a barnstorming display to beat the old enemy 15–9 and open their Six Nations account.

He retained the captaincy for Scotland's summer tour to Argentina and although the side were narrowly beaten in the first of the two Tests in the Stadio Gigante de Arroyito, Blair rallied his troops for the second game at Velez Sarsfield seven days later and with the number nine pulling the strings at number nine, the team pulled off a famous 26–14 win – making Scotland the only side to record a victory south of the equator in a torrid summer for the northern hemisphere teams.

The victory was the fifth game in which Blair had led Scotland out and his 50th cap for his country – a fitting end to a season in which he also featured in four of the side's five World Cup matches and matured into one of the world game's most accomplished scrum-halves.

DANIEL CARTER (NEW ZEALAND)

Getty Images

Dan Carter was back to his best as New Zealand won the Tri-Nations.

When Daniel Carter danced through the Wallaby defence in Brisbane in September to score the try that clinched an unprecedented fourth consecutive Tri-Nations title for the All Blacks, it was further, if unnecessary, proof the prolific New Zealand number 10 remained at the very top of his game.

The Crusaders fly-half contributed 82 of his side's 152 points during the six games of the tournament and the unerring accuracy of his fabled left boot and his ability to orchestrate the All Black backline were yet again a key component of New Zealand's continuing Tri-Nations dominance.

Handed his Test debut at inside centre against Wales in Hamilton in 2003, Carter has gone on to establish himself as arguably the most influential and feared player in international rugby today and with 825 points from his 54 games to date – an average of more than 15 points per match – he now has Jonny Wilkinson's world record haul of 1,099 firmly in his sights.

Named the IRB Player of the Year in 2005 after helping to destroy the challenge of the British & Irish Lions tourists, Carter was no less destructive in 2008 as he contributed 44 points in the two warm-up Tests against England in June before tackling Australia and South Africa in the annual battle of the southern hemisphere.

His four penalties in the tournament opener against the Springboks in Wellington were pivotal in the All Blacks' 18–9 victory and the points flowed with match-winning regularity as New Zealand bounced back from the shock of back-to-back defeats to clinch their ninth Tri-Nations crown. His solo try in the final game in the Suncorp Stadium was a fitting climax to another superb campaign.

RYAN JONES (WALES)

Getty Images

Ryan Jones proved his worth as a captain, leading Wales to a Grand Slam.

When Ryan Jones led Wales to their famous 29–12 victory over France at the Millennium Stadium to claim the Six Nations Grand Slam, it was a result that drew a triumphant line under a tempestuous six months for both the Ospreys star and Welsh rugby as a whole.

Appointed Wales captain by Warren Gatland in early 2008, Jones had been forced to miss the World Cup with a shoulder injury and while his team-mates failed to qualify for the quarter-finals in France, the No 8 was forced to watch his country's lowest ebb from home, powerless to affect proceedings.

Six months later, Jones consigned his personal disappointment and the Principality's pain firmly to the past as Wales swept all before them in the Championship and the roar that greeted the captain as he lifted the trophy in front of the euphoric Welsh fans in Cardiff was as cathartic as it was celebratory.

First capped in the narrow 38–36 defeat to South Africa in the autumn of 2004, Jones first forged his reputation with the Ospreys as they claimed the Celtic League title in 2004–05 and he played in three of Wales five Championship games in 2005 as the Principality won the Grand Slam.

An ever present in the 2007 Six Nations, he seemed destined to make a huge impact at the World Cup until injury cruelly intervened but Gatland was in no doubt Jones was the man to spearhead the Welsh revival and handed him the captain's armband.

Under his leadership, the team was reborn in 2008 and Jones led from the front with a series of superb performances, galvanising the previously suspect Welsh pack and providing the platform for the side's mercurial back line.

28 SERGIO PARISSE (ITALY)

Getty Images

In 2008 Sergio Parisse proved he is a world-class performer.

It is not often that a player with more than 50 caps to his name can still look forward to the most influential years of his international career but in the case of Sergio Parisse, the next few seasons could be even more eye-catching than his already substantial contribution to the Italian cause.

Appointed the Azzurri captain by Nick Mallett ahead of the 2008 Six Nations, the six foot five inch No 8 led the side with great distinction throughout the Championship and still aged only 25, the Stade FrançÁais star looks destined to be a mainstay of the Italy team for many years to come.

First capped as an 18-year-old against the All Blacks in Hamilton in 2002 – making him the second youngest international in Italian history – Parisse came through his baptism of fire in Test rugby with flying colours and quickly established himself as one of the most dynamic and powerful back row forwards in the European game.

A veteran of his country's 2003 and 2007 World Cup campaigns, he assumed the Azzurri captaincy early in 2008 and although Italy eventually finished bottom of the Six Nations on points difference behind Scotland, the table failed to reflect the side's competitiveness and real improvement under his youthful but impressive leadership.

Although they were well beaten by Grand Slam champions Wales in Cardiff, Italy were only beaten by five points by the Irish in Dublin and there was only four points between them and England when the two sides met in Rome. France were also pushed close in Paris and their 23–20 victory over Scotland at the Stadio Flaminio in their final fixture was no less than Parisse and his team-mates deserved.

SHANE WILLIAMS (WALES)

Getty Images

Shane Williams was confirmed as one of the world's best finishers, in 2008.

In a modern international game bursting at the seams with wings of titanic physical proportions, Shane Williams stands out as a beacon for those who still admire natural flair and a sense of adventure over power and his superb strike rate in Tests is testament to the old adage that rugby is indeed a game for all shapes and sizes.

The Ospreys flyer began his international career in 2000 from the bench in Wales' Six Nations clash with France in Cardiff but it was a fortnight later that he signaled his huge potential with a try on his full debut against Italy at the Millennium Stadium.

Ever since, Williams' blend of searing pace, incisive angles of attack and his mesmerising side step have baffled opposition defences and delighted fans in equal measure.

A key member of the Wales team that claimed the 2005 Grand Slam, Williams was equally influential as the Principality repeated the feat in 2008 and in the process set a personal milestone that earned him a place in the record books.

Beginning the season with an already impressive 35 tries from 51 Tests, the Ospreys star was in the points again with a brace against Scotland in Cardiff. Another brace in the next game against the Italians followed and he once again crossed against Ireland in Dublin to equal Gareth Thomas' record of 40 tries for his country.

The stage was set for Williams to claim the record outright and he duly obliged in the final game against France as Wales claimed a famous Grand Slam.

A try in each of Wales' summer Tests against the Springboks took his personal haul to 43 tries in 58 games and with a few good seasons left in him, the sky remains the limit for the diminutive but dashing wing.

Marty Melville/Getty Images

Who will succeed New Zealand's Afeleke Pelenise as best Sevens player in the world?

THE 2008 IRB AWARDS

OTHER AWARDS

The IRB Player of the Year is one of 13 categories of awards that include the IRB Coach of the Year, IRB Team of the Year, IRB Sevens Player of the Year, IRB Junior Player of the Year and IRB Women's Personality of the Year. The event also recognises outstanding achievement and there are two awards run in conjunction with the International Rugby Players' Association (IRPA); the IRPA Special Merit award and the IRPA Try of the Year.

The shortlist of nominees for the IRB Junior Player of the Year is:

Luke Braid – New Zealand
Chris Smith – New Zealand
Joe Simpson – England

The shortlist of nominees for the IRB Sevens Player of the Year award category is:

DJ Forbes – New Zealand
Uale Mai – Samoa
Fabian Juries – South Africa

Marty Melville/Getty Images

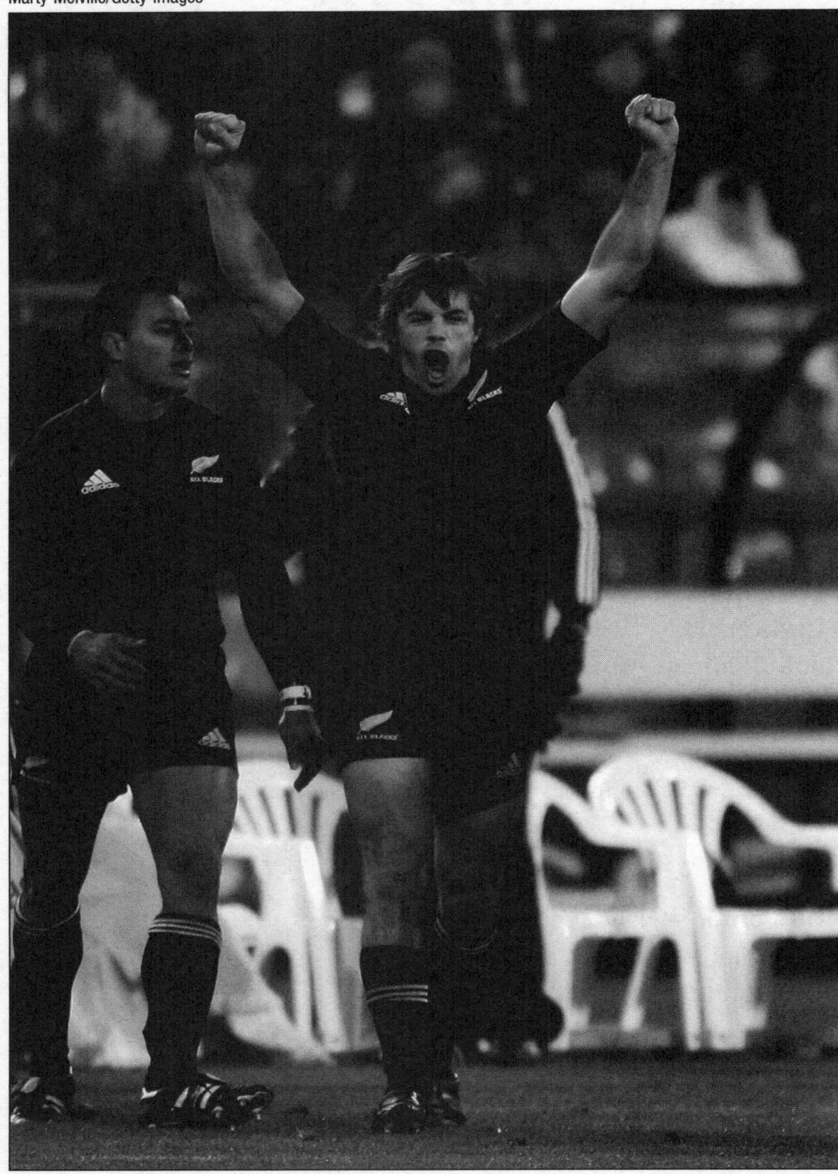

New Zealand are back on top of the world, the top ranked side.

IRB WORLD RANKINGS

TOUGH AT THE TOP

By Dominic Rumbles

While the IRB World Rankings have been the official indicator of international form over the past five years, they took on extra significance in 2008 with the International Rugby Board's announcement that the rankings would determine the seeding of teams for the Rugby World Cup 2011 Pool Allocation Draw.

On 1 December, the 12 directly qualified teams from Rugby World Cup 2007 will be allocated into the top three bands for the random draw using the IRB World Rankings as follows:

Band 1: Top four ranked qualified teams (1 to 4 in IRB World Rankings)

Band 2: Next four ranked qualified teams (5 to 8 in IRB World Rankings)

Band 3: Bottom four ranked qualified teams

As was the case for RWC 2007, the remaining qualifier positions will be randomly allocated into the final two bands:

Band 4: Oceania 1, Europe 1, Europe 2, Americas 1

Band 5: Africa 1, Asia 1, Americas 2, Play-off

At the time of going to print it looked as though New Zealand, South Africa and Australia would be ranked in the top four and therefore each top a pool in New Zealand and importantly avoid each other until at least the quarter-finals. The race to claim the fourth place and final pool topping place was less clear. With Argentina clinging by their fingertips to fourth, England, Wales, France and Ireland were hot in pursuit of the Pumas, hoping to capitalise on any slip ups during November and avoid being placed in a tough pool in New Zealand.

While the jostling within the chasing pack captured the attention, New Zealand firmly put their Rugby World Cup 2007 disappointment behind them to climb ominously to the top of the rankings, reinforcing their status as the Tri-Nations champions and the form team of 2008.

Graham Henry's side won eight of their 10 matches leading up to the November Tests to leapfrog world champions South Africa into top spot. It was the perfect tonic for Henry, who had been under fire heading into the June Test series.

South Africa slipped just one place after a Tri-Nations campaign of peaks and troughs. A change of management and a disappointing Tri-Nations campaign were offset by two wins against Wales, a further victory over Argentina plus a memorable first ever victory over New Zealand at Carisbrook.

Of the top 10 nations, Australia, experiencing a resurgence under Robbie Deans, were the most significant climbers and by the end of the Tri-Nations were established in third and seemingly away from the dangers of the second tier pool lottery.

By contrast Argentina came down to earth after the tremendous highs of a Rugby World Cup that delivered a wonderful third place, the Pumas losing a number of key players, a head coach and matches as they fell from third to fourth, having won just two of their fourth matches.

Defeats in June against Italy and Scotland, both below them in the rankings, did the damage, leaving the Pumas licking their wounds ahead of the November internationals.

England, Wales, France and Ireland all joined the race to topple the Pumas. A Grand Slam meant that Warren Gatland's Wales brushed aside their poor RWC 2007 form to climb from 10th to fifth and give themselves a real shot at the top four. England, despite having fallen one place and having endured a tough summer tour to New Zealand, were left optimistic about leapfrogging Argentina into fourth and a place at the top table. At the time of writing it was a wholly plausible possibility given that a win against New Zealand, Australia or South Africa in a full November schedule would provide the catalyst for Martin Johnson's team.

The IRB Pacific Nations Cup proved as competitive as ever and Japan, with a record victory over RWC 2011 automatic qualifiers Tonga, climbed two places to 16th. Fiji, meanwhile, slipped from ninth to 11th in part due to a defeat by Tonga when both teams were without key European-based players. Tonga, despite an indifferent PNC campaign, remained 13th.

Away from the top 12 teams ranked for the draw, there were significant gains and losses. Notable climbers included Norway, who continued their progress on the European stage, climbing five places to 82nd and Cameroon, who moved up four places to 77. The major fallers were Luxembourg, down 10 places to 90th and Jamaica, who lost all three of their Tests, including one to the lower ranked Bahamas, to slip nine places to 85th.

Inaugurated in October 2003, the IRB World Rankings are published every week on www.irb.com and are calculated using a *points exchange* system in which teams take points off each other based on the match result. Whatever one team wins, the other team loses.

The exchanges are determined by the match result, the relative strength of the team and the margin of victory. There is also an allowance for home advantage.

Ninety-five of the IRB's Member Unions have a rating, typically between 0 and 100. The top side in the world will usually have a rating above 90. Any match that is not a full international between the two countries or a Test against the British & Irish Lions or Pacific Islanders, does not count, as neither teams are in the rankings. The same is true of a match against a country that is not a full member union of the IRB.

For further details and Rankings analysis, visit www.irb.com.

IRB WORLD RANKINGS 22.10.07 - 30.09.08

POSITION	MEMBER UNION	RATING POINTS	
1	NEW ZEALAND	92.04	Up 1
2	SOUTH AFRICA	87.75	Down 1
3	AUSTRALIA	85.69	Up 2
4	ARGENTINA	83.36	Down 1
5	ENGLAND	83.16	Down 1
6	WALES	80.12	Up 4
7	FRANCE	78.99	Down 1
8	IRELAND	77.18	Down 1
9	SCOTLAND	76.92	Down 1
10	ITALY	75.57	Up 1
11	FIJI	75.24	Down 1
12	SAMOA	72.57	
13	TONGA	70.05	
14	GEORGIA	69.43	Up 2
15	CANADA	68.81	
16	JAPAN	67.35	Up 1
17	ROMANIA	67.20	Down 3
18	RUSSIA	63.94	Up 1
19	URUGUAY	63.69	Up 1
20	USA	63.11	Down 2
21	SPAIN	61.55	
22	KOREA	59.02	Up 1
23	PORTUGAL	58.88	Down 1
24	CHILE	57.07	
25	GERMANY	57.05	Up 1
26	NAMIBIA	56.82	Down 1
27	BELGIUM	55.87	Up 5
28	BRAZIL	53.98	Up 5
29	TUNISIA	53.37	Up 7
30	HONG KONG	53.16	Down 2
31	POLAND	52.48	
32	PARAGUAY	52.40	Down 2
33	KAZAKHSTAN	52.31	Up 4
34	MOROCCO	52.25	Down 5
35	CZECH REPUBLIC	51.92	
36	UKRAINE	51.77	Up 2
37	MOLDOVA	51.56	Down 10
38	UGANDA	51.42	Up 4
39	SWEDEN	50.92	Up 1
40	KENYA	50.62	Down 1
41	IVORY COAST	50.09	Down 4
42	CHINA	48.83	Up 1
43	LITHUANIA	47.84	Up 12
44	CROATIA	47.80	Up 4
45	TRINIDAD & TOBAGO	47.79	Up 13
46	MADAGASCAR	47.71	

47	LATVIA	47.38	Down 6
48	NETHERLANDS	47.36	Down 4
49	CHINESE TAIPEI	47.02	Down 7
50	SRI LANKA	46.79	Down 1
51	ARABIAN GULF	46.40	Down 4
52	SWITZERLAND	45.67	Down 1
53	PAPUA NEW GUINEA	45.52	Down 1
54	SINGAPORE	44.91	Down 1
55	ZIMBABWE	44.45	Up 2
56	MALTA	44.07	Down 2
57	COOK ISLANDS	44.03	Down 7
58	VENEZUELA	43.92	Up 2
59	ANDORRA	43.40	Up 3
60	DENMARK	42.67	Down 4
61	NIUE ISLANDS	42.36	Up 7
62	THAILAND	42.34	Up 8
63	BERMUDA	42.26	Up 2
64	CAYMAN	42.12	Down 5
65	COLOMBIA	42.03	Up 1
66	SLOVENIA	41.92	Down 3
67	GUYANA	41.52	Up 5
68	SENEGAL	41.44	Down 1
69	BARBADOS	40.96	Down 8
70	PERU	40.64	Down 6
71	ZAMBIA	40.64	
72	SERBIA	40.11	Up 1
73	HUNGARY	39.74	Down 5
74	BOTSWANA	39.53	Up 5
75	ST. VINCENT & THE GRENADINES	39.30	
76	SOLOMON ISLANDS	39.06	
77	CAMEROON	38.97	Up 4
78	MONACO	38.81	
79	MALAYSIA	38.03	Down 9
80	ST. LUCIA	37.57	Up 3
81	INDIA	37.23	Up 3
82	NORWAY	37.10	Up 4
83	GUAM	36.80	Up 4
84	SWAZILAND	36.68	Down 2
85	JAMAICA	36.61	Down 8
86	AUSTRIA	36.47	Down 1
87	BAHAMAS	36.33	Up 3
88	TAHITI	36.25	
89	NIGERIA	35.29	
90	LUXEMBOURG	35.05	Down 10
91	BULGARIA	34.92	
92	VANUATU	34.77	
93	ISRAEL	33.64	
94	BOSNIA & HERZEGOVINA	32.54	Up 1
95	FINLAND	31.98	Down 1

INTERNATIONAL TOURNAMENTS

WALES STORM TO UNEXPECTED GRAND SLAM

By Scott Quinnell

Getty Images

It's ours! Wales get their hands on the trophy.

I think it's safe to say that only the most partisan and optimistic Welsh fan was expecting the Grand Slam after the team's hugely disappointing performance at the World Cup. Failing to get beyond the group stages in France and losing to Fiji was a real body blow to Welsh rugby but the way in which they bounced back was absolutely sensational.

It is difficult to overstate how much credit the new coaching team of Warren Gatland and Shaun Edwards deserve for the way in which they turned things around. They inherited a demoralised set of players and quickly instilled a self-belief and collective will that was evident in the second-half of the game with England at Twickenham and took them through the rest of the tournament. It was an unbelievable transformation.

I think Gatland's greatest achievement was the way he managed to focus his players on the nuts and bolts – the set pieces and the contact areas – without sacrificing the side's flair and attacking instincts. Edwards worked wonders with the defence and after a shaky opening first 40 minutes against the English, Wales began to look like a complete side that was capable of playing more than one style of rugby.

The Grand Slam of 2005 proved to be a false dawn for Welsh rugby but I believe their 2008 clean sweep will provide a more solid platform for the future. In 2005, the side played a hugely entertaining, expansive brand of rugby but over the next year or so, other teams learnt how to nullify the threat and looked to put Wales on the back foot, forcing them to throw the ball wide at the wrong times.

The 2008 side has more depth. The front five is more competitive and the team was able to grind out results, which was particularly evident when they edged Ireland in a close game at Croke Park. It wasn't pretty but it was effective.

In terms of personnel, Wales benefited enormously from the competition between James Hook and Stephen Jones for the number 10 shirt. The battle kept both players on their toes and it gave the side superb tactical options.

Gatland also pulled off a masterstroke in persuading Martyn Williams to come out of international retirement and he gave the team the balance it needed. Ryan Jones was hugely effective as both a player and captain and with Shane Williams in arguably the form of his life; Wales eventually emerged as worthy champions.

It was a truly bizarre tournament for England and their Jekyll and Hyde performances throughout ultimately cost Brian Ashton his job, even though they pipped the French for second place.

Expectations were obviously high after reaching the World Cup final and initially it seemed they were going to pick up where they left off with a convincing first-half performance against Wales at Twickenham. The way the wheels came off in the second-half was staggering and I cannot remember watching an England team implode like that, make so many unforced errors and needlessly throw the ball away. Wales pounced but you have to say England handed them the opportunity.

The rest of the campaign was equally inconsistent. They were unconvincing in victory in Rome against Italy, outstanding against the French in Paris and pretty abject in losing to Scotland at Murrayfield. They finished up with a good win at home against Ireland but it couldn't paper over all the cracks.

The major positives for England were the emergence of Danny Cipriani and James Haskell. Cipriani was sensational against Ireland and the way he shook off the furore that surrounded him getting dropped for the Scotland game after his ill-advised nightclub visit spoke volumes about his mental strength. Haskell also impressed me in the back row and after a wave of retirements since the World Cup, England at least have some new talent coming through.

France finished third but you couldn't escape the feeling they still had their minds on their failure to win the World Cup on home soil. Marc Lièvremont was installed as the new coach, replacing Bernard Laporte, and it was obvious from early on he was going to blood as many new players as he could.

I actually don't think Lièvremont will have been too troubled by the side's results. I think he probably got a little too carried away with making wholesale changes between games but he obviously felt it was time to start over again and he was determined to expose new players to international rugby.

Losing to England in Paris will have hurt but the form of the back three of Cédric Heymans, Vincent Clerc and Julien Malzieu in the first couple of games was sensational. Lièvremont also unearthed a gem in the shape of François Trinh-Duc, the young fly-half who looks a great prospect for the future.

For Ireland, it was a demoralising tournament. Everyone associated with Irish rugby was hoping for a backlash after their tame performances at the World Cup but it failed to materialise and Eddie O'Sullivan paid the ultimate price and lost his job.

There were glimpses of the old Ireland at times, particularly in the second-half against France in Paris, but they also looked tired and there's no doubt they are a side in a difficult period of transition.

The writing was on the wall for O'Sullivan after the first match against Italy in Dublin. It was a win but Ireland failed to convince and things didn't really get any better for them.

I felt Ronan O'Gara had a good tournament but losing Gordon D'Arcy early on to injury was a huge setback and it was far from ideal having Paul O'Connell

TRIVIA

Wales' unbeaten season put them in the driving seat when it came to the selection for the **Rugby World Magazine** Team of the Tournament, Ireland being the most under-represented side with just outside centre Andrew Trimble making it into the elite verdict. The team was: Lee Byrne; Vincent Clerc, Andrew Trimble, Andy Henderson, Shane Williams; James Hook, Mike Phillips; Martin Castrogiovanni, Dimitri Szarzewski, Andrew Sheridan, Steve Borthwick, Nathan Hines, Thierry Dusautoir, Martyn Williams and Sergio Parisse.

chasing full fitness in games, rather than coming back into the side at the peak of his powers.

Eoin Reddan, Tommy Bowe and Jamie Heaslip all impressed, however, there is definitely something for the new coach to work with going forward.

Scotland came down to earth with a bump after an encouraging World Cup. Frank Hadden's side looked fitter and stronger in that tournament than any Scotland team I can remember but the Six Nations produced few highlights for them and the gritty win over England at Murrayfield only really flattered to deceive.

Hadden's biggest problem was once again Scotland's lack of depth. He lost Sean Lamont before the start of the competition and got just one game from Rory Lamont before he joined the injury list and Scotland just don't have the resources to cope with losing leading players like that.

There was huge debate about Chris Paterson, who was left on the bench for the heavy defeat to France in Edinburgh in the campaign opener, came in at full-back for the Wales game and finished the Six Nations at fly-half. Paterson's kicking is world class but I can understand why Hadden initially went with Dan Parks at 10 because he was looking to play a more controlled game.

The win over England was a great day for Scotland but losing to Italy in Rome was very significant. They may have avoided finishing bottom on points difference but the game in the Stadio Flaminio was a battle between the season's two weakest teams and Scotland were beaten, which tells its own story.

Italy started the tournament with a new coach in the shape of Nick Mallett and on balance I don't think they really got everything they deserved for how they played. The table will show they ended up with the wooden spoon but they beat Scotland and pushed both England and Ireland close.

As ever, the Italian pack was abrasive and competitive and once again they had very little out wide. Mallett's a good coach but Italy have got to be more incisive going forward if they're really going to push on and start winning two or three Six Nations games a season on a regular basis.

Marco Bortolami was a big loss for them for the first two matches but the forwards again stood tall and Sergio Parisse was outstanding in the back row, deputising for Mauro Bergamasco as skipper and doing a superb job leading from the front. Parisse is a world-class player and he'd push for a place in any of the Six Nations sides on view.

I'd have to say Italy's biggest problem remains the number 10 shirt. They've never managed to settle on a long-term successor to Diego Dominguez and until they find a fly-half who can pull the strings at this level, they're going to be on the back foot.

On balance, it was a tournament which had an experimental feel about it. There were new head coaches and a lot of younger players taking their first steps on the international stage. Wales were definitely the best side in the competition and fully deserved the Grand Slam. Gatland proved to be a great appointment by the WRU and the future looks bright. None of the other five teams will have been particularly pleased with their campaigns and will know there's plenty of room for improvement.

• England's Under-20s, captained by Wasps back row Hugo Ellis, clinched a first ever RBS Six Nations Grand Slam by turning on the style to outgun Ireland with seven sparkling tries at Kingsholm, 43–14.

Coach Nigel Redman said: "The toughest game of the five was France away which was a tight game because of the environment – a brand new stadium full to 20,000 capacity and the full French experience – while Wales, who beat France in the last round, have developed throughout the tournament. It's a very special group – and I include the management as well as the players – and to have completed the five games unbeaten is a fantastic achievement."

• After the completion of the 2008 tournament, former Wales captain David Pickering was elected chairman of the RBS 6 Nations. Pickering, who is also Welsh Rugby Union chairman, takes over from Jacques Laurans and has a three-year term of office He said: "It is an honour to be elected chairman of the Six Nations and a privilege to work with such a dedicated group of people as the Six Nations Council."

Getty Images

Danny Cipriani emerged in 2008 as England achieved their best finish for five years.

FIXTURES 2009

The 2009 RBS 6 Nations schedule has been announced, with matches taking place between Saturday 7 February and Saturday 21 March, and with a match on a Friday for the first time in the Championship's history.

Saturday 7 February
England v **Italy** (3pm)
Ireland v **France** (5pm)

Sunday 8 February
Scotland v **Wales** (3pm)

Saturday 14 February
France v **Scotland** (3pm)
Wales v **England** (5.30pm)

Sunday 15 February
Italy v **Ireland** (2.30pm)

Friday 27 February
France v **Wales** (8pm)

Saturday 28 February
Scotland v **Italy** (3pm)
Ireland v **England** (5.30pm)

Saturday 14 March
Italy v **Wales** (3pm)
Scotland v **Ireland** (5pm)

Sunday 15 March
England v **France** (3pm)

Saturday 21 March
Italy v **France** (1.15pm)
England v **Scotland** (3.30pm)
Wales v **Ireland** (5.30pm)

* All are in UK time – add one hour for matches in **France** and **Italy**
* In the UK all games will be shown live on the BBC

SIX NATIONS 2008 FINAL TABLE

	P	W	D	L	For	Against	Pts
Wales	5	5	0	0	148	66	**10**
England	5	3	0	2	108	83	**6**
France	5	3	0	2	103	93	**6**
Ireland	5	2	0	3	93	99	**4**
Scotland	5	1	0	4	69	123	**2**
Italy	5	1	0	4	74	131	**2**

Points: Win 2; Draw 1; Defeat 0.

There were 595 points scored at an average of 39.7 a match. The Championship record (803 points at an average of 53.5 a match) was set in 2000. Jonny Wilkinson was the leading individual points scorer with 50, 39 points shy of the Championship record he set in 2001. Shane Williams was the Championship's leading try-scorer with six, equalling Maurice Richards's Welsh record for a season set in 1969 and two short of the all-time record shared between England's Cyril Lowe (1914) and Scotland's Ian Smith (1925).

Getty Images

France put the accent on youth in 2008 and had to settle for third place.

2008 MATCH STATS

2 February, Croke Park, Dublin

IRELAND 16 (1G 3PG) ITALY 11 (2PG 1T)

IRELAND: G T Dempsey; A D Trimble, B G O'Driscoll (*captain*), G M D'Arcy, G E A Murphy; R J R O'Gara, E G Reddan; M J Horan, R Best, J J Hayes, D P O'Callaghan, M E O'Kelly, S H Easterby, D P Leamy, D P Wallace *Substitutions:* R D J Kearney for D'Arcy (25 mins); J P R Heaslip for Easterby (59 mins); B J Jackman for Best (61 mins); M R O'Driscoll for O'Kelly (66 mins); T D Buckley for Hayes (73 mins); P A Stringer for Reddan (73 mins)

SCORERS *Try:* Dempsey *Conversion:* O'Gara *Penalty Goals:* O'Gara (3)

ITALY: D Bortolussi; K Robertson, G-J Canale, Mirco Bergamasco, P Canavosio; A Masi, P Travagli; A Lo Cicero, L Ghiraldini, M-L Castrogiovanni, S Dellape, C-A Del Fava, J Sole, S Parisse (*captain*), Mauro Bergamasco *Substitutions:* E Galon for Canavosio (23 mins); A Zanni for Sole (40 mins); C Festuccia for Ghiraldini (54 mins); S Perugini for Lo Cicero (54 mins); A Marcato for Bortolussi (71 mins); T Reato for Del Fava (73 mins); L Cittadini for Castrogiovanni (79 mins)

SCORERS *Try:* Castrogiovanni *Penalty Goals:* Bortolussi (2)

REFEREE J I Kaplan (South Africa)

YELLOW CARDS Dellape (30 mins); Easterby (48 mins)

2 February, Twickenham

ENGLAND 19 (1G 3PG 1DG) WALES 26 (2G 4PG)

ENGLAND: I R Balshaw; P H Sackey, M J Tindall, T Flood, D Strettle; J P Wilkinson, A C T Gomarsall; A J Sheridan, M P Regan, P J Vickery (*captain*), S D Shaw, S W Borthwick, J Haskell, L Narraway, L W Moody *Substitutions:* L Vainikolo for Strettle (12 mins); T Rees for Moody (13 mins); B J Kay for Rees (40 mins); L A Mears for Regan (57 mins); D Cipriani for Tindall (63 mins); M J H Stevens for Vickery 68 mins)

SCORERS *Try:* Flood *Conversion:* Wilkinson *Penalty Goals:* Wilkinson (3) *Dropped Goal:* Wilkinson

WALES: L M Byrne; M A Jones, S T Parker, G L Henson, S M Williams; J Hook, M Phillips; D J Jones, H Bennett, A R Jones, I M Gough, A-W Jones, J Thomas, R P Jones (*captain*), M E Williams *Substitutions:*A J Popham for Thomas (12 mins); G D Jenkins for A R Jones (45 mins); T G L Shanklin for Parker (45 mins); M Rees for Bennett (57 mins); I Evans for A-W Jones (77 mins)

SCORERS *Tries:* Byrne, Phillips *Conversions:* Hook (2) *Penalty Goals:* Hook (4)

REFEREE C Joubert (South Africa)

3 February, Murrayfield

SCOTLAND 6 (1PG 1DG) FRANCE 27 (3G 2PG)

SCOTLAND: R P Lamont; N Walker, N J De Luca, A R Henderson, S L Webster; D A Parks, M R L Blair; A F Jacobsen, R W Ford, E A Murray, N J Hines, J L Hamilton, J P R White (*captain*), D A Callam, J A Barclay *Substitutions:* K D R Brown for Callam (48 mins); S J MacLeod for Hamilton (54 mins); G Kerr for Murray (57 mins); C D Paterson for Parks (60 mins); H F G Southwell for Lamont (60 mins); C P Cusiter for Blair (65 mins); F M A Thomason for Ford (72 mins)

SCORER *Penalty Goal:* Parks *Dropped Goal:* Parks

FRANCE: C Heymans; V Clerc, D Marty, D Traille, J Malzieu; F Trinh-Duc, J-B Elissalde; L Faure, W Servat, J Brugnaut, L Jacquet, L Nallet (*captain*), T Dusautoir, E Vermeulen, F Ouedraogo *Substitutions:* D Szarzewski for Servat (48 mins); N Mas for Brugnaut (48 mins); J Bonnaire for Vermeulen (54 mins); D Skrela for Trinh-Duc (58 mins); A Mela for Jacquet (61 mins); M Parra for Elissalde (65 mins); A Rougerie for Clerc (72 mins)

SCORERS *Tries:* Clerc (2), Malzieu *Conversions:* Elissalde (2), Skrela *Penalty Goals:* Traille (2)

REFEREE A C Rolland (Ireland)

9 February, Millennium Stadium, Cardiff

WALES 30 (3G 3PG) SCOTLAND 15 (5PG)

WALES: L M Byrne; J Roberts, T G L Shanklin, G L Henson, S M Williams; J Hook, M Phillips; D J Jones, H Bennett, A R Jones, I M Gough, I Evans, J Thomas, R P Jones (*captain*), M E Williams *Substitutions:* G D Jenkins for D J Jones (53 mins); S M Jones for Hook (57 mins); D J Peel for Phillips (57 mins); M Rees for Bennett (57 mins); G L Delve for R P Jones (61 mins); D L Jones for Gough (72 mins); S T Parker for Shanklin (72 mins)

SCORERS *Tries:* S M Williams (2), Hook *Conversions:* Hook (2), S M Jones *Penalty Goals:* S M Jones (2), Hook

SCOTLAND: H F G Southwell; N Walker, N J De Luca, A R Henderson, C D Paterson; D A Parks, M R L Blair; A F Jacobsen, R W Ford, E A Murray, N J Hines, J L Hamilton, J P R White (*captain*), K D R Brown, J A Barclay *Substitutions:* A Hogg for White (31 mins); S J MacLeod for Hines (61 mins); G Kerr for Murray (67 mins); S C J Danielli for Parks (67 mins); F M A Thomson for Ford (73 mins); C P Cusiter for Blair (73 mins); G A Morrison for De Luca (73 mins)

SCORER *Penalty Goals:* Paterson (5)

REFEREE B J Lawrence (New Zealand)

YELLOW CARD Hines (15 mins)

9 February, Stade de France, Paris

FRANCE 26 (3G 1T) IRELAND 21 (1G 3PG 1T)

FRANCE: C Heymans; A Rougerie, D Marty, D Traille, V Clerc; D Skrela, J-B Elissalde; L Faure, D Szarzewski, N Mas, L Nallet (*captain*), A Mela, T Dusautoir, J Bonnaire, F Ouedraogo *Substitutions:* J Brugnaut for Faure (46 mins); W Servat for Szarzewski (46 mins); L Jacquet for Mela (temp 16 to 21 mins and 50 mins); L Picamoles for Ouedraogo (61 mins); M Parra for Elissalde (65 mins); F Trinh-Duc for Skrela (75 mins)

SCORERS *Tries:* Clerc (3), Heymans *Conversions:* Elissalde (3)

IRELAND: G T Dempsey; G E A Murphy, B G O'Driscoll (*captain*), A D Trimble, R D J Kearney; R J R O'Gara, E G Reddan; M J Horan, B J Jackman, J J Hayes, D P O'Callaghan, M E O'Kelly, D P Leamy, J P R Heaslip, D P Wallace *Substitutions:* M R O'Driscoll for O'Kelly (53 mins); R Best for Jackman (60 mins); T D Buckley for Hayes (76 mins)

SCORERS *Tries:* penalty try, D Wallace *Conversion:* O'Gara *Penalty Goals:* O'Gara (3)

REFEREE N Owens (Wales)

10 February, Stadio Flaminio, Rome

ITALY 19 (1G 4PG) ENGLAND 23 (2G 3PG)

ITALY: D Bortolussi; K Robertson, G-J Canale, Mirco Bergamasco, E Galon; A Masi, P Travagli; A Lo Cicero, L Ghiraldini, M-L Castrogiovanni, S Dellape, C-A Del Fava, J Sole, S Parisse (*captain*), Mauro Bergamasco *Substitutions:* S Perugini for Lo Cicero (51 mins); S Picone for Travagli (55 mins); C Nieto for Castrogiovanni (59 mins); A Sgarbi for Canale (62 mins); C Festuccia for Ghiraldini (62 mins); A Marcato for Masi (72 mins); A Zanni for Dellape (72 mins)

SCORERS *Try:* Picone *Conversion:* Bortolussi *Penalty Goals:* Bortolussi (4)

ENGLAND: I R Balshaw; P H Sackey, J D Noon, T Flood, L Vainikolo; J P Wilkinson, A C T Gomarsall; T A N Payne, M P Regan, M J S Stevens, S D Shaw, S W Borthwick (*captain*), J Haskell, N Easter, M R Lipman *Substitutions:* L A Mears for Regan (55 mins); R E P Wigglesworth for Gomarsall (59 mins); L Narraway for Easter (64 mins); D Cipriani for Wilkinson (66 mins); B J Kay for Shaw (77 mins); M Tait for Noon (temp 51 to 62 mins)

SCORERS *Tries:* Sackey, Flood *Conversions:* Wilkinson (2) *Penalty Goals:* Wilkinson (3)

REFEREE A C Rolland (Ireland)

23 February, Millennium Stadium, Cardiff

WALES 47 (5G 4PG) ITALY 8 (1PG 1T)

WALES: L M Byrne; M A Jones, T G L Shanklin, G L Henson, S M Williams; S M Jones, D J Peel; G D Jenkins, M Rees, Rhys Thomas, I M Gough, I Evans, J Thomas, R P Jones (*captain*), M E Williams *Substitutions:* M Phillips for Peel (42 mins); H Bennett for Rees (54 mins); J Hook for S M Jones (66 mins); D J Jones for Rhys Thomas (66 mins); D L Jones for Evans (66 mins); G L Delve for M E Williams (69 mins); S T Parker for Henson (69 mins)

SCORERS *Tries:* S M Williams (2), Byrne (2), Shanklin *Conversions:* S M Jones (3), Hook (2) *Penalty Goals:* S M Jones (4)

ITALY: A Marcato; A Sgarbi, G-J Canale, Mirco Bergamasco, E Galon; A Masi, S Picone; S Perugini, L Ghiraldini, M-L Castrogiovanni, S Dellape, C-A Del Fava, J Sole, S Parisse (*captain*), Mauro Bergamasco *Substitutions:* A Lo Cicero for Castrogiovanni (temp 19 to 28 mins) and for Perugini (49 mins); M Bortolami for Dellape (49 mins); P Buso for Masi (52 mins); P Travagli for Picone (58 mins); A Zanni for Sole (60 mins); C Festuccia for Ghiraldini (69 mins); Perugini back for Castrogiovanni (70 mins)

SCORERS *Try:* Castrogiovanni *Penalty Goal:* Marcato

REFEREE D Pearson (England)

YELLOW CARD Mirco Bergamasco (49 mins)

23 February, Croke Park, Dublin

IRELAND 34 (3G 1PG 2T) SCOTLAND 13 (1G 2PG)

IRELAND: G E A Murphy; T J Bowe, B G O'Driscoll (*captain*), A D Trimble, R D J Kearney; R J R O'Gara, E G Reddan; M J Horan, B J Jackman, J J Hayes, D P O'Callaghan, M R O'Driscoll, D P Leamy, J P R Heaslip, D P Wallace *Substitutions:* R Best for Jackman (43 mins); P J O'Connell for M R O'Driscoll (54 mins); S P Horgan for B G O'Driscoll (69 mins); S H Easterby for Heaslip (69 mins); P A Stringer for Reddan (71 mins); T D Buckley for Hayes (72 mins); P W Wallace for O'Gara (76 mins)

SCORERS *Tries:* Bowe (2), D Wallace, Kearney, Horan *Conversions:* O'Gara (3) *Penalty Goal:* O'Gara

SCOTLAND: H F G Southwell; R P Lamont, S L Webster, A R Henderson, N Walker; C D Paterson, M R L Blair (*captain*); A F Jacobsen, R W Ford, E A Murray, N J Hines, S J MacLeod, A K Strokosch, K D R Brown, A Hogg *Substitutions:* R M Rennie for Brown (45 mins); J L Hamilton for Hines (63 mins); D A Parks for Southwell (66 mins); F M A Thomson for Ford (69 mins); N J De Luca for Walker (temp 61 to 66 mins) and for Henderson (69 mins); G Kerr for Jacobsen (71 mins); C P Cusiter for Blair (71 mins); R W Ford back for Murray (75 mins)

SCORERS *Try:* Webster *Conversion:* Paterson *Penalty Goals:* Paterson (2)

REFEREE C Berdos (France)

23 February, Stade de France, Paris

FRANCE 13 (1G 2PG)
ENGLAND 24 (1G 3PG 1DG 1T)

FRANCE: C Heymans; A Rougerie, D Marty, D Traille, V Clerc; F Trinh-Duc, M Parra; L Faure, D Szarzewski, N Mas, P Papé, L Nallet (*captain*), T Dusautoir, L Picamoles, J Bonnaire *Substitutions:* J-B Poux for Mas (55 mins); W Servat for Szarzewski (58 mins); J Thion for Papé (58 mins); D Yachvili for Parra (65 mins); D Skrela for Trinh-Duc (65 mins); A Floch for Rougerie (65 mins); F Ouedraogo for Picamoles (76 mins)

SCORERS *Try:* Nallet *Conversion:* Traille *Penalty Goals:* Parra, Yachvili

ENGLAND: I R Balshaw; P H Sackey, J D Noon, T Flood, L Vainikolo; J P Wilkinson, R E P Wigglesworth; A J Sheridan, M P Regan, P J Vickery (*captain*), S D Shaw, S W Borthwick, J Haskell, N Easter, M R Lipman *Substitutions:* T Croft for Haskell (20 mins); L A Mears for Regan (48 mins); B J Kay for Shaw (68 mins); M Tait for Noon (69 mins); M J S Stevens for Sheridan (71 mins)

SCORERS *Tries:* Sackey, Wigglesworth *Conversion:* Wilkinson *Penalty Goals:* Wilkinson (3) *Dropped Goal:* Wilkinson

REFEREE S R Walsh (New Zealand)

8 March, Croke Park, Dublin

IRELAND 12 (4PG) WALES 16 (1G 3PG)

IRELAND: R D J Kearney; S P Horgan, B G O'Driscoll (*captain*), A D Trimble, T J Bowe; R J R O'Gara, E G Reddan; M J Horan, R Best, J J Hayes, D P O'Callaghan, P J O'Connell, D P Leamy, J P R Heaslip, D P Wallace *Substitutions:* B J Jackman for Best (70 mins); T D Buckley for Hayes (70 mins); L Fitzgerald for B O'Driscoll (70 mins)

SCORER *Penalty Goals:* O'Gara (4)

WALES: L M Byrne; M A Jones, T G L Shanklin, G L Henson, S M Williams; S M Jones, M Phillips; G D Jenkins, M Rees, A R Jones, I M Gough, A-W.Jones, J Thomas, R P Jones (*captain*), M E Williams *Substitutions:* J Hook for S M Jones (64 mins); D J Jones for A R Jones (71 mins); G L Delve for R P Jones (74 mins)

SCORERS *Try:* S M Williams *Conversion:* S M Jones *Penalty Goals:* S M Jones (2), Hook

REFEREE W Barnes (England)

YELLOW CARDS M Phillips (38 mins); M E Williams (61 mins)

8 March, Murrayfield

SCOTLAND 15 (5PG) ENGLAND 9 (3PG)

SCOTLAND: H F G Southwell; R P Lamont, S L Webster, G A Morrison, N Walker; C D Paterson, M R L Blair (*captain*); A F Jacobsen, R W Ford, E A Murray, N J Hines, S J MacLeod, A K Strokosch, S M Taylor, A Hogg *Substitutions:* D A Parks for Lamont (20 mins); F M A Thomson for Ford (24 mins); J P R White for MacLeod (62 mins); A G Dickinson for Jacobsen (64 mins); C J Smith for Murray (69 mins); K D R Brown for Hogg (71 mins); R G M Lawson for Blair (75 mins)

SCORERS *Penalty Goals:* Paterson (4), Parks

ENGLAND: I R Balshaw; P H Sackey, J D Noon, T Flood, L Vainikolo; J P Wilkinson, R E P Wigglesworth; A J Sheridan, L A Mears, P J Vickery (*captain*), S D Shaw, S W Borthwick, T Croft, N Easter, M R Lipman *Substitutions:* B J Kay for Shaw (66 mins); G S Chuter for Mears (66 mins); M Tait for Flood (66 mins); M J S Stevens for Vickery (69 mins); C C Hodgson for Wilkinson (69 mins); L Narraway for Lipman (73 mins)

SCORER *Penalty Goals:* Wilkinson (3)

REFEREE J I Kaplan (South Africa)

9 March, Stade de France, Paris

FRANCE 25 (2G 2PG 1T) ITALY 13 (1G 2PG)

FRANCE: A Floch; A Rougerie, Y David, Y Jauzion, J Malzieu; F Trinh-Duc, D Yachvili; F Barcella, D Szarzewski, N Mas, L Nallet (*captain*), J Thion, I Diarra, L Picamoles, F Ouedraogo *Substitutions:* J Bonnaire for Diarra (49 mins); J-B Poux for Mas (61 mins); G Guirado for Szarzewski (62 mins); D Traille for David (64 mins); A Mela for Thion (67 mins); J Tomas for Yachvili (70 mins); V Clerc for Floch (temp 53 to 61 mins)

SCORERS *Tries:* Floch, Jauzion, Rougerie *Conversions:* Yachvili (2) *Penalty Goals:* Yachvili (2)

ITALY: A Marcato; K Robertson, G-J Canale, Mirco Bergamasco, E Galon; A Masi, S Picone; A Lo Cicero, L Ghiraldini, M-L Castrogiovanni, C-A Del Fava, M Bortolami, J Sole, S Parisse (*captain*), A Zanni *Substitutions:* F Ongaro for Ghiraldini (55 mins); S Perugini for Lo Cicero (55 mins); C Nieto for Castrogiovanni (58 mins); P Travagli for Picone (68 mins); E Patrizio for Canale (74 mins); J Erasmus for Bortolami (temp 6 to 14 mins) and for Del Fava (temp 35 to 40 mins)

SCORERS *Try:* Castrogiovanni *Conversion:* Marcato *Penalty Goals:* Marcato (2)

REFEREE D A Lewis (Ireland)

15 March, Stadio Flaminio, Rome

ITALY 23 (2G 2PG 1DG) SCOTLAND 20 (2G 2PG)

ITALY: R de Marigny; K Robertson, E Galon, Mirco Bergamasco, M Pratichetti; R Pez, A Troncon; S Perugini, C Festuccia, C Nieto, S Dellape, M Bortolami (*captain*), A Zanni, S Parisse, M Zaffiri *Substitutions:* J Sole for Zaffiri (2 mins); A Scanavacca for Pez (40 mins); F Staibano for Perugini (52 mins); M Barbini for Galon (62 mins); V Bernabo for Parisse (65 mins); S Perugini for Nieto (67 mins); P Griffen for Troncon (79 mins); L Ghiraldini for Festuccia (79 mins)

SCORERS *Tries:* Bortolami, De Marigny *Conversion:* Scanavacca *Penalty Goals:* Pez (2) *Dropped Goals:* Pez (2)

IRELAND: G T Dempsey; S P Horgan, B G O'Driscoll (*captain*), G M D'Arcy, D A Hickie; R J R O'Gara, P A Stringer; M J Horan, R Best, J J Hayes, D F O'Callaghan, M R O'Driscoll, S H Easterby, D P Leamy, D P Wallace *Substitutions:* T Hogan for M O'Driscoll (53 mins); A Trimble for B O'Driscoll (59 mins); J Flannery for R Best (60 mins); S J Best for Horan (65 mins); M J Horan for S Best (79 mins)

SCORERS *Tries:* Dempsey (2), Hickie (2), Easterby, D'Arcy, Horgan, O'Gara *Conversions:* O'Gara (4) *Penalty Goal:* O'Gara

REFEREE J I Kaplan (South Africa)

15 March, Twickenham

ENGLAND 33 (3G 4PG) IRELAND 10 (1G 1PG)

ENGLAND: I R Balshaw; P H Sackey, J D Noon, T Flood, L Vainikolo; D Cipriani, R E P Wigglesworth; A J Sheridan, L A Mears, P J Vickery (*captain*), S D Shaw, S W Borthwick, T Croft, N Easter, M R Lipman *Substitutions:* J P Wilkinson for Flood (52 mins); M J S Stevens for Vickery (60 mins); B J Kay for Shaw (60 mins); J Haskell for Lipman (64 mins); M Tait for Sackey (temp 47 to 57 mins and 64 mins); P Hodgson for Wigglesworth (73 mins); G S Chuter for Mears (75 mins);

SCORERS *Tries:* Sackey, Tait, Noon *Conversions:* Cipriani (3) *Penalty Goals:* Cipriani (4)

IRELAND: G E A Murphy; T J Bowe, A D Trimble, S P Horgan, R D J Kearney; R J R O'Gara (*captain*), E G Reddan; M J Horan, R Best, J J Hayes, D P O'Callaghan, P J O'Connell, D P Leamy, J P R Heaslip, D P Wallace *Substitutions:* S H Easterby for Leamy (11 mins); L Fitzgerald for Murphy (34 mins); T D Buckley for Horan (66 mins); M R O'Driscoll for D P Wallace (66 mins); P A Stringer for Reddan (70 mins); B J Jackman for Best (70 mins); P W Wallace for Horgan (76 mins)

SCORERS *Try:* Kearney *Conversion:* O'Gara *Penalty Goal:* O'Gara

REFEREE S J Dickinson (Australia)

15 March, Millennium Stadium, Cardiff

WALES 29 (2G 5PG)
FRANCE 12 (4PG)

WALES: L M Byrne; M A Jones, T G L Shanklin, G L Henson, S M Williams; J Hook, M Phillips; G D Jenkins, H Bennett, A R Jones, I M Gough, A-W.Jones, J Thomas, R P Jones (*captain*), M E Williams *Substitutions:* M Rees for Bennett (56 mins); S M Jones for Hook (56 mins); D J Jones for Jenkins (temp 47 to 52 mins) and for A R Jones (70 mins); I Evans for Gough (70 mins)

SCORERS *Tries:* S M Williams, M E Williams *Conversions:* S M Jones (2) *Penalty Goals:* Hook (3), S M Jones (2)

FRANCE: A Floch; V Clerc, Y Jauzion, D Traille, J Malzieu; D Skrela, J-B Elissalde; F Barcella, D Szarzewski, N Mas, L Nallet (*captain*), J Thion, T Dusautoir, J Bonnaire, F Ouedraogo *Substitutions:* W Servat for Szarzewski (43 mins); E Vermeulen for Ouedraogo (60 mins); J-B Poux for Mas (60 mins); D Yachvili for Elissalde (62 mins); F Trinh-Duc for Skrela (62 mins); C Heymans for Floch (66 mins); A Mela for Thion (74 mins)

SCORERS *Penalty Goals:* Elissalde (3), Yachvili

REFEREE M Jonker (South Africa)

YELLOW CARD G L Henson (39 mins)

Getty Images

Italy had to wait until the final game for their only victory, but it was a glorious one, against Scotland.

INTERNATIONAL CHAMPIONSHIP RECORDS 1883–2008

PREVIOUS WINNERS

1883 England	1884 England	1885 Not completed
1886 England & Scotland	1887 Scotland	1888 Not completed
1889 Not completed	1890 England & Scotland	1891 Scotland
1892 England	1893 Wales	1894 Ireland
1895 Scotland	1896 Ireland	1897 Not completed
1898 Not completed	1899 Ireland	1900 Wales
1901 Scotland	1902 Wales	1903 Scotland
1904 Scotland	1905 Wales	1906 Ireland & Wales
1907 Scotland	1908 Wales	1909 Wales
1910 England	1911 Wales	1912 England & Ireland
1913 England	1914 England	1920 England & Scotland & Wales
1921 England	1922 Wales	1923 England
1924 England	1925 Scotland	1926 Scotland & Ireland
1927 Scotland & Ireland	1928 England	1929 Scotland
1930 England	1931 Wales	1932 England & Ireland & Wales
1933 Scotland	1934 England	1935 Ireland
1936 Wales	1937 England	1938 Scotland
1939 England & Ireland & Wales	1947 England & Wales	1948 Ireland
1949 Ireland	1950 Wales	1951 Ireland
1952 Wales	1953 England	1954 England & Wales & France
1955 Wales & France	1956 Wales	1957 England
1958 England	1959 France	1960 England & France
1961 France	1962 France	1963 England
1964 Scotland & Wales	1965 Wales	1966 Wales
1967 France	1968 France	1969 Wales
1970 Wales & France	1971 Wales	1972 Not completed
1973 Five Nations tie	1974 Ireland	1975 Wales
1976 Wales	1977 France	1978 Wales
1979 Wales	1980 England	1981 France
1982 Ireland	1983 Ireland & France	1984 Scotland
1985 Ireland	1986 Scotland & France	1987 France
1988 Wales & France	1989 France	1990 Scotland
1991 England	1992 England	1993 France
1994 Wales	1995 England	1996 England
1997 France	1998 France	1999 Scotland
2000 England	2001 England	2002 France
2003 England	2004 France	2005 Wales
2006 France	2007 France	2008 Wales

England have won the title outright 25 times; Wales 24; France 16; Scotland 14; Ireland 10; Italy 0.

TRIPLE CROWN WINNERS

England (23 times) 1883, 1884, 1892, 1913, 1914, 1921, 1923, 1924, 1928, 1934, 1937, 1954, 1957, 1960, 1980, 1991, 1992, 1995, 1996, 1997, 1998, 2002, 2003.

Wales (19 times) 1893, 1900, 1902, 1905, 1908, 1909, 1911, 1950, 1952, 1965, 1969, 1971, 1976, 1977, 1978, 1979, 1988, 2005, 2008.

Scotland (10 times) 1891, 1895, 1901, 1903, 1907, 1925, 1933, 1938, 1984, 1990.

Ireland (Nine times) 1894, 1899, 1948, 1949, 1982, 1985, 2004, 2006, 2007.

GRAND SLAM WINNERS

England (12 times) 1913, 1914, 1921, 1923, 1924, 1928, 1957, 1980, 1991, 1992, 1995, 2003.

Wales (Ten times) 1908, 1909, 1911, 1950, 1952, 1971, 1976, 1978, 2005, 2008.

France (Eight times) 1968, 1977, 1981, 1987, 1997, 1998, 2002, 2004.

Scotland (Three times) 1925, 1984, 1990.

Ireland (Once) 1948.

THE SIX NATIONS CHAMPIONSHIP 2000–2008

COMPOSITE NINE-SEASON TABLE

	P	W	D	L	Pts
France	45	33	0	12	**66**
Ireland	45	31	0	14	**62**
England	45	30	0	15	**60**
Wales	45	20	2	23	**42**
Scotland	45	13	1	31	**27**
Italy	45	6	1	38	**13**

CHIEF RECORDS

RECORD	DETAIL		SET
Most team points in season	229 by England	in five matches	2001
Most team tries in season	29 by England	in five matches	2001
Highest team score	80 by England	80–23 v Italy	2001
Biggest team win	57 by England	80–23 v Italy	2001
Most team tries in match	12 by Scotland	v Wales	1887
Most appearances	56 for Ireland	C M H Gibson	1964 - 1979
Most points in matches	479 for England	J P Wilkinson	1998 - 2008
Most points in season	89 for England	J P Wilkinson	2001
Most points in match	35 for England	J P Wilkinson	v Italy, 2001
Most tries in matches	24 for Scotland	I S Smith	1924 - 1933
Most tries in season	8 for England	C N Lowe	1914
	8 for Scotland	I S Smith	1925
Most tries in match	5 for Scotland	G C Lindsay	v Wales, 1887
Most cons in matches	81 for England	J P Wilkinson	1998 - 2008
Most cons in season	24 for England	J P Wilkinson	2001
Most cons in match	9 for England	J P Wilkinson	v Italy, 2001
Most pens in matches	93 for Wales	N R Jenkins	1991 - 2001
Most pens in season	18 for England	S D Hodgkinson	1991
	18 for England	J P Wilkinson	2000
	18 for France	G Merceron	2002
Most pens in match	7 for England	S D Hodgkinson	v Wales, 1991
	7 for England	C R Andrew	v Scotland, 1995
	7 for England	J P Wilkinson	v France, 1999
	7 for Wales	N R Jenkins	v Italy, 2000
	7 for France	G Merceron	v Italy, 2002
	7 for Scotland	C D Paterson	v Wales, 2007
Most drops in matches	9 for France	J-P Lescarboura	1982 - 1988
	9 for England	C R Andrew	1985 – 1997
	9 for England	J P Wilkinson	1998 - 2008
Most drops in season	5 for France	G Camberabero	1967
	5 for Italy	D Dominguez	2000
	5 for Wales	N R Jenkins	2001
	5 for England	J P Wilkinson	2003
Most drops in match	3 for France	P Albaladejo	v Ireland, 1960
	3 for France	J-P Lescarboura	v England, 1985
	3 for Italy	D Dominguez	v Scotland 2000
	3 for Wales	N R Jenkins	v Scotland 2001

FOUR IN A ROW

By Iain Spragg

New Zealand staged a stunning second-half fightback against Australia in a dramatic denouement to the Tri-Nations season in Brisbane to triumph in the Suncorp Stadium and maintain their virtual monopoly on the southern hemisphere's most prized title.

The 13th Tri-Nations was only decided in the final game of the campaign with the All Blacks and Wallabies both in contention to be crowned champions and after 80 minutes of enthralling, high octane action in Brisbane, it was the All Blacks who finally emerged victorious.

Trailing 17–7 early in the second half, Graham Henry's side's previously unchallenged grip on the title seemed to be slipping but inspired by man of the match Dan Carter, New Zealand rallied to score 21 unanswered points in 17 devastating minutes to wreck the Wallaby dream, claim a 28–24 win and, in the process, retain both the Tri-Nations and the Bledisloe Cup.

Victory gave the all-conquering Kiwis an unprecedented fourth consecutive Tri-Nations title, their ninth in total, and no doubt helped dull the pain of their World Cup disappointment. For Australia, who had begun the season with such promise, the wait for their first crown since 2001 goes on.

"This result definitely ranks right up there," said Carter after the match. "We had a pretty new-look side and a lot of new faces. After the start of the tournament and a couple of losses early on, we had our backs against the wall. To fight back like we did and come away with three really big wins is great.

"It was tough out there. We weren't really playing in the first half. We were taking the easy route and we really had to step up the intensity and keep the self-belief.

"It was great to get the win and hold onto a couple of trophies that mean a lot to this side and the country. There are some pretty happy guys in the changing room."

The chances of the All Blacks celebrating another Tri-Nations triumph had seemed distinctly remote after the tournament's early exchanges. Their opener in early July against South Africa in Wellington certainly went according to plan – Jerome Kaino's try and 14 points from Carter's left boot securing a 19–8 win at the Westpac Stadium and extending the side's record unbeaten run on home soil to 30 matches – but the victory was to prove deceptive.

Seven days later the two sides crossed swords again, this time at Carisbrook, but the Springboks were clearly stung by defeat in Wellington and the first blemish on their record as world champions.

The All Blacks were only able to muster a solitary try from replacement Sione Lauaki but seemed to have been rescued by Carter once again, who kicked 23 points, only to have the game ripped from their grasp at the death. Trailing 28–23 with four minutes left, South Africa delivered the knockout blow with a stunning solo try from scrum half Ricky Januarie, calmly converted by Francois Steyn, and despite two late but wayward drop goal attempts from Carter, the Springboks held out for a famous 30–28 win. The All Blacks winning run at home was finally at an end and South Africa had their first victory in Dunedin in a century of trying.

"It took us 100 years to win here and it might take us another 100 years to win another one, but we're ecstatic," said Jean de Villiers. "The guys have been working hard on what we did wrong last week in the first match and we seemed to get it right today. When we scored that try we told ourselves we were in the same position three years ago and let it slip, so we stuck to our guns today."

South African joy, however, was short-lived as they crossed the Tasman Sea to face Australia in Perth a week later and were brought down to earth with an abrupt bump. The Springboks looked fatigued in the Subiaco Oval and while the Wallabies only found any rhythm in sporadic bursts, tries from Lote Tuqiri and skipper Stirling Mortlock were enough to see off the visitors and Australia ran out 16–9 winners.

The Wallabies were now the only unbeaten side in the competition, albeit having played just once, and hopes of a first Tri-Nations title in seven years were dramatically raised after the clash with New Zealand in Sydney at the end of July.

Australia had lost six of their seven previous games against their Antipodean neighbours but a superb defensive effort, coupled with an uncharacteristically error-strewn Kiwi performance, set the tone for the game and tries from Ryan Cross, Peter Hynes, Rocky Elsom and James Horwill, all converted by Matt Giteau, were enough to secure a famous 34–19 victory and condemn the All Blacks to back-to-back Test defeats for the first time since 2004.

Gallo Images / Getty Images

South Africa passed the 50-point mark against Australia in Johannesburg.

"It was a great performance and I'm very proud of the lads," said coach Robbie Deans, the imported Kiwi in charge of the Wallabies for the first time in a Bledisloe Cup clash. "A lot was asked of them, we didn't have a lot of possession and we had to defend for long periods. They did that well and created turnovers. When the All Blacks scored after half-time it was a pretty tough mental test but the guys got up and responded and finished well."

The Australians were now buoyant while, by their own high standards, New Zealand were close to disarray but the opportunity for the All Blacks to exact swift revenge came a week later when the old rivals met again in Auckland.

Defeat for the home side would have all but crushed their title aspirations but the All Blacks were in no mood for further humiliation, scoring four tries to secure a bonus point and a comprehensive 39–10 win.

The result threw the tournament wide open and when Henry's side travelled to Cape Town and beat the Springboks 19–0 at Newlands, the All Blacks were back in the driving seat.

There was further disappointment for South Africa in the second of their three home games in the competition. Australia were the opposition in Durban and the Boks knew they needed a bonus point win to stay in title contention. However, it was the Wallabies who held sway in the Absa Stadium from the start.

Giteau landed an early penalty, prop Benn Robinson scored the game's first try and Australia were 10–0 to the good at the break. Two second-half tries from Adrian Jacobs gave South Africa brief hope but further scores for the Wallabies from Tuqiri and Mortlock put pay to the fight-back and the Springboks were beaten 27–15. It was Australia's first Tri-Nations win on the road since 2001 and the end of South Africa's challenge for another season.

The result set up a title decider between Australia and New Zealand in Brisbane in September but before the winner-takes-all clash, the Wallabies had to face the Springboks again. The game at Ellis Park pitted a team desperate for revenge against a side with one eye on future battles and it was to be a hugely one-sided encounter as South Africa ran riot.

Wing Jongi Nokwe made Tri-Nations history in Johannesburg, becoming the first player to score four tries in a single game as the Springboks ran in eight tries to one to emerge 53–8 winners and end their first season as reigning world champions on a high.

"We were under a lot of pressure but the coach stuck with the players and this win feels good after the last three weeks," admitted skipper Victor Matfield. "It's an awesome victory, especially after the last three weeks. I think character comes out when the going gets tough. Today the guys showed they've got a lot of character."

The stage was now set for the battle royal in Brisbane. Australia started the brighter but it was the All Blacks who drew first blood after Jimmy Cowan's quick tap penalty to send Mils Muliaina over. The Wallabies hit back with their first try in first-half injury time when Adam Ashley-Cooper was played in by Peter Hynes and there were only three points separating the two sides at the break.

The next 40 minutes would be pivotal and it was Australia who edged ahead five minutes in after Giteau made a superb break and Horwill was on hand to finish off the move. The score stung the Kiwis into decisive action and they took the game away from their hosts with quick-fire scores from Tony Woodcock, replacement Piri Weepu and a superb Carter solo effort. A late score from Cross ensured the All Blacks were unable to rest on their laurels in the dying minutes, but it was too little too late and New Zealand were the kings of the southern hemisphere again.

"It was a marvellous competition and a great game of rugby which either side could have won," conceded All Black coach Henry after a result which went a long way to justifying the New Zealand Rugby Union's faith in him after the side's World Cup turmoil. "I have a huge amount of respect for what the guys have done. They showed a lot of guts and togetherness to come back from 10 points down, so I am exceptionally proud of the boys."

TRI-NATIONS 2008: FINAL TABLE

	P	W	D	L	F	A	Bonus	Pts
New Zealand	6	4	0	2	152	106	**3**	**19**
Australia	6	3	0	3	119	163	**2**	**14**
South Africa	6	2	0	4	115	117	**2**	**10**

Points: win 4; draw 2; four or more tries, or defeat by seven or fewer points 1

5 July, Westpac Stadium, Wellington

NEW ZEALAND 19 (1G 4PG) SOUTH AFRICA 8 (1PG 1T)

NEW ZEALAND: J M Muliaina; S W Sivivatu, C G Smith, M A Nonu, R N Wulf; D W Carter, A M Ellis; T D Woodcock, A K Hore, G M Somerville, B C Thorn, A J Williams, A J Thomson, J Kaino, R Soíoialo (*captain*) *Substitutions:* S T Lauaki for Thomson (60 mins); L R MacDonald for Sivivatu (68 mins); K F Mealamu for Hore (72 mins); N S Tialata for Somerville (74 mins); Q J Cowan for Ellis (74 mins)

SCORERS *Try*: Kaino *Conversion*: Carter *Penalty Goals*: Carter (4)

SOUTH AFRICA: C A Jantjes; O M Ndungane, A A Jacobs, J de Villiers, B G Habana; A D James, E R Januarie; G G Steenkamp, J W Smit (*captain*), C J van der Linde, J P Botha, V Matfield, J H Smith, J C van Niekerk, S W P Burger *Substitutions:* B W du Plessis for Smit (37 mins); B V Mujati for Van der Linde (46 mins); L A Watson for Van Niekerk (58 mins); F P L Steyn for James (58 mins); P C Montgomery for Jantjes (63 mins); A Bekker for Botha (72 mins); J H J Conradie for Januarie (72 mins)

SCORERS *Try:* Habana *Penalty Goal*: James

REFEREE S J Dickinson (Australia)

12 July, Carisbrook, Dunedin

NEW ZEALAND 28 (1G 6PG 1DG)
SOUTH AFRICA 30 (1G 5PG 1DG 1T)

NEW ZEALAND: J M Muliaina; S W Sivivatu, C G Smith, M A Nonu, R N Wulf; D W Carter, A M Ellis; T D Woodcock, A K Hore, I F Afoa, A F Boric, A J Williams, A J Thomson, J Kaino, R Soíoialo (*captain*) *Substitutions:* K J OíNeill for Williams (28 mins); L R MacDonald for Sivivatu (40 mins); S T Lauaki for Kaino (53 mins); K F Mealamu for Hore (55 mins); N S Tialata for Afoa (69 mins)

SCORERS *Try*: Lauaki *Conversion*: Carter *Penalty Goals*: Carter (6) *Dropped Goal*: Carter

SOUTH AFRICA: P C Montgomery; J-P R Pietersen, A A Jacobs, J de Villiers, B G Habana; A D James, E R Januarie; G G Steenkamp, B W du Plessis, C J van der Linde, J P Botha, V Matfield (*captain*), J H Smith, J C van Niekerk, S W P Burger *Substitutions:* F P L Steyn for Jacobs (46 mins); L A Watson for Van Niekerk (60 mins); C A Jantjes for Montgomery (60 mins); A Bekker for Botha (temp 49 to 60 mins and 66 mins); R Pienaar for James (73 mins); S B Brits for Du Plessis (73 mins); B V Mujati for Steenkamp (temp 53 to 60 mins)

SCORERS *Tries:* Pietersen, Januarie *Conversion*: Steyn *Penalty Goals*: Montgomery (3), James (2) *Dropped Goal*: James

REFEREE M Goddard (Australia)

YELLOW CARD V Matfield (72 mins)

19 July, Subiaco Oval, Perth

AUSTRALIA 16 (1PG 1DG 2T)
SOUTH AFRICA 9 (3PG)

AUSTRALIA: A P Ashley-Cooper; P J Hynes, S A Mortlock (*captain*), B S Barnes, L D Tuqiri; M J Giteau, L Burgess; B A Robinson, S T Moore, A K E Baxter, J E Horwill, N C Sharpe, R D Elsom, W L Palu, G B Smith *Substitutions:* R P Cross for Mortlock (48 mins); S J Cordingley for Burgess (71 mins); T Polota-Nau for Moore (71 mins); M J Dunning for Baxter (71 mins); H J McMeniman for Elsom (temp 21 to 27 mins) and for Sharpe (71 mins); P R Waugh for Elsom (79 mins); D A Mitchell for Palu (79 mins)

SCORERS *Tries*: Tuqiri, Mortlock *Penalty Goal*: Giteau *Dropped Goal*: Barnes

SOUTH AFRICA: C A Jantjes; J-P R Pietersen, F P L Steyn, J de Villiers, B G Habana; A D James, E R Januarie; G G Steenkamp, S B Brits, C J van der Linde, J P Botha, V Matfield (*captain*), J H Smith, P J Spies, S W P Burger *Substitutions:* R Kankowski for Burger (48 mins); J A Strauss for Brits (51 mins); T Mtwarira for Steenkamp (51 mins); A Bekker for Kankowski (temp 61 to 65 mins) and for Botha (65 mins); R Pienaar for Habana (65 mins); P J Grant for James (65 mins); B V Mujati for Van der Linde (77 mins)

SCORERS *Penalty Goals*: Steyn (2), James

REFEREE B J Lawrence (New Zealand)

26 July, ANZ Stadium, Sydney

AUSTRALIA 34 (4G 1PG 1DG)
NEW ZEALAND 19 (2G 1T)

AUSTRALIA: A P Ashley-Cooper; P J Hynes, R P Cross, B S Barnes, L D Tuqiri; M J Giteau, L Burgess; B A Robinson, S T Moore, A K E Baxter, J E Horwill, N C Sharpe, R D Elsom, W L Palu, G B Smith (*captain*) *Substitutions:* T Polota-Nau for Moore (58 mins); P R Waugh for Elsom (58 mins); D J Vickerman for Sharpe (61 mins); M J Dunning for Baxter (75 mins); T Tahu for Giteau (76 mins)

SCORERS *Tries*: Cross, Hynes, Elsom, Horwill *Conversions:* Giteau (4) *Penalty Goal*: Giteau *Dropped Goal*: Giteau

NEW ZEALAND: J M Muliaina; A T Tuitavake, R D Kahui, M A Nonu, S W Sivivatu; D W Carter, A M Ellis; T D Woodcock, A K Hore, G M Somerville, B C Thorn, A J Williams, R Soíoialo (*captain*), J Kaino, D J Braid *Substitutions:* S T Lauaki for Braid (48 mins); K F Mealamu for Hore (48 mins); I F Afoa for Somerville (58 mins); C G Smith for Nonu (62 mins); Q J Cowan for Ellis (temp 44 to 56 mins and 69 mins)

SCORERS *Tries*: Muliaina, Hore, Ellis *Conversions*: Carter (2)

REFEREE C Joubert (South Africa)

YELLOW CARD B C Thorn (5 mins)

2 August, Eden Park, Auckland

NEW ZEALAND 39 (2G 5PG 2T)
AUSTRALIA 10 (1G 1PG)

NEW ZEALAND: J M Muliaina; R D Kahui, C G Smith, M A Nonu, S W Sivivatu; D W Carter, Q J Cowan; T D Woodcock, A K Hore, G M Somerville, B C Thorn, A J Williams, J Kaino, R Soíoialo, R H McCaw (*captain*) *Substitutions:* I F Afoa for Somerville (58 mins); K F Mealamu for Hore (66 mins); A T Tuitavake for Smith (68 mins); P A T Weepu for Cowan (73 mins); A J Thomson for Kaino (74 mins); S R Donald for Kahui (74 mins); A F Boric for Thorn (78 mins)

SCORERS *Tries*: Woodcock (2), Nonu (2) *Conversions*: Carter (2) *Penalty Goals:* Carter (5)

AUSTRALIA: A P Ashley-Cooper; P J Hynes, S A Mortlock (*captain*), B S Barnes, L D Tuqiri; M J Giteau, L Burgess; B A Robinson, S T Moore, A K E Baxter, J E Horwill, N C Sharpe, P R Waugh, W L Palu, G B Smith *Substitutions:* D A Mitchell for Ashley-Cooper (40 mins); T Polota-Nau for Moore (51 mins); D J Vickerman for Sharpe (temp 27 to 37 mins and 51 mins); H J McMeniman for Waugh (58 mins); R P Cross for Barnes (74 mins)

SCORERS *Try*: Ashley-Cooper *Conversion:* Giteau *Penalty Goal*: Giteau

REFEREE S M Lawrence (South Africa)

16 August, Newlands, Cape Town

SOUTH AFRICA 0
NEW ZEALAND 19 (2G 1T)

SOUTH AFRICA: P C Montgomery; J-P R Pietersen, A A Jacobs, J de Villiers, B G Habana; A D James, P F du Preez; T Mtawarira, B W du Plessis, C J van der Linde, A Bekker, V Matfield (*captain*), J H Smith, P J Spies, S W P Burger *Substitutions:* C A Jantjes for Habana (47 mins); F P L Steyn for Montgomery (57 mins); E R Januarie for Du Preez (59 mins); L A Watson for Burger (59 mins); J A Strauss for Du Plessis (75 mins); D J Rossouw for Spies (75 mins); B V Mujati for Van der Linde (76 mins)

NEW ZEALAND: J M Muliaina; R D Kahui, C G Smith, M A Nonu, S W Sivivatu; D W Carter, Q J Cowan; T D Woodcock, A K Hore, G M Somerville, B C Thorn, A J Williams, J Kaino, R Soíoialo, R H McCaw (*captain*) *Substitutions:* I Toeava for Sivivatu (23 mins); I F Afoa for Somerville (48 mins); P A T Weepu for Cowan (52 mins); K F Mealamu for Hore (60 mins); A F Boric for Thorn (77 mins); A J Thomson for Soíoialo (78 mins); S R Donald for Carter (78 mins);

SCORERS *Tries*: Smith, Carter, Mealamu *Conversions*: Carter (2)

REFEREE M Goddard (Australia)

23 August, ABSA Stadium, King's Park, Durban

SOUTH AFRICA 15 (1G 1PG 1T)
AUSTRALIA 27 (3G 2PG)

SOUTH AFRICA: C A Jantjes; J-P R Pietersen, A A Jacobs, J de Villiers, J L Nokwe; A D James, P F du Preez; T Mtawarira, B W du Plessis, C J van der Linde, A Bekker, V Matfield (*captain*), J H Smith, P J Spies, S W P Burger *Substitutions:* P C Montgomery for Pietersen (44 mins); B V Mujati for Mtawarira (55 mins); F P L Steyn for James (55 mins); J C van Niekerk for Spies (56 mins); L A Watson for Smith (62 mins); E R Januarie for Du Preez (62 mins); J A Strauss for Du Plessis (79 mins); P J Spies back for Steyn (temp 59 to 68 mins)

SCORERS *Tries:* Jacobs (2) *Conversion*: Montgomery *Penalty Goal*: James

AUSTRALIA: D A Mitchell; P J Hynes, S A Mortlock (*captain*), B S Barnes, L D Tuqiri; M J Giteau, S J Cordingley; B A Robinson, S T Moore, M J Dunning, J E Horwill, D J Vickerman, R D Elsom, W L Palu, G B Smith *Substitutions:* R P Cross for Barnes (19 mins); D W Mumm for Vickerman (38 mins); A K E Baxter for Dunning (54 mins); B R Sheehan for Cordingley (54 mins); T Tahu for Hynes (56 mins); P R Waugh for Palu (temp 47 to 50 mins and 76 mins); T Polota-Nau for Horwill (79 mins)

SCORERS *Tries*: Robinson, Tuqiri, Mortlock *Conversions:* Giteau (3) *Penalty Goals*: Giteau (2)

REFEREE L E Bray (New Zealand)

30 August, Coca-Cola Ellis Park, Johannesburg

SOUTH AFRICA 53 (5G 1PG 3T) AUSTRALIA 8 (1PG 1T)

SOUTH AFRICA: C A Jantjes; O M Ndungane, A A Jacobs, J de Villiers, J L Nokwe; A D James, P F du Preez; T Mtawarira, B W du Plessis, B V Mujati, A Bekker, V Matfield (*captain*), J H Smith, P J Spies, S W P Burger *Substitutions:* J N du Plessis for Mujati (45 mins); P C Montgomery for Nokwe (51 mins); R Pienaar for James (56 mins); E R Januarie for Du Preez (67 mins); J A Strauss for B W Du Plessis (71 mins); D J Rossouw for Bekker (73 mins); L A Watson for Ndungane (temp 67 to 73 mins) and for Jacobs (73 mins)

SCORERS *Tries:* Nokwe (4), Bekker, Jacobs, Pienaar, Ndungane *Conversions*: James (3), Montgomery (2) *Penalty Goal*: James

AUSTRALIA: A P Ashley-Cooper; P J Hynes, S A Mortlock (*captain*), T Tahu, L D Tuqiri; M J Giteau, S J Cordingley; B A Robinson, T Polota-Nau, M J Dunning, J E Horwill, H J McMeniman, R D Elsom, W L Palu, P R Waugh *Substitutions:* A K E Baxter for Dunning (31 mins); G B Smith for Waugh (45 mins); S T Moore for Polota-Nau (46 mins); R P Cross for Tahu (51 mins); D A Mitchell for Hynes (51 mins); B R Sheehan for Cordingley (53 mins); Dunning back for Robinson (58 mins); D W Mumm for McMeniman (67 mins)

SCORERS *Try*: Mitchell *Penalty Goal*: Giteau

REFEREE B J Lawrence (New Zealand)

13 September, Suncorp Stadium, Brisbane

AUSTRALIA 24 (3G 1PG) NEW ZEALAND 28 (4G)

AUSTRALIA: A P Ashley-Cooper; P J Hynes, R P Cross, S A Mortlock (*captain*), L D Tuqiri; M J Giteau, S J Cordingley; B A Robinson, S T Moore, A K E Baxter, J E Horwill, N C Sharpe, R D Elsom, W L Palu, G B Smith *Substitutions:* R N Brown for Palu (33 mins); H J McMeniman for Elsom (70 mins); A L Freier for Moore (71 mins)

SCORERS *Tries*: Ashley-Cooper, Horwill, Cross *Conversions:* Giteau (3) *Penalty Goal*: Giteau

NEW ZEALAND: J M Muliaina; R D Kahui, C G Smith, M A Nonu, S W Sivivatu; D W Carter, Q J Cowan; T D Woodcock, A K Hore, G M Somerville, B C Thorn, A J Williams, J Kaino, R Soíoialo, R H McCaw (*captain*), *Substitutions:* S R Donald for Nonu (50 mins); K F Mealamu for Hore (50 mins); I F Afoa for Somerville (50 mins); P A T Weepu for Cowan (54 mins); A F Boric for Thorn (78 mins)

SCORERS *Tries*: Muliaina, Woodcock, Weepu, Carter *Conversions*: Carter (4)

REFEREE J I Kaplan (South Africa)

TRI-NATIONS RECORDS 1996–2008

PREVIOUS WINNERS

1996 New Zealand	1997 New Zealand	1998 South Africa	1999 New Zealand
2000 Australia	2001 Australia	2002 New Zealand	2003 New Zealand
2004 South Africa	2005 New Zealand	2006 New Zealand	2007 New Zealand
2008 New Zealand			

GRAND SLAM WINNERS

New Zealand (Three times) 1996, 1997, 2003.

South Africa (Once) 1998.

TEAM RECORD	DETAIL		SET
Most team points in season	179 by N Zealand	in six matches	2006
Most team tries in season	18 by S Africa	in four matches	1997
Highest team score	61 by S Africa	61-22 v Australia (h)	1997
Biggest team win	49 by Australia	49-0 v S Africa (h)	2006
Most team tries in match	8 by S Africa	v Australia	1997
	8 by S Africa	v Australia	2008

INDIVIDUAL RECORD	DETAIL		SET
Most appearances	48 for Australia	G M Gregan	1996 to 2007
Most points in matches	328 for N Zealand	A P Mehrtens	1996 to 2004
Most points in season	99 for N Zealand	D W Carter	2006
Most points in match	29 for N Zealand	A P Mehrtens	v Australia (h) 1999
Most tries in matches	16 for N Zealand	C M Cullen	1996 to 2002
Most tries in season	7 for N Zealand	C M Cullen	2000
Most tries in match	4 for S Africa	J L Nokwe	v Australia (h) 2008
Most cons in matches	37 for N Zealand	D W Carter	2003 to 2008
Most cons in season	14 for N Zealand	D W Carter	2006
Most cons in match	6 for S Africa	J H de Beer	v Australia (h),1997
Most pens in matches	82 for N Zealand	A P Mehrtens	1996 to 2004
Most pens in season	21 for N Zealand	D W Carter	2006
Most pens in match	9 for N Zealand	A P Mehrtens	v Australia (h) 1999

From 1996 to 2008 inclusive, each nation played four matches in a season, except in 2006 and 2008 when the nations each played six matches.

SAXONS CLAIM FOURTH CUP

Getty Images

England are ecstatic at another victory.

England's second string continued their dominance of the Churchill Cup as the Saxons came from behind in the Cup final against Scotland A to run out convincing 36–19 winners and suggest that while the senior team was being mauled by New Zealand thousands of miles away in Christchurch, the future of the English game was at least in safe hands.

It was England's fourth triumph in the tournament in six attempts and their victory at Toyota Park in Chicago was a fitting reward for a side that had amassed 98 points in their two previous games against the USA and an Irish second XV.

"This squad has been an absolute pleasure to work with," said Saxons coach Steve Bates after his side lifted the trophy. "Today was a great all round team performance. By winning the tournament, we've achieved what we set out to do and played some great rugby along the way."

The sixth Churchill Cup was back in Canada for the group stages after England had staged the 2007 event and once again featured the Canucks, the USA, the Saxons, Ireland and Scotland's A sides and an Argentina XV, returning to the competition for the first time since 2005.

The tournament began in early June with the Saxons taking on the USA in Ottawa and the pre-match predictions of an English rout proved wholly accurate as Bates' side ran in nine tries, including a hat-trick from Bath wing Matt Banahan, to record a 64–10 victory that sent out an ominous message to the rest of the sides.

England followed up their resounding victory with another good display against Ireland A at Fletcher's Field in Toronto a week later. The Irish provided stiffer resistance than the Americans but the Saxons still crossed the whitewash six times, this time with a brace from Banahan, to register a 34–12 win and book their place in the Cup final.

In contrast, Scotland's progress to the final was altogether more sedate as the second string battled past Canada in their opener in Ottawa, emerging 24–10 winners thanks to a hat-trick from Steve Jones and then had to hold their nerve in a tense 27–24 victory over Argentina in Kingston, winning a close encounter with the Pumas in which the only difference between the two sides was a Gordon Ross penalty.

Ireland A's defeat to England was preceded by a 46–9 triumph over the USA in Kingston to confirm their place in the Plate final against Argentina while Canada's two reverses against the Saxons and Scotland meant they would face the States for the Churchill Bowl. The six teams relocated to America and Toyota Park, the home of MLS side Chicago Fire, for their respective games and the stage was set for the climax of the tournament.

England went into the final as clear favourites but it was Scotland who were quickest out of the blocks and took an early lead through a Ross drop goal. The Saxons were stung into action and Banahan crashed over for the only try of the first-half to give England a 16–9 lead at the interval.

It was still neck and neck as the second-half unfolded. Colin Gregor crossed after just four minutes of the restart and when Ross converted, the two teams were locked at 16–all. Ross and England number 10 Ryan Lamb traded penalties to take it to 19–19 but unfortunately for the Scots, it was to be the closest they got as the Saxons ran riot in the final 23 minutes to score three more tries from Nick Abendanon, Jordan Crane and Ugo Monye. England had rediscovered their killer instinct at exactly the right time and they were Churchill Cup champions again.

"I'm very proud of the boys and very pleased with the performances they put in," Saxons captain Will Skinner said after lifting the trophy. "The Scots came at us hard especially in the first two minutes and then again at the beginning of the second half, but luckily we were able to hold them out."

Scotland's head coach Rob Moffat conceded his side had not been ruthless enough when they had the Saxons on the back foot.

"We were probably seen as underdogs going into this game but we came here to win the Barclays Churchill Cup. The boys trained very well over the three weeks and performed well at times. We just weren't good enough on the day," Moffat said.

"There were two or three good chances today and we just didn't take them. Throughout the tour we have played the type of rugby that we wanted to play and I'm proud of the players for achieving that."

In the Plate final, the Irish finished the tournament with a flourish to see off Argentina 33–8. Fly-half Jonny Sexton was the star turn for the men in green with a fabled full house of try, conversion, penalty for a personal haul of 18 points and the Man of the Match award. Denis Fogarty, Darren Cave and Ian Kealty also crossed for Ireland and all the Pumas could muster in reply was a try from substitute Gabriel Ascarate and an Ignacio Mieres penalty.

"We are delighted with the effort we put in," said Ireland skipper Bob Casey. "You could see in the first half what we were trying to do and we could have had three or four more tries. In patches during this tournament we have shown the talent that is coming through in Irish rugby."

For Argentina, defeat was far from a disgrace for what was a side of amateurs. "It was very hard because we didn't have the ball in the first half and they scored a lot of points," said captain Juan Ignacio Gauthier. "We played better in the second half but they were just too far ahead.

"This competition was very important for us because we get to compete against professional players and although it was tough, we learnt a lot."

The North American clash for the Bowl between Canada and the USA also served as the annual contest for the Can-Am trophy – played between the two countries since 1976 – and was the definitive game of two halves as the USA dominated the first 40 minutes only to see the Canadians storm back after the interval.

The USA took a 10–0 first-half lead into the dressing room courtesy of a Salesi Sika try but Canada's superior fitness and forward power saw them reply with two tries apiece from Nanyak Dala and Ryan Smith and three conversions from Ander Monro to register a 26–10 win.

"We took it slowly in the first half and had to pump it up in the second," said Dala, who was named Man of the Match. "I think our fitness was a lot better than theirs and we started playing some rugby in the second half.

"Our coach Kieran Crowley has been coaching us to get us trying to move 20 or 30 metres up field rather than just 10. He is getting us to think more about the game and that helps us get into the right positions to score tries."

USA coach Scott Johnson was clear why his side had not managed to protect their lead.

"It boils down to one thing – it's clear that we haven't got the capacity to last the 80 minutes," he said. "They were spent at half-time. I have never seen a team that is leading 10–0 at half-time look so exhausted."

CHURCHILL CUP 2008 RESULTS

GROUP PHASE

7 June, Twin Elm Park, Ottawa	
Scotland A 24	**Canada** 10
England Saxons 64	**USA** 10
11 June, Richardson Stadium, Kingston	
Scotland A 27	**Argentina** A 24
USA 9	**Ireland A** 46
14 June, Fletcher's Field, Toronto	
Ireland A 12	**England Saxons** 34
Canada 16	**Argentina** A 17

GROUP TABLES

POOL A

	P	W	D	L	F	A	BP	Pts
Scotland A	2	2	0	0	53	34	2	10
Argentina XV	2	1	0	1	41	43	2	6
Canada	2	0	0	2	26	43	1	1

POOL B

	P	W	D	L	F	A	BP	Pts
Saxons	2	2	0	0	98	22	2	10
Ireland A	2	1	0	1	58	43	1	5
USA	2	0	0	2	19	110	0	0

CHURCHILL BOWL FINAL

21 June, Toyota Park, Chicago

CANADA 26 (3G, 1T) USA 10 (1G, 1PG)

CANADA: M Pyke; J Mensah Coker, B Keys, R Smith, J Pritchard; A Monro, E Fairhurst (captain); K Tkachuk, P Riordan, S Franklin, T Hotson, L Cudmore, A Kleeberger, N Dala, A Carpenter Substitutions: D Spicer for Mensah Coker (22 mins); S Ault for Cudmore (50 mins); M Pletch for Franklin (63 mins); M Webb for Carpenter (70 mins); H Boydens for Tkachuk (73 mins); A Wilson for Kleeberger (78 mins)

SCORERS *Tries*: Dala (2) Smith (2) *Conversions*: Monro (3)

USA: C Wyles; T Ngwenga, P Emerick, S Sika, G DeBartolo; M Hercus, M Petri; M MacDonald, M Crick, M Moekiola, B Wiedemer, J Giessen, T Clever (captain), J Lett, K Schubert Substitutions: R Shaw for Petrie (63 mins); H Bloomfield for Lett (63 mins); M Laulaupa'alu for Crick (66 mins), V Malifa for Hercus (70 mins); C Slaby for Moekiola (79 mins)

SCORERS *Try*: Sika *Conversion*: Hercus Penalty Goal: Hercus

REFEREE F Cuesta (Argentina)

CHURCHILL PLATE FINAL

21 June, Toyota Park, Chicago

IRELAND A 33 (2G, 2PG, 2T, 1DG)
ARGENTINA A 8 (1PG, 1T)

IRELAND A: D Hurley; M McCrea, D Cave, K Earls, B Tuohy; J Sexton, F Murphy; C Healy, D Fogarty, M Ross, D Ryan, B Casey (captain), N Best, J O'Connor, R Wilson Substitutions: T Hogan for Casey (59 mins); D Pollock for Wilson (64 mins); I Keatley for Sexton (70 mins); S Cronin for Fogarty (72 mins); F McFadden for McCrea (78 mins)

SCORERS *Tries*: Fogarty, Cave, Sexton, Keatley *Conversions*: Sexton (2) *Penalty Goals*: Sexton (2) *Drop Goal*: Sexton

ARGENTINA XV: L Barrera Oro; G Comacho, J Ignacio Gauthier (captain), F Amelong, F Merello; I Mieres, F Albarracin; D Rodriguez, R Maria, JP Orlandi, P Lagarrique, F Aranguren, A Creevy, G Fessia, A Abadie Substitutions: F Genoud for Creevy (54 mins); G Ascarate for Merello (64 mins); F Bettolli for Orlandi (72 mins); Kodela for Rodriguez (78 mins)

SCORERS *Try*: Ascarate *Penalty Goal*: Mieres

REFEREE C Henshall (USA)

CHURCHILL CUP FINAL

21 June, Toyota Park, Chicago

ENGLAND SAXONS 36 (2G, 4PG, 2T)
SCOTLAND A 19 (1G, 3PG, 1DG)

England Saxons: N Abendanon; U Monye, O Smith, A Allen, M Banahan; R Lamb, P Hodgson; A Clarke, G Chuter, J Forster, C Jones, G Skivington, C Robshaw, W Skinner (captain), J Crane Substitutions: T French for Clarke (55 mins); S Armitage for Robshaw (55 mins); S Hooper for Jones (67 mins); A Titterrell for Chuter (75 mins); B Foden for Banahan (79 mins); L Dickson for Hodgson (80 mins)

SCORERS *Tries*: Banahan, Abendanon, Crane, Monye. *Conversions*: Lamb (2) *Penalty Goals*: Lamb (4)

Scotland A: S Jones; M Robertson, R Dewey, C MacRae, R Reid; G Ross, C Gregor; E Kalman, F Thomson (captain), D Young, F Pringle, D Turner, J Eddie, A MacDonald, S Swindall Substitutions: J Dunbar for Pringle (41 mins); M McMillan for Robertson (50 mins); S Corsar for Young (55 mins); A Kelly for Thomson (59 mins); S Newlands for Swindall (65 mins); D Blair for Reid (67 mins)

SCORERS *Try*: Gregor *Conversion*: Ross *Penalty Goals*: Ross (3) *Drop Goal*: Ross

REFEREE S McDowell (Ireland)

KIWIS TRIUMPH AGAIN

By Iain Spragg

Marty Melville / Getty Images

DJ Forbes gets the party started in Hong Kong.

New Zealand produced another masterclass of sevens rugby to retain their IRB Sevens World Series title and underline their undisputed status as the kings of the shortened game. The New Zealanders wrapped up the IRB title at Twickenham on the penultimate weekend of the season to make it eight out of nine and leave the rest of the world trailing.

The Kiwis stamped their authority on the tournament from day one and triumphs in the first five events in Dubai, South Africa, New Zealand, America and Hong King ensured Gordon Tietjens' side were front runners throughout.

The previous season had seen the Kiwis almost surrender their title to Fiji, claiming victory in a tense encounter in Edinburgh on the final day of the campaign. Tietjens' team were crowned champions by a mere two points last year, but in 2007–08 there were no such dramas as they eclipsed second-placed South Africa by an imposing 48 points.

"It's been a huge year for us," the long-serving Teitjens said lifting the trophy. "It's probably one of the best years we've ever had. We've been battered, got a few injuries, lost a few players but it was great to see some of those young guys step up."

For Tietjens, who was appointed in 1994, another title confirmed his reputation as the game's most accomplished sevens coach and his captain DJ Forbes was quick to put his success into context.

"He is one of a kind," Forbes said. "Eight out of nine is unbelievable and it is probably one of the best records that any coach in any world sport has got. He deserves every accolade he gets."

The series kicked off in Dubai, where New Zealand had not triumphed since 2002, but they made it through to the final to face their perennial rivals Fiji. Two first-half tries from Zar Lawrence and a third from Nigel Hunt established a 21–0 advantage at the break but despite having two players sin-binned, the Fijians fought back with scores from Neumi Nanuku, Vereniki Goneva and Akuila Nawerecagi and the Kiwis were thankful for Steven Yates' late try that quelled the islanders' second revival and secured a 31–21 victory.

A week later in South Africa it was again New Zealand and Fiji in the final but this time the Fijians never threatened to upset the defending champions and two tries from young wing Victor Vito helped set up a comprehensive 34–7 win.

Teitjiens' team moved on to Wellington for their home event in February but this time there were new opponents in the final. Fiji were eliminated in the quarter-finals by Samoa, who went on to to beat Tonga in the semis and earn themselves the chance to defend the title they had won in 2007.

The final was a pulsating clash but with the final whistle looming and the two sides locked at 17–17, Vito raced over to give New Zealand their first triumph in Wellington for three years and preserve their 100 per cent record for the season.

The next stop was San Diego and although the Kiwis once again progressed impressively to the final, the big story was Kenya's march to the Cup semi-final. The Africans produced the shock of the season by beating England 17–7 in the quarter-final and although the dream died in the last four after a thumping 50–10 defeat to New Zealand, it was nonetheless a superb performance from Benjamin Ayimba's side.

"I'm proud of the boys," Ayimba said. "They've done very well in this tournament and I thank them for their maturity, playing at the level they've reached this week. The fans are always a huge part in our performance, they're always appreciated. But New Zealand were really on top of their game today and thanks to them they've showed us a few things we need to go away and work on."

South Africa, meanwhile, beat Samoa in the last four to set up a final clash with the All Blacks but once they surrendered a 17–0 first-half lead to the Kiwis, there was no way back for the Springboks and they were eventually beaten 27–12. The result against South Africa made it an unprecedented 34 consecutive wins for New Zealand, and sent them 32 points clear of the Springboks in the overall standings at the halfway point with Samoa in third and Fiji fourth.

It was five Cup triumphs out of five the following month in Hong Kong as New Zealand met South Africa in the final and the Kiwis once again proved too powerful, emerging 26–12 winners to confirm their mastery of the series. It was a spirited performance from the Springboks and coach Paul Treu said: "To come out here and go all the way to the Hong Kong Cup final is an awesome achievement for our young team. One thing that we have to realise is that we will never beat New Zealand physically. We will have to play the game much smarter."

His players certainly heeded his words when they arrived in Australia for the sixth instalment of the series. Both South Africa and New Zealand battled through to the final but this time it was the Africans who were able to celebrate after the final whistle as Fabian Juries' two tries gave the Boks a 15–7 win to end the Kiwis' unbeaten record and consolidate their own position in second place in the rankings.

South Africa's shock victory in Adelaide merely delayed the inevitable. But it did not all go quite according to plan. Comfortable winners of Pool A, New Zealand faced hosts England in the quarter-finals but were ambushed by Ben Ryan's team at Twickenham and lost 17–12. Their disappointment however was to prove short lived as they recovered to beat South Africa 19–12 in the Plate final and confirm themselves as the 2007–08 World Sevens Series champions.

Murrayfield played host to the eighth and final event at the end of the May and New Zealand were to show no signs of complacency in Edinburgh, gaining revenge over England in the final. The Kiwis stormed into a 19–0 lead with tries from Solomon King, David Smith and Chad Tuoro. England hit back with scores from Uche Oduoza and Ollie Phillips but Nigel Hunt scored late on to complete a 24–14 victory.

The Springboks' flying wing Juries finished the season as the competition's top try scorer with 41 while New Zealand's Tomasi Cama was top points scorer with 319.

IRB SEVENS WORLD SERIES 2007–08 POINTS

DUBAI: 30 NOVEMBER - 1 DECEMBER

New Zealand (20), **Fiji** (16), **South Africa** (12), **England** (12), **Argentina** (8), **Samoa** (6), **Kenya** (4), **Scotland** (4), **Australia** (2)

SOUTH AFRICA: 7–8 DECEMBER

New Zealand (20), **Fiji** (16), **South Africa** (12), **Argentina** (12), **Kenya** (8), **USA** (6), **Scotland** (4), **Samoa** (4), **Wales** (2)

NEW ZEALAND: 1–2 FEBRUARY

New Zealand (20), **Samoa** (16), **Australia** (12), **Tonga** (12), **South Africa** (8), **Wales** (6), **Fiji** (4), **Scotland** (4), **England** (2)

USA: 9–10 FEBRUARY

New Zealand (20), **South Africa** (16), **Samoa** (12), **Kenya** (12), **Fiji** (8), **Argentina** (6), **England** (4), **Scotland** (4), **Wales** (2)

HONG KONG: 28–30 MARCH

New Zealand (30), **South Africa** (24), **Fiji** (18), **Samoa** (18), **England** (8), **Kenya** (8), **Australia** (8), **Wales** (8), **France** (4), **Portugal** (4), **Argentina** (3), **Tonga** (2), **Canada** (2), **Russia** (1)

AUSTRALIA: 5–6 APRIL

South Africa (20), **New Zealand** (16), **Fiji** (12), **Samoa** (12), **Tonga** (8), **Kenya** (6), **Cook Islands** (4), **Australia** (4), **Argentina** (2)

ENGLAND: 24–25 MAY

Samoa (20), **Fiji** (16), **Argentina** (12), **England** (12), **New Zealand** (8), **South Africa** (6), **Scotland** (4), **Portugal** (4), **Australia** (2)

SCOTLAND: 31 MAY – 1 JUNE

New Zealand (20), **England** (16), **Wales** (12), **Samoa** (12), **South Africa** (8), **Scotland** (6), **France** (4), **Fiji** (4), **Australia** (2)

FINAL STANDINGS

New Zealand – 154 points	**South Africa** – 106
Samoa – 100	**Fiji** – 94
England – 54	**Argentina** – 43
Kenya – 38	**Australia** – 30
Wales – 30	**Scotland** – 2
Tonga – 22	**France** – 8
USA – 6	**Cook Islands** – 4
Portugal – 4	**Canada** – 2
Russia – 1	

PREVIOUS WINNERS

1990–00: New Zealand
2000–01: New Zealand
2001–02: New Zealand
2002–03: New Zealand
2003–04: New Zealand
2004–05: New Zealand
2005–06: Fiji
2006–07: New Zealand
2007–08: New Zealand

Simon Cross / Getty Images

South Africa, shocked and delighted in Adelaide.

Portugal won the Hannover Sevens in July to capture the title of European champions and lead the charge of the five regional qualifiers to next year's Rugby World Cup Sevens in Dubai.

Portugal, Wales, Georgia, Ireland and Italy all booked their places at the Dubai showpiece on 5–7 March 2009, joining England, France and Scotland, whose Cup quarter-final appearances at the 2005 event in Hong Kong guaranteed them a place in the draw.

The Portuguese lived up to their billing as top seeds at Hannover's AWD Arena, beating Wales by four tries to two to win the Cup final 26–12. The two sides had won through with tight victories over Ireland and Georgia, who also qualified for Dubai by reaching the Cup semi finals.

The fifth qualifying berth went to the winners of the Plate trophy, Italy, who battled first past hosts Germany and then a strong Spain side in the final. This quintet join Uruguay from South America, Samoa and Tonga from Oceania and Hong Kong the most recent qualifiers from Asia.

For the first time in 2009 the 24–team men's competition will run alongside a 16–team women's World Cup Sevens. Brazil, unbeaten in four years, have already qualified from South America, while England, the Netherlands, France, Russia, Spain and Italy have also made it through to the maiden event from Europe. They have since been joined by Australia and New Zeland from Oceania, South Africa and Uganda from Africa and Japan, Thailand and China from Asia.

The remaining regional qualifiers are:

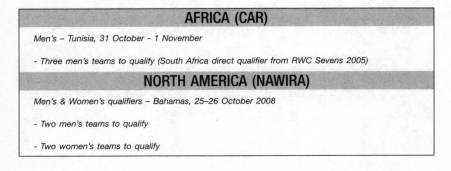

AFRICA (CAR)
Men's – Tunisia, 31 October - 1 November
- Three men's teams to qualify (South Africa direct qualifier from RWC Sevens 2005)
NORTH AMERICA (NAWIRA)
Men's & Women's qualifiers – Bahamas, 25–26 October 2008
- Two men's teams to qualify
- Two women's teams to qualify

BABY BLACKS TRIUMPH

Stu Forster/Getty Images

New Zealand proved too strong for England in the final.

New Zealand's Under-20s side claimed the inaugural Junior World Championship title, comprehensively beating England 38–3 in the final at the Liberty Stadium in Swansea to maintain the All Blacks' unquestioned dominance of the age-grade game.

The Junior World Championship and the parallel, second tier Junior World Trophy were introduced in 2008 by the IRB to replace the Under-19 and Under-21 tournaments. With the Kiwis the last team to lift the Under-19 trophy, it was little surprise that they emerged victorious in the new-look competition held in Wales a year later.

Divided into four pools based in Swansea, Cardiff, Newport and Wrexham, more than 400 young players from the 16 competing countries descended on the Principality in early June to cross swords but it was the irrepressible Baby Blacks who emerged as champions, sweeping all before them in a deluge of points and attacking, free-flowing rugby.

The tournament was a massive success and can only build on its achievements in years to come.

The young Kiwis amassed an incredible 173 points, including 25 tries, in their opening three group games before despatching hosts Wales in the semi-finals. England stood in their way in the final but Nigel Redman's side were unable to offer the New Zealanders any serious resistance and another four tries provided the platform for another convincing victory.

"I'm very confident a lot of our players will jump up to the All Black jersey before too long," New Zealand coach Russel Hilton-Jones said after his side's victory. "We've got a special group. I've been lucky enough to be involved in age-group rugby in New Zealand for six years and this is the best group of players I've had dealings with. We have cycles and this is a special cycle of players coming through from this tournament.

"We've had to work hard for our results. We've probably come home reasonably strongly in all five games we've played. I guess the key thing is we've worn down sides really well."

The Baby Blacks were drawn in Pool A alongside Ireland, Argentina and Tonga and began their campaign with a heavy 48–9 victory over the South Sea Islanders at the Arms Park in Cardiff. Four days later, Ireland were dispatched 65–10 and Argentina fared little better against the rampant Kiwis, who booked their place in the semi-finals with a 60–0 win.

In Pool B, South Africa were in equally impressive form, kicking off their campaign with a 108–18 landslide over the USA at Wrexham's Racecourse Ground, scoring 16 tries in the process. The young South Africans followed up with a 72–3 demolition over Scotland and confirmed their place in the last four with an altogether tighter 16–11 win over Samoa in their final group fixture.

England were drawn in Pool C with Australia, Fiji and Canada. The young Englishmen and their Wallaby counterparts brushed aside the challenge of both Fiji and the Canadians in their opening games to set up an eagerly anticipated group decider at Rodney Parade in Newport. It was a ferocious, keenly-contested clash but England finally emerged the 18–13 victors courtesy of a late try from wing Miles Benjamin to reach the semi-finals.

"It was a Test match played between two full-blooded teams with some brilliant players and at full intensity," said Redman. "There was a lot riding on it, winner takes all and producing a game like that is credit to both teams. It had just about everything."

Hosts Wales found themselves in Pool D and after victories over Italy and Japan, they needed to win against the unbeaten French at the Liberty Stadium to progress to the last four. It was to prove another tense, titanic clash but it was the home side who were celebrating at the final whistle thanks to a superb injury-time try from wing Leigh Halfpenny which wrapped up a dramatic 23–19 win.

"It was a tough game and one which we thought we had lost going into the final 10 minutes," admitted Wales assistant coach Rob Appleyard. "We stuck in there and never stopped trying. We kept going and obviously we were delighted when Leigh went over in the corner. It was a great finish to a very tough game."

The competition now split into two sections with New Zealand, South Africa, England and Wales contesting the semi-finals and the 12 other teams heading to a two-phase, play-off format to determine the final standings.

The first semi-final saw the Baby Blacks tackle Wales in Newport but despite giving the Kiwis their sternest test to date, there was no fairytale victory for the hosts. Halfpenny gave Wales a sixth-minute lead with a penalty but tries from hooker Quentin MacDonald and prop Paea Fa'anunu eased New Zealand into the lead. A second Halfpenny penalty before the break left the home side trailing by a mere four points at half-time but the Kiwis cut loose in the second period and further tries from Nasi Manu and Sean Maitland sealed a 31–6 victory and a place in the final.

"We put pressure on them in the first half when we relied on our defence to produce that pressure," said Wales captain Sam Warburton. "We went in at half time only 10–6 down and that was a huge improvement on last year. But we let it slip a bit in the second half but New Zealand, I think, are hands down the best team in the tournament."

The second semi-final between England and South Africa in Cardiff was a markedly tighter encounter but it was the English who held their nerve at a rain-soaked Arms Park to claim a 26–18 win. With just three minutes left on the clock, England held a precarious 21–18 lead but put the contest beyond doubt when prop Alex Corbisiero crashed over from a lineout drive.

"I am very disappointed but I take my hat off to the boys, they really stuck to their guns and in the second half I think we put ourselves under pressure," said Springbok captain Gerrit Jan van Velze. "We played all the rugby in our own half and we couldn't get into their half and turn it into points. All the best to England in the final."

The South Africans went on to salvage a degree of pride with a 43–18 victory over Wales in their third place play-off clash in Swansea but all eyes were on the final and the rampant Baby Blacks.

England knew it would take a monumental effort to stop the Kiwis but when Kade Poki went over for the first try of the match after 17 minutes, the writing was on the wall for the youngsters in white. Jackson Willison added a second after 20 minutes and although Alex Goode slotted a 26th-minute penalty to get England on the scoreboard, the momentum was firmly with the Kiwis.

Andre Taylor and Ryan Crotty both crossed the whitewash in the second-half for New Zealand and with England unable to trouble the scorers further, the only question was how many points the Baby Blacks would accumulate. To their credit, England dug deep defensively and the final score was 38–3 to the young All Blacks. "It is pretty special," said New Zealand captain Chris Smith. "It is the first ever one of these tournaments and we came here I think with a lot of pressure from a group of us that won the Under-19 tournament last year and we have always thought that we had a good team.

"England provided a great opposition for us, they were really up for the final and they have done well to get to the final. That was a really hard game and we only really pulled away in the last 20 minutes."

England were well beaten but far from disgraced and coach Nigel Redman was quick to pay tribute to the new junior world champions.

"New Zealand have been an awesome side now for two years," he said. "They won the tournament last year by putting 30-points plus on everyone. We knew it would be a very tough final but I would just like to pay credit to the players of England. We have had to play Australia, South Africa and New Zealand all in a week. We have beaten the first two and today was probably a game too far for us."

Elsewhere in the tournament, Australia faced France in the fifth place play-off at the Arms Park and it was the junior Wallabies who were able to call themselves 'the best of the rest' with a highly entertaining 42–21 won over Les Bleus, featuring a sparkling hat-trick from Ratu Nasiganiyavi to take his tally to seven and confirm him as the competition's top try scorer.

RESULTS

POOL A

Round One: **New Zealand** 48 **Tonga** 9, **Argentina** 17 **Ireland** 9. Round Two: **Argentina** 30 **Tonga** 10, **New Zealand** 65 **Ireland** 0. Round Three: **Ireland** 45 **Tonga** 27, **New Zealand** 60 **Argentina** 0

POOL B

Round One: **South Africa** 108 **USA** 18, **Samoa** 29 **Scotland** 17. Round Two: **Samoa** 20 **USA** 6, **South Africa** 72 **Scotland** 3. Round Three: **Scotland** 41 **USA** 14, **South Africa** 16 **Samoa** 11

POOL C

Round One: **Australia** 81 **Canada** 12, **England** 41 **Fiji** 17. Round Two: **England** 60 **Canada** 18, **Australia** 53 **Fiji** 17. Round Three: **Australia** 13 **England** 18, **Fiji** 10 **Canada** 17

POOL D

Round One: **France** 53 **Japan** 17, **Wales** 29 **Italy** 10. Round Two: **France** 32 **Italy** 14, **Wales** 33 **Japan** 10. Round Three: **Japan** 20 **Italy** 24, **Wales** 23 **Italy** 19

WALES 18 (1G, 2PG, 1T) SOUTH AFRICA 43 (4G, 3T)

FINAL

22 June, Liberty Stadium, Swansea

NEW ZEALAND 38 (3G, 4PG, 1T) ENGLAND 3 (1PG)

NEW ZEALAND: T Renata; K Poki, J Willison, R Crotty, Z Guildford; D Kirkpatrick, G Hart; P Fa'anunu, A Dixon, B Afeaki, C Smith (captain), S Whitelock, P Saili, L Braid, N Manu Substitutions: A Smith for Hart (59 mins); S Maitland for Renata (59 mins); J Townsend for Whitelock (67 mins); H Reed for Saili (74 mins); R Ah You for Fa'anunu (74 mins); Q MacDonald for Dixon (75 mins); A Taylor for Poki (77 mins)

SCORERS *Tries*: Poki, Willison, Taylor, Crotty *Conversions*: Renata, Kirkpatrick (2) *Penalty Goals*: Renata (3), Kirkpatrick

ENGLAND: N Cato; M Odejobi, L Eves, J Turner-Hall, M Benjamin; A Goode, J Simpson; N Catt, J Gray, A Corbisiero, B Thomas, G Gillanders, J Fisher, C Clark, H Ellis (captain) Substitutions: B Youngs for Simpson (46 mins); B Moss for Corbisiero (55 mins); S Hobson for Gillanders (55 mins); R Miller for Eves (61 mins); M Cox for Ellis (65 mins); S Freer for Gray (72 mins); S Stegmann for Odejobi (76 mins)

SCORERS Penalty Goal: Goode

YELLOW CARD Smith (70 mins)

RED CARD Clark (72 mins)

REFEREE P Fitzgibbon (Ireland)

FINAL STANDINGS

1. New Zealand	**2. England**
3. South Africa	**4. Wales**
5. Australia	**6. France**
7. Samo	**8. Argentina**
9. Ireland	**10. Scotland**
11. Italy	**12. Canada**
13. Tonga	**14. Fiji**
15. Japan	**16. USA**

URUGUAY SPOIL CHILE'S PARTY

By Dominic Rumbles

Uruguay's young stars were crowned the inaugural IRB Junior World Rugby Trophy champions after coming from behind to defeat hosts Chile 20-8, before a record crowd of nearly 7,000 at the Stade Français Club in Santiago.

As the culmination to a magnificent tournament, the final was always going to be an intriguing affair. The sides had met twice at the IRB Under-19 World Championship in Belfast in 2007 with Uruguay winning both Division B encounters, 30-20 and 21-3.

Chile raced into an 8-0 lead within half an hour courtesy of a Francisco González penalty and try from centre Ricardo Sifri, much to the delight of the partisan home crowd.

However, that was as close as Chile got to the silverware as, despite the best efforts of their fluid backs, a tough tackling and powerful Uruguayan side got to grips with the humid conditions and ran in tries either side of the interval. Second-row Diego Magno was first over the line, and impressive fly-half Germán Albanell followed as they lifted the title and secure promotion to the IRB Junior World Championship 2009 in Japan.

"I am delighted with the win coming at the back of several months of hard work and look forward to Uruguay playing in the IRB Junior World Championship next year. Twelve of the boys are eligible to play in the Under-20s next year," said Bruno Grunwaldt, one of Uruguay's co-coaches along with Martín Mendaro.

To reach the final of the eight-team event had been no easy task for either Chile or Uruguay with no margin for error as only the top side in each pool would progress to the title decider and the likes of Romania, Georgia and Namibia also harbouring their own final aspirations.

Chile sailed through their opening Pool A matches against Cook Islands 33-10 and Namibia 20-6 to set up a showdown with Romania.

When the Romanians took a third minute lead with a penalty from fly half Alin Georgescu, the scene was set for a strong performance. However, roared on by the 5,000 strong crowd, Chile held firm while a man down and ultimately triumphed 14-3 thanks to Felipe Brangier's try and three penalties from fly half González.

It was an historic marker for Chilean rugby and importantly set up the all-South American final against a Uruguay side which had kicked off their impressive charge to the top of Pool B with a 10-try 67-8 defeat of Korea and 82-0 victory over newcomers Jamaica – the first Caribbean side ever to qualify for an IRB international 15-a-side competition.

These wins set up a pool decider against Georgia, one from which Uruguay emerged 20-16 victors owing largely to their sheer guts and determination, although their discipline was also key as they refused to give away kickable penalties – unlike their opponents who had two players sin-binned in the second half.

The final may not have yielded the outcome the hosts had dreamed of, but the tournament was something of a watershed for the Federacion de Rugby de Chile and had put rugby in Chile firmly back on the map, through a combination of a detailed legacy programme and outstanding rugby before large crowds.

Third place was claimed by Georgia after a one-sided 34-10 victory over Romania, but both sets of players would have been bitterly disappointed not to have reached the final and getting within touching distance of promotion to the Junior World Championship, the top tier of Under-20 rugby which replaced the IRB Under-19 and Under-21 World Championships following a restructuring of age grade rugby.

RESULTS

POOL A

Romania 28 **Namibia** 26, **Chile** 33 **Cook Islands** 10, **Romania** 46 **Cook Islands** 7, **Chile** 20 **Namibia** 6, **Namibia** 25 **Cook Islands** 14, **Chile** 14 **Romania** 3.

POOL B

Georgia 90 **Jamaica** 3, **Uruguay** 67 **Korea** 8, **Georgia** 50 **Korea** 31, **Uruguay** 82 **Jamaica** 0, **Korea** 55 **Jamaica** 17, **Uruguay** 20 **Georgia** 16. 7th Place Play-Off: **Cook Islands** 54 **Jamaica** 15. 5th Place Play-Off: **Namibia** 36 **Korea** 29. 3rd Place Play-Off: **Romania** 10 **Georgia** 34

IRB JUNIOR WORLD RUGBY TROPHY FINAL

27 April – Stade Français Club, Santiago

CHILE 8 URUGUAY 20

CHILE: S Fuenzalida; F Brangier, F de la Fuente, R Sifri, D Schachner; F González, M Rochette; A Rios, B Barbosa, L Salamunic, N Lafrentz, T Dahmen, S Aviles, F Yaconi, B Del Solar (Captain).

REPLACEMENTS: P Valladares for Del Solar 51, JJ Ruiz for F Brangier 72, A Oliver for M Rochette 72.

SCORERS: *Try*: Sifri *Penalty*: González

URUGUAY: R Mendez; T Jolivet, G Etcheverry, A Lewis, L Leivas; G Albanell, F Vecino; E Benitez, J Rocco, R Tchilingirbachain, D Magno, F Perez, JM Gaminara, JD Ormaechea, M Fonseca (Captain).

REPLACEMENTS: A Fiorito for E Benitez 51, A Nieto for R Tchilingirbachain 65, M Horta for JD Ormaechea 70, J De Freitas for A Lewis 71, R Espiga for F Perez 72.

SCORERS: *Tries*: Magno, Albanell *Conversions*: Albanell (2) *Penalty*: Etcheverry *Drop goal*: Albanell

REFEREE: J Mancuso (Argentina)

LELOS FULFIL EASTERN PROMISE

By Iain Spragg

Georgia bounced back from the bitter disappointment of missing out on the European Nations Cup on points difference in 2004–06 to lift the 2006–08 incarnation of the competition, frequently referred to as the second tier of the Six Nations, and cap a hugely encouraging run of results for Georgian rugby.

In September 2007 the Lelos were celebrating their maiden victory in the World Cup after beating Namibia 30–0 in the Stade Felix Bollaert in Lens, their first win in seven attempts in the finals, and seven months later the Georgians were once again in party mood after triumphing 22–20 over Spain in Tbilisi to be crowned European Nations Cup champions.

Georgia had come agonisingly close to lifting the trophy in 2006 but conceded the title to Romania on points difference. They made no mistake two years later with a dominant campaign in which they were beaten just once in 10 outings to relegate neighbours Russia into second place.

A fascinating campaign in which Georgia, Russia and Romania emerged as the three strongest sides, leaving Portugal, Czech Republic and newly-promoted Spain in their wake, was finally settled in mid April when the Lelos braved the freezing conditions of Krasnoyarsk in Siberia to beat Russia 18–12 and secure the title with a game to spare.

The season began with a mouth-watering heavyweight clash between Romania and Georgia in Bucharest in February 2007 and the hostilities in the Steaua II Stadium were as fierce as predicted as two of the pre-tournament favourites battled to deliver the early psychological blow in proceedings.

The Lelos were quickest out of the blocks, however, and tries from hooker Akvsenti Giorgadze and No 8 Besso Udesiani, both converted by fly half Merab Kvirikashvili, laid the foundations for a crucial 20–17 win over the Oaks and the right to lift the Antim Cup for the fourth time in its eight-year history.

A week later, Russia established their own title credentials as they flew to Spain for their opening game in Madrid and proved far too strong for their Iberian hosts, running out convincing 39–14 winners.

Spain, however, steeled themselves after a hat-trick of opening defeats to Portugal, Romania and the Russians when Georgia arrived in Madrid the following month and despite all the pre-match talk of the Lelos coming away with the points, it was the home side who produced the shock of the competition to date.

The early omens however were not good. Georgia crossed for the opening try of the match inside the first minute through Davit Bolgashvili but three penalties by Esteban Roqué Segovia hauled Spain back into contention.

The Leones scored their first try early in the second half when David Mota went over under the posts and when Roqué Segovia added the conversion, Spain were 16–5 up. Georgia fought back with a second score from Bolgashvili but the hosts pulled clear with two tries from Victor Marlet to emerge surprise 31–17 winners.

Georgia were stunned but had no time to dwell on their setback as they faced Russia seven days later in Tbilisi. The game produced a stark contrast of styles as the Lelos looked to dominate their visitors in the forward exchanges while Russia tried to put width on the ball and in the end it was Georgian power up front that won the day.

Three first half penalties from fly half Yury Kushnarev gave Russia an early advantage but openside flanker Giorgi Chkhaidze hit back with the first try of the match for the home side moments before half-time and Georgia went in 10–9 ahead.

The second 40 minutes saw Georgia's pack become increasingly influential. A penalty try after Russia collapsed a maul was no less than they deserved and lock Zurab Mtchedlishvili virtually settled the contest with his side's third try. The Georgian backs finally got in on the act to create the space for flanker Grigol Labadze to score the fourth and the Lelos were 21–12 winners.

Elsewhere, the Czech Republic were finding the competition a real struggle and hopes were not high when they faced Georgia in Tbilisi in April.

Boosted by their victory over the Russians, the Lelos showed the Czechs no mercy in front of 10,000 fans in the Boris Paichadze National Stadium and scored 16 unanswered tries, including a hat-trick from hooker David Dadunashvili and centre Malkhaz Urjukasvhvili in an emphatic 98–3 victory.

The win was to be Georgia's last before their World Cup sojourn but Russia maintained the pressure with a 62–6 victory over the Czech Republic followed by a vital 21–13 away win against Portugal in Lisbon to maintain the pressure.

The European Nations Cup shut down for the summer, resuming in November 2007 after Portugal, Romania and Georgia's involvement in the World Cup with the destination of the silverware still very much in doubt.

The Russians were the first of the title contenders to return to the fray with a crucial clash with Romania in Bucharest. Both teams were desperate to overhaul Georgia at the top of the table and it was the visitors who were celebrating at the final whistle after a hard-fought 22–12 triumph over the Oaks. The competition was now looking like a two-horse race between Georgia and Russia.

The Lelos were back in action in February 2008 with a 31–3 home win over Portugal, but the key challenge came a week later with the visit of Romania to Tbilisi. The game represented a new, post World Cup era for the two sides, who had both appointed new coaches.

Romania had installed New Zealander Ellis Meachen as their Director of Rugby while Georgia had secured the services of former Wallaby Tim Lane, who had an impressive CV after stints in France with Clermont Auvergne, Toulon and Brive, as well as spells with both Australia and the Springboks.

"Of course, the Lelos should stick to their traditional strength, that is vigorous forward play, but at the same time the new 15-man game will be introduced step by step," explained Lane when asked about his vision for the Georgia team. "I hope we can start playing a little bit more expansively, which they have never done before."

Lane's expansive plans had to wait, however, as the Lelos reverted to their traditional forward power against the Oaks and although full back Otar Barkalaia contributed four vital penalties, Georgia's only try of the game came from the forwards in the sizeable shape of second row Mamuka Gorgodze, who crashed over to help set up a 22–7 win.

With four games left to play, the Lelos were now firmly in the driving seat and victories over Portugal in Lisbon and the Czech Republic in Prague strengthened their position. Only Russia now stood in their way and victory over their Caucasus neighbours was all that stood between Lane's side and the title.

The game in Krasnoyarsk was delayed by 40 minutes as the pitch had to be swept clear of snow and the pitch markings redrawn in red, but the bitter Siberian conditions were overcome and the game went ahead.

The Lelos drew first blood when flanker Rati Urushadze burst through a tackle after just eight minutes for the opening try and the visitors found themselves 10–0 up when Barkalaia slotted a penalty on 20 minutes. Kushnarev's boot kept Russia in contention and after 68 minutes of battle in the freezing conditions, Georgia held a precarious 13–12 lead. A minute later saw the decisive act of the match, however, when

Lelos centre Davit Kacharava found space to race over and Georgia were 18–12 victors.

Victory meant the Lelos were two points clear of the Russians with the final round of games remaining, but Georgia boasted a superior points difference and even if they lost to Spain in their last match, Russia would have to run up a cricket score against the Czech Republic to overhaul them.

As it transpired, Georgia were already effectively champions. Russia beat the Czechs 49–3 but the result meant the Lelos would have to lose by 58 points to the Spanish to surrender the title. Lane's team were in no mood to snatch defeat from the jaws of victory and held on for a 22–20 win over Spain to confirm their triumph.

Elsewhere in European Nations Cup action, Germany secured a return to the top tier for the first time in two decades by winning the Division 2A on points difference from Belgium. Germany replace the winless Czech Republic, who are relegated to Division 2A for the 2008–2010 competition. Poland, meanwhile, were crowned Division 2B champions ahead of Latvia with seven wins from their eight games with Sweden (Division 3A), Lithuania (3B), Slovenia (3C) and Cyprus (3D), the other divisional champions.

FINAL TABLE

	P	W	PD	Points
Georgia	10	9	+178	28
Russia	10	8	+165	26
Romania	10	6	+133	22
Spain	10	4	-7	18
Portugal	10	3	-22	16
Czech Rep	10	0	-447	10

The next European Nations Cup, which kicked off in September, will double as the region's qualifying process for Rugby World Cup 2011. The first two teams in Division 1 will qualify for RWC 2011 as Europe 1 and Europe 2. The third placed team can still qualify, but must safely negotiate a play-off against another European side and then the Final Place Play-off which will determine the 20th and final qualifier for Rugby World Cup 2011 in New Zealand.

WOMEN'S RUGBY

HAT-TRICK FOR ENGLAND

By Paul Morgan

In the men's game England haven't won an RBS 6 Nations Grand Slam for five years, and it was eight years before that when they completed a clean sweep of victories against the best Europe had to offer. But in the women's game England haven't had as many problems, and in 2008 completed an unprecedented third successive Grand Slam, no side coming within 10 points of Gary Street's side as they dominated in the Championship.

England's 17–7 victory over Ireland clinched the trophy, under captain Catherine Spencer, and came after a 55–0 win over Wales, a 76–6 triumph against Italy, a record away 31–0 victory against France and a 34–5 defeat of Scotland.

Saracens centre Claire Allan led the try-scoring tally with an impressive six touchdowns during the campaign, including a try in the first minute of the game against Ireland.

"It's a great feeling to win the Grand Slam again. For me this is my first one as head coach and I have to say this title is a testament to the hard work of the players on and off the field," said Street.

"We would have liked to put in a better performance against Ireland [in the final game] but really it is all about the performance of this team throughout the championship. The real success story has been the bonding of this squad, from a new coaching team to a relatively new and young squad. We clearly have a very strong squad with a lot of depth and that is going to stand us in very good stead for the future."

Wales finished second in the Championship and saw Louise Rickard win her 100th cap. In doing so Rickard joined former Scotland captain Donna Kennedy as the only women in the select club of 100-cap winners.

Italy – who replaced Spain in 2007 – also won their first Championship match, beating Scotland 20–5. "We only performed poorly against England during the tournament," said coach Gianfranco Ermolli. "The victory against Scotland is really important for whole of Italian women's rugby."

England went from the Six Nations to win the FIRA Women's European championship in Amsterdam, beating Wales 12–6 in the final.

Russia claimed the Group B award, full-back Anastasiya Mukharyamova leading her side to the title with a 31–14 defeat of the France Army in the final.

The 2008–09 season will represent a big breakthrough for the women's game as they will be included – on an equal footing with the men – in the IRB Rugby World Cup Sevens, in March, and would clearly make a compelling case for inclusion in both the Commonwealth and Olympic Games.

As England know domination in Europe means little in the World Cup and Street may secretly be relieved to see so many of his players disappear to Dubai in the early part of 2009, for the IRB Rugby World Cup Sevens, as it will force him to blood some inexperienced players in the backline.

The arrival of the women at the IRB Rugby World Cup Sevens has led to development of the game all over the world, Australia forming their first ever women's sevens team to enable them to qualify.

The appointment of former Eagles captain Alexandra Williams as USA Rugby's first ever Women's High Performance Manager in August has been heralded as a "great step forward in women's rugby" by CEO and President of Operations Nigel Melville.

A veteran of three Women's Rugby World Cups between 1994 and 2002 during her 10 years in the USA national side, Williams is also the assistant coach of the current USA Women's Eagles side and head coach of her former side Berkeley All-Blues.

Kazakhstan scored seven tries to successfully defend their ARFU Women's Championship title with a 39–3 defeat of Japan in the final on home soil at the Locomotive Stadium in Taras, in June.

Trinidad & Tobago's women carried on where their male counterparts left off in their Rugby World Cup qualifying campaign by beating the Cayman Islands in the final to win the 2008 women's Caribbean Championships. Defending champions Jamaica finished third ahead of Cayman, who were playing in their first competitive tournament.

In Africa, Uganda's Lady Cranes emulated the feats of their men's national side in defeating the Kenya 18–7 in Kampala to take the advantage in their 2008 Elgon Cup rivalry.

THE COUNTRIES

IRB
INTERNATIONAL RUGBY BOARD

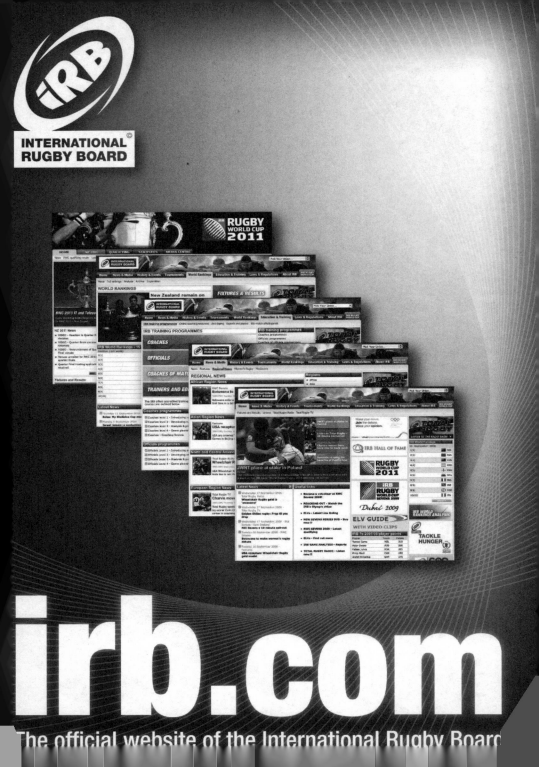

RUGBY WORLD CUP 2011
WORLD RANKINGS
New Zealand remain on
FIXTURES & RESULTS
IRB TRAINING PROGRAMMES
COACHES
OFFICIALS
REGIONAL NEWS
African Region News
Asian Region News
JWRT place at stake in Poland
IRB HALL OF FAME
RUGBY WORLD CUP 2011
RUGBY WORLD CUP SEVENS 2009
Dubai 2009
ELV GUIDE
WITH VIDEO CLIPS
TACKLE HUNGER

INTERNATIONAL RECORDS

RESULTS OF INTERNATIONAL MATCHES

MATCH RECORDS UP TO 30TH SEPTEMBER 2008

Cap matches involving senior executive council member unions only. Years for International Championship matches are for the second half of the season: eg 1972 means season 1971–72. Years for matches against touring teams from the Southern Hemisphere refer to the actual year of the match.
Points-scoring was first introduced in 1886, when an International Board was formed by Scotland, Ireland and Wales. Points values varied among the countries until 1890, when England agreed to join the Board, and uniform values were adopted.

Northern Hemisphere seasons	Try	Conversions	Penalty Goal	Dropped goal	Goal from mark
1890–91	1	2	2	3	3
1891–92 to 1892–93	2	3	3	4	4
1893–94 to 1904–05	3	2	3	4	4
1905–06 to 1947–48	3	2	3	4	3
1948–49 to 1970–71	3	2	3	3	3
1971–72 to 1991–92	4	2	3	3	3*
1992–93 onwards	5	2	3	3	–

**The goal from mark ceased to exist when the free-kick clause was introduced, 1977–78.*

WC indicates a fixture played during the Rugby World Cup finals. LC indicates a fixture played in the Latin Cup. TN indicates a fixture played in the Tri Nations.

ENGLAND V SCOTLAND

Played 125 England won 66, Scotland won 42, Drawn 17
Highest scores England 43–3 in 2001 and 43–22 in 2005, Scotland 33–6 in 1986
Biggest wins England 43–3 in 2001, Scotland 33–6 in 1986

1871 Raeburn Place (Edinburgh) **Scotland** 1G 1T to 1T
1872 The Oval (London) **England** 1G 1DG 2T to 1DG
1873 Glasgow **Drawn** no score
1874 The Oval **England** 1DG to 1T
1875 Raeburn Place **Drawn** no score
1876 The Oval **England** 1G 1T to 0
1877 Raeburn Place **Scotland** 1 DG to 0
1878 The Oval **Drawn** no score
1879 Raeburn Place **Drawn** Scotland 1DG England 1G
1880 Manchester **England** 2G 3T to 1G
1881 Raeburn Place **Drawn** Scotland 1G 1T England 1DG 1T
1882 Manchester **Scotland** 2T to 0
1883 Raeburn Place **England** 2T to 1T
1884 Blackheath (London) **England** 1G to 1T
1885 No Match
1886 Raeburn Place **Drawn** no score
1887 Manchester **Drawn** 1T each
1888 No Match
1889 No Match
1890 Raeburn Place **England** 1G 1T to 0
1891 Richmond (London) **Scotland** 9–3
1892 Raeburn Place **England** 5–0
1893 Leeds **Scotland** 8–0
1894 Raeburn Place **Scotland** 6–0
1895 Richmond **Scotland** 6–3
1896 Glasgow **Scotland** 11–0
1897 Manchester **England** 12–3
1898 Powderhall (Edinburgh) **Drawn** 3–3
1899 Blackheath **Scotland** 5–0
1900 Inverleith (Edinburgh) **Drawn** 0–0
1901 Blackheath **Scotland** 18–3
1902 Inverleith **England** 6–3
1903 Richmond **Scotland** 10–6
1904 Inverleith **Scotland** 6–3
1905 Richmond **Scotland** 8–0
1906 Inverleith **England** 9–3
1907 Blackheath **Scotland** 8–3
1908 Inverleith **Scotland** 16–10
1909 Richmond **Scotland** 18–8
1910 Inverleith **England** 14–5
1911 Twickenham **England** 13–8
1912 Inverleith **Scotland** 8–3
1913 Twickenham **England** 3–0
1914 Inverleith **England** 16–15
1920 Twickenham **England** 13–4
1921 Inverleith **England** 18–0
1922 Twickenham **England** 11–5
1923 Inverleith **England** 8–6
1924 Twickenham **England** 19–0
1925 Murrayfield **Scotland** 14–11
1926 Twickenham **Scotland** 17–9
1927 Murrayfield **Scotland** 21–13
1928 Twickenham **England** 6–0
1929 Murrayfield **Scotland** 12–6
1930 Twickenham **Drawn** 0–0
1931 Murrayfield **Scotland** 28–19
1932 Twickenham **England** 16–3
1933 Murrayfield **Scotland** 3–0
1934 Twickenham **England** 6–3
1935 Murrayfield **Scotland** 10–7
1936 Twickenham **England** 9–8
1937 Murrayfield **England** 6–3
1938 Twickenham **Scotland** 21–16
1939 Murrayfield **England** 9–6
1947 Twickenham **England** 24–5
1948 Murrayfield **Scotland** 6–3
1949 Twickenham **England** 19–3
1950 Murrayfield **Scotland** 13–11
1951 Twickenham **England** 5–3
1952 Murrayfield **England** 19–3
1953 Twickenham **England** 26–8
1954 Murrayfield **England** 13–3
1955 Twickenham **England** 9–6
1956 Murrayfield **England** 11–6
1957 Twickenham **England** 16–3
1958 Murrayfield **Drawn** 3–3
1959 Twickenham **Drawn** 3–3
1960 Murrayfield **England** 21–12
1961 Twickenham **England** 6–0
1962 Murrayfield **Drawn** 3–3
1963 Twickenham **England** 10–8
1964 Murrayfield **Scotland** 15–6

1965 Twickenham **Drawn** 3–3
1966 Murrayfield **Scotland** 6–3
1967 Twickenham **England** 27–14
1968 Murrayfield **England** 8–6
1969 Twickenham **England** 8–3
1970 Murrayfield **Scotland** 14–5
1971 Twickenham **Scotland** 16–15
1971 Murrayfield **Scotland** 26–6
Special centenary match – non-championship
1972 Murrayfield **Scotland** 23–9
1973 Twickenham **England** 20–13
1974 Murrayfield **Scotland** 16–14
1975 Twickenham **England** 7–6
1976 Murrayfield **Scotland** 22–12
1977 Twickenham **England** 26–6
1978 Murrayfield **England** 15–0
1979 Twickenham **Drawn** 7–7
1980 Murrayfield **England** 30–18
1981 Twickenham **England** 23–17
1982 Murrayfield **Drawn** 9–9
1983 Twickenham **Scotland** 22–12
1984 Murrayfield **Scotland** 18–6
1985 Twickenham **England** 10–7
1986 Murrayfield **Scotland** 33–6
1987 Twickenham **England** 21–12
1988 Murrayfield **England** 9–6
1989 Twickenham **Drawn** 12–12
1990 Murrayfield **Scotland** 13–7
1991 Twickenham **England** 21–12
1991 Murrayfield WC **England** 9–6
1992 Murrayfield **England** 25–7
1993 Twickenham **England** 26–12
1994 Murrayfield **England** 15–14
1995 Twickenham **England** 24–12
1996 Murrayfield **England** 18–9
1997 Twickenham **England** 41–13
1998 Murrayfield **England** 34–20
1999 Twickenham **England** 24–21
2000 Murrayfield **Scotland** 19–13
2001 Twickenham **England** 43–3
2002 Murrayfield **England** 29–3
2003 Twickenham **England** 40–9
2004 Murrayfield **England** 35–13
2005 Twickenham **England** 43–22
2006 Murrayfield **Scotland** 18–12
2007 Twickenham **England** 42–20
2008 Murrayfield **Scotland** 15–9

ENGLAND V IRELAND

Played 121 England won 70, Ireland won 43, Drawn 8
Highest scores England 50–18 in 2000, Ireland 43–13 in 2007
Biggest wins England 46–6 in 1997, Ireland 43–13 in 2007

1875 The Oval (London) **England** 1G 1DG 1T to 0
1876 Dublin **England** 1G 1T to 0
1877 The Oval **England** 2G 2T to 0
1878 Dublin **England** 2G 1T to 0
1879 The Oval **England** 2G 1DG 2T to 0
1880 Dublin **England** 1G 1T to 1T
1881 Manchester **England** 2G 2T to 0
1882 Dublin **Drawn** 2T each
1883 Manchester **England** 1G 3T to 1T
1884 Dublin **England** 1G to 0
1885 Manchester **England** 2T to 1T
1886 Dublin **England** 1T to 0
1887 Dublin **Ireland** 2G to 0
1888 No Match
1889 No Match
1890 Blackheath (London) **England** 3T to 0
1891 Dublin **England** 9–0
1892 Manchester **England** 7–0
1893 Dublin **England** 4–0
1894 Blackheath **Ireland** 7–5
1895 Dublin **England** 6–3
1896 Leeds **Ireland** 10–4
1897 Dublin **Ireland** 13–9
1898 Richmond (London) **Ireland** 9–6
1899 Dublin **Ireland** 6–0
1900 Richmond **England** 15–4
1901 Dublin **Ireland** 10–6
1902 Leicester **England** 6–3
1903 Dublin **Ireland** 6–0

1904 Blackheath **England** 19–0
1905 Cork **Ireland** 17–3
1906 Leicester **Ireland** 16–6
1907 Dublin **Ireland** 17–9
1908 Richmond **England** 13–3
1909 Dublin **England** 11–5
1910 Twickenham **Drawn** 0–0
1911 Dublin **Ireland** 3–0
1912 Twickenham **England** 15–0
1913 Dublin **England** 15–4
1914 Twickenham **England** 17–12
1920 Dublin **England** 14–11
1921 Twickenham **England** 15–0
1922 Dublin **England** 12–3
1923 Leicester **England** 23–5
1924 Belfast **England** 14–3
1925 Twickenham **Drawn** 6–6
1926 Dublin **Ireland** 19–15
1927 Twickenham **England** 8–6
1928 Dublin **England** 7–6
1929 Twickenham **Ireland** 6–5
1930 Dublin **Ireland** 4–3
1931 Twickenham **Ireland** 6–5
1932 Dublin **England** 11–8
1933 Twickenham **England** 17–6
1934 Dublin **England** 13–3
1935 Twickenham **England** 14–3
1936 Dublin **Ireland** 6–3
1937 Twickenham **England** 9–8
1938 Dublin **England** 36–14
1939 Twickenham **Ireland** 5–0
1947 Dublin **Ireland** 22–0
1948 Twickenham **Ireland** 11–10
1949 Dublin **Ireland** 14–5
1950 Twickenham **England** 3–0
1951 Dublin **Ireland** 3–0
1952 Twickenham **England** 3–0
1953 Dublin **Drawn** 9–9
1954 Twickenham **England** 14–3
1955 Dublin **Drawn** 6–6
1956 Twickenham **England** 20–0
1957 Dublin **England** 6–0
1958 Twickenham **England** 6–0
1959 Dublin **England** 3–0
1960 Twickenham **England** 8–5
1961 Dublin **Ireland** 11–8
1962 Twickenham **England** 16–0
1963 Dublin **Drawn** 0–0
1964 Twickenham **Ireland** 18–5
1965 Dublin **Ireland** 5–0
1966 Twickenham **Drawn** 6–6
1967 Dublin **England** 8–3
1968 Twickenham **Drawn** 9–9
1969 Dublin **Ireland** 17–15
1970 Twickenham **England** 9–3
1971 Dublin **England** 9–6
1972 Twickenham **Ireland** 16–12
1973 Dublin **Ireland** 18–9
1974 Twickenham **Ireland** 26–21
1975 Dublin **Ireland** 12–9
1976 Twickenham **Ireland** 13–12
1977 Dublin **England** 4–0
1978 Twickenham **England** 15–9
1979 Dublin **Ireland** 12–7
1980 Twickenham **England** 24–9
1981 Dublin **England** 10–6
1982 Twickenham **Ireland** 16–15
1983 Dublin **Ireland** 25–15
1984 Twickenham **England** 12–9
1985 Dublin **Ireland** 13–10
1986 Twickenham **England** 25–20
1987 Dublin **Ireland** 17–0
1988 Twickenham **England** 35–3
1988 Dublin **England** 21–10
Non-championship match
1989 Dublin **England** 16–3
1990 Twickenham **England** 23–0
1991 Dublin **England** 16–7
1992 Twickenham **England** 38–9
1993 Dublin **Ireland** 17–3
1994 Twickenham **Ireland** 13–12
1995 Dublin **England** 20–8
1996 Twickenham **England** 28–15
1997 Dublin **England** 46–6
1998 Twickenham **England** 35–17
1999 Dublin **England** 27–15
2000 Twickenham **England** 50–18
2001 Dublin **Ireland** 20–14
2002 Twickenham **England** 45–11
2003 Dublin **England** 42–6
2004 Twickenham **Ireland** 19–13
2005 Dublin **Ireland** 19–13
2006 Twickenham **Ireland** 28–24
2007 Dublin **Ireland** 43–13
2008 Twickenham **England** 33–10

ENGLAND V WALES

Played 117 England won 53, Wales won 52, Drawn 12
Highest scores England 62–5 in 2007, Wales 34–21 in 1967
Biggest wins England 62–5 in 2007, Wales 25–0 in 1905

1881 Blackheath (London) **England** 7G 1DG 6T to 0
1882 No Match
1883 Swansea **England** 2G 4T to 0
1884 Leeds **England** 1G 2T to 1G
1885 Swansea **England** 1G 4T to 1G 1T
1886 Blackheath **England** 1GM 2T to 1G
1887 Llanelli **Drawn** no score
1888 No Match
1889 No Match
1890 Dewsbury **Wales** 1T to 0
1891 Newport **England** 7–3
1892 Blackheath **England** 17–0
1893 Cardiff **Wales** 12–11
1894 Birkenhead **England** 24–3
1895 Swansea **England** 14–6
1896 Blackheath **England** 25–0
1897 Newport **Wales** 11–0
1898 Blackheath **England** 14–7
1899 Swansea **Wales** 26–3
1900 Gloucester **Wales** 13–3
1901 Cardiff **Wales** 13–0
1902 Blackheath **Wales** 9–8
1903 Swansea **Wales** 21–5
1904 Leicester **Drawn** 14–14
1905 Cardiff **Wales** 25–0
1906 Richmond (London) **Wales** 16–3
1907 Swansea **Wales** 22–0
1908 Bristol **Wales** 28–18
1909 Cardiff **Wales** 8–0
1910 Twickenham **England** 11–6
1911 Swansea **Wales** 15–11
1912 Twickenham **England** 8–0
1913 Cardiff **England** 12–0
1914 Twickenham **England** 10–9
1920 Swansea **Wales** 19–5
1921 Twickenham **England** 18–3
1922 Cardiff **Wales** 28–6
1923 Twickenham **England** 7–3
1924 Swansea **England** 17–9
1925 Twickenham **England** 12–6
1926 Cardiff **Drawn** 3–3
1927 Twickenham **England** 11–9
1928 Swansea **England** 10–8
1929 Twickenham **England** 8–3
1930 Cardiff **England** 11–3
1931 Twickenham **Drawn** 11–11
1932 Swansea **Wales** 12–5
1933 Twickenham **Wales** 7–3
1934 Cardiff **England** 9–0
1935 Twickenham **Drawn** 3–3
1936 Swansea **Drawn** 0–0
1937 Twickenham **England** 4–3
1938 Cardiff **Wales** 14–8
1939 Twickenham **England** 3–0
1947 Cardiff **England** 9–6
1948 Twickenham **Drawn** 3–3
1949 Cardiff **Wales** 9–3
1950 Twickenham **Wales** 11–5
1951 Swansea **Wales** 23–5
1952 Twickenham **Wales** 8–6
1953 Cardiff **England** 8–3
1954 Twickenham **England** 9–6
1955 Cardiff **Wales** 3–0
1956 Twickenham **Wales** 8–3
1957 Cardiff **England** 3–0
1958 Twickenham **Drawn** 3–3
1959 Cardiff **Wales** 5–0
1960 Twickenham **England** 14–6
1961 Cardiff **Wales** 6–3
1962 Twickenham **Drawn** 0–0
1963 Cardiff **England** 13–6
1964 Twickenham **Drawn** 6–6
1965 Cardiff **Wales** 14–3
1966 Twickenham **Wales** 11–6
1967 Cardiff **Wales** 34–21
1968 Twickenham **Drawn** 11–11
1969 Cardiff **Wales** 30–9
1970 Twickenham **Wales** 17–13
1971 Cardiff **Wales** 22–6
1972 Twickenham **Wales** 12–3
1973 Cardiff **Wales** 25–9
1974 Twickenham **England** 16–12
1975 Cardiff **Wales** 20–4
1976 Twickenham **Wales** 21–9
1977 Cardiff **Wales** 14–9

1978 Twickenham **Wales** 9–6
1979 Cardiff **Wales** 27–3
1980 Twickenham **England** 9–8
1981 Cardiff **Wales** 21–19
1982 Twickenham **England** 17–7
1983 Cardiff **Drawn** 13–13
1984 Twickenham **Wales** 24–15
1985 Cardiff **Wales** 24–15
1986 Twickenham **England** 21–18
1987 Cardiff **Wales** 19–12
1987 Brisbane WC **Wales** 16–3
1988 Twickenham **Wales** 11–3
1989 Cardiff **Wales** 12–9
1990 Twickenham **England** 34–6
1991 Cardiff **England** 25–6
1992 Twickenham **England** 24–0
1993 Cardiff **Wales** 10–9
1994 Twickenham **England** 15–8
1995 Cardiff **England** 23–9
1996 Twickenham **England** 21–15
1997 Cardiff **England** 34–13
1998 Twickenham **England** 60–26
1999 Wembley **Wales** 32–31
2000 Twickenham **England** 46–12
2001 Cardiff **England** 44–15
2002 Twickenham **England** 50–10
2003 Cardiff **England** 26–9
2003 Cardiff **England** 43–9
Non-championship match
2003 Brisbane WC **England** 28–17
2004 Twickenham **England** 31–21
2005 Cardiff **Wales** 11–9
2006 Twickenham **England** 47–13
2007 Cardiff **Wales** 27–18
2007 Twickenham **England** 62–5
Non-championship match
2008 Twickenham **Wales** 26–19

ENGLAND V FRANCE

Played 91 England won 49, France won 35, Drawn 7
Highest scores England 48–19 in 2001, France 37–12 in 1972
Biggest wins England 37–0 in 1911, France 37–12 in 1972 and 31–6 in 2006

1906 Paris **England** 35–8
1907 Richmond (London) **England** 41–13
1908 Paris **England** 19–0
1909 Leicester **England** 22–0
1910 Paris **England** 11–3
1911 Twickenham **England** 37–0
1912 Paris **England** 18–8
1913 Twickenham **England** 20–0
1914 Paris **England** 39–13
1920 Twickenham **England** 8–3
1921 Paris **England** 10–6
1922 Twickenham **Drawn** 11–11
1923 Paris **England** 12–3
1924 Twickenham **England** 19–7
1925 Paris **England** 13–11
1926 Twickenham **England** 11–0
1927 Paris **France** 3–0
1928 Twickenham **England** 18–8
1929 Paris **England** 16–6
1930 Twickenham **England** 11–5
1931 Paris **France** 14–13
1947 Twickenham **England** 6–3
1948 Paris **France** 15–0
1949 Twickenham **England** 8–3
1950 Paris **France** 6–3
1951 Twickenham **France** 11–3
1952 Paris **England** 6–3
1953 Twickenham **England** 11–0
1954 Paris **France** 11–3
1955 Twickenham **France** 16–9
1956 Paris **France** 14–9
1957 Twickenham **England** 9–5
1958 Paris **England** 14–0
1959 Twickenham **Drawn** 3–3
1960 Paris **Drawn** 3–3
1961 Twickenham **Drawn** 5–5
1962 Paris **France** 13–0
1963 Twickenham **England** 6–5
1964 Paris **England** 6–3
1965 Twickenham **England** 9–6
1966 Paris **France** 13–0
1967 Twickenham **France** 16–12
1968 Paris **France** 14–9
1969 Twickenham **England** 22–8

1970 Paris **France** 35–13
1971 Twickenham **Drawn** 14–14
1972 Paris **France** 37–12
1973 Twickenham **England** 14–6
1974 Paris **Drawn** 12–12
1975 Twickenham **France** 27–20
1976 Paris **France** 30–9
1977 Twickenham **France** 4–3
1978 Paris **France** 15–6
1979 Twickenham **England** 7–6
1980 Paris **England** 17–13
1981 Twickenham **France** 16–12
1982 Paris **England** 27–15
1983 Twickenham **France** 19–15
1984 Paris **France** 32–18
1985 Twickenham **Drawn** 9–9
1986 Paris **France** 29–10
1987 Twickenham **France** 19–15
1988 Paris **France** 10–9
1989 Twickenham **England** 11–0
1990 Paris **England** 26–7
1991 Twickenham **England** 21–19
1991 Paris WC **England** 19–10
1992 Paris **England** 31–13
1993 Twickenham **England** 16–15
1994 Paris **England** 18–14
1995 Twickenham **England** 31–10
1995 Pretoria WC **France 19–9**
1996 Paris **France** 15–12
1997 Twickenham **France** 23–20
1998 Paris **France** 24–17
1999 Twickenham **England** 21–10
2000 Paris **England** 15–9
2001 Twickenham **England** 48–19
2002 Paris **France** 20–15
2003 Twickenham **England** 25–17
2003 Marseilles **France** 17–16
Non-championship match
2003 Twickenham **England** 45–14
Non-championship match
2003 Sydney WC **England** 24–7
2004 Paris **France** 24–21
2005 Twickenham **France** 18–17
2006 Paris **France** 31–6
2007 Twickenham **England** 26–18
2007 Twickenham **France** 21–15
Non-championship match
2007 Marseilles **France** 22–9
Non-championship match
2007 Paris WC **England** 14–9
2008 Paris **England** 24–13

ENGLAND V SOUTH AFRICA

Played 30 England won 12, South Africa won 17, Drawn 1
Highest scores England 53–3 in 2002, South Africa 58–10 in 2007
Biggest wins England 53–3 in 2002, South Africa 58–10 in 2007

1906 Crystal Palace (London) **Drawn** 3–3
1913 Twickenham **South Africa** 9–3
1932 Twickenham **South Africa** 7–0
1952 Twickenham **South Africa** 8–3
1961 Twickenham **South Africa** 5–0
1969 Twickenham **England** 11–8
1972 Johannesburg **England** 18–9
1984 *1* Port Elizabeth **South Africa** 33–15
2 Johannesburg **South Africa** 35–9
South Africa won series 2–0
1992 Twickenham **England** 33–16
1994 *1* Pretoria **England** 32–15
2 Cape Town **South Africa** 27–9
Series drawn 1–1
1995 Twickenham **South Africa** 24–14
1997 Twickenham **South Africa** 29–11
1998 Cape Town **South Africa** 18–0
1998 Twickenham **England** 13–7
1999 Paris WC **South Africa** 44–21
2000 *1* Pretoria **South Africa** 18–13
2 Bloemfontein **England** 27–22
Series drawn 1–1
2000 Twickenham **England** 25–17
2001 Twickenham **England** 29–9
2002 Twickenham **England** 53–3
2003 Perth WC **England** 25–6
2004 Twickenham **England** 32–16
2006 1 Twickenham **England** 23–21
2 Twickenham **South Africa** 25–14
Series drawn 1–1
2007 1 Bloemfontein **South Africa** 58–10
2 Pretoria **South Africa** 55–22
South Africa won series 2–0
2007 Paris WC **South Africa** 36–0
2007 Paris WC **South Africa** 15–6

ENGLAND V NEW ZEALAND

Played 31 England won 6, New Zealand won 24, Drawn 1
Highest scores England 31–28 in 2002, New Zealand 64–22 in 1998
Biggest wins England 13–0 in 1936, New Zealand 64–22 in 1998

1905 Crystal Palace (London) **New Zealand** 15–0
1925 Twickenham **New Zealand** 17–11
1936 Twickenham **England** 13–0
1954 Twickenham **New Zealand** 5–0
1963 *1* Auckland **New Zealand** 21–11
2 Christchurch **New Zealand** 9–6
New Zealand won series 2–0
1964 Twickenham **New Zealand** 14–0
1967 Twickenham **New Zealand** 23–11
1973 Twickenham **New Zealand** 9–0
1973 Auckland **England** 16–10
1978 Twickenham **New Zealand** 16–6
1979 Twickenham **New Zealand** 10–9
1983 Twickenham **England** 15–9
1985 *1* Christchurch **New Zealand** 18–13
2 Wellington **New Zealand** 42–15
New Zealand won series 2–0
1991 Twickenham WC **New Zealand** 18–12
1993 Twickenham **England** 15–9
1995 Cape Town WC **New Zealand 45–29**
1997 *1* Manchester **New Zealand** 25–8
2 Twickenham **Drawn** 26–26
New Zealand won series 1–0, with 1 draw
1998 *1* Dunedin **New Zealand** 64–22
2 Auckland **New Zealand** 40–10
New Zealand won series 2–0
1999 Twickenham WC **New Zealand** 30–16
2002 Twickenham **England** 31–28
2003 Wellington **England** 15–13
2004 *1* Dunedin **New Zealand** 36–3
2 Auckland **New Zealand** 36–12
New Zealand won series 2–0
2005 Twickenham **New Zealand** 23–19
2006 Twickenham **New Zealand** 41–20
2008 *1* Auckland **New Zealand** 37–20
2 Christchurch **New Zealand** 44–12
New Zealand won series 2–0

ENGLAND V AUSTRALIA

Played 35 England won 14, Australia won 20, Drawn 1
Highest scores England 32–31 in 2002, Australia 76–0 in 1998
Biggest wins England 20–3 in 1973 & 23–6 in 1976, Australia 76–0 in 1998

1909 Blackheath (London) **Australia** 9–3
1928 Twickenham **England** 18–11
1948 Twickenham **Australia** 11–0
1958 Twickenham **England** 9–6
1963 Sydney **Australia** 18–9
1967 Twickenham **Australia** 23–11
1973 Twickenham **England** 20–3
1975 *1* Sydney **Australia** 16–9
2 Brisbane **Australia** 30–21
Australia won series 2–0
1976 Twickenham **England** 23–6
1982 Twickenham **England** 15–11
1984 Twickenham **Australia** 19–3
1987 Sydney WC **Australia** 19–6
1988 *1* Brisbane **Australia** 22–16
2 Sydney **Australia** 28–8
Australia won series 2–0
1988 Twickenham **England** 28–19
1991 Sydney **Australia** 40–15
1991 Twickenham WC **Australia** 12–6
1995 Cape Town WC **England** 25–22
1997 Sydney **Australia** 25–6
1997 Twickenham **Drawn** 15–15
1998 Brisbane **Australia** 76–0
1998 Twickenham **Australia** 12–11
1999 Sydney **Australia** 22–15
2000 Twickenham **England** 22–19
2001 Twickenham **England** 21–15
2002 Twickenham **England** 32–31
2003 Melbourne **England** 25–14

2003	Sydney WC **England** 20–17 (aet)	2006	1 Sydney **Australia** 34–3
2004	Brisbane **Australia** 51–15		2 Melbourne **Australia** 43–18
2004	Twickenham **Australia** 21–19		Australia won series 2–0
2005	Twickenham **England** 26–16	2007	Marseilles WC **England** 12–10

ENGLAND V NEW ZEALAND NATIVES

Played 1 England won 1
Highest score England 7–0 in 1889, NZ Natives 0–7 in 1889
Biggest win England 7–0 in 1889, NZ Natives no win

1889	Blackheath **England** 1G 4T to 0

ENGLAND V RFU PRESIDENT'S XV

Played 1 President's XV won 1
Highest score England 11–28 in 1971, RFU President's XV 28–11 in 1971
Biggest win RFU President's XV 28–11 in 1971

1971	Twickenham **President's XV** 28–11

ENGLAND V ARGENTINA

Played 12 England won 8, Argentina won 3, Drawn 1
Highest scores England 51–0 in 1990, Argentina 33–13 in 1997
Biggest wins England 51–0 in 1990, Argentina 33–13 in 1997

1981	*1* Buenos Aires **Drawn** 19–19	1996	Twickenham **England** 20–18
	2 Buenos Aires **England** 12–6	1997	*1* Buenos Aires **England** 46–20
	England won series 1–0 with 1 draw		*2* Buenos Aires **Argentina** 33–13
1990	*1* Buenos Aires **England** 25–12		Series drawn 1–1
	2 Buenos Aires **Argentina** 15–13	2000	Twickenham **England** 19–0
	Series drawn 1–1	2002	Buenos Aires **England** 26–18
1990	Twickenham **England** 51–0	2006	Twickenham **Argentina** 25–18
1995	Durban WC **England** 24–18		

ENGLAND V ROMANIA

Played 4 England won 4
Highest scores England 134–0 in 2001, Romania 15–22 in 1985
Biggest win England 134–0 in 2001, Romania no win

1985 Twickenham **England** 22–15
1989 Bucharest **England** 58–3
1994 Twickenham **England** 54–3
2001 Twickenham **England** 134–0

ENGLAND V JAPAN

Played 1 England won 1
Highest score England 60–7 in 1987, Japan 7–60 in 1987
Biggest win England 60–7 in 1987, Japan no win

1987 Sydney WC **England** 60–7

ENGLAND V UNITED STATES

Played 5 England won 5
Highest scores England 106–8 in 1999, United States 19–48 in 2001
Biggest win England 106–8 in 1999, United States no win

1987 Sydney WC **England** 34–6
1991 Twickenham WC **England** 37–9
1999 Twickenham **England** 106–8
2001 San Francisco **England** 48–19
2007 Lens WC **England** 28–10

ENGLAND V FIJI

Played 4 England won 4
Highest scores England 58–23 in 1989, Fiji 24–45 in 1999
Biggest win England 58–23 in 1989, Fiji no win

1988 Suva **England** 25–12
1989 Twickenham **England** 58–23
1991 Suva **England** 28–12
1999 Twickenham WC **England** 45–24

ENGLAND V ITALY

Played 14 England won 14
Highest scores England 80–23 in 2001, Italy 23–80 in 2001
Biggest win England 67–7 in 1999, Italy no win

1991	Twickenham WC **England** 36–6	2002	Rome **England** 45–9
1995	Durban WC **England 27–20**	2003	Twickenham **England** 40–5
1996	Twickenham **England** 54–21	2004	Rome **England** 50–9
1998	Huddersfield **England** 23–15	2005	Twickenham **England** 39–7
1999	Twickenham WC **England** 67–7	2006	Rome **England** 31–16
2000	Rome **England** 59–12	2007	Twickenham **England** 20–7
2001	Twickenham **England** 80–23	2008	Rome **England** 23–19

ENGLAND V CANADA

Played 6 England won 6
Highest scores England 70–0 in 2004, Canada 20–59 in 2001
Biggest win England 70–0 in 2004, Canada no win

1992	Wembley **England** 26–13		*2* Burnaby **England** 59–20
1994	Twickenham **England** 60–19		England won series 2–0
1999	Twickenham **England** 36–11	2004	Twickenham **England** 70–0
2001	*1* Markham **England** 22–10		

ENGLAND V SAMOA

Played 5 England won 5
Highest scores England 44–22 in 1995 and 44–22 in 2007, Samoa 22–44 in 1995, 22–35 in 2003 and 22–44 in 2007
Biggest win England 40–3 in 2005, Samoa no win

1995	Durban WC **England** 44–22	2005	Twickenham **England** 40–3
1995	Twickenham **England** 27–9	2007	Nantes WC **England** 44–22
2003	Melbourne WC **England** 35–22		

ENGLAND V THE NETHERLANDS

Played 1 England won 1
Highest scores England 110–0 in 1998, The Netherlands 0–110 in 1998
Biggest win England 110–0 in 1998, The Netherlands no win

1998	Huddersfield **England** 110–0

ENGLAND V TONGA

Played 2 England won 2
Highest scores England 101–10 in 1999, Tonga 20–36 in 2007
Biggest win England 101–10 in 1999, Tonga no win

1999 Twickenham WC **England** 101–10	2007 Paris WC **England** 36–20

ENGLAND V GEORGIA

Played 1 England won 1
Highest scores England 84–6 in 2003, Georgia 6–84 in 2003
Biggest win England 84–6 in 2003, Georgia no win

2003 Perth WC **England** 84–6

ENGLAND V URUGUAY

Played 1 England won 1
Highest scores England 111–13 in 2003, Uruguay 13–111 in 2003
Biggest win England 111–13 in 2003, Uruguay no win

2003 Brisbane WC **England** 111–13

SCOTLAND V IRELAND

Played 122 Scotland won 62, Ireland won 54, Drawn 5, Abandoned 1
Highest scores Scotland 38–10 in 1997, Ireland 44–22 in 2000
Biggest wins Scotland 38–10 in 1997, Ireland 36–6 in 2003

1877 Belfast **Scotland** 4G 2DG 2T to 0
1878 No Match
1879 Belfast **Scotland** 1G 1DG 1T to 0
1880 Glasgow **Scotland** 1G 2DG 2T to 0
1881 Belfast **Ireland** 1DG to 1T
1882 Glasgow **Scotland** 2T to 0
1883 Belfast **Scotland** 1G 1T to 0
1884 Raeburn Place (Edinburgh) **Scotland** 2G 2T to 1T
1885 Belfast **Abandoned** Ireland 0 Scotland 1T
1885 Raeburn Place **Scotland** 1G 2T to 0
1886 Raeburn Place **Scotland** 3G 1DG 2T to 0
1887 Belfast **Scotland** 1G 1GM 2T to 0
1888 Raeburn Place **Scotland** 1G to 0
1889 Belfast **Scotland** 1DG to 0
1890 Raeburn Place **Scotland** 1DG 1T to 0
1891 Belfast **Scotland** 14–0
1892 Raeburn Place **Scotland** 2–0
1893 Belfast **Drawn** 0–0
1894 Dublin **Ireland** 5–0
1895 Raeburn Place **Scotland** 6–0
1896 Dublin **Drawn** 0–0
1897 Powderhall (Edinburgh) **Scotland** 8–3
1898 Belfast **Scotland** 8–0
1899 Inverleith (Edinburgh) **Ireland** 9–3
1900 Dublin **Drawn** 0–0

1901 Inverleith **Scotland** 9–5
1902 Belfast **Ireland** 5–0
1903 Inverleith **Scotland** 3–0
1904 Dublin **Scotland** 19–3
1905 Inverleith **Ireland** 11–5
1906 Dublin **Scotland** 13–6
1907 Inverleith **Scotland** 15–3
1908 Dublin **Ireland** 16–11
1909 Inverleith **Scotland** 9–3
1910 Belfast **Scotland** 14–0
1911 Inverleith **Ireland** 16–10
1912 Dublin **Ireland** 10–8
1913 Inverleith **Scotland** 29–14
1914 Dublin **Ireland** 6–0
1920 Inverleith **Scotland** 19–0
1921 Dublin **Ireland** 9–8
1922 Inverleith **Scotland** 6–3
1923 Dublin **Scotland** 13–3
1924 Inverleith **Scotland** 13–8
1925 Dublin **Scotland** 14–8
1926 Murrayfield **Ireland** 3–0
1927 Dublin **Ireland** 6–0
1928 Murrayfield **Ireland** 13–5
1929 Dublin **Scotland** 16–7
1930 Murrayfield **Ireland** 14–11
1931 Dublin **Ireland** 8–5
1932 Murrayfield **Ireland** 20–8
1933 Dublin **Scotland** 8–6
1934 Murrayfield **Scotland** 16–9
1935 Dublin **Ireland** 12–5
1936 Murrayfield **Ireland** 10–4
1937 Dublin **Ireland** 11–4
1938 Murrayfield **Scotland** 23–14
1939 Dublin **Ireland** 12–3
1947 Murrayfield **Ireland** 3–0
1948 Dublin **Ireland** 6–0
1949 Murrayfield **Ireland** 13–3
1950 Dublin **Ireland** 21–0
1951 Murrayfield **Ireland** 6–5
1952 Dublin **Ireland** 12–8
1953 Murrayfield **Ireland** 26–8
1954 Belfast **Ireland** 6–0
1955 Murrayfield **Scotland** 12–3
1956 Dublin **Ireland** 14–10
1957 Murrayfield **Ireland** 5–3
1958 Dublin **Ireland** 12–6
1959 Murrayfield **Ireland** 8–3
1960 Dublin **Scotland** 6–5
1961 Murrayfield **Scotland** 16–8
1962 Dublin **Scotland** 20–6
1963 Murrayfield **Scotland** 3–0
1964 Dublin **Scotland** 6–3
1965 Murrayfield **Ireland** 16–6
1966 Dublin **Scotland** 11–3
1967 Murrayfield **Ireland** 5–3
1968 Dublin **Ireland** 14–6
1969 Murrayfield **Ireland** 16–0
1970 Dublin **Ireland** 16–11
1971 Murrayfield **Ireland** 17–5
1972 No Match
1973 Murrayfield **Scotland** 19–14
1974 Dublin **Ireland** 9–6
1975 Murrayfield **Scotland** 20–13
1976 Dublin **Scotland** 15–6
1977 Murrayfield **Scotland** 21–18
1978 Dublin **Ireland** 12–9
1979 Murrayfield **Drawn** 11–11
1980 Dublin **Ireland** 22–15
1981 Murrayfield **Scotland** 10–9
1982 Dublin **Ireland** 21–12
1983 Murrayfield **Ireland** 15–13
1984 Dublin **Scotland** 32–9
1985 Murrayfield **Ireland** 18–15
1986 Dublin **Scotland** 10–9
1987 Murrayfield **Scotland** 16–12
1988 Dublin **Ireland** 22–18
1989 Murrayfield **Scotland** 37–21
1990 Dublin **Scotland** 13–10
1991 Murrayfield **Scotland** 28–25
1991 Murrayfield WC **Scotland** 24–15
1992 Dublin **Scotland** 18–10
1993 Murrayfield **Scotland** 15–3
1994 Dublin **Drawn** 6–6
1995 Murrayfield **Scotland** 26–13
1996 Dublin **Scotland** 16–10
1997 Murrayfield **Scotland** 38–10
1998 Dublin **Scotland** 17–16
1999 Murrayfield **Scotland** 30–13
2000 Dublin **Ireland** 44–22
2001 Murrayfield **Scotland** 32–10
2002 Dublin **Ireland** 43–22
2003 Murrayfield **Ireland** 36–6
2003 Murrayfield **Ireland** 29–10
Non-championship match
2004 Dublin **Ireland** 37–16
2005 Murrayfield **Ireland** 40–13
2006 Dublin **Ireland** 15–9
2007 Murrayfield **Ireland** 19–18
2007 Murrayfield **Scotland** 31–21
Non-championship match
2008 Dublin **Ireland** 34–13

SCOTLAND V WALES

Played 113 Scotland won 48, Wales won 62, Drawn 3
Highest scores Scotland 35–10 in 1924, Wales 46–22 in 2005
Biggest wins Scotland 35–10 in 1924, Wales 46–22 in 2005

1883 Raeburn Place (Edinburgh) **Scotland** 3G to 1G
1884 Newport **Scotland** 1DG 1T to 0
1885 Glasgow **Drawn** no score
1886 Cardiff **Scotland** 2G 1T to 0
1887 Raeburn Place **Scotland** 4G 8T to 0
1888 Newport **Wales** 1T to 0
1889 Raeburn Place **Scotland** 2T to 0
1890 Cardiff **Scotland** 1G 2T to 1T
1891 Raeburn Place **Scotland** 15–0
1892 Swansea **Scotland** 7–2
1893 Raeburn Place **Wales** 9–0
1894 Newport **Wales** 7–0
1895 Raeburn Place **Scotland** 5–4
1896 Cardiff **Wales** 6–0
1897 No Match
1898 No Match
1899 Inverleith (Edinburgh) **Scotland** 21–10
1900 Swansea **Wales** 12–3
1901 Inverleith **Scotland** 18–8
1902 Cardiff **Wales** 14–5
1903 Inverleith **Scotland** 6–0
1904 Swansea **Wales** 21–3
1905 Inverleith **Wales** 6–3
1906 Cardiff **Wales** 9–3
1907 Inverleith **Scotland** 6–3
1908 Swansea **Wales** 6–5
1909 Inverleith **Wales** 5–3
1910 Cardiff **Wales** 14–0
1911 Inverleith **Wales** 32–10
1912 Swansea **Wales** 21–6
1913 Inverleith **Wales** 8–0
1914 Cardiff **Wales** 24–5
1920 Inverleith **Scotland** 9–5
1921 Swansea **Scotland** 14–8
1922 Inverleith **Drawn** 9–9
1923 Cardiff **Scotland** 11–8
1924 Inverleith **Scotland** 35–10
1925 Swansea **Scotland** 24–14
1926 Murrayfield **Scotland** 8–5
1927 Cardiff **Scotland** 5–0
1928 Murrayfield **Wales** 13–0
1929 Swansea **Wales** 14–7
1930 Murrayfield **Scotland** 12–9
1931 Cardiff **Wales** 13–8
1932 Murrayfield **Wales** 6–0
1933 Swansea **Scotland** 11–3
1934 Murrayfield **Wales** 13–6
1935 Cardiff **Wales** 10–6
1936 Murrayfield **Wales** 13–3
1937 Swansea **Scotland** 13–6
1938 Murrayfield **Scotland** 8–6
1939 Cardiff **Wales** 11–3
1947 Murrayfield **Wales** 22–8
1948 Cardiff **Wales** 14–0
1949 Murrayfield **Scotland** 6–5
1950 Swansea **Wales** 12–0
1951 Murrayfield **Scotland** 19–0
1952 Cardiff **Wales** 11–0
1953 Murrayfield **Wales** 12–0
1954 Swansea **Wales** 15–3
1955 Murrayfield **Scotland** 14–8
1956 Cardiff **Wales** 9–3
1957 Murrayfield **Scotland** 9–6
1958 Cardiff **Wales** 8–3
1959 Murrayfield **Scotland** 6–5
1960 Cardiff **Wales** 8–0
1961 Murrayfield **Scotland** 3–0
1962 Cardiff **Scotland** 8–3
1963 Murrayfield **Wales** 6–0
1964 Cardiff **Wales** 11–3
1965 Murrayfield **Wales** 14–12
1966 Cardiff **Wales** 8–3
1967 Murrayfield **Scotland** 11–5
1968 Cardiff **Wales** 5–0
1969 Murrayfield **Wales** 17–3
1970 Cardiff **Wales** 18–9
1971 Murrayfield **Wales** 19–18
1972 Cardiff **Wales** 35–12
1973 Murrayfield **Scotland** 10–9
1974 Cardiff **Wales** 6–0
1975 Murrayfield **Scotland** 12–10
1976 Cardiff **Wales** 28–6
1977 Murrayfield **Wales** 18–9
1978 Cardiff **Wales** 22–14
1979 Murrayfield **Wales** 19–13

1980 Cardiff **Wales** 17–6
1981 Murrayfield **Scotland** 15–6
1982 Cardiff **Scotland** 34–18
1983 Murrayfield **Wales** 19–15
1984 Cardiff **Scotland** 15–9
1985 Murrayfield **Wales** 25–21
1986 Cardiff **Wales** 22–15
1987 Murrayfield **Scotland** 21–15
1988 Cardiff **Wales** 25–20
1989 Murrayfield **Scotland** 23–7
1990 Cardiff **Scotland** 13–9
1991 Murrayfield **Scotland** 32–12
1992 Cardiff **Wales** 15–12
1993 Murrayfield **Scotland** 20–0
1994 Cardiff **Wales** 29–6
1995 Murrayfield **Scotland** 26–13
1996 Cardiff **Scotland** 16–14
1997 Murrayfield **Wales** 34–19
1998 Wembley **Wales** 19–13
1999 Murrayfield **Scotland** 33–20
2000 Cardiff **Wales** 26–18
2001 Murrayfield **Drawn** 28–28
2002 Cardiff **Scotland** 27–22
2003 Murrayfield **Scotland** 30–22
2003 Cardiff **Wales** 23–9
Non-championship match
2004 Cardiff **Wales** 23–10
2005 Murrayfield **Wales** 46–22
2006 Cardiff **Wales** 28–18
2007 Murrayfield **Scotland** 21–9
2008 Cardiff **Wales** 30–15

SCOTLAND V FRANCE

Played 81 Scotland won 34, France won 44, Drawn 3
Highest scores Scotland 36–22 in 1999, France 51–16 in 1998 and 51–9 in 2003
Biggest wins Scotland 31–3 in 1912, France 51–9 in 2003

1910 Inverleith (Edinburgh) **Scotland** 27–0
1911 Paris **France** 16–15
1912 Inverleith **Scotland** 31–3
1913 Paris **Scotland** 21–3
1914 No Match
1920 Paris **Scotland** 5–0
1921 Inverleith **France** 3–0
1922 Paris **Drawn** 3–3
1923 Inverleith **Scotland** 16–3
1924 Paris **France** 12–10
1925 Inverleith **Scotland** 25–4
1926 Paris **Scotland** 20–6
1927 Murrayfield **Scotland** 23–6
1928 Paris **Scotland** 15–6
1929 Murrayfield **Scotland** 6–3
1930 Paris **France** 7–3
1931 Murrayfield **Scotland** 6–4
1947 Paris **France** 8–3
1948 Murrayfield **Scotland** 9–8
1949 Paris **Scotland** 8–0
1950 Murrayfield **Scotland** 8–5
1951 Paris **France** 14–12
1952 Murrayfield **France** 13–11
1953 Paris **France** 11–5
1954 Murrayfield **France** 3–0
1955 Paris **France** 15–0
1956 Murrayfield **Scotland** 12–0
1957 Paris **Scotland** 6–0
1958 Murrayfield **Scotland** 11–9
1959 Paris **France** 9–0
1960 Murrayfield **France** 13–11
1961 Paris **France** 11–0
1962 Murrayfield **France** 11–3
1963 Paris **Scotland** 11–6
1964 Murrayfield **Scotland** 10–0
1965 Paris **France** 16–8
1966 Murrayfield **Drawn** 3–3
1967 Paris **Scotland** 9–8
1968 Murrayfield **France** 8–6
1969 Paris **Scotland** 6–3
1970 Murrayfield **France** 11–9
1971 Paris **France** 13–8
1972 Murrayfield **Scotland** 20–9
1973 Paris **France** 16–13
1974 Murrayfield **Scotland** 19–6
1975 Paris **France** 10–9
1976 Murrayfield **France** 13–6
1977 Paris **France** 23–3
1978 Murrayfield **France** 19–16
1979 Paris **France** 21–17

1980 Murrayfield **Scotland** 22–14
1981 Paris **France** 16–9
1982 Murrayfield **Scotland** 16–7
1983 Paris **France** 19–15
1984 Murrayfield **Scotland** 21–12
1985 Paris **France** 11–3
1986 Murrayfield **Scotland** 18–17
1987 Paris **France** 28–22
1987 Christchurch WC **Drawn** 20–20
1988 Murrayfield **Scotland** 23–12
1989 Paris **France** 19–3
1990 Murrayfield **Scotland** 21–0
1991 Paris **France** 15–9
1992 Murrayfield **Scotland** 10–6
1993 Paris **France** 11–3
1994 Murrayfield **France** 20–12
1995 Paris **Scotland** 23–21
1995 Pretoria WC **France** 22–19
1996 Murrayfield **Scotland** 19–14
1997 Paris **France** 47–20
1998 Murrayfield **France** 51–16
1999 Paris **Scotland** 36–22
2000 Murrayfield **France** 28–16
2001 Paris **France** 16–6
2002 Murrayfield **France** 22–10
2003 Paris **France** 38–3
2003 Sydney WC **France** 51–9
2004 Murrayfield **France** 31–0
2005 Paris **France** 16–9
2006 Murrayfield **Scotland** 20–16
2007 Paris **France** 46–19
2008 Murrayfield **France** 27–6

SCOTLAND V SOUTH AFRICA

Played 19 Scotland won 4, South Africa won 15, Drawn 0
Highest scores Scotland 29–46 in 1999, South Africa 68–10 in 1997
Biggest wins Scotland 21–6 in 2002, South Africa 68–10 in 1997

1906 Glasgow **Scotland** 6–0
1912 Inverleith **South Africa** 16–0
1932 Murrayfield **South Africa** 6–3
1951 Murrayfield **South Africa** 44–0
1960 Port Elizabeth **South Africa** 18–10
1961 Murrayfield **South Africa** 12–5
1965 Murrayfield **Scotland** 8–5
1969 Murrayfield **Scotland** 6–3
1994 Murrayfield **South Africa** 34–10
1997 Murrayfield **South Africa** 68–10
1998 Murrayfield **South Africa** 35–10
1999 Murrayfield WC **South Africa** 46–29
2002 Murrayfield **Scotland** 21–6
2003 *1* Durban **South Africa** 29–25
2 Johannesburg **South Africa** 28–19
South Africa won series 2–0
2004 Murrayfield **South Africa** 45–10
2006 1 Durban **South Africa** 36–16
2 Port Elizabeth **South Africa** 29–15
South Africa won series 2–0
2007 Murrayfield **South Africa** 27–3

SCOTLAND V NEW ZEALAND

Played 26 Scotland won 0, New Zealand won 24, Drawn 2
Highest scores Scotland 31–62 in 1996, New Zealand 69–20 in 2000
Biggest wins Scotland no win, New Zealand 69–20 in 2000

1905 Inverleith (Edinburgh) **New Zealand** 12–7
1935 Murrayfield **New Zealand** 18–8
1954 Murrayfield **New Zealand** 3–0
1964 Murrayfield **Drawn** 0–0
1967 Murrayfield **New Zealand** 14–3
1972 Murrayfield **New Zealand** 14–9

1975	Auckland **New Zealand** 24–0	1993	Murrayfield **New Zealand** 51–15
1978	Murrayfield **New Zealand** 18–9	1995	Pretoria WC **New Zealand** 48–30
1979	Murrayfield **New Zealand** 20–6	1996	*1* Dunedin **New Zealand** 62–31
1981	*1* Dunedin **New Zealand** 11–4		*2* Auckland **New Zealand** 36–12
	2 Auckland **New Zealand** 40–15		New Zealand won series 2–0
	New Zealand won series 2–0	1999	Murrayfield WC **New Zealand** 30–18
1983	Murrayfield **Drawn** 25–25	2000	*1* Dunedin **New Zealand** 69–20
1987	Christchurch WC **New Zealand** 30–3		*2* Auckland **New Zealand** 48–14
1990	*1* Dunedin **New Zealand** 31–16		New Zealand won series 2–0
	2 Auckland **New Zealand** 21–18	2001	Murrayfield **New Zealand** 37–6
	New Zealand won series 2–0	2005	Murrayfield **New Zealand** 29–10
1991	Cardiff WC **New Zealand** 13–6	2007	Murrayfield WC **New Zealand** 40–0

SCOTLAND V AUSTRALIA

Played 25 Scotland won 7, Australia won 18, Drawn 0
Highest scores Scotland 24–15 in 1981, Australia 45–3 in 1998
Biggest wins Scotland 24–15 in 1981, Australia 45–3 in 1998

1927	Murrayfield **Scotland** 10–8		Australia won series 2–0
1947	Murrayfield **Australia** 16–7	1996	Murrayfield **Australia** 29–19
1958	Murrayfield **Scotland** 12–8	1997	Murrayfield **Australia** 37–8
1966	Murrayfield **Scotland** 11–5	1998	*1* Sydney **Australia** 45–3
1968	Murrayfield **Scotland** 9–3		*2* Brisbane **Australia** 33–11
1970	Sydney **Australia** 23–3		Australia won series 2–0
1975	Murrayfield **Scotland** 10–3	2000	Murrayfield **Australia** 30–9
1981	Murrayfield **Scotland** 24–15	2003	Brisbane WC **Australia** 33–16
1982	*1* Brisbane **Scotland** 12–7	2004	1 Melbourne **Australia** 35–15
	2 Sydney **Australia** 33–9		2 Sydney **Australia** 34–13
	Series drawn 1–1		Australia won series 2–0
1984	Murrayfield **Australia** 37–12	2004	1 Murrayfield **Australia** 31–14
1988	Murrayfield **Australia** 32–13		2 Glasgow **Australia** 31–17
1992	*1* Sydney **Australia** 27–12		Australia won series 2–0
	2 Brisbane **Australia** 37–13	2006	Murrayfield **Australia** 44–15

SCOTLAND V SRU PRESIDENT'S XV

Played 1 Scotland won 1
Highest scores Scotland 27–16 in 1972, SRU President's XV 16–27 in 1973
Biggest win Scotland 27–16 in 1973, SRU President's XV no win

1973	Murrayfield **Scotland** 27–16

SCOTLAND V ROMANIA

Played 12 Scotland won 10 Romania won 2, Drawn 0
Highest scores Scotland 60–19 in 1999, Romania 28–55 in 1987 & 28–22 in 1984
Biggest wins Scotland 48–6 in 2006 and 42–0 in 2007, Romania 28–22 in 1984 & 18–12 in 1991

1981	Murrayfield **Scotland** 12–6	1995	Murrayfield **Scotland** 49–16
1984	Bucharest **Romania** 28–22	1999	Glasgow **Scotland** 60–19
1986	Bucharest **Scotland** 33–18	2002	Murrayfield **Scotland** 37–10
1987	Dunedin WC **Scotland** 55–28	2005	Bucharest **Scotland** 39–19
1989	Murrayfield **Scotland** 32–0	2006	Murrayfield **Scotland** 48–6
1991	Bucharest **Romania** 18–12	2007	Murrayfield WC **Scotland** 42–0

SCOTLAND V ZIMBABWE

Played 2 Scotland won 2
Highest scores Scotland 60–21 in 1987, Zimbabwe 21–60 in 1987
Biggest win Scotland 60–21 in 1987 & 51–12 in 1991, Zimbabwe no win

1987	Wellington WC **Scotland** 60–21	1991	Murrayfield WC **Scotland** 51–12

SCOTLAND V FIJI

Played 4 Scotland won 3, Fiji won 1
Highest scores Scotland 38–17 in 1989, Fiji 51–26 in 1998
Biggest win Scotland 38–17 in 1989, Fiji 51–26 in 1998

1989	Murrayfield **Scotland** 38–17	2002	Murrayfield **Scotland** 36–22
1998	Suva **Fiji** 51–26	2003	Sydney WC **Scotland** 22–20

SCOTLAND V ARGENTINA

Played 9 Scotland won 2, Argentina won 7, Drawn 0
Highest scores Scotland 49–3 in 1990, Argentina 31–22 in 1999
Biggest wins Scotland 49–3 in 1990, Argentina 31–22 in 1999 and 25–16 in 2001

1990	Murrayfield **Scotland** 49–3	*2* Buenos Aires **Argentina** 19–17
1994	*1* Buenos Aires **Argentina** 16–15	Argentina won series 2–0

1999	Murrayfield **Argentina** 31–22	2008	*1* Rosario **Argentina** 21–15
2001	Murrayfield **Argentina** 25–16		*2* Buenos Aires **Scotland** 26–14
2005	Murrayfield **Argentina** 23–19		Series drawn 1–1
2007	Paris WC **Argentina** 19–13		

SCOTLAND V JAPAN

Played 3 Scotland won 3
Highest scores Scotland 100–8 in 2004, Japan 11–32 in 2003
Biggest win Scotland 100–8 in 2004, Japan no win

1991	Murrayfield WC **Scotland** 47–9	2004	Perth **Scotland** 100–8
2003	Townsville WC **Scotland** 32–11		

SCOTLAND V SAMOA

Played 6 Scotland won 5, Drawn 1
Highest scores Scotland 38–3 in 2004, Samoa 20–35 in 1999
Biggest win Scotland 38–3 in 2004, Samoa no win

1991	Murrayfield WC **Scotland** 28–6	2000	Murrayfield **Scotland** 31–8
1995	Murrayfield **Drawn** 15–15	2004	Wellington (NZ) **Scotland** 38–3
1999	Murrayfield WC **Scotland** 35–20	2005	Murrayfield **Scotland** 18–11

SCOTLAND V CANADA

Played 2 Scotland won 1, Canada won 1
Highest scores Scotland 23–26 in 2002, Canada 26–23 in 2002
Biggest win Scotland 22–6 in 1995, Canada 26–23 in 2002

1995	Murrayfield **Scotland** 22–6	2002	Vancouver **Canada** 26–23

SCOTLAND V IVORY COAST

Played 1 Scotland won 1
Highest scores Scotland 89–0 in 1995, Ivory Coast 0–89 in 1995
Biggest win Scotland 89–0 in 1995, Ivory Coast no win

1995	Rustenburg WC **Scotland 89–0**

SCOTLAND V TONGA

Played 2 Scotland won 2
Highest scores Scotland 43–20 in 2001, Tonga 20–43 in 2001
Biggest win Scotland 41–5 in 1995, Tonga no win

1995 Pretoria WC **Scotland 41–5**	2001 Murrayfield **Scotland** 43–20

SCOTLAND V ITALY

Played 14 Scotland won 9, Italy won 5
Highest scores Scotland 47–15 in 2003, Italy 37–17 in 2007
Biggest wins Scotland 47–15 in 2003, Italy 37–17 in 2007

1996	Murrayfield **Scotland** 29–22		Non-championship match
1998	Treviso **Italy** 25–21	2004	Rome **Italy** 20–14
1999	Murrayfield **Scotland** 30–12	2005	Murrayfield **Scotland** 18–10
2000	Rome **Italy** 34–20	2006	Rome **Scotland** 13–10
2001	Murrayfield **Scotland** 23–19	2007	Murrayfield **Italy** 37–17
2002	Rome **Scotland** 29–12	2007	Saint Etienne WC **Scotland** 18–16
2003	Murrayfield **Scotland** 33–25	2008	Rome **Italy** 23–20
2003	Murrayfield **Scotland** 47–15		

SCOTLAND V URUGUAY

Played 1 Scotland won 1
Highest scores Scotland 43–12 in 1999, Uruguay 12–43 in 1999
Biggest win Scotland 43–12 in 1999, Uruguay no win

1999 Murrayfield WC **Scotland** 43–12

SCOTLAND V SPAIN

Played 1 Scotland won 1
Highest scores Scotland 48–0 in 1999, Spain 0–48 in 1999
Biggest win Scotland 48–0 in 1999, Spain no win

1999 Murrayfield WC **Scotland** 48–0

SCOTLAND V UNITED STATES

Played 3 Scotland won 3
Highest scores Scotland 65–23 in 2002, United States 23–65 in 2002
Biggest win Scotland 53–6 in 2000, United States no win

2000	Murrayfield **Scotland** 53–6	2003	Brisbane WC **Scotland** 39–15
2002	San Francisco **Scotland** 65–23		

SCOTLAND V PACIFIC ISLANDS

Played 1 Scotland won 1
Highest scores Scotland 34–22 in 2006, Pacific Islands 22–34 in 2006
Biggest win Scotland 34–22 in 2006, Pacific Islands no win

2006	Murrayfield **Scotland** 34–22

SCOTLAND V PORTUGAL

Played 1 Scotland won 1
Highest scores Scotland 56–10 in 2007, Portugal 10–56 in 2007
Biggest win Scotland 56–10 in 2007, Portugal no win

2007	Saint Etienne WC **Scotland** 56–10

IRELAND V WALES

Played 113 Ireland won 45, Wales won 62, Drawn 6
Highest scores Ireland 54–10 in 2002, Wales 34–9 in 1976
Biggest wins Ireland 54–10 in 2002, Wales 29–0 in 1907

1882	Dublin **Wales** 2G 2T to 0	1891	Llanelli **Wales** 6–4
1883	No Match	1892	Dublin **Ireland** 9–0
1884	Cardiff **Wales** 1DG 2T to 0	1893	Llanelli **Wales** 2–0
1885	No Match	1894	Belfast **Ireland** 3–0
1886	No Match	1895	Cardiff **Wales** 5–3
1887	Birkenhead **Wales** 1DG 1T to 3T	1896	Dublin **Ireland** 8–4
1888	Dublin **Ireland** 1G 1DG 1T to 0	1897	No Match
1889	Swansea **Ireland** 2T to 0	1898	Limerick **Wales** 11–3
1890	Dublin **Drawn** 1G each	1899	Cardiff **Ireland** 3–0

1900 Belfast **Wales** 3–0
1901 Swansea **Wales** 10–9
1902 Dublin **Wales** 15–0
1903 Cardiff **Wales** 18–0
1904 Belfast **Ireland** 14–12
1905 Swansea **Wales** 10–3
1906 Belfast **Ireland** 11–6
1907 Cardiff **Wales** 29–0
1908 Belfast **Wales** 11–5
1909 Swansea **Wales** 18–5
1910 Dublin **Wales** 19–3
1911 Cardiff **Wales** 16–0
1912 Belfast **Ireland** 12–5
1913 Swansea **Wales** 16–13
1914 Belfast **Wales** 11–3
1920 Cardiff **Wales** 28–4
1921 Belfast **Wales** 6–0
1922 Swansea **Wales** 11–5
1923 Dublin **Ireland** 5–4
1924 Cardiff **Ireland** 13–10
1925 Belfast **Ireland** 19–3
1926 Swansea **Wales** 11–8
1927 Dublin **Ireland** 19–9
1928 Cardiff **Ireland** 13–10
1929 Belfast **Drawn** 5–5
1930 Swansea **Wales** 12–7
1931 Belfast **Wales** 15–3
1932 Cardiff **Ireland** 12–10
1933 Belfast **Ireland** 10–5
1934 Swansea **Wales** 13–0
1935 Belfast **Ireland** 9–3
1936 Cardiff **Wales** 3–0
1937 Belfast **Ireland** 5–3
1938 Swansea **Wales** 11–5
1939 Belfast **Wales** 7–0
1947 Swansea **Wales** 6–0
1948 Belfast **Ireland** 6–3
1949 Swansea **Ireland** 5–0
1950 Belfast **Wales** 6–3
1951 Cardiff **Drawn** 3–3
1952 Dublin **Wales** 14–3
1953 Swansea **Wales** 5–3
1954 Dublin **Wales** 12–9
1955 Cardiff **Wales** 21–3
1956 Dublin **Ireland** 11–3
1957 Cardiff **Wales** 6–5
1958 Dublin **Wales** 9–6
1959 Cardiff **Wales** 8–6
1960 Dublin **Wales** 10–9
1961 Cardiff **Wales** 9–0
1962 Dublin **Drawn** 3–3
1963 Cardiff **Ireland** 14–6
1964 Dublin **Wales** 15–6
1965 Cardiff **Wales** 14–8
1966 Dublin **Ireland** 9–6
1967 Cardiff **Ireland** 3–0
1968 Dublin **Ireland** 9–6
1969 Cardiff **Wales** 24–11
1970 Dublin **Ireland** 14–0
1971 Cardiff **Wales** 23–9
1972 No Match
1973 Cardiff **Wales** 16–12
1974 Dublin **Drawn** 9–9
1975 Cardiff **Wales** 32–4
1976 Dublin **Wales** 34–9
1977 Cardiff **Wales** 25–9
1978 Dublin **Wales** 20–16
1979 Cardiff **Wales** 24–21
1980 Dublin **Ireland** 21–7
1981 Cardiff **Wales** 9–8
1982 Dublin **Ireland** 20–12
1983 Cardiff **Wales** 23–9
1984 Dublin **Wales** 18–9
1985 Cardiff **Ireland** 21–9
1986 Dublin **Wales** 19–12
1987 Cardiff **Ireland** 15–11
1987 Wellington WC **Wales** 13–6
1988 Dublin **Wales** 12–9
1989 Cardiff **Ireland** 19–13
1990 Dublin **Ireland** 14–8
1991 Cardiff **Drawn** 21–21
1992 Dublin **Wales** 16–15
1993 Cardiff **Ireland** 19–14
1994 Dublin **Wales** 17–15
1995 Cardiff **Ireland** 16–12
1995 Johannesburg WC **Ireland** 24–23
1996 Dublin **Ireland** 30–17
1997 Cardiff **Ireland** 26–25
1998 Dublin **Wales** 30–21
1999 Wembley **Ireland** 29–23
2000 Dublin **Wales** 23–19
2001 Cardiff **Ireland** 36–6
2002 Dublin **Ireland** 54–10
2003 Cardiff **Ireland** 25–24
2003 Dublin **Ireland** 35–12
2004 Dublin **Ireland** 36–15
2005 Cardiff **Wales** 32–20
2006 Dublin **Ireland** 31–5
2007 Cardiff **Ireland** 19–9
2008 Dublin **Wales** 16–12

IRELAND V FRANCE

Played 84 Ireland won 28, France won 51, Drawn 5
Highest scores Ireland 31–43 in 2006, France 45–10 in 1996
Biggest wins Ireland 24–0 in 1913, France 44–5 in 2002

1909 Dublin **Ireland** 19–8
1910 Paris **Ireland** 8–3
1911 Cork **Ireland** 25–5
1912 Paris **Ireland** 11–6
1913 Cork **Ireland** 24–0
1914 Paris **Ireland** 8–6
1920 Dublin **France** 15–7
1921 Paris **France** 20–10
1922 Dublin **Ireland** 8–3
1923 Paris **France** 14–8
1924 Dublin **Ireland** 6–0
1925 Paris **Ireland** 9–3
1926 Belfast **Ireland** 11–0
1927 Paris **Ireland** 8–3
1928 Belfast **Ireland** 12–8
1929 Paris **Ireland** 6–0
1930 Belfast **France** 5–0
1931 Paris **France** 3–0
1947 Dublin **France** 12–8
1948 Paris **Ireland** 13–6
1949 Dublin **France** 16–9
1950 Paris **Drawn** 3–3
1951 Dublin **Ireland** 9–8
1952 Paris **Ireland** 11–8
1953 Belfast **Ireland** 16–3
1954 Paris **France** 8–0
1955 Dublin **France** 5–3
1956 Paris **France** 14–8
1957 Dublin **Ireland** 11–6
1958 Paris **France** 11–6
1959 Dublin **Ireland** 9–5
1960 Paris **France** 23–6
1961 Dublin **France** 15–3
1962 Paris **France** 11–0
1963 Dublin **France** 24–5
1964 Paris **France** 27–6
1965 Dublin **Drawn** 3–3
1966 Paris **France** 11–6
1967 Dublin **France** 11–6
1968 Paris **France** 16–6
1969 Dublin **Ireland** 17–9
1970 Paris **France** 8–0
1971 Dublin **Drawn** 9–9
1972 Paris **Ireland** 14–9
1972 Dublin **Ireland** 24–14
Non-championship match
1973 Dublin **Ireland** 6–4
1974 Paris **France** 9–6
1975 Dublin **Ireland** 25–6
1976 Paris **France** 26–3
1977 Dublin **France** 15–6
1978 Paris **France** 10–9
1979 Dublin **Drawn** 9–9
1980 Paris **France** 19–18
1981 Dublin **France** 19–13
1982 Paris **France** 22–9
1983 Dublin **Ireland** 22–16
1984 Paris **France** 25–12
1985 Dublin **Drawn** 15–15
1986 Paris **France** 29–9
1987 Dublin **France** 19–13
1988 Paris **France** 25–6
1989 Dublin **France** 26–21
1990 Paris **France** 31–12
1991 Dublin **France** 21–13
1992 Paris **France** 44–12
1993 Dublin **France** 21–6
1994 Paris **France** 35–15
1995 Dublin **France** 25–7
1995 Durban WC **France 36–12**
1996 Paris **France** 45–10
1997 Dublin **France** 32–15
1998 Paris **France** 18–16
1999 Dublin **France** 10–9
2000 Paris **Ireland** 27–25
2001 Dublin **Ireland** 22–15
2002 Paris **France** 44–5
2003 Dublin **Ireland** 15–12
2003 Melbourne WC **France** 43–21
2004 Paris **France** 35–17
2005 Dublin **France** 26–19
2006 Paris **France** 43–31
2007 Dublin **France** 20–17
2007 Paris WC **France** 25–3
2008 Paris **France** 26–21

IRELAND V SOUTH AFRICA

Played 18 Ireland won 3, South Africa won 14, Drawn 1
Highest scores Ireland 32–15 in 2006, South Africa 38–0 in 1912
Biggest wins Ireland 32–15 in 2006, South Africa 38–0 in 1912

1906	Belfast **South Africa** 15–12
1912	Dublin **South Africa** 38–0
1931	Dublin **South Africa** 8–3
1951	Dublin **South Africa** 17–5
1960	Dublin **South Africa** 8–3
1961	Cape Town **South Africa** 24–8
1965	Dublin **Ireland** 9–6
1970	Dublin **Drawn** 8–8
1981	*1* Cape Town **South Africa** 23–15
	2 Durban **South Africa** 12–10
	South Africa won series 2–0
1998	*1* Bloemfontein **South Africa** 37–13
	2 Pretoria **South Africa** 33–0
	South Africa won series 2–0
1998	Dublin **South Africa** 27–13
2000	Dublin **South Africa** 28–18
2004	1 Bloemfontein **South Africa** 31–17
	2 Cape Town **South Africa** 26–17
	South Africa won series 2–0
2004	Dublin **Ireland** 17–12
2006	Dublin **Ireland** 32–15

IRELAND V NEW ZEALAND

Played 21 Ireland won 0, New Zealand won 20, Drawn 1
Highest scores Ireland 29–40 in 2001, New Zealand 63–15 in 1997
Biggest win Ireland no win, New Zealand 59–6 in 1992

1905	Dublin **New Zealand** 15–0
1924	Dublin **New Zealand** 6–0
1935	Dublin **New Zealand** 17–9
1954	Dublin **New Zealand** 14–3
1963	Dublin **New Zealand** 6–5
1973	Dublin **Drawn** 10–10
1974	Dublin **New Zealand** 15–6
1976	Wellington **New Zealand** 11–3
1978	Dublin **New Zealand** 10–6
1989	Dublin **New Zealand** 23–6
1992	*1* Dunedin **New Zealand** 24–21
	2 Wellington **New Zealand** 59–6
	New Zealand won series 2–0
1995	Johannesburg WC **New Zealand 43–19**
1997	Dublin **New Zealand** 63–15
2001	Dublin **New Zealand** 40–29
2002	*1* Dunedin **New Zealand** 15–6
	2 Auckland **New Zealand** 40–8
	New Zealand won series 2–0
2005	Dublin **New Zealand** 45–7
2006	1 Hamilton **New Zealand** 34–23
	2 Auckland **New Zealand** 27–17
	New Zealand won series 2–0
2008	Wellington **New Zealand** 21–11

IRELAND V AUSTRALIA

Played 27 Ireland won 8, Australia won 19, Drawn 0
Highest scores Ireland 27–12 in 1979, Australia 46–10 in 1999
Biggest wins Ireland 27–12 in 1979 & 21–6 in 2006, Australia 46–10 in 1999

1927	Dublin **Australia** 5–3	1994	*1* Brisbane **Australia** 33–13
1947	Dublin **Australia** 16–3		*2* Sydney **Australia** 32–18
1958	Dublin **Ireland** 9–6		Australia won series 2–0
1967	Dublin **Ireland** 15–8	1996	Dublin **Australia** 22–12
1967	Sydney **Ireland** 11–5	1999	*1* Brisbane **Australia** 46–10
1968	Dublin **Ireland** 10–3		*2* Perth **Australia** 32–26
1976	Dublin **Australia** 20–10		Australia won series 2–0
1979	*1* Brisbane **Ireland** 27–12	1999	Dublin WC **Australia** 23–3
	2 Sydney **Ireland** 9–3	2002	Dublin **Ireland** 18–9
	Ireland won series 2–0	2003	Perth **Australia** 45–16
1981	Dublin **Australia** 16–12	2003	Melbourne WC **Australia** 17–16
1984	Dublin **Australia** 16–9	2005	Dublin **Australia** 30–14
1987	Sydney WC **Australia** 33–15	2006	Perth **Australia** 37–15
1991	Dublin WC **Australia** 19–18	2006	Dublin **Ireland** 21–6
1992	Dublin **Australia** 42–17	2008	Melbourne **Australia** 18–12

IRELAND V NEW ZEALAND NATIVES

Played 1 New Zealand Natives won 1
Highest scores Ireland 4–13 in 1888, Zew Zealand Natives 13–4 in 1888
Biggest win Ireland no win, New Zealand Natives 13–4 in 1888

1888	Dublin **New Zealand Natives** 4G 1T to 1G 1T

IRELAND V IRU PRESIDENT'S XV

Played 1 Drawn 1
Highest scores Ireland 18–18 in 1974, IRFU President's XV 18–18 in 1974

1974	Dublin **Drawn** 18–18

IRELAND V ROMANIA

Played 8 Ireland won 8
Highest scores Ireland 60–0 in 1986, Romania 35–53 in 1998
Biggest win Ireland 60–0 in 1986, Romania no win

1986 Dublin **Ireland** 60–0	2001 Bucharest **Ireland** 37–3
1993 Dublin **Ireland** 25–3	2002 Limerick **Ireland** 39–8
1998 Dublin **Ireland** 53–35	2003 Gosford WC **Ireland** 45–17
1999 Dublin WC **Ireland** 44–14	2005 Dublin **Ireland** 43–12

IRELAND V CANADA

Played 3 Ireland won 2 Drawn 1
Highest scores Ireland 46–19 in 1987, Canada 27–27 in 2000
Biggest win Ireland 46–19 in 1987, Canada no win

1987 Dunedin WC **Ireland** 46–19	2000 Markham **Drawn** 27–27
1997 Dublin **Ireland** 33–11	

IRELAND V TONGA

Played 2 Ireland won 2
Highest scores Ireland 40–19 in 2003, Tonga 19–40 in 2003
Biggest win Ireland 32–9 in 1987, Tonga no win

1987 Brisbane WC **Ireland** 32–9	2003 Nuku'alofa **Ireland** 40–19

IRELAND V SAMOA

Played 4 Ireland won 3, Samoa won 1, Drawn 0
Highest scores Ireland 49–22 in 1988, Samoa 40–25 in 1996
Biggest wins Ireland 49–22 in 1988 and 35–8 in 2001, Samoa 40–25 in 1996

1988 Dublin **Ireland** 49–22	2001 Dublin **Ireland** 35–8
1996 Dublin **Samoa** 40–25	2003 Apia **Ireland** 40–14

IRELAND V ITALY

Played 16 Ireland won 13, Italy won 3, Drawn 0
Highest scores Ireland 61–6 in 2003, Italy 37–29 in 1997 & 37–22 in 1997
Biggest wins Ireland 61–6 in 2003, Italy 37–22 in 1997

1988 Dublin **Ireland** 31–15
1995 Treviso **Italy** 22–12
1997 Dublin **Italy** 37–29
1997 Bologna **Italy** 37–22
1999 Dublin **Ireland** 39–30
2000 Dublin **Ireland** 60–13
2001 Rome **Ireland** 41–22
2002 Dublin **Ireland** 32–17
2003 Rome **Ireland** 37–13
2003 Limerick **Ireland** 61–6
Non-championship match
2004 Dublin **Ireland** 19–3
2005 Rome **Ireland** 28–17
2006 Dublin **Ireland** 26–16
2007 Rome **Ireland** 51–24
2007 Belfast **Ireland** 23–20
Non-championship match
2008 Dublin **Ireland** 16–11

IRELAND V ARGENTINA

Played 10 Ireland won 5 Argentina won 5
Highest scores Ireland 32–24 in 1999, Argentina 34–23 in 2000
Biggest win Ireland 32–24 in 1999, Argentina 16–0 in 2007

1990 Dublin **Ireland** 20–18
1999 Dublin **Ireland** 32–24
1999 Lens WC **Argentina** 28–24
2000 Buenos Aires **Argentina** 34–23
2002 Dublin **Ireland** 16–7
2003 Adelaide WC **Ireland** 16–15
2004 Dublin **Ireland** 21–19
2007 1 Santa Féé **Argentina** 22–20
2 Buenos Aires **Argentina** 16–0
Argentina won series 2–0
2007 Paris WC **Argentina** 30–15

IRELAND V NAMIBIA

Played 4 Ireland won 2, Namibia won 2
Highest scores Ireland 64–7 in 2003, Namibia 26–15 in 1991
Biggest win Ireland 64–7 in 2003, Namibia 26–15 in 1991

1991 *1* Windhoek **Namibia** 15–6
2 Windhoek **Namibia** 26–15
Namibia won series 2–0
2003 Sydney WC **Ireland** 64–7
2007 Bordeaux WC **Ireland** 32–17

INTERNATIONAL RECORDS

IRELAND V ZIMBABWE

Played 1 Ireland won 1
Highest scores Ireland 55–11 in 1991, Zimbabwe 11–55 in 1991
Biggest win Ireland 55–11 in 1991, Zimbabwe no win

1991	Dublin WC **Ireland** 55–11

IRELAND V JAPAN

Played 5 Ireland won 5
Highest scores Ireland 78–9 in 2000, Japan 28–50 in 1995
Biggest win Ireland 78–9 in 2000, Japan no win

1991	Dublin WC **Ireland** 32–16	2005	1 Osaka **Ireland** 44–12
1995	Bloemfontein WC **Ireland 50–28**		2 Tokyo **Ireland** 47–18
2000	Dublin **Ireland** 78–9		Ireland won series 2–0

IRELAND V UNITED STATES

Played 5 Ireland won 5
Highest scores Ireland 83–3 in 2000, United States 18–25 in 1996
Biggest win Ireland 83–3 in 2000, United States no win

1994	Dublin **Ireland** 26–15	2000	Manchester (NH) **Ireland** 83–3
1996	Atlanta **Ireland** 25–18	2004	Dublin **Ireland** 55–6
1999	Dublin WC **Ireland** 53–8		

IRELAND V FIJI

Played 2 Ireland won 2
Highest scores Ireland 64–17 in 2002, Fiji 17–64 in 2002
Biggest win Ireland 64–17 in 2002, Fiji no win

1995	Dublin **Ireland** 44–8	2002	Dublin **Ireland** 64–17

IRELAND V GEORGIA

Played 3 Ireland won 3
Highest scores Ireland 70–0 in 1998, Georgia 14–63 in 2002
Biggest win Ireland 70–0 in 1998, Georgia no win

1998 Dublin **Ireland** 70–0
2002 Dublin **Ireland** 63–14
2007 Bordeaux WC **Ireland** 14–10

IRELAND V RUSSIA

Played 1 Ireland won 1
Highest scores Ireland 35–3 in 2002, Russia 3–35 in 2002
Biggest win Ireland 35–3 in 2002, Russia no win

2002 Krasnoyarsk **Ireland** 35–3

IRELAND V PACIFIC ISLANDS

Played 1 Ireland won 1
Highest scores Ireland 61–17 in 2006, Pacific Islands 17–61 in 2006
Biggest win Ireland 61–17 in 2006, Pacific Islands no win

2006 Dublin **Ireland** 61–17

WALES V FRANCE

Played 85 Wales won 43, France won 39, Drawn 3
Highest scores Wales 49–14 in 1910, France 51–0 in 1998
Biggest wins Wales 47–5 in 1909, France 51–0 in 1998

1908 Cardiff **Wales** 36–4
1909 Paris **Wales** 47–5
1910 Swansea **Wales** 49–14
1911 Paris **Wales** 15–0
1912 Newport **Wales** 14–8
1913 Paris **Wales** 11–8
1914 Swansea **Wales** 31–0
1920 Paris **Wales** 6–5
1921 Cardiff **Wales** 12–4
1922 Paris **Wales** 11–3
1923 Swansea **Wales** 16–8
1924 Paris **Wales** 10–6
1925 Cardiff **Wales** 11–5
1926 Paris **Wales** 7–5
1927 Swansea **Wales** 25–7
1928 Paris **France** 8–3

1929 Cardiff **Wales** 8–3
1930 Paris **Wales** 11–0
1931 Swansea **Wales** 35–3
1947 Paris **Wales** 3–0
1948 Swansea **France** 11–3
1949 Paris **France** 5–3
1950 Cardiff **Wales** 21–0
1951 Paris **France** 8–3
1952 Swansea **Wales** 9–5
1953 Paris **Wales** 6–3
1954 Cardiff **Wales** 19–13
1955 Paris **Wales** 16–11
1956 Cardiff **Wales** 5–3
1957 Paris **Wales** 19–13
1958 Cardiff **France** 16–6
1959 Paris **France** 11–3
1960 Cardiff **France** 16–8
1961 Paris **France** 8–6
1962 Cardiff **Wales** 3–0
1963 Paris **France** 5–3
1964 Cardiff **Drawn** 11–11
1965 Paris **France** 22–13
1966 Cardiff **Wales** 9–8
1967 Paris **France** 20–14
1968 Cardiff **France** 14–9
1969 Paris **Drawn** 8–8
1970 Cardiff **Wales** 11–6
1971 Paris **Wales** 9–5
1972 Cardiff **Wales** 20–6
1973 Paris **France** 12–3
1974 Cardiff **Drawn** 16–16
1975 Paris **Wales** 25–10
1976 Cardiff **Wales** 19–13
1977 Paris **France** 16–9
1978 Cardiff **Wales** 16–7
1979 Paris **France** 14–13
1980 Cardiff **Wales** 18–9
1981 Paris **France** 19–15
1982 Cardiff **Wales** 22–12
1983 Paris **France** 16–9
1984 Cardiff **France** 21–16
1985 Paris **France** 14–3
1986 Cardiff **France** 23–15
1987 Paris **France** 16–9
1988 Cardiff **France** 10–9
1989 Paris **France** 31–12
1990 Cardiff **France** 29–19
1991 Paris **France** 36–3
1991 Cardiff **France** 22–9
Non-championship match
1992 Cardiff **France** 12–9
1993 Paris **France** 26–10
1994 Cardiff **Wales** 24–15
1995 Paris **France** 21–9
1996 Cardiff **Wales** 16–15
1996 Cardiff **France** 40–33
Non-championship match
1997 Paris **France 27–22**
1998 Wembley **France** 51–0
1999 Paris **Wales** 34–33
1999 Cardiff **Wales** 34–23
Non-championship match
2000 Cardiff **France** 36–3
2001 Paris **Wales** 43–35
2002 Cardiff **France** 37–33
2003 Paris **France** 33–5
2004 Cardiff **France** 29–22
2005 Paris **Wales** 24–18
2006 Cardiff **France** 21–16
2007 Paris **France** 32–21
2007 Cardiff **France** 34–7
Non-championship match
2008 Cardiff **Wales** 29–12

WALES V SOUTH AFRICA

Played 22 Wales won 1, South Africa won 20, Drawn 1
Highest scores Wales 36–38 in 2004, South Africa 96–13 in 1998
Biggest win Wales 29–19 in 1999, South Africa 96–13 in 1998

1906 Swansea **South Africa** 11–0
1912 Cardiff **South Africa** 3–0
1931 Swansea **South Africa** 8–3
1951 Cardiff **South Africa** 6–3
1960 Cardiff **South Africa** 3–0
1964 Durban **South Africa** 24–3

1970 Cardiff **Drawn** 6–6
1994 Cardiff **South Africa** 20–12
1995 Johannesburg **South Africa** 40–11
1996 Cardiff **South Africa** 37–20
1998 Pretoria **South Africa** 96–13
1998 Wembley **South Africa** 28–20
1999 Cardiff **Wales** 29–19
2000 Cardiff **South Africa** 23–13
2002 *1* Bloemfontein **South Africa** 34–19
2 Cape Town **South Africa** 19–8
SA won series 2–0
2004 Pretoria **South Africa** 53–18
2004 Cardiff **South Africa** 38–36
2005 Cardiff **South Africa** 33–16
2007 Cardiff **South Africa** 34–12
2008 *1* Bloemfontein **South Africa** 43–17
2 Pretoria **South Africa** 37–21
SA won series 2–0

WALES V NEW ZEALAND

Played 23 Wales won 3, New Zealand won 20, Drawn 0
Highest scores Wales 37–53 in 2003, New Zealand 55–3 in 2003
Biggest wins Wales 13–8 in 1953, New Zealand 55–3 in 2003

1905 Cardiff **Wales** 3–0
1924 Swansea **New Zealand** 19–0
1935 Cardiff **Wales** 13–12
1953 Cardiff **Wales** 13–8
1963 Cardiff **New Zealand** 6–0
1967 Cardiff **New Zealand** 13–6
1969 *1* Christchurch **New Zealand** 19–0
2 Auckland **New Zealand** 33–12
New Zealand won series 2–0
1972 Cardiff **New Zealand** 19–16
1978 Cardiff **New Zealand** 13–12
1980 Cardiff **New Zealand** 23–3
1987 Brisbane WC **New Zealand** 49–6
1988 *1* Christchurch **New Zealand** 52–3
2 Auckland **New Zealand** 54–9
New Zealand won series 2–0
1989 Cardiff **New Zealand** 34–9
1995 Johannesburg WC **New Zealand 34–9**
1997 Wembley **New Zealand** 42–7
2002 Cardiff **New Zealand** 43–17
2003 Hamilton **New Zealand** 55–3
2003 Sydney WC **New Zealand** 53–37
2004 Cardiff **New Zealand** 26–25
2005 Cardiff **New Zealand** 41–3
2006 Cardiff **New Zealand** 45–10

WALES V AUSTRALIA

Played 27 Wales won 9, Australia won 17, Drawn 1
Highest scores Wales 29–29 in 2006, Australia 63–6 in 1991
Biggest wins Wales 28–3 in 1975, Australia 63–6 in 1991

1908 Cardiff **Wales** 9–6
1927 Cardiff **Australia** 18–8
1947 Cardiff **Wales** 6–0
1958 Cardiff **Wales** 9–3
1966 Cardiff **Australia** 14–11
1969 Sydney **Wales** 19–16
1973 Cardiff **Wales** 24–0
1975 Cardiff **Wales** 28–3
1978 *1* Brisbane **Australia** 18–8
2 Sydney **Australia** 19–17
Australia won series 2–0
1981 Cardiff **Wales** 18–13
1984 Cardiff **Australia** 28–9
1987 Rotorua WC **Wales** 22–21
1991 Brisbane **Australia** 63–6
1991 Cardiff WC **Australia** 38–3
1992 Cardiff **Australia** 23–6
1996 *1* Brisbane **Australia** 56–25

2 Sydney **Australia** 42–3	2005 Cardiff **Wales** 24–22
Australia won series 2–0	2006 Cardiff **Drawn** 29–29
1996 Cardiff **Australia 28–19**	2007 1 Sydney **Australia** 29–23
1999 Cardiff WC **Australia** 24–9	2 Brisbane **Australia** 31–0
2001 Cardiff **Australia** 21–13	Australia won series 2–0
2003 Sydney **Australia** 30–10	2007 Cardiff WC **Australia** 32–20

WALES V NEW ZEALAND NATIVES

Played 1 Wales won 1
Highest scores Wales 5–0 in 1888, New Zealand Natives 0–5 in 1888
Biggest win Wales 5–0 in 1888, New Zealand Natives no win

1888 Swansea **Wales** 1G 2T to 0

WALES V NEW ZEALAND ARMY

Played 1 New Zealand Army won 1
Highest scores Wales 3–6 in 1919, New Zealand Army 6–3 in 1919
Biggest win Wales no win, New Zealand Army 6–3 in 1919

1919 Swansea **New Zealand Army** 6–3

WALES V ROMANIA

Played 8 Wales won 6, Romania won 2
Highest scores Wales 81–9 in 2001, Romania 24–6 in 1983
Biggest wins Wales 81–9 in 2001, Romania 24–6 in 1983

1983 Bucharest **Romania** 24–6	2001 Cardiff **Wales** 81–9
1988 Cardiff **Romania** 15–9	2002 Wrexham **Wales** 40–3
1994 Bucharest **Wales** 16–9	2003 Wrexham **Wales** 54–8
1997 Wrexham **Wales** 70–21	2004 Cardiff **Wales** 66–7

WALES V FIJI

Played 7 Wales won 6, Fiji won 1
Highest scores Wales 58–14 in 2002, Fiji 38–34 in 2007
Biggest win Wales 58–14 in 2002, Fiji 38–34 in 2007

1985	Cardiff **Wales** 40–3	2002	Cardiff **Wales** 58–14
1986	Suva **Wales** 22–15	2005	Cardiff **Wales** 11–10
1994	Suva **Wales** 23–8	2007	Nantes WC **Fiji** 38–34
1995	Cardiff **Wales** 19–15		

WALES V TONGA

Played 6 Wales won 6
Highest scores Wales 51–7 in 2001, Tonga 20–27 in 2003
Biggest win Wales 51–7 in 2001, Tonga no win

1986	Nuku'Alofa **Wales** 15–7	1997	Swansea **Wales** 46–12
1987	Palmerston North WC **Wales** 29–16	2001	Cardiff **Wales** 51–7
1994	Nuku'Alofa **Wales** 18–9	2003	Canberra WC **Wales** 27–20

WALES V SAMOA

Played 6 Wales won 3, Samoa won 3, Drawn 0
Highest scores Wales 50–6 in 2000, Samoa 38–31 in 1999
Biggest wins Wales 50–6 in 2000, Samoa 34–9 in 1994

1986	Apia **Wales** 32–14	1994	Moamoa **Samoa** 34–9
1988	Cardiff **Wales** 28–6	1999	Cardiff WC **Samoa** 38–31
1991	Cardiff WC **Samoa** 16–13	2000	Cardiff **Wales** 50–6

WALES V CANADA

Played 10 Wales won 9, Canada won 1, Drawn 0
Highest scores Wales 61–26 in 2006, Canada 26–24 in 1993 & 26–61 in 2006
Biggest wins Wales 60–3 in 2005, Canada 26–24 in 1993

1987	Invercargill WC **Wales** 40–9	1994	Toronto **Wales** 33–15
1993	Cardiff **Canada** 26–24	1997	Toronto **Wales** 28–25

1999	Cardiff **Wales** 33–19	2005	Toronto **Wales** 60–3
2002	Cardiff **Wales** 32–21	2006	Cardiff **Wales** 61–26
2003	Melbourne WC **Wales** 41–10	2007	Nantes WC **Wales** 42–17

WALES V UNITED STATES

Played 6 Wales won 6
Highest scores Wales 77–3 in 2005, United States 23–28 in 1997
Biggest win Wales 77–3 in 2005, United States no win

1987	Cardiff **Wales** 46–0		Wales won series 2–0
1997	Cardiff **Wales** 34–14	2000	Cardiff **Wales** 42–11
1997	*1* Wilmington **Wales** 30–20	2005	Hartford **Wales** 77–3
	2 San Francisco **Wales** 28–23		

WALES V NAMIBIA

Played 3 Wales won 3
Highest scores Wales 38–23 in 1993, Namibia 30–34 in 1990
Biggest win Wales 38–23 in 1993, Namibia no win

1990	*1* Windhoek **Wales** 18–9		Wales won series 2–0
	2 Windhoek **Wales** 34–30	1993	Windhoek **Wales** 38–23

WALES V BARBARIANS

Played 2 Wales won 1, Barbarians won 1
Highest scores Wales 31–10 in 1996, Barbarians 31–24 in 1990
Biggest wins Wales 31–10 in 1996, Barbarians 31–24 in 1990

1990	Cardiff **Barbarians** 31–24	1996	Cardiff **Wales** 31–10

WALES V ARGENTINA

Played 11 Wales won 7, Argentina won 4
Highest scores Wales 44–50 in 2004, Argentina 50–44 in 2004
Biggest win Wales 35–20 in 2004, Argentina 45–27 in 2006

1991	Cardiff WC **Wales** 16–7	2004	1 Tucumáán **Argentina** 50–44
1998	Llanelli **Wales** 43–30		2 Buenos Aires **Wales** 35–20
1999	*1* Buenos Aires **Wales** 36–26		Series drawn 1–1
	2 Buenos Aires **Wales** 23–16	2006	1 Puerto Madryn **Argentina** 27–25
	Wales won series 2–0		2 Buenos Aires **Argentina** 45–27
1999	Cardiff WC **Wales** 23–18		Argentina won series 2–0
2001	Cardiff **Argentina** 30–16	2007	Cardiff **Wales** 27–20

WALES V ZIMBABWE

Played 3 Wales won 3
Highest scores Wales 49–11 in 1998, Zimbabwe 14–35 in 1993
Biggest win Wales 49–11 in 1998, Zimbabwe no win

1993	*1* Bulawayo **Wales** 35–14		Wales won series 2–0
	2 Harare **Wales** 42–13	1998	Harare **Wales** 49–11

WALES V JAPAN

Played 7 Wales won 7
Highest scores Wales 98–0 in 2004, Japan 30–53 in 2001
Biggest win Wales 98–0 in 2004, Japan no win

1993	Cardiff **Wales** 55–5		*2* Tokyo **Wales** 53–30
1995	Bloemfontein WC **Wales 57–10**		Wales won series 2–0
1999	Cardiff WC **Wales** 64–15	2004	Cardiff **Wales** 98–0
2001	*1* Osaka **Wales** 64–10	2007	Cardiff WC **Wales** 72–18

WALES V PORTUGAL

Played 1 Wales won 1
Highest scores Wales 102–11 in 1994, Portugal 11–102 in 1994
Biggest win Wales 102–11 in 1994, Portugal no win

1994	Lisbon **Wales** 102–11

WALES V SPAIN

Played 1 Wales won 1
Highest scores Wales 54–0 in 1994, Spain 0–54 in 1994
Bigegst win Wales 54–0 in 1994, Spain no win

1994 Madrid **Wales** 54–0

WALES V ITALY

Played 15 Wales won 12, Italy won 2, Drawn 1
Highest scores Wales 60–21 in 1999, Italy 30–22 in 2003
Biggest win Wales 60–21 in 1999, Italy 30–22 in 2003

1994 Cardiff **Wales** 29–19
1996 Cardiff **Wales** 31–26
1996 Rome **Wales** 31–22
1998 Llanelli **Wales** 23–20
1999 Treviso **Wales** 60–21
2000 Cardiff **Wales** 47–16
2001 Rome **Wales** 33–23
2002 Cardiff **Wales** 44–20
2003 Rome **Italy** 30–22
2003 Canberra WC **Wales** 27–15
2004 Cardiff **Wales** 44–10
2005 Rome **Wales** 38–8
2006 Cardiff **Drawn** 18–18
2007 Rome **Italy** 23–20
2008 Cardiff **Wales** 47–8

WALES V PACIFIC ISLANDS

Played 1 Wales won 1
Highest scores Wales 38–20 in 2006, Pacific Islands 20–38 in 2006
Biggest win Wales 38–20 in 2006, Pacific Islands no win

2006 Cardiff **Wales** 38–20

BRITISH/IRISH ISLES V SOUTH AFRICA

Played 43 British/Irish won 16, South Africa won 21, Drawn 6
Highest scores: British/Irish 28–9 in 1974, South Africa 35–16 in 1997
Biggest wins: British/Irish 28–9 in 1974, South Africa 34–14 in 1962

1891 *1* Port Elizabeth **British/Irish** 4–0
2 Kimberley **British/Irish** 3–0
3 Cape Town **British/Irish** 4–0
British/Irish won series 3–0
1896 *1* Port Elizabeth **British/Irish** 8–0
2 Johannesburg **British/Irish** 17–8
3 Kimberley **British/Irish** 9–3
4 Cape Town **South Africa** 5–0
British/Irish won series 3–1
1903 *1* Johannesburg **Drawn** 10–10
2 Kimberley **Drawn** 0–0
3 Cape Town **South Africa** 8–0

√

South Africa won series 1–0 with two drawn

1910 *1* Johannesburg **South Africa** 14–10
2 Port Elizabeth **British/Irish** 8–3
3 Cape Town **South Africa** 21–5
South Africa won series 2–1

1924 *1* Durban **South Africa** 7–3
2 Johannesburg **South Africa** 17–0
3 Port Elizabeth **Drawn** 3–3
4 Cape Town **South Africa** 16–9
South Africa won series 3–0, with 1 draw

1938 *1* Johannesburg **South Africa** 26–12
2 Port Elizabeth **South Africa** 19–3
3 Cape Town **British/Irish** 21–16
South Africa won series 2–1

1955 *1* Johannesburg **British/Irish** 23–22
2 Cape Town **South Africa** 25–9
3 Pretoria **British/Irish** 9–6
4 Port Elizabeth **South Africa** 22–8
Series drawn 2–2

1962 *1* Johannesburg **Drawn** 3–3
2 Durban **South Africa** 3–0
3 Cape Town **South Africa** 8–3
4 Bloemfontein **South Africa** 34–14
South Africa won series 3–0, with 1 draw

1968 *1* Pretoria **South Africa** 25–20
2 Port Elizabeth **Drawn** 6–6
3 Cape Town **South Africa** 11–6
4 Johannesburg **South Africa** 19–6
South Africa won series 3–0, with 1 draw

1974 *1* Cape Town **British/Irish** 12–3
2 Pretoria **British/Irish** 28–9
3 Port Elizabeth **British/Irish** 26–9
4 Johannesburg **Drawn** 13–13
British/Irish won series 3–0, with 1 draw

1980 *1* Cape Town **South Africa** 26–22
2 Bloemfontein **South Africa** 26–19
3 Port Elizabeth **South Africa** 12–10
4 Pretoria **British/Irish** 17–13
South Africa won series 3–1

1997 *1* Cape Town **British/Irish** 25–16
2 Durban **British/Irish** 18–15
3 Johannesburg **South Africa** 35–16
British/Irish won series 2–1

BRITISH/IRISH ISLES V NEW ZEALAND

Played 35 British/Irish won 6, New Zealand won 27, Drawn 2
Highest scores: British/Irish 20–7 in 1993, New Zealand 48–18 in 2005
Biggest wins: British/Irish 20–7 in 1993, New Zealand 38–6 in 1983

1904 Wellington **New Zealand** 9–3

1930 *1* Dunedin **British/Irish** 6–3
2 Christchurch **New Zealand** 13–10
3 Auckland **New Zealand** 15–10
4 Wellington **New Zealand** 22–8
New Zealand won series 3–1

1950 *1* Dunedin **Drawn** 9–9
2 Christchurch **New Zealand** 8–0
3 Wellington **New Zealand** 6–3
4 Auckland **New Zealand** 11–8
New Zealand won series 3–0, with 1 draw

1959 *1* Dunedin **New Zealand** 18–17
2 Wellington **New Zealand** 11–8
3 Christchurch **New Zealand** 22–8
4 Auckland **British/Irish** 9–6
New Zealand won series 3–1

1966 *1* Dunedin **New Zealand** 20–3
2 Wellington **New Zealand** 16–12
3 Christchurch **New Zealand** 19–6
4 Auckland **New Zealand** 24–11
New Zealand won series 4–0

1971 *1* Dunedin **British/Irish** 9–3
2 Christchurch **New Zealand** 22–12
3 Wellington **British/Irish** 13–3
4 Auckland **Drawn** 14–14
British/Irish won series 2–1, with 1 draw

1977 *1* Wellington **New Zealand** 16–12
2 Christchurch **British/Irish** 13–9
3 Dunedin **New Zealand** 19–7
4 Auckland **New Zealand** 10–9
New Zealand won series 3–1

1983 *1* Christchurch **New Zealand** 16–12
2 Wellington **New Zealand** 9–0
3 Dunedin **New Zealand** 15–8
4 Auckland **New Zealand** 38–6
New Zealand won series 4–0

1993 *1* Christchurch **New Zealand** 20–18
2 Wellington **British/Irish** 20–7
3 Auckland **New Zealand** 30–13
New Zealand won series 2–1

2005 1 Christchurch **New Zealand** 21–3
2 Wellington **New Zealand** 48–18
3 Auckland **New Zealand** 38–19
New Zealand won series 3–0

ANGLO-WELSH V NEW ZEALAND

Played 3 New Zealand won 2, Drawn 1
Highest scores Anglo Welsh 5–32 in 1908, New Zealand 32–5 in 1908
Biggest win Anglo Welsh no win, New Zealand 29–0 in 1908

1908 *1* Dunedin **New Zealand** 32–5
2 Wellington **Drawn** 3–3
3 Auckland **New Zealand** 29–0
New Zealand won series 2–0 with one drawn

BRITISH/IRISH ISLES V AUSTRALIA

Played 20 British/Irish won 15, Australia won 5, Drawn 0
Highest scores: British/Irish 31–0 in 1966, Australia 35–14 in 2001
Biggest wins: British/Irish 31–0 in 1966, Australia 35–14 in 2001

1899 *1* Sydney **Australia** 13–3
2 Brisbane **British/Irish** 11–0
3 Sydney **British/Irish** 11–10
4 Sydney **British/Irish** 13–0
British/Irish won series 3–1

1904 *1* Sydney **British/Irish** 17–0
2 Brisbane **British/Irish** 17–3
3 Sydney **British/Irish** 16–0
British/Irish won series 3–0

1930 Sydney **Australia** 6–5

1950 *1* Brisbane **British/Irish** 19–6
2 Sydney **British/Irish** 24–3
British/Irish won series 2–0

1959 *1* Brisbane **British/Irish** 17–6
2 Sydney **British/Irish** 24–3
British/Irish won series 2–0

1966 *1* Sydney **British/Irish** 11–8
2 Brisbane **British/Irish** 31–0
British/Irish won series 2–0

1989 *1* Sydney **Australia** 30–12
2 Brisbane **British/Irish** 19–12
3 Sydney **British/Irish** 19–18
British/Irish won series 2–1

2001 *1* Brisbane **British/Irish** 29–13
2 Melbourne **Australia** 35–14
3 Sydney **Australia** 29–23
Australia won series 2–1

BRITISH/IRISH ISLES V ARGENTINA

Played 1 British/Irish won 0, Argentina won 0, Drawn 1
Highest scores: British/Irish 25–25 in 2005, Argentina 25–25 in 2005
Biggest win: British/Irish no win to date, Argentina no win to date

2005 Cardiff **Drawn** 25–25

FRANCE V SOUTH AFRICA

Played 36 France won 10, South Africa won 20, Drawn 6
Highest scores France 36–26 in 2006, South Africa 52–10 in 1997
Biggest wins France 30–10 in 2002, South Africa 52–10 in 1997

1913	Bordeaux **South Africa** 38–5
1952	Paris **South Africa** 25–3
1958	*1* Cape Town **Drawn** 3–3
	2 Johannesburg **France** 9–5
	France won series 1–0, with 1 draw
1961	Paris **Drawn** 0–0
1964	Springs (SA) **France** 8–6
1967	*1* Durban **South Africa** 26–3
	2 Bloemfontein **South Africa** 16–3
	3 Johannesburg **France** 19–14
	4 Cape Town **Drawn** 6–6
	South Africa won series 2–1, with 1 draw
1968	*1* Bordeaux **South Africa** 12–9
	2 Paris **South Africa** 16–11
	South Africa won series 2–0
1971	*1* Bloemfontein **South Africa** 22–9
	2 Durban **Drawn** 8–8
	South Africa won series 1–0, with 1 draw
1974	*1* Toulouse **South Africa** 13–4
	2 Paris **South Africa** 10–8
	South Africa won series 2–0
1975	*1* Bloemfontein **South Africa** 38–25
	2 Pretoria **South Africa** 33–18
	South Africa won series 2–0
1980	Pretoria **South Africa** 37–15
1992	*1* Lyons **South Africa** 20–15
	2 Paris **France** 29–16
	Series drawn 1–1
1993	*1* Durban **Drawn** 20–20
	2 Johannesburg **France** 18–17
	France won series 1–0, with 1 draw
1995	Durban WC **South Africa 19–15**
1996	*1* Bordeaux **South Africa** 22–12
	2 Paris **South Africa** 13–12
	South Africa won series 2–0
1997	*1* Lyons **South Africa** 36–32
	2 Paris **South Africa** 52–10
	South Africa won series 2–0
2001	*1* Johannesburg **France** 32–23
	2 Durban **South Africa** 20–15
	Series drawn 1–1
2001	Paris **France** 20–10
2002	Marseilles **France** 30–10
2005	1 Durban **Drawn** 30–30
	2 Port Elizabeth **South Africa** 27–13
	South Africa won series 1–0, with 1 draw
2005	Paris **France** 26–20
2006	Cape Town **France** 36–26

FRANCE V NEW ZEALAND

Played 46 France won 11, New Zealand won 34, Drawn 1
Highest scores France 43–31 in 1999, New Zealand 61–10 in 2007
Biggest wins France 22–8 in 1994, New Zealand 61–10 in 2007

1906	Paris **New Zealand** 38–8
1925	Toulouse **New Zealand** 30–6
1954	Paris **France** 3–0
1961	*1* Auckland **New Zealand** 13–6
	2 Wellington **New Zealand** 5–3
	3 Christchurch **New Zealand** 32–3
	New Zealand won series 3–0
1964	Paris **New Zealand** 12–3
1967	Paris **New Zealand** 21–15
1968	*1* Christchurch **New Zealand** 12–9
	2 Wellington **New Zealand** 9–3
	3 Auckland **New Zealand** 19–12
	New Zealand won series 3–0
1973	Paris **France** 13–6
1977	*1* Toulouse **France** 18–13
	2 Paris **New Zealand** 15–3

Series drawn 1–1
1979 *1* Christchurch **New Zealand** 23–9
2 Auckland **France** 24–19
Series drawn 1–1
1981 *1* Toulouse **New Zealand** 13–9
2 Paris **New Zealand** 18–6
New Zealand won series 2–0
1984 *1* Christchurch **New Zealand** 10–9
2 Auckland **New Zealand** 31–18
New Zealand won series 2–0
1986 Christchurch **New Zealand** 18–9
1986 *1* Toulouse **New Zealand** 19–7
2 Nantes **France** 16–3
Series drawn 1–1
1987 Auckland WC **New Zealand** 29–9
1989 *1* Christchurch **New Zealand** 25–17
2 Auckland **New Zealand** 34–20
New Zealand won series 2–0
1990 *1* Nantes **New Zealand** 24–3
2 Paris **New Zealand** 30–12
New Zealand won series 2–0
1994 *1* Christchurch **France** 22–8
2 Auckland **France** 23–20
France won series 2–0
1995 *1* Toulouse **France** 22–15
2 Paris **New Zealand** 37–12
Series drawn 1–1
1999 Wellington **New Zealand** 54–7
1999 Twickenham WC **France** 43–31
2000 *1* Paris **New Zealand** 39–26
2 Marseilles **France** 42–33
Series drawn 1–1
2001 Wellington **New Zealand** 37–12
2002 Paris **Drawn** 20–20
2003 Christchurch **New Zealand** 31–23
2003 Sydney WC **New Zealand** 40–13
2004 Paris **New Zealand** 45–6
2006 1 Lyons **New Zealand** 47–3
2 Paris **New Zealand** 23–11
New Zealand won series 2–0
2007 1 Auckland **New Zealand** 42–11
2 Wellington **New Zealand** 61–10
New Zealand won series 2–0
2007 Cardiff WC **France** 20–18

FRANCE V AUSTRALIA

Played 38 France won 16, Australia won 20, Drawn 2
Highest scores France 34–6 in 1976, Australia 48–31 in 1990
Biggest wins France 34–6 in 1976, Australia 40–10 in 2008

1928 Paris **Australia** 11–8
1948 Paris **France** 13–6
1958 Paris **France** 19–0
1961 Sydney **France** 15–8
1967 Paris **France** 20–14
1968 Sydney **Australia** 11–10
1971 *1* Toulouse **Australia** 13–11
2 Paris **France** 18–9
Series drawn 1–1
1972 *1* Sydney **Drawn** 14–14
2 Brisbane **France** 16–15
France won series 1–0, with 1 draw
1976 *1* Bordeaux **France** 18–15
2 Paris **France** 34–6
France won series 2–0
1981 *1* Brisbane **Australia** 17–15
2 Sydney **Australia** 24–14
Australia won series 2–0
1983 *1* Clermont-Ferrand **Drawn** 15–15
2 Paris **France** 15–6
France won series 1–0, with 1 draw
1986 Sydney **Australia** 27–14
1987 Sydney WC **France** 30–24
1989 *1* Strasbourg **Australia** 32–15
2 Lille **France** 25–19
Series drawn 1–1
1990 *1* Sydney **Australia** 21–9
2 Brisbane **Australia** 48–31
3 Sydney **France** 28–19
Australia won series 2–1
1993 *1* Bordeaux **France** 16–13
2 Paris **Australia** 24–3
Series drawn 1–1
1997 *1* Sydney **Australia** 29–15

	2 Brisbane **Australia** 26–19		Australia won series 2–0
	Australia won series 2–0	2004	Paris **France** 27–14
1998	Paris **Australia** 32–21	2005	Brisbane **Australia** 37–31
1999	Cardiff WC **Australia** 35–12	2005	Marseilles **France** 26–16
2000	Paris **Australia** 18–13	2008	*1* Sydney **Australia** 34–13
2001	Marseilles **France** 14–13		*2* Brisbane **Australia** 40–10
2002	*1* Melbourne **Australia** 29–17		Australia won series 2–0
	2 Sydney **Australia** 31–25		

FRANCE V UNITED STATES

Played 7 France won 6, United States won 1, Drawn 0
Highest scores France 41–9 in 1991 and 41–14 in 2003, United States 31–39 in 2004
Biggest wins France 41–9 in 1991, United States 17–3 in 1924

1920	Paris **France** 14–5		*Abandoned after 43 mins
1924	Paris **United States** 17–3		France won series 2–0
1976	Chicago **France** 33–14	2003	Wollongong WC **France** 41–14
1991	*1* Denver **France** 41–9	2004	Hartford **France** 39–31
	2 Colorado Springs **France** 10–3*		

FRANCE V ROMANIA

Played 49 France won 39, Romania won 8, Drawn 2
Highest scores France 67–20 in 2000, Romania 21–33 in 1991
Biggest wins France 59–3 in 1924, Romania 15–0 in 1980

1924	Paris **France** 59–3	1974	Bucharest **Romania** 15–10
1938	Bucharest **France** 11–8	1975	Bordeaux **France** 36–12
1957	Bucharest **France** 18–15	1976	Bucharest **Romania** 15–12
1957	Bordeaux **France** 39–0	1977	Clermont-Ferrand **France** 9–6
1960	Bucharest **Romania** 11–5	1978	Bucharest **France** 9–6
1961	Bayonne **Drawn** 5–5	1979	Montauban **France** 30–12
1962	Bucharest **Romania** 3–0	1980	Bucharest **Romania** 15–0
1963	Toulouse **Drawn** 6–6	1981	Narbonne **France** 17–9
1964	Bucharest **France** 9–6	1982	Bucharest **Romania** 13–9
1965	Lyons **France** 8–3	1983	Toulouse **France** 26–15
1966	Bucharest **France** 9–3	1984	Bucharest **France** 18–3
1967	Nantes **France** 11–3	1986	Lille **France** 25–13
1968	Bucharest **Romania** 15–14	1986	Bucharest **France** 20–3
1969	Tarbes **France** 14–9	1987	Wellington WC **France** 55–12
1970	Bucharest **France** 14–3	1987	Agen **France** 49–3
1971	Bééziers **France** 31–12	1988	Bucharest **France** 16–12
1972	Constanza **France** 15–6	1990	Auch **Romania** 12–6
1973	Valence **France** 7–6	1991	Bucharest **France** 33–21

1991	Bééziers WC **France** 30–3	1997	Bucharest **France** 51–20
1992	Le Havre **France** 25–6	1997	Lourdes LC **France 39–3**
1993	Bucharest **France** 37–20	1999	Castres **France** 62–8
1993	Brive **France** 51–0	2000	Bucharest **France** 67–20
1995	Bucharest **France** 24–15	2003	Lens **France** 56–8
1995	Tucumáán LC **France 52–8**	2006	Bucharest **France** 62–14
1996	Aurillac **France** 64–12		

FRANCE V NEW ZEALAND MAORI

Played 1 New Zealand Maori won 1
Highest scores France 3–12 in 1926, New Zealand Maori 12–3 in 1926
Biggest win France no win, New Zealand Maori 12–3 in 1926

1926	Paris **New Zealand Maori** 12–3

FRANCE V GERMANY

Played 15 France won 13, Germany won 2, Drawn 0
Highest scores France 38–17 in 1933, Germany 17–16 in 1927 & 17–38 in 1933
Biggest wins France 34–0 in 1931, Germany 3–0 in 1938

1927	Paris **France** 30–5	1934	Hanover **France** 13–9
1927	Frankfurt **Germany** 17–16	1935	Paris **France** 18–3
1928	Hanover **France** 14–3	1936	*1* Berlin **France** 19–14
1929	Paris **France** 24–0		*2* Hanover **France** 6–3
1930	Berlin **France** 31–0		France won series 2–0
1931	Paris **France** 34–0	1937	Paris **France** 27–6
1932	Frankfurt **France** 20–4	1938	Frankfurt **Germany** 3–0
1933	Paris **France** 38–17	1938	Bucharest **France** 8–5

FRANCE V ITALY

Played 29 France won 28, Italy won 1, Drawn 0
Highest scores France 60–13 in 1967, Italy 40–32 in 1997
Biggest wins France 60–13 in 1967, Italy 40–32 in 1997

1937	Paris **France** 43–5	1953	Lyons **France** 22–8
1952	Milan **France** 17–8	1954	Rome **France** 39–12

1955 Grenoble **France** 24–0	1995 Buenos Aires LC **France 34–22**
1956 Padua **France** 16–3	1997 Grenoble **Italy** 40–32
1957 Agen **France** 38–6	1997 Auch LC **France 30–19**
1958 Naples **France** 11–3	2000 Paris **France** 42–31
1959 Nantes **France** 22–0	2001 Rome **France** 30–19
1960 Treviso **France** 26–0	2002 Paris **France** 33–12
1961 Chambééry **France** 17–0	2003 Rome **France** 53–27
1962 Brescia **France** 6–3	2004 Paris **France** 25–0
1963 Grenoble **France** 14–12	2005 Rome **France** 56–13
1964 Parma **France** 12–3	2006 Paris **France** 37–12
1965 Pau **France** 21–0	2007 Rome **France** 39–3
1966 Naples **France** 21–0	2008 Paris **France** 25–13
1967 Toulon **France** 60–13	

FRANCE V BRITISH XVS

Played 5 France won 2, British XVs won 3, Drawn 0
Highest scores France 27–29 in 1989, British XV 36–3 in 1940
Biggest wins France 21–9 in 1945, British XV 36–3 in 1940

1940 Paris **British XV** 36–3	1946 Paris **France** 10–0
1945 Paris **France** 21–9	1989 Paris **British XV** 29–27
1945 Richmond **British XV** 27–6	

FRANCE V WALES XVS

Played 2 France won 1, Wales XV won 1
Highest scores France 12–0 in 1946, Wales XV 8–0 in 1945
Biggest win France 12–0 in 1946, Wales XV 8–0 in 1945

1945 Swansea **Wales XV** 8–0	1946 Paris **France** 12–0

FRANCE V IRELAND XVS

Played 1 France won 1
Highest scores France 4–3 in 1946, Ireland XV 3–4 in 1946
Biggest win France 4–3 in 1946, Ireland XV no win

1946 Dublin **France** 4–3

FRANCE V NEW ZEALAND ARMY

Played 1 New Zealand Army won 1
Highest scores France 9–14 in 1946, New Zealand Army 14–9 in 1946
Biggest win France no win, New Zealand Army 14–9 in 1946

1946 Paris **New Zealand Army** 14–9

FRANCE V ARGENTINA

Played 41 France won 30, Argentina won 10, Drawn 1
Highest scores France 47–12 in 1995 & 47–26 in 1999, Argentina 34–10 in 2007
Biggest wins France 47–12 in 1995, Argentina 34–10 in 2007

1949 *1* Buenos Aires **France** 5–0
2 Buenos Aires **France** 12–3
France won series 2–0
1954 *1* Buenos Aires **France** 22–8
2 Buenos Aires **France** 30–3
France won series 2–0
1960 *1* Buenos Aires **France** 37–3
2 Buenos Aires **France** 12–3
3 Buenos Aires **France** 29–6
France won series 3–0
1974 *1* Buenos Aires **France** 20–15
2 Buenos Aires **France** 31–27
France won series 2–0
1975 *1* Lyons **France** 29–6
2 Paris **France** 36–21
France won series 2–0
1977 *1* Buenos Aires **France** 26–3
2 Buenos Aires **Drawn** 18–18
France won series 1–0, with 1 draw
1982 *1* Toulouse **France** 25–12
2 Paris **France** 13–6
France won series 2–0
1985 *1* Buenos Aires **Argentina** 24–16
2 Buenos Aires **France** 23–15
Series drawn 1–1
1986 *1* Buenos Aires **Argentina** 15–13
2 Buenos Aires **France** 22–9
Series drawn 1–1
1988 *1* Buenos Aires **France** 18–15
2 Buenos Aires **Argentina** 18–6
Series drawn 1–1
1988 *1* Nantes **France** 29–9
2 Lille **France** 28–18
France won series 2–0
1992 *1* Buenos Aires **France** 27–12
2 Buenos Aires **France** 33–9
France won series 2–0
1992 Nantes **Argentina** 24–20
1995 Buenos Aires LC **France** 47–12
1996 *1* Buenos Aires **France** 34–27
2 Buenos Aires **France** 34–15
France won series 2–0
1997 Tarbes LC **France** 32–27
1998 *1* Buenos Aires **France** 35–18
2 Buenos Aires **France** 37–12
France won series 2–0
1998 Nantes **France** 34–14
1999 Dublin WC **France** 47–26
2002 Buenos Aires **Argentina** 28–27
2003 *1* Buenos Aires **Argentina** 10–6
2 Buenos Aires **Argentina** 33–32
Argentina won series 2–0
2004 Marseilles **Argentina** 24–14
2006 Paris **France** 27–26
2007 Paris WC **Argentina** 17–12
2007 Paris WC **Argentina** 34–10

FRANCE V CZECHOSLOVAKIA

Played 2 France won 2
Highest scores France 28–3 in 1956, Czechoslovakia 6–19 in 1968
Biggest win France 28–3 in 1956, Czechoslovakia no win

1956 Toulouse **France** 28–3
1968 Prague **France** 19–6

FRANCE V FIJI

Played 7 France won 7
Highest scores France 77–10 in 2001, Fiji 19–28 in 1999
Biggest win France 77–10 in 2001, Fiji no win

1964 Paris **France** 21–3
1987 Auckland WC **France** 31–16
1991 Grenoble WC **France** 33–9
1998 Suva **France** 34–9
1999 Toulouse WC **France** 28–19
2001 Saint Etienne **France** 77–10
2003 Brisbane WC **France** 61–18

FRANCE V JAPAN

Played 2 France won 2
Highest scores France 51–29 in 2003, Japan 29–51 in 2003
Biggest win France 51–29 in 2003, Japan no win

1973 Bordeaux **France** 30–18
2003 Townsville WC **France** 51–29

FRANCE V ZIMBABWE

Played 1 France won 1
Highest scores France 70–12 in 1987, Zimbabwe 12–70 in 1987
Biggest win France 70–12 in 1987, Zimbabwe no win

1987 Auckland WC **France** 70–12

FRANCE V CANADA

Played 7 France won 6, Canada won 1, Drawn 0
Highest scores France 50–6 in 2005, Canada 20–33 in 1999
Biggest wins France 50–6 in 2005, Canada 18–16 in 1994

1991	Agen WC **France** 19–13	2002	Paris **France** 35–3
1994	Nepean **Canada** 18–16	2004	Toronto **France** 47–13
1994	Besançcon **France** 28–9	2005	Nantes **France** 50–6
1999	Béeziers WC **France** 33–20		

FRANCE V TONGA

Played 3 France won 2, Tonga won 1
Highest scores France 43–8 in 2005, Tonga 20–16 in 1999
Biggest win France 43–8 in 2005, Tonga 20–16 in 1999

1995	Pretoria WC **France** 38–10	2005	Toulouse **France** 43–8
1999	Nuku'alofa **Tonga** 20–16		

FRANCE V IVORY COAST

Played 1 France won 1
Highest scores France 54–18 in 1995, Ivory Coast 18–54 in 1995
Biggest win France 54–18 in 1995, Ivory Coast no win

1995	Rustenburg WC **France** 54–18

FRANCE V SAMOA

Played 1 France won 1
Highest scores France 39–22 in 1999, Samoa 22–39 in 1999
Biggest win France 39–22 in 1999, Samoa no win

1999	Apia **France** 39–22

FRANCE V NAMIBIA

Played 2 France won 2
Highest scores France 87–10 in 2007, Namibia 13–47 in 1999
Biggest win France 87–10 in 2007, Namibia no win

1999 Bordeaux WC **France** 47–13
2007 Toulouse WC **France** 87–10

FRANCE V GEORGIA

Played 1 France won 1
Highest scores France 64–7 in 2007, Georgia 7–64 in 2007
Biggest win France 64–7 in 2007, Georgia no win

2007 Marseilles WC **France** 64–7

SOUTH AFRICA V NEW ZEALAND

Played 75 New Zealand won 42, South Africa won 30, Drawn 3
Highest scores New Zealand 55–35 in 1997, South Africa 46–40 in 2000
Biggest wins New Zealand 52–16 in 2003, South Africa 17–0 in 1928

1921 *1* Dunedin **New Zealand** 13–5
2 Auckland **South Africa** 9–5
3 Wellington **Drawn** 0–0
Series drawn 1–1, with 1 draw
1928 *1* Durban **South Africa** 17–0
2 Johannesburg **New Zealand** 7–6
3 Port Elizabeth **South Africa** 11–6
4 Cape Town **New Zealand** 13–5
Series drawn 2–2
1937 *1* Wellington **New Zealand** 13–7
2 Christchurch **South Africa** 13–6
3 Auckland **South Africa** 17–6
South Africa won series 2–1
1949 *1* Cape Town **South Africa** 15–11
2 Johannesburg **South Africa** 12–6
3 Durban **South Africa** 9–3
4 Port Elizabeth **South Africa** 11–8
South Africa won series 4–0
1956 *1* Dunedin **New Zealand** 10–6
2 Wellington **South Africa** 8–3
3 Christchurch **New Zealand** 17–10
4 Auckland **New Zealand** 11–5
New Zealand won series 3–1
1960 *1* Johannesburg **South Africa** 13–0
2 Cape Town **New Zealand** 11–3
3 Bloemfontein **Drawn** 11–11
4 Port Elizabeth **South Africa** 8–3
South Africa won series 2–1, with 1 draw
1965 *1* Wellington **New Zealand** 6–3
2 Dunedin **New Zealand** 13–0
3 Christchurch **South Africa** 19–16
4 Auckland **New Zealand** 20–3
New Zealand won series 3–1
1970 *1* Pretoria **South Africa** 17–6
2 Cape Town **New Zealand** 9–8
3 Port Elizabeth **South Africa** 14–3
4 Johannesburg **South Africa** 20–17
South Africa won series 3–1
1976 *1* Durban **South Africa** 16–7
2 Bloemfontein **New Zealand** 15–9
3 Cape Town **South Africa** 15–10
4 Johannesburg **South Africa** 15–14

	South Africa won series 3–1
1981	*1* Christchurch **New Zealand** 14–9
	2 Wellington **South Africa** 24–12
	3 Auckland **New Zealand** 25–22
	New Zealand won series 2–1
1992	Johannesburg **New Zealand** 27–24
1994	*1* Dunedin **New Zealand** 22–14
	2 Wellington **New Zealand** 13–9
	3 Auckland **Drawn** 18–18
	New Zealand won series 2–0, with 1 draw
1995	Johannesburg WC **South Africa** 15–12 (*aet*)
1996	Christchurch TN **New Zealand** 15–11
1996	Cape Town TN **New Zealand** 29–18
1996	*1* Durban **New Zealand** 23–19
	2 Pretoria **New Zealand** 33–26
	3 Johannesburg **South Africa** 32–22
	New Zealand won series 2–1
1997	Johannesburg TN **New Zealand** 35–32
1997	Auckland TN **New Zealand** 55–35
1998	Wellington TN **South Africa** 13–3
1998	Durban TN **South Africa** 24–23
1999	Dunedin TN **New Zealand** 28–0
1999	Pretoria TN **New Zealand** 34–18
1999	Cardiff WC **South Africa** 22–18
2000	Christchurch TN **New Zealand** 25–12
2000	Johannesburg TN **South Africa** 46–40
2001	Cape Town TN **New Zealand** 12–3
2001	Auckland TN **New Zealand** 26–15
2002	Wellington TN **New Zealand** 41–20
2002	Durban TN **New Zealand** 30–23
2003	Pretoria TN **New Zealand** 52–16
2003	Dunedin TN **New Zealand** 19–11
2003	Melbourne WC **New Zealand** 29–9
2004	Christchurch TN **New Zealand** 23–21
2004	Johannesburg TN **South Africa** 40–26
2005	Cape Town TN **South Africa** 22–16
2005	Dunedin TN **New Zealand** 31–27
2006	Wellington TN **New Zealand** 35–17
2006	Pretoria TN **New Zealand** 45–26
2006	Rustenburg TN **South Africa** 21–20
2007	Durban TN **New Zealand** 26–21
2007	Christchurch TN **New Zealand** 33–6
2008	Wellington TN **New Zealand** 19–8
2008	Dunedin TN **South Africa** 30–28
2008	Cape Town TN **New Zealand** 19–0

SOUTH AFRICA V AUSTRALIA

Played 65 South Africa won 38, Australia won 26, Drawn 1
Highest scores South Africa 61–22 in 1997, Australia 49–0 in 2006
Biggest wins South Africa 53–8 in 2008, Australia 49–0 in 2006

1933	*1* Cape Town **South Africa** 17–3
	2 Durban **Australia** 21–6
	3 Johannesburg **South Africa** 12–3
	4 Port Elizabeth **South Africa** 11–0
	5 Bloemfontein **Australia** 15–4
	South Africa won series 3–2
1937	*1* Sydney **South Africa** 9–5
	2 Sydney **South Africa** 26–17
	South Africa won series 2–0
1953	*1* Johannesburg **South Africa** 25–3
	2 Cape Town **Australia** 18–14
	3 Durban **South Africa** 18–8
	4 Port Elizabeth **South Africa** 22–9
	South Africa won series 3–1
1956	*1* Sydney **South Africa** 9–0
	2 Brisbane **South Africa** 9–0
	South Africa won series 2–0
1961	*1* Johannesburg **South Africa** 28–3
	2 Port Elizabeth **South Africa** 23–11
	South Africa won series 2–0
1963	*1* Pretoria **South Africa** 14–3
	2 Cape Town **Australia** 9–5
	3 Johannesburg **Australia** 11–9
	4 Port Elizabeth **South Africa** 22–6
	Series drawn 2–2
1965	*1* Sydney **Australia** 18–11
	2 Brisbane **Australia** 12–8
	Australia won series 2–0
1969	*1* Johannesburg **South Africa** 30–11
	2 Durban **South Africa** 16–9
	3 Cape Town **South Africa** 11–3
	4 Bloemfontein **South Africa** 19–8
	South Africa won series 4–0
1971	*1* Sydney **South Africa** 19–11

2 Brisbane **South Africa** 14–6
3 Sydney **South Africa** 18–6
South Africa won series 3–0
1992 Cape Town **Australia** 26–3
1993 *1* Sydney **South Africa** 19–12
2 Brisbane **Australia** 28–20
3 Sydney **Australia** 19–12
Australia won series 2–1
1995 Cape Town WC **South Africa** 27–18
1996 Sydney TN **Australia** 21–16
1996 Bloemfontein TN **South Africa** 25–19
1997 Brisbane TN **Australia** 32–20
1997 Pretoria TN **South Africa** 61–22
1998 Perth TN **South Africa** 14–13
1998 Johannesburg TN **South Africa** 29–15
1999 Brisbane TN **Australia** 32–6
1999 Cape Town TN **South Africa** 10–9
1999 Twickenham WC **Australia** 27–21
2000 Melbourne **Australia** 44–23
2000 Sydney TN **Australia** 26–6
2000 Durban TN **Australia** 19–18
2001 Pretoria TN **South Africa** 20–15
2001 Perth TN **Drawn** 14–14
2002 Brisbane TN **Australia** 38–27
2002 Johannesburg TN **South Africa** 33–31
2003 Cape Town TN **South Africa** 26–22
2003 Brisbane TN **Australia** 29–9
2004 Perth TN **Australia** 30–26
2004 Durban TN **South Africa** 23–19
2005 Sydney **Australia** 30–12
2005 Johannesburg **South Africa** 33–20
2005 Pretoria TN **South Africa** 22–16
2005 Perth TN **South Africa** 22–19
2006 Brisbane TN **Australia** 49–0
2006 Sydney TN **Australia** 20–18
2006 Johannesburg TN **South Africa** 24–16
2007 Cape Town TN **South Africa** 22–19
2007 Sydney TN **Australia** 25–17
2008 Perth TN **Australia** 16–9
2008 Durban TN **Australia** 27–15
2008 Johannesburg TN **South Africa** 53–8

SOUTH AFRICA V WORLD XVS

Played 3 South Africa won 3
Highest scores South Africa 45–24 in 1977, World XV 24–45 in 1977
Biggest win South Africa 45–24 in 1977, World XV no win

1977 Pretoria **South Africa** 45–24
1989 *1* Cape Town **South Africa** 20–19
2 Johannesburg **South Africa** 22–16
South Africa won series 2–0

SOUTH AFRICA V SOUTH AMERICA

Played 8 South Africa won 7, South America won 1, Drawn 0
Highest scores South Africa 50–18 in 1982, South America 21–12 in 1982
Biggest wins South Africa 50–18 in 1982, South America 21–12 in 1982

1980 *1* Johannesburg **South Africa** 24–9
2 Durban **South Africa** 18–9
South Africa won series 2–0
1980 *1* Montevideo **South Africa** 22–13
2 Santiago **South Africa** 30–16
South Africa won series 2–0
1982 *1* Pretoria **South Africa** 50–18
2 Bloemfontein **South America** 21–12
Series drawn 1–1
1984 *1* Pretoria **South Africa** 32–15
2 Cape Town **South Africa** 22–13
South Africa won series 2–0

SOUTH AFRICA V UNITED STATES

Played 3 South Africa won 3
Highest scores South Africa 64–10 in 2007, United States 20–43 in 2001
Biggest win South Africa 64–10 in 2007, United States no win

1981 Glenville **South Africa** 38–7
2001 Houston **South Africa** 43–20
2007 Montpellier WC **South Africa** 64–10

SOUTH AFRICA V NEW ZEALAND CAVALIERS

Played 4 South Africa won 3, New Zealand Cavaliers won 1, Drawn 0
Highest scores South Africa 33–18 in 1986, New Zealand Cavaliers 19–18 in 1986
Biggest wins South Africa 33–18 in 1986, New Zealand Cavaliers 19–18 in 1986

1986 *1* Cape Town **South Africa** 21–15
2 Durban **New Zealand Cavaliers** 19–18
3 Pretoria **South Africa** 33–18
4 Johannesburg **South Africa** 24–10
South Africa won series 3–1

SOUTH AFRICA V ARGENTINA

Played 13 South Africa won 13
Highest scores South Africa 63–9 in 2008, Argentina 33–37 in 2000
Biggest wins South Africa 63–9 in 2008, Argentina no win

1993 *1* Buenos Aires **South Africa** 29–26
2 Buenos Aires **South Africa** 52–23
South Africa won series 2–0
1994 *1* Port Elizabeth **South Africa** 42–22
2 Johannesburg **South Africa** 46–26
South Africa won series 2–0
1996 *1* Buenos Aires **South Africa** 46–15
2 Buenos Aires **South Africa** 44–21
South Africa win series 2–0
2000 Buenos Aires **South Africa** 37–33
2002 Springs **South Africa** 49–29
2003 Port Elizabeth **South Africa** 26–25
2004 Buenos Aires **South Africa** 39–7
2005 Buenos Aires **South Africa** 34–23
2007 Paris WC **South Africa** 37–13
2008 Johannesburg **South Africa** 63–9

SOUTH AFRICA V SAMOA

Played 6 South Africa won 6
Highest scores South Africa 60–8 in 1995, 60–18 in 2002 and 60–10 in 2003, Samoa 18–60 in 2002
Biggest win South Africa 60–8 in 1995 and 59–7 in 2007, Samoa no win

1995	Johannesburg **South Africa** 60–8	2003	Brisbane WC **South Africa** 60–10
1995	Johannesburg WC **South Africa** 42–14	2007	Johannesburg **South Africa** 35–8
2002	Pretoria **South Africa** 60–18	2007	Paris WC **South Africa** 59–7

SOUTH AFRICA V ROMANIA

Played 1 South Africa won 1
Highest score South Africa 21–8 in 1995, Romania 8–21 in 1995
Biggest win South Africa 21–8 in 1995, Romania no win

1995	Cape Town WC **South Africa** 21–8

SOUTH AFRICA V CANADA

Played 2 South Africa won 2
Highest scores South Africa 51–18 in 2000, Canada 18–51 in 2000
Biggest win South Africa 51–18 in 2000, Canada no win

1995	Port Elizabeth WC **South Africa** 20–0	2000	East London **South Africa** 51–18

SOUTH AFRICA V ITALY

Played 7 South Africa won 7
Highest scores South Africa 101–0 in 1999, Italy 31–62 in 1997
Biggest win South Africa 101–0 in 1999, Italy no win

1995	Rome **South Africa** 40–21		South Africa won series 2–0
1997	Bologna **South Africa** 62–31	2001	Port Elizabeth **South Africa** 60–14
1999	*1* Port Elizabeth **South Africa** 74–3	2001	Genoa **South Africa** 54–26
	2 Durban **South Africa** 101–0	2008	Cape Town **South Africa** 26–0

SOUTH AFRICA V FIJI

Played 2 South Africa won 2
Highest scores South Africa 43–18 in 1996, Fiji 20–37 in 2007
Biggest win South Africa 43–18 in 1996, Fiji no win

1996	Pretoria **South Africa** 43–18	2007	Marseilles WC **South Africa** 37–20

SOUTH AFRICA V TONGA

Played 2 South Africa won 2
Higest scores South Africa 74–10 in 1997, Tonga 25–30 in 2007
Biggest win South Africa 74–10 in 1997, Tonga no win

1997	Cape Town **South Africa** 74–10	2007	Lens WC **South Africa** 30–25

SOUTH AFRICA V SPAIN

Played 1 South Africa won 1
Highest scores South Africa 47–3 in 1999, Spain 3–47 in 1999
Biggest win South Africa 47–3 in 1999, Spain no win

1999	Murrayfield WC **South Africa** 47–3

SOUTH AFRICA V URUGUAY

Played 3 South Africa won 3
Highest scores South Africa 134–3 in 2005, Uruguay 6–72 in 2003
Biggest win South Africa 134–3 in 2005, Uruguay no win

1999	Glasgow WC **South Africa** 39–3		Perth WC **South Africa** 72–6
2003	Glasgow *WC* **South Africa** 39–3	2005	East London **South Africa** 134–3

SOUTH AFRICA V GEORGIA

Played 1 South Africa won 1
Highest scores South Africa 46–19 in 2003, Georgia 19–46 in 2003
Biggest win South Africa 46–19 in 2003, Georgia no win

2003 Sydney WC **South Africa** 46–19

SOUTH AFRICA V PACIFIC ISLANDS

Played 1 South Africa won 1
Highest scores South Africa 38–24 in 2004, Pacific Islands 24–38 in 2004
Biggest win South Africa 38–24 in 2004, Pacific Islands no win

2004 Gosford (Aus) **South Africa** 38–24

SOUTH AFRICA V NAMIBIA

Played 1 South Africa won 1
Highest scores South Africa 105–13 in 2007, Namibia 13–105 in 2007
Biggest win South Africa 105–13 in 2007, Namibia no win

2007 Cape Town **South Africa** 105–13

NEW ZEALAND V AUSTRALIA

Played 131 New Zealand won 87, Australia won 39, Drawn 5
Highest scores New Zealand 50–21 in 2003, Australia 35–39 in 2000
Biggest wins New Zealand 43–6 in 1996, Australia 28–7 in 1999

1903 Sydney **New Zealand** 22–3
1905 Dunedin **New Zealand** 14–3
1907 *1* Sydney **New Zealand** 26–6
2 Brisbane **New Zealand** 14–5
3 Sydney **Drawn** 5–5
New Zealand won series 2–0, with 1 draw
1910 *1* Sydney **New Zealand** 6–0
2 Sydney **Australia** 11–0
3 Sydney **New Zealand** 28–13
New Zealand won series 2–1
1913 *1* Wellington **New Zealand** 30–5
2 Dunedin **New Zealand** 25–13
3 Christchurch **Australia** 16–5
New Zealand won series 2–1
1914 *1* Sydney **New Zealand** 5–0
2 Brisbane **New Zealand** 17–0
3 Sydney **New Zealand** 22–7
New Zealand won series 3–0

1929 *1* Sydney **Australia** 9–8
2 Brisbane **Australia** 17–9
3 Sydney **Australia** 15–13
Australia won series 3–0

1931 Auckland **New Zealand** 20–13

1932 *1* Sydney **Australia** 22–17
2 Brisbane **New Zealand** 21–3
3 Sydney **New Zealand** 21–13
New Zealand won series 2–1

1934 *1* Sydney **Australia** 25–11
2 Sydney **Drawn** 3–3
Australia won series 1–0, with 1 draw

1936 *1* Wellington **New Zealand** 11–6
2 Dunedin **New Zealand** 38–13
New Zealand won series 2–0

1938 *1* Sydney **New Zealand** 24–9
2 Brisbane **New Zealand** 20–14
3 Sydney **New Zealand** 14–6
New Zealand won series 3–0

1946 *1* Dunedin **New Zealand** 31–8
2 Auckland **New Zealand** 14–10
New Zealand won series 2–0

1947 *1* Brisbane **New Zealand** 13–5
2 Sydney **New Zealand** 27–14
New Zealand won series 2–0

1949 *1* Wellington **Australia** 11–6
2 Auckland **Australia** 16–9
Australia won series 2–0

1951 *1* Sydney **New Zealand** 8–0
2 Sydney **New Zealand** 17–11
3 Brisbane **New Zealand** 16–6
New Zealand won series 3–0

1952 *1* Christchurch **Australia** 14–9
2 Wellington **New Zealand** 15–8
Series drawn 1–1

1955 *1* Wellington **New Zealand** 16–8
2 Dunedin **New Zealand** 8–0
3 Auckland **Australia** 8–3
New Zealand won series 2–1

1957 *1* Sydney **New Zealand** 25–11
2 Brisbane **New Zealand** 22–9
New Zealand won series 2–0

1958 *1* Wellington **New Zealand** 25–3
2 Christchurch **Australia** 6–3
3 Auckland **New Zealand** 17–8
New Zealand won series 2–1

1962 *1* Brisbane **New Zealand** 20–6
2 Sydney **New Zealand** 14–5
New Zealand won series 2–0

1962 *1* Wellington **Drawn** 9–9
2 Dunedin **New Zealand** 3–0
3 Auckland **New Zealand** 16–8
New Zealand won series 2–0, with1 draw

1964 *1* Dunedin **New Zealand** 14–9
2 Christchurch **New Zealand** 18–3
3 Wellington **Australia** 20–5
New Zealand won series 2–1

1967 Wellington **New Zealand** 29–9

1968 *1* Sydney **New Zealand** 27–11
2 Brisbane **New Zealand** 19–18
New Zealand won series 2–0

1972 *1* Wellington **New Zealand** 29–6
2 Christchurch **New Zealand** 30–17
3 Auckland **New Zealand** 38–3
New Zealand won series 3–0

1974 *1* Sydney **New Zealand** 11–6
2 Brisbane **Drawn** 16–16
3 Sydney **New Zealand** 16–6
New Zealand won series 2–0, with 1 draw

1978 *1* Wellington **New Zealand** 13–12
2 Christchurch **New Zealand** 22–6
3 Auckland **Australia** 30–16
New Zealand won series 2–1

1979 Sydney **Australia** 12–6

1980 *1* Sydney **Australia** 13–9
2 Brisbane **New Zealand** 12–9
3 Sydney **Australia** 26–10
Australia won series 2–1

1982 *1* Christchurch **New Zealand** 23–16
2 Wellington **Australia** 19–16
3 Auckland **New Zealand** 33–18
New Zealand won series 2–1

1983 Sydney **New Zealand** 18–8

1984 *1* Sydney **Australia** 16–9
2 Brisbane **New Zealand** 19–15
3 Sydney **New Zealand** 25–24
New Zealand won series 2–1

1985 Auckland **New Zealand** 10–9

1986 *1* Wellington **Australia** 13–12
2 Dunedin **New Zealand** 13–12
3 Auckland **Australia** 22–9
Australia won series 2–1

1987 Sydney **New Zealand** 30–16

1988 *1* Sydney **New Zealand** 32–7
2 Brisbane **Drawn** 19–19
3 Sydney **New Zealand** 30–9
New Zealand won series 2–0, with 1 draw

1989 Auckland **New Zealand** 24–12

1990 *1* Christchurch **New Zealand** 21–6
2 Auckland **New Zealand** 27–17
3 Wellington **Australia** 21–9
New Zealand won series 2–1
1991 *1* Sydney **Australia** 21–12
2 Auckland **New Zealand** 6–3
1991 Dublin WC **Australia** 16–6
1992 *1* Sydney **Australia** 16–15
2 Brisbane **Australia** 19–17
3 Sydney **New Zealand** 26–23
Australia won series 2–1
1993 Dunedin **New Zealand** 25–10
1994 Sydney **Australia** 20–16
1995 Auckland **New Zealand** 28–16
1995 Sydney **New Zealand** 34–23
1996 Wellington TN **New Zealand** 43–6
1996 Brisbane TN **New Zealand** 32–25
New Zealand won series 2–0
1997 Christchurch **New Zealand** 30–13
1997 Melbourne TN **New Zealand** 33–18
1997 Dunedin TN **New Zealand** 36–24
New Zealand won series 3–0
1998 Melbourne TN **Australia** 24–16
1998 Christchurch TN **Australia** 27–23
1998 Sydney Australia 19–14
Australia won series 3–0
1999 Auckland TN **New Zealand** 34–15
1999 Sydney TN **Australia** 28–7
Series drawn 1–1
2000 Sydney TN **New Zealand** 39–35
2000 Wellington TN **Australia** 24–23
Series drawn 1–1
2001 Dunedin TN **Australia** 23–15
2001 Sydney TN **Australia** 29–26
Australia won series 2–0
2002 Christchurch TN **New Zealand** 12–6
2002 Sydney TN **Australia** 16–14
Series drawn 1–1
2003 Sydney TN **New Zealand** 50–21
2003 Auckland TN **New Zealand** 21–17
New Zealand won series 2–0
2003 Sydney WC **Australia** 22–10
2004 Wellington TN **New Zealand** 16–7
2004 Sydney TN **Australia** 23–18
Series drawn 1–1
2005 Sydney TN **New Zealand** 30–13
2005 Auckland TN **New Zealand** 34–24
New Zealand won series 2–0
2006 Christchurch TN **New Zealand** 32–12
2006 Brisbane TN **New Zealand** 13–9
2006 Auckland TN **New Zealand** 34–27
New Zealand won series 3–0
2007 Melbourne TN **Australia** 20–15
2007 Auckland TN **New Zealand** 26–12
Series drawn 1–1
2008 Sydney TN **Australia** 34–19
2008 Auckland TN **New Zealand** 39–10
2008 Brisbane TN **New Zealand** 28–24

NEW ZEALAND V UNITED STATES

Played 2 New Zealand won 2
Highest scores New Zealand 51–3 in 1913, United States 6–46 in 1991
Biggest win New Zealand 51–3 in 1913, United States no win

1913 Berkeley **New Zealand** 51–3
1991 Gloucester WC **New Zealand** 46–6

NEW ZEALAND V ROMANIA

Played 2 New Zealand won 2
Highest score New Zealand 85–8 in 2007, Romania 8–85 in 2007
Biggest win New Zealand 85–8 in 2007, Romania no win

1981 Bucharest **New Zealand** 14–6	2007 Toulouse WC **New Zealand** 85–8

NEW ZEALAND V ARGENTINA

Played 13 New Zealand won 12, Drawn 1
Highest scores New Zealand 93–8 in 1997, Argentina 21–21 in 1985
Biggest win New Zealand 93–8 in 1997, Argentina no win

1985	*1* Buenos Aires **New Zealand** 33–20
	2 Buenos Aires **Drawn** 21–21
	New Zealand won series 1–0, with 1 draw
1987	Wellington *WC* **New Zealand** 46–15
1989	*1* Dunedin **New Zealand** 60–9
	2 Wellington **New Zealand** 49–12
	New Zealand won series 2–0
1991	*1* Buenos Aires **New Zealand** 28–14
	2 Buenos Aires **New Zealand** 36–6
	New Zealand won series 2–0
1997	*1* Wellington **New Zealand** 93–8
	2 Hamilton **New Zealand** 62–10
	New Zealand won series 2–0
2001	Christchurch **New Zealand** 67–19
2001	Buenos Aires **New Zealand** 24–20
2004	Hamilton **New Zealand** 41–7
2006	Buenos Aires **New Zealand** 25–19

NEW ZEALAND V ITALY

Played 9 New Zealand won 9
Highest scores New Zealand 101–3 in 1999, Italy 21–31 in 1991
Biggest win New Zealand 101–3 in 1999, Italy no win

1987	Auckland WC **New Zealand** 70–6
1991	Leicester WC **New Zealand** 31–21
1995	Bologna **New Zealand** 70–6
1999	Huddersfield WC **New Zealand** 101–3
2000	Genoa **New Zealand** 56–19
2002	Hamilton **New Zealand** 64–10
2003	Melbourne WC **New Zealand** 70–7
2004	Rome **New Zealand** 59–10
2007	Marseilles WC **New Zealand** 76–14

NEW ZEALAND V FIJI

Played 4 New Zealand won 4
Highest scores New Zealand 91–0 in 2005, Fiji 18–68 in 2002
Biggest win New Zealand 91–0 in 2005, Fiji no win

1987	Christchurch WC **New Zealand** 74–13	2002	Wellington **New Zealand** 68–18
1997	Albany **New Zealand** 71–5	2005	Albany **New Zealand** 91–0

NEW ZEALAND V CANADA

Played 4 New Zealand won 4
Highest scores New Zealand 73–7 in 1995, Canada 13–29 in 1991 & 13–64 in 2007
Biggest win New Zealand 73–7 in 1995, Canada no win

1991	Lille WC **New Zealand** 29–13	2003	Melbourne WC **New Zealand** 68–6
1995	Auckland **New Zealand** 73–7	2007	Hamilton **New Zealand** 64–13

NEW ZEALAND V WORLD XVS

Played 3 New Zealand won 2, World XV won 1, Drawn 0
Highest scores New Zealand 54–26 in 1992, World XV 28–14 in 1992
Biggest wins New Zealand 54–26 in 1992, World XV 28–14 in 1992

1992	*1* Christchurch **World XV** 28–14	*3* Auckland **New Zealand** 26–15
	2 Wellington **New Zealand** 54–26	New Zealand won series 2–1

NEW ZEALAND V SAMOA

Played 5 New Zealand won 5
Highest scores New Zealand 101–14 in 2008, Samoa 14–101 in 2008
Biggest win New Zealand 101–14 in 2008, Samoa no win

1993	Auckland **New Zealand** 35–13	2001	Albany **New Zealand** 50–6
1996	Napier **New Zealand** 51–10	2008	New Plymouth **New Zealand** 101–14
1999	Albany **New Zealand** 71–13		

NEW ZEALAND V JAPAN

Played 1 New Zealand won 1
Highest scores New Zealand 145–17 in 1995, Japan 17–145 in 1995
Biggest win New Zealand 145–17 in 1995, Japan no win

1995 Bloemfontein WC **New Zealand** 145–17

NEW ZEALAND V TONGA

Played 3 New Zealand won 3
Highest scores New Zealand 102–0 in 2000, Tonga 9–45 in 1999
Biggest win New Zealand 102–0 in 2000, Tonga no win

1999 Bristol WC **New Zealand** 45–9
2000 Albany **New Zealand** 102–0
2003 Brisbane WC **New Zealand** 91–7

NEW ZEALAND V PACIFIC ISLANDS

Played 1 New Zealand won 1
Highest scores New Zealand 41–26 in 2004, Pacific Islands 26–41 in 2004
Biggest win New Zealand 41–26 in 2004, Pacific Islands no win

2004 Albany **New Zealand 41–26**

NEW ZEALAND V PORTUGAL

Played 1 New Zealand won 1
Highest scores New Zealand 108–13 in 2007, Portugal 13–108 in 2007
Biggest win New Zealand 108–13 in 2007, Portugal no win

2007 Lyons WC **New Zealand** 108–13

AUSTRALIA V UNITED STATES

Played 6 Australia won 6
Highest scores Australia 67–9 in 1990, United States 19–55 in 1999
Biggest win Australia 67–9 in 1990, United States no win

1912 Berkeley **Australia** 12–8
1976 Los Angeles **Australia** 24–12
1983 Sydney **Australia** 49–3
1987 Brisbane WC **Australia** 47–12
1990 Brisbane **Australia** 67–9
1999 Limerick WC **Australia** 55–19

AUSTRALIA V NEW ZEALAND XVS

Played 24 Australia won 6, New Zealand XVs won 18, Drawn 0
Highest scores Australia 26–20 in 1926, New Zealand XV 38–11 in 1923 and 38–8 in 1924
Biggest win Australia 17–0 in 1921, New Zealand XV 38–8 in 1924

1920 *1* Sydney **New Zealand XV** 26–15
2 Sydney **New Zealand XV** 14–6
3 Sydney **New Zealand XV** 24–13
New Zealand XV won series 3–0
1921 Christchurch **Australia** 17–0
1922 *1* Sydney **New Zealand XV** 26–19
2 Sydney **Australia** 14–8
3 Sydney **Australia** 8–6
Australia won series 2–1
1923 *1* Dunedin **New Zealand XV** 19–9
2 Christchurch **New Zealand XV** 34–6
3 Wellington **New Zealand XV** 38–11
New Zealand XV won series 3–0
1924 *1* Sydney **Australia** 20–16
2 Sydney **New Zealand XV** 21–5
3 Sydney **New Zealand XV** 38–8
New Zealand XV won series 2–1
1925 *1* Sydney **New Zealand XV** 26–3
2 Sydney **New Zealand XV** 4–0
3 Sydney **New Zealand XV** 11–3
New Zealand XV won series 3–0
1925 Auckland **New Zealand XV** 36–10
1926 *1* Sydney **Australia** 26–20
2 Sydney **New Zealand XV** 11–6
3 Sydney **New Zealand XV** 14–0
4 Sydney **New Zealand XV** 28–21
New Zealand XV won series 3–1
1928 *1* Wellington **New Zealand XV** 15–12
2 Dunedin **New Zealand XV** 16–14
3 Christchurch **Australia** 11–8
New Zealand XV won series 2–1

AUSTRALIA V SOUTH AFRICA XVS

Played 3 South Africa XVs won 3
Highest scores Australia 11–16 in 1921, South Africa XV 28–9 in 1921
Biggest win Australia no win, South Africa XV 28–9 in 1921

1921 *1* Sydney **South Africa XV** 25–10
2 Sydney **South Africa XV** 16–11
3 Sydney **South Africa XV** 28–9
South Africa XV won series 3–0

AUSTRALIA V NEW ZEALAND MAORIS

Played 16 Australia won 8, New Zealand Maoris won 6, Drawn 2
Highest scores Australia 31–6 in 1936, New Zealand Maoris 25–22 in 1922
Biggest wins Australia 31–6 in 1936, New Zealand Maoris 20–0 in 1946

1922	*1* Sydney **New Zealand Maoris** 25–22
	2 Sydney **Australia** 28–13
	3 Sydney **New Zealand Maoris** 23–22
	New Zealand Maoris won series 2–1
1923	*1* Sydney **Australia** 27–23
	2 Sydney **Australia** 21–16
	3 Sydney **Australia** 14–12
	Australia won series 3–0
1928	Wellington **New Zealand Maoris** 9–8
1931	Palmerston North **Australia** 14–3
1936	Palmerston North **Australia** 31–6
1946	Hamilton **New Zealand Maoris** 20–0
1949	*1* Sydney **New Zealand Maoris** 12–3
	2 Brisbane **Drawn** 8–8
	3 Sydney **Australia** 18–3
	Series drawn 1–1, with 1 draw
1958	*1* Brisbane **Australia** 15–14
	2 Sydney **Drawn** 3–3
	3 Melbourne **New Zealand Maoris** 13–6
	Series drawn 1–1, with 1 draw

AUSTRALIA V FIJI

Played 18 Australia won 15, Fiji won 2, Drawn 1
Highest scores Australia 66–20 in 1998, Fiji 28–52 in 1985
Biggest wins Australia 49–0 in 2007, Fiji 17–15 in 1952 & 18–16 in 1954

1952	*1* Sydney **Australia** 15–9
	2 Sydney **Fiji** 17–15
	Series drawn 1–1
1954	*1* Brisbane **Australia** 22–19
	2 Sydney **Fiji** 18–16
	Series drawn 1–1
1961	*1* Brisbane **Australia** 24–6
	2 Sydney **Australia** 20–14
	3 Melbourne **Drawn** 3–3
	Australia won series 2–0, with 1 draw
1972	Suva **Australia** 21–19
1976	*1* Sydney **Australia** 22–6
	2 Brisbane **Australia** 21–9
	3 Sydney **Australia** 27–17
	Australia won series 3–0
1980	Suva **Australia** 22–9
1984	Suva **Australia** 16–3
1985	*1* Brisbane **Australia** 52–28
	2 Sydney **Australia** 31–9
	Australia won series 2–0
1998	Sydney **Australia** 66–20
2007	Perth **Australia** 49–0
2007	Montpellier WC **Australia** 55–12

AUSTRALIA V TONGA

Played 4 Australia won 3, Tonga won 1, Drawn 0
Highest scores Australia 74–0 in 1998, Tonga 16–11 in 1973
Biggest wins Australia 74–0 in 1998, Tonga 16–11 in 1973

1973 *1* Sydney **Australia** 30–12
2 Brisbane **Tonga** 16–11
Series drawn 1–1
1993 Brisbane **Australia** 52–14
1998 Canberra **Australia** 74–0

AUSTRALIA V JAPAN

Played 4 Australia won 4
Highest scores Australia 91–3 in 2007, Japan 25–50 in 1973
Biggest win Australia 91–3 in 2007, Japan no win

1975 *1* Sydney **Australia** 37–7
2 Brisbane **Australia** 50–25
Australia won series 2–0
1987 Sydney WC **Australia** 42–23
2007 Lyons WC **Australia** 91–3

AUSTRALIA V ARGENTINA

Played 17 Australia won 12, Argentina won 4, Drawn 1
Highest scores Australia 53–7 in 1995 & 53–6 in 2000, Argentina 27–19 in 1987
Biggest wins Australia 53–6 in 2000, Argentina 18–3 in 1983

1979 *1* Buenos Aires **Argentina** 24–13
2 Buenos Aires **Australia** 17–12
Series drawn 1–1
1983 *1* Brisbane **Argentina** 18–3
2 Sydney **Australia** 29–13
Series drawn 1–1
1986 *1* Brisbane **Australia** 39–19
2 Sydney **Australia** 26–0
Australia won series 2–0
1987 *1* Buenos Aires **Drawn** 19–19
2 Buenos Aires **Argentina** 27–19
Argentina won series 1–0, with 1 draw
1991 Llanelli WC **Australia** 32–19
1995 *1* Brisbane **Australia** 53–7
2 Sydney **Australia** 30–13
Australia won series 2–0
1997 *1* Buenos Aires **Australia** 23–15
2 Buenos Aires **Argentina** 18–16
Series drawn 1–1
2000 *1* Brisbane **Australia** 53–6
2 Canberra **Australia** 32–25
Australia won series 2–0
2002 Buenos Aires **Australia** 17–6
2003 Sydney WC **Australia** 24–8

AUSTRALIA V SAMOA

Played 4 Australia won 4
Highest scores Australia 74–7 in 2005, Samoa 13–25 in 1998
Biggest win Australia 73–3 in 1994, Samoa no win

1991	Pontypool WC **Australia** 9–3	1998	Brisbane **Australia** 25–13
1994	Sydney **Australia** 73–3	2005	Sydney **Australia** 74–7

AUSTRALIA V ITALY

Played 9 Australia won 9
Highest scores Australia 69–21 in 2005, Italy 21–69 in 2005
Biggest win Australia 55–6 in 1988, Italy no win

1983	Rovigo **Australia** 29–7		Australia won series 2–0
1986	Brisbane **Australia** 39–18	1996	Padua **Australia** 40–18
1988	Rome **Australia** 55–6	2002	Genoa **Australia** 34–3
1994	*1* Brisbane **Australia** 23–20	2005	Melbourne **Australia** 69–21
	2 Melbourne **Australia** 20–7	2006	Rome **Australia** 25–18

AUSTRALIA V CANADA

Played 6 Australia won 6
Highest scores Australia 74–9 in 1996, Canada 16–43 in 1993
Biggest win Australia 74–9 in 1996, Canada no win

1985	*1* Sydney **Australia** 59–3	1995	Port Elizabeth WC **Australia** 27–11
	2 Brisbane **Australia** 43–15	1996	Brisbane **Australia** 74–9
	Australia won series 2–0	2007	Bordeaux WC **Australia** 37–6
1993	Calgary **Australia** 43–16		

AUSTRALIA V KOREA

Played 1 Australia won 1
Highest scores Australia 65–18 in 1987, Korea 18–65 in 1987
Biggest win Australia 65–18 in 1987, Korea no win

1987	Brisbane **Australia** 65–18

AUSTRALIA V ROMANIA

Played 3 Australia won 3
Highest scores Australia 90–8 in 2003, Romania 9–57 in 1999
Biggest win Australia 90–8 in 2003, Romania no win

1995 Stellenbosch WC **Australia** 42–3
1999 Belfast WC **Australia** 57–9
2003 Brisbane WC **Australia** 90–8

AUSTRALIA V SPAIN

Played 1 Australia won 1
Highest scores Australia 92–10 in 2001, Spain 10–92 in 2001
Biggest win Australia 92–10 in 2001, Spain no win

2001 Madrid **Australia** 92–10

AUSTRALIA V NAMIBIA

Played 1 Australia won 1
Highest scores Australia 142–0 in 2003, Namibia 0–142 in 2003
Biggest win Australia 142–0 in 2003, Namibia no win

2003 Adelaide WC **Australia** 142–0

AUSTRALIA V PACIFIC ISLANDS

Played 1 Australia won 1
Highest scores Australia 29–14 in 2004, Pacific Islands 14–29 in 2004
Biggest win Australia 29–14 in 2004, Pacific Islands no win

2004 Adelaide **Australia** 29–14

Getty Images

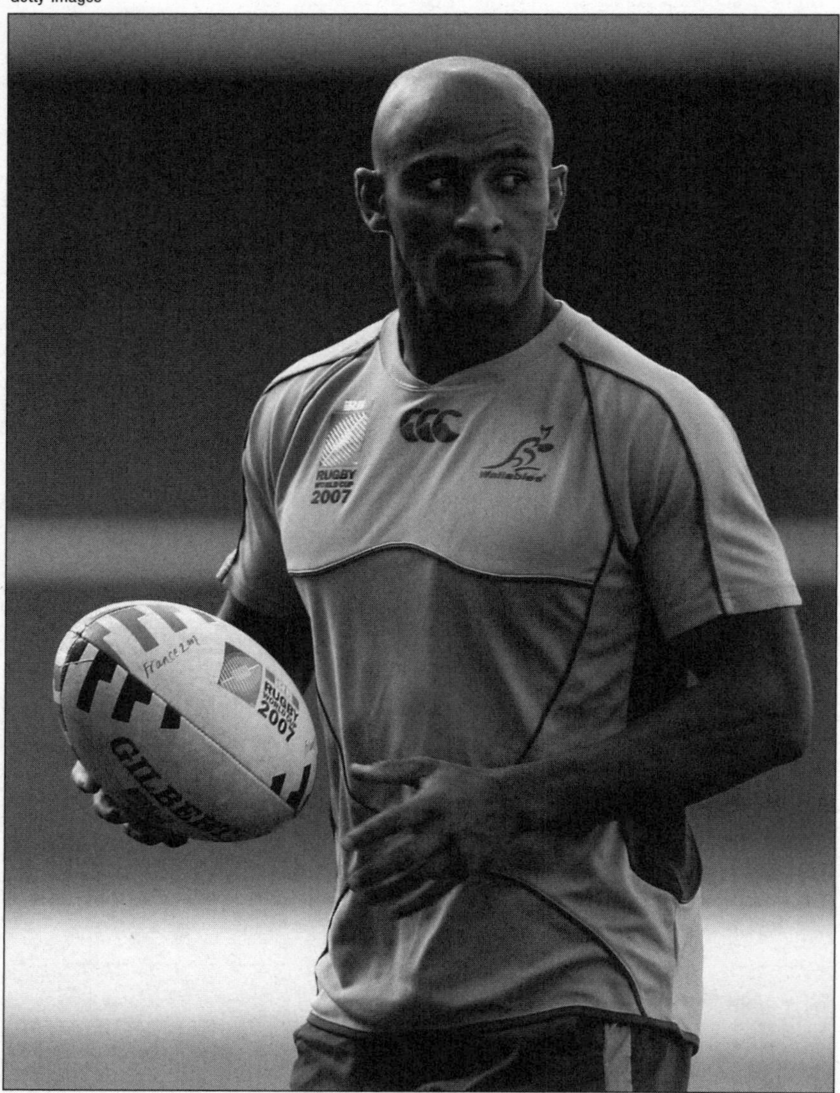

Australia's George Gregan ends 2008 as the world's most-capped player.

INTERNATIONAL WORLD RECORDS

The match and career records cover **official Test matches** *played by the dozen Executive Council Member Unions of the International Board (England, Scotland, Ireland, Wales, France, Italy, South Africa, New Zealand, Australia, Argentina, Canada and Japan) from 1871 up to 30 September 2008. Figures include Test performances for the (British/Irish Isles) Lions and (South American) Jaguars (shown in brackets). Where a world record has been set in a Test match played by another nation in membership of the IRB, this is shown as a footnote to the relevant table.*

MATCH RECORDS

MOST CONSECUTIVE TEST WINS

17 by N Zealand	1965 *SA* 4, 1966 *BI* 1,2,3,4, 1967 *A, E, W, F, S*, 1968 *A* 1,2, *F* 1,2,3, 1969 *W* 1,2
17 by S Africa	1997 *A* 2, *It, F* 1,2, *E, S*, 1998 *I* 1,2, *W* 1, *E* 1, *A* 1, *NZ* 1,2, *A* 2, *W* 2, *S, I* 3

MOST CONSECUTIVE TESTS WITHOUT DEFEAT

Matches	Wins	Draws	Periods
23 by N Zealand	22	1	1987 to 1990
17 by N Zealand	15	2	1961 to 1964
17 by N Zealand	17	0	1965 to 1969
17 by S Africa	17	0	1997 to 1998

MOST POINTS IN A MATCH

BY THE TEAM

Pts.	Opponent	Venue	Year
155 by Japan	Chinese Taipei	Tokyo	2002
152 by Argentina	Paraguay	Mendoza	2002
147 by Argentina	Venezuela	Santiago	2004
145 by N Zealand	Japan	Bloemfontein	1995
144 by Argentina	Paraguay	Montevideo	2003
142 by Australia	Namibia	Adelaide	2003
134 by Japan	Chinese Taipei	Singapore	1998
134 by England	Romania	Twickenham	2001
134 by S Africa	Uruguay	East London	2005
120 by Japan	Chinese Taipei	Tainan	2002

Hong Kong scored 164 points against Singapore at Kuala Lumpur in 1994

BY A PLAYER

Pts.	Player	Opponent	Venue	Year
60 for Japan	T Kurihara	Chinese Taipei	Tainan	2002
50 for Argentina	E Morgan	Paraguay	San Pablo	1973
45 for N Zealand	S D Culhane	Japan	Bloemfontein	1995
45 for Argentina	J-M Nuñez-Piossek	Paraguay	Montevideo	2003
44 for Scotland	A G Hastings	Ivory Coast	Rustenburg	1995
44 for England	C Hodgson	Romania	Twickenham	2001
42 for Australia	M S Rogers	Namibia	Adelaide	2003
40 for Argentina	G M Jorge	Brazil	Sao Paulo	1993
40 for Japan	D Ohata	Chinese Taipei	Tokyo	2002
40 for Scotland	C D Paterson	Japan	Perth	2004
39 for Australia	M C Burke	Canada	Brisbane	1996

MOST TRIES IN A MATCH

BY THE TEAM

Tries	Opponent	Venue	Year
24 by Argentina	Paraguay	Mendoza	2002
24 by Argentina	Paraguay	Montevideo	2003
23 by Japan	Chinese Taipei	Tokyo	2002
23 by Argentina	Venezuela	Santiago	2004
22 by Australia	Namibia	Adelaide	2003
21 by N Zealand	Japan	Bloemfontein	1995
21 by S Africa	Uruguay	East London	2005
20 by Argentina	Brazil	Montevideo	1989
20 by Japan	Ch Taipei	Singapore	1998
20 by England	Romania	Twickenham	2001
19 by Argentina	Brazil	Santiago	1979
19 by Argentina	Paraguay	Asuncion	1985

Hong Kong scored 26 tries against Singapore at Kuala Lumpur in 1994

BY A PLAYER

Tries	Player	Opponent	Venue	Year
11 for Argentina	U O'Farrell	Brazil	Buenos Aires	1951
9 for Argentina	J-M Nuñez-Piossek	Paraguay	Montevideo	2003
8 for Argentina	G M Jorge	Brazil	Sao Paulo	1993
8 for Japan	D Ohata	Chinese Taipei	Tokyo	2002
6 for Argentina	E Morgan	Paraguay	San Pablo	1973
6 for Argentina	G M Jorge	Brazil	Montevideo	1989
6 for N Zealand	M C G Ellis	Japan	Bloemfontein	1995
6 for Japan	T Kurihara	Chinese Taipei	Tainan	2002
6 for S Africa	T Chavhanga	Uruguay	East London	2005
6 for Japan	D Ohata	Hong Kong	Tokyo	2005
5 for Scotland	G C Lindsay	Wales	Raeburn Place	1887
5 for England	D Lambert	France	Richmond	1907
5 for Argentina	H Goti	Brazil	Montevideo	1961
5 for Argentina	M R Jurado	Brazil	Montevideo	1971
5 for England	R Underwood	Fiji	Twickenham	1989
5 for N Zealand	J W Wilson	Fiji	Albany	1997
5 for Japan	T Masuho	Ch Taipei	Singapore	1998
5 for Argentina	P Grande	Paraguay	Asuncion	1998
5 for S Africa	C S Terblanche	Italy	Durban	1999
5 for England	O J Lewsey	Uruguay	Brisbane	2003
5 for Australia	C E Latham	Namibia	Adelaide	2003
5 for Argentina	F Higgs	Venezuela	Santiago	2004

MOST CONVERSIONS IN A MATCH

BY THE TEAM

Cons	Opponent	Venue	Year
20 by N Zealand	Japan	Bloemfontein	1995
20 by Japan	Chinese Taipei	Tokyo	2002
17 by Japan	Chinese Taipei	Singapore	1998
16 by Argentina	Paraguay	Mendoza	2002
16 by Australia	Namibia	Adelaide	2003
16 by Argentina	Venezuela	Santiago	2004
15 by Argentina	Brazil	Santiago	1979
15 by England	Holland	Huddersfield	1998
15 by Japan	Chinese Taipei	Tainan	2002

BY A PLAYER

Cons	Player	Opponent	Venue	Year
20 for N Zealand	S D Culhane	Japan	Bloemfontein	1995
16 for Argentina	J-L Cilley	Paraguay	Mendoza	2002
16 for Australia	M S Rogers	Namibia	Adelaide	2003
15 for England	P J Grayson	Holland	Huddersfield	1998
15 for Japan	T Kurihara	Chinese Taipei	Tainan	2002

MOST PENALTIES IN A MATCH

BY THE TEAM

Pens	Opponent	Venue	Year
9 by Japan	Tonga	Tokyo	1999
9 by N Zealand	Australia	Auckland	1999
9 by Wales	France	Cardiff	1999
9 by N Zealand	France	Paris	2000

Portugal scored nine penalties against Georgia at Lisbon in 2000

BY A PLAYER

Pens	Player	Opponent	Venue	Year
9 for Japan	K Hirose	Tonga	Tokyo	1999
9 for N Zealand	A P Mehrtens	Australia	Auckland	1999
9 for Wales	N R Jenkins	France	Cardiff	1999
9 for N Zealand	A P Mehrtens	France	Paris	2000

Nine penalties were scored for Portugal by T Teixeira against Georgia at Lisbon in 2000

MOST DROPPED GOALS IN A MATCH

BY THE TEAM

Drops	Opponent	Venue	Year
5 by South Africa	England	Paris	1999
4 by South Africa	England	Twickenham	2006
3 by several nations			

BY A PLAYER

Drops	Player	Opponent	Venue	Year
5 for S Africa	J H de Beer	England	Paris	1999
4 for S Africa	A S Pretorius	England	Twickenham	2006
3 for several nations				

CAREER RECORDS

MOST TEST APPEARANCES

Caps	Player	Career Span
139	G M Gregan (Australia)	1994 to 2007
119 (5)	J Leonard (England/Lions)	1990 to 2004
118	F Pelous (France)	1995 to 2007
111	P Sella (France)	1982 to 1995
103 (3)	Gareth Thomas (Wales/Lions)	1995 to 2007
102	S J Larkham (Australia)	1996 to 2007
102	P C Montgomery (S Africa)	1997 to 2008
101	D I Campese (Australia)	1982 to 1996
101	A Troncon (Italy)	1994 to 2007
98	R Ibañez (France)	1996 to 2007
96 (2)	C L Charvis (Wales/Lions)	1996 to 2007
93	S Blanco (France)	1980 to 1991
92	S B T Fitzpatrick (N Zealand)	1986 to 1997
92 (8)	M O Johnson (England/Lions)	1993 to 2003
92	G O Llewellyn (Wales)	1989 to 2004
92	G B Smith (Australia)	2000 to 2008
91 (6)	R Underwood (England/Lions)	1984 to 1996
91 (4)	N R Jenkins (Wales/Lions)	1991 to 2002
91	M E O'Kelly (Ireland)	1997 to 2008

MOST POINTS IN TESTS

Points	Player	Tests	Career Span
1099 (67)	J P Wilkinson (England/Lions)	76 (6)	1998 to 2008
1090 (41)	N R Jenkins (Wales/Lions))	91 (4)	1991 to 2002
1010 (27)	D Dominguez (Italy/Argentina)	76 (2)	1989 to 2003
967	A P Mehrtens (N Zealand)	70	1995 to 2004
911	M P Lynagh (Australia)	72	1984 to 1995
893	P C Montgomery (S Africa)	102	1997 to 2008
878	M C Burke (Australia)	81	1993 to 2004
835 (0)	R J R O'Gara (Ireland/Lions)	85 (1)	2000 to 2008
825	D W Carter (N Zealand)	54	2003 to 2008
733 (66)	A G Hastings (Scotland/Lions)	67 (6)	1986 to 1995

MOST CONSECUTIVE TESTS

Tests	Player	Career span
63	S B T Fitzpatrick (N Zealand)	1986 to 1995
62	J W C Roff (Australia)	1996 to 2001
53	G O Edwards (Wales)	1967 to 1978
52	W J McBride (Ireland)	1964 to 1975
51	C M Cullen (N Zealand)	1996 to 2000

MOST TESTS AS CAPTAIN

Tests	Captain	Career span
59	W D C Carling (England)	1988 to 1996
59	G M Gregan (Australia)	2001 to 2007
55	J A Eales (Australia)	1996 to 2001
52	J W Smit (S Africa)	2003 to 2008
51	S B T Fitzpatrick (N Zealand)	1992 to 1997
49 (1)	B G O'Driscoll (Ireland/Lions)	2002 to 2008
46 (8)	H Porta (Argentina/Jaguars)	1971 to 1990
45 (6)	M O Johnson (England/Lions)	1997 to 2003
42	F Pelous (France)	1997 to 2006
41	L Arbizu (Argentina)	1992 to 2002
41	R Ibañez (France)	1996 to 2007
37	M Giovanelli (Italy)	1992 to 1999
36	N C Farr-Jones (Australia)	1988 to 1992
36	G H Teichmann (S Africa)	1996 to 1999
36	K G M Wood (Ireland)	1996 to 2003

MOST TRIES IN TESTS

Tries	Player	Tests	Career Span
69	D Ohata (Japan)	58	1996 to 2007
64	D I Campese (Australia)	101	1982 to 1996
50 (1)	R Underwood (England/Lions)	91 (6)	1984 to 1996
49	D C Howlett (N Zealand)	62	2000 to 2007
46	C M Cullen (N Zealand)	58	1996 to 2002
44	J W Wilson (N Zealand)	60	1993 to 2001
43	J T Rokocoko (N Zealand)	48	2003 to 2007
43 (0)	S M Williams (Wales/Lions)	60 (2)	2000 to 2008
41 (1)	Gareth Thomas (Wales/Lions)	103 (3)	1995 to 2007
40	C E Latham (Australia)	78	1998 to 2007
38	S Blanco (France)	93	1980 to 1991
38	J H van der Westhuizen (S Africa)	89	1993 to 2003
37	J T Lomu (N Zealand)	63	1994 to 2002
37*	J F Umaga (N Zealand)	74	1999 to 2005
35	J J Kirwan (N Zealand)	63	1984 to 1994
34 (1)	I C Evans (Wales/Lions)	79 (7)	1987 to 1998

* includes a penalty try

MOST CONVERSIONS IN TESTS

Cons	Player	Tests	Career Span
169	A P Mehrtens (N Zealand)	70	1995 to 2004
153	P C Montgomery (S Africa)	102	1997 to 2008
151 (7)	J P Wilkinson (England/Lions)	76 (6)	1998 to 2008
149	D W Carter (N Zealand)	54	2003 to 2008
140	M P Lynagh (Australia)	72	1984 to 1995
133 (6)	D Dominguez (Italy/Argentina)	76 (2)	1989 to 2003
131 (1)	N R Jenkins (Wales/Lions))	91 (4)	1991 to 2002
129 (0)	R J R O'Gara (Ireland/Lions)	85 (1)	2000 to 2008
118	G J Fox (N Zealand)	46	1985 to 1993

MOST PENALTY GOALS IN TESTS

Pens	Player	Tests	Career Span
248 (13)	N R Jenkins (Wales/Lions)	91 (4)	1991 to 2002
225 (16)	J P Wilkinson (England/Lions)	76 (6)	1998 to 2008
214 (5)	D Dominguez (Italy/Argentina)	76 (2)	1989 to 2003
188	A P Mehrtens (N Zealand)	70	1995 to 2004
177	M P Lynagh (Australia)	72	1984 to 1995
174	M C Burke (Australia)	81	1993 to 2004
160 (20)	A G Hastings (Scotland/Lions)	67 (6)	1986 to 1995
158 (0)	R J R O'Gara (Ireland/Lions))	85 (1)	2000 to 2008

MOST DROPPED GOALS IN TESTS

Drops	Player	Tests	Career Span
29 (0)	J P Wilkinson (England/Lions)	76 (6)	1998 to 2008
28 (2)	H Porta (Argentina/Jaguars)	65 (8)	1971 to 1990
23 (2)	C R Andrew (England/Lions)	76 (5)	1985 to 1997
19 (0)	D Dominguez (Italy/Argentina)	76 (2)	1989 to 2003
18	H E Botha (S Africa)	28	1980 to 1992
17	S Bettarello (Italy)	55	1979 to 1988
15	J-P Lescarboura (France)	28	1982 to 1990

ARGENTINA

ARGENTINA'S 2007–08 TEST RECORD

OPPONENTS	DATE	VENUE	RESULT
Chile	15 December	H	**Won** 79–8
Scotland	7 June	H	**Won** 21–15
Scotland	14 June	H	**Lost** 14–26
Italy	28 June	H	**Lost** 12–13
South Africa	9 August	A	**Lost** 9–63

TIME TO REBUILD

By Frankie Deges

As happy as the heights of 2007 were for Argentine rugby, there was always the real possibility that what had been achieved in finishing third in that glorious and never to be forgotten Rugby World Cup in France would not be maintained. By the end of October Los Pumas had only dropped one place on the IRB rankings (to fourth) but the opportunities to defend those points are scarce. Off the field, the numbers have grown and there is a real need for changes to be implemented and structures put in place.

Argentine rugby history is accustomed to bouncing back and this might be another page that will be written with a similar pattern. The game in South America – for it was a regional thing – was not braced for the growth in playing numbers thanks to the performance of Los Pumas, heroes in their country as well as the highlands of Colombia, the big smoke of Sao Paulo or the beaches of Reñaca in Chile. The whole regional rugby fraternity supported the Pumas' World Cup campaign so much that numbers are at an all time high in the CONSUR region.

This support has not diminished in spite of a logical slump in form since 2007. With a number of players calling it quits at Test rugby, the intensity never being the same as a year ago, new Test coaches and the same old availability issues that have and will continue to be a problem, Argentina's Test record for 2008 read: played four, lost three.

The U20s and Argentina A side failed to meet the standards expected, raising a few questions that are being addressed, not at full speed though, by the Argentine Rugby Union (UAR). Argentina Sevens was the only team to have a better season than the previous one.

When new IRB Chairman Bernard Lapasset came to Argentina in May for a four-day visit, he shone as a beacon. Speaking in perfect Spanish and smiling a lot, he met with every relevant official in the country and heard the Argentine story from the horse's mouth. On behalf of the IRB, Lapasset confirmed earlier announcements on the availability of funds for a country that has not yet been able to survive on its own. Most important, Lapasset's announced that Argentina will formally become a Tier One nation from 2012.

Until then, IRB grants will ensure the game continues to grow. The idea is to be self-sufficient by that year and able to compete in an enlarged Southern Hemisphere tournament. There are a number of options available for Argentina.

Movements in the right direction are being made. After slow progress, a High Performance Unit is about to kick-start a new development era and to look after the home-based players, new international competitions are being looked at. It has been confirmed for 2009 that Argentina will play in an enlarged five-team South American Championship (now including Brazil) and will start looking to the North – in the form of USA and Canada – for regular competition. Argentina A will continue to play in the Churchill Cup.

A new professional Board will be set by then although politics – the fight for power between the Buenos Aires Rugby Union (caters for 42% of the players in the country) and the rest of the provinces – have not yet allowed for crucial rewriting of the by-laws. Whatever moves are made will need to be rubber stamped and there is always the risk of politics intervening.

At the end of 2007 one final match was played against Chile, a match with no World Cup players and organised in haste brought a 79–8 win. What was more important was that 20 new players got to play a full international for the first time. Only a handful of them would play again in the ensuing four Tests of 2008.

The New Year began with only three games on the June window agenda. South Africa, one of Argentina's closest allies in world rugby, once again came to the rescue and offered a fourth international in August. That was duly accepted, in spite of the problems it would generate with players' release and holidays.

Marcelo Loffreda, who had guided Los Pumas for eight seasons, soon settled in Leicester (his would be a short stint in the Midlands club), and a new Puma coach was named. Santiago Phelan, a fiery flanker with 44 caps to his name and two World Cups on his battered shoulders, was asked to become the first ever full-time Puma coach. At 34 – born March 31, 1974 – and only four matches in charge of Argentina A as top level coaching background, the gamble was big, but the respect he had as a leader and a player ensured that everybody supported the nomination.

The full backing of the senior players – all of whom had played with him before his retirement in 2003 – was sufficient for him to accept the post. He brought Fabian Turnes, once a gem of a Puma centre and a recent coach of multi-champion Buenos Aires province, as his assistant.

Their task was never going to be easy and the problems with player release ensured their start included a few sleepless nights waiting to see who would be in their team. Eleven World Cup survivors were involved

Shaun Botterill/Getty Images

Argentina will officially be a Tier One nation in 2012.

in the first game. It was confirmed that Leinster's Felipe Contepomi will be the captain of Argentina on the road to RWC 2011.

The first Test against Scotland arrived and at a full Rosario Central stadium – a new Test venue in the country – Los Pumas managed to beat a rudderless Scottish side. Two unanswered tries – the first by 31-year old debutant hooker Alvaro Tejeda, the second with the last move of the match by centre Gonzalo Tiesi – settled the affair with a 21–15 win.

A week later, full of confidence that this Scottish side had no B game plan, Los Pumas made far too many mistakes and failed to contain a visiting team intent on finishing the season with a high. There were few equivalences and the retirement of Ignacio Fernandez Lobbe after thirteen seasons of great service was in defeat. He would score the first Puma try of the 14–26 defeat – the second was a cosmetic one in the last move of the game by Horacio Agulla.

Able to regroup and check on availabilities – with the French LNR semi-finals already played, some stars were be able to return to play for their country – Italy was next, in Cordoba, a fortnight later. The return of Rodrigo Roncero (to captain Argentina for the first time) and Juan Martín Hernández was the big news, yet it would bring no rewards – Hernandez broke a bone in his hand in the 18th minute and too many penalties and indiscipline cost the team dearly. With 14-men and Roncero on the sin-bin, the match was won by Italy with the last kick of the game. Hooker Leonardo Ghiraldini scored at the bottom of a maul a-la-Puma. Andrea Marcato, whose boot had failed to put Italy in the RWC quarter-finals, ended his season with an angled conversion. Argentina was now ranked fourth in the IRB Rankings.

June was extremely busy for Argentine rugby – Argentina U20 finished eighth in the IRB Junior World Championship in Wales. Having beaten Ireland U20 17–9 and Tonga U20 30–10, eventual champions New Zealand annihilated them 0–60. The toll on the team was very high and losses to France U20 6–30 and Samoa 10–30 condemned them to eighth place.

Argentina A, mostly selected from local based amateur players, travelled to Canada and USA to play in the Churchill Cup and their only win was against Canada, a good scalp, by a narrow 17–16. This win was sandwiched by losses to Scotland A 24–27 and Ireland 8–33.

Argentina Sevens recovered from finishing overall tenth in the 2006–2007 season to come in sixth. Not the heights of 2003–04 when they finished third, but a return to form for the Gomez Cora brothers-led team.

The Test season would end with the second biggest loss in Pumas history. Invited to celebrate Nelson Mandela's 90th birthday, Los Pumas went to South Africa where they were duly dispatched by an in-form Springboks by 63–9. Thirty minutes of Puma control were followed by 50 of Springbok domination. It was never going to be easy with the European-based Pumas in pre-season mode and playing for the first time under the ELVs.

Argentina must prove, soon, that it can continue to be competitive and attractive – the crowd in Johannesburg was small for Test standards. The big goal for the November Tests is to maintain the ranking (because of its importance for RWC-seedings) and for the following couple of years it has to be that Argentina continues being an option for the revamped tournaments that SANZAR will put on the table post-RWC 2011.

For that, the task at home is big. The UAR must work on the development of new players and systems that enable them to be competitive whilst staying at home. It is still hard to imagine a local professional competition but Europe is closing its doors more and more to foreigners.

A new National Provincial Championship must be organised and the National Club Championship must also be able to provide a higher standard of rugby for those in the elite. Buenos Aires Rugby Union won the NPC for a third consecutive year, whilst La Plata RC won the NCC.

ARGENTINA INTERNATIONAL STATISTICS

MATCH RECORDS UP TO 30TH SEPTEMBER 2008

WINNING MARGIN

Date	Opponent	Result	Winning Margin
01/05/2002	Paraguay	152–0	**152**
27/04/2003	Paraguay	144–0	**144**
01/05/2004	Venezuela	147–7	**140**
02/10/1993	Brazil	114–3	**111**
09/10/1979	Brazil	109–3	**106**

MOST POINTS IN A MATCH
BY THE TEAM

Date	Opponent	Result	Pts.
01/05/2002	Paraguay	152–0	**152**
01/05/2004	Venezuela	147–7	**147**
27/04/2003	Paraguay	144–0	**144**
02/10/1993	Brazil	114–3	**114**
09/10/1979	Brazil	109–3	**109**

MOST TRIES IN A MATCH
BY THE TEAM

Date	Opponent	Result	Tries
01/05/2002	Paraguay	152–0	**24**
27/04/2003	Paraguay	144–0	**24**
01/05/2004	Venezuela	147–7	**23**
08/10/1989	Brazil	103–0	**20**
21/09/1985	Paraguay	102–3	**19**
09/10/1979	Brazil	109–3	**19**

MOST CONVERSIONS IN A MATCH
BY THE TEAM

Date	Opponent	Result	Cons
01/05/2002	Paraguay	152–0	**16**
01/05/2004	Venezuela	147–7	**16**
09/10/1979	Brazil	109–3	**15**
21/09/1985	Paraguay	102–3	**13**
14/10/1973	Paraguay	98–3	**13**

MOST PENALTIES IN A MATCH
BY THE TEAM

Date	Opponent	Result	Pens
10/10/1999	Samoa	32–16	**8**
10/03/1995	Canada	29–26	**8**
17/06/2006	Wales	45–27	**8**

MOST DROP GOALS IN A MATCH
BY THE TEAM

Date	Opponent	Result	DGs
27/10/1979	Australia	24–13	**3**
02/11/1985	New Zealand	21–21	**3**
26/05/2001	Canada	20–6	**3**
21/09/1975	Uruguay	30–15	**3**
07/08/1971	SA Gazelles	12–0	**3**
30/09/2007	Ireland	30–15	**3**

MOST POINTS IN A MATCH
BY A PLAYER

Date	Player	Opponent	Pts.
14/10/1973	Eduardo Morgan	Paraguay	**50**
27/04/2003	José María Nuñez Piossek	Paraguay	**45**
02/10/1993	Gustavo Jorge	Brazil	**40**
24/10/1977	Martin Sansot	Brazil	**36**
13/09/1951	Uriel O'Farrell	Brazil	**33**

MOST TRIES IN A MATCH BY A PLAYER

Date	Player	Opponent	Tries
13/09/1951	Uriel O'Farrell	Brazil	11
27/04/2003	José María Nuñez Piossek	Paraguay	9
02/10/1993	Gustavo Jorge	Brazil	8
08/10/1989	Gustavo Jorge	Brazil	6
14/10/1973	Eduardo Morgan	Paraguay	6

MOST CONVERSIONS IN A MATCH BY A PLAYER

Date	Player	Opponent	Cons
01/05/2002	Jose Cilley	Paraguay	16
21/09/1985	Hugo Porta	Paraguay	13
14/10/1973	Eduardo Morgan	Paraguay	13
25/09/1975	Eduardo de Forteza	Paraguay	11
	3 Players		10

MOST PENALTIES IN A MATCH BY A PLAYER

Date	Player	Opponent	Pens
10/10/1999	Gonzalo Quesada	Samoa	8
10/03/1995	Santiago Meson	Canada	8
17/06/2006	Federico Todeschini	Wales	8

MOST DROP GOALS IN A MATCH BY A PLAYER

Date	Player	Opponent	DGs
27/10/1979	Hugo Porta	Australia	3
02/11/1985	Hugo Porta	New Zealand	3
07/08/1971	Tomas Harris-Smith	SA Gazelles	3
26/05/2001	Juan Fernández Miranda	Canada	3
30/09/2007	Juan Martín Hernández	Ireland	3

MOST CAPPED PLAYERS

Name	Caps
Lisandro Arbizu	86
Rolando Martin	86
Pedro Sporleder	78
Federico Méndez	73
Agustín Pichot	71

LEADING TRY SCORERS

Name	Tries
José María Nuñez Piossek	29
Diego Cuesta Silva	28
Gustavo Jorge	24
Facundo Soler	18
Rolando Martin	18

LEADING CONVERSIONS SCORERS

Name	Cons
Hugo Porta	84
Gonzalo Quesada	68
Santiago Meson	68
Felipe Contepomi	55
Juan Fernández Miranda	41

LEADING PENALTY SCORERS

Name	Pens
Gonzalo Quesada	103
Hugo Porta	102
Felipe Contepomi	94
Santiago Meson	63
Federico Todeschini	54

LEADING DROP GOAL SCORERS

Name	DGs
Hugo Porta	26
Lisandro Arbizu	11
Tomas Harris-Smith	6
Gonzalo Quesada	6
Juan Fernández Miranda	5

LEADING POINTS SCORERS

Name	Pts.
Hugo Porta	593
Gonzalo Quesada	483
Felipe Contepomi	456
Santiago Meson	370
Federico Todeschini	256

ARGENTINA INTERNATIONAL PLAYERS

UP TO 30TH SEPTEMBER 2008

Note: Years given for International Championship matches are for second half of season; eg 1972 means season 1971–72. Years for all other matches refer to the actual year of the match.

A Abadie 2007 *Ch*
A Abella 1969 *Ur, Ch*
C Abud 1975 *Par, Bra, Ch*
H Achaval 1948 *OCC*
J Aguilar 1983 *Ch, Ur*
A Aguirre 1997 *Par, Ch*
ME Aguirre 1990 *E, S,* 1991 *Sa*
H Agulla 2005 *Sa,* 2006 *Ur, E, It,* 2007 *It, F, Nm, I, S, SA, F,* 2008 *S, It, SA*
P Albacete 2003 *Par, Ur, F, SA, Ur, C, A, R,* 2004 *W, W, NZ, F, I,* 2005 *It, It,* 2006 *E, It, F,* 2007 *W, F, Geo, Nm, I, S, SA, F,* 2008 *SA*
DL Albanese 1995 *Ur, C, E, F,* 1996 *Ur, F, SA, E,* 1997 *NZ, Ur, R, It, F, A, A,* 1998 *F, F, R, US, C, It, F, W,* 1999 *W, W, S, I, W, Sa, J, I, F,* 2000 *I, A, A, SA,* 2001 *NZ, It, W, S, NZ,* 2002 *F, E, SA, A, It, I,* 2003 *F, F, SA, US, C, A, Nm, I*
F Albarracin 2007 *Ch*
M Albina 2001 *Ur, US,* 2003 *Par, Ur, Fj,* 2004 *Ch, Ven, W, W,* 2005 *J*
C Aldao 1961 *Ch, Bra, Ur*
P Alexenicer 1997 *Par, Ch*
C Alfonso 1936 *BI*
H Alfonso 1936 *BI, BI, Ch*
G Allen 1977 *Par*
JG Allen 1981 *C,* 1985 *F, F, Ur, NZ, NZ,* 1986 *F, F, A, A,* 1987 *Ur, Fj, It, NZ, Sp, A, A,* 1988 *F, F, F, F,* 1989 *Bra, Ch, Par, Ur, US*
L Allen 1951 *Ur, Bra, Ch*
M Allen 1990 *C, E, S,* 1991 *NZ, Ch*
A Allub 1997 *Par, Ur, It, F, A, A,* 1998 *F, F, US, C, J, It, F, W,* 1999 *W, W, S, I, W, Sa, J, I, F,* 2000 *I, A, A, SA, E,* 2001 *NZ*
M Alonso 1973 *R, R, S,* 1977 *F, F*
A Altberg 1972 *SAG, SAG,* 1973 *R, R, Par*
J Altube 1998 *Par, Ch, Ur*
C Alvarez 1958 *Per, Ur, Ch,* 1959 *JSB, JSB,* 1960 *F*
GM Alvarez 1975 *Ur, Par, Bra, Ch,* 1976 *Ur, NZ,* 1977 *Bra, Ur, Par, Ch*
R Álvarez Kairelis 1998 *Par, Ch, Ur,* 2001 *Ur, US, C, W, S, NZ,* 2002 *F, E, SA, A, It, I,* 2003 *F, SA, Fj, Ur, C, Nm, I,* 2004 *F, I,* 2006 *W, W, NZ, Ch, Ur,* 2007 *I, It, W, F, Geo, Nm, I, S, SA, F,* 2008 *SA*
F Amelong 2007 *Ch*
LG Amorosino 2007 *Ch*
A Amuchastegui 2002 *Ur, Par, Ch*
GP Angaut 1987 *NZ, Ur, Ch,* 1990 *S,* 1991 *NZ, Sa*
J-J Angelillo 1987 *Ur, Ch, A,* 1988 *F, F, F,* 1989 *It, Bra, Ch, Par, Ur, US,* 1990 *C, US, E, E,* 1994 *US, S, S, US,* 1995 *Par, Ch, R, F*
W Aniz 1960 *F*
R Annichini 1983 *Ch, Ur,* 1985 *F, Ch, Par*
A Anthony 1965 *OCC, Ch,* 1967 *Ur, Ch,* 1968 *W, W,* 1969 *S, S, Ur, Ch,* 1970 *I, I,* 1971 *SAG, SAG, OCC,* 1972 *SAG, SAG,* 1974 *F, F*
F Aranguren 2007 *Ch*
L Arbizu 1990 *I, S,* 1991 *NZ, NZ, Ch, A, W, Sa,* 1992 *F, F, Sp, Sp, R, F,* 1993 *J, J, Bra, Ch, Par, Ur, SA, SA,* 1995 *Ur, A, A, E, Sa, It, Par, Ch, Ur, R, It, F,* 1996 *Ur, US, Ur, C, SA, SA, E,* 1997 *E, E, NZ, NZ, R, It, F, A, A,* 1998 *F, F, R, US, C, It, F, W,* 1999 *W, W, S, I, W, Sa, J, I, F,* 2000 *A, A, SA, E,* 2001 *NZ, It, W, S, NZ*
F Argerich *1979 Ur*
G Aristide *1997 E*
J Arocena Messones *2005 Sa*
E Arriaga *1936 Ch, Ch*
S Artese *2004 SA*
M Avellaneda *1948 OCC, OCC, 1951 Bra, Ch*
M Avramovic *2005 J, Sa, 2006 Ch, Ur, E, It, 2007 I, 2008 It, SA*
M Ayerra *1927 GBR*
MI Ayerza *2004 SA, 2005 J, It, Sa, 2006 W, W, Ch, Ur, E, It, F, 2007 I, I, Geo, F, 2008 S, S, SA*
G Azcarate *2007 Ch*
M Azpiroz *1956 OCC, 1958 Per, Ur, Ch, 1959 JSB, JSB*
J Bach *1975 Par, Bra, Ch*
A Badano *1977 Bra, Ur, Par, Ch*
J Baeck *1983 Par*
M Baeck *1985 Ur, Ch, Par, 1990 US, E, E*
DR Baetti Sabah *1980 WXV, Fj, Fj, 1981 E, E, C, 1983 WXV, 1987 Ur, Par, Ch, 1988 F, F, 1989 It, NZ, NZ*
L Balfour *1977 Bra, Ur, Par, Ch*
C Barrea *1996 Ur, C, SA*
O Bartolucci *1996 US, C, SA, 1998 Ch, Ur, 1999 W, W, S, I, W, Sa, 2000 I, A, A, SA, E, 2001 US, C, 2003 Par, Ur*
E Basile *1983 Ch, Ur*
L Bavio *1954 F*
R Bazan *1951 Ur, Bra, Ch, 1956 OCC*
D Beccar Varela *1975 F, F, 1976 Ur, W, NZ, 1977 F, F*
G Beccar Varela *1976 W, NZ, NZ, 1977 F, F*
M Beccar Varela *1965 Rho, OCC, OCC*
G Begino *2007 Ch*
JW Beith *1936 BI*
J Benzi *1965 Rho, 1969 S, Ur, Ch*
E Bergamaschi *2001 US*
O Bernacchi *1954 F, 1956 OCC, OCC, 1958 Per, Ur, Ch*
G Bernardi *1997 Ch*
O Bernat *1932 JSB*
MM Berro *1964 Ur, Bra, Ch*
MJS Bertranou *1989 It, NZ, NZ, Ch, Par, 1990 C, US, C, E, E, I, E, S, 1993 SA*
E Bianchetti *1959 JSB, JSB*
G Blacksley *1971 SAG*
T Blades *1938 Ch*
G Bocca *1998 J, Par*
C Bofelli *1997 Ur, 1998 Par, 2004 Ch, Ur, Ven*
L Borges *2003 Par, Ch, Ur, 2004 Ch, Ur, Ven, W, W, NZ, F, I, SA, 2005 SA, S, 2006 W, W, Ch, Ur, 2007 W, F, Geo, I, S, SA, 2008 S, It*
C Bori *1975 F*
F Bosch *2004 Ch, SA, 2005 J, Sa*
MA Bosch *1991 A, Sa, 1992 F, F*
MT Bosch *2007 It, 2008 It*
N Bossicovich *1995 Ur, C*
CA Bottarini *1973 Par, Ur, Bra, I, 1974 F, 1975 F, F, 1979 Ur, Ch, Bra, 1983 Ch, Par, Ur*
R Botting *1927 GBR, GBR, GBR*
L Bouza *1992 Sp*

M Bouza *1966 SAG, SAG, 1967 Ur, Ch*
P Bouza *1996 Ur, F, F, E, 1997 E, NZ, NZ, Ur, R, 1998 Ur, 2002 Ur, Par, Ch, 2003 Par, Ch, Ur, US, Ur, Nm, R, 2004 Ch, Ur, Ven, W, NZ, SA, 2005 J, It, It, SA, S, It, 2006 Ch, Ur, 2007 I, I*
N Bozzo *1975 Bra*
JG Braceras *1971 Bra, Par, 1976 W, NZ, 1977 F*
W Braddon *1927 GBR*
EN Branca *1976 Ur, W, NZ, NZ, 1977 F, F, 1980 Fj, 1981 E, E, C, 1983 WXV, A, A, 1985 F, F, Ur, Ch, Par, NZ, NZ, 1986 F, F, A, A, 1987 Ur, Fj, It, NZ, Sp, A, A, 1988 F, F, F, F, 1989 Bra, Par, Ur, 1990 E, E*
M Brandi *1997 Par, Ch, 1998 Par, Ch, Ur*
J Bridger *1932 JSB*
J Brolese *1998 Ch, Ur*
E Brouchou *1975 Ur, Par, Bra, Ch*
F Buabse *1991 Ur, Par, Bra, 1992 Sp*
PM Buabse *1989 NZ, US, 1991 Sa, 1993 Bra, 1995 Ur, C, A*
E Buckley *1938 Ch*
R Bullrich *1991 Ur, Bra, 1992 R, 1993 Bra, Ch, SA, 1994 SA, SA*
S Bunader *1989 US, 1990 C*
K Bush *1938 Ch*
E Bustamante *1927 GBR, GBR, GBR, GBR*
F Bustillo *1977 F, F, Bra, Ur, Par, Ch*
G Bustos *2003 Par, Ur, 2004 Ch, Ven*
E Caffarone *1949 F, F, 1951 Bra, Ch, 1952 I, I, 1954 F, F*
M Caldwell *1956 OCC*
GF Camardon *1990 E, 1991 NZ, Ch, A, W, Sa, 1992 F, F, Sp, R, F, 1993 J, Par, Ur, SA, SA, 1995 A, 1996 Ur, US, Ur, C, SA, E, 1999 W, W, Sa, J, I, F, 2001 US, C, NZ, It, W, S, NZ, 2002 F, E, SA, It, I*
PJ Camerlinckx *1989 Bra, Par, Ur, 1990 C, US, 1994 S, 1995 Ch, 1996 Ur, F, F, US, Ur, C, SA, SA, E, 1997 E, E, NZ, NZ, Ur, R, It, F, A, A, 1998 R, US, C, F, W, 1999 W*
A Cameron *1936 BI, BI, Ch, Ch, 1938 Ch*
R Cameron *1927 GBR, GBR*
J Caminotti *1987 Ur, Par, Ch*
M Campo *1978 E, It, 1979 NZ, NZ, A, A, 1980 WXV, Fj, 1981 E, E, C, 1982 F, F, Sp, 1983 WXV, A, A, 1987 Ur, Fj, NZ*
A Campos *2007 Ch, 2008 S, It*
A Canalda *1999 S, I, F, 2000 A, 2001 Ur, US, C*
R Cano *1997 Par*
J Capalbo *1975 Bra, 1977 Bra, Ur, Ch*
AE Capelletti *1977 F, F, 1978 E, It, 1979 NZ, NZ, A, A, 1980 WXV, Fj, Fj, 1981 E, E*
R Carballo *2006 W, Ch, Ur, 2008 SA*
N Carbone *1969 Ur, Ch, 1971 SAG, 1973 I, S*
PF Cardinali *2001 US, 2002 Ur, Par, 2004 W, 2007 I*
M Carizza *2004 SA, 2005 J, SA, S, It, 2006 W, Ch, Ur, 2007 It, 2008 It*
J Carlos Galvalisi *1983 Par, Ur*
MA Carluccio *1973 R, R, Ur, Bra, I, 1975 F, F, 1976 NZ, 1977 F, F*
M Carmona *1997 Par, Ch*
S Carossio *1985 NZ, 1987 It, NZ*
J Carracedo *1971 Ch, Bra, Par, 1972 SAG, SAG, 1973 R, R, Par, Ur, Bra, Ch, I, S, 1975 F, 1976 W, NZ, NZ, 1977 F*
M Carreras *1991 NZ, NZ, Ch, A, W, Sa, 1992 F*
M Carreras *1987 Par*
M Carrique *1983 Par, Ur*
J Casanegra *1959 JSB, JSB, 1960 F, F*
GF Casas *1971 OCC, 1973 Par, Ch, I, 1975 F, F*
DM Cash *1985 F, F, Ur, Ch, NZ, NZ, 1986 F, F, A, A, 1987 Ur, Fj, It, NZ, Sp, A, A, 1988 F, F, F, F, 1989 It, NZ, NZ, US, 1990 C, US, C, E, I, E, S, 1991 NZ, NZ, Ch, A, Sa, 1992 F, F*
R Castagna *1977 F*
A Castellina *2004 Ch, Ur, Ven*
R Castro *1971 Ch, Bra, Par*
J Cato *1975 Ur, Par*
R Cazenave *1965 Rho, JSB, OCC, Ch, 1966 SAG, SAG*
A Cerioni *1975 F, 1978 E, It, 1979 Ch, Bra*
G Cernegoy *1938 Ch*
H Cespedes *1997 Ur, Ch*
M Chesta *1966 SAG, SAG, 1967 Ur, Ch, 1968 W, W*
W Chiswell *1949 F*
V Christianson *1954 F, F, 1956 OCC*
E Cilley *1932 JSB, JSB*
J Cilley *1936 BI, Ch, Ch, 1938 Ch*
JL Cilley *1994 SA, 1995 Sa, It, Par, Ch, 1996 Ur, F, F, SA, SA, 1999 W, 2000 A, 2002 Par*
J Clement *1987 Par, 1989 Bra*
R Cobelo *1987 Ur, Par, Ch*
I Comas *1951 Bra, Ch, 1958 Per, Ch, 1960 F*
A Conen *1951 Ch, 1952 I, I*
J Conrard *1927 GBR, GBR*
CA Contepomi *1964 Bra, Ch*
F Contepomi *1998 Ch, Ur, F, W, 1999 W, S, I, J, I, F, 2000 I, A, A, SA, E, 2001 Ur, US, C, NZ, It, W, S, NZ, 2002 F, E, SA, A, It, I, 2003 F, F, SA, US, C, A, Nm, I, 2004 W, W, F, I, 2005 It, It, SA, S, It, 2006 W, NZ, E, F, 2007 I, W, F, Geo, Nm, I, S, SA, F, 2008 S, S, SA*
M Contepomi *1998 US, C, It, F, W, 1999 S, I, W, Sa, F, 2003 Ur, F, Fj, Ur, A, R, 2004 Ch, Ur, Ven, W, W, NZ, F, I, SA, 2005 SA, S, 2006 It, F, 2007 I, It, W, F, Nm, I, S, SA, F*
F Conti *1988 F*
GEF Cooke *1927 GBR*
KAM Cookson *1932 JSB*
N Cooper *1936 BI, Ch, Ch*
R Cooper *1927 GBR, GBR, GBR, GBR*
J Copello *1975 Ur, Bra*
C Cordeiro *1983 Par*
J Coria *1987 Ur, Par, Ch, 1989 Bra*
I Corleto *1998 J, F, W, 1999 I, J, I, F, 2000 I, A, SA, E, 2001 W, S, NZ, 2002 F, E, SA, A, It, I, 2003 F, Fj, US, Ur, C, A, I, 2006 It, F, 2007 W, F, Geo, Nm, I, S, SA, F*
ME Corral *1993 J, Bra, Par, Ur, SA, SA, 1994 US, S, SA, SA, 1995 Ur, C, A, A, E, Sa, It*
M Cortese *2005 Sa*
F Cortopasso *2003 Ch, Ur*
A Costa Repetto *2005 Sa*
JD Costante *1971 OCC, OCC, Ch, Bra, Par, Ur, 1976 Ur, W, NZ, 1977 F*
AF Courreges *1979 Ur, Par, Bra, 1982 F, F, Sp, 1983 WXV, A, A, 1987 Sp, A, A, 1988 F*
PH Cox *1938 Ch*
A Creevy *2005 J, Sa, 2006 Ur*
P Cremaschi *1993 J, J, 1995 Par, Ch, Ur, It*
RH Crexell *1990 I, S, 1991 Par, 1992 Sp, 1993 J, 1995 Ur, C, A, E, Sa, It, Par, Ch, Ur*
L Criscuolo *1992 F, F, 1993 Bra, SA, 1996 Ur, F, F*
J Cruz Legora *2002 Par, Ch*
J Cruz Meabe *1997 Par*
AG Cubelli *1977 Bra, Ur, Ch, 1978 E, It, 1979 A, A, 1980 WXV, Fj, 1983 Par, 1985 F, F, Ur, Par, NZ, NZ, 1990 S*
D Cuesta Silva *1983 Ch, Ur, 1985 F, F, Ur, Ch, NZ, NZ, 1986 F, F, A, A, 1987 Ur, Fj, It, Sp, A, A, 1988 F, F, F, F, 1989 It, NZ, NZ, 1990 C, E, E, I, E, S, 1991 NZ, NZ, Ch, A, W, Sa, 1992 F, F, Sp, R, F, 1993 J, J, Bra, Par, Ur, SA, SA, 1994 US, S, S, US, SA, 1995 Ur, C, E, Sa, It, Par, R, It, F*
J Cuesta Silva *1927 GBR, GBR, GBR, GBR*
B Cuezzo *2007 Ch*
M Cutler *1969 Ur, 1971 Ch, Bra, Par, Ur*
A Da Milano *1964 Bra, Ch*
F D'Agnillo *1975 Ur, Bra, 1977 Bra, Ur, Par, Ch*
JL Damioli *1991 Ur, Par, Bra*
H Dande *2001 Ur, C, 2004 Ch, Ven*
J Dartiguelongue *1964 Bra, Ch, 1968 W, W*
S Dassen *1983 Ch, Par, Ur*
H Davel *1936 BI*
R de Abelleyra *1932 JSB, JSB*
L de Chazal *2001 Ur, C, 2004 SA*
E de Forteza *1975 Ur, Par, Bra, Ch*
R de la Arena *1992 F, Sp*
JC De Pablo *1948 OCC*
G de Robertis *2005 Sa, 2006 Ch, Ur*
R de Vedia *1982 F, Sp*
T de Vedia *2007 I, I, 2008 S*
R del Busto *2007 Ch*
F del Castillo *1994 US, SA, 1995 Ur, C, A, 1996 Ur, F, 1997 Par, Ur, 1998 Ur*

GJ del Castillo 1991 NZ, NZ, Ch, A, W, 1993 J, 1994 S, S, US, SA, 1995 C, A
L del Chazal 1983 Ch, Par, Ur
R Dell'Acqua 1956 OCC
S Dengra 1982 F, Sp, 1983 WXV, A, A, 1986 A, 1987 It, NZ, Sp, A, A, 1988 F, F, F, F, 1989 It, NZ, NZ
C Derkheim 1927 GBR
M Devoto 1975 Par, Bra, 1977 Par
PM Devoto 1982 F, F, Sp, 1983 WXV
R Devoto 1960 F
Diaz 1997 Par, Ch, 1998 J, Par, Ch
F Diaz Alberdi 1997 Ur, 1999 S, I, 2000 A, A
J Diez 1956 OCC
R Dillon 1956 OCC
P Dinisio 1989 NZ, 1990 C, US
M Dip 1979 Par, Bra
D Dominguez 1989 Ch, Par
E Dominguez 1949 F, F, 1952 I, I, 1954 F, F
L Dorado 1949 F
J Dumas 1973 R, R, Ur, Bra, S
M Dumas 1966 SAG, SAG
MA Durand 1997 Ch, 1998 Par, Ch, Ur, It, F, W, 2000 SA, 2001 Ur, US, C, It, NZ, 2002 F, SA, A, It, I, 2003 Ch, Ur, Fj, US, Ur, C, A, Nm, R, 2004 Ch, Ur, Ven, W, W, NZ, F, I, SA, 2005 SA, S, It, 2006 W, NZ, Ch, Ur, It, F, 2007 I, I, It, W, F, Geo, I, F, 2008 S, S, It, SA
C Echeverria 1932 JSB
G Ehrman 1948 OCC, 1949 F, F, 1951 Ur, Bra, Ch, 1952 I, I, 1954 F, F
O Elia 1954 F
R Elliot 1936 Bl, Bl, 1938 Ch
J Escalante 1975 Ur, Par, Ch, 1978 It, 1979 Ur, Par, Bra
N Escary 1927 GBR, GBR, 1932 JSB, JSB
R Espagnol 1971 SAG
AM Etchegaray 1964 Ur, Bra, Ch, 1965 Rho, JSB, Ch, 1967 Ur, Ch, 1968 W, W, 1969 S, S, 1971 SAG, OCC, OCC, 1972 SAG, SAG, 1973 Par, Bra, I, 1974 F, F, 1976 Ur, W, NZ, NZ
R Etchegoyen 1991 Ur, Par, Bra
C Ezcurra 1958 Per, Ur, Ch
E Ezcurra 1990 I, E, S
R Fariello 1973 Par, Ur, Ch, S
M Farina 1968 W, W, 1969 S, S
D Farrell 1951 Ur
P Felisari 1956 OCC
JJ Fernandez 1971 SAG, Ch, Bra, Par, Ur, 1972 SAG, SAG, 1973 R, R, Par, Ur, Ch, I, S, 1974 F, F, 1975 F, 1976 Ur, W, NZ, NZ, 1977 F, F
Pablo Fernandez Bravo 1993 SA, SA
E Fernandez del Casal 1951 Ur, Bra, Ch, 1952 I, I, 1956 OCC, OCC
CI Fernandez Lobbe 1996 US, 1997 E, E, 1998 F, F, R, US, Ur, C, J, It, F, 1999 W, W, S, I, W, Sa, J, I, F, 2000 I, A, A, SA, E, 2001 NZ, It, W, S, NZ, 2002 F, E, SA, A, It, I, 2003 F, F, SA, US, C, A, Nm, I, 2004 W, W, NZ, 2005 SA, S, It, 2006 W, W, NZ, E, F, 2007 It, W, F, Nm, I, S, SA, 2008 S, S
JM Fernandez Lobbe 2004 Ur, Ven, 2005 S, It, Sa, 2006 W, W, NZ, E, It, F, 2007 I, I, It, W, F, Geo, Nm, I, S, SA, F, 2008 S, S, SA
N Fernandez Miranda 1994 US, S, S, US, 1995 Ch, Ur, 1996 F, SA, SA, E, 1997 E, E, NZ, NZ, Ur, R, 1998 R, US, C, It, 1999 I, F, 2002 Ur, Ch, It, 2003 Ch, Ur, F, F, SA, US, Ur, Nm, R, 2004 W, NZ, 2005 J, It, It, 2006 W, It, 2007 It, Geo, Nm
JC Fernández Miranda 1997 Ur, R, It, 1998 Ur, It, 2000 I, 2001 US, C, 2002 Ur, Par, Ch, It, I, 2003 Par, Ch, Ur, Fj, US, Nm, R, 2004 W, NZ, SA, 2005 J, Sa, 2006 Ch, Ur, 2007 It
N Ferrari 1992 Sp, Sp
G Fessia 2007 I
R Follett 1948 OCC, OCC, 1952 I, I, 1954 F
G Foster 1971 Ch, Bra, Par, Ur
R Foster 1965 Rho, JSB, OCC, OCC, Ch, 1966 SAG, SAG, 1970 I, I, 1971 SAG, SAG, OCC, 1972 SAG, SAG
P Franchi 1987 Ur, Par, Ch
JL Francombe 1932 JSB, JSB, 1936 Bl, Bl
J Freixas 2003 Ch, Ur
R Frigerio 1948 OCC, OCC, 1954 F
J Frigoli 1936 Bl, Bl, Ch, Ch
P Fuselli 1998 J, Par
E Gahan 1954 F, F
M Gaitán 1998 Ur, 2002 Par, Ch, 2003 Fj, US, Nm, R, 2004 W, 2007 It, W
AM Galindo 2004 Ur, Ven, 2008 S, It, SA
R Gallo 1964 Bra
P Gambarini 2006 W, Ch, Ur, 2007 I, It, Ch, 2008 S
E Garbarino 1992 Sp, Sp
FL Garcia 1994 SA, 1995 A, A, Par, Ch, 1996 Ur, F, F, 1997 NZ, 1998 R, Ur, J
J Garcia 1998 Par, Ur, 2000 A
PT Garcia 1948 OCC
E Garcia Hamilton 1993 Bra
P Garcia Hamilton 1998 Ch
HM Garcia Simon 1990 I, 1992 F
G Garcia-Orsetti 1992 R, F
PA Garreton 1987 Sp, Ur, Ch, A, A, 1988 F, F, F, F, 1989 It, NZ, Bra, Ch, Ur, US, 1990 C, E, E, I, E, S, 1991 NZ, NZ, Ch, A, W, Sa, 1992 F, F, 1993 J, J
P Garzon 1990 C, 1991 Par, Bra
G Gasso 1983 Ch, Par
JM Gauweloose 1975 F, F, 1976 W, NZ, NZ, 1977 F, F, 1981 C
E Gavina 1956 OCC, OCC, 1958 Per, Ur, Ch, 1959 JSB, JSB, 1960 F, F, 1961 Ch, Bra, Ur
FA Genoud 2004 Ch, Ur, Ven, 2005 J, It
J Genoud 1952 I, I, 1956 OCC, OCC
M Gerosa 1987 Ur, Ch
D Giannantonio 1996 Ur, 1997 Par, Ur, It, A, A, 1998 F, F, 2000 A, 2002 E
MC Giargia 1973 Par, Ur, Bra, 1975 Par, Ch
R Giles 1948 OCC, 1949 F, F, 1951 Ur, 1952 I, I
C Giuliano 1959 JSB, JSB, 1960 F
L Glastra 1948 OCC, OCC, 1952 I, I
M Glastra 1979 Ur, Ch, 1981 C
FE Gomez 1985 Ur, 1987 Ur, Fj, It, NZ, 1989 NZ, 1990 C, E, E
JF Gomez 2006 It, 2008 S, S, It
N Gomez 1997 Par, Ch
PM Gomez Cora 2004 NZ, SA, 2005 Sa, 2006 E
D Gonzalez 1988 F, F
D Gonzalez 1987 Par
T Gonzalez 1975 Ur, Ch
S Gonzalez Bonorino 2001 Ur, US, C, 2002 Par, Ch, 2003 F, SA, 2007 I, I, It, W, F, Geo, 2008 S, S
E Gonzalez del Solar 1960 F, 1961 Ch, Bra, Ur
N Gonzalez del Solar 1964 Ur, Bra, Ch, 1965 Rho, JSB, OCC, OCC, Ch
H Goti 1961 Ch, Bra, Ur, 1964 Ur, Bra, Ch, 1965 Rho, 1966 SAG
LM Gradin 1965 OCC, OCC, Ch, 1966 SAG, SAG, 1969 Ch, 1970 I, I, 1973 R, R, Par, Ur, Ch, S
P Grande 1998 Par, Ch, Ur
RD Grau 1993 J, Bra, Ch, 1995 Par, Ch, 1996 F, F, US, Ur, C, SA, SA, E, 1997 E, E, NZ, NZ, A, A, 1998 F, It, F, 1999 W, W, S, I, W, F, 2000 A, SA, E, 2001 NZ, W, S, NZ, 2002 F, E, SA, A, It, 2003 F, SA, US, Ur, C, A, I
L Gravano 1997 Ch, 1998 Ch, Ur
B Grigolon 1948 OCC, 1954 F, F
V Grimoldi 1927 GBR, GBR
J Grondona 1990 C
R Grosse 1952 I, I, 1954 F, F
P Guarrochena 1977 Par
A Guastella 1956 OCC, 1959 JSB, JSB, 1960 F
J Guidi 1958 Per, Ur, Ch, 1959 JSB, 1960 F, 1961 Ch, Bra, Ur
E Guiñazu 2003 Par, Ch, Ur, 2004 Ch, Ur, Ven, W, W, SA, 2005 J, It, 2007 I, It, F
JA Guzman 2007 Ch
D Halle 1989 Bra, Ch, Ur, US, 1990 US
A Hamilton 1936 Bl
R Handley 1966 SAG, SAG, 1968 W, W, 1969 S, S, Ur, Ch, 1970 I, I, 1971 SAG, SAG, 1972 SAG, SAG
G Hardie 1948 OCC

TA Harris-Smith 1969 S, S, 1971 SAG, OCC, OCC, 1973 Par, Ur
V Harris-smith 1936 Bl
O Hasan Jalil 1995 Ur, 1996 Ur, C, SA, SA, 1997 E, E, NZ, R, It, F, A, 1998 F, F, R, US, C, It, F, W, 1999 W, W, S, W, Sa, J, I, 2000 SA, E, 2001 NZ, It, W, S, NZ, 2002 F, E, SA, A, It, I, 2003 US, C, A, R, 2004 W, W, NZ, F, I, 2005 It, It, SA, S, It, 2006 NZ, E, F, 2007 It, Geo, Nm, I, S, SA, F
P Henn 2004 Ch, Ur, Ven, 2005 J, It, 2007 It
M Hernandez 1927 GBR, GBR, GBR
JM Hernández 2003 Par, Ur, F, F, SA, C, A, Nm, R, 2004 F, I, SA, 2005 SA, S, It, 2006 W, W, NZ, E, It, F, 2007 F, Geo, I, S, SA, F, 2008 It
L Herrera 1991 Ur, Par
FA Higgs 2004 Ur, Ven, 2005 J
D Hine 1938 Ch
C Hirsch 1960 F
C Hirsch 1960 F
E Hirsch 1954 F, 1956 OCC
R Hogg 1958 Per, Ur, Ch, 1959 JSB, JSB, 1961 Ch, Bra, Ur
S Hogg 1956 OCC, OCC, 1958 Per, Ur, Ch, 1959 JSB, JSB
E Holmberg 1948 OCC
B Holmes 1949 F, F
E Holmgren 1958 Per, Ur, Ch, 1959 JSB, JSB, 1960 F, F
G Holmgren 1985 NZ, NZ
E Horan 1956 OCC
L Hughes 1936 Ch
M Hughes 1954 F, F
M Hughes 1949 F, F
CA Huntley Robertson 1932 JSB, JSB
A Iachetti 1977 Bra, 1987 Ch
A Iachetti 1975 Ur, Par, 1977 Ur, Par, Ch, 1978 E, It, 1979 NZ, NZ, A, A, 1980 WXV, Fj, Fj, 1981 E, E, 1982 F, F, Sp, 1987 Ur, Par, A, A, 1988 F, F, F, F, 1989 It, NZ, 1990 C, E, E
ME Iachetti 1979 NZ, NZ, A, A
M Iglesias 1973 R, 1974 F, F
G Illia 1965 Rho
JL Imhoff 1967 Ur, Ch
V Inchausti 1936 Bl, Ch, Ch
F Insua 1971 Ch, Bra, Par, Ur, 1972 SAG, SAG, 1973 R, R, Bra, Ch, I, S, 1974 F, F, 1976 Ur, W, NZ, NZ, 1977 F, F
R Iraneta 1974 F, 1976 Ur, W, NZ
FJ Irarrazabal 1991 Sa, 1992 Sp, Sp
S Irazoqui 1993 J, Ch, Par, Ur, 1995 E, Sa, Par
A Irigoyen 1997 Par
C Jacobi 1979 Ch, Par
AG Jacobs 1927 GBR, GBR
AGW Jones 1948 OCC
GM Jorge 1989 Bra, Ch, Par, Ur, 1990 I, E, 1992 F, F, Sp, Sp, R, F, 1993 J, J, Bra, Ch, Ur, SA, SA, 1994 US, S, S, US
J Jose Villar 2001 Ur, US, C, 2002 Par, Ch
E Jurado 1995 A, A, E, Sa, It, Par, Ch, Ur, R, It, F, 1996 SA, E, 1997 E, E, NZ, NZ, Ur, R, It, F, A, A, 1998 F, Ur, C, It, 1999 W
E Karplus 1959 JSB, JSB, 1960 F, F, F
A Ker 1936 Ch, 1938 Ch
E Kossler 1960 F, F, F
EH Laborde 1991 A, W, Sa
G Laborde 1979 Ch, Bra
J Lacarra 1989 Par, Ur
R Lagarde 1956 OCC
A Lalanne 2008 SA
M Lamas 1998 Par, Ch
TR Landajo 1977 F, Bra, Ur, Ch, 1978 E, 1979 A, A, 1980 WXV, Fj, Fj, 1981 E, E
M Lanfranco 1991 Ur, Par, Bra
AR Lanusse 1932 JSB
M Lanusse 1951 Ur, Bra, Ch
J Lanza 1985 F, Ur, Par, NZ, NZ, 1986 F, F, A, A, 1987 Ur, Fj, It, NZ
P Lanza 1983 Ch, Par, Ur, 1985 F, F, Ur, Ch, Par, NZ, NZ, 1986 F, F, A, A, 1987 It, NZ
J Lasalle 1964 Ur
J Lavayen 1961 Ch, Bra, Ur
CG Lazcano Miranda 1998 Ch, 2004 Ch, Ur, Ven, 2005 J
RA le Fort 1990 I, E, 1991 NZ, NZ, Ch, A, W, 1992 R, F, 1993 J, SA, SA, 1995 Ur, It
F Lecot 2003 Par, Ur, 2005 J, 2007 Ch
P Ledesma 2008 It, SA
ME Ledesma Arocena 1996 Ur, C, 1997 NZ, NZ, Ur, R, It, F, A, A, 1998 F, F, Ur, C, J, Ur, F, W, 1999 W, W, Sa, J, I, F, 2000 SA, 2001 It, W, NZ, 2002 F, E, SA, A, It, I, 2003 F, SA, Fj, US, C, A, Nm, R, 2004 W, NZ, F, I, 2005 It, It, SA, S, It, 2006 W, W, NZ, Ch, Ur, E, It, F, 2007 W, F, Geo, I, S, SA, 2008 SA
J Legora 1996 F, F, US, Ur, 1997 Ch, 1998 Par
JM Leguizamón 2005 J, It, It, SA, S, It, 2006 W, NZ, Ch, Ur, E, It, F, 2007 I, I, It, W, F, Geo, Nm, S, SA, F, 2008 S, S, It, SA
GP Leiros 1973 Bra, I
C Lennon 1958 Per, Ur
FJ Leonelli Morey 2001 Ur, 2004 Ur, Ven, 2005 J, It, SA, S, It, 2006 W, W, 2007 I, I, It
M Lerga 1995 Par, Ch, Ur
Lesianado 1948 OCC
I Lewis 1932 JSB
GA Llanes 1990 I, E, S, 1991 NZ, NZ, Ch, A, W, 1992 F, F, Sp, R, F, 1993 Bra, Ch, SA, SA, 1994 US, S, S, SA, SA, 1995 A, A, E, Sa, It, R, It, F, 1996 SA, SA, E, 1997 E, E, NZ, NZ, R, It, F, 1998 F, 2000 A
L Lobrauco 1996 US, 1997 Ch, 1998 J, Ch, Ur
MH Loffreda 1978 E, 1979 NZ, NZ, A, A, 1980 WXV, Fj, Fj, 1981 E, E, C, 1982 F, F, Sp, 1983 WXV, A, A, 1985 Ur, Ch, Par, 1987 Ur, Par, Ch, A, A, 1988 F, F, F, F, 1989 It, NZ, Bra, Ch, Par, Ur, US, 1990 C, US, E, E, 1994 US, S, S, US, SA, SA
G Logan 1936 Bl, Bl
GM Longo Elía 1999 W, W, S, I, W, Sa, I, F, 2000 I, A, A, SA, E, 2001 US, NZ, It, W, S, NZ, 2002 F, E, SA, A, It, I, 2003 F, F, SA, Fj, C, A, I, 2004 W, W, NZ, F, I, 2005 It, It, SA, 2006 W, W, NZ, E, It, F, 2007 W, Nm, I, S, SA, F
L Lopez Fleming 2004 Ur, Ven, W, 2005 Sa
A Lopresti 1997 Par, Ch
J Loures 1954 F
R Loyola 1964 Ur, Ch, 1965 Rho, JSB, OCC, OCC, Ch, 1966 SAG, SAG, 1968 W, W, 1969 S, S, 1970 I, I, 1971 Ch, Bra, Par, Ur
E Lozada 2006 E, It, 2007 I, I, Geo, F, 2008 S, S, It, SA
F Lucioni 1927 GBR
R Lucke 1975 Ur, Par, Bra, Ch, 1976 Ur, 1981 C
J Luna 1995 Par, Ch, Ur, R, It, F, 1997 Par, Ch
P Macadam 1949 F, F
AM Macome 1990 I, E, 1995 Ur, C
RM Madero 1978 E, It, 1979 NZ, NZ, A, A, 1980 WXV, Fj, Fj, 1981 E, E, C, 1982 F, F, Sp, 1983 WXV, A, A, 1985 F, NZ, 1986 A, A, 1987 Ur, It, NZ, Sp, Ur, Par, Ch, A, A, 1988 F, F, F, 1989 It, NZ, NZ, 1990 E, E
L Makin 1927 GBR
A Mamanna 1991 Par, 1997 Par
J Manuel Belgrano 1956 OCC
A Marguery 1991 Ur, Bra, 1993 Ch, Par
R Martin 1938 Ch
RA Martin 1994 US, S, S, US, SA, SA, 1995 Ur, C, A, A, E, Sa, It, Ch, Ur, R, It, F, 1996 Ur, F, F, Ur, C, SA, SA, E, 1997 E, E, NZ, NZ, It, F, A, A, 1998 F, F, R, US, Ur, J, Par, Ch, Ur, It, W, 1999 W, W, S, I, W, Sa, J, I, F, 2000 I, A, A, SA, E, 2001 Ur, US, C, NZ, It, W, S, NZ, 2002 Ur, Par, Ch, F, E, SA, A, It, I, 2003 <
F Martin Aramburu 2004 Ch, Ven, W, NZ, F, I, 2005 It, SA, S, It, 2006 NZ, 2007 Geo, F, 2008 S, SA
J Martin Copella 1989 Ch, Par
Martinez 1969 Ur, Ch, 1970 I, I
E Martinez 1971 Ch, Bra, Ur
O Martinez Basante 1954 F
M Martinez Mosquera 1971 Ch
RC Mastai 1975 F, 1976 Ur, W, NZ, NZ, 1977 F, F, Bra, Ur, Par, Ch, 1980 WXV
R Matarazzo 1971 SAG, SAG, Par, Ur, 1972 SAG, SAG, 1973 R, R, Par, Ur, Ch, I, S, 1974 F, F
H Maurer 1932 JSB, JSB
L Maurette 1948 OCC, OCC
C Mazzini 1977 F, F

G McCormick *1964 Bra, Ch, 1965 Rho, OCC, OCC, Ch, 1966 SAG, SAG*
M McCormick *1927 GBR*
A Memoli *1979 Ur, Par, Bra*
FJ Mendez *1991 Ur, Par, Bra, 1992 Sp, Sp*
H Mendez *1967 Ur, Ch*
L Mendez *1958 Per, Ur, Ch, 1959 JSB*
FE Méndez *1990 I, E, 1991 NZ, NZ, Ch, A, W, 1992 F, F, Sp, Sp, R, F, 1994 S, US, SA, SA, 1995 Ur, C, A, A, E, Sa, It, Par, Ch, Ur, R, It, F, 1996 SA, SA, 1997 E, 1998 F, F, R, US, Ur, C, It, F, W, 1999 W, W, 2000 I, A, A, SA, E, 2001 NZ, It, W, S, NZ, 2002 Ur, Ch, F, E, SA, A, 2003 F, F, SA, Fj, Ur, Nm, I, 2004 Ch, Ur, W, W, NZ, SA*
CI Mendy *1987 Ur, Par, Ch, A, A, 1988 F, F, F, F, 1989 It, NZ, NZ, US, 1990 C, 1991 Ur, Bra*
FJ Merello *2007 Ch*
I Merlo *1993 Bra, Ch*
P Merlo *1985 Ch, Par*
SE Meson *1987 Par, 1989 Bra, Par, Ur, US, 1990 US, C, S, 1991 NZ, NZ, Ch, Sa, 1992 F, F, Sp, R, F, 1993 J, Bra, Par, Ur, SA, SA, 1994 US, S, S, US, 1995 Ur, C, A, A, 1996 US, C, 1997 Ch*
Mieres *2007 Ch*
BH Miguens *1983 WXV, A, A, 1985 F, F, NZ, NZ, 1986 F, F, A, A, 1987 Sp*
E Miguens *1975 Ur, Par, Ch*
H Miguens *1969 S, S, Ur, Ch, 1970 I, I, 1971 OCC, 1972 SAG, SAG, 1973 R, R, Par, Ur, Bra, Ch, I, S, 1975 F*
J Miguens *1982 F, 1985 F, F, 1986 F, F, A, A*
GE Milano *1982 F, F, Sp, 1983 WXV, A, A, 1985 F, F, Ur, Ch, Par, NZ, NZ, 1986 F, F, A, A, 1987 Ur, Fj, Sp, Ur, Ch, A, A, 1988 F, F, F, 1989 It, NZ, NZ*
A Mimesi *1998 J, Par, Ch*
B Minguez *1975 Par, Bra, Ch, 1979 Ur, Ch, Par, 1983 WXV, A, A, 1985 Ur, Ch*
B Mitchelstein *1936 BI*
E Mitchelstein *1956 OCC, 1960 F, F*
LE Molina *1985 Ch, 1987 Ur, Fj, It, NZ, 1989 NZ, NZ, Bra, Ch, Par, 1990 C, E, 1991 W*
M Molina *1998 Par, Ch, Ur*
G Montes de Oca *1961 Ch, Bra, Ur*
E Montpelat *1948 OCC, OCC*
G Morales Oliver *2001 Ur, US, C*
C Morea *1951 Ur, Bra, Ch*
FR Morel *1979 A, A, 1980 WXV, Fj, Fj, 1981 E, E, C, 1982 F, 1985 F, F, Ur, Par, NZ, NZ, 1986 F, F, A, 1987 Ur, Fj*
A Moreno *1998 Par, Ch, Ur*
D Morgan *1967 Ch, 1970 I, I, 1971 SAG, SAG, OCC, OCC, 1972 SAG, SAG*
E Morgan *1969 S, S, 1972 SAG, SAG, 1973 R, R, Par, Ur, Bra, Ch, I, S, 1975 F, F*
G Morgan *1977 Bra, Ur, Par, Ch, 1979 Ur, Par, Bra*
M Morgan *1971 SAG, OCC, OCC*
JS Morganti *1951 Ur, Bra, Ch*
J Mostany *1987 Ur, Fj, NZ*
E Muliero *1997 Ch*
S Muller *1927 GBR*
R Muniz *1975 Par, Bra, Ch*
M Nannini *2002 Ur, Par, Ch, 2003 Par, Ch*
A Navajas *1932 JSB, JSB*
E Naveyra *1998 Ch*
G Nazassi *1997 Ch*
ML Negri *1979 Ch, Bra*
E Neri *1960 F, F, 1961 Ch, Bra, Ur, 1964 Ur, Bra, Ch, 1965 Rho, JSB, OCC, 1966 SAG, SAG*
CM Neyra *1975 F, F, 1976 W, NZ, NZ, 1983 WXV*
A Nicholson *1979 Ur, Par, Bra*
HM Nicola *1971 SAG, OCC, OCC, Ch, Bra, Par, Ur, 1975 F, F, 1978 E, It, 1979 NZ, NZ*
EP Noriega *1991 Par, 1992 Sp, Sp, R, F, 1993 J, J, Ch, Par, Ur, SA, SA, 1994 US, S, S, US, SA, SA, 1995 Ur, C, A, A, E, Sa, It*
JM Nuñez Piossek *2001 Ur, NZ, 2002 Ur, Par, Ch, A, 2003 Par, Ur, F, SA, Ur, C, A, R, I, 2004 Ch, Ur, W, W, 2005 It, It, 2006 W, W, NZ, E, F, 2008 S, SA*
R Ochoa *1956 OCC*
M Odriozola *1961 Ch, Ur*
J O'Farrell *1948 OCC, 1951 Ur, Bra, 1956 OCC*
U O'Farrell *1951 Ur, Bra, Ch*
C Ohanian *1998 Par, Ur*
C Olivera *1958 Per, Ur, Ch, 1959 JSB, JSB*
R Olivieri *1960 F, F, F, 1961 Ch, Bra, Ur*
J Orengo *1996 Ur, 1997 Ur, R, It, 1998 F, F, R, US, C, F, W, 1999 W, 2000 A, SA, E, 2001 Ur, US, C, NZ, W, S, NZ, 2002 F, E, SA, A, It, I, 2003 F, SA, Ur, C, A, I, 2004 W, W*
C Orti *1949 F, F*
L Ortiz *2003 Par, Ch, Ur*
A Orzabal *1974 F, F*
L Ostiglia *1999 W, W, S, I, W, J, F, 2001 NZ, It, W, S, 2002 E, SA, 2003 Par, Ch, Ur, F, F, SA, Nm, I, 2004 W, W, NZ, F, I, SA, 2007 F, Nm, I, S, SA*
B Otaño *1960 F, F, F, 1961 Ch, Bra, Ur, 1964 Ur, Bra, Ch, 1965 Rho, JSB, OCC, OCC, Ch, 1966 SAG, SAG, 1968 W, W, 1969 S, S, Ur, Ch, 1970 I, I, 1971 SAG, OCC, OCC*
J Otaola *1970 I, 1971 Ch, Bra, Par, Ur, 1974 F, F*
M Pacheco *1938 Ch*
A Palma *1949 F, F, 1952 I, I, 1954 F, F*
JMC Palma *1982 F, Sp, 1983 WXV, A, A*
R Palma *1985 Ch, Par*
M Palou *1996 US, Ur*
M Parra *1975 Ur, Bra, Ch*
A Pasalagua *1927 GBR, GBR*
M Pascual *1965 Rho, JSB, OCC, OCC, Ch, 1966 SAG, SAG, 1967 Ur, Ch, 1968 W, W, 1969 S, S, Ur, Ch, 1970 I, I, 1971 SAG, SAG, OCC, OCC*
HR Pascuali *1936 BI*
H Pasman *1936 Ch*
R Passaglia *1977 Bra, Ur, Ch, 1978 E, It*
G Paz *1979 Ur, Ch, Par, Bra, 1983 Ch, Par, Ur*
JJ Paz *1991 Ur, Bra*
S Peretti *1993 Bra, Par, SA*
N Perez *1968 W*
RN Perez *1992 F, F, Sp, R, F, 1993 Bra, Par, Ur, SA, 1995 Ur, R, It, F, 1996 US, Ur, C, SA, SA, 1998 Ur, 1999 I*
J Perez Cobo *1979 NZ, NZ, 1980 Fj, 1981 E, E, C*
M Peri Brusa *1998 Ch*
R Pesce *1958 Per, Ur, Ch*
TA Petersen *1978 E, It, 1979 NZ, NZ, A, A, 1980 Fj, Fj, 1981 E, E, C, 1982 F, 1983 WXV, A, A, 1985 F, F, Ur, Ch, Par, NZ, NZ, 1986 F, F, A*
AD Petrilli *2004 SA, 2005 J*
J Petrone *1949 F, F*
R Petti *1995 Par, Ch*
M Pfister *1994 SA, SA, 1996 F, 1998 R, Ur, J*
S Phelan *1997 Ur, Ch, R, It, 1998 F, F, R, US, C, It, 1999 S, I, W, Sa, J, I, F, 2000 I, A, A, SA, E, 2001 NZ, It, W, S, NZ, 2002 Ur, Par, Ch, F, E, SA, A, It, I, 2003 Ch, Ur, F, SA, Fj, C, A, R*
A Phillips *1948 OCC, 1949 F, F*
JP Piccardo *1981 E, 1983 Ch, Par, Ur*
A Pichot *1995 A, R, It, F, 1996 Ur, F, F, 1997 It, F, A, A, 1998 F, F, R, It, F, W, 1999 W, W, S, I, W, Sa, J, I, F, 2000 I, A, A, SA, E, 2001 Ur, US, C, NZ, It, W, S, NZ, 2002 F, E, SA, A, It, I, 2003 Ur, C, A, R, I, 2004 F, I, SA, 2005 It, SA, S, It, 2006 W, W, NZ, Ch, Ur, E, F, 2007 W, F, Nm, I, S, SA, F*
G Pimentel *1971 Bra*
R Pineo *1954 F*
E Pittinari *1991 Ur, Par, Bra*
E Poggi *1965 JSB, OCC, OCC, Ch, 1966 SAG, 1967 Ur, 1969 Ur*
C Pollano *1927 GBR*
S Ponce *2007 Ch*
R Pont Lezica *1951 Ur, Bra, Ch*
H Porta *1971 Ch, Bra, Par, Ur, 1972 SAG, SAG, 1973 R, R, Ur, Bra, Ch, I, S, 1974 F, F, 1975 F, F, 1976 Ur, W, NZ, NZ, 1977 F, F, 1978 E, It, 1979 NZ, NZ, A, A, 1980 WXV, Fj, Fj, 1981 E, E, C, 1982 F, F, Sp, 1983 A, A, 1985 F, F, Ur, Ch, Par, NZ, NZ, 1986 F, F, A, 1987 Fj, It, NZ, Sp, A, A, 1990 I, E, S*
O Portillo *1995 Par, Ch, 1997 Par, Ch*
J Posse *1977 Par*
S Posse *1991 Par, 1993 Bra, Ch, Ur*
C Promanzio *1995 C, 1996 Ur, F, F, E, 1997 E, E, NZ, Ur, 1998 R, J*

U Propato 1956 OCC
A Puccio 1979 Ch, Par, Bra
M Puigdeval 1964 Ur, Bra
J Pulido 1960 F
JC Queirolo 1964 Ur, Bra, Ch
G Quesada 1996 US, Ur, C, SA, E, 1997 E, E, NZ, NZ, 1998 F, R, US, C, It, 1999 W, S, I, W, Sa, J, I, F, 2000 I, SA, E, 2001 NZ, It, NZ, 2002 F, E, SA, 2003 F, SA, Ur, C, Nm, R, I
E Quetglas 1965 Ch
G Quinones 2004 Ur, Ven
R Raimundez 1959 JSB, JSB
C Ramallo 1979 Ur, Ch, Par
S Ratcliff 1936 Ch
F Rave 1997 Par
M Reggiardo 1996 Ur, F, F, E, 1997 E, E, NZ, NZ, R, F, A, A, 1998 F, F, R, US, Ur, C, It, W, 1999 W, W, S, I, W, Sa, J, I, F, 2000 I, SA, 2001 NZ, It, W, S, NZ, 2002 F, E, SA, A, It, I, 2003 F, SA, Fj, US, Ur, A, Nm, I
C Reyes 1927 GBR, GBR, GBR
M Ricci 1987 Sp
A Riganti 1927 GBR, GBR, GBR
MA Righentini 1989 NZ
J Rios 1960 F, F
G Rivero 1996 Ur, US, Ur
T Roan 2007 Ch
F Robson 1927 GBR
M Roby 1992 Sp, 1993 J
A Rocca 1989 US, 1990 C, US, C, E, 1991 Ur, Bra
O Rocha 1974 F, F
D Rodriguez 1998 J, Par, Ch, Ur
D Rodriguez 2002 Ur, Par, Ch
EE Rodriguez 1979 NZ, NZ, A, A, 1980 WXV, Fj, Fj, 1981 E, E, C, 1983 WXV, A, A
F Rodriguez 2007 Ch
A Rodriguez Jurado 1927 GBR, GBR, GBR, GBR, 1932 JSB, JSB, 1936 Ch, Ch
M Rodriguez Jurado 1971 SAG, OCC, Ch, Bra, Par, Ur
A Rodriguez-Jurado 1965 JSB, OCC, OCC, Ch, 1966 SAG, SAG, 1968 W, W, 1969 S, Ch, 1970 I, 1971 SAG, 1973 R, Par, Bra, Ch, I, S, 1974 F, F, 1975 F, F, 1976 Ur
L Roldan 2001 Ur, C
AS Romagnoli 2004 Ch, Ur, Ven
R Roncero 1998 J, 2002 Ur, Par, Ch, 2003 Fj, US, Nm, R, 2004 W, W, NZ, F, I, 2005 It, SA, S, It, 2006 W, W, NZ, 2007 W, F, Nm, I, S, SA, F, 2008 It, SA
S Rondinelli 2005 Sa
S Rosatti 1977 Par, Ch
M Rospide 2003 Par, Ch, Ur
F Rossi 1991 Ur, Par, Bra, 1998 F
D Rotondo 1997 Par, Ch
MA Ruiz 1997 NZ, Ch, R, It, F, A, A, 1998 F, F, R, US, Ur, C, J, It, F, W, 1999 W, Sa, J, F, 2002 Ur, Par, Ch
C Sainz Trapaga 1979 Ur, Par, Bra
A Salinas 1954 F, 1956 OCC, 1958 Ur, Ch, 1960 F, F
S Salvat 1987 Ur, Fj, It, 1988 F, 1989 It, NZ, 1990 C, US, C, E, E, 1991 Ur, Par, Bra, 1992 Sp, F, 1993 Bra, Ch, Par, Ur, SA, SA, 1994 SA, SA, 1995 Ur, C, A, A, E, Sa, It, Par, Ch, Ur, R, It, F
T Salzman 1936 Bl, Ch, Ch
M Sambucetti 2001 Ur, US, C, 2002 Ur, Ch, 2003 Par, Ch, Fj, 2005 It, Sa
T Sanderson 1932 JSB
D Sanes 1985 Ch, Par, 1986 F, F, 1987 Ur, Par, Ch, 1989 Bra, Ch, Ur
EJ Sanguinetti 1975 Ur, Par, Ch, 1978 It, 1979 A, 1982 F, F, Sp
G Sanguinetti 1979 Ur, Ch, Par, Bra
J Sansot 1948 OCC
M Sansot 1975 F, F, 1976 Ur, W, NZ, NZ, 1977 Bra, Ch, 1978 E, It, 1979 NZ, NZ, A, A, 1980 WXV, Fj, 1983 WXV
Jm Santamarina 1991 NZ, NZ, Ch, A, W, Sa, 1992 F, Sp, R, F, 1993 J, J, 1994 US, S, US, 1995 A, A, E, Sa, It, Ur, R, It, F
J Santiago 1948 OCC, 1952 I, I
JR Sanz 1973 Par, Ur, Bra, Ch, 1974 F, F, 1976 Ur, 1977 F, F
S Sanz 2003 US, 2004 Ch, Ven, 2005 It, Sa, 2007 Ch
M Sarandon 1948 OCC, OCC, 1949 F, F, 1951 Ur, Bra, Ch, 1952 I, I, 1954 F
J Sartori 1979 Ch, Par, Bra
R Sauze 1983 Par
JM Scelzo 1996 US, SA, 1997 R, It, F, A, 1998 F, US, Ur, C, Ch, F, 1999 I, Sa, I, F, 2000 I, A, A, 2003 F, F, Fj, Ur, C, Nm, R, I, 2005 SA, S, It, 2006 W, W, NZ, Ch, Ur, E, It, F, 2007 W, F, Nm, I, S, SA
F Schacht 1989 Bra, Ch, Par, Ur, US, 1990 C
E Scharemberg 1961 Ch, Bra, Ur, 1964 Ur, Bra, 1965 Rho, JSB, OCC, OCC, 1967 Ur, Ch
AM Schiavio 1983 Ch, Ur, 1986 A, 1987 Fj, It, NZ
E Schiavio 1936 Bl, Bl, Ch, Ch
R Schmidt 1960 F, F, F, 1961 Bra, 1964 Ur, 1965 JSB
G Schmitt 1964 Ur, Ch
M Schusterman 2003 Par, Fj, 2004 W, W, NZ, F, 2005 It, It, SA, S, 2006 W, Ch, Ur, E, 2007 I, It, Geo
AA Scolni 1983 Ch, Par, Ur, 1985 F, 1987 Sp, A, 1988 F, F, F, F, 1989 NZ, US, 1990 C, US, E, E, I, E, S
J Seaton 1968 W, W, 1969 Ur, Ch
R Seaton 1967 Ur, Ch
H Senillosa 2002 Ur, Par, Ch, 2003 Par, Ch, Ur, F, SA, Fj, US, Nm, R, 2004 Ch, Ur, Ven, W, W, NZ, F, I, 2005 It, It, 2006 Ch, It, F, 2007 I, I, F, Geo, Nm, I, S, F, 2008 It
R Serra 1927 GBR, GBR, GBR
F Serra Miras 2003 Ch, 2005 J, 2006 W, Ch, Ur, 2007 I, It, W, Nm, 2008 S
C Serrano 1978 It, 1980 Fj, 1983 Ch, Par, Ur
R Sharpe 1948 OCC
HL Silva 1965 JSB, OCC, 1967 Ur, Ch, 1968 W, W, 1969 S, S, Ur, Ch, 1970 I, I, 1971 SAG, SAG, OCC, OCC, Ur, 1978 E, 1979 NZ, NZ, A, A, 1980 WXV
R Silva 1998 J
F Silvestre 1988 F, 1989 Bra, Par, Ur, US, 1990 C, US
D Silvetti 1993 J
J Simes 1989 Bra, Ch, 1990 C, US, 1993 J, J, 1996 Ur, F, F, US, C
HG Simon 1991 NZ, NZ, A, W, Sa
E Simone 1996 US, SA, SA, E, 1997 E, E, NZ, NZ, R, F, A, A, 1998 F, F, US, Ur, C, J, It, F, W, 1999 W, S, I, W, Sa, J, I, F, 2000 I, SA, 2001 Ur, US, It, 2002 Ur, Ch
A Soares-Gache 1978 It, 1979 NZ, NZ, 1981 C, 1982 F, Sp, 1983 WXV, A, A, 1987 Sp, A, A, 1988 F
T Solari 1996 Ur, C, SA, 1997 E, E, NZ, NZ
F Soler 1996 Ur, F, F, SA, SA, 1997 E, E, NZ, NZ, Ur, R, It, F, 1998 F, F, R, US, C, It, W, 2001 Ur, US, 2002 Ur, Par, Ch
JS Soler Valls 1989 It, Bra, Par, Ur
H Solveira 1951 Ur
J Sommer 1927 GBR
E Sorhaburu 1958 Per, Ur, 1960 F, 1961 Ch, Ur
E Spain 1965 JSB, OCC, OCC, Ch, 1967 Ur, Ch
PL Sporleder 1990 I, E, S, 1991 NZ, NZ, Ch, A, W, Sa, 1992 F, F, Sp, Sp, R, F, 1993 J, J, Bra, Ch, Par, Ur, SA, SA, 1994 US, S, S, US, SA, SA, 1995 A, A, E, Sa, It, 1996 Ur, F, F, Ur, C, SA, SA, E, 1997 E, E, NZ, NZ, Par, Ur, R, It, F, A, A, 1998 F, R, US, Ur, C, Ur, It, F, W, 1999 W, W, J, 2002 Ur, Par, Ch, It, I, 2003 Par, Ch, Ur, F, Fj
J Stanfield 1932 JSB
A Stewart 1936 Bl
J Stewart 1932 JSB, JSB
BM Stortoni 1998 J, Par, 2001 Ur, US, C, NZ, It, NZ, 2002 Ur, Par, Ch, 2003 F, Fj, US, 2005 It, It, S, It, 2007 I, 2008 S, S, It, SA
J Stuart 2007 Ch, 2008 S, It
M Sugasti 1995 Par, Ch
W Sutton 1936 Ch
C Swain 1948 OCC, 1949 F, F, 1951 Ur, Bra, Ch, 1952 I, I
J Tagliabue 1936 Ch, Ch
L Tahier 1964 Ur, Ch
F Talbot 1936 Bl, Bl, 1938 Ch
H Talbot 1936 Bl, Bl, Ch, Ch, 1938 Ch
A Tejeda 2008 S, S, It
EG Teran 1977 Bra, Ur, Par, 1979 Ch, Par, Bra
G Teran 1988 F
MJ Teran 1991 NZ, NZ, Ch, A, W, Sa, 1992 F, Sp, R, F, 1993

J, J, Ur, SA, SA, 1994 US, S, S, US, SA, SA, 1995 A, A, E, Sa, It, Ur, R, It, F
GP Tiesi 2004 SA, 2005 J, It, Sa, 2006 W, W, NZ, Ch, Ur, E, 2007 Geo, Nm, SA, 2008 S, S
FJ Todeschini 1998 R, Ur, 2005 J, It, It, S, 2006 W, W, NZ, Ch, Ur, E, It, F, 2007 I, W, Geo, Nm, 2008 S, S
A Tolomei 1991 Par, Bra, 1993 Bra, Ch, Par
N Tompkins 1948 OCC, 1949 F, F, 1952 I, I
JA Topping 1938 Ch
E Torello 1983 Par, 1989 Ch
F Torino 1927 GBR, GBR
NC Tozer 1932 JSB, JSB
AA Travaglini 1967 Ur, Ch, 1968 W, 1969 S, S, 1970 I, I, 1971 SAG, SAG, OCC, OCC, 1972 SAG, SAG, 1973 R, Par, Ur, Bra, Ch, I, S, 1974 F, F, 1975 F, F, 1976 Ur, W, NZ, NZ
G Travaglini 1978 E, It, 1979 NZ, NZ, A, A, 1980 WXV, Fj, Fj, 1981 E, E, 1982 F, F, Sp, 1983 WXV, A, 1987 Ur, Fj, It, NZ
R Travaglini 1996 US, Ur, C, 1997 NZ, R, F, 1998 Ur, C
J Trucco 1977 Bra, Ur, Par, Ch
A Turner 1932 JSB, JSB
FA Turnes 1985 F, F, Ur, NZ, NZ, 1986 F, F, A, A, 1987 Ur, Fj, NZ, Sp, A, A, 1988 F, F, F, F, 1989 It, NZ, NZ, 1997 Ur, F, A, A
G Ugartemendia 1991 Ur, 1993 J, Ch, Par, Ur, SA, SA, 1994 US, SA, SA, 1997 Ur, 1998 Par, 2000 E
M Urbano 1991 Ur, Bra, 1995 Par, Ch, R, It, F
B Urdapilleta 2007 Ch, 2008 SA
EM Ure 1980 WXV, Fj, Fj, 1981 E, E, 1982 F, F, Sp, 1983 A, 1985 F, F, NZ, NZ, 1986 F, F, A
J Uriarte 1986 A, 1987 Par
E Valesani 1986 A, A
MR Valesani 1989 It, NZ, NZ, Ch, Par, Ur, US, 1990 C, US, C
GB Varela 1979 Ur, Ch
L Varela 1961 Ch, Bra, Ur
F Varella 1960 F
GM Varone 1982 F
C Vazquez 1927 GBR, GBR, GBR
A Velazquez 1971 Ch, Par
R Ventura 1975 Ur, Bra, Ch, 1977 Bra, Ur, 1978 It, 1979 Ur, Ch, Par, 1983 Ch, Par, Ur
E Verardo 1958 Ch, 1959 JSB, JSB, 1964 Ur, Bra, Ch, 1967 Ur, Ch
N Vergallo 2005 Sa, 2006 Ch, Ur, 2007 I, I, Ch, 2008 S, S, It, SA
AV Vernet Basualdo 2004 SA, 2005 J, 2006 It, 2007 I, Geo, Nm, I, F, 2008 SA
G Veron 1997 Par
J Vibart 1960 F
H Vidou 1960 F, 1961 Bra
H Vidou 1987 Par, 1990 C, US, E, E, 1991 NZ
C Viel Temperley 1993 Bra, Ch, Par, Ur, 1994 US, S, S, US, SA, SA, 1995 Ur, C, A, A, E, Sa, It, Par, Ur, R, It, F, 1996 SA, 1997 E, NZ
E Vila 1975 Ur, Par, Ch
D Villen 1998 J, Par
M Viola 1993 Bra
J Virasoro 1973 R, R, Ur, Bra, Ch, S
JL Visca 1985 Par
J Walther 1971 OCC
M Walther 1967 Ur, Ch, 1968 W, W, 1969 S, S, Ur, Ch, 1970 I, I, 1971 SAG, OCC, OCC, 1973 Bra, Ch, 1974 F, F
F Werner 1996 US, 1997 Ur
Wessek 1960 F
R Wilkins 1936 Ch, Ch
J Wittman 1971 SAG, SAG, OCC, OCC, Ur, 1972 SAG, SAG, 1973 R
L Yanez 1965 Rho, JSB, OCC, OCC, Ch, 1966 SAG, SAG, 1968 W, W, 1969 S, S, Ur, Ch, 1970 I, I, 1971 SAG, OCC, OCC, Ur
EP Yanguela 1956 OCC
M Yanguela 1987 It
B Yustini 1954 F, 1956 OCC
R Zanero 1990 C
E Zapiola 1998 Par
A Zappa 1927 GBR

AUSTRALIA

AUSTRALIA'S 2008 TEST RECORD

OPPONENTS	DATE	VENUE	RESULT
Ireland	14 June	H	**Won** 18–12
France	28 June	H	**Won** 34–13
France	5 July	H	**Won** 40–10
South Africa	19 July	H	**Won** 16–9
New Zealand	26 July	H	**Won** 34–19
New Zealand	2 August	A	**Lost** 10–39
South Africa	23 August	A	**Won** 27–15
South Africa	30 August	A	**Lost** 8–53
New Zealand	13 September	H	**Lost** 24–28

MIXED BAG FOR NEW BOY DEANS

By Iain Spragg

The Wallabies found themselves in uncharted territory in late 2007 when they ventured to New Zealand. For this trip was not for a Bledisloe Cup clash with their old foe the All Blacks but rather a mission to recruit their new head coach and when ARU officials returned home having secured the services of the Crusaders' Robbie Deans there was no little surprise on either side of the Tasman Sea.

When Deans put pen to paper on a contract taking him through to 2011 and the next World Cup, he became the first non-Australian to be entrusted with the Wallaby reins in over a century of Test match rugby. It was an appointment without precedent Down Under and a move which ultimately materialised as a result of other factors.

Many in New Zealand had expected Graham Henry to be replaced after overseeing another All Black failure at the World Cup in France but he held onto his job. Deans was widely acknowledged as the heir apparent by virtue of his superb Super-14 record with the Crusaders but with the top job unavailable and Australia looking for fresh direction after the departure of John Connolly, Deans decided his future lay nearer to Canberra than Christchurch.

"The decision to leave and coach overseas has undoubtedly been one of the most difficult of my professional career," he conceded when his appointment was made public. "While the rugby marketplace has been global ever since rugby went professional, it is probably only now that I truly appreciate the thought process and the 'what ifs?' that so many others have gone through before reaching this point.

"To go is a big decision but I am ready to coach internationally. After serving for 11 years as a Super rugby manager and coach here, I feel I cannot afford to forgo the position offered to me in Australia. It is both flattering and humbling that I have been afforded this opportunity."

His switch across the Tasman, however, was not immediate. The ARU agreed to let Deans fulfill his Crusaders commitments and he made the most of his swansong season by guiding the side to a Super-14 final victory over the Waratahs in May – his fifth Super title – before finally heading to Australia and the job of rebuilding the Wallabies.

Wallaby supporters hoping for fresh impetus under the new coach were not disappointed. In June, he announced his squad for the 2008 campaign and Deans included seven uncapped players – Luke Burgess,

Cameron Spencer / Getty Images

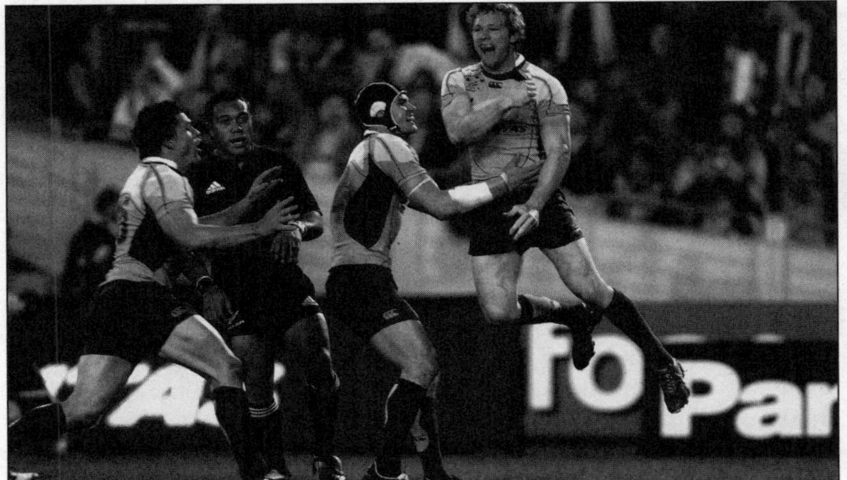

The high point of the Tri-Nations campaign arrived with a sensational 34–19 win over New Zealand

Dean Mumm, Lachie Turner, Ryan Cross, Richard Brown, Peter Hynes and Ben Alexander – in his 30-man line-up. The adopted Kiwi was obviously keen to make his mark.

"There are a lot of new faces in this squad," Deans said. "Our ultimate goal is the 2011 Rugby World Cup in New Zealand, but that is a long way into the future. In the interim there is a lot of hard work to be done."

The first challenge awaiting the revamped Wallabies came in June with the arrival of Ireland for a one-off Test in Melbourne. Deans handed debuts to Hynes on the wing and Burgess at scrum-half but the game was a classic encounter between a side with little match practice in the shape of Australia against a well-oiled but tired Irish team at the end of a long, arduous season.

Berrick Barnes went over after only six minutes but the floodgates failed to open and even though James Horwill added a second midway through the first-half, the Wallabies were unable pull away from the tourists and at the final whistle they were relieved to have battled their way to a 18–12 win.

A fortnight later the opposition was France in the first of their two-Test tour. Les Bleus arrived in Australia with a hugely inexperienced squad, shorn of the players from France's leading four clubs who were still in domestic action, and the Wallabies showed them little mercy when the two teams met in Sydney.

An early try from Matt Giteau established a platform and although the tourists battled manfully in the first half, the Wallabies cut loose after the break. Nathan Sharpe, Rocky Elsom and captain Stirling Mortlock all added to the first try and with Giteau converting all four scores, Australia cantered to a 34–13 win that undoubtedly boosted morale but hardly answered any serious questions about the team's potential.

"That was an improved performance," argued Deans after the final whistle. "We sustained our attack for longer than we did against Ireland. We made a few mistakes in the first half but showed a bit more patience in the second and were able to profit from that."

The venue for the second Test seven days later was Brisbane but although the backdrop had changed, the storyline of the match was essentially the same as Australia cut through the under-strength French almost at will to record a handsome 40–10 win.

The home side's deluge of points, a record against the French, began when Giteau carved out an opportunity for Hynes and there was no way back for the tourists. Horwill added a second try before the break and at half-time Deans decided to bring on rugby league convert Cross for his second cap and the former Sydney Roosters star amply repaid the coach's faith with two tries to complete the rout. The start of the Tri-Nations was only two weeks away and the Wallabies appeared in fine fettle, even if they had not yet been really extended.

"We're very conscious that the next arena will be very different," Deans admitted. "It will be another level, there's no doubt about that. I think France were looking forward to their vacation. That's harsh but fair. We created opportunities and we took those opportunities and there were many more that we didn't take as well."

Australia had won the last of their two Tri-Nations titles in 2001 but after slugging their way to an opening 16–9 win over the Springboks at the Subiaco Oval courtesy of tries from Mortlock and Lote Tuqiri, hopes of reviving former glories grew.

They reached fever pitch a week later. The All Blacks were in Sydney to renew old hostilities but Deans was lurking in the background to spring a nasty surprise on his compatriots.

The Wallabies came flying out of the blocks and tries from Cross, on his full debut, and Hynes established a 17–12 half-time lead. New Zealand crossed the whitewash through Mils Muliaina, Andrew Hore and Andy Ellis but Australia held their nerve and late tries from Elsom and Horwill secured a 34–19 win and extended Deans' winning run as coach to five from five.

"It was great to be here," Deans said. "A lot was asked of them. We didn't have a lot of possession there for long periods and we had to defend for long periods. I suspect part of their thinking was they thought they could move us around and fatigue us that way. At times it was tenuous but overall it worked for us."

The Kiwis ensured Australian euphoria was abruptly dampened seven days later with a clinical 39–10 win at Eden Park but Deans' side remained very much in title contention as they headed to South Africa for back-to-back Tests against the Springboks.

The first match in Durban saw the Wallabies looking for their first win away from home in the tournament since 2001 – a miserable losing streak of 15 games – but the confidence imbued by beating New Zealand was in evidence from the start and Australia turned in a strong and professional performance, scored three tries through Benn Robinson, Tuqiri and Mortlock and emerged surprisingly comfortable 27–15 winners.

Australia had two games left but their victory in Durban ensured the climax of the competition against New Zealand in September would determine the destination of the silverware irrespective of the result of their second clash with the Springboks and it was a distinctly distracted Wallabies team that took to the field in Johannesburg.

The sense of disinterest cost Deans' team dearly. Bent on a face-saving victory, South Africa tore into the visitors and they met with little resistance as they ran in eight tries to one and claimed a crushing 53–8 win.

The real business was now at hand as Australia headed to home to Brisbane and the denouement of the campaign.

The clash in the Suncorp Stadium saw New Zealand surge into an early lead with a Mils Muliaina try but the Wallabies hit back with scores from Adam Ashley-Cooper and Horwill either side of half-time to get their noses in front.

The emphasis was now on the All Blacks to play catch-up rugby and they did this with irresistible force as Tony Woodcock, substitute Piri Weepu and Dan Carter all crossed in a pivotal 17 minutes. Australia hit back with a try from Cross but the clock was against them and the Kiwis held out for a 28–24 victory, the Bledisloe Cup and the Tri-Nations trophy. The Wallabies had fallen at the final hurdle but Deans had certainly made his mark in his debut season at the helm.

"We gave it a fair crack and came up just short," he conceded after the final whistle. "I was delighted with their effort tonight to build a lot of pressure but we couldn't convert that into points. We're not happy losing but the players gave it everything and it could have been different. To win the Tri-Nations you have to be that much better."

AUSTRALIA INTERNATIONAL STATISTICS

MATCH RECORDS UP TO 30TH SEPTEMBER 2008

MOST CONSECUTIVE TEST WINS

10 1991 Arg, WS, W, I, NZ, E, 1992 S 1,2, NZ 1,2
10 1998 NZ 3, Fj, Tg, Sm, F, E 2, 1999 I 1,2, E, SA 1
10 1999 NZ 2, R, I 3, US,W, SA 3, F, 2000 Arg 1,2, SA 1

MOST CONSECUTIVE TESTS WITHOUT DEFEAT

Matches	Wins	Draws	Periods
10	10	0	1991 to 1992
10	10	0	1998 to 1999
10	10	0	1999 to 2000

MOST POINTS IN A MATCH

BY THE TEAM

Pts.	Opponents	Venue	Year
142	Namibia	Adelaide	2003
92	Spain	Madrid	2001
91	Japan	Lyons	2007
90	Romania	Brisbane	2003
76	England	Brisbane	1998
74	Canada	Brisbane	1996
74	Tonga	Canberra	1998
74	W Samoa	Sydney	2005
73	W Samoa	Sydney	1994
69	Italy	Melbourne	2005
67	United States	Brisbane	1990

BY A PLAYER

Pts.	Player	Opponents	Venue	Year
42	M S Rogers	Namibia	Adelaide	2003
39	M C Burke	Canada	Brisbane	1996
30	E J Flatley	Romania	Brisbane	2003
29	S A Mortlock	South Africa	Melbourne	2000
28	M P Lynagh	Argentina	Brisbane	1995
27	M J Giteau	Fiji	Montpellier	2007
25	M C Burke	Scotland	Sydney	1998
25	M C Burke	France	Cardiff	1999
25	M C Burke	British/Irish Lions	Melbourne	2001
25	E J Flatley*	Ireland	Perth	2003
25	C E Latham	Namibia	Adelaide	2003
24	M P Lynagh	United States	Brisbane	1990
24	M P Lynagh	France	Brisbane	1990
24	M C Burke	New Zealand	Melbourne	1998
24	M C Burke	South Africa	Twickenham	1999

* includes a penalty try

MOST TRIES IN A MATCH

BY THE TEAM

Tries	Opponents	Venue	Year
22	Namibia	Adelaide	2003
13	South Korea	Brisbane	1987
13	Spain	Madrid	2001
13	Romania	Brisbane	2003
13	Japan	Lyons	2007
12	United States	Brisbane	1990
12	Wales	Brisbane	1991
12	Tonga	Canberra	1998
12	Samoa	Sydney	2005
11	Western Samoa	Sydney	1994
11	England	Brisbane	1998
11	Italy	Melbourne	2005

BY A PLAYER

Tries	Player	Opponents	Venue	Year
5	C E Latham	Namibia	Adelaide	2003
4	G Cornelsen	New Zealand	Auckland	1978
4	D I Campese	United States	Sydney	1983
4	J S Little	Tonga	Canberra	1998
4	C E Latham	Argentina	Brisbane	2000
4	L D Tuqiri	Italy	Melbourne	2005

MOST CONVERSIONS IN A MATCH

BY THE TEAM

Cons	Opponents	Venue	Year
16	Namibia	Adelaide	2003
12	Spain	Madrid	2001
11	Romania	Brisbane	2003
10	Japan	Lyons	2007
9	Canada	Brisbane	1996
9	Fiji	Parramatta	1998
8	Italy	Rome	1988
8	United States	Brisbane	1990
7	Canada	Sydney	1985
7	Tonga	Canberra	1998
7	Samoa	Sydney	2005
7	Italy	Melbourne	2005

BY A PLAYER

Cons	Player	Opponents	Venue	Year
16	M S Rogers	Namibia	Adelaide	2003
11	E J Flatley	Romania	Brisbane	2003
10	M C Burke	Spain	Madrid	2001
9	M C Burke	Canada	Brisbane	1996
9	J A Eales	Fiji	Parramatta	1998
8	M P Lynagh	Italy	Rome	1988
8	M P Lynagh	United States	Brisbane	1990
7	M P Lynagh	Canada	Sydney	1985
7	S A Mortlock	Japan	Lyons	2007

MOST PENALTIES IN A MATCH

BY THE TEAM

Pens	Opponents	Venue	Year
8	South Africa	Twickenham	1999
7	New Zealand	Sydney	1999
7	France	Cardiff	1999
7	Wales	Cardiff	2001
6	New Zealand	Sydney	1984
6	France	Sydney	1986
6	England	Brisbane	1988
6	Argentina	Buenos Aires	1997
6	Ireland	Perth	1999
6	France	Paris	2000
6	British/Irish Lions	Melbourne	2001
6	New Zealand	Sydney	2004

BY A PLAYER

Pens	Player	Opponents	Venue	Year
8	M C Burke	South Africa	Twickenham	1999
7	M C Burke	New Zealand	Sydney	1999
7	M C Burke	France	Cardiff	1999
7	M C Burke	Wales	Cardiff	2001
6	M P Lynagh	France	Sydney	1986
6	M P Lynagh	England	Brisbane	1988
6	D J Knox	Argentina	Buenos Aires	1997
6	M C Burke	France	Paris	2000
6	M C Burke	British/Irish Lions	Melbourne	2001

MOST DROPPED GOALS IN A MATCH

BY THE TEAM

Drops	Opponents	Venue	Year
3	England	Twickenham	1967
3	Ireland	Dublin	1984
3	Fiji	Brisbane	1985

BY A PLAYER

Drops	Player	Opponent	Venue	Year
3	P F Hawthorne	England	Twickenham	1967
2	M G Ella	Ireland	Dublin	1984
2	D J Knox	Fiji	Brisbane	1985

CAREER RECORDS

MOST CAPPED PLAYERS

Caps	Player	Career Span
139	G M Gregan	1994 to 2007
102	S J Larkham	1996 to 2007
101	D I Campese	1982 to 1996
92	G B Smith	2000 to 2008
86	J A Eales	1991 to 2001
86	J W C Roff	1995 to 2004
81	M C Burke	1993 to 2004
80	T J Horan	1989 to 2000
79	D J Wilson	1992 to 2000
78	C E Latham	1998 to 2007
75	J S Little	1989 to 2000
74	P R Waugh	2000 to 2008
72	M P Lynagh	1984 to 1995
72	J A Paul	1998 to 2006
71	S A Mortlock	2000 to 2008
70	N C Sharpe	2002 to 2008
67	P N Kearns	1989 to 1999
67	D J Herbert	1994 to 2002
66	L D Tuqiri	2003 to 2008
63	N C Farr Jones	1984 to 1993
63	M J Cockbain	1997 to 2003
60	R S T Kefu	1997 to 2003
60	M J Giteau	2002 to 2008
60	A K E Baxter	2003 to 2008
59	S P Poidevin	1980 to 1991

MOST CONSECUTIVE TESTS

Tests	Player	Career Span
62	J W C Roff	1996 to 2001
46	P N Kearns	1989 to 1995
44	G B Smith	2003 to 2006
42	D I Campese	1990 to 1995
37	P G Johnson	1959 to 1968

MOST TESTS AS CAPTAIN

Tests	Captain	Career Span
59	G M Gregan	2001 to 2007
55	J A Eales	1996 to 2001
36	N C Farr Jones	1988 to 1992
20	S A Mortlock	2006 to 2008
19	A G Slack	1984 to 1987
16	J E Thornett	1962 to 1967
16	G V Davis	1969 to 1972

MOST POINTS IN TESTS

Pts	Player	Tests	Career Span
911	M P Lynagh	72	1984 to 1995
878	M C Burke	81	1993 to 2004
478	S A Mortlock	71	2000 to 2008
352	M J Giteau	60	2002 to 2008
315	D I Campese	101	1982 to 1996
260	P E McLean	30	1974 to 1982
249*	J W Roff	86	1995 to 2004
200	C E Latham	78	1998 to 2007
187*	E J Flatley	38	1997 to 2005
173	J A Eales	86	1991 to 2001

* Roff and Flatley's totals include a penalty try

MOST TRIES IN TESTS

Tries	Player	Tests	Career Span
64	D I Campese	101	1982 to 1996
40	C E Latham	78	1998 to 2007
31*	J W Roff	86	1995 to 2004
30	T J Horan	80	1989 to 2000
30	L D Tuqiri	66	2003 to 2008
29	M C Burke	81	1993 to 2004
28	S A Mortlock	71	2000 to 2008
25	S J Larkham	102	1996 to 2007
24	B N Tune	47	1996 to 2006
21	J S Little	75	1989 to 2000
21	M J Giteau	60	2002 to 2008

* Roff's total includes a penalty try

MOST CONVERSIONS IN TESTS

Cons	Player	Tests	Career Span
140	M P Lynagh	72	1984 to 1995
104	M C Burke	81	1993 to 2004
61	S A Mortlock	71	2000 to 2008
59	M J Giteau	60	2000 to 2008
31	J A Eales	86	1991 to 2001
30	E J Flatley	38	1997 to 2005
27	P E McLean	30	1974 to 1982
27	M S Rogers	45	2002 to 2006
20	J W Roff	86	1995 to 2004
19	D J Knox	13	1985 to 1997

MOST PENALTY GOALS IN TESTS

Pens	Player	Tests	Career Span
177	M P Lynagh	72	1984 to 1995
174	M C Burke	81	1993 to 2004
72	S A Mortlock	71	2000 to 2008
62	P E McLean	30	1974 to 1982
41	M J Giteau	60	2002 to 2008
34	J A Eales	86	1991 to 2001
34	E J Flatley	38	1997 to 2005
23	M C Roebuck	23	1991 to 1993

MOST DROPPED GOALS IN TESTS

Drops	Player	Tests	Career Span
9	P F Hawthorne	21	1962 to 1967
9	M P Lynagh	72	1984 to 1995
8	M G Ella	25	1980 to 1984
4	P E McLean	30	1974 to 1982

TRI-NATIONS RECORDS

RECORD	DETAIL	HOLDER	SET
Most points in season	133	in six matches	2006
Most tries in season	14	in six matches	2006
	14	in six matches	2008
Highest Score	49	49-0 v S Africa (h)	2006
Biggest win	49	49-0 v S Africa (h)	2006
Highest score conceded	61	22-61 v S Africa (a)	1997
Biggest defeat	45	8-53 v S Africa (a)	2008
Most points in matches	271	M C Burke	1996 to 2004
Most points in season	71	S A Mortlock	2000
Most points in match	24	M C Burke	v N Zealand (h) 1998
Most tries in matches	9	J W C Roff	1996 to 2003
	9	S A Mortlock	2000 to 2008
	9	L D Tuqiri	2003 to 2008
Most tries in season	4	S A Mortlock	2000
Most tries in match	2	B N Tune	v S Africa (h) 1997
	2	S J Larkham	v N Zealand (a) 1997
	2	M C Burke	v N Zealand (h) 1998
	2	J W C Roff	v S Africa (h) 1999
	2	S A Mortlock	v N Zealand (h) 2000
	2	C E Latham	v S Africa (h) 2002
	2	M J Giteau	v S Africa (h) 2006
	2	L D Tuqiri	v N Zealand (a) 2006
Most cons in matches	21	S A Mortlock	2000 to 2008
Most cons in season	12	S A Mortlock	2006
Most cons in match	5	S A Mortlock	v S Africa (h) 2006
Most pens in matches	65	M C Burke	1996 to 2004
Most pens in season	14	M C Burke	2001
Most pens in match	7	M C Burke	v N Zealand (h) 1999

MISCELLANEOUS RECORDS

RECORD	HOLDER	DETAIL
Longest Test Career	G M Cooke	1932-1948
Youngest Test Cap	B W Ford	18 yrs 90 days in 1957
Oldest Test Cap	A R Miller	38 yrs 113 days in 1967

CAREER RECORDS OF AUSTRALIA INTERNATIONAL PLAYERS (UP TO 30 SEPTEMBER 2008)

PLAYER BACKS	DEBUT	CAPS	T	C	P	D	PTS
A P Ashley-Cooper	2005 v SA	19	6	0	0	0	30
B S Barnes	2007 v J	11	3	0	0	3	24
L Burgess	2008 v I	6	0	0	0	0	0
S J Cordingley	2000 v Arg	21	0	0	0	0	0
R P Cross	2008 v F	8	4	0	0	0	20
M A Gerrard	2005 v It	23	9	0	0	0	45
M J Giteau	2002 v E	60	21	59	41	2	352
P J Hynes	2008 v I	9	2	0	0	0	10
D N Ioane	2007 v W	1	1	0	0	0	5
D A Mitchell	2005 v SA	25	15	0	0	0	75
S A Mortlock	2000 v Arg	71	28	61	72	0	478
S H Norton-Knight	2007 v W	2	1	0	0	0	5
C Rathbone	2004 v S	26	8	0	0	0	40
B R Sheehan	2006 v SA	3	0	0	0	0	0
C B Shepherd	2006 v E	9	3	2	0	0	19
T Tahu	2008 v NZ	3	0	0	0	0	0
L D Tuqiri	2003 v I	66	30	0	0	0	150
L D Turner	2008 v F	1	0	0	0	0	0
J J Valentine	2006 v E	4	0	0	0	0	0
FORWARDS:							
B Alexander	2008 v F	2	0	0	0	0	0
A K E Baxter	2003 v NZ	60	1	0	0	0	5
R C Blake	2006 v E	7	1	0	0	0	5
R N Brown	2008 v NZ	1	0	0	0	0	0
M D Chisholm	2004 v S	35	5	0	0	0	25
M J Dunning	2003 v Nm	41	0	0	0	0	0
R D Elsom	2005 v Sm	40	7	0	0	0	35
A L Freier	2002 v Arg	24	2	0	0	0	10
S A Hoiles	2004 v S	16	3	0	0	0	15
J E Horwill	2007 v Fj	10	4	0	0	0	20
H J McMeniman	2005 v Sm	17	0	0	0	0	0
S T Moore	2005 v Sm	28	1	0	0	0	5
D W Mumm	2008 v I	5	0	0	0	0	0

W L Palu	2006 v E	25	1	0	0	0	5
T Polota-Nau	2005 v E	8	0	0	0	0	0
B A Robinson	2006 v SA	15	1	0	0	0	5
N C Sharpe	2002 v F	70	7	0	0	0	35
G T Shepherdson	2006 v I	18	1	0	0	0	5
G B Smith	2000 v F	92	9	0	0	0	45
D J Vickerman	2002 v F	55	0	0	0	0	0
P R Waugh	2000 v E	74	4	0	0	0	20

Dave Rogers/Getty Images

Nathan Sharpe moved into the 70–cap club in 2008.

AUSTRALIA INTERNATIONAL PLAYERS

UP TO 30TH SEPTEMBER 2008

Note: Years given for International Championship matches are for second half of season; eg 1972 means season 1971-72. Years for all other matches refer to the actual year of the match. Entries in square brackets denote matches played in RWC Finals.

Abrahams, A M F (NSW) 1967 NZ, 1968 NZ 1, 1969 W
Adams, N J (NSW) 1955 NZ 1
Adamson, R W (NSW) 1912 US
Alexander, B (ACT) 2008 F1(R),2(R)
Allan, T (NSW) 1946 NZ 1, M, NZ 2, 1947 NZ 2, S, I, W, 1948 E, F, 1949 M 1,2,3, NZ 1,2
Anderson, R P (NSW) 1925 NZ 1
Anlezark, E A (NSW) 1905 NZ
Armstrong, A R (NSW) 1923 NZ 1,2
Ashley-Cooper, A P (ACT) 2005 SA4(R), 2007 W1,2,Fj,SA1(R),NZ1,SA2,NZ2, [J,Fj,C,E], 2008 F1(R),2,SA1,NZ1,2,SA3,NZ3
Austin, L R (NSW) 1963 E

Baker, R L (NSW) 1904 BI 1,2
Baker, W H (NSW) 1914 NZ 1,2,3
Ballesty, J P (NSW) 1968 NZ 1,2, F, I, S, 1969 W, SA 2,3,4,
Bannon, D P (NSW) 1946 M
Bardsley, E J (NSW) 1928 NZ 1,3, M (R)
Barker, H S (NSW) 1952 Fj 1,2, NZ 1,2, 1953 SA 4, 1954 Fj 1,2
Barnes, B S (Q) 2007 [J(R),W,Fj,E], 2008 I,F1,2,SA1,NZ1,2,SA2
Barnett, J T (NSW) 1907 NZ 1,2,3, 1908 W, 1909 E
Barry, M J (Q) 1971 SA 3
Bartholomeusz, M A (ACT) 2002 It (R)
Barton, R F D (NSW) 1899 BI 3
Batch, P G (Q) 1975 S, W, 1976 E, Fj 1,2,3, F 1,2, 1978 W 1,2, NZ 1,2,3, 1979 Arg 2
Batterham, R P (NSW) 1967 NZ, 1970 S
Battishall, B R (NSW) 1973 E
Baxter, A J (NSW) 1949 M 1,2,3, NZ 1,2, 1951 NZ 1,2, 1952 NZ 1,2
Baxter, A K E (NSW) 2003 NZ 2(R), [Arg,R,I(R),S(R),NZ(R),E], 2004 S1,2,E1,PI,NZ1,SA1,NZ2,SA2,S3,F,S4,E2, 2005 It,F1,SA1,2,3(R),NZ1,SA4,NZ2,F2,E,I(R),W(R), 2006 E1(R),2(R),I1(R),NZ1(R),SA1(R),NZ3(R),SA3(R),W,It,I2,S(R), 2007 Fj,SA1(R),NZ1(R),SA2(R),NZ2(R), [J,W(R),C,E(R)], 2008 I(R),F1,2,SA1,NZ1,2,SA2(R),3(R),NZ3
Baxter, T J (Q) 1958 NZ 3
Beith, B McN (NSW) 1914 NZ 3, 1920 NZ 1,2,3
Bell, K R (Q) 1968 S
Bell, M D NSW) 1996 C
Bennett, W G (Q) 1931 M, 1933 SA 1,2,3,
Bermingham, J V (Q) 1934 NZ 1,2, 1937 SA 1
Berne, J E (NSW) 1975 S
Besomo, K S (NSW) 1979 I 2
Betts, T N (Q) 1951 NZ 2,3, 1954 Fj 2
Biilmann, R R (NSW) 1933 SA 1,2,3,4
Birt, R S W (Q) 1914 NZ 2
Black, J W (NSW) 1985 C 1,2, NZ, Fj 1
Blackwood, J G (NSW) 1922 M 1, NZ 1,2,3, 1923 M 1, NZ 1,2,3, 1924 NZ 1,2,3, 1925 NZ 1,4, 1926 NZ 1,2,3, 1927 I, W, S, 1928 E, F
Blades, A T (NSW) 1996 S, I, W 3, 1997 NZ 1(R), E 1(R), SA 1(R), NZ 3, SA 2, Arg 1,2, E 2, S, 1998 E 1, S 1,2, NZ 1, SA 1, NZ 2, SA 2, NZ 3, Fj, WS, F, E 2, 1999 I 1(R), SA 2, NZ 2, [R, I 3, W, SA 3, F]
Blades, C D (NSW) 1997 E 1
Blake, R C (Q) 2006 E1,2, NZ2,SA2,NZ3,SA3,W
Blair, M R (NSW) 1928 F, 1931 M, NZ
Bland, G V (NSW) 1928 NZ 3, M, 1932 NZ 1,2,3, 1933 SA 1,2,4,5
Blomley, J (NSW) 1949 M 1,2,3, NZ 1,2, 1950 BI 1,2
Boland, S B (Q) 1899 BI 3,4, 1903 NZ
Bond, G S G (ACT) 2001 SA 2(R), Sp (R), E (R), F, W
Bond, J H (NSW) 1920 NZ 1,2,3, 1921 NZ
Bondfield, C (NSW) 1925 NZ 2
Bonis, E T (Q) 1929 NZ 1,2,3, 1930 BI, 1931 M, NZ, 1932 NZ 1,2,3, 1933 SA 1,2,3,4,5, 1934 NZ 1,2, 1936 NZ 1,2, M, 1937 SA 1, 1938 NZ 1
Bonner, J E (NSW) 1922 NZ 1,2,3, 1923 M 1,2,3, 1924 NZ 1,2
Bosler, J M (NSW) 1953 SA 1
Bouffler, R G (NSW) 1899 BI 3
Bourke, T K (Q) 1947 NZ 2
Bowden, R (NSW) 1926 NZ 4
Bowen, S (NSW) 1993 SA 1,2,3, 1995 [R], NZ 1,2, 1996 C, NZ 1, SA 2
Bowers, A J A (NSW) 1923 M 2(R),3, NZ, 3, 1925 NZ 1,4, 1926 NZ 1, 1927 I
Bowman, T M (NSW) 1998 E 1, S 1,2, NZ 1, SA 1, NZ 2, SA 2, NZ 3, Fj, WS, F, E 2, 1999 I 1,2, SA 2, [US]
Boyce, E S (NSW) 1962 NZ 1,2, 1964 NZ 1,2,3, 1965 SA 1,2, 1966 W, S, 1967 E, I 1, F, I 2
Boyce, J S (NSW) 1962 NZ 3,4,5, 1963 E, SA 1,2,3,4, 1964 NZ 1,3, 1965 SA 1,2
Boyd, A (NSW) 1899 BI 3
Boyd, A F McC (Q) 1958 M 1
Brass, J E (NSW) 1966 BI 2, W, S, 1967 E, I 1, F, I 2, NZ, 1968 NZ 1, F, I, S
Breckenridge, J W (NSW) 1925 NZ 2(R),3, 1927 I, W, S, 1928 E, F, 1929 NZ 1,2,3, 1930 BI
Brial, M C (NSW) 1993 F 1(R), 2, 1996 W 1(R), 2, C, NZ 1, SA 1, NZ 2, SA 2, It, I, W 3, 1997 NZ 2
Bridle, O L (V) 1931 M, 1932 NZ 1,2,3, 1933 SA 3,4,5, 1934 NZ 1,2, 1936 NZ 1,2, M
Broad, E G (Q) 1949 M 1
Brockhoff, J D (NSW) 1949 M 2,3, NZ 1,2, 1950 BI 1,2, 1951 NZ 2,3
Brown, B R (Q) 1972 NZ 1,3
Brown, J V (NSW) 1956 SA 1,2, 1957 NZ 1,2, 1958 W, I, E, S, F
Brown, R C (NSW) 1975 E 1,2
Brown, R N (WF) 2008 NZ3(R)
Brown, S W (NSW) 1953 SA 2,3,4
Bryant, H (NSW) 1925 NZ 1,3,4
Buchan, A J (NSW) 1946 NZ 1,2, 1947 NZ 1,2, S, I, W, 1948 E, F, 1949 M 3
Buchanan, P N (NSW) 1923 M 2(R),3
Bull, D (NSW) 1928 M
Buntine, H (NSW) 1923 NZ 1(R), 1924 NZ 2
Burdon, A (NSW) 1903 NZ, 1904 BI 1,2, 1905 NZ
Burge, A B (NSW) 1907 NZ 3, 1908 W
Burge, P H (NSW) 1907 NZ 1,2,3
Burge, R (NSW) 1928 NZ 1,2,3(R), M (R)
Burgess, L (NSW) 2008 I,F1,2,SA1,NZ1,2
Burke, B T (NSW) 1988 S (R)
Burke, C T (NSW) 1946 NZ 2, 1947 NZ 1,2, S, I, W, 1948 E, F, 1949 M 2,3, NZ 1,2, 1950 BI 1,2, 1951 NZ 1,2,3, 1953 SA 2,3,4, 1954 Fj 1, 1955 NZ 1,2,3, 1956 SA 1,2,
Burke, M C (NSW) 1993 SA 3(R), F 1, 1994 I 1,2, It 1,2, 1995 [C, R, E], NZ 1,2, 1996 W 1,2, C, NZ 1, SA 1, NZ 2, SA 2, It, S, I, W 3, 1997 E 1, NZ 2 , 1998 E 1, S 1,2, NZ 1, SA 1, NZ 2, SA 2, NZ 3, 1999 I 2(R), E (R), SA 1, NZ 1, SA 2, NZ 2, [R, I 3, US, W, SA 3, F], 2000 F, S, E, 2001 BI 1(R),2,3, SA 1, NZ 1, SA 2, NZ 2, Sp, E, F, W, 2002 F 1,2, NZ 1, SA 1, NZ 2, SA 2, Arg, I, E, It, 2003 SA 1, NZ 1, SA 2(R), NZ 2(R),[Arg,R,Nm(R),I], 2004 S1(R),PI(R),SA1(R),NZ2(t&R),SA2(R)
Burke, M P (NSW) 1984 E (R), I, 1985 C 1,2, NZ, Fj 1,2, 1986 It (R), F, Arg 1,2, NZ 1,2,3, 1987 SK, [US, J, I, F, W], NZ, Arg 1,2
Burnet, D R (NSW) 1972 F 1,2, NZ 1,2,3, Fj
Butler, O F (NSW) 1969 SA 1,2, 1970 S, 1971 SA 2,3, F 1,2

Calcraft, W J (NSW) 1985 C 1, 1986 It, Arg 2
Caldwell, B C (NSW) 1928 NZ 3
Cameron, A S (NSW) 1951 NZ 1,2,3, 1952 Fj 1,2, NZ 1,2, 1953 SA 1,2,3,4, 1954 Fj 1,2, 1955 NZ 1,2,3, 1956 SA 1,2, 1957 NZ 1, 1958 I
Campbell, A M (ACT) 2005 F1(R), 2006 It(R),I2(R),S
Campbell, J D (NSW) 1910 NZ 1,2,3
Campbell, W A (Q) 1984 Fj, 1986 It, F, Arg 1,2, NZ 1,2,3, 1987 SK, [E, US, J (R), I, F], NZ, 1988 E, 1989 BI 1,2,3, NZ, 1990 NZ 2,3
Campese, D I (ACT, NSW) 1982 NZ 1,2,3, 1983 US, Arg 1,2, NZ, It, F 1,2, 1984 Fj, NZ 1,2,3, E, I, W, S, 1985 Fj 1,2, 1986 It, F, Arg 1,2, NZ 1,2,3, 1987 [E, US, J, I, F, W], NZ, 1988 E 1,2, NZ 1,2,3, E, S, It, 1989 BI 1,2,3, NZ, F 1,2, 1990 F 2,3, US, NZ 1,2,3, 1991 W, E, NZ 1,2, [Arg, WS, W, I, NZ, E], 1992 S 1,2, NZ 1,2,3, SA, I, W, 1993 Tg, NZ, SA 1,2,3, C, F 1,2, 1994 I 1,2, It 1,2, WS, NZ, 1995 Arg 1,2, [SA, C, E], NZ 2(R), 1996 W 1,2, C, NZ 1, SA 1, NZ 2, SA 2, It, W3
Canniffe, W D (Q) 1907 NZ 2
Cannon, B J (NSW, WF) 2001 BI 2(R), NZ 1(R), Sp (R), F (R), W (R), 2002 F 1(R),2, SA 1(t),2(R), I (t), It (R), 2003 I (R), W (R), E (R), SA 1, NZ 1, SA 2, NZ 2, [Arg,R,I,S,NZ,E], 2004 S1,2,E1,PI,NZ1,2,SA2,S3(R),4(R), 2005 NZ1(R),SA4,NZ2,F2,E,I,W, 2006 W(R),It
Caputo, M E (ACT) 1996 W 1,2, 1997 F 1,2, NZ 1
Carberry, C M (NSW, Q) 1973 Tg 2, E, 1976 I, US, Fj 1,2,3, 1981 F 1,2, I, W, S, 1982 E
Cardy, A M (NSW) 1966 BI 1,2, W, S, 1967 E, I 1, F, 1968 NZ 1,2
Carew, P J (Q) 1899 BI 1,2,3,4
Carmichael, P (Q) 1904 BI 2, 1907 NZ 1, 1908 W, 1909 E
Carozza, P V (Q) 1990 F 1,2,3, NZ 2,3, 1992 S 1,2, NZ 1,2,3, SA, I, W, 1993 Tg, NZ
Carpenter, M G (V) 1938 NZ 1,2,
Carr, E T A (NSW) 1913 NZ 1,2,3, 1914 NZ 1,2,3
Carr, E W (NSW) 1921 SA 1,2,3, NZ (R)
Carroll, D B (NSW) 1908 W, 1912 US
Carroll, J C (NSW) 1953 SA 1
Carroll, J H (NSW) 1958 M 2,3, NZ 1,2,3, 1959 BI 1,2
Carson, J (NSW) 1899 BI 1
Carson, P J (NSW) 1979 NZ, 1980 NZ 3
Carter, D G (NSW) 1988 E 1,2, NZ 1, 1989 F 1,2
Casey, T V (NSW) 1963 SA 2,3,4, 1964 NZ 1,2,3
Catchpole, K W (NSW) 1961 Fj 1,2,3, SA 1,2, F, 1962 NZ 1,2,4, 1963 SA 2,3,4, 1964 NZ 1,2,3, 1965 SA 1,2, 1966 BI 1,2, W, S, 1967 E, I 1, F, I 2, NZ, 1968 NZ 1
Cawsey, R M (NSW) 1949 M 1, NZ 1,2
Cerutti, W H (NSW) 1928 NZ 1,2,3, M, 1929 NZ 1,2,3, 1930 BI, 1931 M, NZ, 1932 NZ 1,2,3, 1933 SA 1,2,3,4,5, 1936 M, 1937 SA 1,2
Challoner, R L (NSW) 1899 BI 2
Chambers, R (NSW) 1920 NZ 1,3
Chapman, G A (NSW) 1962 NZ 3,4,5
Chisholm, M D (ACT) 2004 S3(R), 2005 Sm,It,F1,SA1,2,3(R),NZ1(R),2,F2,E(t&R),I(R),W(R), 2006 E1(R),2,I1,NZ1,SA1(R),NZ2(R),SA2(R),NZ3(t&R),SA3(R),W(R),It,I 2,S(t&R), 2007 W1,2(R),Fj,SA1(R),NZ1(R),2(R), [W(R),Fj,C]
Clark, J G (Q) 1931 M, NZ, 1932 NZ 1,2, 1933 SA 1
Clarken, J C (NSW) 1905 NZ, 1910 NZ 1,2,3
Cleary, M A (NSW) 1961 Fj 1,2,3, SA 1,2, F
Clements, P (NSW) 1982 NZ 3
Clifford, M (NSW) 1938 NZ 3
Cobb, W G (NSW) 1899 BI 3,4
Cockbain, M J (Q) 1997 F 2(R), NZ 1, SA 1,2, 1998 E 1, S 1,2, NZ 1, SA 1, NZ 2, SA 2, NZ 3, Fj, Tg (R), WS, F, E 2, 1999 I 1,2, E, SA 1, NZ 1, SA 2, NZ 2, [US (t&R), W, SA 3, F], 2000 Arg 1,2, SA 2(t&R),3(t&R), F, S, E (R), 2001 BI 1(R),2(R),3(R), SA 1(R), NZ 1(R), SA 2(R), NZ 2(R), Sp (R), E (R), F (t+R), W, 2002 F 1(R),2(R), NZ 1(R), SA 1(R), NZ 2(R), SA 2(R), Arg, I, E, It, 2003 [Arg(R),R(R),Nm(R),I(R),S(R), NZ(R),E(R)]
Cocks, M R (NSW, Q) 1972 F 1,2, NZ 2,3, Fj, 1973 Tg 1,2, W, E, 1975 J 1
Codey, D (NSW Country, Q) 1983 Arg 1, 1984 E, W, S, 1985 C 2, NZ, 1986 F, Arg 1, 1987 [US, J, F (R), W], NZ
Cody, E W (NSW) 1913 NZ 1,2,3
Coker, T (Q, ACT) 1987 [E, US, F, W], 1991 NZ 2, [Arg, WS, NZ, E], 1992 NZ 1,2,3, W (R), 1993 Tg, NZ, 1995 Arg 2, NZ 1(R), 1997 F 1(R), 2, NZ 1, E 1, NZ 2(R), SA 1(R), NZ 3, SA 2, Arg 1,2
Colbert, R (NSW) 1952 Fj 2, NZ 1,2, 1953 SA 2,3,4
Cole, J W (NSW) 1968 NZ 1,2, F, I, S, 1969 W, SA 1,2,3,4, 1970 S, 1971 SA 1,2,3, F 1,2, 1972 NZ 1,2,3, 1973 Tg 1,2, 1974 NZ 1,2,3
Collins, P K (NSW) 1937 SA 2, 1938 NZ 2,3
Colton, A J (Q) 1899 BI 1,3
Colton, T (Q) 1904 BI 1,2
Comrie-Thomson, I R (NSW) 1926 NZ 4, 1928 NZ 1,2,3 M
Connor, D M (Q) 1958 W, I, E, S, F, M 2,3, NZ 1,2,3, 1959 BI 1,2
Connors, M R (Q) 1999 SA 1(R), NZ 1(R), SA 2(R), NZ 2, [R (R), I 3, US, W (R), SA 3(R), F(R)], 2000 Arg 1(R),2(R), SA 1, NZ 1, SA 2, NZ 2(t&R), SA 3, F (R), S (R), E (R)
Constable, R (Q) 1994 I 2(t & R)
Cook, M T (Q) 1986 F, 1987 SK, [J], 1988 E 1,2, NZ 1,2,3, E, S, It
Cooke, B P (Q) 1979 I 1
Cooke, G M (Q) 1932 NZ 1,2,3, 1933 SA 1,2,3, 1946 NZ 2, 1947 NZ 2, S, I, W, 1948 E, F
Coolican, J E (NSW) 1982 NZ 1, 1983 It, F 1,2
Cooney, R C (NSW) 1922 M 2
Cordingley, S J (Q) 2000 Arg 1(R), SA 1(R), F, S, E, 2006 E2,I1(R),NZ1(R),SA1(R),NZ2(R),SA2(R), 2007 Fj(R), [Fj(R),C], 2008 I(R),F1(R),2(t&R),SA1(R),2,3,NZ3
Corfe, A C (Q) 1899 BI 2
Cornelsen, G (NSW) 1974 NZ 2,3, 1975 J 2, S, W, 1976 E, F 1,2, 1978 W 1,2, NZ 1,2,3, 1979 I 1,2, NZ, Arg 1,2, 1980 NZ 1,2,3, 1981 I, W, S, 1982 E
Cornes, J R (Q) 1972 Fj
Cornforth, R G W (NSW) 1947 NZ 1, 1950 BI 2
Cornish, P (ACT) 1990 F 2,3, NZ 1
Costello, P P S (Q) 1950 BI 2
Cottrell, N V (Q) 1949 M 1,2,3, NZ 1,2, 1950 BI 1,2, 1951 NZ 1,2,3, 1952 Fj 1,2, NZ 1,2
Cowper, D L (V) 1931 NZ, 1932 NZ 1,2,3, 1933 SA 1,2,3,4,5
Cox, B P (NSW) 1952 Fj 1,2, NZ 1,2, 1954 Fj 2, 1955 NZ 1, 1956 SA 2, 1957 NZ 1,2
Cox, M H (NSW) 1981 W, S
Cox, P A (NSW) 1979 Arg 1,2, 1980 Fj, NZ 1,2, 1981 W (R), S, 1982 S 1,2, NZ 1,2,3, 1984 Fj, NZ 1,2,3
Craig, R R (NSW) 1908 W
Crakanthorp, J S (NSW) 1923 NZ 3
Cremin, J F (NSW) 1946 NZ 1,2, 1947 NZ 1
Crittle, C P (NSW) 1962 NZ 4,5, 1963 SA 2,3,4, 1964 NZ 1,2,3, 1965 SA 1,2, 1966 BI 1,2, S, 1967 E, I
Croft, B H D (NSW) 1928 M
Croft, D N (Q) 2002 Arg (t&R), I (R), E (t&R), It (R), 2003 [Nm]
Cross, J R (NSW) 1955 NZ 1,2,3
Cross, K A (NSW) 1949 M 1, NZ 1,2, 1950 BI 1,2, 1951 NZ 2,3, 1952 NZ 1, 1953 SA 1,2,3,4, 1954 Fj 1,2, 1955 NZ 3, 1956 SA 1,2, 1957 NZ 1,2
Cross, R P (WF) 2008 F1(R),2(R),SA1(R),NZ1,2(R),SA2(R),3(R),NZ3
Crossman, O C (NSW) 1923 M 1(R),2,3, 1924, NZ 1,2,3, 1925 NZ 1,3,4, 1926 NZ 1,2,3,4, 1929 NZ 2, 1930 BI
Crowe, P J (NSW) 1976 F 2, 1978 W 1,2, 1979 I 2, NZ, Arg 1
Crowley, D J (Q) 1989 BI 1,2,3, 1991 [WS], 1992 I, W, 1993 C (R), 1995 Arg 1,2, [SA, E], NZ 1, 1996 W 2(R), C, NZ 1, SA 1,2, I, W 3, 1998 E 1(R), S 1(R),2(R), NZ 1(R), SA 1, NZ 2, SA 2, NZ 3, Tg, WS, 1999 I 1,2(R), E (R), SA 1, NZ 1(R), [R (R), I 3(t&R), US, F(R)]
Curley, T G P (NSW) 1957 NZ 1,2, 1958 W, I, E, S, F, M 1, NZ 1,2,3
Curran, D J (NSW) 1980 NZ 3, 1981 F 1,2, W, 1983 Arg 1
Currie, E W (Q) 1899 BI 2
Cutler, S A G (NSW) 1982 NZ 2(R), 1984 NZ 1,2,3, E, I, W, S, 1985 C 1,2, NZ, Fj 1,2, 1986 It, F, NZ 1,2,3, 1987 SK, [E, J, I, F, W], NZ, Arg 1,2, 1988 E 1,2, NZ 1,2,3, E, S, It, 1989 BI 1,2,3, NZ, 1991 [WS]

Daly, A J (NSW) 1989 NZ, F 1,2, 1990 F 1,2,3, US, NZ 1,2,3, 1991 W, E, NZ 1,2, [Arg, W, I, NZ, E], 1992 S 1,2, NZ 1,2,3, SA, 1993 Tg, NZ, SA 1,2,3, C, F 1,2, 1994 I 1,2, It 1,2, WS, NZ, 1995 [C, R]
D'Arcy, A M (Q) 1980 Fj, NZ 3, 1981 F 1,2, I, W, S, 1982 E, S 1,2
Darveniza, P (NSW) 1969 W, SA 2,3,4
Darwin, B J (ACT) 2001 BI 1(R), SA 1(R), NZ 1(R), SA 2(R), NZ 2(t&R), Sp, E, F, W, 2002 NZ 1(R), SA 1(R), NZ 2(R), SA 2, Arg (R), I (R), E (R), It (R), 2003 I (R), W (t&R), E (R), SA 1(R), NZ 1(R), [Arg(R),R(R),Nm,I,S,NZ]
Davidson, R A L (NSW) 1952 Fj 1,2, NZ 1,2, 1953 SA 1, 1957 NZ 1,2, 1958 W, I, E, S, F, M 1
Davis, C C (NSW) 1949 NZ 1, 1951 NZ 1,2,3

AUSTRALIA

Davis, E H (V) 1947 S, W, 1949 M 1,2
Davis, G V (NSW) 1963 E, SA 1,2,3,4, 1964 NZ 1,2,3, 1965 SA 1, 1966 BI 1,2, W, S, 1967 E, I 1, F, I 2, NZ, 1968 NZ 1,2, F, I, S, 1969 W, SA 1,2,3,4, 1970 S, 1971 SA 1,2,3, F 1,2, 1972 F 1,2, NZ 1,2,3
Davis, G W G (NSW) 1955 NZ 2,3
Davis, R A (NSW) 1974 NZ 1,2,3
Davis, T S R (NSW) 1920 NZ 1,2,3, 1921 SA 1,2,3, NZ, 1922 M 1,2,3, NZ 1,2,3, 1923 M 3, NZ 1,2,3, 1924 NZ 1,2, 1925 NZ 1
Davis, W (NSW) 1899 BI 1,3,4
Dawson, W L (NSW) 1946 NZ 1,2
Diett, L J (NSW) 1959 BI 1,2
Dix, W (NSW) 1907 NZ 1,2,3, 1909 E
Dixon, E J (Q) 1904 BI 3
Donald, K J (Q) 1957 NZ 1, 1958 W, I, E, S, M 2,3, 1959 BI 1,2
Dore, E (Q) 1904 BI 1
Dore, M J (Q) 1905 NZ
Dorr, R W (V) 1936 M, 1937 SA 1
Douglas, J A (V) 1962 NZ 3,4,5
Douglas, W A (NSW) 1922 NZ 3(R)
Dowse, J H (NSW) 1961 Fj 1,2, SA 1,2
Dunbar, A R (NSW) 1910 NZ 1,2,3, 1912 US
Duncan, J L (NSW) 1926 NZ 4
Dunlop, E E (V) 1932 NZ 3, 1934 NZ 1
Dunn, P K (NSW) 1958 NZ 1,2,3, 1959 BI 1,2
Dunn, V A (NSW) 1920 NZ 1,2,3, 1921 SA 1,2,3, NZ
Dunning, M J (NSW) 2003 [Nm,E(R)], 2004 S1(R),2(R),E1(R),NZ1(R),SA1(R),NZ2(t&R),SA2(R),S3(R),F(R),S4(R),E2(R), 2005 Sm,It(R),F1(t&R),SA1(R),2(R),3,NZ1(t&R),SA4(t&R),NZ2(R),F2,E,W, 2007 W1,2(R),Fj,SA1,NZ1,SA2,NZ2, [J,W,Fj,E], 2008 I,SA1(R),NZ1(R),SA2,3
Dunworth, D A (Q) 1971 F 1,2, 1972 F 1,2, 1976 Fj 2
Dwyer, L J (NSW) 1910 NZ 1,2,3, 1912 US, 1913 NZ 3, 1914 NZ 1,2,3
Dyson, F J (Q) 2000 Arg 1,2, SA 1, NZ 1, SA 2, NZ 2, SA 3, F, S, E

Eales, J A (Q) 1991 W, E, NZ 1,2, [Arg, WS, W, I, NZ, E], 1992 S 1,2, NZ 1,2,3, SA, I, 1994 I 1,2, It 1,2, WS, NZ, 1995 Arg 1,2, [SA, C, R, E], NZ 1,2, 1996 W 1,2, C, NZ 1, SA 1, NZ 2, SA 2, It, S, I, 1997 F 1,2, NZ 1, E 1, NZ 2, SA 1, Arg 1,2, E 2, S, 1998 E 1, S 1,2, NZ 1, SA 1, NZ 2, SA 2, NZ 3, Fj, Tg, WS, F, E 2, 1999 [R, I 3, W, SA 3, F], 2000 Arg 1,2, SA 1, NZ 1, SA 2, NZ 2, SA 3, F, S, E, 2001 BI 1,2,3, SA 1, NZ 1, SA 2, NZ 2
Eastes, C C (NSW) 1946 NZ 1,2, 1947 NZ 1,2, 1949 M 1,2
Edmonds, M H M (NSW) 1998 Tg, 2001 SA 1(R)
Egerton, R H (NSW) 1991 W, E, NZ 1,2, [Arg, W, I, NZ, E]
Ella, G A (NSW) 1982 NZ 1,2, 1983 F 1,2, 1988 E 2, NZ 1
Ella, G J (NSW) 1982 S 1, 1983 It, 1985 C 2(R), Fj 2
Ella, M G (NSW) 1980 NZ 1,2,3, 1981 F 2, S, 1982 E, S 1, NZ 1,2,3, 1983 US, Arg 1,2, NZ, It, F 1,2, 1984 Fj, NZ 1,2,3, E, I, W, S
Ellem, M A (NSW) 1976 Fj 3(R)
Elliott, F M (NSW) 1957 NZ 1
Elliott, R E (NSW) 1920 NZ 1, 1921 NZ, 1922 M 1,2, NZ 1(R),2,3, 1923 M 1,2,3, NZ 1,2,3
Ellis, C S (NSW) 1899 BI 1,2,3,4
Ellis, K J (NSW) 1958 NZ 1,2,3, 1959 BI 1,2
Ellwood, B J (NSW) 1958 NZ 1,2,3, 1961 Fj 2,3, SA 1, F, 1962 NZ 1,2,3,4,5, 1963 SA 1,2,3,4, 1964 NZ 3, 1965 SA 1,2, 1966 BI 1
Elsom, R D (NSW) 2005 Sm,It,F1,SA1,2,3(R),4,NZ2,F2, 2006 E1,2,I1,NZ1,SA1,NZ2,SA2,NZ3,SA3,W,It,I2,S, 2007 W1,2,SA1,NZ1,SA2,NZ2, [J,W,Fj,E], 2008 I,F1,2,SA1,NZ1,SA2,3,NZ3
Emanuel, D M (NSW) 1957 NZ 2, 1958 W, I, E, S, F, M 1,2,3
Emery, N A (NSW) 1947 NZ 2, S, I, W, 1948 E, F, 1949 M 2,3, NZ 1,2
Erasmus, D J (NSW) 1923 NZ 1,2
Erby, A B (NSW) 1923 M 1,2, NZ 2,3, 1925 NZ 2
Evans, L J (Q) 1903 NZ, 1904 BI 1,3
Evans, W T (Q) 1899 BI 1,2

Fahey, E J (NSW) 1912 US, 1913 NZ 1,2, 1914 NZ 3
Fairfax, R L (NSW) 1971 F 1,2, 1972 F 1,2, NZ 1, Fj, 1973 W, E
Farmer, E H (Q) 1910 NZ 1
Farquhar, C R (NSW) 1920 NZ 2
Farr-Jones, N C (NSW) 1984 E, I, W, S, 1985 C 1,2, NZ, Fj 1,2, 1986 It, F, Arg 1,2, NZ 1,2,3, 1987 SK, [E, I, F, W (R)], NZ, Arg 2, 1988 E 1,2, NZ 1,2,3, E, S, It, 1989 BI 1,2,3, NZ, F 1,2, 1990 F 1,2,3, US, NZ 1,2,3, 1991 W, E, NZ 1,2, [Arg, WS, I, NZ, E], 1992 S 1,2, NZ 1,2,3, SA, 1993 NZ, SA 1,2,3
Fava, S G (ACT, WF) 2005 E(R),I(R), 2006 NZ1(R),SA1,NZ2
Fay, G (NSW) 1971 SA 2, 1972 NZ 1,2,3, 1973 Tg 1,2, W, E, 1974 NZ 1,2,3, 1975 E 1,2, J 1, S, W, 1976 I, US, 1978 W 1,2, NZ 1,2,3, 1979 I 1
Fenwicke, P T (NSW) 1957 NZ 1, 1958 W, I, E, 1959 BI 1,2
Ferguson, R T (NSW) 1922 M 3, NZ 1, 1923 M 3, NZ 3
Fihelly, J A (Q) 1907 NZ 2
Finau, S F (NSW) 1997 NZ 3
Finegan, O D A (ACT) 1996 W 1,2, C, NZ 1, SA 1(t), S, W 3, 1997 SA 1, NZ 3, SA 2, Arg 1,2, E 2, S, 1998 E 1(R), S 1(t + R),2(t + R), NZ 1(R), SA 1(t),2(R), NZ 3(R), Fj (R), Tg, WS (t + R), F (R), E 2(R), 1999 NZ 2(R), [R, I 3(R), US, W (R), SA 3(R), F (R)], 2001 BI 1,2,3, SA 1, NZ 1, SA 2, NZ 2, Sp, E, F, W, 2002 F 1,2, NZ 1, SA 1, NZ 2, SA 2, I, 2003 SA 1(t&R), NZ 1(R), SA 2(R), NZ 2(R)
Finlay, A N (NSW) 1926 NZ 1,2,3, 1927 I, W, S, 1928 E, F, 1929 NZ 1,2,3, 1930 BI
Finley, F G (NSW) 1904 BI 3
Finnane, S C (NSW) 1975 E 1, J 1,2, 1976 E, 1978 W 1,2
Fitter, D E S (ACT) 2005 I,W
FitzSimons, P (NSW) 1989 F 1,2, 1990 F 1,2,3, US, NZ 1
Flanagan, P (Q) 1907 NZ 1,2
Flatley, E J (Q) 1997 E 2, S, 2000 S (R), 2001 BI 1(R),2(R),3, SA 1, NZ 1(R),2(R), Sp (R), F (R), W, 2002 F 1(R),2(R), NZ 1(t+R), SA 1(R), NZ 2(t), Arg (R), I (R), E, It, 2003 I, W, SA 1, NZ 1, SA 2, NZ 2, [Arg,R,I,S,NZ,E], 2004 S3(R),F(R),S4(R),E2, 2005 NZ1(R)
Flett, J A (NSW) 1990 US, NZ 2,3, 1991 [WS]
Flynn, J P (Q) 1914 NZ 1,2
Fogarty, J R (Q) 1949 M 2,3
Foley, M A (Q) 1995 [C (R), R], 1996 W 2(R), NZ 1, SA 1, NZ 2, SA 2, It, S, I, W 3, 1997 NZ 1(R), E 1, NZ 2, SA 1, NZ 3, SA 2, Arg 1,2, E 2, S, 1998 Tg (R), F (R), E 2(R), 1999 NZ 2(R), [US, W, SA 3, F], 2000 Arg 1,2, SA 1, NZ 1, SA 2, NZ 2, SA 3, F, S, E, 2001 BI 1(R),2,3, SA 1, NZ 1, SA 2, NZ 2, Sp, E, F, W
Foote, R H (NSW) 1924 NZ 2,3, 1926 NZ 2
Forbes, C F (Q) 1953 SA 2,3,4, 1954 Fj 1, 1956 SA 1,2
Ford, B (Q) 1957 NZ 2
Ford, E E (NSW) 1927 I, W, S, 1928 E, F, 1929 NZ 1,3
Ford, J A (NSW) 1925 NZ 4, 1926 NZ 1,2, 1927 I, W, S, 1928 E, 1929 NZ 1,2,3, 1930 BI
Forman, T R (NSW) 1968 I, S, 1969 W, SA 1,2,3,4
Fowles, D G (NSW) 1921 SA 1,2,3, 1922 M 2,3, 1923 M 2,3
Fox, C L (NSW) 1920 NZ 1,2,3, 1921 SA 1, NZ, 1922 M 1,2, NZ 1, 1924 NZ 1,2,3, 1925 NZ 1,2,3, 1926 NZ 1,3, 1928 F
Fox, O G (NSW) 1958 F
Francis, E (Q) 1914 NZ 1,2
Frawley, D (Q, NSW) 1986 Arg 2(R), 1987 Arg 1,2, 1988 E 1,2, NZ 1,2,3, S, It
Freedman, J E (NSW) 1962 NZ 3,4,5, 1963 SA 1
Freeman, E (NSW) 1946 NZ 1(R), M
Freier, A L (NSW) 2002 Arg (R), I, E (R), It, 2003 SA 1(R), NZ 1(t), 2005 NZ2(R), 2006 E2, 2007 W1(R),2(R),Fj,SA1(R), NZ1(R),SA2,NZ2(R), [J(R),W(R),Fj(R),C,E(R)], 2008 I(R),F1(R),2(R),NZ3(R)
Freney, M E (Q) 1972 NZ 1,2,3, 1973 Tg 1, W, E (R)
Friend, W S (NSW) 1920 NZ 3, 1921 SA 1,2,3, 1922 NZ 1,2,3, 1923 M 1,2,3
Furness, D C (NSW) 1946 M
Futter, F C (NSW) 1904 BI 3

Gardner, J M (Q) 1987 Arg 2, 1988 E 1, NZ 1, E
Gardner, W C (NSW) 1950 BI 1
Garner, R L (NSW) 1949 NZ 1,2
Gavin, K A (NSW) 1909 E
Gavin, T B (NSW) 1988 NZ 2,3, S, It (R), 1989 NZ (R), F 1,2, 1990 F 1,2,3, US, NZ 1,2,3, 1991 W, E, NZ 1, 1992 S 1,2, SA, I, W, 1993 Tg, NZ, SA 1,2,3, C, F 1,2, 1994 I 1,2, It 1,2, WS, NZ, 1995 Arg 1,2, [SA, C, R, E], NZ 1,2, 1996 NZ 2(R), SA 2, W 3
Gelling, A M (NSW) 1972 NZ 1, Fj
George, H W (NSW) 1910 NZ 1,2,3, 1912 US, 1913 NZ 1,3, 1914 NZ 1,3
George, W G (NSW) 1923 M 1,3, NZ 1,2, 1924 NZ 3, 1925 NZ 2,3, 1926 NZ 4, 1928 NZ 1,2,3, M
Gerrard, M A (ACT) 2005 It(R),SA1(R),NZ1,2,E,I,W, 2006

E1,2,I1,NZ1,SA1,NZ2,SA2,NZ3(t),SA3(R),I2,S, 2007 W1,2(R),SA2,NZ2, [J(R)]
Gibbons, E de C (NSW) 1936 NZ 1,2, M
Gibbs, P R (V) 1966 S
Giffin, D T (ACT) 1996 W 3, 1997 F 1,2, 1999 I 1,2, E, SA 1, NZ 1, SA 2, NZ 2, [R, I 3, US (R), W, SA 3, F], 2000 Arg 1,2, SA 1, NZ 1, SA 2, NZ 2, SA 3, F, S, E, 2001 BI 1,2, SA 1, NZ 2, Sp, E, F, W, 2002 Arg (R), I, E (R), It (R), 2003 I, W, E, SA 1, NZ 1, SA 2, NZ 2, [Arg,Nm(R),I,NZ(t&R),E(R)]
Gilbert, H (NSW) 1910 NZ 1,2,3
Girvan, B (ACT) 1988 E
Giteau, M J (ACT, WF) 2002 E (R), It (R), 2003 SA 2(R), NZ 2(R), [Arg(R),R(R),Nm,I(R),S(R),E(t)], 2004 S1,E1,PI, NZ1,SA1,NZ2,SA2,S3,F,S4,E2, 2005 Sm,It,F1,SA1,2,3, NZ1,SA4,F2,E(t&R), 2006 NZ1(R),SA1,NZ2,SA2,NZ3, SA3,W,It,I2,S, 2007 W1,2,SA1,NZ1,SA2,NZ2, [J,W,Fj,E], 2008 I,F1,2,SA1,NZ1,2,SA2,3,NZ3
Gordon, G C (NSW) 1929 NZ 1
Gordon, K M (NSW) 1950 BI 1,2
Gould, R G (Q) 1980 NZ 1,2,3, 1981 I, W, S, 1982 S 2, NZ 1,2,3, 1983 US, Arg 1, F 1,2, 1984 NZ 1,2,3, E, I, W, S, 1985 NZ, 1986 It, 1987 SK, [E]
Gourley, S R (NSW) 1988 S, It, 1989 BI 1,2,3
Graham, C S (Q) 1899 BI 2
Graham, R (NSW) 1973 Tg 1,2, W, E, 1974 NZ 2,3, 1975 E 2, J 1,2, S, W, 1976 I, US, Fj 1,2,3, F 1,2
Gralton, A S I (Q) 1899 BI 1,4, 1903 NZ
Grant, J C (NSW) 1988 E 1, NZ 2,3, E
Graves, R H (NSW) 1907 NZ 1(R)
Greatorex, E N (NSW) 1923 M 3, NZ 3, 1924 NZ 1,2,3, 1925 NZ 1, 1928 E, F
Gregan, G M (ACT) 1994 It 1,2, WS, NZ, 1995 Arg 1,2, [SA, C (R), R, E], 1996 W 1, C (t), SA 1, NZ 2, SA 2, It, I, W 3, 1997 F 1,2, NZ 1, E 1, NZ 2, SA 1, NZ 3, SA 2, Arg 1,2, E 2, S, 1998 E 1, S 1,2, NZ 1, SA 1, NZ 2, SA 2, NZ 3, Fj, WS, F, E 2, 1999 I 1,2, E, SA 1, NZ 1, SA 2, NZ 2, [R, I 3, W, SA 3, F], 2000 Arg 1,2, SA 1, NZ 1, SA 2, NZ 2, SA 3, 2001 BI 1,2,3, SA 1, NZ 1, SA 2, NZ 2, Sp, E, F, W, 2002 F 1,2, NZ 1, SA 1, NZ 2, SA 2, Arg, I, E, It, 2003 I, W, E, SA 1, NZ 1, SA 2, NZ 2, [Arg,R,I,S,NZ,E], 2004 S1,2,E1,PI,SA1,NZ2, SA2,S3,F,S4,E2, 2005 It,F1,SA1,2,3,NZ1,SA4,NZ2,F2,E,I,W, 2006 E1,2(R),I1,NZ1,SA1,NZ2,SA2,NZ3,SA3, 2007 W1(R),2(R),Fj,SA1,NZ1,SA2,NZ2, [J,W,Fj,C(R),E]
Gregory, S C (Q) 1968 NZ 3, F, I, S, 1969 SA 1,3, 1971 SA 1,3, F 1,2, 1972 F 1,2, 1973 Tg 1,2, W, E
Grey, G O (NSW) 1972 F 2(R), NZ 1,2,3, Fj (R)
Grey, N P (NSW) 1998 S 2(R), SA 2(R), Fj (R), Tg (R), F, E 2, 1999 I 1(R),2(R), E, SA 1, NZ 1, SA 2, NZ 2(t&R), [R (R), I 3(R), US, SA 3(R), F (R)], 2000 S (R), E (R), 2001 BI 1,2,3, SA 1, NZ 1, SA 2, NZ 2, Sp, E, F, 2003 I (R), W (R), E, [Nm,NZ(t)]
Griffin, T S (NSW) 1907 NZ 1,3, 1908 W, 1910 NZ 1,2, 1912 US
Grigg, P C (Q) 1980 NZ 3, 1982 S 2, NZ 1,2,3, 1983 Arg 2, NZ, 1984 Fj, W, S, 1985 C 1,2, NZ, Fj 1,2, 1986 Arg 1,2, NZ 1,2, 1987 SK, [E, J, I, F, W]
Grimmond, D N (NSW) 1964 NZ 2
Gudsell, K E (NSW) 1951 NZ 1,2,3
Guerassimoff, J (Q) 1963 SA 2,3,4, 1964 NZ 1,2,3, 1965 SA 2, 1966 BI 1,2, 1967 E, I, F
Gunther, W J (NSW) 1957 NZ 2

Hall, D (Q) 1980 Fj, NZ 1,2,3, 1981 F 1,2, 1982 S 1,2, NZ 1,2, 1983 US, Arg 1,2, NZ, It
Hamalainen, H A (Q) 1929 NZ 1,2,3
Hamilton, B G (NSW) 1946 M
Hammand, C A (NSW) 1908 W, 1909 E
Hammon, J D C (V) 1937 SA 2
Handy, C B (Q) 1978 NZ 3, 1979 NZ, Arg 1,2, 1980 NZ 1,2
Hanley, R G (Q) 1983 US (R), It (R), 1985 Fj 2(R)
Hardcastle, P A (NSW) 1946 NZ 1, M, NZ 2, 1947 NZ 1, 1949 M 3
Hardcastle, W R (NSW) 1899 BI 4, 1903 NZ
Harding, M A (NSW) 1983 It
Hardman, S P (Q) 2002 F 2(R), 2006 SA1(R), 2007 SA2(t&R), [C(R)]
Hardy, M D (ACT) 1997 F 1(t), 2(R), NZ 1(R), 3(R), Arg 1(R), 2(R), 1998 Tg, WS
Harrison, J B (ACT, NSW) 2001 BI 3, NZ 1, SA 2, Sp, E, F, W (R), 2002 F 1,2, NZ 1, SA 1, NZ 2, SA 2, Arg, I (R), E, It, 2003 [R(R),Nm,S,NZ,E], 2004 S1,2,E1,PI,NZ1,SA1, NZ2,SA2,S3,F,S4,E2
Harry, R L L (NSW) 1996 W 1,2, NZ 1, SA 1(t), NZ 2, It, S, 1997 F 1,2, NZ 1,2, SA 1, NZ 3, SA 2, Arg 1,2, E 2, S, 1998 E 1, S 1,2, NZ 1, Fj, 1999 SA 2, NZ 2, [R, I 3, W, SA 3, F], 2000 Arg 1,2, SA 1, NZ 1, SA 2, NZ 2, SA 3
Hartill, M N (NSW) 1986 NZ 1,2,3, 1987 SK, [J], Arg 1, 1988 NZ 1,2, E, It, 1989 BI 1(R), 2,3, F 1,2, 1995 Arg 1(R), 2(R), [C], NZ 1,2
Harvey, P B (Q) 1949 M 1,2
Harvey, R M (NSW) 1958 F, M 3
Hatherell, W I (Q) 1952 Fj 1,2
Hauser, R G (Q) 1975 J 1(R), 2, W (R), 1976 E, I, US, Fj 1,2,3, F 1,2, 1978 W 1,2, 1979 I 1,2
Hawker, M J (NSW) 1980 Fj, NZ 1,2,3, 1981 F 1,2, I, W, 1982 E, S 1,2, NZ 1,2,3, 1983 US, Arg 1,2, NZ, It, F 1,2, 1984 NZ 1,2,3, 1987 NZ
Hawthorne, P F (NSW) 1962 NZ 3,4,5, 1963 E, SA 1,2,3,4, 1964 NZ 1,2,3, 1965 SA 1,2, 1966 BI 1,2, W, 1967 E, I 1, F, I 2, NZ
Hayes, E S (Q) 1934 NZ 1,2, 1938 NZ 1,2,3
Heath, A (NSW) 1996 C, SA 1, NZ 2, SA 2, It, 1997 NZ 2, SA 1, E 2(R)
Heenan, D P (Q, ACT) 2003 W, 2006 E1
Heinrich, E L (NSW) 1961 Fj 1,2,3, SA 2, F, 1962 NZ 1,2,3, 1963 E, SA 1
Heinrich, V W (NSW) 1954 Fj 1,2
Heming, R J (NSW) 1961 Fj 2,3, SA 1,2, F, 1962 NZ 2,3,4,5, 1963 SA 2,3,4, 1964 NZ 1,2,3, 1965 SA 1,2, 1966 BI 1,2, W, 1967 F
Hemingway, W H (NSW) 1928 NZ 2,3, 1931 M, NZ, 1932 NZ 3
Henderson, N J (ACT) 2004 PI(R), 2005 Sm(R), 2006 It(R)
Henjak, M T (ACT) 2004 E1(R),NZ1(R), 2005 Sm(R),I(R)
Henry, A R (Q) 1899 BI 2
Herbert, A G (Q) 1987 SK (R), [F (R)], 1990 F 1(R), US, NZ 2,3, 1991 [WS], 1992 NZ 3(R), 1993 NZ (R), SA 2(R)
Herbert, D J (Q) 1994 I 2, It 1,2, WS (R), 1995 Arg 1,2, [SA, R], 1996 C, SA 2, It, S, I, 1997 NZ 1, 1998 E 1, S 1,2, NZ 1, SA 1, NZ 2, SA 2, Fj, Tg, WS, F, E 2, 1999 I 1,2, E, SA 1, NZ 1, SA 2, NZ 2, [R, I 3, W, SA 3, F], 2000 Arg 1,2, SA 1, NZ 1, SA 2, NZ 2, SA 3, F, S, E, 2001 BI 1,2,3, SA 1, NZ 1, SA 2, NZ 2, Sp, E, 2002 F 1,2, NZ 1, SA 1, NZ 2, SA 2, Arg, I, E, It
Herd, H V (NSW) 1931 M
Hickey, J (NSW) 1908 W, 1909 E
Hill, J (NSW) 1925 NZ 1
Hillhouse, D W (Q) 1975 S, 1976 E, Fj 1,2,3, F 1,2, 1978 W 1,2, 1983 US, Arg 1,2, NZ, It, F 1,2
Hills, E F (V) 1950 BI 1,2
Hindmarsh, J A (Q) 1904 BI 1
Hindmarsh, J C (NSW) 1975 J 2, S, W, 1976 US, Fj 1,2,3, F 1,2
Hipwell, J N B (NSW) 1968 NZ 1(R), 2, F, I, S, 1969 W, SA 1,2,3,4, 1970 S, 1971 SA 1,2, F 1,2, 1972 F 1,2, 1973 Tg 1, W, E, 1974 NZ 1,2,3, 1975 E 1,2, J 1, S, W, 1978 NZ 1,2,3, 1981 F 1,2, I, W, 1982 E
Hirschberg, W A (NSW) 1905 NZ
Hodgins, C H (NSW) 1910 NZ 1,2,3
Hodgson, A J (NSW) 1933 SA 2,3,4, 1934 NZ 1, 1936 NZ 1,2, M, 1937 SA 2, 1938 NZ 1,2,3
Hoiles, S A (NSW, ACT) 2004 S4(R),E2(R), 2006 W(R), 2007 W1(R),2(R),Fj(R),SA1(R),NZ1(R),SA2,NZ2, [J(R),W(R),Fj(R),C(R),E(R)] 2006 W(R), 2007. W1(R),2(R),Fj(R),SA1(R),NZ1(R),SA2,NZ2, [J(R),W(R),Fj(R),C(R),E(R)], 2008 F2
Holbeck, J C (ACT) 1997 NZ 1(R), E 1, NZ 2, SA 1, NZ 3, SA 2, 2001 BI 3(R)
Holdsworth, J W (NSW) 1921 SA 1,2,3, 1922 M 2,3, NZ 1(R)
Holmes, G S (Q) 2005 F2(R),E(t&R),I, 2006 E1,2,I1,NZ1,SA1,NZ2,SA2,NZ3, 2007 [Fj(R),C]
Holt, N C (Q) 1984 Fj
Honan, B D (Q) 1968 NZ 1(R), 2, F, I, S, 1969 SA 1,2,3,4
Honan, R E (Q) 1964 NZ 1,2
Horan, T J (Q) 1989 NZ, F 1,2, 1990 F 1, NZ 1,2,3, 1991 W, E, NZ 1,2, [Arg, WS, W, I, NZ, E], 1992 S 1,2, NZ 1,2,3, SA, I, W, 1993 Tg, NZ, SA 1,2,3, C, F 1,2, 1995 [C, R, E], NZ 1,2, 1996 W 1,2, C, NZ 1, SA 1, It, S, I, W 3, 1997 F 1,2, NZ 1, E 1, NZ 2, Arg 1,2, E 2, S, 1998 E 1, S 1,2, NZ 1, SA 1, NZ 2, SA 2, NZ 3, Fj, Tg, WS, 1999 I 1,2, E, SA 1, NZ 1, SA 2, NZ 2, [R, I 3, W, SA 3, F], 2000 Arg 1
Horodam, D J (Q) 1913 NZ 2
Horsley, G R (Q) 1954 Fj 2

AUSTRALIA

Horton, P A (NSW) 1974 NZ 1,2,3, 1975 E 1,2, J 1,2, S, W, 1976 E, F 1,2, 1978 W 1,2, NZ 1,2,3, 1979 NZ, Arg 1
Horwill, J E (Q) 2007 Fj, 2008 I,F1,2,SA1,NZ1,2,SA2,3,NZ3
Hoskins, J E (NSW) 1924 NZ 1,2,3
How, R A (NSW) 1967 I 2
Howard, J (Q) 1938 NZ 1,2
Howard, J L (NSW) 1970 S, 1971 SA 1, 1972 F 1(R), NZ 2, 1973 Tg 1,2, W
Howard, P W (Q, ACT) 1993 NZ, 1994 WS, NZ, 1995 NZ 1(R), 2(t), 1996 W 1,2, SA 1, NZ 2, SA 2, It, S, W 3, 1997 F 1,2, NZ 1, Arg 1,2, E 2, S
Howell, M L (NSW) 1946 NZ 1(R), 1947 NZ 1, S, I, W
Hughes, B D (NSW) 1913 NZ 2,3
Hughes, J C (NSW) 1907 NZ 1,3
Hughes, N McL (NSW) 1953 SA 1,2,3,4, 1955 NZ 1,2,3, 1956 SA 1,2, 1958 W, I, E, S, F
Humphreys, O W (NSW) 1920 NZ 3, 1921 NZ, 1922 M 1,2,3, 1925 NZ 1
Hutchinson, E E (NSW) 1937 SA 1,2
Hutchinson, F E (NSW) 1936 NZ 1,2, 1938 NZ 1,3
Huxley, J L (ACT) 2007 W1,2,Fj,SA1,NZ1,SA2, [W(R),Fj(R),C]
Hynes, P J (Q) 2008 I,F1,2,SA1,NZ1,2,SA2,3,NZ3

Ide, W P J (Q) 1938 NZ 2,3
Ioane, D N (WF) 2007 W2
Ives, W N (NSW) 1926 NZ 1,2,3,4, 1929 NZ 3

James, P M (Q) 1958 M 2,3
James, S L (NSW) 1987 SK (R), [E (R)], NZ, Arg 1,2, 1988 NZ 2(R)
Jamieson, A E (NSW) 1925 NZ 3(R)
Jaques, T (ACT) 2000 SA 1(R), NZ 1(R)
Jessep, E M (V) 1934 NZ 1,2
Johansson, L D T (Q) 2005 NZ2(R),F2(R),E(R)
Johnson, A P (NSW) 1946 NZ 1, M
Johnson, B B (NSW) 1952 Fj 1,2, NZ 1,2, 1953 SA 2,3,4, 1955 NZ 1,2
Johnson, P G (NSW) 1959 BI 1,2, 1961 Fj 1,2,3, SA 1,2, F, 1962 NZ 1,2,3,4,5, 1963 E, SA 1,2,3,4, 1964 NZ 1,2,3, 1965 SA 1,2, 1966 BI 1,2, W, S, 1967 E, I 1, F, I 2, NZ, 1968 NZ 1,2, F, I, S, 1970 S, 1971 SA 1,2, F 1,2
Johnstone, B (Q) 1993 Tg (R)
Jones, G G (Q) 1952 Fj 1,2, 1953 SA 1,2,3,4, 1954 Fj 1,2, 1955 NZ 1,2,3, 1956 SA 1
Jones, H (NSW) 1913 NZ 1,2,3
Jones, P A (NSW) 1963 E, SA 1
Jorgensen, P (NSW) 1992 S 1(R), 2(R)
Joyce, J E (NSW) 1903 NZ
Judd, H A (NSW) 1903 NZ, 1904 BI 1,2,3, 1905 NZ
Judd, P B (NSW) 1925 NZ 4, 1926 NZ 1,2,3,4, 1927 I, W, S, 1928 E, 1931 M, NZ
Junee, D K (NSW) 1989 F 1(R), 2(R), 1994 WS (R), NZ (R)

Kafer, R B (ACT) 1999 NZ 2, [R, US (R)], 2000 Arg 1(R),2, SA 1, NZ 1(t&R), SA 2(R),3(R), F, S, E
Kahl, P R (Q) 1992 W
Kanaar, A (NSW) 2005 NZ2(R)
Kassulke, N (Q) 1985 C 1,2
Kay, A R (V) 1958 NZ 2, 1959 BI 2
Kay, P (NSW) 1988 E 2
Kearney, K H (NSW) 1947 NZ 1,2, S, I, W, 1948 E, F
Kearns, P N (NSW) 1989 NZ, F 1,2, 1990 F 1,2,3, US, NZ 1,2,3, 1991 W, E, NZ 1,2, [Arg, WS, W, I, NZ, E], 1992 S 1,2, NZ 1,2,3, SA, I, W, 1993 Tg, NZ, SA 1,2,3, C, F 1,2, 1994 I 1,2, It 1,2, WS, NZ, 1995 Arg 1,2, [SA, C, E], NZ 1,2, 1998 E 1, S 1,2, NZ 1, SA 1, NZ 2, SA 2, NZ 3, Fj, WS, F, E 2, 1999 I 2(R), SA 1(R),2, NZ 2, [R, I 3]
Kefu, R S T (Q) 1997 SA 2(R), 1998 E 1, S 1,2, NZ 1, SA 1, NZ 2, SA 2, NZ 3, Fj (R), Tg, WS (R), F, E 2, 1999 I 1,2, E, SA 1, NZ 1(R), SA 2, NZ 2, [R, I 3, SA 3, F], 2000 SA 1(t&R), NZ 1(R), SA 2(R), NZ 2, SA 3(R), F, S, E, 2001 BI 1,2,3, SA 1, NZ 1, SA 2, NZ 2, Sp, E, F, W, 2002 F 1, NZ 1, SA 1, NZ 2, SA 2, Arg, I, E, It, 2003 I, W, E, SA 1, NZ 1, SA 2, NZ 2
Kefu, S (Q) 2001 W (R), 2003 I, W, E, SA 1, NZ 1(R)
Kelaher, J D (NSW) 1933 SA 1,2,3,4,5, 1934 NZ 1,2, 1936 NZ 1,2, M, 1937 SA 1,2, 1938 NZ 3
Kelaher, T P (NSW) 1992 NZ 1, I (R), 1993 NZ
Kelleher, R J (Q) 1969 SA 2,3
Keller, D H (NSW) 1947 NZ 1, S, I, W, 1948 E, F
Kelly, A J (NSW) 1899 BI 1
Kelly, R L F (NSW) 1936 NZ 1,2, M, 1937 SA 1,2, 1938 NZ 1,2
Kent, A (Q) 1912 US
Kerr, F R (V) 1938 NZ 1
King, S C (NSW) 1926 NZ 1,2,3,4(R), 1927 W, S, 1928 E, F, 1929 NZ 1,2,3, 1930 BI, 1932 NZ 1,2
Knight, M (NSW) 1978 W 1,2, NZ 1
Knight, S O (NSW) 1969 SA 2,4, 1970 S, 1971 SA 1,2,3
Knox, D J (NSW, ACT) 1985 Fj 1,2, 1990 US (R), 1994 WS, NZ, 1996 It, S, I, 1997 SA 1, NZ 3, SA 2, Arg 1,2
Kraefft, D F (NSW) 1947 NZ 2, S, I, W, 1948 E, F
Kreutzer, S D (Q) 1914 NZ 2

Lamb, J S (NSW) 1928 NZ 1,2, M
Lambie, J K (NSW) 1974 NZ 1,2,3, 1975 W
Lane, R E (NSW) 1921 SA 1
Lane, T A (Q) 1985 C 1,2, NZ
Lang, C W P (V) 1938 NZ 2,3
Langford, J F (ACT) 1997 NZ 3, SA 2, E 2, S
Larkham, S J (ACT) 1996 W 2(R), 1997 F 1,2, NZ 1,2(R), SA 1, NZ 3, SA 2, Arg 1,2, E 2, S, 1998 E 1, S 1,2, NZ 1, SA 1, NZ 2, SA 2, NZ 3, Fj, Tg (t), WS, F, E 2, 1999 [I 3, US, W, SA 3, F], 2000 Arg 1,2, SA 1, NZ 1, SA 2, NZ 2, SA 3, 2001 BI 1,2, NZ 1, SA 2, NZ 2, Sp, E, F, W, 2002 F 1,2, NZ 1, SA 1, NZ 2, SA 2, Arg, I, E, 2003 SA 1(R), NZ 1, SA 2, NZ 2,[Arg,R,I,S,NZ,E], 2004S1,2,E1,PI,NZ1,SA1,NZ2,SA2,S3,F,S4, 2005 Sm(R),It,F1,SA1,2,3, 2006 E1,2,I1,NZ1,SA1,NZ2, SA2,NZ3,SA3,W,It,I2,S, 2007 W2,Fj,SA1,NZ1,SA2,NZ2, [J]
Larkin, E R (NSW) 1903 NZ
Larkin, K K (Q) 1958 M 2,3
Latham, C E (Q) 1998 F, E 2, 1999 I 1,2, E, [US], 2000 Arg 1,2, SA 1, NZ 1, SA 2, NZ 2, SA 3, F, S, E, 2001 BI 1,2(R), SA 1(R), NZ 1(R), SA 2, NZ 2, Sp, E, F, W (R), 2002 F 1,2, NZ 1, SA 1, NZ 2, SA 2, 2003 I, W, E, NZ 1(R), SA 2, NZ 2,[Nm], 2004 S1(R),2(R),E1(R),PI(t&R),NZ1,SA1,NZ2,SA2,S3,F,S4,E2, 2005 Sm,F1,SA2,3,F2,E,I,W, 2006 E1,2,I1,NZ1,SA1,NZ2,SA2,NZ3,SA3,W,It,I2,S, 2007 NZ2(R), [J,W,Fj,C,E]
Latimer, N B (NSW) 1957 NZ 2
Lawton, R (Q) 1988 E 1, NZ 2(R), 3, S
Lawton, T (NSW, Q) 1920 NZ 1,2, 1925 NZ 4, 1927 I, W, S, 1928 E, F, 1929 NZ 1,2,3, 1930 BI, 1932 NZ 1,2
Lawton, T A (Q) 1983 F 1(R), 2, 1984 Fj, NZ 1,2,3, E, I, W, S, 1985 C 1,2, NZ, Fj 1, 1986 It, F, Arg 1,2, NZ 1,2,3, 1987 SK, [E, US, I, F, W], NZ, Arg 1,2, 1988 E 1,2, NZ 1,2,3, E, S, It, 1989 BI 1,2,3
Laycock, W M B (NSW) 1925 NZ 2,3,4, 1926 NZ 2
Leeds, A J (NSW) 1986 NZ 3, 1987 [US, W], NZ, Arg 1,2, 1988 E 1,2, NZ 1,2,3, E, S, It
Lenehan, J K (NSW) 1958 W, E, S, F, M 1,2,3, 1959 BI 1,2, 1961 SA 1,2, F, 1962 NZ 2,3,4,5, 1965 SA 1,2, 1966 W, S, 1967 E, I 1, F, I 2
L'Estrange, R D (Q) 1971 F 1,2, 1972 NZ 1,2,3, 1973 Tg 1,2, W, E, 1974 NZ 1,2,3, 1975 S, W, 1976 I, US
Lewis, L S (Q) 1934 NZ 1,2, 1936 NZ 2, 1938 NZ 1
Lidbury, S (NSW) 1987 Arg 1, 1988 E 2
Lillicrap, C P (Q) 1985 Fj 2, 1987 [US, I, F, W], 1989 BI 1, 1991 [WS]
Lindsay, R T G (Q) 1932 NZ 3
Lisle, R J (NSW) 1961 Fj 1,2,3, SA 1
Little, J S (Q, NSW) 1989 F 1,2, 1990 F 1,2,3, US, 1991 W, E, NZ 1,2, [Arg, W, I, NZ, E], 1992 NZ 1,2,3, SA, I, W, 1993 Tg, NZ, SA 1,2,3, C, F 1,2, 1994 WS, NZ, 1995 Arg 1,2, [SA, C, E], NZ 1,2, 1996 It (R), I, W 3, 1997 F 1,2, E 1, NZ 2, SA 1, NZ 3, SA 2, 1998 E 1(R), S 2(R), NZ 2, SA 2(R), NZ 3, Fj, Tg, WS, F, E 2, 1999 I 1(R),2, SA 2(R), NZ 2, [R, I 3(t&R), US, W (R), SA 3(t&R), F (R)], 2000 Arg 1(R),2(R), SA 1(R), NZ 1, SA 2, NZ 2, SA 3
Livermore, A E (Q) 1946 NZ 1, M
Loane, M E (Q) 1973 Tg 1,2, 1974 NZ 1, 1975 E 1,2, J 1, 1976 E, I, Fj 1,2,3, F 1,2, 1978 W 1,2, 1979 I 1,2, NZ, Arg 1,2, 1981 F 1,2, I, W, S, 1982 E, S 1,2
Logan, D L (NSW) 1958 M 1
Loudon, D B (NSW) 1921 NZ, 1922 M 1,2,3
Loudon, R B (NSW) 1923 NZ 1(R), 2,3, 1928 NZ 1,2,3, M, 1929 NZ 2, 1933 SA 2,3,4,5, 1934 NZ 2
Love, E W (NSW) 1932 NZ 1,2,3
Lowth, D R (NSW) 1958 NZ 1
Lucas, B C (Q) 1905 NZ
Lucas, P W (NSW) 1982 NZ 1,2,3
Lutge, D (NSW) 1903 NZ, 1904 BI 1,2,3
Lynagh, M P (Q) 1984 Fj, E, I, W, S, 1985 C 1,2, NZ, 1986 It, F, Arg 1,2, NZ 1,2,3, 1987 [E, US, J, I, F, W], Arg 1,2, 1988 E 1,2, NZ 1,3(R), E, S, It, 1989 BI 1,2,3, NZ, F 1,2, 1990 F 1,2,3, US, NZ 1,2,3, 1991 W, E, NZ 1,2, [Arg, WS, W, I, NZ,

E], 1992 S 1,2, NZ 1,2,3, SA, I, 1993 Tg, C, F 1,2, 1994 I 1,2, It 1, 1995 Arg 1,2, [SA, C, E]
Lyons, D J (NSW) 2000 Arg 1(t&R),2(R), 2001 BI 1(R), SA 1(R), 2002 F 1(R),2, NZ 1(R), SA 1(R), NZ 2(R), SA 2(t+R), 2003 I, W, E, SA 1, [Arg,R,Nm,I,S,NZ,E], 2004 S1,2,E1,PI,NZ1,SA1, NZ2,SA2,S3(R),F(R),S4,E2, 2005 Sm,It,F1,SA1,2,NZ1,SA4, 2006 S, 2007 Fj,SA2(R), [C]

McArthur, M (NSW) 1909 E
McBain, M I (Q) 1983 It, F 1, 1985 Fj 2, 1986 It (R), 1987 [J], 1988 E 2(R), 1989 BI 1(R)
MacBride, J W T (NSW) 1946 NZ 1, M, NZ 2, 1947 NZ 1,2, S, I, W, 1948 E, F
McCabe, A J M (NSW) 1909 E
McCall, R J (Q) 1989 F 1,2, 1990 F 1,2,3, US, NZ 1,2,3, 1991 W, E, NZ 1,2, [Arg, W, I, NZ, E], 1992 S 1,2, NZ 1,2,3, SA, I, W, 1993 Tg, NZ, SA 1,2,3, C, F 1,2, 1994 It 2, 1995 Arg 1,2, [SA, R, E]
McCarthy, F J C (Q) 1950 BI 1
McCowan, R H (Q) 1899 BI 1,2,4
McCue, P A (NSW) 1907 NZ 1,3, 1908 W, 1909 E
McDermott, L C (Q) 1962 NZ 1,2
McDonald, B S (NSW) 1969 SA 4, 1970 S
McDonald, J C (Q) 1938 NZ 2,3
Macdougall, D G (NSW) 1961 Fj 1, SA 1
Macdougall, S G (NSW, ACT) 1971 SA 3, 1973 E, 1974 NZ 1,2,3, 1975 E 1,2, 1976 E
McGhie, G H (Q) 1929 NZ 2,3, 1930 BI
McGill, A N (NSW) 1968 NZ 1,2, F, 1969 W, SA 1,2,3,4, 1970 S, 1971 SA 1,2,3, F 1,2, 1972 F 1,2, NZ 1,2,3, 1973 Tg 1,2
McIntyre, A J (Q) 1982 NZ 1,2,3, 1983 F 1,2, 1984 Fj, NZ 1,2,3, E, I, W, S, 1985 C 1,2, NZ, Fj 1,2, 1986 It, F, Arg 1,2, 1987 [E, US, I, F, W], NZ, Arg 2, 1988 E 1,2, NZ 1,2,3, E, S, It, 1989 NZ
McIsaac, T P (WF) 2006 E1,I1,NZ1,2(R),SA2,3(R),W,I2
McKay, G R (NSW) 1920 NZ 2, 1921 SA 2,3, 1922 M 1,2,3
MacKay, L J (NSW) 2005 NZ2(R)
McKenzie, E J A (NSW, ACT) 1990 F 1,2,3, US, NZ 1,2,3, 1991 W, E, NZ 1,2, [Arg, W, I, NZ, E], 1992 S 1,2, NZ 1,2,3, SA, I, W, 1993 Tg, NZ, SA 1,2,3, C, F 1,2, 1994 I 1,2, It 1,2, WS, NZ, 1995 Arg 1,2, [SA, C (R), R, E], NZ 2, 1996 W 1,2, 1997 F 1,2, NZ 1, E 1
McKid, W A (NSW) 1976 E, Fj 1, 1978 NZ 2,3, 1979 I 1,2
McKinnon, A (Q) 1904 BI 2
McKivat, C H (NSW) 1907 NZ 1,3, 1908 W, 1909 E
McLaren, S D (NSW) 1926 NZ 4
McLaughlin, R E M (NSW) 1936 NZ 1,2
McLean, A D (Q) 1933 SA 1,2,3,4,5, 1934 NZ 1,2, 1936 NZ 1,2, M
McLean, J D (Q) 1904 BI 2,3, 1905 NZ
McLean, J J (Q) 1971 SA 2,3, F 1,2, 1972 F 1,2, NZ 1,2,3, Fj, 1973 W, E, 1974 NZ 1
McLean, P E (Q) 1974 NZ 1,2,3, 1975 J 1,2, S, W, 1976 E, I, Fj 1,2,3, F 1,2, 1978 W 1,2, NZ 2, 1979 I 1,2, NZ, Arg 1,2, 1980 Fj, 1981 F 1,2, I, W, S, 1982 E, S 2
McLean, P W (Q) 1978 NZ 1,2,3, 1979 I 1,2, NZ, Arg 1,2, 1980 Fj (R), NZ 3, 1981 I, W, S, 1982 E, S 1,2
McLean, R A (NSW) 1971 SA 1,2,3, F 1,2
McLean, W M (Q) 1946 NZ 1, M, NZ 2, 1947 NZ 1,2
McMahon, M J (Q) 1913 NZ 1
McMaster, R E (Q) 1946 NZ 1, M, NZ 2, 1947 NZ 1,2, I, W
McMeniman, H J (Q) 2005 Sm(R),It(R),F2(R),E,I,W, 2007 SA2(R),NZ2(R), [J(R),Fj(R),C,E(t&R)], 2008 F2(R),SA1(t&R),NZ2(R),SA3,NZ3(R)
MacMillan, D I (Q) 1950 BI 1,2
McMullen, K V (NSW) 1962 NZ 3,5, 1963 E, SA 1
McShane, J M S (NSW) 1937 SA 1,2
Mackay, G (NSW) 1926 NZ 4
Mackney, W A R (NSW) 1933 SA 1,5, 1934 NZ 1,2
Magrath, E (NSW) 1961 Fj 1, SA 2, F
Maguire, D J (Q) 1989 BI 1,2,3
Malcolm, S J (NSW) 1927 S, 1928 E, F, NZ 1,2, M, 1929 NZ 1,2,3, 1930 BI, 1931 NZ, 1932 NZ 1,2,3, 1933 SA 4,5, 1934 NZ 1,2
Malone, J H (NSW) 1936 NZ 1,2, M, 1937 SA 2
Malouf, B P (NSW) 1982 NZ 1
Mandible, E F (NSW) 1907 NZ 2,3, 1908 W
Manning, J (NSW) 1904 BI 2
Manning, R C S (Q) 1967 NZ
Mansfield, B W (NSW) 1975 J 2
Manu, D T (NSW) 1995 [R (t)], NZ 1,2, 1996 W 1,2(R), SA 1, NZ 2, It, S, I, 1997 F 1, NZ 1(t), E 1, NZ 2, SA 1
Marks, H (NSW) 1899 BI 1,2
Marks, R J P (Q) 1962 NZ 4,5, 1963 E, SA 2,3,4, 1964 NZ 1,2,3, 1965 SA 1,2, 1966 W, S, 1967 E, I 1, F, I 2
Marrott, R (NSW) 1920 NZ 1,3
Marrott, W J (NSW) 1922 NZ 2,3, 1923 M 1,2,3, NZ 1,2
Marshall, J S (NSW) 1949 M 1
Martin, G J (Q) 1989 BI 1,2,3, NZ, F 1,2, 1990 F 1,3(R), NZ 1
Martin, M C (NSW) 1980 Fj, NZ 1,2, 1981 F 1,2, W (R)
Massey-Westropp, M (NSW) 1914 NZ 3
Mathers, M J (NSW) 1980 Fj, NZ 2(R)
Maund, J W (NSW) 1903 NZ
Mayne, A V (NSW) 1920 NZ 1,2,3, 1922 M 1
Meadows, J E C (V, Q) 1974 NZ 1, 1975 S, W, 1976 I, US, Fj 1,3, F 1,2, 1978 NZ 1,2,3, 1979 I 1,2, 1981 I, S, 1982 E, NZ 2,3, 1983 US, Arg 2, NZ
Meadows, R W (NSW) 1958 M 1,2,3, NZ 1,2,3
Meagher, F W (NSW) 1923 NZ 3, 1924 NZ 3, 1925 NZ 4, 1926 NZ 1,2,3, 1927 I, W
Meibusch, J H (Q) 1904 BI 3
Meibusch, L S (Q) 1912 US
Melrose, T C (NSW) 1978 NZ 3, 1979 I 1,2, NZ, Arg 1,2
Merrick, S (NSW) 1995 NZ 1,2
Messenger, H H (NSW) 1907 NZ 2,3
Middleton, S A (NSW) 1909 E, 1910 NZ 1,2,3
Miller, A R (NSW) 1952 Fj 1,2, NZ 1,2, 1953 SA 1,2,3,4, 1954 Fj 1,2, 1955 NZ 1,2,3, 1956 SA 1,2, 1957 NZ 1,2, 1958 W, E, S, F, M 1,2,3, 1959 BI 1,2, 1961 Fj 1,2,3, SA 2, F, 1962 NZ 1,2, 1966 BI 1,2, W, S, 1967 I 1, F, I 2, NZ
Miller, J M (NSW) 1962 NZ 1, 1963 E, SA 1, 1966 W, S, 1967 E
Miller, J S (Q) 1986 NZ 2,3, 1987 SK, [US, I, F], NZ, Arg 1,2, 1988 E 1,2, NZ 2,3, E, S, It, 1989 BI 1,2,3, NZ, 1990 F 1,3, 1991 W, [WS, W, I]
Miller, S W J (NSW) 1899 BI 3
Mingey, N (NSW) 1920 NZ 3, 1921 SA 1,2,3, 1923 M 1, NZ 1,2
Mitchell, D A (Q, WF) 2005 SA1(R),2(R),3(R),NZ1,SA4,NZ2, F2(R),E,I,W, 2007 W1,2,Fj,SA1,2(R),NZ2, [J(R),W,Fj,C,E(R)], 2008 SA1(R),NZ2(R),SA2,3(R)
Monaghan, L E (NSW) 1973 E, 1974 NZ 1,2,3, 1975 E 1,2, S, W, 1976 E, I, US, F 1, 1978 W 1,2, NZ 1, 1979 I 1,2
Monti, C I A (Q) 1938 NZ 2
Moon, B J (Q) 1978 NZ 2,3, 1979 I 1,2, NZ, Arg 1,2, 1980 Fj, NZ 1,2,3, 1981 F 1,2, I, W, S, 1982 E, S 1,2, 1983 US, Arg 1,2, NZ, It, F 1,2, 1984 Fj, NZ 1,2,3, E, 1986 It, F, Arg 1,2
Mooney, T P (Q) 1954 Fj 1,2
Moore, R C (ACT, NSW) 1999 [US], 2001 BI 2,3, SA 1, NZ 1, SA 2, NZ 2, Sp (R), E (R), F (R), W (R), 2002 F 1(R),2(R), SA 2(R)
Moore, S T (Q) 2005 Sm(R),It(R),F1(R),SA2(R),3(R),F2(t&R), 2006 It(t),I2(R),S, 2007 W1,2,Fj(R),SA1,NZ1,2, [J,W,Fj,E], 2008 I,F1,2,SA1,NZ1,2,SA2,3(R),NZ3
Moran, H M (NSW) 1908 W
Morgan, G (Q) 1992 NZ 1(R), 3(R), W, 1993 Tg, NZ, SA 1,2,3, C, F 1,2, 1994 I 1,2, It 1, WS, NZ, 1996 W 1,2, C, NZ 1, SA 1, NZ 2, 1997 E 1, NZ 2
Morrissey, C V (NSW) 1925 NZ 2,3,4, 1926 NZ 2,3
Morrissey, W (Q) 1914 NZ 2
Mortlock, S A (ACT) 2000 Arg 1,2, SA 1, NZ 1, SA 2, NZ 2, SA 3, F, S, E, 2002 F 1,2, NZ 1, SA 1, NZ 2, SA 2, Arg, I, E, It, 2003 [R(R),Nm,S,NZ,E], 2004 S2,E1,PI,NZ1,SA1,NZ2, SA2,S3,F,S4, 2005 Sm,It,F1,SA2,3(R),NZ1, 2006 E1,2,I1,NZ1,SA1,NZ2,SA2,NZ3,SA3,It,I2,S, 2007 W1,2,Fj(R),SA1,NZ1,SA2,NZ2, [J,W,E], 2008 I,F1,2,SA1,NZ2,SA2,3,NZ3
Morton, A R (NSW) 1957 NZ 1,2, 1958 F, M 1,2,3, NZ 1,2,3, 1959 BI 1,2
Mossop, R P (NSW) 1949 NZ 1,2, 1950 BI 1,2, 1951 NZ 1
Moutray, I E (NSW) 1963 SA 2
Mulligan, P J (NSW) 1925 NZ 1(R)
Mumm, D W (NSW) 2008 I(t&R),F1(R),2,SA2(R),3(R)
Munsie, A (NSW) 1928 NZ 2
Murdoch, A R (NSW) 1993 F 1, 1996 W 1
Murphy, P J (Q) 1910 NZ 1,2,3, 1913 NZ 1,2,3, 1914 NZ 1,2,3
Murphy, W (Q) 1912 US

Nasser, B P (Q) 1989 F 1,2, 1990 F 1,2,3, US, NZ 2, 1991 [WS]
Newman, E W (NSW) 1922 NZ 1
Nicholson, F C (Q) 1904 BI 3
Nicholson, F V (Q) 1903 NZ, 1904 BI 1
Niuqila, A S (NSW) 1988 S, It, 1989 BI 1

Noriega, E P (ACT, NSW) 1998 F, E 2, 1999 I 1,2, E, SA 1, NZ 1, SA 2(R), NZ 2(R), 2002 F 1,2, NZ 1, SA 1, NZ 2, Arg, I, E, It, 2003 I, W, E, SA 1, NZ 1, SA 2
Norton-Knight, S H (NSW) 2007 W1,Fj(R)
Nothling, O E (NSW) 1921 SA 1,2,3, NZ, 1922 M 1,2,3, NZ 1,2,3, 1923 M 1,2,3, NZ 1,2,3, 1924 NZ 1,2,3
Nucifora, D V (Q) 1991 [Arg (R)], 1993 C (R)

O'Brien, F W H (NSW) 1937 SA 2, 1938 NZ 3
O'Connor, J A (NSW) 1928 NZ 1,2,3, M
O'Connor, M (ACT) 1994 I 1
O'Connor, M D (ACT, Q) 1979 Arg 1,2, 1980 Fj, NZ 1,2,3, 1981 F 1,2, I, 1982 E, S 1,2
O'Donnell, C (NSW) 1913 NZ 1,2
O'Donnell, I C (NSW) 1899 BI 3,4
O'Donnell, J B (NSW) 1928 NZ 1,3, M
O'Donnell, J M (NSW) 1899 BI 4
O'Gorman, J F (NSW) 1961 Fj 1, SA 1,2, F, 1962 NZ 2, 1963 E, SA 1,2,3,4, 1965 SA 1,2, 1966 W, S, 1967 E, I 1, F, I 2
O'Neill, D J (Q) 1964 NZ 1,2
O'Neill, J M (Q) 1952 NZ 1,2, 1956 SA 1,2
Ofahengaue, V (NSW) 1990 NZ 1,2,3, 1991 W, E, NZ 1,2, [Arg, W, I, NZ, E], 1992 S 1,2, SA, I, W, 1994 WS, NZ, 1995 Arg 1,2(R), [SA, C, E], NZ 1,2, 1997 Arg 1(t + R), 2(R), E 2, S, 1998 E 1(R), S 1(R),2(R), NZ 1(R), SA 1(R), NZ 2(R), SA 2(R), NZ 3(R), Fj, WS, F (R)
Ormiston, I W L (NSW) 1920 NZ 1,2,3
Osborne, D H (V) 1975 E 1,2, J 1
Outterside, R (NSW) 1959 BI 1,2
Oxenham, A McE (Q) 1904 BI 2, 1907 NZ 2
Oxlade, A M (Q) 1904 BI 2,3, 1905 NZ, 1907 NZ 2
Oxlade, B D (Q) 1938 NZ 1,2,3

Palfreyman, J R L (NSW) 1929 NZ 1, 1930 BI, 1931 NZ, 1932 NZ 3
Palu, W L (NSW) 2006 E2(t&R),I1(R),SA2,NZ3,SA3,W,It,I2,S(R), 2007 W1,2,SA1,NZ1, [J,W,Fj,E], 2008 I,F1,SA1,NZ1,2, SA2,3,NZ3
Panoho, G M (Q) 1998 SA 2(R), NZ 3(R), Fj (R), Tg, WS (R), 1999 I 2, E, SA 1(R), NZ 1, 2000 Arg 1(R),2(R), SA 1(R), NZ 1(R), SA 2(R),3(R), F (R), S (R), E (R), 2001 BI 1, 2003 SA 2(R), NZ 2
Papworth, B (NSW) 1985 Fj 1,2, 1986 It, Arg 1,2, NZ 1,2,3, 1987 [E, US, J (R), I, F], NZ, Arg 1,2
Parker, A J (Q) 1983 Arg 1(R), 2, NZ
Parkinson, C E (Q) 1907 NZ 2
Pashley, J J (NSW) 1954 Fj 1,2, 1958 M 1,2,3
Paul, J A (ACT) 1998 S 1(R), NZ 1(R), SA 1(t), Fj (R), Tg, 1999 I 1,2, E, SA 1, NZ 1, [R (R), I 3(R), W (t), F (R)], 2000 Arg 1(R),2(R), SA 1(R), NZ 1(R), SA 2(R), NZ 2(R), SA 3(R), F (R), S (R), E (R), 2001 BI 1, 2002 F 1, NZ 1, SA 1, NZ 2, SA 2, Arg, E, 2003 I, W, E, SA 2(t&R), NZ2(R),[Arg(R),R(R),Nm, I(R),S(R),NZ(R),E(R)], 2004 S1(R),2(R),E1(R),PI(R),NZ1(t&R), SA1,NZ2(R),SA2(R),S3,F,S4,E2, 2005 Sm,It,F1,SA1,2,3, NZ1,2006 E1(R),2(R),I1(R),NZ1(R),SA1,NZ2,SA2(R),NZ3,SA3
Pauling, T P (NSW) 1936 NZ 1, 1937 SA 1
Payne, S J (NSW) 1996 W 2, C, NZ 1, S, 1997 F 1(t), NZ 2(R), Arg 2(t)
Pearse, G K (NSW) 1975 W (R), 1976 I, US, Fj 1,2,3, 1978 NZ 1,2,3
Penman, A P (NSW) 1905 NZ
Perrin, P D (Q) 1962 NZ 1
Perrin, T D (NSW) 1931 M, NZ
Phelps, R (NSW) 1955 NZ 2,3, 1956 SA 1,2, 1957 NZ 1,2, 1958 W, I, E, S, F, M 1, NZ 1,2,3, 1961 Fj 1,2,3, SA 1,2, F, 1962 NZ 1,2
Phipps, J A (NSW) 1953 SA 1,2,3,4, 1954 Fj 1,2, 1955 NZ 1,2,3, 1956 SA 1,2
Phipps, W J (NSW) 1928 NZ 2
Piggott, H R (NSW) 1922 M 3(R)
Pilecki, S J (Q) 1978 W 1,2, NZ 1,2, 1979 I 1,2, NZ, Arg 1,2, 1980 Fj, NZ 1,2, 1982 S 1,2, 1983 US, Arg 1,2, NZ
Pini, M (Q) 1994 I 1, It 2, WS, NZ, 1995 Arg 1,2, [SA, R (t)]
Piper, B J C (NSW) 1946 NZ 1, M, NZ 2, 1947 NZ 1, S, I, W, 1948 E, F, 1949 M, 1,2,3
Poidevin, S P (NSW) 1980 Fj, NZ 1,2,3, 1981 F 1,2, I, W, S, 1982 E, NZ 1,2,3, 1983 US, Arg 1,2, NZ, It, F 1,2, 1984 Fj, NZ 1,2,3, E, I, W, S, 1985 C 1,2, NZ, Fj 1,2, 1986 It, F, Arg 1,2, NZ 1,2,3, 1987 SK, [E, J, I, F, W], Arg 1, 1988 NZ 1,2,3, 1989 NZ, 1991 E, NZ 1,2, [Arg, W, I, NZ, E]
Polota-Nau, T (NSW) 2005 E(R),I(R), 2006 S(R), 2008 SA1(R),NZ1(R),2(R),SA2(R),3
Pope, A M (Q) 1968 NZ 2(R)
Potter, R T (Q) 1961 Fj 2
Potts, J M (NSW) 1957 NZ 1,2, 1958 W, I, 1959 BI 1
Prentice, C W (NSW) 1914 NZ 3
Prentice, W S (NSW) 1908 W, 1909 E, 1910 NZ 1,2,3, 1912 US
Price, R A (NSW) 1974 NZ 1,2,3, 1975 E 1,2, J 1,2, 1976 US
Primmer, C J (Q) 1951 NZ 1,3
Proctor, I J (NSW)) 1967 NZ
Prosser, R B (NSW) 1967 E, I 1,2, NZ, 1968 NZ 1,2, F, I, S, 1969 W, SA 1,2,3,4, 1971 SA 1,2,3, F 1,2, 1972 F 1,2, NZ 1,2,3, Fj
Pugh, G H (NSW) 1912 US
Purcell, M P (Q) 1966 W, S, 1967 I 2
Purkis, E M (NSW) 1958 S, M 1
Pym, J E (NSW) 1923 M 1

Rainbow, A E (NSW) 1925 NZ 1
Ramalli, C (NSW) 1938 NZ 2,3
Ramsay, K M (NSW) 1936 M, 1937 SA 1, 1938 NZ 1,3
Rankin, R (NSW) 1936 NZ 1,2, M, 1937 SA 1,2, 1938 NZ 1,2
Rathbone, C (ACT) 2004 S1,2(R),E1,PI,NZ1,SA1,NZ2, SA2,S3,F,S4, 2005 Sm,NZ1(R),SA4,NZ2, 2006E1(R),2(R), I1(R),SA1(R),NZ2(R),SA2(R),NZ3,SA3,W,It,I2
Rathie, D S (Q) 1972 F 1,2
Raymond, R L (NSW) 1920 NZ 1,2, 1921 SA 2,3, NZ, 1922 M 1,2,3, NZ 1,2,3, 1923 M 1,2
Redwood, C (Q) 1903 NZ, 1904 BI 1,2,3
Reid, E J (NSW) 1925 NZ 2,3,4
Reid, T W (NSW) 1961 Fj 1,2,3, SA 1, 1962 NZ 1
Reilly, N P (Q) 1968 NZ 1,2, F, I, S, 1969 W, SA 1,2,3,4
Reynolds, L J (NSW) 1910 NZ 2(R), 3
Reynolds, R J (NSW) 1984 Fj, NZ 1,2,3, 1985 Fj 1,2, 1986 Arg 1,2, NZ 1, 1987 [J]
Richards, E W (Q) 1904 BI 1,3, 1905 NZ, 1907 NZ 1(R), 2
Richards, G (NSW) 1978 NZ 2(R), 3, 1981 F 1
Richards, T J (Q) 1908 W, 1909 E, 1912 US
Richards, V S (NSW) 1936 NZ 1,2(R), M, 1937 SA 1, 1938 NZ 1
Richardson, G C (Q) 1971 SA 1,2,3, 1972 NZ 2,3, Fj, 1973 Tg 1,2, W
Rigney, W A (NSW) 1925 NZ 2,4, 1926 NZ 4
Riley, S A (NSW) 1903 NZ
Ritchie, E V (NSW) 1924 NZ 1,3, 1925 NZ 2,3
Roberts, B T (NSW) 1956 SA 2
Roberts, H F (Q) 1961 Fj 1,3, SA 2, F
Robertson, I J (NSW) 1975 J 1,2
Robinson, B A (NSW) 2006 SA3,I2(R),S, 2007 W1(R),2,Fj(R), 2008 I,F1,2,SA1,NZ1,2,SA2,3,NZ3
Robinson, B J (ACT) 1996 It (R), S (R), I (R), 1997 F 1,2, NZ 1, E 1, NZ 2, SA 1(R), NZ 3(R), SA 2(R), Arg 1,2, E 2, S, 1998 Tg
Roche, C (Q) 1982 S 1,2, NZ 1,2,3, 1983 US, Arg 1,2, NZ, It, F 1,2, 1984 Fj, NZ 1,2,3, I
Rodriguez, E E (NSW) 1984 Fj, NZ 1,2,3, E, I, W, S, 1985 C 1,2, NZ, Fj 1, 1986 It, F, Arg 1,2, NZ 1,2,3, 1987 SK, [E, J, W (R)], NZ, Arg 1,2Roe, J A (Q) 2003 [Nm(R)], 2004 E1(R), SA1(R),NZ2(R),SA2(t&R),S3,F, 2005 Sm(R),It(R),F1(R),SA1(R),3, NZ1,SA4(t&R),NZ2(R),F2(R),E,I,W
Roebuck, M C (NSW) 1991 W, E, NZ 1,2, [Arg, WS, W, I, NZ, E], 1992 S 1,2, NZ 2,3, SA, I, W, 1993 Tg, SA 1,2,3, C, F 2
Roff, J W (ACT) 1995 [C, R], NZ 1,2, 1996 W 1,2, NZ 1, SA 1, NZ 2, SA 2(R), S, I, W 3, 1997 F 1,2, NZ 1, E 1, NZ 2, SA 1, NZ 3, SA 2, Arg 1,2, E 2, S, 1998 E 1, S 1,2, NZ 1, SA 1, NZ 2, SA 2, NZ 3, Fj, Tg, WS, F, E 2, 1999 I 1,2, E, SA 1, NZ 1, SA 2, NZ 2(R), [R (R), I 3, US (R), W, SA 3, F], 2000 Arg 1,2, SA 1, NZ 1, SA 2, NZ 2, SA 3, F, S, E, 2001 BI 1,2,3, SA 1, NZ 1, SA 2, NZ 2, Sp, E, F, W, 2003 I, W, E, SA 1, [Arg,R,I,S(R),NZ(t&R),E(R)], 2004 S1,2,E1,PI
Rogers, M S (NSW) 2002 F 1(R),2(R), NZ 1(R), SA 1(R), NZ 2(R), SA 2(t&R), Arg, 2003 E (R), SA 1, NZ 1, SA 2, NZ 2, [Arg,R,Nm,I,S,NZ,E],2004S3(R),F(R),S4(R),E2(R), 2005 Sm(R),It,F1(R),SA1,4,NZ2,F2,E,I,W, 2006 E1,2,I1,NZ1,SA1(R), NZ2(R),SA2(R),NZ3(R),W,It,I2(R),S(R)
Rose, H A (NSW), 1967 I 2, NZ, 1968 NZ 1,2, F, I, S, 1969 W, SA 1,2,3,4, 1970 S
Rosenblum, M E (NSW) 1928 NZ 1,2,3, M
Rosenblum, R G (NSW) 1969 SA 1,3, 1970 S
Rosewell, J S H (NSW) 1907 NZ 1,3
Ross, A W (NSW) 1925 NZ 1,2,3, 1926 NZ 1,2,3, 1927 I, W, S, 1928 E, F, 1929 NZ 1, 1930 BI, 1931 M, NZ, 1932 NZ 2,3, 1933 SA 5, 1934 NZ 1,2

Ross, W S (Q) 1979 I 1,2, Arg 2, 1980 Fj, NZ 1,2,3, 1982 S 1,2, 1983 US, Arg 1,2, NZ
Rothwell, P R (NSW) 1951 NZ 1,2,3, 1952 Fj 1
Row, F L (NSW) 1899 BI 1,3,4
Row, N E (NSW) 1907 NZ 1,3, 1909 E, 1910 NZ 1,2,3
Rowles, P G (NSW) 1972 Fj, 1973 E
Roxburgh, J R (NSW) 1968 NZ 1,2, F, 1969 W, SA 1,2,3,4, 1970 S
Ruebner, G (NSW) 1966 BI 1,2
Russell, C J (NSW) 1907 NZ 1,2,3, 1908 W, 1909 E
Ryan, J R (NSW) 1975 J 2, 1976 I, US, Fj 1,2,3
Ryan, K J (Q) 1958 E, M 1, NZ 1,2,3
Ryan, P F (NSW) 1963 E, SA 1, 1966 BI 1,2
Rylance, M H (NSW) 1926 NZ 4(R)

Sailor, W J (Q) 2002 F 1,2, Arg (R), I, E, It, 2003 I, W, E, SA 1, NZ 1, SA 2, NZ 2, [Arg,R,I,S,NZ,E], 2004 S1,2,NZ1(R),2(R),SA2(R),S3(R),F(R),S4(R),E2, 2005 Sm,It,F1,SA1,2,3,F2,I(R),W(R)
Samo, R U (ACT) 2004 S1,2,E1,PI,NZ1,S4(R)
Sampson, J H (NSW) 1899 BI 4
Sayle, J L (NSW) 1967 NZ
Schulte, B G (Q) 1946 NZ 1, M
Scott, P R I (NSW) 1962 NZ 1,2
Scott-Young, S J (Q) 1990 F 2,3(R), US, NZ 3, 1992 NZ 1,2,3
Shambrook, G G (Q) 1976 Fj 2,3
Sharpe, N C (Q, WF) 2002 F 1,2, NZ 1, SA 1, NZ 2, SA 2, 2003 I, W, E, SA 1(R), NZ 1(R), SA 2(R), NZ 2(R),[Arg,R,Nm,I,S,NZ,E], 2004 S1,2,E1,PI,NZ1,SA1,NZ2,SA2, 2005 Sm,It,F1,SA1,2,3,NZ1,SA4,NZ2,F2,E,I,W, 2006 E1,2,I1,NZ1,SA1,NZ2,SA2,NZ3,SA3,W,It,I2,S, 2007 W1,2,SA1,NZ1,SA2,NZ2, [J,W,C,E], 2008 I,F1,SA1,NZ1,2,3
Shaw, A A (Q) 1973 W, E, 1975 E 1,2, J 2, S, W, 1976 E, I, US, Fj 1,2,3, F 1,2, 1978 W 1,2, NZ 1,2,3, 1979 I 1,2, NZ, Arg 1,2, 1980 Fj, NZ 1,2,3, 1981 F 1,2, I, W, S, 1982 S 1,2
Shaw, C (NSW) 1925 NZ 2,3,4(R)
Shaw, G A (NSW) 1969 W, SA 1(R), 1970 S, 1971 SA 1,2,3, F 1,2, 1973 W, E, 1974 NZ 1,2,3, 1975 E 1,2, J 1,2, W, 1976 E, I, US, Fj 1,2,3, F 1,2, 1979 NZ
Sheehan, B R (ACT) 2006 SA3(R), 2008 SA2(R),3(R)
Sheehan, W B J (NSW) 1921 SA 1,2,3, 1922 NZ 1,2,3, 1923 M 1,2, NZ 1,2,3, 1924 NZ 1,2, 1926 NZ 1,2,3, 1927 W, S
Shehadie, N M (NSW) 1947 NZ 2, 1948 E, F, 1949 M 1,2,3, NZ 1,2, 1950 BI 1,2, 1951 NZ 1,2,3, 1952 Fj 1,2, NZ 2, 1953 SA 1,2,3,4, 1954 Fj 1,2, 1955 NZ 1,2,3, 1956 SA 1,2, 1957 NZ 2, 1958 W, I
Sheil, A G R (Q) 1956 SA 1
Shepherd, C B (WF) 2006 E1(R),2(R),I1(R),SA3,W, 2007 [C], 2008 I,F1,2(R)
Shepherd, D J (V) 1964 NZ 3, 1965 SA 1,2, 1966 BI 1,2
Shepherdson, G T (ACT) 2006 I1,NZ1,SA1,NZ2(R), SA2(R),It,I2,S, 2007 W1,2,SA1,NZ1,SA2,NZ2, [J(R),W,Fj,E]
Shute, J L (NSW) 1920 NZ 3, 1922 M 2,3
Simpson, R J (NSW) 1913 NZ 2
Skinner, A J (NSW) 1969 W, SA 4, 1970 S
Slack, A G (Q) 1978 W 1,2, NZ 1,2, 1979 NZ, Arg 1,2, 1980 Fj, 1981 I, W, S, 1982 E, S 1, NZ 3, 1983 US, Arg 1,2 NZ, It, 1984 Fj, NZ 1,2,3, E, I, W, S, 1986 It, F, NZ 1,2,3, 1987 SK, [E, US, J, I, F, W]
Slater, S H (NSW) 1910 NZ 3
Slattery, P J (Q) 1990 US (R), 1991 W (R), E (R), [WS (R), W, I (R)], 1992 I, W, 1993 Tg, C, F 1,2, 1994 I 1,2, It 1(R), 1995 [C, R (R)]
Smairl, A M (NSW) 1928 NZ 1,2,3
Smith, B A (Q) 1987 SK, [US, J, I (R), W], Arg 1
Smith, D P (Q) 1993 SA 1,2,3, C, F 2, 1994 I 1,2, It 1,2, WS, NZ, 1995 Arg 1,2, [SA, R, E], NZ 1,2, 1998 SA 1(R), NZ 3(R), Fj
Smith, F B (NSW) 1905 NZ, 1907 NZ 1,2,3
Smith, G B (ACT) 2000 F, S, E, 2001 BI 1,2,3, SA 1, NZ 1, SA 2, NZ 2, Sp, E, F (R), W (R), 2002 F 1,2, NZ 1, SA 1, NZ 2, SA 2, Arg, I, E, It, 2003 I, NZ 1, SA 2, NZ 2, [Arg,R,Nm,I,S,NZ,E], 2004 S1,2(R),E1(t&R),PI(R),NZ1(R),SA1,NZ2,SA2,S3,F,S4,E2, 2005 Sm,It,F1,SA1,2,3,NZ1,SA4(R),NZ2,F2,E,I,W, 2006 E1,2,I1,NZ1,SA1,NZ2,SA2,NZ3(t),SA3(R),It,I2(R),S, 2007 W1(R),2,Fj(R),SA1,NZ1,SA2,NZ2, [J,W,C,E], 2008 I,F1,2(R),SA1,NZ1,2,SA2,3(R),NZ3
Smith, L M (NSW) 1905 NZ
Smith, N C (NSW) 1922 NZ 2,3, 1923 NZ 1, 1924 NZ 1,3(R), 1925 NZ 2,3
Smith, P V (NSW) 1967 NZ, 1968 NZ 1,2, F, I, S, 1969 W, SA 1
Smith, R A (NSW) 1971 SA 1,2, 1972 F 1,2, NZ 1,2(R), 3, Fj, 1975 E 1,2, J 1,2, S, W, 1976 E, I, US, Fj 1,2,3, F 1,2
Smith, T S (NSW) 1921 SA 1,2,3, NZ, 1922 M 2,3, NZ 1,2,3, 1925 NZ 1,3,4
Snell, H W (NSW) 1925 NZ 2,3, 1928 NZ 3
Solomon, H J (NSW) 1949 M 3, NZ 2, 1950 BI 1,2, 1951 NZ 1,2, 1952 Fj 1,2, NZ 1,2, 1953 SA 1,2,3, 1955 NZ 1
Spooner, N R (Q) 1999 I 1,2
Spragg, S A (NSW) 1899 BI 1,2,3,4
Staniforth, S N G (NSW,WF) 1999 [US], 2002 I, It, 2006 SA3(R),I2(R),S, 2007 Fj,NZ1(R),SA2(R),NZ2(R), [W(R),Fj(R)]
Stanley, R G (NSW) 1921 NZ, 1922 M 1,2,3, NZ 1,2,3, 1923 M 2,3, NZ 1,2,3, 1924 NZ 1,3
Stapleton, E T (NSW) 1951 NZ 1,2,3, 1952 Fj 1,2, NZ 1,2, 1953 SA 1,2,3,4, 1954 Fj 1, 1955 NZ 1,2,3, 1958 NZ 1
Steggall, J C (Q) 1931 M, NZ, 1932 NZ 1,2,3, 1933 SA 1,2,3,4,5
Stegman, T R (NSW) 1973 Tg 1,2
Stephens, O G (NSW) 1973 Tg 1,2, W, 1974 NZ 2,3
Stewart, A A (NSW) 1979 NZ, Arg 1,2
Stiles, N B (Q) 2001 BI 1,2,3, SA 1, NZ 1, SA 2, NZ 2, Sp, E, F, W, 2002 I
Stone, A H (NSW) 1937 SA 2, 1938 NZ 2,3
Stone, C G (NSW) 1938 NZ 1
Stone, J M (NSW) 1946 M, NZ 2
Storey, G P (NSW) 1926 NZ 4, 1927 I, W, S, 1928 E, F, 1929 NZ 3(R), 1930 BI
Storey, K P (NSW) 1936 NZ 2
Storey, N J D (NSW) 1962 NZ 1
Strachan, D J (NSW) 1955 NZ 2,3
Strauss, C P (NSW) 1999 I 1(R),2(R), E (R), SA 1(R), NZ 1, SA 2(R), NZ 2(R), [R (R), I 3(R), US, W]
Street, N O (NSW) 1899 BI 2
Streeter, S F (NSW) 1978 NZ 1
Stuart, R (NSW) 1910 NZ 2,3
Stumbles, B D (NSW) 1972 NZ 1(R), 2,3, Fj
Sturtridge, G S (V) 1929 NZ 2, 1932 NZ 1,2,3, 1933 SA 1,2,3,4,5
Sullivan, P D (NSW) 1971 SA 1,2,3, F 1,2, 1972 F 1,2, NZ 1,2, Fj, 1973 Tg 1,2, W
Summons, A J (NSW) 1958 W, I, E, S, M 2, NZ 1,2,3, 1959 BI 1,2
Suttor, D C (NSW) 1913 NZ 1,2,3
Swannell, B I (NSW) 1905 NZ
Sweeney, T L (Q) 1953 SA 1

Taafe, B S (NSW) 1969 SA 1, 1972 F 1,2
Tabua, I (Q) 1993 SA 2,3, C, F 1, 1994 I 1,2, It 1,2, 1995 [C, R]
Tahu, T (NSW) 2008 NZ1(R),SA2(R),3
Tancred, A J (NSW) 1927 I, W, S
Tancred, H E (NSW) 1923 M 1,2
Tancred, J L (NSW) 1926 NZ 3,4, 1928 F
Tanner, W H (Q) 1899 BI 1,2
Tarleton, K (NSW) 1925 NZ 2,3
Tasker, W G (NSW) 1913 NZ 1,2,3, 1914 NZ 1,2,3
Tate, M J (NSW) 1951 NZ 3, 1952 Fj 1,2, NZ 1,2, 1953 SA 1, 1954 Fj 1,2
Taylor, D A (Q) 1968 NZ 1,2, F, I, S
Taylor, H C (NSW) 1923 NZ 1,2,3, 1924 NZ 4
Taylor, J I (NSW) 1971 SA 1, 1972 F 1,2, Fj
Taylor, J M (NSW) 1922 M 1,2
Teitzel, R G (Q) 1966 W, S, 1967 E, I 1, F, I 2, NZ
Telford, D G (NSW) 1926 NZ 3(R)
Thompson, C E (NSW) 1922 M 1, 1923 M 1,2, NZ 1, 1924 NZ 2,3
Thompson, E G (Q) 1929 NZ 1,2,3, 1930 BI
Thompson, F (NSW) 1913 NZ 1,2,3, 1914 NZ 1,3
Thompson, J (Q) 1914 NZ 1, 2
Thompson, P D (Q) 1950 BI 1
Thompson, R J (WA) 1971 SA 3, F 2(R), 1972 Fj
Thorn, A M (NSW) 1921 SA 1,2,3, NZ, 1922 M 1,3
Thorn, E J (NSW) 1922 NZ 1,2,3, 1923 NZ 1,2,3, 1924 NZ 1,2,3, 1925 NZ 1,2, 1926 NZ 1,2,3,4
Thornett, J E (NSW) 1955 NZ 1,2,3, 1956 SA 1,2, 1958 W, I, S, F, M 2,3, NZ 2,3, 1959 BI 1,2, 1961 Fj 2,3, SA 1,2, F, 1962 NZ 2,3,4,5, 1963 E, SA 1,2,3,4, 1964 NZ 1,2,3, 1965 SA 1,2, 1966 BI 1,2, 1967 F
Thornett, R N (NSW) 1961 Fj 1,2,3, SA 1,2, F, 1962 NZ 1,2,3,4,5
Thorpe, A C (NSW) 1929 NZ 1(R)

Timbury, F R V (Q) 1910 NZ 1,2,
Tindall, E N (NSW) 1973 Tg 2
Toby, A E (NSW) 1925 NZ 1,4
Tolhurst, H A (NSW) 1931 M, NZ
Tombs, R C (NSW) 1992 S 1,2, 1994 I 2, It 1, 1996 NZ 2
Tonkin, A E J (NSW) 1947 S, I, W, 1948 E, F, 1950 BI 2
Tooth, R M (NSW) 1951 NZ 1,2,3, 1954 Fj 1,2, 1955 NZ 1,2,3, 1957 NZ 1,2
Towers, C H T (NSW) 1926 NZ 1,3(R),4, 1927 I, 1928 E, F, NZ 1,2,3, M, 1929 NZ 1,3, 1930 BI, 1931 M, NZ, 1934 NZ 1,2, 1937 SA 1,2
Trivett, R K (Q) 1966 BI 1,2
Tune, B N (Q) 1996 W 2, C, NZ 1, SA 1, NZ 2, SA 2, 1997 F 1,2, NZ 1, E 1, NZ 2, SA 1, NZ 3, SA 2, Arg, 1,2, E 2, S, 1998 E 1, S 1,2, NZ 1, SA 1,2, NZ 3, 1999 I 1, E, SA 1, NZ 1, SA 2, NZ 2, [R, I 3, W, SA 3, F], 2000 SA 2(R), NZ 2(t&R), SA 3(R), 2001 F (R), W, 2002 NZ 1, SA 1, NZ 2, SA 2, Arg, 2006 NZ1(R)
Tuqiri, L D (NSW) 2003 I (R), W (R), E (R), SA 1(R), NZ 1, SA 2, NZ 2, [Arg(R),R(R),Nm,I(R),S,NZ,E], 2004 S1,2,E1,PI,NZ1,SA1,NZ2,SA2,S3,F,S4,E2, 2005 It,F1,SA1,2,3,NZ1,SA4,NZ2,F2,E,I,W, 2006 E1,2,I1,NZ1,SA1,NZ2,SA2,NZ3,W,It,I2,S, 2007 Fj,SA1,NZ1, [J,W,Fj,C,E], 2008 I,F1,SA1,NZ1,2,SA2,3,NZ3
Turinui, M P (NSW) 2003 I, W, E, 2003 [Nm(R)], 2004 S1(R),2,E2, 2005 Sm,It(R),F1(R),SA1,2(t&R),3,NZ1,SA4,NZ2,F2,E,I,W
Turnbull, A (V) 1961 Fj 3
Turnbull, R V (NSW) 1968 I
Turner, L D (NSW) 2008 F2
Tuynman, S N (NSW) 1983 F 1,2, 1984 E, I, W, S, 1985 C 1,2, NZ, Fj 1,2, 1986 It, F, Arg 1,2, NZ 1,2,3, 1987 SK, [E, US, J, I, W], NZ, Arg 1(R), 2, 1988 E, It, 1989 BI 1,2,3, NZ, 1990 NZ 1
Tweedale, E (NSW) 1946 NZ 1,2, 1947 NZ 2, S, I, 1948 E, F, 1949 M 1,2,3

Valentine, J J (Q) 2006 E1(R),W(R),I2(R),S(R)
Vaughan, D (NSW) 1983 US, Arg 1, It, F 1,2
Vaughan, G N (V) 1958 E, S, F, M 1,2,3
Verge, A (NSW) 1904 BI 1,2
Vickerman, D J (ACT, NSW) 2002 F 2(R), Arg, E, It, 2003 I (R), W (R), E (R), SA 1, NZ 1, SA 2, NZ 2, [Arg(R),R,I(R),S(R)], 2004 S1(t&R),2(R),E1(R),PI(R),NZ1(R),SA1(R),NZ2(R),SA2(R), S3,F,S4,E2, 2005 SA2(R),3,NZ1,SA4, 2006 E1,2,I1,NZ1, SA1,NZ2,SA2,NZ3,SA3,W, 2007 W1(R),2,Fj,SA1,NZ1,SA2, NZ2, [J,W,Fj,E], 2008 NZ1(R),2(t&R),SA2

Walden, R J (NSW) 1934 NZ 2, 1936 NZ 1,2, M
Walker, A K (NSW) 1947 NZ 1, 1948 E, F, 1950 BI 1,2
Walker, A M (ACT) 2000 NZ 1(R), 2001 BI 1,2,3, SA 1, NZ 1,2(R)
Walker, A S B (NSW) 1912 US, 1920 NZ 1,2, 1921 SA 1,2,3, NZ, 1922 M 1,3, NZ 1,2,3, 1923 M 2,3, 1924 NZ 1,2
Walker, L F (NSW) 1988 NZ 2,3, S, It, 1989 BI 1,2,3, NZ
Walker, L R (NSW) 1982 NZ 2,3
Wallace, A C (NSW) 1921 NZ, 1926 NZ 3,4, 1927 I, W, S, 1928 E, F
Wallace, T M (NSW) 1994 It 1(R), 2
Wallach, C (NSW) 1913 NZ 1,3, 1914 NZ 1,2,3
Walsh, J J (NSW) 1953 SA 1,2,3,4
Walsh, P B (NSW) 1904 BI 1,2,3
Walsham, K P (NSW) 1962 NZ 3, 1963 E
Ward, P G (NSW) 1899 BI 1,2,3,4
Ward, T (Q) 1899 BI 2
Watson, G W (Q) 1907 NZ 1
Watson, W T (NSW) 1912 US, 1913 NZ 1,2,3, 1914 NZ 1, 1920 NZ 1,2,3
Waugh, P R (NSW) 2000 E (R), 2001 NZ 1(R), SA 2(R), NZ 2(R), Sp (R), E (R), F, W, 2003 I (R), W, E, SA 1, NZ 1, SA 2, NZ2, [Arg,R,I,S,NZ,E], 2004 S1(R),2,E1,PI,NZ1,SA1,NZ2, SA2,S3,F,S4,E2,2005 SA1(R),2(R),3,NZ1(R),SA4,NZ2,F2,E,I,W, 2006 E1(R),2(R),I1(R),NZ1(R),SA1(R),NZ2(R),SA2(R),NZ3, SA3,W,I2,S(R), 2007 W1,2(R),Fj,SA1(R),NZ1(R),SA2(R),NZ2(R) , [W(R),Fj,C(R),E(R)], 2008 I(R),F1(R),2,SA1(R),NZ1(R),2, SA2(t&R),3
Waugh, W W (NSW, ACT) 1993 SA 1, 1995 [C], NZ 1,2, 1996 S, I, 1997 Arg 1,2
Weatherstone, L J (ACT) 1975 E 1,2, J 1,2, S (R), 1976 E, I
Webb, W (NSW) 1899 BI 3,4
Welborn J P (NSW) 1996 SA 2, It, 1998 Tg, 1999 E, SA 1, NZ 1
Wells, B G (NSW) 1958 M 1
Westfield, R E (NSW) 1928 NZ 1,2,3, M, 1929 NZ 2,3
Whitaker, C J (NSW) 1998 SA 2(R), Fj (R), Tg, 1999 NZ 2(R), [R (R), US, F (R)], 2000 S (R), 2001 Sp (R), W (R), 2002 Arg (R), It (R), 2003 I (R), W (R), SA 2(R),[Arg(R),Nm,S(R)], 2004 PI(R),NZ1, 2005 Sm,It(R),F1(R),SA1(R),2(R),NZ1(t&R),SA4(R), NZ2(R),F2(R),E(R),W(R)
White, C J B (NSW) 1899 BI 1, 1903 NZ, 1904 BI 1
White, J M (NSW) 1904 BI 3
White, J P L (NSW) 1958 NZ 1,2,3, 1961 Fj 1,2,3, SA 1,2, F, 1962 NZ 1,2,3,4,5, 1963 E, SA 1,2,3,4, 1964 NZ 1,2,3, 1965 SA 1,2
White, M C (Q) 1931 M, NZ 1932 NZ 1,2, 1933 SA 1,2,3,4,5
White, S W (NSW) 1956 SA 1,2, 1958 I, E, S, M 2,3
White, W G S (Q) 1933 SA 1,2,3,4,5, 1934 NZ 1,2, 1936 NZ 1,2, M
White, W J (NSW) 1928 NZ 1, M, 1932 NZ 1
Wickham, S M (NSW) 1903 NZ, 1904 BI 1,2,3, 1905 NZ
Williams, D (Q) 1913 NZ 3, 1914 NZ 1,2,3
Williams, I M (NSW) 1987 Arg 1,2, 1988 E 1,2, NZ 1,2,3, 1989 BI 2,3, NZ, F 1,2, 1990 F 1,2,3, US, NZ 1
Williams, J L (NSW) 1963 SA 1,3,4
Williams, R W (ACT) 1999 I 1(t&R),2(t&R), E (R), [US], 2000 Arg 1,2, SA 1, NZ 1, SA 2, NZ 2, SA 3, F (R), S (R), E
Williams, S A (NSW) 1980 Fj, NZ 1,2, 1981 F 1,2, 1982 E, NZ 1,2,3, 1983 US, Arg 1(R), 2, NZ, It, F 1,2, 1984 NZ 1,2,3, E, I, W, S, 1985 C 1,2, NZ, Fj 1,2
Wilson, B J (NSW) 1949 NZ 1,2
Wilson, C R (Q) 1957 NZ 1, 1958 NZ 1,2,3
Wilson, D J (Q) 1992 S 1,2, NZ 1,2,3, SA, I, W, 1993 Tg, NZ, SA 1,2,3, C, F 1,2, 1994 I 1,2, It 1,2, WS, NZ, 1995 Arg 1,2, [SA, R, E], 1996 W 1,2, C, NZ 1, SA 1, NZ 2, SA 2, It, S, I, W 3, 1997 F 1,2, NZ 1, E 1(t + R), NZ 2(R), SA 1, NZ 3, SA 2, E 2(R), S (R), 1998 E 1, S 1,2, NZ 1, SA 1, NZ 2, SA 2, NZ 3, Fj, WS, F, E 2, 1999 I 1,2, E, SA 1, NZ 1, SA 2, NZ 2, [R, I 3, W, SA 3, F], 2000 Arg 1,2, SA 1, NZ 1, SA 2, NZ 2, SA 3
Wilson, V W (Q) 1937 SA 1,2, 1938 NZ 1,2,3
Windon, C J (NSW) 1946 NZ 1,2, 1947 NZ 1, S, I, W, 1948 E, F, 1949 M 1,2,3, NZ 1,2, 1951 NZ 1,2,3, 1952 Fj 1,2, NZ 1,2
Windon, K S (NSW) 1937 SA 1,2, 1946 M
Windsor, J C (Q) 1947 NZ 2
Winning, K C (Q) 1951 NZ 1
Wogan, L W (NSW) 1913 NZ 1,2,3, 1914 NZ 1,2,3, 1920 NZ 1,2,3, 1921 SA 1,2,3, NZ, 1922 M 3, NZ 1,2,3, 1923 M 1,2, 1924 NZ 1,2,3
Wood, F (NSW) 1907 NZ 1,2,3, 1910 NZ 1,2,3, 1913 NZ 1,2,3, 1914 NZ 1,2,3
Wood, R N (Q) 1972 Fj
Woods, H F (NSW) 1925 NZ 4, 1926 NZ 1,2,3, 1927 I, W, S, 1928 E
Wright, K J (NSW) 1975 E 1,2, J 1, 1976 US, F 1,2, 1978 NZ 1,2,3
Wyld, G (NSW) 1920 NZ 2

Yanz, K (NSW) 1958 F
Young, W K (ACT, NSW) 2000 F, S, E, 2002 F 1,2, NZ 1, SA 1, NZ 2, SA 2, Arg, E, It, 2003 I, W, E, SA 1, NZ 1, SA 2, NZ 2, [Arg,R,I,S,NZ,E], 2004 S1,2,E1,PI,NZ1,SA1,NZ2,SA2, S3,F,S4,E2, 2005 Sm,It,F1,SA1,2,3,NZ1,SA4,NZ2

CANADA

CANADA'S 2008 RECORD

OPPONENTS	DATE	VENUE	RESULT
Scotland A	7 June	H	**Lost** 10–26
Argentina A	14 June	H	**Lost** 16–17
USA	21 June	A	**Won** 26–10
French Barbarians	28 June	H	**Lost** 7–17
Gloucester	9 August	H	**Lost** 12–34

CANADA LOOK FOR ALL BLACK MAGIC

By Doug Crosse

The year proved to be one of the busiest seasons for Canada, outside a World Cup, and provided a number of challenges for the variety of teams that play under the Maple Leaf through the course of the calendar year.

It saw Canadian rugby begin to chart a new course with the men's side, as former All Black Kieran Crowley accepted the challenge of leading the team for the next three years to the 2011 World Cup. The former Taranaki coach took the helm in March 2008 – with his first game being part of the Barclays Churchill Cup where Canada took on Scotland A to open the tournament.

On an extremely hot day in Ottawa, Canada kept it close and were unlucky not to have the lead going into the break. They trailed 5–3 before a hat-trick from Scotland full-back Steve Jones saw them pull away for a 26–10 win. Justin Mensah-Coker scored the lone Canadian try late in the game, breaking free to dot down untouched.

A week later in Toronto it was a much more physical encounter with Argentina A that left fans begging for more as a good Canadian effort saw the South Americans manage a slim 17–16 victory. With 10 minutes to go and down by 17–9, Canada brought on replacement second row and debutant Tyler Hotson. A moment later he was the benefactor of a great run by 6ft 7in Luke Cudmore, who broke for the Pumas line before getting tackled five metres out. He off-loaded to a trailing Hotson, who came in off Cudmore's hip to take a flat pass across for the score. The James Pritchard conversion left Canada just one point adrift, but the legendary Argentinean mauling saw the ball stay away from Canada possession for the remainder of the game to leave them winless in the Barclays Churchill Cup.

On to Chicago, for finals day of the tournament, with all six teams in attendance at Toyota Park, home to the Fire of Major League Soccer. Canada was left facing its normal foes the USA to determine fifth and sixth place.

It was a unique situation as two first-year coaches, Australia's Scott Johnson squaring off against Crowley, were both in their third matches in charge, and seeking their first win. In the early going it appeared the Americans might have the upper hand taking a 10–0 lead into the changing rooms. However, flanker Nanyak Dala was the spark plug Canada needed, the Nigerian born, Saskatchewan resident scoring a try in the opening minute of the second half, followed by a second effort in the 75th minute to garner man of the match honours. Ryan Smith also scored twice to help Canada to a 26–10 win. A relieved Crowley said of the efforts by Smith and Dala: "They finished strongly on some great work by the forwards, and yeah, they did a good job, but it was hard work by everyone that made it happen."

For most teams the finals in Chicago marked a break in the summer series, but for Canada it was re-assembly time on Canada's West Coast in Victoria, BC, to take on the French Barbarians in a one-off friendly. The match was played on a temporary pitch in Esquimalt, with 3,400 fans packing Bullen Park in 30° temperatures to play the tourists. With a number of changes and player unavailability to the Canadians Crowley picked some young players, mixed with some faces from the past including prop Jon Thiel, who had last played for Canada in the World Cup the previous year. Tries from former All Black prop Kees Meeuws and Yoan Audrin saw the visitors take a 12–0 lead at half time. Canadian defence remained stout in the stifling heat that saw the Barbarians empty their bench through in the second half. A late try by Bryn Keys gave Canada a scoreline to be proud of – with a final 17–7 victory by the French.

Canada captain Pat Riordan was clearly disappointed at the loss, but more so because his team made so many trips to the French end and came away empty-handed.

"For sure we were hanging in there with them [the French] so that was very frustrating to not convert more of those efforts," said Riordan.

The Canadian summer campaign took a one-month break and then re-assembled in Toronto in August for a first ever match against Guinness Premiership side Gloucester, who conducted part of their pre-season training camp in Canada. A rare Friday night fixture at York Stadium produced a pleasing spectacle that saw a very young Canuck squad take a 12–8 lead courtesy of a pair of dropped-goals through scrum-half Phil Mack and U20 fly-half Matt Evans. Evans also kicked a penalty before an injury knocked him out of the game, but overall it was a creditable performance by the youngster who plays rugby at Hartpury College in the UK.

The second half saw Gloucester get the measure of the Canadians, the 2007/08 Guinness Premiership table toppers pulling away for a 34–12 win.

Canada's Sevens programme continues to act as a litmus test for the 15-a-side game. Former Sevens player Shane Thompson, in his second year as a coach, selected a number of fresh faces in 2008, including Phil Mackenzie, Ciaran Hearn and Bryn Keys to name a few. Of the rookies, it was Newfoundland's Hearn that caught the most attention, scoring three tries in his first tournament in Wellington. He continued to impress in San Diego, where he scored another pair, and showed the pace and confidence that would eventually net him selection to the full Canada squad later in the year.

In the end it was a disappointing IRB Sevens World Series for Canada, scoring only two points in Hong Kong, in the Plate semi-finals. In 2008–09 Canada will only take part in six of the eight events, dropping Dubai and South Africa from the schedule.

Canada's senior women, meanwhile, took part in the inaugural Nation's Cup in England during August. The hosts England beat both the USA and Canadian women in the opening rounds of the tournament, with Canada beating the Eagles 15–0. After falling to England 43–0 in the Nations Cup, Canada tightened its defence to allow only a 24–0 win by the English in the post-tournament encounter.

The U20 women hosted the junior version of the Nations Cup in July, with England taking the honours in a competition that also included Wales and two squads from Canada.

Canada's U20 men played in its first IRB Junior World Championship under the new age format, and struggled through losses to Australia (81–12) and England 60–18 before downing Fiji 17–10 for a key win to keep them in the top competition in 2009. Canada then lost to Scotland (15–10) and Italy (33–10) to finish 12th of the 16 teams.

In the Rugby Canada Super League the Newfoundland Rock were undefeated in the East at 5–0 and hosted the Calgary Mavericks, who last won the Mactier Cup at home in 2003. On a dreary day in St. John's, Rock rolled over the Mavs for a 30–6 win and a third national title – the first time ever a Newfoundland provincial sports team of any stripe has managed such a feat.

At the National Festival in Ottawa in August all four age categories featured British Columbia v Ontario finals. On the men's side BC's U16 and U18 sides prevailed with big wins, while on the women's side Ontario's U17 and U19 squads bettered their BC counterparts.

CANADA INTERNATIONAL STATISTICS

MATCH RECORDS UP TO 30TH SEPTEMBER 2008

WINNING MARGIN

Date	Opponent	Result	Winning Margin
24/06/2006	Barbados	69–3	**66**
14/10/1999	Namibia	72–11	**61**
12/08/2006	USA	56–7	**49**
06/07/1996	Hong Kong	57–9	**48**
15/07/2000	Japan	62–18	**44**

MOST POINTS IN A MATCH

BY THE TEAM

Date	Opponent	Result	Pts.
14/10/1999	Namibia	72–11	**72**
24/06/2006	Barbados	69–3	**69**
15/07/2000	Japan	62–18	**62**
06/07/1996	Hong Kong	57–9	**57**
12/08/2006	USA	56–7	**56**

MOST TRIES IN A MATCH

BY THE TEAM

Date	Opponent	Result	Tries
24/06/2006	Barbados	69–3	**11**
14/10/1999	Namibia	72–11	**9**
11/05/1991	Japan	49–26	**8**
15/07/2000	Japan	62–18	**8**

MOST CONVERSIONS IN A MATCH

BY THE TEAM

Date	Opponent	Result	Cons
14/10/1999	Namibia	72–11	**9**
15/07/2000	Japan	62–18	**8**
24/06/2006	Barbados	69–3	**7**
02/06/2007	USA	52–10	**7**
11/05/1991	Japan	49–26	**7**

MOST PENALTIES IN A MATCH

BY THE TEAM

Date	Opponent	Result	Pens
25/05/1991	Scotland	24–19	**8**
22/08/1998	Argentina	28–54	**7**

MOST DROP GOALS IN A MATCH

BY THE TEAM

Date	Opponent	Result	DGs
08/11/1986	USA	27–16	**2**
04/07/2001	Fiji	23–52	**2**
08/06/1980	USA	16–0	**2**
24/05/1997	Hong Kong	35–27	**2**

MOST POINTS IN A MATCH

BY A PLAYER

Date	Player	Opponent	Pts.
12/08/2006	James Pritchard	USA	**36**
24/06/2006	James Pritchard	Barbados	**29**
14/10/1999	Gareth Rees	Namibia	**27**
13/07/1996	Bobby Ross	Japan	**26**
25/05/1991	Mark Wyatt	Scotland	**24**

MOST TRIES IN A MATCH

BY A PLAYER

Date	Player	Opponent	Tries
15/07/2000	Kyle Nichols	Japan	**4**
24/06/2006	James Pritchard	Barbados	**3**
12/08/2006	James Pritchard	USA	**3**
10/05/1987	Steve Gray	USA	**3**

MOST CONVERSIONS IN A MATCH

BY A PLAYER

Date	Player	Opponent	Cons
14/10/1999	Gareth Rees	Namibia	9
15/07/2000	Jared Barker	Japan	8
24/06/2006	James Pritchard	Barbados	7
02/06/2007	James Pritchard	USA	7
11/05/1991	Mark Wyatt	Japan	7

LEADING CONVERSIONS SCORERS

Name	Cons
Bobby Ross	52
Gareth Rees	51
James Pritchard	42
Jared Barker	24
Mark Wyatt	24

MOST PENALTIES IN A MATCH

BY A PLAYER

Date	Player	Opponent	Pens
225/05/1991	Mark Wyatt	Scotland	8
22/08/1998	Gareth Rees	Argentina	7
	5 Players		6

LEADING PENALTY SCORERS

Name	Pens
Gareth Rees	110
Bobby Ross	84
Mark Wyatt	64
Jared Barker	55
James Pritchard	29

MOST DROP GOALS IN A MATCH

BY A PLAYER

Date	Player	Opponent	DGs
04/07/2001	Bobby Ross	Fiji	2
24/05/1997	Bobby Ross	Hong Kong	2

LEADING DROP GOAL SCORERS

Name	DGs
Bobby Ross	10
Gareth Rees	9
Mark Wyatt	5

MOST CAPPED PLAYERS

Name	Caps
Al Charron	76
Winston Stanley	66
Scott Stewart	64
Rod Snow	62
Bobby Ross	58

LEADING POINTS SCORERS

Name	Pts.
Gareth Rees	491
Bobby Ross	421
Mark Wyatt	263
Jared Barker	226
James Pritchard	211

LEADING TRY SCORERS

Name	Tries
Winston Stanley	24
Morgan Williams	13
Pat Palmer	10
Kyle Nichols	10
John Graf	9
Al Charron	9

CANADIAN INTERNATIONAL PLAYERS
UP TO 30TH SEPTEMBER 2008

Note: Years given for International Championship matches are for second half of season; eg 1972 means season 1971–72. Years for all other matches refer to the actual year of the match. Entries in square brackets denote matches played in RWC Finals.

AD Abrams 2003 *US, NZ, Tg*, 2004 *US, J, E, US, F, It, E*, 2005 *US, J, W, E, US, Ar, F, R*, 2006 *S, E, US, It*
MJ Alder 1976 *Bb*
P Aldous 1971 *W*
AS Arthurs 1988 *US*
M Ashton 1971 *W*
F Asselin 1999 *Fj*, 2000 *Tg, US, SA*, 2001 *Ur, Ar, Fj*, 2002 *S, US, US, Ur, Ur, Ch, W, F*
O Atkinson 2005 *J, Ar*, 2006 *E, US, It*
S Ault 2006 *W, It*, 2008 *US*
JC Bain 1932 *J*
RG Banks 1999 *J, Fj, Sa, US, Tg, W, E, F, Nm*, 2000 *US, SA, I, J, It*, 2001 *US, Ur, Ar, E, Fj, J*, 2002 *S, US, US, Ur, Ch, Ur, Ch, W, F*, 2003 *E, US, M, M, Ur, NZ, It*
S Barber 1973 *W*, 1976 *Bb*
M Barbieri 2006 *E, US*
B Barker 1966 *BI*, 1971 *W*
J Barker 2000 *Tg, J, It*, 2002 *S, US, US, Ur, Ch, Ur, Ch, W*, 2003 *US, NZ, It*, 2004 *US, J, F, It*
T Bauer 1977 *US, E*, 1978 *US, F*, 1979 *US*
D Baugh 1998 *J, HK, US, HK, J, Ur, Ar*, 1999 *J, Fj, Sa, US, Tg, W, E, F, Fj, Nm*, 2000 *US, SA, I, It*, 2001 *E, E*, 2002 *S, US, Ur, Ch*
A Bianco 1966 *BI*
AJ Bibby 1979 *US, F*, 1980 *W, US, NZ*, 1981 *US, Ar*
R Bice 1996 *US, A*, 1997 *US, J, HK, US, W, I*, 1998 *US, US, HK, J, Ur, US, Ar*, 1999 *J, Fj, Sa, US, Tg, W, F*
P Bickerton 2004 *US, J*
D Biddle 2006 *S, E, Bar*, 2007 *M, W, Fj, A*
JM Billingsley 1974 *Tg*, 1977 *US*, 1978 *F*, 1979 *US*, 1980 *W*, 1983 *US, It, It*, 1984 *US*
WG Bjarneson 1962 *Bb*
TJH Blackwell 1973 *W*
B Bonenberg 1983 *US, It, It*
J Boone 1932 *J, J*
T Bourne 1967 *E*
R Breen 1986 *US*, 1987 *W*, 1990 *US*, 1991 *J, S, US, R*, 1993 *E, US*
R Breen 1983 *E*, 1987 *US*
R Brewer 1967 *E*
STT Brown 1989 *I, US*
N Browne 1973 *W*, 1974 *Tg*
S Bryan 1996 *Ur, US, Ar*, 1997 *HK, J, US, W*, 1998 *HK, J, US, Ar*, 1999 *Fj, Sa, US, Tg, W, E, F, Fj, Nm*
M Burak 2004 *US, J, E, US, F, It, E*, 2005 *E, US, Ar, F, R*, 2006 *US, Bar, W*, 2007 *IrA, M, NZ, Pt, W, Fj, J, A*
C Burford 1970 *Fj*
D Burgess 1962 *Bb, W23*
D Burleigh 2001 *Ur, Ar, E, E*
JB Burnham 1966 *BI*, 1967 *E*, 1970 *Fj*, 1971 *W*
H Buydens 2006 *E*, 2008 *US*
GE Cameron 1932 *J*
JWD Cannon 2001 *US, Ar, E, E, Fj, J*, 2002 *S, US, Ur, Ch, Ur, Ch, W, F*, 2003 *E, M, M, Ur, US, Ar, NZ, It*, 2004 *US, F, It, E*, 2005 *W, E, US, F*
R Card 1996 *US, A, Ur, US, Ar*, 1997 *US, J, HK*
ME Cardinal 1986 *US*, 1987 *US, Tg, I, US*, 1991 *S*, 1993 *A*, 1994 *US, F, E, F*, 1995 *S, Fj, NZ, R, SA*, 1996 *US, US, HK, J, A, HK, J*, 1997 *US, US, W, I*, 1998 *US, HK*, 1999 *Fj, US, W, E, Fj, Nm*
LAG Carlson 2002 *Ur, W*, 2003 *E*
A Carpenter 2005 *US, J, E, US, Ar, F, R*, 2006 *S, E, US, W, It*, 2007 *IrA, M, US, NZ, Pt, W, Fj, J, A*, 2008 *US*
NS Carr 1985 *A, A*
DJ Carson 1980 *W, US, NZ*, 1981 *US, Ar*, 1982 *J, E, US*, 1983 *It, It*
SFB Carson 1977 *E*
MP Chambers 1962 *Bb, W23*, 1966 *BI*
AJ Charron 1990 *Ar, US, Ar*, 1991 *J, S, Fj, F, NZ*, 1992 *US*, 1993 *E, E, US, A, W*, 1994 *US, F, W*, 1995 *Fj, NZ, R, A, SA, US*, 1996 *US, US, A, HK, J, Ur, US, Ar*, 1997 *US, J, HK, HK, J, US, W, I*, 1998 *US, HK, J, Ur, US, Ar*, 1999 *Fj, Sa, US, Tg, W, E, F, Fj, Nm*, 2000 *Tg, US, SA, Sa, Fj, J, It*, 2001 *Ur, Ar, E, E*, 2002 *S, US, US, Ur, Ch, Ur, Ch, F*, 2003 *W*
L Chung 1978 *F*
N Clapinson 1995 *US*, 1996 *US*
RM Clark 1962 *Bb*
D Clarke 1996 *A*
ME Clarkin 1985 *A, A*
B Collins 2004 *US, J*
W Collins 1977 *US, E*
GG Cooke 2000 *Tg, US*, 2001 *Fj, J*, 2003 *E, US, M, M, Ur, US, Ar, W, NZ, Tg*, 2004 *E, US, It, E*, 2005 *US, J, W, Ar, F, R*, 2006 *US*
I Cooper 1993 *W*
JA Cordle 1998 *HK, J*, 1999 *J, Fj, Sa*, 2001 *J*
GER Cox 1932 *J*
S Creagh 1988 *US*
J Cudmore 2002 *US, Ch, W, F*, 2003 *E, US, W, NZ, It, Tg*, 2004 *US, F, It, E*, 2005 *W, F*, 2006 *US*, 2007 *Pt, W, Fj*
L Cudmore 2008 *US*
C Culpan 2006 *E*, 2007 *IrA, M, US, NZ, Pt, W, Fj, J*
TJ Cummings 1966 *BI*, 1973 *W*
Z Cvitak 1983 *E*
N Dala 2007 *IrA, US*, 2008 *US*
MJW Dandy 1977 *E, E*
M Danskin 2001 *J*, 2004 *E, F*
D Daypuck 2004 *E, F, It, E*, 2005 *US, J, W, E, Ar, F, R*, 2006 *S, US, US, W, It*, 2007 *IrA, M, A*
H de Goede 1976 *Bb*, 1977 *US, E, E*, 1978 *US*, 1979 *US, F*, 1980 *W, US, NZ*, 1981 *US*, 1982 *J, J, E, US*, 1984 *US*, 1985 *US*, 1986 *J, US*, 1987 *US, Tg, I, W*
HW de Goede 1974 *Tg*
F Deacy 1973 *W*
J Delaney 1983 *E*
P Densmore 2005 *E*
JD Devlin 1985 *US*, 1986 *US*
M di Girolamo 2001 *Ur, Ar*, 2002 *US, Ur, Ch, Ur, W, F*, 2003 *US, M, M, Ur, W, NZ, It, Tg*, 2004 *E, US, F, It, E*
GA Dixon 2000 *US, SA, I, Sa, Fj, J, It*, 2001 *US, Ar, E, E*
D Docherty 1973 *W*
WJ Donaldson 1978 *F*, 1979 *US, F*, 1980 *W, US, NZ*, 1981 *US*, 1982 *E, US*, 1983 *US, It, It*, 1984 *US*
A Douglas 1974 *Tg*
JT Douglas 2003 *M, M, Ur, US, Ar, NZ, It*, 2004 *US, F*
A du Temple 1932 *J, J*

G Dukelow *1980 W, US, NZ, 1981 US, 1982 J, J, E, US, 1983 US, It, It, E, 1984 US, 1990 US*
PJ Dunkley *1998 J, HK, US, HK, J, US, Ar, 1999 J, Fj, Sa, US, Tg, E, F, Fj, Nm, 2000 Tg, SA, I, Sa, Fj, 2001 US, Ar, E, Fj, J, 2002 S, US, US, Ur, Ch, W, F, 2003 M, M, Ur, Ar, 2005 W*
C Dunning *2005 E, US, Ar, F, R*
B Ebl *1995 NZ, 1998 J, HK*
DC Eburne *1977 US, E, E*
MA Eckardt *1974 Tg, 1977 US, E, E, 1978 US*
IJ Edwards *1967 E*
G Ellwand *1973 W*
GD Ennis *1986 J, US, 1987 US, Tg, I, W, 1988 US, 1989 I, US, 1990 Ar, US, Ar, 1991 J, S, US, Fj, R, F, NZ, 1993 E, E, 1994 US, W, 1995 Fj, NZ, R, A, SA, 1998 J, HK, US, US*
EA Evans *1986 US, 1987 US, Tg, I, US, 1989 I, US, 1990 Ar, Ar, 1991 J, S, US, Fj, R, F, NZ, 1992 US, E, 1993 E, E, 1994 US, F, W, E, F, 1995 S, Ur, Ar, Fj, NZ, R, A, SA, 1996 J, HK, J, 1997 US, J, HK, J, US, W, I, 1998 J, HK, US, US, US, Ar*
I Exner *2005 E, US*
EG Fairhurst *2001 US, Ar, 2002 US, Ur, Ch, Ur, Ch, W, F, 2003 E, M, M, US, NZ, Tg, 2004 US, J, E, US, F, It, E, 2005 US, W, E, US, F, 2006 S, E, US, Bar, US, W, It, 2007 IrA, M, US, NZ, Pt, W, A, 2008 US*
SC Fauth *2000 Tg, US, SA, I, Sa, Fj, J, It, 2001 US, Ar, E, E, Fj, J, 2002 S, US, US, Ur, Ch, Ch, W, F, 2003 US, M, Ur, US, Ar, NZ, Tg*
M Felix *1985 A, A, 1996 Ur, US*
P Fleck *2004 US, J, It, E, 2005 US, W*
I Fleming *1976 Bb*
AC Forbes *1932 J, J*
F Forster *1983 US, It, It*
AE Foster *1970 Fj, 1976 Bb, 1977 US, E, E*
C Fowler *1988 US, 1990 US*
TE Fraine *1967 E*
RP Frame *1986 J, 1987 US, Tg, I, W, US*
S Franklin *2007 IrA, M, US, NZ, J, 2008 US*
G Fraser *1983 E*
P Frize *1962 Bb, W23*
GW Fumano *1967 E, 1970 Fj*
QA Fyffe *2003 E, US, NZ, It, Tg, 2004 US, J, E, US, F, It, 2005 US, J, W, Ar*
F Gainer *2004 US, J, E, US, F, It, E, 2005 J, W, E, US, F, R, 2006 W, It*
A Godziek *1982 J, E, US, 1983 US, It, It, E, 1984 US*
G Gonis *1978 US*
GG Gonis *1977 US, E, E*
I Gordon *1991 S, 1992 US, E, 1993 US, A, W, 1994 F, W, E, F, 1995 S, R, SA, US, 1996 US, HK, J, A, HK, 1997 US, J, HK, 1998 J, HK, US, J, US, Ar*
JD Graf *1989 I, US, 1990 Ar, 1991 S, R, 1992 US, E, 1993 E, E, US, A, 1994 US, F, W, E, F, 1995 S, Ur, Ar, Fj, NZ, R, A, SA, US, 1996 US, HK, J, A, HK, J, 1997 US, J, HK, HK, US, W, I, 1998 J, HK, US, US, HK, J, Ur, US, Ar, 1999 J, Fj, Sa, US, Tg, F, Nm*
W Granleese *1962 W23*
G Grant *1977 E, E, 1978 US, 1979 US, F, 1980 W*
I Grant *1983 US, It, It, E*
PR Grantham *1962 Bb, W23, 1966 BI*
SD Gray *1984 US, 1987 US, W, US, 1989 I, 1990 Ar, US, Ar, 1991 J, S, Fj, F, NZ, 1992 US, E, 1993 E, E, US, A, W, 1994 US, F, W, E, F, 1995 S, Ar, Fj, NZ, R, A, SA, US, 1996 US, US, HK, J, A, HK, J, US, Ar, 1997 US, J, HK, J, US*
GR Greig *1973 W*
J Greig *1977 US, E*
JR Grieg *1978 US, 1979 US, F, 1980 W, US, NZ, 1981 Ar*
J Grout *1995 Ur*
G Gudmundseth *1973 W*
N Hadley *1987 US, 1989 I, US, 1990 Ar, 1991 S, US, Fj, R, F, NZ, 1992 US, E, 1993 E, 1994 E, F*
J Haley *1996 Ur*
J Hall *1996 US, 1997 HK, 1998 J, HK, J, US, Ar*
WT Handson *1985 A, A, US, 1986 J, US, 1987 US, Tg, I, W*
JP Hawthorn *1982 J, J, E, 1983 US, It, It*
A Healy *1996 HK, J, HK, J, Ur, US, Ar, 1997 US, HK, HK, I, 1998 HK, J, Ur, 1999 J*
AR Heaman *1988 US*
B Henderson *2005 J, F, R*
S Hendry *1996 Ur, US, Ar*
G Henrikson *1971 W*
L Hillier *1973 W*
RE Hindson *1974 Tg*
RE Hindson *1973 W, 1976 Bb, 1977 US, E, E, 1978 US, F, 1979 US, F, 1980 W, US, NZ, 1981 US, Ar, 1982 J, J, E, US, 1983 US, It, It, 1984 US, 1985 A, A, US, 1986 J, 1987 US, I, W, 1990 Ar*
G Hirayama *1977 E, E, 1978 US, 1979 US, F, 1980 W, US, NZ, 1981 US, 1982 J, E, US*
N Hirayama *2007 M*
M Holmes *1987 US*
T Hotson *2008 US*
P Howlett *1974 Tg*
BM Hunnings *1932 J, J*
E Hunt *1966 BI, 1967 E*
S Hunter *2005 R*
J Hutchinson *1993 E, A, W, 1995 S, Ar, Fj, A, SA, US, 1996 US, US, HK, J, A, HK, J, Ur, US, Ar, 1997 US, J, HK, HK, J, US, W, I, 1998 J, HK, US, US, HK, J, Ur, US, Ar, 1999 J, Fj, Sa, US, Tg, W, E, F, Fj, Nm, 2000 US, Sa, Fj, J*
I Hyde-Lay *1986 J, 1987 US, 1988 US*
M Irvine *2000 Tg, SA, I, Sa, Fj, J, 2001 US, Ar*
DC Jackart *1991 J, S, US, Fj, R, F, 1992 US, E, 1993 E, E, US, A, W, 1994 US, F, W, E, F, 1995 S, Ar, Fj*
J Jackson *2003 Ur, US, Ar, W, It, Tg, 2004 E, US, It, E, 2005 W, US, Ar, R, 2006 S, 2007 IrA, M, US, NZ, J*
RO Jackson *1970 Fj, 1971 W*
MB James *1994 US, F, W, E, F, 1995 S, Ur, Ar, Fj, NZ, R, A, US, 1996 US, US, HK, J, A, HK, J, 1997 J, US, W, I, 1998 US, US, Ur, US, Ar, 1999 Sa, W, E, F, Fj, Nm, 2000 It, 2002 S, US, US, Ur, Ch, W, F, 2003 M, M, Ur, US, Ar, W, Tg, 2005 F, 2006 US, 2007 Pt, W, Fj, J, A*
G Jennings *1981 Ar, 1983 US, It, It, E*
O Johnson *1970 Fj*
G Johnston *1978 F*
RR Johnstone *2001 Ur, Fj, J, 2002 Ch, Ur, Ch, 2003 E*
C Jones *1983 E, 1987 US*
EL Jones *1982 J, 1983 US*
TK Kariya *1967 E, 1970 Fj, 1971 W*
A Kennedy *1985 A, A*
I Kennedy *1993 A, W*
ED Kettleson *1985 US*
B Keys *2008 US*
MMG King *2002 US, Ur, 2003 M, US, Ar, NZ, 2005 US, J, W, E, US, Ar*
A Kingham *1974 Tg*
A Kleeberger *2005 F, R, 2006 S, E, US, Bar, It, 2007 IrA, M, US, NZ, Pt, J, 2008 US*
ERP Knaggs *2000 Tg, US, SA, I, Sa, Fj, J, 2001 US, Ur, Ar, E, E, Fj, J, 2002 S, 2003 E, Ur, Ar, NZ*
JD Knauer *1992 E, 1993 E, E, US, W*
MJ Kokan *1984 US, 1985 US*
P Kyle *1984 US*
A La Carte *2004 US, J*
M Langley *2004 E, 2005 Ar*
MJ Lawson *2002 US, Ur, Ch, Ur, Ch, F, 2003 E, US, M, M, Ur, US, Ar, W, It, Tg, 2004 F, It, E, 2005 US, J, F, R, 2006 US, W*
P le Blanc *1994 F, 1995 Ur, Fj, NZ*
CE le Fevre *1976 Bb*
J Lecky *1962 Bb, W23*
JL Lecky *1982 J, US, 1983 US, It, It, 1984 US, 1985 A, US, 1986 J, US, 1987 I, W, US, 1991 J, S, Fj, R*
GB Legh *1973 W, 1974 Tg, 1976 Bb*
LSF Leroy *1932 J*
J Lorenz *1966 BI, 1970 Fj, 1971 W*
DC Lougheed *1990 Ar, 1991 J, US, 1992 US, E, 1993 E, E, US, 1994 F, W, E, F, 1995 Fj, NZ, R, A, SA, 1996 A, HK, 1997 J, W, I, 1998 US, Ar, 1999 US, Tg, W, E, F, Fj, Nm, 2003 W, It*
J Loveday *1993 E, E, US, A, 1996 HK, J, 1998 J, Ur, 1999 Sa, US*
B Luke *2004 US, J*

M Luke *1974 Tg, 1976 Bb, 1977 US, E, E, 1978 US, F, 1979 US, F, 1980 W, US, NZ, 1981 US, 1982 J, US*
S Lytton *1995 Ur, Ar, US, 1996 US, HK, J, J, US, Ar*
G MacDonald *1970 Fj*
GDT MacDonald *1998 HK*
I MacKay *1993 A, W*
GI MacKinnon *1985 US, 1986 J, 1988 US, 1989 I, US, 1990 Ar, Ar, 1991 J, S, Fj, R, F, NZ, 1992 US, E, 1993 E, 1994 US, F, W, E, F, 1995 S, Ur, Ar, Fj, NZ, A, SA*
S MacKinnon *1992 US, 1995 Ur, Ar, Fj*
C MacLachlan *1981 Ar, 1982 J, E*
P Maclean *1983 US, It, It, E*
I Macmillan *1981 Ar, 1982 J, J, E, US*
B Major *2001 Fj, J*
D Major *1999 E, Fj, Nm, 2000 Tg, US, SA, I, Fj, 2001 Ur, E, E*
A Marshall *1997 J, 1998 Ur*
P Mason *1974 Tg*
B McCarthy *1996 US, Ar, 1998 J, HK, J*
J McDonald *1974 Tg*
RN McDonald *1966 Bl, 1967 E, 1970 Fj*
AG McGann *1985 A, A*
R McGeein *1973 W*
RI McInnes *1979 F, 1980 NZ, 1981 US, Ar, 1982 J, J, E, US, 1983 US, It, It, 1984 US, 1985 US*
B Mckee *1966 Bl, 1970 Fj*
B McKee *1962 Bb, W23*
S McKeen *2004 US, J, E, US, F, It, E, 2005 US, J, W, E, F, R, 2006 S, US, US, W, It, 2007 IrA, US, NZ*
JR McKellar *1985 A, A, 1986 J, 1987 W*
JH McKenna *1967 E*
C McKenzie *1992 US, E, 1993 E, US, A, W, 1994 US, F, W, E, F, 1995 S, Ur, Ar, Fj, NZ, R, SA, 1996 US, HK, J, J, 1997 J, HK, I*
SG McTavish *1970 Fj, 1971 W, 1976 Bb, 1977 US, E, E, 1978 US, F, 1979 US, F, 1980 W, US, 1981 US, Ar, 1982 J, J, E, US, 1985 US, 1987 US, Tg, I*
R McWhinney *2005 F, R*
J Mensah-Coker *2006 S, E, US, Bar, US, W, It, 2007 US, NZ, Pt, J, A, 2008 US*
C Michaluk *1995 SA, 1996 US, J, 1997 US, HK*
N Milau *2000 US, J*
DRW Milne *1966 Bl, 1967 E*
AB Mitchell *1932 J, J*
P Monaghan *1982 J*
A Monro *2006 E, US, Bar, US, W, It, 2007 M, W, A, 2008 US*
D Moonlight *2003 E, 2004 E, E, 2005 US*
DL Moore *1962 Bb, W23*
K Morgan *1997 HK, HK, J, W*
VJP Moroney *1962 Bb*
B Mosychuk *1996 Ur, 1997 J*
J Moyes *1981 Ar, 1982 J, J, E, US*
PT Murphy *2000 Tg, US, SA, I, Sa, Fj, J, 2001 Fj, J, 2002 S, US, US, Ur, Ch, W, F, 2003 US, M, M, 2004 F*
WA Murray *1932 J*
K Myhre *1970 Fj*
J Newton *1962 W23*
GN Niblo *1932 J, J*
K Nichols *1996 Ur, 1998 J, HK, US, US, Ur, 1999 J, Fj, Sa, US, Tg, Fj, Nm, 2000 Tg, US, SA, I, Sa, Fj, J, It, 2001 Ur, E, Fj, J, 2002 S*
D Nikas *1995 Ur*
S O'Leary *2004 US, J, E, E, 2005 J*
S Pacey *2005 W*
C Pack *2006 S, US*
J Pagano *1997 I, 1998 J, HK, US, HK, J, US, 1999 J, Fj, Nm*
DV Pahl *1971 W*
P Palmer *1983 E, 1984 US, 1985 A, 1986 J, US, 1987 Tg, I, W, 1988 US, 1990 Ar, US, 1991 J, US, Fj, R, F, 1992 US*
K Parfrey *2005 J*
A Pasutto *2004 US, J*
K Peace *1978 F, 1979 US, F, 1980 W, US*
J Penaluna *1996 Ur*
DN Penney *1995 US, 1996 US, A, US, Ar, 1997 HK, 1999 E*
JM Phelan *1980 NZ, 1981 Ar, 1982 J, J, 1985 A, A*
M Phinney *2006 S, E*
EC Pinkham *1932 J*
C Plater *2003 E*
D Pletch *2004 US, J, E, It, E, 2005 US, J, W, E, 2006 S, E, US, Bar, US, W, It, 2007 IrA, M, US, NZ, Pt, W, Fj, J, A*
M Pletch *2005 Ar, 2006 S, E, US, Bar, W, It, 2007 IrA, M, US, NZ, Pt, W, J, A, 2008 US*
J Pritchard *2003 M, M, Ur, US, Ar, W, Tg, 2006 S, US, Bar, US, W, 2007 IrA, M, US, NZ, Pt, W, Fj, J, A, 2008 US*
G Puil *1962 Bb, W23*
M Pyke *2004 US, J, US, It, 2005 US, F, R, 2006 S, E, US, Bar, US, W, It, 2007 IrA, M, US, NZ, Pt, W, Fj, J, A, 2008 US*
DLJ Quigley *1976 Bb, 1979 F*
RE Radu *1985 A, 1986 US, 1987 US, Tg, I, US, 1988 US, 1989 I, US, 1990 Ar, Ar, 1991 US*
D Ramsey *2005 US*
GL Rees *1986 US, 1987 US, Tg, I, W, US, 1989 I, US, 1990 Ar, Ar, 1991 J, S, US, Fj, R, F, NZ, 1992 US, E, 1993 E, E, US, W, 1994 US, F, W, E, F, 1995 S, Fj, NZ, R, A, SA, 1996 HK, J, 1997 US, J, HK, J, US, W, I, 1998 US, US, Ur, US, Ar, 1999 Sa, Tg, W, E, F, Fj, Nm*
J Reid *2003 M, US, Ar, NZ, Tg*
G Relph *1974 Tg*
S Richmond *2004 E, US, F, It, E, 2005 US, W, E, US*
PD Riordan *2003 E, 2004 US, J, E, US, 2006 S, E, US, Bar, US, W, It, 2007 IrA, M, US, NZ, Pt, W, Fj, J, A, 2008 US*
JR Robertsen *1985 A, A, US, 1986 US, 1987 Tg, US, 1989 I, US, 1990 Ar, US, Ar, 1991 Fj, F*
C Robertson *1997 HK, 1998 US, US, HK, J, Ur, 2001 Ur*
AK Robinson *1998 HK*
G Robinson *1966 Bl*
R Robson *1998 HK, US, 1999 J, Tg*
S Rodgers *2005 US*
RP Ross *1989 I, US, 1990 US, 1995 Ar, NZ, 1996 US, US, HK, J, A, HK, J, Ur, US, Ar, 1997 US, J, HK, HK, J, US, W, 1998 J, HK, US, US, HK, J, Ur, US, 1999 J, Fj, Sa, US, W, E, F, Nm, 2001 Ur, E, E, Fj, J, 2002 S, US, US, Ur, Ch, Ur, Ch, F, 2003 E, US, M, Ur, Ar, W, Tg*
JG Rowland *1932 J, J*
G Rowlands *1995 Ar, NZ, A, US, 1996 US, US*
RJ Russell *1979 US, 1983 E, 1985 A, A*
JB Ryan *1966 Bl, 1967 E*
IH Saundry *1932 J, J*
MD Schiefler *1981 US, Ar, 1982 J, E, US, 1983 US, 1984 US*
MD Schielfer *1980 US, NZ*
M Schmid *1996 Ur, US, Ar, 1997 US, J, US, W, I, 1998 US, HK, J, Ur, Ar, 1999 Sa, US, W, E, F, Fj, Nm, 2001 US, Ur, E, E*
T Scott *1976 Bb*
S Selkirk *1932 J*
JD Shaw *1978 F*
CJ Shergold *1980 US, NZ, 1981 US*
DM Shick *1970 Fj, 1971 W*
DC Sinnott *1979 F, 1981 US, Ar*
FG Skillings *1932 J, J*
DM Slater *1971 W*
C Smith *1995 Ur, US, 1996 HK, J, Ur, US, Ar, 1997 US, 1998 J, HK, US, HK, Ur, 1999 J, Fj, Sa, US, Tg, W, E, F*
RJ Smith *2003 E, M, M, Ur, US, Ar, W, NZ, Tg, 2004 US, J, E, US, F, It, E, 2005 US, J, W, E, US, Ar, F, R, 2006 S, Bar, US, W, It, 2007 IrA, M, US, NZ, Pt, W, Fj, J, 2008 US*
C Smythe *1997 J, HK*
RGA Snow *1995 Ar, NZ, R, A, SA, US, 1996 HK, J, A, HK, J, 1997 US, HK, J, W, I, 1998 US, US, US, Ar, 1999 J, Fj, Sa, US, W, E, F, Fj, Nm, 2000 I, J, It, 2001 US, Ar, E, E, Fj, J, 2002 S, US, US, Ur, Ch, Ur, Ch, W, F, 2003 Ur, US, Ar, W, NZ, It, Tg, 2006 US, Bar, US, 2007 Pt, W, Fj, J, A*
DA Speirs *1988 US, 1989 I, US, 1991 Fj, NZ*
D Spicer *2004 E, 2005 R, 2006 S, E, US, Bar, US, W, 2007 IrA, US, NZ, Pt, W, Fj, J, 2008 US*
WE Spofford *1981 Ar*
W Stanley *1994 US, F, 1995 S, Ur, Ar, R, A, SA, US, 1996 US, US, A, HK, J, 1997 US, J, HK, HK, US, W, I, 1998 US, US, HK, Ur, US, Ar, 1999 J, Fj, Sa, US, Tg, W, E, F, Fj, Nm,*

2000 Tg, US, SA, I, Sa, Fj, J, It, 2001 E, E, 2002 S, US, US, Ur, Ch, Ur, Ch, W, F, 2003 E, US, M, M, Ur, US, Ar, W, It, Tg
AI Stanton 1971 W, 1973 W, 1974 Tg
E Stapleton 1978 US, F
D Steen 1966 BI
SM Stephen 2005 E, US, 2006 S, E, US, Bar, US, W, 2007 US, NZ, Pt, W, Fj, A
C Stewart 1991 S, US, Fj, R, F, NZ, 1994 E, F, 1995 S, Fj, NZ, R, A, SA
DS Stewart 1989 US, 1990 Ar, 1991 US, Fj, R, F, NZ, 1992 E, 1993 E, E, US, A, W, 1994 US, F, W, E, F, 1995 S, Fj, NZ, R, A, SA, US, 1996 US, US, A, HK, J, Ur, US, Ar, 1997 US, J, HK, HK, J, US, W, I, 1998 US, J, Ur, Ar, 1999 Sa, US, Tg, W, E, F, Fj, Nm, 2000 US, SA, I, Sa, Fj, It, 2001 US, Ur, Ar, E, E
R Stewart 2005 R
B Stoikos 2001 Ur
G Stover 1962 Bb
R Strang 1983 E
C Strubin 2004 E
IC Stuart 1984 US, 1985 A, A, 1986 J, 1987 US, Tg, I, W, US, 1988 US, 1989 US, 1990 Ar, US, Ar, 1992 E, 1993 A, W, 1994 US, F, W, E
JD Stubbs 1962 Bb, W23
FJ Sturrock 1971 W
CW Suter 1932 J
KF Svoboda 1985 A, A, US, 1986 J, US, 1987 W, 1990 Ar, US, Ar, 1991 J, US, R, F, 1992 US, E, 1993 E, E, US, 1994 F, W, F, 1995 Fj, A, US
P Szabo 1989 I, US, 1990 Ar, US, Ar, 1991 NZ, 1993 US, A, W
JN Tait 1997 US, J, HK, HK, J, US, W, I, 1998 US, Ur, Ar, 1999 J, Fj, Sa, US, Tg, W, E, F, Fj, Nm, 2000 Tg, US, SA, I, Sa, Fj, J, It, 2001 US, Ur, Ar, E, E, 2002 US, W, F
L Tait 2005 US, J, W, E, 2006 S, E, US, Bar, US, W, It, 2007 M, US, NZ, Pt, W, Fj, A
WG Taylor 1978 F, 1979 US, F, 1980 W, US, NZ, 1981 US, Ar, 1983 US, It
J Thiel 1998 HK, J, Ur, 1999 J, Fj, Sa, US, Tg, W, E, F, Fj, Nm, 2000 SA, I, Sa, Fj, J, 2001 US, Ar, E, E, 2002 S, US, US, Ur, Ch, Ur, W, F, 2003 Ur, US, Ar, W, It, 2004 F, 2007 Pt, W, Fj, J, A
S Thompson 2001 Fj, J
W Thomson 1970 Fj
K Tkachuk 2000 Tg, US, SA, Sa, Fj, It, 2001 Fj, J, 2002 Ch, Ur, Ch, W, F, 2003 E, US, M, M, Ur, US, Ar, W, NZ, It, Tg, 2004 E, US, F, It, E, 2005 US, J, W, Ar, F, R, 2006 US, W, It, 2007 IrA, M, US, NZ, 2008 US
H Toews 1997 HK, 1998 J, HK, HK, Ur, 1999 Tg, 2000 US, Sa, J, It, 2001 Fj, J
R Toews 1993 W, 1994 US, F, W, E, 1995 S, Ur, Ar, Fj, 1996 US, HK, J, A, 1997 US, I
J Tomlinson 1996 A, 2001 Ur
N Trenkel 2007 A
DM Tucker 1985 A, A, US, 1986 US, 1987 US, W
A Tyler 2005 Ar
A Tynan 1995 Ur, Ar, US, 1997 J
CJ Tynan 1987 US, 1988 US, 1990 Ar, US, Ar, 1991 J, US, Fj, F, NZ, 1992 US, 1993 E, E, US, W, 1995 NZ, 1996 US, J, 1997 HK, J, 1998 US
DN Ure 1962 Bb, W23
PC Vaesen 1985 US, 1986 J, 1987 US, Tg, US
D van Camp 2005 J, R, 2006 It, 2007 IrA, M, US, NZ
R van den Brink 1986 US, 1987 Tg, 1988 US, 1991 J, US, R, F, NZ
D van der Merwe 2006 Bar, It, 2007 Pt, W, Fj, J, A
D Van Eeuwen 1978 F, 1979 US
A van Staveren 2000 Tg, Sa, Fj, 2002 US, US, Ur, Ch, Ur, Ch, W, F, 2003 E, US, M, M, Ur, US, W, NZ, Tg
J Verstraten 2000 US, SA, Fj, J
J Vivian 1983 E, 1984 US
KC Walt 1976 Bb, 1977 US, E, E, 1978 US, F
JM Ward 1962 W23
M Webb 2004 US, J, US, F, It, 2005 US, J, W, E, US, Ar, F, 2006 US, W, It, 2007 M, J, A, 2008 US
M Weingart 2004 J, 2005 J, E, US, F, R, 2007 Pt
GJM Wessels 1962 W23
WR Wharton 1932 J, J
K Whitley 1995 S
C Whittaker 1993 US, A, 1995 Ur, 1996 A, 1997 J, 1998 J, HK, US, US, HK, J, US, Ar, 1999 J, Fj, US
LW Whitty 1967 E
DW Whyte 1974 Tg, 1977 US, E, E
RR Wickland 1966 BI, 1967 E
JP Wiley 1977 US, E, E, 1978 US, F, 1979 US, 1980 W, US, NZ, 1981 US
K Wilke 1971 W, 1973 W, 1976 Bb, 1978 US
K Wilkinson 1976 Bb, 1978 F, 1979 F
BN Williams 1962 W23
J Williams 2001 US, Ur, Ar, Fj, J
M Williams 1992 E, 1993 A, W
M Williams 1999 Tg, W, E, F, Fj, Nm, 2000 Tg, SA, I, Sa, Fj, J, It, 2001 E, E, Fj, J, 2002 S, US, US, Ur, Ch, W, F, 2003 E, US, M, M, Ur, US, Ar, W, It, Tg, 2004 E, US, F, 2005 W, Ar, F, R, 2006 E, US, Bar, US, W, It, 2007 IrA, M, US, NZ, W, Fj, J, A
MH Williams 1982 J
MH Williams 1978 US, F, 1980 US
A Wilson 2008 US
PG Wilson 1932 J, J
RS Wilson 1962 Bb
K Wirachowski 1992 E, 1993 US, 1996 US, HK, Ur, US, Ar, 1997 US, HK, 2000 It, 2001 Ur, E, Fj, J, 2002 S, Ch, 2003 E, US, M
T Wish 2004 US, J
K Witkowski 2005 E, Ar, 2006 E
N Witkowski 1998 US, J, 2000 Tg, US, SA, I, Sa, Fj, J, It, 2001 US, E, E, 2002 S, US, US, Ur, Ch, Ur, Ch, W, F, 2003 E, US, M, M, Ur, Ar, W, NZ, Tg, 2005 E, US, 2006 E
AH Woller 1967 E
S Wood 1977 E
TA Woods 1984 US, 1986 J, US, 1987 US, Tg, I, W, 1988 US, 1989 I, US, 1990 Ar, US, 1991 S, F, NZ, 1996 US, US, 1997 US, J
MA Wyatt 1982 J, J, E, US, 1983 US, It, It, E, 1985 A, A, US, 1986 J, US, 1987 Tg, I, W, US, 1988 US, 1989 I, US, 1990 Ar, US, Ar, 1991 J, S, US, R, F, NZ
H Wyndham 1973 W
JJ Yeganegi 1996 US, 1998 J
C Yukes 2001 Ur, Fj, J, 2002 S, US, Ur, Ur, 2003 E, US, M, M, US, Ar, W, NZ, It, Tg, 2004 US, J, E, US, F, It, E, 2005 W, E, US, 2006 Bar, US, 2007 IrA, US, NZ, Pt, W, Fj, J, A

ENGLAND

ENGLAND'S 2008 TEST RECORD

OPPONENTS	DATE	VENUE	RESULT
Wales	2 February	H	**Lost** 19–26
Italy	10 February	A	**Won** 23–19
France	23 February	A	**Won** 24–13
Scotland	8 March	A	**Lost** 9–15
Ireland	15 March	H	**Won** 33–10
New Zealand	14 June	A	**Lost** 20–37
New Zealand	21 June	A	**Lost** 12–44

TURBULENT YEAR FOR ENGLAND

By Iain Spragg

Dave Rogers / Getty Images

England's best win in the Six Nations came in Paris, Richard Wigglesworth (above) getting the final try.

England have experienced so many false dawns amidst the malaise created by their World Cup triumph of 2003 that it's a moot point whether their supporters held out much hope for their embattled side as they welcomed in 2008 and looked ahead, with no little trepidation, to another Six Nations campaign and an intimidating two-Test tour of New Zealand.

There were, of course, causes for optimism. The side's gritty, turbulent progress to the World Cup final in Paris against the Springboks was as inspiring as it was surprising and their defeat to South Africa did little to diminish the hope that England had finally begun to put their house in order.

The rumours about dressing room unrest over Brian Ashton's leadership and coaching were conveniently forgotten and England prepared for the Championship with renewed confidence and purpose.

Just five short months later, however, and they were once again in disarray. Ashton was removed as head coach at the end of the tournament despite guiding the side to second place – their best finish for five years – and World Cup-winning captain Martin Johnson was installed as the new team manager.

Ashton paid a heavy price for his side's abject second-half capitulation against Wales at Twickenham and a dire display again against the Scots at Murrayfield. But the way his dismissal was handled, as the RFU attempted to entice Johnson in the full glare of the attendant media while the incumbent coach waited forlornly in the wings, left a decidedly bitter taste in the mouth.

Worse was to follow in the summer as England headed to New Zealand. Rob Andrew, the RFU's elite rugby director, temporarily took up the touring reins as Johnson remained at home to be at the birth of his second child and while their new boss waited to assume control, England ensured a torrid time.

On the pitch, the team were blown away in both Tests by the All Blacks while off it, an unsavoury controversy engulfed the squad to cast an even longer shadow on the trip. England had suffered many demoralising tours to the southern hemisphere after their famous triumph in Sydney in 2003 but their 2008 foray to New Zealand was without doubt their lowest ebb yet.

The irony was that the first 40 minutes of the year had promised so much. Looking for their first win at Twickenham for 20 years, Wales were in London for the Six Nations opener and at half-time England were sitting on 16–6 lead and in a position of dominance. It was as the two teams emerged from the tunnel for the second-half that the wheels began to come for Ashton and his players, both in the match and eventually their season as a whole.

England simply froze. Basic errors, a lack of invention and an inability to inject pace into their play all contrived to hand the initiative to Wales and the visitors gratefully accepted the opportunity, scoring tries from Lee Byrne and Mike Phillips to turn the game on its head and record a 26–19 win. England had choked horribly in front of their own supporters.

"It is difficult to get my head around exactly what went on in the second-half," Ashton admitted in the aftermath. "A lack of clarity of thought and how to play under pressure cost us and we helped Wales along the way. We just didn't make correct decisions. Wales didn't have to work particularly hard for their points."

The side were hardly any more convincing a week later in Rome against the Italians. Sitting on a 20–6 half-time lead after tries from Paul Sackey and Toby Flood, England once again toiled aimlessly

Dave Rogers / Getty Images

The victory over Ireland brought a great end to England's Six Nations campaign.

after the break and in the end were relieved to hang on for a 23–19 win.

England's next destination was the Stade de France to meet France in a repeat of the sides' World Cup semi-final clash. The English had not recorded a Championship victory in Paris for eight years and after the underwhelming performances against Wales and Italy, their prospects of breaking the sequence looked remote.

No-one however appeared to tell the England players. They took the lead with a Sackey try, which Wilkinson converted and when the fly-half landed a penalty, the visitors were 10–0 up. A youthful-looking France side hit back with a converted Lionel Nallet try but a second Wilkinson penalty gave England a 13–7 half-time advantage.

The anticipated French second-half fightback fizzled out quickly as England's pack began to exert more control. Wilkinson landed a drop goal to surpass Hugo Porta's long-standing record of 28 in international rugby and when scrum-half Richard Wigglesworth darted over late on, Ashton's side were 24–13 victors.

"Some of the rugby perhaps was not fantastic, but the endeavour, will and commitment was fantastic," said skipper Phil Vickery. "Everyone worked extremely hard for 80 minutes."

England's post Paris euphoria was not to last long. Scotland lay in wait at Murrayfield and in 80 horrendous minutes in Edinburgh, all the good work at the Stade de France was spectacularly undone.

The wind and rain at Murrayfield made the match something of a lottery but while the Scots adapted to the conditions, England looked like fish out of water and four Chris Paterson penalties and a fifth from Dan Parks were more than enough to send the auld enemy back south with their tail firmly between their legs.

"Patience is the biggest virtue a coach can have, but that starts to wear thin after a while," Ashton said ominously after the game. "We have to think really seriously about what happened today and what's going to happen in the future. Their kicking game and their discipline was better and you're highly unlikely to win games of international rugby if you don't compete in those areas."

A face-saving 33–10 win over at Ireland at Twickenham steered England to second place in the Championship but the speculation about Ashton's future was already rampant and as the days and weeks past, it seemed it was merely a matter of time before the RFU hierarchy dispensed with his services.

Confirmation came in April when the iconic Johnson was finally unveiled as the new England team manager and Ashton was officially removed as head coach. It was the worst kept secret in the game and although the majority of fans welcomed Johnson's appointment, there was also great sympathy for Ashton and the way the axe had been wielded, the coach being kept in the dark for much of the process.

"I am passionate about the England team and delivering success for it," Johnson said after taking the job. "While I cannot take up my position until July for personal reasons I will be working closely with Rob [Andrew] and the England coaching team on selection for the Barbarians match and the New Zealand tour."

The clash with the Barbarians at Twickenham provided few crumbs of comfort as a second string England side limped to an uninspiring 17–14 win and the squad, containing six uncapped players and captained by Steve Borthwick in the absence of the injured Vickery, flew out to New Zealand more in hope than expectation.

The first Test against the All Blacks in Auckland merely confirmed what many England supporters had feared. England did take a 6–3 first-half lead but their frailties were cruelly exposed by the Kiwis and tries from Conrad Smith and Dan Carter, Mils Muliaina and Sitiveni Sivivatu rubbed salt into the wound. Debutant wing Topsy Ojo scored tries either side of half-time but there was an element of luck in both scores and the final 37–20 scoreline flattered the visitors. England had been exposed as defensively vulnerable and bereft of ideas going forward.

Dave Rogers / Getty Images

England suffered on and off the field in New Zealand, losing both Tests.

"Test match rugby is a brutal place and if you make simple mistakes then you will be punished," Andrew admitted "We're disappointed with the end result and really, when you analyse it, they were better with the ball than we were and that was the difference."

Preparations for the second Test in Christchurch were dominated by lurid allegations in the media about the players' post-match behaviour in Auckland. It cast a shadow over the whole England camp and it almost went unnoticed when Andrew announced he was making six changes, five in the backs, for the game.

An investigation into the allegations of sexual misconduct on that tour to New Zealand, on the part of some players, exonerated all of them bar Ojo and full-back Mike Brown, who were both fined after being found guilty of misconduct.

Brown was reprimanded and fined £1,000 for "staying out all night during an England rugby tour" and missing a physio appointment.

Ojo was reprimanded and fined £500 after admitting staying out until after 7am on Sunday morning, the day after the Test.

England desperately needed a much-improved performance in the Jade Stadium to end their season on something resembling a high but the All Blacks were not in a merciful mood, running in five tries in 44–12 drubbing that drew the curtain on an ill-fated tour that started badly and got steadily worse.

"You can have a great week's training but it comes down to the 80 minutes," said Borthwick, the beleaguered stand-in skipper. "The last two games we've been found wanting against very strong opponents. We had some opportunities in the first half but we didn't take them and ultimately that cost us."

In truth, England were totally out thought and outplayed by the Kiwis and if Johnson, sitting at home watching his television, still had any lingering illusions of the size of the task ahead of him, they will have been decisively dispelled by what he saw unfold in New Zealand.

Johnson made his first coaching appointment in July when London Irish's Director of Rugby, Brian Smith, was put in charge of the nation's backline. A new deal with the clubs also means increased access to the players from the 2008–09 season and although 2008 is probably best forgotten, on and off the field, many in the game believe the future could still be bright for England.

ENGLAND INTERNATIONAL STATISTICS

MATCH RECORDS UP TO 30TH SEPTEMBER 2008

MOST CONSECUTIVE TEST WINS

14 2002 W,It,Arg,NZ,A,SA, 2003 F1,W1,It,S,I, NZ,A, W2
11 2000 SA 2,A,Arg,SA3, 2001 W,It,S,F,C1,2,US
10 1882 W, 1883 I,S, 1884 W,I,S, 1885 W,I, 1886 W,I
10 1994 R,C, 1995 I,F,W,S, Arg, It, WS, A
10 2003 F,Gg,SA,Sm,U,W,F,A, 2004 It,S

MOST CONSECUTIVE TESTS WITHOUT DEFEAT

Matches	Wins	Draws	Periods
14	14	0	2002 to 2003
12	10	2	1882 to 1887
11	10	1	1922 to 1924
11	11	0	2000 to 2001

MOST POINTS IN A MATCH

BY THE TEAM

Pts.	Opponents	Venue	Year
134	Romania	Twickenham	2001
111	Uruguay	Brisbane	2003
110	Netherlands	Huddersfield	1998
106	U S A	Twickenham	1999
101	Tonga	Twickenham	1999
84	Georgia	Perth	2003
80	Italy	Twickenham	2001

BY A PLAYER

Pts.	Player	Opponents	Venue	Year
44	C Hodgson	Romania	Twickenham	2001
36	P J Grayson	Tonga	Twickenham	1999
35	J P Wilkinson	Italy	Twickenham	2001
32	J P Wilkinson	Italy	Twickenham	1999
30	C R Andrew	Canada	Twickenham	1994
30	P J Grayson	Netherlands	Huddersfield	1998
30	J P Wilkinson	Wales	Twickenham	2002
29	D J H Walder	Canada	Burnaby	2001
27	C R Andrew	South Africa	Pretoria	1994
27	J P Wilkinson	South Africa	Bloemfontein	2000
27	C C Hodgson	South Africa	Twickenham	2004
27	J P Wilkinson	Scotland	Twickenham	2007
26	J P Wilkinson	United States	Twickenham	1999

MOST TRIES IN A MATCH

BY THE TEAM

Tries	Opponents	Venue	Year
20	Romania	Twickenham	2001
17	Uruguay	Brisbane	2003
16	Netherlands	Huddersfield	1998
16	United States	Twickenham	1999
13	Wales	Blackheath	1881
13	Tonga	Twickenham	1999
12	Georgia	Perth	2003
12	Canada	Twickenham	2004
10	Japan	Sydney	1987
10	Fiji	Twickenham	1989
10	Italy	Twickenham	2001

BY A PLAYER

Tries	Player	Opponents	Venue	Year
5	D Lambert	France	Richmond	1907
5	R Underwood	Fiji	Twickenham	1989
5	O J Lewsey	Uruguay	Brisbane	2003
4	G W Burton	Wales	Blackheath	1881
4	A Hudson	France	Paris	1906
4	R W Poulton	France	Paris	1914
4	C Oti	Romania	Bucharest	1989
4	J C Guscott	Netherlands	Huddersfield	1998
4	N A Back	Netherlands	Huddersfield	1998
4	J C Guscott	United States	Twickenham	1999
4	J Robinson	Romania	Twickenham	2001
4	N Easter	Wales	Twickenham	2007

MOST CONVERSIONS IN A MATCH

BY THE TEAM

Cons	Opponents	Venue	Year
15	Netherlands	Huddersfield	1998
14	Romania	Twickenham	2001
13	United States	Twickenham	1999
13	Uruguay	Brisbane	2003
12	Tonga	Twickenham	1999
9	Italy	Twickenham	2001
9	Georgia	Perth	2003
8	Romania	Bucharest	1989
7	Wales	Blackheath	1881
7	Japan	Sydney	1987
7	Argentina	Twickenham	1990
7	Wales	Twickenham	1998
7	Wales	Twickenham	2007

BY A PLAYER

Cons	Player	Opponents	Venue	Year
15	P J Grayson	Netherlands	Huddersfield	1998
14	C Hodgson	Romania	Twickenham	2001
13	J P Wilkinson	United States	Twickenham	1999
12	P J Grayson	Tonga	Twickenham	1999
11	P J Grayson	Uruguay	Brisbane	2003
9	J P Wilkinson	Italy	Twickenham	2001
8	S D Hodgkinson	Romania	Bucharest	1989
7	J M Webb	Japan	Sydney	1987
7	S D Hodgkinson	Argentina	Twickenham	1990
7	P J Grayson	Wales	Twickenham	1998
7	J P Wilkinson	Wales	Twickenham	2007

MOST PENALTIES IN A MATCH

BY THE TEAM

Pens	Opponents	Venue	Year
8	South Africa	Bloemfontein	2000
7	Wales	Cardiff	1991
7	Scotland	Twickenham	1995
7	France	Twickenham	1999
7	Fiji	Twickenham	1999
7	South Africa	Paris	1999
7	South Africa	Twickenham	2001
6	Wales	Twickenham	1986
6	Canada	Twickenham	1994
6	Argentina	Durban	1995
6	Scotland	Murrayfield	1996
6	Ireland	Twickenham	1996
6	South Africa	Twickenham	2000
6	Australia	Twickenham	2002
6	Wales	Brisbane	2003

BY A PLAYER

Pens	Player	Opponents	Venue	Year
8	J P Wilkinson	South Africa	Bloemfontein	2000
7	S D Hodgkinson	Wales	Cardiff	1991
7	C R Andrew	Scotland	Twickenham	1995
7	J P Wilkinson	France	Twickenham	1999
7	J P Wilkinson	Fiji	Twickenham	1999
7	J P Wilkinson	South Africa	Twickenham	2001
6	C R Andrew	Wales	Twickenham	1986
6	C R Andrew	Canada	Twickenham	1994
6	C R Andrew	Argentina	Durban	1995
6	P J Grayson	Scotland	Murrayfield	1996
6	P J Grayson	Ireland	Twickenham	1996
6	P J Grayson	South Africa	Paris	1999
6	J P Wilkinson	South Africa	Twickenham	2000
6	J P Wilkinson	Australia	Twickenham	2002
6	J P Wilkinson	Wales	Brisbane	2003

MOST DROPPED GOALS IN A MATCH

BY THE TEAM

Drops	Opponents	Venue	Year
3	France	Sydney	2003
2	Ireland	Twickenham	1970
2	France	Paris	1978
2	France	Paris	1980
2	Romania	Twickenham	1985
2	Fiji	Suva	1991
2	Argentina	Durban	1995
2	France	Paris	1996
2	Australia	Twickenham	2001
2	Wales	Cardiff	2003
2	Ireland	Dublin	2003
2	South Africa	Perth	2003
2	Samoa	Nantes	2007
2	Tonga	Paris	2007

BY A PLAYER

Drops	Player	Opponents	Venue	Year
3	J P Wilkinson	France	Sydney	2003
2	R Hiller	Ireland	Twickenham	1970
2	A G B Old	France	Paris	1978
2	J P Horton	France	Paris	1980
2	C R Andrew	Romania	Twickenham	1985
2	C R Andrew	Fiji	Suva	1991
2	C R Andrew	Argentina	Durban	1995
2	P J Grayson	France	Paris	1996
2	J P Wilkinson	Australia	Twickenham	2001
2	J P Wilkinson	Wales	Cardiff	2003
2	J P Wilkinson	Ireland	Dublin	2003
2	J P Wilkinson	South Africa	Perth	2003
2	J P Wilkinson	Samoa	Nantes	2007
2	J P Wilkinson	Tonga	Paris	2007

CAREER RECORDS

MOST CAPPED PLAYERS

Caps	Player	Career Span
114	J Leonard	1990 to 2004
85	R Underwood	1984 to 1996
85	L B N Dallaglio	1995 to 2007
84	M O Johnson	1993 to 2003
77	M J S Dawson	1995 to 2006
75	M J Catt	1994 to 2007
72	W D C Carling	1988 to 1997
71	C R Andrew	1985 to 1997
71	R A Hill	1997 to 2004
70	J P Wilkinson	1998 to 2008
69	D J Grewcock	1997 to 2007
67	J P R Worsley	1999 to 2008
66	N A Back	1994 to 2003
65	J C Guscott	1989 to 1999
64	B C Moore	1987 to 1995
64	M E Corry	1997 to 2007
64	P J Vickery	1998 to 2008
60	B J Kay	2001 to 2008
58	P J Winterbottom	1982 to 1993
57	B C Cohen	2000 to 2006
56	M J Tindall	2000 to 2008
55	W A Dooley	1985 to 1993
55	W J H Greenwood	1997 to 2004
55	O J Lewsey	1998 to 2007
54	G C Rowntree	1995 to 2006
53	L W Moody	2001 to 2008
51	A S Healey	1997 to 2003
51	K P P Bracken	1993 to 2003
51	J T Robinson	2001 to 2007

MOST CONSECUTIVE TESTS

Tests	Player	Span
44	W D C Carling	1989 to 1995
40	J Leonard	1990 to 1995
36	J V Pullin	1968 to 1975
33	W B Beaumont	1975 to 1982
30	R Underwood	1992 to 1996

MOST TESTS AS CAPTAIN

Tests	Player	Span
59	W D C Carling	1988 to 1996
39	M O Johnson	1998 to 2003
22	L B N Dallaglio	1997 to 2004
21	W B Beaumont	1978 to 1982
17	M E Corry	2005 to 2007
15	P J Vickery	2002 to 2008
13	W W Wakefield	1924 to 1926
13	N M Hall	1949 to 1955
13	E Evans	1956 to 1958
13	R E G Jeeps	1960 to 1962
13	J V Pullin	1972 to 1975

MOST POINTS IN TESTS

Points	Player	Tests	Career
1032	J P Wilkinson	70	1998 to 2008
400	P J Grayson	32	1995 to 2004
396	C R Andrew	71	1985 to 1997
296	J M Webb	33	1987 to 1993
259	C C Hodgson	31	2001 to 2008
240	W H Hare	25	1974 to 1984
210	R Underwood	85	1984 to 1996

MOST TRIES IN TESTS

Tries	Player	Tests	Career
49	R Underwood	85	1984 to 1996
31	W J H Greenwood	55	1997 to 2004
31	B C Cohen	57	2000 to 2006
30	J C Guscott	65	1989 to 1999
28	J T Robinson	51	2001 to 2007
24	D D Luger	38	1998 to 2003
22	O J Lewsey	55	1998 to 2007
18	C N Lowe	25	1913 to 1923
17	L B N Dallaglio	85	1995 to 2007
16	N A Back	66	1994 to 2003
16	M J S Dawson	77	1995 to 2006
15	A S Healey	51	1997 to 2003
13	T Underwood	27	1992 to 1998
13	M J Tindall	56	2000 to 2008
13	M J Cueto	24	2004 to 2007
13	I R Balshaw	35	2000 to 2008

MOST CONVERSIONS IN TESTS

Cons	Player	Tests	Career
144	J P Wilkinson	70	1998 to 2008
78	P J Grayson	32	1995 to 2004
44	C C Hodgson	31	2001 to 2008
41	J M Webb	33	1987 to 1993
35	S D Hodgkinson	14	1989 to 1991
33	C R Andrew	71	1985 to 1997
17	L Stokes	12	1875 to 1881

MOST DROPPED GOALS IN TESTS

Drops	Player	Tests	Career
29	J P Wilkinson	70	1998 to 2008
21	C R Andrew	71	1985 to 1997
6	P J Grayson	32	1995 to 2004
4	J P Horton	13	1978 to 1984
4	L Cusworth	12	1979 to 1988

MOST PENALTY GOALS IN TESTS

Pens	Player	Tests	Career
209	J P Wilkinson	70	1998 to 2008
86	C R Andrew	71	1985 to 1997
72	P J Grayson	32	1995 to 2004
67	W H Hare	25	1974 to 1984
66	J M Webb	33	1987 to 1993
44	C C Hodgson	31	2001 to 2008
43	S D Hodgkinson	14	1989 to 1991

INTERNATIONAL CHAMPIONSHIP RECORDS

RECORD	DETAIL		SET
Most points in season	229	in five matches	2001
Most tries in season	29	in five matches	2001
Highest Score	80	80–23 v Italy	2001
Biggest win	57	80–23 v Italy	2001
Highest score conceded	43	13–43 v Ireland	2007
Biggest defeat	30	13–43 v Ireland	2007
Most appearances	54	J Leonard	1991–2004
Most points in matches	479	J P Wilkinson	1998–2008
Most points in season	89	J P Wilkinson	2001
Most points in match	35	J P Wilkinson	v Italy, 2001
Most tries in matches	18	C N Lowe	1913–1923
	18	R Underwood	1984–1996
Most tries in season	8	C N Lowe	1914
Most tries in match	4	R W Poulton	v France, 1914
Most cons in matches	81	J P Wilkinson	1998–2008
Most cons in season	24	J P Wilkinson	2001
Most cons in match	9	J P Wilkinson	v Italy, 2001
Most pens in matches	90	J P Wilkinson	1998–2008
Most pens in season	18	S D Hodgkinson	1991
	18	J P Wilkinson	2000
Most pens in match	7	S D Hodgkinson	v Wales, 1991
	7	C R Andrew	v Scotland, 1995
	7	J P Wilkinson	v France, 1999
Most drops in matches	9	C R Andrew	1985–1997
	9	J P Wilkinson	1998–2008
Most drops in season	5	J P Wilkinson	2003
Most drops in match	2	R Hiller	v Ireland, 1970
	2	A G B Old	v France, 1978
	2	J P Horton	v France, 1980
	2	P J Grayson	v France, 1996
	2	J P Wilkinson	v Wales, 2003
	2	J P Wilkinson	v Ireland, 2003

MISCELLANEOUS RECORDS

RECORD	HOLDER	DETAIL
Longest Test Career	J Leonard	1990 to 2004
Youngest Test Cap	H C C Laird	18 yrs 134 days in 1927
Oldest Test Cap	F Gilbert	38 yrs 362 days in 1923

CAREER RECORDS OF ENGLAND INTERNATIONAL PLAYERS (UP TO 30 SEPTEMBER 2008)

PLAYER BACKS	DEBUT	CAPS	T	C	P	D	PTS
N Abendanon	2007 v SA	2	0	0	0	0	0
A Allen	2006 v NZ	2	0	0	0	0	0
I R Balshaw	2000 v I	35	13	0	0	0	65
O J Barkley	2001 v US	23	2	9	18	0	82
M Brown	2007 v SA	3	0	0	0	0	0
D Care	2008 v NZ	2	1	0	0	0	5
D Cipriani	2008 v W	3	0	3	4	0	18
B C Cohen	2000 v I	57	31	0	0	0	155
M J Cueto	2004 v C	24	13	0	0	0	65
H A Ellis	2004 v SA	18	3	0	0	0	15
A Farrell	2007 v S	8	1	0	0	0	5
T Flood	2006 v Arg	18	3	2	5	1	37
S Geraghty	2007 v F	2	0	1	1	0	5
A C T Gomarsall	1996 v It	35	6	2	0	1	37
A J Goode	2005 v It	9	0	7	10	1	47
D Hipkiss	2007 v W	6	0	0	0	0	0
C C Hodgson	2001 v R	31	6	44	44	3	259
P Hodgson	2008 v I	1	0	0	0	0	0
O J Lewsey	1998 v NZ	55	22	0	0	0	110
O Morgan	2007 v S	2	0	0	0	0	0
J D Noon	2001 v C	33	7	0	0	0	35
T Ojo	2008 v NZ	2	2	0	0	0	10
S Perry	2006 v NZ	14	2	0	0	0	10
P C Richards	2006 v A	13	0	0	0	0	0
J T Robinson	2001 v It	51	28	0	0	0	140
P H Sackey	2006 v NZ	15	8	0	0	0	40
D G R Scarbrough	2003 v W	2	1	0	0	0	5
J D Simpson-Daniel	2002 v NZ	10	3	0	0	0	15
D Strettle	2007 v I	6	1	0	0	0	5
M Tait	2005 v W	24	3	0	0	0	15
M J Tindall	2000 v I	56	13	2	0	0	69
L Vainikolo	2008 v W	5	0	0	0	0	0
T W Varndell	2005 v Sm	4	3	0	0	0	15
R E P Wigglesworth	2008 v It	5	1	0	0	0	5
J P Wilkinson	1998 v I	70	6	144	209	29	1032

FORWARDS

S W Borthwick	2001 v F	39	2	0	0	0	10
A Brown	2006 v A	3	0	0	0	0	0
M I Cairns	2007 v SA	1	0	0	0	0	0
G S Chuter	2006 v A	21	1	0	0	0	5
M E Corry	1997 v Arg	64	6	0	0	0	30
T Croft	2008 v F	4	0	0	0	0	0
L B N Dallaglio	1995 v SA	85	17	0	0	0	85
L P Deacon	2005 v Sm	8	0	0	0	0	0
N Easter	2007 v It	16	4	0	0	0	20
P T Freshwater	2005 v Sm	10	0	0	0	0	0
D J Grewcock	1997 v Arg	69	2	0	0	0	10
J Haskell	2007 v W	8	0	0	0	0	0
A R Hazell	2004 v C	7	1	0	0	0	5
J Hobson	2008 v NZ	1	0	0	0	0	0
C M Jones	2004 v It	12	1	0	0	0	5
B J Kay	2001 v C	60	2	0	0	0	10
M R Lipman	2004 v NZ	7	0	0	0	0	0
M B Lund	2006 v A	10	1	0	0	0	5
L A Mears	2005 v Sm	25	0	0	0	0	0
L W Moody	2001 v C	53	9	0	0	0	45
L Narraway	2008 v W	5	0	0	0	0	0
D Paice	2008 v NZ	2	0	0	0	0	0
T Palmer	2001 v US	10	0	0	0	0	0
T A N Payne	2004 v A	8	0	0	0	0	0
T Rees	2007 v S	11	1	0	0	0	5
M P Regan	1995 v SA	46	3	0	0	0	15
P H Sanderson	1998 v NZ	16	1	0	0	0	5
D Schofield	2007 v SA	2	0	0	0	0	0
S D Shaw	1996 v It	48	2	0	0	0	10
A J Sheridan	2004 v C	25	0	0	0	0	0
B Skirving	2007 v SA	1	0	0	0	0	0
M J H Stevens	2004 v NZ	28	0	0	0	0	0
A J Titterrell	2004 v NZ	5	0	0	0	0	0
S C Turner	2007 v W	3	0	0	0	0	0
P J Vickery	1998 v W	64	2	0	0	0	10
J M White	2000 v SA	44	0	0	0	0	0
R A Winters	2007 v SA	2	0	0	0	0	0
J P R Worsley	1999 v Tg	67	9	0	0	0	45
K P Yates	1997 v Arg	4	0	0	0	0	0

ENGLAND INTERNATIONAL PLAYERS

UP TO 30TH SEPTEMBER 2008

Note: Years given for International Championship matches are for second half of season; eg 1972 means season 1971-72. Years for all other matches refer to the actual year of the match. Entries in square brackets denote matches played in RWC Finals.

Aarvold, C D (Cambridge U, W Hartlepool, Headingley, Blackheath) 1928 A, W, I, F, S, 1929 W, I, F, 1931 W, S, F, 1932 SA, W, I, S, 1933 W
Abbott, S R (Wasps, Harlequins) 2003 W2, F3, [Sm, U, W(R)], 2004 NZ1(t&R), 2, 2006 I, A2(R)
Abendanon, N (Bath) 2007 SA2(R),F2
Ackford, P J (Harlequins) 1988 A, 1989 S, I, F, W, R, Fj, 1990 I, F, W, S, Arg 3, 1991 W, S, I, F, A, [NZ, It, F, S, A]
Adams, A A (London Hospital) 1910 F
Adams, F R (Richmond) 1875 I, S, 1876 S, 1877 I, 1878 S, 1879 S, I
Adebayo, A A (Bath) 1996, It, 1997 Arg 1,2, A 2, NZ 1, 1998 S
Adey, G J (Leicester) 1976 I, F
Adkins, S J (Coventry) 1950 I, F, S, 1953 W, I, F, S
Agar, A E (Harlequins) 1952 SA, W, S, I, F, 1953 W, I
Alcock, A (Guy's Hospital) 1906 SA
Alderson, F H R (Hartlepool R) 1891 W, I, S, 1892 W, S, 1893 W
Alexander, H (Richmond) 1900 I, S, 1901 W, I, S, 1902 W, I
Alexander, W (Northern) 1927 F
Allen, A (Gloucester) 2006 NZ,Arg
Allison, D F (Coventry) 1956 W, I, S, F, 1957 W, 1958 W, S
Allport, A (Blackheath) 1892 W, 1893 I, 1894 W, I, S
Anderson, S (Rockcliff) 1899 I
Anderson, W F (Orrell) 1973 NZ 1
Anderton, C (Manchester FW) 1889 M
Andrew, C R (Cambridge U, Nottingham, Wasps, Toulouse, Newcastle) 1985 R, F, S, I, W, 1986 W, S, I, F, 1987 I, F, W, [J (R), US], 1988 S, I 1,2, A 1,2, Fj, A, 1989 S, I, F, W, R, Fj, 1990 I, F, W, S, Arg 3, 1991 W, S, I, F, Fj, A, [NZ, It, US, F, S, A], 1992 S, I, F, W, C, SA, 1993 F, W, NZ, 1994 S, I, F, W, SA 1,2, R, C, 1995 I, F, W, S, [Arg, It, A, NZ, F], 1997 W (R)
Appleford, G N (London Irish) 2002 Arg
Archer, G S (Bristol, Army, Newcastle) 1996 S, I, 1997 A 2, NZ 1, SA, NZ 2, 1998 F, W, S, I, A 1, NZ 1, H, It, 1999 Tg, Fj, 2000 I, F, W, It, S
Archer, H (Bridgwater A) 1909 W, F, I
Armstrong, R (Northern) 1925 W
Arthur, T G (Wasps) 1966 W, I
Ashby, R C (Wasps) 1966 I, F, 1967 A
Ashcroft, A (Waterloo) 1956 W, I, S, F, 1957 W, I, F, S, 1958 W, A, I, F, S, 1959 I, F, S
Ashcroft, A H (Birkenhead Park) 1909 A
Ashford, W (Richmond) 1897 W, I, 1898 S, W
Ashworth, A (Oldham) 1892 I
Askew, J G (Cambridge U) 1930 W, I, F
Aslett, A R (Richmond) 1926 W, I, F, S, 1929 S, F
Assinder, E W (O Edwardians) 1909 A, W
Aston, R L (Blackheath) 1890 S, I
Auty, J R (Headingley) 1935 S

Back, N A (Leicester) 1994 S, I, 1995 [Arg (t), It, WS], 1997 NZ 1(R), SA, NZ 2, 1998 F, W, S, I, H, It, A 2, SA 2, 1999 S, I, F, W, A, US, C, [It, NZ, Fj, SA], 2000 I, F, W, It, S, SA 1,2, A, Arg, SA 3, 2001 W, It, S, F, I, A, R, SA, 2002 S, I, F, W, It, NZ (t + R), A, SA, 2003 F 1, W 1, S, I, NZ, A, F 3, [Gg, SA, Sm, W, F, A]
Bailey, M D (Cambridge U, Wasps) 1984 SA 1,2, 1987 [US], 1989 Fj, 1990 I, F, S (R)
Bainbridge, S (Gosforth, Fylde) 1982 F, W, 1983 F, W, S, I, NZ, 1984 S, I, F, W, 1985 NZ 1,2, 1987 F, W, S, [J, US]
Baker, D G S (OMTs) 1955 W, I, F, S
Baker, E M (Moseley) 1895 W, I, S, 1896 W, I, S, 1897 W
Baker, H C (Clifton) 1887 W
Balshaw, I R (Bath, Leeds, Gloucester) 2000 I (R), F (R), It (R), S (R), A (R), Arg, SA 3(R), 2001 W, It, S, F, I, 2002 S (R), I (R), 2003 F2,3, [Sm, U, A(R)], 2004 It, S, I, 2005 It, S, 2006 A1, 2, NZ,Arg, 2007 It,SA1, 2008 W,It,F,S,I
Bance, J F (Bedford) 1954 S
Barkley, O J (Bath) 2001 US (R), 2004 It(R), I(t), W, F, NZ2(R), A1(R), 2005 W(R), F, I, It, S, A(R), Sm(R), 2006 A1, 2(R), 2007 F2,3(R), [US,Sm,Tg], 2008 NZ1,2(R)
Barley, B (Wakefield) 1984 I, F, W, A, 1988 A 1,2, Fj
Barnes, S (Bristol, Bath) 1984 A, 1985 R (R), NZ 1,2, 1986 S (R), F (R), 1987 I (R), 1988 Fj, 1993 S, I
Barr, R J (Leicester) 1932 SA, W, I
Barrett, E I M (Lennox) 1903 S
Barrington, T J M (Bristol) 1931 W, I
Barrington-Ward, L E (Edinburgh U) 1910 W, I, F, S
Barron, J H (Bingley) 1896 S, 1897 W, I
Bartlett, J T (Waterloo) 1951 W
Bartlett, R M (Harlequins) 1957 W, I, F, S, 1958 I, F, S
Barton, J (Coventry) 1967 I, F, W, 1972 F
Batchelor, T B (Oxford U) 1907 F
Bates, S M (Wasps) 1989 R
Bateson, A H (Otley) 1930 W, I, F, S
Bateson, H D (Liverpool) 1879 I
Batson, T (Blackheath) 1872 S, 1874 S, 1875 I
Batten, J M (Cambridge U) 1874 S
Baume, J L (Northern) 1950 S
Baxendell, J J N (Sale) 1998 NZ 2, SA 1
Baxter, J (Birkenhead Park) 1900 W, I, S
Bayfield, M C (Northampton) 1991 Fj, A, 1992 S, I, F, W, C, SA, 1993 F, W, S, I, 1994 S, I, SA 1,2, R, C, 1995 I, F, W, S, [Arg, It, A, NZ, F], SA, WS, 1996 F, W
Bazley, R C (Waterloo) 1952 I, F, 1953 W, I, F, S, 1955 W, I, F, S
Beal, N D (Northampton) 1996 Arg, 1997 A 1, 1998 NZ 1,2, SA 1, H (R), SA 2, 1999 S, F (R), A (t), C (R), [It (R), Tg (R), Fj, SA]
Beaumont, W B (Fylde) 1975 I, A 1(R),2, 1976 A, W, S, I, F, 1977 S, I, F, W, 1978 F, W, S, I, NZ, 1979 S, I, F, W, NZ, 1980 I, F, W, S, 1981 W, S, I, F, Arg 1,2, 1982 A, S
Bedford, H (Morley) 1889 M, 1890 S, I
Bedford, L L (Headingley) 1931 W, I
Beer, I D S (Harlequins) 1955 F, S
Beese, M C (Liverpool) 1972 W, I, F
Beim, T D (Sale) 1998 NZ 1(R),2
Bell, D S C (Bath) 2005 It(R), S
Bell, F J (Northern) 1900 W
Bell, H (New Brighton) 1884 I
Bell, J L (Darlington) 1878 I
Bell, P J (Blackheath) 1968 W, I, F, S
Bell, R W (Northern) 1900 W, I, S
Bendon, G J (Wasps) 1959 W, I, F, S
Bennett, N O (St Mary's Hospital, Waterloo) 1947 W, S, F, 1948 A, W, I, S
Bennett, W N (Bedford, London Welsh) 1975 S, A1, 1976 S (R), 1979 S, I, F, W

Bennetts, B B (Penzance) 1909 A, W
Bentley, J (Sale, Newcastle) 1988 I 2, A 1, 1997 A 1, SA
Bentley, J E (Gipsies) 1871 S, 1872 S
Benton, S (Gloucester) 1998 A 1
Berridge, M J (Northampton) 1949 W, I
Berry, H (Gloucester) 1910 W, I, F, S
Berry, J (Tyldesley) 1891 W, I, S
Berry, J T W (Leicester) 1939 W, I, S
Beswick, E (Swinton) 1882 I, S
Biggs, J M (UCH) 1878 S, 1879 I
Birkett, J G G (Harlequins) 1906 S, F, SA, 1907 F, W, S, 1908 F, W,I , S, 1910 W, I, S, 1911 W, F, I , S, 1912 W, I , S, F
Birkett L (Clapham R) 1875 S, 1877 I, S
Birkett, R H (Clapham R) 1871 S, 1875 S, 1876 S, 1877 I
Bishop, C C (Blackheath) 1927 F
Black, B H (Blackheath) 1930 W, I, F, S, 1931 W, I, S, F, 1932 S, 1933 W
Blacklock, J H (Aspatria) 1898 I, 1899 I
Blakeway, P J (Gloucester) 1980 I, F, W, S, 1981 W, S, I, F, 1982 I, F, W, 1984 I, F, W, SA 1, 1985 R, F, S, I
Blakiston, A F (Northampton) 1920 S, 1921 W, I, S, F, 1922 W, 1923 S, F, 1924 W, I, F, S, 1925 NZ, W, I, S, F
Blatherwick, T (Manchester) 1878 I
Body, J A (Gipsies) 1872 S, 1873 S
Bolton, C A (United Services) 1909 F
Bolton, R (Harlequins) 1933 W, 1936 S, 1937 S, 1938 W, I
Bolton, W N (Blackheath) 1882 I, S, 1883 W, I, S, 1884 W, I, S, 1885 I, 1887 I, S
Bonaventura, M S (Blackheath) 1931 W
Bond, A M (Sale) 1978 NZ, 1979 S, I, NZ, 1980 I, 1982 I
Bonham-Carter, E (Oxford U) 1891 S
Bonsor, F (Bradford) 1886 W, I, S, 1887 W, S, 1889 M
Boobbyer, B (Rosslyn Park) 1950 W, I, F, S, 1951 W, F, 1952 S, I, F
Booth, L A (Headingley) 1933 W, I, S, 1934 S, 1935 W, I, S
Borthwick, S W (Bath) 2001 F, C 1,2(R), US, R, 2003 A(t), W 2(t), F 2, 2004 I, F(R), NZ1(R), 2, A1, C, SA, A2, 2005 W(R), It(R), S(R), A, NZ, Sm, 2006 W, It, S, F, I, 2007 W2,F3, [SA1(t&R),Sm(R),Tg], 2008 W,It,F,S,I,NZ1,2
Botting, I J (Oxford U) 1950 W, I
Boughton, H J (Gloucester) 1935 W, I, S
Boyle, C W (Oxford U) 1873 S
Boyle, S B (Gloucester) 1983 W, S, I
Boylen, F (Hartlepool R) 1908 F, W, I, S
Bracken, K P P (Bristol, Saracens) 1993 NZ, 1994 S, I, C, 1995 I, F, W, S, [It, WS (t)], SA, 1996 It (R), 1997 Arg 1,2, A 2, NZ 1,2, 1998 F, W, 1999 S(R), I, F, A, 2000 SA 1,2, A, 2001 It (R), S (R), F (R), C 1,2, US, I (R), A, R (R), SA, 2002 S, I, F, W, It, 2003 W 1, It(R), I(t), NZ, A, F3, [SA, U(R), W(R), F(t&R)]
Bradby, M S (United Services) 1922 I, F
Bradley, R (W Hartlepool) 1903 W
Bradshaw, H (Bramley) 1892 S, 1893 W, I, S, 1894 W, I, S
Brain, S E (Coventry) 1984 SA 2, A (R), 1985 R, F, S, I, W, NZ 1,2, 1986 W, S, I, F
Braithwaite, J (Leicester) 1905 NZ
Braithwaite-Exley, B (Headingley) 1949 W
Brettargh, A T (Liverpool OB) 1900 W, 1903 I, S, 1904 W, I, S, 1905 I, S
Brewer, J (Gipsies) 1876 I
Briggs, A (Bradford) 1892 W, I, S
Brinn, A (Gloucester) 1972 W, I, S
Broadley, T (Bingley) 1893 W, S, 1894 W, I, S, 1896 S
Bromet, W E (Richmond) 1891 W, I, 1892 W, I, S, 1893 W, I, S, 1895 W, I, S, 1896 I
Brook, P W P (Harlequins) 1930 S, 1931 F, 1936 S
Brooke, T J (Richmond) 1968 F, S
Brooks, F G (Bedford) 1906 SA
Brooks, M J (Oxford U) 1874 S
Brophy, T J (Liverpool) 1964 I, F, S, 1965 W, I, 1966 W, I, F
Brough, J W (Silloth) 1925 NZ, W
Brougham, H (Harlequins) 1912 W, I, S, F
Brown A (Gloucester) 2006 A1, 2007 SA1,2
Brown, A A (Exeter) 1938 S
Brown, L G (Oxford U, Blackheath) 1911 W, F, I, S, 1913 SA, W, F, I, S, 1914 W, I, S, F, 1921 W, I, S, F, 1922 W
Brown, M (Harlequins) 2007 SA1,2, 2008 NZ1
Brown S P (Richmond) 1998 A 1, SA 1
Brown, T W (Bristol) 1928 S, 1929 W, I, S, F, 1932 S, 1933 W, I, S
Brunton, J (N Durham) 1914 W, I, S
Brutton, E B (Cambridge U) 1886 S
Bryden, C C (Clapham R) 1876 I, 1877 S
Bryden, H A (Clapham R) 1874 S
Buckingham, R A (Leicester) 1927 F
Bucknall, A L (Richmond) 1969 SA, 1970 I, W, S, F, 1971 W, I, F, S (2[1C])
Buckton, J R D (Saracens) 1988 A (R), 1990 Arg 1,2
Budd, A J (Blackheath) 1878 I, 1879 S, I, 1881 W, S
Budworth, R T D (Blackheath) 1890 W, 1891 W, S
Bull, A G (Northampton) 1914 W
Bullough, E (Wigan) 1892 W, I, S
Bulpitt, M P (Blackheath) 1970 S
Bulteel, A J (Manchester) 1876 I
Bunting, W L (Moseley) 1897 I, S, 1898 I, S, W, 1899 S, 1900 S, 1901 I, S
Burland, D W (Bristol) 1931 W, I, F, 1932 I, S, 1933 W, I, S
Burns, B H (Blackheath) 1871 S
Burton, G W (Blackheath) 1879 S, I, 1880 S, 1881 I, W, S
Burton, H C (Richmond) 1926 W
Burton, M A (Gloucester) 1972 W, I, F, S, SA, 1974 F, W, 1975 S, A 1,2, 1976 A, W, S, I, F, 1978 F, W
Bush, J A (Clifton) 1872 S, 1873 S, 1875 S, 1876 I, S
Butcher, C J S (Harlequins) 1984 SA 1,2, A
Butcher, W V (Streatham) 1903 S, 1904 W, I, S, 1905 W, I, S
Butler, A G (Harlequins) 1937 W, I
Butler, P E (Gloucester) 1975 A 1, 1976 F
Butterfield, J (Northampton) 1953 F, S, 1954 W, NZ, I, S, F, 1955 W, I, F, S, 1956 W, I, S, F, 1957 W, I, F, S, 1958 W, A, I, F, S, 1959 W, I, F, S
Byrne, F A (Moseley) 1897 W
Byrne, J F (Moseley) 1894 W, I, S, 1895 I, S, 1896 I, 1897 W, I, S, 1898 I, S, W, 1899 I

Cain, J J (Waterloo) 1950 W
Cairns, M I (Saracens) 2007 SA1(R)
Callard, J E B (Bath) 1993 NZ, 1994 S, I, 1995 [WS], SA
Campbell, D A (Cambridge U) 1937 W, I
Candler, P L (St Bart's Hospital) 1935 W, 1936 NZ, W, I, S, 1937 W, I, S, 1938 W, S
Cannell, L B (Oxford U, St Mary's Hospital) 1948 F, 1949 W, I, F, S, 1950 W, I, F, S, 1952 SA, W, 1953 W, I, F, 1956 I, S, F, 1957 W, I
Caplan, D W N (Headingley) 1978 S, I
Cardus, R M (Roundhay) 1979 F, W
Care, D (Harlequins) 2008 NZ1(R),2
Carey, G M (Blackheath) 1895 W, I, S, 1896 W, I
Carleton, J (Orrell) 1979 NZ, 1980 I, F, W, S, 1981 W, S, I, F, Arg 1,2, 1982 A, S, I, F, W, 1983 F, W, S, I, NZ, 1984 S, I, F, W, A
Carling, W D C (Durham U, Harlequins) 1988 F, W, S, I 1,2, A2, Fj, A, 1989 S, I, F, W, Fj, 1990 I, F, W, S, Arg 1,2,3, 1991 W, S, I, F, Fj, A, [NZ, It, US, F, S, A], 1992 S, I, F, W, C, SA, 1993 F, W, S, I, NZ, 1994 S, I, F, W, SA 1,2, R, C, 1995 I, F, W, S, [Arg, WS, A, NZ, F], SA, WS, 1996 F, W, S, I, It, Arg, 1997 S, I, F, W
Carpenter, A D (Gloucester) 1932 SA
Carr, R S L (Manchester) 1939 W, I, S
Cartwright, V H (Nottingham) 1903 W, I, S, 1904 W, S, 1905 W, I, S, NZ, 1906 W, I, S, F, SA
Catcheside, H C (Percy Park) 1924 W, I, F, S, 1926 W, I, 1927 I, S
Catt, M J (Bath, London Irish) 1994 W (R), C (R), 1995 I, F, W, S, [Arg, It, WS, A, NZ, F], SA, WS, 1996 F, W, S, I, It, Arg, 1997 W, Arg 1, A 1,2, NZ 1, SA, 1998 F, W (R), I, A 2(R), SA 2, 1999 S, F, W, A, C (R), [Tg (R), Fj, SA (R)], 2000 I, F, W, It, S, SA 1,2, A, Arg, 2001 W, It, S, F, I, A, R (R), SA, 2003 [Sm(R), U, W(R), F, A(R)], 2004 W(R), F(R), NZ1, A1, 2006 A1, 2, 2007 F1,W1,F2, [US,SA1,A,F,SA2]
Cattell, R H B (Blackheath) 1895 W, I, S, 1896 W, I, S, 1900 W
Cave, J W (Richmond) 1889 M
Cave, W T C (Blackheath) 1905 W

Challis, R (Bristol) 1957 I, F, S
Chambers, E L (Bedford) 1908 F, 1910 W, I
Chantrill, B S (Bristol) 1924 W, I, F, S
Chapman, C E (Cambridge U) 1884 W
Chapman D E (Richmond) 1998 A 1(R)
Chapman, F E (Hartlepool) 1910 W, I, F, S, 1912 W, 1914 W, I
Cheesman, W I (OMTs) 1913 SA, W, F, I
Cheston, E C (Richmond) 1873 S, 1874 S, 1875 I, S, 1876 S
Chilcott, G J (Bath) 1984 A, 1986 I, F, 1987 F (R), W, [J, US, W (R)], 1988 I 2(R), Fj, 1989 I (R), F, W, R
Christophers, P D (Bristol) 2002 Arg, SA, 2003 W 1 (R)
Christopherson, P (Blackheath) 1891 W, S
Chuter, G S (Leicester) 2006 A1(R), 2, NZ, Arg, SA1,2(R), 2007 S,It,I,F1,W1,2(R), [US(R),SA1(R),Sm,Tg,A(R),F(R), SA2(R)], 2008 S(R),I(R)
Cipriani, D (Wasps) 2008 W(R),It(R),I
Clark, C W H (Liverpool) 1876 I
Clarke, A J (Coventry) 1935 W, I, S, 1936 NZ, W, I
Clarke, B B (Bath, Richmond) 1992 SA, 1993 F, W, S, I, NZ, 1994 S, F, W, SA 1,2, R, C, 1995 I, F, W, S, [Arg, It, A, NZ, F], SA, WS, 1996 F, W, S, I, Arg (R), 1997 W, Arg 1,2, A 1(R), 1998 A 1(t),NZ 1,2, SA 1, H, It, 1999 A (R)
Clarke, S J S (Cambridge U, Blackheath) 1963 W, I, F, S, NZ 1,2, A, 1964 NZ, W, I, 1965 I, F, S
Clayton, J H (Liverpool) 1871 S
Clements, J W (O Cranleighans) 1959 I, F, S
Cleveland, C R (Blackheath) 1887 W, S
Clibborn, W G (Richmond) 1886 W, I, S, 1887 W, I, S
Clough, F J (Cambridge U, Orrell) 1986 I, F, 1987 [J (R), US]
Coates, C H (Yorkshire W) 1880 S, 1881 S, 1882 S
Coates, V H M (Bath) 1913 SA, W, F, I, S
Cobby, W (Hull) 1900 W
Cockerham, A (Bradford Olicana) 1900 W
Cockerill, R (Leicester) 1997 Arg 1(R),2, A 2(t+R), NZ 1, SA, NZ 2, 1998 W, S, I, A 1, NZ 1,2, SA 1, H, It, A 2, SA 2, 1999 S, I, F, W, A, C (R), [It, NZ, Tg (R), Fj (R)]
Codling, A J (Harlequins) 2002 Arg
Cohen, B C (Northampton) 2000 I, F, W, It, S, SA 2, Arg, SA 3, 2001 W, It, S, F, R, 2002 S, I, F, W, It, NZ, A, SA, 2003 F 1, W 1, S, I, NZ, A, F2, 3, [Gg, SA, Sm, W, F, A], 2004 It, S, I, W, F, NZ1, 2, A1,C(R), A2(R), 2005 F(R), A, NZ, 2006 W, It, S, F, I, NZ,Arg, SA1, 2
Colclough, M J (Angoulîme, Wasps, Swansea) 1978 S, I, 1979 NZ, 1980 F, W, S, 1981 W, S, I, F, 1982 A, S, I, F, W, 1983 F, NZ, 1984 S, I, F, W, 1986 W, S, I, F
Coley, E (Northampton) 1929 F, 1932 W
Collins, P J (Camborne) 1952 S, I, F
Collins, W E (O Cheltonians) 1874 S, 1875 I, S, 1876 I, S
Considine, S G U (Bath) 1925 F
Conway, G S (Cambridge U, Rugby, Manchester) 1920 F, I, S, 1921 F, 1922 W, I, F, S, 1923 W, I, S, F, 1924 W, I, F, S, 1925 NZ, 1927 W
Cook, J G (Bedford) 1937 S
Cook, P W (Richmond) 1965 I, F
Cooke, D A (Harlequins) 1976 W, S, I, F
Cooke, D H (Harlequins) 1981 W, S, I, F, 1984 I, 1985 R, F, S, I, W, NZ 1,2
Cooke, P (Richmond) 1939 W, I
Coop, T (Leigh) 1892 S
Cooper, J G (Moseley) 1909 A, W
Cooper, M J (Moseley) 1973 F, S, NZ 2(R), 1975 F, W, 1976 A, W, 1977 S, I, F, W
Coopper, S F (Blackheath) 1900 W, 1902 W, I, 1905 W, I, S, 1907 W
Corbett, L J (Bristol) 1921 F, 1923 W, I, 1924 W, I, F, S, 1925 NZ, W, I, S, F, 1927 W, I, S, F
Corless, B J (Coventry, Moseley) 1976 A, I (R), 1977 S, I, F, W, 1978 F, W, S, I
Corry, M E (Bristol, Leicester) 1997 Arg 1,2, 1998 H, It, SA 2(t), 1999 F(R), A, C (t), [It (R), NZ (t+R), SA (R)], 2000 I (R), F (R), W (R), It (R), S (R), Arg (R), SA 3(t), 2001 W (R), It (R), F (t), C 1, I, 2002 F (t+R), W (t), 2003 W 2, F 2,3, [U], 2004 A1(R), C, SA, A2, 2005 F, I, It, S, A, NZ, Sm, 2006 W, It, S, F, I, NZ,Arg, SA1,2, 2007 S,It,I,F1,W1,2,F2(R),3, [US(R),SA1,Sm,Tg,A,F,SA2]
Cotton, F E (Loughborough Colls, Coventry, Sale) 1971 S (2[1C]), P, 1973 W, I, F, S, NZ 2, A, 1974 S, I, 1975 I, F, W, 1976 A, W, S, I, F, 1977 S, I, F, W, 1978 S, I, 1979 NZ, 1980 I, F, W, S, 1981 W
Coulman, M J (Moseley) 1967 A, I, F, S, W, 1968 W, I, F, S
Coulson, T J (Coventry) 1927 W, 1928 A, W
Court, E D (Blackheath) 1885 W
Coverdale, H (Blackheath) 1910 F, 1912 I, F, 1920 W
Cove-Smith, R (OMTs) 1921 S, F, 1922 I, F, S, 1923 W, I, S, F, 1924 W, I, S, F, 1925 NZ, W, I, S, F, 1927 W, I, S, F, 1928 A, W, I, F, S, 1929 W, I
Cowling, R J (Leicester) 1977 S, I, F, W, 1978 F, NZ, 1979 S, I
Cowman, A R (Loughborough Colls, Coventry) 1971 S (2[1C]), P, 1973 W, I
Cox, N S (Sunderland) 1901 S
Cranmer, P (Richmond, Moseley) 1934 W, I, S, 1935 W, I, S, 1936 NZ, W, I, S, 1937 W, I, S, 1938 W, I, S
Creed, R N (Coventry) 1971 P
Cridlan, A G (Blackheath) 1935 W, I, S
Croft, T (Leicester) 2008 F(R),S,I,NZ2(R)
Crompton, C A (Blackheath) 1871 S
Crompton, D E (Bristol) 2007 SA1(R)
Crosse, C W (Oxford U) 1874 S, 1875 I
Cueto, M J (Sale) 2004 C, SA, A2, 2005 W, F, I, It, S, A, NZ, Sm, 2006 W, It, S, F, I, SA1,2, 2007 W1,F3, [US,Sm,Tg,SA2]
Cumberlege, B S (Blackheath) 1920 W, I, S, 1921 W, I, S, F, 1922 W
Cumming, D C (Blackheath) 1925 S, F
Cunliffe, F L (RMA) 1874 S
Currey, F I (Marlborough N) 1872 S
Currie, J D (Oxford U, Harlequins, Bristol) 1956 W, I, S, F, 1957 W, I, F, S, 1958 W, A, I, F, S, 1959 W, I, F, S, 1960 W, I, F, S, 1961 SA, 1962 W, I, F
Cusani, D A (Orrell) 1987 I
Cusworth, L (Leicester) 1979 NZ, 1982 F, W, 1983 F, W, NZ, 1984 S, I, F, W, 1988 F, W

D'Aguilar, F B G (Royal Engineers) 1872 S
Dallaglio, L B N (Wasps) 1995 SA (R), WS, 1996 F, W, S, I, It, Arg, 1997 S, I, F, A 1,2, NZ 1, SA, NZ 2, 1998 F, W, S, I, A 2, SA 2, 1999 S, I, F, W, US, C, [It, NZ, Tg, Fj, SA], 2000 I, F, W, It, S, SA 1,2, A, Arg, SA 3, 2001 W, It, S, F, 2002 It (R), NZ, A (t), SA(R), 2003 F 1 (R), W 1, It, S, I, NZ, A, [Gg, SA, Sm, U, W, F, A], 2004 It, S, I, W, F, NZ1, 2, A1,2006 W(t&R), It(R), S(R), F(R), 2007 W2(R),F2,3(R), [US,Tg(R),A(R),F(R),SA2(R)]
Dalton, T J (Coventry) 1969 S(R)
Danby, T (Harlequins) 1949 W
Daniell, J (Richmond) 1899 W, 1900 I, S, 1902 I, S, 1904 I, S
Darby, A J L (Birkenhead Park) 1899 I
Davenport, A (Ravenscourt Park) 1871 S
Davey, J (Redruth) 1908 S, 1909 W
Davey, R F (Teignmouth) 1931 W
Davidson, Jas (Aspatria) 1897 S, 1898 S, W, 1899 I, S
Davidson, Jos (Aspatria) 1899 W, S
Davies, G H (Cambridge U, Coventry, Wasps) 1981 S, I, F, Arg 1,2, 1982 A, S, I, 1983 F, W, S, 1984 S, SA 1,2, 1985 R (R), NZ 1,2, 1986 W, S, I, F
Davies, P H (Sale) 1927 I
Davies, V G (Harlequins) 1922 W, 1925 NZ
Davies, W J A (United Services, RN) 1913 SA, W, F, I, S, 1914 I, S, F, 1920 F, I, S, 1921 W, I, S, F, 1922 I, F, S, 1923 W, I, S, F
Davies, W P C (Harlequins) 1953 S, 1954 NZ, I, 1955 W, I, F, S, 1956 W, 1957 F, S, 1958 W
Davis, A M (Torquay Ath, Harlequins) 1963 W, I, S, NZ 1,2, 1964 NZ, W, I, F, S, 1966 W, 1967 A, 1969 SA, 1970 I, W, S
Dawe, R G R (Bath) 1987 I, F, W, [US], 1995 [WS]
Dawson, E F (RIEC) 1878 I
Dawson, M J S (Northampton, Wasps) 1995 WS, 1996 F, W, S, I, 1997 A 1, SA, NZ 2(R), 1998 W (R), S, I, NZ 1,2, SA 1, H, It, A 2, SA 2, 1999 S, F(R), W, A(R), US, C, [It, NZ, Tg, Fj (R), SA], 2000 I, F, W, It, S, A (R), Arg, SA 3, 2001 W, It, S, F, I, 2002 W (R), It (R), NZ, A, SA, 2003 It, S, I,

A(R), F3(R), [Gg, Sm, W, F, A], 2004It(R), S(R), I, W, F, NZ1, 2(R), A1(R), 2005 W, F(R), I(R), It(R), S(R), A, NZ, 2006 W(R), It(R), S(t&R), F, I(R)
Day, H L V (Leicester) 1920 W, 1922 W, F, 1926 S
Deacon, L P (Leicester) 2005 Sm, 2006 A1, 2(R), 2007 S,It,I,F1(R),W1(R)
Dean, G J (Harlequins) 1931 I
Dee, J M (Hartlepool R) 1962 S, 1963 NZ 1
Devitt, Sir T G (Blackheath) 1926 I, F, 1928 A, W
Dewhurst, J H (Richmond) 1887 W, I, S, 1890 W
De Glanville, P R (Bath) 1992 SA (R), 1993 W (R), NZ, 1994 S, I, F, W, SA 1,2, C (R), 1995 [Arg (R), It, WS], SA (R), 1996 W (R), I (R), It, 1997 S, I, F, W, Arg 1,2, A 1,2, NZ 1,2, 1998 W (R), S (R), I (R), A 2, SA 2, 1999 A (R), US, [It, NZ, Fj (R), SA]
De Winton, R F C (Marlborough N) 1893 W
Dibble, R (Bridgwater A) 1906 S, F, SA, 1908 F, W, I, S, 1909 A, W, F, I, S, 1910 S, 1911 W, F, S, 1912 W, I, S
Dicks, J (Northampton) 1934 W, I, S, 1935 W, I, S, 1936 S, 1937 I
Dillon, E W (Blackheath) 1904 W, I, S, 1905 W
Dingle, A J (Hartlepool R) 1913 I, 1914 S, F
Diprose, A J (Saracens) 1997 Arg 1,2, A 2, NZ 1, 1998 W (R), S (R), I, A 1, NZ 2, SA 1
Dixon, P J (Harlequins, Gosforth) 1971 P, 1972 W, I, F, S, 1973 I, F, S, 1974 S, I, F, W, 1975 I, 1976 F, 1977 S, I, F, W, 1978 F, S, I, NZ
Dobbs, G E B (Devonport A) 1906 W, I
Doble, S A (Moseley) 1972 SA, 1973 NZ 1, W
Dobson, D D (Newton Abbot) 1902 W, I, S, 1903 W, I, S
Dobson, T H (Bradford) 1895 S
Dodge, P W (Leicester) 1978 W, S, I, NZ, 1979 S, I, F, W, 1980 W, S, 1981 W, S, I, F, Arg 1,2, 1982 A, S, F, W, 1983 F, W, S, I, NZ, 1985 R, F, S, I, W, NZ 1,2
Donnelly, M P (Oxford U) 1947 I
Dooley, W A (Preston Grasshoppers, Fylde) 1985 R, F, S, I, W, NZ 2(R), 1986 W, S, I, F, 1987 F, W, [A, US, W], 1988 F, W, S, I 1,2, A 1,2, Fj, A, 1989 S, I, F, W, R, Fj, 1990 I, F, W, S, Arg 1,2,3, 1991 W, S, I, F, [NZ, US, F, S, A], 1992 S, I, F, W, C, SA, 1993 W, S, I
Dovey, B A (Rosslyn Park) 1963 W, I
Down, P J (Bristol) 1909 A
Dowson, A O (Moseley) 1899 S
Drake-Lee, N J (Cambridge U, Leicester) 1963 W, I, F, S, 1964 NZ, W, I, 1965 W
Duckett, H (Bradford) 1893 I, S
Duckham, D J (Coventry) 1969 I, F, S, W, SA, 1970 I, W, S, F, 1971 W, I, F, S (2[1C]), P, 1972 W, I, F, S, 1973 NZ 1, W, I, F, S, NZ 2, A, 1974 S, I, F, W, 1975 I, F, W, 1976 A, W, S
Dudgeon, H W (Richmond) 1897 S, 1898 I, S, W, 1899 W, I, S
Dugdale, J M (Ravenscourt Park) 1871 S
Dun, A F (Wasps) 1984 W
Duncan, R F H (Guy's Hospital) 1922 I, F, S
Duncombe, N S (Harlequins) 2002 S (R), I (R)
Dunkley, P E (Harlequins) 1931 I, S, 1936 NZ, W, I, S
Duthie, J (W Hartlepool) 1903 W
Dyson, J W (Huddersfield) 1890 S, 1892 S, 1893 I, S

Easter, N (Harlequins) 2007 It,F1,SA1,2,W2,F3, [SA1,Sm,Tg, A,F,SA2], 2008 It,F,S,I
Ebdon, P J (Wellington) 1897 W, I
Eddison, J H (Headingley) 1912 W, I, S, F
Edgar, C S (Birkenhead Park) 1901 S
Edwards, R (Newport) 1921 W, I, S, F, 1922 W, F, 1923 W, 1924 W, F, S, 1925 NZ
Egerton, D W (Bath) 1988 I 2, A 1, Fj (R), A, 1989 Fj, 1990 I, Arg 2(R)
Elliot, C H (Sunderland) 1886 W
Elliot, E W (Sunderland) 1901 W, I, S, 1904 W
Elliot, W (United Services, RN) 1932 I, S, 1933 W, I, S, 1934 W, I
Elliott, A E (St Thomas's Hospital) 1894 S
Ellis, H A (Leicester) 2004 SA(R), A2(R), 2005 W(R), F, I, It, S, Sm, 2006 W, It, S, F(R), I, 2007 S,It,I,F1,W1
Ellis, J (Wakefield) 1939 S
Ellis, S S (Queen's House) 1880 I
Emmott, C (Bradford) 1892 W
Enthoven, H J (Richmond) 1878 I
Estcourt, N S D (Blackheath) 1955 S
Evans, B J (Leicester) 1988 A 2, Fj
Evans, E (Sale) 1948 A, 1950 W, 1951 I, F, S, 1952 SA, W, S, I, F, 1953 I, F, S, 1954 W, NZ, I, F, 1956 W, I, S, F, 1957 W, I, F, S, 1958 W, A, I, F, S
Evans, G W (Coventry) 1972 S, 1973 W (R), F, S, NZ 2, 1974 S, I, F, W
Evans, N L (RNEC) 1932 W, I, S, 1933 W, I
Evanson, A M (Richmond) 1883 W, I, S, 1884 S
Evanson, W A D (Richmond) 1875 S, 1877 S, 1878 S, 1879 S, I
Evershed, F (Blackheath) 1889 M, 1890 W, S, I, 1892 W, I, S, 1893 W, I, S
Eyres, W C T (Richmond) 1927 I

Fagan, A R St L (Richmond) 1887 I
Fairbrother, K E (Coventry) 1969 I, F, S, W, SA, 1970 I, W, S, F, 1971 W, I, F
Faithfull, C K T (Harlequins) 1924 I, 1926 F, S
Fallas, H (Wakefield T) 1884 I
Farrell, A (Saracens) 2007 S,It,I,W2,F3, [US(R),SA1,Tg(R)]
Fegan, J H C (Blackheath) 1895 W, I, S
Fernandes, C W L (Leeds) 1881 I, W, S
Fidler, J H (Gloucester) 1981 Arg 1,2, 1984 SA 1,2
Fidler, R J (Gloucester) 1998 NZ 2, SA 1
Field, E (Middlesex W) 1893 W, I
Fielding, K J (Moseley, Loughborough Colls) 1969 I, F, S, SA, 1970 I, F, 1972 W, I, F, S
Finch, R T (Cambridge U) 1880 S
Finlan, J F (Moseley) 1967 I, F, S, W, NZ, 1968 W, I, 1969 I, F, S, W, 1970 F, 1973 NZ 1
Finlinson, H W (Blackheath) 1895 W, I, S
Finney, S (RIE Coll) 1872 S, 1873 S
Firth, F (Halifax) 1894 W, I, S
Flatman, D L (Saracens) 2000 SA 1(t),2(t+R), A (t), Arg (t+R), 2001 F (t), C 2(t+R), US (t+R), 2002 Arg
Fletcher, N C (OMTs) 1901 W, I, S, 1903 S
Fletcher, T (Seaton) 1897 W
Fletcher, W R B (Marlborough N) 1873 S, 1875 S
Flood, T (Newcastle) 2006 Arg(R),SA2(R), 2007 S(R),It(R), F1,W1,SA1,2,W2(t), [A(R),F(R),SA2(R)], 2008 W,It,F,S, I,NZ2
Fookes, E F (Sowerby Bridge) 1896 W, I, S, 1897 W, I, S, 1898 I, W, 1899 I, S
Ford, P J (Gloucester) 1964 W, I, F, S
Forrest, J W (United Services, RN) 1930 W, I, F, S, 1931 W, I, S, F, 1934 I, S
Forrest, R (Wellington) 1899 W, 1900 S, 1902 I, S, 1903 I, S
Forrester, J (Gloucester) 2005 W(t), Sm(t&R)
Foulds, R T (Waterloo) 1929 W, I
Fowler, F D (Manchester) 1878 S, 1879 S
Fowler, H (Oxford U) 1878 S, 1881 W, S
Fowler, R H (Leeds) 1877 I
Fox, F H (Wellington) 1890 W, S
Francis, T E S (Cambridge U) 1926 W, I, F, S
Frankcom, G P (Cambridge U, Bedford) 1965 W, I, F, S
Fraser, E C (Blackheath) 1875 I
Fraser, G (Richmond) 1902 W, I, S, 1903 W, I
Freakes, H D (Oxford U) 1938 W, 1939 W, I
Freeman, H (Marlborough N) 1872 S, 1873 S, 1874 S
French, R J (St Helens) 1961 W, I, F, S
Freshwater, P T (Perpignan) 2005 v Sm(R), 2006 S(t&R), I(R),Arg, 2007 S,It,I,F3, [SA1(R),Sm(R)]
Fry, H A (Liverpool) 1934 W, I, S
Fry, T W (Queen's House) 1880 I, S, 1881 W
Fuller, H G (Cambridge U) 1882 I, S, 1883 W, I, S, 1884 W

Gadney, B C (Leicester, Headingley) 1932 I, S, 1933 I, S, 1934 W, I, S, 1935 S, 1936 NZ, W, I, S, 1937 S, 1938 W
Gamlin, H T (Blackheath) 1899 W, S, 1900 W, I, S, 1901 S, 1902 W, I, S, 1903 W, I, S, 1904 W, I, S
Gardner, E R (Devonport Services) 1921 W, I, S, 1922 W, I, F, 1923 W, I, S, F
Gardner, H P (Richmond) 1878 I
Garforth, D J (Leicester) 1997 W (R), Arg 1,2, A 1, NZ 1, SA,

NZ 2, 1998 F, W (R), S, I, H, It, A 2, SA 2, 1999 S, I, F, W, A, C (R), [It (R), NZ (R), Fj], 2000 It
Garnett, H W T (Bradford) 1877 S
Gavins, M N (Leicester) 1961 W
Gay, D J (Bath) 1968 W, I, F, S
Gent, D R (Gloucester) 1905 NZ, 1906 W, I, 1910 W, I
Genth, J S M (Manchester) 1874 S, 1875 S
George, J T (Falmouth) 1947 S, F, 1949 I
Geraghty, S (London Irish) 2007 F1(R),W1(R)
Gerrard, R A (Bath) 1932 SA, W, I, S, 1933 W, I, S, 1934 W, I, S, 1936 NZ, W, I, S
Gibbs, G A (Bristol) 1947 F, 1948 I
Gibbs, J C (Harlequins) 1925 NZ, W, 1926 F, 1927 W, I, S, F
Gibbs, N (Harlequins) 1954 S, F
Giblin, L F (Blackheath) 1896 W, I, 1897 S
Gibson, A S (Manchester) 1871 S
Gibson, C O P (Northern) 1901 W
Gibson, G R (Northern) 1899 W, 1901 S
Gibson, T A (Northern) 1905 W, S
Gilbert, F G (Devonport Services) 1923 W, I
Gilbert, R (Devonport A) 1908 W, I, S
Giles, J L (Coventry) 1935 W, I, 1937 W, I, 1938 I, S
Gittings, W J (Coventry) 1967 NZ
Glover, P B (Bath) 1967 A, 1971 F, P
Godfray, R E (Richmond) 1905 NZ
Godwin, H O (Coventry) 1959 F, S, 1963 S, NZ 1,2, A, 1964 NZ, I, F, S, 1967 NZ
Gomarsall, A C T (Wasps, Bedford, Gloucester, Harlequins) 1996 It, Arg, 1997 S, I, F, Arg 2(R) 2000 It (R), 2002 Arg, SA(R), 2003 F 1, W 1(R),2, F2(R), [Gg(R), U], 2004 It, S, NZ1(R), 2, A1, C, SA, A2, 2007 SA1,2,F2(R),3(R), [SA1(R),Sm,Tg,A,F,SA2], 2008 W,It
Goode, A J (Leicester) 2005 It(R), S(R), 2006 W(R), F(R), I, A1(R), 2, SA1(R),2
Gordon-Smith, G W (Blackheath) 1900 W, I, S
Gotley, A L H (Oxford U) 1910 F, S, 1911 W, F, I, S
Graham, D (Aspatria) 1901 W
Graham, H J (Wimbledon H) 1875 I, S, 1876 I, S
Graham, J D G (Wimbledon H) 1876 I
Gray, A (Otley) 1947 W, I, S
Grayson, P J (Northampton) 1995 WS, 1996 F, W, S, I, 1997 S, I, F, A 2(t), SA (R), NZ 2, 1998 F, W, S, I, H, It, A 2, 1999 I, [NZ (R), Tg, Fj (R), SA], 2003 S(R), I(t), F2, 3(R), [Gg(R), U], 2004 It, S, I
Green, J (Skipton) 1905 I, 1906 S, F, SA, 1907 F, W, I, S
Green, J F (West Kent) 1871 S
Green, W R (Wasps) 1997 A 2, 1998 NZ 1(t+R), 1999 US (R), 2003 W 2(R)
Greening, P B T (Gloucester, Wasps) 1996 It (R), 1997 W (R), Arg 1 1998 NZ 1(R),2(R), 1999 A (R), US, C, [It (R), NZ (R), Tg, Fj, SA], 2000 I, F, W, It, S, SA 1,2, A, SA 3, 2001 F, I
Greenstock, N J J (Wasps) 1997 Arg 1,2, A 1, SA
Greenwell, J H (Rockcliff) 1893 W, I
Greenwood, J E (Cambridge U, Leicester) 1912 F, 1913 SA, W, F, I, S, 1914 W, S, F, 1920 W, F, I, S
Greenwood, J R H (Waterloo) 1966 I, F, S, 1967 A, 1969 I
Greenwood, W J H (Leicester, Harlequins) 1997 A 2, NZ 1, SA, NZ 2, 1998 F, W, S, I, H, It, 1999 C, [It, Tg, Fj, SA], 2000 Arg (R), SA 3, 2001 W, It, S, F, I, A, R, SA, 2002 S, I, F, W, It, NZ, A, SA, 2003 F 1, W 1, It, S, I, NZ, A, F3, [Gg, SA, U(R), W, F, A], 2004 It, S, I, W, F, C(R), SA(R), A2(R)
Greg, W (Manchester) 1876 I, S
Gregory, G G (Bristol) 1931 I, S, F, 1932 SA, W, I, S, 1933 W, I, S, 1934 W, I, S
Gregory, J A (Blackheath) 1949 W
Grewcock, D J (Coventry, Saracens, Bath) 1997 Arg 2, SA, 1998 W (R), S (R), I (R), A 1, NZ 1, SA 2(R), 1999 S (R), A (R), US, C, [It, NZ, Tg (R), SA], 2000 SA 1,2, A, Arg, SA 3, 2001 W, It, S, I, A, R (R), SA, 2002 S (R), I (R), F (R), W, It, NZ, SA (R), 2003 F 1 (R), W 1 (R), It, S (R), I (t), W 2, F 2, [U], 2004 It, S, W, F, NZ1, 2(R), C, SA, A2, 2005 W, F, I, It, S, A, NZ, 2006 W, It, S, F, I(R),NZ, Arg, 2007 S, It, I
Grylls, W M (Redruth) 1905 I
Guest, R H (Waterloo) 1939 W, I, S, 1947 W, I, S, F, 1948 A, W, I, S, 1949 F, S
Guillemard, A G (West Kent) 1871 S, 1872 S
Gummer, C H A (Plymouth A) 1929 F
Gunner, C R (Marlborough N) 1876 I
Gurdon, C (Richmond) 1880 I, S, 1881 I, W, S, 1882 I, S, 1883 S, 1884 W, S, 1885 I, 1886 W, I, S
Gurdon, E T (Richmond) 1878 S, 1879 I, 1880 S, 1881 I, W, S, 1882 S, 1883 W, I, S, 1884 W, I, S, 1885 W, I, 1886 S
Guscott, J C (Bath) 1989 R, Fj, 1990 I, F, W, S, Arg 3, 1991 W, S, I, F, Fj, A, [NZ, It, F, S, A], 1992 S, I, F, W, C, SA, 1993 F, W, S, I, 1994 R, C, 1995 I, F, W, S, [Arg, It, A, NZ, F], SA, WS, 1996 F, W, S, I, Arg, 1997 I (R), W (R), 1998 F, W, S, I, H, It, A 2, SA 2, 1999 S, I, F, A, US, C, [It (R), NZ, Tg]

Haag, M (Bath) 1997 Arg 1,2
Haigh, L (Manchester) 1910 W, I, S, 1911 W, F, I, S
Hale, P M (Moseley) 1969 SA, 1970 I, W
Hall, C (Gloucester) 1901 I, S
Hall, J (N Durham) 1894 W, I, S
Hall, J P (Bath) 1984 S (R), I, F, SA 1,2, A, 1985 R, F, S, I, W, NZ 1,2, 1986 W, S, 1987 I, F, W, S, 1990 Arg 3, 1994 S
Hall, N M (Richmond) 1947 W, I, S, F, 1949 W, I, 1952 SA, W, S, I, F, 1953 W, I, F, S, 1955 W, I
Halliday, S J (Bath, Harlequins) 1986 W, S, 1987 S, 1988 S, I 1,2, A 1, A, 1989 S, I, F, W, R, Fj (R), 1990 W, S, 1991 [US, S, A], 1992 S, I, F, W
Hamersley, A St G (Marlborough N) 1871 S, 1872 S, 1873 S, 1874 S
Hamilton-Hill, E A (Harlequins) 1936 NZ, W, I
Hamilton-Wickes, R H (Cambridge U) 1924 I, 1925 NZ, W, I, S, F, 1926 W, I, S, 1927 W
Hammett, E D G (Newport) 1920 W, F, S, 1921 W, I, S, F, 1922 W
Hammond, C E L (Harlequins) 1905 S, NZ, 1906 W, I, S, F, 1908 W, I
Hancock, A W (Northampton) 1965 F, S, 1966 F
Hancock, G E (Birkenhead Park) 1939 W, I, S
Hancock, J H (Newport) 1955 W, I
Hancock, P F (Blackheath) 1886 W, I, 1890 W
Hancock, P S (Richmond) 1904 W, I, S
Handford, F G (Manchester) 1909 W, F, I, S
Hands, R H M (Blackheath) 1910 F, S
Hanley, J (Plymouth A) 1927 W, S, F, 1928 W, I, F, S
Hanley, S M (Sale) 1999 W
Hannaford, R C (Bristol) 1971 W, I, F
Hanvey, R J (Aspatria) 1926 W, I, F, S
Harding, E H (Devonport Services) 1931 I
Harding, R M (Bristol) 1985 R, F, S, 1987 S, [A, J, W], 1988 I 1(R),2, A 1,2, Fj
Harding, V S J (Saracens) 1961 F, S, 1962 W, I, F, S
Hardwick, P F (Percy Park) 1902 I, S, 1903 W, I, S, 1904 W, I, S
Hardwick, R J K (Coventry) 1996 It (R)
Hardy, E M P (Blackheath) 1951 I, F, S
Hare, W H (Nottingham, Leicester) 1974 W, 1978 F, NZ, 1979 NZ, 1980 I, F, W, S, 1981 W, S, Arg 1,2, 1982 F, W, 1983 F, W, S, I, NZ, 1984 S, I, F, W, SA 1,2
Harper, C H (Exeter) 1899 W
Harriman, A T (Harlequins) 1988 A
Harris, S W (Blackheath) 1920 I, S
Harris, T W (Northampton) 1929 S, 1932 I
Harrison, A C (Hartlepool R) 1931 I, S
Harrison, A L (United Services, RN) 1914 I, F
Harrison, G (Hull) 1877 I, S, 1879 S, I, 1880 S, 1885 W, I
Harrison, H C (United Services, RN) 1909 S, 1914 I, S, F
Harrison, M E (Wakefield) 1985 NZ 1,2, 1986 S, I, F, 1987 I, F, W, S, [A, J, US, W], 1988 F, W
Hartley, B C (Blackheath) 1901 S, 1902 S
Haskell, J (Wasps) 2007 W1,F2, 2008 W,It,F,I(R),NZ1,2
Haslett, L W (Birkenhead Park) 1926 I, F
Hastings, G W D (Gloucester) 1955 W, I, F, S, 1957 W, I, F, S, 1958 W, A, I, F, S
Havelock, H (Hartlepool R) 1908 F, W, I
Hawcridge, J J (Bradford) 1885 W, I
Hayward, L W (Cheltenham) 1910 I
Hazell, A R (Gloucester) 2004 C, SA(t&R), 2005 W, F(t), It(R), S(R), 2007 SA1
Hazell, D St G (Leicester) 1955 W, I, F, S
Healey, A S (Leicester) 1997 I (R), W, A 1(R),2(R), NZ 1(R), SA (R), NZ 2, 1998 F, W, S, I, A 1, NZ 1,2, H, It, A 2, SA

2(R), 1999 US, C, [It, NZ, Tg, Fj, SA (R)], 2000 I, F, W, It, S, SA 1,2, A, SA 3(R), 2001 W (R), It, S, F, I (R), A, R, SA, 2002 S, I, F, W, It (R), NZ (R), A (R), SA(R), 2003 F2

Hearn, R D (Bedford) 1966 F, S, 1967 I, F, S, W

Heath, A H (Oxford U) 1876 S

Heaton, J (Waterloo) 1935 W, I, S, 1939 W, I, S, 1947 I, S, F

Henderson, A P (Edinburgh Wands) 1947 W, I, S, F, 1948 I, S, F, 1949 W, I

Henderson, R S F (Blackheath) 1883 W, S, 1884 W, S, 1885 W

Heppell, W G (Devonport A) 1903 I

Herbert, A J (Wasps) 1958 F, S, 1959 W, I, F, S

Hesford, R (Bristol) 1981 S (R), 1982 A, S, F (R), 1983 F (R), 1985 R, F, S, I, W

Heslop, N J (Orrell) 1990 Arg 1,2,3, 1991 W, S, I, F, [US, F], 1992 W (R)

Hetherington, J G G (Northampton) 1958 A, I, 1959 W, I, F, S

Hewitt, E N (Coventry) 1951 W, I, F

Hewitt, W W (Queen's House) 1881 I, W, S, 1882 I

Hickson, J L (Bradford) 1887 W, I, S, 1890 W, S, I

Higgins, R (Liverpool) 1954 W, NZ, I, S, 1955 W, I, F, S, 1957 W, I, F, S, 1959 W

Hignell, A J (Cambridge U, Bristol) 1975 A 2, 1976 A, W, S, I, 1977 S, I, F, W, 1978 W, 1979 S, I, F, W

Hill, B A (Blackheath) 1903 I, S, 1904 W, I, 1905 W, NZ, 1906 SA, 1907 F, W

Hill, R A (Saracens) 1997 S, I, F, W, A 1,2, NZ 1, SA, NZ 2, 1998 F, W, H (R), It (R), A 2, SA 2, 1999 S, I, F, W, A, US, C, [It, NZ, Tg, Fj (R), SA], 2000 I, F, W, It, S, SA 1,2, A, Arg, SA 3, 2001 W, It, S, F, I, A, SA, 2002 S, I, F, W, It, NZ, A, SA, 2003 F 1, W 1, It, S, I, NZ, A, F 3, [Gg, F, A], 2004 It, S, I, W, F, NZ1, 2, A1

Hill, R J (Bath) 1984 SA 1,2, 1985 I (R), NZ 2(R), 1986 F (R), 1987 I, F, W, [US], 1989 Fj, 1990 I, F, W, S, Arg 1,2,3, 1991 W, S, I, F, Fj, A, [NZ, It, US, F, S, A]

Hillard, R J (Oxford U) 1925 NZ

Hiller, R (Harlequins) 1968 W, I, F, S, 1969 I, F, S, W, SA, 1970 I, W, S, 1971 I, F, S (2[1C]), P, 1972 W, I

Hind, A E (Leicester) 1905 NZ, 1906 W

Hind, G R (Blackheath) 1910 S, 1911 I

Hipkiss, D (Leicester) 2007 W2,F3, [Sm(R),Tg(R),F(R),SA2(R)]

Hobbs, R F A (Blackheath) 1899 S, 1903 W

Hobbs, R G S (Richmond) 1932 SA, W, I, S

Hobson, J (Bristol) 2008 NZ2(R)

Hodges, H A (Nottingham) 1906 W, I

Hodgkinson, S D (Nottingham) 1989 R, Fj, 1990 I, F, W, S, Arg 1,2,3, 1991 W, S, I, F, [US]

Hodgson, C C (Sale) 2001 R, 2002 S (R), I (R), It (R), Arg, 2003 F 1, W 1, It (R), 2004 NZ1, 2, A1, C, SA, A2, 2005 W, F, I, It, S, A, NZ, Sm, 2006 W, It, S, F,NZ, Arg, SA1, 2008 S(R),NZ1

Hodgson, J McD (Northern) 1932 SA, W, I, S, 1934 W, I, 1936 I

Hodgson, P (London Irish) 2008 I(R)

Hodgson, S A M (Durham City) 1960 W, I, F, S, 1961 SA, W, 1962 W, I, F, S, 1964 W

Hofmeyr, M B (Oxford U) 1950 W, F, S

Hogarth, T B (Hartlepool R) 1906 F

Holford, G (Gloucester) 1920 W, F

Holland, D (Devonport A) 1912 W, I, S

Holliday, T E (Aspatria) 1923 S, F, 1925 I, S, F, 1926 F, S

Holmes, C B (Manchester) 1947 S, 1948 I, F

Holmes, E (Manningham) 1890 S, I

Holmes, W A (Nuneaton) 1950 W, I, F, S, 1951 W, I, F, S, 1952 SA, S, I, F, 1953 W, I, F, S

Holmes, W B (Cambridge U) 1949 W, I, F, S

Hook, W G (Gloucester) 1951 S, 1952 SA, W

Hooper, C A (Middlesex W) 1894 W, I, S

Hopley, D P (Wasps) 1995 [WS (R)], SA, WS

Hopley, F J V (Blackheath) 1907 F, W, 1908 I

Horak, M J (London Irish) 2002 Arg

Hordern, P C (Gloucester) 1931 I, S, F, 1934 W

Horley, C H (Swinton) 1885 I

Hornby, A N (Manchester) 1877 I, S, 1878 S, I, 1880 I, 1881 I, S, 1882 I, S

Horrocks-Taylor, J P (Cambridge U, Leicester, Middlesbrough) 1958 W, A, 1961 S, 1962 S, 1963 NZ 1,2, A, 1964 NZ, W

Horsfall, E L (Harlequins) 1949 W

Horton, A L (Blackheath) 1965 W, I, F, S, 1966 F, S, 1967 NZ

Horton, J P (Bath) 1978 W, S, I, NZ, 1980 I, F, W, S, 1981 W, 1983 S, I, 1984 SA 1,2

Horton, N E (Moseley, Toulouse) 1969 I, F, S, W, 1971 I, F, S, 1974 S, 1975 W, 1977 S, I, F, W, 1978 F, W, 1979 S, I, F, W, 1980 I

Hosen, R W (Bristol, Northampton) 1963 NZ 1,2, A, 1964 F, S, 1967 A, I, F, S, W

Hosking, G R d'A (Devonport Services) 1949 W, I, F, S, 1950 W

Houghton, S (Runcorn) 1892 I, 1896 W

Howard, P D (O Millhillians) 1930 W, I, F, S, 1931 W, I, S, F

Hubbard, G C (Blackheath) 1892 W, I

Hubbard, J C (Harlequins) 1930 S

Hudson, A (Gloucester) 1906 W, I, F, 1908 F, W, I, S, 1910 F

Hughes, G E (Barrow) 1896 S

Hull, P A (Bristol, RAF) 1994 SA 1,2, R, C

Hulme, F C (Birkenhead Park) 1903 W, I, 1905 W, I

Hunt, J T (Manchester) 1882 I, S, 1884 W

Hunt, R (Manchester) 1880 I, 1881 W, S, 1882 I

Hunt, W H (Manchester) 1876 S, 1877 I, S, 1878 I

Hunter, I (Northampton) 1992 C, 1993 F, W, 1994 F, W, 1995 [WS, F]

Huntsman, R P (Headingley) 1985 NZ 1,2

Hurst, A C B (Wasps) 1962 S

Huskisson, T F (OMTs) 1937 W, I, S, 1938 W, I, 1939 W, I, S

Hutchinson, F (Headingley) 1909 F, I, S

Hutchinson, J E (Durham City) 1906 I

Hutchinson, W C (RIE Coll) 1876 S, 1877 I

Hutchinson, W H H (Hull) 1875 I, 1876 I

Huth, H (Huddersfield) 1879 S

Hyde, J P (Northampton) 1950 F, S

Hynes, W B (United Services, RN) 1912 F

Ibbitson, E D (Headingley) 1909 W, F, I, S

Imrie, H M (Durham City) 1906 NZ, 1907 I

Inglis, R E (Blackheath) 1886 W, I, S

Irvin, S H (Devonport A) 1905 W

Isherwood, F W (Ravenscourt Park) 1872 S

Jackett, E J (Leicester, Falmouth) 1905 NZ, 1906 W, I, S, F, SA, 1907 W, I, S, 1909 W, F, I, S

Jackson, A H (Blackheath) 1878 I, 1880 I

Jackson, B S (Broughton Park) 1970 S (R), F

Jackson, P B (Coventry) 1956 W, I, F, 1957 W, I, F, S, 1958 W, A, F, S, 1959 W, I, F, S, 1961 S, 1963 W, I, F, S

Jackson, W J (Halifax) 1894 S

Jacob, F (Cambridge U) 1897 W, I, S, 1898 I, S, W, 1899 W, I

Jacob, H P (Blackheath) 1924 W, I, F, S, 1930 F

Jacob, P G (Blackheath) 1898 I

Jacobs, C R (Northampton) 1956 W, I, S, F, 1957 W, I, F, S, 1958 W, A, I, F, S, 1960 W, I, F, S, 1961 SA, W, I, F, S, 1963 NZ 1,2, A, 1964 W, I, F, S

Jago, R A (Devonport A) 1906 W, I, SA, 1907 W, I

Janion, J P A G (Bedford) 1971 W, I, F, S (2[1C]), P, 1972 W, S, SA, 1973 A, 1975 A 1,2

Jarman, J W (Bristol) 1900 W

Jeavons, N C (Moseley) 1981 S, I, F, Arg 1,2, 1982 A, S, I, F, W, 1983 F, W, S, I

Jeeps, R E G (Northampton) 1956 W, 1957 W, I, F, S, 1958 W, A, I, F, S, 1959 I, 1960 W, I, F, S, 1961 SA, W, I, F, S, 1962 W, I, F, S

Jeffery, G L (Blackheath) 1886 W, I, S, 1887 W, I, S

Jennins, C R (Waterloo) 1967 A, I, F

Jewitt, J (Hartlepool R) 1902 W

Johns, W A (Gloucester) 1909 W, F, I, S, 1910 W, I, F

Johnson, M O (Leicester) 1993 F, NZ, 1994 S, I, F, W, R, C, 1995 I, F, W, S, [Arg, It, WS, A, NZ, F], SA, WS, 1996 F, W, S, I, It, Arg, 1997 S, I, F, W, A 2, NZ 1,2, 1998 F, W, S, I, H, It, A 2, SA 2, 1999 S, I, F, W, A, US, C, [It, NZ, Tg, Fj, SA], 2000 SA 1,2, A, Arg, SA 3, 2001 W, It, S, F, SA, 2002 S, I, F, It (t+R), NZ, A, SA, 2003 F 1, W 1, S, I, NZ, A, F 3, [Gg, SA, Sm, U(R),W, F, A]

Johnston, J B (Saracens) 2002 Arg, NZ (R)

Johnston, W R (Bristol) 1910 W, I, S, 1912 W, I, S, F, 1913 SA, W, F, I, S, 1914 W, I, S, F

Jones, C M (Sale) 2004 It(R), S, I(R), W, NZ1, 2005 W, 2006 A1(R), 2, SA1(R),2, 2007 SA1, 2(R)
Jones, F P (New Brighton) 1893 S
Jones, H A (Barnstaple) 1950 W, I, F
Jorden, A M (Cambridge U, Blackheath, Bedford) 1970 F, 1973 I, F, S, 1974 F, 1975 W, S
Jowett, D (Heckmondwike) 1889 M, 1890 S, I, 1891 W, I, S
Judd, P E (Coventry) 1962 W, I, F, S, 1963 S, NZ 1,2, A, 1964 NZ, 1965 I, F, S, 1966 W, I, F, S, 1967 A, I, F, S, W, NZ

Kay, B J (Leicester) 2001 C 1,2, A, R, SA (t+R), 2002 S, I, F, W, It, Arg, NZ (R), A, SA, 2003 F 1, W 1, It, S, I, NZ, A, F 3, [Gg, SA, Sm, W, F, A], 2004 It, S, I, W, F, C(R), SA(R), 2005 W, F, I, It, S, 2006 A2, NZ, Arg, SA1,2(R), 2007 F2, [US,SA1,Sm,Tg,A,F,SA2], 2008 W(R),It(R),F(R),S(R),I(R), NZ1(R),2(R)
Kayll, H E (Sunderland) 1878 S
Keeling, J H (Guy's Hospital) 1948 A, W
Keen, B W (Newcastle U) 1968 W, I, F, S
Keeton, G H (Leicester) 1904 W, I, S
Kelly, G A (Bedford) 1947 W, I, S, 1948 W
Kelly, T S (London Devonians) 1906 W, I, S, F, SA, 1907 F, W, I, S, 1908 F, I, S
Kemble, A T (Liverpool) 1885 W, I, 1887 I
Kemp, D T (Blackheath) 1935 W
Kemp, T A (Richmond) 1937 W, I, 1939 S, 1948 A, W
Kendall, P D (Birkenhead Park) 1901 S, 1902 W, 1903 S
Kendall-Carpenter, J MacG K (Oxford U, Bath) 1949 I, F, S, 1950 W, I, F, S, 1951 I, F, S, 1952 SA, W, S, I, F, 1953 W, I, F, S, 1954 W, NZ, I, F
Kendrew, D A (Leicester) 1930 W, I, 1933 I, S, 1934 S, 1935 W, I, 1936 NZ, W, I
Kennedy, R D (Camborne S of M) 1949 I, F, S
Kent, C P (Rosslyn Park) 1977 S, I, F, W, 1978 F (R)
Kent, T (Salford) 1891 W, I, S, 1892 W, I, S
Kershaw, C A (United Services, RN) 1920 W, F, I, S, 1921 W, I, S, F, 1922 W, I, F, S, 1923 W, I, S, F
Kewley, E (Liverpool) 1874 S, 1875 S, 1876 I, S, 1877 I, S, 1878 S
Kewney, A L (Leicester) 1906 W, I, S, F, 1909 A, W, F, I, S, 1911 W, F, I, S, 1912 I, S, 1913 SA
Key, A (O Cranleighans) 1930 I, 1933 W
Keyworth, M (Swansea) 1976 A, W, S, I
Kilner, B (Wakefield T) 1880 I
Kindersley, R S (Exeter) 1883 W, 1884 S, 1885 W
King, A D (Wasps) 1997 Arg 2(R), 1998 SA 2(R), 2000 It (R), 2001 C 2(R), 2003 W2
King, I (Harrogate) 1954 W, NZ, I
King, J A (Headingley) 1911 W, F, I, S, 1912 W, I, S, 1913 SA, W, F, I, S
King, Q E M A (Army) 1921 S
Kingston, P (Gloucester) 1975 A 1,2, 1979 I, F, W
Kitching, A E (Blackheath) 1913 I
Kittermaster, H J (Harlequins) 1925 NZ, W, I, 1926 W, I, F, S
Knight, F (Plymouth) 1909 A
Knight, P M (Bristol) 1972 F, S, SA
Knowles, E (Millom) 1896 S, 1897 S
Knowles, T C (Birkenhead Park) 1931 S
Krige, J A (Guy's Hospital) 1920 W

Labuschagne, N A (Harlequins, Guy's Hospital) 1953 W, 1955 W, I, F, S
Lagden, R O (Richmond) 1911 S
Laird, H C C (Harlequins) 1927 W, I, S, 1928 A, W, I, F, S, 1929 W, I
Lambert, D (Harlequins) 1907 F, 1908 F, W, S, 1911 W, F, I
Lampkowski, M S (Headingley) 1976 A, W, S, I
Lapage, W N (United Services, RN) 1908 F, W, I, S
Larter, P J (Northampton, RAF) 1967 A, NZ, 1968 W, I, F, S, 1969 I, F, S, W, SA, 1970 I, W, F, S, 1971 W, I, F, S (2[1C]), P, 1972 SA, 1973 NZ 1, W
Law, A F (Richmond) 1877 S
Law, D E (Birkenhead Park) 1927 I
Lawrence, Hon H A (Richmond) 1873 S, 1874 S, 1875 I, S
Lawrie, P W (Leicester) 1910 S, 1911 S
Lawson, R G (Workington) 1925 I
Lawson, T M (Workington) 1928 A, W
Leadbetter, M M (Broughton Park) 1970 F
Leadbetter, V H (Edinburgh Wands) 1954 S, F
Leake, W R M (Harlequins) 1891 W, I, S
Leather, G (Liverpool) 1907 I
Lee, F H (Marlborough N) 1876 S, 1877 I
Lee, H (Blackheath) 1907 F
Le Fleming, J (Blackheath) 1887 W
Leonard, J (Saracens, Harlequins) 1990 Arg 1,2,3, 1991 W, S, I, F, Fj, A, [NZ, It, US, F, S, A], 1992 S, I, F, W, C, SA, 1993 F, W, S, I, NZ, 1994 S, I, F, W, SA 1,2, R, C, 1995 I, F, W, S, [Arg, It, A, NZ, F], SA, WS, 1996 F, W, S, I, It, Arg, 1997 S, I, F, W, A 2, NZ 1, SA, NZ 2, 1998 F, W, S, I, H, It, A 2 SA 2, 1999 S, I, F, W, A, C (R), [It, NZ, Fj, SA], 2000 I, F, W, It, S, SA 1,2, A, Arg, SA 3, 2001 W, It, S, F, I, R, 2002 S (R), I (R), F (R), It (R), A, SA, 2003 F 1, S, I, NZ, W 2, F 2(t+R), 3(R), [Gg(t&R), SA(R), Sm, U, W, F(t&R), A(R)], 2004 It(R)
Leslie-Jones, F A (Richmond) 1895 W, I
Lewis, A O (Bath) 1952 SA, W, S, I, F, 1953 W, I, F, S, 1954 F
Lewsey, O J (Wasps) 1998 NZ 1,2, SA 1, 2001 C 1,2, US, 2003 It, S, I, NZ, A, F2, 3(t+R), [Gg, SA, U, F, A], 2004 It, S, I, W, F, NZ1, 2, A1, C, SA, A2, 2005 W, F, I, It, S, A, NZ, Sm, 2006 W, S, F,Arg(R), SA1,2, 2007 S,It,I,F1,2,3, [US,SA1,Sm,Tg,A,F]
Leyland, R (Waterloo) 1935 W, I, S
Linnett, M S (Moseley) 1989 Fj
Lipman, M R (Bath) 2004 NZ2(R), A1(R), 2006 A2, 2008 It,F,S,I
Livesay, R O'H (Blackheath) 1898 W, 1899 W
Lloyd, L D (Leicester) 2000 SA 1(R),2(R), 2001 C 1,2, US
Lloyd, R H (Harlequins) 1967 NZ, 1968 W, I, F, S
Locke, H M (Birkenhead Park) 1923 S, F, 1924 W, F, S, 1925 W, I, S, F, 1927 W, I, S
Lockwood, R E (Heckmondwike) 1887 W, I, S, 1889 M, 1891 W, I, S, 1892 W, I, S, 1893 W, I, 1894 W, I
Login, S H M (RN Coll) 1876 I
Lohden, F C (Blackheath) 1893 W
Long, A E (Bath) 1997 A 2, 2001 US (R)
Longland, R J (Northampton) 1932 S, 1933 W, S, 1934 W, I, S, 1935 W, I, S, 1936 NZ, W, I, S, 1937 W, I, S, 1938 W, I, S
Lowe, C N (Cambridge U, Blackheath) 1913 SA, W, F, I, S, 1914 W, I, S, F, 1920 W, F, I, S, 1921 W, I, S, F, 1922 W, I, F, S, 1923 W, I, S, F
Lowrie, F W (Wakefield T) 1889 M, 1890 W
Lowry, W M (Birkenhead Park) 1920 F
Lozowski, R A P (Wasps) 1984 A
Luddington, W G E (Devonport Services) 1923 W, I, S, F, 1924 W, I, F, S, 1925 W, I, S, F, 1926 W
Luger, D D (Harlequins, Saracens) 1998 H, It, SA 2, 1999 S, I, F, W, A, US, C, [It, NZ, Tg, Fj, SA], 2000 SA 1, A, Arg, SA 3, 2001 W, I, A, R, SA, 2002 F (R), W, It, 2003 F 1, W 1, It, S (R), I (R), NZ(R), W 2, [Gg(R), SA(R), U, W]
Lund, M B (Sale) 2006 A1, 2(R), NZ(R), Arg(t&R), 2007 S, It, I, F1(R),W1(R), SA2
Luscombe, F (Gipsies) 1872 S, 1873 S, 1875 I, S, 1876 I, S
Luscombe, J H (Gipsies) 1871 S
Luxmoore, A F C C (Richmond) 1900 S, 1901 W
Luya, H F (Waterloo, Headingley) 1948 W, I, S, F, 1949 W
Lyon, A (Liverpool) 1871 S
Lyon, G H d'O (United Services, RN) 1908 S, 1909 A

McCanlis, M A (Gloucester) 1931 W, I
McCarthy, N (Gloucester) 1999 I (t), US (R), 2000 It (R)
McFadyean, C W (Moseley) 1966 I, F, S, 1967 A, I, F, S, W, NZ, 1968 W, I
MacIlwaine, A H (United Services, Hull & E Riding) 1912 W, I, S, F, 1920 I
Mackie, O G (Wakefield T, Cambridge U) 1897 S, 1898 I
Mackinlay, J E H (St George's Hospital) 1872 S, 1873 S, 1875 I
MacLaren, W (Manchester) 1871 S
MacLennan, R R F (OMTs) 1925 I, S, F
McLeod, N F (RIE Coll) 1879 S, I
Madge, R J P (Exeter) 1948 A, W, I, S
Malir, F W S (Otley) 1930 W, I, S

Mallett, J A (Bath) 1995 [WS (R)]
Mallinder, J (Sale) 1997 Arg 1,2
Mangles, R H (Richmond) 1897 W, I
Manley, D C (Exeter) 1963 W, I, F, S
Mann, W E (United Services, Army) 1911 W, F, I
Mantell, N D (Rosslyn Park) 1975 A 1
Mapletoft, M S (Gloucester) 1997 Arg 2
Markendale, E T (Manchester R) 1880 I
Marques, R W D (Cambridge U, Harlequins) 1956 W, I, S, F, 1957 W, I, F, S, 1958 W, A, I, F, S, 1959 W, I, F, S, 1960 W, I, F, S, 1961 SA, W
Marquis, J C (Birkenhead Park) 1900 I, S
Marriott, C J B (Blackheath) 1884 W, I, S, 1886 W, I, S, 1887 I
Marriott, E E (Manchester) 1876 I
Marriott, V R (Harlequins) 1963 NZ 1,2, A, 1964 NZ
Marsden, G H (Morley) 1900 W, I, S
Marsh, H (RIE Coll) 1873 S
Marsh, J (Swinton) 1892 I
Marshall, H (Blackheath) 1893 W
Marshall, M W (Blackheath) 1873 S, 1874 S, 1875 I, S, 1876 I, S, 1877 I, S, 1878 S, I
Marshall, R M (Oxford U) 1938 I, S, 1939 W, I, S
Martin, C R (Bath) 1985 F, S, I, W
Martin, N O (Harlequins) 1972 F (R)
Martindale, S A (Kendal) 1929 F
Massey, E J (Leicester) 1925 W, I, S
Mather, B-J (Sale) 1999 W
Mathias, J L (Bristol) 1905 W, I, S, NZ
Matters, J C (RNE Coll) 1899 S
Matthews, J R C (Harlequins) 1949 F, S, 1950 I, F, S, 1952 SA, W, S, I, F
Maud, P (Blackheath) 1893 W, I
Maxwell, A W (New Brighton, Headingley) 1975 A 1, 1976 A, W, S, I, F, 1978 F
Maxwell-Hyslop, J E (Oxford U) 1922 I, F, S
Maynard, A F (Cambridge U) 1914 W, I, S
Mears, L A (Bath) 2005 Sm(R), 2006 W(R), It(R), F(R), I, A1, 2(R), NZ(R), Arg(R), SA1(R),2, 2007 S(R),It(R),I(R),W1(R), F2(R),3(R), [Tg(R)], 2008 W(R),It(R),F(R),S,I,NZ1,2
Meikle, G W C (Waterloo) 1934 W, I, S
Meikle, S S C (Waterloo) 1929 S
Mellish, F W (Blackheath) 1920 W, F, I, S, 1921 W, I
Melville, N D (Wasps) 1984 A, 1985 I, W, NZ 1,2, 1986 W, S, I, F, 1988 F, W, S, I 1
Merriam, L P B (Blackheath) 1920 W, F
Michell, A T (Oxford U) 1875 I, S, 1876 I
Middleton, B B (Birkenhead Park) 1882 I, 1883 I
Middleton, J A (Richmond) 1922 S
Miles, J H (Leicester) 1903 W
Millett, H (Richmond) 1920 F
Mills, F W (Marlborough N) 1872 S, 1873 S
Mills, S G F (Gloucester) 1981 Arg 1,2, 1983 W, 1984 SA 1, A
Mills, W A (Devonport A) 1906 W, I, S, F, SA, 1907 F, W, I, S, 1908 F, W
Milman, D L K (Bedford) 1937 W, 1938 W, I, S
Milton, C H (Camborne S of M) 1906 I
Milton, J G (Camborne S of M) 1904 W, I, S, 1905 S, 1907 I
Milton, W H (Marlborough N) 1874 S, 1875 I
Mitchell, F (Blackheath) 1895 W, I, S, 1896 W, I, S
Mitchell, W G (Richmond) 1890 W, S, I, 1891 W, I, S, 1893 S
Mobbs, E R (Northampton) 1909 A, W, F, I, S, 1910 I, F
Moberley, W O (Ravenscourt Park) 1872 S
Moody, L W (Leicester) 2001 C 1,2, US, I (R), R, SA (R), 2002 I (R), W, It, Arg, NZ, A, SA, 2003 F 1, W 2, F 2, 3(R), [Gg(R), SA, Sm(R), U, W, F(R), A(R)], 2004 C, SA, A2, 2005 F, I, It, S, A, NZ, Sm, 2006 W, It, S, F, I, A1, NZ, Arg, SA1(R),2(R),W2(R), 2007 [US(R),SA1(R),Sm(R),Tg,A,F,SA2], 2008 W
Moore, B C (Nottingham, Harlequins) 1987 S, [A, J, W], 1988 F, W, S, I 1,2, A 1, 2, Fj, A, 1989 S, I, F, W, R, Fj, 1990 I, F, W, S, Arg 1,2, 1991 W, S, I, F, Fj, A, [NZ, It, F, S, A], 1992 S, I, F, W, SA, 1993 F, W, S, I, NZ, 1994 S, I, F, W, SA 1,2, R, C, 1995 I, F, W, S, [Arg, It, WS (R), A, NZ, F]
Moore, E J (Blackheath) 1883 I, S
Moore, N J N H (Bristol) 1904 W, I, S
Moore, P B C (Blackheath) 1951 W
Moore, W K T (Leicester) 1947 W, I, 1949 F, S, 1950 I, F, S
Mordell, R J (Rosslyn Park) 1978 W
Morfitt, S (W Hartlepool) 1894 W, I, S, 1896 W, I, S
Morgan, J R (Hawick) 1920 W
Morgan, O (Gloucester) 2007 S,I
Morgan, W G D (Medicals, Newcastle) 1960 W, I, F, S, 1961 SA, W, I, F, S
Morley, A J (Bristol) 1972 SA, 1973 NZ 1, W, I, 1975 S, A 1,2
Morris, A D W (United Services, RN) 1909 A, W, F
Morris, C D (Liverpool St Helens, Orrell) 1988 A, 1989 S, I, F, W, 1992 S, I, F, W, C, SA, 1993 F, W, S, I, 1994 F, W, SA 1,2, R, 1995 S (t), [Arg, WS, A, NZ, F]
Morris, R (Northampton) 2003 W 1, It
Morrison, P H (Cambridge U) 1890 W, S, I, 1891 I
Morse, S (Marlborough N) 1873 S, 1874 S, 1875 S
Mortimer, W (Marlborough N) 1899 W
Morton, H J S (Blackheath) 1909 I, S, 1910 W, I
Moss, F (Broughton) 1885 W, I, 1886 W
Mullins, A R (Harlequins) 1989 Fj
Mycock, J (Sale) 1947 W, I, S, F, 1948 A
Myers, E (Bradford) 1920 I, S, 1921 W, I, 1922 W, I, F, S, 1923 W, I, S, F, 1924 W, I, F, S, 1925 S, F
Myers, H (Keighley) 1898 I

Nanson, W M B (Carlisle) 1907 F, W
Narraway, L (Gloucester) 2008 W,It(R),S(R),NZ1,2
Nash, E H (Richmond) 1875 I
Neale, B A (Rosslyn Park) 1951 I, F, S
Neale, M E (Blackheath) 1912 F
Neame, S (O Cheltonians) 1879 S, I, 1880 I, S
Neary, A (Broughton Park) 1971 W, I, F, S (2[1C]), P, 1972 W, I, F, S, SA, 1973 NZ 1, W, I, F, S, NZ 2, A, 1974 S, I, F, W, 1975 I, F, W, S, A 1, 1976 A, W, S, I, F, 1977 I, 1978 F (R), 1979 S, I, F, W, NZ, 1980 I, F, W, S
Nelmes, B G (Cardiff) 1975 A 1,2, 1978 W, S, I, NZ
Newbold, C J (Blackheath) 1904 W, I, S, 1905 W, I, S
Newman, S C (Oxford U) 1947 F, 1948 A, W
Newton, A W (Blackheath) 1907 S
Newton, P A (Blackheath) 1882 S
Newton-Thompson, J O (Oxford U) 1947 S, F
Nichol, W (Brighouse R) 1892 W, S
Nicholas, P L (Exeter) 1902 W
Nicholson, B E (Harlequins) 1938 W, I
Nicholson, E S (Leicester) 1935 W, I, S, 1936 NZ, W
Nicholson, E T (Birkenhead Park) 1900 W, I
Nicholson, T (Rockcliff) 1893 I
Ninnes, B F (Coventry) 1971 W
Noon, J D (Newcastle) 2001 C 1,2, US, 2003 W 2, F 2(t+R), 2005 W, F, I, It, S, A, NZ, 2006 W, It, S, F, I, 2006 A1(R), 2, NZ, Arg, SA1,2, 2007 SA2, F2, [US, SA1], 2008 It,F, S,I,NZ1(R),2
Norman, D J (Leicester) 1932 SA, W
North, E H G (Blackheath) 1891 W, I, S
Northmore, S (Millom) 1897 I
Novak, M J (Harlequins) 1970 W, S, F
Novis, A L (Blackheath) 1929 S, F, 1930 W, I, F, 1933 I, S

Oakeley, F E (United Services, RN) 1913 S, 1914 I, S, F
Oakes, R F (Hartlepool R) 1897 W, I, S, 1898 I, S, W, 1899 W, S
Oakley, L F L (Bedford) 1951 W
Obolensky, A (Oxford U) 1936 NZ, W, I, S
Ojo, T (London Irish) 2008 NZ1,2
Ojomoh, S O (Bath, Gloucester) 1994 I, F, SA 1(R),2, R, 1995 S (R), [Arg, WS, A (t), F], 1996 F, 1998 NZ 1
Old, A G B (Middlesbrough, Leicester, Sheffield) 1972 W, I, F, S, SA, 1973 NZ 2, A, 1974 S, I, F, W, 1975 I, A 2, 1976 S, I, 1978 F
Oldham, W L (Coventry) 1908 S, 1909 A
Olver, C J (Northampton) 1990 Arg 3, 1991 [US], 1992 C
O'Neill, A (Teignmouth, Torquay A) 1901 W, I, S
Openshaw, W E (Manchester) 1879 I
Orwin, J (Gloucester, RAF, Bedford) 1985 R, F, S, I, W, NZ 1,2, 1988 F, W, S, I 1,2, A 1,2
Osborne, R R (Manchester) 1871 S
Osborne, S H (Oxford U) 1905 S

Oti, C (Cambridge U, Nottingham, Wasps) 1988 S, I 1, 1989 S, I, F, W, R, 1990 Arg 1,2, 1991 Fj, A, [NZ, It]
Oughtred, B (Hartlepool R) 1901 S, 1902 W, I, S, 1903 W, I
Owen, J E (Coventry) 1963 W, I, F, S, A, 1964 NZ, 1965 W, I, F, S, 1966 I, F, S, 1967 NZ
Owen-Smith, H G O (St Mary's Hospital) 1934 W, I, S, 1936 NZ, W, I, S, 1937 W, I, S

Page, J J (Bedford, Northampton) 1971 W, I, F, S, 1975 S
Paice, D (London Irish) 2008 NZ1(R),2(R)
Pallant, J N (Notts) 1967 I, F, S
Palmer, A C (London Hospital) 1909 I, S
Palmer, F H (Richmond) 1905 W
Palmer, G V (Richmond) 1928 I, F, S
Palmer, J A (Bath) 1984 SA 1,2, 1986 I (R)
Palmer, T (Leeds, Wasps) 2001 US (R), 2006 Arg(R), SA1,2, 2007 It(R), I(R), F1, W1, 2008 NZ1,2
Pargetter, T A (Coventry) 1962 S, 1963 F, NZ 1
Parker, G W (Gloucester) 1938 I, S
Parker, Hon S (Liverpool) 1874 S, 1875 S
Parsons, E I (RAF) 1939 S
Parsons, M J (Northampton) 1968 W, I, F, S
Patterson, W M (Sale) 1961 SA, S
Pattisson, R M (Blackheath) 1883 I, S
Paul, H R (Gloucester) 2002 F(R), 2004 It(t&R), S(R), C, SA, A2
Paul, J E (RIE Coll) 1875 S
Payne, A T (Bristol) 1935 I, S
Payne, C M (Harlequins) 1964 I, F, S, 1965 I, F, S, 1966 W, I, F, S
Payne, J H (Broughton) 1882 S, 1883 W, I, S, 1884 I, 1885 W, I
Payne, T A N (Wasps) 2004 A1, 2006 A1(R), 2(R), 2007 F1, W1, 2008 It,NZ1(R),2
Pearce, G S (Northampton) 1979 S, I, F, W, 1981 Arg 1,2, 1982 A, S, 1983 F, W, S, I, NZ, 1984 S, SA 2, A, 1985 R, F, S, I, W, NZ 1,2, 1986 W, S, I, F, 1987 I, F, W, S, [A, US, W], 1988 Fj, 1991 [US]
Pears, D (Harlequins) 1990 Arg 1,2, 1992 F (R), 1994 F
Pearson, A W (Blackheath) 1875 I, S, 1876 I, S, 1877 S, 1878 S, I
Peart, T G A H (Hartlepool R) 1964 F, S
Pease, F E (Hartlepool R) 1887 I
Penny, S H (Leicester) 1909 A
Penny, W J (United Hospitals) 1878 I, 1879 S, I
Percival, L J (Rugby) 1891 I, 1892 I, 1893 S
Periton, H G (Waterloo) 1925 W, 1926 W, I, F, S, 1927 W, I, S, F, 1928 A, I, F, S, 1929 W, I, S, F, 1930 W, I, F, S
Perrott, E S (O Cheltonians) 1875 I
Perry, D G (Bedford) 1963 F, S, NZ 1,2, A 1964 NZ, W, I, 1965 W, I, F, S, 1966 W, I, F
Perry, M B (Bath) 1997 A 2, NZ 1, SA, NZ 2, 1998 W, S, I, A 1, NZ 1,2, SA 1, H, It, A 2, 1999 I, F, W, A US, C, [It, NZ, Tg, Fj, SA], 2000 I, F, W, It, S, SA 1,2, A, SA 3, 2001 W (R), F (R)
Perry, S (Bristol) 2006 NZ,Arg,SA1(R),2(R), 2007 I(R),F1(R), W1(R),SA1(R),2(R),W2,
F2,3, [US,SA1]
Perry, S V (Cambridge U, Waterloo) 1947 W, I, 1948 A, W, I, S, F
Peters, J (Plymouth) 1906 S, F, 1907 I, S, 1908 W
Phillips, C (Birkenhead Park) 1880 S, 1881 I, S
Phillips, M S (Fylde) 1958 A, I, F, S, 1959 W, I, F, S, 1960 W, I, F, S, 1961 W, 1963 W, I, F, S, NZ 1,2, A, 1964 NZ, W, I, F, S
Pickering, A S (Harrogate) 1907 I
Pickering, R D A (Bradford) 1967 I, F, S, W, 1968 F, S
Pickles, R C W (Bristol) 1922 I, F
Pierce, R (Liverpool) 1898 I, 1903 S
Pilkington, W N (Cambridge U) 1898 S
Pillman, C H (Blackheath) 1910 W, I, F, S, 1911 W, F, I, S, 1912 W, F, 1913 SA, W, F, I, S, 1914 W, I, S
Pillman, R L (Blackheath) 1914 F
Pinch, J (Lancaster) 1896 W, I, 1897 S
Pinching, W W (Guy's Hospital) 1872 S
Pitman, I J (Oxford U) 1922 S
Plummer, K C (Bristol) 1969 W, 1976 S, I, F
Pool-Jones, R J (Stade Francais) 1998 A 1
Poole, F O (Oxford U) 1895 W, I, S
Poole, R W (Hartlepool R) 1896 S
Pope, E B (Blackheath) 1931 W, S, F
Portus, G V (Blackheath) 1908 F, I
Potter, S (Leicester) 1998 A 1(t)
Poulton, R W (later Poulton Palmer) (Oxford U, Harlequins, Liverpool) 1909 F, I, S, 1910 W, 1911 S, 1912 W, I, S, 1913 SA, W, F, I, S, 1914 W, I, S, F
Powell, D L (Northampton) 1966 W, I, 1969 I, F, S, W, 1971 W, I, F, S (2[1C])
Pratten, W E (Blackheath) 1927 S, F
Preece, I (Coventry) 1948 I, S, F, 1949 F, S, 1950 W, I, F, S, 1951 W, I, F
Preece, P S (Coventry) 1972 SA, 1973 NZ 1, W, I, F, S, NZ 2, 1975 I, F, W, A 2, 1976 W (R)
Preedy, M (Gloucester) 1984 SA 1
Prentice, F D (Leicester) 1928 I, F, S
Prescott, R E (Harlequins) 1937 W, I, 1938 I, 1939 W, I, S
Preston, N J (Richmond) 1979 NZ, 1980 I, F
Price, H L (Harlequins) 1922 I, S, 1923 W, I
Price, J (Coventry) 1961 I
Price, P L A (RIE Coll) 1877 I, S, 1878 S
Price, T W (Cheltenham) 1948 S, F, 1949 W, I, F, S
Probyn, J A (Wasps, Askeans) 1988 F, W, S, I 1,2, A 1, 2, A, 1989 S, I, R (R), 1990 I, F, W, S, Arg 1,2,3, 1991 W, S, I, F, Fj, A, [NZ, It, F, S, A], 1992 S, I, F, W, 1993 F, W, S, I
Prout, D H (Northampton) 1968 W, I
Pullin, J V (Bristol) 1966 W, 1968 W, I, F, S, 1969 I, F, S, W, SA, 1970 I, W, S, F, 1971 W, I, F, S (2[1C]), P, 1972 W, I, F, S, SA, 1973 NZ 1, W, I, F, S, NZ 2, A, 1974 S, I, F, W, 1975 I, W (R), S, A 1,2, 1976 F
Purdy, S J (Rugby) 1962 S
Pyke, J (St Helens Recreation) 1892 W
Pym, J A (Blackheath) 1912 W, I, S, F

Quinn, J P (New Brighton) 1954 W, NZ, I, S, F

Rafter, M (Bristol) 1977 S, F, W, 1978 F, W, S, I, NZ, 1979 S, I, F, W, NZ, 1980 W(R), 1981 W, Arg 1,2
Ralston, C W (Richmond) 1971 S (C), P, 1972 W, I, F, S, SA, 1973 NZ 1, W, I, F, S, NZ 2, A, 1974 S, I, F, W, 1975 I, F, W, S
Ramsden, H E (Bingley) 1898 S, W
Ranson, J M (Rosslyn Park) 1963 NZ 1,2, A, 1964 W, I, F, S
Raphael, J E (OMTs) 1902 W, I, S, 1905 W, S, NZ, 1906 W, S, F
Ravenscroft, J (Birkenhead Park) 1881 I
Ravenscroft, S C W (Saracens) 1998 A 1, NZ 2(R)
Rawlinson, W C W (Blackheath) 1876 S
Redfern, S P (Leicester) 1984 I (R)
Redman, N C (Bath) 1984 A, 1986 S (R), 1987 I, S, [A, J, W], 1988 Fj, 1990 Arg 1,2, 1991 Fj, [It, US], 1993 NZ, 1994 F, W, SA 1,2, 1997 Arg 1, A 1
Redmond, G F (Cambridge U) 1970 F
Redwood, B W (Bristol) 1968 W, I
Rees, D L (Sale) 1997 A 2, NZ 1, SA, NZ 2, 1998 F, W, SA 2(R), 1999 S, I, F, A
Rees, G W (Nottingham) 1984 SA 2(R), A, 1986 I, F, 1987 F, W, S, [A, J, US, W], 1988 S (R), I 1,2, A 1,2, Fj, 1989 W (R), R (R), Fj (R), 1990 Arg 3(R), 1991 Fj, [US]
Rees, T (Wasps) 2007 S(R), It(R), I(R), F1, W1, F3, [US, SA1], 2008 W(R),NZ1,2
Reeve, J S R (Harlequins) 1929 F, 1930 W, I, F, S, 1931 W, I, S
Regan, M (Liverpool) 1953 W, I, F, S, 1954 W, NZ, I, S, F, 1956 I, S, F
Regan, M P (Bristol, Bath, Leeds) 1995 SA, WS, 1996 F, W, S, I, It, Arg, 1997 S, I, F, W, A 1, NZ 2(R), 1998 F, 2000 SA 1(t), A(R), Arg, SA 3(t), 2001 It(R), S(R), C 2(R), R, 2003 F 1(t), It(R), W 2, [Gg(R), Sm], 2004 It(R), I(R), NZ1(R), 2, A1, 2007 SA1,2,W2,F2,3, [US,SA1,A,F,SA2], 2008 W,It,F
Rendall, P A G (Wasps, Askeans) 1984 W, SA 2, 1986 W, S, 1987 I, F, S, [A, J, W], 1988 F, W, S, I 1,2, A 1,2, A, 1989 S, I, F, W, R, 1990 I, F, W, S, 1991 [It (R)]
Rew, H (Blackheath) 1929 S, F, 1930 F, S, 1931 W, S, F, 1934 W, I, S
Reynolds, F J (O Cranleighans) 1937 S, 1938 I, S

Reynolds, S (Richmond) 1900 W, I, S, 1901 I
Rhodes, J (Castleford) 1896 W, I, S
Richards, D (Leicester) 1986 I, F, 1987 S, [A, J, US, W], 1988 F, W, S, I 1, A 1,2, Fj, A, 1989 S, I, F, W, R, 1990 Arg 3, 1991 W, S, I, F, Fj, A, [NZ, It, US], 1992 S (R), F, W, C, 1993 NZ, 1994 W, SA 1, C, 1995 I, F, W, S, [WS, A, NZ], 1996 F (t), S, I
Richards, E E (Plymouth A) 1929 S, F
Richards, J (Bradford) 1891 W, I, S
Richards, P C (Gloucester, London Irish) 2006 A1, 2,NZ(R), Arg(R), SA1,2, 2007 [US(R),SA1(R),Tg(R),A(t),F(R),SA2(R)], 2008 NZ2(R)
Richards, S B (Richmond) 1965 W, I, F, S, 1967 A, I, F, S, W
Richardson, J V (Birkenhead Park) 1928 A, W, I, F, S
Richardson, W R (Manchester) 1881 I
Rickards, C H (Gipsies) 1873 S
Rimmer, G (Waterloo) 1949 W, I, 1950 W, 1951 W, I, F, 1952 SA, W, 1954 W, NZ, I, S
Rimmer, L I (Bath) 1961 SA, W, I, F, S
Ripley, A G (Rosslyn Park) 1972 W, I, F, S, SA, 1973 NZ 1, W, I, F, S, NZ 2, A, 1974 S, I, F, W, 1975 I, F, S, A 1,2, 1976 A, W, S
Risman, A B W (Loughborough Coll) 1959 W, I, F, S, 1961 SA, W, I, F
Ritson, J A S (Northern) 1910 F, S, 1912 F, 1913 SA, W, F, I, S
Rittson-Thomas, G C (Oxford U) 1951 W, I, F
Robbins, G L (Coventry) 1986 W, S
Robbins, P G D (Oxford U, Moseley, Coventry) 1956 W, I, S, F, 1957 W, I, F, S, 1958 W, A, I, S, 1960 W, I, F, S, 1961 SA, W, 1962 S
Roberts, A D (Northern) 1911 W, F, I, S, 1912 I, S, F, 1914 I
Roberts, E W (RNE Coll) 1901 W, I, 1905 NZ, 1906 W, I, 1907 S
Roberts, G D (Harlequins) 1907 S, 1908 F, W
Roberts, J (Sale) 1960 W, I, F, S, 1961 SA, W, I, F, S, 1962 W, I, F, S, 1963 W, I, F, S, 1964 NZ
Roberts, R S (Coventry) 1932 I
Roberts, S (Swinton) 1887 W, I
Roberts, V G (Penryn, Harlequins) 1947 F, 1949 W, I, F, S, 1950 I, F, S, 1951 W, I, F, S, 1956 W, I, S, F
Robertshaw, A R (Bradford) 1886 W, I, S, 1887 W, S
Robinson, A (Blackheath) 1889 M, 1890 W, S, I
Robinson, E T (Coventry) 1954 S, 1961 I, F, S
Robinson, G C (Percy Park) 1897 I, S, 1898 I, 1899 W, 1900 I, S, 1901 I, S
Robinson, J T (Sale) 2001 It (R), S (R), F (R), I, A, R, SA, 2002 S, I, F, It, NZ, A, SA, 2003 F 1, W 1, S, I, NZ, A, F 3, [Gg, SA, Sm, U(R), W, F, A], 2004 It, S, I, W, F, C, SA, A2, 2005 W, F, I, 2007 S,It,F1,W1,SA1,W2,F3, [US,SA1,A,F,SA2]
Robinson, J J (Headingley) 1893 S, 1902 W, I, S
Robinson, R A (Bath) 1988 A 2, Fj, A, 1989 S, I, F, W, 1995 SA
Robson, A (Northern) 1924 W, I, F, S, 1926 W
Robson, M (Oxford U) 1930 W, I, F, S
Rodber, T A K (Army, Northampton) 1992 S, I, 1993 NZ, 1994 I, F, W, SA 1,2, R, C, 1995 I, F, W, S, [Arg, It, WS (R), A, NZ, F], SA, WS, 1996 W, S (R), I (t), It, Arg, 1997 S, I, F, W, A 1, 1998 H (R), It (R), A 2, SA 2, 1999 S, I, F, W, A, US (R), [NZ (R), Fj (R)]
Rogers, D P (Bedford) 1961 I, F, S, 1962 W, I, F, 1963 W, I, F, S, NZ 1,2, A, 1964 NZ, W, I, F, S, 1965 W, I, F, S, 1966 W, I, F, S, 1967 A, S, W, NZ, 1969 I, F, S, W
Rogers, J H (Moseley) 1890 W, S, I, 1891 S
Rogers, W L Y (Blackheath) 1905 W, I
Rollitt, D M (Bristol) 1967 I, F, S, W, 1969 I, F, S, W, 1975 S, A 1,2
Roncoroni, A D S (West Herts, Richmond) 1933 W, I, S
Rose, W M H (Cambridge U, Coventry, Harlequins) 1981 I, F, 1982 A, S, I, 1987 I, F, W, S, [A]
Rossborough, P A (Coventry) 1971 W, 1973 NZ 2, A, 1974 S, I, 1975 I, F
Rosser, D W A (Wasps) 1965 W, I, F, S, 1966 W
Rotherham, Alan (Richmond) 1883 W, S, 1884 W, S, 1885 W, I, 1886 W, I, S, 1887 W, I, S
Rotherham, Arthur (Richmond) 1898 S, W, 1899 W, I, S
Roughley, D (Liverpool) 1973 A, 1974 S, I
Rowell, R E (Leicester) 1964 W, 1965 W
Rowley, A J (Coventry) 1932 SA
Rowley, H C (Manchester) 1879 S, I, 1880 I, S, 1881 I, W, S, 1882 I, S
Rowntree, G C (Leicester) 1995 S (t), [It, WS], WS, 1996 F, W, S, I, It, Arg, 1997 S, I, F, W, A 1, 1998 A 1, NZ 1, 2, SA 1, H (R), It (R), 1999 US, C, [It (R), Tg, Fj (R)], 2001 C 1,2, US, I(R), A, R, SA, 2002 S, I, F, W, It, 2003 F 1(R), W 1, It, S, I, NZ, F 2, 2004 C, SA, A2, 2005 W, F, I, It, 2006 A1, 2
Royds, P M R (Blackheath) 1898 S, W, 1899 W
Royle, A V (Broughton R) 1889 M
Rudd, E L (Liverpool) 1965 W, I, S, 1966 W, I, S
Russell, R F (Leicester) 1905 NZ
Rutherford, D (Percy Park, Gloucester) 1960 W, I, F, S, 1961 SA, 1965 W, I, F, S, 1966 W, I, F, S, 1967 NZ
Ryalls, H J (New Brighton) 1885 W, I
Ryan, D (Wasps, Newcastle) 1990 Arg 1,2, 1992 C, 1998 S
Ryan, P H (Richmond) 1955 W, I

Sackey, P H (Wasps) 2006 NZ,Arg, 2007 F2,3(R), [SA1,Sm,Tg,A,F,SA2], 2008 W,It,F,S,I
Sadler, E H (Army) 1933 I, S
Sagar, J W (Cambridge U) 1901 W, I
Salmon, J L B (Harlequins) 1985 NZ 1,2, 1986 W, S, 1987 I, F, W, S, [A, J, US, W]
Sample, C H (Cambridge U) 1884 I, 1885 I, 1886 S
Sampson, P C (Wasps) 1998 SA 1, 2001 C 1,2
Sanders, D L (Harlequins) 1954 W, NZ, I, S, F, 1956 W, I, S, F
Sanders, F W (Plymouth A) 1923 I, S, F
Sanderson, A (Sale) 2001 R (R), 2002 Arg, 2003 It(t + R), W 2(R), F 2
Sanderson, P H (Sale, Harlequins, Worcester) 1998 NZ 1,2, SA 1, 2001 C 1(R),2(R), US(t+R), 2005 A, NZ, Sm, 2006 A1, 2, NZ, Arg, SA1,2, 2007 SA1(R)
Sandford, J R P (Marlborough N) 1906 I
Sangwin, R D (Hull and E Riding) 1964 NZ, W
Sargent, G A F (Gloucester) 1981 I (R)
Savage, K F (Northampton) 1966 W, I, F, S, 1967 A, I, F, S, W, NZ, 1968 W, F, S
Sawyer, C M (Broughton) 1880 S, 1881 I
Saxby, L E (Gloucester) 1932 SA, W
Scarbrough, D G R (Leeds, Saracens) 2003 W 2, 2007 SA2
Schofield, D (Sale) 2007 SA1,2(R)
Schofield, J W (Manchester) 1880 I
Scholfield, J A (Preston Grasshoppers) 1911 W
Schwarz, R O (Richmond) 1899 S, 1901 W, I
Scorfield, E S (Percy Park) 1910 F
Scott, C T (Blackheath) 1900 W, I, 1901 W, I
Scott, E K (St Mary's Hospital, Redruth) 1947 W, 1948 A, W, I, S
Scott, F S (Bristol) 1907 W
Scott, H (Manchester) 1955 F
Scott, J P (Rosslyn Park, Cardiff) 1978 F, W, S, I, NZ, 1979 S (R), I, F, W, NZ, 1980 I, F, W, S, 1981 W, S, I, F, Arg 1,2, 1982 I, F, W, 1983 F, W, S, I, NZ, 1984 S, I, F, W, SA 1,2
Scott, J S M (Oxford U) 1958 F
Scott, M T (Cambridge U) 1887 I, 1890 S, I
Scott, W M (Cambridge U) 1889 M
Seddon, R L (Broughton R) 1887 W, I, S
Sellar, K A (United Services, RN) 1927 W, I, S, 1928 A, W, I, F
Sever, H S (Sale) 1936 NZ, W, I, S, 1937 W, I, S, 1938 W, I, S
Shackleton, I R (Cambridge U) 1969 SA, 1970 I, W, S
Sharp, R A W (Oxford U, Wasps, Redruth) 1960 W, I, F, S, 1961 I, F, 1962 W, I, F, 1963 W, I, F, S, 1967 A
Shaw, C H (Moseley) 1906 S, SA, 1907 F, W, I, S
Shaw, F (Cleckheaton) 1898 I
Shaw, J F (RNE Coll) 1898 S, W
Shaw, S D (Bristol, Wasps) 1996 It, Arg, 1997 S, I, F, W, A 1, SA (R), 2000 I, F, W, It, S, SA 1(R),2(R), 2001 C 1(R), 2, US, I, 2003 It (R), W 2, F 2(R), 3(R), 2004 It(t&R), S(R), NZ1, 2, A1, 2005 Sm(R), 2006 W(R), It(R), S(R), F(R), I, 2007 W2,F2,3, [US, SA1,Sm,A,F,SA2], 2008 W,It,F,S,I
Sheasby, C M A (Wasps) 1996 It, Arg, 1997 W (R), Arg 1(R),2(R), SA (R), NZ 2(t)

Sheppard, A (Bristol) 1981 W (R), 1985 W
Sheridan, A J (Sale) 2004 C(R), 2005 A, NZ, Sm, 2006 W, It, S, F(R), I, NZ, SA1, 2007 W2, F2, [US, SA1, Sm, Tg, A, F, SA2], 2008 W,F,S,I,NZ1
Sherrard, C W (Blackheath) 1871 S, 1872 S
Sherriff, G A (Saracens) 1966 S, 1967 A, NZ
Shewring, H E (Bristol) 1905 I, NZ, 1906 W, S, F, SA, 1907 F, W, I, S
Shooter, J H (Morley) 1899 I, S, 1900 I, S
Shuttleworth, D W (Headingley) 1951 S, 1953 S
Sibree, H J H (Harlequins) 1908 F, 1909 I, S
Silk, N (Harlequins) 1965 W, I, F, S
Simms, K G (Cambridge U, Liverpool, Wasps) 1985 R, F, S, I, W, 1986 I, F, 1987 I, F, W, [A, J, W], 1988 F, W
Simpson, C P (Harlequins) 1965 W
Simpson, P D (Bath) 1983 NZ, 1984 S, 1987 I
Simpson, T (Rockcliff) 1902 S, 1903 W, I, S, 1904 I, S, 1905 I, S, 1906 S, SA, 1909 F
Simpson-Daniel, J D (Gloucester) 2002 NZ, A, 2003 W 1(t + R), It, W 2, 2004 I(R), NZ1, 2005 Sm, 2006 It(R), 2007 SA1(R)
Sims, D (Gloucester) 1998 NZ 1(R),2, SA 1
Skinner, M G (Harlequins) 1988 F, W, S, I 1,2, 1989 Fj, 1990 I, F, W, S, Arg 1,2, 1991 Fj (R), [US, F, S, A], 1992 S, I, F, W
Skirving, B (Saracens) 2007 SA2
Sladen, G M (United Services, RN) 1929 W, I, S
Sleightholme, J M (Bath) 1996 F, W, S, I, It, Arg, 1997 S, I, F, W, Arg 1,2
Slemen, M A C (Liverpool) 1976 I, F, 1977 S, I, F, W, 1978 F, W, S, I, NZ, 1979 S, I, F, W, NZ, 1980 I, F, W, S, 1981 W, S, I, F, 1982 A, S, I, F, W, 1983 NZ, 1984 S
Slocock, L A N (Liverpool) 1907 F, W, I, S, 1908 F, W, I, S
Slow, C F (Leicester) 1934 S
Small, H D (Oxford U) 1950 W, I, F, S
Smallwood, A M (Leicester) 1920 F, I, 1921 W, I, S, F, 1922 I, S, 1923 W, I, S, F, 1925 I, S
Smart, C E (Newport) 1979 F, W, NZ, 1981 S, I, F, Arg 1,2, 1982 A, S, I, F, W, 1983 F, W, S, I
Smart, S E J (Gloucester) 1913 SA, W, F, I, S, 1914 W, I, S, F, 1920 W, I, S
Smeddle, R W (Cambridge U) 1929 W, I, S, 1931 F
Smith, C C (Gloucester) 1901 W
Smith, D F (Richmond) 1910 W, I
Smith, J V (Cambridge U, Rosslyn Park) 1950 W, I, F, S
Smith, K (Roundhay) 1974 F, W, 1975 W, S
Smith, M J K (Oxford U) 1956 W
Smith, O J (Leicester) 2003 It (R), W 2(R), F 2, 2005 It(R), S(R)
Smith, S J (Sale) 1973 I, F, S, A, 1974 I, F, 1975 W (R), 1976 F, 1977 F (R), 1979 NZ, 1980 I, F, W, S, 1981 W, S, I, F, Arg 1,2, 1982 A, S, I, F, W, 1983 F, W, S
Smith, S R (Richmond) 1959 W, F, S, 1964 F, S
Smith, S T (Wasps) 1985 R, F, S, I, W, NZ 1,2, 1986 W, S
Smith, T H (Northampton) 1951 W
Soane, F (Bath) 1893 S, 1894 W, I, S
Sobey, W H (O Millhillians) 1930 W, F, S, 1932 SA, W
Solomon, B (Redruth) 1910 W
Sparks, R H W (Plymouth A) 1928 I, F, S, 1929 W, I, S, 1931 I, S, F
Speed, H (Castleford) 1894 W, I, S, 1896 S
Spence, F W (Birkenhead Park) 1890 I
Spencer, J (Harlequins) 1966 W
Spencer, J S (Cambridge U, Headingley) 1969 I, F, S, W, SA, 1970 I, W, S, F, 1971 W, I, S (2[1C]), P
Spong, R S (O Millhillians) 1929 F, 1930 W, I, F, S, 1931 F, 1932 SA, W
Spooner, R H (Liverpool) 1903 W
Springman, H H (Liverpool) 1879 S, 1887 S
Spurling, A (Blackheath) 1882 I
Spurling, N (Blackheath) 1886 I, S, 1887 W
Squires, P J (Harrogate) 1973 F, S, NZ 2, A, 1974 S, I, F, W, 1975 I, F, W, S, A 1,2, 1976 A, W, 1977 S, I, F, W, 1978 F, W, S, I, NZ, 1979 S, I, F, W
Stafford R C (Bedford) 1912 W, I, S, F
Stafford, W F H (RE) 1874 S
Stanbury, E (Plymouth A) 1926 W, I, S, 1927 W, I, S, F, 1928 A, W, I, F, S, 1929 W, I, S, F
Standing, G (Blackheath) 1883 W, I
Stanger-Leathes, C F (Northern) 1905 I
Stark, K J (O Alleynians) 1927 W, I, S, F, 1928 A, W, I, F, S
Starks, A (Castleford) 1896 W, I
Starmer-Smith, N C (Harlequins) 1969 SA, 1970 I, W, S, F, 1971 S (C), P
Start, S P (United Services, RN) 1907 S
Steeds, J H (Saracens) 1949 F, S, 1950 I, F, S
Steele-Bodger, M R (Cambridge U) 1947 W, I, S, F, 1948 A, W, I, S, F
Steinthal, F E (Ilkley) 1913 W, F
Stephenson, M (Newcastle) 2001 C 1,2, US
Stevens, C B (Penzance-Newlyn, Harlequins) 1969 SA, 1970 I, W, S, 1971 P, 1972 W, I, F, S, SA, 1973 NZ 1, W, I, F, S, NZ 2, A, 1974 S, I, F, W, 1975 I, F, W, S
Stevens, M J H (Bath) 2004 NZ1(R), 2(t), 2005 I, It, S, NZ(R), Sm, 2006 W, It, F, 2007 SA2, W2(R), F2, 3(R), [US(R), SA1, Sm, Tg, A(R), F(R), SA2(R)], 2008 W(R),It,F(R),S(R),I(R),NZ1,2
Still, E R (Oxford U, Ravenscourt P) 1873 S
Stimpson, T R G (Newcastle, Leicester) 1996 It, 1997 S, I, F, W, A 1, NZ 2(t+R), 1998 A 1, NZ 1,2(R), SA 1(R), 1999 US (R), C (R), 2000 SA 1, 2001 C 1(t),2(R), 2002 W (R), Arg, SA (R)
Stirling, R V (Leicester, RAF, Wasps) 1951 W, I, F, S, 1952 SA, W, S, I, F, 1953 W, I, F, S, 1954 W, NZ, I, S, F
Stoddart, A E (Blackheath) 1885 W, I, 1886 W, I, S, 1889 M, 1890 W, I, 1893 W, S
Stoddart, W B (Liverpool) 1897 W, I, S
Stokes, F (Blackheath) 1871 S, 1872 S, 1873 S
Stokes, L (Blackheath) 1875 I, 1876 S, 1877 I, S, 1878 S, 1879 S, I, 1880 I, S, 1881 I, W, S
Stone, F le S (Blackheath) 1914 F
Stoop, A D (Harlequins) 1905 S, 1906 S, F, SA, 1907 F, W, 1910 W, I, S, 1911 W, F, I, S, 1912 W, S
Stoop, F M (Harlequins) 1910 S, 1911 F, I, 1913 SA
Stout, F M (Richmond) 1897 W, I, 1898 I, S, W, 1899 I, S, 1903 S, 1904 W, I, S, 1905 W, I, S
Stout, P W (Richmond) 1898 S, W, 1899 W, I, S
Strettle, D (Harlequins) 2007 I,F1,W1,2, 2008 W,NZ1
Stringer, N C (Wasps) 1982 A (R), 1983 NZ (R), 1984 SA 1(R), A, 1985 R
Strong, E L (Oxford U) 1884 W, I, S
Sturnham B (Saracens) 1998 A 1, NZ 1(t),2(t)
Summerscales, G E (Durham City) 1905 NZ
Sutcliffe, J W (Heckmondwike) 1889 M
Swarbrick, D W (Oxford U) 1947 W, I, F, 1948 A, W, 1949 I
Swayne, D H (Oxford U) 1931 W
Swayne, J W R (Bridgwater) 1929 W
Swift, A H (Swansea) 1981 Arg 1,2, 1983 F, W, S, 1984 SA 2
Syddall, J P (Waterloo) 1982 I, 1984 A
Sykes, A R V (Blackheath) 1914 F
Sykes, F D (Northampton) 1955 F, S, 1963 NZ 2, A
Sykes, P W (Wasps) 1948 F, 1952 S, I, F, 1953 W, I, F
Syrett, R E (Wasps) 1958 W, A, I, F, 1960 W, I, F, S, 1962 W, I, F

Tait, M (Newcastle) 2005 W, 2006 A1, 2,SA1,2,2007 It(R),I(R),F1(R),W1,SA1,2,W2, [US(R),SA1(R),Sm,Tg,A,F, SA2], 2008 It(t),F(R),S(R),I(t&R), NZ2
Tallent, J A (Cambridge U, Blackheath) 1931 S, F, 1932 SA, W, 1935 I
Tanner, C C (Cambridge U, Gloucester) 1930 S, 1932 SA, W, I, S
Tarr, F N (Leicester) 1909 A, W, F, 1913 S
Tatham, W M (Oxford U) 1882 S, 1883 W, I, S, 1884 W, I, S
Taylor, A S (Blackheath) 1883 W, I, 1886 W, I
Taylor, E W (Rockcliff) 1892 I, 1893 I, 1894 W, I, S, 1895 W, I, S, 1896 W, I, 1897 W, I, S, 1899 I
Taylor, F (Leicester) 1920 F, I
Taylor, F M (Leicester) 1914 W
Taylor, H H (Blackheath) 1879 S, 1880 S, 1881 I, W, 1882 S
Taylor, J T (W Hartlepool) 1897 I, 1899 I, 1900 I, 1901 W, I, 1902 W, I, S, 1903 W, I, 1905 S
Taylor, P J (Northampton) 1955 W, I, 1962 W, I, F, S
Taylor, R B (Northampton) 1966 W, 1967 I, F, S, W, NZ, 1969 F, S, W, SA, 1970 I, W, S, F, 1971 S (2[1C])

Taylor, W J (Blackheath) 1928 A, W, I, F, S
Teague, M C (Gloucester, Moseley) 1985 F (R), NZ 1, 2, 1989 S, I, F, W, R, 1990 F, W, S, 1991 W, S, I, F, Fj, A, [NZ, It, F, S, A], 1992 SA, 1993 F, W, S, I
Teden, D E (Richmond) 1939 W, I, S
Teggin, A (Broughton R) 1884 I, 1885 W, 1886 I, S, 1887 I, S
Tetley, T S (Bradford) 1876 S
Thomas, C (Barnstaple) 1895 W, I, S, 1899 I
Thompson, P H (Headingley, Waterloo) 1956 W, I, S, F, 1957 W, I, F, S, 1958 W, A, I, F, S, 1959 W, I, F, S
Thompson, S G (Northampton) 2002 S, I, F, W, It, Arg, NZ, A, SA, 2003 F 1, W 1, It, S, I, NZ, A, F 2(R), 3, [Gg, SA, Sm(R), W, F, A], 2004 It, S, I, W, F, NZ1, A1(R), C, SA, A2, 2005 W, F, I, It, S, A, NZ, Sm, 2006 W, It, S, F, I(R)
Thomson, G T (Halifax) 1878 S, 1882 I, S, 1883 W, I, S, 1884 I, S, 1885 I
Thomson, W B (Blackheath) 1892 W, 1895 W, I, S
Thorne, J D (Bristol) 1963 W, I, F
Tindall, M J (Bath, Gloucester) 2000 I, F, W, It, S, SA 1,2, A Arg, SA 3, 2001 W (R), R, SA (R), 2002 S, I, F, W, It, NZ, A, SA, 2003 It, S, I, NZ, A, F 2, [Gg, SA, Sm, W, F(R), A], 2004 W, F, NZ1, 2, A1, C, SA, A2, 2005 A, NZ, Sm, 2006 W, It, S, F, I(t&R), 2007 S,It,I,F1, 2008 W,NZ1,2
Tindall, V R (Liverpool U) 1951 W, I, F, S
Titterrell, A J (Sale) 2004 NZ2(R), C(R), 2005 It(R), S(R), 2007 SA2(R)
Tobin, F (Liverpool) 1871 S
Todd, A F (Blackheath) 1900 I, S
Todd, R (Manchester) 1877 S
Toft, H B (Waterloo) 1936 S, 1937 W, I, S, 1938 W, I, S, 1939 W, I, S
Toothill, J T (Bradford) 1890 S, I, 1891 W, I, 1892 W, I, S, 1893 W, I, S, 1894 W, I
Tosswill, L R (Exeter) 1902 W, I, S
Touzel, C J C (Liverpool) 1877 I, S
Towell, A C (Bedford) 1948 F, 1951 S
Travers, B H (Harlequins) 1947 W, I, 1948 A, W, 1949 F, S
Treadwell, W T (Wasps) 1966 I, F, S
Trick, D M (Bath) 1983 I, 1984 SA 1
Tristram, H B (Oxford U) 1883 S, 1884 W, S, 1885 W, 1887 S
Troop, C L (Aldershot S) 1933 I, S
Tucker, J S (Bristol) 1922 W, 1925 NZ, W, I, S, F, 1926 W, I, F, S, 1927 W, I, S, F, 1928 A, W, I, F, S, 1929 W, I, F, 1930 W, I, F, S, 1931 W
Tucker, W E (Blackheath) 1894 W, I, 1895 W, I, S
Tucker, W E (Blackheath) 1926 I, 1930 W, I
Turner, D P (Richmond) 1871 S, 1872 S, 1873 S, 1874 S, 1875 I, S
Turner, E B (St George's Hospital) 1876 I, 1877 I, 1878 I
Turner, G R (St George's Hospital) 1876 S
Turner, H J C (Manchester) 1871 S
Turner, M F (Blackheath) 1948 S, F
Turner, S C (Sale) 2007 W1(R), SA1,2(R)
Turquand-Young, D (Richmond) 1928 A, W, 1929 I, S, F
Twynam, H T (Richmond) 1879 I, 1880 I, 1881 W, 1882<j> I, 1883 I, 1884 W, I, S

Ubogu, V E (Bath) 1992 C, SA, 1993 NZ, 1994 S, I, F, W, SA 1,2, R, C, 1995 I, F, W, S, [Arg, WS, A, NZ, F], SA, 1999 F (R), W (R), A (R)
Underwood, A M (Exeter) 1962 W, I, F, S, 1964 I
Underwood, R (Leicester, RAF) 1984 I, F, W, A, 1985 R, F, S, I, W, 1986 W, I, F, 1987 I, F, W, S, [A, J, W], 1988 F, W, S, I 1,2, A 1,2, Fj, A, 1989 S, I, F, W, R, Fj, 1990 I, F, W, S, Arg 3, 1991 W, S, I, F, Fj, A, [NZ, It, US, F, S, A], 1992 S, I, F, W, SA, 1993 F, W, S, I, NZ, 1994 S, I, F, W, SA 1,2, R, C, 1995 I, F, W, S, [Arg, It, WS, A, NZ, F], SA, WS, 1996 F, W, S, I
Underwood, T (Leicester, Newcastle) 1992 C, SA, 1993 S, I, NZ, 1994 S, I, W, SA 1,2, R, C, 1995 I, F, W, S, [Arg, It, A, NZ], 1996 Arg, 1997 S, I, F, W, 1998 A 2, SA 2
Unwin, E J (Rosslyn Park, Army) 1937 S, 1938 W, I, S
Unwin, G T (Blackheath) 1898 S
Uren, R (Waterloo) 1948 I, S, F, 1950 I
Uttley, R M (Gosforth) 1973 I, F, S, NZ 2, A, 1974 I, F, W, 1975 F, W, S, A 1,2, 1977 S, I, F, W, 1978 NZ 1979 S, 1980 I, F, W, S
Vainikolo, L (Gloucester) 2008 W(R),It,F,S,I
Valentine J (Swinton) 1890 W, 1896 W, I, S
Vanderspar, C H R (Richmond) 1873 S
Van Gisbergen, M C (Wasps) 2005 A(t)
Van Ryneveld, C B (Oxford U) 1949 W, I, F, S
Varley, H (Liversedge) 1892 S
Varndell, T W (Leicester) 2005 Sm(R), 2006 A1,2, 2008 NZ2
Vassall, H (Blackheath) 1881 W, S, 1882 I, S, 1883 W
Vassall, H H (Blackheath) 1908 I
Vaughan, D B (Headingley) 1948 A, W, I, S, 1949 I, F, S, 1950 W
Vaughan-Jones, A (Army) 1932 I, S, 1933 W
Verelst, C L (Liverpool) 1876 I, 1878 I
Vernon, G F (Blackheath) 1878 S, I, 1880 I, S, 1881 I
Vickery, G (Aberavon) 1905 I
Vickery, P J (Gloucester, Wasps) 1998 W, A 1, NZ 1,2, SA 1, 1999 US, C, [It, NZ, Tg, SA], 2000 I, F, W, S, A, Arg (R), SA 3(R), 2001 W, It, S, A, SA, 2002 I, F, Arg, NZ, A, SA, 2003 NZ(R), A, [Gg, SA, Sm(R), U, W, F, A], 2004 It, S, I, W, F, 2005 W(R), F, A, NZ, 2006 SA1(R),2, 2007 S, It, I, W2, F2(R),3, [US, Tg(R), A, F, SA2], 2008 W,F,S,I
Vivyan, E J (Devonport A) 1901 W, 1904 W, I, S
Voyce, A T (Gloucester) 1920 I, S, 1921 W, I, S, F, 1922 W, I, F, S, 1923 W, I, S, F, 1924 W, I, F, S, 1925 NZ, W, I, S, F, 1926 W, I, F, S
Voyce, T M D (Bath, Wasps) 2001 US (R), 2004 NZ2, A1, 2005 Sm, 2006 W(R), It, F(R), I, A1
Vyvyan, H D (Saracens) 2004 C(R)

Wackett, J A S (Rosslyn Park) 1959 W, I
Wade, C G (Richmond) 1883 W, I, S, 1884 W, S, 1885 W, 1886 W, I
Wade, M R (Cambridge U) 1962 W, I, F
Wakefield, W W (Harlequins) 1920 W, F, I, S, 1921 W, I, S, F, 1922 W, I, F, S, 1923 W, I, S, F, 1924 W, I, F, S, 1925 NZ, W, I, S, F, 1926 W, I, F, S, 1927 S, F
Walder, D J H (Newcastle) 2001 C 1,2, US, 2003 W 2(R)
Walker, G A (Blackheath) 1939 W, I
Walker, H W (Coventry) 1947 W, I, S, F, 1948 A, W, I, S, F
Walker, R (Manchester) 1874 S, 1875 I, 1876 S, 1879 S, 1880 S
Wallens, J N S (Waterloo) 1927 F
Walshe, N P J (Bath) 2006 A1(R), 2(R)
Walton, E J (Castleford) 1901 W, I, 1902 I, S
Walton, W (Castleford) 1894 S
Ward, G (Leicester) 1913 W, F, S, 1914 W, I, S
Ward, H (Bradford) 1895 W
Ward, J I (Richmond) 1881 I, 1882 I
Ward, J W (Castleford) 1896 W, I, S
Wardlow, C S (Northampton) 1969 SA (R), 1971 W, I, F, S (2[1C])
Warfield, P J (Rosslyn Park, Durham U) 1973 NZ 1, W, I, 1975 I, F, S
Warr, A L (Oxford U) 1934 W, I
Waters, F H H (Wasps) 2001 US, 2004 NZ2(R), A1(R)
Watkins, J A (Gloucester) 1972 SA, 1973 NZ 1, W, NZ 2, A, 1975 F, W
Watkins, J K (United Services, RN) 1939 W, I, S
Watson, F B (United Services, RN) 1908 S, 1909 S
Watson, J H D (Blackheath) 1914 W, S, F
Watt, D E J (Bristol) 1967 I, F, S, W
Webb, C S H (Devonport Services, RN) 1932 SA, W, I, S, 1933 W, I, S, 1935 S, 1936 NZ, W, I, S
Webb, J M (Bristol, Bath) 1987 [A (R), J, US, W], 1988 F, W, S, I 1,2, A 1,2, A, 1989 S, I, F, W, 1991 Fj, A, [NZ, It, F, S, A], 1992 S, I, F, W, C, SA, 1993 F, W, S, I
Webb, J W G (Northampton) 1926 F, S, 1929 S
Webb, R E (Coventry) 1967 S, W, NZ, 1968 I, F, S, 1969 I, F, S, W, 1972 I, F
Webb, St L H (Bedford) 1959 W, I, F, S
Webster, J G (Moseley) 1972 W, I, SA, 1973 NZ 1, W, NZ 2, 1974 S, W, 1975 I, F, W
Wedge, T G (St Ives) 1907 F, 1909 W
Weighill, R H G (RAF, Harlequins) 1947 S, F, 1948 S, F
Wells, C M (Cambridge U, Harlequins) 1893 S, 1894 W, S, 1896 S, 1897 W, S
West, B R (Loughborough Colls, Northampton) 1968 W, I, F, S, 1969 SA, 1970 I, W, S

West, D E (Leicester) 1998 F (R), S (R), 2000 Arg (R), 2001 W, It, S, F (t), C 1,2, US, I (R), A, SA, 2002 F (R), W (R), It (R), 2003 W 2(R), F 2,3(t+R), [U, F(R)]
West, R (Gloucester) 1995 [WS]
Weston, H T F (Northampton) 1901 S
Weston, L E (W of Scotland) 1972 F, S
Weston, M P (Richmond, Durham City) 1960 W, I, F, S, 1961 SA, W, I, F, S, 1962 W, I, F, 1963 W, I, F, S, NZ 1,2, A, 1964 NZ, W, I, F, S, 1965 F, S, 1966 S, 1968 F, S
Weston, W H (Northampton) 1933 I, S, 1934 I, S, 1935 W, I, S, 1936 NZ, W, S, 1937 W, I, S, 1938 W, I, S
Wheatley, A A (Coventry) 1937 W, I, S, 1938 W, S
Wheatley, H F (Coventry) 1936 I, 1937 S, 1938 W, S, 1939 W, I, S
Wheeler, P J (Leicester) 1975 F, W, 1976 A, W, S, I, 1977 S, I, F, W, 1978 F, W, S, I, NZ, 1979 S, I, F, W, NZ, 1980 I, F, W, S, 1981 W, S, I, F, 1982 A, S, I, F, W, 1983 F, S, I, NZ, 1984 S, I, F, W
White, C (Gosforth) 1983 NZ, 1984 S, I, F
White, D F (Northampton) 1947 W, I, S, 1948 I, F, 1951 S, 1952 SA, W, S, I, F, 1953 W, I, S
White, J M (Saracens, Bristol, Leicester) 2000 SA 1,2, Arg, SA 3, 2001 F, C 1,2, US, I, R (R), 2002 S, W, It, 2003 F 1(R), W 2, F 2,3, [Sm, U(R)], 2004 W(R), F(R), NZ1,2, A1,C, SA, A2, 2005 W, 2006 W(R), It(R), S, F, I, A1,2, NZ, Arg, SA1,2, 2007 S(R), It(R), I(R),F1, W1
White-Cooper, S (Harlequins) 2001 C 2, US
Whiteley, E C P (O Alleynians) 1931 S, F
Whiteley, W (Bramley) 1896 W
Whitely, H (Northern) 1929 W
Wightman, B J (Moseley, Coventry) 1959 W, 1963 W, I, NZ 2, A
Wigglesworth, H J (Thornes) 1884 I
Wigglesworth, R E P (Sale) 2008 It(R),F,S,I,NZ1
Wilkins, D T (United Services, RN, Roundhay) 1951 W, I, F, S, 1952 SA, W, S, I, F, 1953 W, I, F, S
Wilkinson, E (Bradford) 1886 W, I, S, 1887 W, S
Wilkinson, H (Halifax) 1929 W, I, S, 1930 F
Wilkinson, H J (Halifax) 1889 M
Wilkinson, J P (Newcastle) 1998 I (R), A 1, NZ 1, 1999 S, I, F, W, A, US, C, [It, NZ, Fj, SA (R)], 2000 I, F, W, It, S, SA 2, A, Arg, SA 3, 2001 W, It, S, F, I, A, SA, 2002 S, I, F, W, It, NZ, A, SA, 2003 F 1, W 1, It, S, I, NZ, A, F 3, [Gg, SA, Sm, W, F, A], 2007 S,It,I,SA1,2,W2,F2(R),F3, [Sm,Tg,A,F, SA2], 2008 W,It,F,S,I(R)
Wilkinson, P (Law Club) 1872 S
Wilkinson, R M (Bedford) 1975 A 2, 1976 A, W, S, I, F
Willcocks, T J (Plymouth) 1902 W
Willcox, J G (Oxford U, Harlequins) 1961 I, F, S, 1962 W, I, F, S, 1963 W, I, F, S, 1964 NZ, W, I, F, S
William-Powlett, P B R W (United Services, RN) 1922 S
Williams, C G (Gloucester, RAF) 1976 F
Williams, C S (Manchester) 1910 F
Williams, J E (O Millhillians, Sale) 1954 F, 1955 W, I, F, S, 1956 I, S, F, 1965 W
Williams, J M (Penzance-Newlyn) 1951 I, S
Williams, P N (Orrell) 1987 S, [A, J, W]
Williams, S G (Devonport A) 1902 W, I, S, 1903 I, S, 1907 I, S
Williams, S H (Newport) 1911 W, F, I, S
Williamson, R H (Oxford U) 1908 W, I, S, 1909 A, F
Wilson, A J (Camborne S of M) 1909 I
Wilson, C E (Blackheath) 1898 I
Wilson, C P (Cambridge U, Marlborough N) 1881 W
Wilson, D S (Met Police, Harlequins) 1953 F, 1954 W, NZ, I, S, F, 1955 F, S
Wilson, G S (Tyldesley) 1929 W, I
Wilson, K J (Gloucester) 1963 F
Wilson, R P (Liverpool OB) 1891 W, I, S
Wilson, W C (Richmond) 1907 I, S
Winn, C E (Rosslyn Park) 1952 SA, W, S, I, F, 1954 W, S, F
Winterbottom, P J (Headingley, Harlequins) 1982 A, S, I, F, W, 1983 F, W, S, I, NZ, 1984 S, F, W, SA 1,2, 1986 W, S, I, F, 1987 I, F, W, [A, J, US, W], 1988 F, W, S, 1989 R, Fj, 1990 I, F, W, S, Arg 1,2,3, 1991 W, S, I, F, A, [NZ, It, F, S, A], 1992 S, I, F, W, C, SA, 1993 F, W, S, I
Winters, R A (Bristol) 2007 SA1(R),2
Wintle, T C (Northampton) 1966 S, 1969 I, F, S, W
Wodehouse, N A (United Services, RN) 1910 F, 1911 W, F, I, S, 1912 W, I, S, F, 1913 SA, W, F, I, S
Wood, A (Halifax) 1884 I
Wood, A E (Gloucester, Cheltenham) 1908 F, W, I
Wood, G W (Leicester) 1914 W
Wood, M B (Wasps) 2001 C 2(R), US (R)
Wood, R (Liversedge) 1894 I
Wood, R D (Liverpool OB) 1901 I, 1903 W, I
Woodgate, E E (Paignton) 1952 W
Woodhead, E (Huddersfield) 1880 I
Woodman, T J (Gloucester) 1999 US (R), 2000 I (R), It (R), 2001 W (R), It (R), 2002 NZ, 2003 S (R), I(t + R), A, F 3, [Gg, SA, W(R), F, A], 2004 It, S, I, W, F, NZ1, 2
Woodruff, C G (Harlequins) 1951 W, I, F, S
Woods, S M J (Cambridge U, Wellington) 1890 W, S, I, 1891 W, I, S, 1892 I, S, 1893 W, I, 1895 W, I, S
Woods, T (Bridgwater) 1908 S
Woods, T (United Services, RN) 1920 S, 1921 W, I, S, F
Woodward, C R (Leicester) 1980 I (R), F, W, S, 1981 W, S, I, F, Arg 1,2, 1982 A, S, I, F, W, 1983 I, NZ, 1984 S, I, F, W
Woodward, J E (Wasps) 1952 SA, W, S, 1953 W, I, F, S, 1954 W, NZ, I, S, F, 1955 W, I, 1956 S
Wooldridge, C S (Oxford U, Blackheath) 1883 W, I, S, 1884 W, I, S, 1885 I
Wordsworth, A J (Cambridge U) 1975 A 1(R)
Worsley, J P R (Wasps) 1999 [Tg, Fj], 2000 It (R), S (R), SA 1(R),2(R), 2001 It (R), S (R), F (R), C 1,2, US, A, R, SA, 2002 S, I, F, W (t+R), Arg, 2003 W 1(R), It, S(R), I(t), NZ(R), A(R), W 2, [SA(t), Sm, U], 2004 It, I, W(R), F, NZ1(R), 2, A1, SA, A2, 2005 W, F, I, It, S, 2006 W, It, S, F, I, A1(R), 2, SA1,2, 2007 S, I, F1,W1,2, F2,3(R), [US, Sm,A(R), F(R), SA2(R)], 2008 NZ1(R),2(R)
Worsley, M A (London Irish, Harlequins) 2003 It(R), 2004 A1(R), 2005 S(R)
Worton, J R B (Harlequins, Army) 1926 W, 1927 W
Wrench, D F B (Harlequins) 1964 F, S
Wright, C C G (Cambridge U, Blackheath) 1909 I, S
Wright, F T (Edinburgh Acady, Manchester) 1881 S
Wright, I D (Northampton) 1971 W, I, F, S (R)
Wright. J C (Met Police) 1934 W
Wright, J F (Bradford) 1890 W
Wright, T P (Blackheath) 1960 W, I, F, S, 1961 SA, W, I, F, S, 1962 W, I, F, S
Wright, W H G (Plymouth) 1920 W, F
Wyatt, D M (Bedford) 1976 S (R)

Yarranton, P G (RAF, Wasps) 1954 W, NZ, I, 1955 F, S
Yates, K P (Bath, Saracens) 1997 Arg 1,2, 2007 SA1,2
Yiend, W (Hartlepool R, Gloucester) 1889 M, 1892 W, I, S, 1893 I, S
Young, A T (Cambridge U, Blackheath, Army) 1924 W, I, F, S, 1925 NZ, F, 1926 I, F, S, 1927 I, S, F, 1928 A, W, I, F, S, 1929 I
Young, J R C (Oxford U, Harlequins) 1958 I, 1960 W, I, F, S, 1961 SA, W, I, F
Young, M (Gosforth) 1977 S, I, F, W, 1978 F, W, S, I, NZ, 1979 S
Young, P D (Dublin Wands) 1954 W, NZ, I, S, F, 1955 W, I, F, S
Youngs, N G (Leicester) 1983 I, NZ, 1984 S, I, F, W

DALLAGLIO MEETS HIS DESTINY

Dave Rogers/ Getty Images

Ian McGeechan, Lawrence Dallaglio and Shaun Edwards celebrate the crowning of London Wasps as English champions

Wasps displayed their miraculous powers of recovery once again to claim the Guinness Premiership title for a fourth time in six seasons with victory over arch rivals Leicester in the Play-Off final and in the process ensured Lawrence Dallaglio's last game for the club fittingly ended in triumph.

The former England captain was making his 339th and final appearance for the Londoners and his illustrious 15-year career ended on high as Wasps beat the Tigers 26–16 at Twickenham in front of a world record crowd of 81,600 supporters for a club game.

Victory represented a remarkable achievement for Ian McGeechan's side, who were crippled at the start of their campaign by the number of their players on World Cup duty and won just two of their opening eight Premiership fixtures to leave the side in 10th place in the table in December.

An unseemly relegation battle had suddenly become a real possibility but Wasps' famed ability to find their form at the business end of the season did not desert them and 10 victories in their final 11 league games lifted them into second in the table behind Gloucester and into the play-offs.

Defeat for Leicester in the final however was a depressingly familiar experience and completed a hat-trick of recent losses to Wasps on the big stage after falling to the Londoners in the 2007 Heineken Cup final and the Premiership final of 2005.

"This was not about me, it was a wonderful squad effort," Dallaglio said after lifting the trophy at Twickenham. "We were 10th in the table around Christmas time, so this is probably our greatest achievement.

"This win is testament to all the staff, players, coaches and fans of this great club. We're not blessed with the greatest of resources but we have heart and soul. We played a mighty opponent today in Leicester and we always knew it was going to be tough. They came back at us but we held on and performed heroically."

Wasps head coach Shaun Edwards was quick to pay tribute to Dallaglio after leading the side to victory and completing the club's improbable reversal of fortune.

"It's a fitting way for him to go out," he said. "The reception from the crowd shows how much respect he has in the game, even among away fans.

"We've basically been playing play-off rugby since November. It was just a matter of trying to win the next game. I think we really started to believe during the Six Nations when we got into a run of winning games without the internationals. That's something we haven't done in the last two or three years."

The Premiership season kicked off in September and while Wasps struggled it was Dean Ryan's Gloucester and Steve Meehan's Bath who made the early running.

The Cherry and Whites had suffered the bitter disappointment of topping the table the previous season only to be blown away by the Tigers in the final but emerged for the new campaign invigorated and eight wins in their opening nine games sent out a clear message of intent.

Bath were equally impressive in the early phase of the campaign, winning seven of their first nine fixtures and by Christmas the two West Country sides were firmly in the driving seat.

The New Year however was to see a seismic shift in the balance of power. Wasps' 42–34 victory over Bath at the Rec in February was the catalyst for an eight-match winning streak and while McGeechan's side blossomed, the others began to stumble.

The final round of league games in May saw Bath and Gloucester already assured of a play-off place but Wasps were now in third and vying

Dave Rogers / Getty Images

Gloucester finished top of the table in the regular season but lost out in the play-offs, again!

with Sale, Harlequins and Leicester for the other two semi-final spots.

The Sharks had their destiny in their own hands but were beaten 17–7 by London Irish at Edgeley Park. Wasps' 45–28 victory at Leeds Carnegie saw them safely through and it was left to the Tigers and Quins to battle it out for the final place and in the end it was Leicester who prevailed with a dramatic 31–28 win courtesy of Tom Varndell's late try and Andy Goode's conversion.

The first semi-final saw Wasps entertain Bath at Adams Park and although it was Meehan's side who enjoyed the lions' share of territory and possession, the home side proved the more clinical when their chances came and tries from Fraser Waters, Riki Flutey and Tom Palmer set up a hard-fought 21–10 victory.

The win was marred by a serious ankle injury to their young England fly-half Danny Cipriani but Wasps were a least through to the final.

"To win a game in which we had so little possession showed that the defensive performance was quite remarkable," McGeechan said after the game. "We have played without a lot of our frontline players at various times in the season so to get to another Premiership final is very satisfying."

The second semi-final between Gloucester and Leicester was to provide much more drama as the two sides slugged it out at Kingsholm and with 70 minutes on the clock, the Tigers held a precarious 23–22 advantage.

Full-back Willie Walker appeared to have stolen it for the Cherry and

Whites with a drop goal with just five minutes to play but Gloucester's ecstasy turned to despair three minutes later when Goode landed a drop of his own and Leicester were 26–25 winners.

"I don't think it was about temperament," said Ryan after his side's defeat. "I think we made stupid choices. For the last few weeks we have been very smart and the best side around. We have taken Wasps away and beaten Bath at home, and we could and should have beaten Leicester today."

The build-up to the eagerly-anticipated Premiership final was dominated by talk of Dallaglio's emotional swansong and the early exchanges at Twickenham strongly suggested the gnarled No 8 would indeed sign off with another winner's medal.

Mark van Gisbergen and Goode traded penalties inside the first 10 minutes but when flanker Tom Rees drove over the line on 11 minutes, Wasps found themselves firmly in the ascendancy while the Tigers looked uncharacteristically toothless.

An incisive break from Josh Lewsey saw Wasps cross for a second time four minutes before the break and as the two sides disappeared into the changing rooms, the Londoners had already established an imposing 23–6 lead.

Leicester rallied in the second-half and tries from Varndell and Harry Ellis gave them brief hope but Wasps were in no mood to surrender their advantage. Dallaglio left the field after 67 minutes to huge cheers from the record Twickenham crowd and watched from the bench as his team-mates closed out the game.

Defeat was a body blow for Leicester after the heartbreak of losing the Heineken Cup final 12 months earlier but Tigers skipper Martin Corry was still magnanimous in defeat.

"You can just see by all the column inches he has had leading up to this game how highly Lawrence is regarded," he said. "All the plaudits he has had this week have been richly deserved. He has been magnificent for Wasps and England. As a competitor he has been a great man to play against and we have always had some great battles."

Elsewhere in England, Northampton made quick amends for their relegation from the Premiership the previous season by clinching the National League One title and earning themselves an immediate return to the top-flight.

The Saints were simply irresistible throughout their campaign, winning all 30 of their league outings, averaging 44 points per game and confirmed their promotion in March with an 18–8 victory over Exeter at Franklin's Gardens.

"We are glad to be back in the Premiership and of course we will have to raise our game again, but it's been an enjoyable season," said former All Black Carlos Spencer. "The six-hour coach journeys back home from wherever and a few quiet beers in the coach have been a great bonding experience. The season has been good for us as a group of players."

In National League Two, Otley held their nerve in a dramatic cross Pennine battle with Manchester to claim the title by a single point. The Yorkshire side beat Waterloo 37–15 in their final game of the season and although Manchester also won, beating Blackheath 29–3, Otley's bonus point victory was enough to ensure they were crowned champions.

Tynedale were the dominant force in National League Three North, suffering just one defeat in their 26 outings to land the title by an imposing 29 points while Mounts Bay were similarly untroubled as they walked away with the National League Three South honours.

In the Bill Beaumont Cup final (County Championship) at Twickenham, Yorkshire ended Devon's recent dominance of the competition with a 33–13 victory. The defending champions, Devon were appearing in their fifth successive final and looking for a fourth triumph but were blown away by the men from Yorkshire in a repeat of the final in 2000. Otley wing Robin Kitching was the star turn for the new champions, scoring a try, two conversions and three penalties for a match-winning haul of 18 points.

Laurence Griffiths / Getty Images

Northampton roared back into the Guinness Premiership by dominating National One

GUINNESS PREMIERSHIP 2007–08 RESULTS

September 15: **Bath** 29 **Worcester** 15, **Harlequins** 35 **London Irish** 27, **Wasps** 19 **Saracens** 29. September 16: **Bristol** 13 **Leicester** 26, **Leeds** 24 **Gloucester** 49, **Newcastle** 33 **Sale** 12. September 22: **Leicester** 26 **Bath** 16, **Harlequins** 39 **Leeds** 15, **Worcester** 24 **Wasps** 24. September 23: **London Irish** 19 **Newcastle** 0, **Sale** 20 **Bristol** 6, **Saracens** 31 **Gloucester** 38. September 29: **Bath** 21 **Sale** 19, **Gloucester** 29 **Worcester** 7, **Newcastle** 19 **Harlequins** 12. September 30: **Bristol** 14 **London Irish** 11, **Leeds** 7 **Saracens** 31, **Wasps** 17 **Leicester** 20. **October** 5: **Sale** 16 **Wasps** 0, **London Irish** 20 **Bath** 22, **Newcastle** 21 **Leeds** 19. October 6: **Harlequins** 24 **Bristol** 18, **Worcester** 16 **Saracens** 21, **Leicester** 17 **Gloucester** 30, October 12: **Leeds** 26 **Worcester** 21. October 13: **Bath** 25 **Harlequins** 10, **Gloucester** 21 **Sale** 12. October 14: **Bristol** 23 **Newcastle** 16, **Wasps** 28 **London Irish** 14, **Saracens** 26 **Leicester** 19. October 19: **Sale** 34 **Saracens** 30. October 20: **Harlequins** 26 **Wasps** 25, **Leicester** 28 **Worcester** 20. October 21: **Newcastle** 20 **Bath** 33, **Bristol** 39 **Leeds** 13, **London Irish** 15 **Gloucester** 10. November 23: **Worcester** 15 **Sale** 34. November 24: **Bath** 28 **Bristol** 13, **Leeds** 6 **Leicester** 29, **Gloucester** 27 **Harlequins** 25. November 25: **Wasps** 35 **Newcastle** 12, **Saracens** 24 **London Irish** 20. December 22: **Bath** 41 **Leeds** 10, **Bristol** 23 **Wasps** 23, **Harlequins** 20 **Saracens** 27. December 23: **Sale** 20 **Leicester** 14, **London Irish** 23 **Worcester** 16, **Newcastle** 13 **Gloucester** 20. December 29: **Leicester** 25 **London Irish** 17, **Wasps** 25 **Bath** 10, **Gloucester** 27 **Bristol** 0, **Worcester** 7 **Harlequins** 10. December 30: **Leeds** 20 **Sale** 34, **Saracens** 19 **Newcastle** 22. January 4: **Bath** 10 **Gloucester** 5. January 5: **Wasps** 25 **Leeds** 17. January 6: **Harlequins** 13 **Leicester** 42, **Bristol** 18 **Saracens** 3, **London Irish** 20 **Sale** 12, **Newcastle** 15 **Worcester** 12. January 25: **Sale** 20 **Harlequins** 13. January 26: **Gloucester** 18 **Wasps** 17, **Leicester** 41 **Newcastle** 14, **Worcester** 25 **Bristol** 5. January 27: **Saracens** 26 **Bath** 20, **Leeds** 24 **London Irish** 36. February 9: **Gloucester** 13 **Leicester** 20. February 10: **Saracens** 19 **Worcester** 6. February 15: **Sale** 29 **Leeds** 3. February 16: **Bath** 34 **Wasps** 42, **Harlequins** 36 **Worcester** 15. February 17: **London Irish** 22 **Leicester** 13, **Bristol** 29 **Gloucester** 26, **Newcastle** 16 **Saracens** 14, February 22: **Worcester** 11 **London Irish** 12. February 23: **Gloucester** 28 **Newcastle** 20, **Leicester** 11 **Sale** 14, **Wasps** 32 **Bristol** 30 February 24: **Leeds** 15 **Bath** 34, **Saracens** 6 **Harlequins** 15. February 29: **Sale** 15 **Worcester** 22. March 1: **London Irish** 27 **Saracens** 24, **Harlequins** 30 **Gloucester** 25, **Leicester** 34 **Leeds** 21. March 2: **Bristol** 9 **Bath** 19. March 8: **Bath** 22 **Newcastle** 11, **Worcester** 23 **Leicester** 19, **Gloucester** 34 **London Irish** 14. March 9: **Leeds** 13 **Bristol** 30, **Wasps** 29 **Harlequins** 25, **Saracens** 24 **Sale** 20. March 14: **Sale** 22 **Gloucester** 16. March 15: **Leicester** 36 **Saracens** 23. March 16: **Worcester** 10 **Leeds** 10, **Harlequins** 22 **Bath** 16, **London Irish** 16 **Wasps** 22, **Newcastle** 8 **Bristol** 28. March 21: **Leeds** 16 **Newcastle** 15. March 22: **Bath** 19 **London Irish** 16. March 23: **Bristol** 15 **Harlequins** 28. March 28: **Sale** 22 **Bath** 6. March 29: **Leicester** 19 **Wasps** 24, **Harlequins** 15 **Newcastle** 9, **Worcester** 17 **Gloucester** 14. March 30: **London Irish** 28 **Bristol** 8, **Saracens** 66 **Leeds** 7. April 11: **Bristol** 17 **Sale** 24. April 12: **Gloucester** 39 **Saracens** 15, **Wasps** 49 **Worcester** 12. April 13: **Leeds** 6 **Harlequins** 32, **Newcastle** 8 **London Irish** 13. April 15: **Wasps** 29 **Sale** 19, **Bath** 26 **Leicester** 12. April 19: **London Irish** 13 **Harlequins** 6, **Gloucester** 39 **Leeds** 16, **Leicester** 32 **Bristol** 14, **Worcester** 20 **Bath** 23. April 20: **Saracens** 29 **Wasps** 40, **Sale** 53 **Newcastle** 10. May 3: **Bristol** 21 **Worcester** 22, **Bath** 66 **Saracens** 21. May 4: **Harlequins** 16 **Sale** 23, **London Irish** 43 **Leeds** 20, **Wasps** 17 **Gloucester** 25, **Newcastle** 28 **Leicester** 25. May 7: **Newcastle** 13 **Wasps** 32. May 10: **Gloucester** 8 **Bath** 6, **Leeds** 28 **Wasps** 45, **Leicester** 31 **Harlequins** 28, **Sale** 7 **London Irish** 17, **Saracens** 25 **Bristol** 20, **Worcester** 51 **Newcastle** 10

THE 2007–08 FINAL TABLE

	P	W	D	L	For	A	Pts
Gloucester	22	15	0	7	551	377	74
Wasps	22	14	2	6	599	459	70
Bath	22	15	0	7	526	387	69
Leicester	22	13	0	9	539	428	64
Sale	22	14	0	8	481	374	63
Harlequins	22	12	0	10	480	440	63
London Irish	22	13	0	9	433	382	59
Saracens	22	11	0	11	533	525	52
Bristol	22	7	1	14	393	473	37
Worcester	22	6	2	14	387	472	36
Newcastle	22	7	0	15	333	542	34
Leeds	22	2	1	19	336	732	12

PREVIOUS ENGLISH CHAMPIONS

1987/1988: Leicester
1988/1989: Bath
1989/1990: Wasps
1990/1991: Bath
1991/1992: Bath
1992/1993: Bath
1993/1994: Bath
1994/1995: Leicester
1995/1996: Bath
1996/1997: Wasps
1997/1998: Newcastle
1998/1999: Leicester
1999/2000: Leicester
2000/2001: Leicester
2001/2002: Leicester
2002/2003: Wasps
2003/2004: Wasps
2004/2005: Wasps
2005/2006: Sale
2006/2007: Leicester
2007/2008: London Wasps

2007–08 PLAY-OFFS SEMI-FINALS

18 May, Adams Park, High Wycombe

WASPS 21 (3G) BATH 10 (1G, 1PG)

WASPS: J Leswey; P Sackey, F Waters, R Flutey, T Voyce; D Cipriani, E Reddan; T Payne, J Ward, P Barnard, S Shaw, T Palmer, J Haskell, T Rees, L Dallaglio (*captain*) *Substitutions:* J Buckland for Ward (28 mins); M van Gisbergen for Cipriani (55 mins); M McMillan for Voyce (62 mins);T French for Barnard (63 mins); R Birkett for Rees (temp 65 to 71 mins); J Worsley for Payne (66 mins); J Hart for Dallaglio (66 mins); Birkett for Haskell (76 mins)

SCORERS Tries: Waters, Flutey, Palmer *Conversions:* Cipriani (2), van Gisbergen

BATH: J Maddock; A Higgins, A Crockett, O Barkley, M Banahan; B James, M Claassens; D Barnes, P Dixon, M Stevens, S Borthwick (*captain*), D Grewcock, J Faamatuainu, M Lipman, D Browne

SUBSTITUTIONS: P Short for Lipman (30 mins); N Abendanon for Maddock (65 mins); S Berne for Crockett (65 mins); D Flatman for Barnes (65 mins); D Bell for Stevens (73 mins); R Hawkins for Dixon (78 mins)

SCORERS *Try:* Crockett Conversion: Barkley Penalty Goal: Barkley

YELLOW CARD Waters (80 mins)

REFEREE C White (Gloucestershire)

18 May, Kingsholm, Gloucester

GLOUCESTER 25 (1G, 5PG, 1DG) LEICESTER 26(2G, 3PG, 1DG)

GLOUCESTER: W Walker; I Balshaw, J Simpson-Daniel, A Allen, L Vainikolo; R Lamb, R Lawson; N Wood, A Titterrell, C Nieto, M Bortolami (captain), A Brown, A Strokosch, A Qera, G Delve *Substitutions:* O Azam for Titterrell (55 mins); W James for Bortolami (66 mins)

SCORERS *Try:* Simpson-Daniel Conversion: Lamb *Penalty Goals:* Lamb (5) *Drop Goal:* Walker

LEICESTER: G Murphy; A Tuilagi, D Hipkiss, A Mauger, T Varndell; A Goode, H Ellis; B Stankovich, M Davies, J White, M Wentzel, B Kay, M Corry (*captain*), B Herring, J Crane *Substitutions:* S Vesty for Murphy (temp 29 to 36 mins); M Ayerza for Stankovich (55 mins); T Croft for Herring (55 mins); G Chuter for Davies (60 mins); R Blaze for Wentzel (80 mins)

SCORERS *Tries:* Tuilagi, Mauger *Conversions:* Goode (2) *Penalty Goals:* Goode (3) *Drop Goal:* Goode

YELLOW CARD Crane (28 mins) Ellis (39 mins)

REFEREE D Pearson (Northumberland)

FINAL

31 May, Twickenham, London

WASPS 26 (2G, 4PG) LEICESTER 16 (2PG, 2T)

WASPS: M van Gisbergen; P Sackey, F Waters, D Waldouck , J Lewsey; R Flutey, E Reddan; T Payne, R Ibanez, P Vickery, S Shaw, T Palmer, J Haskell, T Rees, L Dallaglio (*captain*) *Substitutions:* P Barnard for Vickery (40 mins); J Worsley for Payne (61 mins); J Ward for Ibanez (61 mins); J Hart for Dallaglio (67 mins); J Staunton for Waldouck (79 mins); R Birkett for Reddan (79 mins)

SCORERS *Tries:* Rees, Lewsey *Conversions:* van Gisbergen (2) *Penalty Goals:* van Gisbergen (4)

Leicester: G Murphy; T Varndell, D Hipkiss, A Mauger, A Tuilagi; A Goode, H Ellis; B Stankovich, M Davies, J White, M Wentzel, B Kay, M Corry (*captain*), B Herring, J Crane *Substitutions:* A Erinle for Hipkiss (41 mins); B Kayser for Davies (46 mins); R Blaze for Wentzel (54 mins); C Laussucq for Ellis (79 mins)

SCORERS *Tries:* Varndell, Ellis *Penalty Goals:* Goode (2)

REFEREE W Barnes (England)

OTHER MAJOR DOMESTIC WINNERS

NATIONAL ONE

Northampton Saints

NATIONAL TWO

Otley

NATIONAL THREE NORTH

Tynedale

NATIONAL THREE SOUTH

Mounts Bay

NORTH ONE

Kendal

SOUTH WEST ONE

Chinnor

MIDLANDS ONE

Loughborough Students

LONDON ONE

Richmond

FIJI

FIJI'S 2008 RECORD

OPPONENTS	DATE	VENUE	RESULT
Samoa	7 June	H	**Won** 34–17
NZ Maori	14 June	H	**Lost** 7–11
Japan	22 June	A	**Won** 24–12
Australia A	29 June	A	**Lost** 13–50
Tonga	5 July	A	**Lost** 16–27

TOUGH ACT TO FOLLOW

By Jeremy Duxbury

The glorious feats achieved by the Flying Fijians at the 2007 Rugby World Cup in Nantes and Marseille were always going to be hard to follow. Suddenly, the world would expect coach Ilivasi Tabua and his men to do the business over other teams in the Pacific region with ease. But when Fiji humbled Wales and brought eventual world champions South Africa to their knees, Tabua was able to field his best, best line-up. Fiji's sub-par finish in the 2008 IRB Pacific Nations Cup, therefore, highlighted the chronic lack of local player depth in the islands.

At the 2007 Rugby World Cup, Leicester centre Seru Rabeni had caused havoc all over the field; Clermont's Vilimoni Delasau scored two amazing tries; and Nicky Little and Seremaia Bai kicked every penalty goal and conversion that came their way. And in reserve for the quarter-finals came Sireli Bobo, one of the best finishers you could find.

In the forwards, Padova's big No.8 Sisa Koyamaibole had shown how wrong former coach Wayne Pivac had been to leave him out of even the 2006 back-up squad; and the form of rampant Gloucester flanker Akapusi Qera was simply scintillating.

Qera went from the World Cup to becoming one of the best players in the Guinness Premiership and due to his knee injury Gloucester missed his influence at the start of the 2008-09 season.

Yet come the latter stages of the Pacific Nations Cup this year, none of the above-mentioned stars was available for Fiji. Club commitment, suspension or injury had taken them out of the picture. For the crucial clash with Tonga in Nuku'alofa – where victory would have seen Fiji climb up the IRB rankings – even skipper Moses Rauluni (unavailable) and Semisi Naevo (injured) were missing.

All told, only three of the starting players against Tonga had been regular starters during the World Cup – lock Kele Leawere and front-rowers Graham Dewes and Sunia Koto. And clearly, Fiji just does not at present have the strength in depth to be able to field a second-string team and expect the same results.

Injury had kept out Koyamaibole, whilst Rabeni was still under suspension for gouging at club level in England. But other than that, the Union could rightly be disappointed. Some professional players didn't make the trip at all, others were allowed to be selective with the matches they played.

The annihilation of Samoa in Lautoka had been a long time coming. At 31–0 after an hour's play, Fiji should really have kept piling up the points and tried to emulate the 1996 feat by Brad Johnstone's team when Fiji defeated the Samoans 60–0 in Suva.

But, as is Fiji's want, they took their foot off the gas, sat back and conceded three late tries to make it appear that Samoa had been in the game with a final score of 34–17.

Fiji had done a similar thing at the World Cup against Japan and Canada, letting them back into the game after early domination – and against Wales too when Fiji led 25–3 after half an hour. It seems the friendly Fijians are far too nice at times for their own good. When opponents are on their knees, professional teams have no hesitation in putting the boot in. But in Fiji, it's like the boys want to help them get back up and make a game of it.

And in this opening Pacific Nations Cup match at Churchill Park, Fiji found yet another wing for the future – young Timoci Nagusa, who scored two good tries on his Test debut at age 20.

Also enjoying an impressive, and long-awaited, Test debut was former Sevens star Sireli Naqelevuki. At 1m 89 (6'3") and 105kg, the South Africa based centre punched holes in Samoa's defence at will.

The down point in the match was the knee injury to Qera that ruled him out of action for six months – and he only came on as sub with half an hour to go.

The amazing battle against the New Zealand Maoris at the same venue will be remembered by everyone present long into their pensioner years.

It wasn't just the 80 minutes of spellbinding rugby that made it so memorable, it was the thunder storm, torrential flood, the roof flying off the temporary stand, and the unbelievable atmosphere created by the 12,500 spectators hungry for a first win over the Maori in 50 years.

Alas, it was not to be. Despite Fiji's domination of territory, possession and scoring opportunities, somehow the Kiwis still sneaked a narrow 11–7 win.

Rauluni's men looked shattered at the final whistle. They knew they could and should have won against a team laden with All Blacks. They had out-played their opponents right across the park, except in lineouts and crucially, goal-kicking.

Even the Maori try came from a slip from a Fijian lineout that wrong-footed Aussie ref Matt Goddard, who was thus too late to see that lanky lock Jason Eaton had been held up and never actually grounded the ball (no TV Match Officials in the islands).

And poor Rauluni, who had begun the month wonderfully with a try against Samoa (his first for Fiji in eight years), was kicking himself for giving away a needless penalty towards the end that put Fiji four points behind and thus prevented his team from taking the winning kick when given the chance in front of the sticks in stoppage time.

One wonders how long Fiji will have to wait to get another chance like that to beat the Maori?

Fiji travelled to Tokyo without Rauluni or Delasau and made hard work of Japan, though that has become a bit of a habit lately. Japan led 9–3 at the break and were still in with a shout at 12–17 with a minute to play before replacement wing Vereniki Goneva dotted down a try to seal the match 24–12.

Fiji had enough golden chances to get a bonus point but again lacked that killer instinct.

By the time the team had reached Brisbane, they were looking a little stretched. Qera was out, Delasau gone, flanker Aca Ratuva was also out with injury, and there were doubts over top players Naqelevuki and Kameli Ratuvou.

The fine performances in Lautoka seemed an age ago as the Fijians struggled to keep shape on the field against another experienced Australian XV with a dozen Wallabies in their ranks. Perhaps tiredness was taking its toll?

Bar two beautiful tries to Dewes and Ratuvou, Fiji looked sore and never truly managed to compete against the team they had shared a 14–14 draw with in Suva 12 months earlier. This time, Australia A coasted to a 50–13 victory.

And so to Nuku'alofa to face a Tongan side that had lost all their previous PNC games, including a 35–13 thrashing at the hands of Japan and a horrific 90–6 demolition by the Aussies.

Were Fiji complacent, over-confident or under-prepared? Probably all three. Instead of putting the match beyond reach in the first half, the Fijians allowed Tonga to stay in touch then gifted them three tries in the closing quarter, just like they had done against Samoa.

Even with two minutes left on the clock, Fiji led 16–15. But late tries to Nili Latu and Epi Taione saw Tonga home 27–16.

So, it was a tough time for coach Tabua, who must find a way to field his best Test side on every occasion. It is tough to see Fiji performing miracles at the World Cup and then a few months later struggling to win a Test match.

This year's PNC tournament highlighted the urgent need for Fiji to grow more depth and not be so reliant on the overseas-based players.

The IRB-supported High Performance Unit has been around for near-on three years, but Fiji's HPU teams in general fared very poorly in 2008. The Fiji Warriors and Fiji Barbarians finished last and second-last, respectively, in the IRB Pacific Rugby Cup. The most needs to be made of such a facility.

The Fiji sevens team came under the control of HPU manager Peter Murphy in November 2007 but failed to win a single tournament; and the Fiji U20s finished a disappointing 14th out of 16 at the Junior World Championship in Wales.

On the domestic front, the Crusaders won their first Colonial Cup with a cracking 16–15 victory in April over surprise finalists, the Knights, at Ratu Cakobau Park in Nausori. Defending champions Stallions bombed out before the semi-finals for the first time, whilst the Sharks from the North turned Fiji rugby upside down by finishing top after the round-robin.

On the provincial scene, powerhouses Nadi and Nadroga contested the Digicel Cup Final after brushing aside the challenges of Suva and Tailevu, whilst the two provinces' junior sides were also going head-to head in the U19 final.

With some help from a rotund winger by the name of Rupeni Caucau, Tailevu clung onto the Sullivan-Farebrother Trophy through three tough challenges, including a 16–16 draw with Lautoka, and a 17–14 victory over Nadroga. Caucau scored five tries in his four appearances.

FIJI INTERNATIONAL STATISTICS

MATCH RECORDS UP TO 30TH SEPTEMBER 2008

WINNING MARGIN

Date	Opponent	Result	Winning Margin
10/09/1983	Niue Island	120–4	**116**
21/08/1969	Solomon Islands	113–13	**100**
08/09/1983	Solomon Islands	86–0	**86**
30/08/1979	Papua New Guinea	86–0	**86**
23/08/1969	Papua New Guinea	88–3	**85**

MOST TRIES IN A MATCH BY THE TEAM

Date	Opponent	Result	Tries
21/08/1969	Solomon Islands	113–13	**25**
10/09/1983	Niue Island	120–4	**21**
18/08/1969	Papua New Guinea	79–0	**19**
30/08/1979	Papua New Guinea	86–0	**18**
08/09/1983	Solomon Islands	86–0	**16**

MOST POINTS IN A MATCH BY THE TEAM

Date	Opponent	Result	Pts.
10/09/1983	Niue Island	120–4	**120**
21/08/1969	Solomon Islands	113–13	**113**
23/08/1969	Papua New Guinea	88–3	**88**
08/09/1983	Solomon Islands	86–0	**86**
30/08/1979	Papua New Guinea	86–0	**86**

MOST CONVERSIONS IN A MATCH BY THE TEAM

Date	Opponent	Result	Cons
21/08/1969	Solomon Islands	113–13	**19**
10/09/1983	Niue Island	120–4	**18**
18/08/1969	Papua New Guinea	79–0	**11**
07/10/1989	Belgium	74–0	**11**
01/10/1999	Namibia	67–18	**8**

MOST PENALTIES IN A MATCH BY THE TEAM

Date	Opponent	Result	Pens
08/07/2001	Samoa	28–17	7
26/05/2000	Tonga	25–22	6
05/10/1996	Hong Kong	37–16	6
25/05/2001	Tonga	26–31	6
08/07/1967	Tonga	18–6	6

MOST DROP GOALS IN A MATCH BY THE TEAM

Date	Opponent	Result	DGs
02/07/1994	Samoa	20–13	3
12/10/1991	Romania	15–17	3

MOST POINTS IN A MATCH BY A PLAYER

Date	Player	Opponent	Pts.
10/09/1983	Severo Koroduadua	Niue Island	36
07/10/1989	Waisale Serevi	Belgium	26
28/08/1999	Nicky Little	Italy	25
30/08/1979	Tevita Makutu	Papua New Guinea	24
29/09/1996	Nicky Little	Hong Kong	24
21/08/1969	Semesa Sikivou	Solomon Islands	24

MOST TRIES IN A MATCH BY A PLAYER

Date	Player	Opponent	Tries
30/08/1979	Tevita Makutu	Papua New Guinea	6
18/08/1969	George Sailosi	Papua New Guinea	5
	8 Players		4

MOST CONVERSIONS IN A MATCH BY A PLAYER

Date	Player	Opponent	Cons
10/09/1983	Severo Koroduadua	Niue Island	18
21/08/1969	Semesa Sikivou	Solomon Islands	12
07/10/1989	Waisale Serevi	Belgium	11
01/10/1999	Waisale Serevi	Namibia	8
30/08/1979	Kemueli Musunamasi	Papua New Guinea	7
21/08/1969	Asaeli Batibasaga	Solomon Islands	7

MOST PENALTIES IN A MATCH BY A PLAYER

Date	Player	Opponent	Pens
08/07/2001	Nicky Little	Samoa	7
26/05/2000	Nicky Little	Tonga	6
25/05/2001	Nicky Little	Tonga	6
05/10/1996	Nicky Little	Hong Kong	6
08/07/1967	Inoke Tabualevu	Tonga	6

MOST DROP GOALS IN A MATCH BY A PLAYER

Date	Player	Opponent	Pens
02/07/1994	Opeti Turuva	Samoa	3
12/10/1991	Tomasi Rabaka	Romania	2

MOST CAPPED PLAYERS

Name	Caps
Nicky Little	63
Jacob Rauluni	50
Joeli Veitayaki	49
Emori Katalau	47
Ifereimi Tawake	46

LEADING TRY SCORERS

Name	Tries
Senivalati Laulau	19
Norman Ligairi	16
Viliame Satala	16
Fero Lasagavibau	16
Aisea Tuilevu	13

LEADING CONVERSIONS SCORERS

Name	Cons
Nicky Little	113
Waisale Serevi	51
Severo Koroduadua	43
Seremaia Baikeinuku	20
Isimeli Batibasaga	17

LEADING PENALTY SCORERS

Name	Pens
Nicky Little	133
Severo Koroduadua	37
Waisale Serevi	27
Seremaia Baikeinuku	18

LEADING DROP GOAL SCORERS

Name	DGs
Opeti Turuva	5
Severo Koroduadua	5
Waisale Serevi	3
Tomasi Rabaka	2
Pio Tikoisuva	2
Nicky Little	2

LEADING POINTS SCORERS

Name	Pts.
Nicky Little	641
Waisale Serevi	239
Severo Koroduadua	212
Seremaia Baikeinuku	117

FRANCE

FRANCE'S 2008 TEST RECORD

OPPONENTS	DATE	VENUE	RESULT
Scotland	3 February	A	**Won** 27–6
Ireland	9 February	H	**Won** 26–21
England	23 February	H	**Lost** 13–24
Italy	9 March	H	**Won** 25–13
Wales	15 March	A	**Lost** 12–29
Australia	28 June	A	**Lost** 13–34
Australia	5 July	A	**Lost** 10–40

BAPTISM OF FIRE

By Iain Spragg

Cameron Spencer/Getty Images

New France coach Marc Lièvremont shook up the team in 2008.

French rugby rarely does anything by the book and so it proved once again when the FFR surveyed the wreckage of Les Bleus' Rugby World Cup 2007 campaign and swiftly announced the appointment of Marc Lièvremont as the side's new head coach.

Just five days after France's meek surrender to Argentina in the third place play-off in Paris, the FFR sprung a major surprise when they decided to hand the 38-year-old former international flanker the reins, bringing to an end Bernard Laporte's colourful and frequently controversial eight-year tenure in charge.

Laporte headed off for a new career in French politics, leaving his successor to mastermind a new era for Les Bleus. The FFR's decision was nothing if not bold and with Sale's Philippe Saint-Andre, Stade Francais' Fabien Galthie and Toulouse's Guy Noves all appearing to boast more impressive CVs, Lièvremont found himself having to defend his appointment even before a ball had been kicked or a tackle made.

"I realise that I am at the centre of a lot of attention and of hopes for the future," Lièvremont said as he faced the media for the first time. "I also understand that some people are disappointed, legitimately or not, but I consider myself to be a man with convictions surrounding both the sport and on the human front. I have not asked for anything from anyone. I respect all the coaches who were viable candidates for the post, but it is not for me to justify what has happened."

It would be three months and the start of the Six Nations before Lièvremont was presented with the opportunity to finally make his mark and when he unveiled his 22-man squad for the tournament opener against Scotland at Murrayfield, it was immediately obvious the new coach was looking firmly to the future.

Only 11 of France's 30-strong World Cup contingent survived the cut and six uncapped players were drafted in to invigorate the side.

"We selected those players with the 2011 World Cup in mind and we also wanted a team that could be competitive," Lièvremont explained. "We believe that we have the potential to play a more ambitious style of rugby, more in tune with our own culture.

"We want a team of players with an attacking mind-set, guys who have the courage to attack and to take individual initiatives on the field. But to do that, they must not be afraid of making mistakes, and we want to give them the confidence that will allow them to take risks."

The initial signs were encouraging and although their 27–6 victory in Edinburgh was not exactly a vintage French performance, it was undeniably brimming with the adventure Lièvremont craved and two tries from the superb Vincent Clerc and a third from Julien Malzieu were more than enough to subdue the Scots.

It was, however, to prove the highlight of France's season. Lièvremont made six changes to his starting line-up for the visit of Ireland to Paris the following week despite his side's victory and although his selection gamble initially seemed to have paid off, the team's 26–21 victory over the Irish ultimately asked more questions than it answered.

France began the match in spectacular style and Clerc's scintillating first-half hat-trick illuminated the Stade de France and when Cédric Heymans cross early in the second-half, Les Bleus were on course for a crushing, crowd-pleasing victory. But Ireland had other ideas and clawed their way back into the game and when the final whistle sounded, France's winning margin of just five points felt distinctly underwhelming. The alarm bells were not yet ringing but France's new era was already looking like a work very much in progress.

The arrival of the English in Paris a fortnight later presented France with the chance to avenge their World Cup semi-final defeat and with two wins from their opening two games under their belt, the Grand Slam was still on the cards.

Lièvremont pulled another selection rabbit out of the hat when he named the inexperienced half-back pairing of scrum-half, Morgan Parra, and outside-half François Trinh-Duc in his starting line-up and his decision badly backfired as England won the tactical battle in Paris. Paul Sackey drew first blood with an early score and although captain Lionel Nallet reduced his side's arrears with a try, France went in at half-time 13–7 down. The second period saw England's pack exert more and more pressure and although the visitors were never able to rest on their laurels, Richard Wrigglesworth's late try was enough to secure a 24–13 win.

On paper, the visit of the Italians to Paris two weeks later should have handed France with the ideal opportunity to exorcise the demons of defeat to the old enemy. Once again, Lièvremont could not resist the temptation to make bold changes to his side, naming the uncapped trio of centre Yann David, prop Fabien Barcella and flanker Ibrahim Diarra in the team to face the Azzurri but the new faces failed to add the required spark.

A first try from full-back Anthony Floch was followed by further scores from Yannick Jauzion and Aurélien Rougerie after the break but the anticipated riot of running rugby failed to materialise and the final scoreline of 25–13 to the home side told its own story.

There was, however, the possibility of salvation on the horizon. England's shock defeat to Scotland the day before ruled Brian Ashton's side out of title contention and although France's dreams of the Grand Slam were over, a big victory over unbeaten Wales in Cardiff in their final fixture would give Lièvremont's side the Championship.

They needed to win by 20 clear points in the Millennium Stadium but after what had been a patchy campaign, claiming the title would have represented a superb return.

France had not lost a Championship game in Cardiff since 1996 but with the Grand Slam tantalisingly close, Wales were in no mood to allow the visitors to extend the sequence. Three first-half James Hook penalties to one from the recalled Jean-Baptiste Élissalde gave the home side the early advantage but the defining moment of the match came on the hour when Shane Williams capitalised on a French handling error for the games' first try. Les Blues chipped away at Wales' lead with a penalty from substitute Dimitri Yachvili but when Martyn Williams went over three minutes from time, the contest was over and Wales were 29–12 winners and Grand Slam champions.

Stu Forster/Getty Images

Toulouse were once again confirmed as the best club side in France.

France's spirit was be severely tested in the summer on France's two-Test tour of Australia. With the climax of the Top 14 campaign denying Lièvremont of the services of players from Perpignan, Clermont Auvergne, Toulouse and Stade Francais, the coach was forced to name an experimental squad to head Down Under and 11 of the 26 players he eventually named were uncapped rookies.

The first Test in Sydney offered little hiding place for his depleted troops and although France batted bravely in defence, particularly in the first 40 minutes, the Wallabies cruised into a 34–6 lead with tries from Matt Giteau, Nathan Sharpe, Rocky Elsom and Stirling Mortlock and although debutant wing Alexis Palisson saved some face with a late score, France were overpowered and outclassed.

France's hopes of salvaging pride in the second Test in Brisbane looked remote and so it proved in the Suncorp Stadium as Australia ran riot and Les Bleus ended their first season under Lièvremont in desperately disappointing style.

The floodgates opened when wing Peter Hynes scored in the first-half and Australia ran in a further three tries in a crushing 40–10 victory. Fly-half Trinh-Duc scored a late consolation but there was no disguising the gulf in class between the Wallabies and France's demoralised second string.

Toulouse lifted the famous Bouclier de Brennus for a record 17th time after overcoming perennial bridesmaids Clermont Auvergne in the

Top 14 final in Paris, claiming their first French Championship for seven years and repeating their triumph over the hapless Jaunards in the 2001 final.

Six weeks after the bitter disappointment of narrowly losing to Munster in the Heineken Cup final, Toulouse held their nerve in the Stade de France to emerge 26–20 victors and condemn Clermont to get another final heartache.

The 2007 final had seen the Jaunards lead Stade Francais until the 78th minute only to surrender their advantage at the death and although their 26–20 reverse to the Rouge et Noir in 2008 was not as close as the final score line suggests, defeat in Paris was the ninth time the club had fallen at the final hurdle in their bid to be crowned French champions. It was also the fourth time Toulouse had delivered the fatal coup de grace.

Clermont had headed the Top 14 table at the end of the regular season, finishing five points clear of Toulouse, and barely broke sweat in their 21–7 victory over Perpignan in the semi-final. They beat Guy Noves' side home and away in the process but were unable to rediscover that form when it really mattered.

For Toulouse, victory in the Stade de France was the perfect riposte to the club's detractors who had been quick to criticise after the side's indifferent performances in the previous campaign.

"The players have shown magnificent character in this final," Noves said after the final whistle in Saint-Denis. "This is my 10th final and my players continue to surprise me. I didn't think they would be able to find the energy to get through all the difficulties that we have experienced this season.

For Clermont, defeat in the final was a depressingly familiar feeling and the club's 97-year wait to claim the Top 14 title goes on.

"I am proud of the run the players have gone on this year," said coach Vern Cotter. "But we didn't get into this match and we know we can play better than that.

That is two finals we have lost now and that is enough. When I look back at the season as a whole, the team has grown. But we just weren't there in the final."

FRANCE INTERNATIONAL STATISTICS

MATCH RECORDS UP TO 30TH SEPTEMBER 2008

MOST CONSECUTIVE TEST WINS

10 1931 E,G, 1932 G, 1933 G, 1934 G, 1935 G, 1936 G1,2, 1937 G,It
8 1998 E, S, I, W, Arg 1,2, Fj, Arg 3
8 2001 SA 3 A, Fj 2002 It, W, E, S,I
8 2004 I, It, W, S, E, US, C, A

MOST CONSECUTIVE TESTS WITHOUT DEFEAT

Matches	Wins	Draws	Period
10	10	0	1931 to 1938
10	8	2	1958 to 1959
10	9	1	1986 to 1987

MOST POINTS IN A MATCH

BY THE TEAM

Pts.	Opponents	Venue	Year
87	Namibia	Toulouse	2007
77	Fiji	Saint Etienne	2001
70	Zimbabwe	Auckland	1987
67	Romania	Bucharest	2000
64	Romania	Aurillac	1996
64	Georgia	Marseilles	2007
62	Romania	Castres	1999
62	Romania	Bucharest	2006
61	Fiji	Brisbane	2003
60	Italy	Toulon	1967
59	Romania	Paris	1924
56	Romania	Lens	2003
56	Italy	Rome	2005

BY A PLAYER

Pts.	Player	Opponents	Venue	Year
30	D Camberabero	Zimbabwe	Auckland	1987
28	C Lamaison	New Zealand	Twickenham	1999
28	F Michalak	Scotland	Sydney	2003
27	J-B Elissalde	Namibia	Toulouse	2007
27	G Camberabero	Italy	Toulon	1967
27	C Lamaison	New Zealand	Marseilles	2000
27	G Merceron	South Africa	Johannesburg	2001
26	T Lacroix	Ireland	Durban	1995
26	F Michalak	Fiji	Brisbane	2003
25	J-P Romeu	United States	Chicago	1976
25	P Berot	Romania	Agen	1987
25	T Lacroix	Tonga	Pretoria	1995

MOST TRIES IN A MATCH

BY THE TEAM

Tries	Opponents	Venue	Year
13	Romania	Paris	1924
13	Zimbabwe	Auckland	1987
13	Namibia	Toulouse	2007
12	Fiji	Saint Etienne	2001
11	Italy	Toulon	1967
10	Romania	Aurillac	1996
10	Romania	Bucharest	2000

BY A PLAYER

Tries	Player	Opponents	Venue	Year
4	A Jauréguy	Romania	Paris	1924
4	M Celhay	Italy	Paris	1937

MOST CONVERSIONS IN A MATCH

BY THE TEAM

Cons	Opponents	Venue	Year
11	Namibia	Toulouse	2007
9	Italy	Toulon	1967
9	Zimbabwe	Auckland	1987
8	Romania	Wellington	1987
8	Romania	Lens	2003

BY A PLAYER

Cons	Player	Opponents	Venue	Year
11	J-B Elissalde	Namibia	Toulouse	2007
9	G Camberabero	Italy	Toulon	1967
9	D Camberabero	Zimbabwe	Auckland	1987
8	G Laporte	Romania	Wellington	1987

MOST PENALTIES IN A MATCH

BY THE TEAM

Pens	Opponents	Venue	Year
8	Ireland	Durban	1995
7	Wales	Paris	2001
7	Italy	Paris	2002
6	Argentina	Buenos Aires	1977
6	Scotland	Paris	1997
6	Italy	Auch	1997
6	Ireland	Paris	2000
6	South Africa	Johannesburg	2001
6	Argentina	Buenos Aires	2003
6	Fiji	Brisbane	2003
6	England	Twickenham	2005
6	Wales	Paris	2007
6	England	Twickenham	2007

BY A PLAYER

Pens	Player	Opponents	Venue	Year
8	T Lacroix	Ireland	Durban	1995
7	G Merceron	Italy	Paris	2002
6	J-M Aguirre	Argentina	Buenos Aires	1977
6	C Lamaison	Scotland	Paris	1997
6	C Lamaison	Italy	Auch	1997
6	G Merceron	Ireland	Paris	2000
6	G Merceron	South Africa	Johannesburg	2001
6	D Yachvili	England	Twickenham	2005
6	F Michalak	Fiji	Brisbane	2003

MOST DROPPED GOALS IN A MATCH

BY THE TEAM

Drops	Opponents	Venue	Year
3	Ireland	Paris	1960
3	England	Twickenham	1985
3	New Zealand	Christchurch	1986
3	Australia	Sydney	1990
3	Scotland	Paris	1991
3	New Zealand	Christchurch	1994

BY A PLAYER

Drops	Player	Opponents	Venue	Year
3	P Albaladejo	Ireland	Paris	1960
3	J-P Lescarboura	England	Twickenham	1985
3	J-P Lescarboura	New Zealand	Christchurch	1986
3	D Camberabero	Australia	Sydney	1990

CAREER RECORDS

MOST CAPPED PLAYERS

Caps	Player	Career Span
118	F Pelous	1995 to 2007
111	P Sella	1982 to 1995
98	R Ibañez	1996 to 2007
93	S Blanco	1980 to 1991
89	O Magne	1997 to 2007
78	A Benazzi	1990 to 2001
71	J-L Sadourny	1991 to 2001
71	O Brouzet	1994 to 2003
71	C Califano	1994 to 2007
71	S Marconnet	1998 to 2007
69	R Bertranne	1971 to 1981
69	P Saint-André	1990 to 1997
69	P de Villiers	1999 to 2007
67	C Dominici	1998 to 2007
64	F Galthié	1991 to 2003
64	D Traille	2001 to 2008
63	M Crauste	1957 to 1966
63	B Dauga	1964 to 1972
63	S Betsen	1997 to 2007

MOST CONSECUTIVE TESTS

Tests	Player	Career Span
46	R Bertranne	1973 to 1979
45	P Sella	1982 to 1987
44	M Crauste	1960 to 1966
35	B Dauga	1964 to 1968

MOST TESTS AS CAPTAIN

Tests	Captain	Span
42	F Pelous	1997 to 2006
41	R Ibanez	1998 to 2007
34	J-P Rives	1978 to 1984
34	P Saint-André	1994 to 1997
25	D Dubroca	1986 to 1988
25	F Galthié	1999 to 2003
24	G Basquet	1948 to 1952
22	M Crauste	1961 to 1966

MOST POINTS IN TESTS

Pts	Player	Tests	Career
380	C Lamaison	37	1996 to 2001
367	T Lacroix	43	1989 to 1997
354	D Camberabero	36	1982 to 1993
267	G Merceron	32	1999 to 2003
265	J-P Romeu	34	1972 to 1977
258	D Yachvili	38	2002 to 2008
247	T Castaignède	54	1995 to 2007
246	F Michalak	50	2001 to 2007
233	S Blanco	93	1980 to 1991
214	J-B Elissalde	33	2000 to 2008
200	J-P Lescarboura	28	1982 to 1990

MOST TRIES IN TESTS

Tries	Player	Tests	Career
38	S Blanco	93	1980 to 1991
33	P Saint-André	69	1990 to 1997
30	P Sella	111	1982 to 1995
26	E Ntamack	46	1994 to 2000
26	P Bernat Salles	41	1992 to 2001
25	C Dominici	67	1998 to 2007
23	C Darrouy	40	1957 to 1967

MOST CONVERSIONS IN TESTS

Cons	Player	Tests	Career
59	C Lamaison	37	1996 to 2001
48	D Camberabero	36	1982 to 1993
45	M Vannier	43	1953 to 1961
42	T Castaignède	54	1995 to 2007
40	J-B Elissalde	33	2000 to 2008
37	D Yachvili	38	2002 to 2008
36	R Dourthe	31	1995 to 2001
36	G Merceron	32	1999 to 2003
36	F Michalak	50	2001 to 2007
32	T Lacroix	43	1989 to 1997
29	P Villepreux	34	1967 to 1972

MOST PENALTY GOALS IN TESTS

Pens	Player	Tests	Career
89	T Lacroix	43	1989 to 1997
78	C Lamaison	37	1996 to 2001
59	D Camberabero	36	1982 to 1993
57	G Merceron	32	1999 to 2003
56	J-P Romeu	34	1972 to 1977
56	D Yachvili	38	2002 to 2008
38	F Michalak	50	2001 to 2007
38	J-B Elissalde	33	2000 to 2008
33	P Villepreux	34	1967 to 1972
33	P Bérot	19	1986 to 1989

MOST DROPPED GOALS IN TESTS

Drops	Player	Tests	Career
15	J-P Lescarboura	28	1982 to 1990
12	P Albaladejo	30	1954 to 1964
11	G Camberabero	14	1961 to 1968
11	D Camberabero	36	1982 to 1993
9	J-P Romeu	34	1972 to 1977

INTERNATIONAL CHAMPIONSHIP RECORDS

RECORD	DETAIL		SET
Most points in season	156	in five matches	2002
Most tries in season	18	in four matches	1998
	18	in five matches	2006
Highest Score	56	56-13 v Italy	2005
Biggest win	51	51 - 0 v Wales	1998
Highest score conceded	49	14-49 v Wales	1910
Biggest defeat	37	0-37 v England	1911
Most appearances	50	P Sella	1983 - 1995
Most points in matches	180	D Yachvili	2003 - 2008
Most points in season	80	G Merceron	2002
Most points in match	24	S Viars	v Ireland, 1992
	24	C Lamaison	v Scotland, 1997
	24	J-B Elissalde	v Wales, 2004
Most tries in matches	14	S Blanco	1981 – 1991
	14	P Sella	1983 – 1995
Most tries in season	5	P Estève	1983
	5	E Bonneval	1987
	5	E Ntamack	1999
	5	P Bernat Salles	2001
	5	V Clerc	2008
Most tries in match	3	M Crauste	v England, 1962
	3	C Darrouy	v Ireland, 1963
	3	E Bonneval	v Scotland, 1987
	3	D Venditti	v Ireland, 1997
	3	E Ntamack	v Wales, 1999
	3	V Clerc	v Ireland, 2008
Most cons in matches	25	D Yachvili	2003 – 2008
Most cons in season	9	C Lamaison	1998
	9	G Merceron	2002
	9	D Yachvili	2003
Most cons in match	6	D Yachvili	v Italy, 2003
Most pens in matches	40	D Yachvili	2003 – 2008
Most pens in season	18	G Merceron	2002
Most pens in match	7	G Merceron	v Italy, 2002
Most drops in matches	9	J-P Lescarboura	1982 – 1988
Most drops in season	5	G Camberabero	1967
Most drops in match	3	P Albaladejo	v Ireland, 1960
	3	J-P Lescarboura	v England, 1985

MISCELLANEOUS RECORDS

RECORD	HOLDER	DETAIL
Longest Test Career	F Haget	1974 to 1987
	C Califano	1994 to 2007
Youngest Test Cap	C Dourthe	18 yrs 7 days in 1966
Oldest Test Cap	A Roques	37 yrs 329 days in 1963

CAREER RECORDS OF FRANCE INTERNATIONAL PLAYERS (UP TO 30 SEPTEMBER 2008)

PLAYER BACKS	DEBUT	CAPS	T	C	P	D	PTS
L Beauxis	2007 v It	12	1	16	14	0	79
B Boyet	2006 v I	5	0	1	3	0	11
T Castaignède	1995 v R	54	17	42	21	5	247
V Clerc	2002 SA	33	20	0	0	0	100
J-F Coux	2007 v NZ	2	1	0	0	0	5
Y David	2008 v It	1	0	0	0	0	0
C Dominici	1998 v E	67	25	0	0	0	125
N Durand	2007 v NZ	2	0	0	0	0	0
P Elhorga	2001 v NZ	19	3	0	0	0	15
J-B Elissalde	2000 v S	33	4	40	38	0	214
A Floch	2008 v E	3	1	0	0	0	5
M Forest	2007 v NZ	2	0	0	0	0	0
F Fritz	2005 v SA	13	3	0	0	2	21
J-P Grandclaude	2005 v E	3	0	0	0	0	0
C Heymans	2000 v It	41	11	0	0	0	55
D Janin	2008 v A	2	0	0	0	0	0
Y Jauzion	2001 v SA	52	17	0	0	1	88
T Lacroix	2008 v A	2	0	0	0	0	0
J Laharrague	2005 v W	12	4	0	0	0	20
N Laharrague	2007 v NZ	2	0	0	0	0	0
J Malzieu	2008 v S	3	1	0	0	0	5
D Marty	2005 v It	22	8	0	0	0	40
L Mazars	2007 v NZ	1	0	0	0	0	0
M Mermoz	2008 v A	1	0	0	0	0	0
F Michalak	2001 v SA	50	9	36	38	5	246
A Mignardi	2007 v NZ	2	0	0	0	0	0
P Mignoni	1997 v R	28	6	0	0	0	30
A Palisson	2008 v A	2	1	0	0	0	5
M Parra	2008 v S	3	0	0	1	0	3
J-B Peyras	2008 v A	1	0	0	0	0	0
C Poitrenaud	2001 v SA	32	6	0	0	0	30
A Rougerie	2001 v SA	55	21	0	0	0	105
D Skrela	2001 v NZ	15	0	8	21	0	79
B Thiéry	2007 v NZ	4	0	0	0	0	0
S Tillous-Borde	2008 v A	2	0	0	0	0	0
J Tomas	2008 v It	1	0	0	0	0	0
D Traille	2001 v SA	64	12	8	12	1	115
F Trinh-Duc	2008 v S	7	1	1	1	0	10
L Valbon	2004 v US	5	1	0	0	0	5
D Yachvili	2002 v C	38	2	37	56	2	258

FORWARDS							
B August	2007 v W	1	0	0	0	0	0
F Barcella	2008 v It	2	0	0	0	0	0
S Betsen	1997 v It	63	9	0	0	0	45
J Bonnaire	2004 v S	42	6	0	0	0	30
R Boyoud	2008 v A	2	0	0	0	0	0
J Brugnaut	2008 v S	2	0	0	0	0	0
S Bruno	2002 v W	26	4	0	0	0	20
Y Caballero	2008 v A	1	0	0	0	0	0
C Califano	1994 v NZ	71	6	0	0	0	30
S Chabal	2000 v S	39	5	0	0	0	25
D Chouly	2007 v NZ	2	0	0	0	0	0
P Correia	2008 v A	1	0	0	0	0	0
D Couzinet	2004 v US	3	0	0	0	0	0
P de Villiers	1999 v W	69	2	0	0	0	10
I Diarra	2008 v It	1	0	0	0	0	0
T Dusautoir	2006 v R	14	3	0	0	0	15
L Faure	2008 v S	4	0	0	0	0	0
G Guirado	2008 v It	1	0	0	0	0	0
I Harinordoquy	2002 v W	48	10	0	0	0	50
R Ibañez	1996 v W	98	8	0	0	0	40
L Jacquet	2006 v NZ	4	0	0	0	0	0
B Kayser	2008 v A	2	0	0	0	0	0
G Lamboley	2005 v S	13	1	0	0	0	5
G Le Corvec	2007 v NZ	1	0	0	0	0	0
B Lecouls	2008 v A	2	0	0	0	0	0
M Lièvremont	2008 v A	2	0	0	0	0	0
O Magne	1997 v W	89	14	0	0	0	70
S Marconnet	1998 v Arg	71	3	0	0	0	15
R Martin	2002 v E	21	3	0	0	0	15
N Mas	2003 v NZ	19	0	0	0	0	0
A Mela	2008 v S	4	0	0	0	0	0
O Milloud	2000 v R	50	1	0	0	0	5
F Montanella	2007 v NZ	1	0	0	0	0	0
L Nallet	2000 v R	39	6	0	0	0	30
Y Nyanga	2004 v US	25	4	0	0	0	20
O Olibeau	2007 v NZ	2	0	0	0	0	0
F Ouedraogo	2007 v NZ	8	0	0	0	0	0
P Papé	2004 v I	20	2	0	0	0	10
F Pelous	1995 v R	118	8	0	0	0	40
L Picamoles	2008 v I	5	0	0	0	0	0
J Pierre	2007 v NZ	2	0	0	0	0	0
J-B Poux	2001 v Fj	23	3	0	0	0	15
W Servat	2004 v I	20	0	0	0	0	0
O Sourgens	2007 v NZ	1	0	0	0	0	0
D Szarzewski	2004 v C	27	3	0	0	0	15
J Thion	2003 v Arg	45	1	0	0	0	5
E Vermeulen	2001 v SA	10	1	0	0	0	5

FRENCH INTERNATIONAL PLAYERS

UP TO 30TH SEPTEMBER 2008

Note: Years given for International Championship matches are for second half of season; eg 1972 means season 1971-72. Years for all other matches refer to the actual year of the match. Entries in square brackets denote matches played in RWC Finals.

Abadie, A (Pau) 1964 I
Abadie, A (Graulhet) 1965 R, 1967 SA 1,3,4, NZ, 1968 S, I
Abadie, L (Tarbes) 1963 R
Accoceberry, G (Bègles) 1994 NZ 1,2, C 2, 1995 W, E, S, I, R 1, [Iv, S], It, 1996 I, W 1, R, Arg 1, W 2(R), SA 2, 1997 S, It 1
Aguerre, R (Biarritz O) 1979 S
Aguilar, D (Pau) 1937 G
Aguirre, J-M (Bagnères) 1971 A 2, 1972 S, 1973 W, I, J, R, 1974 I, W, Arg 2, R, SA 1, 1976 W (R), E, US, A 2, R, 1977 W, E, S, I, Arg 1,2, NZ 1,2, R, 1978 E, S, I, W, R, 1979 I, W, E, S, NZ 1,2, R, 1980 W, I
Ainciart, E (Bayonne) 1933 G, 1934 G, 1935 G, 1937 G, It, 1938 G 1
Albaladéjo, P (Dax) 1954 E, It, 1960 W, I, It, R, 1961 S, SA, E, W, I, NZ 1,2, A, 1962 S, E, W, I, 1963 S, I, E, W, It, 1964 S, NZ, W, It, I, SA, Fj
Albouy, A (Castres) 2002 It (R)
Alvarez, A-J (Tyrosse) 1945 B2, 1946 B, I, K, W, 1947 S, I, W, E, 1948 I, A, S, W, E, 1949 I, E, W, 1951 S, E, W
Amand, H (SF) 1906 NZ
Ambert, A (Toulouse) 1930 S, I, E, G, W
Amestoy, J-B (Mont-de-Marsan) 1964 NZ, E
André, G (RCF) 1913 SA, E, W, I, 1914 I, W, E
Andrieu, M (Nîmes) 1986 Arg 2, NZ 1, R 2, NZ 2, 1987 [R, Z], R, 1988 E, S, I, W, Arg 1,2,3,4, R, 1989 I, W, E, S, NZ 2, B, A 2, 1990 W, E, I (R)
Anduran, J (SCUF) 1910 W
Aqua, J-L (Toulon) 1999 R, Tg, NZ 1(R)
Araou, R (Narbonne) 1924 R
Arcalis, R (Brive) 1950 S, I, 1951 I, E, W
Arino, M (Agen) 1962 R
Aristouy, P (Pau) 1948 S, 1949 Arg 2, 1950 S, I, E, W
Arlettaz, P (Perpignan) 1995 R 2
Armary, L (Lourdes) 1987 [R], R, 1988 S, I, W, Arg 3,4, R, 1989 W, S, A 1,2, 1990 W, E, S, I, A 1,2,3, NZ 1, 1991 W 2, 1992 S, I, R, Arg 1,2, SA 1,2, Arg, 1993 E, S, I, W, SA 1,2, R 2, A 1,2, 1994 I, W, NZ 1(t),2(t), 1995 I, R 1 [Tg, I, SA]
Arnal, J-M (RCF) 1914 I, W
Arnaudet, M (Lourdes) 1964 I, 1967 It, W
Arotca, R (Bayonne) 1938 R
Arrieta, J (SF) 1953 E, W
Arthapignet, P (see Harislur-Arthapignet)
Artiguste, E (Castres) 1999 WS
Astre, R (Béziers) 1971 R, 1972 I 1, 1973 E (R), 1975 E, S, I, SA 1,2, Arg 2, 1976 A 2, R
Attoub, D (Castres) 2006 R
Aucagne, D (Pau) 1997 W (R), S, It 1, R 1(R), A 1, R 2(R), SA 2(R), 1998 S (R), W (R), Arg 2(R), Fj (R), Arg 3, A, 1999 W 1(R), S (R)
Audebert, A (Montferrand) 2000 R, 2002 W (R)
Aué, J-M (Castres) 1998 W (R)
Augé, J (Dax) 1929 S, W
Augras-Fabre, L (Agen) 1931 I, S, W
August, B (Biarritz) 2007 W1(R)
Auradou, D (SF) 1999 E (R), S (R), WS (R), Tg, NZ 1, W 2(R), [Arg (R)], 2000 A (R), NZ 1,2, 2001 S, I, It, W, E (R), SA 1,2, NZ (R), SA 3, A, Fj, 2002 It, E, I (R), C (R), 2003 S (R), It (R), W (R), Arg, 1,2, NZ (R), R (R), E 2(R),3, [J(R),US,NZ] , 2004 I(R),It(R),S(R),E(R)
Averous, J-L (La Voulte) 1975 S, I, SA 1,2, 1976 I, W, E, US, A 1,2, R, 1977 W, E, S, I, Arg 1, R, 1978 E, S, I, 1979 NZ 1,2, 1980 E, S, 1981 A 2
Avril, D (Biarritz) 2005 A1
Azam, O (Montferrand, Gloucester) 1995 R 2, Arg (R), 2000 A (R), NZ 2(R), 2001 SA 2(R), NZ, 2002 E (R), I (R), Arg (R), A 1
Azarete, J-L (Dax, St Jean-de-Luz) 1969 W, R, 1970 S, I, W, R, 1971 S, I, E, SA 1,2, A 1, 1972 E, W, I 2, A 1, R, 1973 NZ, W, I, R, 1974 I, R, SA 1,2, 1975 W

Baby, B (Toulouse) 2005 I,SA2(R),A1
Bacqué, N (Pau) 1997 R 2
Bader, E (Primevères) 1926 M, 1927 I, S
Badin, C (Chalon) 1973 W, I, 1975 Arg 1
Baillette, M (Perpignan) 1925 I, NZ, S, 1926 W, M, 1927 I, W, G 2, 1929 G, 1930 S, I, E, G, 1931 I, S, E, 1932 G
Baladie, G (Agen) 1945 B 1,2, W, 1946 B, I, K
Ballarin, J (Tarbes) 1924 E, 1925 NZ, S
Baquey, J (Toulouse) 1921 I
Barbazanges, A (Roanne) 1932 G, 1933 G
Barcella, F (Auch) 2008 It,W
Barrau, M (Beaumont, Toulouse) 1971 S, E, W, 1972 E, W, A 1,2, 1973 S, NZ, E, I, J, R, 1974 I, S
Barrau, M (Agen) 2004 US,C(R),NZ(R)
Barrère, P (Toulon) 1929 G, 1931 W
Barrière, R (Béziers) 1960 R
Barthe, E (SBUC) 1925 W, E
Barthe, J (Lourdes) 1954 Arg 1,2, 1955 S, 1956 I, W, It, E, Cz, 1957 S, I, E, W, R 1,2, 1958 S, E, A, W, It, I, SA 1,2, 1959 S, E, It, W
Basauri, R (Albi) 1954 Arg 1
Bascou, P (Bayonne) 1914 E
Basquet, G (Agen) 1945 W, 1946 B, I, K, W, 1947 S, I, W, E, 1948 I, A, S, W, E, 1949 S, I, E, W, Arg 1, 1950 S, I, E, W, 1951 S, I, E, W, 1952 S, I, SA, W, E, It
Bastiat, J-P (Dax) 1969 R, 1970 S, I, W, 1971 S, I, SA 2, 1972 S, A 1, 1973 E, 1974 Arg 1,2, SA 2, 1975 W, Arg 1,2, R, 1976 S, I, W, E, A 1,2, R, 1977 W, E, S, I, 1978 E, S, I, W
Baudry, N (Montferrand) 1949 S, I, W, Arg 1,2
Baulon, R (Vienne, Bayonne) 1954 S, NZ, W, E, It, 1955 I, E, W, It, 1956 S, I, W, It, E, Cz, 1957 S, I, It
Baux, J-P (Lannemezan) 1968 NZ 1,2, SA 1,2
Bavozet, J (Lyon) 1911 S, E, W
Bayard, J (Toulouse) 1923 S, W, E, 1924 W, R, US
Bayardon, J (Chalon) 1964 S, NZ, E
Beaurin-Gressier, C (SF) 1907 E, 1908 E
Beauxis, L (SF) 2007 It(R),I(R),W1(R),E1(R),S,W2, [Nm(R),I(R),Gg,NZ,E,Arg 2(R)]
Bégu, J (Dax) 1982 Arg 2(R), 1984 E, S
Béguerie, C (Agen) 1979 NZ 1
Béguet, L (RCF) 1922 I, 1923 S, W, E, I, 1924 S, I, E, R, US
Béhotéguy, A (Bayonne, Cognac) 1923 E, 1924 S, I, E, W, R, US, 1926 E, 1927 E, G 1,2, 1928 A, I, E, G, W, 1929 S, W, E
Béhotéguy, H (RCF, Cognac) 1923 W, 1928 A, I, E, G, W
Bélascain, C (Bayonne) 1977 R, 1978 E, S, I, W, R, 1979 I, W, E, S, 1982 W, E, S, I, 1983 E, S, I, W

Belletante, G (Nantes) 1951 I, E, W
Belot, F (Toulouse) 2000 I (R)
Benazzi, A (Agen) 1990 A 1,2,3, NZ 1,2, 1991 E, US 1(R),2, [R, Fj, C], 1992 SA 1(R),2, Arg, 1993 E, S, I, W, A 1,2, 1994 I, W, E, S, C 1, NZ 1,2, C 2, 1995 W, E, S, I, [Tg, Iv, S, I, SA, E], NZ 1,2, 1996 E, S, I, W 1, Arg 1,2, W 2, SA 1,2, 1997 I, W, E, S, R 1, A 1,2, It 2, R 2(R), Arg, SA 1,2, 1999 R, WS, W 2, [C, Nm (R), Fj, Arg, NZ 2, A], 2000 W, E, I, It (R), R, 2001 S (R), I (t&R), E
Bénésis, R (Narbonne) 1969 W, R, 1970 S, I, W, E, R, 1971 S, I, E, W, A 2, R, 1972 S, I 1, E, W, I 2, A 1, R, 1973 NZ, E, W, I, J, R, 1974 I, W, E, S
Benetière, J (Roanne) 1954 It, Arg 1
Benetton, P (Agen) 1989 B, 1990 NZ 2, 1991 US 2, 1992 Arg 1,2(R), SA 1(R),2, Arg, 1993 E, S, I, W, SA 1,2, R 2, A 1,2, 1994 I, W, E, S, C 1, NZ 1,2, C 2, 1995 W, E, S, I, [Tg, Iv (R), S], It, R 2(R), Arg, NZ 1,2, 1996 Arg 1,2, W 2, SA 1,2, 1997 I, It 1,2(R), R 2, Arg, SA 1,2 1998 E, S (R), I (R), W (R), Arg 1(R),2(R), Fj (R), 1999 I, W 1, S (R)
Benezech, L (RCF) 1994 E, S, C 1, NZ 1,2, C 2, 1995 W, E, [Iv, S, E], R 2, Arg, NZ 1,2
Berbizier, P (Lourdes, Agen) 1981 S, I, W, E, NZ 1,2, 1982 I, R, 1983 S, I, 1984 S (R), NZ 1,2, 1985 Arg 1,2, 1986 S, I, W, E, R 1, Arg 1, A, NZ 1, R 2, NZ 2,3, 1987 W, E, S, I, [S, R, Fj, A, NZ], R, 1988 E, S, I, W, Arg 1,2, 1989 I, W, E, S, NZ 1,2, B, A 1, 1990 W, E, 1991 S, I, W 1, E
Berejnoï, J-C (Tulle) 1963 R, 1964 S, W, It, I, SA, Fj, R, 1965 S, I, E, W, It, R, 1966 S, I, E, W, It, R, 1967 S, A, E, It, W, I, R
Bergès, B (Toulouse) 1926 I
Berges-Cau, R (Lourdes) 1976 E (R)
Bergese, F (Bayonne) 1936 G 2, 1937 G, It, 1938 G 1, R, G 2
Bergougnan, Y (Toulouse) 1945 B 1, W, 1946 B, I, K, W, 1947 S, I, W, E, 1948 S, W, E, 1949 S, E, Arg 1,2
Bernard, R (Bergerac) 1951 S, I, E, W
Bernat-Salles, P (Pau, Bègles-Bordeaux, Biarritz) 1992 Arg, 1993 R 1, SA 1,2, R 2, A 1,2, 1994 I, 1995 E, S, 1996 E (R), 1997 R 1, A 1,2, 1998 E, S, I, W, Arg 1,2, Fj, Arg 3(R), A 1999 I, W 1, R, Tg, [Nm, Fj, Arg, NZ 2, A], 2000 I, It, NZ 1(R),2, 2001 S, I, It, W, E
Bernon, J (Lourdes) 1922 I, 1923 S
Bérot, J-L (Toulouse) 1968 NZ 3, A, 1969 S, I, 1970 E, R, 1971 S, I, E, W, SA 1,2, A 1,2, R, 1972 S, I 1, E, W, A 1, 1974 I
Bérot, P (Agen) 1986 R 2, NZ 2,3, 1987 W, E, S, I, R, 1988 E, S, I, Arg 1,2,3,4, R, 1989 S, NZ 1,2
Bertrand, P (Bourg) 1951 I, E, W, 1953 S, I, E, W, It
Bertranne, R (Bagnères) 1971 E, W, SA 2, A 1,2, 1972 S, I 1, 1973 NZ, E, J, R, 1974 I, W, E, S, Arg 1,2, R, SA 1,2, 1975 W, E, S, I, SA 1,2, Arg 1,2, R, 1976 S, I, W, E, US, A 1,2, R, 1977 W, E, S, I, Arg 1,2, NZ 1,2, R, 1978 E, S, I, W, R, 1979 I, W, E, S, R, 1980 W, E, S, I, SA, R, 1981 S, I, W, E, R, NZ 1,2
Berty, D (Toulouse) 1990 NZ 2, 1992 R (R), 1993 R 2, 1995 NZ 1(R), 1996 W 2(R), SA 1
Besset, E (Grenoble) 1924 S
Besset, L (SCUF) 1914 W, E
Besson, M (CASG) 1924 I, 1925 I, E, 1926 S, W, 1927 I
Besson, P (Brive) 1963 S, I, E, 1965 R, 1968 SA 1
Betsen, S (Biarritz) 1997 It 1(R), 2000 W (R), E (R), A (R), NZ 1(R),2(R), 2001 S (R), I (R), It (R), W (R), SA 3(R), A, Fj, 2002 It, W, E, S, I, Arg, A 1,2, SA, NZ, C, 2003 E 1, S, I, It, W, R, E 2, [Fj,J,S,I,E], 2004 I,It,W,S,E,A,Arg,NZ, 2005 E,W,I,It, 2006 SA,
NZ2(R),Arg(R), 2007 It,I,W1,E1,S,E2,W2, [Arg 1,I,Gg,NZ,E]
Bianchi, J (Toulon) 1986 Arg 1
Bichindaritz, J (Biarritz O) 1954 It, Arg 1,2
Bidabé, P (Biarritz) 2004 C, 2006 R
Bidart, L (La Rochelle) 1953 W
Biémouret, P (Agen) 1969 E, W, 1970 I, W, E, 1971 W, SA 1,2, A 1, 1972 E, W, I 2, A 2, R, 1973 S, NZ, E, W, I
Biénès, R (Cognac) 1950 S, I, E, W, 1951 S, I, E, W, 1952 S, I, SA, W, E, It, 1953 S, I, E, 1954 S, I, NZ, W, E, Arg 1,2, 1956 S, I, W, It, E
Bigot, C (Quillan) 1930 S, E, 1931 I, S
Bilbao, L (St Jean-de-Luz) 1978 I, 1979 I
Billac, E (Bayonne) 1920 S, E, W, I, US, 1921 S, W, 1922 W, 1923 E
Billière, M (Toulouse) 1968 NZ 3
Bioussa, A (Toulouse) 1924 W, US, 1925 I, NZ, S, E, 1926 S, I, E, 1928 E, G, W, 1929 I, S, W, E, 1930 S, I, E, G, W
Bioussa, C (Toulouse) 1913 W, I, 1914 I
Biraben, M (Dax) 1920 W, I, US, 1921 S, W, E, I, 1922 S, E, I
Blain, A (Carcassonne) 1934 G
Blanco, S (Biarritz O) 1980 SA, R, 1981 S, W, E, A 1,2, R, NZ 1,2, 1982 W, E, S, I, R, Arg 1,2, 1983 E, S, I, W, 1984 I, W, E, S, NZ 1,2, R, 1985 E, S, I, W, Arg 1,2, 1986 S, I, W, E, R 1, Arg 2, A, NZ 1, R 2, NZ 2,3, 1987 W, E, S, I, [S, R, Fj, A, NZ], R, 1988 E, S, I, W, Arg 1,2,3,4, R, 1989 I, W, E, S, NZ 1,2, B, A 1, 1990 E, S, I, R, A 1,2,3, NZ 1,2, 1991 S, I, W 1, E, R, US 1,2, W 2, [R, Fj, C, E]
Blond, J (SF) 1935 G, 1936 G 2, 1937 G, 1938 G 1, R, G 2
Blond, X (RCF) 1990 A 3, 1991 S, I, W 1, E, 1994 NZ 2(R)
Boffelli, V (Aurillac) 1971 A 2, R, 1972 S, I 1, 1973 J, R, 1974 I, W, E, S, Arg 1,2, R, SA 1,2, 1975 W, S, I
Bonal, J-M (Toulouse) 1968 E, W, Cz, NZ 2,3, SA 1,2, R, 1969 S, I, E, R, 1970 W, E
Bonamy, R (SB) 1928 A, I
Bondouy, P (Narbonne, Toulouse) 1997 S (R), It 1, A 2(R), R 2, 2000 R (R)
Bonetti, S (Biarritz) 2001 It, W, NZ (R)
Boniface, A (Mont-de-Marsan) 1954 I, NZ, W, E, It, Arg 1,2, 1955 S, I, 1956 S, I, W, It, Cz, 1957 S, I, W, R 2, 1958 S, E, 1959 E, 1961 NZ 1,3, A, R, 1962 E, W, I, It, R, 1963 S, I, E, W, It, R, 1964 S, NZ, E, W, It, 1965 W, It, R, 1966 S, I, E, W
Boniface, G (Mont-de-Marsan) 1960 W, I, It, R, Arg 1,2,3, 1961 S, SA, E, W, It, I, NZ 1,2,3, R, 1962 R, 1963 S, I, E, W, It, R, 1964 S, 1965 S, I, E, W, It, R, 1966 S, I, E, W
Bonnaire, J (Bourgoin, Clermont-Auvergne) 2004 S(t&R),A(R),NZ(R), 2005 S,E,W,I,It,SA1,2,A1,C,Tg,SA3, 2006 S,I,It(R),E(R),W,R,SA(R),NZ1,2,Arg, 2007 It,I(R),W1,E1,S,E2,3(R), [Arg1(R),Nm,I,Gg,NZ,E], 2008 S(R),I,E,It(R),W
Bonnes, E (Narbonne) 1924 W, R, US
Bonneval, E (Toulouse) 1984 NZ 2(R), 1985 W, Arg 1, 1986 W, E, R 1, Arg 1,2, A, R 2, NZ 2,3, 1987 W, E, S, I, [Z], 1988 E
Bonnus, F (Toulon) 1950 S, I, E, W
Bonnus, M (Toulon) 1937 It, 1938 G 1, R, G 2, 1940 B
Bontemps, D (La Rochelle) 1968 SA 2
Borchard, G (RCF) 1908 E, 1909 E, W, I, 1911 I
Borde, F (RCF) 1920 I, US, 1921 S, W, E, 1922 S, W, 1923 S, I, 1924 E, 1925 I, 1926 E
Bordenave, L (Toulon) 1948 A, S, W, E, 1949 S
Bory, D (Montferrand) 2000 I, It, A, NZ 1, 2001 S, I, SA 1,2,3, A, Fj, 2002 It, E, S, I, C, 2003 [US,NZ]
Boubée, J (Tarbes) 1921 S, E, I, 1922 E, W, 1923 E, I, 1925 NZ, S
Boudreaux, R (SCUF) 1910 W, S
Bouet, D (Dax) 1989 NZ 1,2, B, A 2, 1990 A 3
Bouguyon, G (Grenoble) 1961 SA, E, W, It, I, NZ 1,2,3, A
Bouic, G (Agen) 1996 SA 1
Bouilhou, J (Toulouse) 2001 NZ, 2003 Arg 1
Boujet, C (Grenoble) 1968 NZ 2, A (R), SA 1
Bouquet, J (Bourgoin, Vienne) 1954 S, 1955 E, 1956 S, I, W, It, E, Cz, 1957 S, E, W, R 2, 1958 S, E, 1959 S, It, W, I, 1960 S, E, W, I, R, 1961 S, SA, E, W, It, I, R, 1962 S, E, W, I
Bourdeu, J R (Lourdes) 1952 S, I, SA, W, E, It, 1953 S, I, E
Bourgarel, R (Toulouse) 1969 R, 1970 S, I, E, R, 1971 W, SA 1,2, 1973 S
Bourguignon, G (Narbonne) 1988 Arg 3, 1989 I, E, B, A 1, 1990 R
Bousquet, A (Béziers) 1921 E, I, 1924 R
Bousquet, R (Albi) 1926 M, 1927 I, S, W, E, G 1, 1929 W, E, 1930 W
Bousses, G (Bourgoin) 2006 S(R)
Boyau, M (SBUC) 1912 I, S, W, E, 1913 W, I
Boyer, P (Toulon) 1935 G
Boyet, B (Bourgoin) 2006 I(R), 2007 NZ1,2, 2008 A1,2(R)
Boyoud, R (Dax) 2008 A1(R),2
Branca, G (SF) 1928 S, 1929 I, S
Branlat, A (RCF) 1906 NZ, E, 1908 W
Bréjassou, R (Tarbes) 1952 S, I, SA, W, E, 1953 W, E, 1954 S, I, NZ, 1955 S, I, E, W, It

Brèthes, R (St Séver) 1960 Arg 2
Bringeon, A (Biarritz O) 1925 W
Brouzet, O (Grenoble, Bègles, Northampton, Montferrand) 1994 S, NZ 2(R), 1995 E, S, I, R 1, [Tg, Iv, E (t)], It, Arg (R), 1996 W 1(R), 1997 R 1, A 1,2, It 2, Arg, SA 1,2, 1998 E, S, I, W, Arg 1,2, Fj, Arg 3, A, 1999 I, W 1, E, S, R, [C (R), Nm, Fj (R), Arg, NZ 2(R), A (R)], 2000 W, E, S, I, It, A, NZ 1(R),2(R), 2001 SA 1,2, NZ, 2002 W, E, S, I, Arg, A 1(R),2, SA, NZ, C, 2003 E 1, S, I, It, W, E 3, [Fj(R),J,S(R),US,I(R)]
Bru, Y (Toulouse) 2001 A (R), Fj (R), 2002 It, 2003 Arg 2, NZ, R, E 2,3(R), [J,S(R),US,I(t&R),NZ], 2004 I(R),It(R),W(R),S(R),E(R)
Brugnaut, J (Dax) 2008 S,I(R)
Brun, G (Vienne) 1950 E, W, 1951 S, E, W, 1952 S, I, SA, W, E, It, 1953 E, W, It
Bruneau, M (SBUC) 1910 W, E, 1913 SA, E
Brunet, Y (Perpignan) 1975 SA 1, 1977 Arg 1
Bruno, S (Béziers, Sale) 2002 W (R), 2004 A(R),NZ(t&R), 2005 S(R),E,W,I,It,SA1,2(R),A1(R),2(R),C,SA3(R), 2006 S(R),I(R), 2007 I(R),E1(R),NZ1,2,E3(R),W2(R), [Gg,Arg 2(t&R)], 2008 A1,2
Brusque, N (Pau, Biarritz) 1997 R 2(R), 2002 W, E, S, I, Arg, A 2, SA, NZ, C, 2003 E 2, [Fj,S,I,E,NZ(R)], 2004 I,It,W,S,E,A,Arg, 2005 SA1(R),2,A1, 2006 S
Buchet, E (Nice) 1980 R, 1982 E, R (R), Arg 1,2
Buisson, H (see Empereur-Buisson)
Buonomo, Y (Béziers) 1971 A 2, R, 1972 I 1
Burgun, M (RCF) 1909 I, 1910 W, S, I, 1911 S, E, 1912 I, S, 1913 S, E, 1914 E
Bustaffa, D (Carcassonne) 1977 Arg 1,2, NZ 1,2, 1978 W, R, 1980 W, E, S, SA, R
Buzy, C-E (Lourdes) 1946 K, W, 1947 S, I, W, E, 1948 I, A, S, W, E, 1949 S, I, E, W, Arg 1,2

Caballero, Y (Montauban) 2008 A2(R)
Cabanier, J-M (Montauban) 1963 R, 1964 S, Fj, 1965 S, I, W, It, R, 1966 S, I, E, W, It, R, 1967 S, A, E, It, W, I, SA 1,3, NZ, R, 1968 S, I
Cabannes, L (RCF, Harlequins) 1990 NZ 2(R), 1991 S, I, W 1, E, US 2, W 2, [R, Fj, C, E], 1992 W, E, S, I, R, Arg 2, SA 1,2, 1993 E, S, I, W, R 1, SA 1,2, 1994 E, S, C 1, NZ 1,2, 1995 W, E, S, R 1, [Tg (R), Iv, S, I, SA, E], 1996 E, S, I, W 1, 1997 It 2, Arg, SA 1,2
Cabrol, H (Béziers) 1972 A 1(R),2, 1973 J, 1974 SA 2
Cadenat, J (SCUF) 1910 S, E, 1911 W, I, 1912 W, E, 1913 I
Cadieu, J-M (Toulouse) 1991 R, US 1, [R, Fj, C, E], 1992 W, I, R, Arg 1,2, SA 1
Cahuc, F (St Girons) 1922 S
Califano, C (Toulouse, Saracens, Gloucester) 1994 NZ 1,2, C 2, 1995 W, E, S, I, [Iv, S, I, SA, E], It, Arg, NZ 1,2, 1996 E, S, I, W 1, R, Arg 1,2, SA 1,2, 1997 I, W, E, A 1,2, It 2, R 2(R), Arg, SA 1,2, 1998 E, S, I, W, 1999 I, W 1, E (R), S, WS, Tg (R), NZ 1, W 2, [C, Nm, Fj], 2000 W, E, S, I, It, R, A, NZ 1,2(R), 2001 S (R), I (R), It, W, SA 1(R),2(R), NZ, 2003 E 1, S (R), I (R), 2007 NZ1,2
Cals, R (RCF) 1938 G 1
Calvo, G (Lourdes) 1961 NZ 1,3
Camberabero, D (La Voulte, Béziers) 1982 R, Arg 1,2, 1983 E, W, 1987 [R (R), Z, Fj (R), A, NZ], 1988 I, 1989 B, A 1, 1990 W, S, I, R, A 1,2,3, NZ 1,2, 1991 S, I, W 1, E, R, US 1,2, W 2, [R, Fj, C], 1993 E, S, I
Camberabero, G (La Voulte) 1961 NZ 3, 1962 R, 1964 R, 1967 A, E, It, W, I, SA 1,3,4, 1968 S, E, W
Camberabero, L (La Voulte) 1964 R, 1965 S, I, 1966 E, W, 1967 A, E, It, W, I, 1968 S, E, W
Cambré, T (Oloron) 1920 E, W, I, US
Camel, A (Toulouse) 1928 S, A, I, E, G, W, 1929 W, E, G, 1930 S, I, E, G, W, 1935 G
Camel, M (Toulouse) 1929 S, W, E
Camicas, F (Tarbes) 1927 G 2, 1928 S, I, E, G, W, 1929 I, S, W, E
Camo, E (Villeneuve) 1931 I, S, W, E, G, 1932 G
Campaès, A (Lourdes) 1965 W, 1967 NZ, 1968 S, I, E, W, Cz, NZ 1,2, A, 1969 S, W, 1972 R, 1973 NZ
Campan, O (Agen) 1993 SA 1(R),2(R), R 2(R), 1996 I, W 1, R
Candelon, J (Narbonne) 2005 SA1,A1(R)
Cantoni, J (Béziers) 1970 W, R, 1971 S, I, E, W, SA 1,2, R, 1972 S, I 1, 1973 S, NZ, W, I, 1975 W (R)
Capdouze, J (Pau) 1964 SA, Fj, R, 1965 S, I, E
Capendeguy, J-M (Bègles) 1967 NZ, R
Capitani, P (Toulon) 1954 Arg 1,2
Capmau, J-L (Toulouse) 1914 E
Carabignac, G (Agen) 1951 S, I, 1952 SA, W, E, 1953 S, I
Carbonne, J (Perpignan) 1927 W
Carbonneau, P (Toulouse, Brive, Pau) 1995 R 2, Arg, NZ 1,2, 1996 E, S, R (R), Arg 2, W 2, SA 1, 1997 I (R), W, E, S (R), R 1(R), A 1,2, 1998 E, S, I, W, Arg 1,2, Fj, Arg 3, A, 1999 I, W 1, E, S, 2000 NZ 2(R), 2001 I
Carminati, A (Béziers, Brive) 1986 R 2, NZ 2, 1987 [R, Z], 1988 I, W, Arg 1,2, 1989 I, W, S, NZ 1(R),2, A 2, 1990 S, 1995 It, R 2, Arg, NZ 1,2 Caron, L (Lyon O, Castres) 1947 E, 1948 I, A, W, E, 1949 S, I, E, W, Arg 1
Carpentier, M (Lourdes) 1980 E, SA, R, 1981 S, I, A 1, 1982 E, S
Carrère, C (Toulon) 1966 R, 1967 S, A, E, W, I, SA 1,3,4, NZ, R, 1968 S, I, E, W, Cz, NZ 3, A, R, 1969 S, I, 1970 S, I, W, E, 1971 E, W
Carrère, J (Vichy, Toulon) 1956 S, 1957 E, W, R 2, 1958 S, SA 1,2, 1959 I
Carrère, R (Mont-de-Marsan) 1953 E, It
Casadei, D (Brive) 1997 S, R 1, SA 2(R)
Casaux, L (Tarbes) 1959 I, It, 1962 S
Cassagne, P (Pau) 1957 It
Cassayet-Armagnac, A (Tarbes, Narbonne) 1920 S, E, W, US, 1921 W, E, I, 1922 S, E, W, 1923 S, W, E, I, 1924 S, E, W, R, US, 1925 I, NZ, S, W, 1926 S, I, E, W, M, 1927 I, S, W
Cassiède, M (Dax) 1961 NZ 3, A, R
Castaignède, S (Mont-de-Marsan) 1999 W 2, [C (R), Nm (R), Fj, Arg (R), NZ 2(R), A (R)]
Castaignède, T (Toulouse, Castres, Saracens) 1995 R 2, Arg, NZ 1,2, 1996 E, S, I, W 1, Arg 1,2, 1997 I, A 1,2, It 2, 1998 E, S, I, W, Arg 1,2, Fj, 1999 I, W 1, E, S, R, WS, Tg (R), NZ 1, W 2, [C], 2000 W, E, S, It, 2002 SA, NZ, C, 2003 E 1(R), S (R), It, W, Arg 1, 2005 A2(R),C,Tg,SA3, 2006 It,E,W,R,SA(R), 2007 NZ1,2
Castel, R (Toulouse, Béziers) 1996 I, W 1, W 2, SA 1(R),2, 1997 I (R), W, E (R), S (R), A 1(R), 1998 Arg 3(R), A (R), 1999 W 1(R), E, S
Castets, J (Toulon) 1923 W, E, I
Caujolle, J (Tarbes) 1909 E, 1913 SA, E, 1914 W, E
Caunègre, R (SB) 1938 R, G 2
Caussade, A (Lourdes) 1978 R, 1979 I, W, E, NZ 1,2, R, 1980 W, E, S, 1981 S (R), I
Caussarieu, G (Pau) 1929 I
Cayrefourcq, E (Tarbes) 1921 E
Cazalbou, J (Toulouse) 1997 It 2(R), R 2, Arg, SA 2(R)
Cazals, P (Mont-de-Marsan) 1961 NZ 1, A, R
Cazenave, A (Pau) 1927 E, G 1, 1928 S, A, G
Cazenave, F (RCF) 1950 E, 1952 S, 1954 I, NZ, W, E
Cécillon, M (Bourgoin) 1988 I, W, Arg 2,3,4, R, 1989 I, E, NZ 1,2, A 1, 1991 S, I, E (R), R, US 1, W 2, [E], 1992 W, E, S, I, R, Arg 1,2, SA 1,2, 1993 E, S, I, W, R 1, SA 1,2, R 2, A 1,2, 1994 I, W, NZ 1(R), 1995 I, R 1, [Tg, S (R), I, SA]
Celaya, M (Biarritz O, SBUC) 1953 E, W, It, 1954 I, E, It, Arg 1,2, 1955 S, I, E, W, It, 1956 S, I, W, It, E, Cz 1957 S, I, E, W, R 2, 1958 S, E, A, W, It, 1959 S, E, 1960 S, E, W, I, R, Arg 1,2,3, 1961 S, SA, E, W, It, I, NZ 1,2,3, A, R
Celhay, M (Bayonne) 1935 G, 1936 G 1, 1937 G, It, 1938 G 1, 1940 B
Cermeno, F (Perpignan) 2000 R
Cessieux, N (Lyon) 1906 NZ
Cester, E (TOEC, Valence) 1966 S, I, E, 1967 W, 1968 S, I, E, W, Cz, NZ 1,3, A, SA 1,2, R, 1969 S, I, E, W, 1970 S, I, W, E, 1971 A 1, 1972 R, 1973 S, NZ, W, I, J, R, 1974 I, W, E, S
Chabal, S (Bourgoin, Sale) 2000 S, 2001 SA 1,2, NZ (R), Fj (R), 2002 Arg (R), A 2, SA (R), NZ (t), C (R), 2003 E 1(R), S (R), I (R), Arg 2, NZ (R), E 2(R),3, [J(R),US,NZ], 2005 S,E,A2(R),Tg, 2007 It,I,E1,NZ1,2,E2(R),W2, [Arg 1(R),Nm,I,NZ(R),E(R),Arg 2(R)], 2008 A1,2
Chaban-Delmas, J (CASG) 1945 B 2
Chabowski, H (Nice, Bourgoin) 1985 Arg 2, 1986 R 2, NZ 2, 1989 B (R)

FRANCE

Chadebech, P (Brive) 1982 R, Arg 1,2, 1986 S, I
Champ, E (Toulon) 1985 Arg 1,2, 1986 I, W, E, R 1, Arg 1,2, A, NZ 1, R 2, NZ 2,3, 1987 W, E, S, I, [S, R, Fj, A, NZ], R, 1988 E, S, Arg 1,3,4, R, 1989 W, S, A 1,2, 1990 W, E, NZ 1, 1991 R, US 1, [R, Fj, C, E]
Chapuy, L (SF) 1926 S
Charpentier, G (SF) 1911 E, 1912 W, E
Charton, P (Montferrand) 1940 B
Charvet, D (Toulouse) 1986 W, E, R 1, Arg 1, A, NZ 1,3, 1987 W, E, S, I, [S, R, Z, Fj, A, NZ], R, 1989 E (R), 1990 W, E, 1991 S, I
Chassagne, J (Montferrand) 1938 G 1
Chatau, A (Bayonne) 1913 SA
Chaud, E (Toulon) 1932 G, 1934 G, 1935 G
Chazalet, A (Bourgoin) 1999 Tg
Chenevay, C (Grenoble) 1968 SA 1
Chevallier, B (Montferrand) 1952 S, I, SA, W, E, It, 1953 E, W, It, 1954 S, I, NZ, W, Arg 1, 1955 S, I, E, W, It, 1956 S, I, W, It, E, Cz, 1957 S
Chiberry, J (Chambéry) 1955 It
Chilo, A (RCF) 1920 S, W, 1925 I, NZ
Cholley, G (Castres) 1975 E, S, I, SA 1,2, Arg 1,2, R, 1976 S, I, W, E, A 1,2, R, 1977 W, E, S, I, Arg 1,2, NZ 1,2, R, 1978 E, S, I, W, R, 1979 I, S
Chouly, D (Brive) 2007 NZ1(R),2
Choy J (Narbonne) 1930 S, I, E, G, W, 1931 I, 1933 G, 1934 G, 1935 G, 1936 G 2
Cigagna, A (Toulouse) 1995 [E]
Cimarosti, J (Castres) 1976 US (R)
Cistacq, J-C (Agen) 2000 R (R)
Clady, A (Lezignan) 1929 G, 1931 I, S, E, G
Clarac, H (St Girons) 1938 G 1
Claudel, R (Lyon) 1932 G, 1934 G
Clauzel, F (Béziers) 1924 E, W, 1925 W
Clavé, J (Agen) 1936 G 2, 1938 R, G 2
Claverie, H (Lourdes) 1954 NZ, W
Cléda, T (Pau) 1998 E (R), S (R), I (R), W (R), Arg 1(R), Fj (R), Arg 3(R), 1999 I (R), S
Clément, G (RCF) 1931 W
Clément, J (RCF) 1921 S, W, E, 1922 S, E, W, I, 1923 S, W, I
Clemente, M (Oloron) 1978 R, 1980 S, I
Clerc, V (Toulouse) 2002 SA, NZ, C, 2003 E 1, S, I, It (R), W (R), Arg 2, NZ, 2004 I,It,W, 2005 SA2,Tg, 2006 SA, 2007 I,W1,E1,S,E2,W2, [Nm,I,Gg(R),NZ,E,Arg 2(R)], 2008 S,I,E,It(t),W
Cluchague, L (Biarritz O) 1924 S, 1925 E
Coderc, J (Chalon) 1932 G, 1933 G, 1934 G, 1935 G, 1936 G 1
Codorniou, D (Narbonne) 1979 NZ 1,2, R, 1980 W, E, S, I, 1981 S, W, E, A 2, 1983 E, S, I, W, A 1,2, R, 1984 I, W, E, S, NZ 1,2, R, 1985 E, S, I, W, Arg 1,2
Coeurveille, C (Agen) 1992 Arg 1(R),2
Cognet, L (Montferrand) 1932 G, 1936 G 1,2, 1937 G, It
Collazo, P (Bègles) 2000 R
Colombier, J (St Junien) 1952 SA, W, E
Colomine, G (Narbonne) 1979 NZ 1
Comba, F (SF) 1998 Arg 1,2, Fj, Arg 3, 1999 I, W 1, E, S, 2000 A, NZ 1,2, 2001 S, I
Combe, J (SF) 1910 S, E, I, 1911 S
Combes, G (Fumel) 1945 B 2
Communeau, M (SF) 1906 NZ, E, 1907 E, 1908 E, W, 1909 E, W, I, 1910 S, E, I, 1911 S, E, I, 1912 I, S, W, E, 1913 SA, E, W
Condom, J (Boucau, Biarritz O) 1982 R, 1983 E, S, I, W, A 1,2, R, 1984 I, W, E, S, NZ 1,2, R, 1985 E, S, I, W, Arg 1,2, 1986 S, I, W, E, R 1, Arg 1,2, NZ 1, R 2, NZ 2,3, 1987 W, E, S, I, [S, R, Z, A, NZ], R, 1988 E, S, W, Arg 1,2,3,4, R, 1989 I, W, E, S, NZ 1,2, A 1, 1990 I, R, A 2,3(R)
Conilh de Beyssac, J-J (SBUC) 1912 I, S, 1914 I, W, E
Constant, G (Perpignan) 1920 W
Correia, P (Albi) 2008 A2
Coscolla, G (Béziers) 1921 S, W
Costantino, J (Montferrand) 1973 R
Costes, A (Montferrand) 1994 C 2, 1995 R 1, [Iv], 1997 It 1, 1999 WS, Tg (R), NZ 1, [Nm (R), Fj (R), Arg (R), NZ 2(R), A (t&R)], 2000 S (R), I
Costes, F (Montferrand) 1979 E, S, NZ 1,2, R, 1980 W, I
Couffignal, H (Colomiers) 1993 R 1
Coulon, E (Grenoble) 1928 S
Courtiols, M (Bègles) 1991 R, US 1, W 2
Coux, J-F (Bourgoin) 2007 NZ1,2
Couzinet, D (Biarritz) 2004 US,C(R), 2008 A1(R)
Crabos, R (RCF) 1920 S, E, W, I, US, 1921 S, W, E, I, 1922 S, E, W, I, 1923 S, I, 1924 S, I
Crampagne, J (Bègles) 1967 SA 4
Crancée, R (Lourdes) 1960 Arg 3, 1961 S
Crauste, M (RCF, Lourdes) 1957 R 1,2, 1958 S, E, A, W, It, I, 1959 E, It, W, I, 1960 S, E, W, I, It, R, Arg 1,3, 1961 S, SA, E, W, It, I, NZ 1,2,3, A, R, 1962 S, E, W, I, It, R, 1963 S, I, E, W, It, R, 1964 S, NZ, E, W, It, I, SA, Fj, R, 1965 S, I, E, W, It, R, 1966 S, I, E, W, It
Cremaschi, M (Lourdes) 1980 R, 1981 R, NZ 1,2, 1982 W, S, 1983 A 1,2, R, 1984 I, W
Crenca, J-J (Agen) 1996 SA 2(R), 1999 R, Tg, WS (R), NZ 1(R), 2001 SA 1,2, NZ (R), SA 3, A, Fj, 2002 It, W, E, S, I, Arg, A 2, SA, NZ, C, 2003 E 1, S, I, It, W, R, E 2, [Fj,J(t&R),S,I,E,NZ(R)], 2004 I(R),It(R),W(R),S(R),E(R)
Crichton, W H (Le Havre) 1906 NZ, E
Cristina, J (Montferrand) 1979 R
Cussac, P (Biarritz O) 1934 G
Cutzach, A (Quillan) 1929 G

Daguerre, F (Biarritz O) 1936 G 1
Daguerre, J (CASG) 1933 G
Dal Maso, M (Mont-de-Marsan, Agen, Colomiers) 1988 R (R), 1990 NZ 2, 1996 SA 1(R),2, 1997 I, W, E, S, It 1, R 1(R), A 1,2, It 2, Arg, SA 1,2, 1998 W (R), Arg 1(t), Fj (R), 1999 R (R), WS (R), Tg, NZ 1(R), W 2(R), [Nm (R), Fj (R), Arg (R), A (R)], 2000 W, E, S, I, It
Danion, J (Toulon) 1924 I
Danos, P (Toulon, Béziers) 1954 Arg 1,2, 1957 R 2, 1958 S, E, W, It, I, SA 1,2, 1959 S, E, It, W, I, 1960 S, E
Dantiacq, D (Pau) 1997 R 1
Darbos, P (Dax) 1969 R
Darracq, R (Dax) 1957 It
Darrieussecq, A (Biarritz O) 1973 E
Darrieussecq, J (Mont-de-Marsan) 1953 It
Darrouy, C (Mont-de-Marsan) 1957 I, E, W, It, R 1, 1959 E, 1961 R, 1963 S, I, E, W, It, 1964 NZ, E, W, It, I, SA, Fj, R, 1965 S, I, E, It, R, 1966 S, I, E, W, It, R, 1967 S, A, E, It, W, I, SA 1,2,4
Daudé, J (Bourgoin) 2000 S
Daudignon, G (SF) 1928 S
Dauga, B (Mont-de-Marsan) 1964 S, NZ, E, W, It, I, SA, Fj, R, 1965 S, I, E, W, It, R, 1966 S, I, E, W, It, R, 1967 S, A, E, It, W, I, SA 1,2,3,4, NZ, R, 1968 S, I, NZ 1,2,3, A, SA 1,2, R, 1969 S, I, E, R, 1970 S, I, W, E, R, 1971 S, I, E, W, SA 1,2, A 1,2, R, 1972 S, I 1, W
Dauger, J (Bayonne) 1945 B 1,2, 1953 S
Daulouède, P (Tyrosse) 1937 G, It, 1938 G 1, 1940 B
David, Y (Bourgoin) 2008 It
Debaty, V (Perpignan) 2006 R(R)
De Besombes, S (Perpignan) 1998 Arg 1(R), Fj (R)
Decamps, P (RCF) 1911 S
Dedet, J (SF) 1910 S, E, I, 1911 W, I, 1912 S, 1913 E, I
Dedeyn, P (RCF) 1906 NZ
Dedieu, P (Béziers) 1963 E, It, 1964 W, It, I, SA, Fj, R, 1965 S, I, E, W
De Gregorio, J (Grenoble) 1960 S, E, W, I, It, R, Arg 1,2, 1961 S, SA, E, W, It, I, 1962 S, E, W, 1963 S, W, It, 1964 NZ, E
Dehez, J-L (Agen) 1967 SA 2, 1969 R
De Jouvencel, E (SF) 1909 W, I
De Laborderie, M (RCF) 1921 I, 1922 I, 1925 W, E
Delage, C (Agen) 1983 S, I
De Malherbe, H (CASG) 1932 G, 1933 G
De Malmann, R (RCF) 1908 E, W, 1909 E, W, I, 1910 E, I
De Muizon, J J (SF) 1910 I
Delaigue, G (Toulon) 1973 J, R
Delaigue, Y (Toulon, Toulouse, Castres) 1994 S, NZ 2(R), C 2, 1995 I, R 1, [Tg, Iv], It, R 2(R), 1997 It 1, 2003 Arg 1,2, 2005 S,E,W,I,It,A2(R),Tg,SA3(R)
Delmotte, G (Toulon) 1999 R, Tg
Delque, A (Toulouse) 1937 It, 1938 G 1, R, G 2
De Rougemont, M (Toulon) 1995 E (t), R 1(t), [Iv], NZ 1,2, 1996 I (R), Arg 1,2, W 2, SA 1, 1997 E (R), S (R), It 1

Desbrosse, C (Toulouse) 1999 [Nm (R)], 2000 I
Descamps, P (SB) 1927 G 2
Desclaux, F (RCF) 1949 Arg 1,2, 1953 It
Desclaux, J (Perpignan) 1934 G, 1935 G, 1936 G 1,2, 1937 G, It, 1938 G 1, R, G 2, 1945 B 1
Deslandes, C (RCF) 1990 A 1, NZ 2, 1991 W 1, 1992 R, Arg 1,2
Desnoyer, L (Brive) 1974 R
Destarac, L (Tarbes) 1926 S, I, E, W, M, 1927 W, E, G 1,2
Desvouges, R (SF) 1914 W
Detrez, P-E (Nîmes) 1983 A 2(R), 1986 Arg 1(R),2, A (R), NZ1
Devergie, T (Nîmes) 1988 R, 1989 NZ 1,2, B, A 2, 1990 W, E, S, I, R, A 1,2,3, 1991 US 2, W 2, 1992 R (R), Arg 2(R)
De Villiers, P (SF) 1999 W 2, [Arg (R), NZ 2(R), A (R)], 2000 W (R), E (R), S (R), I (R), It (R), NZ 1(R),2, 2001 S, I, It, W, E, SA 1,2, NZ (R), SA 3, A, Fj, 2002 It, W, E, I, SA, NZ, C, 2003 Arg 1,2, NZ (R), 2004 I,It,W,S,E,US,C,NZ, 2005 S,I(R),It(R),SA1(R),2,A1(R),2,C,Tg(R),SA3, 2006 S,I,It,E,W,SA,NZ1,2,Arg, 2007 It,I,E1,S,W2, [Arg1,Nm,I,NZ,E]
Deygas, M (Vienne) 1937 It
Deylaud, C (Toulouse) 1992 R, Arg 1,2, SA 1, 1994 C 1, NZ 1,2, 1995 W, E, S, [Iv (R), S, I, SA], It, Arg
Diarra, I (Montauban) 2008 It
Dintrans, P (Tarbes) 1979 NZ 1,2, R, 1980 E, S, I, SA, R, 1981 S, I, W, E, A 1,2, R, NZ 1,2, 1982 W, E, S, I, R, Arg 1,2, 1983 E, W, A 1,2, R, 1984 I, W, E, S, NZ 1,2, R, 1985 E, S, I, W, Arg 1,2, 1987 [R], 1988 Arg 1,2,3, 1989 W, E, S, 1990 R
Dispagne, S (Toulouse) 1996 I (R), W 1
Dizabo, P (Tyrosse) 1948 A, S, E, 1949 S, I, E, W, Arg 2, 1950 S, I, 1960 Arg 1,2,3
Domec, A (Carcassonne) 1929 W
Domec, H (Lourdes) 1953 W, It, 1954 S, I, NZ, W, E, It, 1955 S, I, E, W, 1956 I, W, It, 1958 E, A, W, It, I
Domenech, A (Vichy, Brive) 1954 W, E, It, 1955 S, I, E, W, 1956 S, I, W, It, E, Cz, 1957 S, I, E, W, It, R 1,2, 1958 S, E, It, 1959 It, 1960 S, E, W, I, It, R, Arg 1,2,3, 1961 S, SA, E, W, It, I, NZ 1,2,3, A, R, 1962 S, E, W, I, It, R, 1963 W, It
Domercq, J (Bayonne) 1912 I, S
Dominici, C (SF) 1998 E, S, Arg 1,2, 1999 E, S, WS, NZ 1, W 2, [C, Fj, Arg, NZ 2, A], 2000 W, E, S, R, 2001 I (R), It, W, E, SA 1,2, NZ, Fj, 2003 Arg 1, R, E 2,3, [Fj,J,S,I,E], 2004 I,It,W,S,E,A(R),NZ(R), 2005 S,E,W,I,It, 2006 S,I,It,E,W,NZ1,2(R),Arg, 2007 It,I,W1,E1,S(R),E3,W2(R), [Arg 1,Gg,NZ(R),E(R),Arg 2]
Dorot, J (RCF) 1935 G
Dospital, P (Bayonne) 1977 R, 1980 I, 1981 S, I, W, E, 1982 I, R, Arg 1,2, 1983 E, S, I, W, 1984 E, S, NZ 1,2, R, 1985 E, S, I, W, Arg 1
Dourthe, C (Dax) 1966 R, 1967 S, A, E, W, I, SA 1,2,3, NZ, 1968 W, NZ 3, SA 1,2, 1969 W, 1971 SA 2(R), R, 1972 I 1,2, A 1,2, R, 1973 S, NZ, E, 1974 I, Arg 1,2, SA 1,2, 1975 W, E, S
Dourthe, M (Dax) 2000 NZ 2(t)
Dourthe, R (Dax, SF, Béziers) 1995 R 2, Arg, NZ 1,2, 1996 E, R, 1996 Arg 1,2, W 2, SA 1,2, 1997 W, A 1, 1999 I, W 1,2, [C, Nm, Fj, Arg, NZ 2, A], 2000 W, E, It, R, A, NZ 1,2, 2001 S, I
Doussau, E (Angoulêlme) 1938 R
Droitecourt, M (Montferrand) 1972 R, 1973 NZ (R), E, 1974 E, S, Arg 1, SA 2, 1975 SA 1,2, Arg 1,2, R, 1976 S, I, W, A 1, 1977 Arg 2
Dubertrand, A (Montferrand) 1971 A 1,2, R, 1972 I 2, 1974 I, W, E, SA 2, 1975 Arg 1,2, R, 1976 S, US
Dubois, D (Bègles) 1971 S
Dubroca, D (Agen) 1979 NZ 2, 1981 NZ 2(R), 1982 E, S, 1984 W, E, S, 1985 Arg 2, 1986 S, I, W, E, R 1, Arg 2, A, NZ 1, R 2, NZ 2,3, 1987 W, E, S, I, [S, Z, Fj, A, NZ], R, 1988 E, S, I, W
Duché, A (Limoges) 1929 G
Duclos, A (Lourdes) 1931 S
Ducousso, J (Tarbes) 1925 S, W, E
Dufau, G (RCF) 1948 I, A, 1949 I, W, 1950 S, E, W, 1951 S, I, E, W, 1952 SA, W, 1953 S, I, E, W, 1954 S, I, NZ, W, E, It, 1955 S, I, E, W, It, 1956 S, I, W, It, 1957 S, I, E, W, It, R 1
Dufau, J (Biarritz) 1912 I, S, W, E
Duffaut, Y (Agen) 1954 Arg 1,2
Duffour, R (Tarbes) 1911 W
Dufourcq, J (SBUC) 1906 NZ, E, 1907 E, 1908 W
Duhard, Y (Bagnères) 1980 E
Duhau, J (SF) 1928 I,1930 I, G, 1931 I, S, W, 1933 G
Dulaurens, C (Toulouse) 1926 I, 1928 S, 1929 W
Duluc, A (Béziers) 1934 G
Du Manoir, Y le P (RCF) 1925 I, NZ, S, W, E, 1926 S, 1927 I, S
Dupont, C (Lourdes) 1923 S, W, I, 1924 S, I, W, R, US, 1925 S, 1927 E, G 1,2, 1928 A, G, W, 1929 I
Dupont, J-L (Agen) 1983 S
Dupont, L (RCF) 1934 G, 1935 G, 1936 G 1,2, 1938 R, G 2
Dupouy, A (SB) 1924 W, R
Duprat, B (Bayonne) 1966 E, W, It, R, 1967 S, A, E, SA 2,3, 1968 S, I, 1972 E, W, I 2, A 1
Dupré, P (RCF) 1909 W
Dupuy, J (Tarbes) 1956 S, I, W, It, E, Cz, 1957 S, I, E, W, It, R 2, 1958 S, E, SA 1,2, 1959 S, E, It, W, I, 1960 W, I, It, Arg 1,3, 1961 S, SA, E, NZ 2, R, 1962 S, E, W, I, It, 1963 W, It, R, 1964 S
Durand, N (Perpignan) 2007 NZ1,2
Dusautoir, T (Biarritz, Toulouse) 2006 R,SA,NZ1, 2007 E3,W2(R), [Nm,I,NZ,E,Arg 2], 2008 S,I,E,W
Du Souich, C J (see Judas du Souich)
Dutin, B (Mont-de-Marsan) 1968 NZ 2, A, SA 2, R
Dutour, F X (Toulouse) 1911 E, I, 1912 S, W, E, 1913 S
Dutrain, H (Toulouse) 1945 W, 1946 B, I, 1947 E, 1949 I, E, W, Arg 1
Dutrey, J (Lourdes) 1940 B
Duval, R (SF) 1908 E, W, 1909 E, 1911 E, W, I

Echavé, L (Agen) 1961 S
Elhorga, P (Agen) 2001 NZ, 2002 A 1,2, 2003 Arg 2, NZ (R), R, [Fj(R),US,I(R),NZ], 2004 I(R),It(R),S,E, 2005 S,E, 2006 NZ2,Arg, 2008 A1
Elissalde, E (Bayonne) 1936 G 2, 1940 B
Elissalde, J-B (La Rochelle, Toulouse) 2000 S (R), R (R), 2003 It (R), W (R), 2004 I,It,W,A,Arg, 2005 SA1,2(R),A1,2,SA3, 2006 S,I,It,W(R),NZ1(R),2, 2007 E2(R),3,W2(R), [Arg 1(R),Nm,I,Gg(R),NZ,E,Arg 2], 2008 S,I,W
Elissalde, J-P (La Rochelle) 1980 SA, R, 1981 A 1,2, R
Empereur-Buisson, H (Béziers) 1931 E, G
Erbani, D (Agen) 1981 A 1,2, NZ 1,2, 1982 Arg 1,2, 1983 S (R), I, W, A 1,2, R, 1984 W, E, R, 1985 E, W (R), Arg 2, 1986 S, I, W, E, R 1, Arg 2, NZ 1,2(R),3, 1987 W, E, S, I, [S, R, Fj, A, NZ], 1988 E, S, 1989 I (R), W, E, S, NZ 1, A 2, 1990 W, E
Escaffre, P (Narbonne) 1933 G, 1934 G
Escommier, M (Montelimar) 1955 It
Esponda, J-M (RCF) 1967 SA 1,2, R, 1968 NZ 1,2, SA 2, R, 1969 S, I (R), E
Estève, A (Béziers) 1971 SA 1, 1972 I 1, E, W, I 2, A 2, R, 1973 S, NZ, E, I, 1974 I, W, E, S, R, SA 1,2, 1975 W, E
Estève, P (Narbonne, Lavelanet) 1982 R, Arg 1,2, 1983 E, S, I, W, A 1,2, R, 1984 I, W, E, S, NZ 1,2, R, 1985 E, S, I, W, 1986 S, I, 1987 [S, Z]
Etcheberry, J (Rochefort, Cognac) 1923 W, I, 1924 S, I, E, W, R, US, 1926 S, I, E, M, 1927 I, S, W, G 2
Etchenique, J-M (Biarritz O) 1974 R, SA 1, 1975 E, Arg 2
Etchepare, A (Bayonne) 1922 I
Etcheverry, M (Pau) 1971 S, I
Eutrope, A (SCUF) 1913 I

Fabre, E (Toulouse) 1937 It, 1938 G 1,2
Fabre, J (Toulouse) 1963 S, I, E, W, It, 1964 S, NZ, E
Fabre, L (Lezignan) 1930 G
Fabre, M (Béziers) 1981 A 1, R, NZ 1,2, 1982 I, R
Failliot, P (RCF) 1911 S, W, I, 1912 I, S, E, 1913 E, W
Fargues, G (Dax) 1923 I
Fauré, F (Tarbes) 1914 I, W, E
Faure, L (Sale) 2008 S,I,E,A1
Fauvel, J-P (Tulle) 1980 R
Favre, M (Lyon) 1913 E, W
Ferrand, L (Chalon) 1940 B

Ferrien, R (Tarbes) 1950 S, I, E, W
Finat, R (CASG) 1932 G, 1933 G
Fite, R (Brive) 1963 W, It
Floch, A (Clermont-Auvergne) 2008 E(R),It,W
Forest, M (Bourgoin) 2007 NZ1(R),2(R)
Forestier, J (SCUF) 1912 W
Forgues, F (Bayonne) 1911 S, E, W, 1912 I, W, E, 1913 S, SA, W, 1914 I, E
Fort, J (Agen) 1967 It, W, I, SA 1,2,3,4
Fourcade, G (BEC) 1909 E, W
Foures, H (Toulouse) 1951 S, I, E, W
Fournet, F (Montferrand) 1950 W
Fouroux, J (La Voulte) 1972 I 2, R, 1974 W, E, Arg 1,2, R, SA 1,2, 1975 W, Arg 1, R, 1976 S, I, W, E, US, A 1, 1977 W, E, S, I, Arg 1,2, NZ 1,2, R
Francquenelle, A (Vaugirard) 1911 S, 1913 W, I
Fritz, F (Toulouse) 2005 SA1,A2,SA3, 2006 S,I,It,E,W,SA,NZ1,2,Arg, 2007 It
Froment, R (Castres) 2004 US(R)
Furcade, R (Perpignan) 1952 S

Gabernet, S (Toulouse) 1980 E, S, 1981 S, I, W, E, A 1,2, R, NZ 1,2, 1982 I, 1983 A 2, R
Gachassin, J (Lourdes) 1961 S, I, 1963 R, 1964 S, NZ, E, W, It, I, SA, Fj, R, 1965 S, I, E, W, It, R, 1966 S, I, E, W, 1967 S, A, It, W, I, NZ, 1968 I, E, 1969 S, I
Galasso, A (Toulon, Montferrand) 2000 R (R), 2001 E (R)
Galau, H (Toulouse) 1924 S, I, E, W, US
Galia, J (Quillan) 1927 E, G 1,2, 1928 S, A, I, E, W, 1929 I, E, G, 1930 S, I, E, G, W, 1931 S, W, E, G
Gallart, P (Béziers) 1990 R, A 1,2(R),3, 1992 S, I, R, Arg 1,2, SA 1,2, Arg, 1994 I, W, E, 1995 I (t), R 1, [Tg]
Gallion, J (Toulon) 1978 E, S, I, W, 1979 I, W, E, S, NZ 2, R, 1980 W, E, S, I, 1983 A 1,2, R, 1984 I, W, E, S, R, 1985 E, S, I, W, 1986 Arg 2
Galthié, F (Colomiers, SF) 1991 R, US 1, [R, Fj, C, E], 1992 W, E, S, R, Arg, 1994 I, W, E, 1995 [SA, E], 1996 W 1(R), 1997 I, It 2, SA 1,2, 1998 W (R), Fj (R), 1999 R, WS (R), Tg, NZ 1(R), [Fj (R), Arg, NZ 2, A], 2000 W, E, A, NZ 1,2, 2001 S, It, W, E, SA 1,2, NZ, SA 3, A, Fj, 2002 E, S, I, SA, NZ, C, 2003 E 1, S, Arg 1,2, NZ, R, E 2, [Fj,J,S,I,E]
Galy, J (Perpignan) 1953 W
Garbajosa, X (Toulouse) 1998 I, W, Arg 2(R), Fj, 1999 W 1(R), E, S, WS, NZ 1, W 2, [C, Nm (R), Fj (R), Arg, NZ 2, A], 2000 A, NZ 1,2, 2001 S, I, E, 2002 It (R), W, SA (R), C (R), 2003 E 1, S, I, It, W, E 3
Garuet-Lempirou, J-P (Lourdes) 1983 A 1,2, R, 1984 I, NZ 1,2, R, 1985 E, S, I, W, Arg 1, 1986 S, I, W, E, R 1, Arg 1, NZ 1, R 2, NZ 2,3, 1987 W, E, S, I, [S, R, Fj, A, NZ], 1988 E, S, Arg 1,2, R, 1989 E (R), S, NZ 1,2, 1990 W, E
Gasc, J (Graulhet) 1977 NZ 2
Gasparotto, G (Montferrand) 1976 A 2, R
Gauby, G (Perpignan) 1956 Cz
Gaudermen, P (RCF) 1906 E
Gayraud, W (Toulouse) 1920 I
Gelez, F (Agen) 2001 SA 3, 2002 I (R), A 1, SA, NZ, C (R), 2003 S, I
Geneste, R (BEC) 1945 B 1, 1949 Arg 2
Genet, J-P (RCF) 1992 S, I, R
Gensane, R (Béziers) 1962 S, E, W, I, It, R, 1963 S
Gérald, G (RCF) 1927 E, G 2, 1928 S, 1929 I, S, W, E, G, 1930 S, I, E, G, W, 1931 I, S, E, G
Gérard, D (Bègles) 1999 Tg
Gérintes, G (CASG) 1924 R, 1925 I, 1926 W
Geschwind, P (RCF) 1936 G 1,2
Giacardy, M (SBUC) 1907 E
Gimbert, P (Bègles) 1991 R, US 1, 1992 W, E
Giordani, P (Dax) 1999 E, S
Glas, S (Bourgoin) 1996 S (t), I (R), W 1, R, Arg 2(R), W 2, SA 1,2, 1997 I, W, E, S, It 2(R), R 2, Arg, SA 1,2, 1998 E, S, I, W, Arg 1,2, Fj, Arg 3, A, 1999 W 2, [C,Nm, Arg (R), NZ 2(R), A (t&R)], 2000 I, 2001 E, SA 1,2, NZ
Gomès, A (SF) 1998 Arg 1,2, Fj, Arg 3, A, 1999 I (R)
Gommes, J (RCF) 1909 I
Gonnet, C-A (Albi) 1921 E, I, 1922 E, W, 1924 S, E, 1926 S, I, E, W, M, 1927 I, S, W, E, G 1
Gonzalez, J-M (Bayonne) 1992 Arg 1,2, SA 1,2, Arg, 1993 R 1, SA 1,2, R 2, A 1,2, 1994 I, W, E, S, C 1, NZ 1,2, C 2, 1995 W, E, S, I, R 1, [Tg, S, I, SA, E], It, Arg, 1996 E, S, I, W 1
Got, R (Perpignan) 1920 I, US, 1921 S, W, 1922 S, E, W, I, 1924 I, E, W, R, US
Gourdon, J-F (RCF, Bagnères) 1974 S, Arg 1,2, R, SA 1,2, 1975 W, E, S, I, R, 1976 S, I, W, E, 1978 E, S, 1979 W, E, S, R, 1980 I
Gourragne, J-F (Béziers) 1990 NZ 2, 1991 W 1
Goutta, B (Perpignan) 2004 C
Goyard, A (Lyon U) 1936 G 1,2, 1937 G, It, 1938 G 1, R, G 2
Graciet, R (SBUC) 1926 I, W, 1927 S, G 1, 1929 E, 1930 W
Grandclaude, J-P (Perpignan) 2005 E(R),W(R), 2007 NZ1
Graou, S (Auch, Colomiers) 1992 Arg (R), 1993 SA 1,2, R 2, A 2(R), 1995 R 2, Arg (t), NZ 2(R)
Gratton, J (Agen) 1984 NZ 2, R, 1985 E, S, I, W, Arg 1,2, 1986 S, NZ 1
Graule, V (Arl Perpignan) 1926 I, E, W, 1927 S, W, 1931 G
Greffe, M (Grenoble) 1968 W, Cz, NZ 1,2, SA 1
Griffard, J (Lyon U) 1932 G, 1933 G, 1934 G
Gruarin, A (Toulon) 1964 W, It, I, SA, Fj, R, 1965 S, I, E, W, It, 1966 S, I, E, W, It, R, 1967 S, A, E, It, W, I, NZ, 1968 S, I
Guélorget, P (RCF) 1931 E, G
Guichemerre, A (Dax) 1920 E, 1921 E, I, 1923 S
Guilbert, A (Toulon) 1975 E, S, I, SA 1,2, 1976 A 1, 1977 Arg 1,2, NZ 1,2, R, 1979 I, W, E
Guillemin, P (RCF) 1908 E, W, 1909 E, I, 1910 W, S, E, I, 1911 S, E, W
Guilleux, P (Agen) 1952 SA, It
Guirado, G (Perpignan) 2008 It(R)
Guiral, M (Agen) 1931 G, 1932 G, 1933 G
Guiraud, H (Nîmes) 1996 R

Haget, A (PUC) 1953 E, 1954 I, NZ, E, Arg 2, 1955 E, W, It, 1957 I, E, It, R 1, 1958 It, SA 2
Haget, F (Agen, Biarritz O) 1974 Arg 1,2, 1975 SA 2, Arg 1,2, R, 1976 S, 1978 S, I, W, R, 1979 I, W, E, S, NZ 1,2, R, 1980 W, S, I, 1984 S, NZ 1,2, R, 1985 E, S, I, 1986 S, I, W, E, R 1, Arg 1, A, NZ 1, 1987 S, I, [R, Fj]
Haget, H (CASG) 1928 S, 1930 G
Halet, R (Strasbourg) 1925 NZ, S, W
Hall, S (Béziers) 2002 It, W
Harinordoquy, I (Pau, Biarritz)) 2002 W, E, S, I, A 1,2, SA, NZ, C, 2003 E 1, S, I, It, W, Arg 1(R),2, NZ, R, E 2,3(R), [Fj,S,I,E], 2004 I,It,W,E,A,Arg,NZ, 2005 W(R),2006 R(R),SA, 2007 It(R),I,W1(R),E1(R),S,E3,W2, [Arg 1,Nm(R),NZ(R),E(R), Arg 2], 2008 A1,2
Harislur-Arthapignet, P (Tarbes) 1988 Arg 4(R)
Harize, D (Cahors, Toulouse) 1975 SA 1,2, 1976 A 1,2, R, 1977 W, E, S, I
Hauc, J (Toulon) 1928 E, G, 1929 I, S, G
Hauser, M (Lourdes) 1969 E
Hedembaigt, M (Bayonne) 1913 S, SA, 1914 W
Hericé, D (Bègles) 1950 I
Herrero, A (Toulon) 1963 R, 1964 NZ, E, W, It, I, SA, Fj, R, 1965 S, I, E, W, 1966 W, It, R, 1967 S, A, E, It, I, R
Herrero, B (Nice) 1983 I, 1986 Arg 1
Heyer, F (Montferrand) 1990 A 2
Heymans, C (Agen, Toulouse) 2000 It (R) R, 2002 A 2(R), SA, NZ, 2004 W(R),US,C(R),A,Arg,NZ, 2005 I,It,SA1,2,A1,2,C,SA3, 2006 S,I,W(R),R,SA,NZ2,Arg, 2007 It,I(R),E1(R),S,E3,W2, [Arg 1,Nm,I,NZ,E], 2008 S,I,E,W(R)
Hiquet, J-C (Agen) 1964 E
Hoche, M (PUC) 1957 I, E, W, It, R 1
Hondagné-Monge, M (Tarbes) 1988 Arg 2(R)
Hontas, P (Biarritz) 1990 S, I, R, 1991 R, 1992 Arg, 1993 E, S, I, W
Hortoland, J-P (Béziers) 1971 A 2
Houblain, H (SCUF) 1909 E, 1910 W
Houdet, R (SF) 1927 S, W, G 1, 1928 G, W, 1929 I, S, E, 1930 S, E
Hourdebaigt, A (SBUC) 1909 I, 1910 W, S, E, I
Hubert, A (ASF) 1906 E, 1907 E, 1908 E, W, 1909 E, W, I
Hueber, A (Lourdes, Toulon) 1990 A 3, NZ 1, 1991 US 2, 1992 I, Arg 1,2, SA 1,2, 1993 E, S, I, W, R 1, SA 1,2, R 2, A 1,2, 1995 [Tg, S (R), I], 2000 It, R

Hutin, R (CASG) 1927 I, S, W
Hyardet, A (Castres) 1995 It, Arg (R)

Ibañez, R (Dax, Perpignan, Castres, Saracens, Wasps) 1996 W 1(R), 1997 It 1(R), R 1, It 2(R), R 2, SA 2(R), 1998 E, S, I, W, Arg 1,2, Fj, Arg 3, A, 1999 I, W 1, E, S, R, WS, Tg (R), NZ 1, W 2, [C, Nm, Fj, Arg, NZ 2, A], 2000 W (R), E (R), S (R), I (R), It (R), R, 2001 S, I, It, W, E, SA 1,2, NZ (R), SA 3, A, Fj, 2002 It (R), W, E, S, I, Arg, A 1(R),2, SA, NZ, C, 2003 E 1, S, I, It, W, R (R), E 2(R),3, [Fj,J(R),S,I,E,NZ(R)], 2005 C(R),Tg, 2006 I,It,E,W,R,SA(R), NZ1(R),2,Arg, 2007 It,I,W1,E1,S,NZ1(R),2(R),E2,3, [Arg 1,Nm(R),I,NZ,E,Arg 2]
Icard, J (SF) 1909 E, W
Iguiniz, E (Bayonne) 1914 E
Ihingoué, D (BEC) 1912 I, S
Imbernon, J-F (Perpignan) 1976 I, W, E, US, A 1, 1977 W, E, S, I, Arg 1,2, NZ 1,2, 1978 E, R, 1979 I, 1981 S, I, W, E, 1982 I, 1983 I, W
Iraçabal, J (Bayonne) 1968 NZ 1,2, SA 1, 1969 S, I, W, R, 1970 S, I, W, E, R, 1971 W, SA 1,2, A 1, 1972 E, W, I 2, A 2, R, 1973 S, NZ, E, W, I, J, 1974 I, W, E, S, Arg 1,2, SA 2(R)
Isaac, H (RCF) 1907 E, 1908 E
Ithurra, E (Biarritz O) 1936 G 1,2, 1937 G

Jacquet, L (Clermont-Auvergne) 2006 NZ2(R),Arg, 2008 S,I(t&R)
Janeczek, T (Tarbes) 1982 Arg 1,2, 1990 R
Janik, K (Toulouse) 1987 R
Janin, D (Bourgoin) 2008 A1(R),2
Jarasse, A (Brive) 1945 B 1
Jardel, J (SB) 1928 I, E
Jauréguy, A (RCF, Toulouse, SF) 1920 S, E, W, I, US, 1922 S, W, 1923 S, W, E, I, 1924 S, W, R, US, 1925 I, NZ, 1926 S, E, W, M, 1927 I, E, 1928 S, A, E, G, W, 1929 I, S, E
Jauréguy, P (Toulouse) 1913 S, SA, W, I
Jauzion, Y (Colomiers, Toulouse) 2001 SA 1,2, NZ, 2002 A 1(R),2(R), 2003 Arg 2, NZ, R, E 2,3, [Fj,S,I,E], 2004 I,It,W,S,E,A,Arg,NZ(t), 2005 W,I,It,SA1,2,A1,2,C,Tg(R),SA3, 2006 R,SA,NZ1,2,Arg, 2007 It,I,W1,E1,S,E3,W2, [Arg 1,Nm(R),I(R),Gg,NZ,E], 2008 It,W
Jeangrand, M-H (Tarbes) 1921 I
Jeanjean, N (Toulouse) 2001 SA 1,2, NZ, SA 3(R), A (R), Fj (R), 2002 It, Arg, A 1
Jeanjean, P (Toulon) 1948 I
Jérôme, G (SF) 1906 NZ, E
Joinel, J-L (Brive) 1977 NZ 1, 1978 R, 1979 I, W, E, S, NZ 1,2, R, 1980 W, E, S, I, SA, 1981 S, I, W, E, R, NZ 1,2, 1982 E, S, I, R, 1983 E, S, I, W, A 1,2, R, 1984 I, W, E, S, NZ 1,2, 1985 S, I, W, Arg 1, 1986 S, I, W, E, R 1, Arg 1,2, A, 1987 [Z]
Jol, M (Biarritz O) 1947 S, I, W, E, 1949 S, I, E, W, Arg 1,2
Jordana, J-L (Pau, Toulouse) 1996 R (R), Arg 1(t),2, W 2, 1997 I (t), W, S (R)
Judas du Souich, C (SCUF) 1911 W, I
Juillet, C (Montferrand, SF) 1995 R 2, Arg, 1999 E, S, WS, NZ 1, [C, Fj, Arg, NZ 2, A], 2000 A, NZ 1,2, 2001 S, I, It, W
Junquas, L (Tyrosse) 1945 B 1,2, W, 1946 B, I, K, W, 1947 S, I, W, E, 1948 S, W

Kaczorowski, D (Le Creusot) 1974 I (R)
Kaempf, A (St Jean-de-Luz) 1946 B
Kayser, B (Leicester) 2008 A1(R),2(R)

Labadie, P (Bayonne) 1952 S, I, SA, W, E, It, 1953 S, I, It, 1954 S, I, NZ, W, E, Arg 2, 1955 S, I, E, W, 1956 I, 1957 I
Labarthète, R (Pau) 1952 S
Labazuy, A (Lourdes) 1952 I, 1954 S, W, 1956 E, 1958 A, W, I, 1959 S, E, It, W
Labit, C (Toulouse) 1999 S, R (R), WS (R), Tg, 2000 R (R), 2002 Arg, A 1(R), 2003 Arg 1,2, NZ (R), R (R), E 3, [Fj(R),J,US,E(R),NZ]
Laborde, C (RCF) 1962 It, R, 1963 R, 1964 SA, 1965 E
Labrousse, T (Brive) 1996 R, SA 1
Lacans, P (Béziers) 1980 SA, 1981 W, E, A 2, R, 1982 W
Lacassagne, H (SBUC) 1906 NZ, 1907 E
Lacaussade, R (Bègles) 1948 A, S
Lacaze, C (Lourdes, AngoulêÎme) 1961 NZ 2,3, A, R, 1962 E, W, I, It, 1963 W, R, 1964 S, NZ, E, 1965 It, R, 1966 S, I, E, W, It, R, 1967 S, E, SA 1,3,4, R, 1968 S, E, W, Cz, NZ 1, 1969 E
Lacaze, H (Périgueux) 1928 I, G, W, 1929 I, W
Lacaze, P (Lourdes) 1958 SA 1,2, 1959 S, E, It, W, I
Lacazedieu, C (Dax) 1923 W, I, 1928 A, I, 1929 S
Lacombe, B (Agen) 1989 B, 1990 A 2
Lacome, M (Pau) 1960 Arg 2
Lacoste, R (Tarbes) 1914 I, W, E
Lacrampe, F (Béziers) 1949 Arg 2
Lacroix, P (Mont-de-Marsan, Agen) 1958 A, 1960 W, I, It, R, Arg 1,2,3, 1961 S, SA, E, W, I, NZ 1,2,3, A, R, 1962 S, E, W, I, R, 1963 S, I, E, W
Lacroix, T (Dax, Harlequins) 1989 A 1(R),2, 1991 W 1(R),2(R), [R, C (R), E], 1992 SA 2, 1993 E, S, I, W, SA 1,2, R 2, A 1,2, 1994 I, W, E, S, C 1, NZ 1,2, C 2, 1995 W, E, S, R 1, [Tg, Iv, S, I, SA, E], 1996 E, S, I, 1997 It 2, R 2, Arg, SA 1,2
Lacroix, T (Albi) 2008 A1(R),2
Lafarge, Y (Montferrand) 1978 R, 1979 NZ 1, 1981 I (R)
Laffitte, R (SCUF) 1910 W, S
Laffont, H (Narbonne) 1926 W
Lafond, A (Bayonne) 1922 E
Lafond, J-B (RCF) 1983 A 1, 1985 Arg 1,2 1986 S, I, W, E, R 1, 1987 I (R), 1988 W, 1989 I, W, E, 1990 W, A 3(R), NZ 2, 1991 S, I, W 1, E, R, US 1, W 2, [R (R), Fj, C, E], 1992 W, E, S, I (R), SA 2, 1993 E, S, I, W
Lagisquet, P (Bayonne) 1983 A 1,2, R, 1984 I, W, NZ 1,2, 1986 R 1(R), Arg 1,2, A, NZ 1, 1987 [S, R, Fj, A, NZ], R, 1988 S, I, W, Arg 1,2,3,4, R, 1989 I, W, E, S, NZ 1,2, B, A 1,2, 1990 W, E, S, I, A 1,2,3, 1991 S, I, US 2, [R]
Lagrange, J-C (RCF) 1966 It
Laharrague, J (Brive, Perpignan, Sale) 2005 W,I,It,SA1,A1, 2,C(R),Tg, 2006 R(R),SA,NZ1, 2007 NZ2
Laharrague, N (Perpignan) 2007 NZ1(R),2(R)
Lalande, M (RCF) 1923 S, W, I
Lalanne, F (Mont-de-Marsan) 2000 R
Lamaison, C (Brive, Agen) 1996 SA 1(R),2, 1997 W, E, S, R 1, A 2, It 2, R 2, Arg, SA 1,2, 1998 E, S, I, W, Arg 3(R), A, 1999 R, WS (R), Tg, NZ 1(R), W 2(R), [C (R), Nm, Fj, Arg, NZ 2, A], 2000 W, A, NZ 1,2, 2001 S, I, It, W (R)
Lamboley, G (Toulouse) 2005 S(R),E(R),W(R),I(R),It(R), SA1(R),2(R),A1,2(R),C(R),Tg,SA3(R), 2007 W1(R)
Landreau, F (SF) 2000 A, NZ 1,2, 2001 E (R)
Lane, G (RCF) 1906 NZ, E, 1907 E, 1908 E, W, 1909 E, W, I, 1910 W, E, 1911 S, W, 1912 I, W, E, 1913 S
Langlade, J-C (Hyères) 1990 R, A 1, NZ 1
Laperne, D (Dax) 1997 R 1(R)
Laporte, G (Graulhet) 1981 I, W, E, R, NZ 1,2, 1986 S, I, W, E, R 1, Arg 1, A (R), 1987 [R, Z (R), Fj]
Larreguy, G (Bayonne) 1954 It
Larribau, J (Périgueux) 1912 I, S, W, E, 1913 S, 1914 I, E
Larrieu, J (Tarbes) 1920 I, US, 1921 W, 1923 S, W, E, I
Larrieux, M (SBUC) 1927 G 2
Larrue, H (Carmaux) 1960 W, I, It, R, Arg 1,2,3
Lasaosa, P (Dax) 1950 I, 1952 S, I, E, It, 1955 It
Lascubé, G (Agen) 1991 S, I, W 1, E, US 2, W 2, [R, Fj, C, E], 1992 W, E
Lassegue, J-B (Toulouse) 1946 W, 1947 S, I, W, 1948 W, 1949 I, E, W, Arg 1
Lasserre, F (René) (Bayonne, Cognac, Grenoble) 1914 I, 1920 S, 1921 S, W, I, 1922 S, E, W, I, 1923 W, E, 1924 S, I, R, US
Lasserre, J-C (Dax) 1963 It, 1964 S, NZ, E, W, It, I, Fj, 1965 W, It, R, 1966 R, 1967 S
Lasserre, M (Agen) 1967 SA 2,3, 1968 E, W, Cz, NZ 3, A, SA 1,2, 1969 S, I, E, 1970 E, 1971 E, W
Laterrade, G (Tarbes) 1910 E, I, 1911 S, E, I
Laudouar, J (Soustons, SBUC) 1961 NZ 1,2, R, 1962 I, R
Lauga, P (Vichy) 1950 S, I, E, W
Laurent, A (Biarritz O) 1925 NZ, S, W, E, 1926 W
Laurent, J (Bayonne) 1920 S, E, W
Laurent, M (Auch) 1932 G, 1933 G, 1934 G, 1935 G, 1936 G 1

FRANCE

Laussucq, C (SF) 1999 S (R), 2000 W (R), S, I
Lavail, G (Perpignan) 1937 G, 1940 B
Lavaud, R (Carcassonne) 1914 I, W
Lavergne, P (Limoges) 1950 S
Lavigne, B (Agen) 1984 R, 1985 E
Lavigne, J (Dax) 1920 E, W
Laziès, H (Auch) 1954 Arg 2, 1955 It, 1956 E, 1957 S
Le Bourhis, R (La Rochelle) 1961 R
Lecointre, M (Nantes) 1952 It
Le Corvec, G (Perpignan) 2007 NZ1
Lecouls, B (Biarritz) 2008 A1,2(R)
Le Droff, J (Auch) 1963 It, R, 1964 S, NZ, E, 1970 E, R, 1971 S, I
Lefèvre, R (Brive) 1961 NZ 2
Leflamand, L (Bourgoin) 1996 SA 2, 1997 W, E, S, It 2, Arg, SA 1,2(R)
Lefort, J-B (Biarritz O) 1938 G 1
Le Goff, R (Métro) 1938 R, G 2
Legrain, M (SF) 1909 I, 1910 I, 1911 S, E, W, I, 1913 S, SA, E, I, 1914 I, W
Lemeur, Y (RCF) 1993 R 1
Lenient, J-J (Vichy) 1967 R
Lepatey, J (Mazamet) 1954 It, 1955 S, I, E, W
Lepatey, L (Mazamet) 1924 S, I, E
Lescarboura, J-P (Dax) 1982 W, E, S, I, 1983 A 1,2, R, 1984 I, W, E, S, NZ 1,2, R, 1985 E, S, I, W, Arg 1,2, 1986 Arg 2, A, NZ 1, R 2, NZ 2, 1988 S, W, 1990 R
Lesieur, E (SF) 1906 E, 1908 E, W, 1909 E, W, I, 1910 S, E, I, 1911 E, I, 1912 W
Leuvielle, M (SBUC) 1908 W, 1913 S, SA, E, W, 1914 W, E
Levasseur, R (SF) 1925 W, E
Levée, H (RCF) 1906 NZ
Lewis, E W (Le Havre) 1906 E
Lhermet, J-M (Montferrand) 1990 S, I, 1993 R 1
Libaros, G (Tarbes) 1936 G 1, 1940 B
Liebenberg, B (SF) 2003 R (R), E 2(R),3, [US,I(R),NZ(R)], 2004 I(R),US,C,NZ, 2005 S,E
Lièvremont, M (Perpignan, SF) 1995 It, R 2, Arg (R), NZ 2(R), 1996 R, Arg 1(R), SA 2(R), 1997 R 1, A 2(R), 1998 E (R), S, I, W, Arg 1,2, Fj, Arg 3, A, 1999 W 2, [C, Nm, Fj, Arg, NZ 2, A]
Lièvremont, M (Dax) 2008 A1(R),2
Lièvremont, T (Perpignan, SF, Biarritz) 1996 W 2(R), 1998 E, S, I, W, Arg 1,2, Fj, Arg 3, A, 1999 I, W 1, E, W 2, [Nm], 2000 W (R), E (R), S (R), I, It, 2001 E (R), 2004 I(R),It(R),W,S,US,C, 2005 A2,C,Tg(t&R),SA3(R), 2006 S(R),It,E,W
Lira, M (La Voulte) 1962 R, 1963 I, E, W, It, R, 1964 W, It, I, SA, 1965 S, I, R
Llari, R (Carcassonne) 1926 S
Lobies, J (RCF) 1921 S, W, E
Lombard, F (Narbonne) 1934 G, 1937 It
Lombard, T (SF) 1998 Arg 3, A, 1999 I, W 1, S (R), 2000 W, E, S, A, NZ 1, 2001 It, W
Lombarteix, R (Montferrand) 1938 R, G 2
Londios, J (Montauban) 1967 SA 3
Loppy, L (Toulon) 1993 R 2
Lorieux, A (Grenoble, Aix) 1981 A 1, R, NZ 1,2, 1982 W, 1983 A 2, R, 1984 I, W, E, 1985 Arg 1,2(R), 1986 R 2, NZ 2,3, 1987 W, E, [S, Z, Fj, A, NZ], 1988 S, I, W, Arg 1,2,4, 1989 W, A 2
Loury, A (RCF) 1927 E, G 1,2, 1928 S, A, I
Loustau, L (Perpignan) 2004 C
Loustau, M (Dax) 1923 E
Lubin-Lebrère, M-F (Toulouse) 1914 I, W, E, 1920 S, E, W, I, US, 1921 S, 1922 S, E, W, 1924 W, US, 1925 I
Lubrano, A (Béziers) 1972 A 2, 1973 S
Lux, J-P (Tyrosse, Dax) 1967 E, It, W, I, SA 1,2,4, R, 1968 I, E, Cz, NZ 3, A, SA 1,2, 1969 S, I, E, 1970 S, I, W, E, R, 1971 S, I, E, W, A 1,2, 1972 S, I 1, E, W, I 2, A 1,2, R, 1973 S, NZ, E, 1974 I, W, E, S, Arg 1,2, 1975 W

Macabiau, A (Perpignan) 1994 S, C 1
Maclos, P (SF) 1906 E, 1907 E
Magne, O (Dax, Brive, Montferrand, Clermont-Auvergne, London Irish) 1997 W (R), E, S, R 1(R), A 1,2, It 2(R), R 2, Arg (R), 1998 E, S, I, W, Arg 1,2, Fj, Arg 3, A, 1999 I, R, WS, NZ 1, W 2, [C, Nm, Fj, Arg, NZ 2, A], 2000 W, E, S, It, R, A, NZ 1,2, 2001 S, I, It, W, E, SA 1,2, NZ, SA 3, A, Fj, 2002 It, E, S, I, Arg, A 1,2(R), SA, NZ, C, 2003 E 1, S, I, It, W, R, E 2,3(R), [Fj,J,S,I,E,NZ(R)], 2004 I,It,W(R),S,E,A,Arg,NZ, 2005 SA1,2(R),A1, 2006 I,It,E,W(R), 2007 NZ1,2
Magnanou, C (RCF) 1923 E, 1925 W, E, 1926 S, 1929 S, W, 1930 S, I, E, W
Magnol, L (Toulouse) 1928 S, 1929 S, W, E
Magois, H (La Rochelle) 1968 SA 1,2, R
Majérus, R (SF) 1928 W, 1929 I, S, 1930 S, I, E, G, W
Malbet, J-C (Agen) 1967 SA 2,4
Maleig, A (Oloron) 1979 W, E, NZ 2, 1980 W, E, SA, R
Mallier, L (Brive) 1999 R, W 2(R), [C (R)], 2000 I (R), It
Malquier, Y (Narbonne) 1979 S
Malzieu, J (Clermont-Auvergne) 2008 S,It,W
Manterola, T (Lourdes) 1955 It, 1957 R 1
Mantoulan, C (Pau) 1959 I
Marcet, J (Albi) 1925 I, NZ, S, W, E, 1926 I, E
Marchal, J-F (Lourdes) 1979 S, R, 1980 W, S, I
Marconnet, S (SF) 1998 Arg 3, A, 1999 I (R), W 1(R), E, S (R), R, Tg, 2000 A, NZ 1,2, 2001 S, I, It (R), W (R), E, 2002 S (R), Arg (R), A 1,2, SA (R), C (R), 2003 E 1(R), S, I, It, W, Arg 1(t+R),2, NZ, R, E 2,3(t+R), [S,US(R),I,E,NZ], 2004 I,It,W,S,E,A,Arg,NZ, 2005 S,E,W,I,It,SA1,2,A1(R),2(R),C,Tg,SA3(R), 2006 S,I(R),It(R),E,W,R,SA,NZ1,2(R),Arg(R), 2007 It(R),I,W1(R)
Marchand, R (Poitiers) 1920 S, W
Marfaing, M (Toulouse) 1992 R, Arg 1
Marlu, J (Montferrand, Biarritz)) 1998 Fj (R), 2002 S (R), I (R), 2005 E
Marocco, P (Montferrand) 1968 S, I, W, E, R 1, Arg 1,2, A, 1988 Arg 4, 1989 I, 1990 E (R), NZ 1(R), 1991 S, I, W 1, E, US 2, [R, Fj, C, E]
Marot, A (Brive) 1969 R, 1970 S, I, W, 1971 SA 1, 1972 I 2, 1976 A 1
Marquesuzaa, A (RCF) 1958 It, SA 1,2, 1959 S, E, It, W, 1960 S, E, Arg 1
Marracq, H (Pau) 1961 R
Marsh, T (Montferrand) 2001 SA 3, A, Fj, 2002 It, W, E, S, I, Arg, A 1,2, 2003 [Fj,J,S,I,E,NZ], 2004 C,A,Arg,NZ
Martin, C (Lyon) 1909 I, 1910 W, S
Martin, H (SBUC) 1907 E, 1908 W
Martin, J-L (Béziers) 1971 A 2, R, 1972 S, I 1
Martin, L (Pau) 1948 I, A, S, W, E, 1950 S
Martin, R (SF) 2002 E (t+R), S (R), I (R), 2005 SA1(t&R),2,A1,2,C,SA3, 2006 S,I(t&R),R,SA(R),NZ1(R),2,Arg, 2007 E2,W2, [Arg 1,Gg(R),Arg 2(R)]
Martine, R (Lourdes) 1952 S, I, It, 1953 It, 1954 S, I, NZ, W, E, It, Arg 2, 1955 S, I, W, 1958 A, W, It, I, SA 1,2, 1960 S, E, Arg 3, 1961 S, It
Martinez, A (Narbonne) 2002 A 1, 2004 C
Martinez, G (Toulouse) 1982 W, E, S, Arg 1,2, 1983 E, W
Marty, D (Perpignan) 2005 It,C,Tg, 2006 I,It(R),R(R),NZ1(R), Arg(R), 2007 I,W1,E1,S,E2, [Nm,I,Gg,NZ,E,Arg 2], 2008 S,I,E
Mas, F (Béziers) 1962 R, 1963 S, I, E, W
Mas, N (Perpignan) 2003 NZ, 2005 E,W,I,It, 2007 W1,NZ1,2(R),E2(R),3(R),W2, [Nm(R),Gg(R),Arg 2], 2008 S(R),I,E,It,W
Maso, J (Perpignan, Narbonne) 1966 It, R, 1967 S, R, 1968 S, W, Cz, NZ 1,2,3, A, R, 1969 S, I, W, 1971 SA 1,2, R, 1972 E, W, A 2, 1973 W, I, J, R
Massare, J (PUC) 1945 B 1,2, W, 1946 B, I, W
Massé, A (SBUC) 1908 W, 1909 E, W, 1910 W, S, E, I
Masse, H (Grenoble) 1937 G
Matheu-Cambas, J (Agen) 1945 W, 1946 B, I, K, W, 1947 S, I, W, E, 1948 I, A, S, W, E, 1949 S, I, E, W, Arg 1,2, 1950 E, W, 1951 S, I
Matiu, L (Biarritz) 2000 W, E
Mauduy, G (Périgueux) 1957 It, R 1,2, 1958 S, E, 1961 W, It
Mauran, J (Castres) 1952 SA, W, E, It, 1953 I, E
Mauriat, P (Lyon) 1907 E, 1908 E, W, 1909 W, I, 1910 W, S, E, I, 1911 S, E, W, I, 1912 I, S, 1913 S, SA, W, I
Maurin, G (ASF) 1906 E
Maury, A (Toulouse) 1925 I, NZ, S, W, E, 1926 S, I, E
Mayssonnié, A (Toulouse) 1908 E, W, 1910 W

Mazars, L (Narbonne) 2007 NZ2
Mazas, L (Colomiers, Biarritz) 1992 Arg, 1996 SA 1
Mela, A (Albi) 2008 S(R),I,It(R),W(R)
Melville, E (Toulon) 1990 I (R), A 1,2,3, NZ 1, 1991 US 2
Menrath, R (SCUF) 1910 W
Menthiller, Y (Romans) 1964 W, It, SA, R, 1965 E
Merceron, G (Montferrand) 1999 R (R), Tg, 2000 S, I, R, 2001 S (R), W, E, SA 1,2, NZ (R), Fj, 2002 It, W, E, S, I, Arg, A 2, C, 2003 E 1, It (R), W (R), NZ (t+R), R (R), E 3, [Fj(R),J(R),S(R),US,E(R),NZ]
Meret, F (Tarbes) 1940 B
Mericq, S (Agen) 1959 I, 1960 S, E, W, 1961 I
Merle, O (Grenoble, Montferrand) 1993 SA 1,2, R 2, A 1,2, 1994 I, W, E, S, C 1, NZ 1,2, C 2, 1995 W, I, R 1, [Tg, S, I, SA, E], It, R 2, Arg, NZ 1,2, 1996 E, S, R, Arg 1,2, W 2, SA 2, 1997 I, W, E, S, It 1, R 1, A 1,2, It 2, R 2, SA 1(R),2
Mermoz, M (Toulouse) 2008 A2
Merquey, J (Toulon)1950 S, I, E, W
Mesnel, F (RCF) 1986 NZ 2(R),3, 1987 W, E, S, I, [S, Z, Fj, A, NZ], R, 1988 E, Arg 1,2,3,4, R, 1989 I, W, E, S, NZ 1, A 1,2, 1990 E, S, I, A 2,3, NZ 1,2, 1991 S, I, W 1, E, R, US 1,2, W 2, [R, Fj, C, E], 1992 W, E, S, I, SA 1,2, 1993 E (R), W, 1995 I, R 1, [Iv, E]
Mesny, P (RCF, Grenoble) 1979 NZ 1,2, 1980 SA, R, 1981 I, W (R), A 1,2, R, NZ 1,2, 1982 I, Arg 1,2
Meyer, G-S (Périgueux) 1960 S, E, It, R, Arg 2
Meynard, J (Cognac) 1954 Arg 1, 1956 Cz
Mias, L (Mazamet) 1951 S, I, E, W, 1952 I, SA, W, E, It, 1953 S, I, W, It, 1954 S, I, NZ, W, 1957 R 2, 1958 S, E, A, W, I, SA 1,2, 1959 S, It, W, I
Michalak, F (Toulouse) 2001 SA 3(R), A, Fj (R), 2002 It, A 1,2, 2003 It, W, Arg 2(R), NZ, R, E 2, [Fj,J,S,I,E,NZ(R)], 2004 I,W,S,E,A,Arg,NZ, 2005 S(R),E(R),W(R),I(R),It(R), SA1,2,A1,2,C,Tg(R),SA3, 2006 S,I,It,E,W, 2007 E2(R),3, [Arg1(t&R),Nm,I,NZ(R),E(R),Arg 2]
Mignardi, A (Agen) 2007 NZ1,2
Mignoni, P (Béziers, Clermont-Auvergne)) 1997 R 2(R), Arg (t), 1999 R (R), WS, NZ 1, W 2(R), [C, Nm], 2002 W, E (R), I (R), Arg, A 2(R), 2005 S,It(R),C(R), 2006 R, 2007 It,I,W1,E1(R),S,E2,3(R),W2, [Arg 1,Gg,Arg 2(R)]
Milhères, C (Biarritz) 2001 E
Milliand, P (Grenoble) 1936 G 2, 1937 G, It
Millo-Chlusky, R (Toulouse) 2005 SA1
Milloud, O (Bourgoin) 2000 R (R), 2001 NZ, 2002 W (R), E (R), 2003 It (R), W (R), Arg 1, R (R), E 2(t+R),3, [J,S(R),US,I(R),E(R)], 2004 US,C(R),A,Arg,NZ(R), 2005 S(R),E(R),W(R),SA1,2(R),A1,2,C(R),Tg,SA3,2006 S(R),I,It,E(R),W(R),NZ1(R),2,Arg, 2007 It,I(R),W1,E1,S,E2,3, [Arg 1,I,Gg,NZ,E]
Minjat, R (Lyon) 1945 B 1
Miorin, H (Toulouse) 1996 R, SA 1, 1997 I, W, E, S, It 1, 2000 It (R), R (R)
Mir, J-H (Lourdes) 1967 R, 1968 I
Mir, J-P (Lourdes) 1967 A
Modin, R (Brive) 1987 [Z]
Moga, A-M-A (Bègles) 1945 B 1,2, W, 1946 B, I, K, W, 1947 S, I, W, E, 1948 I, A, S, W, E, 1949 S, I, E, W, Arg 1,2
Mola, U (Dax, Castres) 1997 S (R), 1999 R (R), WS, Tg (R), NZ 1, W 2, [C, Nm, Fj, Arg (R), NZ 2(R), A (R)]
Momméjat, B (Cahors, Albi) 1958 It, I, SA 1,2, 1959 S, E, It, W, I, 1960 S, E, I, R, 1962 S, E, W, I, It, R, 1963 S, I, W
Moncla, F (RCF, Pau) 1956 Cz, 1957 I, E, W, It, R 1, 1958 SA 1,2, 1959 S, E, It, W, I, 1960 S, E, W, I, It, R, Arg 1,2,3, 1961 S, SA, E, W, It, I, NZ 1,2,3
Moni, C (Nice, SF) 1996 R, 2000 A, NZ 1,2, 2001 S, I, It, W
Monié, R (Perpignan) 1956 Cz, 1957 E
Monier, R (SBUC) 1911 I, 1912 S
Monniot, M (RCF) 1912 W, E
Montade, A (Perpignan) 1925 I, NZ, S, W, 1926 W
Montanella, F (Auch) 2007 NZ1(R)
Montlaur, P (Agen) 1992 E (R), 1994 S (R)
Moraitis, B (Toulon) 1969 E, W
Morel, A (Grenoble) 1954 Arg 2
Morère, J (Toulouse) 1927 E, G 1, 1928 S, A
Moscato, V (Bègles) 1991 R, US 1, 1992 W, E
Mougeot, C (Bègles) 1992 W, E, Arg
Mouniq, P (Toulouse) 1911 S, E, W, I,1912 I, E, 1913 S, SA, E
Moure, H (SCUF) 1908 E
Moureu, P (Béziers) 1920 I, US, 1921 W, E, I, 1922 S, W, I, 1923 S, W, E, I, 1924 S, I, E, W, 1925 E
Mournet, A (Bagnères) 1981 A 1(R)
Mouronval, F (SF) 1909 I
Muhr, A H (RCF) 1906 NZ, E, 1907 E
Murillo, G (Dijon) 1954 It, Arg 1

Nallet, L (Bourgoin, Castres) 2000 R, 2001 E, SA 1(R),2(R), NZ, SA 3(R), A (R), Fj (R), 2003 NZ, 2005 A2(R),C,Tg(R), SA3, 2006 I(R),It(R),E(R),W(R),R,SA(R),NZ1(R),2,Arg, 2007 It,I,W1,E1,S,E3(R), [Nm,I(R),Gg,Arg 2], 2008 S,I,E,It,W, A1,2
Namur, R (Toulon) 1931 E, G
Noble, J-C (La Voulte) 1968 E, W, Cz, NZ 3, A, R
Normand, A (Toulouse) 1957 R 1
Novès, G (Toulouse) 1977 NZ 1,2, R, 1978 W, R, 1979 I, W
Ntamack, E (Toulouse) 1994 W, C 1, NZ 1,2, C 2, 1995 W, I, R 1, [Tg, S, I, SA, E], It, R 2, Arg, NZ 1,2, 1996 E, S, I, W 1, R (R), Arg 1,2, W 2, 1997 I, 1998 Arg 3, 1999 I, W 1, E, S, WS, NZ 1, W 2(R), [C (R), Nm, Fj, Arg, NZ 2, A], 2000 W, E, S, I, It
Ntamack F (Colomiers) 2001 SA 3
Nyanga, Y (Béziers, Toulouse) 2004 US,C, 2005 S(R),E(R),W,I,It,SA1,2,A1(R),2,C(t&R),Tg,SA3, 2006 S,I,It,E,W, 2007 E2(R),3, [Nm,I(R),Gg,Arg 2]

Olibeau, O (Perpignan) 2007 NZ1(R),2(R)
Olive, D (Montferrand) 1951 I, 1952 I
Ondarts, P (Biarritz O) 1986 NZ 3, 1987 W, E, S, I, [S, Z, Fj, A, NZ], R, 1988 E, I, W, Arg 1,2,3,4, R, 1989 I, W, E, NZ 1,2, A 2, 1990 W, E, S, I, R (R), NZ 1,2, 1991 S, I, W 1, E, US 2, W 2, [R, Fj, C, E]
Orso, J-C (Nice, Toulon) 1982 Arg 1,2, 1983 E, S, A 1, 1984 E (R), S, NZ 1, 1985 I (R), W, 1988 I
Othats, J (Dax) 1960 Arg 2,3
Ouedraogo, F (Montpellier) 2007 NZ2(R), 2008 S,I,E(R),It,W,A1,2
Ougier, S (Toulouse) 1992 R, Arg 1, 1993 E (R), 1997 It 1

Paco, A (Béziers) 1974 Arg 1,2, R, SA 1,2, 1975 W, E, Arg 1,2, R, 1976 S, I, W, E, US, A 1,2, R, 1977 W, E, S, I, NZ 1,2, R, 1978 E, S, I, W, R, 1979 I, W, E, S, 1980 W
Palat, J (Perpignan) 1938 G 2
Palisson, A (Brive) 2008 A1,2
Palmié, M (Béziers) 1975 SA 1,2, Arg 1,2, R, 1976 S, I, W, E, US, 1977 W, E, S, I, Arg 1,2, NZ 1,2, R, 1978 E, S, I, W
Paoli, R (see Simonpaoli)
Paparemborde, R (Pau) 1975 SA 1,2, Arg 1,2, R, 1976 S, I, W, E, US, A 1,2, R, 1977 W, E, S, I, Arg 1, NZ 1,2, 1978 E, S, I, W, R, 1979 I, W, E, S, NZ 1,2, R, 1980 W, E, S, SA, R, 1981 S, I, W, E, A 1,2, R, NZ 1,2, 1982 W, I, R, Arg 1,2 1983 E, S, I, W
Papé, P (Bourgoin, Castres, SF) 2004 I,It,W,S,E,C,NZ(R), 2005 I(R),It(R),SA1,2,A1, 2006 NZ1,2, 2007 It(R),I,S(R),NZ1,2, 2008 E
Pardo, L (Hendaye) 1924 I, E
Pardo, L (Bayonne) 1980 SA, R, 1981 S, I, W, E, A 1, 1982 W, E, S, 1983 A 1(R), 1985 S, I, Arg 2
Pargade, J-H (Lyon U) 1953 It
Pariès, L (Biarritz O) 1968 SA 2, R, 1970 S, I, W, 1975 E, S, I
Parra, M (Bourgoin) 2008 S(R),I(R),E
Pascalin, P (Mont-de-Marsan) 1950 I, E, W, 1951 S, I, E, W
Pascarel, J-R (TOEC) 1912 W, E, 1913 S, SA, E, I
Pascot, J (Perpignan) 1922 S, E, I, 1923 S, 1926 I, 1927 G 2
Paul, R (Montferrand) 1940 B
Pauthe, G (Graulhet) 1956 E
Pebeyre, E-J (Fumel, Brive) 1945 W, 1946 I, K, W, 1947 S, I, W, E
Pebeyre, M (Vichy, Montferrand) 1970 E, R, 1971 I, SA 1,2, A 1, 1973 W
Péclier, A (Bourgoin) 2004 US,C

Pécune, J (Tarbes) 1974 W, E, S, 1975 Arg 1,2, R, 1976 I, W, E, US
Pédeutour, P (Bègles) 1980 I
Pellissier, L (RCF) 1928 A, I, E, G, W
Pelous, F (Dax, Toulouse) 1995 R 2, Arg, NZ 1,2, 1996 E, S, I, R (R), Arg 1,2, W 2, SA 1,2, 1997 I, W, E, S, It 1, R 1, A 1,2, It 2, R 2, Arg, SA 1,2(R), 1998 E, S, I, W, Arg 1,2, Fj, Arg 3, A, 1999 I, W 1, E, R (R), WS, Tg (R), NZ 1, W 2, [C, Nm, Fj, NZ 2, A], 2000 W, E, S, I, It, A, NZ 1,2, 2001 S, I, It, W, E, 2002 It (R), W (R), E (R), S, I, Arg, A 1,2, SA, NZ, C, 2003 E 1, S, I, It, W, R, E 2,3(R), [Fj,J,S,I,E,NZ(R)], 2004 I,It,W,S,E,US,C,A,Arg,NZ, 2005 S,E,W,I,It,A2, 2006 S,I,It,E,W,R,SA,NZ1, 2007 E2,3,W2(R), [Arg1,Nm(R),Gg(R),NZ,E]
Penaud, A (Brive, Toulouse) 1992 W, E, S, I, R, Arg 1,2, SA 1,2, Arg, 1993 R 1, SA 1,2, R 2, A 1,2, 1994 I, W, E, 1995 NZ 1,2, 1996 S, R, Arg 1,2, W 2, 1997 I, E, R 1, A 2, 2000 W (R), It
Périé, M (Toulon) 1996 E, S, I (R)
Péron, P (RCF) 1975 SA 1,2
Perrier, P (Bayonne) 1982 W, E, S, I (R)
Pesteil, J-P (Béziers) 1975 SA 1, 1976 A 2, R
Petit, C (Lorrain) 1931 W
Peyras, J-B (Bayonne) 2008 A2(R)
Peyrelade, H (Tarbes) 1940 B
Peyrelongue, J (Biarritz) 2004 It,S(R),C(R),A(R),Arg(R),NZ
Peyroutou, G (Périgueux) 1911 S, E
Phliponeau, J-F (Montferrand) 1973 W, I
Piazza, A (Montauban) 1968 NZ 1, A
Picamoles, L (Montpellier) 2008 I(R),E,It,A1,2(t&R)
Picard, T (Montferrand) 1985 Arg 2, 1986 R 1(R), Arg 2
Pierre, J (Bourgoin) 2007 NZ1,2
Pierrot, G (Pau) 1914 I, W, E
Pilon, J (Périgueux) 1949 E, 1950 E
Piqué, J (Pau) 1961 NZ 2,3, A, 1962 S, It, 1964 NZ, E, W, It, I, SA, Fj, R, 1965 S, I, E, W, It
Piquemal, M (Tarbes) 1927 I, S, 1929 I, G, 1930 S, I, E, G, W
Piquiral, E (RCF) 1924 S, I, E, W, R, US, 1925 E, 1926 S, I, E, W, M, 1927 I, S, W, E, G 1,2, 1928 E
Piteu, R (Pau) 1921 S, W, E, I, 1922 S, E, W, I, 1923 E, 1924 E, 1925 I, NZ, W, E, 1926 E
Plantefol, A (RCF) 1967 SA 2,3,4, NZ, R, 1968 E, W, Cz, NZ 2, 1969 E, W
Plantey, S (RCF) 1961 A, 1962 It
Podevin, G (SF) 1913 W, I
Poeydebasque, F (Bayonne) 1914 I, W
Poirier, A (SCUF) 1907 E
Poitrenaud, C (Toulouse) 2001 SA 3, A, Fj, 2003 E 1, S, I, It, W, Arg 1, NZ, E 3, [J,US,E(R),NZ], 2004 E(R),US,C,Arg(R),NZ, 2006 R, 2007 It,I,W1,E1,S,E2,3, [Nm,I,Gg,Arg 2]
Pomathios, M (Agen, Lyon U, Bourg) 1948 I, A, S, W, E, 1949 S, I, E, W, Arg 1,2, 1950 S, I, W, 1951 S, I, E, W, 1952 W, E, 1953 S, I, W, 1954 S
Pons, P (Toulouse) 1920 S, E, W, 1921 S, W, 1922 S
Porcu, C (Agen) 2002 Arg (R), A 1,2(R)
Porra, M (Lyon) 1931 I
Porthault, A (RCF) 1951 S, E, W, 1952 I, 1953 S, I, It
Portolan, C (Toulouse) 1986 A, 1989 I, E
Potel, A (Begles) 1932 G
Poux, J-B (Narbonne, Toulouse) 2001 Fj (R), 2002 S, I (R), Arg, A 1(R),2(R), 2003 E 3, [Fj,J,US,NZ], 2007 E2,3,W2(R), [Nm,I(R),Gg,NZ(R),E(R),Arg 2], 2008 E(R),It(R),W(R)
Prat, J (Lourdes) 1945 B 1,2, W, 1946 B, I, K, W, 1947 S, I, W, E, 1948 I, A, S, W, E, 1949 S, I, E, W, Arg 1,2, 1950 S, I, E, W, 1951 S, E, W, 1952 S, I, SA, W, E, It, 1953 S, I, E, W, It, 1954 S, I, NZ, W, E, It, 1955 S, I, E, W, It
Prat, M (Lourdes) 1951 I, 1952 S, I, SA, W, E, 1953 S, I, E, 1954 I, NZ, W, E, It, 1955 S, I, E, W, It, 1956 I, W, It, Cz, 1957 S, I, W, It, R 1, 1958 A, W, I
Prévost, A (Albi) 1926 M, 1927 I, S, W
Prin-Clary, J (Cavaillon, Brive) 1945 B 1,2, W, 1946 B, I, K, W, 1947 S, I, W
Privat, T (Béziers, Clermont-Auvergne) 2001 SA 3, A, Fj, 2002 It, W, S (R), SA (R), 2003 [NZ], 2005 SA2,A1(R)
Puech, L (Toulouse) 1920 S, E, I, 1921 E, I
Puget, M (Toulouse) 1961 It, 1966 S, I, It, 1967 SA 1,3,4, NZ, 1968 Cz, NZ 1,2, SA 1,2, R, 1969 E, R, 1970 W
Puig, A (Perpignan) 1926 S, E
Pujol, A (SOE Toulouse) 1906 NZ
Pujolle, M (Nice) 1989 B, A 1, 1990 S, I, R, A 1,2, NZ 2

Quaglio, A (Mazamet) 1957 R 2, 1958 S, E, A, W, I, SA 1,2, 1959 S, E, It, W, I
Quilis, A (Narbonne) 1967 SA 1,4, NZ, 1970 R, 1971 I

Rabadan, P (SF) 2004 US(R),C(R)
Ramis, R (Perpignan) 1922 E, I, 1923 W
Rancoule, H (Lourdes, Toulon, Tarbes) 1955 E, W, It, 1958 A, W, It, I, SA 1, 1959 S, It, W, 1960 I, It, R, Arg 1,2, 1961 SA, E, W, It, NZ 1,2, 1962 S, E, W, I, It
Rapin, A (SBUC) 1938 R
Raymond, F (Toulouse) 1925 S, 1927 W, 1928 I
Raynal, F (Perpignan) 1935 G, 1936 G 1,2, 1937 G, It
Raynaud, F (Carcassonne) 1933 G
Raynaud, M (Narbonne) 1999 W 1, E (R)
Razat, J-P (Agen) 1962 R, 1963 S, I, R
Rebujent, R (RCF) 1963 E
Revailler, D (Graulhet) 1981 S, I, W, E, A 1,2, R, NZ 1,2, 1982 W, S, I, R, Arg 1
Revillon, J (RCF) 1926 I, E, 1927 S
Ribère, E (Perpignan, Quillan) 1924 I, 1925, I, NZ, S, 1926 S, I, W, M, 1927 I, S, W, E, G 1,2, 1928 S, A, I, E, G, W, 1929 I, E, G, 1930 S, I, E, W, 1931 I, S, W, E, G, 1932 G, 1933 G
Rives, J-P (Toulouse, RCF) 1975 E, S, I, Arg 1,2, R, 1976 S, I, W, E, US, A 1,2, R, 1977 W, E, S, I, Arg 1,2, R, 1978 E, S, I, W, R, 1979 I, W, E, S, NZ 1,2, R, 1980 W, E, S, I, SA, 1981 S, I, W, E, A 2, 1982 W, E, S, I, R, 1983 E, S, I, W, A 1,2, R, 1984 I, W, E, S
Rochon, A (Montferrand) 1936 G 1
Rodrigo, M (Mauléon) 1931 I, W
Rodriguez, L (Mont-de-Marsan, Montferrand, Dax) 1981 A 1,2, R, NZ 1,2, 1982 W, E, S, I, R, 1983 E, S, 1984 I, NZ 1,2, R, 1985 E, S, I, W, 1986 Arg 1, A, R 2, NZ 2,3, 1987 W, E, S, I, [S, Z, Fj, A, NZ], R, 1988 E, S, I, W, Arg 1,2,3,4, R, 1989 I, E, S, NZ 1,2, B, A 1, 1990 W, E, S, I, NZ 1
Rogé, L (Béziers) 1952 It, 1953 E, W, It, 1954 S, Arg 1,2, 1955 S, I, 1956 W, It, E, 1957 S, 1960 S, E
Rollet, J (Bayonne) 1960 Arg 3, 1961 NZ 3, A, 1962 It, 1963 I
Romero, H (Montauban) 1962 S, E, W, I, It, R, 1963 E
Romeu, J-P (Montferrand) 1972 R, 1973 S, NZ, E, W, I, R, 1974 W, E, S, Arg 1,2, R, SA 1,2(R), 1975 W, SA 2, Arg 1,2, R, 1976 S, I, W, E, US, 1977 W, E, S, I, Arg 1,2, NZ 1,2, R
Roques, A (Cahors) 1958 A, W, It, I, SA 1,2, 1959 S, E, W, I, 1960 S, E, W, I, It, Arg 1,2,3, 1961 S, SA, E, W, It, I, 1962 S, E, W, I, It, 1963 S
Roques, J-C (Brive) 1966 S, I, It, R
Rossignol, J-C (Brive) 1972 A 2
Rouan, J (Narbonne) 1953 S, I
Roucariès, G (Perpignan) 1956 S
Rouffia, L (Narbonne) 1945 B 2, W, 1946 W, 1948 I
Rougerie, A (Montferrand, Clermont-Auvergne) 2001 SA 3, A, Fj (R), 2002 It, W, E, S, I, Arg, A 1,2, 2003 E 1, S, I, It, W, Arg 1,2, NZ, R, E 2,3(R), [Fj,J,S,I,E], 2004 US,C,A,Arg,NZ, 2005 S,W,A2,C,Tg,SA3, 2006 I,It,E,W, NZ1,2, 2007 E2,W2, [Arg1,Nm(R),I(R),Gg,Arg 2], 2008 S(R),I,E,It
Rougerie, J (Montferrand) 1973 J
Rougé-Thomas, P (Toulouse) 1989 NZ 1,2
Roujas, F (Tarbes) 1910 I
Roumat, O (Dax) 1989 NZ 2(R), B, 1990 W, E, S, I, R, A 1,2,3, NZ 1,2, 1991 S, I, W 1, E, R, US 1, W 2, [R, Fj, C, E], 1992 W (R), E (R), S, I, SA 1,2, Arg, 1993 E, S, I, W, R 1, SA 1,2, R 2, A 1,2, 1994 I, W, E, C 1, NZ 1,2, C 2, 1995 W, E, S, [Iv, S, I, SA, E], 1996 E, S, I, W 1, Arg 1,2
Rousie, M (Villeneuve) 1931 S, G, 1932 G, 1933 G
Rousset, G (Béziers) 1975 SA 1, 1976 US
Rué, J-B (Agen) 2002 SA (R), C (R), 2003 E 1(R), S (R), It (R), W (R), Arg 1,2(R)
Ruiz, A (Tarbes) 1968 SA 2, R

Rupert, J-J (Tyrosse) 1963 R, 1964 S, Fj, 1965 E, W, It, 1966 S, I, E, W, It, 1967 It, R, 1968 S

Sadourny, J-L (Colomiers) 1991 W 2(R), [C (R)], 1992 E (R), S, I, Arg 1(R),2, SA 1,2, 1993 R 1, SA 1,2, R 2, A 1,2, 1994 I, W, E, S, C 1, NZ 1,2, C 2, 1995 W, E, S, I, R 1, [Tg, S, I, SA, E], It, R 2, Arg, NZ 1,2, 1996 E, S, I, W 1, Arg 1,2, W 2, SA 1,2, 1997 I, W, E, S, It 1, R 1, A 1,2, It 2, R 2, Arg, SA 1,2, 1998 E, S, I, W, 1999 R, Tg, NZ 1(R), 2000 NZ 2, 2001 It, W, E
Sagot, P (SF) 1906 NZ, 1908 E, 1909 W
Sahuc, A (Métro) 1945 B 1,2
Sahuc, F (Toulouse) 1936 G 2
Saint-André, P (Montferrand, Gloucester) 1990 R, A 3, NZ 1,2, 1991 I (R), W 1, E, US 1,2, W 2, [R, Fj, C, E], 1992 W, E, S, I, R, Arg 1,2, SA 1,2, 1993 E, S, I, W, SA 1,2, A 1,2, 1994 I, W, E, S, C 1, NZ 1,2, C 2, 1995 W, E, S, I, R 1, [Tg, Iv, S, I, SA, E], It, R 2, Arg, NZ 1,2, 1996 E, S, I, W 1, R, Arg 1,2, W 2, 1997 It 1,2, R 2, Arg, SA 1,2
Saisset, O (Béziers) 1971 R, 1972 S, I 1, A 1,2, 1973 S, NZ, E, W, I, J, R, 1974 I, Arg 2, SA 1,2, 1975 W
Salas, P (Narbonne) 1979 NZ 1,2, R, 1980 W, E, 1981 A 1, 1982 Arg 2
Salinié, R (Perpignan) 1923 E
Sallefranque, M (Dax) 1981 A 2, 1982 W, E, S
Salut, J (TOEC) 1966 R, 1967 S, 1968 I, E, Cz, NZ 1, 1969 I
Samatan, R (Agen) 1930 S, I, E, G, W, 1931 I, S, W, E, G
Sanac, A (Perpignan) 1952 It, 1953 S, I, 1954 E, 1956 Cz, 1957 S, I, E, W, It
Sangalli, F (Narbonne) 1975 I, SA 1,2, 1976 S, A 1,2, R, 1977 W, E, S, I, Arg 1,2, NZ 1,2
Sanz, H (Narbonne) 1988 Arg 3,4, R, 1989 A 2, 1990 S, I, R, A 1,2, NZ 2, 1991 W 2
Sappa, M (Nice) 1973 J, R, 1977 R
Sarrade, R (Pau) 1929 I
Sarraméa, O (Castres) 1999 R, WS (R), Tg, NZ 1
Saux, J-P (Pau) 1960 W, It, Arg 1,2, 1961 SA, E, W, It, I, NZ 1,2,3, A, 1962 S, E, W, I, It, 1963 S, I, E, It
Savitsky, M (La Voulte) 1969 R
Savy, M (Montferrand) 1931 I, S, W, E, 1936 G 1
Sayrou, J (Perpignan) 1926 W, M, 1928 E, G, W, 1929 S, W, E, G
Scohy, R (BEC) 1931 S, W, E, G
Sébedio, J (Tarbes) 1913 S, E, 1914 I, 1920 S, I, US, 1922 S, E, 1923 S
Séguier, N (Béziers) 1973 J, R
Seigne, L (Agen, Merignac) 1989 B, A 1, 1990 NZ 1, 1993 E, S, I, W, R 1, A 1,2, 1994 S, C 1, 1995 E (R), S
Sella, P (Agen) 1982 R, Arg 1,2, 1983 E, S, I, W, A 1,2, R, 1984 I, W, E, S, NZ 1,2, R, 1985 E, S, I, W, Arg 1,2, 1986 S, I, W, E, R 1, Arg 1,2, A, NZ 1, R 2, NZ 2,3, 1987 W, E, S, I, [S, R, Z (R), Fj, A, NZ], 1988 E, S, I, W, Arg 1,2,3,4, R, 1989 I, W, E, S, NZ 1,2, B, A 1,2, 1990 W, E, S, I, A 1,2,3, 1991 W 1, E, R, US 1,2, W 2, [Fj, C, E], 1992 W, E, S, I, Arg, 1993 E, S, I, W, R 1, SA 1,2, R 2, A 1,2, 1994 I, W, E, S, C 1, NZ 1,2, C 2, 1995 W, E, S, I, [Tg, S, I, SA, E]
Semmartin, J (SCUF) 1913 W, I
Sénal, G (Béziers) 1974 Arg 1,2, R, SA 1,2, 1975 W
Sentilles, J (Tarbes) 1912 W, E, 1913 S, SA
Serin, L (Béziers) 1928 E, 1929 W, E, G, 1930 S, I, E, G, W, 1931 I, W, E
Serre, P (Perpignan) 1920 S, E
Serrière, P (RCF) 1986 A, 1987 R, 1988 E
Servat, W (Toulouse) 2004 I,It,W,S,E,US,C,A,Arg,NZ 2005 S,E(R),W(R),It(R),SA1(R),2, 2008 S,I(R),E(R),W(R)
Servole, L (Toulon) 1931 I, S, W, E, G, 1934 G, 1935 G
Sicart, N (Perpignan) 1922 I
Sillières, J (Tarbes) 1968 R, 1970 S, I, 1971 S, I, E, 1972 E, W
Siman, M (Montferrand) 1948 E, 1949 S, 1950 S, I, E, W
Simon, S (Bègles) 1991 R, US 1
Simonpaoli, R (SF) 1911 I, 1912 I, S
Sitjar, M (Agen) 1964 W, It, I, R, 1965 It, R, 1967 A, E, It, W, I, SA 1,2
Skrela, D (Colomiers, SF) 2001 NZ, 2007 It,I,W1,E1,2,3(R),W2, [Arg 1,Gg(R),Arg 2], 2008 S(R),I,E(R),W
Skrela, J-C (Toulouse) 1971 SA 2, A 1,2, 1972 I 1(R), E, W, I 2, A 1, 1973 W, J, R, 1974 W, E, S, Arg 1, R, 1975 W (R), E, S, I, SA 1,2, Arg 1,2, R, 1976 S, I, W, E, US, A 1,2, R, 1977 W, E, S, I, Arg 1,2, NZ 1,2, R, 1978 E, S, I, W
Soler, M (Quillan) 1929 G
Soro, R (Lourdes, Romans) 1945 B 1,2, W, 1946 B, I, K, 1947 S, I, W, E, 1948 I, A, S, W, E, 1949 S, I, E, W, Arg 1,2
Sorondo, L-M (Montauban) 1946 K, 1947 S, I, W, E, 1948 I
Soulette, C (Béziers, Toulouse) 1997 R 2, 1998 S (R), I (R), W (R), Arg 1,2, Fj, 1999 W 2(R), [C (R), Nm (R), Arg, NZ 2, A]
Soulié, E (CASG) 1920 E, I, US, 1921 S, E, I, 1922 E, W, I
Sourgens, J (Bègles) 1926 M
Sourgens, O (Bourgoin) 2007 NZ2
Souverbie, J-M (Bègles) 2000 R
Spanghero, C (Narbonne) 1971 E, W, SA 1,2, A 1,2, R, 1972 S, E, W, I 2, A 1,2, 1974 I, W, E, S, R, SA 1, 1975 E, S, I
Spanghero, W (Narbonne) 1964 SA, Fj, R, 1965 S, I, E, W, It, R, 1966 S, I, E, W, It, R, 1967 S, A, E, SA 1,2,3,4, NZ, 1968 S, I, E, W, NZ 1,2,3, A, SA 1,2, R, 1969 S, I, W, 1970 R, 1971 E, W, SA 1, 1972 E, I 2, A 1,2, R, 1973 S, NZ, E, W, I
Stener, G (PUC) 1956 S, I, E, 1958 SA 1,2
Struxiano, P (Toulouse) 1913 W, I, 1920 S, E, W, I, US
Sutra, G (Narbonne) 1967 SA 2, 1969 W, 1970 S, I
Swierczinski, C (Bègles) 1969 E, 1977 Arg 2
Szarzewski, D (Béziers, SF) 2004 C(R), 2005 I(R),A1,2, SA3, 2006 S,E(R),W(t&R),R(R),SA,NZ1,2(R),Arg(R), 2007 It(R),E2(R),W2,[Arg1(R),Nm,I(R),Gg(R),NZ(R),E(R)], 2008 S(R),I,E,It,W

Tabacco, P (SF) 2001 SA 1,2, NZ, SA 3, A, Fj, 2003 It (R), W (R), Arg 1, NZ, E 2(R),3, [S(R),US,I(R),NZ], 2004 US, 2005 S
Tachdjian, M (RCF) 1991 S, I, E
Taffary, M (RCF) 1975 W, E, S, I
Taillantou, J (Pau) 1930 I, G, W
Tarricq, P (Lourdes) 1958 A, W, It, I
Tavernier, H (Toulouse) 1913 I
Téchoueyres, W (SBUC) 1994 E, S, 1995 [Iv]
Terreau, M-M (Bourg) 1945 W, 1946 B, I, K, W, 1947 S, I, W, E, 1948 I, A, W, E, 1949 S, Arg 1,2, 1951 S
Theuriet, A (SCUF) 1909 E, W, 1910 S, 1911 W, 1913 E
Thevenot, M (SCUF) 1910 W, E, I
Thierry, R (RCF) 1920 S, E, W, US
Thiers, P (Montferrand) 1936 G 1,2, 1937 G, It, 1938 G 1,2, 1940 B, 1945 B, 1,2
Thiéry, B (Bayonne, Biarritz) 2007 NZ1,2(R), 2008 A1,2
Thion, J (Perpignan, Biarritz) 2003 Arg 1,2, NZ, R, E 2, [Fj,S,I,E], 2004 A,Arg,NZ 2005 S,E,W,I,It,A2,C,Tg,SA3, 2006 S,I,It,E,W,R(R),SA, 2007 It,I(R),W1,E1,S,E2,3,W2, [Arg 1,I,Gg,NZ,E,Arg 2], 2008 E(R),It,W
Tignol, P (Toulouse) 1953 S, I
Tilh, H (Nantes) 1912 W, E, 1913 S, SA, E, W
Tillous-Borde, S (Castres) 2008 A1(R),2
Tolot, J-L (Agen) 1987 [Z]
Tomas, J (Clermont-Auvergne) 2008 It(R)
Tordo, J-F (Nice) 1991 US 1(R), 1992 W, E, S, I, R, Arg 1,2, SA 1, Arg, 1993 E, S, I, W, R 1
Torossian, F (Pau) 1997 R 1
Torreilles, S (Perpignan) 1956 S
Tournaire, F (Narbonne, Toulouse) 1995 It, 1996 I, W 1, R, Arg 1,2(R), W 2, SA 1,2, 1997 I, E, S, It 1, R 1, A 1,2, It 2, R 2, Arg, SA 1,2, 1998 E, S, I, W, Arg 1,2, Fj, Arg 3, A, 1999 I, W 1, E, S, R (R), WS, NZ 1, [C, Nm, Fj, Arg, NZ 2, A], 2000 W, E, S, I, It, A (R)
Tourte, R (St Girons) 1940 B
Traille, D (Pau, Biarritz) 2001 SA 3, A, Fj, 2002 It, W, E, S, I, Arg, A 1,2, SA, NZ, C, 2003 E 1, S, I, It, W, Arg, 1,2, NZ, R, E 2, [Fj(R),J,S(R),US,NZ], 2004 I,It,W,S,E, 2005 S,E,W,It(R),SA1(R),2,A1(R), 2006 It,E,W,R,SA,NZ1,2,Arg, 2007 S(R),E2,3,W2(R), [Arg 1,Nm,I,NZ,E], 2008 S,I,E,It(R),W,A1
Trillo, J (Bègles) 1967 SA 3,4, NZ, R, 1968 S, I, NZ 1,2,3, A, 1969 I, E, W, R, 1970 E, R, 1971 S, I, SA 1,2, A 1,2, 1972 S, A 1,2, R, 1973 S, E
Trinh-Duc, F (Montpellier) 2008 S,I(R),E,It,W(R),A1,2

Triviaux, R (Cognac) 1931 E, G
Tucco-Chala, M (PUC) 1940 B

Ugartemendia, J-L (St Jean-de-Luz) 1975 S, I

Vaills, G (Perpignan) 1928 A, 1929 G
Valbon, L (Brive) 2004 US, 2005 S(R), 2006 S,E(R), 2007 NZ1(R)
Vallot, C (SCUF) 1912 S
Van Heerden, A (Tarbes) 1992 E, S
Vannier, M (RCF, Chalon) 1953 W, 1954 S, I, Arg 1,2, 1955 S, I, E, W, It, 1956 S, I, W, It, E, 1957 S, I, E, W, It, R 1,2, 1958 S, E, A, W, It, I, 1960 S, E, W, I, It, R, Arg 1,3, 1961 SA, E, W, It, I, NZ 1, A
Vaquer, F (Perpignan) 1921 S, W, 1922 W
Vaquerin, A (Béziers) 1971 R, 1972 S, I 1, A 1, 1973 S, 1974 W, E, S, Arg 1,2, R, SA 1,2, 1975 W, E, S, I, 1976 US, A 1(R),2, R, 1977 Arg 2, 1979 W, E, 1980 S, I
Vareilles, C (SF) 1907 E, 1908 E, W, 1910 S, E
Varenne, F (RCF) 1952 S
Varvier, T (RCF) 1906 E, 1909 E, W, 1911 E, W, 1912 I
Vassal, G (Carcassonne) 1938 R, G 2
Vaysse, J (Albi) 1924 US, 1926 M
Vellat, E (Grenoble) 1927 I, E, G 1,2, 1928 A
Venditti, D (Bourgoin, Brive) 1996 R, SA 1(R),2, 1997 I, W, E, S, R 1, A 1, SA 2, 2000 W (R), E, S, It (R)
Vergé, L (Bègles) 1993 R 1(R)
Verger, A (SF) 1927 W, E, G 1, 1928 I, E, G, W
Verges, S-A (SF) 1906 NZ, E, 1907 E
Vermeulen, E (Brive, Montferrand, Clermont-Auvergne) 2001 SA 1(R),2(R), 2003 NZ, 2006 NZ1,2,Arg, 2007 W1,S(R), 2008 S,W(R)
Viard, G (Narbonne) 1969 W, 1970 S, R, 1971 S, I
Viars, S (Brive) 1992 W, E, I, R, Arg 1,2, SA 1,2(R), Arg, 1993 R 1, 1994 C 1(R), NZ 1(t), 1995 E (R), [Iv], 1997 R 1(R), A 1(R),2
Vigerie, M (Agen) 1931 W
Vigier, R (Montferrand) 1956 S, W, It, E, Cz, 1957 S, E, W, It, R 1,2, 1958 S, E, A, W, It, I, SA 1,2, 1959 S, E, It, W, I
Vigneau, A (Bayonne) 1935 G
Vignes, C (RCF) 1957 R 1,2, 1958 S, E
Vila, E (Tarbes) 1926 M
Vilagra, J (Vienne) 1945 B 2
Villepreux, P (Toulouse) 1967 It, I, SA 2, NZ, 1968 I, Cz, NZ 1,2,3, A, 1969 S, I, E, W, R, 1970 S, I, W, E, R, 1971 S, I, E, W, A 1,2, R, 1972 S, I 1, E, W, I 2, A 1,2
Viviès, B (Agen) 1978 E, S, I, W, 1980 SA, R, 1981 S, A 1, 1983 A 1(R)
Volot, M (SF) 1945 W, 1946 B, I, K, W

Weller, S (Grenoble) 1989 A 1,2, 1990 A 1, NZ 1
Wolf, J-P (Béziers) 1980 SA, R, 1981 A 2, 1982 E

Yachvili, D (Biarritz) 2002 C (R), 2003 S (R), I, It, W, R (R), E 3, [US,NZ], 2004 I(R),It(R),W(R),S,E, 2005 S(R),E,W,I,It, SA1(R),2,C,Tg, 2006 S(R),I(R),It(R),E,W,SA, NZ1,2(R),Arg, 2007 E1, 2008 E(R),It,W(R),A1,2(R)
Yachvili, M (Tulle, Brive) 1968 E, W, Cz, NZ 3, A, R, 1969 S, I, R, 1971 E, SA 1,2 A 1, 1972 R, 1975 SA 2

Zago, F (Montauban) 1963 I, E

GEORGIA

GEORGIA'S 2008 RECORD

OPPONENTS	DATE	VENUE	RESULT
Portugal	2 February	H	**Won** 31–3
Romania	9 February	H	**Won** 22–7
Portugal	23 February	A	**Won** 11–6
Czech Republic	29 March	A	**Won** 22–3
Russia	12 April	A	**Won** 18–12
Spain	26 April	H	**Won** 22–20
Emerging SA	11 June	A (NC)	**Lost** 3–11
Uruguay	15 June	A (NC)	**Won** 20–18
Italy A	20 June	A (NC)	**Won** 25–3

BUILDING ON THE WORLD CUP

By Frankie Deges

Shaun Botterill/Getty Images

Georgia's rugby team celebrated another crown in 2008.

If the RBS Six Nations had in place a promotion-relegation system, then the Georgian Lelos would be gracing the hallowed fields of Twickenham and Murrayfield, the Millenium Stadium and the Stade de France in the next couple of seasons. If such a scenario was in place, then as winners of the 2007–2008 European Nations Cup, Georgia would take the place of Italy, bottom-placed in the last Six Nations.

The boost such a move would represent to the Eastern European nation is impossible to imagine, although the idea of having a "new" nation in the oldest of international tournaments would make a few uncomfortable in the knowledge that their presence alone would ensure other nations in the so called Six Nations B would work harder to shorten the gap in the hope of playing in the Six Nations. Even a repechage with Scotland or Italy would be a wonderful match, worth travelling to Tbilisi for.

Remember that night at the Stade Chaban-Delmas in Bordeaux, during RWC 2007? That could have been the biggest ever upset in the history of international rugby. Georgia could and should have beaten Ireland. The 10–14 final score only reflected the difference in experience between both teams. The hunger and drive was there, evident also in their first ever RWC-finals win against Namibia, a few days earlier.

Politically, Georgia is a new nation, having become independent in 1991 after the Soviet Union collapsed. The Georgian Rugby Union, in times of trouble, took an active role, being involved in the distribution of humanitarian aid to refugees from South Ossetia living in Tbilisi.

In fact, on their march towards winning the European Nations Cup, there was a much-celebrated win against their fiercest rivals Russia under the thick snow of Krasnoyarsk, Siberia. The fact that on the back of a good Rugby World Cup they could maintain the good work and win its six matches, showed a lot of character. Almost all of those games were tight and needed every bit of Georgian strength. In spite of having many new players in the team, they all came through.

During the World Cup that former Wallaby and much travelled coach Tim Lane was approached to join the Georgian Rugby Union. With an impressive coaching CV (with the Wallabies, in South Africa, Italy and France), it was a mayor coup for the game in the country. Lane arrived in Tbilisi at the end of January; there was no looking back for him or the team.

The 2008 international season opened for the Georgian Lelos a week later at home with a solid 31–3, five-try win against fellow RWC participants Portugal. That win showed how much the team grew after the experience gained four months earlier and how the new message was filtering through. An under-strength Portuguese XV was torn apart in the forwards.

A week later, again at home, a 22–7 win against Romania was much celebrated, Georgia keeping the Antim Iverianu Transitional Cup put on display when both teams meet. With a few new names in the team, it was one of the best displays of the season. The February treble was completed with a hard away win against the Portuguese Lobos in Lisbon 11–6.

The second part of the European Nations Cup season came with similar success. The Czech Republic were beaten in Prague (22–3) in Georgia's 100th official Test match, before the long trip to Siberia where in a snow-covered field, the 18–12 win against a Russia XV coached by former Lelo's coach Claude Saurel – massive fight included – secured the Nations Cup and was much celebrated.

The final match of the ENC, at home in Tbilisi's National Stadium, was played in front of 25,000 supporters. Spain, in the first year of the tournament's two-year cycle, had been the only team to beat them. This time it was, again, not easy, Georgia needing to come back from 0–17. Two tries by Mamuka "Gulliver" Gorgodze left the halftime score at 12–17. Eventually, Rati Urushadze scored the winning try.

The 22–20 victory brought congratulations from the highest national office. Attending the match against Spain was Georgian Prime Minister Lado Gurgenidze. "We have approved a totally new programme to support and develop rugby in our country," he told Total Rugby at the time. "We hope to finance the building of 15 new stadiums as well as supporting the federation through the next four years up to the World Cup.

"This will also include making the funds available for a professional league. We'll do everything possible to fully develop this sport in Georgia," he said. Those promises were made in times of peace; hopefully, the government will be able to fully support a sport that is attracting more and more fans and players and will soon compete for public interest with soccer and wrestling.

In this respect, rugby festivals were organised throughout the year in the nation's capital, Tbilisi, and elsewhere around the country in a bid to boost the 2,300 youth players currently playing the game in the 36 clubs nationwide.

"We have massive potential, at the moment I would say we are only tapping into about three to four per cent of the potential that is apparent in the age groups," said the country's Development officer Tamaz Mgeladze.

"When we can get that figure up to about 30 per cent then we will be able to compete on equal terms with the biggest nations in rugby. I really do believe that we can achieve that goal in about 10 years."

Under an Australian coach, it was natural that the national team would change the forward-oriented game-plan. "We are now starting to play a little bit more expansively, which they have never done before. We have picked a lot of young backs especially that have come on pretty well," said Lane.

"Hopefully, over the next two years of qualifications for the World Cup, the top two teams in our Seven Nations go through. Obviously, that's our goal."

On arriving in Tbilisi, Lane soon had to unearth new talent due to the retirement of some of the World Cup heroes. He thus started with a young team with some 20–21 year olds and an average age of about 23, 24 years, with a handful of forwards in their late 20s.

A solid scrum and the natural strength of the forwards were given a new dimension with the backs given the reigns and options to operate in a more expansive game plan. What hasn't changed is the difficulty of keeping the best players within the Georgian frontiers and training time is very precious.

Tim Lane said: "The more time we spend together the better it is going to be. We only usually get together three days before a Test match so it's not a lot of time to prepare. We don't always get our strongest team as some clubs don't release our players."

Captain Irakli Abuseridze believes there are some positives of having about 80 or 90 per cent of the players in France. "Thanks to the 'legionnaires' the level of the rugby team is where it is now. We are a small team but from the big family. We can achieve a lot when we work as a team together."

In the absence of national coach Tim Lane, the two Georgian coaches, Nikoloz Chavchavadze and Levan Miasashvili – who coached Georgia U20 to third position in the IRB Junior World Rugby Trophy in Chile – must be comfortable with the depth of talent on display. It has worked as in nine matches in 2008 only one was lost, against a strong Emerging South African side and by a small margin, 3–11. That was at the start of the IRB Nations Cup in Romania.

They then went on to beat the Uruguayan Teros 20–18 and Italy A 25–3 to claim second place in the Bucharest tournament.

This mix of experience and youth will be crucial in the build-up to the qualifying rounds for RWC 2011. Georgia U20 had travelled in April to Santiago de Chile where they failed in their quest to return to the A Division, only managing third place. A number of those players showed sufficient talent to be in the mix for the next few years.

Georgia will also compete in the Rugby World Cup Sevens after qualifying at the European finals in Hanover, Germany.

Women's rugby gained momentum; the Georgian "Gadflies" finishing tenth in the European Sevens Championship.

Kochebi RC, a Tbilisi-based club, dominated, winning the 2007 Georgian Championship and Cup.

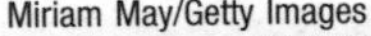

Miriam May/Getty Images

Giorgi Chkhaidze celebrates Georgia's Sevens success in Hannover.

GEORGIA INTERNATIONAL RECORDS

MATCH RECORDS UP TO 30TH SEPTEMBER 2008

WINNING MARGIN

Date	Opponent	Result	Winning Margin
07/04/2007	Czech Republic	98–3	**95**
03/02/2002	Netherlands	88–0	**88**
26/02/2005	Ukraine	65–0	**65**

MOST DROP GOALS IN A MATCH BY THE TEAM

Date	Opponent	Result	DGs
20/10/1996	Russia	29–20	**2**
21/11/1991	Ukraine	19–15	**2**
15/07/1992	Ukraine	15–0	**2**
04/06/1994	Switzerland	22–21	**2**

MOST POINTS IN A MATCH BY THE TEAM

Date	Opponent	Result	Pts.
07/04/2007	Czech Republic	98–3	**98**
03/02/2002	Netherlands	88–0	**88**
12/06/2005	Czech Republic	75–10	**75**

MOST POINTS IN A MATCH BY A PLAYER

Date	Player	Opponent	Pts.
08/03/2003	Pavle Jimsheladze	Russia	**23**
07/04/2007	Merab Kvirikashvili	Czech Republic	**23**
12/06/2005	Malkhaz Urjukashvili	Czech Republic	**20**

MOST TRIES IN A MATCH BY THE TEAM

Date	Opponent	Result	Tries
07/04/2007	Czech Republic	98–3	**16**
03/02/2002	Netherlands	88–0	**14**

MOST TRIES IN A MATCH BY A PLAYER

Date	Player	Opponent	Tries
23/03/1995	Pavle Jimsheladze	Bulgaria	**3**
23/03/1995	Archil Kavtarashvili	Bulgaria	**3**
12/06/2005	Mamuka Gorgodze	Czech Republic	**3**
07/04/2007	David Dadunashvili	Czech Republic	**3**
26/04/2008	Mamuka Gorgodze	Spain	**3**
07/04/2007	Malkhaz Urjukashvili	Czech Republic	**3**

MOST CONVERSIONS IN A MATCH BY THE TEAM

Date	Opponent	Result	Cons
03/02/2002	Netherlands	88–0	**9**
07/04/2007	Czech Republic	98–3	**9**
12/06/2005	Czech Republic	75–10	**7**

MOST CONVERSIONS IN A MATCH BY A PLAYER

Date	Player	Opponent	Cons
03/02/2002	Pavle Jimsheladze	Netherlands	**9**
07/04/2007	Merab Kvirikashvili	Czech Republic	**9**
12/06/2005	Malkhaz Urjukashvili	Czech Republic	**7**

MOST PENALTIES IN A MATCH BY THE TEAM

Date	Opponent	Result	Pens
08/03/2003	Russia	23–7	6

MOST PENALTIES IN A MATCH BY A PLAYER

Date	Player	Opponent	Pens
08/03/2003	Pavle Jimsheladze	Russia	6

MOST DROP GOALS IN A MATCH BY A PLAYER

Date	Player	Opponent	DGs
15/07/1992	Davit Chavleishvili	Ukraine	2

MOST CAPPED PLAYERS

Player	Caps
Pavle Jimsheladze	57
Malkhaz Urjukashvili	56
Irakli Abuseridze	53
Besiki Khamashuridze	53

LEADING TRY SCORERS

Player	Tries
Malkhaz Urjukashvili	15
Ilia Zedginidze	13
Mamuka Gorgodze	12
Besiki Khamashuridze	12

LEADING CONVERSIONS SCORERS

Player	Cons
Pavle Jimsheladze	61
Malkhaz Urjukashvili	40
Merab Kvirikashvili	22
Nugzar Dzagnidze	9

LEADING PENALTY SCORERS

Player	Pens
Pavle Jimsheladze	48
Malkhaz Urjukashvili	37
Nugzar Dzagnidze	22
Merab Kvirikashvili	14

LEADING DROP GOAL SCORERS

Player	DGs
Kakha Machitidze	4
Nugzar Dzagnidze	3
Pavle Jimsheladze	3

LEADING POINTS SCORERS

Player	Pts.
Pavle Jimsheladze	320
Malkhaz Urjukashvili	269
Nugzar Dzagnidze	105

GEORGIA INTERNATIONAL PLAYERS
UP TO 30TH SEPTEMBER 2008

Note: Years given for International Championship matches are for second half of season; eg 1972 means season 1971–72. Years for all other matches refer to the actual year of the match.

V Abashidze 1998 *It, Ukr, I*, 1999 *Tg, Tg*, 2000 *It, Mor, Sp*, 2001 *H, Pt, Rus, Sp, R*, 2006 *J*
N Abdaladze 1997 *Cro, De*
I Abuseridze 2000 *It, Pt, Mor, Sp, H, R*, 2001 *H, Pt, Rus, Sp, R*, 2002 *Pt, Rus, Sp, R, I, Rus*, 2003 *Pt, Rus, CZR, R, It, E, Sa, SA*, 2004 *Rus*, 2005 *Pt, Ukr, R*, 2006 *Rus, R, Pt, Ukr, J, R, Sp, Pt, Pt*, 2007 *R, Rus, CZR, Nm, ESp, ItA, Ar, I, Nm, F*, 2008 *Pt, R, Pt, Rus, Sp*
V Akhvlediani 2007 *CZR*
K Alania 1993 *Lux*, 1994 *Swi*, 1996 *CZR, CZR, Rus*, 1997 *Pt, Pol, Cro, De*, 1998 *It*, 2001 *H, Pt, Sp, F, SA*, 2002 *H, Pt, Rus, Sp, R, I, Rus*, 2003 *Rus*, 2004 *Pt, Sp*
N Andghuladze 1997 *Pol*, 2000 *It, Pt, Mor, Sp, H, R*, 2004 *Sp, Rus, CZR, R*
D Ashvetia 1998 *Ukr*, 2005 *Pt*, 2006 *R*, 2007 *Sp*
K Asieshvili 2008 *ItA*
G Babunashvili 1992 *Ukr, Ukr, Lat*, 1993 *Rus, Pol, Lux*, 1996 *CZR*
Z Bakuradze 1989 *Z*, 1990 *Z*, 1991 *Ukr, Ukr*, 1993 *Rus, Pol*
D Baramidze 2000 *H*
O Barkalaia 2002 *I*, 2004 *Sp, Rus, CZR, R, Ur, Ch, Rus*, 2005 *Pt, Ukr, R, CZR, Ch*, 2006 *Rus, R, Pt, Ukr, J, Bb, R, Sp*, 2007 *Nm, ItA, I, F*, 2008 *Pt, R, Pt, Rus, Sp, Ur, ItA*
D Basilaia 2008 *Pt, R, Pt, CZR, Rus, Sp*
R Belkania 2004 *Sp*, 2005 *Ch*, 2007 *Sp, Rus*
G Beriashvili 1993 *Rus, Pol*, 1995 *Ger*
M Besselia 1991 *Ukr*, 1993 *Rus, Pol*, 1996 *Rus*, 1997 *Pt*
D Bolgashvili 2000 *It, Pt, H, R*, 2001 *H, Pt, Rus, Sp, R, F, SA*, 2002 *H, Pt, Rus, I*, 2003 *Pt, Sp, Rus, CZR, R, E, Sa, SA*, 2004 *Rus, Ur, Ch, Rus*, 2005 *CZR*, 2007 *Sp*
J Bregvadze 2008 *ItA*
G Buguianishvili 1996 *CZR, Rus*, 1997 *Pol*, 1998 *It, Rus, I, R*, 2000 *Sp, H, R*, 2001 *H, F, SA*, 2002 *Rus*
D Chavleishvili 1990 *Z, Z*, 1992 *Ukr, Ukr, Lat*, 1993 *Pol, Lux*
M Cheishvili 1989 *Z*, 1990 *Z, Z*, 1995 *H*
Chichua 2008 *CZR*
I Chikava 1993 *Pol, Lux*, 1994 *Swi*, 1995 *Bul, Mol, H*, 1996 *CZR, CZR*, 1997 *Pol*, 1998 *I*
R Chikvaidze 2004 *Ur, Ch*
L Chikvinidze 1994 *Swi*, 1995 *Bul, Mol, Ger, H*, 1996 *CZR, Rus*
G Chkhaidze 2002 *H, R, I, Rus*, 2003 *Pt, CZR, It, E, SA, Ur*, 2004 *CZR, R*, 2006 *Pt, Ukr*, 2007 *R, Rus, CZR, Nm, ESp, ItA, Ar, I, Nm, F*, 2008 *R, Pt, CZR, Rus, Sp*
S Chkhenkeli 1997 *Pol*
I Chkhikvadze 2005 *Ch*, 2007 *Sp*, 2008 *Pt, R, Pt, CZR, Rus, Ur, ItA*
I Chkonia 2007 *ESp, ItA*
D Dadunashvili 2003 *It, E, SA, Ur*, 2004 *Sp, Rus, CZR, R*, 2005 *Ch*, 2007 *Sp, Rus, CZR, Nm, ItA*, 2008 *Pt, R, Pt, CZR, Rus, Sp*
L Datunashvili 2004 *Sp*, 2005 *Pt, Ukr, R, CZR*, 2006 *Rus, R, Pt, Ukr, J, Bb, CZR, Pt, Pt*, 2007 *R, Rus, Nm, ESp, ItA, I, Nm, F*, 2008 *Pt, Pt*
V Didebulidze 1991 *Ukr*, 1994 *Kaz*, 1995 *Bul, Mol*, 1996 *CZR*, 1997 *De*, 1999 *Tg*, 2000 *H*, 2001 *H, Pt, Rus, Sp, R, F, SA*, 2002 *H, Pt, Rus, Sp, R, I, Rus*, 2003 *Pt, Sp, Rus, CZR, R, It, E, Sa, SA*, 2004 *Rus*, 2005 *Pt*, 2006 *R, R*, 2007 *R, Sp, Rus, CZR, Nm, ESp, ItA, Ar, Nm, F*
E Dzagnidze 1992 *Ukr, Ukr, Lat*, 1993 *Rus, Pol*, 1995 *Bul, Mol, Ger, H*, 1998 *I*
N Dzagnidze 1989 *Z*, 1990 *Z, Z*, 1991 *Ukr*, 1992 *Ukr, Ukr, Lat*, 1993 *Rus, Pol*, 1994 *Swi*, 1995 *Ger, H*
D Dzneladze 1992 *Ukr, Lat*, 1993 *Lux*, 1994 *Kaz*
P Dzotsenidze 1995 *Ger, H*, 1997 *Pt, Pol*
G Elizbarashvili 2002 *Rus*, 2003 *Sp*, 2004 *Ch*, 2005 *CZR*, 2006 *Pt, Ukr, J, Bb, CZR, Sp, Pt*, 2007 *R, Sp, Rus, I, F*
O Eloshvili 2002 *H*, 2003 *SA*, 2006 *Bb, CZR*, 2007 *Sp, CZR, Nm, ESp, ItA, I, F*
S Essakia 1999 *Tg, Tg*, 2000 *It, Mor, Sp, H*, 2004 *CZR, R*
M Gagnidze 1991 *Ukr, Ukr*
D Gasviani 2004 *Sp, Rus*, 2005 *CZR, Ch*, 2006 *Ukr, J*, 2007 *Rus, CZR*, 2008 *Ur, ItA*
A Ghibradze 1992 *Ukr, Ukr, Lat*, 1994 *Swi*, 1995 *Bul, Mol, Ger*, 1996 *CZR*
D Ghudushauri 1989 *Z*, 1991 *Ukr, Ukr*
L Ghvaberidze 2004 *Pt*
R Gigauri 2006 *Ukr, J, Bb, CZR, Sp, Pt, Pt*, 2007 *R, Nm, ESp, ItA, Ar, Nm, F*, 2008 *Pt, R, Pt, Rus, Sp, Ur*
A Giorgadze 1996 *CZR*, 1998 *It, Ukr, Rus, R*, 1999 *Tg, Tg*, 2000 *It, Pt, Mor, H, R*, 2001 *H, Pt, Rus, Sp, R, F, SA*, 2002 *H, Pt, Rus, Sp, R, I, Rus*, 2003 *Pt, Sp, Rus, R, It, E, Sa, SA, Ur*, 2005 *Pt, Ukr, R, CZR*, 2006 *Rus, R, Pt, Bb, CZR, Sp, Pt*, 2007 *R, Ar, I, Nm, F*
I Giorgadze 2001 *F, SA*, 2003 *Pt, Sp, Rus, R, It, E, Sa, Ur*, 2004 *Rus*, 2005 *Pt, R, CZR*, 2006 *Rus, R, Pt, Bb, CZR, R, Sp, Pt, Pt*, 2007 *R, Sp, Rus, CZR, Ar, Nm, F*, 2008 *R*
M Gorgodze 2003 *Sp, Rus*, 2004 *Pt, Sp, Rus, CZR, R, Ur, Ch, Rus*, 2005 *Pt, Ukr, R, CZR, Ch*, 2006 *Rus, Pt, Bb, CZR, R, Sp, Pt, Pt*, 2007 *Ar, I, Nm*, 2008 *R, Rus, Sp*
E Gueguchadze 1990 *Z, Z*
L Gugava 2004 *Sp, Rus, CZR, Ur, Ch, Rus*, 2005 *Pt, Ukr*, 2006 *Bb, CZR*
I Guiorkhelidze 1998 *R*, 1999 *Tg, Tg*
G Guiunashvili 1989 *Z*, 1990 *Z*, 1991 *Ukr, Ukr*, 1992 *Ukr, Ukr, Lat*, 1993 *Rus, Pol, Lux*, 1994 *Swi*, 1996 *Rus*, 1997 *Pt*
K Guiunashvili 1990 *Z, Z*, 1991 *Ukr, Ukr*, 1992 *Ukr, Ukr, Lat*
S Gujaraidze 2003 *SA, Ur*
I Gundishvili 2002 *I*, 2003 *Pt, Sp, Rus, CZR*, 2008 *Ur, ItA*
D Gurgenidze 2007 *Sp, ItA*
A Gusharashvili 1998 *Ukr*
D Iobidze 1993 *Rus, Pol*
E Iovadze 1993 *Lux*, 1994 *Kaz*, 1995 *Bul, Mol, Ger, H*, 2001 *Sp, F, SA*, 2002 *H, Rus, Sp, R, I*
A Issakadze 1989 *Z*
N Iurini 1991 *Ukr*, 1994 *Swi*, 1995 *Ger, H*, 1996 *CZR, CZR, Rus*, 1997 *Pt, Pol, Cro, De*, 1998 *Ukr, Rus*, 2000 *It, Sp, H, R*
S Janelidze 1991 *Ukr, Ukr*, 1993 *Rus*, 1994 *Kaz*, 1995 *Ger*, 1997 *Pt*, 1998 *Ukr, I, R*, 1999 *Tg*, 2000 *R*
R Japarashvili 1992 *Ukr, Ukr, Lat*, 1993 *Pol, Lux*, 1996 *CZR*, 1997 *Pt*
L Javelidze 1997 *Cro*, 1998 *I*, 2001 *H, R, F, SA*, 2002 *H, R*, 2004 *R*, 2005 *Ukr*, 2007 *Sp*
G Jgenti 2007 *Nm, ESp, ItA*
D Jghenti 2004 *CZR, R*
D Jhamutashvili 2005 *Ch*
G Jhghenti 2004 *Ur*, 2005 *Ch*, 2007 *Sp, CZR*

P Jimsheladze 1995 *Bul, Mol, H,* 1996 *CZR, CZR, Rus,* 1997 *De,* 1998 *It, Ukr, Rus, I, R,* 1999 *Tg, Tg,* 2000 *Pt, Mor, Sp, H, R,* 2001 *H, Pt, Rus, Sp, R, F, SA,* 2002 *H, Pt, Rus, Sp, I, Rus,* 2003 *Pt, Sp, Rus, CZR, R, It, E, Sa, SA, Ur,* 2004 *Rus,* 2005 *R,* 2006 *Rus, R, Pt, Ukr, J, Bb, CZR, Pt, Pt,* 2007 *R, Rus, CZR, Ar*
K Jintcharadze 1993 *Rus, Pol,* 2000 *It, Mor*
D Kacharava 2006 *Ukr, J, R, Sp, Pt,* 2007 *R, Sp, Rus, CZR, Nm, ESp, ItA, I, Nm,* 2008 *Pt, R, Pt, CZR, Rus, Sp*
G Kacharava 2005 *Ukr,* 2006 *J, Bb, CZR, R,* 2007 *Sp,* 2008 *CZR*
G Kakhiani 1995 *Bul, Mol*
V Katsadze 1997 *Pol,* 1998 *It, Ukr, Rus, I, R,* 1999 *Tg, Tg,* 2000 *Pt, Mor, Sp, H, R,* 2001 *H, Pt, Rus, Sp, R,* 2002 *Pt, Rus, Sp, R, I, Rus,* 2003 *Pt, Sp, CZR, R, E, Sa, SA, Ur,* 2004 *Sp,* 2005 *Ukr*
A Kavtarashvili 1994 *Swi,* 1995 *Bul, Mol, Ger,* 1996 *CZR, Rus,* 1997 *Pt, Cro, De,* 1998 *It, Rus, I, R,* 1999 *Tg, Tg,* 2000 *It, H, R,* 2001 *H,* 2003 *SA, Ur*
I Kerauli 1991 *Ukr, Ukr,* 1992 *Ukr, Ukr*
L Khachirashvili 2005 *Ukr*
T Khakhaleishili 1994 *Kaz*
B Khamashuridze 1989 *Z*
B Khamashuridze 1998 *It, Ukr, Rus, I, R,* 1999 *Tg, Tg,* 2000 *It, Pt, Sp, H, R,* 2001 *Pt, Rus, Sp, R, F, SA,* 2002 *H, Pt, Rus, Sp, R, I, Rus,* 2003 *Pt, CZR, R, It, E, Sa, SA, Ur,* 2004 *Pt, Rus, Rus,* 2005 *Pt, Ukr, Ch,* 2006 *Rus, R, Pt, R, Sp, Pt, Pt,* 2007 *Rus, CZR, ESp, Ar, Nm, F,* 2008 *Pt*
M Kharshiladze 1991 *Ukr*
B Khekhelashvili 1999 *Tg, Tg,* 2000 *It, Pt, Mor, Sp, H, R,* 2001 *H, Pt, R, F, SA,* 2002 *H, Pt, Rus, Sp, R, I,* 2003 *Sp, Rus, CZR, R, E, Sa,* 2004 *Sp*
D Khinchagashvili 2003 *Sp, CZR,* 2004 *Pt, Sp, Rus,* 2006 *Bb, CZR, Sp, Pt, Pt,* 2007 *R, Rus, Nm, ESp, ItA, Ar, I, Nm*
L Khmaladze 2008 *ItA*
G Khonelidze 2003 *SA*
G Khositashvili 2008 *Ur, ItA*
N Khuade 1989 *Z,* 1990 *Z, Z,* 1991 *Ukr, Ukr,* 1993 *Rus, Pol, Lux,* 1994 *Swi,* 1995 *Ger*
Z Khutsishvili 1993 *Lux,* 1994 *Kaz, Swi,* 1995 *Bul,* 1996 *CZR*
A Khvedelidze 1989 *Z,* 1990 *Z, Z,* 1991 *Ukr, Ukr,* 1992 *Ukr, Ukr, Lat,* 1993 *Rus, Pol*
I Kiasashvili 2008 *Pt, CZR, Ur*
D Kiknadze 2004 *Rus,* 2005 *Pt, Ukr*
A Kobakhidze 1997 *Cro,* 1998 *I*
K Kobakhidze 1995 *Ger, H,* 1996 *Rus,* 1997 *Pt,* 1998 *It, Ukr, Rus, I, R,* 1999 *Tg,* 2000 *It*
Z Koberidze 2004 *Ur*
V Kolelishvili 2008 *ItA*
A Kopaleishvili 2004 *Ur*
A Kopaliani 2003 *It, SA, Ur,* 2004 *Pt,* 2005 *Ukr, R,* 2006 *Rus, R, Ukr, J, Bb, CZR, R, Sp, Pt,* 2007 *R, Sp, Rus, CZR, Ar, I, Nm, F*
D Kubriashvili 2008 *Pt, R, Pt, Rus, Sp*
E Kuparadze 2007 *ESp*
G Kutarashvili 2004 *Pt, Sp, CZR, R,* 2005 *Ch,* 2006 *Rus, R, Pt, Ukr, J, R*
B Kvinikhidze 2002 *R,* 2004 *Pt, Sp, CZR, R,* 2005 *Ch*
M Kvirikashvili 2003 *Pt, Sp, CZR, E, Sa, SA, Ur,* 2004 *Rus, CZR, R, Ch,* 2005 *CZR, Ch,* 2007 *R, Sp, Rus, CZR, Nm, ESp, ItA, Ar, I, Nm, F,* 2008 *Pt, CZR, Rus, Sp*
G Labadze 1996 *CZR, Rus,* 1997 *Pt, Pol, Cro, De,* 1998 *It, Ukr, Rus, I, R,* 1999 *Tg, Tg,* 2000 *It, Pt, Sp, H, R,* 2001 *H, Pt, Rus, Sp, F, SA,* 2002 *Pt, Rus, Sp, R, Rus,* 2003 *Rus, CZR, R, It, E, Sa,* 2004 *Rus,* 2005 *R,* 2006 *Rus, R, Pt, J, R, Pt, Pt,* 2007 *Rus, Ar, Nm*
I Lezhava 1991 *Ukr, Ukr,* 1992 *Ukr,* 1995 *Bul*
Z Lezhava 1991 *Ukr,* 1995 *Ger,* 1996 *CZR, CZR, Rus,* 1997 *Pt, Cro, De,* 1998 *It, Rus, R,* 1999 *Tg*
B Liluashvili 1989 *Z,* 1990 *Z, Z*
L Liluashvili 1997 *Pt*
O Liparteliani 1989 *Z,* 1990 *Z, Z*
S Liparteliani 1991 *Ukr,* 1994 *Kaz, Swi,* 1996 *CZR*
Z Liparteliani 1994 *Kaz, Swi,* 1995 *Bul, Mol, Ger, H*
M Lossaberidze 1989 *Z*
K Machitidze 1989 *Z,* 1993 *Rus,* 1995 *Bul, Mol, Ger, H,* 1996 *CZR, CZR, Rus,* 1997 *Pt, Pol, Cro, De,* 1998 *It, Ukr, Rus, R,* 1999 *Tg*
I Machkhaneli 2002 *H, R,* 2003 *It, E, Sa, SA, Ur,* 2004 *Pt, Ur, Ch, Rus,* 2005 *Pt, Ukr, R, CZR, Ch,* 2006 *Rus, R, Pt, Bb, CZR, R, Pt,* 2007 *R, Ar, I, Nm*
M Magrakvelidze 1998 *Ukr,* 2000 *Mor,* 2001 *F,* 2002 *Pt, Sp, R,* 2004 *Rus,* 2005 *Pt, R,* 2006 *Bb, CZR, Pt, Pt,* 2007 *R, CZR, Nm, ESp, ItA, I, F*
I Maisuradze 1997 *Cro,* 1998 *It, Ukr,* 1999 *Tg, Tg,* 2004 *Rus, R,* 2005 *CZR,* 2006 *Bb, CZR, R, Pt, Pt,* 2007 *R, Sp, Rus, CZR, ESp, ItA, I, F*
S Maisuradze 2008 *Pt, CZR, Rus, Sp, Ur, ItA*
Z Maisuradze 2004 *Pt, Sp, CZR, Ur, Ch, Rus,* 2005 *Ukr, R,* 2006 *Rus, R, Pt, Ukr, J, Bb, CZR, Sp,* 2007 *Nm, ESp, ItA, Ar, I, F,* 2008 *Pt*
L Malaguradze 2008 *Pt, R, Pt, CZR, Rus, Sp, Ur, ItA*
K Margvelashvili 2003 *It, E, Sa, SA*
M Marjanishvili 1990 *Z, Z,* 1992 *Ukr, Ukr, Lat,* 1993 *Rus, Pol, Lux*
A Matchutadze 1993 *Lux,* 1994 *Kaz,* 1995 *Bul, Mol,* 1997 *Pt, Pol, Cro, De*
Z Matiashvili 2003 *Sp,* 2005 *Ch*
G Mchedlishvili 2008 *CZR*
S Melikidze 2008 *CZR, Sp, ItA*
L Mgueladze 1992 *Ukr, Ukr*
N Mgueladze 1995 *Bul, Mol, H,* 1997 *Pol*
I Modebadze 2003 *SA, Ur,* 2004 *Sp*
S Modebadze 1994 *Kaz,* 1995 *Mol,* 1996 *CZR, CZR, Rus,* 1997 *Pt, Pol, Cro, De,* 1998 *It, Ukr, Rus,* 1999 *Tg,* 2000 *It, Pt,* 2001 *Sp, F, SA,* 2002 *H, Pt, Rus, Sp, R*
A Mtchedlishvili 2004 *Ur, Ch,* 2008 *CZR*
S Mtchedlishvili 2000 *It,* 2007 *Sp*
Z Mtchedlishvili 1995 *Mol,* 1996 *CZR,* 1997 *Cro, De,* 1998 *It, Ukr, Rus, I, R,* 1999 *Tg, Tg,* 2000 *Pt, Mor, Sp, H, R,* 2001 *Rus, Sp, R, F, SA,* 2002 *H, Pt, Rus, I, Rus,* 2003 *Pt, Sp, Rus, CZR, R, It, E, Sa, Ur,* 2004 *Pt, Rus,* 2005 *Pt,* 2006 *J,* 2007 *Rus, CZR, Nm, ESp, ItA, F*
M Mtiulishvili 1991 *Ukr,* 1994 *Kaz,* 1996 *CZR, CZR, Rus,* 1997 *Pt, Pol, Cro, De,* 1998 *It, Ukr, Rus, R,* 2001 *H, Pt, Rus, Sp, R,* 2002 *H, Pt, Rus, Sp, R, I,* 2003 *Rus, CZR, R,* 2004 *Rus, CZR, R*
V Nadiradze 1994 *Kaz, Swi,* 1995 *H,* 1996 *Rus,* 1997 *Pt, De,* 1998 *I, R,* 1999 *Tg,* 2000 *Pt, Mor, Sp, H, R,* 2001 *H, Pt, Rus, Sp, R, F, SA,* 2002 *H, Pt, Rus, Sp, R, I, Rus,* 2003 *Rus, CZR, R, It, E, Sa*
A Natchqebia 1990 *Z, Z*
I Natriashvili 2008 *Ur, ItA*
I Natriashvili 2006 *Ukr, J,* 2007 *ItA,* 2008 *Pt, R, Pt, Rus, Sp*
N Natroshvili 1992 *Ukr, Ukr, Lat*
G Nemsadze 2005 *Ch,* 2006 *Ukr,* 2007 *Sp,* 2008 *CZR, Sp, Ur, ItA*
A Nijaradze 2008 *CZR*
I Nikolaenko 1999 *Tg, Tg,* 2000 *It, Mor, Sp, H, R,* 2001 *R, F,* 2003 *Pt, Sp, E, Sa, SA, Ur*
I Ninidze 2004 *Ur, Ch*
D Oboladze 1993 *Rus, Pol, Lux,* 1994 *Swi,* 1995 *Bul, Mol, Ger, H,* 1996 *CZR, CZR, Rus,* 1997 *Pt, Pol,* 1998 *It, Ukr*
T Odisharia 1989 *Z,* 1994 *Kaz*
S Papashvili 2001 *SA,* 2004 *CZR, R,* 2006 *Bb, CZR,* 2007 *Sp*
S Partsikanashvili 1994 *Kaz,* 1996 *CZR, Rus,* 1997 *Pol,* 1999 *Tg, Tg,* 2000 *It, Pt, Mor*
Peikrishvili 2008 *Pt, Pt*
G Peradze 1991 *Ukr*
Z Peradze 1997 *Pol,* 1998 *Rus*
D Pinchukovi 2004 *CZR*
L Pirpilashvili 2004 *Rus, CZR, R, Ur, Ch,* 2005 *Ukr, R, CZR*
G Pirtskhalava 1989 *Z,* 1995 *Ger,* 1996 *CZR, Rus,* 1997 *Pt, Pol*
T Pkhakadze 1989 *Z,* 1990 *Z, Z,* 1993 *Rus, Pol, Lux,* 1994 *Kaz,* 1996 *CZR*
G Rapava-Ruskini 1990 *Z,* 1992 *Ukr, Lat,* 1994 *Kaz,* 1996 *Rus,* 1997 *Pt, Cro, De,* 1998 *It, Ukr, Rus, R,* 1999 *Tg*

T Ratianidze 2000 *It*, 2001 *H*, *Pt*, *Sp*, *R*, *SA*, 2002 *Pt*, *Rus*, *Sp*, *R*, *I*, *Rus*, 2003 *Pt*, *Sp*, *Rus*, *CZR*, *R*
Z Rekhviashvili 1995 *H*, 1997 *Pt*, *Pol*
G Rokhvadze 2008 *ItA*
S Sakandelidze 1996 *CZR*, 1998 *Ukr*
B Samkharadze 2004 *Pt*, *Sp*, *Rus*, *CZR*, *R*, *Ur*, *Ch*, 2005 *CZR*, *Ch*, 2006 *Rus*, *R*, *Pt*, *Ukr*, *Bb*, *CZR*, *R*, *Sp*, *Pt*, *Pt*, 2007 *R*, *Sp*, *Rus*, *CZR*, *Nm*, *ESp*, *Ar*, *I*, *Nm*, *F*, 2008 *Pt*, *R*, *Pt*, *Sp*, *Ur*, *ItA*
A Sanadze 2004 *Ch*
P Saneblidze 1994 *Kaz*
G Sanikidze 2004 *Ur*, *Ch*
B Sardanashvili 2004 *Ch*
V Satseradze 1989 *Z*, 1990 *Z*, 1991 *Ukr*, 1992 *Ukr*, *Ukr*, *Lat*
E Shanidze 1994 *Swi*
G Shkinin 2004 *CZR*, *R*, *Ch*, 2005 *Ch*, 2006 *Rus*, *R*, *Ukr*, *J*, *R*, *Sp*, *Pt*, *Pt*, 2007 *R*, *Sp*, *Rus*, *CZR*, *Nm*, *ESp*, *ItA*, *Ar*, *I*, *Nm*, 2008 *R*, *Pt*, *CZR*, *Rus*, *Sp*, *Ur*, *ItA*
B Shvanguiradze 1990 *Z*, *Z*, 1992 *Ukr*, *Ukr*, *Lat*, 1993 *Rus*, *Pol*, *Lux*
G Shvelidze 1998 *I*, *R*, 1999 *Tg*, *Tg*, 2000 *It*, *Pt*, *Sp*, *H*, *R*, 2001 *H*, *Pt*, *Sp*, *F*, *SA*, 2002 *H*, *Rus*, *I*, *Rus*, 2003 *Pt*, *Sp*, *Rus*, *CZR*, *R*, *It*, *E*, *Sa*, *Ur*, 2004 *Rus*, 2005 *Pt*, *CZR*, 2006 *Rus*, *R*, *Pt*, *R*, *Sp*, *Pt*, *Pt*, 2007 *Ar*, *I*, *Nm*, *F*, 2008 *Pt*, *R*, *Pt*, *CZR*, *Rus*
I Sikharulidze 1994 *Kaz*
T Sokhadze 2005 *CZR*, 2006 *Rus*, *R*, *Pt*, *Ukr*, *J*, *Pt*, *Pt*
M Sujashvili 2004 *Pt*, *Rus*, 2005 *Pt*, *Ukr*, *R*, *CZR*, 2006 *Pt*, *Ukr*, *J*, *Bb*, *CZR*
S Sultanishvili 1998 *Ukr*
S Sutiashvili 2005 *Ch*, 2006 *Ukr*, 2007 *CZR*, *Nm*, *ESp*, 2008 *Pt*, *R*, *CZR*, *Rus*
P Svanidze 1992 *Ukr*
T Tavadze 1991 *Ukr*, *Ukr*
N Tchavtchavadze 1998 *It*, *Ukr*, 2004 *CZR*, *R*, *Ur*, *Ch*
B Tepnadze 1995 *H*, 1996 *CZR*, 1997 *Cro*, 1998 *I*, *R*, 1999 *Tg*
Todua 2008 *CZR*, *Rus*, *Sp*, *Ur*, *ItA*
P Tqabladze 1993 *Lux*, 1995 *Bul*
L Tsabadze 1994 *Kaz*, *Swi*, 1995 *Bul*, *Ger*, *H*, 1996 *CZR*, *Rus*, 1997 *Cro*, *De*, 1998 *It*, *Rus*, *I*, *R*, 1999 *Tg*, *Tg*, 2000 *Pt*, *Mor*, *Sp*, *R*, 2001 *H*, *Pt*, *Rus*, *Sp*, *R*, *F*, *SA*, 2002 *H*, *Pt*, *Rus*, *Sp*, *R*, *I*, *Rus*
B Tsiklauri 2008 *ItA*
G Tsiklauri 2003 *SA*, *Ur*
D Tskhvediani 1998 *Ukr*
V Tskitishvili 1994 *Swi*, 1995 *Bul*, *Mol*
T Turdzeladze 1989 *Z*, 1990 *Z*, *Z*, 1991 *Ukr*, 1995 *Ger*, *H*
K Uchava 2002 *Sp*, 2004 *Sp*, 2008 *Pt*, *R*, *Pt*, *Rus*, *Sp*, *Ur*, *ItA*
B Udesiani 2001 *Sp*, *F*, 2002 *H*, 2004 *Pt*, *Sp*, *CZR*, *R*, *Rus*, 2005 *Pt*, *Ukr*, *R*, *CZR*, *Ch*, 2006 *Rus*, *R*, *Ukr*, *J*, *Bb*, *CZR*, *R*, *Sp*, *Pt*, *Pt*, 2007 *R*, *Rus*, *CZR*, *Ar*, *Nm*, 2008 *CZR*, *Sp*, *Ur*, *ItA*
M Urjukashvili 1997 *Cro*, *De*, 1998 *Ukr*, *Rus*, *R*, 1999 *Tg*, *Tg*, 2000 *It*, *Pt*, *Mor*, *Sp*, 2001 *Pt*, *Rus*, *Sp*, *R*, *F*, *SA*, 2002 *H*, *Pt*, *Sp*, *R*, *I*, *Rus*, 2003 *Pt*, *Sp*, *Rus*, *R*, *It*, *E*, *Sa*, *Ur*, 2004 *Pt*, *Rus*, *Ur*, *Ch*, *Rus*, 2005 *Pt*, *R*, *CZR*, 2006 *Rus*, *R*, *Pt*, *Ukr*, *J*, *R*, *Sp*, 2007 *Rus*, *CZR*, *Nm*, *ESp*, *ItA*, *Ar*, *I*, *Nm*, *F*, 2008 *Sp*
R Urushadze 1997 *Pol*, 2002 *R*, 2004 *Pt*, *Rus*, *Rus*, 2005 *Pt*, *Ukr*, *R*, *CZR*, *Ch*, 2006 *Rus*, *R*, *Pt*, *Bb*, *CZR*, *R*, *Sp*, *Pt*, *Pt*, 2007 *Nm*, *ESp*, *ItA*, *I*, *Nm*, *F*, 2008 *Pt*, *R*, *Pt*, *Rus*, *Sp*
Z Valishvili 2004 *Ch*
D Vartaniani 1991 *Ukr*, *Ukr*, 1992 *Ukr*, *Ukr*, *Lat*, 1997 *Pol*, 2000 *Sp*, *H*, *R*
L Vashadze 1991 *Ukr*, 1992 *Ukr*, *Ukr*, *Lat*
G Yachvili 2001 *H*, *Pt*, *R*, 2003 *Pt*, *Sp*, *Rus*, *CZR*, *R*, *It*, *E*, *Sa*, *Ur*
I Zedginidze 1998 *I*, 2000 *It*, *Pt*, *Mor*, *Sp*, *H*, *R*, 2001 *H*, *Pt*, *Rus*, *Sp*, *R*, 2002 *H*, *Rus*, *Sp*, *I*, *Rus*, 2003 *Pt*, *Sp*, *Rus*, *CZR*, *R*, *It*, *Sa*, *SA*, *Ur*, 2004 *Pt*, *Sp*, *Rus*, *CZR*, *R*, *Rus*, 2005 *Pt*, *Ukr*, *R*, *CZR*, 2006 *Rus*, *R*, *Pt*, *Ukr*, *CZR*, *R*, *Sp*, *Pt*, *Pt*, 2007 *R*, *Ar*, *I*
T Zibzibadze 2000 *It*, *Pt*, *Mor*, *Sp*, 2001 *H*, *Pt*, *Rus*, *Sp*, *R*, *F*, *SA*, 2002 *H*, *Pt*, *Rus*, *Sp*, *R*, *I*, *Rus*, 2003 *Pt*, *Sp*, *Rus*, *CZR*, *R*, *It*, *E*, *Sa*, *Ur*, 2004 *Pt*, *Sp*, *Rus*, *CZR*, *R*, *Rus*, 2005 *Pt*, *Ukr*, *R*, *CZR*
D Zirakashvili 2004 *Ur*, *Ch*, *Rus*, 2005 *Ukr*, *R*, *CZR*, 2006 *Rus*, *R*, *Pt*, *R*, *Sp*, *Pt*, 2007 *R*, *Ar*, *Nm*, *F*, 2008 *R*

IRELAND

IRELAND'S 2008 TEST RECORD

OPPONENTS	DATE	VENUE	RESULT
Italy	2 February	H	**Won** 16-11
France	9 February	A	**Lost** 21-26
Scotland	23 February	H	**Won** 34-13
Wales	8 March	H	**Lost** 12-16
England	15 March	A	**Lost** 10-33
New Zealand	7 June	A	**Lost** 11-21
Australia	14 June	A	**Lost** 12-18

O'SULLIVAN QUITS AS IRISH STRUGGLE

Shaun Botterill / Getty Images

The high point for Ireland in the 2008 Six Nations was the win over Scotland

When their side crashed out of the World Cup, failing to make the knockout stages for the first time in the tournament's 20-year history, optimistic Ireland fans hoped it would prove a temporary, albeit demoralising aberration rather than evidence of a once powerful side in terminal decline.

Judging on the evidence of the side's subsequent Six Nations campaign and summer foray to New Zealand and Australia, their optimism may have been misplaced.

Ireland were truly woeful at the World Cup but the anticipated resurgence in the Six Nations failed to materialise, ultimately costing Eddie O'Sullivan his job after seven years as head coach, and although they were competitive in both their one-off Tests against the All Blacks and

Wallabies, the sense that the side was in urgent need of dismantling so it could be rebuilt was inescapable.

The national side's frailties were the more frustrating given the successes of the provincial teams. Munster lifted the Heineken Cup after a heroic effort against Toulouse and Leinster claimed the Magners League title for the second time and still the Ireland team struggled. The pieces of the jigsaw were there but O'Sullivan and his players could not solve the puzzle.

Ireland and O'Sullivan began the season acutely aware of the pressure they were under. The head coach had escaped the wrath of his employers despite the team's dismal displays at the World Cup and kept his job but there was no doubt the axe was being discreetly sharpened in the wings. Ireland simply had to perform or the coach would pay the ultimate price.

The Six Nations campaign began at Croke Park against the Italians and although Ireland eventually emerged 16-11 winners, it was not the convincing performance that the coach had wanted. A solitary try from Girvan Dempsey and three penalties from Ronan O'Gara were enough to secure victory but the Azzurri could have snatched it late on and the performance raised more questions than it answered.

"It was a long, drawn-out, ugly affair and we had to work very hard for the win," O'Sullivan conceded. "I'd have preferred if we hit the ground running but I have to be sensible and know that winning the first game is hard.

"In the first half we showed some great flashes and played some good rugby after the initial shadowboxing, but we didn't finish things off and the danger is that the opposition come back into the game."

Ireland travelled to Paris a week later to tackle France, looking for their first win in the French capital since 2000 but a hat-trick of first-half tries from wing Vincent Clerc put pay to their challenge almost before it had began and the visitors trailed 19-6 at the break.

The second half, however, was a different story and a penalty try and a further score from flanker David Wallace gave O'Sullivan's side hope of pulling off a sensational comeback but they could not quite produce the knockout blow and a visibly relieved France clung on for a 26-21 win.

"When you lose a game, the initial feeling is disappointment," said skipper Brian O'Driscoll after his side's near miss. "But when I think about it more, the overriding feeling now is huge pride in the team. We really felt we owed ourselves a performance and the coach a performance."

Two weeks later the Irish welcomed Scotland to Croke Park and it was to prove the most comfortable fixture of their Championship as they ran in five tries, including a brace from Tommy Bowe, in a 34-13 triumph. It was still not vintage Ireland but the green shoots of recovery were nonetheless in evidence.

Wales, however, were to trample all over them at Croke Park in early March as they claimed the Triple Crown. Four O'Gara penalties gave Ireland a glimmer of hope but a Shane Williams try in the second-half gave Wales the edge and it was the visitors who held out for a narrow 16-12 win. Irish hopes of a concerted revival had been blown off course.

O'Sullivan's side's Six Nations campaign ended in London against England and with Ireland looking for their third consecutive win at Twickenham, their was confidence they could end the tournament on a high. The loss of O'Driscoll with a hamstring injury sustained in the Wales game was a blow but with England licking their wounds after defeat in Scotland, Ireland knew their hosts were vulnerable.

The early exchanges heightened Irish expectation when Rob Kearney crashed over in the fourth minute. O'Gara converted and added a penalty and Ireland were 10-0 to the good. It was Ireland's best period of the game but when England came storming back into contention, they could find no answer to the challenge and tries from Paul Sackey, Matthew Tait and Jamie Noon, plus 18 points from young fly-half Danny Cipriani on debut, steered the home side to a crushing 33-10 victory. Ireland's Championship has ended with a whimper rather than a bang. The team's fourth place finish was the first time they had finished outside the top three since the Six Nations' inception in 2000.

Almost as soon as the final whistle sounded at Twickenham, the fevered speculation about O'Sullivan's future began among the fans and the media alike, although the coach himself refused to be drawn on the prospects of losing his job.

"We have to let the dust settle," he said "There is a lot of emotion straight after a defeat in the Six Nations. We will sit down and review the tournament in the cold light of day. I certainly want to be around."

Four days later, however, O'Sullivan seemingly accepted the inevitable and fell on his own sword. It was a sad end for Ireland's most successful ever coach and the man who guided the side to three Triple Crowns but after the lows of the World Cup and Six Nations, it was inevitable that the Irish RFU would begin the search for a new man.

It took them two months to find a successor and they turned to 48-year-old Munster coach Declan Kidney, handing him a four-year contract up to the 2011 World Cup. It was the logical choice and a popular one among Ireland fans.

"There is no greater honour for any coach than to lead his own country," Kidney said. "There is no doubt that we have the talent in Ireland to be successful at the highest level."

The only problem was Kidney would be involved with Munster and the Heineken Cup and with the summer tour to New Zealand and Australia looming, Ireland appointed Connacht's Michael Bradley as caretaker coach and with a 39-14 warm-up victory over the Barbarians at Kingsholm under their belts, they set off for the southern hemisphere.

Bradley named a side to face the All Blacks in Wellington containing seven Munster forwards and four Leinster backs as Ireland looked for their first ever win on Kiwi soil in 103 years of trying.

Driving rain and icy winds made conditions in the Westpac Stadium virtually impossible but it was the All Blacks who adapted quicker, drawing first blood with a Sitiveni Sivivatu score but Ireland held firm and Paddy Wallace's try ensured the tourists went in at half-time level at 8-8.

The second period was equally treacherous as the first but New Zealand claimed the all-important try courtesy of Ma'a Nonu and although Ireland fought valiantly until the end, they could not overhaul the home side and went down 21-11. It was a creditable performance but victory against New Zealand had proved as elusive as ever.

"It's hugely disappointing," O'Driscoll said. "We came so close but we don't seem to be able to finish these games. We were well in the game after 60 minutes but we couldn't finish it off."

Ireland decamped to Melbourne to tackle the Wallabies a week later as Bradley made the decision to draft in veteran scrum-half Peter Stringer in place of Eoin Reddan.

It was the climax of what had been a difficult season but once again Ireland were only able to gain respectability rather than the breakthrough victory against a southern hemisphere power away from home, fighting all the way before succumbing to an 18-12 defeat.

In many ways the clash in the Telstra Dome was a mirror image of their loss to the All Blacks. Australia struck first with an early Berrick Barnes try, Ireland hit back through Denis Leamy, only to let the Wallabies restore their cushion courtesy of James Horwill's score. O'Driscoll gave his side genuine hope with a 61st minute try to make it 18-12 but once again Ireland could not find the extra gear in the last 20 minutes and Australia were home and dry.

"We could have had two wins," said Bradley as he reflected on a tour that promised much but ultimately failed to deliver. "The feeling is of disappointment rather than frustration. We raised the bar but the victories did not come. It is not a case of gallant losses but under-achievement."

IRELAND INTERNATIONAL STATISTICS

MATCH RECORDS UP TO 30TH SEPTEMBER 2008

MOST CONSECUTIVE TEST WINS

10	2002 R,Ru,Gg,A,Fj,Arg,	2003 S1,It1,F,W1
8	2003 Tg, Sm,W2 ,It2, S2, R ,Nm, Arg	
6	1968 S,W,A,	1969 F,E,S
6	2004 SA,US,Arg,	2005 It,S,E

MOST CONSECUTIVE TEST WITHOUT DEFEAT

Matches	Wins	Draws	Period
10	10	0	2002 to 2003
8	8	0	2003
7	6	1	1968 to 1969
6	6	0	2004 to 2005

MOST POINTS IN A MATCH

BY THE TEAM

Pts.	Opponents	Venue	Year
83	United States	Manchester (NH)	2000
78	Japan	Dublin	2000
70	Georgia	Dublin	1998
64	Fiji	Dublin	2002
64	Namibia	Sydney	2003
63	Georgia	Dublin	2002
61	Italy	Limerick	2003
61	Pacific Islands	Dublin	2006
60	Romania	Dublin	1986
60	Italy	Dublin	2000
55	Zimbabwe	Dublin	1991
55	United States	Dublin	2004
54	Wales	Dublin	2002
53	Romania	Dublin	1998
53	United States	Dublin	1999
51	Italy	Rome	2007
50	Japan	Bloemfontein	1995

BY A PLAYER

Pts.	Player	Opponents	Venue	Year
32	R J R O'Gara	Samoa	Apia	2003
30	R J R O'Gara	Italy	Dublin	2000
26	D G Humphreys	Scotland	Murrayfield	2003
26	D G Humphreys	Italy	Limerick	2003
26	P Wallace	Pacific Islands	Dublin	2006
24	P A Burke	Italy	Dublin	1997
24	D G Humphreys	Argentina	Lens	1999
23	R P Keyes	Zimbabwe	Dublin	1991
23	R J R O'Gara	Japan	Dublin	2000
22	D G Humphreys	Wales	Dublin	2002
21	S O Campbell	Scotland	Dublin	1982
21	S O Campbell	England	Dublin	1983
21	R J R O'Gara	Italy	Rome	2001
21	R J R O'Gara	Argentina	Dublin	2004
21	R J R O'Gara	England	Dublin	2007
20	M J Kiernan	Romania	Dublin	1986
20	E P Elwood	Romania	Dublin	1993
20	S J P Mason	Samoa	Dublin	1996
20	E P Elwood	Georgia	Dublin	1998
20	K G M Wood	United States	Dublin	1999
20	D A Hickie	Italy	Limerick	2003
20	D G Humphreys	United States	Dublin	2004

MOST TRIES IN A MATCH

BY THE TEAM

Tries	Opponents	Venue	Year
13	United States	Manchester (NH)	2000
11	Japan	Dublin	2000
10	Romania	Dublin	1986
10	Georgia	Dublin	1998
10	Namibia	Sydney	2003
9	Fiji	Dublin	2003
8	Western Samoa	Dublin	1988
8	Zimbabwe	Dublin	1991
8	Georgia	Dublin	2002
8	Italy	Limerick	2003
8	Pacific Islands	Dublin	2006
8	Italy	Rome	2007
7	Japan	Bloemfontein	1995
7	Romania	Dublin	1998
7	United States	Dublin	1999
7	United States	Dublin	2004
7	Japan	Tokyo	2005

BY A PLAYER

Tries	Player	Opponents	Venue	Year
4	B F Robinson	Zimbabwe	Dublin	1991
4	K G M Wood	United States	Dublin	1999
4	D A Hickie	Italy	Limerick	2003
3	R Montgomery	Wales	Birkenhead	1887
3	J P Quinn	France	Cork	1913
3	E O'D Davy	Scotland	Murrayfield	1930
3	S J Byrne	Scotland	Murrayfield	1953
3	K D Crossan	Romania	Dublin	1986
3	B J Mullin	Tonga	Brisbane	1987
3	M R Mostyn	Argentina	Dublin	1999
3	B G O'Driscoll	France	Paris	2000
3	M J Mullins	United States	Manchester (NH)	2000
3	D A Hickie	Japan	Dublin	2000
3	R A J Henderson	Italy	Rome	2001
3	B G O'Driscoll	Scotland	Dublin	2002
3	K M Maggs	Fiji	Dublin	2002

MOST CONVERSIONS IN A MATCH

BY THE TEAM

Cons	Opponents	Venue	Year
10	Georgia	Dublin	1998
10	Japan	Dublin	2000
9	United States	Manchester (NH)	2000
7	Romania	Dublin	1986
7	Georgia	Dublin	2002
7	Namibia	Sydney	2003
7	United States	Dublin	2004
6	Japan	Bloemfontein	1995
6	Romania	Dublin	1998
6	United States	Dublin	1999
6	Italy	Dublin	2000
6	Italy	Limerick	2003
6	Japan	Tokyo	2005
6	Pacific Islands	Dublin	2006

BY A PLAYER

Cons	Player	Opponents	Venue	Year
10	E P Elwood	Georgia	Dublin	1998
10	R J R O'Gara	Japan	Dublin	2000
8	R J R O'Gara	United States	Manchester (NH)	2000
7	M J Kiernan	Romania	Dublin	1986
7	R J R O'Gara	Namibia	Sydney	2003
7	D G Humphreys	United States	Dublin	2004
6	P A Burke	Japan	Bloemfontein	1995
6	R J R O'Gara	Italy	Dublin	2000
6	D G Humphreys	Italy	Limerick	2003
6	D G Humphreys	Japan	Tokyo	2005
6	P Wallace	Pacific Islands	Dublin	2006
5	M J Kiernan	Canada	Dunedin	1987
5	E P Elwood	Romania	Dublin	1999
5	R J R O'Gara	Georgia	Dublin	2002
5	D G Humphreys	Fiji	Dublin	2002
5	D G Humphreys	Romania	Dublin	2005

MOST PENALTIES IN A MATCH

BY THE TEAM

Pens	Opponents	Venue	Year
8	Italy	Dublin	1997
7	Argentina	Lens	1999
6	Scotland	Dublin	1982
6	Romania	Dublin	1993
6	United States	Atlanta	1996
6	Western Samoa	Dublin	1996
6	Italy	Dublin	2000
6	Wales	Dublin	2002
6	Australia	Dublin	2002
6	Samoa	Apia	2003
6	Japan	Osaka	2005

BY A PLAYER

Pens	Player	Opponents	Venue	Year
8	P A Burke	Italy	Dublin	1997
7	D G Humphreys	Argentina	Lens	1999
6	S O Campbell	Scotland	Dublin	1982
6	E P Elwood	Romania	Dublin	1993
6	S J P Mason	Western Samoa	Dublin	1996
6	R J R O'Gara	Italy	Dublin	2000
6	D G Humphreys	Wales	Dublin	2002
6	R J R O'Gara	Australia	Dublin	2002

MOST DROPPED GOALS IN A MATCH

BY THE TEAM

Drops	Opponents	Venue	Year
2	Australia	Dublin	1967
2	France	Dublin	1975
2	Australia	Sydney	1979
2	England	Dublin	1981
2	Canada	Dunedin	1987
2	England	Dublin	1993
2	Wales	Wembley	1999
2	New Zealand	Dublin	2001
2	Argentina	Dublin	2004
2	England	Dublin	2005

BY A PLAYER

Drops	Player	Opponents	Venue	Year
2	C M H Gibson	Australia	Dublin	1967
2	W M McCombe	France	Dublin	1975
2	S O Campbell	Australia	Sydney	1979
2	E P Elwood	England	Dublin	1993
2	D G Humphreys	Wales	Wembley	1999
2	D G Humphreys	New Zealand	Dublin	2001
2	R J R O'Gara	Argentina	Dublin	2004
2	R J R O'Gara	England	Dublin	2005

MOST CAPPED PLAYERS

Caps	Player	Career Span
91	M E O'Kelly	1997 to 2008
86	J J Hayes	2000 to 2008
85	B G O'Driscoll	1999 to 2008
84	R J R O'Gara	2000 to 2008
84	P A Stringer	2000 to 2008
81	G T Dempsey	1998 to 2008
72	D G Humphreys	1996 to 2005
70	K M Maggs	1997 to 2005
69	C M H Gibson	1964 to 1979
65	S H Easterby	2000 to 2008
63	W J McBride	1962 to 1975
63	S P Horgan	2000 to 2008
62	A G Foley	1995 to 2005
62	D A Hickie	1997 to 2007
61	J F Slattery	1970 to 1984
59	P S Johns	1990 to 2000
58	P A Orr	1976 to 1987
58	K G M Wood	1994 to 2003
58	G E A Murphy	2000 to 2008
58	M J Horan	2000 to 2008
55	B J Mullin	1984 to 1995
54	T J Kiernan	1960 to 1973
54	P M Clohessy	1993 to 2002
54	P J O'Connell	2002 to 2008
52	D G Lenihan	1981 to 1992
51	M I Keane	1974 to 1984

MOST CONSECUTIVE TESTS

Tests	Player	Span
52	W J McBride	1964 to 1975
49	P A Orr	1976 to 1986
43	D G Lenihan	1981 to 1989
39	M I Keane	1974 to 1981
38	P A Stringer	2003 to 2007
37	G V Stephenson	1920 to 1929

MOST TESTS AS CAPTAIN

Tests	Captain	Span
48	B G O'Driscoll	2002 to 2008
36	K G M Wood	1996 to 2003
24	T J Kiernan	1963 to 1973
19	C F Fitzgerald	1982 to 1986
17	J F Slattery	1979 to 1981
17	D G Lenihan	1986 to 1990

MOST POINTS IN TESTS

Pts	Player	Tests	Career
835	R J R O'Gara	84	2000 to 2008
565*	D G Humphreys	72	1996 to 2005
308	M J Kiernan	43	1982 to 1991
296	E P Elwood	35	1993 to 1999
217	S O Campbell	22	1976 to 1984
172	B G O'Driscoll	85	1999 to 2008
158	T J Kiernan	54	1960 to 1973
145	D A Hickie	62	1997 to 2007
113	A J P Ward	191978 to 1987	

* Humphreys's total includes a penalty try against Scotland in 1999

MOST TRIES IN TESTS

Tries	Player	Tests	Career
32	B G O'Driscoll	85	1999 to 2008
29	D A Hickie	62	1997 to 2007
20	S P Horgan	63	2000 to 2008
19	G T Dempsey	81	1998 to 2008
18	G E A Murphy	58	2000 to 2008
17	B J Mullin	55	1984 to 1995
15	K G M Wood	58	1994 to 2003
15	K M Maggs	70	1997 to 2005
14	G V Stephenson	42	1920 to 1930
14	R J R O'Gara	84	2000 to 2008
12	K D Crossan	41	1982 to 1992
11	A T A Duggan	25	1963 to 1972
11	S P Geoghegan	37	1991 to 1996

MOST CONVERSIONS IN TESTS

Cons	Player	Tests	Career
129	R J R O'Gara	84	2000 to 2008
88	D G Humphreys	72	1996 to 2005
43	E P Elwood	35	1993 to 1999
40	M J Kiernan	43	1982 to 1991
26	T J Kiernan	54	1960 to 1973
16	R A Lloyd	19	1910 to 1920
15	S O Campbell	22	1976 to 1984

MOST PENALTY GOALS IN TESTS

Pens	Player	Tests	Career
158	R J R O'Gara	84	2000 to 2008
110	D G Humphreys	72	1996 to 2005
68	E P Elwood	35	1993 to 1999
62	M J Kiernan	43	1982 to 1991
54	S O Campbell	22	1976 to 1984
31	T J Kiernan	54	1960 to 1973
29	A J P Ward	19	1978 to 1987

MOST DROPPED GOALS IN TESTS

Drops	Player	Tests	Career
11	R J R O'Gara	84	2000 to 2008
8	D G Humphreys	72	1996 to 2005
7	R A Lloyd	19	1910 to 1920
7	S O Campbell	22	1976 to 1984
6	C M H Gibson	69	1964 to 1979
6	B J McGann	25	1969 to 1976
6	M J Kiernan	43	1982 to 1991

INTERNATIONAL CHAMPIONSHIP RECORDS

RECORD	DETAIL		SET
Most points in season	168	in five matches	2000
Most tries in season	17	in five matches	2000
	17	in five matches	2004
	17	in five matches	2007
Highest Score	60	60-13 v Italy	2000
Biggest win	47	60-13 v Italy	2000
Highest score conceded	50	18-50 v England	2000
Biggest defeat	40	6-46 v England	1997
Most appearances	56	C M H Gibson	1964 - 1979
Most points in matches	443	R J R O'Gara	2000 – 2008
Most points in season	82	R J R O'Gara	2007
Most points in match	30	R J R O'Gara	v Italy, 2000
Most tries in matches	17	B G O'Driscoll	2000 – 2008
Most tries in season	5	J E Arigho	1928
	5	B G O'Driscoll	2000
Most tries in match	3	R Montgomery	v Wales, 1887
	3	J P Quinn	v France, 1913
	3	E O'D Davy	v Scotland, 1930
	3	S J Byrne	v Scotland, 1953
	3	B G O'Driscoll	v France, 2000
	3	R A J Henderson	v Italy, 2001
	3	B G O'Driscoll	v Scotland, 2002
Most cons in matches	61	R J R O'Gara	2000 – 2008
Most cons in season	11	R J R O'Gara	2000
	11	R J R O'Gara	2004
Most cons in match	6	R J R O'Gara	v Italy, 2000
Most pens in matches	89	R J R O'Gara	2000 – 2008
Most pens in season	17	R J R O'Gara	2006
Most pens in match	6	S O Campbell	v Scotland, 1982
	6	R J R O'Gara	v Italy, 2000
	6	D G Humphreys	v Wales, 2002
Most drops in matches	7	R A Lloyd	1910 – 1920
Most drops in season	2	on several	Occasions
Most drops in match	2	W M McCombe	v France, 1975
	2	E P Elwood	v England, 1993
	2	D G Humphreys	v Wales, 1999
	2	R J R O'Gara	v England, 2005

MISCELLANEOUS RECORDS

RECORD	HOLDER	DETAIL
Longest Test Career	A J F O'Reilly	1955 to 1970
	C M H Gibson	1964 to 1979
Youngest Test Cap	F S Hewitt	17 yrs 157 days in 1924
Oldest Test Cap	C M H Gibson	36 yrs 195 days in 1979

CAREER RECORDS OF IRELAND INTERNATIONAL PLAYERS (UP TO 30 SEPTEMBER 2008)

PLAYER BACKS	DEBUT	CAPS	T	C	P	D	PTS
I J Boss	2006 v NZ	12	2	0	0	0	10
T J Bowe	2004 v US	15	5	0	0	0	25
B B Carney	2007 v Arg	4	1	0	0	0	5
G M D'Arcy	1999 v R	37	4	0	0	0	20
G T Dempsey	1998 v Gg	81	19	0	0	0	95
G W Duffy	2004 v SA	8	3	0	1	0	18
L Fitzgerald	2006 v PI	4	0	0	0	0	0
S P Horgan	2000 v S	63	20	0	0	0	100
R D J Kearney	2007 v Arg	8	2	0	0	0	10
K P Lewis	2005 v J	3	0	0	0	0	0
B J Murphy	2007 v Arg	2	0	0	0	0	0
G E A Murphy	2000 v US	58	18	1	1	1	98
B G O'Driscoll	1999 v A	85	32	0	0	4	172
R J R O'Gara	2000 v S	84	14	129	158	11	835
T G O'Leary	2007 v Arg	1	0	0	0	0	0
E G Reddan	2006 F	12	0	0	0	0	0
J W Staunton	2001 v Sm	5	1	2	4	0	21
P A Stringer	2000 v S	84	6	0	0	0	30
A D Trimble	2005 v A	24	8	0	0	0	40
P W Wallace	2006 v SA	10	2	10	6	0	48

FORWARDS							
N A Best	2005 v NZ	18	2	0	0	0	10
R Best	2005 v NZ	24	3	0	0	0	15
T D Buckley	2007 v Arg	9	0	0	0	0	0
L F M Cullen	2002 v NZ	19	0	0	0	0	0
S H Easterby	2000 v S	65	8	0	0	0	40
S Ferris	2006 v PI	5	0	0	0	0	0
J P Flannery	2005 v R	23	3	0	0	0	15
K D Gleeson	2002 v W	27	4	0	0	0	20
J J Hayes	2000 v S	86	2	0	0	0	10
J P R Heaslip	2006 v PI	10	0	0	0	0	0
T Hogan	2005 v J	4	0	0	0	0	0
M J Horan	2000 v US	58	6	0	0	0	30
B J Jackman	2005 v J	9	0	0	0	0	0
S Jennings	2007 v Arg	3	0	0	0	0	0
D P Leamy	2004 v US	34	2	0	0	0	10
D P O'Callaghan	2003 v W	47	1	0	0	0	5
P J O'Connell	2002 v W	54	6	0	0	0	30
J H O'Connor	2004 v SA	12	1	0	0	0	5
M R O'Driscoll	2001 v R	15	0	0	0	0	0
M E O'Kelly	1997 v NZ	91	8	0	0	0	40
A N Quinlan	1999 v R	25	5	0	0	0	25
F J Sheahan	2000 v US	29	5	0	0	0	25
D P Wallace	2000 v Arg	47	9	0	0	0	45
B G Young	2006 v NZ	8	0	0	0	0	0

Phil Walter/Getty Images

John Hayes (middle) is closing in on his 90th cap for Ireland, the most for a front row forward in Irish history.

IRELAND INTERNATIONAL PLAYERS

UP TO 30TH SEPTEMBER 2008

Note: Years given for International Championship matches are for second half of season; eg 1972 means season 1971-72. Years for all other matches refer to the actual year of the match. Entries in square brackets denote matches played in RWC Finals.

Abraham, M (Bective Rangers) 1912 E, S, W, SA, 1914 W
Adams, C (Old Wesley), 1908 E, 1909 E, F, 1910 F, 1911 E, S, W, F, 1912 S, W, SA, 1913 W, F, 1914 F, E, S
Agar, R D (Malone) 1947 F, E, S, W, 1948 F, 1949 S, W, 1950 F, E, W
Agnew, P J (CIYMS) 1974 F (R), 1976 A
Ahearne, T (Queen's Coll, Cork) 1899 E
Aherne, L F P (Dolphin, Lansdowne) 1988 E 2, WS, It, 1989 F, W, E, S, NZ, 1990 E, S, F, W (R), 1992 E, S, F, A
Alexander, R (NIFC, Police Union) 1936 E, S, W, 1937 E, S, W, 1938 E, S, 1939 E, S, W
Allen, C E (Derry, Liverpool) 1900 E, S, W, 1901 E, S, W, 1903 S, W, 1904 E, S, W, 1905 E, S, W, NZ, 1906 E, S, W, SA, 1907 S, W
Allen, G G (Derry, Liverpool) 1896 E, S, W, 1897 E, S, 1898 E, S, 1899 E, W
Allen, T C (NIFC) 1885 E, S 1
Allen, W S (Wanderers) 1875 E
Allison, J B (Edinburgh U) 1899 E, S, 1900 E, S, W, 1901 E, S, W, 1902 E, S, W, 1903 S
Anderson, F E (Queen's U, Belfast, NIFC) 1953 F, E, S, W, 1954 NZ, F, E, S, W, 1955 F, E, S, W
Anderson, H J (Old Wesley) 1903 E, S, 1906 E, S
Anderson, W A (Dungannon) 1984 A, 1985 S, F, W, E, 1986 F, S, R, 1987 E, S, F, W, [W, C, Tg, A], 1988 S, F, W, E 1,2, 1989 F, W, E, NZ, 1990 E, S
Andrews, G (NIFC) 1875 E, 1876 E
Andrews, H W (NIFC) 1888 M, 1889 S, W
Archer, A M (Dublin U, NIFC) 1879 S
Arigho, J E (Lansdowne) 1928 F, E, W, 1929 F, E, S, W, 1930 F, E, S, W, 1931 F, E, S, W, SA
Armstrong, W K (NIFC) 1960 SA, 1961 E
Arnott, D T (Lansdowne) 1876 E
Ash, W H (NIFC) 1875 E, 1876 E, 1877 S
Aston, H R (Dublin U) 1908 E, W
Atkins, A P (Bective Rangers) 1924 F
Atkinson, J M (NIFC) 1927 F, A
Atkinson, J R (Dublin U) 1882 W, S

Bagot, J C (Dublin U, Lansdowne) 1879 S, E, 1880 E, S, 1881 S
Bailey, A H (UC Dublin, Lansdowne) 1934 W, 1935 E, S, W, NZ, 1936 E, S, W, 1937 E, S, W, 1938 E, S
Bailey, N (Northampton) 1952 E
Bardon, M E (Bohemians) 1934 E
Barlow, M (Wanderers) 1875 E
Barnes, R J (Dublin U, Armagh) 1933 W
Barr, A (Methodist Coll, Belfast) 1898 W, 1899 S, 1901 E, S
Barry, N J (Garryowen) 1991 Nm 2(R)
Beamish, C E St J (RAF, Leicester) 1933 W, S, 1934 S, W, 1935 E, S, W, NZ, 1936 E, S, W, 1938 W
Beamish, G R (RAF, Leicester) 1925 E, S, W, 1928 F, E, S, W, 1929 F, E, S, W, 1930 F, S, W, 1931 F, E, S, W, SA, 1932 E, S, W, 1933 E, W, S
Beatty, W J (NIFC, Richmond) 1910 F, 1912 F, W
Becker, V A (Lansdowne) 1974 F, W
Beckett, G G P (Dublin U) 1908 E, S, W
Bell, J C (Ballymena, Northampton, Dungannon) 1994 A 1,2, US, 1995 S, It, [NZ, W, F], Fj, 1996 US, S, F, W, E, WS, A, 1997 It 1, F, W, E, S, 1998 Gg, R, SA 3, 1999 F, W, S It (R), A 2, [US (R), A 3(R), R], 2001 R (R), 2003 Tg, Sm, It 2(R)
Bell, R J (NIFC) 1875 E, 1876 E
Bell, W E (Belfast Collegians) 1953 F, E, S, W
Bennett, F (Belfast Collegians) 1913 S
Bent, G C (Dublin U) 1882 W, E
Berkery, P J (Lansdowne) 1954 W, 1955 W, 1956 S, W, 1957 F, E, S, W, 1958 A, E, S
Bermingham, J J C (Blackrock Coll) 1921 E, S, W, F
Best, N A (Ulster) 2005 NZ(R),R, 2006 NZ1,2,A1,SA,A2, 2007 F(R),E(R),S1(R),Arg1,2(R),S2,It2, [Nm(R),Gg(R),F(R), Arg(t&R]
Best, R (Ulster) 2005 NZ(R),A(t), 2006 W(R),A1(R),SA,A2,PI(R), 2007 W,F,E,S1,It1,S2(R),It2, [Nm,Gg,Arg(R)], 2008 It,F(R),S(R), W,E,NZ1(R),A
Best, S J (Belfast Harlequins, Ulster) 2003 Tg (R), W 2, S 2(R), 2003 [Nm(R)], 2004 W(R),US(R), 2005 J1,2,NZ(R),R, 2006 F(R), W(R),PI(R), 2007 E(R),S1,It1(R),Arg1,2,S2,It2(R), [Nm(R), Gg(R),F(R)]
Bishop, J P (London Irish) 1998 SA, 1,2, Gg, R, SA 3, 1999 F, W, E, S, It, A 1,2, Arg 1, [US, A 3, Arg 2], 2000 E, Arg, C, 2002 NZ 1,2, Fj, Arg, 2003 W 1, E
Blackham, J C (Queen's Coll, Cork) 1909 S, W, F, 1910 E, S, W
Blake-Knox, S E F (NIFC) 1976 E, S, 1977 F (R)
Blayney, J J (Wanderers) 1950 S
Bond, A T W (Derry) 1894 S, W
Bornemann, W W (Wanderers) 1960 E, S, W, SA
Boss, I J (Ulster) 2006 NZ2(R),A1(R),SA(R),A2,PI(R), 2007 F,E(R),Arg1,S2,It2(R), [Gg(R),Arg(R)]
Bowe, T J (Ulster) 2004 US, 2005 J1,2,NZ,A,R, 2006 It,F, 2007 Arg1,S2, 2008 S,W,E,NZ1,A
Bowen, D St J (Cork Const) 1977 W, E, S
Boyd, C A (Dublin U) 1900 S, 1901 S, W
Boyle, C V (Dublin U) 1935 NZ, 1936 E, S, W, 1937 E, S, W, 1938 W, 1939 W
Brabazon, H M (Dublin U) 1884 E, 1885 S 1, 1886 E
Bradley, M J (Dolphin) 1920 W, F, 1922 E, S, W, F, 1923 E, S, W, F, 1925 F, S, W, 1926 F, E, S, W, 1927 F, W
Bradley, M T (Cork Constitution) 1984 A, 1985 S, F, W, E, 1986 F, W, E, S, R, 1987 E, S, F, W, [W, C, Tg, A], 1988 S, F, W, E 1, 1990 W, 1992 NZ 1,2, 1993 S, F, W, E, R, 1994 F, W, E, S, A 1,2, US, 1995 S, F, [NZ]
Bradshaw, G (Belfast Collegians) 1903 W
Bradshaw, R M (Wanderers) 1885 E, S 1,2
Brady, A M (UC Dublin, Malone) 1966 S, 1968 E, S, W
Brady, J A (Wanderers) 1976 E, S
Brady, J R (CIYMS) 1951 S, W, 1953 F, E, S, W, 1954 W, 1956 W, 1957 F, E, S, W
Bramwell, T (NIFC) 1928 F
Brand, T N (NIFC) 1924 NZ
Brennan, J I (CIYMS) 1957 S, W
Brennan, T (St Mary's Coll, Barnhall) 1998 SA 1(R),2(R), 1999 F (R), S (R), It, A 2, Arg 1, [US, A 3], 2000 E (R), 2001 W (R), E (R), Sm (R)
Bresnihan, F P K (UC Dublin, Lansdowne, London Irish) 1966 E, W, 1967 A 1, E, S, W, F, 1968 F, E, S, W, A, 1969 F, E, S, W, 1970 SA, F, E, S, W, 1971 F, E, S, W
Brett, J T (Monkstown) 1914 W
Bristow, J R (NIFC) 1879 E

Brophy, N H (Blackrock Coll, UC Dublin, London Irish) 1957 F, E, 1959 E, S, W, F, 1960 F, SA, 1961 S, W, 1962 E, S, W, 1963 E, W, 1967 E, S, W, F, A 2
Brown, E L (Instonians) 1958 F
Brown, G S (Monkstown, United Services) 1912 S, W, SA
Brown, H (Windsor) 1877 E
Brown, T (Windsor) 1877 E, S
Brown, W H (Dublin U) 1899 E
Brown, W J (Malone) 1970 SA, F, S, W
Brown, W S (Dublin U) 1893 S, W, 1894 E, S, W
Browne, A W (Dublin U) 1951 SA
Browne, D (Blackrock Coll) 1920 F
Browne, H C (United Services and RN) 1929 E, S, W
Browne, W F (United Services and Army) 1925 E, S, W, 1926 S, W, 1927 F, E, S, W, A, 1928 E, S
Browning, D R (Wanderers) 1881 E, S
Bruce, S A M (NIFC) 1883 E, S, 1884 E
Brunker, A A (Lansdowne) 1895 E, W
Bryant, C H (Cardiff) 1920 E, S
Buchanan, A McM (Dublin U) 1926 E, S, W, 1927 S, W, A
Buchanan, J W B (Dublin U) 1882 S, 1884 E, S
Buckley, J H (Sunday's Well) 1973 E, S
Buckley, T D (Munster) 2007 Arg1(R),2(R), 2008 It(R),F(R),S(R), W(R),E(R),NZ1(R),A(R)
Bulger, L Q (Lansdowne) 1896 E, S, W, 1897 E, S, 1898 E, S, W
Bulger, M J (Dublin U) 1888 M
Burges, J H (Rosslyn Park) 1950 F, E
Burgess, R B (Dublin U) 1912 SA
Burke, P A (Cork Constitution, Bristol, Harlequins) 1995 E, S, W (R), It, [J], Fj, 1996 US (R), A, 1997 It 1, S (R), 2001 R (R), 2003 S 1(R), Sm (R)
Burkitt, J C S (Queen's Coll, Cork) 1881 E
Burns, I J (Wanderers) 1980 E (R)
Butler, L G (Blackrock Coll) 1960 W
Butler, N (Bective Rangers) 1920 E
Byers, R M (NIFC) 1928 S, W, 1929 E, S, W
Byrne, E (St Mary's Coll) 2001 It (R), F (R), S (R), W (R), E (R), Sm, NZ (R), 2003 A (R), Sm (R)
Byrne, E M J (Blackrock Coll) 1977 S, F, 1978 F, W, E, NZ
Byrne, J S (Blackrock Coll, Leinster, Saracens) 2001 R (R), 2002 W (R), E (R), S (R), It, NZ 2(R), R, Ru (R), Gg, A, Arg, 2003 S 1, It 1, F, W 1, E, A, Tg, Sm, W 2(R), It 2, S2(R), [R(R),Nm(R)], 2004 F,W,E,It,S,SA1,2,3,Arg, 2005 It,S,E,F,W, NZ,A,R
Byrne, N F (UC Dublin) 1962 F
Byrne, S J (UC Dublin, Lansdowne) 1953 S, W, 1955 F
Byron, W G (NIFC) 1896 E, S, W, 1897 E, S, 1898 E, S, W, 1899 E, S, W

Caddell, E D (Dublin U, Wanderers) 1904 S, 1905 E, S, W, NZ, 1906 E, S, W, SA, 1907 E, S, 1908 S, W
Cagney, S J (London Irish) 1925 W, 1926 F, E, S, W, 1927 F, 1928 E, S, W, 1929 F, E, S, W
Callan, C P (Lansdowne) 1947 F, E, S, W, 1948 F, E, S, W, 1949 F, E
Cameron, E D (Bective Rangers) 1891 S, W
Campbell, C E (Old Wesley) 1970 SA
Campbell, E F (Monkstown) 1899 S, W, 1900 E, W
Campbell, K P (Ulster) 2005 J1(R),2(R),R
Campbell, S B B (Derry) 1911 E, S, W, F, 1912 F, E, S, W, SA, 1913 E, S, F
Campbell, S O (Old Belvedere) 1976 A, 1979 A 1,2, 1980 E, S, F, W, 1981 F, W, E, S, SA 1, 1982 W, E, S, F, 1983 S, F, W, E, 1984 F, W
Canniffe, D M (Lansdowne) 1976 W, E
Cantrell, J L (UC Dublin, Blackrock Coll) 1976 A, F, W, E, S, 1981 S, SA 1,2, A
Carey, R W (Dungannon) 1992 NZ 1,2
Carney, B B (Munster) 2007 Arg1,2,S2,It2(R)
Carpendale, M J (Monkstown) 1886 S, 1887 W, 1888 W, S
Carr, N J (Ards) 1985 S, F, W, E, 1986 W, E, S, R, 1987 E, S, W
Carroll, C (Bective Rangers) 1930 F
Carroll, R (Lansdowne) 1947 F, 1950 S, W
Casement, B N (Dublin U) 1875 E, 1876 E, 1879 E
Casement, F (Dublin U) 1906 E, S, W
Casey, J C (Young Munster) 1930 S, 1932 E
Casey, P J (UC Dublin, Lansdowne) 1963 F, E, S, W, NZ, 1964 E, S, W, F, 1965 F, E, S
Casey, R E (Blackrock Coll) 1999 [A 3(t), Arg 2(R)], 2000 E, US (R), C (R)
Chambers, J (Dublin U) 1886 E, S, 1887 E, S, W
Chambers, R R (Instonians) 1951 F, E, S, W, 1952 F, W
Clancy, T P J (Lansdowne) 1988 W, E 1,2, WS, It, 1989 F, W, E, S
Clarke, A T H (Northampton, Dungannon) 1995 Fj (R), 1996 W, E, WS, 1997 F (R), It 2(R), 1998 Gg (R), R
Clarke, C P (Terenure Coll) 1993 F, W, E, 1998 W, E
Clarke, D J (Dolphin) 1991 W, Nm 1,2, [J, A], 1992 NZ 2(R)
Clarke, J A B (Bective Rangers) 1922 S, W, F, 1923 F, 1924 E, S, W
Clegg, R J (Bangor) 1973 F, 1975 E, S, F, W
Clifford, J T (Young Munster) 1949 F, E, S, W, 1950 F, E, S, W, 1951 F, E, SA, 1952 F, S, W
Clinch, A D (Dublin U, Wanderers) 1892 S, 1893 W, 1895 E, S, W, 1896 E, S, W, 1897 E, S
Clinch, J D (Wanderers, Dublin U) 1923 W, 1924 F, E, S, W, NZ, 1925 F, E, S, 1926 E, S, W, 1927 F, 1928 F, E, S, W, 1929 F, E, S, W, 1930 F, E, S, W, 1931 F, E, S, W, SA
Clohessy, P M (Young Munster) 1993 F, W, E, 1994 F, W, E, S, A 1,2, US, 1995 E, S, F, W, 1996 S, F, 1997 It 2, 1998 F (R), W (R), SA 2(R), Gg, R, SA 3, 1999 F, W, E, S, It, A 1,2 Arg 1, [US, A 3(R)], 2000 E, S, It, F, W, Arg, J, SA, 2001 It, F, R, S, W, E, Sm (R), NZ, 2002 W, E, S, It, F
Clune, J J (Blackrock Coll) 1912 SA, 1913 W, F, 1914 F, E, W
Coffey, J J (Lansdowne) 1900 E, 1901 W, 1902 E, S, W, 1903 E, S, W, 1905 E, S, W, NZ, 1906 E, S, W, SA, 1907 E, 1908 W, 1910 F
Cogan, W St J (Queen's Coll, Cork) 1907 E, S
Collier, S R (Queen's Coll, Belfast) 1883 S
Collins, P C (Lansdowne, London Irish) 1987 [C], 1990 S (R)
Collis, W R F (KCH, Harlequins) 1924 F, W, NZ, 1925 F, E, S, 1926 F
Collis, W S (Wanderers) 1884 W
Collopy, G (Bective Rangers) 1891 S, 1892 S
Collopy, R (Bective Rangers) 1923 E, S, W, F, 1924 F, E, S, W, NZ, 1925 F, E, S, W
Collopy, W P (Bective Rangers) 1914 F, E, S, W, 1921 E, S, W, F, 1922 E, S, W, F, 1923 S, W, F, 1924 F, E, S, W
Combe, A (NIFC) 1875 E
Condon, H C (London Irish) 1984 S (R)
Cook, H G (Lansdowne) 1884 W
Coote, P B (RAF, Leicester) 1933 S
Corcoran, J C (London Irish) 1947 A, 1948 F
Corken, T S (Belfast Collegians) 1937 E, S, W
Corkery, D S (Cork Constitution, Bristol) 1994 A 1,2, US, 1995 E, [NZ, J, W, F], Fj, 1996 US, S, F, W, E, WS, A, 1997 It 1, F, W, E, S, 1998 S, F, W, E, 1999 A 1(R),2(R)
Corley, H H (Dublin U, Wanderers) 1902 E, S, W, 1903 E, S, W, 1904 E, S
Cormac, H S T (Clontarf) 1921 E, S, W
Corrigan, R (Greystones, Lansdowne, Leinster) 1997 C (R), It 2, 1998 S, F, W, E, SA 3(R), 1999 A 1(R),2(R), [Arg 2], 2002 NZ 1,2, R, Ru, Gg, A, Fj (R), Arg, 2003 S 1, It 1, A, Tg, Sm, W 2, It 2, S 2, [R,Arg,A,F], 2004 F,W,E,It,S,SA1,2,3,Arg, 2005 It,S,E,F,W,
J1(R),2(R), 2006 F
Costello, P (Bective Rangers) 1960 F
Costello, R A (Garryowen) 1993 S
Costello, V C P (St Mary's Coll, London Irish) 1996 US, F, W, E. WS (R), 1997 C, It 2(R), 1998 S (R), F, W, E, SA 1,2, Gg, R, SA 3, 1999 F, W (R), E, S (R), It, A 1, 2002 R (R), A, Arg, 2003 S 1, It 1, F, E, A, It 2, S 2, [R,Arg,F], 2004 F(R),W(R),It(R), S(R)
Cotton, J (Wanderers) 1889 W
Coulter, H H (Queen's U, Belfast) 1920 E, S, W
Courtney, A W (UC Dublin) 1920 S, W, F, 1921 E, S, W, F
Cox, H L (Dublin U) 1875 E, 1876 E, 1877 E, S
Craig, R G (Queen's U, Belfast) 1938 S, W
Crawford, E C (Dublin U) 1885 E, S 1
Crawford, W E (Lansdowne) 1920 E, S, W, F, 1921 E, S, W, F, 1922 E, S, 1923 E, S, W, F, 1924 F, E, W, NZ, 1925 F, E, S, W, 1926 F, E, S, W, 1927 F, E, S, W
Crean, T J (Wanderers) 1894 E, S, W, 1895 E, S, W, 1896 E, S, W
Crichton, R Y (Dublin U) 1920 E, S, W, F, 1921 F, 1922 E, 1923 W, F, 1924 F, E, S, W, NZ, 1925 E, S

Croker, E W D (Limerick) 1878 E
Cromey, G E (Queen's U, Belfast) 1937 E, S, W, 1938 E, S, W, 1939 E, S, W
Cronin, B M (Garryowen) 1995 S, 1997 S
Cronyn, A P (Dublin U, Lansdowne) 1875 E, 1876 E, 1880 S
Crossan, K D (Instonians) 1982 S, 1984 F, W, E, S, 1985 S, F, W, E, 1986 E, S, R, 1987 E, S, F, W, [W, C, Tg, A], 1988 S, F, W, E 1, WS, It, 1989 W, S, NZ, 1990 E, S, F, W, Arg, 1991 E, S, Nm 2 [Z, J, S], 1992 W
Crotty, D J (Garryowen) 1996 A, 1997 It 1, F, W, 2000 C
Crowe, J F (UC Dublin) 1974 NZ
Crowe, L (Old Belvedere) 1950 E, S, W
Crowe, M P (Lansdowne) 1929 W, 1930 E, S, W, 1931 F, S, W, SA, 1932 S, W, 1933 W, S, 1934 E
Crowe, P M (Blackrock Coll) 1935 E, 1938 E
Cullen, L F M (Blackrock Coll, Leinster, Leicester) 2002 NZ 2(R), R (R), Ru (R), Gg (R), A (R), Fj, Arg (R), 2003 S 1(R), It 1(R), F (R), W 1, Tg, Sm, It 2, 2004 US(R), 2005 J1,2,R, 2007 Arg2
Cullen, T J (UC Dublin) 1949 F
Cullen, W J (Monkstown and Manchester) 1920 E
Culliton, M G (Wanderers) 1959 E, S, W, F, 1960 E, S, W, F, SA, 1961 E, S, W, F, 1962 S, F, 1964 E, S, W, F
Cummins, W E A (Queen's Coll, Cork) 1879 S, 1881 E, 1882 E
Cunningham, D McC (NIFC) 1923 E, S, W, 1925 F, E, W
Cunningham, M J (UC Cork) 1955 F, E, S, W, 1956 F, S, W
Cunningham, V J G (St Mary's Coll) 1988 E 2, It, 1990 Arg (R), 1991 Nm 1,2, [Z, J(R)], 1992 NZ 1,2, A, 1993 S, F, W, E, R, 1994 F
Cunningham, W A (Lansdowne) 1920 W, 1921 E, S, W, F, 1922 E, 1923 S, W
Cuppaidge, J L (Dublin U) 1879 E, 1880 E, S
Currell, J (NIFC) 1877 S
Curtis, A B (Oxford U) 1950 F, E, S
Curtis, D M (London Irish) 1991 W, E, S, Nm 1,2, [Z, J, S, A], 1992 W, E, S (R), F
Cuscaden, W A (Dublin U, Bray) 1876 E
Cussen, D J (Dublin U) 1921 E, S, W, F, 1922 E, 1923 E, S, W, F, 1926 F, E, S, W, 1927 F, E

Daly, J C (London Irish) 1947 F, E, S, W, 1948 E, S, W
Daly, M J (Harlequins) 1938 E
Danaher, P P A (Lansdowne, Garryowen) 1988 S, F, W, WS, It, 1989 F, NZ (R), 1990 F, 1992 S, F, NZ 1, A, 1993 S, F, W, E, R, 1994 F, W, E, S, A 1,2, US, 1995 E, S, F, W
D'Arcy, G M (Lansdowne, Leinster) 1999 [R (R)], 2002 Fj (R), 2003 Tg (R), Sm (R), W 2(R), 2004 F,W,E,It,S,SA1, 2005 It,NZ,A,R, 2006 It,F,W,S,E,NZ1,2,A1,SA,A2,PI(R), 2007 W,F,E,S1,It1,2, [Nm,Gg,F,Arg], 2008 It
Dargan, M J (Old Belvedere) 1952 S, W
Davidson, C T (NIFC) 1921 F
Davidson, I G (NIFC) 1899 E, 1900 S, W, 1901 E, S, W, 1902 E, S, W
Davidson, J C (Dungannon) 1969 F, E, S, W, 1973 NZ, 1976 NZ
Davidson, J W (Dungannon, London Irish, Castres) 1995 Fj, 1996 S, F, W, E, WS, A, 1997 It 1, F, W, E, S, 1998 Gg (R), R (R), SA 3(R), 1999 F, W, E, S, It, A 1,2(R), Arg 1, [US,R (R), Arg 2], 2000 S (R), W (R), US, C, 2001 It (R), S
Davies, F E (Lansdowne) 1892 S, W, 1893 E, S, W
Davis, J L (Monkstown) 1898 E, S
Davis, W J N (Edinburgh U, Bessbrook) 1890 S, W, E, 1891 E, S, W, 1892 E, S, 1895 S
Davison, W (Belfast Academy) 1887 W
Davy, E O'D (UC Dublin, Lansdowne) 1925 W, 1926 F, E, S, W, 1927 F, E, S, W, A, 1928 F, E, S, W, 1929 F, E, S, W, 1930 F, E, S, W, 1931 F, E, S, W, SA, 1932 E, S, W, 1933 E, W, S, 1934 E
Dawson, A R (Wanderers) 1958 A, E, S, W, F, 1959 E, S, W, F, 1960 F, SA, 1961 E, S, W, F, SA, 1962 S, F, W, 1963 F, E, S, W, NZ, 1964 E, S, F
Dawson, K (London Irish) 1997 NZ, C, 1998 S, 1999 [R, Arg 2], 2000 E, S, It, F, W, J, SA, 2001 R, S, W (R), E (R), Sm, 2002 Fj, 2003 Tg, It 2(R), S 2(R)
Dean, P M (St Mary's Coll) 1981 SA 1,2, A, 1982 W, E, S, F, 1984 A, 1985 S, F, W, E, 1986 F, W, R, 1987 E, S, F, W, [W, A], 1988 S, F, W, E 1,2, WS, It, 1989 F, W, E, S
Deane, E C (Monkstown) 1909 E
Deering, M J (Bective Rangers) 1929 W
Deering, S J (Bective Rangers) 1935 E, S, W, NZ, 1936 E, S, W, 1937 E, S
Deering, S M (Garryowen, St Mary's Coll) 1974 W, 1976 F, W, E, S, 1977 W, E, 1978 NZ
De Lacy, H (Harlequins) 1948 E, S
Delany, M G (Bective Rangers) 1895 W
Dempsey, G T (Terenure Coll, Leinster) 1998 Gg (R). SA 3, 1999 F, E, S, It, A 2, 2000 E (R), S, It, F, W, SA, 2001 It, F, S, W, E, NZ, 2002 W, E, S, It, F, NZ 1,2, R, Ru, Gg, A, Arg, 2003 S 1, E (R), A, Sm, W 2(R), It 2, S 2(R),[R,Nm,Arg,A,F], 2004 F,W, E,It,S, SA1,2,3,US(R),Arg, 2005 It(R),S,E,F,W,J1,2, NZ(R),R(R), 2006 E(R),NZ1(R),2(t&R),A1,SA,A2(R),PI, 2007 W,F,E,S1,It1,2, [Nm,Gg,F], 2008 It,F,A(R)
Dennison, S P (Garryowen) 1973 F, 1975 E, S
Dick, C J (Ballymena) 1961 W, F, SA, 1962 W, 1963 F, E, S, W
Dick, J S (Queen's U, Belfast) 1962 E
Dick, J S (Queen's U, Cork) 1887 E, S, W
Dickson, J A N (Dublin U) 1920 E, W, F
Doherty, A E (Old Wesley) 1974 P (R)
Doherty, W D (Guy's Hospital) 1920 E, S, W, 1921 E, S, W, F
Donaldson, J A (Belfast Collegians) 1958 A, E, S, W
Donovan, T M (Queen's Coll, Cork) 1889 S
Dooley, J F (Galwegians) 1959 E, S, W
Doran, B R W (Lansdowne) 1900 S, W, 1901 E, S, W, 1902 E, S, W
Doran, E F (Lansdowne) 1890 S, W
Doran, G P (Lansdowne) 1899 S, W, 1900 E, S, 1902 S, W, 1903 W, 1904 E
Douglas, A C (Instonians) 1923 F, 1924 E, S, 1927 A, 1928 S
Downing, A J (Dublin U) 1882 W
Dowse, J C A (Monkstown) 1914 F, S, W
Doyle, J A P (Greystones) 1984 E, S
Doyle, J T (Bective Rangers) 1935 W
Doyle, M G (Blackrock Coll, UC Dublin, Cambridge U, Edinburgh Wands) 1965 F, E, S, W, SA, 1966 F, E, S, W, 1967 A 1, E, S, W, F, A 2, 1968 F, E, S, W, A
Doyle, T J (Wanderers) 1968 E, S, W
Duffy, G W (Harlequins, Connacht) 2004 SA 2(R), 2005 S(R),J1,2, 2007 Arg1,2,S2, [Arg(R)]
Duggan, A T A (Lansdowne) 1963 NZ, 1964 F, 1966 W, 1967 A 1, S, W, A 2, 1968 F, E, S, W, 1969 F, E, S, W, 1970 SA, F, E, S, W, 1971 F, E, S, W, 1972 F 2
Duggan, W (UC Cork) 1920 S, W
Duggan, W P (Blackrock Coll) 1975 E, S, F, W, 1976 A, F, W, S, NZ, 1977 W, E, S, F, 1978 S, F, W, E, NZ, 1979 E, S, A 1,2, 1980 E, 1981 F, W, E, S, SA 1,2, A, 1982 W, E, S, 1983 S, F, W, E, 1984 F, W, E, S
Duignan, P (Galwegians) 1998 Gg, R
Duncan, W R (Malone) 1984 W, E
Dunlea, F J (Lansdowne) 1989 W, E, S
Dunlop, R (Dublin U) 1889 W, 1890 S, W, E, 1891 E, S, W, 1892 E, S, 1893 W, 1894 W
Dunn, P E F (Bective Rangers) 1923 S
Dunn, T B (NIFC) 1935 NZ
Dunne, M J (Lansdowne) 1929 F, E, S, 1930 F, E, S, W, 1932 E, S, W, 1933 E, W, S, 1934 E, S, W
Dwyer, P J (UC Dublin) 1962 W, 1963 F, NZ, 1964 S, W

Easterby, S H (Llanelli Scarlets) 2000 S, It, F, W, Arg, US, C, 2001 S, Sm (R), 2002 W, E (R), S (R), It, F, NZ 1,2, R, Ru, Gg, 2003 Tg, Sm, It 2, S 2(t+R), [Nm,Arg,A,F], 2004 F,W,E,It,S,SA1,2,3,US,Arg, 2005 It,S,E,F,W,NZ,A, 2006 It,F,W,S,E,SA(R),A2(R),PI, 2007 W,F,E,S1,It1,2, [Nm,Gg,F,Arg], 2008 It,S(R),E(R)
Easterby, W G (Ebbw Vale, Ballynahinch, Llanelli, Leinster) 2000 US, C (R), 2001 R (R), S, W (R), Sm (R), 2002 W (R), S (R), R (R), Ru (R), Gg (R), Fj, 2003 S 1(R), It 1(R), Tg, Sm, W 2(R), It 2, S 2(R), [R(R),Nm(R),F(R)], 2004 W(R),It(R),S(R),SA2(R), US, 2005 S(R)
Edwards, H G (Dublin U) 1877 E, 1878 E
Edwards, R W (Malone) 1904 W
Edwards, T (Lansdowne) 1888 M, 1890 S, W, E, 1892 W, 1893 E
Edwards, W V (Malone) 1912 F, E
Egan, J D (Bective Rangers) 1922 S
Egan, J T (Cork Constitution) 1931 F, E, SA
Egan, M S (Garryowen) 1893 E, 1895 S

Ekin, W (Queen's Coll, Belfast) 1888 W, S
Elliott, W R J (Bangor) 1979 S
Elwood, E P (Lansdowne, Galwegians) 1993 W, E, R, 1994 F, W, E, S, A 1,2, 1995 F, W, [NZ, W, F], 1996 US, S, 1997 F, W, E, NZ, C, It 2(R), 1998 F, W, E, SA 1,2, Gg, R, SA 3, 1999 It, Arg 1(R), [US (R), A 3(R), R]
English, M A F (Lansdowne, Limerick Bohemians) 1958 W, F, 1959 E, S, F, 1960 E, S, 1961 S, W, F, 1962 F, W, 1963 E, S, W, NZ
Ennis, F N G (Wanderers) 1979 A 1(R)
Ensor, A H (Wanderers) 1973 W, F, 1974 F, W, E, S, P, NZ, 1975 E, S, F, W, 1976 A, F, W, E, NZ, 1977 E, 1978 S, F, W, E
Entrican, J C (Queen's U, Belfast) 1931 S
Erskine, D J (Sale) 1997 NZ (R), C, It 2

Fagan, G L (Kingstown School) 1878 E
Fagan, W B C (Wanderers) 1956 F, E, S
Farrell, J L (Bective Rangers) 1926 F, E, S, W, 1927 F, E, S, W, A, 1928 F, E, S, W, 1929 F, E, S, W, 1930 F, E, S, W, 1931 F, E, S, W, SA, 1932 E, S, W
Feddis, N (Lansdowne) 1956 E
Feighery, C F P (Lansdowne) 1972 F 1, E, F 2
Feighery, T A O (St Mary's Coll) 1977 W, E
Ferris, H H (Queen's Coll, Belfast) 1901 W
Ferris, J H (Queen's Coll, Belfast) 1900 E, S, W
Ferris, S (Ulster) 2006 PI, 2007 Arg1(R),2,S2, 2008 A(R)
Field, M J (Malone) 1994 E, S, A 1(R), 1995 F (R), W (t), It (R), [NZ(t + R), J], Fj, 1996 F (R), W, E, A (R), 1997 F, W, E, S
Finlay, J E (Queen's Coll, Belfast) 1913 E, S, W, 1920 E, S, W
Finlay, W (NIFC) 1876 E, 1877 E, S, 1878 E, 1879 S, E, 1880 S, 1882 S
Finn, M C (UC Cork, Cork Constitution) 1979 E, 1982 W, E, S, F, 1983 S, F, W, E, 1984 E, S, A, 1986 F, W
Finn, R G A (UC Dublin) 1977 F
Fitzgerald, C C (Glasgow U, Dungannon) 1902 E, 1903 E, S
Fitzgerald, C F (St Mary's Coll) 1979 A 1,2, 1980 E, S, F, W, 1982 W, E, S, F, 1983 S, F, W, E, 1984 F, W, A, 1985 S, F, W, E, 1986 F, W, E, S
Fitzgerald, D C (Lansdowne, De La Salle Palmerston) 1984 E, S, 1986 W, E, S, R, 1987 E, S, F, W, [W, C, A], 1988 S, F, W, E 1, 1989 NZ (R), 1990 E, S, F, W, Arg, 1991 F, W, E, S, Nm 1,2, [Z, S, A], 1992 W, S (R)
Fitzgerald, J (Wanderers) 1884 W
Fitzgerald, J J (Young Munster) 1988 S, F, 1990 S, F, W, 1991 F, W, E, S, [J], 1994 A 1,2
Fitzgerald, L (Leinster) 2006 PI, 2007 Arg2(R), 2008 W(R),E(R)
Fitzgibbon, M J J (Shannon) 1992 W, E, S, F, NZ 1,2
Fitzpatrick, J M (Dungannon) 1998 SA 1,2 Gg (R), R (R), SA 3, 1999 F (R), W (R), E (R), It, Arg 1(R), [US (R), A 3, R, Arg 2(t&R)], 2000 S (R), It (R), Arg (R), US, C, SA (t&R), 2001 R (R), 2003 W 1(R), E (R), Tg, W 2(R), It 2(R)
Fitzpatrick, M P (Wanderers) 1978 S, 1980 S, F, W, 1981 F, W, E, S, A, 1985 F (R)
Flannery, J P (Munster) 2005 R(R), 2006 It,F,W,S,E,NZ1,2,A1, 2007 W(R),F(R),E(R),S1(R),It1(R),Arg1,S2,It2(R), [Nm(R),Gg(R), F,Arg], 2008 NZ1,A(R)
Flavin, P (Blackrock Coll) 1997 F (R), S
Fletcher, W W (Kingstown) 1882 W, S, 1883 E
Flood, R S (Dublin U) 1925 W
Flynn, M K (Wanderers) 1959 F, 1960 F, 1962 E, S, F, W, 1964 E, S, W, F, 1965 F, E, S, W, SA, 1966 F, E, S, 1972 F 1, E, F 2, 1973 NZ
Fogarty, T (Garryowen) 1891 W
Foley, A G (Shannon, Munster) 1995 E, S, F, W, It, [J(t + R)], 1996 A, 1997 It 1, E (R), 2000 E, S, It, F, W, Arg, C, J, SA, 2001 It, F, R, S, W, E, Sm, NZ, 2002 W, E, S, It, F, NZ 1,2, R, Ru, Gg, A, Fj, Arg, 2003 S 1, It 1, F, W 1, E, W 2, [R,A], 2004 F,W,E,It,S,
SA1,2,3,US(R),Arg, 2005 It,S,E,F,W
Foley, B O (Shannon) 1976 F, E, 1977 W (R), 1980 F, W, 1981 F, E, S, SA 1,2, A
Forbes, R E (Malone) 1907 E
Forrest, A J (Wanderers) 1880 E, S, 1881 E, S, 1882 W, E, 1883 E, 1885 S 2
Forrest, E G (Wanderers) 1888 M, 1889 S, W, 1890 S, E, 1891 E, 1893 S, W, 1894 E, S, W, 1895 W, 1897 E, S
Forrest, H (Wanderers) 1893 S, W
Fortune, J J (Clontarf) 1963 NZ, 1964 E
Foster, A R (Derry) 1910 E, S, F, 1911 E, S, W, F, 1912 F, E, S, W, 1914 E, S, W, 1921 E, S, W
Francis, N P J (Blackrock Coll, London Irish, Old Belvedere) 1987 [Tg, A], 1988 WS, It, 1989 S, 1990 E, F, W, 1991 E, S, Nm 1,2, [Z, J, S, A], 1992 W, E, S, 1993 F, R, 1994 F, W, E, S, A 1,2, US, 1995 E, [NZ, J, W, F], Fj, 1996 US, S
Franks, J G (Dublin U) 1898 E, S, W
Frazer, E F (Bective Rangers) 1891 S, 1892 S
Freer, A E (Lansdowne) 1901 E, S, W
Fulcher, G M (Cork Constitution, London Irish) 1994 A 2, US, 1995 E (R), S, F, W, It, [NZ, W, F], Fj, 1996 US, S, F, W, E, A, 1997 It 1, W (R), 1998 SA 1(R)
Fulton, J (NIFC) 1895 S, W, 1896 E, 1897 E, 1898 W, 1899 E, 1900 W, 1901 E, 1902 E, S, W, 1903 E, S, W, 1904 E, S
Furlong, J N (UC Galway) 1992 NZ 1,2

Gaffikin, W (Windsor) 1875 E
Gage, J H (Queen's U, Belfast) 1926 S, W, 1927 S, W
Galbraith, E (Dublin U) 1875 E
Galbraith, H T (Belfast Acad) 1890 W
Galbraith, R (Dublin U) 1875 E, 1876 E, 1877 E
Galwey, M J (Shannon) 1991 F, W, Nm 2(R), [J], 1992 E, S, F, NZ 1,2, A, 1993 F, W, E, R, 1994 F, W, E, S, A 1, US (R), 1995 E, 1996 WS, 1998 F (R), 1999 W (R), 2000 E (R), S, It, F, W, Arg, C, 2001 It, F, R, W, E, Sm, NZ, 2002 W, E, S
Ganly, J B (Monkstown) 1927 F, E, S, W, A, 1928 F, E, S, W, 1929 F, S, 1930 F
Gardiner, F (NIFC) 1900 E, S, 1901 E, W, 1902 E, S, W, 1903 E, W, 1904 E, S, W, 1906 E, S, W, 1907 S, W, 1908 S, W, 1909 E, S, F
Gardiner, J B (NIFC) 1923 E, S, W, F, 1924 F, E, S, W, NZ, 1925 F, E, S, W
Gardiner, S (Belfast Albion) 1893 E, S
Gardiner, W (NIFC) 1892 E, S, 1893 E, S, W, 1894 E, S, W, 1895 E, S, W, 1896 E, S, W, 1897 E, S, 1898 W
Garry, M G (Bective Rangers) 1909 E, S, W, F, 1911 E, S, W
Gaston, J T (Dublin U) 1954 NZ, F, E, S, W, 1955 W 1956 F, E
Gavin, T J (Moseley, London Irish) 1949 F, E
Geoghegan, S P (London Irish, Bath) 1991 F, W, E, S, Nm 1, [Z, S, A], 1992 E, S, F, A, 1993 S, F, W, E, R, 1994 F, W, E, S, A 1,2, US, 1995 E, S, F, W, [NZ, J, W, F], Fj, 1996 US, S, W, E
Gibson, C M H (Cambridge U, NIFC) 1964 E, S, W, F, 1965 F, E, S, W, SA, 1966 F, E, S, W, 1967 A 1, E, S, W, F, A 2, 1968 E, S, W, A, 1969 E, S, W, 1970 SA, F, E, S, W, 1971 F, E, S, W, 1972 F 1, E, F 2, 1973 NZ, E, S, W, F, 1974 F, W, E, S, P, 1975 E, S, F, W, 1976 A, F, W, E, S, NZ, 1977 W, E, S, F, 1978 F, W, E, NZ, 1979 S, A 1,2
Gibson, M E (Lansdowne, London Irish) 1979 F, W, E, S, 1981 W (R), 1986 R, 1988 S, F, W, E 2
Gifford, H P (Wanderers) 1890 S
Gillespie, J C (Dublin U) 1922 W, F
Gilpin, F G (Queen's U, Belfast) 1962 E, S, F
Glass, D C (Belfast Collegians) 1958 F, 1960 W, 1961 W, SA
Gleeson, K D (St Mary's Coll, Leinster) 2002 W (R), F (R), NZ 1,2, R, Ru, Gg, A, Arg, 2003 S 1, It 1, F, W 1, E, A, W 2, [R,A,F], 2004 F,W,E,It, 2006 NZ1(R),A1(R), 2007 Arg1,S2(R)
Glennon, B T (Lansdowne) 1993 F (R)
Glennon, J J (Skerries) 1980 E, S, 1987 E, S, F, [W (R)]
Godfrey, R P (UC Dublin) 1954 S, W
Goodall, K G (City of Derry, Newcastle U) 1967 A 1, E, S, W, F, A 2, 1968 F, E, S, W, A, 1969 F, E, S, 1970 SA, F, E, S, W
Gordon, A (Dublin U) 1884 S
Gordon, T G (NIFC) 1877 E, S, 1878 E
Gotto, R P C (NIFC) 1906 SA
Goulding, W J (Cork) 1879 S
Grace, T O (UC Dublin, St Mary's Coll) 1972 F 1, E, 1973 NZ, E, S, W, 1974 E, S, P, NZ, 1975 E, S, F, W, 1976 A, F, W, E, S, NZ, 1977 W, E, S, F, 1978 S
Graham, R I (Dublin U) 1911 F
Grant, E L (CIYMS) 1971 F, E, S, W
Grant, P J (Bective Rangers) 1894 S, W
Graves, C R A (Wanderers) 1934 E, S, W, 1935 E, S, W, NZ, 1936 E, S, W, 1937 E, S, 1938 E, S, W
Gray, R D (Old Wesley) 1923 E, S, 1925 F, 1926 F
Greene, E H (Dublin U, Kingstown) 1882 W, 1884 W, 1885 E, S 2, 1886 E
Greer, R (Kingstown) 1876 E

Greeves, T J (NIFC) 1907 E, S, W, 1909 W, F
Gregg, R J (Queen's U, Belfast) 1953 F, E, S, W, 1954 F, E, S
Griffin, C S (London Irish) 1951 F, E
Griffin, J L (Wanderers) 1949 S, W
Griffiths, W (Limerick) 1878 E
Grimshaw, C (Queen's U, Belfast) 1969 E (R)
Guerin, B N (Galwegians) 1956 S
Gwynn, A P (Dublin U) 1895 W
Gwynn, L H (Dublin U) 1893 S, 1894 E, S, W, 1897 S, 1898 E, S

Hakin, R F (CIYMS) 1976 W, S, NZ, 1977 W, E, F
Hall, R O N (Dublin U) 1884 W
Hall, W H (Instonians) 1923 E, S, W, F, 1924 F, S
Hallaran, C F G T (Royal Navy) 1921 E, S, W, 1922 E, S, W, 1923 E, F, 1924 F, E, S, W, 1925 F, 1926 F, E
Halpin, G F (Wanderers, London Irish) 1990 E, 1991 [J], 1992 E, S, F, 1993 R, 1994 F (R), 1995 It, [NZ, W, F]
Halpin, T (Garryowen) 1909 S, W, F, 1910 E, S, W, 1911 E, S, W, F, 1912 F, E, S
Halvey, E O (Shannon) 1995 F, W, It, [J, W (t), F (R)], 1997 NZ, C (R)
Hamilton, A J (Lansdowne) 1884 W
Hamilton, G F (NIFC) 1991 F, W, E, S, Nm 2, [Z, J, S, A], 1992 A
Hamilton, R L (NIFC) 1926 F
Hamilton, R W (Wanderers) 1893 W
Hamilton, W J (Dublin U) 1877 E
Hamlet, G T (Old Wesley) 1902 E, S, W, 1903 E, S, W, 1904 S, W, 1905 E, S, W, NZ, 1906 SA, 1907 E, S, W, 1908 E, S, W, 1909 E, S, W, F, 1910 E, S, F, 1911 E, S, W, F
Hanrahan, C J (Dolphin) 1926 S, W, 1927 E, S, W, A, 1928 F, E, S, 1929 F, E, S, W, 1930 F, E, S, W, 1931 F, 1932 S, W
Harbison, H T (Bective Rangers) 1984 W (R), E, S, 1986 R, 1987 E, S, F, W
Hardy, G G (Bective Rangers) 1962 S
Harman, G R A (Dublin U) 1899 E, W
Harper, J (Instonians) 1947 F, E, S
Harpur, T G (Dublin U) 1908 E, S, W
Harrison, T (Cork) 1879 S, 1880 S, 1881 E
Harvey, F M W (Wanderers) 1907 W, 1911 F
Harvey, G A D (Wanderers) 1903 E, S, 1904 W, 1905 E, S
Harvey, T A (Dublin U) 1900 W, 1901 S, W, 1902 E, S, W, 1903 E, W
Haycock, P P (Terenure Coll) 1989 E
Hayes, J J (Shannon, Munster) 2000 S, It, F, W, Arg, C, J, SA, 2001 It, F, R, S, W, E, Sm, NZ, 2002 W, E, S, It, F, NZ 1,2, R, Ru, Gg, A, Fj, Arg, 2003 S 1, It 1, F, W 1, E, [R(R),Nm,Arg,A,F], 2004 F,W,E,It,S,SA1,2,3,US,Arg, 2005 It,S,E,F,W,NZ,A,R(R), 2006 It,F,W,S,E,NZ1,2,A1,SA,A2,PI, 2007 W,F,E,S1,It1,S2(R),It2, [Nm,Gg,F,Arg], 2008 It,F,S,W,E,NZ1,A
Headon, T A (UC Dublin) 1939 S, W
Healey, P (Limerick) 1901 E, S, W, 1902 E, S, W, 1903 E, S, W, 1904 S
Heaslip, J P R (Leinster) 2006 PI, 2007 Arg1,S2, 2008 It(R),F,S,W,E,NZ1,A
Heffernan, M R (Cork Constitution) 1911 E, S, W, F
Hemphill, R (Dublin U) 1912 F, E, S, W
Henderson, N J (Queen's U, Belfast, NIFC) 1949 S, W, 1950 F, 1951 F, E, S, W, SA, 1952 F, S, W, E, 1953 F, E, S, W, 1954 NZ, F, E, S, W, 1955 F, E, S, W, 1956 S, W, 1957 F, E, S, W, 1958 A, E, S, W, F, 1959 E, S, W, F
Henderson R A J (London Irish, Wasps, Young Munster) 1996 WS, 1997 NZ, C, 1998 F, W, SA 1(R),2(R), 1999 F (R), E, S (R), It, 2000 S (R), It (R), F, W, Arg, US, J (R), SA, 2001 It, F, 2002 W (R), E (R), F, R (R), Ru (t), Gg (R), 2003 It 1(R),2
Henebrey, G J (Garryowen) 1906 E, S, W, SA, 1909 W, F
Heron, A G (Queen's Coll, Belfast) 1901 E
Heron, J (NIFC) 1877 S, 1879 E
Heron, W T (NIFC) 1880 E, S
Herrick, R W (Dublin U) 1886 S
Heuston, F S (Kingstown) 1882 W, 1883 E, S
Hewitt, D (Queen's U, Belfast, Instonians) 1958 A, E, S, F, 1959 S, W, F, 1960 E, S, W, F, 1961 E, S, W, F, 1962 S, F, 1965 W
Hewitt, F S (Instonians) 1924 W, NZ, 1925 F, E, S, 1926 E, 1927 E, S, W
Hewitt, J A (NIFC) 1981 SA 1(R),2(R)
Hewitt, T R (Queen's U, Belfast) 1924 W, NZ, 1925 F, E, S, 1926 F, E, S, W
Hewitt, V A (Instonians) 1935 S, W, NZ, 1936 E, S, W
Hewitt, W J (Instonians) 1954 E, 1956 S, 1959 W, 1961 SA
Hewson, F T (Wanderers) 1875 E
Hickie, D A (St Mary's Coll, Leinster) 1997 W, E, S, NZ, C, It 2, 1998 S, F, W, E, SA 1,2, 2000 S, It, F, W, J, SA, 2001 F, R, S, W, E, NZ, 2002 W, E, S, It, F, R, Ru, Gg, A, 2003 S 1, It 1, F, W 1, E, It 2, S 2, [R,Nm,Arg,A], 2004 SA3,Arg, 2005 It,S,E,F,W, 2006 A2,PI, 2007 W,F,E,S1,It1,2, [Nm,Gg,Arg]
Hickie, D J (St Mary's Coll) 1971 F, E, S, W, 1972 F 1, E
Higgins, J A D (Civil Service) 1947 S, W, A, 1948 F, S, W
Higgins, W W (NIFC) 1884 E, S
Hillary, M F (UC Dublin) 1952 E
Hingerty, D J (UC Dublin) 1947 F, E, S, W
Hinton, W P (Old Wesley) 1907 W, 1908 E, S, W, 1909 E, S, 1910 E, S, W, F, 1911 E, S, W, 1912 F, E, W
Hipwell, M L (Terenure Coll) 1962 E, S, 1968 F, A, 1969 F (R), S (R), W, 1971 F, E, S, W, 1972 F 2
Hobbs, T H M (Dublin U) 1884 S, 1885 E
Hobson, E W (Dublin U) 1876 E
Hogan, N A (Terenure Coll, London Irish) 1995 E, W, [J, W, F], 1996 F, W, E, WS, 1997 F, W, E, It 2
Hogan, P (Garryowen) 1992 F
Hogan, T (Munster, Leinster) 2005 J1(R),2(R), 2007 It1(R),Arg1
Hogg, W (Dublin U) 1885 S 2
Holland, J J (Wanderers) 1981 SA 1,2, 1986 W
Holmes, G W (Dublin U) 1912 SA, 1913 E, S
Holmes, L J (Lisburn) 1889 S, W
Hooks, K J (Queen's U, Belfast, Ards, Bangor) 1981 S, 1989 NZ, 1990 F, W, Arg, 1991 F
Horan, A K (Blackheath) 1920 E, W
Horan, M J (Shannon, Munster) 2000 US (R), 2002 Fj, Arg (R), 2003 S 1(R), It 1(R), F, W 1, E, A, Sm, It 2, S 2, [R,Nm,Arg(t&R), A(R),F(R)], 2004 It(R),S(R),SA1(R),2(t&R),3(R),US, 2005 It(R), S(R),E(R),F(R),W(R),J1,2,NZ,A,R, 2006 It,W,S,E,NZ1,2,A1,SA, A2(R), 2007 W,F,E,It1,2, [Nm,Gg,F,Arg], 2008 It,F,S,W,E,NZ1, A
Horgan, A P (Cork Const, Munster) 2003 Sm, W 2, S 2, 2004 F(R), 2005 J1,2,NZ
Horgan, S P (Lansdowne, Leinster) 2000 S, It, W, Arg, C, J, SA (R), 2001 It, S, W, E, NZ, 2002 S, It, F, A, Fj, Arg, 2003 S 1, [R,Nm,Arg,A,F], 2004 F,W,E,It,S,SA1,2,3,US,Arg, 2005 It,S,E,NZ,A,R, 2006 It,F,W,S,E,NZ1,2,A1,SA,A2,PI, 2007 F,E,S1,It1, [Gg,F,Arg], 2008 S(R),W,E,NZ1,A
Houston, K J (Oxford U, London Irish) 1961 SA, 1964 S, W, 1965 F, E, SA
Howe, T G (Dungannon, Ballymena, Ulster) 2000 US, J, SA, 2001 It, F, R, Sm, 2002 It (R), 2003 Tg, W 2, 2004 F,W,E, SA2
Hughes, R W (NIFC) 1878 E, 1880 E, S, 1881 S, 1882 E, S, 1883 E, S, 1884 E, S, 1885 E, 1886 E
Humphreys, D G (London Irish, Dungannon, Ulster) 1996 F, W, E, WS, 1997 E (R), S, It 2, 1998 S, E (R), SA 2(t + R), R (R), 1999 F, W, E, S, A 1,2, Arg 1, [US, A 3, Arg 2], 2000 E, S (R), F (t&R), W (R), Arg, US (R), C, J (R), SA (R), 2001 It (R), R, S (R), W, E, NZ, 2002 W, E, S, It, F, NZ 1(R),2(R), R (t+R), Ru (R), Gg (R), Fj, 2003 S 1, It 1, F, W 1, E, A, W 2, It 2, S 2(R), [R,Arg,A(R),F(R)], 2004W(R),It(R),S(R),SA2(R),US, 2005 S(R),W(R),J1,2,NZ(R),A(R),R
Hunt, E W F de Vere (Army, Rosslyn Park) 1930 F, 1932 E, S, W, 1933 E
Hunter, D V (Dublin U) 1885 S 2
Hunter, L M (Civil Service) 1968 W, A
Hunter, W R (CIYMS) 1962 E, S, W, F, 1963 F, E, S, 1966 F, E, S
Hurley, H D (Old Wesley, Moseley) 1995 Fj (t), 1996 WS
Hutton, S A (Malone) 1967 S, W, F, A 2

Ireland J (Windsor) 1876 E, 1877 E
Irvine, H A S (Collegians) 1901 S
Irwin, D G (Queen's U, Belfast, Instonians) 1980 F, W, 1981 F, W, E, S, SA 1,2, A, 1982 W, 1983 S, F, W, E, 1984 F, W, 1987 [Tg, A (R)], 1989 F, W, E, S, NZ, 1990 E, S
Irwin, J W S (NIFC) 1938 E, S, 1939 E, S, W
Irwin, S T (Queen's Coll, Belfast) 1900 E, S, W, 1901 E, W, 1902 E, S, W, 1903 S

Jack, H W (UC Cork) 1914 S, W, 1921 W

Jackman, B J (Leinster) 2005 J1(R),2(R), 2007 Arg1(R),2(R), 2008 It(R),F,S,W(R), E(R)
Jackson, A R V (Wanderers) 1911 E, S, W, F, 1913 W, F, 1914 F, E, S, W
Jackson, F (NIFC) 1923 E
Jackson, H W (Dublin U) 1877 E
Jameson, J S (Lansdowne) 1888 M, 1889 S, W, 1891 W, 1892 E, W, 1893 S
Jeffares, E W (Wanderers) 1913 E, S
Jennings, S (Leicester, Leinster) 2007 Arg 2, 2008 NZ1(R),A
Johns, P S (Dublin U, Dungannon, Saracens) 1990 Arg, 1992 NZ 1,2, A, 1993 S, F, W, E, R, 1994 F, W, E, S, A 1,2, US, 1995 E, S, W, It, [NZ, J, W, F], Fj, 1996 US, S, F, WS, 1997 It 1(R), F, W, E, S, NZ, C, It 2, 1998 S, F, W, E, SA 1,2, Gg, R, SA 3, 1999 F, W, E, S, It, A 1,2, Arg 1, [US, A 3, R], 2000 F (R), J
Johnston, J (Belfast Acad) 1881 S, 1882 S, 1884 S, 1885 S 1,2, 1886 E, 1887 E, S, W
Johnston, M (Dublin U) 1880 E, S, 1881 E, S, 1882 E, 1884 E, S, 1886 E
Johnston, R (Wanderers) 1893 E, W
Johnston, R W (Dublin U) 1890 S, W, E
Johnston, T J (Queen's Coll, Belfast) 1892 E, S, W, 1893 E, S, 1895 E
Johnstone, W E (Dublin U) 1884 W
Johnstone-Smyth, T R (Lansdowne) 1882 E

Kavanagh, J R (UC Dublin, Wanderers) 1953 F, E, S, W, 1954 NZ, S, W, 1955 F, E, 1956 E, S, W, 1957 F, E, S, W, 1958 A, E, S, W, 1959 E, S, W, F, 1960 E, S, W, F, SA, 1961 E, S, W, F, SA, 1962 F
Kavanagh, P J (UC Dublin, Wanderers) 1952 E, 1955 W
Keane, K P (Garryowen) 1998 E (R)
Keane, M I (Lansdowne) 1974 F, W, E, S, P, NZ, 1975 E, S, F, W, 1976 A, F, W, E, S, NZ, 1977 W, E, S, F, 1978 S, F, W, E, NZ, 1979 F, W, E, S, A 1,2, 1980 E, S, F, W, 1981 F, W, E, S, 1982 W, E, S, F, 1983 S, F, W, E, 1984 F, W, E, S
Kearney, R D J (Leinster) 2007 Arg 2, 2008 It(R),F,S,W,E,NZ1,A
Kearney, R K (Wanderers) 1982 F, 1984 A, 1986 F, W
Keeffe, E (Sunday's Well) 1947 F, E, S, W, A, 1948 F
Kelly, H C (NIFC) 1877 E, S, 1878 E, 1879 S, 1880 E, S
Kelly, J C (UC Dublin) 1962 F, W, 1963 F, E, S, W, NZ, 1964 E, S, W, F
Kelly, J P (Cork Constitution) 2002 It, NZ 1,2, R, Ru, Gg, A (R), 2003 It 1, F, A, Tg, Sm, It 2, [R(R),Nm(R),A(R),F]
Kelly, S (Lansdowne) 1954 S, W, 1955 S, 1960 W, F
Kelly, W (Wanderers) 1884 S
Kennedy, A G (Belfast Collegians) 1956 F
Kennedy, A P (London Irish) 1986 W, E
Kennedy, F (Wanderers) 1880 E, 1881 E, 1882 W
Kennedy, F A (Wanderers) 1904 E, W
Kennedy, H (Bradford) 1938 S, W
Kennedy, J M (Wanderers) 1882 W, 1884 W
Kennedy, K W (Queen's U, Belfast, London Irish) 1965 F, E, S, W, SA, 1966 F, E, W, 1967 A 1, E, S, W, F, A 2, 1968 F, A, 1969 F, E, S, W, 1970 SA, F, E, S, W, 1971 F, E, S, W, 1972 F 1, E, F 2, 1973 NZ, E, S, W, F, 1974 F, W, E, S, P, NZ, 1975 F, W
Kennedy, T J (St Mary's Coll) 1978 NZ, 1979 F, W, E (R), A 1,2, 1980 E, S, F, W, 1981 SA 1,2, A
Kenny, P (Wanderers) 1992 NZ 2(R)
Keogh, F S (Bective Rangers) 1964 W, F
Keon, J J (Limerick) 1879 E
Keyes, R P (Cork Constitution) 1986 E, 1991 [Z, J, S, A], 1992 W, E, S
Kidd, F W (Dublin U, Lansdowne) 1877 E, S, 1878 E
Kiely, M D (Lansdowne) 1962 W, 1963 F, E, S, W
Kiernan, M J (Dolphin, Lansdowne) 1982 W (R), E, S, F, 1983 S, F, W, E, 1984 E, S, A, 1985 S, F, W, E, 1986 F, W, E, S, R, 1987 E, S, F, W, [W, C, A], 1988 S, F, W, E 1,2, WS, 1989 F, W, E, S, 1990 E, S, F, W, Arg, 1991 F
Kiernan, T J (UC Cork, Cork Const) 1960 E, S, W, F, SA, 1961 E, S, W, F, SA, 1962 E, W, 1963 F, S, W, NZ, 1964 E, S, 1965 F, E, S, W, SA, 1966 F, E, S, W, 1967 A 1, E, S, W, F, A 2, 1968 F, E, S, W, A, 1969 F, E, S, W, 1970 SA, F, E, S, W, 1971 F, 1972 F 1, E, F 2, 1973 NZ, E, S
Killeen, G V (Garryowen) 1912 E, S, W, 1913 E, S, W, F, 1914 E, S, W
King, H (Dublin U) 1883 E, S
Kingston, T J (Dolphin) 1987 [W, Tg, A], 1988 S, F, W, E 1, 1990 F, W, 1991 [J], 1993 F, W, E, R, 1994 F, W, E, S, 1995 F, W, It, [NZ, J (R), W, F], Fj, 1996 US, S, F
Knox, J H (Dublin U, Lansdowne) 1904 W, 1905 E, S, W, NZ, 1906 E, S, W, 1907 W, 1908 S
Kyle, J W (Queen's U, Belfast, NIFC) 1947 F, E, S, W, A, 1948 F, E, S, W, 1949 F, E, S, W, 1950 F, E, S, W, 1951 F, E, S, W, SA, 1952 F, S, W, E, 1953 F, E, S, W, 1954 NZ, F, 1955 F, E, W, 1956 F, E, S, W, 1957 F, E, S, W, 1958 A, E, S

Lambert, N H (Lansdowne) 1934 S, W
Lamont, R A (Instonians) 1965 F, E, SA, 1966 F, E, S, W, 1970 SA, F, E, S, W
Landers, M F (Cork Const) 1904 W, 1905 E, S, W, NZ
Lane, D J (UC Cork) 1934 S, W, 1935 E, S
Lane, M F (UC Cork) 1947 W, 1949 F, E, S, W, 1950 F, E, S, W, 1951 F, S, W, SA, 1952 F, S, 1953 F, E
Lane, P (Old Crescent) 1964 W
Langan, D J (Clontarf) 1934 W
Langbroek, J A (Blackrock Coll) 1987 [Tg]
Lavery, P (London Irish) 1974 W, 1976 W
Lawlor, P J (Clontarf) 1951 S, SA, 1952 F, S, W, E, 1953 F, 1954 NZ, E, S, 1956 F, E
Lawlor, P J (Bective Rangers) 1935 E, S, W, 1937 E, S, W
Lawlor, P J (Bective Rangers) 1990 Arg, 1992 A, 1993 S
Leahy, K T (Wanderers) 1992 NZ 1
Leahy, M W (UC Cork) 1964 W
Leamy, D P (Munster) 2004 US, 2005 It,J2,NZ,A,R, 2006 It,F,W,S,E,NZ1,2,A1,SA,A2,PI(R), 2007 W,F,E,S1,It1,2, [Nm, Gg,F,Arg], 2008 It,F,S,W,E,NZ1,A
Lee, S (NIFC) 1891 E, S, W, 1892 E, S, W, 1893 E, S, W, 1894 E, S, W, 1895 E, W, 1896 E, S, W, 1897 E, 1898 E
Le Fanu, V C (Cambridge U, Lansdowne) 1886 E, S, 1887 E, W, 1888 S, 1889 W, 1890 E, 1891 E, 1892 E, S, W
Lenihan, D G (UC Cork, Cork Const) 1981 A, 1982 W, E, S, F, 1983 S, F, W, E, 1984 F, W, E, S, A, 1985 S, F, W, E, 1986 F, W, E, S, R, 1987 E, S, F, W, [W, C, Tg, A], 1988 S, F, W, E 1,2, WS, It, 1989 F, W, E, S, NZ, 1990 S, F, W, Arg, 1991 Nm 2, [Z, S, A], 1992 W
L'Estrange, L P F (Dublin U) 1962 E
Levis, F H (Wanderers) 1884 E
Lewis, K P (Leinster) 2005 J2(R), 2007 Arg1,2(R)
Lightfoot, E J (Lansdowne) 1931 F, E, S, W, SA, 1932 E, S, W, 1933 E, W, S
Lindsay, H (Dublin U, Armagh) 1893 E, S, W, 1894 E, S, W, 1895 E, 1896 E, S, W, 1898 E, S, W
Little, T J (Bective Rangers) 1898 W, 1899 S, W, 1900 S, W, 1901 E, S
Lloyd, R A (Dublin U, Liverpool) 1910 E, S, 1911 E, S, W, F, 1912 F, E, S, W, SA, 1913 E, S, W, F, 1914 F, E, 1920 E, F
Longwell, G W (Ballymena) 2000 J (R), SA, 2001 F (R), R, S (R), Sm, NZ (R), 2002 W (R), E (R), S (R), It, F, NZ 1,2, R, Ru, Gg, A, Arg, 2003 S 1, It 1, F, E, A, It 2, 2004 It(R)
Lydon, C T J (Galwegians) 1956 S
Lyle, R K (Dublin U) 1910 W, F
Lyle, T R (Dublin U) 1885 E, S 1,2, 1886 E, 1887 E, S
Lynch, J F (St Mary's Coll) 1971 F, E, S, W, 1972 F 1, E, F 2, 1973 NZ, E, S, W, 1974 F, W, E, S, P, NZ
Lynch, L M (Lansdowne) 1956 S
Lytle, J H (NIFC) 1894 E, S, W, 1895 W, 1896 E, S, W, 1897 E, S, 1898 E, S, 1899 S
Lytle, J N (NIFC) 1888 M, 1889 W, 1890 E, 1891 E, S, 1894 E, S, W
Lyttle, V J (Collegians, Bedford) 1938 E, 1939 E, S

McAleese, D R (Ballymena) 1992 F
McAllan, G H (Dungannon) 1896 S, W
Macauley, J (Limerick) 1887 E, S
McBride, W D (Malone) 1988 W, E 1, WS, It, 1989 S, 1990 F, W, Arg, 1993 S, F, W, E, R, 1994 W, E, S, A 1(R), 1995 S, F, [NZ, W, F], Fj (R), 1996 W, E, WS, A, 1997 It 1(R), F, W, E, S
McBride, W J (Ballymena) 1962 E, S, F, W, 1963 F, E, S, W, NZ, 1964 E, S, F, 1965 F, E, S, W, SA, 1966 F, E, S, W, 1967 A 1, E, S, W, F, A 2, 1968 F, E, S, W, A, 1969 F, E, S, W, 1970 SA, F, E, S, W, 1971 F, E, S, W, 1972 F 1, E, F 2, 1973 NZ, E, S, W, F, 1974 F, W, E, S, P, NZ, 1975 E, S, F, W
McCahill, S A (Sunday's Well) 1995 Fj (t)
McCall, B W (London Irish) 1985 F (R), 1986 E, S
McCall, M C (Bangor, Dungannon, London Irish) 1992 NZ

1(R),2, 1994 W, 1996 E (R), A, 1997 It 1, NZ, C, It 2, 1998 S, E, SA 1,2
McCallan, B (Ballymena) 1960 E, S
McCarten, R J (London Irish) 1961 E, W, F
McCarthy, E A (Kingstown) 1882 W
McCarthy, J S (Dolphin) 1948 F, E, S, W, 1949 F, E, S, W, 1950 W, 1951 F, E, S, W, SA, 1952 F, S, W, E, 1953 F, E, S, 1954 NZ, F, E, S, W, 1955 F, E
McCarthy, P D (Cork Const) 1992 NZ 1,2, A, 1993 S, R (R)
MacCarthy, St G (Dublin U) 1882 W
McCarthy, T (Cork) 1898 W
McClelland, T A (Queen's U, Belfast) 1921 E, S, W, F, 1922 E, W, F, 1923 E, S, W, F, 1924 F, E, S, W, NZ
McClenahan, R O (Instonians) 1923 E, S, W
McClinton, A N (NIFC) 1910 W, F
McCombe, W McM (Dublin U, Bangor) 1968 F, 1975 E, S, F, W
McConnell, A A (Collegians) 1947 A, 1948 F, E, S, W, 1949 F, E
McConnell, G (Derry, Edinburgh U) 1912 F, E, 1913 W, F
McConnell, J W (Lansdowne) 1913 S
McCormac, F M (Wanderers) 1909 W, 1910 W, F
McCormick, W J (Wanderers) 1930 E
McCoull, H C (Belfast Albion) 1895 E, S, W, 1899 E
McCourt, D (Queen's U, Belfast) 1947 A
McCoy, J J (Dungannon, Bangor, Ballymena) 1984 W, A, 1985 S, F, W, E, 1986 F, 1987 [Tg], 1988 E 2, WS, It, 1989 F, W, E, S, NZ
McCracken, H (NIFC) 1954 W
McCullen, A (Lansdowne) 2003 Sm
McCullough, M T (Ulster) 2005 J1,2,NZ(R),A(R)
McDermott, S J (London Irish) 1955 S, W
Macdonald, J A (Methodist Coll, Belfast) 1875 E, 1876 E, 1877 S, 1878 E, 1879 S, 1880 E, 1881 S, 1882 E, S, 1883 E, S, 1884 E, S
McDonald, J P (Malone) 1987 [C], 1990 E (R), S, Arg
McDonnell, A C (Dublin U) 1889 W, 1890 S, W, 1891 E
McDowell, J C (Instonians) 1924 F, NZ
McFarland, B A T (Derry) 1920 S, W, F, 1922 W
McGann, B J (Lansdowne) 1969 F, E, S, W, 1970 SA, F, E, S, W, 1971 F, E, S, W, 1972 F 1, E, F 2, 1973 NZ, E, S, W, 1976 F, W, E, S, NZ
McGowan, A N (Blackrock Coll) 1994 US
McGown, T M W (NIFC) 1899 E, S, 1901 S
McGrath, D G (UC Dublin, Cork Const) 1984 S, 1987 [W, C, Tg, A]
McGrath, N F (Oxford U, London Irish) 1934 W
McGrath, P J (UC Cork) 1965 E, S, W, SA, 1966 F, E, S, W, 1967 A 1, A 2
McGrath, R J M (Wanderers) 1977 W, E, F (R), 1981 SA 1,2, A, 1982 W, E, S, F, 1983 S, F, W, E, 1984 F, W
McGrath, T (Garryowen) 1956 W, 1958 F, 1960 E, S, W, F, 1961 SA
McGuinness, C D (St Mary's Coll) 1997 NZ, C, 1998 F, W, E, SA 1,2, Gg, R (R), SA 3, 1999 F, W, E, S
McGuire, E P (UC Galway) 1963 E, S, W, NZ, 1964 E, S, W, F
MacHale, S (Lansdowne) 1965 F, E, S, W, SA, 1966 F, E, S, W, 1967 S, W, F
McHugh, M (St Mary's Coll) 2003 Tg
McIldowie, G (Malone) 1906 SA, 1910 E, S, W
McIlrath, J A (Ballymena) 1976 A, F, NZ, 1977 W, E
McIlwaine, E H (NIFC) 1895 S, W
McIlwaine, E N (NIFC) 1875 E, 1876 E
McIlwaine, J E (NIFC) 1897 E, S, 1898 E, S, W, 1899 E, W
McIntosh, L M (Dublin U) 1884 S
MacIvor, C V (Dublin U) 1912 F, E, S, W, 1913 E, S, F
McIvor, S C (Garryowen) 1996 A, 1997 It 1, S (R)
McKay, J W (Queen's U, Belfast) 1947 F, E, S, W, A, 1948 F, E, S, W, 1949 F, E, S, W, 1950 F, E, S, W, 1951 F, E, S, W, SA, 1952 F
McKee, W D (NIFC) 1947 A, 1948 F, E, S, W, 1949 F, E, S, W, 1950 F, E, 1951 SA
McKeen, A J W (Lansdowne) 1999 [R (R)]
McKelvey, J M (Queen's U, Belfast) 1956 F, E
McKenna, P (St Mary's Coll) 2000 Arg
McKibbin, A R (Instonians, London Irish) 1977 W, E, S, 1978 S, F, W, E, NZ, 1979 F, W, E, S, 1980 E, S
McKibbin, C H (Instonians) 1976 S (R)
McKibbin, D (Instonians) 1950 F, E, S, W, 1951 F, E, S, W
McKibbin, H R (Queen's U, Belfast) 1938 W, 1939 E, S, W
McKinney, S A (Dungannon) 1972 F 1, E, F 2, 1973 W, F, 1974 F, E, S, P, NZ, 1975 E, S, 1976 A, F, W, E, S, NZ, 1977 W, E, S, 1978 S (R), F, W, E
McLaughlin, J H (Derry) 1887 E, S, 1888 W, S
McLean, R E (Dublin U) 1881 S, 1882 W, E, S, 1883 E, S, 1884 E, S, 1885 E, S 1
Maclear, B (Cork County, Monkstown) 1905 E, S, W, NZ, 1906 E, S, W, SA, 1907 E, S, W
McLennan, A C (Wanderers) 1977 F, 1978 S, F, W, E, NZ, 1979 F, W, E, S, 1980 E, F, 1981 F, W, E, S, SA 1,2
McLoughlin, F M (Northern) 1976 A
McLoughlin, G A J (Shannon) 1979 F, W, E, S, A 1,2, 1980 E, 1981 SA 1,2, 1982 W, E, S, F, 1983 S, F, W, E, 1984 F
McLoughlin, R J (UC Dublin, Blackrock Coll, Gosforth) 1962 E, S, F, 1963 E, S, W, NZ, 1964 E, S, 1965 F, E, S, W, SA, 1966 F, E, S, W, 1971 F, E, S, W, 1972 F 1, E, F 2, 1973 NZ, E, S, W, F, 1974 F, W, E, S, P, NZ, 1975 E, S, F, W
McMahon, L B (Blackrock Coll, UC Dublin) 1931 E, SA, 1933 E, 1934 E, 1936 E, S, W, 1937 E, S, W, 1938 E, S
McMaster, A W (Ballymena) 1972 F 1, E, F 2, 1973 NZ, E, S, W, F, 1974 F, E, S, P, 1975 F, W, 1976 A, F, W, NZ
McMordie, J (Queen's Coll, Belfast) 1886 S
McMorrow, A (Garryowen) 1951 W
McMullen, A R (Cork) 1881 E, S
McNamara, V (UC Cork) 1914 E, S, W
McNaughton, P P (Greystones) 1978 S, F, W, E, 1979 F, W, E, S, A 1,2, 1980 E, S, F, W, 1981 F
MacNeill, H P (Dublin U, Oxford U, Blackrock Coll, London Irish) 1981 F, W, E, S, A, 1982 W, E, S, F, 1983 S, F, W, E, 1984 F, W, E, A, 1985 S, F, W, E, 1986 F, W, E, S, R, 1987 E, S, F, W, [W, C, Tg, A], 1988 S (R), E 1,2
McQuilkin, K P (Bective Rangers, Lansdowne) 1996 US, S, F, 1997 F (t & R), S
MacSweeney, D A (Blackrock Coll) 1955 S
McVicker, H (Army, Richmond) 1927 E, S, W, A, 1928 F
McVicker, J (Collegians) 1924 F, E, S, W, NZ, 1925 F, E, S, W, 1926 F, E, S, W, 1927 F, E, S, W, A, 1928 W, 1930 F
McVicker, S (Queen's U, Belfast) 1922 E, S, W, F
McWeeney, J P J (St Mary's Coll) 1997 NZ
Madden, M N (Sunday's Well) 1955 E, S, W
Magee, A M (Louis) (Bective Rangers, London Irish) 1895 E, S, W, 1896 E, S, W, 1897 E, S, 1898 E, S, W, 1899 E, S, W, 1900 E, S, W, 1901 E, S, W, 1902 E, S, W, 1903 E, S, W, 1904 W
Magee, J T (Bective Rangers) 1895 E, S
Maggs, K M (Bristol, Bath, Ulster) 1997 NZ (R), C, It 2, 1998 S, F, W, E, SA 1,2, Gg, R (R), SA 3, 1999 F, W, E, S, It, A 1,2, Arg 1, [US, A 3, Arg 2], 2000 E, F, Arg, US (R), C, 2001 It (R), F (R), R, S (R), W, E, Sm, NZ, 2002 W, E, S, R, Ru, Gg, A, Fj, Arg, 2003 S 1, It 1, F, W 1, E, A, W 2, S 2, [R,Nm,Arg,A,F], 2004 F,W(R),E(R),It(R),S(R),SA1(R),2, US, 2005 S,F,W,J1
Maginiss, R M (Dublin U) 1875 E, 1876 E
Magrath, R M (Cork Constitution) 1909 S
Maguire, J F (Cork) 1884 S
Mahoney, J (Dolphin) 1923 E
Malcolmson, G L (RAF, NIFC) 1935 NZ, 1936 E, S, W, 1937 E, S, W
Malone, N G (Oxford U, Leicester) 1993 S, F, 1994 US (R)
Mannion, N P (Corinthians, Lansdowne, Wanderers) 1988 WS, It, 1989 F, W, E, S, NZ, 1990 E, S, F, W, Arg, 1991 Nm 1(R),2, [J], 1993 S
Marshall, B D E (Queen's U, Belfast) 1963 E
Mason, S J P (Orrell, Richmond) 1996 W, E, WS
Massey-Westropp, R H (Limerick, Monkstown) 1886 E
Matier, R N (NIFC) 1878 E, 1879 S
Matthews, P M (Ards, Wanderers) 1984 A, 1985 S, F, W, E, 1986 R, 1987 E, S, F, W, [W, Tg, A], 1988 S, F, W, E 1,2, WS, It, 1989 F, W, E, S, NZ, 1990 E, S, 1991 F, W, E, S, Nm 1 [Z, S, A], 1992 W, E, S
Mattsson, J (Wanderers) 1948 E
Mayne, R B (Queen's U, Belfast) 1937 W, 1938 E, W, 1939 E, S, W
Mayne, R H (Belfast Academy) 1888 W, S
Mayne, T (NIFC) 1921 E, S, F
Mays, K M A (UC Dublin) 1973 NZ, E, S, W
Meares, A W D (Dublin U) 1899 S, W, 1900 E, W
Megaw, J (Richmond, Instonians) 1934 W, 1938 E

Millar, A (Kingstown) 1880 E, S, 1883 E
Millar, H J (Monkstown) 1904 W, 1905 E, S, W
Millar, S (Ballymena) 1958 F, 1959 E, S, W, F, 1960 E, S, W, F, SA, 1961 E, S, W, F, SA, 1962 E, S, F, 1963 F, E, S, W, 1964 F, 1968 F, E, S, W, A, 1969 F, E, S, W, 1970 SA, F, E, S, W
Millar, W H J (Queen's U, Belfast) 1951 E, S, W, 1952 S, W
Miller, E R P (Leicester, Tererure Coll, Leinster) 1997 It 1, F, W, E, NZ, It 2, 1998 S, W (R), Gg, R, 1999 F, W, E (R), S, Arg 1(R), [US (R), A 3(t&R), Arg 2(R)], 2000 US, C (R), SA, 2001 R, W, E, Sm, NZ, 2002 E, S, It (R), Fj (R), 2003 W 1(t+R), Tg, Sm, It 2, S 2, [Nm,Arg(R),A(t&R),F(R)], 2004 SA3(R), US,Arg(R), 2005 It(R),S(R),F(R),W(R), J1(R),2
Miller, F H (Wanderers) 1886 S
Milliken, R A (Bangor) 1973 E, S, W, F, 1974 F, W, E, S, P, NZ, 1975 E, S, F, W
Millin, T J (Dublin U) 1925 W
Minch, J B (Bective Rangers) 1912 SA, 1913 E, S, 1914 E, S
Moffat, J (Belfast Academy) 1888 W, S, M, 1889 S, 1890 S, W, 1891 S
Moffatt, J E (Old Wesley) 1904 S, 1905 E, S, W
Moffett, J W (Ballymena) 1961 E, S
Molloy, M G (UC Galway, London Irish) 1966 F, E, 1967 A 1, E, S, W, F, A 2, 1968 F, E, S, W, A, 1969 F, E, S, W, 1970 F, E, S, W, 1971 F, E, S, W, 1973 F, 1976 A
Moloney, J J (St Mary's Coll) 1972 F 1, E, F 2, 1973 NZ, E, S, W, F, 1974 F, W, E, S, P, NZ, 1975 E, S, F, W, 1976 S, 1978 S, F, W, E, 1979 A 1,2, 1980 S, W
Moloney, L A (Garryowen) 1976 W (R), S, 1978 S (R), NZ
Molony, J U (UC Dublin) 1950 S
Monteith, J D E (Queen's U, Belfast) 1947 E, S, W
Montgomery, A (NIFC) 1895 S
Montgomery, F P (Queen's U, Belfast) 1914 E, S, W
Montgomery, R (Cambridge U) 1887 E, S, W, 1891 E, 1892 W
Moore, C M (Dublin U) 1887 S, 1888 W, S
Moore, D F (Wanderers) 1883 E, S, 1884 E, W
Moore, F W (Wanderers) 1884 W, 1885 E, S 2, 1886 S
Moore, H (Windsor) 1876 E, 1877 S
Moore, H (Queen's U, Belfast) 1910 S, 1911 W, F, 1912 F, E, S, W, SA
Moore, T A P (Highfield) 1967 A 2, 1973 NZ, E, S, W, F, 1974 F, W, E, S, P, NZ
Moore, W D (Queen's Coll, Belfast) 1878 E
Moran, F G (Clontarf) 1936 E, 1937 E, S, W, 1938 S, W, 1939 E, S, W
Morell, H B (Dublin U) 1881 E, S, 1882 W, E
Morgan, G J (Clontarf) 1934 E, S, W, 1935 E, S, W, NZ, 1936 E, S, W, 1937 E, S, W, 1938 E, S, W, 1939 E, S, W
Moriarty, C C H (Monkstown) 1899 W
Moroney, J C M (Garryowen) 1968 W, A, 1969 F, E, S, W
Moroney, R J M (Lansdowne) 1984 F, W, 1985 F
Moroney, T A (UC Dublin) 1964 W, 1967 A 1, E
Morphy, E McG (Dublin U) 1908 E
Morris, D P (Bective Rangers) 1931 W, 1932 E, 1935 E, S, W, NZ
Morrow, J W R (Queen's Coll, Belfast) 1882 S, 1883 E, S, 1884 E, W, 1885 S 1,2, 1886 E, S, 1888 S
Morrow, R D (Bangor) 1986 F, E, S
Mortell, M (Bective Rangers, Dolphin) 1953 F, E, S, W, 1954 NZ, F, E, S, W
Morton, W A (Dublin U) 1888 S
Mostyn, M R (Galwegians) 1999 A 1, Arg 1, [US, A 3, R, Arg 2]
Moyers, L W (Dublin U) 1884 W
Moylett, M M F (Shannon) 1988 E 1
Mulcahy, W A (UC Dublin, Bective Rangers, Bohemians) 1958 A, E, S, W, F, 1959 E, S, W, F, 1960 E, S, W, SA, 1961 E, S, W, SA, 1962 E, S, F, W, 1963 F, E, S, W, NZ, 1964 E, S, W, F, 1965 F, E, S, W, SA
Mullan, B (Clontarf) 1947 F, E, S, W, 1948 F, E, S, W
Mullane, J P (Limerick Bohemians) 1928 W, 1929 F
Mullen, K D (Old Belvedere) 1947 F, E, S, W, A, 1948 F, E, S, W, 1949 F, E, S, W, 1950 F, E, S, W, 1951 F, E, S, W, SA, 1952 F, S, W
Mulligan, A A (Wanderers) 1956 F, E, 1957 F, E, S, W, 1958 A, E, S, F, 1959 E, S, W, F, 1960 E, S, W, F, SA, 1961 W, F, SA
Mullin, B J (Dublin U, Oxford U, Blackrock Coll, London Irish) 1984 A, 1985 S, W, E, 1986 F, W, E, S, R, 1987 E, S, F, W, [W, C, Tg, A], 1988 S, F, W, E 1,2, WS, It, 1989 F, W, E, S, NZ, 1990 E, S, W, Arg, 1991 F, W, E, S, Nm 1,2, [J, S, A], 1992 W, E, S, 1994 US, 1995 E, S, F, W, It, [NZ, J, W, F]
Mullins, M J (Young Munster, Old Crescent) 1999 Arg 1(R), [R], 2000 E, S, It, Arg (t&R), US, C, 2001 It, R, W (R), E (R), Sm (R), NZ (R), 2003 Tg, Sm
Murphy, B J (Munster) 2007 Arg1(R),2
Murphy, C J (Lansdowne) 1939 E, S, W, 1947 F, E
Murphy, G E A (Leicester) 2000 US, C (R), J, 2001 R, S, Sm, 2002 W, E, NZ 1,2, Fj, 2003 S 1(R), It 1, F, W 1, E, A, W 2, It 2(R), S 2, 2004 It,S,SA1,3,US,Arg, 2005 It,S,E,F,W,NZ,A,R, 2006 It,F,W,S,E,NZ1,2,A1(R),SA(R),A2, 2007 W(t&R),F, Arg1(t&R),2,S2,It2, [Nm(R),Arg], 2008 It,F,S,E,NZ1(R),A(R)
Murphy, J G M W (London Irish) 1951 SA, 1952 S, W, E, 1954 NZ, 1958 W
Murphy, J J (Greystones) 1981 SA 1, 1982 W (R), 1984 S
Murphy, J N (Greystones) 1992 A
Murphy, K J (Cork Constitution) 1990 E, S, F, W, Arg, 1991 F, W (R), S (R), 1992 S, F, NZ 2(R)
Murphy, N A A (Cork Constitution) 1958 A, E, S, W, F, 1959 E, S, W, F, 1960 E, S, W, F, SA, 1961 E, S, W, 1962 E, 1963 NZ, 1964 E, S, W, F, 1965 F, E, S, W, SA, 1966 F, E, S, W, 1967 A 1, E, S, W, F, 1969 F, E, S, W
Murphy, N F (Cork Constitution) 1930 E, W, 1931 F, E, S, W, SA, 1932 E, S, W, 1933 E
Murphy-O'Connor, J (Bective Rangers) 1954 E
Murray, H W (Dublin U) 1877 S, 1878 E, 1879 E
Murray, J B (UC Dublin) 1963 F
Murray, P F (Wanderers) 1927 F, 1929 F, E, S, 1930 F, E, S, W, 1931 F, E, S, W, SA, 1932 E, S, W, 1933 E, W, S
Murtagh, C W (Portadown) 1977 S
Myles, J (Dublin U) 1875 E

Nash, L C (Queen's Coll, Cork) 1889 S, 1890 W, E, 1891 E, S, W
Neely, M R (Collegians) 1947 F, E, S, W
Neill, H J (NIFC) 1885 E, S 1,2, 1886 S, 1887 E, S, W, 1888 W, S
Neill, J McF (Instonians) 1926 F
Nelson, J E (Malone) 1947 A, 1948 E, S, W, 1949 F, E, S, W, 1950 F, E, S, W, 1951 F, E, W, 1954 F
Nelson, R (Queen's Coll, Belfast) 1882 E, S, 1883 S, 1886 S
Nesdale, R P (Newcastle) 1997 W, E, S, NZ (R), C, 1998 F (R), W (R), Gg, SA 3(R), 1999 It, A 2(R), [US (R), R]
Nesdale, T J (Garryowen) 1961 F
Neville, W C (Dublin U) 1879 S, E
Nicholson, P C (Dublin U) 1900 E, S, W
Norton, G W (Bective Rangers) 1949 F, E, S, W, 1950 F, E, S, W, 1951 F, E, S
Notley, J R (Wanderers) 1952 F, S
Nowlan, K W (St Mary's Coll) 1997 NZ, C, It 2

O'Brien, B (Derry) 1893 S, W
O'Brien, B A P (Shannon) 1968 F, E, S
O'Brien, D J (London Irish, Cardiff, Old Belvedere) 1948 E, S, W, 1949 F, E, S, W, 1950 F, E, S, W, 1951 F, E, S, W, SA, 1952 F, S, W, E
O'Brien, K A (Broughton Park) 1980 E, 1981 SA 1(R),2
O'Brien-Butler, P E (Monkstown) 1897 S, 1898 E, S, 1899 S, W, 1900 E
O'Callaghan, C T (Carlow) 1910 W, F, 1911 E, S, W, F, 1912 F
O'Callaghan, D P (Cork Const, Munster) 2003 W 1(R), Tg (R), Sm (R), W 2(R), It2(R), [R(R),A(t&R)], 2004 F(t&R),W,It,S(t&R), SA2(R),US, 2005 It(R),S(R),W(R),NZ,A,R, 2006 It(R),F(R),W, S(R),E(R),NZ1,2,A1,SA,A2,PI(R), 2007 W,F,E,S1,It1,2, [Nm,Gg,F, Arg], 2008 It,F,S,W,E,NZ1,A
O'Callaghan, M P (Sunday's Well) 1962 W, 1964 E, F
O'Callaghan, P (Dolphin) 1967 A 1, E, A 2, 1968 F, E, S, W, 1969 F, E, S, W, 1970 SA, F, E, S, W, 1976 F, W, E, S, NZ
O'Connell, K D (Sunday's Well) 1994 F, E (t)
O'Connell, P (Bective Rangers) 1913 W, F, 1914 F, E, S, W
O'Connell, P J (Young Munster, Munster) 2002 W, It (R), F (R), NZ 1, 2003 E (R), A (R), Tg, Sm, W 2, S 2, [R(R),A(t&R)], 2004 F(t&R),W,It,S(t&R),SA1(R),US, 2005 It(R),S(R),W(R),NZ, A,R, 2006 It(R),F(R),W,S(R),E(R),NZ1,2,A1, SA,A2,PI, 2007 W,F, E,S1,2,It2, [Nm,Gg,F,Arg], 2008 S(R),W,E, NZ1,A
O'Connell, W J (Lansdowne) 1955 F
O'Connor, H S (Dublin U) 1957 F, E, S, W

O'Connor, J (Garryowen) 1895 S
O'Connor, J H (Bective Rangers) 1888 M, 1890 S, W, E, 1891 E, S, 1892 E, W, 1893 E, S, 1894 E, S, W, 1895 E, 1896 E, S, W
O'Connor, J H (Wasps) 2004 SA3,Arg, 2005 S,E,F,W,J1,NZ,A,R, 2006 W(R),E(t&R)
O'Connor, J J (Garryowen) 1909 F
O'Connor, J J (UC Cork) 1933 S, 1934 E, S, W, 1935 E, S, W, NZ, 1936 S, W, 1938 S
O'Connor, P J (Lansdowne) 1887 W
O'Cuinneagain, D (Sale, Ballymena) 1998 SA 1,2, Gg (R), R (R), SA 3, 1999 F, W, E, S, It, A 1,2, Arg 1, [US, A 3, R, Arg 2], 2000 E, It (R)
Odbert, R V M (RAF) 1928 F
O'Donnell, R C (St Mary's Coll) 1979 A 1,2, 1980 S, F, W
O'Donoghue, P J (Bective Rangers) 1955 F, E, S, W, 1956 W, 1957 F, E, 1958 A, E, S, W
O'Driscoll, B G (Blackrock Coll, Leinster) 1999 A 1,2, Arg 1, [US, A 3, R (R), Arg 2], 2000 E, S, It, F, W, J, SA, 2001 F, S, W, E, Sm, NZ, 2002 W, E, S, It, F, NZ 1,2, R, Ru, Gg, A, Fj, Arg, 2003 S 1, It 1, F, W 1, E, W 2, It 2, S 2, [R,Nm,Arg,A,F], 2004 W,E,It,S,SA1,2,3,US,Arg, 2005 It,E,F,W, 2006 It,F,W,S, E,NZ1,2,A1,SA,A2,PI, 2007 W,E,S1,It1,S2, [Nm,Gg,F,Arg], 2008 It,F,S,W,NZ1,A
O'Driscoll, B J (Manchester) 1971 F (R), E, S, W
O'Driscoll, J B (London Irish, Manchester) 1978 S, 1979 A 1,2, 1980 E, S, F, W, 1981 F, W, E, S, SA 1,2, A, 1982 W, E, S, F, 1983 S, F, W, E, 1984 F, W, E, S
O'Driscoll, M R (Cork Const, Munster) 2001 R (R), 2002 Fj (R), 2005 R(R), 2006 W(R),NZ1(R),2(R),A1(R), 2007 E(R),It1, Arg1(t&R),2, 2008 It(R),F(R),S,E(R)
O'Flanagan, K P (London Irish) 1947 A
O'Flanagan, M (Lansdowne) 1948 S
O'Gara, R J R (Cork Const, Munster) 2000 S, It, F, W, Arg (R), US, C (R), J, SA, 2001 It, F, S, W (R), E (R), Sm, 2002 W (R), E (R), S (R), It (t), F (R), NZ 1,2, R, Ru, Gg, A, Arg, 2003 W 1(R), E (R), A (t+R), Tg, Sm, S 2, [R(R),Nm,Arg(R),A,F], 2004 F,W,E,It, S,SA1,2,3,Arg, 2005 It,S,E,F,W,NZ,A,R(R), 2006 It, F,W,S,E,NZ1,2,A1,SA,A2,PI(R), 2007 W,F,E,S1,It1,S2(R),It2, [Nm,Gg,F,Arg], 2008 It,F,S,W,E,NZ1,A
O'Grady, D (Sale) 1997 It 2
O'Hanlon, B (Dolphin) 1947 E, S, W, 1948 F, E, S, W, 1949 F, E, S, W, 1950 F
O'Hara, P T J (Sunday's Well, Cork Const) 1988 WS (R), 1989 F, W, E, NZ, 1990 E, S, F, W, 1991 Nm 1, [J], 1993 F, W, E, 1994 US
O'Kelly, M E (London Irish, St Mary's Coll, Leinster) 1997 NZ, C, It 2, 1998 S, F, W, E, SA 1,2, Gg, R, SA 3, 1999 A 1(R),2, Arg 1(R), [US (R), A 3, R, Arg 2], 2000 E, S, It, F, W, Arg, US, J, SA, 2001 It, F, S, W, E, NZ, 2002 E, S, It, F, NZ 1(R),2, R, Ru, Gg, A, Fj, Arg, 2003 S 1, It 1, F, W 1, E, A, W 2, S 2, [R,Nm,Arg,A,F], 2004 F,W(R),E,It,S, SA1,2,3,Arg, 2005 It,S,E,F, W,NZ,A, 2006 It,F,W,S,E,SA(R),A2(R),PI, 2007 Arg1,2(R),S2, It2(R), [F(R),Arg(R)], 2008 It,F
O'Leary, A (Cork Constitution) 1952 S, W, E
O'Leary, T G (Munster) 2007 Arg1(R)
O'Loughlin, D B (UC Cork) 1938 E, S, W, 1939 E, S, W
O'Mahony, D W (UC Dublin, Moseley, Bedford) 1995 It, [F], 1997 It 2, 1998 R
O'Mahony, David (Cork Constitution) 1995 It
O'Meara, B T (Cork Constitution) 1997 E (R), S, NZ (R), 1998 S, 1999 [US (R), R (R)], 2001 It (R), 2003 Sm (R), It 2(R)
O'Meara, J A (UC Cork, Dolphin) 1951 F, E, S, W, SA, 1952 F, S, W, E, 1953 F, E, S, W, 1954 NZ, F, E, S, 1955 F, E, 1956 S, W, 1958 W
O'Neill, H O'H (Queen's U, Belfast, UC Cork) 1930 E, S, W, 1933 E, S, W
O'Neill, J B (Queen's U, Belfast) 1920 S
O'Neill, W A (UC Dublin, Wanderers) 1952 E, 1953 F, E, S, W, 1954 NZ
O'Reilly, A J F (Old Belvedere, Leicester) 1955 F, E, S, W, 1956 F, E, S, W, 1957 F, E, S, W, 1958 A, E, S, W, F, 1959 E, S, W, F, 1960 E, 1961 E, F, SA, 1963 F, S, W, 1970 E
Orr, P A (Old Wesley) 1976 F, W, E, S, NZ, 1977 W, E, S, F, 1978 S, F, W, E, NZ, 1979 F, W, E, S, A 1,2, 1980 E, S, F, W, 1981 F, W, E, S, SA 1,2, A, 1982 W, E, S, F, 1983 S, F, W, E, 1984 F, W, E, S, A, 1985 S, F, W, E, 1986 F, S, R, 1987 E, S, F, W, [W, C, A]
O'Shea, C M P (Lansdowne, London Irish) 1993 R, 1994 F, W, E, S, A 1,2, US, 1995 E, S, [J, W, F], 1997 It 1, F, S (R), 1998 S, F, SA 1,2, Gg, R, SA 3, 1999 F, W, E, S, It, A 1, Arg 1, [US, A 3, R, Arg 2], 2000 E
O'Sullivan, A C (Dublin U) 1882 S
O'Sullivan, J M (Limerick) 1884 S, 1887 S
O'Sullivan, P J A (Galwegians) 1957 F, E, S, W, 1959 E, S, W, F, 1960 SA, 1961 E, S, 1962 F, W, 1963 F, NZ
O'Sullivan, W (Queen's Coll, Cork) 1895 S
Owens, R H (Dublin U) 1922 E, S

Parfrey, P (UC Cork) 1974 NZ
Parke, J C (Monkstown) 1903 W, 1904 E, S, W, 1905 W, NZ, 1906 E, S, W, SA, 1907 E, S, W, 1908 E, S, W, 1909 E, S, W, F
Parr, J S (Wanderers) 1914 F, E, S, W
Patterson, C S (Instonians) 1978 NZ, 1979 F, W, E, S, A 1,2, 1980 E, S, F, W
Patterson, R d'A (Wanderers) 1912 F, S, W, SA, 1913 E, S, W, F
Payne, C T (NIFC) 1926 E, 1927 F, E, S, A, 1928 F, E, S, W, 1929 F, E, W, 1930 F, E, S, W
Pedlow, A C (CIYMS) 1953 W, 1954 NZ, F, E, 1955 F, E, S, W, 1956 F, E, S, W, 1957 F, E, S, W, 1958 A, E, S, W, F, 1959 E, 1960 E, S, W, F, SA, 1961 S, 1962 W, 1963 F
Pedlow, J (Bessbrook) 1882 S, 1884 W
Pedlow, R (Bessbrook) 1891 W
Pedlow, T B (Queen's Coll, Belfast) 1889 S, W
Peel, T (Limerick) 1892 E, S, W
Peirce, W (Cork) 1881 E
Phipps, G C (Army) 1950 E, W, 1952 F, W, E
Pike, T O (Lansdowne) 1927 E, S, W, A, 1928 F, E, S, W
Pike, V J (Lansdowne) 1931 E, S, W, SA, 1932 E, S, W, 1933 E, W, S, 1934 E, S, W
Pike, W W (Kingstown) 1879 E, 1881 E, S, 1882 E, 1883 S
Pinion, G (Belfast Collegians) 1909 E, S, W, F
Piper, O J S (Cork Constitution) 1909 E, S, W, F, 1910 E, S, W, F
Polden, S E (Clontarf) 1913 W, F, 1914 F, 1920 F
Popham, I (Cork Constitution) 1922 S, W, F, 1923 F
Popplewell, N J (Greystones, Wasps, Newcastle) 1989 NZ, 1990 Arg, 1991 Nm 1,2, [Z, S, A], 1992 W, E, S, F, NZ 1,2, A, 1993 S, F, W, E, R, 1994 F, W, E, S, US, 1995 E, S, F, W, It, [NZ, J, W, F], Fj, 1996 US, S, F, W, E, A, 1997 It 1, F, W, E, NZ, C, 1998 S (t), F (R)
Potterton, H N (Wanderers) 1920 W
Pratt, R H (Dublin U) 1933 E, W, S, 1934 E, S
Price, A H (Dublin U) 1920 S, F
Pringle, J C (NIFC) 1902 S, W
Purcell, N M (Lansdowne) 1921 E, S, W, F
Purdon, H (NIFC) 1879 S, E, 1880 E, 1881 E, S
Purdon, W B (Queen's Coll, Belfast) 1906 E, S, W
Purser, F C (Dublin U) 1898 E, S, W

Quinlan, A N (Shannon, Munster) 1999 [R (R)], 2001 It, F, 2002 NZ 2(R), Ru (R), Gg (R), A (R), Fj, Arg (R), 2003 S 1(R), It 1(R), F (R), W 1, E (R), A, W 2, [R(R),Nm,Arg], 2004 SA1(R),2(R), 2005 J1,2(t&R), 2007 Arg2,S2(t&R)
Quinlan, D P (Northampton) 2005 J1(R),2
Quinlan, S V J (Blackrock Coll) 1956 F, E, W, 1958 W
Quinn, B T (Old Belvedere) 1947 F
Quinn, F P (Old Belvedere) 1981 F, W, E
Quinn, J P (Dublin U) 1910 E, S, 1911 E, S, W, F, 1912 E, S, W, 1913 E, W, F, 1914 F, E, S
Quinn, K (Old Belvedere) 1947 F, A, 1953 F, E, S
Quinn, M A M (Lansdowne) 1973 F, 1974 F, W, E, S, P, NZ, 1977 S, F, 1981 SA 2
Quirke, J M T (Blackrock Coll) 1962 E, S, 1968 S

Rainey, P I (Ballymena) 1989 NZ
Rambaut, D F (Dublin U) 1887 E, S, W, 1888 W
Rea, H H (Edinburgh U) 1967 A 1, 1969 F
Read, H M (Dublin U) 1910 E, S, 1911 E, S, W, F, 1912 F, E, S, W, SA, 1913 E, S
Reardon, J V (Cork Constitution) 1934 E, S
Reddan, E G (Wasps) 2006 F(R), 2007 Arg2,S2(R), [F,Arg], 2008 It,F,S,W,E,NZ1,A(R)
Reid, C (NIFC) 1899 S, W, 1900 E, 1903 W
Reid, J L (Richmond) 1934 S, W
Reid, P J (Garryowen) 1947 A, 1948 F, E, W

Reid, T E (Garryowen) 1953 E, S, W, 1954 NZ, F, 1955 E, S, 1956 F, E, 1957 F, E, S, W
Reidy, C J (London Irish) 1937 W
Reidy, G F (Dolphin, Lansdowne) 1953 W, 1954 F, E, S, W
Richey, H A (Dublin U) 1889 W, 1890 S
Ridgeway, E C (Wanderers) 1932 S, W, 1935 E, S, W
Rigney, B J (Greystones) 1991 F, W, E, S, Nm 1, 1992 F, NZ 1(R),2
Ringland, T M (Queen's U, Belfast, Ballymena) 1981 A, 1982 W, E, F, 1983 S, F, W, E, 1984 F, W, E, S, A, 1985 S, F, W, E, 1986 F, W, E, S, R, 1987 E, S, F, W, [W, C, Tg, A], 1988 S, F, W, E 1
Riordan, W F (Cork Constitution) 1910 E
Ritchie, J S (London Irish) 1956 F, E
Robb, C G (Queen's Coll, Belfast) 1904 E, S, W, 1905 NZ, 1906 S
Robbie, J C (Dublin U, Greystones) 1976 A, F, NZ, 1977 S, F, 1981 F, W, E, S
Robinson, B F (Ballymena, London Irish) 1991 F, W, E, S, Nm 1,2, [Z, S, A], 1992 W, E, S, F, NZ 1,2, A, 1993 W, E, R, 1994 F, W, E, S, A 1,2
Robinson, T T H (Wanderers) 1904 E, S, 1905 E, S, W, NZ, 1906 SA, 1907 E, S, W
Roche, J (Wanderers) 1890 S, W, E, 1891 E, S, W, 1892 W
Roche, R E (UC Galway) 1955 E, S, 1957 S, W
Roche, W J (UC Cork) 1920 E, S, F
Roddy, P J (Bective Rangers) 1920 S, F
Roe, R (Lansdowne) 1952 E, 1953 F, E, S, W, 1954 F, E, S, W, 1955 F, E, S, W, 1956 F, E, S, W, 1957 F, E, S, W
Rolland, A C (Blackrock Coll) 1990 Arg, 1994 US (R), 1995 It (R)
Rooke, C V (Dublin U) 1891 E, W, 1892 E, S, W, 1893 E, S, W, 1894 E, S, W, 1895 E, S, W, 1896 E, S, W, 1897 E, S
Ross, D J (Belfast Academy) 1884 E, 1885 S 1,2, 1886 E, S
Ross, G R P (CIYMS) 1955 W
Ross, J F (NIFC) 1886 S
Ross, J P (Lansdowne) 1885 E, S 1,2, 1886 E, S
Ross, N G (Malone) 1927 F, E
Ross, W McC (Queen's U, Belfast) 1932 E, S, W, 1933 E, W, S, 1934 E, S, 1935 NZ
Russell, J (UC Cork) 1931 F, E, S, W, SA, 1933 E, W, S, 1934 E, S, W, 1935 E, S, W, 1936 E, S, W, 1937 E, S
Russell, P (Instonians) 1990 E, 1992 NZ 1,2, A
Rutherford, W G (Tipperary) 1884 E, S, 1885 E, S 1, 1886 E, 1888 W
Ryan, E (Dolphin) 1937 W, 1938 E, S
Ryan, J (Rockwell Coll) 1897 E, 1898 E, S, W, 1899 E, S, W, 1900 S, W, 1901 E, S, W, 1902 E, 1904 E
Ryan, J G (UC Dublin) 1939 E, S, W
Ryan, M (Rockwell Coll) 1897 E, S, 1898 E, S, W, 1899 E, S, W, 1900 E, S, W, 1901 E, S, W, 1903 E, 1904 E, S

Saunders, R (London Irish) 1991 F, W, E, S, Nm 1,2, [Z, J, S, A], 1992 W, 1994 F (t)
Saverimutto, C (Sale) 1995 Fj, 1996 US, S
Sayers, H J M (Lansdowne) 1935 E, S, W, 1936 E, S, W, 1938 W, 1939 E, S, W
Scally, C J (U C Dublin) 1998 Gg (R), R, 1999 S (R), It
Schute, F (Wanderers) 1878 E, 1879 E
Schute, F G (Dublin U) 1912 SA, 1913 E, S
Scott, D (Malone) 1961 F, SA, 1962 S
Scott, R D (Queen's U, Belfast) 1967 E, F, 1968 F, E, S
Scovell, R H (Kingstown) 1883 E, 1884 E
Scriven, G (Dublin U) 1879 S, E, 1880 E, S, 1881 E, 1882 S, 1883 E, S
Sealy, J (Dublin U) 1896 E, S, W, 1897 S, 1899 E, S, W, 1900 E, S
Sexton, J F (Dublin U, Lansdowne) 1988 E 2, WS, It, 1989 F
Sexton, W J (Garryowen) 1984 A, 1988 S, E 2
Shanahan, T (Lansdowne) 1885 E, S 1,2, 1886 E, 1888 S, W
Shaw, G M (Windsor) 1877 S
Sheahan, F J (Cork Const, Munster) 2000 US (R), 2001 It (R), R, W (R), Sm, 2002 W, E, S, Gg (R), A (t+R), Fj, 2003 S 1(R), It 1(R), 2004 F(R),W(R),It(R),S(R),SA1(R),US, 2005 It(R),S(R), W(R),J1,2, 2006 SA(R),A2(R),PI, 2007 Arg2, [F(t&R)]
Sheehan, M D (London Irish) 1932 E
Sherry, B F (Terenure Coll) 1967 A 1, E, S, A 2, 1968 F, E
Sherry, M J A (Lansdowne) 1975 F, W
Shields, P M (Ballymena) 2003 Sm (R), It 2(R)
Siggins, J A E (Belfast Collegians) 1931 F, E, S, W, SA, 1932 E, S, W, 1933 E, W, S, 1934 E, S, W, 1935 E, S, W, NZ, 1936 E, S, W, 1937 E, S, W
Slattery, J F (UC Dublin, Blackrock Coll) 1970 SA, F, E, S, W, 1971 F, E, S, W, 1972 F 1, E, F 2, 1973 NZ, E, S, W, F, 1974 F, W, E, S, P, NZ, 1975 E, S, F, W, 1976 A, 1977 S, F, 1978 S, F, W, E, NZ, 1979 F, W, E, S, A 1,2, 1980 E, S, F, W, 1981 F, W, E, S, SA 1,2, A, 1982 W, E, S, F, 1983 S, F, W, E, 1984 F
Smartt, F N B (Dublin U) 1908 E, S, 1909 E
Smith, B A (Oxford U, Leicester) 1989 NZ, 1990 S, F, W, Arg, 1991 F, W, E, S
Smith, J H (London Irish) 1951 F, E, S, W, SA, 1952 F, S, W, E, 1954 NZ, W, F
Smith, R E (Lansdowne) 1892 E
Smith, S J (Ballymena) 1988 E 2, WS, It, 1989 F, W, E, S, NZ, 1990 E, 1991 F, W, E, S, Nm 1,2, [Z, S, A], 1992 W, E, S, F, NZ 1,2, 1993 S
Smithwick, F F S (Monkstown) 1898 S, W
Smyth, J T (Queen's U, Belfast) 1920 F
Smyth, P J (Belfast Collegians) 1911 E, S, F
Smyth, R S (Dublin U) 1903 E, S, 1904 E
Smyth, T (Malone, Newport) 1908 E, S, W, 1909 E, S, W, 1910 E, S, W, F, 1911 E, S, W, 1912 E
Smyth, W S (Belfast Collegians) 1910 W, F, 1920 E
Solomons, B A H (Dublin U) 1908 E, S, W, 1909 E, S, W, F, 1910 E, S, W
Spain, A W (UC Dublin) 1924 NZ
Sparrow, W (Dublin U) 1893 W, 1894 E
Spillane, B J (Bohemians) 1985 S, F, W, E, 1986 F, W, E, 1987 F, W, [W, C, A (R)], 1989 E (R)
Spring, D E (Dublin U) 1978 S, NZ, 1979 S, 1980 S, F, W, 1981 W
Spring, R M (Lansdowne) 1979 F, W, E
Spunner, H F (Wanderers) 1881 E, S, 1884 W
Stack, C R R (Dublin U) 1889 S
Stack, G H (Dublin U) 1875 E
Staples, J E (London Irish, Harlequins) 1991 W, E, S, Nm 1,2, [Z, J, S, A], 1992 W, E, NZ 1,2, A, 1995 F, W, It, [NZ], Fj, 1996 US, S, F, A, 1997 W, E, S
Staunton, J W (Garryowen, Wasps) 2001 Sm, 2005 J1(R),2(R), 2006 A1(R), 2007 Arg2
Steele, H W (Ballymena) 1976 E, 1977 F, 1978 F, W, E, 1979 F, W, E, A 1,2
Stephenson, G V (Queen's U, Belfast, London Hosp) 1920 F, 1921 E, S, W, F, 1922 E, S, W, F, 1923 E, S, W, F, 1924 F, E, S, W, NZ, 1925 F, E, S, W, 1926 F, E, S, W, 1927 F, E, S, W, A, 1928 F, E, S, W, 1929 F, E, W, 1930 F, E, S, W
Stephenson, H W V (United Services) 1922 S, W, F, 1924 F, E, S, W, NZ, 1925 F, E, S, W, 1927 A, 1928 E
Stevenson, J (Dungannon) 1888 M, 1889 S
Stevenson, J B (Instonians) 1958 A, E, S, W, F
Stevenson, R (Dungannon) 1887 E, S, W, 1888 M, 1889 S, W, 1890 S, W, E, 1891 W, 1892 W, 1893 E, S, W
Stevenson, T H (Belfast Acad) 1895 E, W, 1896 E, S, W, 1897 E, S
Stewart, A L (NIFC) 1913 W, F, 1914 F
Stewart, J W (Queen's U, Belfast, NIFC) 1922 F, 1924 S, 1928 F, E, S, W, 1929 F, E, S, W
Stoker, E W (Wanderers) 1888 W, S
Stoker, F O (Wanderers) 1886 S, 1888 W, M, 1889 S, 1891 W
Stokes, O S (Cork Bankers) 1882 E, 1884 E
Stokes, P (Garryowen) 1913 E, S, 1914 F, 1920 E, S, W, F, 1921 E, S, F, 1922 W, F
Stokes, R D (Queen's Coll, Cork) 1891 S, W
Strathdee, E (Queen's U, Belfast) 1947 E, S, W, A, 1948 W, F, 1949 E, S, W
Stringer, P A (Shannon, Munster) 2000 S, It, F, W, Arg, C, J, SA, 2001 It, F, R, S (R), W, E, Sm, NZ, 2002 W, E, S, It, F, NZ 1,2, R, Ru, Gg, A, Arg, 2003 S 1, It 1, F, W 1, E, A, W 2, S 2, [R,Nm,Arg,A,F], 2004 F,W,E,It,S,SA1,2,3,US(R),Arg, 2005 It,S,E,F,W, J1,2,NZ,A,R(R), 2006 It,F,W,S,E,NZ1,2, A1,SA,A2(R),PI, 2007 W,E,S1,It1,2, [Nm,Gg], 2008 It(R),S(R), E(R),NZ1(R),A
Stuart, C P (Clontarf) 1912 SA
Stuart, I M B (Dublin U) 1924 E, S
Sugars, H S (Dublin U) 1905 NZ, 1906 SA, 1907 S
Sugden, M (Wanderers) 1925 F, E, S, W, 1926 F, E, S, W, 1927 E, S, W, A, 1928 F, E, S, W, 1929 F, E, S, W, 1930 F, E, S, W, 1931 F, E, S, W

Sullivan, D B (UC Dublin) 1922 E, S, W, F
Sweeney, J A (Blackrock Coll) 1907 E, S, W
Symes, G R (Monkstown) 1895 E
Synge, J S (Lansdowne) 1929 S

Taggart, T (Dublin U) 1887 W
Taylor, A S (Queen's Coll, Belfast) 1910 E, S, W, 1912 F
Taylor, D R (Queen's Coll, Belfast) 1903 E
Taylor, J (Belfast Collegians) 1914 E, S, W
Taylor, J W (NIFC) 1879 S, 1880 E, S, 1881 S, 1882 E, S, 1883 E, S
Tector, W R (Wanderers) 1955 F, E, S
Tedford, A (Malone) 1902 E, S, W, 1903 E, S, W, 1904 E, S, W, 1905 E, S, W, NZ, 1906 E, S, W, SA, 1907 E, S, W, 1908 E, S, W
Teehan, C (UC Cork) 1939 E, S, W
Thompson, C (Belfast Collegians) 1907 E, S, 1908 E, S, W, 1909 E, S, W, F, 1910 E, S, W, F
Thompson, J A (Queen's Coll, Belfast) 1885 S 1,2
Thompson, J K S (Dublin U) 1921 W, 1922 E, S, F, 1923 E, S, W, F
Thompson, R G (Lansdowne) 1882 W
Thompson, R H (Instonians) 1951 SA, 1952 F, 1954 NZ, F, E, S, W, 1955 F, S, W, 1956 W
Thornhill, T (Wanderers) 1892 E, S, W, 1893 E
Thrift, H (Dublin U) 1904 W, 1905 E, S, W, NZ, 1906 E, W, SA, 1907 E, S, W, 1908 E, S, W, 1909 E, S, W, F
Tierney, D (UC Cork) 1938 S, W, 1939 E
Tierney, T A (Garryowen) 1999 A 1,2, Arg 1, [US, A 3, R, Arg 2], 2000 E
Tillie, C R (Dublin U) 1887 E, S, 1888 W, S
Todd, A W P (Dublin U) 1913 W, F, 1914 F
Topping, J A (Ballymena) 1996 WS, A, 1997 It 1, F, E, 1999 [R], 2000 US, 2003 A
Torrens, J D (Bohemians) 1938 W, 1939 E, S, W
Trimble, A D (Ulster) 2005 A,R, 2006 F(R),W,S,E,NZ1,2,A1,SA, 2007 W,F(R),E(R),It1(R),Arg1,S2(R),It2, [Nm,F], 2008 It,F,S,W,E
Tucker, C C (Shannon) 1979 F, W, 1980 F (R)
Tuke, B B (Bective Rangers) 1890 E, 1891 E, S, 1892 E, 1894 E, S, W, 1895 E, S
Turley, N (Blackrock Coll) 1962 E
Tweed, D A (Ballymena) 1995 F, W, It, [J]
Tydings, J J (Young Munster) 1968 A
Tyrrell, W (Queen's U, Belfast) 1910 F, 1913 E, S, W, F, 1914 F, E, S, W

Uprichard, R J H (Harlequins, RAF) 1950 S, W

Waide, S L (Oxford U, NIFC) 1932 E, S, W, 1933 E, W
Waites, J (Bective Rangers) 1886 S, 1888 M, 1889 W, 1890 S, W, E, 1891 E
Waldron, O C (Oxford U, London Irish) 1966 S, W, 1968 A
Walker, S (Instonians) 1934 E, S, 1935 E, S, W, NZ, 1936 E, S, W, 1937 E, S, W, 1938 E, S, W
Walkington, D B (NIFC) 1887 E, W, 1888 W, 1890 W, E, 1891 E, S, W
Walkington, R B (NIFC) 1875 E, 1876 E, 1877 E, S, 1878 E, 1879 S, 1880 E, S, 1882 E, S
Wall, H (Dolphin) 1965 S, W
Wallace, D P (Garryowen, Munster) 2000 Arg, US, 2001 It, F, R (R), S (R), W, E, NZ, 2002 W, E, S, It, F, 2003 Tg (R), Sm (R), W 2(t+R), S 2, 2004 S,SA1,2, 2005 J2, 2006 It,F,W,S,E,NZ1,2,A1,SA,A2, 2007 W,F,E,S1,It1, [Nm,Gg,F,Arg], 2008 It,F,S,W,E,NZ1
Wallace, Jas (Wanderers) 1904 E, S
Wallace, Jos (Wanderers) 1903 S, W, 1904 E, S, W, 1905 E, S, W, NZ, 1906 W
Wallace, P S (Blackrock Coll, Saracens) 1995 [J], Fj, 1996 US, W, E, WS, A, 1997 It 1, F, W, E, S, NZ, C, 1998 S, F, W, E, SA 1,2, Gg, R, 1999 F, W, E, S, It (R), 1999 A 1,2, Arg 1, [US, A 3, R, Arg 2], 2000 E, US, C (R), 2002 W (R), E (R), S (R), It (R), F (R), NZ 2(R), Ru (R), Gg (R)
Wallace, P W (Ulster) 2006 SA(R),PI, 2007 E(R),Arg1,S2, [Nm(R)], 2008 S(R),E(R), NZ1,A
Wallace, R M (Garryowen, Saracens) 1991 Nm 1(R), 1992 W, E, S, F, A, 1993 S, F, W, E, R, 1994 F, W, E, S, 1995 W, It, [NZ, J, W], Fj, 1996 US, S, F, WS, 1998 S, F, W, E
Wallace, T H (Cardiff) 1920 E, S, W
Wallis, A K (Wanderers) 1892 E, S, W, 1893 E, W
Wallis, C O'N (Old Cranleighans, Wanderers) 1935 NZ
Wallis, T G (Wanderers) 1921 F, 1922 E, S, W, F
Wallis, W A (Wanderers) 1880 S, 1881 E, S, 1882 W, 1883 S
Walmsley, G (Bective Rangers) 1894 E
Walpole, A (Dublin U) 1888 S, M
Walsh, E J (Lansdowne) 1887 E, S, W, 1892 E, S, W, 1893 E
Walsh, H D (Dublin U) 1875 E, 1876 E
Walsh, J C (UC Cork, Sunday's Well) 1960 S, SA, 1961 E, S, F, SA, 1963 E, S, W, NZ, 1964 E, S, W, F, 1965 F, S, W, SA, 1966 F, S, W, 1967 E, S, W, F, A 2
Ward, A J (Ballynahinch) 1998 F, W, E, SA 1,2, Gg, R, SA 3, 1999 W, E, S, It (R), A 1,2, Arg 1, [US, A 3, R, Arg 2], 2000 F (R), W (t&R), Arg (R), US (R), C, J, SA (R), 2001 It (R), F (R)
Ward, A J P (Garryowen, St Mary's Coll, Greystones) 1978 S, F, W, E, NZ, 1979 F, W, E, S, 1981 W, E, S, A, 1983 E (R), 1984 E, S, 1986 S, 1987 [C, Tg]
Warren, J P (Kingstown) 1883 E
Warren, R G (Lansdowne) 1884 W, 1885 E, S 1,2, 1886 E, 1887 E, S, W, 1888 W, S, M, 1889 S, W, 1890 S, W, E
Watson, R (Wanderers) 1912 SA
Wells, H G (Bective Rangers) 1891 S, W, 1894 E, S
Westby, A J (Dublin U) 1876 E
Wheeler, G H (Queen's Coll, Belfast) 1884 S, 1885 E
Wheeler, J R (Queen's U, Belfast) 1922 E, S, W, F, 1924 E
Whelan, P C (Garryowen) 1975 E, S, 1976 NZ, 1977 W, E, S, F, 1978 S, F, W, E, NZ, 1979 F, W, E, S, 1981 F, W, E
White, M (Queen's Coll, Cork) 1906 E, S, W, SA, 1907 E, W
Whitestone, A M (Dublin U) 1877 E, 1879 S, E, 1880 E, 1883 S
Whittle, D (Bangor) 1988 F
Wilkinson, C R (Malone) 1993 S
Wilkinson, R W (Wanderers) 1947 A
Williamson, F W (Dolphin) 1930 E, S, W
Willis, W J (Lansdowne) 1879 E
Wilson, F (CIYMS) 1977 W, E, S
Wilson, H G (Glasgow U, Malone) 1905 E, S, W, NZ, 1906 E, S, W, SA, 1907 E, S, W, 1908 E, S, W, 1909 E, S, W, 1910 W
Wilson, R G (Ulster) 2005 J1
Wilson, W H (Bray) 1877 E, S
Withers, H H C (Army, Blackheath) 1931 F, E, S, W, SA
Wolfe, E J (Armagh) 1882 E
Wood, G H (Dublin U) 1913 W, 1914 F
Wood, B G M (Garryowen) 1954 E, S, 1956 F, E, S, W, 1957 F, E, S, W, 1958 A, E, S, W, F, 1959 E, S, W, F, 1960 E, S, W, F, SA, 1961 E, S, W, F, SA
Wood, K G M (Garryowen, Harlequins) 1994 A 1,2, US, 1995 E, S, [J], 1996 A, 1997 It 1, F, 1997 NZ, It 2, 1998 S, F, W, E, SA 1,2, R (R), SA 3, 1999 F, W, E, S, It (R), A 1,2, Arg 1, [US, A 3, R (R), Arg 2], 2000 E, S, It, F, W, Arg, US, C, J, SA, 2001 It, F, S, W, E, NZ, 2002 F, NZ 1,2, Ru, 2003 W 2, S 2, [R,Nm,Arg,A,F]
Woods, D C (Bessbrook) 1888 M, 1889 S
Woods, N K P J (Blackrock Coll, London Irish) 1994 A 1,2, 1995 E, F, 1996 F, W, E, 1999 W
Wright, R A (Monkstown) 1912 S

Yeates, R A (Dublin U) 1889 S, W
Young, B G (Ulster) 2006 NZ2(R),A1(R),SA(R),A2,PI, 2007 Arg1,2,S2
Young, G (UC Cork) 1913 E
Young, R M (Collegians) 1965 F, E, S, W, SA, 1966 F, E, S, W, 1967 W, F, 1968 W, A, 1969 F, E, S, W, 1970 SA, F, E, S, W, 1971 F, E, S, W, 1971 F, E, S, W

CON COME UP TRUMPS

Cork Constitution finally translated their irresistible league form into silverware after beating Garryowen in the AIB League Division One final at Musgrave Park. They exacted revenge over their Munster rivals after an agonising 16–15 defeat in the final, 12 months earlier.

Jeremy Manning was the Con hero, landing five penalties and a drop goal in his side's 18–8 triumph, earning himself the man of the match award and Cork's first league title in nine years.

In their previous seven campaigns, Con had topped the league table four times at the end of the regular season only to stumble in the play-offs but made no mistake in 2008 as Brian Walsh's side, who had been beaten just once in their 15 games going into the knockout phases, were crowned Irish champions for the first time since 1999 and for only the third time in the club's history.

"These titles are incredibly hard to win," said Walsh, a veteran of Con's two previous triumphs in 1999 and 1991. "I played on that team in '91 as a young fella and thought "there'll be loads more of these" but it never happened. So it's great to have done it. We were so determined to make up for last year and I think that was evident on the pitch.

"It is always great to beat Garryowen in a final because we have huge respect for them. It wasn't a free flowing game but hard work and commitment won it for us. We needed to win this game more than anything else."

The AIB season began in late October and it was clear from the early skirmishes that Cork, Garryowen – the domestic double winners in 2007 – and Shannon would once again be the three teams for the rest to beat.

In the end, Con topped the table by two points from Shannon. Garryowen were third and Clontarf finished fourth to secure the final play-off place.

The first semi-final between Cork and Clontarf at Temple Hill never threatened to produce a shock after Daragh O'Shea missed an early penalty chance for the visitors and when Cronan Healy scored a pulsating breakaway try on 27 minutes, Con were firmly in the ascendancy.

Clontarf were on the scoreboard early in the second-half when O'Shea found his range with a penalty but any hopes Andy Wood's side had of mounting a comeback were crushed when Con prop Tim Ryan crashed over and the contest was well and truly over 10 minutes from the final whistle when full-back Richie Lane grabbed the Leesiders' third try of the match to seal a 17–3 victory.

The second semi-final was a surprisingly one-sided affair as Garryowen kept their hopes of defending their crown alive with a comprehensive 31–6 win over Shannon at Coonagh – the Parishmen's first ever defeat in the last four of the competition.

With the wind behind their backs in the first half, the visitors built a crucial 14–3 half-time lead courtesy of three penalties from Conor Kilroy and a David Sherry try and although a penalty from Shannon wing David O'Donovan after the break cut the deficit to eight points, Mick Galwey's side were put to the sword by the impressive Garryowen pack and further tries from Kieran Lewis, Conan Doyle and Keith Earls saw the visitors pull decisively clear, record a 31-win and set up a repeat of the 2007 final.

Revenge was clearly on the Con agenda as the two sides emerged for the final at Musgrave Park but it was Garryowen who struck first when Kilroy landed a third-minute penalty. Manning hit back with three penalties his own and at half-time, Cork held a 9–3 lead.

The second 40 minutes proved to be a cagey, tense affair and Con relied heavily on the boot of Manning, who landed two more penalties and a drop goal to extend his side's advantage to 18–3. There was a glimmer of hope for Garryowen when Cork hooker Des Murray was yellow carded and when Lorcan Bourke touched down in the 74th minute for the only try of the match, the deficit was only 10 points. Con however held on and the trophy was heading to Temple Hill.

Manning's 18-point haul ensured the fly-half was the headline act but Walsh was quick to pay tribute to his back row trio of Frank Cogan, Billy Holland and Brendan Cutriss after the final whistle.

"We had identified Garryowen's back row as one of their main threats," Walsh said. "I was delighted with the effort of our three boys. Their work rate was tremendous and that applies to the whole team."

In the AIB Cup, Shannon gained a degree of consolation for their failure to regain the league title with an enthralling 12–9 victory in the final over Blackrock College at Dubarry Park.

The Parishmen had never lifted the cup before but followed in the recent footsteps of Cork and Garryowen in taking the cup to Munster after a titanic struggle with Rock that failed to produce any tries but was not found wanting in terms of drama and excitement.

"It was a typical cup match," said Mick Galwey after his side's triumph. "We've been down that road before and we had the experience."

AIB DIVISION ONE 2007–08 RESULTS

27 October: **Ballymena** 3 **Garryowen** 26, **Cork Constitution** 18 **Blackrock** 5, **Dolphin** 23 **Greystones** 14, **Dungannon** 31 **Terenure College** 30, **Galwegians** 10 **St Mary's** 8, **Lansdowne** 15 **Clontarf** 10, **Old Belvedere** 13 **Shannon** 15, **Bohemians** 16 **UCD** 8. 3 November: **Galwegians** 25 **Ballymena** 18, **Garryowen** 6 **Shannon** 8, **Greystones** 10 **Cork Constitution** 19, **St Mary's** 15 **Clontarf** 31, **Terenure College** 24 **Blackrock** 23, **Bohemians** 19 **Lansdowne** 6, **UCD** 23 **Dungannon** 13. 4 November: **Dolphin** 28 **Old Belvedere** 24. 10 November: **Blackrock** 29 **Dungannon** 22, **Clontarf** 22 **Ballymena** 23, **Cork Constitution** 18 **Old Belvedere** 7, **Garryowen** 19 **Dolphin** 18, **Greystones** 10 **Lansdowne** 35, **Shannon** 16 **Bohemians** 6, Terenure 7 **Galwegians** 5, **UCD**, 16 **St Mary's** 15. 17 November: **Ballymena** 19 **UCD** 0, **Clontarf** 16 **Shannon** 23, **Cork Constitution** 12 **Garryowen** 12, **Dungannon** 14 **Greystones** 16, **Lansdowne** 8 **Blackrock** 24, **Old Belvedere** 21 **Terenure College** 15, **Bohemians** 10 **St Mary's** 3. 18 November: **Dolphin** 23 **Galwegians** 22. 1 December: **Dolphin** 21 **Lansdowne** 5, **Galwegians** 0 **Bohemians** 18, **Garryowen** 8 **Clontarf** 19, **Greystones** 0 **Ballymena** 27, **Shannon** 26 **Blackrock** 7, **St Mary's** 26 **Dungannon** 3, **Terenure College** 16 **Cork Constitution** 23, **UCD** 24 **Old Belvedere** 22. 8 December: **Ballymena** 20 **Lansdowne** 0, **Blackrock** 17 **Old Belvedere** 11, **Clontarf** 20 **Dolphin** 12, **Cork Constitution** 20 **Bohemians** 3, **Garryowen** 19 **Dungannon** 5, **Greystones** 15 **Galwegians** 23, **St Mary's** 10 **Shannon** 8 **UCD** 18 **Terenure College.** 15 December: **Ballymena** 22 **St Mary's** 34, **Blackrock** 15 **Garryowen** 17, **Clontarf** 17 **Terenure College** 3, **Cork Constitution** 46 **UCD** 13, **Dungannon** 12 **Galwegians** 12, **Lansdowne** 19 **Shannon** 45, **Old Belvedere** 20 **Greystones** 19, **Bohemians** 34 **Dolphin** 7. 12 January: **Blackrock College** 25 **Dolphin** 9, **Galwegians** 3 **Lansdowne** 3, **Garryowen** 20 **St Mary's** 6, **Old Belvedere** 15 **Ballymena** 3, **Shannon** 3 **Cork Constitution** 0, **Terenure College** 16 **Greystones** 18, **UCD** 8 **Clontarf** 14. 19 January: **Dungannon** 25 **Shannon** 18, **Ballymena** 12 **Blackrock** 17, **Dolphin** 30 **Terenure College** 6, **Lansdowne** 13 **Cork Constitution** 20, **Old Belvedere** 14 **Clontarf** 16, **St Mary's** 13 **Greystones** 9, **Bohemians** 14 **Garryowen** 19, **UCD** 10 **Galwegians** 0. 26 January: **Clontarf** 10 **Bohemians** 8, **Cork Constitution** 40 **Dungannon** 12, **Dolphin** 19 **Ballymena** 12, **Garryowen** 12 **Terenure College** 10, **Greystones** 23 **Blackrock** 22, **Lansdowne** 16 **UCD** 29, **Shannon** 16 **Galwegians** 5, **St Mary's** 23 **Old Belvedere** 22. 16 February: **Clontarf** 7 **Cork Constitution** 36, **Dungannon** 12 **Old Belvedere** 29, **Galwegians** 14 **Blackrock** 17, **Greystones** 5 **Garryowen** 38 **Shannon** 28 **Ballymena** 21, **St Mary's** 13 **Lansdowne** 9, **Terenure College** 9 **Bohemians** 25, **UCD** 23 **Dolphin** 28. 1 March: **Blackrock** 29 **UCD** 38, **Clontarf** 27 **Greystones** 18, **Cork Constitution** 19 **St Mary's** 8, **Dolphin** 19 **Dungannon** 12, **Lansdowne** 5 **Garryowen** 11, **Old Belvedere** 24 **Galwegians** 26, **Shannon** 27 **Terenure College** 12, **Bohemians** 11 **Ballymena** 15. 8 March: **Dungannon** 24 **Bohemians** 12. 22 March: **Ballymena** 16 **Cork Constitution** 18, **Dungannon** 19 **Clontarf** 23, **Galwegians** 7 **Garryowen** 20, **Greystones** 25 **UCD** 18, **Old Belvedere** 35 **Lansdowne Road** 14, **Bohemians** 20 **Blackrock** 23, **St Mary's** 20 **Terenure College** 31. 23 March: **Dolphin** 18 **Shannon** 13. 29 March: **Blackrock** 17 **Clontarf** 16, **Galwegians** 5 **Cork Constitution** 13, **Garryowen** 34 **Old Belvedere** 17, **Greystones** 15 **Bohemians** 38, **Lansdowne** 6 **Dungannon** 0, **Terenure College** 14 **Ballymena** 12, **UCD** 14 **Shannon** 45. 6 April: **St Mary's** 19 **Dolphin** 11. 19 April: **Ballymena** 7 **Dungannon** 38, **Blackrock** 49 **St Mary's** 27, **Clontarf** 37 **Galwegians** 14, **Cork Constitution** 25 **Dolphin** 3, **Garryowen** 34 **UCD** 13, **Old Belvedere** 33 **Bohemians** 18, **Shannon** 38 **Greystones** 5, **Terenure College** 20 **Lansdowne** 27

FINAL TABLE

	P	W	D	L	For	A	Pts
Cork Constitution	15	13	1	1	327	133	58
Shannon	15	12	0	3	327	177	56
Garryowen	15	12	1	2	295	157	55
Clontarf	15	10	0	5	285	233	47
Blackrock	15	9	0	6	319	285	43
Dolphin	15	9	0	6	269	273	39
Bohemians	15	7	0	8	252	205	35
Old Belvedere	15	6	0	9	307	282	34
St Mary's	15	7	0	8	240	270	33
UCD	15	7	0	8	255	335	33
Ballymena	15	5	0	10	230	267	27
Terenure	15	4	0	11	225	304	25
Dungannon	15	4	1	10	242	309	24
Galwegians	15	4	2	9	171	241	23
Lansdowne	15	4	1	10	176	280	22
Greystones	15	4	0	11	202	371	18

PLAY-OFF SEMI-FINALS

3 May, 2008

Cork Constitution 17 **Clontarf** 3

Shannon 6 **Garryowen** 31

PLAY-OFF FINAL

11 May, Musgrave Park, Cork

CORK CONSTITUTION 18 (5PG, 1DG) GARRYOWEN 8 (IPG, IT)

CORK CONSTITUTION: R Lane; J Kelly, T Gleeson, E Ryan, C Healy; J Manning, J Stringer; D Hurley, D Murray, T Ryan, M O'Connell (*captain*), S O'Connor, F Cogan, B Cuttriss, B Holland Substitutions: D Lyons for Kelly (65 mins); E Leamy for Cogan (65 mins); R Quinn for Cuttriss (76 mins); C Murphy for Ryan (79 mins); D O'Leary for Stringer (79 mins)
SCORERS *Penalty Goals:* Manning (5) Drop Goal: Manning

GARRYOWEN: C Kilroy; C O'Boyle, K Lewis, C Doyle, K Earls; W Staunton, G Hurley; R Brosnan, D Varley, E McGovern, M Melbourne, F McKenna, P Neville (*captain*), A Kavanagh, P Malone Substitutions: D Sherry for McKenna (56 mins); D Lavery for Brosnan (64 mins); L Bourke for Kilroy (65 mins); B O'Mahony for Kavanagh (68 mins); F Quaglia for Staunton (68 mins)
SCORERS *Try:* Bourke; Penalty *Goal:* Kilroy **YELLOW CARD** Murray (73 mins)
REFEREE G Clancy (Ireland)

AIB Division Two: Winners: UCC
AIB Division Three: Winners: Instonians

AIB CUP 2007–08 RESULTS

Quarter-Finals: **Clontarf** 23 **Garryowen** 11, **Blackrock** 33 **UCD** 7, **Galwegians** 53 **Malone** 0, **St Mary's** 15 **Shannon** 28

Semi-Finals: **Blackrock** 34 **Clontarf** 17, **Galwegians** 5 **Shannon** 8

FINAL

12 April, Dubarry Park, Dublin

SHANNON 12 (2PG, 2DG) BLACKROCK 9 (3PG)

SHANNON: A Finn; D O'Donovan, M Kinsella, J Clogan, S Kelly; M Lawlor, F O'Loughlin; K O'Neill, S Cronin, K Griffin, P O'Brien, D Ryan, P O'Connor, C McMahon, D Quinlan (*captain*) Substitutions: L Hogan for O'Neill (55 mins); L Mullane for O'Connor (67 mins); J Maunel for Kinsella (70 mins)
SCORERS *Penalty Goals:* O'Donovan (2) *Drop Goals:* Lawlor (2)

BLACKROCK COLLEGE: F Carr; S Monahan, B Canavan, S Morrissey, D Rowan; K Tonetti, D Madigan; K Moloney, Shane Byrne, R Burke Flynn, D Dillon (*captain*), P Huntley, P Ryan, Z Farivarz, P Graham Substitutions: D Moore for Madigan (54 mins); J Hill for Graham (59 mins); Sean Byrne for Burke Flynn (79 mins)
SCORERS *Penalty Goals:* Carr (3) **YELLOW CARD** O'Connor (19 mins)
REFEREE S McDowell (IRFU)

THE IRB/EMIRATES AIRLINE RUGBY PHOTOGRAPH OF THE YEAR 2008

In its third year, the IRB/Emirates Airline Rugby Photograph of the Year competition continues to go from strength to strength.

This year hundreds of entries were received from all over the world, from professional and amateur photographers alike, providing the judging panel with an extremely difficult task of selecting a shortlist of six pictures and, eventually, a winner based on the theme of the 'Spirit of Rugby'.

This year's judging panel was: Paul Morgan, editor of the IRB World Rugby Yearbook and Rugby World magazine; Dominic Rumbles, communications manager, IRB; Lynda Glennon, graphic designer, IRB; Barry Newcombe, Sports Journalist's Association; Bob Aylott, features editor at Amateur Photographer magazine; Joelle Watkins, corporate communications manager, Emirates Airline; Toby Trotman, Vision Sports Publishing.

The prize for the winner is a trophy, plus a trip for two to the Emirates Dubai Sevens, courtesy of Emirates Airlines.

For details of how to enter the 2009 competition, see the back page of this picture section.

THE RUNNERS-UP: IN NO PARTICULAR ORDER

◀ Reaching Out
(Hans Wilink)
Hans Wilink says: "This picture, taken during the New Zealand v Romania game at the Rugby World Cup, is special to me because it shows clearly that, no matter how fantastic it is to attend a match, it is always even better to touch the ball yourself."

Sportsmanship ▲
(Eugene Smalberger)

Eugene Smalberger says: "This picture stood out for me as it shows a scene that all those who have played the game can empathise with. Two props who have been going at each other all game – tired, unable to give anymore – helping each other to their feet. It shows the spirit of respect and sportsmanship that is unique to rugby union."

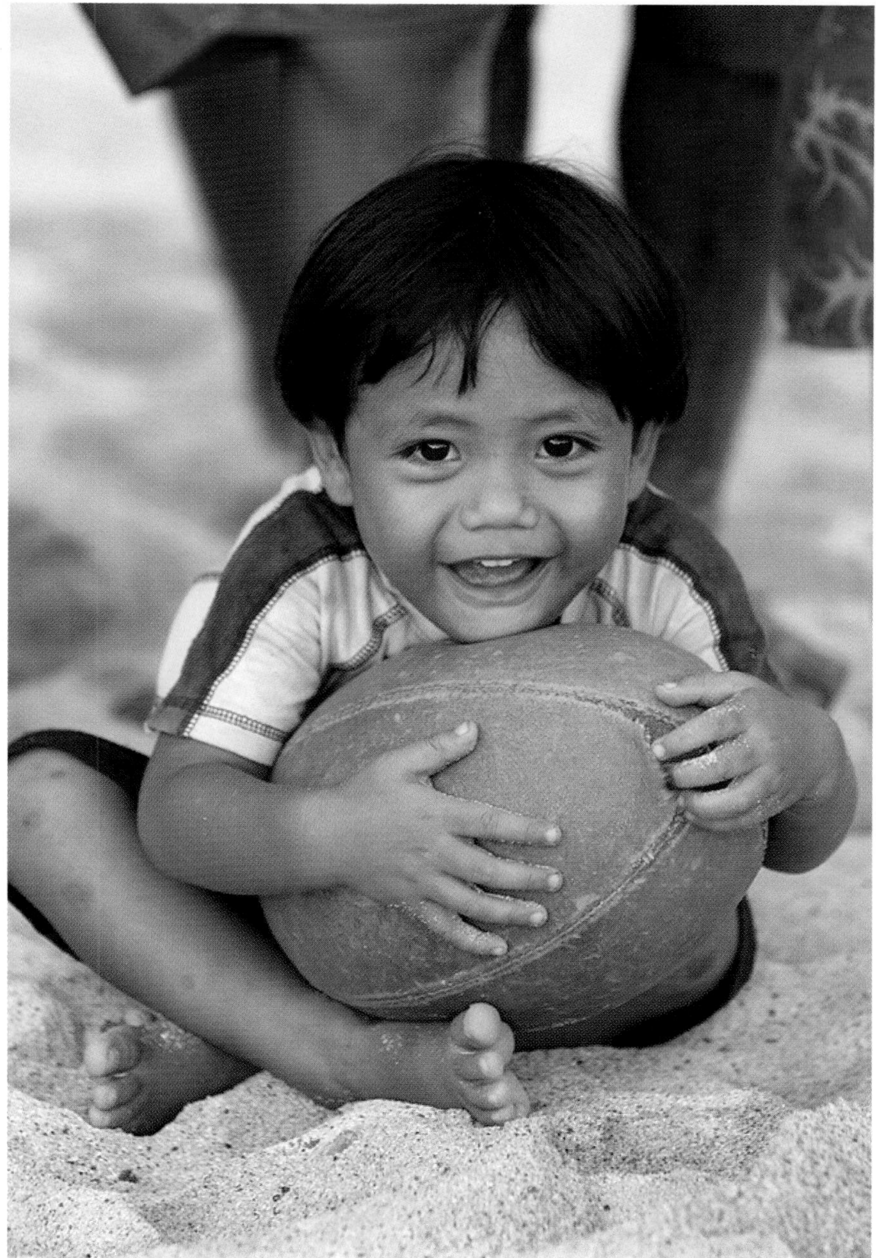

My Turn Next (Bruce Southwick)

Bruce Southwick says: "To me this picture, taken in Samoa, highlights the sheer joy that rugby brings to the people of the Pacific Islands. It was his character and enthusiasm to follow play that stood out to me. In the end he got what he wanted – a game of rugby with the older kids!"

Well done mate! (Chas Williamson)

Chas Williamson says: "The picture is of Olly Barkley leaving the field after the European Challenge Cup Final which ended Bath's ten year trophy drought. It was also Barkley's last game for the club and captures the sheer friendship, camaraderie and spirit that exists between a 'band of brothers."

End of the Line (Andre Paton)

Andre Paton says: "It was a beautiful evening in Galway, Connacht were playing Ospreys, and I knew the sun was coming down and there are only a few moments when the conditions are perfect for this kind of shot. I waited for the lineout and got it. The energy within the team is almost palpable."

AND THE WINNER IS...

Gladiator **Matthew Impey**

Matthew Impey says: "I was actually covering Leicester attack at the start of the Guinness Premiership Final, but as Wasps tore into them for the opening ten minutes I changed ends and within a couple of minutes Wasps were bearing down on the Leicester line. Flanker Tom Rees went over from close range to score the first Wasps try which didn't make much of a picture but, with the bulk of the players still getting up from the pitch, Raphael Ibanez came into the frame celebrating and looking like a Roman gladiator. You can see from the look in his face how important to Wasps scoring the first try of the match was and that they were determined not to lose in Lawrence Dallaglio's final match at a packed Twickenham."

THE IRB/EMIRATES AIRLINE RUGBY PHOTOGRAPH OF THE YEAR 2009

The IRB/Emirates Airline Rugby Photograph of the Year competition is open to all photographers, professional or amateur, and the subject matter can be from any level of the game – from mini-rugby to the Rugby World Cup Final.

To request an entry form for next year's competition, send an e-mail to:

dominic.rumbles@irb.com

Or write to:
IRB/Emirates Airline Rugby Photograph of the Year Competition
c/o Dominic Rumbles
IRB
Huguenot House
35-38 St Stephen's Green
Dublin 2, Ireland

www.irb.com

ITALY

ITALY'S 2008 TEST RECORD

OPPONENTS	DATE	VENUE	RESULT
Ireland	2 Feb	A	**Lost** 11–16
England	10 Feb	H	**Lost** 19–23
Wales	23 Feb	A	**Lost** 8–47
France	09 Mar	A	**Lost** 13–25
Scotland	15 Mar	H	**Won** 23–20
South Africa	21 Jun	A	**Lost** 0–26
Argentina	28 Jun	A	**Won** 13–12

MALLETT HERALDS NEW ERA

By Gianluca Barca

Michael Steele/Getty Images

Nick Mallett took over as Italy coach in 2008

There was life after St-Etienne, after all. Italy gathered themselves together and started the 2007–08 season just a week after their painful defeat at the hands of Scotland in France. Coach Pierre Berbizier had long before the start of the World Cup announced that he would be leaving the job after the end of the tournament. The Italian Federation (FIR) had signed his replacement, South African Nick Mallett, at the beginning of September. As soon as the Azzurri were knocked out of the French tournament, the FIR was quick to announce his appointment and the new season began with no looking back.

Mallett knew that Italy's main problems lay with the half backs, so he wasted no time in starting his worldwide search for the long sought-after replacements for Diego Dominguez and the more recently retired Alessandro Troncon. Mallett saw the best solution to his problem as being to import a few young talents from overseas and make them eligible for national duty through residency or Italian ancestry, if possible.

FIR president Giancarlo Dondi viewed the matter differently. He said he was looking to develop an Italian flavour in the squad and Mallett would have to fish nearer home. Berbizier had already taken South Africans, Kiwis, Argentineans and even a Fijian to the World Cup and Dondi, who is now a member of the IRB Executive Committee, the first Italian ever, thought that was enough.

Mallett knew one of Italy's weaknesses was scoring tries so he decided that the best way to start would be for his team to give away as few as possible.

With this in mind, he picked out heavyweight Andrea Masi for the fly-half job even if the player was a regular for French club Biarritz at wing and sometimes at centre. He went for defensive skills over attacking ability and this tipped the balance in favour of Masi over Andrea Marcato, 25, a perennial youngster and the only other possible option for the job. Marcato wasn't helped either by the fact that South African Marius Goosen was often selected instead of him for the Treviso XV.

The Masi v Marcato debate was one of the talking points of the season in Italy.

To mark the start of a new era Mallett also appointed No 8 Sergio Parisse as skipper in place of Marco Bortolami who had served under John Kirwan and Berbizier. Parisse was to rise to the job with a series of outstanding performances, and finished as one of the players of the 2008 Six Nations.

The 2008 Six Nations opening game saw the Azzurri playing in Dublin against an Ireland side, which was also under heavy scrutiny after their World Cup failure.

The match was scrappy and the Irish just managed to keep their noses ahead. Masi's instructions were to keep the ball tight and Italy's only try came from a pushover by the forwards. Ireland won 16–11

There were mixed feelings in the Italian camp after the game: they had conceded a try and scored one themselves and the margin of their defeat was the tightest ever in Dublin in the Six Nations. However their play had lacked the flair or lines to cut through the Ireland defence and Masi had looked uncomfortable in his new position, especially with his boot. Far from being an international No 10 Pietro Travagli, picked at scrum-half didn't shine either.

England in Rome was the next step. Mallett named an almost unchanged team for his debut at the Stadio Flaminio and when Paul Sackey scored for England only three minutes into the game the supporters feared the worst. Toby Flood added another soon after and Italy went in at half time, 6–20 down. But the home team managed to regroup and when Picone, in for Travagli, picked up a try in injury time, after Danny Cipriani had a kick charged down. The feeling in Italy was that with a bit more time on the clock the Azzurri might just have snatched it. Italy lost 19–23, their best result against England, but again it was their attack that let them down with the No 10 still looking at odds with his role and Marcato waiting for his chance on the bench.

Mallett stood firm reminding his critics of the size of recent defeats Italy had suffered against the English and that progress had been made.

Then high-flying Wales brushed the Azzurri effortlessly aside at the Millennium, 47–8, and in Paris, against a second string France, Italy lost 25–13. It was the lowest moment of the season for the new coach and his staff: in four games the Azzurri had only scored four tries, three by the forwards. To add salt to the wound, flanker Mauro Bergamasco was banned for several weeks following a citing after the Welsh game.

Meanwhile full-back David Bortolussi was out through injury and Marcato given a chance at 15, with Mallett keeping faith in Masi at 10.

There was a lot resting on the Scotland game when the tournament came to its last day, not only did Italy want to avenge themselves for their World Cup defeat, but another loss would also mean they would finish the tournament winless: a big step backwards, after the enthusiasm of their record two wins in the 2007 Six Nations.

A penalty try awarded by the referee when the Scotland scrum collapsed five meters from the try line, gave Italy an early advantage, but as the game progressed the result hung very much in the balance and it was only a last minute drop goal by the much debated Andrea Marcato, finally moved to fly-half from full-back, that sealed it for the home team, 23–20.

It was a result that swung things in Mallett's favour and eased the pressure on him ahead of the summer tour to South Africa and Argentina, in June.

As soon as the Six Nations ended it became clear however that the Masi experiment would not continue while the summer tour would start without many key players due to injury and club commitment.

As the domestic season progressed and Calvisano climbed steadily to the top, Kiwi fly-half Gerard Fraser emerged as the main candidate for Italy's vacant No 10 spot. He had married an Italian and was awaiting his Italian passport. Its issue unfortunately however co-incided with a serious injury that wrote him off until the end of the summer. Mallett's gaze switched then to another Calvisano import, young Aussie full-back Luke Mclean, whose grandparents had moved to Australia from Italy. Standing 1.90m and weighing 95 kilos, with a powerful boot, Mclean, 21, looked to fit the bill perfectly. Just one snag: in Calvisano he was played at full-back, making him, along with Marcato at 15, another player that Mallett would be asking to play out of position.

Without Martin Castrogiovanni and Marco Bortolami, both injured, and with Andrea Lo Cicero, the Bergamascos, skipper Sergio Parisse and Gonzalo Canale all tied up with the French play-offs, the tour to South Africa and Argentina loomed menacingly. Mallett boldly gave the captaincy to young hooker Leonardo Ghiraldini, 23, who had just led Calvisano to their league title, and had even to recall veteran prop Alex Moreno, 35, from the Leicester Tigers, to reinforce the front row. He could at least count on emerging centre Gonzalo Garcia, also from Calvisano, who had been called up contemporarily both by his home country Argentina and Italy, home of his ancestors. He chose to play for the Azzurri.

In South Africa, on a wet rainy day, with Luke Mclean and Gonzalo Garcia both winning their first caps and Masi finally picked at centre, Italy managed to limit the damage against the World champions, losing 26–0. Meanwhile Stade Francais were beaten by Toulouse in the French semi-finals and Parisse and co were quickly flown out to Argentina for the Azzurri's next game against the Pumas.

In Cordoba, the match was marred by an astronomical number of errors on both sides and Argentina entered the final quarter leading 12–6. Once again however it was the Italian forwards that led the way and on the final whistle they crashed over the line with hooker Leonardo Ghiraldini scoring the decisive try. Full-back Andrea Marcato converted to give Italy a much hoped for victory 13–12.

Mallett's first season with the Azzurri ended with two wins out of seven games, five of those played away. More worrying was the number of tries scored: only seven in total, four of which by front rowers, Italy's best weapon to date.

On the domestic scene, Calvisano, a tiny village, in the north of Italy, managed to halt Treviso's dominance in a hard fought league that saw six teams contending the top four places for the play-off right down to the last minute of the regular season. Calvisano beat the defending champions Treviso in the final, 20–3, with tries by Aussie lock Cameron Treloar and Italy back Matteo Pratichetti. The number of foreign imports however stayed sky high among the clubs and while Mallett is doing his best to try and develop a group of young Italian talents the foreign players in Italy, at present, continue to be his best resource for the national squad's survival in the international arena.

ITALY INTERNATIONAL STATISTICS

MATCH RECORDS UP TO 30TH SEPTEMBER 2008

WINNING MARGIN

Date	Opponent	Result	Winning Margin
18/05/1994	Czech Republic	104–8	**96**
07/10/2006	Portugal	83–0	**83**
17/06/1993	Croatia	76–11	**65**
19/06/1993	Morocco	70–9	**61**
02/03/1996	Portugal	64–3	**61**

MOST POINTS IN A MATCH BY THE TEAM

Date	Opponent	Result	Pts.
18/05/1994	Czech Republic	104–8	**104**
07/10/2006	Portugal	83–0	**83**
17/06/1993	Croatia	76–11	**76**
19/06/1993	Morocco	70–9	**70**

MOST TRIES IN A MATCH BY THE TEAM

Date	Opponent	Result	Tries
18/05/1994	Czech Republic	104–8	**16**
07/10/2006	Portugal	83–0	**13**
18/11/1998	Netherlands	67–7	**11**
17/06/1993	Croatia	76–11	**11**

MOST CONVERSIONS IN A MATCH BY THE TEAM

Date	Opponent	Result	Cons
18/05/1994	Czech Republic	104–8	**12**
19/06/1993	Morocco	70–9	**10**
17/06/1993	Croatia	76–11	**9**
07/10/2006	Portugal	83–0	**9**
14/10/2006	Russia	67–7	**8**
07/05/1994	Spain	62–15	**8**

MOST PENALTIES IN A MATCH BY THE TEAM

Date	Opponent	Result	Pens
01/10/1994	Romania	24–6	**8**
10/11/2001	Fiji	66–10	**7**
	9 Matches		**6**

MOST DROP GOALS IN A MATCH BY THE TEAM

Date	Opponent	Result	DGs
07/10/1990	Romania	29–21	**3**
05/02/2000	Scotland	34–20	**3**
11/07/1973	Transvaal	24–28	**3**
	9 Matches		**2**

MOST POINTS IN A MATCH BY A PLAYER

Date	Player	Opponent	Pts.
10/11/2001	Diego Dominguez	Fiji	**29**
05/02/2000	Diego Dominguez	Scotland	**29**
01/07/1983	Stefano Bettarello	Canada	**29**
21/05/1994	Diego Dominguez	Netherlands	**28**
20/12/1997	Diego Dominguez	Ireland	**27**
10/11/2001	Diego Dominguez	Fiji	**29**

MOST TRIES IN A MATCH BY A PLAYER

Date	Player	Opponent	Tries
19/06/1993	Ivan Francescato	Morocco	**4**
10/10/1937	Renzo Cova	Belgium	**4**
	14 Players		**3**

MOST CONVERSIONS IN A MATCH BY A PLAYER

Date	Player	Opponent	Cons
18/05/1994	Luigi Troiani	Czech Republic	**12**
19/06/1993	Gabriel Filizzola	Morocco	**10**
17/06/1993	Luigi Troiani	Croatia	**9**
07/05/1994	Luigi Troiani	Spain	**8**
07/10/2006	David Bortolussi	Portugal	**8**
14/10/2006	David Bortolussi	Russia	**8**

MOST PENALTIES IN A MATCH BY A PLAYER

Date	Player	Opponent	Pens
01/10/1994	Diego Dominguez	Romania	8
10/11/2001	Diego Dominguez	Fiji	7
	9 Players		6

MOST DROP GOALS IN A MATCH BY A PLAYER

Date	Player	Opponent	DGs
05/02/2000	Diego Dominguez	Scotland	3
11/07/1973	Rocco Caligiuri	Transvaal	3
	7 Players		2

MOST CAPPED PLAYERS

Player	Caps
Alessandro Troncon	101
Carlo Checchinato	83
Andrea Lo Cicero	76
Diego Dominguez	74
Cristian Stoica	71

LEADING TRY SCORERS

Player	Tries
Marcello Cuttitta	25
Paolo Vaccari	22
Manrico Marchetto	21
Carlo Checchinato	21
Alessandro Troncon	19

LEADING CONVERSIONS SCORERS

Player	Cons
Diego Dominguez	127
Luigi Troiani	57
Stefano Bettarello	46
David Bortolussi	35
Ramiro Pez	33

LEADING PENALTY SCORERS

Player	Pens
Diego Dominguez	209
Stefano Bettarello	106
Luigi Troiani	57
Ramiro Pez	52
Ennio Ponzi	31

LEADING DROP GOAL SCORERS

Player	DGs
Diego Dominguez	19
Stefano Bettarello	15
Ramiro Pez	6
Oscar Collodo	5
Massimo Bonomi	5

LEADING POINT SCORERS

Player	Pts.
Diego Dominguez	983
Stefano Bettarello	483
Luigi Troiani	294
Ramiro Pez	260
David Bortolussi	153

ITALY INTERNATIONAL PLAYERS
UP TO 30TH SEPTEMBER 2008

Note: Years given for International Championship matches are for second half of season; eg 1972 means season 1971–72. Years for all other matches refer to the actual year of the match.

E Abbiati 1968 *WGe*, 1970 *R*, 1971 *Mor*, *F*, 1972 *Pt*, *Sp*, *Sp*, *Yug*, 1973 *Pt*, *ETv*, 1974 *Leo*
A Agosti 1933 *Cze*
M Aguero 2005 *Tg*, *Ar*, *Fj*, 2006 *Fj*, 2007 *Ur*, *Ar*, *I*, *Pt*
A Agujari 1967 *Pt*
E Aio 1974 *WGe*
G Aiolfi 1952 *Sp*, *Ger*, *F*, 1953 *F*, 1955 *Ger*, *F*
A Alacevich 1939 *R*
A Albonico 1934 *R*, 1935 *F*, 1936 *Ger*, *R*, 1937 *Ger*, *R*, *Bel*, *Ger*, *F*, 1938 *Ger*
N Aldorvandi 1994 *Sp*, *CZR*, *H*
M Alfonsetti 1994 *F*
E Allevi 1929 *Sp*, 1933 *Cze*
I Aloisio 1933 *Cze*, *Cze*, 1934 *Cat*, *R*, 1935 *Cat*, 1936 *Ger*, *R*
A Altigeri 1973 *Rho*, *WTv*, *Bor*, *NEC*, *Nat*, *Leo*, *FS*, *Tva*, *Cze*, *Yug*, *A*, 1974 *Pt*, *WGe*, 1975 *F*, *E*, *Pol*, *H*, *Sp*, 1976 *F*, *R*, *J*, 1978 *Ar*, *USS*, *Sp*, 1979 *F*, *Pol*, *R*
T Altissimi 1929 *Sp*
V Ambron 1962 *Ger*, *R*, 1963 *F*, 1964 *Ger*, *F*, 1965 *F*, *Cze*, 1966 *F*, *Ger*, *R*, 1967 *Pt*, *R*, 1968 *Pt*, *WGe*, *Yug*, 1969 *Bul*, *Sp*, *Bel*, 1970 *Mad*, *Mad*, *R*, 1971 *Mor*, 1972 *Sp*, *Sp*
R Ambrosio 1987 *NZ*, *USS*, *Sp*, 1988 *F*, *R*, *A*, *I*, 1989 *R*, *Sp*, *Ar*, *Z*, *USS*
B Ancillotti 1978 *Sp*, 1979 *F*, *Pol*, *R*
E Andina 1952 *F*, 1955 *F*
C Angelozzi 1979 *E*, *Mor*, 1980 *Coo*
A Angioli 1960 *Ger*, *F*, 1961 *Ger*, *F*, 1962 *F*, *Ger*, *R*, 1963 *F*
A Angrisiani 1979 *Mor*, *F*, *Pol*, *USS*, *Mor*, 1980 *Coo*, 1984 *Tun*
S Annibal 1980 *Fj*, *Coo*, *Pol*, *Sp*, 1981 *F*, *WGe*, 1982 *R*, *E*, *WGe*, 1983 *F*, *USS*, *Sp*, *Mor*, *F*, *A*, 1984 *F*, 1985 *F*, *Z*, *Z*, 1986 *Tun*, *F*, *Pt*, 1990 *F*
JM Antoni 2001 *Nm*, *SA*
C Appiani 1976 *Sp*, 1977 *Mor*, *Pol*, *Sp*, 1978 *USS*
S Appiani 1985 *R*, 1986 *Pt*, 1988 *A*, 1989 *F*
O Arancio 1993 *Rus*, 1994 *CZR*, *H*, *A*, *A*, *R*, *W*, *F*, 1995 *S*, *I*, *Sa*, *E*, *Ar*, *F*, *R*, *NZ*, *SA*, 1996 *W*, *Pt*, *W*, *A*, *E*, *S*, 1997 *I*, *I*, 1998 *S*, *Ar*, *E*, 1999 *F*, *W*, *I*, *SA*, *E*, *NZ*
D Armellin 1965 *Cze*, 1966 *Ger*, 1968 *Pt*, *WGe*, *Yug*, 1969 *Bul*, *Sp*, *Bel*, *F*
A Arrigoni 1949 *Cze*
G Artuso 1977 *Pol*, *R*, 1978 *Sp*, 1979 *F*, *E*, *NZ*, *Mor*, 1980 *F*, *R*, *JAB*, 1981 *F*, 1982 *F*, *E*, *Mor*, 1983 *F*, *R*, *USS*, *C*, *C*, 1984 *USS*, 1985 *R*, *E*, *USS*, *R*, 1986 *Tun*, *F*, *Tun*, 1987 *Pt*, *F*, *R*, *NZ*
E Augeri 1962 *F*, *Ger*, *R*, 1963 *F*
A Autore 1961 *Ger*, *F*, 1962 *F*, 1964 *Ger*, 1966 *Ger*, 1968 *Pt*, *WGe*, *Yug*, 1969 *Bul*, *Sp*, *Bel*, *F*
L Avigo 1959 *F*, 1962 *F*, *Ger*, *R*, 1963 *F*, 1964 *Ger*, *F*, 1965 *F*, *Cze*, 1966 *Ger*, *R*
R Aymonod 1933 *Cze*, 1934 *Cat*, *R*, 1935 *F*
A Azzali 1981 *WGe*, 1982 *F*, *R*, *WGe*, 1983 *F*, *R*, *USS*, *Sp*, *Mor*, *F*, 1984 *F*, *Mor*, *R*, 1985 *R*, *E*, *Sp*
S Babbo 1996 *Pt*
A Balducci 1929 *Sp*
F Baraldi 1973 *Cze*, *Yug*, 1974 *Mid*, *Sus*, *Oxo*, 1975 *E*, *Pol*, *H*, *Sp*, 1976 *F*, *R*, *A*, 1977 *F*, *Mor*, *Cze*
R Baraldi 1971 *R*
A Barattin 1996 *A*, *E*
S Barba 1985 *R*, *E*, 1986 *E*, *A*, 1987 *Pt*, *F*, *R*, *Ar*, *Fj*, 1988 *R*, *USS*, *A*, 1990 *F*, *Pol*, *Sp*, *H*, *R*, *USS*, 1991 *F*, *R*, *Nm*, *Nm*, *US*, *E*, *USS*, 1992 *Sp*, *F*, *R*, *R*, *S*, 1993 *Sp*, *F*, *Cro*, *Mor*, *Sp*
RJ Barbieri 2006 *J*, *Fj*, *Pt*, 2007 *Ur*, *Ar*, *I*, 2008 *SA*
G Barbini 1978 *USS*
M Barbini 2002 *NZ*, *Sp*, *Ar*, *A*, 2003 *I*, *NZ*, 2004 *F*, *I*, *R*, *J*, *NZ*, *US*, 2005 *W*, *E*, 2007 *I*
N Barbini 1953 *Ger*, *R*, 1954 *Sp*, *F*, 1955 *Ger*, *F*, *Sp*, *Cze*, 1956 *Ger*, 1957 *Ger*, 1958 *R*, 1960 *Ger*, *F*
F Bargelli 1979 *E*, *Sp*, *Mor*, *F*, *Pol*, *USS*, *NZ*, *Mor*, 1980 *F*, *R*, *Fj*, *Sp*, 1981 *F*, *R*
S Barilari 1948 *Cze*, 1953 *Ger*, *R*
M Baroni 1999 *F*, *W*, *I*, *SA*, *SA*, 2000 *C*
V Barzaghi 1929 *Sp*, 1930 *Sp*, 1933 *Cze*
JL Basei 1979 *E*, *Sp*, *Mor*, *F*, *Pol*, *USS*, *NZ*, *Mor*, 1980 *F*, *R*, *Fj*, *JAB*, *Coo*, *USS*, 1981 *R*
A Battagion 1948 *F*, *Cze*
F Battaglini 1948 *F*
M Battaglini 1940 *R*, *Ger*, 1951 *Sp*, 1953 *F*, *R*
A Becca 1937 *R*, 1938 *Ger*, 1939 *R*, 1940 *Ger*
E Bellinazzo 1958 *R*, 1959 *F*, 1960 *Ger*, *F*, 1961 *Ger*, *F*, 1962 *F*, *Ger*, 1964 *Ger*, *F*, 1966 *F*, *Ger*, *R*, 1967 *F*
A Benatti 2001 *Fj*, *SA*, *Sa*, 2002 *W*, 2003 *NZ*
C Bentivoglio 1977 *Pol*
D Beretta 1993 *S*
A Bergamasco 1973 *Bor*, *Tva*, 1977 *Pol*, 1978 *USS*
M Bergamasco 2002 *F*, *S*, *W*, *Ar*, *A*, 2003 *W*, *I*, *E*, *F*, *S*, *S*, *Geo*, *NZ*, *C*, 2004 *E*, *F*, *S*, *I*, *W*, 2005 *I*, *W*, *S*, *Tg*, *Ar*, *Fj*, 2006 *I*, *E*, *F*, *W*, *S*, *J*, *Fj*, *Pt*, *Rus*, *A*, *Ar*, *C*, 2007 *F*, *E*, *S*, *W*, *I*, *J*, *I*, *NZ*, *R*, *S*, 2008 *I*, *E*, *W*, *F*, *S*, *Ar*
M Bergamasco 1998 *H*, *E*, 1999 *SA*, *E*, 2000 *S*, *W*, *I*, *E*, *F*, *C*, 2001 *I*, *E*, *F*, *S*, *W*, *Fj*, *SA*, *Sa*, 2002 *F*, *S*, *W*, *I*, *E*, *NZ*, *Sp*, *R*, *A*, 2003 *W*, *I*, *S*, *I*, *Geo*, *NZ*, *W*, 2004 *J*, *C*, *NZ*, 2005 *I*, *W*, *Ar*, *A*, *Ar*, *Fj*, 2006 *I*, *E*, *F*, *J*, *Fj*, *Pt*, *Rus*, *A*, *Ar*, *C*, 2007 *F*, *S*, *W*, *J*, *NZ*, *R*, *Pt*, *S*, 2008 *I*, *E*, *W*, *Ar*
L Bernabo 1970 *Mad*, *Mad*, *R*, 1972 *Sp*, *Sp*
V Bernabò 2004 *US*, 2005 *Tg*, *Fj*, 2007 *E*, *S*, *W*, *I*, *Ur*, *Ar*, *J*, *I*, *NZ*, *R*
F Berni 1985 *R*, *Sp*, *Z*, *Z*, 1986 *E*, *A*, 1987 *R*, *NZ*, 1988 *A*, 1989 *F*
Bertoli 1967 *R*
V Bertolotto 1936 *Ger*, *R*, 1937 *Ger*, *R*, 1942 *R*, 1948 *F*
O Bettarello 1958 *F*, 1959 *F*, 1961 *Ger*
R Bettarello 1953 *Ger*, *R*
S Bettarello 1979 *Pol*, *E*, *Sp*, *F*, *NZ*, *Mor*, 1980 *F*, *R*, *Fj*, *JAB*, *Coo*, *Pol*, *USS*, *Sp*, 1981 *F*, *R*, *USS*, *WGe*, 1982 *F*, *R*, *E*, *WGe*, *Mor*, 1983 *F*, *R*, *USS*, *C*, *Sp*, *Mor*, *F*, *A*, 1984 *F*, *Mor*, *R*, *Tun*, *USS*, 1985 *F*, *R*, *E*, *Sp*, *Z*, *USS*, *R*, 1986 *Tun*, *F*, *Pt*, *E*, *A*, *Tun*, *USS*, 1987 *R*, *USS*, *Sp*, 1988 *USS*, *A*
L Bettella 1969 *Sp*, *Bel*, *F*
R Bevilacqua 1937 *Bel*, *Ger*, *F*, 1938 *Ger*, 1939 *Ger*, *R*, 1940 *R*, *Ger*, 1942 *R*
C Bezzi 2003 *W*, *I*, *E*, *F*, *S*, *I*, *NZ*, *W*, 2004 *US*, 2005 *Ar*, *A*
G Biadene 1958 *R*, 1959 *F*
G Bigi 1930 *Sp*, 1933 *Cze*
M Bimbati 1989 *Z*
M Birtig 1998 *H*, 1999 *F*
F Blessano 1975 *F*, *R*, *Pol*, *H*, *Sp*, 1976 *F*, *R*, *J*, 1977 *F*, *Mor*, *Pol*, *R*, *Cze*, *R*, *Sp*, 1978 *F*, *Ar*, *Sp*, 1979 *F*, *Pol*, *R*
L Boccaletto 1969 *Bul*, *Bel*, *F*, 1970 *Cze*, *Mad*, *Mad*, *R*, 1971 *F*, *R*, 1972 *Pt*, *Sp*, *Sp*, 1975 *E*

S Boccazzi 1985 *Z*, 1988 *USS*
M Bocconelli 1967 *R*
M Bollesan 1963 *F*, 1964 *F*, 1965 *F*, 1966 *F*, *Ger*, 1967 *F*, *Pt*, 1968 *Pt*, *WGe*, *Yug*, 1969 *Bul*, *Sp*, *Bel*, *F*, 1970 *Cze*, *Mad*, *Mad*, *R*, 1971 *Mor*, *F*, *R*, 1972 *Pt*, *Pt*, *Sp*, *Sp*, *Yug*, 1973 *Pt*, *Rho*, *WTv*, *Bor*, *NEC*, *Nat*, *ETv*, *Leo*, *FS*, *Tva*, *Yug*, *A*, 1974 *Pt*, *Mid*, *Sus*, *Oxo*, *WGe*, *Leo*, 1975 *F*, *Sp*, *Cze*
A Bona 1972 *Sp*, *Yug*, 1973 *Rho*, *WTv*, *Bor*, *NEC*, *Nat*, *ETv*, *Leo*, *FS*, *Tva*, *Cze*, *Yug*, *A*, 1974 *Pt*, *WGe*, *Leo*, 1975 *F*, *Sp*, *R*, *Cze*, *E*, *Pol*, *H*, *Sp*, 1976 *F*, *R*, *J*, *A*, *Sp*, 1977 *F*, *Mor*, 1978 *Ar*, *USS*, *Sp*, 1979 *F*, *Sp*, *Mor*, *F*, *Pol*, *USS*, *NZ*, *Mor*, 1980 *F*, *R*, *Fj*, *JAB*, *Pol*, *Sp*, 1981 *F*
L Bonaiti 1979 *R*, 1980 *Pol*
G Bonati 1939 *Ger*, *R*
S Bonetti 1972 *Yug*, 1973 *Rho*, *WTv*, *Bor*, *NEC*, *Nat*, *ETv*, *Leo*, *FS*, *Tva*, 1974 *Pt*, *Mid*, *Sus*, *Oxo*, *Leo*, 1975 *F*, *Sp*, *R*, *Cze*, *E*, *Pol*, *H*, *Sp*, 1976 *R*, *J*, *A*, *Sp*, 1977 *F*, *Mor*, *R*, *Sp*, 1978 *F*, 1979 *F*, 1980 *USS*
S Bonfante 1936 *Ger*, *R*
G Bonino 1949 *F*
M Bonomi 1988 *F*, *R*, 1990 *Sp*, *H*, *R*, *USS*, 1991 *F*, *R*, *Nm*, *Nm*, *E*, *NZ*, *USS*, 1992 *R*, *R*, 1993 *Cro*, *Mor*, *Sp*, *F*, *S*, 1994 *Sp*, *R*, *H*, *A*, *A*, *W*, 1995 *S*, *I*, *Sa*, *F*, *Ar*, *R*, *NZ*, 1996 *W*
S Bordon 1990 *R*, *USS*, 1991 *Nm*, *USS*, 1992 *F*, *R*, 1993 *Sp*, *F*, *Pt*, *Rus*, *F*, 1994 *R*, *A*, *A*, *R*, *W*, *F*, 1995 *I*, *E*, *Ar*, *F*, *Ar*, *NZ*, *SA*, 1996 *W*, *A*, *E*, 1997 *I*, *F*
L Borsetto 1977 *Pol*
V Borsetto 1948 *F*, *Cze*
M Bortolami 2001 *Nm*, *SA*, *Fj*, *SA*, *Sa*, 2002 *F*, *S*, *W*, *I*, *E*, *NZ*, *Sp*, *R*, *Ar*, *A*, 2003 *W*, *I*, *E*, *S*, *Geo*, *Tg*, *C*, 2004 *E*, *F*, *S*, *I*, *W*, *R*, *J*, *C*, *NZ*, 2005 *I*, *W*, *S*, *E*, *F*, *Ar*, *Ar*, *A*, *Tg*, *Ar*, *Fj*, 2006 *I*, *E*, *F*, *W*, *S*, *J*, *Fj*, *Pt*, *Rus*, *A*, *Ar*, *C*, 2007 *F*, *E*, *S*, *W*, *I*, *J*, *I*, *NZ*, *R*, *Pt*, 2008 *W*, *F*, *S*
G Bortolini 1933 *Cze*, 1934 *Cat*
D Bortolussi 2006 *J*, *Fj*, *Pt*, *Rus*, *Ar*, *C*, 2007 *Ur*, *Ar*, *J*, *I*, *NZ*, *R*, *Pt*, *S*, 2008 *I*, *E*
L Boscaino 1967 *Pt*
L Bossi 1940 *R*, *Ger*
A Bottacchiara 1991 *NZ*, *USS*, 1992 *Sp*, *F*, *R*, *R*
G Bottacin 1956 *Cze*
O Bottonelli 1929 *Sp*, 1934 *R*, 1935 *Cat*, *F*, 1937 *Ger*, 1939 *Ger*
L Bove 1948 *Cze*, 1949 *F*, *Cze*
O Bracaglia 1939 *R*
M Braga 1958 *R*
L Bricchi 1929 *Sp*, 1930 *Sp*, 1933 *Cze*
L Brighetti 1934 *Cat*
A Brunelli 1969 *Bel*, 1970 *Mad*, 1971 *F*
M Brunello 1988 *I*, 1989 *F*, 1990 *F*, *Sp*, *H*, *R*, *USS*, 1993 *Pt*
S Brusin 1957 *Ger*
CS Burton 2007 *Ur*, *Ar*
P Buso 2008 *W*
G Busson 1957 *Ger*, 1958 *R*, 1959 *F*, 1960 *Ger*, *F*, 1961 *Ger*, *F*, 1962 *F*, *Ger*, 1963 *F*
F Caccia-Dominioni 1935 *F*, 1937 *Ger*
C Caione 1995 *R*, 1996 *Pt*, 1997 *F*, *R*, 1998 *Rus*, *Ar*, *H*, *E*, 1999 *F*, *S*, *SA*, *Ur*, *Sp*, *Fj*, *Tg*, *NZ*, 2000 *Sa*, *Fj*, *C*, *R*, *NZ*, 2001 *I*, *E*, *S*, *Fj*
R Caligiuri 1969 *F*, 1973 *Pt*, *Rho*, *WTv*, *NEC*, *Nat*, *ETv*, *Leo*, *FS*, *Tva*, 1975 *E*, *Pol*, *H*, *Sp*, 1976 *F*, *R*, *J*, *A*, *Sp*, 1978 *F*, *Ar*, *USS*, *Sp*, 1979 *F*, *Pol*, *R*
A Caluzzi 1970 *R*, 1971 *Mor*, *F*, 1972 *Pt*, *Pt*, *Sp*, *Sp*, 1973 *Pt*, 1974 *Oxo*, *WGe*, *Leo*
P Camiscioni 1975 *E*, 1976 *R*, *J*, *A*, *Sp*, 1977 *F*, 1978 *F*
M Campagna 1933 *Cze*, 1934 *Cat*, 1936 *Ger*, *R*, 1937 *Ger*, *R*, *Bel*, 1938 *Ger*
G-J Canale 2003 *S*, *Geo*, *NZ*, *Tg*, *C*, *W*, 2004 *S*, *I*, *W*, *R*, *J*, *C*, 2005 *I*, *Ar*, *Ar*, *A*, *Tg*, *Ar*, *Fj*, 2006 *I*, *E*, *F*, *W*, *S*, *A*, *Ar*, *C*, 2007 *F*, *E*, *S*, *W*, *J*, *I*, *R*, *Pt*, *S*, 2008 *I*, *E*, *W*, *F*, *S*
PL Canavosio 2005 *A*, *Tg*, *Fj*, 2006 *I*, *E*, *F*, *W*, *S*, *Fj*, *Pt*, *Rus*, *A*, *Ar*, 2007 *Ar*, *J*, *I*, *Pt*, 2008 *I*, *SA*, *Ar*
C Cantoni 1956 *Ger*, *F*, *Cze*, 1957 *Ger*
L Capitani 1989 *F*, *R*, *Sp*, *Ar*, *Z*, *USS*
M Capuzzoni 1993 *Cro*, 1995 *I*
A Caranci 1989 *R*
M Carli 1955 *Sp*, *Cze*
C Carloni 1935 *F*
D Carpente 2004 *R*, *J*
T Carraro 1937 *R*
T Casagrande 1977 *R*
U Cassellato 1990 *Sp*, 1992 *R*, *S*, 1993 *Sp*, *F*, *Pt*, *Cro*, *Mor*, *F*, *S*
R Cassina 1992 *R*, *S*
A Castellani 1994 *CZR*, 1995 *Ar*, *R*, 1996 *W*, *S*, 1997 *Ar*, *R*, *I*, 1998 *S*, *W*, *Rus*, *H*, *E*, 1999 *F*, *W*, *Ur*, *Sp*, *Fj*, *Tg*, *NZ*
LM Castrogiovanni 2002 *NZ*, *Sp*, *R*, *Ar*, *A*, 2003 *I*, *E*, *F*, *S*, *I*, *Geo*, *NZ*, *Tg*, *C*, *W*, 2004 *E*, *F*, *S*, *I*, *W*, *J*, 2005 *I*, *W*, *S*, *E*, *F*, *Ar*, *A*, *Ar*, *Fj*, 2006 *I*, *E*, *F*, *W*, *S*, *Pt*, *Rus*, *A*, *Ar*, *C*, 2007 *F*, *E*, *S*, *J*, *I*, *NZ*, *R*, *Pt*, *S*, 2008 *I*, *E*, *W*, *F*, *S*
L Catotti 1979 *Pol*, *E*
A Cazzini 1933 *Cze*, *Cze*, 1934 *Cat*, *R*, 1935 *Cat*, *F*, 1936 *Ger*, *R*, 1937 *Ger*, *R*, *Bel*, *Ger*, *F*, 1939 *R*, 1942 *R*
G Cecchetto 1955 *F*
A Cecchetto-Milani 1952 *Sp*, *Ger*, *F*
G Cecchin 1970 *Cze*, *R*, 1971 *F*, *R*, 1972 *Pt*
G Ceccotti 1972 *Pt*, *Sp*
A Centinari 1930 *Sp*
R Centinari 1935 *F*, 1936 *Ger*, *R*, 1937 *Bel*, *F*, 1939 *Ger*
A Cepolino 1999 *Ur*, *Sp*, *Fj*, *Tg*, *NZ*
L Cesani 1929 *Sp*, 1930 *Sp*, 1935 *Cat*, *F*
F Ceselin 1989 *F*, *R*
C Checchinato 1990 *Sp*, 1991 *Nm*, *Nm*, *US*, *NZ*, *USS*, 1992 *Sp*, *F*, *R*, *S*, 1993 *Pt*, *Cro*, *Sp*, *F*, *Rus*, *F*, *S*, 1994 *Sp*, *R*, *CZR*, *A*, *A*, *R*, *W*, *F*, 1995 *Sa*, *F*, *Ar*, *R*, *NZ*, 1996 *W*, *E*, 1997 *I*, *F*, *Ar*, *R*, *SA*, *I*, 1998 *Rus*, *Ar*, *H*, *E*, 1999 *F*, *S*, *SA*, *SA*, *Ur*, *Fj*, *E*, *Tg*, *NZ*, 2000 *S*, *W*, *I*, *E*, *F*, *Sa*, *Fj*, 2001 *I*, *E*, *F*, *S*, *W*, *Nm*, *SA*, *Ur*, *Ar*, *Fj*, *SA*, *Sa*, 2002 *F*, *S*, *W*, *Sp*, *R*
***G Chechinato** 1973 Cze, Yug, A, 1974 WGe, Leo*
***G Cherubini** 1949 Cze, 1951 Sp*
***T Ciccio** 1992 R, 1993 Sp, F, Mor, F*
***E Cicognani** 1940 Ger*
***R Cinelli** 1968 Pt, 1969 Sp*
***G Cinti** 1973 Rho, WTv, ETv*
***F Cioni** 1967 Pt, R, 1968 Pt, 1969 Bul, Sp, Bel, 1970 Cze, Mad, Mad, R*
***L Cittadini** 2008 I*
***L Clerici** 1939 Ger*
***A Colella** 1983 R, USS, C, C, Sp, Mor, F, A, USS, 1984 R, Tun, USS, 1985 F, R, E, Sp, Z, Z, USS, R, 1986 Tun, F, Pt, E, A, Tun, USS, 1987 Pt, F, Ar, Fj, USS, Sp, 1988 F, R, USS, 1989 R, Sp, Ar, 1990 Pol, R*
***O Collodo** 1977 Pol, Cze, R, Sp, 1978 F, 1986 Pt, E, A, USS, 1987 Pt, F, R, NZ, Ar, Fj*
***S Colombini** 1971 R*
***F Colombo** 1933 Cze*
***G Colussi** 1957 F, 1958 F, 1964 Ger, F, 1965 F, Cze, 1968 Pt*
***C Colusso** 1982 F*
***A Comin** 1955 Ger, F, Sp, F, Cze, 1956 F, Cze, 1958 F*
***U Conforto** 1965 Cze, 1966 Ger, R, 1967 F, R, 1968 Pt, WGe, Yug, 1969 Bul, Sp, Bel, F, 1970 Cze, 1971 Mor, F, 1972 Yug, 1973 Pt*
***F Coppio** 1993 F, Pt, Cro, Mor, Sp*
***L Cornella** 1999 Sp*
***R Corvo** 1985 F, Sp, Z*
***U Cossara** 1971 Mor, F, R, 1972 Pt, Sp, 1973 Pt, Rho, NEC, Nat, Leo, FS, Tva, Cze, 1975 F, Sp, R, Cze, E, Pol, H, 1976 F, J, A, 1977 Pol*
***A Costa** 1940 R, Ger, 1942 R*
***S Costanzo** 2004 R, C, NZ, US*
***E Cottafava** 1973 Pt*
***R Cova** 1937 Bel, Ger, F, 1938 Ger, 1939 Ger, R, 1942 R*
***C Covi** 1988 F, R, USS, A, I, 1989 F, R, Sp, Ar, Z, USS, 1990 F, Pol, R, 1991 F, R, Nm, Nm, 1996 E*
***F Crepaz** 1972 Pt*
***M Crescenzo** 1984 R*
***U Crespi** 1933 Cze, Cze, 1934 Cat, R, 1935 Cat, 1937 Ger*
***W Cristofoletto** 1992 R, 1993 Mor, Sp, F, 1996 Pt, A, E, S, 1997 I, F, F, Ar, SA, I, 1998 S, W, Rus, Ar, E, 1999 F, S, W, I, SA, SA, Sp, Fj, E, NZ, 2000 E, F*
***G Croci** 1990 Sp, H, R, USS, 1991 F, R, Nm, US, E, NZ, USS, 1992 Sp, F, 1993 S, 1996 S, 1997 I, F, F, Ar, R, SA, I, 1998 S, W*
***R Crotti** 1993 S, 1995 SA*
***L Cuccharelli** 1966 R, 1967 R*

G Cucchiella *1973 A, 1974 Sus, 1979 Sp, F, Pol, USS, NZ, Mor, 1980 F, R, Fj, JAB, Coo, 1985 USS, R, 1986 Tun, F, Pt, E, 1987 Pt, F, Fj*
M Cuttitta *1987 Pt, F, R, NZ, Ar, Fj, USS, Sp, 1988 F, R, 1989 Z, USS, 1990 Pol, R, 1991 F, R, Nm, US, E, NZ, USS, 1992 Sp, F, R, R, S, 1993 Sp, F, Mor, Sp, F, F, 1994 Sp, R, H, A, A, F, 1995 S, I, Sa, 1996 S, 1997 I, F, F, Ar, R, SA, I, 1998 S, W, Rus, Ar, 1999 F*
M Cuttitta *1990 Pol, R, Sp, H, R, USS, 1991 F, Nm, Nm, US, E, NZ, USS, 1992 Sp, F, R, R, S, 1993 Sp, F, Pt, Cro, Mor, Sp, F, Rus, F, S, 1994 Sp, R, CZR, H, A, A, W, F, 1995 S, I, Sa, E, Ar, F, Ar, R, NZ, SA, 1996 W, Pt, W, E, S, 1997 I, F, F, Ar, SA, I, 1998 W, Rus, Ar, H, E, 1999 F, S, W, 2000 S, W, I, E*
G Dagnini *1949 F*
D Dal Maso *2000 Sa, Fj, 2001 I, E, 2004 J, C, NZ, US, 2005 I, W, S, E, F, A*
M Dal Sie *1993 Pt, 1994 R, W, F, 1995 F, Ar, 1996 A*
A D'Alberton *1966 F, Ger, R, 1967 F, R*
D Daldoss *1979 Pol, R, E, Sp, Mor*
C D'Alessio *1937 R, Bel, F, 1938 Ger, 1939 Ger*
D Dallan *1999 F, S, W, 2000 S, W, I, E, F, C, R, NZ, 2001 I, E, F, W, Fj, SA, Sa, 2002 F, S, I, E, NZ, Sp, R, 2003 W, I, E, F, S, Tg, C, W, 2004 E, F, S, I, W, C, 2006 J, 2007 F, E*
M Dallan *1997 Ar, R, I, 1998 Ar, H, E, 1999 SA, SA, 2000 S, Sa, C, 2001 F, S, 2003 Tg, C, 2004 E, F, S*
A Danieli *1955 Ger, F, Sp, F, Cze*
V D'Anna *1993 Rus*
P Dari *1951 Sp, 1952 Sp, Ger, F, 1953 Ger, R, 1954 Sp, F*
G De Angelis *1934 Cat, R, 1935 Cat, F, 1937 R*
E De Anna *1972 Yug, 1973 Cze, A, 1975 F, Sp, R, Cze, E, Pol, H, Sp, 1976 F, R, 1978 Ar, USS, Sp, 1979 F, R, Sp, Mor, F, USS, NZ, 1980 F, R, Fj, JAB*
R De Bernardo *1980 USS, Sp, 1981 F, R, USS, WGe, 1982 R, E, 1983 R, USS, C, C, Sp, Mor, F, A, USS, 1984 F, USS, 1985 R, E, 1988 I, 1989 Ar, Z*
CF De Biase *1987 Sp, 1988 F, A*
G De Carli *1996 W, 1997 R, 1998 S, Rus, Ar, H, E, 1999 F, I, SA, SA, Ur, Fj, 2000 S, Sa, Fj, 2001 I, E, W, SA, Ur, Fj, SA, Sa, 2002 F, S, W, I, E, 2003 W, I, E*
B de Jager *2006 J*
L De Joanni *1983 C, Mor, F, A, USS, 1984 R, Tun, USS, 1985 F, R, E, Sp, Z, 1986 A, Tun, 1989 F, R, Sp, Ar, Z, 1990 R*
R De Marchis *1935 F*
H De Marco *1993 Pt*
JR de Marigny *2004 E, F, S, I, W, US, 2005 I, W, S, 2007 F, E, S, W, I, Ur, J, I, NZ, Pt*
A de Rossi *1999 Ur, Sp, E, 2000 I, E, F, Sa, C, R, NZ, 2001 SA, Ur, Ar, 2002 I, E, NZ, Sp, R, 2003 W, I, E, F, S, I, Geo, Tg, C, W, 2004 E, F, S, I, W, R*
C De Rossi *1994 Sp, H, R*
L De Santis *1952 Sp*
M De Stefani *1989 Z*
C De Vecchi *1948 F*
G Degli Antoni *1963 F, 1965 F, 1966 F, Ger, R, 1967 F*
G Del Bono *1951 Sp*
M Del Bono *1960 Ger, F, 1961 Ger, F, 1962 F, Ger, R, 1963 F, 1964 Ger, F*
CA Del Fava *2004 W, R, J, 2005 I, W, S, E, F, Tg, Ar, Fj, 2006 I, E, F, W, S, J, Fj, Pt, 2007 Ur, Ar, Pt, S, 2008 I, E, W, F, S, SA, Ar*
C Della Valle *1968 WGe, Yug, 1969 F, 1970 Mad, Mad, 1971 F*
S Dellapè *2002 F, S, I, E, NZ, Sp, Ar, 2003 F, S, S, Geo, Tg, C, W, 2004 E, F, S, I, W, C, NZ, 2005 I, W, S, E, F, Ar, 2006 I, E, W, S, J, Fj, Pt, Rus, A, Ar, C, 2007 F, E, S, W, I, J, NZ, R, S, 2008 I, E, W, SA, Ar*
G Delli Ficorilli *1969 F*
A Di Bello *1930 Sp, 1933 Cze, Cze, 1934 Cat*
F Di Carlo *1975 Sp, R, Cze, Sp, 1976 F, Sp, 1977 Pol, R, Pol, 1978 Ar, USS*
B Di Cola *1973 A*
G Di Cola *1972 Sp, Sp, 1973 A*
F Di Maura *1971 Mor*
A Di Zitti *1958 R, 1960 Ger, 1961 Ger, F, 1962 F, Ger, R, 1964 Ger, F, 1965 F, Cze, 1966 F, Ger, R, 1967 F, Pt, R, 1969 Bul, Sp, Bel, 1972 Pt, Sp*
R Dolfato *1985 F, 1986 A, 1987 Pt, Fj, USS, Sp, 1988 F, R, USS*
D Dominguez *1991 F, R, Nm, Nm, US, E, NZ, USS, 1992 Sp, F, R, S, 1993 Sp, F, Rus, F, S, 1994 R, H, R, W, 1995 S, I, Sa, E, Ar, SA, 1996 W, Pt, W, A, E, S, 1997 I, F, F, Ar, R, SA, I, 1998 S, W, Rus, Ar, H, E, 1999 F, S, W, I, Ur, Sp, Fj, E, Tg, NZ, 2000 S, W, I, E, F, 2001 F, S, W, Fj, SA, Sa, 2002 F, S, I, E, Ar, 2003 W, I*
D Donadona *1929 Sp, 1930 Sp*
G Dora *1929 Sp*
R D'Orazio *1969 Bul*
M Dotti IV *1939 R, 1940 R, Ger*
F Dotto *1971 Mor, F, 1972 Pt, Pt, Sp*
P Dotto *1993 Sp, Cro, 1994 Sp, R*
J Erasmus *2008 F, S, SA*
U Faccioli *1948 F*
A Falancia *1975 E, Pol*
G Faliva *1999 SA, 2002 NZ, Ar, A*
G Faltiba *1993 Pt*
G Fanton *1979 Pol*
P Farina *1987 F, NZ, Fj*
P Farinelli *1940 R, 1949 F, Cze, 1951 Sp, 1952 Sp*
T Fattori *1936 Ger, R, 1937 R, Ger, F, 1938 Ger, 1939 Ger, R, 1940 R, Ger*
E Fava *1948 F, Cze*
P Favaretto *1951 Sp*
R Favaro *1988 F, USS, A, I, 1989 F, R, Sp, Ar, Z, USS, 1990 F, Pol, R, H, R, USS, 1991 F, R, Nm, Nm, US, E, NZ, USS, 1992 Sp, F, R, 1993 Sp, F, Cro, Sp, F, 1994 CZR, A, A, R, W, F, 1995 S, I, Sa, 1996 Pt*
G Favretto *1948 Cze, 1949 Cze*
A Fedrigo *1972 Yug, 1973 Pt, Rho, WTv, Bor, NEC, Nat, ETv, Leo, FS, Cze, Yug, A, 1974 Pt, Mid, Sus, Oxo, WGe, Leo, 1975 F, Sp, R, Cze, E, Pol, H, Sp, 1976 F, J, A, Sp, 1977 F, Pol, R, Cze, R, Sp, 1978 F, Ar, 1979 Pol, R*
P Fedrigo *1973 Pt*
P Ferracin *1975 R, Cze, E, Pol, H, Sp, 1976 F, 1977 Mor, Pol, 1978 USS*
C Festuccia *2003 W, I, E, F, S, S, I, Geo, NZ, Tg, C, W, 2004 E, F, S, I, 2005 F, Ar, Ar, A, Tg, Ar, 2006 E, F, W, S, Pt, Rus, A, Ar, C, 2007 F, E, S, W, I, Ur, Ar, J, NZ, R, S, 2008 I, E, W*
G Figari *1940 R, Ger, 1942 R*
EG Filizzola *1993 Pt, Mor, Sp, F, Rus, F, S, 1994 Sp, CZR, A, 1995 R, NZ*
M Finocchi *1968 Yug, 1969 F, 1970 Cze, Mad, Mad, R, 1971 Mor, R*
G Fornari *1952 Sp, Ger, F, 1953 F, Ger, R, 1954 Sp, F, 1955 Ger, F, Sp, F, Cze, 1956 Ger, F, Cze*
B Francescato *1977 Cze, R, Sp, 1978 F, Sp, 1979 F, 1981 R*
I Francescato *1990 R, USS, 1991 F, R, US, E, NZ, USS, 1992 R, S, 1993 Mor, F, 1994 Sp, H, R, W, F, 1995 S, I, Sa, E, Ar, F, Ar, R, NZ, SA, 1996 W, Pt, W, A, E, S, 1997 F, F, Ar, R, SA*
N Francescato *1972 Yug, 1973 Rho, WTv, Bor, NEC, Nat, ETv, Leo, 1974 Pt, 1976 J, A, Sp, 1977 F, Mor, Pol, R, R, Sp, 1978 F, Ar, USS, Sp, 1979 F, R, E, Sp, Mor, F, Pol, USS, NZ, 1980 F, R, Fj, JAB, Coo, Pol, USS, Sp, 1981 F, R, 1982 Mor*
R Francescato *1976 Sp, 1978 Ar, USS, 1979 Sp, F, Pol, USS, NZ, Mor, 1980 F, R, Fj, JAB, Coo, Pol, USS, Sp, 1981 F, R, 1982 WGe, 1983 F, R, USS, C, C, Sp, Mor, F, A, 1984 Mor, R, Tun, 1985 F, Sp, Z, USS, 1986 Tun, F*
G Franceschini *1975 H, Sp, 1976 F, J, 1977 F, Pol, Pol, Cze, R, Sp*
A Francese *1939 R, 1940 R*
J Francesio *2000 W, I, Sa, 2001 Ur*
F Frati *2000 C, NZ, 2001 I, S*
F Frelich *1955 Cze, 1957 F, Ger, 1958 F, R*
M Fumei *1984 F*
A Fusco *1982 E, 1985 R, 1986 Tun, F, Tun*
E Fusco *1960 Ger, F, 1961 F, 1962 F, Ger, R, 1963 F, 1964 Ger, F, 1965 F, 1966 F*
R Gabanella *1951 Sp, 1952 Sp*
P Gabrielli *1948 Cze, 1949 F, Cze, 1951 Sp, 1954 F*
F Gaetaniello *1980 Sp, 1982 E, 1984 USS, 1985 R, Sp, Z,*

Z, USS, R, 1986 Pt, E, A, Tun, USS, 1987 Pt, F, NZ, Ar, Fj, USS, Sp, 1988 F, 1990 F, R, Sp, H, 1991 Nm, US, E, NZ
F Gaetaniello 1975 H, 1976 R, A, Sp, 1977 F, Pol, R, Pol, R, Sp, 1978 Sp, 1979 Pol, R, E, Sp, Mor, F, Pol, USS, NZ, Mor, 1980 Fj, JAB, Sp, 1981 F, R, USS, WGe, 1982 F, R, E, WGe, Mor, 1983 F, R, USS, C, C, Sp
A Galante 2007 Ur, Ar
A Galeazzo 1985 Sp, 1987 Pt, R, Ar, USS
M Galletto 1972 Pt, Sp, Yug
E Galon 2001 I, 2005 Tg, Ar, Fj, 2006 W, S, Rus, 2007 I, Ur, Ar, I, NZ, R, S, 2008 I, E, W, F, S
R Ganzerla 1973 Bor, NEC
G Garcia 2008 SA, Ar
M Gardin 1981 USS, WGe, 1982 Mor, 1983 F, R, 1984 Mor, R, USS, 1985 E, USS, R, 1986 Tun, F, Pt, Tun, USS, 1987 Pt, F, R, NZ, Ar, Fj, USS, Sp, 1988 R
JM Gardner 1992 R, S, 1993 Rus, F, 1994 Sp, R, H, F, 1995 S, I, Sa, E, Ar, 1996 W, 1997 I, F, SA, I, 1998 S, W
P Gargiullo 1973 FS, 1974 Mid, Sus, Oxo
F Garguillo 1972 Yug
F Garguilo 1967 F, Pt, 1968 Yug, 1974 Sus
S Garozzo 2001 Ur, Ar, 2002 Ar
M Gatto 1967 Pt, R
G Gattoni 1933 Cze, Cze
A Gerardo 1968 Yug, 1969 Sp, 1970 Cze, Mad, 1971 R, 1972 Sp
F Geremia 1980 JAB, Pol
G Geremia 1956 Cze
E Gerosa 1952 Sp, Ger, F, 1953 F, Ger, R, 1954 Sp
M Gerosa 1994 CZR, A, A, R, W, 1995 E, Ar
C Ghezzi 1938 Ger, 1939 Ger, R, 1940 R, Ger
A Ghini 1981 USS, WGe, 1982 F, R, E, Mor, 1983 F, R, C, Mor, F, A, USS, 1984 F, Mor, R, USS, 1985 F, R, E, Z, Z, USS, 1987 Fj, 1988 R, USS
L Ghiraldini 2006 J, Fj, 2007 I, J, Pt, 2008 I, E, W, F, S, SA, Ar
S Ghizzoni 1977 F, Mor, Pol, R, Pol, Cze, R, Sp, 1978 F, Ar, USS, 1979 F, Pol, Sp, Mor, F, Pol, 1980 R, Fj, JAB, Coo, Pol, USS, Sp, 1981 F, 1982 F, R, E, WGe, Mor, 1983 F, USS, C, C, Sp, Mor, F, A, USS, 1984 F, Mor, R, Tun, USS, 1985 F, R, E, Z, Z, USS, R, 1986 F, E, A, Tun, USS, 1987 Pt, F, R, NZ
M Giacheri 1992 R, 1993 Sp, F, Pt, Rus, F, S, 1994 Sp, R, CZR, H, A, A, F, 1995 S, I, E, Ar, F, Ar, R, NZ, SA, 1996 W, 1999 S, W, I, Ur, Fj, E, Tg, NZ, 2001 Nm, SA, Ur, Ar, SA, 2002 F, S, W, I, E, NZ, A, 2003 E, F, S, I
G Giani 1966 Ger, R, 1967 F, Pt, R
G Gini 1968 Pt, WGe, Yug, 1969 Bul, Sp, Bel, F, 1970 Cze, Mad, Mad, R, 1971 Mor, F, 1972 Pt, Pt, 1974 Mid, Oxo
G Giorgio 1968 Pt, WGe
M Giovanelli 1989 Z, USS, 1990 Pol, Sp, H, R, USS, 1991 F, R, Nm, E, NZ, USS, 1992 Sp, F, S, 1993 Sp, F, Pt, Cro, Mor, Sp, F, 1994 R, CZR, H, A, A, 1995 F, Ar, R, NZ, SA, 1996 A, E, S, 1997 F, F, Ar, R, SA, I, 1998 S, W, Rus, Ar, H, E, 1999 S, W, I, SA, SA, Ur, Sp, Fj, E, Tg, NZ, 2000 S
E Giugovaz 1965 Cze, 1966 F
R Giuliani 1951 Sp
M Gorni 1939 R, 1940 R, Ger
M Goti 1990 H
G Grasselli 1952 Ger
G Grespan 1989 F, Sp, USS, 1990 F, R, 1991 R, NZ, USS, 1992 R, S, 1993 Sp, F, Cro, Sp, F, Rus, 1994 Sp, CZR, R, W
PR Griffen 2004 E, F, S, I, W, R, J, C, NZ, US, 2005 W, S, F, Ar, Ar, A, Tg, Ar, Fj, 2006 I, E, F, W, S, J, Fj, Rus, A, Ar, C, 2007 F, I, Ur, Ar, I, NZ, R, Pt
A Gritti 1996 Pt, 2000 S, W, I, E, F, Sa, Fj, C, R, NZ, 2001 E, F, S, W
G Guidi 1996 Pt, E, 1997 F, Ar, R
M Innocenti 1981 WGe, 1982 F, R, E, WGe, Mor, 1983 F, USS, C, C, Mor, F, A, USS, 1984 F, Mor, Tun, USS, 1985 F, R, E, Sp, USS, R, 1986 Tun, F, Pt, E, A, Tun, USS, 1987 Pt, F, R, NZ, Ar, Fj, USS, Sp, 1988 F, R, A
G Intoppa 2004 R, J, C, NZ, 2005 I, W, E
C Jannone 1981 USS, 1982 F, R
S Lanfranchi 1949 F, Cze, 1953 F, Ger, R, 1954 Sp, F, 1955 F, 1956 Ger, Cze, 1957 F, 1958 F, 1959 F, 1960 F, 1961 F, 1962 F, Ger, R, 1963 F, 1964 Ger, F
G Lanzi 1998 Ar, H, E, 1999 Sp, 2000 S, W, I, 2001 I
G Lari 1972 Yug, 1973 Yug, A, 1974 Pt, Mid, Sus, Oxo, Leo
E Lazzarini 1970 Cze, 1971 Mor, F, R, 1972 Pt, Pt, Sp, Sp, 1973 Pt, Rho, WTv, Bor, NEC, Leo, FS, Tva, Cze, Yug, A, 1974 Pt, Mid, Sus, Oxo, WGe
U Levorato 1956 Ger, F, 1957 F, 1958 F, R, 1959 F, 1961 Ger, F, 1962 F, Ger, R, 1963 F, 1964 Ger, F, 1965 F
A Lijoi 1977 Pol, R, 1978 Sp, 1979 R, Mor
G Limone 1979 E, Mor, USS, Mor, 1980 JAB, Sp, 1981 USS, WGe, 1982 E, 1983 USS
A Lo Cicero 2000 E, F, Sa, Fj, C, R, NZ, 2001 I, E, F, S, W, Fj, SA, Sa, 2002 F, S, W, Sp, R, A, 2003 F, S, S, I, Geo, Tg, C, W, 2004 E, F, S, I, W, R, J, C, NZ, US, 2005 I, W, S, E, F, Ar, Ar, A, Tg, Ar, 2006 E, F, W, S, J, Fj, Pt, Rus, A, Ar, C, 2007 F, E, S, W, Ur, Ar, J, NZ, R, Pt, S, 2008 I, E, W, F, S
C Loranzi 1973 Nat, ETv, Leo, FS, Tva
F Lorigiola 1979 Sp, F, Pol, USS, NZ, Mor, 1980 F, R, Fj, JAB, Pol, USS, Sp, 1981 F, R, USS, 1982 WGe, 1983 R, USS, C, Sp, 1984 Tun, 1985 Sp, 1986 Pt, E, A, Tun, USS, 1987 Pt, F, R, NZ, Ar, 1988 F
G Luchini 1973 Rho, Nat
L Luise 1955 Ger, F, Sp, F, Cze, 1956 Ger, F, Cze, 1957 Ger, 1958 F
R Luise III 1959 F, 1960 Ger, F, 1961 Ger, F, 1962 F, Ger, R, 1965 F, Cze, 1966 F, 1971 R, 1972 Pt, Sp, Sp
T Lupini 1987 R, NZ, Ar, Fj, USS, Sp, 1988 F, R, USS, A, 1989 R
O Maestri 1935 Cat, F, 1937 Ger
R Maffioli 1933 Cze, Cze, 1934 Cat, R, 1935 Cat, 1936 Ger, R, 1937 Ger, R, Bel, Ger
R Maini 1948 F, Cze
G Malosti 1953 F, 1954 Sp, 1955 F, 1956 Ger, F, 1957 F, 1958 F
G Mancini 1952 Ger, F, 1953 F, Ger, R, 1954 Sp, F, 1955 Cze, 1956 Ger, F, Cze, 1957 F
R Mandelli 2004 I, W, R, J, US, 2007 F, E, Ur, Ar
A Mannato 2004 US, 2005 Ar, A
E Manni 1976 J, A, Sp, 1977 Mor
L Manteri 1996 W, A, E, S
A Marcato 2006 J, Pt, 2008 I, E, W, F, S, SA, Ar
M Marchetto 1972 Yug, 1973 Pt, Cze, Yug, 1974 Pt, Mid, Sus, WGe, Leo, 1975 F, Sp, R, Cze, E, Pol, H, Sp, 1976 F, R, J, A, Sp, 1977 F, Mor, Pol, R, Cze, R, Sp, 1978 F, USS, Sp, 1979 F, Pol, R, E, Pol, USS, NZ, Mor, 1980 F, Coo, 1981 USS
A Marescalchi 1933 Cze, 1935 F, 1937 R
P Mariani 1976 R, A, Sp, 1977 F, Pol, 1978 F, Ar, USS, Sp, 1979 F, Pol, R, Sp, F, Pol, USS, NZ, Mor, 1980 F, R, Fj, JAB
P Marini 1949 F, Cze, 1951 Sp, 1953 F, Ger, R, 1955 Ger
L Martin 1997 F, R, 1998 S, W, Rus, H, E, 1999 F, S, W, I, SA, SA, Ur, Sp, Fj, E, 2000 S, W, I, E, F, Sa, Fj, C, R, NZ, 2001 I, E, S, W, SA, Ar, Fj, SA, Sa, 2002 F, S
F Martinenghi 1952 Sp, Ger
R Martinez-Frugoni 2002 NZ, Sp, R, 2003 W, I, E, F, S, S, NZ
G Martini 1965 F, 1967 F, 1968 Pt
R Martini 1959 F, 1960 Ger, F, 1961 Ger, F, 1964 Ger, F, 1965 F, 1968 WGe, Yug
P Masci 1948 Cze, 1949 F, Cze, 1952 Sp, Ger, F, 1953 F, 1954 Sp, 1955 F
M Mascioletti 1977 Mor, Pol, 1978 Ar, USS, Sp, 1979 Pol, E, Sp, Mor, F, Pol, USS, NZ, Mor, 1980 F, R, Fj, 1981 WGe, 1982 F, R, WGe, 1983 F, R, USS, C, C, Sp, Mor, F, A, USS, 1984 F, Mor, Tun, 1985 F, R, Z, Z, USS, R, 1986 Tun, F, Pt, E, Tun, USS, 1987 NZ, Ar, Fj, 1989 Sp, Ar, Z, USS, 1990 Pol
A Masi 1999 Sp, 2003 E, F, S, S, I, NZ, Tg, C, W, 2004 E, I, W, R, J, C, 2005 I, W, S, E, F, Ar, Ar, A, 2006 J, Fj, Pt, Rus, 2007 F, S, J, NZ, R, Pt, S, 2008 I, E, W, F, S, SA
L Mastrodomenico 2000 Sa, C, NZ, 2001 Nm, Ar
I Matacchini 1948 F, Cze, 1949 F, Cze, 1954 Sp, 1955 Ger, F, Sp, F
L Mattarolo 1973 Bor, Nat, ETv, Leo, FS, Tva, Cze

M Mattei 1967 R
R Mattei 1978 F, USS
F Mazzantini 1965 Cze, 1966 F, 1967 F
M Mazzantini 2000 S, 2001 S, W, 2002 E, NZ, 2003 E, F, Geo, NZ, C
F Mazzariol 1995 F, Ar, R, NZ, 1996 Pt, 1997 F, R, SA, 1998 Ar, H, 1999 F, SA, SA, Sp, E, NZ, 2000 Fj, C, 2001 Nm, SA, Ur, Ar, Fj, SA, 2002 W, NZ, Sp, 2003 S, I, NZ, C, W, 2004 R
G Mazzi 1998 H, 1999 SA, SA, Ur, Sp
N Mazzucato 1995 SA, 1996 Pt, S, 1997 I, 1999 Sp, E, Tg, NZ, 2000 F, Sa, Fj, R, 2001 Nm, SA, Ur, Ar, 2002 W, I, E, NZ, Sp, R, Ar, A, 2003 E, F, S, I, NZ, Tg, W, 2004 E, F, S, I, W, R, J
I Mazzucchelli 1965 F, Cze, 1966 F, Ger, R, 1967 F, 1968 Pt, WGe, 1969 Bul, F, 1971 F, 1972 Pt, Sp, 1974 WGe, 1975 F, R, Cze, Pol, 1976 F, R
McLean 2008 SA, Ar
P Menapace 1996 Pt
E Michelon 1969 Bel, F, 1970 Cze, Mad, Mad, R, 1971 R
A Miele 1968 Yug, 1970 Mad, 1971 R, 1972 Pt, Sp
GE Milano 1990 USS
A Mioni 1955 Ger, F, F, 1957 F
A Modonesi 1929 Sp
L Modonesi 1966 Ger, R, 1967 F, Pt, R, 1968 Pt, WGe, 1970 Cze, Mad, Mad, R, 1971 F, 1974 Leo, 1975 F, Sp, R, Cze
N Molari 1957 F, 1958 R
F Molinari 1973 NEC
G Molinari 1948 F
P Monfeli 1970 R, 1971 Mor, F, 1972 Pt, 1976 J, A, Sp, 1977 F, R, Cze, R, Sp, 1978 F
G Morelli 1981 WGe, 1982 R, E, Mor, 1983 USS, 1984 F
G Morelli 1976 F, 1982 F, R, Mor, 1983 R, C, Sp, A, USS, 1984 Mor, R, USS, 1985 R, E, Z, Z, USS, R, 1986 Tun, F, E, A, Tun, USS, 1987 F, NZ
G Morelli 1988 I, 1989 F, R
A Moreno 1999 Tg, NZ, 2002 F, S, 2008 Ar
A Moretti 1997 R, 1998 Rus, 1999 Ur, Sp, Tg, NZ, 2002 E, NZ, Sp, R, Ar, A, 2005 Ar
U Moretti 1933 Cze, 1934 R, 1935 Cat, 1937 R, Ger, F, 1942 R
A Morimondi 1930 Sp, 1933 Cze, 1934 Cat, 1935 Cat
A Moscardi 1993 Pt, 1995 R, 1996 S, 1998 Ar, H, E, 1999 F, S, W, I, SA, SA, Ur, Fj, E, Tg, NZ, 2000 S, W, I, E, F, Sa, Fj, C, R, NZ, 2001 I, E, F, S, W, Nm, SA, Ur, Ar, Fj, SA, Sa, 2002 F, S, W, I, E
A Muraro 2000 C, R, NZ, 2001 I, E, Nm, SA, Ur, Ar, Fj, SA, Sa, 2002 F
E Nathan 1930 Sp
G Navarini 1957 Ger, 1958 R
M Nicolosi 1982 R
C Nieto 2002 E, 2005 Ar, Ar, A, Tg, Ar, Fj, 2006 I, E, F, W, J, Fj, A, Ar, C, 2007 F, S, W, I, Ar, 2008 E, F, S, SA, Ar
A Nisti 1929 Sp, 1930 Sp
L Nitoglia 2004 C, NZ, US, 2005 I, W, S, E, F, Ar, Tg, Ar, Fj, 2006 I, E, F, W, S
F Ongaro 2000 C, 2001 Nm, SA, Ur, Ar, 2002 Ar, A, 2003 E, F, S, I, Geo, NZ, Tg, C, W, 2004 E, F, S, I, W, R, J, C, NZ, US, 2005 I, W, S, E, F, Tg, Ar, Fj, 2006 I, E, F, W, S, J, Fj, Pt, Rus, Ar, C, 2007 F, S, Ur, Ar, I, NZ, S, 2008 F, S, SA, Ar
C Orlandi 1992 S, 1993 Sp, F, Mor, F, Rus, F, S, 1994 Sp, CZR, H, A, A, R, W, 1995 S, I, Sa, E, Ar, F, Ar, R, NZ, SA, 1996 W, Pt, W, A, E, S, 1997 I, F, F, Ar, R, SA, I, 1998 S, W, 2000 W, F
S Orlando 2004 E, S, W, C, NZ, US, 2005 E, F, Ar, A, 2006 J, 2007 Ur, Ar, Pt
L Orquera 2004 C, NZ, US, 2005 I, W, S, E, F, Ar, Tg
A Osti 1981 F, R, USS, 1982 E, Mor, 1983 R, C, A, USS, 1984 R, USS, 1985 F, 1986 Tun, 1988 R
S Pace 2001 SA, Sa, 2005 Fj
S Pace 1977 Mor, 1984 R, Tun
P Pacifici 1969 Bul, Sp, F, 1970 Cze, Mad, Mad, R, 1971 Mor, F
R Paciucci 1937 R, Ger, F
F Paganelli 1972 Sp
S Palmer 2002 Ar, A, 2003 I, E, F, S, S, NZ, C, W, 2004 I, R
P Paoletti 1972 Pt, Sp, Yug, 1973 Pt, Rho, WTv, Bor, NEC, Nat, ETv, Leo, FS, Tva, 1974 Mid, Oxo, WGe, Leo, 1975 F, Sp, 1976 R
T Paoletti 2000 S, W, I, E, F, Sa, C, R, NZ, 2001 F, Nm, Ur, Ar, Fj, SA
G Paolin 1929 Sp
S Parisse 2002 NZ, Sp, R, Ar, A, 2003 S, I, Geo, NZ, Tg, C, W, 2004 E, F, S, 2005 I, W, S, E, F, Ar, Ar, A, Tg, Ar, Fj, 2006 I, E, F, W, S, Fj, Pt, Rus, A, Ar, C, 2007 F, E, S, W, I, J, I, NZ, R, Pt, S, 2008 I, E, W, F, S, Ar
E Parmiggiani 1942 R, 1948 Cze
P Paseli 1929 Sp, 1930 Sp, 1933 Cze
E Passarotto 1975 Sp
E Patrizio 2007 Ur, 2008 F, S, SA
R Pavan 2008 SA
A Pavanello 2007 Ar
E Pavanello 2002 R, Ar, A, 2004 R, J, C, NZ, US, 2005 Ar, A
P Pavesi 1977 Pol, 1979 Mor, 1980 USS
M Pavin 1980 USS, 1986 F, Pt, E, A, Tun, USS, 1987 Ar
R Pedrazzi 2001 Nm, Ar, 2002 F, S, W, 2005 S, E, F
P Pedroni 1989 Z, USS, 1990 F, Pol, R, 1991 F, R, Nm, 1993 Rus, F, 1994 Sp, R, CZR, H, 1995 I, Sa, E, Ar, F, Ar, R, NZ, SA, 1996 W, W
G Peens 2002 W, I, E, NZ, Sp, R, Ar, A, 2003 E, F, S, S, I, Geo, NZ, 2004 NZ, 2005 E, F, Ar, Ar, A, 2006 Pt, A
L Pelliccione 1983 Sp, Mor, F
L Pelliccione 1977 Pol
M Percudani 1952 F, 1954 F, 1955 Ger, Sp, F, Cze, 1956 Cze, 1957 F, 1958 R
F Perrini 1955 Sp, F, Cze, 1956 Ger, F, Cze, 1957 F, 1958 F, 1959 F, 1962 R, 1963 F
F Perrone 1951 Sp
AR Persico 2000 S, W, E, F, Sa, Fj, 2001 F, S, W, Nm, SA, Ur, Ar, Fj, SA, Sa, 2002 F, S, W, I, E, NZ, Sp, R, Ar, A, 2003 W, I, E, F, S, I, Geo, Tg, C, W, 2004 E, F, S, I, W, R, J, C, NZ, 2005 I, W, S, E, F, Ar, Ar, Tg, Ar, 2006 I, E
J Pertile 1994 R, 1995 Ar, 1996 W, A, E, S, 1997 I, F, SA, 1998 Rus, 1999 S, W, I, SA, SA
S Perugini 2000 I, F, Sa, Fj, 2001 S, W, Nm, SA, Ur, Ar, 2002 W, I, 2003 W, S, Geo, NZ, Tg, W, 2004 E, F, I, W, C, NZ, US, 2005 I, W, S, E, F, 2006 I, E, F, W, S, Pt, Rus, 2007 F, E, S, W, I, J, I, NZ, Pt, S, 2008 I, E, W, F, S
L Perziano 1993 Pt
M Perziano 2000 NZ, 2001 F, S, W, Nm, SA, Ur, Ar, Fj, SA
V Pesce 1988 I, 1989 R
P Pescetto 1956 Ger, Cze, 1957 F
G Petralia 1984 F
R Pez 2000 Sa, Fj, C, R, NZ, 2001 I, 2002 S, W, E, A, 2003 I, E, F, S, S, Geo, 2005 Ar, A, Tg, Ar, Fj, 2006 I, E, F, W, S, J, Fj, Pt, Rus, A, Ar, 2007 F, E, S, W, I, J, R, S
M Phillips 2002 F, S, W, I, E, 2003 W, I, E, F, S, S, I, NZ, W
G Pianna 1934 R, 1935 Cat, F, 1936 Ger, R, 1938 Ger
A Piazza 1990 USS
F Piccini 1963 F, 1964 Ger, 1966 F
S Picone 2004 I, W, 2005 F, 2006 E, F, S, J, Pt, Rus, Ar, C, 2008 E, W, F, S, SA, Ar
F Pietroscanti 1987 USS, Sp, 1988 A, I, 1989 F, R, Sp, Ar, Z, USS, 1990 F, Pol, R, H, 1991 Nm, Nm, 1992 Sp, F, R, 1993 Sp, Mor, Sp, F, Rus, F
F Pignotti 1968 WGe, Yug, 1969 Bul, Sp, Bel
C Pilat 1997 I, 1998 S, W, 2000 E, Sa, 2001 I, W
MJ Pini 1998 H, E, 1999 F, Ur, Fj, E, Tg, NZ, 2000 S, W, I, F
M Piovan 1973 Pt, 1974 Pt, Mid, Sus, Oxo, 1976 A, 1977 F, Mor, R, 1979 F
R Piovan 1996 Pt, 1997 R, 2000 R, NZ
M Piovene 1995 NZ
E Piras 1971 R
M Pisaneschi 1948 Cze, 1949 Cze, 1953 F, Ger, R, 1954 Sp, F, 1955 Ger, F, Sp, F, Cze
F Pitorri 1948 Cze, 1949 F
M Pitorri 1973 NEC
G Pivetta 1979 R, E, Mor, 1980 Coo, USS, 1981 R, USS, WGe, 1982 F, R, WGe, Mor, 1983 F, USS, C, Sp, Mor, F, USS, 1984 F, Mor, R, Tun, 1985 F, R, Sp, Z, Z, 1986 Pt, 1987 Sp, 1989 R, Sp, 1990 F, Pol, R, Sp, R, USS, 1991 F,

R, Nm, Nm, US, E, NZ, USS, 1992 Sp, F, R, R, 1993 Cro, Mor, Sp
M Platania 1994 F, 1995 F, R, 1996 Pt
I Ponchia 1955 F, Sp, F, Cze, 1956 F, 1957 Ger, 1958 F
E Ponzi 1973 Cze, A, 1974 WGe, 1975 F, Sp, R, Cze, E, Pol, H, Sp, 1976 F, R, J, A, Sp, 1977 F, Mor, Pol, R
G Porcellato 1989 R
G Porzio 1970 Cze, Mad, Mad
C Possamai 1970 Cze, Mad, Mad
W Pozzebon 2001 I, E, F, S, W, Nm, SA, Ur, Ar, Fj, SA, Sa, 2002 NZ, Sp, 2004 R, J, C, NZ, US, 2005 W, E, 2006 C
C Pratichetti 1988 R, 1990 Pol
M Pratichetti 2004 NZ, 2007 E, W, I, Ur, Ar, I, Pt, 2008 SA, Ar
G Preo 1999 I, 2000 I, E, Sa, Fj, R, NZ
P Presutti 1974 Mid, Sus, Oxo, 1977 Pol, Cze, R, Sp, 1978 F
FP Properzi-Curti 1990 Pol, Sp, H, R, 1991 F, Nm, Nm, US, E, NZ, 1992 Sp, F, R, 1993 Cro, Mor, F, Rus, F, S, 1994 Sp, R, H, A, A, 1995 S, I, Sa, E, Ar, NZ, SA, 1996 W, Pt, W, A, E, 1997 I, F, F, Ar, SA, 1998 Ar, 1999 S, W, I, SA, SA, Ur, E, Tg, NZ, 2001 F, S, W
C Prosperini 1966 R, 1967 F, Pt, R
F Pucciarello 1999 Sp, Fj, E, 2002 S, W, I, E, Ar
G Puglisi 1971 F, 1972 Yug, 1973 Cze
M Pulli 1968 Pt, 1972 Pt, Pt
A Puppo 1972 Pt, Pt, Sp, Sp, 1973 Pt, Rho, WTv, Bor, NEC, Nat, ETv, Leo, FS, Tva, 1974 Mid, Sus, Oxo, WGe, Leo, 1977 R
I Quaglio 1970 R, 1971 R, 1972 Pt, Sp, 1973 WTv, Bor, NEC, Nat, Leo, FS, Tva, 1975 H, Sp, 1976 F, R
M Quaglio 1984 Tun, 1988 F, R
JM Queirolo 2000 Sa, Fj, 2001 E, F, Fj, 2002 NZ, Sp, A, 2003 Geo
P Quintavala 1958 R
C Raffo 1929 Sp, 1930 Sp, 1933 Cze, Cze, 1937 R, Bel
G Raineri 1998 H, 2000 Fj, R, NZ, 2001 I, E, S, W, Nm, SA, Ur, Ar, 2002 W, I, E, NZ, 2003 W, I, E, F, S, Geo
G Raisi 1956 Ger, F, 1957 F, Ger, 1960 Ger, 1964 Ger, F
R Rampazzo 1996 W, 1999 I
M Ravazzolo 1993 Cro, Sp, F, F, S, 1994 Sp, R, CZR, H, 1995 S, I, Sa, F, Ar, NZ, 1996 W, Pt, W, A, 1997 F, Ar, R, SA
A Re Garbagnati 1936 Ger, R, 1937 Ger, Bel, Ger, F, 1938 Ger, 1939 Ger, R, 1940 R, Ger, 1942 R
P Reale 1987 USS, Sp, 1988 USS, A, I, 1989 Z, 1992 S
T Reato 2008 I, SA, Ar
G Riccardi 1955 Ger, F, Sp, F, Cze, 1956 F, Cze
G Ricci 1967 Pt, 1969 Bul, Sp, Bel, F
G Ricciarelli 1962 Ger
L Riccioni 1951 Sp, 1952 Sp, Ger, F, 1953 F, Ger, 1954 F
S Rigo 1992 S, 1993 Sp, F, Pt
A Rinaldo 1977 Mor, Pol, R, Cze
W Rista 1968 Yug, 1969 Bul, Sp, Bel, F
M Rivaro 2000 S, W, I, 2001 E
M Rizzo 2005 A, 2008 SA
G Rizzoli 1935 F, 1936 Ger, R
C Robazza 1978 Ar, Sp, 1979 F, Pol, R, E, Sp, F, Pol, USS, NZ, Mor, 1980 F, R, Fj, JAB, Coo, Pol, Sp, 1981 F, R, USS, WGe, 1982 E, WGe, 1983 F, USS, C, Mor, F, 1984 F, Tun, 1985 F
KP Robertson 2004 R, J, C, NZ, US, 2005 I, W, S, F, Ar, Ar, A, 2006 Pt, Rus, 2007 F, E, S, W, I, Ur, Ar, J, I, NZ, R, S, 2008 I, E, F, S, SA, Ar
A Rocca 1973 WTv, Bor, NEC, 1977 R
G Romagnoli 1965 F, Cze, 1967 Pt, R
S Romagnoli 1982 Mor, 1984 R, Tun, USS, 1985 F, Z, Z, 1986 Tun, Pt, A, Tun, USS, 1987 Pt, F, Fj
G Romano 1942 R
P Romano 1942 R
F Roselli 1995 F, R, 1996 W, 1998 Rus, Ar, H, E, 1999 F, S, W, I, SA, SA, Ur, Fj, Tg
P Rosi 1948 F, Cze, 1949 F, Cze, 1951 Sp, 1952 Ger, F, 1953 F, Ger, R, 1954 Sp, F
G Rossi 1981 USS, WGe, 1982 E, WGe, Mor, 1983 F, R, USS, C, C, Mor, F, A, USS, 1984 Mor, 1985 F, R, E, Sp, Z, USS, R, 1986 Tun, F, E, A, Tun, USS, 1987 R, NZ, Ar, USS, Sp, 1988 USS, A, I, 1989 F, R, Sp, Ar, Z, USS, 1990 F, R, 1991 R
N Rossi 1973 Yug, 1974 Pt, Mid, Sus, Oxo, WGe, Leo, 1975 Sp, Cze, E, H, 1976 J, A, Sp, 1977 Cze, 1980 USS
Z Rossi 1959 F, 1961 Ger, F, 1962 F, Ger, R
E Rossini 1948 F, Cze, 1949 F, Cze, 1951 Sp, 1952 Ger
I Rouyet 2008 SA, Ar
B Rovelli 1960 Ger, F, 1961 Ger, F
A Russo 1986 E
D Sacca 2003 I
R Saetti 1988 USS, I, 1989 F, R, Sp, Ar, Z, USS, 1990 F, Sp, H, R, USS, 1991 R, Nm, Nm, US, E, 1992 R
R Saetti 1957 Ger, 1958 F, R, 1959 F, 1960 F, 1961 Ger, F, 1964 Ger, F
A Sagramora 1970 Mad, Mad, 1971 R
E Saibene 1957 F, Ger
C Salmasco 1965 F, 1967 F
L Salsi 1971 Mor, 1972 Pt, Sp, Yug, 1973 Pt, Rho, WTv, Nat, ETv, Leo, FS, Tva, Cze, Yug, A, 1974 Pt, Oxo, WGe, Leo, 1975 Sp, R, Sp, 1977 R, Pol, Cze, R, Sp, 1978 F
F Salvadego 1985 Z
R Salvan 1973 Yug, 1974 Pt
L Salvati 1987 USS, 1988 USS, I
R Santofadre 1952 Sp, Ger, F, 1954 Sp, F
F Sartorato 1956 Ger, F, 1957 F
M Savi 2004 R, J, 2005 E
S Saviozzi 1998 Rus, H, 1999 W, I, SA, SA, Ur, Fj, Tg, NZ, 2000 C, NZ, 2002 NZ, Sp
D Scaglia 1994 R, W, 1995 S, 1996 W, A, 1999 W
E Scalzotto 1974 Mid, Sus, Oxo
A Scanavacca 1999 Ur, 2001 E, 2002 Sp, R, 2004 US, 2006 Ar, C, 2007 F, E, S, I
R Sciacol 1965 Cze
I Scodavolpe 1954 Sp
F Screnci 1977 Cze, R, Sp, 1978 F, 1979 Pol, R, E, 1982 F, 1984 Mor
A Selvaggio 1973 Rho, WTv, ETv, Leo, FS, Tva
M Sepe 2006 J, Fj
D Sesenna 1992 R, 1993 Cro, Mor, F, 1994 R
G Sessa 1930 Sp
G Sessi 1942 R
A Sgarbi 2008 E, W
E Sgorbati 1968 WGe, Yug
E Sgorbati 1933 Cze, 1934 Cat, R, 1935 Cat, F, 1936 Ger, 1937 Ger, 1938 Ger, 1939 Ger, 1940 R, Ger, 1942 R
A Sgorlon 1993 Pt, Mor, Sp, F, Rus, F, S, 1994 CZR, R, W, 1995 S, E, Ar, F, Ar, R, NZ, SA, 1996 W, Pt, W, A, E, S, 1997 I, F, F, Ar, R, SA, I, 1998 S, W, Rus, 1999 F, S, W
P Sguario 1958 R, 1959 F, 1960 Ger, F, 1961 Ger, 1962 R
M Silini 1955 Ger, Sp, F, Cze, 1956 Cze, 1957 Ger, 1958 F, 1959 F
S Silvestri 1954 F
U Silvestri 1967 Pt, R, 1968 Pt, WGe
U Silvestri 1949 F, Cze
L Simonelli 1956 Ger, F, Cze, 1958 F, 1960 Ger, F
F Sinitich 1980 Fj, Coo, Pol, Sp, 1981 R, 1983 USS
JW Sole 2005 Ar, Tg, Ar, 2006 I, E, F, W, S, J, Fj, Rus, A, Ar, C, 2007 F, E, I, Ur, Ar, J, I, R, S, 2008 I, E, W, F, S, SA, Ar
F Soro 1965 Cze, 1966 F, Ger, R
A Spagnoli 1973 Rho
E Speziali 1965 Cze
W Spragg 2006 C
F Staibano 2006 J, Fj, 2007 W, I, Ur, Ar
MP Stanojevic 2006 Pt, Rus, A, Ar, C, 2007 J, NZ
U Stenta 1937 Bel, Ger, F, 1938 Ger, 1939 Ger, R, 1940 R, Ger, 1942 R
P Stievano 1948 F, 1952 F, 1953 F, Ger, R, 1954 Sp, F, 1955 Ger
S Stocco 1998 H, 1999 S, I, 2000 Fj
CA Stoica 1997 I, F, SA, I, 1998 S, W, Rus, Ar, H, E, 1999 S, W, SA, SA, Ur, Sp, Fj, E, Tg, NZ, 2000 S, W, I, E, F, Sa, Fj, C, R, NZ, 2001 I, E, F, S, W, Fj, SA, Sa, 2002 F, S, W, I, E, Sp, R, Ar, A, 2003 W, I, S, I, Geo, Tg, C, W, 2004 E, F, S, I, W, US, 2005 S, Tg, Ar, 2006 I, E, F, W, S, 2007 Ur, Ar
L Tagliabue 1930 Sp, 1933 Cze, Cze, 1934 Cat, R, 1935 F, 1937 Ger

S Tartaglini *1948 Cze, 1949 F, Cze, 1951 Sp, 1952 Sp, Ger, F, 1953 F*
A Tassin *1973 A*
A Taveggia *1954 F, 1955 Ger, F, Sp, F, 1956 Ger, F, Cze, 1957 F, Ger, 1958 F, R, 1959 F, 1960 Ger, F, 1967 Pt*
D Tebaldi *1985 Z, Z, 1987 R, Ar, Fj, USS, Sp, 1988 F, A, I, 1989 F, 1990 F, Pol, R, 1991 Nm*
Tedeschi *1948 F*
G Testoni *1937 Bel, 1938 Ger, 1942 R*
C Tinari *1980 JAB, Coo, Pol, USS, Sp, 1981 USS, WGe, 1982 F, WGe, 1983 R, USS, C, C, Sp, Mor, A, USS, 1984 Mor, R*
M Tommasi *1990 Pol, 1992 R, S, 1993 Pt, Cro, Sp, F*
C Torresan *1980 F, R, Fj, Coo, Pol, USS, 1981 R, USS, 1982 R, Mor, 1983 C, F, A, USS, 1984 F, Mor, Tun, USS, 1985 Z, Z, USS*
F Tozzi *1933 Cze*
P Travagli *2004 C, NZ, 2008 I, E, W, F, S*
L Travini *1999 SA, Ur, Sp, Fj, 2000 I*
F Trebbi *1933 Cze, Cze*
F Trentin *1979 Mor, F, Pol, USS, 1981 R*
M Trevisiol *1988 F, USS, A, I, 1989 F, Ar, USS, 1994 R*
M Trippiteli *1979 Pol, 1980 Pol, Sp, 1981 F, R, 1982 F, E, WGe, 1984 Tun*
L Troiani *1985 R, 1986 Tun, F, Pt, A, USS, 1987 Pt, F, 1988 R, USS, A, I, 1989 Sp, Ar, Z, USS, 1990 F, Pol, R, Sp, H, R, USS, 1991 F, R, Nm, Nm, US, E, 1992 Sp, F, R, R, S, 1993 Sp, F, Cro, Rus, F, 1994 Sp, CZR, A, A, F, 1995 S, E, Ar*
A Troncon *1994 Sp, R, CZR, H, A, A, R, W, F, 1995 S, I, Sa, E, Ar, F, Ar, R, NZ, SA, 1996 W, W, A, E, S, 1997 I, F, F, Ar, SA, I, 1998 S, W, Rus, Ar, H, E, 1999 F, S, W, I, Ur, Sp, Fj, E, Tg, NZ, 2000 S, W, I, E, F, R, NZ, 2001 I, F, Nm, SA, Ur, Ar, Fj, SA, Sa, 2002 F, S, W, I, E, Sp, R, Ar, A, 2003 W, I, E, F, S, S*
G Troncon *1962 F, Ger, R, 1963 F, 1964 Ger, F, 1965 Cze, 1966 F, R, 1967 F, 1968 Yug, 1972 Pt*
L Turcato *1952 Sp, Ger, F, 1953 Ger, R*
M Turcato *1949 F, 1951 Sp*
P Vaccari *1991 Nm, Nm, US, E, NZ, USS, 1992 Sp, F, R, R, S, 1993 Mor, Sp, F, Rus, F, S, 1994 Sp, R, CZR, H, A, A, R, W, F, 1995 I, Sa, E, Ar, F, Ar, R, NZ, SA, 1996 W, W, E, S, 1997 I, F, F, Ar, R, SA, I, 1998 S, W, Ar, 1999 Ur, Sp, E, Tg, NZ, 2001 Fj, 2002 F, S, Ar, A, 2003 W, I, E, F, S*
V Vagnetti *1939 R, 1940 R*
F Valier *1968 Yug, 1969 F, 1970 Cze, R, 1971 Mor, R, 1972 Pt*
L Valtorta *1957 Ger, 1958 F*
O Vene *1966 F*
E Venturi *1983 C, 1985 E, Sp, 1986 Tun, Pt, 1988 USS, A, 1989 F, R, Sp, Ar, USS, 1990 F, Pol, R, Sp, H, R, USS, 1991 F, R, NZ, USS, 1992 Sp, F, R, 1993 Sp, F*
P Vezzani *1973 Yug, 1975 F, Sp, R, Cze, E, Pol, H, Sp, 1976 F*
F Vialetto *1972 Yug*
V Viccariotto *1948 F*
S Vigliano *1937 R, Bel, Ger, F, 1939 R, 1942 R*
L Villagra *2000 Sa, Fj*
E Vinci I *1929 Sp*
P Vinci II *1929 Sp, 1930 Sp, 1933 Cze*
F Vinci III *1929 Sp, 1930 Sp, 1934 Cat, R, 1935 Cat, F, 1936 Ger, R, 1937 Ger, R, Ger, F, 1939 Ger, R, 1940 Ger*
P Vinci IV *1929 Sp, 1930 Sp, 1933 Cze, Cze, 1934 Cat, R, 1935 Cat, F, 1937 Ger, Bel, Ger, F, 1939 Ger*
A Visentin *1970 R, 1972 Pt, Sp, 1973 Rho, WTv, Bor, NEC, Nat, ETv, Leo, FS, Tva, Cze, Yug, A, 1974 Pt, Leo, 1975 F, Sp, R, Cze, 1976 R, 1978 Ar*
G Visentin *1935 Cat, F, 1936 R, 1937 Ger, Bel, Ger, F, 1938 Ger, 1939 Ger*
T Visentin *1996 W*
W Visser *1999 I, SA, SA, 2000 S, W, I, F, C, R, NZ, 2001 I, E, F, S, W, Nm, SA, Ur, Ar, Fj, SA, Sa*
F Vitadello *1985 Sp, 1987 Pt*
C Vitelli *1973 Cze, Yug, 1974 Pt, Sus*
I Vittorini *1969 Sp*
RMS Vosawai *2007 J, I, NZ, R, Pt*
RS Wakarua *2003 Tg, C, W, 2004 E, F, S, W, J, C, NZ, 2005 Fj*
F Williams *1995 SA*
M Zaffiri *2000 Fj, R, NZ, 2001 W, 2003 S, 2005 Tg, Fj, 2006 W, S, C, 2007 E, S, W, I*
R Zanatta *1954 Sp, F*
G Zanchi *1953 Ger, R, 1955 Sp, Cze, 1957 Ger*
A Zanella *1977 Mor*
M Zanella *1976 J, Sp, 1977 R, Pol, Cze, 1978 Ar, 1980 Pol, USS*
E Zanetti *1942 R*
F Zani *1960 Ger, F, 1961 Ger, F, 1962 F, R, 1963 F, 1964 F, 1965 F, 1966 Ger, R*
G Zani *1934 R*
A Zanni *2005 Tg, Ar, Fj, 2006 F, W, S, Pt, Rus, A, Ar, C, 2007 S, W, I, Ur, I, NZ, 2008 I, E, W, F, S, SA, Ar*
C Zanoletti *2001 Sa, 2002 E, NZ, R, Ar, A, 2005 A*
G Zanon *1981 F, R, USS, WGe, 1982 R, E, WGe, Mor, 1983 F, R, USS, C, C, Sp, Mor, F, A, USS, 1984 F, Mor, R, USS, 1985 F, R, E, Sp, Z, Z, USS, 1986 USS, 1987 R, Ar, USS, 1989 Sp, Ar, 1990 F, Pol, R, Sp, H, R, USS, 1991 Nm, US, E*
M Zingarelli *1973 A*
N Zisti *1999 E, NZ, 2000 E, F*
G Zoffoli *1936 Ger, R, 1937 Ger, R, Ger, 1938 Ger, 1939 R*
S Zorzi *1985 R, 1986 Tun, F, 1988 F, R, USS, 1992 R*
A Zucchelo *1956 Ger, F*
C Zucchi *1952 Sp, 1953 F*
L Zuin *1977 Cze, 1978 Ar, USS, Sp, 1979 F, Pol, R*

JAPAN

JAPAN'S 2008 RECORD

OPPONENTS	DATE	VENUE	RESULT
Korea	26 April	A	**Won** 39–17
Arabian Gulf	3 May	H	**Won** 114–6
Kazakhstan	11 May	A	**Won** 82–6
Hong Kong	18 May	H	**Won** 75–29
Australia A	8 June	H	**Lost** 21–42
Tonga	15 June	H	**Won** 35–13
Fiji	22 June	H	**Lost** 12–24
New Zealand Maori	28 June	A	**Lost** 22–65
Samoa	5 July	A	**Lost** 31–37

BUILDING FOR THE FUTURE

By Rich Freeman

In naming his squad for 2008, Japan coach John Kirwan made it very clear what he expected.

"This year should be a transition year," he said. "So we have picked a mix of older, experienced players and younger players. By the end of the season I hope we have the formation of a team heading to the next World Cup and one that confirms Japan's status in world rugby and moving up the ranking ladder."

Japan did move up the ladder, finishing the year 16th in the world rankings – having reached a best-ever 15th at one stage – and won more Tests than they lost. A point not lost on the Japan Rugby Football Union which said it had reached an agreement with the former All Black to extend his contract beyond the 2011 Rugby World Cup.

Kirwan, though, is a perfectionist when it comes to rugby and accepts nothing but success.

"We had some success last year," he said prior to the 2008–09 Top League season. "But we need to keep building to the next World Cup. I have told the players the transition period is over."

Success came in the inaugural HSBC Asian Five Nations, where Japan won all four games. But losses to Fiji and Samoa – games Kirwan said the Brave Blossoms "could and should have won" – meant Japan only finished fifth in the IRB Pacific Nations Cup.

Kirwan had said following the World Cup that the only way Japan could improve was if they played the likes of New Zealand and Australia, rather than their regular Asian opponents.

But he also knows the importance of developing the game in an area that still hopes to play host to the World Cup in 2015 or 2019.

"We feel we have a responsibility to Asia," he said prior to the Asian Five Nations opener against Korea. "So we are taking a full team and doing all we can to win the tournament."

The opening game was, as expected, the title decider and although Japan won 39–17, it was a far from impressive performance.

"They outplayed us in the second half and lived off our mistakes. I think their coach can go away happy," Kirwan said.

In the following weeks, however, Japan showed how much better they are than the rest of Asia when they ran in 18 tries in a 114–6 thrashing of the Arabian Gulf in Osaka, crossed 12 times in an 82–6 win over Kazakhstan in Almaty, before sealing the title by beating Hong Kong 75–29 to finish the competition with a maximum 24 points from their four games.

Aware that the IRB Pacific Nations Cup was a step up, Kirwan invited the Classic All Blacks to Tokyo to play a Japan XV.

In a game that was hardly a classic; the Kiwis won 15–13, though it was Japan that scored the two best tries through Kosuke Endo and Hirotoki Onozawa.

Scoring great tries is all well and good but you need to stop the opposition from scoring.

The hosts may have "won" the second half of their PNC opener in Fukuoka, but first-half defensive frailties meant Japan went down 42–21 to Australia A, having turned around 28–3 down.

No such problems seven days later though as Japan picked up a bonus point for the first time in the three-year history of the tournament, courtesy of a 35–13 win over Tonga.

But they were unable to build on that, as heavy rain meant neither Fiji nor Japan were able to show off their handling skills and Fiji left Tokyo a week later with a 24–12 victory under their belt.

"We threw the game away through errors and turnovers," said Kirwan. "We had ample opportunity to win today."

Errors also played a role a week later at Napier's McLean Park, although they were probably more to do with exhaustion.

Japan led the New Zealand Maori 22–17 at half-time. However, Japan's defensive effort was unable to last the distance and with tackles being missed and handling errors creeping into their game, the Maori took full advantage, running in 48 unanswered points to win 65–22.

To their credit, heads didn't drop and the Brave Blossoms were able to finish in fifth place in the Pacific Nations Cup following a battling 37–31 loss to Samoa.

Once again Kirwan knew his players should have left Samoa with more than two bonus points. "It was a very unfortunate result," said Kirwan. "But we have begun to give countries in the Pacific Nations Cup competitive games. This confirms without a doubt that we are improving and getting stronger."

One reason for that development has been the improvement in the Top League.

Despite losing twice in the regular season, Suntory Sungoliath took the silverware beating the previously unbeaten Sanyo Wild Knights 14–10 in the Microsoft Cup final.

Sanyo got their revenge a month later in the season-concluding All-Japan Championship, winning 40–18. But the club was still seething at having played the best rugby of the year only to be out-thought in the league play-offs.

JAPAN INTERNATIONAL RECORDS

Does not include 2008 Asian 5 Nations results

WINNING MARGIN

Date	Opponent	Result	Winning Margin
06/07/2002	Chinese Taipei	155–3	**152**
27/10/1998	Chinese Taipei	134–6	**128**
21/07/2002	Chinese Taipei	120–3	**117**
08/05/2005	Hong Kong	91–3	**88**

MOST POINTS IN A MATCH

BY THE TEAM

Date	Opponent	Result	Pts.
06/07/2002	Chinese Taipei	155–3	**155**
27/10/1998	Chinese Taipei	134–6	**134**
21/07/2002	Chinese Taipei	120–3	**120**
08/05/2005	Hong Kong	91–3	**91**

MOST TRIES IN A MATCH

BY THE TEAM

Date	Opponent	Result	Tries
06/07/2002	Chinese Taipei	155–3	**23**
27/10/1998	Chinese Taipei	134–6	**20**
21/07/2002	Chinese Taipei	120–3	**18**

MOST CONVERSIONS IN A MATCH

BY THE TEAM

Date	Opponent	Result	Cons
06/07/2002	Chinese Taipei	155–3	**20**
27/10/1998	Chinese Taipei	134–6	**17**
21/07/2002	Chinese Taipei	120–3	**15**

MOST PENALTIES IN A MATCH

BY THE TEAM

Date	Opponent	Result	Pens
08/05/1999	Tonga	44–17	**9**
08/04/1990	Tonga	28–16	**6**

MOST DROP GOALS IN A MATCH

BY THE TEAM

Date	Opponent	Result	DGs
15/09/1998	Argentina	44–29	**2**

MOST POINTS IN A MATCH

BY A PLAYER

Date	Player	Opponent	Pts.
21/07/2002	Toru Kurihara	Chinese Taipei	**60**
06/07/2002	Daisuke Ohata	Chinese Taipei	**40**
16/06/2002	Toru Kurihara	Korea	**35**
08/05/1999	Keiji Hirose	Tonga	**34**
08/05/2005	Keiji Hirose	Hong Kong	**31**

MOST TRIES IN A MATCH

BY A PLAYER

Date	Player	Opponent	Tries
06/07/2002	Daisuke Ohata	Chinese Taipei	**8**
21/07/2002	Toru Kurihara	Chinese Taipei	**6**
08/05/2005	Daisuke Ohata	Hong Kong	**6**
27/10/1998	Terunori Masuho	Chinese Taipei	**5**

MOST CONVERSIONS IN A MATCH BY A PLAYER

Date	Player	Opponent	Cons
21/07/2002	Toru Kurihara	Chinese Taipei	15
06/07/2002	Andy Miller	Chinese Taipei	12
16/06/2002	Toru Kurihara	Korea	11
08/05/2005	Keiji Hirose	Hong Kong	11

MOST PENALTIES IN A MATCH BY A PLAYER

Date	Player	Opponent	Pens
08/05/1999	Keiji Hirose	Tonga	9
08/04/1990	Takahiro Hosokawa	Tonga	6

MOST DROP GOALS IN A MATCH BY A PLAYER

Date	Player	Opponent	DGs
15/09/1998	Kensuke Iwabuchi	Argentina	2

MOST CAPPED PLAYERS

Name	Caps
Yukio Motoki	79
Takeomi Ito	62
Daisuke Ohata	58
Masahiro Kunda	48
Terunori Masuho	47

LEADING TRY SCORERS

Name	Tries
Daisuke Ohata	69
Terunori Masuho	28
Hirotoki Onozawa	26
Toru Kurihara	20
Yoshihito Yoshida	17

LEADING CONVERSIONS SCORERS

Name	Cons
Keiji Hirose	77
Toru Kurihara	71

LEADING PENALTY SCORERS

Name	Pens
Keiji Hirose	76
Toru Kurihara	35
Takahiro Hosokawa	24
Wataru Ikeda	12
Kyohei Morita	12

LEADING DROP GOAL SCORERS

Name	DGs
Kyohei Morita	5

LEADING POINTS SCORERS

Name	Pts.
Keiji Hirose	413
Toru Kurihara	347
Daisuke Ohata	345
Terunori Masuho	142
Hirotoki Onozawa	130

JAPAN INTERNATIONAL PLAYERS
UP TO 30TH SEPTEMBER 2008

Note: Years given for International Championship matches are for second half of season; eg 1972 means season 1971–72. Years for all other matches refer to the actual year of the match.

T Adachi 1932 *C, C*
M Aizawa 1984 *Kor*, 1986 *US, C, S, E, Kor*, 1987 *A, NZ, NZ*, 1988 *Kor*
H Akama 1973 *F*, 1975 *A, W*, 1976 *S, E, It, Kor*, 1977 *S*
T Akatsuka 1994 *Fj*, 1995 *Tg, NZ*, 2005 *Sp*, 2006 *HK, Kor*
J Akune 2001 *W, C*
M Amino 2000 *Kor, C*, 2003 *Rus, AuA, Kor, E, E, S, Fj, US*
E Ando 2006 *AG, Kor, Geo, Tg, Sa, JAB, Fj*, 2007 *HK, Fj, Tg, Sa, JAB, It*
D Anglesey 2002 *Tg, Tai, Tai*
T Aoi 1959 *BCo, BCo*, 1963 *BCo*
S Aoki 1989 *S*, 1990 *Fj*, 1991 *US, C*, 1993 *W*
Y Aoki 2007 *Kor, AuA, JAB*, 2008 *Kor, Kaz, HK, Tg, Fj, Sa*
S Arai 1959 *BCo, BCo*
JA Arlidge 2007 *Kor*, 2008 *Kor, AG, Kaz, HK, Tg, Fj, Sa*
G Aruga 2006 *HK, Kor*, 2007 *Kor, HK, AuA, Sa, JAB, It, Fj, C*, 2008 *Kor, HK*
K Aruga 1974 *NZU*, 1975 *A, A, W, W*, 1976 *S, E, It, Kor*
R Asano 2003 *AuA, AuA, F, Fj*, 2005 *Ar, HK, Kor, R, C, I, I, Sp*, 2006 *Kor, Geo, Tg, It, HK, Kor*, 2007 *Kor, It, W*
M Atokawa 1969 *HK*, 1970 *Tha, BCo*, 1971 *E, E*
H Atou 1976 *BCo*
T Baba 1932 *C*
GTM Bachop 1999 *C, Tg, Sa, Fj, Sp, Sa, W, Ar*
I Basiyalo 1997 *HK, US, US, C, HK*
D Bickle 1996 *HK, HK, C, US, US, C*
KCC Chang 1930 *BCo*, 1932 *C, C*
T Chiba 1930 *BCo*
M Chida 1980 *Kor*, 1982 *HK, C, C, Kor*, 1983 *W*, 1984 *F, F, Kor*, 1985 *US, I, I, F, F*, 1986 *US, C, S, E, Kor*, 1987 *US, E*
H Daimon 2004 *S, W*
K Endo 2004 *It*, 2006 *AG, Kor, Geo, Tg, It, JAB, Fj*, 2007 *HK, Fj, Tg, AuA, Sa, It, Fj, W, C*, 2008 *Tg, Fj*
J Enomoto 2005 *Sp*
R Enomoto 1959 *BCo, BCo*
B Ferguson 1993 *W*, 1994 *Fj, Fj, HK, Kor*, 1995 *Tg, Tg, R, W, I, NZ*, 1996 *HK, HK, C, US, US, C*
K Fijii 2000 *Sa*
S Fuchigami 2000 *I*, 2002 *Rus, Tai*, 2003 *US, Rus*
A Fuji 1959 *BCo, BCo*
M Fujii 1930 *BCo*
M Fujikake 1993 *W*, 1994 *HK*, 1995 *Tg*
T Fujimoto-Kamohara 1969 *HK*, 1970 *BCo*, 1971 *E, E*, 1972 *HK*, 1973 *W*
T Fujita 1980 *H, F*, 1983 *W*, 1984 *F, F, Kor*, 1985 *US, I, I, F, F*, 1986 *US, C, S, E*, 1987 *US, E, A, NZ, NZ*, 1989 *S*, 1990 *Fj, Tg, Kor, Sa*, 1991 *US, US, I*
M Fujiwara 1973 *W*, 1974 *NZU*, 1975 *A, A, W, W*, 1976 *S, E, It*, 1977 *S*, 1978 *F, Kor*, 1979 *HK, E*, 1980 *H, F*
K Fukumuro 1990 *Kor*
K Fukuoka 2000 *Fj*
S Fukuoka 1990 *Kor*
R Fukurodate 1976 *BCo, Kor*, 1979 *E, E*, 1980 *H, F, Kor*
T Fumihara 2000 *I*
T Goda 1990 *Fj, Tg, Kor, Sa, US, Kor*, 1991 *US*, 1995 *Tg*
WR Gordon 1997 *HK, C, US, US*, 1998 *C, US, HK, HK, US, C*, 1999 *C, Sa, Fj, Sp, Sa, W, Ar*
A Goromaru 2005 *Ur, R, C, I*
S Goto 2005 *Ur, Ar, Kor, R, C, I, I*, 2006 *HK*
M Hagimoto 1987 *E*
T Hagiwara-Maekawa 1930 *BCo*
K Hamabe 1996 *C, US, US, C, Kor*, 1997 *HK, C, US, US, C*, 2001 *Sa, C*
T Haneda 1995 *Tg*
S Hara 1970 *BCo*, 1971 *E, E*, 1973 *W, F*, 1974 *NZU, SL*, 1975 *A, W*, 1976 *E*
T Harada 1959 *BCo*
S Hasegawa 1997 *HK*, 1998 *C, US, HK, HK, US, C, Ar, Kor, Tai, HK, Kor*, 1999 *C, Tg, Sa, Fj, US, Sa, W*, 2000 *Fj, US, Tg, Sa, C*, 2001 *W, W, Sa, C*, 2002 *Tg, Kor, Tai, Kor*, 2003 *US, AuA, E, S, F, Fj, US*
T Hatakeyama 1976 *It, Kor*, 1977 *S*, 1978 *F, Kor*, 1979 *HK, E, E*
T Hayashi 1980 *F*, 1982 *C, C, Kor*, 1983 *W*, 1984 *F, F*, 1985 *US, I, I, F, F*, 1986 *US, C, S, E, Kor*, 1987 *US, E, A, NZ, NZ*, 1990 *Tg, Sa*, 1991 *US, C, HK, S, I, Z*, 1992 *HK*
T Hayashi 1989 *S*
T Higashida 1983 *W*
T Hirai 1980 *Kor*, 1982 *HK*
S Hirao 1932 *C, C*
S Hirao 1983 *W*, 1984 *F, F*, 1985 *US, I, I*, 1986 *US, C, S, E*, 1987 *US, E, A, NZ, NZ*, 1988 *Kor*, 1989 *S*, 1990 *Fj, Tg, Kor, US, Kor*, 1991 *US, C, HK, S, I, Z*, 1995 *R, W, I*
T Hirao 1998 *Kor*, 1999 *Tg, Sa, W*, 2001 *Tai, Sa, C*, 2004 *Kor, Rus, C, It*
T Hirata 2000 *US, C*
J Hiratsuka 1999 *US*
K Hirose 1994 *Kor*, 1995 *Tg, NZ*, 1996 *HK, HK, C, US, US, Kor*, 1998 *HK, HK, US, C, Kor, Tai, HK, Kor*, 1999 *C, Tg, Sa, Fj, US, Sp, Sa, W, Ar*, 2000 *Fj, US, Kor, C, I*, 2003 *AuA, AuA, Kor, E, E, S*, 2005 *HK, I, Sp*
T Hirose 1988 *Kor*
T Hirose 2007 *HK*
E Hirotsu 1995 *Tg*
Y Hisadomi 2002 *Rus*, 2003 *Rus, AuA, Kor, E*, 2004 *Kor, C, It, S, R*, 2005 *Sp*, 2006 *AG, Kor, Geo, Tg, It, Sa, JAB, Fj, HK, Kor*
M Hohokabe 1978 *F, Kor*
RK Holani 2008 *Kaz, HK, Fj, Sa*
K Honjo 1982 *C, C*, 1985 *US, I, F*
K Horaguchi 1979 *E, E*, 1980 *F*, 1982 *HK, C, C, Kor*, 1983 *W*, 1984 *F*, 1985 *US, I, I, F, F*, 1987 *US, E*
M Horikoshi 1988 *Kor*, 1989 *S*, 1990 *Fj, Tg, Kor, US, Kor*, 1991 *US, C, HK, I, Z*, 1992 *HK*, 1993 *Ar, Ar*, 1994 *Kor*, 1995 *Tg, R, W, I*, 1997 *C*, 1998 *C, US, Tai, HK, Kor*
S Hoshino 1975 *W*, 1976 *S*, 1978 *Kor*, 1979 *HK*
T Hosokawa 1990 *Tg, Kor, Sa, US*, 1991 *US, S, I, Z*, 1993 *Ar, Ar*
S Iburi 1972 *HK*
M Iguchi 1973 *F*, 1974 *NZU*, 1975 *A, A, W*
H Ijyuin 1932 *C, C*
W Ikeda 2004 *Kor, Rus, C, It, S, R, W*, 2005 *Sp*, 2006 *AG, Geo, Tg, It, JAB, Fj*
Y Ikeda 1980 *Kor*, 1983 *W*, 1984 *F, F*
Y Ikegaya 2008 *AG, HK*

H Ikuta 1987 *US, A, NZ*
K Imaizumi 1988 *Kor*, 1994 *Fj, HK*, 1996 *US*, 1997 *C, US, US, C*
k Imakoma 1988 *Kor*
K Imamura 1959 *BCo, BCo*
R Imamura 1959 *BCo, BCo*
Y Imamura 2006 *AG, Geo, It, Sa, Fj*, 2007 *HK, Fj, Tg, AuA, Sa, JAB, It, Fj, W, C*, 2008 *AG, Kaz, HK*
R Imazato 1969 *HK*, 1970 *Tha, BCo*, 1971 *E, E*, 1972 *HK*, 1973 *W, F*, 1975 *A, A, W, W*, 1976 *S, E, It*
T Inokuchi 2007 *It, A, W*, 2008 *AG, HK*
Y Inose 2008 *AG, Kaz, Tg, Sa*
M Inoue 1982 *C, C, Kor*
R Ishi 1999 *Sp*
K Ishii 1986 *S*
J Ishiyama 1980 *H, F, Kor*, 1982 *HK, C, Kor*, 1983 *W*, 1985 *US, I, I, F, F*
K Ishizuka 1963 *BCo*
T Ishizuka 1974 *NZU, SL*, 1975 *A, W, W*, 1978 *F, Kor*, 1979 *HK, E, E*, 1980 *H, F, Kor*, 1982 *HK, C, C, Kor*
H Ito 2004 *Kor, Rus*
M Ito 1969 *HK*
M Ito 2000 *Tg, Sa, Kor, C, I*, 2004 *Kor, C*, 2006 *AG, Kor, Geo, Tg, Sa, Fj, HK, Kor*
T Ito 1996 *HK, HK, C, US, US, C, Kor*, 1997 *HK, C, US, US*, 1998 *C, US, HK, HK, US, C, Ar, Kor, Tai, HK, Kor*, 1999 *Tg, Sa, Fj, US, Sp, Sa, W, Ar*, 2000 *I*, 2001 *Kor, W, Sa, C*, 2002 *Rus, Tg, Kor, Tai, Kor, Tai*, 2003 *US, Rus, AuA, AuA, Kor, E, E, S, F, Fj, US*, 2004 *Kor, Rus, C, It*, 2005 *Ur, Ar, R, C, I, Sp*
T Ito 1963 *BCo*, 1969 *HK*, 1970 *Tha, BCo*, 1971 *E*, 1972 *HK*, 1973 *W, F*, 1974 *NZU*
T Ito 1980 *H, F*, 1982 *HK, C, Kor*
K Iwabuchi 1997 *HK, C, US, US, C, HK*, 1998 *C, US, Ar, Tai, HK*, 1999 *C*, 2001 *Tai, W, W, Sa*, 2002 *Tg, Kor, Tai, Kor*
Y Iwama 2000 *US, Tg, Sa, Kor, C*, 2001 *Tai*
H Iwashita 1930 *BCo*
Y Izawa 1970 *Tha, BCo*, 1971 *E, E*, 1972 *HK*, 1973 *W, F*, 1974 *NZU*, 1975 *A, A, W*, 1976 *S, E, It*
K Izawa-Nakamura 1995 *Tg, Tg, I, NZ*, 1996 *US, Kor*, 1997 *HK, C, US, US, C, HK*, 1998 *Ar, Kor, Tai, HK, Kor*
JW Joseph 1999 *C, Tg, Sa, Fj, US, Sp, Sa, W, Ar*
H Kajihara 1989 *S*, 1990 *Fj, Tg, Kor, Sa, US, Kor*, 1991 *US, US, HK, S, I, Z*, 1993 *Ar, Ar*, 1994 *Fj, Fj, Kor*, 1995 *Tg, R, W, I, NZ*, 1996 *HK, HK, C, US, US, C, Kor*, 1997 *C*
S Kaleta 1992 *HK*, 1993 *Ar, Ar, W*
K Kamata 1970 *BCo*
F Kanaya 1980 *F*, 1982 *HK, C, C*, 1983 *W*, 1984 *F, F, Kor*, 1985 *US*
Kanbara 1971 *E*
H Kaneshiro 1993 *Ar*
H Kano 1974 *SL*, 1982 *Kor*
T Kasahara 1932 *C, C*
K Kasai 1999 *C*, 2005 *Ar, HK, Kor, R, C, I, I*, 2006 *AG, Tg*
Y Kasai 1985 *F, F*
Y Katakura 1959 *BCo*
A Kato 2001 *Tai*
H Kato 1993 *Ar, Ar*
D Katsuno 2002 *Kor*
T Katsuraguchi 1970 *Tha*
H Kawachi 1980 *H, Kor*, 1982 *C*, 1983 *W*, 1984 *F, F, Kor*
K Kawachi 1984 *Kor*
R Kawai 2000 *I*
K Kawasaki 1963 *BCo*
M Kawasaki 1970 *Tha*
T Kawasaki 2000 *US, Tg*
Y Kawase 1983 *W*, 1985 *US, I, I, F*, 1986 *Kor*, 1987 *A*
T Kikutani 2005 *Sp*, 2006 *AG, Kor, Geo, Tg, It, Sa, JAB, Fj, Kor*, 2008 *Kor, AG, Tg, Fj, Sa*
CW Kim 2007 *W, C*
K Kimura 1996 *C*
T Kimura 1984 *F, F, Kor*, 1985 *US*, 1986 *E, Kor*, 1987 *E, A, NZ*
T Kinashita 2002 *Tg, Kor*
T Kinoshita 1932 *C, C*
H Kiso 2001 *Kor, Tai*, 2003 *AuA, AuA, Kor, E, E, S, Fj, US*, 2004 *S, R, W*, 2005 *HK, I, Sp*, 2006 *AG, Kor, Geo, It, Sa, JAB, Fj, HK, Kor*, 2007 *Kor, Fj, AuA, A, W, C*
T Kitagawa 2006 *HK*, 2007 *HK, A*
T Kitagawa 2005 *Sp*, 2006 *AG, Kor, Tg, Sa, JAB*, 2008 *Kor, AG, Kaz, HK, Tg, Fj, Sa*
Y Kitagawa 2007 *Kor*
T Kitahara 1978 *Kor*, 1979 *HK*
H Kitajima 1963 *BCo*
T Kitano 1930 *BCo*, 1932 *C, C*
S Kitaoka 1959 *BCo*
H Kobayashi 1983 *W*, 1984 *F, Kor*, 1985 *I, F*, 1986 *Kor*
I Kobayashi 1975 *A, A, W, W*, 1976 *BCo, S, E, It, Kor*, 1977 *S*, 1978 *F, Kor*, 1979 *HK, E, E*
K Kobayashi 1959 *BCo, BCo*
K Koizumi 1997 *US, C, HK*, 2000 *Fj, US, Tg, Sa, C*, 2001 *W, C*, 2002 *Tg, Tai*
J Komura 1992 *HK*, 1998 *Kor*, 2000 *Kor, C*
GN Konia 2003 *US, AuA, AuA, F, Fj, US*
K Konishi 1986 *US, Kor*
Y Konishi 1980 *F, Kor*, 1982 *HK, Kor*, 1983 *W*, 1984 *F, F, Kor*, 1985 *US, I, I, F, F*, 1986 *US, C, S, E, Kor*, 1987 *NZ*
M Koshiyama 1984 *F, F, Kor*, 1985 *US, I, I*, 1986 *C, Kor*, 1987 *NZ, NZ*
T Kouda 1988 *Kor*
O Koyabu 1974 *SL*
K Kubo 2000 *I*, 2001 *Kor, W, Sa, C*, 2002 *Rus, Kor, Tai, Kor, Kor*, 2003 *US, Rus, E, F, Fj*, 2004 *Kor, C, It*
K Kubota 2004 *S, R, W*
T Kudo-Nakayama 1979 *E*
T Kumagae 2004 *Kor, Rus, C, It, S, R, W*, 2005 *Ur, Ar, Kor, R, C, I, I, Sp*, 2006 *AG, Kor, Geo, It, Sa, Fj*, 2007 *HK, Fj, AuA, Sa, A*
N Kumagai 1977 *S*, 1978 *F*, 1979 *HK*
M Kunda 1990 *Sa, US, Kor*, 1991 *C, HK, S, I, Z*, 1992 *HK*, 1993 *Ar, Ar, W*, 1994 *Fj, Fj, HK, Kor*, 1995 *Tg, R, W, I, NZ*, 1996 *HK, HK, C, US, US*, 1997 *HK, C, US, US*, 1998 *C, US, HK, HK, US, C, Ar, Kor, Tai, HK, Kor*, 1999 *Sa, Fj, US, Sp, Sa, W, Ar*
S Kurihara 1986 *S, E*, 1987 *E*
S Kurihara 1974 *SL*
T Kurihara 2000 *Fj, US, Tg, Sa, Kor, C*, 2001 *Kor, W, W, Sa, C*, 2002 *Rus, Tg, Kor, Tai, Kor, Tai*, 2003 *US, Rus, AuA, AuA, E, E, S, F, Fj, US*
M Kurokawa 1998 *Tai, HK, Kor*, 2000 *Fj, Tg, Sa, Kor, C*
T Kurosaka 1970 *BCo*, 1974 *SL*, 1975 *A, A, W, W*
M Kusatsu 1963 *BCo*
T Kusumi 2007 *A, W*, 2008 *Kor*
E Kutsuki 1985 *F*, 1986 *US, C, S, E*, 1987 *US, E, A, NZ, NZ*, 1989 *S*, 1990 *Fj, Tg, Kor, Sa, US, Kor*, 1991 *US, US, C, HK, S, I, Z*, 1992 *HK*, 1993 *W*, 1994 *Fj, Fj, HK*
S Latu 1993 *W*, 1994 *Fj, Fj, HK, Kor*, 1995 *Tg, R, W, I*
S Latu 1987 *US, A, NZ, NZ*, 1989 *S*, 1990 *Fj, Tg, Kor, Sa, US, Kor*, 1991 *US, C, HK, S, I, Z*, 1992 *HK*, 1993 *Ar, Ar*, 1994 *Fj, Fj, HK, Kor*, 1995 *Tg, Tg, R, W, I, NZ*
CED Loamanu 2005 *Ur, HK*, 2007 *Kor, Fj, Tg, Sa, JAB, It, Fj, W, C*, 2008 *Tg, Fj, Sa*
ET Luaiufi 1990 *Fj, Kor, US, Kor*, 1991 *US, US, C, HK, S, I, Z*
T Madea 1991 *US, C, HK*, 1995 *Tg*
HAW Makiri 2005 *Ur, Ar, HK, Kor, R, I, I*, 2006 *AG, Tg, Sa, JAB*, 2007 *Kor, Tg, AuA, Sa, JAB, It, A, Fj, W, C*, 2008 *Tg, Fj, Sa*
M Mantani 1969 *HK*, 1970 *Tha, BCo*, 1971 *E, E*, 1972 *HK*
G Marsh 2007 *AuA, Sa, JAB*
T Masuho 1991 *US, C, HK, S, I, Z*, 1993 *Ar, Ar*, 1994 *Fj, Fj, Kor*, 1995 *Tg, W*, 1996 *HK, C, US, US, C*, 1997 *HK, C, US, C, HK*, 1998 *C, US, HK, HK, US, C, Ar, Kor, Tai, HK*, 1999 *C, US, Sp, Sa*, 2000 *Fj, US, Tg, Sa, Kor, C*, 2001 *Kor, W, Sa, C*
Y Masutome 1986 *Kor*
K Matsubara 1930 *BCo*
T Matsubara 1932 *C, C*
Y Matsubara 2004 *Kor, Rus, C, It*, 2005 *Sp*, 2006 *AG, Kor, Geo, Tg, It, Sa, JAB, Fj, Kor*, 2007 *Kor, Fj, Tg, Sa, JAB, It, Fj, W, C*
T Matsuda 1992 *HK*, 1993 *W*, 1994 *Fj, HK, Kor*, 1995 *Tg*,

R, W, I, NZ, 1996 *HK, HK, C, US, US, C, Kor*, 1998 *US, HK, HK, US, C, Ar, Kor, Tai, HK, Kor*, 1999 *C, Fj, US, Sp, Sa, Ar*, 2001 *Kor, Tai, W*, 2003 *US, AuA, Kor, E, S, Fj, US*

J Matsumoto 1977 *S*, 1978 *F*, 1980 *H*, 1982 *C, C*

T Matsunaga 1985 *F, F*

Y Matsunobu 1963 *BCo*

H Matsuo 2003 *AuA, AuA, Kor, E, E*

K Matsuo 1986 *US, C, S, E, Kor*, 1987 *E, NZ*, 1988 *Kor*, 1990 *Tg, Kor, Sa, US*, 1991 *US, HK, S, I, Z*, 1993 *Ar, Ar*, 1994 *Fj, Fj, HK*, 1995 *Tg*

Y Matsuo 1974 *SL*, 1976 *BCo, E, It, Kor*, 1977 *S*, 1979 *HK, E, E*, 1982 *HK, C, C*, 1983 *W*, 1984 *F, F, Kor*

S Matsuoka 1963 *BCo*, 1970 *Tha*

F Mau 2004 *Rus, C, It, S, R, W*

AF McCormick 1996 *HK, HK, US*, 1997 *HK, C, US, US, C, HK*, 1998 *C, US, HK, Ar, Kor, Tai, HK*, 1999 *C, Tg, Sa, Fj, US, Sp, Sa, W, Ar*

R Miki 1999 *Sp*, 2002 *Tg, Tai, Kor, Tai, Kor*, 2004 *S, R, W*

A Miller 2002 *Rus, Kor, Tai, Kor, Tai*, 2003 *Kor, S, F, Fj, US*

S Miln 1998 *C, US, HK, HK, US*

Y Minamikawa 1976 *BCo*, 1978 *F, Kor*, 1979 *HK, E, E*, 1980 *H, F, Kor*, 1982 *HK, C, C, Kor*

M Mishima 1930 *BCo*, 1932 *C, C*

T Miuchi 2002 *Rus, Kor, Kor, Tai, Kor*, 2003 *US, Rus, AuA, Kor, E, E, S, F, Fj, US*, 2004 *Rus, C, It, S, R, W*, 2005 *Ur, Ar, HK, Kor, R, C, I, I*, 2006 *HK, Kor*, 2007 *Kor, HK, Fj, Tg, Sa, It, Fj, W, C*, 2008 *Kor, AG, Kaz, HK, Tg, Fj, Sa*

S Miura 1963 *BCo*

K Miyai 1959 *BCo, BCo*, 1963 *BCo*

K Miyaji 1969 *HK*

K Miyajima 1959 *BCo, BCo*

H Miyaji-Yoshizawa 1930 *BCo*

T Miyake 2005 *Sp*, 2006 *Sa, JAB, Fj*

K Miyamoto 1986 *S, E*, 1987 *US, E, A*, 1988 *Kor*, 1991 *I*

K Miyata 1971 *E, E*, 1972 *HK*

M Miyauchi 1975 *W*, 1976 *It, Kor*

K Mizobe 1997 *C*

K Mizoguchi 1997 *C*

K Mizube 1997 *HK*

H Mizuno 2004 *R*, 2005 *HK, Kor, R, C, I*, 2006 *AG, Geo, Tg, It, Sa, JAB*

M Mizutani 1970 *Tha*, 1971 *E*

N Mizuyama 2008 *Tg, Sa*

S Mori 1974 *NZU, SL*, 1975 *A, A, W, W*, 1976 *BCo, S, E, It, Kor*, 1977 *S*, 1978 *F*, 1979 *HK, E, E*, 1980 *H, F, Kor*

K Morioka 1982 *Kor*

K Morita 2004 *C, It*, 2005 *Ur, Ar, Kor, R, C, I*

A Moriya 2006 *Tg, It, Sa, JAB, Fj*, 2008 *AG, Kaz*

Y Motoki 1991 *US, US, C*, 1992 *HK*, 1993 *Ar, Ar*, 1994 *Fj, Fj, Kor*, 1995 *Tg, Tg, R, W, I, NZ*, 1996 *HK, HK, C, US, US, C, Kor*, 1997 *HK, C, US, US, C, HK*, 1998 *C, US, HK, HK, US, C, Ar, Kor, HK, Kor*, 1999 *C, Tg, Sa, Fj, US, Sp, Sa, W, Ar*, 2001 *W, W, Sa, C*, 2002 *Rus, Tg, Kor, Tai, Kor, Tai, Kor*, 2003 *Kor, E, E, S, Fj, US*, 2004 *Kor, Rus, C, It, S, R, W*, 2005 *Ur*, <EM

K Motoyoshi 2001 *Tai*

S Mukai 1985 *I, I, F*, 1986 *US, C, E, Kor*, 1987 *US, A, NZ, NZ*

M Mukoyama 2004 *Kor, C, It, S, R, W*

K Muraguchi 1976 *S, Kor*

D Murai 1985 *I, I, F, F*, 1987 *E*

K Murata 1963 *BCo*

W Murata 1991 *US, S*, 1995 *Tg, NZ*, 1996 *HK, HK, C, US, US, C, Kor*, 1997 *HK, C, US, US, HK*, 1998 *HK, HK, US, C, Ar, Kor, Kor*, 1999 *US, W*, 2001 *W, W, Sa*, 2002 *Rus, Tg, Kor, Tai, Kor, Tai*, 2003 *US, AuA, E*, 2005 *Ur, Ar, Kor, I, I*

Y Murata 1971 *E, E*, 1972 *HK*, 1973 *W*, 1974 *NZU, SL*

M Nagai 1988 *Kor*

Y Nagatomo 1993 *W*, 1994 *Fj, HK*, 1995 *Tg*, 1996 *US, US*, 1997 *C*

M Nakabayashi 2005 *HK, Kor, R, I*

T Nakai 2005 *Ur, HK, C, I, I, Sp*, 2006 *AG, Kor, Geo, Tg, It, Fj*

T Nakamichi 1996 *HK, HK, US, US, C*, 1998 *Ar, Kor*, 1999 *C, Sa, Fj, Sp, W, Ar*, 2000 *Fj, US, Tg*

N Nakamura 1998 *C, US, HK, HK, US, C, Ar, Kor, Tai, HK, Kor*, 1999 *C, Tg, Sa, Fj, US, Sp, W, Ar*, 2000 *I*

S Nakashima 1989 *S*, 1990 *Fj, Tg, Kor, Sa, US*, 1991 *US, US, C, HK, S*

T Nakayama 1976 *BCo*, 1978 *F*, 1979 *E*, 1980 *H*, 1982 *C, C*

Y Nakayama 2008 *Kor, AG, Kaz, HK, Tg*

H Namba 2000 *Fj, US, Tg, Sa, Kor, C, I*, 2001 *Tai, W, W, C*, 2002 *Rus, Tg, Kor, Tai, Kor*, 2003 *US, Rus, AuA, AuA, Kor, E, E, F*

R Nicholas 2008 *Kor, Kaz, HK, Tg, Fj, Sa*

H Nishida 1994 *Fj*

S Nishigaki 1932 *C, C*

T Nishiura 2004 *W*, 2006 *HK, Kor*, 2007 *Kor, Fj, Tg, Sa, It, Fj, W, C*, 2008 *Kor, HK, Tg, Fj, Sa*

H Nishizumi 1963 *BCo*

M Niwa 1932 *C*

I Nogami 1932 *C*

T Nozawa 2000 *Tg, Sa, Kor, C*

M Oda 2000 *US, Tg, Sa, Kor, I*

H Ogasawara 1969 *HK*, 1970 *Tha, BCo*, 1971 *E, E*, 1973 *F*, 1974 *NZU*, 1975 *A, A, W, W*, 1977 *S*

K Oguchi 1997 *US, C, HK*, 1998 *Tai*, 1999 *Sa, Ar*, 2000 *Fj, Tg, Sa, Kor*

K Ohara 1998 *Kor, Tai*, 2000 *Kor, C, I*

D Ohata 1996 *Kor*, 1997 *HK, C, US*, 1998 *HK, C, Ar, Kor, HK*, 1999 *C, Tg, Sa, Fj, US, Sp, Sa, W, Ar*, 2000 *Fj, US, Kor, C, I*, 2002 *Rus, Kor, Tai, Kor, Tai, Kor*, 2003 *US, Rus, AuA, AuA, Kor, E, E, S, F, Fj, US*, 2004 *Kor, Rus, C, It*, 2005 *Ur, Ar, HK, Kor, R, C, I, I*, 2006 *AG, Kor, Geo, Tg, HK, Kor*

K Ohigashi 1973 *W, F*, 1974 *NZU, SL*

K Ohigashi 2004 *Kor, Rus, C*, 2007 *Kor, HK, AuA, JAB*

K Ohotsuka 1959 *BCo*

S Oikawa 1980 *H*

E Okabe 1963 *BCo*

Y Okada 1932 *C, C*

M Okidoi 1987 *A, NZ, NZ*

N Okubo 1999 *Tg, Sa, Fj, US, Sp, Sa, W, Ar*, 2000 *Fj, US, Tg, Sa, Kor, C*, 2002 *Rus, Tg, Kor, Tai, Kor, Tai*, 2003 *US, Rus, S, F, Fj, US*, 2004 *S, R, W*

T Omata 1970 *BCo*

S Onishi 2000 *Fj, US, Tg, Sa, Kor, C*, 2001 *Kor, Tai, W, C*, 2005 *Sp*, 2006 *AG, Kor, Geo, Tg, It, JAB, HK, Kor*, 2007 *HK, Tg, AuA, Sa, JAB, It, Fj, W, C*, 2008 *Kor, AG, HK, Sa*

H Ono 2004 *Kor, Rus, C, S*, 2005 *Ar, Kor, I*, 2006 *Kor, Geo, It, Sa, JAB, Fj, HK, Kor*, 2007 *Kor, Fj, Tg, Sa, JAB, It, Fj, W, C*, 2008 *Kor, AG, Tg, Fj*

K Ono 2007 *Kor, AuA, JAB, It, A*

S Ono 1932 *C, C*

H Onozawa 2001 *W, Sa, C*, 2002 *Rus, Kor, Tai, Kor*, 2003 *Rus, AuA, AuA, Kor, E, E, S, F, Fj, US*, 2004 *Kor, Rus, C, It*, 2005 *Ur, Ar, HK, Kor, R, C, I, Sp*, 2006 *HK, Kor*, 2007 *Kor, Tg, AuA, JAB, A, Fj, W, C*, 2008 *Kor, AG, Kaz, HK, Tg, Fj, Sa*

S Onuki 1984 *F, F, Kor*, 1985 *US, I, I, F, F*, 1986 *US, C, S, E, Kor*, 1987 *US, E*

PD O'Reilly 2005 *Kor*, 2006 *JAB, Fj, HK, Kor*, 2007 *It, Fj, C*

G Ota 1930 *BCo*

O Ota 1986 *US, S*, 1989 *S*, 1990 *Fj, Tg, Kor, Sa, US, Kor*, 1991 *US, C, HK, S, I, Z*, 1992 *HK*, 1993 *Ar, Ar, W*, 1994 *Fj, HK, Kor*, 1995 *Tg, R, W, I, NZ*

T Otao 2004 *W*

L Oto 1992 *HK*, 1995 *R, W, I, NZ*, 1996 *C*, 1997 *C, HK*

M Oto 1972 *HK*

N Oto 2001 *Kor, Tai, W, Sa*, 2005 *Sp*, 2006 *Kor, Tg, It, Sa, JAB, Fj*, 2007 *A*

K Otukolo 2005 *HK, Kor, C*

F Ouchi 1991 *US*

H Ouchi 1990 *Kor*, 1993 *Ar, W*, 1994 *HK*

N Owashi 1992 *HK*

M Oyabu 1998 *Kor*

A Oyagi 1983 *W*, 1984 *F, F, Kor*, 1985 *US, I, I, F, F*, 1986

US, *C*, 1987 *US*, *E*, *NZ*, *NZ*, 1988 *Kor*, 1989 *S*, 1990 *Fj*, *Tg*, *Kor*, *Sa*, *US*, *Kor*, 1991 *US*, *C*, *I*, *Z*
J Oyamada 1997 *HK*, *US*
A Ozaki 2008 *Kor*, *AG*, *HK*
M Ozaki 1963 *BCo*, 1969 *HK*
H Ozeki 1996 *HK*, *HK*, *US*, *C*, *Kor*
A Parker 2002 *Rus*, *Tg*, *Kor*, *Tai*, *Kor*, *Tai*, 2003 *US*, *Rus*, *AuA*, *AuA*, *Kor*, *E*, *E*, *S*, *F*, *Fj*, *US*, 2004 *It*
R Parkinson 2003 *Rus*, *AuA*, *E*, *S*, *Fj*, 2005 *Ur*, *Ar*, *HK*, *I*, *I*
BB Robins 2007 *Kor*, *Fj*, *Tg*, *AuA*, *Sa*, *JAB*, *It*, *Fj*, *W*, *C*, 2008 *Kor*, *AG*, *Kaz*, *HK*, *Tg*, *Fj*, *Sa*
K Sagawa 1977 *S*
Y Saito 2001 *Tai*, *W*, *W*, *Sa*, *C*, 2002 *Rus*, *Kor*, *Tai*, *Kor*, 2003 *Kor*, *E*, *E*, *US*, 2004 *Kor*
M Sakamoto 1978 *F*, *Kor*, 1980 *Kor*
M Sakata 1996 *C*, *C*, *Kor*, 1997 *US*, *US*, *C*, *HK*, 1998 *HK*, 1999 *C*, *Tg*, *US*, *Sp*, *Sa*, *W*, *Ar*, 2001 *W*, *W*, *Sa*, *C*, 2002 *Rus*, *Tg*, *Kor*, *Tai*, *Kor*, 2003 *US*, *Rus*, *AuA*, *S*, *F*, *Fj*
Y Sakata 1969 *HK*, 1970 *Tha*, *BCo*, 1971 *E*, *E*, 1972 *HK*
Y Sakuraba 1986 *S*, *E*, 1987 *A*, *NZ*, *NZ*, 1988 *Kor*, 1992 *HK*, 1993 *Ar*, *Ar*, *W*, 1994 *Fj*, *HK*, *Kor*, 1995 *Tg*, *R*, *W*, *I*, *NZ*, 1996 *HK*, *Kor*, 1997 *C*, *US*, *C*, *HK*, 1998 *C*, *US*, *HK*, *HK*, *US*, *C*, *Ar*, *Kor*, *Tai*, *HK*, *Kor*, 1999 *C*, *Tg*, *Sa*, *Fj*, *W*, *Ar*
L Samurai Vatuvei 2001 *Kor*, *Tai*, *W*, *W*, *Sa*, *C*, 2002 *Rus*, *Tg*, *Kor*, *Kor*, *Tai*, 2003 *US*, *Rus*, *AuA*, 2004 *Kor*, *Rus*, *C*, *It*, 2006 *HK*, *Kor*, 2007 *It*, *A*, *C*
T Saruta 1969 *HK*
M Sasada 1976 *BCo*, *E*, *It*, *Kor*, 1977 *S*, 1979 *HK*, *E*
Y Sasada 1973 *W*, *F*
T Sasaki 2007 *HK*, *Fj*, *Tg*, *AuA*, *JAB*, *A*
K Sato 1996 *US*, *US*, *C*, 1997 *C*
T Sato 2008 *Kor*, *AG*, *Kaz*, *HK*
T Sato 2008 *AG*, *Kaz*, *HK*
T Sato 2005 *Sp*, 2006 *AG*, *Kor*, *Geo*, *Tg*, *Sa*, *Fj*, 2007 *Kor*, *AuA*
Y Sato 1994 *Fj*, 1995 *Tg*, 1996 *C*
T Sawaguchi 2002 *Kor*
K Sawaki 1998 *Ar*, *Tai*, *Kor*, 1999 *Sa*, 2004 *S*, 2006 *HK*, *Kor*
K Segawa 1982 *HK*
K Sejimo 1980 *H*, *F*, 1982 *HK*, *C*, *C*, *Kor*
K Shibata 1972 *HK*, 1973 *W*, 1974 *SL*, 1975 *A*, 1976 *BCo*, *S*, *E*
M Shichinohe 2002 *Tai*, *Kor*
S Shiga 1959 *BCo*, *BCo*
F Shimazaki 1970 *Tha*, *BCo*, 1971 *E*, *E*, 1972 *HK*, 1973 *W*, *F*
S Shimizu 1996 *Kor*
S Shimizu 1930 *BCo*
M Shimoji 1979 *HK*
S Shimomura 2004 *S*, *R*, 2007 *HK*
M Shimosono 1970 *Tha*, 1971 *E*, *E*, 1972 *HK*, 1973 *F*
Y Shinomiya 2003 *US*, *AuA*, *Kor*
K Shinozuka 2008 *Kor*, *AG*, *Kaz*, *HK*
K Shomen 2002 *Kor*, 2006 *Kor*
G Smith 1998 *C*, *US*, *HK*, *HK*, *US*, *C*, *Ar*, *Kor*, *HK*, 1999 *C*, *Tg*, *Sa*, *Fj*, *US*, *Sa*, *W*, *Ar*
T Soma 2005 *Sp*, 2006 *AG*, *Kor*, *Geo*, *Tg*, *It*, 2007 *Kor*, *HK*, *Fj*, *Tg*, *AuA*, *Sa*, *JAB*, *It*, *Fj*, *W*, *C*, 2008 *Kor*, *Kaz*, *Tg*, *Fj*, *Sa*
Y Sonoda 2000 *Fj*, *US*, *Tg*, 2001 *Tai*, *W*, *C*, 2002 *Rus*, *Kor*, 2003 *US*, *Rus*, *AuA*, *Kor*, *E*, *E*, *S*, *F*, *Fj*, *US*
H Sugarwara 2000 *Fj*, *US*, *Tg*, *I*, 2001 *Tai*, *W*
T Sugata 1998 *Kor*
H Suzuki 1930 *BCo*
G Tachikawa 1999 *C*, *Tg*, 2005 *Ur*, *Ar*, *Kor*, *R*, *C*, *I*, *I*, *Sp*, 2007 *Kor*, *Fj*, *Tg*
H Taione 1986 *US*, *C*, *S*, 1988 *Kor*
K Taira 2007 *Kor*, *Fj*, *AuA*, *A*, *Fj*, *W*, *C*, 2008 *Tg*, *Fj*
H Takafumi 1999 *Fj*
S Takagi 2005 *Ur*, *HK*, *R*, *I*, *I*
H Takahashi 2005 *Ur*, *Ar*, *Kor*, *C*, *I*
K Takahashi 1990 *Fj*, *Sa*, *Kor*, 1991 *US*, *US*, *C*, 1992 *HK*, 1993 *Ar*, *Ar*, *W*, 1994 *Fj*, *HK*, 1995 *Tg*, *W*, *NZ*, 1996 *HK*, *HK*, *C*, 1997 *US*, *C*, *HK*
T Takata 1974 *NZU*, 1975 *A*, *A*, *W*, *W*, 1976 *BCo*, *S*, *E*, *It*, *Kor*, 1977 *S*
K Takayangi 2001 *Kor*, *Tai*
K Takei 2004 *It*, 2006 *AG*, *Kor*, *Geo*, *It*, *Fj*
T Takeyama 1994 *Kor*, 1995 *Tg*
M Takura 1989 *S*, 1990 *Fj*, *Tg*, *Kor*, *Sa*, *US*, 1991 *US*, *HK*, *S*, *I*, *Z*, 1994 *Fj*, *Kor*, 1995 *Tg*, *R*, *I*
H Tamura 1998 *HK*, *US*, *C*, *Ar*, *Kor*, *Tai*, *HK*, *Kor*, 1999 *C*
F Tanaka 2008 *AG*, *HK*, *Tg*, *Fj*, *Sa*
K Tanaka 2004 *S*, *R*, *W*
N Tanaka 1974 *SL*, 1975 *A*, *W*, 1976 *BCo*, *S*, *E*, 1977 *S*, 1980 *F*, *Kor*, 1982 *HK*, *Kor*
S Tanaka 1959 *BCo*, *BCo*
N Tanifuji 1979 *HK*, *E*, *E*, 1982 *C*, *C*, 1983 *W*, 1984 *F*, *Kor*, 1985 *US*
Y Tanigawa 1969 *HK*
T Taniguchi 2006 *Tg*, *It*, *JAB*, 2008 *Kor*, *Kaz*, *HK*, *Tg*, *Fj*
H Tanuma 1996 *Kor*, 1997 *HK*, *C*, *US*, *US*, *HK*, 1998 *C*, *US*, *HK*, 1999 *Sa*, *Fj*, *US*, *Sp*, *Sa*, *W*, *Ar*, 2000 *Fj*, *US*, *Tg*, *Sa*, *Kor*, *C*, *I*, 2001 *Kor*, *Tai*, *W*, *W*, *Sa*, *C*, 2002 *Kor*, 2003 *AuA*, *E*, *F*
M Tatsukawa 2000 *Sa*
N Taumoefolau 1985 *F*, *F*, 1986 *US*, *C*, *S*, *E*, *Kor*, 1987 *US*, *E*, *A*, *NZ*, 1988 *Kor*, 1989 *S*, 1990 *Fj*
T Terai 1969 *HK*, 1970 *Tha*, 1971 *E*, *E*, 1972 *HK*, 1973 *W*, *F*, 1974 *NZU*, 1975 *A*, *W*, *W*, 1976 *S*, *E*, *It*, *Kor*
S Teramura 1930 *BCo*
LM Thompson 2007 *HK*, *Fj*, *Tg*, *Sa*, *JAB*, *It*, *Fj*, *W*, *C*, 2008 *Sa*
R Thompson 1998 *C*, *US*, *HK*, *HK*, *US*, *C*
Z Toba-Nakajima 1930 *BCo*, 1932 *C*
K Todd 2000 *Fj*, *Sa*, *I*
H Tominaga 1959 *BCo*, *BCo*
T Tomioka 2005 *I*, *I*
T Toshi 1932 *C*, *C*
H Toshima 1980 *H*, *F*, 1982 *HK*, *C*, *C*, 1984 *F*, *F*, *Kor*
N Toyoda 1982 *HK*
S Toyoda 1974 *SL*
T Toyoda 1978 *Kor*
K Toyoyama 1976 *BCo*, 1979 *E*, *E*, 1980 *H*
M Toyoyama 2000 *Fj*, *US*, *Sa*, *C*, 2001 *Kor*, *W*, *W*, *Sa*, *C*, 2002 *Rus*, *Kor*, *Tai*, *Kor*, *Tai*, 2003 *US*, *Rus*, *AuA*, *Kor*, *E*, *E*, *S*, *Fj*, *US*
M Tsuchida 1985 *F*
T Tsuchiya 1959 *BCo*, *BCo*
E Tsuji 1980 *Kor*, 1982 *Kor*
T Tsuji 2003 *S*, *Fj*, *US*, 2005 *HK*, *R*, *C*, 2006 *Kor*
Y Tsujimoto 2001 *Kor*
K Tsukagoshi 2002 *Kor*, 2005 *Ur*, *Ar*, *HK*, *Kor*, *R*, *C*, *I*, *I*
S Tsukda 2001 *Kor*, *C*, 2002 *Tg*, *Tai*, *Kor*, *Tai*, *Kor*, 2003 *AuA*, *E*
T Tsuyama 1976 *BCo*, *Kor*
P Tuidraki 1997 *HK*, *C*, 1998 *C*, *US*, *HK*, *HK*, *US*, *C*, *Tai*, 1999 *Tg*, *Sa*, *Fj*, *Sa*, *W*, *Ar*, 2000 *I*, 2001 *Tai*, *W*, *W*
M Uchida 1969 *HK*
A Ueda 1975 *W*, 1978 *Kor*, 1979 *E*, *E*
S Ueki 1963 *BCo*
N Ueyama 1973 *F*, 1974 *NZU*, *SL*, 1975 *A*, *A*, *W*, *W*, 1976 *BCo*, *E*, *It*, *Kor*, 1978 *F*, 1980 *Kor*
H Ujino 1976 *BCo*, 1977 *S*, 1978 *F*, *Kor*, 1979 *HK*, *E*, *E*, 1980 *H*, *Kor*, 1982 *HK*, *Kor*
Y Uryu 2000 *Sa*, 2001 *Kor*
K Wada 1997 *HK*, *US*, *US*, *C*, *HK*
S Wada 1930 *BCo*
T Wada 1975 *A*, 1976 *S*, 1979 *E*, *E*
J Washington 2005 *Ur*, *Ar*, *HK*, *Kor*, *R*, *C*, *I*
M Washiya 2000 *Kor*, *C*
H Watanabe 1990 *Sa*
T Watanabe 2002 *Kor*
Y Watanabe 1996 *HK*, *HK*, 1998 *C*, *US*, *HK*, *Ar*, *Kor*, *Tai*, *HK*, 1999 *C*, *Tg*, *US*, *Sp*, *Sa*, 2000 *Fj*, *US*, 2003 *Rus*, *AuA*, *AuA*, *E*, *S*, 2004 *Kor*, 2005 *HK*, *R*, *C*, 2007 *HK*, *Fj*, *Tg*, *Sa*, *JAB*, *A*, *W*
S Webb 2008 *AG*, *Kaz*, *HK*, *Tg*, *Fj*, *Sa*
IM Williams 1993 *W*
T Yagai 1930 *BCo*
T Yajima 1978 *Kor*, 1979 *E*
K Yamada 1963 *BCo*
T Yamaguchi 2004 *S*, *R*, *W*

Y Yamaguchi 1970 *Tha*, *BCo*, 1971 *E*, *E*, 1972 *HK*
E Yamamoto 2001 *Kor*, *W*, 2002 *Tg*, *Kor*
I Yamamoto 1973 *W*
M Yamamoto 2002 *Rus*, *Kor*, *Tai*, *Kor*, 2003 *Rus*, *AuA*, *AuA*, *Kor*, *E*, *E*, *Fj*, *US*, 2004 *Kor*, *Rus*, *C*, *S*, *R*, *W*, 2006 *Sa*, *JAB*, *Fj*, 2007 *HK*, *Fj*, *AuA*, *JAB*, *A*
M Yamamoto 2004 *C*, *S*, *W*, 2006 *HK*, *Kor*, 2007 *HK*, *Fj*, *Tg*, *AuA*, *Sa*
T Yamamoto 1988 *Kor*, 1989 *S*, 1990 *Fj*
R Yamamura 2002 *Tg*, *Tai*, *Tai*, 2003 *AuA*, *F*, 2004 *Kor*, *Rus*, *C*, *It*, *S*, *R*, *W*, 2005 *Ur*, *Ar*, *HK*, *Kor*, *R*, *C*, *I*, *I*, *Sp*, 2006 *Kor*, *Geo*, *It*, *Sa*, *JAB*, *Fj*, *HK*, *Kor*, 2007 *Kor*, *Tg*, *AuA*, *Sa*, *JAB*, *It*, *A*, *Fj*, *W*, *C*
T Yamaoka 2004 *It*, *S*, *R*, *W*, 2005 *Sp*, 2006 *AG*, *Kor*, *Geo*, *Tg*, *It*, *Sa*, *JAB*, *Fj*
O Yamashita 1974 *SL*
M Yasuda 1984 *F*
N Yasuda 2000 *Kor*, *I*
T Yasui 1976 *S*, *E*, 1977 *S*, 1978 *F*, *Kor*, 1979 *HK*, *E*
K Yasumi 1986 *C*, 1987 *US*, *NZ*
Y Yatomi 2006 *Kor*, 2007 *HK*, *Fj*, *Tg*, *AuA*, *Sa*, *JAB*, *A*, *Fj*
O Yatsuhashi 1996 *US*, *C*, 1998 *US*, *HK*, *HK*, *US*, *C*, *Ar*, *Tai*, *Kor*, 2000 *Kor*, *C*
A Yokoi 1969 *HK*, 1970 *Tha*, *BCo*, 1971 *E*, 1972 *HK*, 1973 *W*, *F*
A Yoshida 1995 *R*, *W*, *I*, *NZ*, 1996 *C*, *US*, *C*, *Kor*, 1997 *US*, *HK*, 1999 *Sa*, 2000 *Fj*, *US*, *Tg*, *Sa*, *Kor*, *C*
H Yoshida 2001 *Sa*, *C*, 2002 *Tg*, *Tai*, 2004 *R*, *W*, 2006 *AG*, *Kor*, *Geo*, *Tg*, *Sa*, *JAB*, *Fj*, *HK*, *Kor*
H Yoshida 2008 *Kor*, *AG*, *Kaz*
J Yoshida 1973 *W*, *F*
M Yoshida 1974 *NZU*, 1975 *A*, *A*, *W*, 1976 *BCo*, *S*, *E*, *It*, *Kor*, 1977 *S*, 1978 *F*, *Kor*
T Yoshida 2002 *Tg*, *Tai*, *Kor*, 2003 *E*
T Yoshida 2007 *Kor*, *Fj*, *Tg*, *Sa*, *It*, *Fj*, *W*, *C*, 2008 *Kor*, *Kaz*, *Tg*, *Sa*
Y Yoshida 1988 *Kor*, 1989 *S*, 1990 *Fj*, *Tg*, *Kor*, *Sa*, *US*, *Kor*, 1991 *US*, *US*, *C*, *HK*, *S*, *I*, *Z*, 1992 *HK*, 1993 *Ar*, *Ar*, *W*, 1994 *Fj*, *Fj*, *HK*, *Kor*, 1995 *Tg*, *Tg*, *R*, *I*, *NZ*, 1996 *HK*
K Yoshinaga 1986 *Kor*, 1987 *US*, *A*, *NZ*, 1990 *Sa*
K Yoshino 1973 *W*
T Yoshino 1985 *US*, *I*, *I*, *F*, *F*, 1986 *Kor*, 1987 *NZ*

NAMIBIA

NAMIBIA'S 2008 RECORD

OPPONENTS	DATE	VENUE	RESULT
Western Province	7 June	H	**Lost** 45–6
Senegal	14 June	A	**Won** 13–10
South Africa Universities	26 July	H	**Lost** 39–37
Zimbabwe	2 August	H	**Won** 35–21

THE LONG ROAD TO 2011

By Helge Schutz

Shaun Botterill/Getty Images

Namibia were courageous, committed and passionate at the Rugby World Cup.

After enthralling the rugby world with some courageous performances at the 2007 Rugby World Cup in France, Namibia nearly suffered the ignominy of being eliminated at the first hurdle during this year's qualifying stages for the 2011 World Cup.

They took on Senegal away in Dakar in their first qualifying match and just managed to win 13–10 after a late try by captain Jacques Nieuwenhuis.

Namibia were a bit more convincing in their next qualifier, beating Zimbabwe 35–21 at home to remain in contention for 2011, but overall, the promise shown in France had largely made way to the realisation that qualification would be much tougher this time around.

After Namibia's World Cup campaign came to an end, the national selectors decided to start anew with a new coaching staff.

Namibia's coach at the World Cup, Hakkies Husselmann, was not reappointed and instead two local coaches, Johan Diergaardt and

Hakkies Louw were appointed as the caretaker coaches of the national team.

At the end of March, John Williams of South Africa was appointed as the new head coach. Williams has coached at various levels in South Africa, rising to head coach of the Falcons in 2005/06, while he was a member of Namibia's technical team at the World Cup.

"My aim is to put the pride back into Namibian rugby and to start winning some trophies... My ultimate aim will be to finish amongst the top eight teams at the 2011 World Cup. But all the smaller nations have become more professional, and we will have to become semi-professional by 2011 as well," he said at his appointment.

Williams and the Namibian team were however quickly brought back down to earth when they took on Senegal in their opening World Cup qualifying match in June.

Before that, though, the NRU managed to organise a home friendly against Vodacom Western Province on June 7.

A Namibian Invitation team gave a spirited performance, but ran out of steam as Province ran in four late tries to run out 45–6 winners.

Western Province dominated possession, winning the lineouts and the scrums at will, but Namibia defended bravely until the final minutes.

Namibia's loose trio of Jacques Nieuwenhuis, Tinus du Plessis and PJ van Lill gave an excellent defensive display, but it was worrying that Namibia could not do much on the attack and could not breach the visitors' try line once.

It was evident that the backline, which included two new caps in fly-half Jaco van Zyl, and centre David Philander had little penetration, while Namibia's World Cup stars like winger Ryan Witbooi and TC Losper were also ineffective on attack.

The following week, Namibia's qualifying campaign got off to a shaky start when they had to come from behind to beat Senegal in Dakar.

Senegal held the lead for most of the match and seemed to be heading for a shock victory before a try by captain Jacques Nieuwenhuis with three minutes to go gave Namibia a late victory.

Coach Williams said the conditions in Dakar were very difficult, both on and off the pitch, but admitted that Namibia's finishing was poor.

"It was a tough game but I'm proud of the guys who managed to pull through in the end. It was quite an eye opener for us to play in

Africa where the conditions were not good, from the accommodation to the pitch, everything was below par and not what we are accustomed to," he said.

Namibia's points came via a penalty by fullback TC Losper and tries by prop Johnny Redelinghuys and Nieuwenhuis.

In July, Namibia narrowly lost 39–37 to South African Universities in a friendly match which served as preparation for the next World Cup qualifier, against Zimbabwe on August 2.

Namibia seemed to be heading for a comfortable victory when they went ahead 31–22 in the second half, but the Universities rallied strongly and fly-half Steven Jacobs scored the winning try in injury time.

Despite the defeat, Namibia gave a committed performance while several debutants made a good impression.

Chrysander Botha, who represented Namibia at the IRB Junior World Rugby Trophy competition in Chile in April, had a great debut at full-back, scoring two scintillating tries and three conversions for a personal tally of 16 points.

Right wing Luwayne Winckler marked his debut with a fine opportunistic try, while Tinus Venter gave a steady performance at centre.

Namibia scored tries through Botha (2), Jurie van Tonder, Llewellyn Winckler and Tinus du Plessis, while Botha added three conversions and TC Losper two penalties.

Mindful of their near-defeat to Senegal, Namibia selected its strongest possible side for the Zimbabwean encounter. Namibia fielded a strong pack which included World Cup stalwarts like Jane du Toit, Hugo Horn, Nico Esterhuyse, Wacca Kazombiaze and Jacques Nieuwenhuis, while Namibia's inspirational No 8 Jacques Burger was especially flown in for the match. Burger still came on as a sub for the Blue Bulls against the Falcons the previous evening, before flying to Namibia the next morning for the World Cup qualifier.

Namibia's pack applied a lot of pressure in the early stages and wore Zimbabwe down with strong scrumming and driving mauls.

Zimbabwe's defence finally succumbed to the pressure midway through the first half when they infringed in the scrum and the referee awarded a penalty try to Namibia, which was converted by fullback Chrysander Botha.

Namibia's forwards kept up their relentless pressure, and they ran in three more first half tries through fly-half Jaco van Zyl, flanker Tinus du Plessis and centre Tinus Venter, all converted by Botha for a comfortable 28–0 half time lead.

Namibia seemed to be heading for a big score, but it was a different story in the second half.

First Zimbabwean centre Paul Stark cut through Namibia's backline for a try that he converted himself and then substitute Costa Dinha crashed over for a try from a maul which Stark once again converted.

With the score at 28–14 Zimbabwe were on the verge of a remarkable comeback and winger Gerald Sibanda led the charge with an attack down the left wing. But Burger showed tremendous pace to haul him in with a great try-saving tackle about five metres from the tryline.

Namibia however stretched their lead when substitute hooker Shaun Esterhuizen scored from a counterattack, while Zimbabwean substitute Manasa Sita scored in injury time after an intercept, to make the final score 35–21 in Namibia's favour.

Coach Williams expressed his satisfaction after the game, but admitted that the players relaxed too much in the second half.

"We did very well in the first half and had at least three more try scoring opportunities that we did not take. But the players were more relaxed in the second half and took their foot off the pedal, while their fitness was not up to standard," he said.

"But overall I am satisfied with the performance. We dominated the tight exchanges and one could see that the professional players made a

Julian Finney/Getty Images

Namibian fans will be hoping to follow their team at the World Cup in 2011, after a testing qualification process.

big difference. I am not so concerned about playing attractive rugby at the moment, I am just concerned about the result at this stage," he added.

The victory put Namibia through to the semi-finals of the African qualifying competition, which will be contested in 2009.

They were joined in the semi-finals by Uganda who beat Madagascar 32–22 in Kampala to top Pool D; Tunisia, who beat Kenya 44–15 in Tunis to proceed from Pool C; and the Ivory Coast who shocked Morocco with a 21–9 victory in Casablanca to top Pool A.

Meanwhile, the IRB increased Namibia's annual grant after an IRB delegation met the NRU in Windhoek at the beginning of August.

Three executive members of the IRB, Bruce Cook, Alan Solomons and Cliffie Booysen held talks with the NRU which resulted in increased financial assistance for the NRU, amounting to about £1 million over four years.

This amount included support for High Performance of the national team (eg specialised coaching and preparation of national players) and local development programmes (eg training of referees, coaching of coaches and coaching clinics, as well as regional competitions.)

Namibia's performance at the World Cup largely contributed to the increase of the High Performance fund.

On the domestic scene, the MTC Premier League expanded from six to nine clubs, with Jaguars from Windhoek, Kudus from Walvis Bay and the northern town of Grootfontein competing amongst the elite for the first time.

These teams made use of their opportunity in the top flight and provided some memorable upsets throughout the season.

Kudus set the tone with a shock 28–24 home victory against powerhouses Wanderers on the opening day of the season on March 29, while they beat United 10–0 on July 5.

Jaguars also pulled off a stunning 23–19 victory against Western Suburbs on August 2 and then beat the University of Namibia (Unam) 26–23 two weeks later.

By mid-September the defending champions Reho Falcon were leading the log, followed closely by Wanderers and Western Suburbs. Traditional powerhouse, United, had a disappointing season and were battling it out with Rehoboth, Unam and Kudus for the final semifinal spot.

At junior level, Namibia's U20 team competed in the IRB Junior World Trophy in Chile in April.

Namibia lost its opening two matches, losing 28–26 to Romania and 20–6 to the hosts, Chile, before they won their final match, beating the Cook Islands 25–14.

Namibia then beat Korea 36–29 in the fifth place play-off. By finishing fifth, Namibia failed to gain automatic entry into the 2009 tournament and had to once again compete in the Confederation of African Rugby Youth Cup, which took place in Tunisia in August.

Namibia beat Morocco 15–5 and Kenya 26–19 to qualify for the final where they beat Zimbabwe 16–13. It was the second successive year that Namibia had beaten Zimbabwe in the African qualifiers, following their 23–20 victory in Kampala, Uganda in 2007.

NAMIBIA INTERNATIONAL RECORDS

UP TO 30TH SEPTEMBER 2008

WINNING MARGIN

Date	Opponent	Result	Winning Margin
15/06/2002	Madagascar	112–0	**112**
21/04/1990	Portugal	86–9	**77**
27/05/2006	Kenya	82–12	**70**
26/05/2007	Zambia	80–10	**70**

MOST POINTS IN A MATCH BY THE TEAM

Date	Opponent	Result	Pts.
15/06/2002	Madagascar	112–0	**112**
21/04/1990	Portugal	86–9	**86**
31/08/2003	Uganda	82–13	**82**
27/05/2006	Kenya	82–12	**82**

MOST TRIES IN A MATCH BY THE TEAM

Date	Opponent	Result	Tries
15/06/2002	Madagascar	112–0	**18**
21/04/1990	Portugal	86–9	**16**
17/10/1999	Germany	79–13	**13**

MOST CONVERSIONS IN A MATCH BY THE TEAM

Date	Opponent	Result	Cons
15/06/2002	Madagascar	112–0	**11**
21/04/1990	Portugal	86–9	**11**
31/08/2003	Uganda	82–13	**11**
27/05/2006	Kenya	82–12	**11**

MOST PENALTIES IN A MATCH BY THE TEAM

Date	Opponent	Result	Pens
22/06/1991	Italy	33–19	**5**
23/01/1998	Portugal	36–19	**5**
30/06/1990	France A	20–25	**5**

MOST DROP GOALS IN A MATCH BY THE TEAM

1 on 7 Occasions

MOST POINTS IN A MATCH BY A PLAYER

Date	Player	Opponent	Pts.
06/07/1993	Jaco Coetzee	Kenya	**35**
26/05/2007	Justinus van der Westhuizen	Zambia	**33**
21/04/1990	Moolman Olivièr	Portugal	**26**
15/06/2002	Riaan van Wyk	Madagascar	**25**

MOST TRIES IN A MATCH BY A PLAYER

Date	Player	Opponent	Tries
21/04/1990	Gerhard Mans	Portugal	**6**
15/06/2002	Riaan van Wyk	Madagascar	**5**
16/05/1992	Eden Meyer	Zimbabwe	**4**
16/08/2003	Melrick Africa	Kenya	**4**

MOST CONVERSIONS IN A MATCH

BY A PLAYER

Date	Player	Opponent	Cons
21/04/1990	Moolman Olivier	Portugal	11
27/05/2006	Morne Schreuder	Kenya	11
26/05/2007	Justinus van der Westhuizen	Zambia	9

LEADING CONVERSIONS SCORERS

Name	Cons
Jaco Coetzee	84
Morne Schreuder	36
Rudi van Vuuren	26

MOST PENALTIES IN A MATCH

BY A PLAYER

Date	Player	Opponent	Pens
22/06/1991	Jaco Coetzee	Italy	5
23/01/1998	Rudi van Vuuren	Portugal	5
30/06/1990	Shaun McCulley	France A	5

LEADING PENALTY SCORERS

Name	Pens
Jaco Coetzee	46
Morne Schreuder	18
Rudi van Vuuren	14

MOST DROP GOALS IN A MATCH

BY A PLAYER

1 on 7 Occasions

LEADING DROP GOAL SCORERS

Name	DGs
Jaco Coetzee	3

MOST CAPPED PLAYERS

Name	Caps
Herman Lindvelt	32
Jaco Coetzee	28
Casper Derks	28

LEADING POINTS SCORERS

Name	Pts.
Jaco Coetzee	344
Morne Schreuder	146
Gerhard Mans	118
Rudi van Vuuren	109

LEADING TRY SCORERS

Name	Tries
Gerhard Mans	27
Eden Meyer	21
Melrick Africa	12

NAMIBIA INTERNATIONAL PLAYERS

UP TO 30TH SEPTEMBER 2008

Note: Years given for International Championship matches are for second half of season; eg 1972 means season 1971–72. Years for all other matches refer to the actual year of the match. Entries in square brackets denote matches played in RWC Finals.

MJ Africa 2003 *Sa, Ken, Uga, Ar, I, A,* 2005 *Mad, Mor,* 2006 *Ken, Tun, Ken, Tun, Mor, Mor,* 2007 *Za, Geo, R, Uga, SA, I, F, Ar, Geo*
W Alberts 1991 *Sp, Pt, It, It, Z, Z, I, I, Z, Z, Z,* 1995 *Z,* 1996 *Z, Z*
H Amakali 2005 *Mad*
J Augustyn 1991 *Z,* 1998 *Iv, Mor, Z*
RS Bardenhorst 2007 *Geo, R*
J Barnard 1990 *Z, Pt, W, W, F, F,* 1991 *Sp, Pt, It, It, Z, Z, I, I, Z, Z, Z,* 1992 *Z, Z*
D Beukes 2000 *Z, Ur,* 2001 *Z, Z*
E Beukes 1990 *Z, F, WGe*
J Beukes 1994 *Z, Mor,* 1995 *Z*
AJ Blaauw 1996 *Z, Z,* 1997 *Tg,* 1998 *Pt, Tun, Z, Iv, Mor, Z,* 1999 *Z, Fj, F, C, Ger,* 2000 *Z, Z, Ur,* 2001 *It,* 2003 *Ar, I, A, R,* 2004 *Mor*
J Bock 2005 *Mad, Mor*
JH Bock 2005 *Mad, Mor,* 2006 *Ken, Tun, Ken, Tun, Mor, Mor,* 2007 *Za, R, SA, I, F, Ar, Geo*
J Booysen 2003 *Sa, Ken, Ar, A,* 2007 *Uga*
M Booysen 1993 *W, AG, Z,* 1994 *Rus, Z, HK,* 1996 *Z, Z*
LW Botes 2006 *Ken, Mor,* 2007 *Za, Geo, R, Uga, SA, F*
Botha 2008 *Z*
HP Botha 2000 *Z, Z, Ur*
H Breedt 1998 *Tun, Z*
H Brink 1992 *Z, Z,* 1993 *W, Ken, Z,* 1994 *Rus, Z, Iv, Mor, HK*
J Britz 1996 *Z*
B Buitendag 1990 *W, W, F, F, WGe,* 1991 *Sp, Pt, It, It, Z, Z, I, I, Z, Z, Z,* 1992 *Z, Z,* 1993 *W, AG, Ken, Z*
J Burger 2004 *Za, Ken, Z, Mor,* 2006 *Tun, Tun, Mor, Mor,* 2007 *Za, Geo, R, SA, I, F, Ar, Geo,* 2008 *Z*
B Calitz 1995 *Z*
C Campbell 2008 *Z*
DJ Coetzee 1990 *Pt, W, F, F, WGe,* 1991 *Sp, Pt, It, It, Z, Z, I, I, Z, Z, Z,* 1992 *Z, Z,* 1993 *W, AG, Ken, Z,* 1994 *Z, Iv, Mor, HK,* 1995 *Z, Z*
JC Coetzee 1990 *W*
M Couw 2006 *Ken*
B Cronjé 1994 *Rus*
J Dames 1998 *Tun, Z*
D de Beer 2000 *Z*
S de Beer 1995 *Z,* 1997 *Tg,* 1998 *Tun, Z, Iv, Mor, Z,* 1999 *Ger*
H de Waal 1990 *Z, Pt*
N de Wet 2000 *Ur*
R Dedig 2004 *Mor, Za, Ken, Z, Mor*
CJH Derks 1990 *Z, Pt, W, W, F, F, WGe,* 1991 *Sp, Pt, It, It, Z, Z, I, I, Z, Z, Z,* 1992 *Z, Z,* 1993 *W, AG, Z,* 1994 *Rus, Z, Iv, Mor, HK*
J Deysel 1990 *Z, Pt, W, W,* 1991 *Sp, Pt, It, It, Z, Z, I, I, Z, Z, Z,* 1992 *Z*
V Dreyer 2002 *Z,* 2003 *Ar, I*
J Drotsky 2006 *Ken*
I du Plessis 2005 *Mor*
M du Plessis 2001 *Z,* 2005 *Mor*
N du Plessis 1993 *Ken,* 1994 *Rus,* 1995 *Z*
T du Plessis 2006 *Ken, Tun, Mor, Mor,* 2007 *Geo, R, Uga, SA, I, F, Ar, Geo,* 2008 *Z*
P du Plooy 1992 *Z, Z,* 1994 *Z, Mor, HK*
S du Rand 2007 *Geo, R, Uga*
JA du Toit 2007 *Za, Geo, R, Uga, SA, I, F, Geo,* 2008 *Z*
N du Toit 2002 *Tun,* 2003 *Sa, Ar, I, A, R*
V du Toit 1990 *Pt, W, W, F*
JH Duvenhage 2000 *Z, Z,* 2001 *It, Z, Z,* 2002 *Mad,* 2003 *Sa, Uga, Ar, I, R,* 2007 *Za, R, Uga*
A Engelbrecht 2000 *Z*
J Engelbrecht 1990 *WGe,* 1994 *Rus, Z, Iv, Mor, HK,* 1995 *Z, Z*
N Engelbrecht 1996 *Z*
H Engels 1990 *F, WGe*
E Erasmus 1997 *Tg*
N Esterhuize 2006 *Ken, Tun, Mor,* 2007 *Za, Geo, R, Uga, SA, I, F, Ar, Geo,* 2008 *Z*
G Esterhuizen 2008 *Z*
SF Esterhuizen 2008 *Z*
D Farmer 1997 *Tg,* 1998 *Pt, Iv, Mor, Z,* 1999 *Z, Fj, Ger*
F Fisch 1999 *Z, Ger*
S Furter 1999 *Z, Fj, F, C, Ger,* 2001 *It,* 2002 *Mad, Z, Tun, Tun,* 2003 *Sa, Ken, Uga, Ar, I, A, R,* 2004 *Mor,* 2006 *Ken, Tun, Ken*
E Gaoab 2005 *Mad, Mor*
I Gaya 2004 *Za, Ken*
J Genis 2000 *Z, Z, Ur,* 2001 *Z*
N Genis 2006 *Mor*
R Gentz 2001 *It*
R Glundeung 2006 *Ken*
CJ Goosen 1991 *Sp, Pt, It, It,* 1993 *W*
D Gouws 2000 *Z, Z, Ur,* 2001 *It, Z, Z*
T Gouws 2003 *Ken, Uga,* 2004 *Za, Ken,* 2006 *Ken, Tun*
A Graham 2001 *It, Z, Z,* 2002 *Mad, Tun,* 2003 *Ken, Uga, I,* 2004 *Mor*
A Greeff 1997 *Tg*
D Grobelaar 2008 *Z*
DP Grobler 2001 *Z,* 2002 *Mad, Tun, Tun,* 2003 *Sa, Ken, Uga, Ar, I, A, R,* 2004 *Mor, Za, Ken, Z, Mor,* 2006 *Ken, Tun, Ken,* 2007 *Za, Geo, R, SA, Ar*
HJ Grobler 1990 *Z, Pt, W, W, F, F, WGe,* 1991 *Sp, Pt, It, It, Z, Z, I, I, Z, Z, Z,* 1992 *Z, Z*
T Grünewald 1990 *Z*
D Grunschloss 2003 *A, R*
F Hartung 1996 *Z, Z*
L Holtzhausen 1997 *Tg,* 1998 *Pt, Tun, Z, Iv, Mor, Z,* 1999 *Ger*
F Horn 2005 *Mad, Mor,* 2006 *Ken*
H Horn 1997 *Tg,* 1998 *Pt, Iv, Mor, Z,* 1999 *Z, Fj, F, C, Ger,* 2001 *It,* 2002 *Mad, Z, Tun,* 2003 *Sa,* 2007 *Za, Geo, R, Uga, SA, I, F, Ar, Geo,* 2008 *Z*
K Horn 1997 *Tg,* 1998 *Pt*
Q Hough 1995 *Z, Z,* 1998 *Pt, Tun, Z, Iv, Mor, Z,* 1999 *Z, Fj, F, C*
D Husselman 1993 *AG,* 1994 *Z, Mor,* 2002 *Mad, Z, Tun,* 2003 *Sa, Ar, I, A*
JJ Husselman 2004 *Za, Ken*
E Isaacs 1993 *Ken,* 1994 *Iv*
P Isaacs 2000 *Z, Z, Ur,* 2001 *Z, Z,* 2003 *A,* 2005 *Mad, Mor*
E Izaacs 1998 *Pt,* 1999 *Z, Ger,* 2000 *Z, Z, Ur,* 2001 *It, Z, Z,* 2002 *Mad, Z, Tun, Tun,* 2003 *Sa, Ken, Ar, A, R*
M Jacobs 1999 *Z, Fj, F, Ger*
E Jansen 2006 *Ken*
EA Jantjies 2006 *Ken, Tun, Ken, Tun,* 2007 *Za, Geo, R, Uga, SA, I, F, Ar, Geo,* 2008 *Z*

R Jantjies 1994 *HK*, 1995 *Z*, *Z*, 1996 *Z*, 1998 *Pt*, *Tun*, *Iv*, *Mor*, *Z*, 1999 *Z*, *Fj*, *F*, *C*, 2000 *Z*, *Z*
M Jeary 2003 *Uga*, 2004 *Ken*, *Z*, *Mor*
R Jeary 2000 *Z*, *Ur*
D Jeffrey 1990 *F*
J Jenkins 2002 *Mad*, *Tun*, 2003 *Ken*
D Kamonga 2004 *Mor*, *Za*, *Ken*, *Z*, *Mor*, 2007 *Uga*, *Geo*
M Kapitako 2000 *Z*, *Z*, 2001 *It*, *Z*, *Z*, 2003 *Uga*, 2004 *Za*, 2006 *Tun*
M Katjiuanjo 2005 *Mad*, *Mor*
M Kazombiaze 2006 *Ken*, *Tun*
U Kazombiaze 2006 *Ken*, *Tun*, *Mor*, *Mor*, 2007 *Za*, *Uga*, *SA*, *I*, *F*, *Ar*, *Geo*, 2008 *Z*
DPW Koen 2006 *Tun*
A Kotze 1991 *Z*, *Z*, *I*, *I*, 1993 *W*, *AG*, *Z*
D Kotze 1993 *W*, *AG*, *Ken*, *Z*, 1994 *Rus*, *HK*
J Kotze 1995 *Z*, *Z*, 1996 *Z*, *Z*, 2000 *Z*, *Z*, 2001 *It*, *Z*, *Z*, 2002 *Mad*, *Z*, *Tun*, *Tun*, 2004 *Za*, *Ken*, *Z*, *Mor*
P Kotze 2001 *It*
P Kotze 1996 *Z*
L Kotzee 2008 *Z*
JL Kruger 2001 *It*, *Z*, *Z*
R Kruger 2003 *Ken*, *Uga*, 2005 *Mad*, *Mor*
R Kruger 2004 *Mor*, *Za*, *Ken*, *Mor*
SO Lambert 2000 *Z*, *Ur*, 2001 *It*, *Z*, *Z*, 2003 *Ken*, *Uga*, 2004 *Mor*, 2005 *Mad*, 2006 *Ken*, *Tun*, *Ken*
B Langenhoven 2007 *SA*, *I*, *F*, *Ar*, *Geo*, 2008 *Z*
G Lensing 2002 *Mad*, *Z*, *Tun*, *Tun*, 2003 *Sa*, *Ar*, *I*, *A*, *R*, 2004 *Mor*, 2006 *Ken*, *Mor*, *Mor*, 2007 *R*, *SA*, *I*, *F*, *Ar*, *Geo*
C Lesch 2005 *Mad*, *Mor*
HD Lindvelt 1998 *Iv*, *Z*, 1999 *F*, *C*, *Ger*, 2001 *It*, *Z*, *Z*, 2002 *Mad*, *Z*, *Tun*, *Tun*, 2003 *Sa*, *Ken*, *Uga*, *Ar*, *I*, *A*, 2004 *Mor*, *Za*, *Ken*, *Z*, *Mor*, 2006 *Ken*, *Tun*, *Mor*, *Mor*, 2007 *Za*, *Geo*, *SA*, *F*, *Ar*
J Lombaard 1996 *Z*
H Loots 1990 *Z*
J Losper 2005 *Mor*
S Losper 1990 *Z*, *Pt*, *W*, *W*, *F*, *F*, *WGe*, 1991 *Sp*, *Pt*, *It*, *It*, *Z*, *Z*, *I*, *I*, *Z*, *Z*, *Z*
TC Losper 2007 *Za*, *Geo*, *R*, *Uga*, *SA*, *I*, *F*
W Lötter 1990 *Z*
RC Loubser 1999 *F*, 2005 *Mad*, *Mor*
O Louw 1993 *Ken*, *Z*, 1994 *Z*, *Iv*, 1996 *Z*
M MacKenzie 2004 *Mor*, 2006 *Ken*, *Tun*, 2007 *Uga*, *I*, *F*, *Ar*
B Malgas 1991 *Z*, *Z*, *Z*, 1993 *W*, *AG*, *Ken*, *Z*, 1994 *Rus*, *Z*, *Iv*, *Mor*, *HK*, 1995 *Z*, *Z*, 1996 *Z*
G Mans 1990 *Z*, *Pt*, *W*, *W*, *F*, 1991 *Sp*, *Pt*, *It*, *It*, *Z*, *Z*, *I*, *I*, *Z*, *Z*, *Z*, 1992 *Z*, *Z*, 1993 *W*, *AG*, *Ken*, *Z*, 1994 *Rus*, *Z*, *Iv*, *Mor*, *HK*
M Marais 1992 *Z*, 1993 *W*, *AG*, *Z*
W Maritz 1990 *Z*, 1991 *Z*, *Z*, *I*, *I*, *Z*, *Z*, *Z*
S McCulley 1990 *W*, *W*, *F*, *WGe*
E Meyer 1991 *Sp*, *Pt*, *It*, *It*, *Z*, *Z*, *I*, *I*, *Z*, *Z*, *Z*, 1992 *Z*, *Z*, 1993 *W*, 1994 *Z*, *Iv*, *Mor*, *HK*, 1995 *Z*, *Z*, 1996 *Z*
H Meyer 2004 *Za*, *Ken*, *Z*, *Mor*
JM Meyer 2003 *Ken*, *Uga*, *Ar*, *I*, *R*, 2006 *Ken*, *Tun*, *Tun*, *Mor*, *Mor*, 2007 *Uga*, *SA*, *I*, *F*, *Ar*, *Geo*
P Meyer 2005 *Mad*
DA Mouton 1999 *Z*, *Fj*, *Ger*, 2000 *Z*, *Z*, *Ur*, 2002 *Mad*, *Z*, *Tun*, 2003 *Sa*, *Ken*, *Uga*, *Ar*, *I*, *A*, *R*, 2004 *Mor*, 2005 *Mad*, *Mor*, 2006 *Tun*, *Ken*, *Tun*, *Mor*, 2007 *Ar*
H Mouton 2000 *Z*
P Mouton 2005 *Mad*, *Mor*
H Neethling 1993 *Ken*
G Nel 2006 *Mor*, *Mor*
S Nell 2000 *Z*, *Z*
J Nienaber 1998 *Pt*, *Tun*, *Z*, *Mor*, *Z*
J Nieuwenhuis 2007 *Za*, *Geo*, *R*, *Uga*, *SA*, *I*, *F*, *Geo*, 2008 *Z*
J Olivier 1999 *Z*, *Fj*, *Ger*, 2000 *Z*, *Z*, *Ur*
M Olivier 1990 *Pt*, *F*
LT Oosthuizen 1990 *Z*, *Pt*, *W*, *W*, *F*, *F*, *WGe*
J Opperman 1999 *Z*, *Fj*, *F*, *C*, *Ger*
T Opperman 2002 *Mad*, *Z*
WJ Otto 1993 *AG*, *Z*, 1994 *Rus*
R Pedro 1998 *Z*, 1999 *Ger*, 2000 *Ur*, 2001 *It*, *Z*, *Z*, 2003 *Sa*, *Ken*, *Uga*, *Ar*, *I*, *A*, *R*, 2004 *Mor*
F Pienaar 2006 *Ken*
L Plaath 2001 *It*, *Z*, *Z*
CJ Powell 2001 *It*, *Z*, *Z*, 2002 *Mad*, *Z*, *Tun*, *Tun*, 2003 *Sa*, *Ken*, *Uga*, *Ar*, *I*, *R*, 2004 *Mor*, *Ken*, *Z*, *Mor*, 2006 *Ken*, *Tun*, *Tun*, *Mor*, *Mor*, 2007 *Za*, *Geo*, *R*, *Ar*, *Geo*
JH Redelinghuys 2006 *Ken*, *Tun*, *Mor*, 2007 *Za*, *Geo*, *R*, *Uga*, *SA*, *I*, *F*, *Ar*, *Geo*, 2008 *Z*
C Redlinghaus 2001 *It*
H Reinders 1996 *Z*
G Rich 1993 *W*
C Roets 1995 *Z*
P Rossouw 2004 *Za*, *Ken*, *Z*, *Mor*, 2005 *Mad*, *Mor*, 2006 *Mor*, *Mor*, 2007 *Za*, *Geo*, *R*
A Samuelson 1995 *Z*, 1996 *Z*, *Z*, 1997 *Tg*, 1998 *Pt*, *Tun*, *Z*, *Iv*, *Mor*, *Z*, 1999 *Z*, *Fj*, *F*, *C*, *Ger*
M Schreuder 2002 *Mad*, *Z*, *Tun*, *Tun*, 2003 *Sa*, *Ken*, *Uga*, *I*, *A*, *R*, 2004 *Mor*, *Za*, *Ken*, *Z*, *Mor*, 2006 *Ken*, *Ken*, 2007 *Ar*, *Geo*
C Schumacher 1995 *Z*
JH Senekal 1998 *Iv*, *Mor*, *Z*, 1999 *Z*, *Fj*, *F*, *C*, *Ger*, 2002 *Mad*, *Z*, 2003 *Sa*, *Ken*, *Uga*, *Ar*, *I*, *A*, *R*, 2005 *Mad*, 2006 *Ken*, *Mor*, *Mor*, 2007 *Geo*, *R*, *Uga*, *I*, *Ar*, *Geo*
A Skinner 1990 *Z*, *Pt*, *W*, *W*, *F*, *F*, *WGe*
G Smit 1990 *F*
E Smith 1998 *Tun*, *Iv*, *Mor*, *Z*, 1999 *Fj*, *F*, *C*, 2002 *Mad*
P Smith 1993 *Ken*, 1994 *Iv*, 1995 *Z*, *Z*
S Smith 1990 *Pt*, *W*, *W*, *F*, 1992 *Z*, *Z*, 1993 *W*, *AG*, *Ken*, *Z*, 1994 *Rus*, *Z*, *Iv*, *Mor*, *HK*, 1996 *Z*
W Smith 2002 *Mad*, *Z*, *Tun*
D Snyders 2003 *Uga*, 2005 *Mad*
H Snyman 1990 *F*, *F*, 1991 *Sp*, *Pt*, *It*, *It*, *Z*, *Z*, *I*, *I*, *Z*, *Z*, *Z*, 1992 *Z*, *Z*, 1993 *W*, *AG*, *Ken*, *Z*, 1994 *Z*, *Iv*, *Mor*, *HK*, 1995 *Z*, *Z*, 1996 *Z*, *Z*
M Snyman 1994 *Rus*, *Z*, *Iv*, *Mor*, *HK*
D Spangenberg 2005 *Mad*, *Mor*
A Steenkamp 1994 *Iv*, *Mor*
C Steenkamp 2007 *Uga*
T Steenkamp 1992 *Z*, *Z*, 1993 *Ken*, 1994 *Rus*, *Iv*, 1995 *Z*, 1996 *Z*, 1998 *Pt*, *Tun*, *Z*
P Steyn 1996 *Z*, *Z*, 1997 *Tg*, 1998 *Pt*, *Tun*, *Z*, *Iv*, *Mor*, 1999 *Z*, *Fj*, *F*, *C*
A Stoop 1990 *Z*, *Pt*, *W*, 1991 *Sp*, *Pt*, *It*, *It*, *Z*, *I*, *I*, *Z*
L Stoop 1994 *Iv*
G Suze 2005 *Mad*
N Swanepoel 2003 *Ken*, *Ar*, *I*, *A*, *R*, 2004 *Mor*, *Za*, *Ken*, *Z*, *Mor*
H Swart 1995 *Z*, 1996 *Z*, 1997 *Tg*, 1998 *Pt*, *Tun*, *Z*
JL Swart 1990 *F*, *WGe*
BM Swartz 1990 *W*, *W*, *F*, *F*, *WGe*
R Theart 1998 *Pt*
J Theron 1998 *Iv*, *Mor*, *Z*, 1999 *Fj*, *F*, *C*, *Ger*, 2004 *Mor*
RHR Thompson 2004 *Za*, *Ken*, *Mor*, 2005 *Mad*, 2006 *Ken*, *Tun*, *Ken*, *Tun*, *Mor*, *Mor*
D Tredoux 2001 *Z*
H Undveld 2006 *Ken*
L van Coller 1993 *AG*, *Ken*, 1994 *Rus*, *Iv*
GE van der Berg 2005 *Mor*, 2006 *Ken*, *Tun*, *Tun*, *Mor*
L van der Linde 2006 *Tun*
A van der Merwe 1990 *Pt*, *W*, *W*, *F*, *F*, *WGe*, 1991 *Sp*, *Pt*, *It*, *It*, *Z*, *Z*, *I*, *I*, *Z*, *Z*, *Z*, 1992 *Z*, *Z*
D van der Merwe 1990 *WGe*
S van der Merwe 1997 *Tg*, 1998 *Iv*, *Mor*, *Z*, 1999 *Z*, *Fj*, *F*, *C*, 2002 *Z*, *Tun*, *Tun*, 2003 *Sa*, *Ken*, *Ar*, *I*, *A*, *R*, 2004 *Za*, *Ken*, *Z*, *Mor*, 2006 *Tun*, *Mor*
J van der Westhuizen 2007 *Za*, *Geo*
L van Dyk 1998 *Tun*, *Z*, *Iv*, *Mor*, *Z*, 1999 *Fj*, *F*, *C*, *Ger*, 2002 *Mad*
JA van Lill 2002 *Mad*, *Tun*, *Tun*, 2003 *Sa*, *Ar*, *I*, *A*, *R*, 2004 *Mor*, 2006 *Tun*, 2007 *Za*
PJ van Lill 2006 *Ken*, 2008 *Z*
F van Rensburg 1995 *Z*, 1996 *Z*, *Z*, 1997 *Tg*, 1998 *Tun*, *Z*, 1999 *Z*, *Fj*, *F*, *C*, *Ger*, 2000 *Z*, 2001 *It*, *Z*, *Z*
SJ van Rensburg 1998 *Z*, *Iv*, *Mor*, *Z*, 1999 *Z*, *Fj*, *F*, *Ger*, 2000 *Z*, *Ur*
S van Rooi 2003 *Uga*, *A*, 2004 *Mor*, 2005 *Mor*

A van Rooyen 1991 *Sp, Pt, It, It, I,* 1992 *Z, Z*
M van Rooyen 1996 *Z,* 1998 *Pt, Tun, Z, Mor, Z,* 1999 *Z, F, C*
C van Schalkwyk 1993 *AG, Z*
A Van Tonder 1995 *Z*
CJ van Tonder 2002 *Tun,* 2003 *Sa, Ken, Uga, I, A, R,* 2004 *Mor, Za, Ken, Z, Mor,* 2006 *Ken, Ken,* 2007 *Za*
JH van Tonder 2004 *Mor, Ken, Z, Mor,* 2006 *Ken, Tun,* 2007 *Uga, SA, I, F, Ar, Geo,* 2008 *Z*
N van Vuuren 1993 *AG*
RJ van Vuuren 1997 *Tg,* 1998 *Pt, Tun, Z,* 1999 *Z, Ger,* 2000 *Z, Z, Ur,* 2002 *Mad, Z,* 2003 *Ken, Uga, R*
A van Wyk 1993 *W, Ken,* 1994 *Iv, HK*
G van Wyk 1999 *Z, Fj, F, C,* 2000 *Z, Z, Ur,* 2001 *It*
L van Wyk 2004 *Mor*
R van Wyk 2004 *Za, Ken, Z, Mor*
R van Wyk 2002 *Mad, Z, Tun, Tun,* 2003 *Sa,* 2004 *Mor, Za, Ken, Z, Mor*
P van Zyl 2007 *SA, I, F, Ar, Geo,* 2008 *Z*
R van Zyl 1997 *Tg,* 1998 *Tun, Z, Iv, Mor, Z*
T Venter 2003 *Uga,* 2004 *Mor,* 2008 *Z*
D Vermaak 1998 *Z*
JJ Vermaak 1990 *Pt,* 1994 *Rus,* 1996 *Z*
B Vermeulen 1995 *Z*
D Vermeulen 1996 *Z, Z,* 1997 *Tg,* 1998 *Pt*
G Vermeulen 1991 *Z*
M Visser 2007 *Za, Geo, R, Uga, SA, Ar, Geo*
P von Wielligh 1991 *It, Z,* 1992 *Z,* 1993 *AG, Z,* 1994 *Iv, Mor,* 1995 *Z,* 1996 *Z*
G Walters 2008 *Z*
W Wentzel 1991 *Z, Z*
E Wessels 2002 *Tun, Tun,* 2003 *Sa, Ar, I, A, R,* 2006 *Tun, Mor, Mor,* 2007 *SA, I, F*
Winkler 2008 *Z*
RC Witbooi 2004 *Za, Z,* 2005 *Mor,* 2006 *Ken, Tun, Ken,* 2007 *Za, Geo, R, Uga, I, F, Geo*
J Wohler 2005 *Mad, Mor*
J Zaayman 1997 *Tg,* 1998 *Pt, Tun, Z, Iv, Mor, Z,* 1999 *Z, Fj, F, C, Ger*

Dave Rogers/Getty Images

Jurie van Tonder, in Rugby World Cup action for Namibia.

NEW ZEALAND

NEW ZEALAND'S 2008 TEST RECORD

OPPONENTS	DATE	VENUE	RESULT
Ireland	7 June	H	**Won** 21–11
England	14 June	H	**Won** 37–20
England	21 June	H	**Won** 44–12
South Africa	5 July	H	**Won** 19–8
South Africa	12 July	H	**Lost** 28–30
Australia	26 July	A	**Lost** 19–34
Australia	2 August	H	**Won** 39–10
South Africa	16 August	A	**Won** 19–0
Samoa	3 September	H	**Won** 101–14
Australia	13 September	A	**Won** 28–24

HENRY REPAYS THE FAITH

Ross Land / Getty Images

There was plenty for the All Blacks to shout about in 2008

There are few debates in world rugby as contentious or as fierce as that which rages when the All Blacks begin the heavily-scrutinised search for a new head coach and so it was in 2007 as New Zealand poured over the wreckage of their World Cup campaign and turned their thoughts to the appointment of the man to lead them into 2008 and beyond.

The incumbent – Graham Henry – was forced to re-apply for the top job after his side's quarter-final defeat to France at the Millennium Stadium in October 2007 but as the NZRU met in December to discuss their options, it seemed certain they would draw a line under Henry's successful but ultimately tainted reign.

For many it was presumed a new man would be in charge by the time Ireland and England arrived in the land of the long white cloud the following June. A New Zealand coach had never held onto his position in the immediate wake of failing to lift the Webb Ellis trophy and with the highly-regarded Crusaders coach Robbie Deans, the Hurricanes' Colin Cooper and the Chiefs' Ian Foster on the shortlist of possible replacements, they were not short of alternative choices.

What followed stunned much of the Kiwi rugby fraternity. Deans was the hot favourite with a glittering track record with the Crusaders in the Super-14 but the NZRU opted for continuity and reappointed Henry, handing the 61-year-old a new, two-year contract. His record of 42 wins in 48 Tests, a hat-trick of Tri-Nations titles and a whitewash of the British & Irish Lions in 2005 had saved him, while Deans went across the Tasman to coach Australia.

NZRU acting Chairman Mike Eagle said the New Zealand Board was very impressed with the interviews and discussions with all four candidates, which underscored the depth of coaching talent in New Zealand rugby.

"At the end of the process, the Board concluded that Graham Henry was the best candidate for the position," he said.

"We are all disappointed not to have won the Rugby World Cup. In that regard, the NZRU Board accepts it was jointly responsible and accountable for the result and the planning that went into the campaign. We are committed to learning the key lessons."

Eagle said the appointment decision was based on Graham's remarkable results over a four-year tenure.

"Graham's record, both on and off the field, is among the best in All Blacks rugby history. He has set a very high standard in coaching, player management, and integration with the wider New Zealand rugby community. We believe that in the best interests of New Zealand rugby, Graham and his team were the right choice."

"I'm very grateful for the chance to continue," Henry confessed as he faced the media after the announcement. "We have been a strong and successful team over the last few years but we were hugely disappointed we didn't bring the World Cup back for New Zealanders.

"We have learnt lessons from this campaign and we now look forward to being able to build on those learnings and the experience we have. But I would hope that we continue to try to push out the boundaries of how the game is played, which will be exciting and stimulating for the players."

The first major challenge facing Henry was that of rebuilding his squad. The team's failure in France was the catalyst for a player exodus to clubs in Europe and the lucrative contracts on offer and leading lights such as Luke McAllister, Carl Hayman, Aaron Mauger, Chris Jack, Anton Oliver, Byron Kelleher and Doug Howlett all decided to effectively bring the curtain down on their international careers and head north. The NZRU refused to countenance changing their policy of picking non resident players and Henry began the process of replenishing the ranks.

The first game of the new All Black season saw them cross swords with Ireland in Wellington in early June and only six of the side who had started against France in the World Cup quarter-final were in the starting XV for the clash at the Westpac Stadium.

Freezing conditions and heavy rain made a spectacle of running rugby impossible but it was New Zealand who adapted to the difficult conditions better and eventually saw off the challenge of a tenacious Irish side.

Wing Sitiveni Sivivatu scored a fine early try but Ireland hit back midway through the first-half through Paddy Wallace and it required a typically abrasive score from Ma'a Nonu after 64 minutes to see off the tourists and set up a 21–11 win.

The following week England were the opposition in Auckland for the first of a two-Test series. The visitors arrived with a young, inexperienced squad and a caretaker manager, in Rob Andrew, but the All Blacks' disjointed performance against Ireland led some to predict a rare English victory on Kiwi soil.

The pre-match predictions seemed to hold water when Olly Barkley landed two early penalties to give the tourists a 6–3 lead but it was as close as they got to the All Blacks, who began to find their rhythm and eventually cut the English to shreds.

New Zealand's ability to strike off first phase possession was deadly and reflected the way they had studied the attritional style of the Guinness Premiership.

Centre Conrad Smith began the demolition job with New Zealand's first try, Dan Carter added a second before the break and further scores from Mils Muliaina and Sivivatu settled the contest. England helped themselves to a late consolation try but the Kiwis' superiority could not be denied and they ran out 37–20 winners.

"In no way can we get too comfortable," said Carter after the game. "We'll have to pick it up and play better next week. England will head down to Christchurch with self-belief they can really put us under pressure after that performance."

Despite Carter's charitable analysis of the tourists' performance, the second Test at the Jade Stadium served only to emphasise the gulf between the two sides and once debutant Richard Kahui had sliced through the white defence, it was a procession for Henry's team. Carter, Nonu, Sione Lauaki and Jimmy Cowan all helped themselves to tries and England were simply blown away.

“When you win 44–12, it’s not a bad result,” Henry argued. “It’s a pretty good England side but you just have to enjoy the moment, enjoy the occasion but recognise we have some work to do.

“We’re scoring tries from the set piece, which is very positive, but there is a lot to work on at the breakdown. I think we got better defensively as the game went on but there is still some work to do there though. We’re not where we want to be yet.”

There was little time for Henry to iron out the perceived imperfections in his side’s display. A fortnight later, the All Blacks began the defence of their Tri-Nations crown against the Springboks in Wellington. The victories over Ireland and England had been encouraging but Henry was acutely aware he would be judged on his team’s results against southern hemisphere opposition.

The ubiquitous rain in Wellington transformed the Springboks game into a war of attrition and while both sides were able to muster a try apiece through Jerome Kaino and Bryan Habana respectively, the match was settled by the battle between the two kickers and Carter’s four successful penalties gave the All Blacks a hard-fought 19–8 victory and in the process handed South Africa their first defeat since being crowned world champions. They won without skipper Richie McCaw, injured against England, coach Henry handing the captain’s armband to Rodney So’oialo.

“This was a very important match for us,” said So’oialo. “We worked very hard for this all week and we got the result we wanted. The first 15 minutes of the second half were crucial. They were hard to crack but we managed to get on top and to stay there.”

A week later in Dunedin in the rematch, the game appeared to be following a similar script as New Zealand led the Springboks 28–23 in the closing minutes at Carisbrook, only for the Kiwis to be stunned by a superb solo try by scrum-half Ricky Januarie, which was converted to give South Africa a 30–28 triumph and their first win in New Zealand for a decade. It also brought to an end the All Blacks’ record of 30 consecutive home wins and was South Africa’s first win in Dunedin after 87 years of trying!

“We showed lot of skill in the second-half and we just didn’t get enough points in the finish,” Henry said. “It was a marvellous game of rugby but a disappointing result.

“I am deeply proud of our guys. They showed huge attitude and played the best half of rugby this year after half-time. Unfortunately we didn’t quite clinch it, but these guys will have grown from this experience.”

Worse was to follow a fortnight later when the team crossed the Tasman Sea to face Australia in Sydney.

The All Blacks had not lost back-to-back Tests in four years but found the Wallabies in irresistible form in the Telstra Stadium. The Kiwis scored three tries but Australia created four of their own and emerged 34–19 winners, to pour the pressure on coach Henry's shoulders, especially as Australia were now being coached by Robbie Deans.

With two defeats from three Tri-Nations games, the pressure on Henry was phenomenal but his side rescued him in the next game when the Wallabies headed to Eden Park for the return match.

A clearly more determined All Blacks were in no mood to suffer a hat-trick of reverses and two tries apiece from Tony Woodcock and Nonu were enough to dispatch Australia 39–10.

"We certainly weren't happy after last week," admitted returning skipper McCaw, proving just how valuable the Crusader is to this side. "It's not very nice when you know you have been out-muscled and the boys have been hurting all week. When you lose two in a row, it's a measure of how you get back on the horse and we can't afford to go back. We have to continue on from here and get better."

The captain and his team-mates were certainly true to his word. New Zealand flew to South Africa for their fifth game of the campaign and although the Springboks battled bravely for the first hour, the Kiwis

Sandra Mu / Getty Images

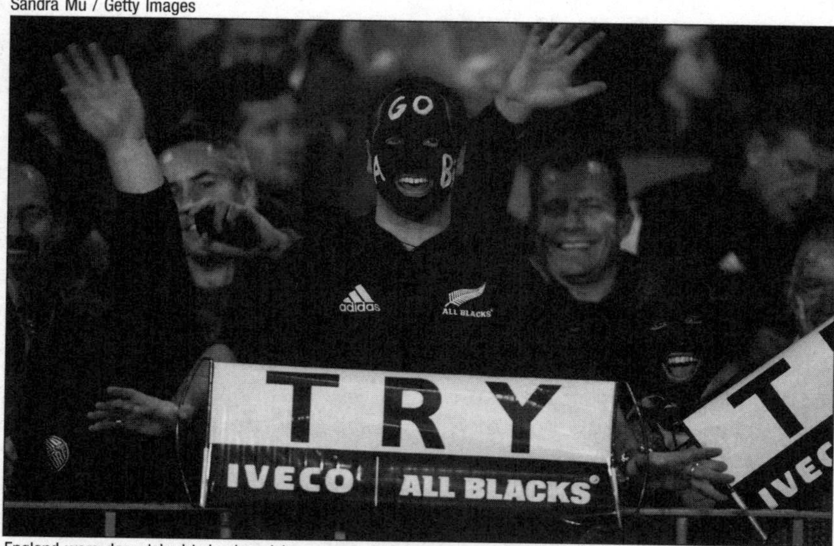

England were despatched twice in quick succession, in June

pulled away in the last 20 minutes with tries from Carter and Keven Mealamu to record a 19–0 win.

The victory set up a Tri-Nations title decider with Australia in Brisbane in September, a month away. A friendly against Samoa at the Yarrow Stadium 10 days before the big showdown kept the Kiwis in the groove and a hat-trick from Muliaina was the pick of their 101–14 rout of the South Sea Islanders. It was now time for the moment of truth in the Suncorp Stadium.

The match began at a frenetic pace and it was New Zealand who drew first blood with a Muliaina try. The Wallabies stormed back with scores from Adam Ashley-Cooper and James Horwill in quick succession either side of the break but the All Blacks were not behind for long and effectively settled the contest in an effervescent 17-minute second-half burst in which they crossed three times through Woodcock, substitute Piri Weepu and Carter. Australia ensured a grandstand finish when Ryan Cross scored late on but the Kiwis held firm as the partisan crowd bayed for one last push and at the final whistle New Zealand were 28–24 to the good.

Victory gave Henry and his side an unprecedented fourth consecutive Tri-Nations title and after the uncertainty and controversy that had surrounded his reappointment, was arguably his greatest achievement at the All Black helm.

"It's a very sweet feeling," the coach said. "This is the fourth Tri-Nations the guys have won in a row and the Bledisloe Cup. A large number of new guys hadn't played in this competition before. Everybody feels like they contributed. The guys that came on all made a difference, they all increased our intensity and our skill level."

McCaw is staying put in New Zealand, and coach Henry is relieved to know that although Dan Carter will move to Perpignan for the early part of 2008 he will only miss a Super 14 campaign and not any Test matches. He was imperious in the victory that brought the Tri-Nations title and stood like a colossus over the tournament, along with McCaw when the flanker was fit.

Carter went on to pay tribute to the Class of 2008, who could easily have folded following two successive victories. But they showed exactly how good they are by bouncing back with an improbable four successive wins to lift the Tri-Nations trophy and Bledisloe Cup.

"It's right up there for the team and me individually. I've been pretty lucky through my career to have these trophies right from my first year. This definitely ranks right up there, a pretty new look side with a lot of new faces," Carter said.

Cameron Spencer / Getty Images

New Zealand ended the Tri-Nations with a win over Australia

"The way we started the Tri-Nations with a couple of losses, we had our backs against the wall and to fight back with three very big wins is great for this bunch of guys."

NEW ZEALAND INTERNATIONAL STATISTICS

MATCH RECORDS UP TO 30TH SEPTEMBER 2008

MOST CONSECUTIVE TEST WINS

17 1965 SA 4, 1966 BI 1,2,3,4, 1967 A,E,W,F,S, 1968 A 1,2, F 1,2,3, 1969 W 1,2

15 2005 A 1, SA 2, A 2, W,I E,S, 2006 I 1,2, Arg, A 1, SA 1, A 2, 3, SA 2

12 1988 A 3, 1989 F 1,2, Arg 1,2, A,W,I, 1990 S 1,2, A 1,2

MOST CONSECUTIVE TESTS WITHOUT DEFEAT

Matches	Wins	Draws	Periods
23	22	1	1987 to 1990
17	17	0	1965 to 1969
17	15	2	1961 to 1964
15	15	0	2005 to 2006

MOST POINTS IN A MATCH

BY THE TEAM

Pts.	Opponent	Venue	Year
145	Japan	Bloemfontein	1995
108	Portugal	Lyons	2007
102	Tonga	Albany	2000
101	Italy	Huddersfield	1999
101	Samoa	N Plymouth	2008
93	Argentina	Wellington	1997
91	Tonga	Brisbane	2003
91	Fiji	Albany	2005
85	Romania	Toulouse	2007
76	Italy	Marseilles	2007
74	Fiji	Christchurch	1987
73	Canada	Auckland	1995
71	Fiji	Albany	1997
71	Samoa	Albany	1999

BY A PLAYER

Pts.	Player	Opponent	Venue	Year
45	S D Culhane	Japan	Bloemfontein	1995
36	T E Brown	Italy	Huddersfield	1999
33	C J Spencer	Argentina	Wellington	1997
33	A P Mehrtens	Ireland	Dublin	1997
33	D W Carter	British/Irish	Wellington	2005
33	N J Evans	Portugal	Lyons	2007
32	T E Brown	Tonga	Albany	2000
30	M C G Ellis	Japan	Bloemfontein	1995
30	T E Brown	Samoa	Albany	2001
29	A P Mehrtens	Australia	Auckland	1999
29	A P Mehrtens	France	Paris	2000
29	L R MacDonald	Tonga	Brisbane	2003
29	D W Carter	Canada	Hamilton	2007

MOST TRIES IN A MATCH

BY THE TEAM

Tries	Opponent	Venue	Year
21	Japan	Bloemfontein	1995
16	Portugal	Lyons	2007
15	Tonga	Albany	2000
15	Fiji	Albany	2005
15	Samoa	N Plymouth	2008
14	Argentina	Wellington	1997
14	Italy	Huddersfield	1999
13	U S A	Berkeley	1913
13	Tonga	Brisbane	2003
13	Romania	Toulouse	2007
12	Italy	Auckland	1987
12	Fiji	Christchurch	1987

BY A PLAYER

Tries	Player	Opponent	Venue	Year
6	M C G Ellis	Japan	Bloemfontein	1995
5	J W Wilson	Fiji	Albany	1997
4	D McGregor	England	Crystal Palace	1905
4	C I Green	Fiji	Christchurch	1987
4	J A Gallagher	Fiji	Christchurch	1987
4	J J Kirwan	Wales	Christchurch	1988
4	J T Lomu	England	Cape Town	1995
4	C M Cullen	Scotland	Dunedin	1996
4	J W Wilson	Samoa	Albany	1999
4	J M Muliaina	Canada	Melbourne	2003
4	S W Sivivatu	Fiji	Albany	2005

MOST CONVERSIONS IN A MATCH

BY THE TEAM

Cons	Opponent	Venue	Year
20	Japan	Bloemfontein	1995
14	Portugal	Lyons	2007
13	Tonga	Brisbane	2003
13	Samoa	N Plymouth	2008
12	Tonga	Albany	2000
11	Italy	Huddersfield	1999
10	Fiji	Christchurch	1987
10	Argentina	Wellington	1997
10	Romania	Toulouse	2007
9	Canada	Melbourne	2003
9	Italy	Marseilles	2007
8	Italy	Auckland	1987
8	Wales	Auckland	1988
8	Fiji	Albany	1997
8	Italy	Hamilton	2003
8	Fiji	Albany	2005

BY A PLAYER

Cons	Player	Opponent	Venue	Year
20	S D Culhane	Japan	Bloemfontein	1995
14	N J Evans	Portugal	Lyons	2007
12	T E Brown	Tonga	Albany	2000
12	L R MacDonald	Tonga	Brisbane	2003
11	T E Brown	Italy	Huddersfield	1999
10	G J Fox	Fiji	Christchurch	1987
10	C J Spencer	Argentina	Wellington	1997
9	D W Carter	Canada	Melbourne	2003
8	G J Fox	Italy	Auckland	1987
8	G J Fox	Wales	Auckland	1988
8	A P Mehrtens	Italy	Hamilton	2002

MOST DROPPED GOALS IN A MATCH

BY THE TEAM

Drops	Opponent	Venue	Year
3	France	Christchurch	1986

BY A PLAYER

Drops	Player	Opponent	Venue	Year
2	O D Bruce	Ireland	Dublin	1978
2	F M Botica	France	Christchurch	1986
2	A P Mehrtens	Australia	Auckland	1995

MOST PENALTIES IN A MATCH

BY THE TEAM

Pens	Opponent	Venue	Year
9	Australia	Auckland	1999
9	France	Paris	2000
7	Western Samoa	Auckland	1993
7	South Africa	Pretoria	1999
7	South Africa	Wellington	2006
7	Australia	Auckland	2007
6	British/Irish Lions	Dunedin	1959
6	England	Christchurch	1985
6	Argentina	Wellington	1987
6	Scotland	Christchurch	1987
6	France	Paris	1990
6	South Africa	Auckland	1994
6	Australia	Brisbane	1996
6	Ireland	Dublin	1997
6	South Africa	Cardiff	1999
6	Scotland	Murrayfield	2001
6	South Africa	Christchurch	2004
6	Australia	Sydney	2004
6	South Africa	Dunedin	2008

BY A PLAYER

Pens	Player	Opponent	Venue	Year
9	A P Mehrtens	Australia	Auckland	1999
9	A P Mehrtens	France	Paris	2000
7	G J Fox	Western Samoa	Auckland	1993
7	A P Mehrtens	South Africa	Pretoria	1999
7	D W Carter	South Africa	Wellington	2006
7	D W Carter	Australia	Auckland	2007
6	D B Clarke	British/Irish Lions	Dunedin	1959
6	K J Crowley	England	Christchurch	1985
6	G J Fox	Argentina	Wellington	1987
6	G J Fox	Scotland	Christchurch	1987
6	G J Fox	France	Paris	1990
6	S P Howarth	South Africa	Auckland	1994
6	A P Mehrtens	Australia	Brisbane	1996
6	A P Mehrtens	Ireland	Dublin	1997
6	A P Mehrtens	South Africa	Cardiff	1999
6	A P Mehrtens	Scotland	Murrayfield	2001
6	D W Carter	South Africa	Dunedin	2008

Phil Walter / Getty Images

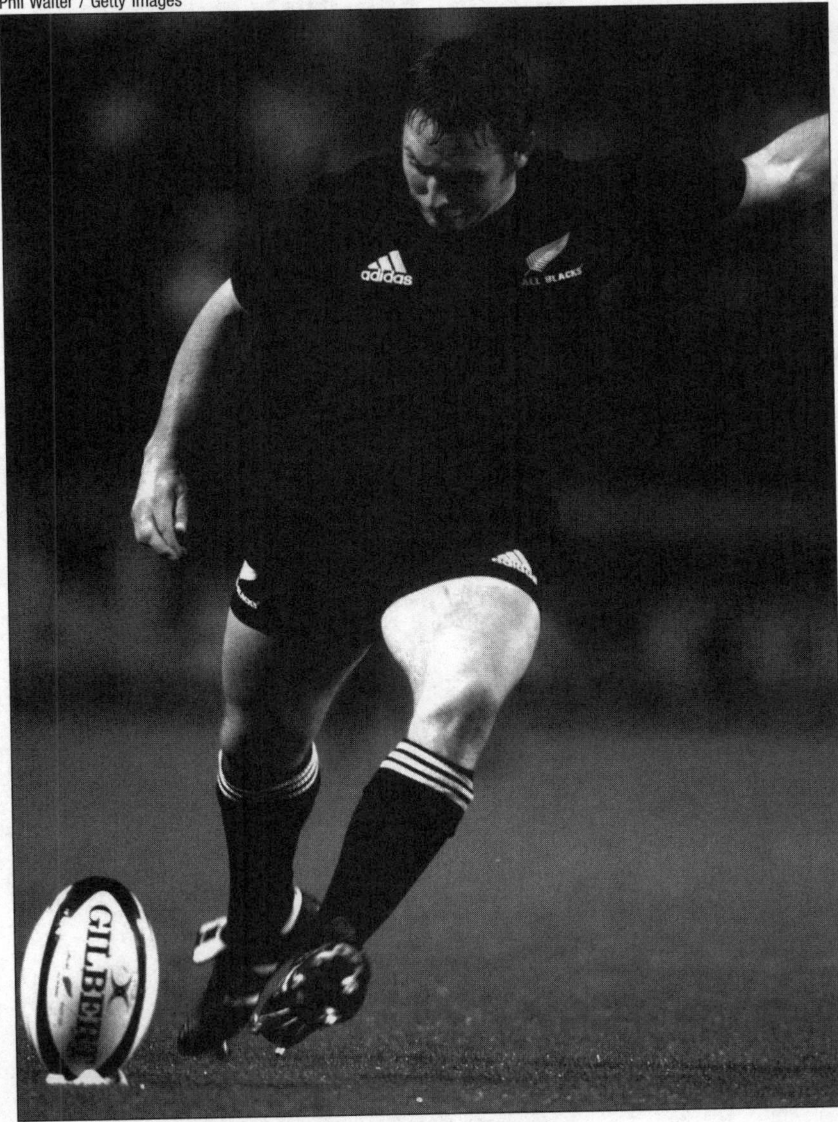

Andrew Mehrtens' record of nine penalties in a match is still a Kiwi record

CAREER RECORDS

MOST CAPPED PLAYERS

Caps	Player	Career Span
92	S B T Fitzpatrick	1986 to 1997
81	J W Marshall	1995 to 2005
79	I D Jones	1990 to 1999
74	J F Umaga	1997 to 2005
70	A P Mehrtens	1995 to 2004
67	C R Jack	2001 to 2007
65	R H McCaw	2001 to 2008
65	J M Muliaina	2003 to 2008
65	G M Somerville	2000 to 2008
63	J J Kirwan	1984 to 1994
63	J T Lomu	1994 to 2002
62	R M Brooke	1992 to 1999
62	D C Howlett	2000 to 2007
60	C W Dowd	1993 to 2001
60	J W Wilson	1993 to 2001
60	K F Mealamu	2002 to 2008
59	A D Oliver	1997 to 2007
58	G W Whetton	1981 to 1991
58	Z V Brooke	1987 to 1997
58	C M Cullen	1996 to 2002
57	B T Kelleher	1999 to 2007
56	O M Brown	1992 to 1998
56	L R MacDonald	2000 to 2008
56	A J Williams	2002 to 2008
55	C E Meads	1957 to 1971
55	F E Bunce	1992 to 1997
55	M N Jones	1987 to 1998

MOST CONSECUTIVE TESTS

Tests	Player	Career span
63	S B T Fitzpatrick	1986 to 1995
51	C M Cullen	1996 to 2000
49	R M Brooke	1995 to 1999
41	J W Wilson	1996 to 1999
40	G W Whetton	1986 to 1991

MOST TESTS AS CAPTAIN

Tests	Player	Career span
51	S B T Fitzpatrick	1992 to 1997
30	W J Whineray	1958 to 1965
29	R H McCaw	2004 to 2008
23	R D Thorne	2002 to 2007
22	T C Randell	1998 to 2002
21	J F Umaga	2004 to 2005
19	G N K Mourie	1977 to 1982
18	B J Lochore	1966 to 1970
17	A G Dalton	1981 to 1985

MOST POINTS IN TESTS

Points	Player	Tests	Career
967	A P Mehrtens	70	1995 to 2004
825	D W Carter	54	2003 to 2008
645	G J Fox	46	1985 to 1993
291	C J Spencer	35	1997 to 2004
245	D C Howlett	62	2000 to 2007
236	C M Cullen	58	1996 to 2002
234	J W Wilson	60	1993 to 2001
215	J T Rokocoko	48	2003 to 2007
207	D B Clarke	31	1956 to 1964
201	A R Hewson	19	1981 to 1984
185	J T Lomu	63	1994 to 2002
185	J F Umaga	74	1997 to 2005

MOST TRIES IN TESTS

Tries	Player	Tests	Career
49	D C Howlett	62	2000 to 2007
46	C M Cullen	58	1996 to 2002
44	J W Wilson	60	1993 to 2001
43	J T Rokocoko	48	2003 to 2007
37	J T Lomu	63	1994 to 2002
37*	J F Umaga	74	1999 to 2005
35	J J Kirwan	63	1984 to 1994
25	D W Carter	54	2003 to 2008
24	J W Marshall	81	1995 to 2005
23	S W Sivivatu	30	2005 to 2008
22	J M Muliaina	65	2003 to 2008
20	F E Bunce	55	1992 to 1997
19	S S Wilson	34	1977 to 1983
19*	T J Wright	30	1986 to 1991

* Umaga and Wright's hauls each include a penalty try

MOST CONVERSIONS IN TESTS

Cons	Player	Tests	Career
169	A P Mehrtens	70	1995 to 2004
149	D W Carter	54	2003 to 2008
118	G J Fox	46	1985 to 1993
49	C J Spencer	35	1997 to 2004
43	T E Brown	18	1999 to 2001
33	D B Clarke	31	1956 to 1964
32	S D Culhane	6	1995 to 1996

MOST PENALTY GOALS IN TESTS

Penalties	Player	Tests	Career
188	A P Mehrtens	70	1995 to 2004
132	D W Carter	54	2003 to 2008
128	G J Fox	46	1985 to 1993
43	A R Hewson	19	1981 to 1984
41	C J Spencer	35	1997 to 2004
38	D B Clarke	31	1956 to 1964
24	W F McCormick	16	1965 to 1971

MOST DROPPED GOALS IN TESTS

Drops	Player	Tests	Career
10	A P Mehrtens	70	1995 to 2004
7	G J Fox	46	1985 to 1993
5	D B Clarke	31	1956 to 1964
5	M A Herewini	10	1962 to 1967
5	O D Bruce	14	1976 to 1978

TRI-NATIONS RECORDS

RECORD	DETAIL	HOLDER	SET
Most points in season	179	in six matches	2006
Most tries in season	17	in four matches	1997
	17	in four matches	2003
	17	in six matches	2006
Highest Score	55	55-35 v S Africa (h)	1997
Biggest win	37	43-6 v Australia (h)	1996
Highest score conceded	46	40-46 v S Africa (a)	2000
Biggest defeat	21	7-28 v Australia (a)	1999
Most points in matches	328	A P Mehrtens	1996 to 2004
Most points in season	99	D W Carter	2006
Most points in match	29	A P Mehrtens	v Australia (h) 1999
Most tries in matches	16	C M Cullen	1996 to 2002
Most tries in season	7	C M Cullen	2000
Most tries in match	3	J T Rokocoko	v Australia (a) 2003
	3	D C Howlett	v Australia (h) 2005
Most cons in matches	37	D W Carter	2003 to 2008
Most cons in season	14	D W Carter	2006
Most cons in match	4	C J Spencer	v S Africa (h) 1997
	4	A P Mehrtens	v Australia (a) 2000
	4	A P Mehrtens	v S Africa (a) 2000
	4	C J Spencer	v S Africa (a) 2003
	4	D W Carter	v S Africa (a) 2006
	4	D W Carter	v Australia (a) 2008
Most pens in matches	82	A P Mehrtens	1996 to 2004
Most pens in season	21	D W Carter	2006
Most pens in match	9	A P Mehrtens	v Australia (h) 1999

MISCELLANEOUS RECORDS

RECORD	HOLDER	DETAIL
Longest Test Career	E Hughes/C E Meads	1907-21/1957-71
Youngest Test Cap	J T Lomu	19 yrs 45 days in 1994
Oldest Test Cap	E Hughes	40 yrs 123 days in 1921

CAREER RECORDS OF NEW ZEALAND INTERNATIONAL PLAYERS (UP TO 30TH SEPTEMBER 2008)

PLAYER BACKS	DEBUT	CAPS	T	C	P	D	PTS
D W Carter	2003 v W	54	25	149	132	2	825
Q J Cowan	2004 v It	17	2	0	0	0	10
S R Donald	2008 v E	6	1	8	0	0	21
A M Ellis	2006 v E	10	2	0	0	0	10
N J Evans	2004 v E	16	5	30	6	0	103
R L Gear	2004 v PI	19	11	0	0	0	55
R D Kahui	2008 v E	6	3	0	0	0	15
B G Leonard	2007 v F	9	2	0	0	0	10
C L McAlister	2005 v BI	22	7	23	13	0	120
L R MacDonald	2000 v S	56	15*	25	7	0	146
A J D Mauger	2001 v I	45	13	8	1	2	90
J M Muliaina	2003 v E	65	22	0	0	0	110
M A Nonu	2003 v E	28	7	0	0	0	35
J T Rokocoko	2003 v E	48	43	0	0	0	215
S W Sivivatu	2005 v Fj	30	23	0	0	0	115
C G Smith	2004 v It	21	10	0	0	0	50
I Toeava	2005 v S	17	6	0	0	0	30
A T Tuitavake	2008 v I	5	0	0	0	0	0
P A T Weepu	2004 v W	24	5	1	1	0	30
R N Wulf	2008 v E	4	0	0	0	0	0

FORWARDS							
I F "John" Afoa	2005 v I	9	0	0	0	0	0
A F Boric	2008 v E	7	0	0	0	0	0
D J Braid	2002 v W	4	1	0	0	0	5
C D Dermody	2006 v I	3	1	0	0	0	5
J J Eaton	2005 v I	10	1	0	0	0	5
R A Filipo	2007 v C	3	0	0	0	0	0
A K Hore	2002 v E	35	4	0	0	0	20
C R Jack	2001 v Arg	67	5	0	0	0	25
J Kaino	2006 v I	11	2	0	0	0	10
S T Lauaki	2005 v Fj	17	3	0	0	0	15
R H McCaw	2001 v I	65	13	0	0	0	65
M C Masoe	2005 v W	20	3	0	0	0	15
K F Mealamu	2002 v W	60	9	0	0	0	45
K J O'Neill	2008 v SA	1	0	0	0	0	0
G P Rawlinson	2006 v I	4	0	0	0	0	0
J A C Ryan	2005 v Fj	9	0	0	0	0	0
J E Schwalger	2007 v C	2	1	0	0	0	5
G M Somerville	2000 v Tg	65	1	0	0	0	5
R So'oialo	2002 v W	51	6	0	0	0	30
A J Thomson	2008 v I	7	1	0	0	0	5
B C Thorn	2003 v W	20	2	0	0	0	10
N S Tialata	2005 v W	27	1	0	0	0	5
A J Williams	2002 v E	56	7	0	0	0	35
T D Woodcock	2002 v W	45	5	0	0	0	25

NB MacDonald's figures include a penalty try awarded against South Africa in 2001.

NEW ZEALAND INTERNATIONAL PLAYERS

UP TO 30TH SEPTEMBER 2008

Note: Years given for International Championship matches are for second half of season; eg 1972 means season 1971-72. Years for all other matches refer to the actual year of the match. Entries in square brackets denote matches played in RWC Finals.

Abbott, H L (Taranaki) 1906 F
Afoa, I F (Auckland) 2005 I,S, 2006 E(R), 2008 I1,SA2,A1(R),2(R),SA3(R),A3(R)
Aitken, G G (Wellington) 1921 SA 1,2
Alatini, P F (Otago) 1999 F 1(R), [It, SA 3(R)], 2000 Tg, S 1, A 1, SA 1, A 2, SA 2, It, 2001 Sm, Arg 1, F, SA 1, A 1, SA 2, A 2
Allen, F R (Auckland) 1946 A 1,2, 1947 A 1,2, 1949 SA 1,2
Allen, M R (Taranaki, Manawatu) 1993 WS (t), 1996 S 2 (t), 1997 Arg 1(R),2(R), SA 2(R), A 3(R), E 2, W (R)
Allen, N H (Counties) 1980 A 3, W
Alley, G T (Canterbury) 1928 SA 1,2,3
Anderson, A (Canterbury) 1983 S, E, 1984 A 1,2,3, 1987 [Fj]
Anderson, B L (Wairarapa-Bush) 1986 A 1
Anesi, S R (Waikato) 2005 Fj(R)
Archer, W R (Otago, Southland) 1955 A 1,2, 1956 SA 1,3
Argus, W G (Canterbury) 1946 A 1,2, 1947 A 1,2
Arnold, D A (Canterbury) 1963 I, W, 1964 E, F
Arnold, K D (Waikato) 1947 A 1,2
Ashby, D L (Southland) 1958 A 2
Asher, A A (Auckland) 1903 A
Ashworth, B G (Auckland) 1978 A 1,2
Ashworth, J C (Canterbury, Hawke's Bay) 1978 A 1,2,3, 1980 A 1,2,3, 1981 SA 1,2,3, 1982 A 1,2, 1983 BI 1,2,3,4, A, 1984 F 1,2, A 1,2,3, 1985 E 1,2, A
Atiga, B A C (Auckland) 2003 [Tg(R)]
Atkinson, H (West Coast) 1913 A 1
Avery, H E (Wellington) 1910 A 1,2,3

Bachop, G T M (Canterbury) 1989 W, I, 1990 S 1,2, A 1,2,3, F 1,2, 1991 Arg 1,2, A 1,2, [E, US, C, A, S], 1992 Wld 1, 1994 SA 1,2,3, A, 1995 C, [I, W, S, E, SA], A 1,2
Bachop, S J (Otago) 1994 F 2, SA 1,2,3, A
Badeley, C E O (Auckland) 1921 SA 1,2
Baird, J A S (Otago) 1913 A 2
Ball, N (Wellington) 1931 A, 1932 A 2,3, 1935 W, 1936 E
Barrett, J (Auckland) 1913 A 2,3
Barry, E F (Wellington) 1934 A 2
Barry, L J (North Harbour) 1995 F 2
Bates, S P (Waikato) 2004 It(R)
Batty, G B (Wellington, Bay of Plenty) 1972 W, S, 1973 E 1, I, F, E 2, 1974 A 1,3, I, 1975 S, 1976 SA 1,2,3,4, 1977 BI 1
Batty, W (Auckland) 1930 BI 1,3,4, 1931 A
Beatty, G E (Taranaki) 1950 BI 1
Bell, R H (Otago) 1951 A 3, 1952 A 1,2
Bellis, E A (Wanganui) 1921 SA 1,2,3
Bennet, R (Otago) 1905 A
Berghan, T (Otago) 1938 A 1,2,3
Berry, M J (Wairarapa-Bush) 1986 A 3(R)
Berryman, N R (Northland) 1998 SA 2(R)
Bevan, V D (Wellington) 1949 A 1,2, 1950 BI 1,2,3,4
Birtwistle, W M (Canterbury) 1965 SA 1,2,3,4, 1967 E, W, S
Black, J E (Canterbury) 1977 F 1, 1979 A, 1980 A 3
Black, N W (Auckland) 1949 SA 3
Black, R S (Otago) 1914 A 1
Blackadder, T J (Canterbury) 1998 E 1(R),2, 2000 Tg, S 1,2, A 1, SA 1, A 2, SA 2, F 1,2, It
Blair, B A (Canterbury) 2001 S (R), Arg 2, 2002 E, W
Blake, A W (Wairarapa) 1949 A 1
Blowers, A F (Auckland) 1996 SA 2(R),4(R), 1997 I, E 1(R), W (R), 1999 F 1(R), SA 1, A 1(R), SA 2, A 2(R), [It]
Boggs, E G (Auckland) 1946 A 2, 1949 SA 1
Bond, J G (Canterbury) 1949 A 2
Booth, E E (Otago) 1906 F, 1907 A 1,3
Boric, A F (North Harbour) 2008 E1(R),2(R),SA2,A2(R), SA3(R),Sm,A3(R)
Boroevich, K G (Wellington) 1986 F 1, A 1, F 3(R)
Botica, F M (North Harbour) 1986 F 1, A 1,2,3, F 2,3, 1989 Arg 1(R)
Bowden, N J G (Taranaki) 1952 A 2
Bowers, R G (Wellington) 1954 I, F
Bowman, A W (Hawke's Bay) 1938 A 1,2,3
Braid, D J (Auckland) 2002 W, 2003 [C(R),Tg], 2008 A1
Braid, G J (Bay of Plenty) 1983 S, E
Bremner, S G (Auckland, Canterbury) 1952 A 2, 1956 SA 2
Brewer, M R (Otago, Canterbury) 1986 F 1, A 1,2,3, F 2,3, 1988 A 1, 1989 A, W, I, 1990 S 1,2, A 1,2,3, F 1,2, 1992 I 2, A 1, 1994 F 1,2, SA 1,2,3, A, 1995 C, [I, W, E, SA], A 1,2
Briscoe, K C (Taranaki) 1959 BI 2, 1960 SA 1,2,3,4, 1963 I, W, 1964 E, S
Brooke, R M (Auckland) 1992 I 2, A 1,2,3, SA, 1993 BI 1,2,3, A, WS, 1994 SA 2,3, 1995 C, [J, S, E, SA], A 1,2, It, F 1,2, 1996 WS, S 1,2, A 1, SA 1, A 2, SA 2,3,4,5, 1997 Fj, Arg 1,2, A 1, SA 1, A 2, SA 2, A 3, I, E 1, W, E 2, 1998 E 1,2, A 1, SA 1, A 2, SA 2, A 3, 1999 WS, F 1, SA 1, A 1, SA 2, A 2, [Tg, E, It (R), S, F 2]
Brooke, Z V (Auckland) 1987 [Arg], 1989 Arg 2(R), 1990 A 1,2,3, F 1(R), 1991 Arg 2, A 1,2, [E, It, C, A, S], 1992 A 2,3, SA, 1993 BI 1,2,3(R), WS (R), S, E, 1994 F 2, SA 1,2,3, A, 1995 [J, S, E, SA], A 1,2, It, F 1,2, 1996 WS, S 1,2, A 1, SA 1, A 2, SA 2,3,4,5, 1997 Arg 1,2, A 1, SA 1, A 2, SA 2, A 3, I, E 1, W, E 2
Brooke-Cowden, M (Auckland) 1986 F 1, A 1, 1987 [W]
Broomhall, S R (Canterbury) 2002 SA 1(R),2(R), E, F
Brown, C (Taranaki) 1913 A 2,3
Brown, O M (Auckland) 1992 I 2, A 1,2,3, SA, 1993 BI 1,2,3, A, S, E, 1994 F 1,2, SA 1,2,3, A, 1995 C, [I, W, S, E, SA], A 1,2, It, F 1,2, 1996 WS, S 1,2, A 1, SA 1, A 2, SA 2,3,4,5, 1997 Fj, Arg 1,2, A 1, SA 1, A 2, SA 2, A 3, I, E 1, W, E 2, 1998 E 1,2, A 1, SA 1, A 2, SA 2
Brown, R H (Taranaki) 1955 A 3, 1956 SA 1,2,3,4, 1957 A 1,2, 1958 A 1,2,3, 1959 BI 1,3, 1961 F 1,2,3, 1962 A 1
Brown, T E (Otago) 1999 WS, F 1(R), SA 1(R), A 1(R),2(R), [E (R), It, S (R)], 2000 Tg, S 2(R), A 1(R), SA 1(R), A 2(R), 2001 Sm, Arg 1(R), F, SA 1, A 1
Brownlie, C J (Hawke's Bay) 1924 W, 1925 E, F
Brownlie, M J (Hawke's Bay) 1924 I, W, 1925 E, F, 1928 SA 1,2,3,4
Bruce, J A (Auckland) 1914 A 1,2
Bruce, O D (Canterbury) 1976 SA 1,2,4, 1977 BI 2,3,4, F 1,2, 1978 A 1,2, I, W, E, S
Bryers, R F (King Country) 1949 A 1
Budd, T A (Southland) 1946 A 2, 1949 A 2
Bullock-Douglas, G A H (Wanganui) 1932 A 1,2,3, 1934 A 1,2
Bunce, F E (North Harbour) 1992 Wld 1,2,3, I 1,2, A 1,2,3, SA, 1993 BI 1,2,3, A, WS, S, E, 1994 F 1,2, SA 1,2,3, A, 1995 C, [I, W, S, E, SA], A 1,2, It, F 1,2, 1996 WS, S 1,2, A1, SA 1, A 2, SA 2,3,4,5, 1997 Fj, Arg 1,2, A 1, SA 1, A 2, SA 2, A 3, I, E 1, W, E 2
Burgess, G A J (Auckland) 1981 SA 2
Burgess, G F (Southland) 1905 A
Burgess, R E (Manawatu) 1971 BI 1,2,3, 1972 A 3, W, 1973 I, F
Burke, P S (Taranaki) 1955 A 1, 1957 A 1,2

Burns, P J (Canterbury) 1908 AW 2, 1910 A 1,2,3, 1913 A 3
Bush, R G (Otago) 1931 A
Bush, W K (Canterbury) 1974 A 1,2, 1975 S, 1976 I, SA, 2,4, 1977 BI 2,3,4(R), 1978 I, W, 1979 A
Buxton, J B (Canterbury) 1955 A 3, 1956 SA 1

Cain, M J (Taranaki) 1913 US, 1914 A 1,2,3
Callesen, J A (Manawatu) 1974 A 1,2,3, 1975 S
Cameron, D (Taranaki) 1908 AW 1,2,3
Cameron, L M (Manawatu) 1980 A 3, 1981 SA 1(R),2,3, R
Carleton, S R (Canterbury) 1928 SA 1,2,3, 1929 A 1,2,3
Carrington, K R (Auckland) 1971 BI 1,3,4
Carter, D W (Canterbury) 2003 W, F, A 1(R),[It,C,Tg,SA(R),F(R)], 2004 E1,2,PI,A1,SA1,A2,It,W,F, 2005 Fj,BI1,2,SA1,A1,W,E, 2006 Arg,A1,SA1,A2,3, SA2,3,E,F1,2,W, 2007 F1,C,SA1,A1,SA2,A2, [It,S,F], 2008 I1,E1,2,SA1,2,A1,2,SA3,Sm,A3
Carter, M P (Auckland) 1991 A 2, [It, A], 1997 Fj (R), A 1(R), 1998 E 2(R), A 2
Casey, S T (Otago) 1905 S, I, E, W, 1907 A 1,2,3, 1908 AW 1
Cashmore, A R (Auckland) 1996 S 2(R), 1997 A 2(R)
Catley, E H (Waikato) 1946 A 1, 1947 A 1,2, 1949 SA 1,2,3,4
Caughey, T H C (Auckland) 1932 A 1,3, 1934 A 1,2, 1935 S, I, 1936 E, A 1, 1937 SA 3
Caulton, R W (Wellington) 1959 BI 2,3,4, 1960 SA 1,4, 1961 F 2, 1963 E 1,2, I, W, 1964 E, S, F, A 1,2,3
Cherrington, N P (North Auckland) 1950 BI 1
Christian, D L (Auckland) 1949 SA 4
Clamp, M (Wellington) 1984 A 2,3
Clark, D W (Otago) 1964 A 1,2
Clark, W H (Wellington) 1953 W, 1954 I, E, S, 1955 A 1,2, 1956 SA 2,3,4
Clarke, A H (Auckland) 1958 A 3, 1959 BI 4, 1960 SA 1
Clarke, D B (Waikato) 1956 SA 3,4, 1957 A 1,2, 1958 A 1,3, 1959 BI 1,2,3,4, 1960 SA 1,2,3,4, 1961 F 1,2,3, 1962 A 1,2,3,4,5, 1963 E 1,2, I, W, 1964 E, S, F, A 2,3
Clarke, E (Auckland) 1992 Wld 2,3, I 1,2, 1993 BI 1,2, S (R), E, 1998 SA 2, A 3
Clarke, I J (Waikato) 1953 W, 1955 A 1,2,3, 1956 SA 1,2,3,4, 1957 A 1,2, 1958 A 1,3, 1959 BI 1,2, 1960 SA 2,4, 1961 F 1,2,3, 1962 A 1,2,3, 1963 E 1,2
Clarke, R L (Taranaki) 1932 A 2,3
Cobden, D G (Canterbury) 1937 SA 1
Cockerill, M S (Taranaki) 1951 A 1,2,3
Cockroft, E A P (South Canterbury) 1913 A 3, 1914 A 2,3
Codlin, B W (Counties) 1980 A 1,2,3
Collins, A H (Taranaki) 1932 A 2,3, 1934 A 1
Collins, J (Wellington) 2001 Arg 1, 2003 E (R), W, F, SA 1, A 1, SA 2, A 2,[It,W,SA,A,F], 2004 E2(R),Arg,PI(R),A1(R), SA1,It,F, 2005 Fj,BI1,2,3,SA1,A1,SA2,W,E, 2006 Arg,A1,2,3, SA2(R),3,F1,2,W, 2007 F2,C,SA1,A1,SA2(R),A2, [It,Pt,R,F]
Collins, J L (Poverty Bay) 1964 A 1, 1965 SA 1,4
Colman, J T H (Taranaki) 1907 A 1,2, 1908 AW 1,3
Connor, D M (Auckland) 1961 F 1,2,3, 1962 A 1,2,3,4,5, 1963 E 1,2, 1964 A 2,3
Conway, R J (Otago, Bay of Plenty) 1959 BI 2,3,4, 1960 SA 1,3,4, 1965 SA 1,2,3,4
Cooke, A E (Auckland, Wellington) 1924 I, W, 1925 E, F, 1930 BI 1,2,3,4
Cooke, R J (Canterbury) 1903 A
Cooksley, M S B (Counties, Waikato) 1992 Wld 1, 1993 BI 2,3(R), A, 1994 F 1,2, SA 1,2, A, 2001 A 1(R), SA 2(t&R)
Cooper, G J L (Auckland, Otago) 1986 F 1, A 1,2, 1992 Wld 1,2,3, I 1
Cooper, M J A (Waikato) 1992 I 2, SA (R), 1993 BI 1(R),3(t), WS (t), S, 1994 F 1,2
Corner, M M N (Auckland) 1930 BI 2,3,4, 1931 A, 1934 A 1, 1936 E
Cossey, R R (Counties) 1958 A 1
Cottrell, A I (Canterbury) 1929 A 1,2,3, 1930 BI 1,2,3,4, 1931 A, 1932 A 1,2,3
Cottrell, W D (Canterbury) 1968 A 1,2, F 2,3, 1970 SA 1, 1971 BI 1,2,3,4
Couch, M B R (Wairarapa) 1947 A 1, 1949 A 1,2
Coughlan, T D (South Canterbury) 1958 A 1
Cowan, Q J (Southland) 2004 It(R), 2005 W(R),I(R),S(R), 2006 I1(R),SA1(R),A2(R),SA2(R),3, 2008 E1(R),2(R),SA1(R), A1(t&R),2,SA3,Sm,A3
Creighton, J N (Canterbury) 1962 A 4
Cribb, R T (North Harbour) 2000 S 1,2, A 1, SA 1, A 2, SA 2, F 1,2, It, 2001 Sm, F, SA 1, A 1, SA 2, A 2
Crichton, S (Wellington) 1983 S, E
Cross, T (Canterbury) 1904 BI, 1905 A
Crowley, K J (Taranaki) 1985 E 1,2, A, Arg 1,2, 1986 A 3, F 2,3, 1987 [Arg], 1990 S 1,2, A 1,2,3, F 1,2, 1991 Arg 1,2, [A]
Crowley, P J B (Auckland) 1949 SA 3,4, 1950 BI 1,2,3,4
Culhane, S D (Southland) 1995 [J], It, F 1,2, 1996 SA 3,4
Cullen C M (Manawatu, Central Vikings, Wellington) 1996 WS, S 1,2, A 1, SA 1, A 2, SA 2,3,4,5, 1997 Fj, Arg 1,2, A 1, SA 1, A 2, SA 2, A 3, I, E 1, W, E 2, 1998 E 1,2, A 1, SA 1, A 2, SA 2, A 3, 1999 WS, F 1, SA 1, A 1, SA 2, A 2, [Tg, E, It (R), S, F 2, SA 3], 2000 Tg, S 1,2, A 1, SA 1, A 2, SA 2, F 1,2, It, 2001 A 2(R), 2002 It, Fj, A 1, SA 1, A 2, F
Cummings, W (Canterbury) 1913 A 2,3
Cundy, R T (Wairarapa) 1929 A 2(R)
Cunningham, G R (Auckland) 1979 A, S, E, 1980 A 1,2
Cunningham, W (Auckland) 1905 S, I, 1906 F, 1907 A 1,2,3, 1908 AW 1,2,3
Cupples, L F (Bay of Plenty) 1924 I, W
Currie, C J (Canterbury) 1978 I, W
Cuthill, J E (Otago) 1913 A 1, US

Dalley, W C (Canterbury) 1924 I, 1928 SA 1,2,3,4
Dalton, A G (Counties) 1977 F 2, 1978 A 1,2,3, I, W, E, S, 1979 F 1,2, S, 1981 S 1,2, SA 1,2,3, R, F 1,2, 1982 A 1,2,3, 1983 BI 1,2,3,4, A, 1984 F 1,2, A 1,2,3, 1985 E 1,2, A
Dalton, D (Hawke's Bay) 1935 I, W, 1936 A 1,2, 1937 SA 1,2,3, 1938 A 1,2
Dalton, R A (Wellington) 1947 A 1,2
Dalzell, G N (Canterbury) 1953 W, 1954 I, E, S, F
Davie, M G (Canterbury) 1983 E (R)
Davies, W A (Auckland, Otago) 1960 SA 4, 1962 A 4,5
Davis, K (Auckland) 1952 A 2, 1953 W, 1954 I, E, S, F, 1955 A 2, 1958 A 1,2,3
Davis, L J (Canterbury) 1976 I, 1977 BI 3,4
Davis, W L (Hawke's Bay) 1967 A, E, W, F, S, 1968 A 1,2, F 1, 1969 W 1,2, 1970 SA 2
Deans, I B (Canterbury) 1988 W 1,2, A 1,2,3, 1989 F 1,2, Arg 1,2, A
Deans, R G (Canterbury) 1905 S, I, E, W, 1908 AW 3
Deans, R M (Canterbury) 1983 S, E, 1984 A 1(R),2,3
Delamore, G W (Wellington) 1949 SA 4
Dermody, C (Southland) 2006 I1,2,E(R)
Devine, S J (Auckland) 2002 E, W 2003 E (R), W, F, SA 1, A 1(R), [C,SA(R),F]
Dewar, H (Taranaki) 1913 A 1, US
Diack, E S (Otago) 1959 BI 2
Dick, J (Auckland) 1937 SA 1,2, 1938 A 3
Dick, M J (Auckland) 1963 I, W, 1964 E, S, F, 1965 SA 3, 1966 BI 4, 1967 A, E, W, F, 1969 W 1,2, 1970 SA 1,4
Dixon, M J (Canterbury) 1954 I, E, S, F, 1956 SA 1,2,3,4, 1957 A 1,2
Dobson, R L (Auckland) 1949 A 1
Dodd, E H (Wellington) 1905 A
Donald, A J (Wanganui) 1983 S, E, 1984 F 1,2, A 1,2,3
Donald, J G (Wairarapa) 1921 SA 1,2
Donald, Q (Wairarapa) 1924 I, W, 1925 E, F
Donald, S R (Waikato) 2008 E1(R),2(R),A2(R),SA3(R), Sm(R),A3(R)
Donaldson, M W (Manawatu) 1977 F 1,2, 1978 A 1,2,3, I, E, S, 1979 F 1,2, A, S (R), 1981 SA 3(R)
Dougan, J P (Wellington) 1972 A 1, 1973 E 2
Dowd, C W (Auckland) 1993 BI 1,2,3, A, WS, S, E, 1994 SA 1(R), 1995 C, [I, W, J, E, SA], A 1,2, It, F 1,2, 1996 WS, S 1,2, A 1, SA 1, A 2, SA 2,3,4,5, 1997 Fj, Arg 1,2, A 1, SA 1, A 2, SA 2, A 3, I, E 1, W, 1998 E 1,2, A 1, SA 1, A 2,3(R), 1999 SA 2(R), A 2(R), [Tg (R), E, It, S, F 2, SA 3], 2000 Tg, S 1(R),2(R), A 1(R), SA 1(R), A 2(R)
Dowd, G W (North Harbour) 1992 I 1(R)
Downing, A J (Auckland) 1913 A 1, US, 1914 A 1,2,3

Dave Rogers / Getty Images

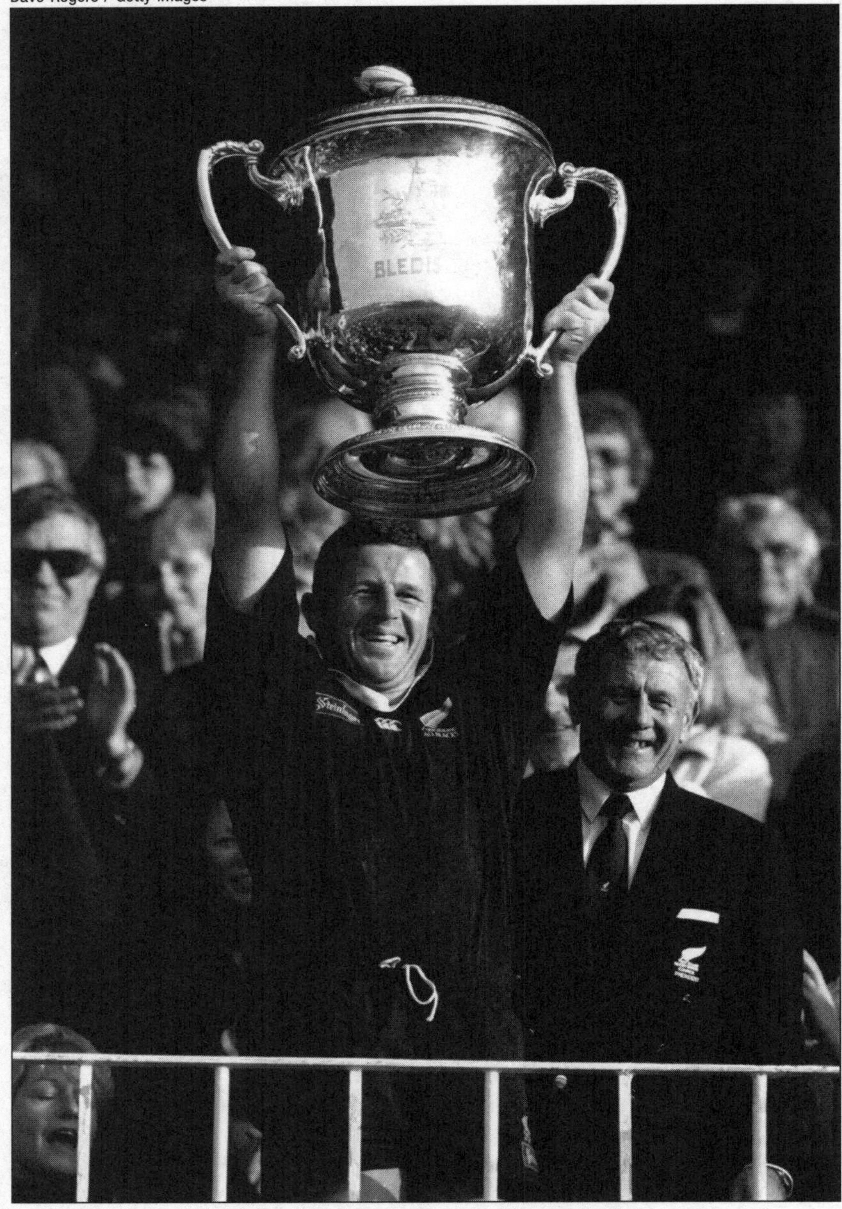

Sean Fitzpatrick's record (right) is incredible, playing in a staggering 63 consecutive Tests

Drake, J A (Auckland) 1986 F 2,3, 1987 [Fj, Arg, S, W, F], A
Duff, R H (Canterbury) 1951 A 1,2,3, 1952 A 1,2, 1955 A 2,3, 1956 SA 1,2,3,4
Duggan, R J L (Waikato) 1999 [It (R)]
Duncan, J (Otago) 1903 A
Duncan, M G (Hawke's Bay) 1971 BI 3(R),4
Duncan, W D (Otago) 1921 SA 1,2,3
Dunn, E J (North Auckland) 1979 S, 1981 S 1
Dunn, I T W (North Auckland) 1983 BI 1,4, A
Dunn, J M (Auckland) 1946 A 1

Earl, A T (Canterbury) 1986 F 1, A 1, F 3(R), 1987 [Arg], 1989 W, I, 1991 Arg 1(R),2, A 1, [E (R), US, S], 1992 A 2,3(R)
Eastgate, B P (Canterbury) 1952 A 1,2, 1954 S
Eaton, J J (Taranaki) 2005 I,E(t),S(R), 2006 Arg,A1,2(R),3, SA3(R),F1(R),2(R)
Elliott, K G (Wellington) 1946 A 1,2
Ellis, A M (Canterbury) 2006 E(R),F2(R), 2007 [Pt(R),R], 2008 I1,E1,2,SA1,2,A1
Ellis, M C G (Otago) 1993 S, E, 1995 C, [I (R), W, J, S, SA (R)]
Elsom, A E G (Canterbury) 1952 A 1,2, 1953 W, 1955 A 1,2,3
Elvidge, R R (Otago) 1946 A 1,2, 1949 SA 1,2,3,4, 1950 BI 1,2,3
Erceg, C P (Auckland) 1951 A 1,2,3, 1952 A 1
Evans, D A (Hawke's Bay) 1910 A 2
Evans, N J (North Harbour, Otago) 2004 E1(R),2,Arg,PI(R), 2005 I,S, 2006 F2(R),W(R), 2007 F1(R),2,SA2(R),A2(R), [Pt,S(R),R,F(R)]
Eveleigh, K A (Manawatu) 1976 SA 2,4, 1977 BI 1,2

Fanning, A H N (Canterbury) 1913 A 3
Fanning, B J (Canterbury) 1903 A, 1904 BI
Farrell, C P (Auckland) 1977 BI 1,2
Fawcett, C L (Auckland) 1976 SA 2,3
Fea, W R (Otago) 1921 SA 3
Feek, G E (Canterbury) 1999 WS (R), A 1(R), SA 2, [E (t), It], 2000 F 1,2, It, 2001 I, S
Filipo, R A (Wellington) 2007 C,SA1(R),A1(R)
Finlay, B E L (Manawatu) 1959 BI 1
Finlay, J (Manawatu) 1946 A 1
Finlayson, I (North Auckland) 1928 SA 1,2,3,4, 1930 BI 1,2
Fitzgerald, J T (Wellington) 1952 A 1
Fitzpatrick, B B J (Wellington) 1953 W, 1954 I, F
Fitzpatrick, S B T (Auckland) 1986 F 1, A 1, F 2,3, 1987 [It, Fj, Arg, S, W, F], A, 1988 W 1,2, A 1,2,3, 1989 F 1,2, Arg 1,2, A, W, I, 1990 S 1,2, A 1,2,3, F 1,2, 1991 Arg 1,2, A 1,2, [E, US, It, C, A, S], 1992 Wld 1,2,3, I 1,2, A 1,2,3, SA, 1993 BI 1,2,3, A, WS, S, E, 1994 F 1,2, SA 1,2,3, A, 1995 C, [I, W, S, E, SA], A 1,2, It, F 1,2, 1996 WS, S 1,2, A 1, SA 1, A 2, SA 2,3,4,5, 1997 Fj, Arg 1,2, A 1, SA 1, A 2, SA 2, A 3, W (R)
Flavell, T V (North Harbour, Auckland) 2000 Tg, S 1(R), A 1(R), SA 1,2(t), F 1(R),2(R), It, 2001 Sm, Arg 1, F, SA 1, A 1, SA 2, A 2, 2006 I1(R),2, 2007 F1(R),2(R),C,SA1,A1
Fleming, J K (Wellington) 1979 S, E, 1980 A 1,2,3
Fletcher, C J C (North Auckland) 1921 SA 3
Flynn, C R (Canterbury) 2003 [C(R),Tg], 2004 It(R)
Fogarty, R (Taranaki) 1921 SA 1,3
Ford, B R (Marlborough) 1977 BI 3,4, 1978 I, 1979 E
Forster, S T (Otago) 1993 S, E, 1994 F 1,2, 1995 It, F 1
Fox, G J (Auckland) 1985 Arg 1, 1987 [It, Fj, Arg, S, W, F], A, 1988 W 1,2, A 1,2,3, 1989 F 1,2, Arg 1,2, A, W, I, 1990 S 1,2, A 1,2,3, F 1,2, 1991 Arg 1,2, A 1,2, [E, It, C, A], 1992 Wld 1,2(R), A 1,2,3, SA, 1993 BI 1,2,3, A, WS
Francis, A R H (Auckland) 1905 A, 1907 A 1,2,3, 1908 AW 1,2,3, 1910 A 1,2,3
Francis, W C (Wellington) 1913 A 2,3, 1914 A 1,2,3
Fraser, B G (Wellington) 1979 S, E, 1980 A 3, W, 1981 S 1,2, SA 1,2,3, R, F 1,2, 1982 A 1,2,3, 1983 BI 1,2,3,4, A, S, E, 1984 A 1
Frazer, H F (Hawke's Bay) 1946 A 1,2, 1947 A 1,2, 1949 SA 2
Fryer, F C (Canterbury) 1907 A 1,2,3, 1908 AW 2
Fuller, W B (Canterbury) 1910 A 1,2
Furlong, B D M (Hawke's Bay) 1970 SA 4

Gallagher, J A (Wellington) 1987 [It, Fj, S, W, F], A, 1988 W 1,2, A 1,2,3, 1989 F 1,2, Arg 1,2, A, W, I
Gallaher, D (Auckland) 1903 A, 1904 BI, 1905 S, E, W, 1906 F
Gard, P C (North Otago) 1971 BI 4
Gardiner, A J (Taranaki) 1974 A 3
Gear, R L (North Harbour, Nelson Bays, Tasman) 2004 PI,It, 2005 BI1(R),2,3,SA1,A1,SA2,W,S, 2006 Arg,A1,2,SA2,3(R), E,W, 2007 C(R),A1
Geddes, J H (Southland) 1929 A 1
Geddes, W McK (Auckland) 1913 A 2
Gemmell, B McL (Auckland) 1974 A 1,2
George, V L (Southland) 1938 A 1,2,3
Gibbes, J B (Waikato) 2004 E1,2,Arg(R),PI,A1,2,SA2, 2005 BI2(R)
Gibson, D P E (Canterbury) 1999 WS, F 1, SA 1, A 1, SA 2, A 2, [Tg (R), E (R), It, S (R), F 2(R)], 2000 F 1,2, 2002 It, I 1(R),2(R), Fj, A 2(R), SA 2(R)
Gilbert, G D M (West Coast) 1935 S, I, W, 1936 E
Gillespie, C T (Wellington) 1913 A 2
Gillespie, W D (Otago) 1958 A 3
Gillett, G A (Canterbury, Auckland) 1905 S, I, E, W, 1907 A 2,3, 1908 AW 1,3
Gillies, C C (Otago) 1936 A 2
Gilray, C M (Otago) 1905 A
Glasgow, F T (Taranaki, Southland) 1905 S, I, E, W, 1906 F, 1908 AW 3
Glenn, W S (Taranaki) 1904 BI, 1906 F
Goddard, M P (South Canterbury) 1946 A 2, 1947 A 1,2, 1949 SA 3,4
Going, S M (North Auckland) 1967 A, F, 1968 F 3, 1969 W 1,2, 1970 SA 1(R),4, 1971 BI 1,2,3,4, 1972 A 1,2,3, W, S, 1973 E 1, I, F, E 2, 1974 I, 1975 S, 1976 I (R), SA 1,2,3,4, 1977 BI 1,2
Gordon, S B (Waikato) 1993 S, E
Graham, D J (Canterbury) 1958 A 1,2, 1960 SA 2,3, 1961 F 1,2,3, 1962 A 1,2,3,4,5, 1963 E 1,2, I, W, 1964 E, S, F, A 1,2,3
Graham, J B (Otago) 1913 US, 1914 A 1,3
Graham, W G (Otago) 1979 F 1(R)
Grant, L A (South Canterbury) 1947 A 1,2, 1949 SA 1,2
Gray, G D (Canterbury) 1908 AW 2, 1913 A 1, US
Gray, K F (Wellington) 1963 I, W, 1964 E, S, F, A 1,2,3, 1965 SA 1,2,3,4, 1966 BI 1,2,3,4, 1967 W, F, S, 1968 A 1, F 2,3, 1969 W 1,2
Gray, W N (Bay of Plenty) 1955 A 2,3, 1956 SA 1,2,3,4
Green, C I (Canterbury) 1983 S (R), E, 1984 A 1,2,3, 1985 E 1,2, A, Arg 1,2, 1986 A 2,3, F 2,3, 1987 [It, Fj, S, W, F], A
Grenside, B A (Hawke's Bay) 1928 SA 1,2,3,4, 1929 A 2,3
Griffiths, J L (Wellington) 1934 A 2, 1935 S, I, W, 1936 A 1,2, 1938 A 3
Guy, R A (North Auckland) 1971 BI 1,2,3,4

Haden, A M (Auckland) 1977 BI 1,2,3,4, F 1,2, 1978 A 1,2,3, I, W, E, S, 1979 F 1,2, A, S, E, 1980 A 1,2,3, W, 1981 S 2, SA 1,2,3, R, F 1,2, 1982 A 1,2,3, 1983 BI 1,2,3,4, A, 1984 F 1,2, 1985 Arg 1,2
Hadley, S (Auckland) 1928 SA 1,2,3,4
Hadley, W E (Auckland) 1934 A 1,2, 1935 S, I, W, 1936 E, A 1,2
Haig, J S (Otago) 1946 A 1,2
Haig, L S (Otago) 1950 BI 2,3,4, 1951 A 1,2,3, 1953 W, 1954 E, S
Hales, D A (Canterbury) 1972 A 1,2,3, W
Hamilton, D C (Southland) 1908 AW 2
Hamilton, S E (Canterbury) 2006 Arg,SA1
Hammett, M G (Canterbury) 1999 F 1(R), SA 2(R), [It, S (R), SA 3], 2000 Tg, S 1(R),2(t&R), A 1(R), SA 1(R), A 2(R), SA 2(R), F 2(R), It (R), 2001 Arg 1(t), 2002 It (R), I 1,2, A 1, SA 1,2(R), 2003 SA 1(R), A 1(R), SA 2, [It(R),C,W(R),SA(R),F(R)]
Hammond, I A (Marlborough) 1952 A 2
Harper, E T (Canterbury) 1904 BI, 1906 F
Harding, S (Otago) 2002 Fj
Harris, P C (Manawatu) 1976 SA 3
Hart, A H (Taranaki) 1924 I
Hart, G F (Canterbury) 1930 BI 1,2,3,4, 1931 A, 1934 A 1, 1935 S, I, W, 1936 A 1,2

Harvey, B A (Wairarapa-Bush) 1986 F 1
Harvey, I H (Wairarapa) 1928 SA 4
Harvey, L R (Otago) 1949 SA 1,2,3,4, 1950 BI 1,2,3,4
Harvey, P (Canterbury) 1904 BI
Hasell, E W (Canterbury) 1913 A 2,3
Hayman, C J (Otago) 2001 Sm (R), Arg 1, F (R), A 1(R), SA 2(R), A 2(R), 2002 F (t), W, 2004 E1,2,PI,A1,2,SA2,It,W(R),F, 2005 BI1,SA1,A1,SA2,A2,W,E, 2006 I1,2,A1,SA1,A2,3,SA3, E,F1,2,W, 2007 F1,2,SA1,A1,SA2,A2, [It,Pt(R),S,F]
Hayward, H O (Auckland) 1908 AW 3
Hazlett, E J (Southland) 1966 BI 1,2,3,4, 1967 A, E
Hazlett, W E (Southland) 1928 SA 1,2,3,4, 1930 BI 1,2,3,4
Heeps, T R (Wellington) 1962 A 1,2,3,4,5
Heke, W R (North Auckland) 1929 A 1,2,3
Hemi, R C (Waikato) 1953 W, 1954 I, E, S, F, 1955 A 1,2,3, 1956 SA 1,3,4, 1957 A 1,2, 1959 BI 1,3,4
Henderson, P (Wanganui) 1949 SA 1,2,3,4, 1950 BI 2,3,4
Henderson, P W (Otago) 1991 Arg 1, [C], 1992 Wld 1,2,3, I 1, 1995 [J]
Herewini, M A (Auckland) 1962 A 5, 1963 I, 1964 S, F, 1965 SA 4, 1966 BI 1,2,3,4, 1967 A
Hewett, D N (Canterbury) 2001 I (R), S (R), Arg 2, 2002 It (R), I 1,2, A 1, SA 1, A 2, SA 2, 2003 E, F, SA 1, A 1, SA 2, A 2, [It,Tg(R),W,SA,A,F]
Hewett, J A (Auckland) 1991 [It]
Hewitt, N J (Southland) 1995 [I (t), J], 1996 A 1(R), 1997 SA 1(R), I, E 1, W, E 2, 1998 E 2(t + R)
Hewson, A R (Wellington) 1981 S 1,2, SA 1,2,3, R, F 1,2, 1982 A 1,2,3, 1983 BI 1,2,3,4, A, 1984 F 1,2, A 1
Higginson, G (Canterbury, Hawke's Bay) 1980 W, 1981 S 1, SA 1, 1982 A 1,2, 1983 A
Hill, D W (Waikato) 2006 I2(R)
Hill, S F (Canterbury) 1955 A 3, 1956 SA 1,3,4, 1957 A 1,2, 1958 A 3, 1959 BI 1,2,3,4
Hines, G R (Waikato) 1980 A 3
Hobbs, M J B (Canterbury) 1983 BI 1,2,3,4, A, S, E, 1984 F 1,2, A 1,2,3, 1985 E 1,2, A, Arg 1,2, 1986 A 2,3, F 2,3
Hoeft, C H (Otago) 1998 E 2(t + R), A 2(R), SA 2, A 3, 1999 WS, F 1, SA 1, A 1,2, [Tg,E, S, F 2, SA 3(R)], 2000 S 1,2, A 1, SA 1, A 2, SA 2, 2001 Sm, Arg 1, F, SA 1, A 1, SA 2, A 2, 2003 W, [C,F(R)]
Holah, M R (Waikato) 2001 Sm, Arg 1(t&R), F (R), SA 1(R), A 1(R), SA 2(R), A 2(R), 2002 It, I 2(R), A 2(t), E, F, W (R), 2003 W, F (R), A 1(R), SA 2, [It(R),C,Tg(R),W(R),SA(t&R), A(R),F(t&R)], 2004 E1(R),2,Arg(R),PI,A1,SA1,A2,SA2, 2005 BI3(R),A1(R), 2006 I1,SA3(t)
Holder, E C (Buller) 1934 A 2
Hook, L S (Auckland) 1929 A 1,2,3
Hooper, J A (Canterbury) 1937 SA 1,2,3
Hopkinson, A E (Canterbury) 1967 S, 1968 A 2, F 1,2,3, 1969 W 2, 1970 SA 1,2,3
Hore, A K (Taranaki) 2002 E, F, 2004 E1(t),2(R),Arg,A1(t), 2005 W(R),I(R),S(R), 2006 I2(R),Arg(R),A1(R),SA1(R),A2(R),SA3, E(R),F2(R),W(R), 2007 F1(R),C,SA2(R), [Pt,S(R),R(R),F(R)], 2008 I1,E1,2,SA1,2,A1,2,SA3,Sm,A3
Hore, J (Otago) 1930 BI 2,3,4, 1932 A 1,2,3, 1934 A 1,2, 1935 S, 1936 E
Horsley, R H (Wellington) 1960 SA 2,3,4
Hotop, J (Canterbury) 1952 A 1,2, 1955 A 3
Howarth, S P (Auckland) 1994 SA 1,2,3, A
Howlett, D C (Auckland) 2000 Tg (R), F 1,2, It, 2001 Sm, Arg 1(R), F (R), SA 1, A 1,2, I, S, Arg 2, 2002 It, I 1,2(R), Fj, A 1, SA 1, A 2, SA 2, E, F, W, 2003 E, W, F, SA 1, A 1, SA 2, A 2, [It,C(R),Tg,W,SA,A,F], 2004 E1,A1,SA1,A2,SA2,W,F, 2005 Fj,BI1,A2,I,E, 2006 I1,2,SA1,A3,SA3, 2007 F2(R),C, SA2,A2, [It,S,R(R)]
Hughes, A M (Auckland) 1949 A 1,2, 1950 BI 1,2,3,4
Hughes, E (Southland, Wellington) 1907 A 1,2,3, 1908 AW 1, 1921 SA 1,2
Hunter, B A (Otago) 1971 BI 1,2,3
Hunter, J (Taranaki) 1905 S, I, E, W, 1906 F, 1907 A 1,2,3, 1908 AW 1,2,3
Hurst, I A (Canterbury) 1973 I, F, E 2, 1974 A 1,2

Ieremia, A (Wellington) 1994 SA 1,2,3, 1995 [J], 1996 SA 2(R),5(R), 1997 A 1(R), SA 1(R), A 2, SA 2, A 3, I, E 1, 1999 WS, F 1, SA 1, A 1, SA 2, A 2, [Tg, E, S, F 2, SA 3], 2000 Tg, S 1,2, A 1,2, SA 2
Ifwersen, K D (Auckland) 1921 SA 3
Innes, C R (Auckland) 1989 W, I, 1990 A 1,2,3, F 1,2, 1991 Arg 1,2, A 1,2, [E, US, It, C, A, S]
Innes, G D (Canterbury) 1932 A 2
Irvine, I B (North Auckland) 1952 A 1
Irvine, J G (Otago) 1914 A 1,2,3
Irvine, W R (Hawke's Bay, Wairarapa) 1924 I, W, 1925 E, F, 1930 BI 1
Irwin, M W (Otago) 1955 A 1,2, 1956 SA 1, 1958 A 2, 1959 BI 3,4, 1960 SA 1

Jack, C R (Canterbury, Tasman) 2001 Arg 1(R), SA 1(R),2, A 2, I, S, Arg 2, 2002 I 1,2, A 1, SA 1, A 2, SA 2, 2003 E, W, F, SA 1, A 1, SA 2(R), A 2, [It,C,SA,A,F], 2004 E1,2,Arg,PI, A1,SA1,A2,SA2,It,W,F, 2005 Fj(R),BI1,2,3,SA1,A1,SA2, A2,W,E,S, 2006 I1,2,A1,SA1,A2,3,SA2(R),3,E,F2, 2007 F1,2,A1,SA2,A2, [It,Pt,S(R),R(R),F(R)]
Jackson, E S (Hawke's Bay) 1936 A 1,2, 1937 SA 1,2,3, 1938 A 3
Jaffray, J L (Otago, South Canterbury) 1972 A 2, 1975 S, 1976 I, SA 1, 1977 BI 2, 1979 F 1,2
Jarden, R A (Wellington) 1951 A 1,2, 1952 A 1,2, 1953 W, 1954 I, E, S, F, 1955 A 1,2,3, 1956 SA 1,2,3,4
Jefferd, A C R (East Coast) 1981 S 1,2, SA 1
Jessep, E M (Wellington) 1931 A, 1932 A 1
Johnson, L M (Wellington) 1928 SA 1,2,3,4
Johnston, W (Otago) 1907 A 1,2,3
Johnstone, B R (Auckland) 1976 SA 2, 1977 BI 1,2, F 1,2, 1978 I, W, E, S, 1979 F 1,2, S, E
Johnstone, C R (Canterbury) 2005 Fj(R),BI2(R),3(R)
Johnstone, P (Otago) 1949 SA 2,4, 1950 BI 1,2,3,4, 1951 A 1,2,3
Jones, I D (North Auckland, North Harbour) 1990 S 1,2, A 1,2,3, F 1,2, 1991 Arg 1,2, A 1,2, [E, US, It, C, A, S], 1992 Wld 1,2,3, I 1,2, A 1,2,3, SA, 1993 BI 1,2(R),3, WS, S, E, 1994 F 1,2, SA 1,3, A, 1995 C, [I, W, S, E, SA], A 1,2, It, F 1,2, 1996 WS, S 1,2, A 1, SA 1, A 2, SA 2,3,4,5, 1997 Fj, Arg 1,2, A 1, SA 1, A 2, SA 2, A 3, I, E 1, W, E 2, 1998 E 1,2, A 1, SA 1, A 2,3(R), 1999 F 1(R), [It, S (R)]
Jones, M G (North Auckland) 1973 E 2
Jones, M N (Auckland) 1987 [It, Fj, S, F], A, 1988 W 1,2, A 2,3, 1989 F 1,2, Arg 1,2, 1990 F 1,2, 1991 Arg 1,2, A 1,2, [E, US, S], 1992 Wld 1,3, I 2, A 1,3, SA, 1993 BI 1,2,3, A, WS, 1994 SA 3(R), A, 1995 A 1(R),2, It, F 1,2, 1996 WS, S 1,2, A 1, SA 1, A 2, SA 2,3,4,5, 1997 Fj, 1998 E 1, A 1, SA 1, A 2
Jones, P F H (North Auckland) 1954 E, S, 1955 A 1,2, 1956 SA 3,4, 1958 A 1,2,3, 1959 BI 1, 1960 SA 1
Joseph, H T (Canterbury) 1971 BI 2,3
Joseph, J W (Otago) 1992 Wld 2,3(R), I 1, A 1(R),3, SA, 1993 BI 1,2,3, A, WS, S, E, 1994 SA 2(t), 1995 C, [I, W, J (R), S, SA (R)]

Kahui, R D (Waikato) 2008 E2,A1,2,SA3,Sm,A3
Kaino, J (Auckland) 2006 I1(R),2, 2008 I1,E1,SA1,2,A1,2,SA3,Sm,A3
Karam, J F (Wellington, Horowhenua) 1972 W, S, 1973 E 1, I, F, 1974 A 1,2,3, I, 1975 S
Katene, T (Wellington) 1955 A 2
Kearney, J C (Otago) 1947 A 2, 1949 SA 1,2,3
Kelleher, B T (Otago, Waikato) 1999 WS (R), SA 1(R), A 2(R), [Tg (R), E (R), It, F 2], 2000 S 1, A 1(R),2(R), It (R), 2001 Sm, F (R), A 1(R), SA 2, A 2, I, S, 2002 It, I 2(R), Fj, SA 1(R),2(R), 2003 F (R), [A(R)], 2004 Arg,PI(R),SA1(R),2(R),It, W(R),F, 2005 Fj,BI1(R),2,3,SA1,W,E, 2006 I1,2,A1,2,3,SA3(R),E,F1(R),2,W, 2007 F2,C,SA1,A1,2, [It,S,F]
Kelly, J W (Auckland) 1949 A 1,2
Kember, G F (Wellington) 1970 SA 4
Ketels, R C (Counties) 1980 W, 1981 S 1,2, R, F 1
Kiernan, H A D (Auckland) 1903 A
Kilby, F D (Wellington) 1932 A 1,2,3, 1934 A 2
Killeen, B A (Auckland) 1936 A 1
King, R M (Waikato) 2002 W
King, R R (West Coast) 1934 A 2, 1935 S, I, W, 1936 E, A 1,2, 1937 SA 1,2,3, 1938 A 1,2,3
Kingstone, C N (Taranaki) 1921 SA 1,2,3

Kirk, D E (Auckland) 1985 E 1,2, A, Arg 1, 1986 F 1, A 1,2,3, F 2,3, 1987 [It, Fj, Arg, S, W, F], A

Kirkpatrick, I A (Canterbury, Poverty Bay) 1967 F, 1968 A 1(R),2, F 1,2,3, 1969 W 1,2, 1970 SA 1,2,3,4, 1971 BI 1,2,3,4, 1972 A 1,2,3, W, S, 1973 E 1, I, F, E 2, 1974 A 1,2,3, I 1975 S, 1976 I, SA 1,2,3,4, 1977 BI 1,2,3,4

Kirton, E W (Otago) 1967 E, W, F, S, 1968 A 1,2, F 1,2,3, 1969 W 1,2, 1970 SA 2,3

Kirwan, J J (Auckland) 1984 F 1,2, 1985 E 1,2, A, Arg 1,2, 1986 F 1, A 1,2,3, F 2,3, 1987 [It, Fj, Arg, S, W, F], A, 1988 W 1,2, A 1,2,3, 1989 F 1,2, Arg 1,2, A, 1990 S 1,2, A 1,2,3, F 1,2, 1991 Arg 2, A 1,2, [E, It, C, A, S], 1992 Wld 1,2(R),3, I 1,2, A 1,2,3, SA, 1993 BI 2,3, A, WS, 1994 F 1,2, SA 1,2,3

Kivell, A L (Taranaki) 1929 A 2,3

Knight, A (Auckland) 1934 A 1

Knight, G A (Manawatu) 1977 F 1,2, 1978 A 1,2,3, E, S, 1979 F 1,2, A, 1980 A 1,2,3, W, 1981 S 1,2, SA 1,3, 1982 A 1,2,3, 1983 BI 1,2,3,4, A, 1984 F 1,2, A 1,2,3, 1985 E 1,2, A, 1986 A 2,3

Knight, L G (Poverty Bay) 1977 BI 1,2,3,4, F 1,2

Koteka, T T (Waikato) 1981 F 2, 1982 A 3

Kreft, A J (Otago) 1968 A 2

Kronfeld, J A (Otago) 1995 C, [I, W, S, E, SA], A 1,2(R) 1996 WS, S 1,2, A 1, SA 1, A 2, SA 2,3,4,5, 1997 Fj, Arg 1,2, A 1, SA 1, A 2, SA 2, A 3, I (R), E 1, W, E 2, 1998 E 1,2, A 1, SA 1,2 A 3, 1999 WS, F 1, SA 1, A 1, SA 2, A 2, [Tg, E, S, F 2, SA 3], 2000 Tg, S 1(R),2, A 1(R), SA 1, A 2, SA 2

Laidlaw, C R (Otago, Canterbury) 1964 F, A 1, 1965 SA 1,2,3,4, 1966 BI 1,2,3,4, 1967 E, W, S, 1968 A 1,2, F 1,2, 1970 SA 1,2,3

Laidlaw, K F (Southland) 1960 SA 2,3,4

Lambert, K K (Manawatu) 1972 S (R), 1973 E 1, I, F, E 2, 1974 I, 1976 SA 1,3,4, 1977 BI 1,4

Lambourn, A (Wellington) 1934 A 1,2, 1935 S, I, W, 1936 E, 1937 SA 1,2,3, 1938 A 3

Larsen, B P (North Harbour) 1992 Wld 2,3, I 1, 1994 F 1,2, SA 1,2,3, A (t), 1995 [I, W, J, E(R)], It, F 1, 1996 S 2(t), SA 4(R)

Lauaki, S T (Waikato) 2005 Fj(R),BI1(R),2(R),3,A2,I,S, 2007 [It(R),Pt,S(R),R], 2008 E1(R),2(R),SA1(R),2(R),A1(R),Sm(R)

Laulala, C D E (Canterbury) 2004 W, 2006 I2

Le Lievre, J M (Canterbury) 1962 A 4

Lee, D D (Otago) 2002 E (R), F

Lendrum, R N (Counties) 1973 E 2

Leonard, B G (Waikato) 2007 F1(R),2(R),SA2(R),A2(R), [It(R),Pt,S(R),R(R),F(R)]

Leslie, A R (Wellington) 1974 A 1,2,3, I, 1975 S, 1976 I, SA 1,2,3,4

Leys, E T (Wellington) 1929 A 3

Lilburne, H T (Canterbury, Wellington) 1928 SA 3,4, 1929 A 1,2,3, 1930 BI 1,4, 1931 A, 1932 A 1, 1934 A 2

Lindsay, D F (Otago) 1928 SA 1,2,3

Lineen, T R (Auckland) 1957 A 1,2, 1958 A 1,2,3, 1959 BI 1,2,3,4, 1960 SA 1,2,3

Lister, T N (South Canterbury) 1968 A 1,2, F 1, 1969 W 1,2, 1970 SA 1,4, 1971 BI 4

Little, P F (Auckland) 1961 F 2,3, 1962 A 2,3,5, 1963 I, W, 1964 E, S, F

Little, W K (North Harbour) 1990 S 1,2, A 1,2,3, F 1,2, 1991 Arg 1,2, A 1, [It, S], 1992 Wld 1,2,3, I 1,2, A 1,2,3, SA, 1993 BI 1, WS (R), 1994 SA 2(R), A, 1995 C, [I, W, S, E, SA], A 1,2, It, F 1,2, 1996 S 2, A 1, SA 1, A 2, SA 2,3,4,5, 1997 W, E 2, 1998 E 1, A 1, SA 1, A 2

Loader, C J (Wellington) 1954 I, E, S, F

Lochore, B J (Wairarapa) 1964 E, S, 1965 SA 1,2,3,4, 1966 BI 1,2,3,4, 1967 A, E, W, F, S, 1968 A 1, F 2,3, 1969 W 1,2, 1970 SA 1,2,3,4, 1971 BI 3

Loe, R W (Waikato, Canterbury) 1987 [It, Arg], 1988 W 1,2, A 1,2,3, 1989 F 1,2, Arg 1,2, A, W, I, 1990 S 1,2, A 1,2,3, F 1,2, 1991 Arg 1,2, A 1,2, [E, It, C, A, S], 1992 Wld 1,2,3, I 1, A 1,2,3, SA, 1994 F 1,2, SA 1,2,3, A, 1995 [J, S, SA (R)], A 2(t), F 2(R)

Lomu, J T (Counties Manukau, Wellington) 1994 F 1,2, 1995 [I, W, S, E, SA], A 1,2, It, F 1,2, 1996 WS, S 1, A 1, SA 1, A 2, 1997 E 1, W, E 2, 1998 E 1,2, A 1(R), SA 1, A 2, SA 2, A 3, 1999 WS (R), SA 1(R), A 1(R), SA 2(R), A 2(R), [Tg, E, It, S, F 2, SA 3], 2000 Tg, S 1,2, A 1, SA 1, A 2, SA 2, F 1, 2001 Arg 1, F, SA 1, A 1, SA 2, A 2, I, S, Arg 2, 2002 It (R), I 1(R),2, Fj, SA 1(R), E, F, W

Long, A J (Auckland) 1903 A

Loveridge, D S (Taranaki) 1978 W, 1979 S, E, 1980 A 1,2,3, W, 1981 S 1,2, SA 1,2,3, R, F 1,2, 1982 A 1,2,3, 1983 BI 1,2,3,4, A, 1985 Arg 2

Lowen, K R (Waikato) 2002 E

Lucas, F W (Auckland) 1924 I, 1925 F, 1928 SA 4, 1930 BI 1,2,3,4

Lunn, W A (Otago) 1949 A 1,2

Lynch, T W (South Canterbury) 1913 A 1, 1914 A 1,2,3

Lynch, T W (Canterbury) 1951 A 1,2,3

McAlister, C L (North Harbour) 2005 BI3,SA1(R),A1(R), SA2(R),A2(R), 2006 I1,2,SA1(R),A3,SA2,F1,W, 2007 F2,C,SA1(R),A1,SA2,A2, [It,S,R,F]

McAtamney, F S (Otago) 1956 SA 2

McCahill, B J (Auckland) 1987 [Arg, S (R), W (R)], 1989 Arg 1(R),2(R), 1991 A 2, [E, US, C, A]

McCaw, R H (Canterbury) 2001 I, S, Arg 2, 2002 I 1,2, A 1, SA 1, A 2, SA 2, 2003 E, F, SA 1, A 1,2, [It,C(R),Tg(R), W,SA,A,F], 2004 E1,Arg,It,W,F, 2005 Fj,BI1,2,SA1,A1, SA2,A2,W(R),I,S, 2006 I1,2,A1,SA1,A2,3,SA2,3,E,F1,2,W, 2007 F1,2,C(R),SA1,A1,SA2,A2, [It,S,R(R),F], 2008 I1,E1,2,A2,SA3,A3

McCaw, W A (Southland) 1951 A 1,2,3, 1953 W, 1954 F

McCool, M J (Wairarapa-Bush) 1979 A

McCormick, W F (Canterbury) 1965 SA 4, 1967 E, W, F, S, 1968 A 1,2, F 1,2,3, 1969 W 1,2, 1970 SA 1,2,3, 1971 BI 1

McCullough, J F (Taranaki) 1959 BI 2,3,4

McDonald, A (Otago) 1905 S, I, E, W, 1907 A 1, 1908 AW 1, 1913 A 1, US

Macdonald, A J (Auckland) 2005 W(R),S

Macdonald, H H (Canterbury, North Auckland) 1972 W, S, 1973 E 1, I, F, E 2, 1974 I, 1975 S, 1976 I, SA 1,2,3

MacDonald, L R (Canterbury) 2000 S 1(R),2(R), SA 1(t),2(R), 2001 Sm, Arg 1, F, SA 1(R), A 1(R), SA 2, A 2, I, S, 2002 I 1,2, Fj (R), A 2(R), SA 2, 2003 A 2(R),[It(R),C,Tg,W,SA,A,F], 2005 BI1,2(R),SA1,2,A2,W(R),I,E(R),S(R), 2006 Arg,A1, SA1,A2,3(R),SA2,F1,2, 2007 F1,2,C(R),SA1(R), [It,Pt(R),S,F], 2008 I1(R),E1(R),2,SA1(R),2(R)

McDonnell, J M (Otago) 2002 It, I 1(R),2(R), Fj, SA 1(R), A 2(R), E, F

McDowell, S C (Auckland, Bay of Plenty) 1985 Arg 1,2, 1986 A 2,3, F 2,3, 1987 [It, Fj, S, W, F], A, 1988 W 1,2, A 1,2,3, 1989 F 1,2, Arg 1,2, A, W, I, 1990 S 1,2, A 1,2,3, F 1,2, 1991 Arg 1,2, A 1,2, [E, US, It, C, A, S], 1992 Wld 1,2,3, I 1,2

McEldowney, J T (Taranaki) 1977 BI 3,4

MacEwan, I N (Wellington) 1956 SA 2, 1957 A 1,2, 1958 A 1,2,3, 1959 BI 1,2,3, 1960 SA 1,2,3,4, 1961 F 1,2,3, 1962 A 1,2,3,4

McGrattan, B (Wellington) 1983 S, E, 1985 Arg 1,2, 1986 F 1, A 1

McGregor, A J (Auckland) 1913 A 1, US

McGregor, D (Canterbury, Southland) 1903 A, 1904 BI, 1905 E, W

McGregor, N P (Canterbury) 1924 W, 1925 E

McGregor, R W (Auckland) 1903 A, 1904 BI

McHugh, M J (Auckland) 1946 A 1,2, 1949 SA 3

McIntosh, D N (Wellington) 1956 SA 1,2, 1957 A 1,2

McKay, D W (Auckland) 1961 F 1,2,3, 1963 E 1,2

McKechnie, B J (Southland) 1977 F 1,2, 1978 A 2(R),3, W (R), E, S, 1979 A, 1981 SA 1(R), F 1

McKellar, G F (Wellington) 1910 A 1,2,3

McKenzie, R J (Wellington) 1913 A 1, US, 1914 A 2,3

McKenzie, R McC (Manawatu) 1934 A 1, 1935 S, 1936 A 1, 1937 SA 1,2,3, 1938 A 1,2,3

McLachlan, J S (Auckland) 1974 A 2

McLaren, H C (Waikato) 1952 A 1

McLean, A L (Bay of Plenty) 1921 SA 2,3

McLean, H F (Wellington, Auckland) 1930 BI 3,4, 1932 A 1,2,3, 1934 A 1, 1935 I, W, 1936 E

McLean, J K (King Country, Auckland) 1947 A 1, 1949 A 2

McLeod, B E (Counties) 1964 A 1,2,3, 1965 SA 1,2,3,4, 1966

BI 1,2,3,4, 1967 E, W, F, S, 1968 A 1,2, F 1,2,3, 1969 W 1,2, 1970 SA 1,2

McLeod, S J (Waikato) 1996 WS, S 1, 1997 Fj (R), Arg 2(t + R), I (R), E 1(R), W (t), E 2(R), 1998 A 1, SA 1(R)

McMinn, A F (Wairarapa, Manawatu) 1903 A, 1905 A

McMinn, F A (Manawatu) 1904 BI

McMullen, R F (Auckland) 1957 A 1,2, 1958 A 1,2,3, 1959 BI 1,2,3, 1960 SA 2,3,4

McNab, J R (Otago) 1949 SA 1,2,3, 1950 BI 1,2,3

McNaughton, A M (Bay of Plenty) 1971 BI 1,2,3

McNeece, J (Southland) 1913 A 2,3, 1914 A 1,2,3

McPhail, B E (Canterbury) 1959 BI 1,4

Macpherson, D G (Otago) 1905 A

MacPherson, G L (Otago) 1986 F 1

MacRae, I R (Hawke's Bay) 1966 BI 1,2,3,4, 1967 A, E, W, F, S, 1968 F 1,2, 1969 W 1,2, 1970 SA 1,2,3,4

McRae, J A (Southland) 1946 A 1(R),2

McWilliams, R G (Auckland) 1928 SA 2,3,4, 1929 A 1,2,3, 1930 BI 1,2,3,4

Mackrell, W H C (Auckland) 1906 F

Macky, J V (Auckland) 1913 A 2

Maguire, J R (Auckland) 1910 A 1,2,3

Mahoney, A (Bush) 1935 S, I, W, 1936 E

Mains, L W (Otago) 1971 BI 2,3,4, 1976 I

Major, J (Taranaki) 1967 A

Maka, I (Otago) 1998 E 2(R), A 1(R), SA 1(R),2

Maling, T S (Otago) 2002 It, I 2(R), Fj, A 1, SA 1, A 2, SA 2, 2004 Arg,A1,SA1,2

Manchester, J E (Canterbury) 1932 A 1,2,3, 1934 A 1,2, 1935 S, I, W, 1936 E

Mannix, S J (Wellington) 1994 F 1

Marshall, J W (Southland, Canterbury) 1995 F 2, 1996 WS, S 1,2, A 1, SA 1, A 2, SA 2,3,4,5, 1997 Fj, Arg 1,2, A 1, SA 1, A 2, SA 2, A 3, I, E 1, W, E 2, 1998 A 1, SA 1, A 2, SA 2, A 3, 1999 WS, F 1, SA 1, A 1, SA 2, A 2, [Tg, E, S, F 2(R), SA 3], 2000 Tg, S 2, A 1, SA 1, A 2, SA 2, F 1,2, It, 2001 Arg 1, F, SA 1, A 1,2(R), 2002 I 1,2, Fj (R), A 1, SA 1, A 2, SA 2, 2003 E, SA 1(R), A 1, SA 2, A 2, [It,Tg,W,SA,A], 2004 E1,2,PI,A1,SA1,A2,SA2, 2005 Fj(R), BI1,2(R),3(R)

Masoe, M C (Taranaki, Wellington) 2005 W,E, 2006Arg,A1(R),SA1(R),A2(R),3(R),SA2,E,F2(R), 2007 F1,2(R),C,A1(R),SA2(R), [It(R),Pt,S,R,F(R)]

Mason, D F (Wellington) 1947 A 2(R)

Masters, R R (Canterbury) 1924 I, W, 1925 E, F

Mataira, H K (Hawke's Bay) 1934 A 2

Matheson, J D (Otago) 1972 A 1,2,3, W, S

Mauger, A J D (Canterbury) 2001 I, S, Arg 2, 2002 It (R), I 1,2, Fj, A 1, SA 1, A 2, SA 2, 2003 SA 1, A 1, SA 2, A 2, [W,SA,A,F], 2004 SA2(R),It(R),W,F(R), 2005 Fj,BI1,2,SA1,A1, SA2,A2,I,E, 2006 I1,2,A1,2,SA3,E, 2007 F1,C,SA1,A1, [It(R),Pt,R]

Max, D S (Nelson) 1931 A, 1934 A 1,2

Maxwell, N M C (Canterbury) 1999 WS, F 1, SA 1, A 1, SA 2, A 2, [Tg, E, S, F 2, SA 3], 2000 S 1,2, A 1, SA 1(R), A 2, SA 2, F 1,2, It (R), 2001 Sm, Arg 1, F, SA 1, A 1, SA 2, A2, I, S, Arg 2, 2002 It, I 1,2, Fj, 2004 It,F

Mayerhofler, M A (Canterbury) 1998 E 1,2, SA 1, A 2, SA 2, A 3

Meads, C E (King Country) 1957 A 1,2, 1958 A 1,2,3, 1959 BI 2,3,4, 1960 SA 1,2,3,4, 1961 F 1,2,3, 1962 A 1,2,3,5, 1963 E 1,2, I, W, 1964 E, S, F, A 1,2,3, 1965 SA 1,2,3,4, 1966 BI 1,2,3,4, 1967 A, E, W, F, S, 1968 A 1,2, F 1,2,3, 1969 W 1,2, 1970 SA 3,4, 1971 BI 1,2,3,4

Meads, S T (King Country) 1961 F 1, 1962 A 4,5, 1963 I, 1964 A 1,2,3, 1965 SA 1,2,3,4, 1966 BI 1,2,3,4

Mealamu, K F (Auckland) 2002 W, 2003 E (R), W, F (R), SA 1, A 1, SA 2(R), A 2,[It,W,SA,A,F], 2004 E1,2,PI,A1,SA1, A2,SA2,W,F(R), 2005 Fj(R),BI1,2,3,SA1,A1,SA2,A2,I,E, 2006 I1,2,A1,2,3,SA2(R),E,F1(R),2, 2007 F1,2(R),SA1(R),A1(R), SA2,A2(R), [It,Pt(R),R], 2008 I1(R),E1(t&R),2(t&R),SA1(R), 2(R),A1(R),2(R),SA3(R),Sm(R),A3(R)

Meates, K F (Canterbury) 1952 A 1,2

Meates, W A (Otago) 1949 SA 2,3,4, 1950 BI 1,2,3,4

Meeuws, K J (Otago, Auckland) 1998 A 3, 1999 WS, F 1, SA 1, A 1, SA 2, A 2, [Tg, It (R), S (R), F 2(R), SA 3], 2000 Tg (R), S 2, A 1, SA 1, A 2, SA 2, 2001 Arg 2, 2002 It, Fj, E, F, W (R), 2003 W, F (R), SA 1(R), A 1(R), SA 2, [It(R),C,Tg, W(R),SA(R),A(R)],2004 E1,2,PI,A1,SA1,A2,SA2

Mehrtens, A P (Canterbury) 1995 C, [I, W, S, E, SA], A 1,2, 1996 WS, S 1,2, A 1, SA 1, A 2, SA 2,5, 1997 Fj, SA 2(R), I, E 1, W, E 2, 1998 E 1,2, A 1, SA 1(R), A 2, SA 2, A 3, 1999 F 1, SA 1, A 1, SA 2, A 2, [Tg, E, S, F 2, SA 3], 2000 S 1,2, A 1, SA 1, A 2, SA 2, F 1,2, It (R), 2001 Arg 1, A 1(R), SA 2, A 2, I, S, Arg 2, 2002 It, I 1,2, Fj (R), A 1, SA 1, A 2, SA 2, E (R), F, W, 2004 E2(R),Arg,A2(R), SA2

Metcalfe, T C (Southland) 1931 A, 1932 A 1

Mexted, G G (Wellington) 1950 BI 4

Mexted, M G (Wellington) 1979 S, E, 1980 A 1,2,3, W, 1981 S 1,2, SA 1,2,3, R, F 1,2, 1982 A 1,2,3, 1983 BI 1,2,3,4, A, S, E, 1984 F 1,2, A 1,2,3, 1985 E 1,2, A, Arg 1,2

Mika, B M (Auckland) 2002 E (R), F, W (R)

Mika, D G (Auckland) 1999 WS, F 1, SA 1(R), A 1,2, [It, SA 3(R)]

Mill, J J (Hawke's Bay, Wairarapa) 1924 W, 1925 E, F, 1930 BI 1

Milliken, H M (Canterbury) 1938 A 1,2,3

Milner, H P (Wanganui) 1970 SA 3

Mitchell, N A (Southland, Otago) 1935 S, I, W, 1936 E, A 2, 1937 SA 3, 1938 A 1,2

Mitchell, T W (Canterbury) 1976 SA 4(R)

Mitchell, W J (Canterbury) 1910 A 2,3

Mitchinson, F E (Wellington) 1907 A 1,2,3, 1908 AW 1,2,3, 1910 A 1,2,3, 1913 A 1(R), US

Moffitt, J E (Wellington) 1921 SA 1,2,3

Moore, G J T (Otago) 1949 A 1

Moreton, R C (Canterbury) 1962 A 3,4, 1964 A 1,2,3, 1965 SA 2,3

Morgan, J E (North Auckland) 1974 A 3, I, 1976 SA 2,3,4

Morris, T J (Nelson Bays) 1972 A 1,2,3

Morrison, T C (South Canterbury) 1938 A 1,2,3

Morrison, T G (Otago) 1973 E 2(R)

Morrissey, P J (Canterbury) 1962 A 3,4,5

Mourie, G N K (Taranaki) 1977 BI 3,4, F 1,2, 1978 I, W, E, S, 1979 F 1,2, A, S, E, 1980 W, 1981 S 1,2, F 1,2, 1982 A 1,2,3

Muliaina, J M (Auckland, Waikato) 2003 E (R), W, F, SA 1, A 1, SA 2, A 2, [It,C,Tg,W,SA,A,F], 2004 E1,2,Arg,PI,A1,SA1,A2,SA2,It,W,F, 2005 Fj,BI1(R),2,3,SA1,A1,SA2,A2,W,E, 2006 I1,2,A1,SA1,A2,3,SA2,3,E,F1(R),2,W, 2007 C,SA1,A1,SA2,A2, [It,Pt,F], 2008 I1,E1,2(t),SA1,2,A1,2,SA3,Sm,A3

Muller, B L (Taranaki) 1967 A, E, W, F, 1968 A 1, F 1, 1969 W 1, 1970 SA 1,2,4, 1971 BI 1,2,3,4

Mumm, W J (Buller) 1949 A 1

Murdoch, K (Otago) 1970 SA 4, 1972 A 3, W

Murdoch, P H (Auckland) 1964 A 2,3, 1965 SA 1,2,3

Murray, H V (Canterbury) 1913 A 1, US, 1914 A 2,3

Murray, P C (Wanganui) 1908 AW 2

Myers, R G (Waikato) 1978 A 3

Mynott, H J (Taranaki) 1905 I, W, 1906 F, 1907 A 1,2,3, 1910 A 1,3

Nathan, W J (Auckland) 1962 A 1,2,3,4,5, 1963 E 1,2, W, 1964 F, 1966 BI 1,2,3,4, 1967 A

Nelson, K A (Otago) 1962 A 4,5

Nepia, G (Hawke's Bay, East Coast) 1924 I, W, 1925 E, F, 1929 A 1, 1930 BI 1,2,3,4

Nesbit, S R (Auckland) 1960 SA 2,3

Newby, C A (North Harbour) 2004 E2(t),SA2(R), 2006 I2(R)

Newton, F (Canterbury) 1905 E, W, 1906 F

Nicholls, H E (Wellington) 1921 SA 1

Nicholls, M F (Wellington) 1921 SA 1,2,3, 1924 I, W, 1925 E, F, 1928 SA 4, 1930 BI 2,3

Nicholson, G W (Auckland) 1903 A, 1904 BI, 1907 A 2,3

Nonu, M A (Wellington) 2003 E, [It(R),C,Tg(R)], 2004 It(R), W(R),F(R), 2005 BI2(R),W(R),I,S(R), 2006 I1,E,F1(R),2,W(R), 2007 F1(R),2(R), 2008 I1,E1,2,SA1,2,A1,2,SA3,Sm,A3

Norton, R W (Canterbury) 1971 BI 1,2,3,4, 1972 A 1,2,3, W, S, 1973 E 1, I, F, E 2, 1974 A 1,2,3, I, 1975 S, 1976 I, SA 1,2,3,4, 1977 BI 1,2,3,4

O'Brien, J G (Auckland) 1914 A 1
O'Callaghan, M W (Manawatu) 1968 F 1,2,3
O'Callaghan, T R (Wellington) 1949 A 2
O'Donnell, D H (Wellington) 1949 A 2
O'Halloran, J D (Wellington) 2000 It (R)
Old, G H (Manawatu) 1981 SA 3, R (R), 1982 A 1(R)
O'Leary, M J (Auckland) 1910 A 1,3, 1913 A 2,3
Oliver, A D (Otago) 1997 Fj (t), 1998 E 1,2, A 1, SA 1, A 2, SA 2, A 3, 1999 WS, F 1, SA 1, A 1, SA 2, A 2, [Tg, E, S, F 2, SA 3(R)], 2000 Tg (R), S 1,2, A 1, SA 1, A 2, SA 2, F 1,2, It, 2001 Sm, Arg 1, F, SA 1, A 1, SA 2, A 2, I, S, Arg 2, 2003 E, F, 2004 It,F, 2005 W,S, 2006 Arg,SA1,2,3(R),F1,W, 2007 F2,SA1,A1,2, [It(R),Pt(R),S,F]
Oliver, C J (Canterbury) 1929 A 1,2, 1934 A 1, 1935 S, I, W, 1936 E
Oliver, D J (Wellington) 1930 BI 1,2
Oliver, D O (Otago) 1954 I, F
Oliver, F J (Southland, Otago, Manawatu) 1976 SA 4, 1977 BI 1,2,3,4, F 1,2, 1978 A 1,2,3, I, W, E, S, 1979 F 1,2, 1981 SA 2
O'Neill, K J (Canterbury) 2008 SA2(R)
Orr, R W (Otago) 1949 A 1
Osborne, G M (North Harbour) 1995 C, [I, W, J, E, SA], A 1,2, F 1(R),2, 1996 SA 2,3,4,5, 1997 Arg 1(R), A 2,3, I, 1999 [It]
Osborne, W M (Wanganui) 1975 S, 1976 SA 2(R),4(R), 1977 BI 1,2,3,4, F 1(R),2, 1978 I, W, E, S, 1980 W, 1982 A 1,3
O'Sullivan, J M (Taranaki) 1905 S, I, E, W, 1907 A 3
O'Sullivan, T P A (Taranaki) 1960 SA 1, 1961 F 1, 1962 A 1,2

Page, J R (Wellington) 1931 A, 1932 A 1,2,3, 1934 A 1,2
Palmer, B P (Auckland) 1929 A 2, 1932 A 2,3
Parker, J H (Canterbury) 1924 I, W, 1925 E
Parkhill, A A (Otago) 1937 SA 1,2,3, 1938 A 1,2,3
Parkinson, R M (Poverty Bay) 1972 A 1,2,3, W, S, 1973 E 1,2
Paterson, A M (Otago) 1908 AW 2,3, 1910 A 1,2,3
Paton, H (Otago) 1910 A 1,3
Pene, A R B (Otago) 1992 Wld 1(R),2,3, I 1,2, A 1,2(R), 1993 BI 3, A, WS, S, E, 1994 F 1,2(R), SA 1(R)
Phillips, W J (King Country) 1937 SA 2, 1938 A 1,2
Philpott, S (Canterbury) 1991 [It (R), S (R)]
Pickering, E A R (Waikato) 1958 A 2, 1959 BI 1,4
Pierce, M J (Wellington) 1985 E 1,2, A, Arg 1, 1986 A 2,3, F 2,3, 1987 [It, Arg, S, W, F], A, 1988 W 1,2, A 1,2,3, 1989 F 1,2, Arg 1,2, A, W, I
Pokere, S T (Southland, Auckland) 1981 SA 3, 1982 A 1,2,3, 1983 BI 1,2,3,4, A, S, E, 1984 F 1,2, A 2,3, 1985 E 1,2, A
Pollock, H R (Wellington) 1932 A 1,2,3, 1936 A 1,2
Porter, C G (Wellington) 1925 F, 1929 A 2,3, 1930 BI 1,2,3,4
Preston, J P (Canterbury, Wellington) 1991 [US, S], 1992 SA (R), 1993 BI 2,3, A, WS, 1996 SA 4(R), 1997 I (R), E 1(R)
Procter, A C (Otago) 1932 A 1
Purdue, C A (Southland) 1905 A
Purdue, E (Southland) 1905 A
Purdue, G B (Southland) 1931 A, 1932 A 1,2,3
Purvis, G H (Waikato) 1991 [US], 1993 WS
Purvis, N A (Otago) 1976 I

Quaid, C E (Otago) 1938 A 1,2

Ralph, C S (Auckland, Canterbury) 1998 E 2, 2002 It, I 1,2, A 1, SA 1, A 2, SA 2, 2003 E, A 1(R), [C,Tg,SA(R),F(t&R)]
Ranby, R M (Waikato) 2001 Sm (R)
Randell, T C (Otago) 1997 Fj, Arg 1,2, A 1, SA 1, A 2, SA 2, A 3, I, E 1, W, E 2, 1998 E 1,2, A 1, SA 1, A 2, SA 2, A 3, 1999 WS, F 1, SA 1, A 1, SA 2, A 2, [Tg, E, It, S, F 2, SA 3], 2000 Tg, S 1,2(R), A 1, SA 1, A 2, SA 2, F 2(R), It (R), 2001 Arg 1, F, SA 1, A 1, SA 2, A 2, 2002 It, Fj, E, F, W
Rangi, R E (Auckland) 1964 A 2,3, 1965 SA 1,2,3,4, 1966 BI 1,2,3,4
Rankin, J G (Canterbury) 1936 A 1,2, 1937 SA 2
Rawlinson, G P (North Harbour) 2006 I1,2(R),SA2, 2007 SA1
Reedy, W J (Wellington) 1908 AW 2,3
Reid, A R (Waikato) 1952 A 1, 1956 SA 3,4, 1957 A 1,2
Reid, H R (Bay of Plenty) 1980 A 1,2, W, 1983 S, E, 1985 Arg 1,2, 1986 A 2,3
Reid, K H (Wairarapa) 1929 A 1,3
Reid, S T (Hawke's Bay) 1935 S, I, W, 1936 E, A 1,2, 1937 SA 1,2,3
Reihana, B T (Waikato) 2000 F 2, It
Reside, W B (Wairarapa) 1929 A 1
Rhind, P K (Canterbury) 1946 A 1,2
Richardson, J (Otago, Southland) 1921 SA 1,2,3, 1924 I, W, 1925 E, F
Rickit, H (Waikato) 1981 S 1,2
Riechelmann, C C (Auckland) 1997 Fj (R), Arg 1(R), A 1(R), SA 2(t), I (R), E 2(t)
Ridland, A J (Southland) 1910 A 1,2,3
Roberts, E J (Wellington) 1914 A 1,2,3, 1921 SA 2,3
Roberts, F (Wellington) 1905 S, I, E, W, 1907 A 1,2,3, 1908 AW 1,3, 1910 A 1,2,3
Roberts, R W (Taranaki) 1913 A 1, US, 1914 A 1,2,3
Robertson, B J (Counties) 1972 A 1,3, S, 1973 E 1, I, F, 1974 A 1,2,3, I, 1976 I, SA 1,2,3,4, 1977 BI 1,3,4, F 1,2, 1978 A 1,2,3, W, E, S, 1979 F 1,2, A, 1980 A 2,3, W, 1981 S 1,2
Robertson, D J (Otago) 1974 A 1,2,3, I, 1975 S, 1976 I, SA 1,3,4, 1977 BI 1
Robertson, S M (Canterbury) 1998 A 2(R), SA 2(R), A 3(R), 1999 [It (R)], 2000 Tg (R), S 1,2(R), A 1, SA 1(R),2(R), F 1,2, It, 2001 I, S, Arg 2, 2002 I 1,2, Fj (R), A 1, SA 1, A 2, SA 2
Robilliard, A C C (Canterbury) 1928 SA 1,2,3,4
Robinson, C E (Southland) 1951 A 1,2,3, 1952 A 1,2
Robinson, K J (Waikato) 2002 E, F (R), W, 2004 E1,2,PI, 2006 E,W, 2007 SA2,A2, [R,F]
Robinson, M D (North Harbour) 1998 E 1(R), 2001 S (R), Arg 2
Robinson, M P (Canterbury) 2000 S 2, SA 1, 2002 It, I 2, A 1, SA 1, E (t&R), F, W (R)
Rokocoko, J T (Auckland) 2003 E, W, F, SA 1, A 1, SA 2, A 2, [It,W,SA,A,F], 2004 E1,2,Arg,PI,A1,SA1,A2,SA2,It,W,F, 2005 SA1(R),A1,SA2,A2,W,E(R),S, 2006 I1,2,A1,2,3,SA3,E, F1,2, 2007 F1,2,SA1,A1,SA2,A2, [Pt,R,F]
Rollerson, D L (Manawatu) 1980 W, 1981 S 2, SA 1,2,3, R, F 1(R),2
Roper, R A (Taranaki) 1949 A 2, 1950 BI 1,2,3,4
Rowley, H C B (Wanganui) 1949 A 2
Rush, E J (North Harbour) 1995 [W (R), J], It, F 1,2, 1996 S 1(R),2, A 1(t), SA 1(R)
Rush, X J (Auckland) 1998 A 3, 2004 E1,2,PI,A1,SA1,A2, SA2
Rutledge, L M (Southland) 1978 A 1,2,3, I, W, E, S, 1979 F 1,2, A, 1980 A 1,2,3
Ryan, J (Wellington) 1910 A 2, 1914 A 1,2,3
Ryan, J A C (Otago) 2005 Fj,BI3(R),A1(R),SA2(R),A2(R),W,S, 2006 F1,W(R)

Sadler, B S (Wellington) 1935 S, I, W, 1936 A 1,2
Salmon, J L B (Wellington) 1981 R, F 1,2(R)
Savage, L T (Canterbury) 1949 SA 1,2,4
Saxton, C K (South Canterbury) 1938 A 1,2,3
Schuler, K J (Manawatu, North Harbour) 1990 A 2(R), 1992 A 2, 1995 [I (R), J]
Schuster, N J (Wellington) 1988 A 1,2,3, 1989 F 1,2, Arg 1,2, A, W, I
Schwalger, J E (Wellington) 2007 C, 2008 I1(R)
Scott, R W H (Auckland) 1946 A 1,2, 1947 A 1,2, 1949 SA 1,2,3,4, 1950 BI 1,2,3,4, 1953 W, 1954 I, E, S, F
Scown, A I (Taranaki) 1972 A 1,2,3, W (R), S
Scrimshaw, G (Canterbury) 1928 SA 1
Seear, G A (Otago) 1977 F 1,2, 1978 A 1,2,3, I, W, E, S, 1979 F 1,2, A
Seeling, C E (Auckland) 1904 BI, 1905 S, I, E, W, 1906 F, 1907 A 1,2, 1908 AW 1,2,3
Sellars, G M V (Auckland) 1913 A 1, US
Senio, K (Bay of Plenty) 2005 A2(R)
Shaw, M W (Manawatu, Hawke's Bay) 1980 A 1,2,3(R), W, 1981 S 1,2, SA 1,2, R, F 1,2, 1982 A 1,2,3, 1983 BI 1,2,3,4, A, S, E, 1984 F 1,2, A 1, 1985 E 1,2, A, Arg 1,2, 1986 A 3
Shelford, F N K (Bay of Plenty) 1981 SA 3, R, 1984 A 2,3
Shelford, W T (North Harbour) 1986 F 2,3, 1987 [It, Fj, S, W, F], A, 1988 W 1,2, A 1,2,3, 1989 F 1,2, Arg 1,2, A, W, I, 1990 S 1,2
Siddells, S K (Wellington) 1921 SA 3
Simon, H J (Otago) 1937 SA 1,2,3

Simpson, J G (Auckland) 1947 A 1,2, 1949 SA 1,2,3,4, 1950 BI 1,2,3
Simpson, V L J (Canterbury) 1985 Arg 1,2
Sims, G S (Otago) 1972 A 2
Sivivatu, S W (Waikato) 2005 Fj,BI1,2,3,I,E, 2006 SA2,3,E(R),F1,2,W, 2007 F1,2,C,SA1,A1(R), [It,S,R,F], 2008 I1,E1,2,SA1,2,A1,2,SA3,A3
Skeen, J R (Auckland) 1952 A 2
Skinner, K L (Otago, Counties) 1949 SA 1,2,3,4, 1950 BI 1,2,3,4, 1951 A 1,2,3, 1952 A 1,2, 1953 W, 1954 I, E, S, F, 1956 SA 3,4
Skudder, G R (Waikato) 1969 W 2
Slater, G L (Taranaki) 2000 F 1(R),2(R), It (R)
Sloane, P H (North Auckland) 1979 E
Smith, A E (Taranaki) 1969 W 1,2, 1970 SA 1
Smith, B W (Waikato) 1984 F 1,2, A 1
Smith, C G (Wellington) 2004 It,F, 2005 Fj(R),BI3,W,S, 2006 F1,W, 2007 SA2(R), [Pt,S,R(R)], 2008 I1,E1,SA1,2,A1(R), 2,SA3,Sm,A3
Smith, G W (Auckland) 1905 S, I
Smith, I S T (Otago, North Otago) 1964 A 1,2,3, 1965 SA 1,2,4, 1966 BI 1,2,3
Smith, J B (North Auckland) 1946 A 1, 1947 A 2, 1949 A 1,2
Smith, R M (Canterbury) 1955 A 1
Smith, W E (Nelson) 1905 A
Smith, W R (Canterbury) 1980 A 1, 1982 A 1,2,3, 1983 BI 2,3, S, E, 1984 F 1,2, A 1,2,3, 1985 E 1,2, A, Arg 2
Snow, E M (Nelson) 1929 A 1,2,3
Solomon, F (Auckland) 1931 A, 1932 A 2,3
Somerville, G M (Canterbury) 2000 Tg, S 1, SA 2(R), F 1,2, It, 2001 Sm, Arg 1(R), F, SA 1, A 1, SA 2, A 2, I, S, Arg 2(t+R), 2002 I 1,2, A 1, SA 1, A 2, SA 2, 2003 E, F, SA 1, A 1, SA 2(R), A 2, [It,Tg,W,SA,A,F], 2004 Arg,SA1,A2(R), SA2(R),It(R),W,F(R), 2005 Fj,BI1(R)2,3,SA1(R),A1(R),SA2(R), A2(R), 2006 Arg,A1(R),SA1(R),A2(R),3(R),SA2, 2007 [Pt,R], 2008 E1,2,SA1,A1,2,SA3,Sm,A3
Sonntag, W T C (Otago) 1929 A 1,2,3
So'oialo, R (Wellington) 2002 W, 2003 E, SA 1(R), [It(R),C,Tg, W(t)], 2004 W,F, 2005 Fj,BI1,2,3,SA1,A1,SA2,A2,W,I(R),E, 2006 I1,2,A1,SA1,A2,3,SA3,E(R),F1,2,W, 2007 F1(R),2,SA1, A1,SA2,A2, [It,Pt(R),S,F], 2008 I1,E1,2,SA1,2,A1,2,SA3, Sm,A3
Speight, M W (Waikato) 1986 A 1
Spencer, C J (Auckland) 1997 Arg 1,2, A 1, SA 1, A 2, SA 2, A 3, E 2(R), 1998 E 2(R), A 1(R), SA 1, A 3(R), 2000 F 1(t&R), It, 2002 E, 2003 E, W, F, SA 1, A 1, SA 2, A 2, [It,C,Tg,W,SA,A,F], 2004 E1,2,PI,A1,SA1,A2
Spencer, J C (Wellington) 1905 A, 1907 A 1(R)
Spiers, J E (Counties) 1979 S, E, 1981 R, F 1,2
Spillane, A P (South Canterbury) 1913 A 2,3
Stanley, J T (Auckland) 1986 F 1, A 1,2,3, F 2,3, 1987 [It, Fj, Arg, S, W, F], A, 1988 W 1,2, A 1,2,3, 1989 F 1,2, Arg 1,2, A, W, I, 1990 S 1,2
Stead, J W (Southland) 1904 BI, 1905 S, I, E, 1906 F, 1908 AW 1,3
Steel, A G (Canterbury) 1966 BI 1,2,3,4, 1967 A, F, S, 1968 A 1,2
Steel, J (West Coast) 1921 SA 1,2,3, 1924 W, 1925 E, F
Steele, L B (Wellington) 1951 A 1,2,3
Steere, E R G (Hawke's Bay) 1930 BI 1,2,3,4, 1931 A, 1932 A 1
Steinmetz, P C (Wellington) 2002 W (R)
Stensness, L (Auckland) 1993 BI 3, A, WS, 1997 Fj, Arg 1,2, A 1, SA 1
Stephens, O G (Wellington) 1968 F 3
Stevens, I N (Wellington) 1972 S, 1973 E 1, 1974 A 3
Stewart, A J (Canterbury, South Canterbury) 1963 E 1,2, I, W, 1964 E, S, F, A 3
Stewart, J D (Auckland) 1913 A 2,3
Stewart, K W (Southland) 1973 E 2, 1974 A 1,2,3, I, 1975 S, 1976 I, SA 1,3, 1979 S, E, 1981 SA 1,2
Stewart, R T (South Canterbury, Canterbury) 1928 SA 1,2,3,4, 1930 BI 2
Stohr, L B (Taranaki) 1910 A 1,2,3
Stone, A M (Waikato, Bay of Plenty) 1981 F 1,2, 1983 BI 3(R), 1984 A 3, 1986 F 1, A 1,3, F 2,3
Storey, P W (South Canterbury) 1921 SA 1,2
Strachan, A D (Auckland, North Harbour) 1992 Wld 2,3, I 1,2, A 1,2,3, SA, 1993 BI 1, 1995 [J, SA (t)]
Strahan, S C (Manawatu) 1967 A, E, W, F, S, 1968 A 1,2, F 1,2,3, 1970 SA 1,2,3, 1972 A 1,2,3, 1973 E 2
Strang, W A (South Canterbury) 1928 SA 1,2, 1930 BI 3,4, 1931 A
Stringfellow, J C (Wairarapa) 1929 A 1(R),3
Stuart, K C (Canterbury) 1955 A 1
Stuart, R C (Canterbury) 1949 A 1,2, 1953 W, 1954 I, E, S, F
Stuart, R L (Hawke's Bay) 1977 F 1(R)
Sullivan, J L (Taranaki) 1937 SA 1,2,3, 1938 A 1,2,3
Sutherland, A R (Marlborough) 1970 SA 2,4, 1971 BI 1, 1972 A 1,2,3, W, 1973 E 1, I, F
Svenson, K S (Wellington) 1924 I, W, 1925 E, F
Swain, J P (Hawke's Bay) 1928 SA 1,2,3,4

Tanner, J M (Auckland) 1950 BI 4, 1951 A 1,2,3, 1953 W
Tanner, K J (Canterbury) 1974 A 1,2,3, I, 1975 S, 1976 I, SA 1
Taumoepeau, S (Auckland) 2004 It, 2005 I(R),S
Taylor, G L (Northland) 1996 SA 5(R)
Taylor, H M (Canterbury) 1913 A 1, US, 1914 A 1,2,3
Taylor, J M (Otago) 1937 SA 1,2,3, 1938 A 1,2,3
Taylor, M B (Waikato) 1979 F 1,2, A, S, E, 1980 A 1,2
Taylor, N M (Bay of Plenty, Hawke's Bay) 1977 BI 2,4(R), F 1,2, 1978 A 1,2,3, I, 1982 A 2
Taylor, R (Taranaki) 1913 A 2,3
Taylor, W T (Canterbury) 1983 BI 1,2,3,4, A, S, 1984 F 1,2, A 1,2, 1985 E 1,2, A, Arg 1,2, 1986 A 2, 1987 [It, Fj, S, W, F], A, 1988 W 1,2
Tetzlaff, P L (Auckland) 1947 A 1,2
Thimbleby, N W (Hawke's Bay) 1970 SA 3
Thomas, B T (Auckland, Wellington) 1962 A 5, 1964 A 1,2,3
Thomson, A J (Otago) 2008 I1(t&R),E2,SA1,2,A2(R),SA3(R),Sm
Thomson, H D (Wellington) 1908 AW 1
Thorn, B C (Canterbury) 2003 W (R), F (R), SA 1(R), A 1(R), SA 2,[It,C,Tg,W,SA(R),A(R),F(R)], 2008 I1,E1,2,SA1,A1,2, SA3,A3
Thorne, G S (Auckland) 1968 A 1,2, F 1,2,3, 1969 W 1, 1970 SA 1,2,3,4
Thorne, R D (Canterbury) 1999 SA 2(R), [Tg, E, S, F 2, SA 3], 2000 Tg, S 2, A 2(R), F 1,2, 2001 Sm, Arg 1, F, SA 1, A 1, I, S, Arg 2, 2002 It, I 1,2, Fj, A 1, SA 1, A2, SA 2, 2003 E, W, F, SA 1, A 1, SA 2, A 2, [It,C,Tg,W,SA,A,F], 2006 SA1,2,E,W(R), 2007 F1,C,SA2, [S,R]
Thornton, N H (Auckland) 1947 A 1,2, 1949 SA 1
Tialata, N S (Wellington) 2005 W,E(t),S(R), 2006 I1(R),2(R), Arg(R),SA1,2,3(R),F1(R),2(R),W, 2007 F1(R),2(R),C, A1(R),SA2(R), [It(t&R),Pt,S(R),R], 2008 I1,E1,2,SA1(R), 2(R),Sm(R)
Tiatia, F I (Wellington) 2000 Tg (R), It
Tilyard, J T (Wellington) 1913 A 3
Timu, J K R (Otago) 1991 Arg 1, A 1,2, [E, US, C, A], 1992 Wld 2, I 2, A 1,2,3, SA, 1993 BI 1,2,3, A, WS, S, E, 1994 F 1,2, SA 1,2,3, A
Tindill, E W T (Wellington) 1936 E
Toeava, I (Auckland) 2005 S, 2006 Arg,A1(t&R),A3,SA2(R), 2007 F1,2,SA1,2,A2, [It(R),Pt,S(R),R,F(R)], 2008 SA3(R), Sm(R)
Tonu'u, O F J (Auckland) 1997 Fj (R), A 3(R), 1998 E 1,2, SA 1(R)
Townsend, L J (Otago) 1955 A 1,3
Tremain, K R (Canterbury, Hawke's Bay) 1959 BI 2,3,4, 1960 SA 1,2,3,4, 1961 F 2,3 1962 A 1,2,3, 1963 E 1,2, I, W, 1964 E, S, F, A 1,2,3, 1965 SA 1,2,3,4, 1966 BI 1,2,3,4, 1967 A, E, W, S, 1968 A 1, F 1,2,3
Trevathan, D (Otago) 1937 SA 1,2,3
Tuck, J M (Waikato) 1929 A 1,2,3
Tuiali'i, M M (Auckland) 2004 Arg,A2(R),SA2(R),It,W, 2005 I,E(R),S(R), 2006 Arg
Tuigamala, V L (Auckland) 1991 [US, It, C, S], 1992 Wld 1,2,3, I 1, A 1,2,3, SA, 1993 BI 1,2,3, A, WS, S, E
Tuitavake, A T (North Harbour) 2008 I1,E1,A1,2(R),Sm
Tuitupou, S (Auckland) 2004 E1(R),2(R),Arg,SA1(R),A2(R),SA2, 2006 Arg,SA1,2(R)
Turner, R S (North Harbour) 1992 Wld 1,2(R)
Turtill, H S (Canterbury) 1905 A
Twigden, T M (Auckland) 1980 A 2,3

Tyler, G A (Auckland) 1903 A, 1904 BI, 1905 S, I, E, W, 1906 F

Udy, D K (Wairarapa) 1903 A
Umaga, J F (Wellington) 1997 Fj, Arg 1,2, A 1, SA 1,2, 1999 WS, F 1, SA 1, A 1, SA 2, A 2, [Tg, E, S, F 2, SA 3], 2000 Tg, S 1,2, A 1, SA 1, A 2, SA 2, F 1,2, It, 2001 Sm, Arg 1, F, SA 1, A 1, SA 2, A 2, I, S, Arg 2, 2002 I 1, Fj, SA 1(R), A 2, SA 2, E, F, W, 2003 E, W, F, SA 1, A 1, SA 2, A 2, [It], 2004 E1,2,Arg,PI,A1,SA1,A2,SA2,It,F, 2005 Fj,BI1,2,3,SA1,A1,SA2,A2,W,E,S
Urbahn, R J (Taranaki) 1959 BI 1,3,4
Urlich, R A (Auckland) 1970 SA 3,4
Uttley, I N (Wellington) 1963 E 1,2

Vidiri, J (Counties Manukau) 1998 E 2(R), A 1
Vincent, P B (Canterbury) 1956 SA 1,2
Vodanovich, I M H (Wellington) 1955 A 1,2,3

Wallace, W J (Wellington) 1903 A, 1904 BI, 1905 S, I, E, W, 1906 F, 1907 A 1,2,3, 1908 AW 2
Waller, D A G (Wellington) 2001 Arg 2(t)
Walsh, P T (Counties) 1955 A 1,2,3, 1956 SA 1,2,4, 1957 A 1,2, 1958 A 1,2,3, 1959 BI 1, 1963 E 2
Ward, R H (Southland) 1936 A 2, 1937 SA 1,3
Waterman, A C (North Auckland) 1929 A 1,2
Watkins, E L (Wellington) 1905 A
Watt, B A (Canterbury) 1962 A 1,4, 1963 E 1,2, W, 1964 E, S, A 1
Watt, J M (Otago) 1936 A 1,2
Watt, J R (Wellington) 1958 A 2, 1960 SA 1,2,3,4, 1961 F 1,3, 1962 A 1,2
Watts, M G (Taranaki) 1979 F 1,2, 1980 A 1,2,3(R)
Webb, D S (North Auckland) 1959 BI 2
Weepu, P A T (Wellington) 2004 W, 2005 SA1(R),A1,SA2,A2,I, E(R),S, 2006 Arg,A1(R),SA1,A3(R),SA2,F1,W(R), 2007 F1, C(R),SA1(R),A1(R),SA2, 2008 A2(R),SA3(R),Sm(R),A3(R)
Wells, J (Wellington) 1936 A 1,2
West, A H (Taranaki) 1921 SA 2,3
Whetton, A J (Auckland) 1984 A 1(R),3(R), 1985 A (R), Arg 1(R), 1986 A 2, 1987 [It, Fj, Arg, S, W, F], A, 1988 W 1,2, A 1,2,3, 1989 F 1,2, Arg 1,2, A, 1990 S 1,2, A 1,2,3, F 1,2, 1991 Arg 1, [E, US, It, C, A]
Whetton, G W (Auckland) 1981 SA 3, R, F 1,2, 1982 A 3, 1983 BI 1,2,3,4, 1984 F 1,2, A 1,2,3, 1985 E 1,2, A, Arg 2, 1986 A 2,3, F 2,3, 1987 [It, Fj, Arg, S, W, F], A, 1988 W 1,2, A 1,2,3, 1989 F 1,2, Arg 1,2, A, W, I, 1990 S 1,2, A 1,2,3, F 1,2, 1991 Arg 1,2, A 1,2, [E, US, It, C, A, S]
Whineray, W J (Canterbury, Waikato, Auckland) 1957 A 1,2, 1958 A 1,2,3, 1959 BI 1,2,3,4, 1960 SA 1,2,3,4, 1961 F 1,2,3, 1962 A 1,2,3,4,5, 1963 E 1,2, I, W, 1964 E, S, F, 1965 SA 1,2,3,4
White, A (Southland) 1921 SA 1, 1924 I, 1925 E, F
White, H L (Auckland) 1954 I, E, F, 1955 A 3
White, R A (Poverty Bay) 1949 A 1,2, 1950 BI 1,2,3,4, 1951 A 1,2,3, 1952 A 1,2, 1953 W, 1954 I, E, S, F, 1955 A 1,2,3, 1956 SA 1,2,3,4
White, R M (Wellington) 1946 A 1,2, 1947 A 1,2
Whiting, G J (King Country) 1972 A 1,2, S, 1973 E 1, I, F
Whiting, P J (Auckland) 1971 BI 1,2,4, 1972 A 1,2,3, W, S, 1973 E 1, I, F, 1974 A 1,2,3, I, 1976 I, SA 1,2,3,4
Williams, A J (Auckland) 2002 E, F, W, 2003 E, W, F, SA 1, A 1, SA 2, A 2, [Tg,W,SA,A,F], 2004 SA1(R),A2,It(R),W,F(R), 2005 Fj,BI1,2,3,SA1,A1,SA2,A2,I,E, 2006 Arg,A1(R),SA1, A2,3(R),SA2,3,F1,2,W, 2007 F1,2, [It,Pt,S,F], 2008 I1,E1,2, SA1,2,A1,2,SA3,Sm,A3
Williams, B G (Auckland) 1970 SA 1,2,3,4, 1971 BI 1,2,4, 1972 A 1,2,3, W, S, 1973 E 1, I, F, E 2, 1974 A 1,2,3, I, 1975 S, 1976 I, SA 1,2,3,4, 1977 BI 1,2,3,4, F 1, 1978 A 1,2,3, I (R), W, E, S
Williams, G C (Wellington) 1967 E, W, F, S, 1968 A 2
Williams, P (Otago) 1913 A 1
Williment, M (Wellington) 1964 A 1, 1965 SA 1,2,3, 1966 BI 1,2,3,4, 1967 A
Willis, R K (Waikato) 1998 SA 2, A 3, 1999 SA 1(R), A 1(R), SA 2(R), A 2(R), [Tg (R), E (R), It, F 2(R), SA 3], 2002 SA 1(R)
Willis, T E (Otago) 2002 It, Fj, SA 2(R), A 2, SA 2
Willocks, C (Otago) 1946 A 1,2, 1949 SA 1,3,4
Wilson, B W (Otago) 1977 BI 3,4, 1978 A 1,2,3, 1979 F 1,2, A
Wilson, D D (Canterbury) 1954 E, S
Wilson, H W (Otago) 1949 A 1, 1950 BI 4, 1951 A 1,2,3
Wilson, J W (Otago) 1993 S, E, 1994 A, 1995 C, [I, J, S, E, SA], A 1,2, It, F 1, 1996 WS, S 1,2, A 1, SA 1, A 2, SA 2,3,4,5, 1997 Fj, Arg 1,2, A 1, SA 1, A 2, SA 2, A 3, I, E 1, W, E 2, 1998 E 1,2, A 1, SA 1, A 2, SA 2, A 3, 1999 WS, F 1, SA 1, A 1, SA 2, A 2, [Tg, E, It, S, F 2, SA 3], 2001 Sm, Arg 1, F, SA 1, A 1, SA 2
Wilson, N A (Wellington) 1908 AW 1,2, 1910 A 1,2,3, 1913 A 2,3, 1914 A 1,2,3
Wilson, N L (Otago) 1951 A 1,2,3
Wilson, R G (Canterbury) 1979 S, E
Wilson, S S (Wellington) 1977 F 1,2, 1978 A 1,2,3, I, W, E, S, 1979 F 1,2, A, S, E, 1980 A 1, W, 1981 S 1,2, SA 1,2,3, R, F 1,2, 1982 A 1,2,3, 1983 BI 1,2,3,4, A, S, E
Witcombe, D J C (Auckland) 2005 Fj,BI1(R),2(R),SA1(R),A1(R)
Wolfe, T N (Wellington, Taranaki) 1961 F 1,2,3, 1962 A 2,3, 1963 E 1
Wood, M E (Canterbury, Auckland) 1903 A, 1904 BI
Woodcock, T D (North Harbour) 2002 W, 2004 E1(t&R), 2(t&R),Arg,W,F, 2005 Fj,BI1,2,3,SA1,A1,SA2,A2,W(R),I,E, 2006 Arg,A1,2,3,SA2(R),3,E,F1,2,W(R), 2007 F1,2,SA1,A1, SA2,A2, [It,Pt(R),S,F], 2008 E2(R),SA1,2,A1,2,SA3,Sm,A3
Woodman, F A (North Auckland) 1981 SA 1,2, F 2
Wrigley, E (Wairarapa) 1905 A
Wright, T J (Auckland) 1986 F 1, A 1, 1987 [Arg], 1988 W 1,2, A 1,2,3, 1989 F 1,2, Arg 1,2, A, W, I, 1990 S 1,2, A 1,2,3, F 1,2, 1991 Arg 1,2, A 1,2, [E, US, It, S]
Wulf, R N (North Harbour) 2008 E2,SA1,2,Sm(R)
Wylie, J T (Auckland) 1913 A 1, US
Wyllie, A J (Canterbury) 1970 SA 2,3, 1971 BI 2,3,4, 1972 W, S, 1973 E 1, I, F, E 2

Yates, V M (North Auckland) 1961 F 1,2,3
Young, D (Canterbury) 1956 SA 2, 1958 A 1,2,3, 1960 SA 1,2,3,4, 1961 F 1,2,3, 1962 A 1,2,3,5, 1963 E 1,2, I, W, 1964 E, S, F

NEW ZEALAND DOMESTIC RUGBY

By Gregor Paul

Ross Land / Getty Images

Wellington's capture of the Ranfurly Shield was one of the higlights of the year

It was a tumultuous year for provincial rugby in New Zealand with most of the action taking place off the field.

A crisis meeting was called in March to discuss ways in which the Air New Zealand Cup should be revamped in 2009. The meeting was called after a number of provinces ended 2007 in financial strife.

Bay of Plenty lost almost $1 million (£375,000), Northland $350,000 (£130,000) and even Canterbury, one of the strongest and most successful teams in the country, lost more than $500,000 (£187,000).

It was agreed at the meeting that the New Zealand Rugby Union needed to conduct a full review of the 14-team competition and suggest ways in which it could be restructured to become financially viable as well as better engage supporters, broadcasters and sponsors.

The NZRU recommended in July that it would cut the competition in 2009 to 12 teams and would assess every union on a range of criteria that included such things as their playing history, financial governance and development systems, and eliminate the two unions with the lowest score.

By the end of the process it was declared that Tasman – the union that came into existence in 2006 when Nelson Bays and Marlborough merged – and Northland, would be relegated to the amateur Heartland Championship at the end of the season.

Tasman had little choice but to accept their fate as the union was only able to see out its obligations in 2008 thanks to a $300,000 (£112,000) loan from the NZRU. The alliance between Nelson Bays and Marlborough was broken with the latter deciding they would rather split and return to the Heartland Championship.

Northland, on the other hand, were outraged by the decision and opted to mount a ferocious legal challenge to have it overturned. An outcome from the law courts was not expected until early 2009.

All that drama off the field took much of the gloss away from an intriguing domestic season that saw Auckland lose the Ranfurly Shield to Wellington.

Auckland had taken the Shield from Canterbury on their way to an undefeated 2007, where they were crowned provincial champions.

They were badly hit by the dreaded player exodus, though, losing 15 of their 2007 squad, including Isa Nacewa (Leinster), Brent Ward (Racing Metro), Saimone Taumeopeau (Toulon) and Sam Tuitupou (Worcester).

That forced Auckland coach Pat Lam – who was awarded the top job with the Blues shortly before the Air NZ Cup began leading to his assistant Shane Howarth taking over mid-way through the campaign – to call up a host of unknown youngsters. They struggled to beat Poverty Bay 54–3 in their first defence – the modern tradition is for the Shield holder to offer two challenges to Heartland unions – before clicking into form against North Otago, whom they beat 113–3.

When the stiffer challenges came, Auckland made hard work of beating Taranaki 22–6 and then required a bit of help from the officials to see off Manawatu 26–3, the game-breaker coming when the home side were awarded a penalty try that was generous to say the least.

Southland came perilously close to winning the Shield for the first time since 1959 when they came to Eden Park on September 7, but just couldn't score in the closing minutes to overturn the 13–9 deficit.

Auckland's unconvincing form meant a rampant Wellington side arrived at Eden Park on September 21 as favourites. The Lions were unbeaten and they soaked up some relentless Auckland pressure in the first half hour before striking twice on the counter-attack to reach the break 10–0 ahead. With 20 minutes remaining the visitors were in total control, dominating every facet of the game and they won 27–0 to claim the Shield for the first time since 1982.

Wellington were expecting to learn before the end of the year whether they would have to defend the Shield under a new format in 2009. The existing rules state that all home Air New Zealand Cup round robin games double as Shield challenges. The NZRU proposed that in 2009, after four successful home defences, the Shield would go on the line every time the holders played.

The NZRU also proposed limiting the number of overseas players that could be included in the match-day 22 after seeing an influx of foreigners in 2008.

The pick of the new arrivals was Ospreys centre Jonathan Spratt, who made a strong impression at Taranaki scoring a hat-trick against Northland. Bath's Martin Purdy settled well in the second row for North Harbour and would have been joined by England cap Dave Walder at Harbour if a broken leg had not prevented the Wasps fly-half from travelling south.

Several unions opted to look offshore for players as the New Zealand market was again left drained by the number of its own promising stars who were lured by the bright lights of Europe.

The 2008 campaign saw a number of long-serving provincial heavy-weights call it quits. Former All Black and New Zealand Maori captain Jono Gibbes retired as Waikato captain due to a knee injury and took up a role as assistant coach at Leinster. Otago captain and former All Black Craig Newby joined Leicester and two other former All Black loose forwards also left; Chris Masoe saw out the campaign with Wellington before jetting off to join Castres and Canterbury No 8 Mose Tuilai'I went east to Japan.

And it wasn't just on the playing side that New Zealand was feeling light on resource. The country's most experienced referee, Paul Honiss, hung up his whistle and was followed into retirement by Lyndon Bray, leaving New Zealand with just three professional referees.

There was also significant change in 2008 to the country's two largest grounds – Eden Park and AMI Stadium.

Auckland had to play their games with demolition of the South Stand in full progress. Renovation of the famous ground began in August as the stadium is being rebuilt to host the semi-finals and final of the 2011 Rugby World Cup.

Canterbury also had to get used to playing on a construction site as AMI Stadium also began a project to transform itself into a 43,000 set venue that will host two quarter-finals in 2011.

PORTUGAL

PORTUGAL'S 2007–08 TEST RECORD

OPPONENTS	DATE	VENUE	RESULT
Romania	1 December	H	**Lost** 8–23
Georgia	2 February	A	**Lost** 3–31
Czech Republic	16 February	H	**Won** 42–6
Georgia	23 February	H	**Lost** 6–11
Russia	1 March	A	**Won** 41–26
Romania	8 March	A	**Lost** 15–21
Spain	10 May	A	**Lost** 17–21

A NEW CHAPTER BEGINS

By Frankie Deges

Vasco Uva test-drives a Mercedes Benz E 220 and is asked if that has been his best try. "Whilst seated . . ." he answers with a crisp smile. The ad campaign ran strongly on prime time Portuguese television for a couple of months post-Rugby World Cup 2007. That the captain of Os Lobos (The Wolves) was chosen by a big brand to be the star of such a campaign shows the new profile the game of rugby enjoyed in Portugal after France 2007.

Before their departure to France, thanks to the much needed support of the Portuguese government and of the small rugby community, the game in the country was starting to become well known thanks to their gutsy qualification to play amongst the best in the world.

It was a superb tournament for the Portuguese team. They were hoping for a win that understandably never came – a close 10–14 loss against Romania the tournament highlight.

Under the captaincy of Uva, one of the standout players of the World Cup, Portugal knew their ride was about pride, emotion, and taking the game to new heights at home. This they did and upon returning home to Lisbon, they were hailed as heroes, huge crowds waiting for them at the airport and the team was paraded for a few days from television show to television show.

Once the dust of celebrity settled, they all went back to their normal life. A squad of doctors, lawyers, dentists, teachers and students returned to their day-to-day grind, one that had been put aside for some five months as the Rugby World Cup goal was pursued.

New sponsors, bigger television coverage, a renewed organisation and more interest in the game were all positive changes for Portuguese rugby. The new Rugby World Cup cycle, one that will hopefully give Portugal another taste of the biggest showdown, in New Zealand within three years, soon started.

Again at the helm and leading the ride with the brain of a senior statesman is Tomaz Morais. A year ago in this IRB World Rugby Yearbook we reflected how Portugal's Mr Rugby had failed to enjoy the World Cup. "His newborn daughter had complications," said the 2008 edition, explaining how Morais, 38, had shuttled backwards and forwards to be by his wife and ailing daughter.

A year later, Morais is able to give his 100 per cent focus to the game he loves – his daughter in full health. He has become a de-facto spokesperson for the game and, holding the job of national coach at 15s and Sevens, he is also in high demand in workshops and has helped spread the rugby gospel.

Expectedly, whilst the playing numbers grew and the game had to be ready to receive so many new kids wanting to play rugby, the World Cup did mean the end of the road for a handful of loyal players, while a few others were given professional opportunities in France and Italy.

There is a new dawn awaiting Portugal.

Thanks to an agreement with the government and with the support of the International Rugby Board, new development structures are being put in place, and a High Performance Centre is in the making. The IRB is again assisting with coaching and implementing a raft of programmes as Portugal also sees some front-loading to enable the development of High Performance infrastructure. It will receive £875,000 over a four-year cycle.

A squad of 30 players has been put on a programme that will assist them financially – whilst not being full-time players, it will allow them to devout sufficient time to preparing for the game.

"We are a lot better as a rugby nation. We had a post-RWC increase of about 40 per cent more children," says Uva. Major sponsors have been signed, amongst them Canterbury is now providing the kit for the national team.

Notwithstanding these moves in the right direction, there is a shortage of rugby fields in the country and it is an issue that must be tackled soon.

"We had to select a new pack of forwards and it wasn't easy," said Morais "We had to experiment with new players and had some good matches but we were overall not competitive enough." This meant that for the first time since 2002 they finished fifth of six teams in the European Nations Cup.

The second part of a tournament that had started in 2007 brought Romania to Lisbon in December. Unlike the match in Paris a couple of months earlier, the Oaks found it easier to control the Portuguese and inflicted on them an 8–23 loss.

The next game, which had to be rescheduled due to the political situation in Georgia, came in February at the Mikheil Meskhi Stadium, Tbilisi, where the Georgian Lelos, who would win the European Nations Cup, tore Os Lobos apart.

Release problems typical of nations that don't have their players under contracts, and the need to select from outside the RWC squad saw Portugal offer no answers to a fired-up Lelos, who scored five tries and three drop goals against a solitary penalty by the visiting XV.

The 31–3 losing margin would be reduced when both teams met again in Lisbon, a fortnight later.

With a good 42–6, five-try, home win against the Czech Republic sandwiched between matches, Os Lobos showed their teeth against Georgia and came painstakingly close to a win, the 11–6 final score a reflection of how, in a short space of time, Morais managed to work his team into regaining confidence. Playing at home was also important in their return to form.

The next Test was a better performance, yet not one that brought a win. When the Wolves travelled to the cold of Krasnodar, it was always going to be difficult, the problems starting on arrival, which required the assistance of the Portuguese Government. Russia won the high tempo match 41–26. New captain Joao Correia scored one of the two tries (Francisco Mira the other scorer) – the remaining 16 points coming from the boot of fly-half Pedro Cabral.

The next game, in Bucharest against Romania, brought a last minute loss – the 21–15 score an unfair reflection of what happened on the field. "We were unlucky in this one," recalled Morais.

Then came the loss that hurt the most, against arch-rivals Spain, in Madrid. "We played very badly against the Spaniards," laments Morais of his team's 21–17 loss. With 20 minutes to turn the tables, they failed to break the solid Spanish defence – the home side upstaged the Portuguese to finish overall fourth in the ENC.

"It wasn't an easy year," reflects Vasco Uva, who was not available for the whole ENC campaign. Having joined his younger brother Gonçalo in Montpellier, in the French National Ligue, he struggled to be released for Test duty and had to relinquish the captaincy. "About ten players were unavailable because of retirement and unavailability. That some of us were offered professional contracts in France and Italy was a reflection of our World Cup campaign."

Uva will return to Portugal after his short French experience and is aiming for a place in the squad that qualified for Rugby World Cup Sevens. Playing and coaching resources are tight in Portugal and it was again the Morais-Uva combo that led the campaign that booked them a place in Dubai.

"The problem is that the qualifying rounds for RWC 2011 start at around the same time as Dubai and we will have to plan very well if we want to do both things right," said Morais who coaches both national teams.

The strength of Portugal in sevens rugby cannot be underestimated. Handsomely beating Wales 26–12 in Hannover to capture the title of European champions they lead the charge of the five regional qualifiers Dubai. The Portuguese lived up to their billing as top seeds in the European championship, this being the sixth European win in seven seasons.

Coach Morais said: "We were able to work out our problems with courage. It was our 19th win in the European Circuit; we won three tournaments and scored more than 500 points."

The sevens seasons had brought few smiles from their IRB Sevens trip to Hong Kong (one win and three losses) but reached the quarter-finals in London, where a win against Australia 28–12 was a highlight of the season.

C.F. Os Belenenses won the Honour Division, the First Division Championship in a tight final, beating Agronomía 22–21. It needed a last gasp try to settle the affair. Agronomía had been the best side of the season, but was unable to control the eventual champions in those last few seconds.

The future at club level seems bright, with an Iberian League ready to start as soon as 2009. Ten franchises – four of which will be based in Portugal – will compete in a format similar to that in the Celtic League.

The Portuguese Federation has in principle agreed to support the new venture and provide four franchises, which will involve the eight First Division clubs. Two will be in Lisbon, where the majority of the close to 10,000 registered players live, the other two in the north (the Oporto region) and in the south (the Algarve, where the strong English ex-pat community will be targeted for its support).

PORTUGAL INTERNATIONAL RECORDS

MATCH RECORDS UP TO 30TH SEPTEMBER 2008

WINNING MARGIN

Date	Opponent	Result	Winning Margin
23/11/1996	Portugal	55–11	**44**
30/05/1998	Portugal	53–11	**42**
28/02/1981	Portugal	39–0	**39**

MOST CONVERSIONS IN A MATCH BY THE TEAM

Date	Opponent	Result	Cons
23/11/1996	Portugal	55–11	**6**
13/05/2006	Portugal	52–14	**6**

MOST POINTS IN A MATCH BY THE TEAM

Date	Opponent	Result	Pts.
23/11/1996	Portugal	55–11	**55**
30/05/1998	Portugal	53–11	**53**
13/05/2006	Portugal	52–14	**52**

MOST PENALTIES IN A MATCH BY THE TEAM

Date	Opponent	Result	Pens
06/02/2000	Portugal	30–32	**9**
20/02/2000	Portugal	21–19	**7**
23/03/2003	Portugal	35–16	**7**

MOST TRIES IN A MATCH BY THE TEAM

Date	Opponent	Result	Tries
15/05/1981	Portugal	45–16	9
23/11/1996	Portugal	55–11	8
13/05/2006	Portugal	52–14	8
30/05/1998	Portugal	53–11	8

MOST DROP GOALS IN A MATCH BY THE TEAM

Date	Opponent	Result	DGs
05/05/1990	Portugal	24–12	2
17/03/1985	Portugal	12–6	2

MOST POINTS IN A MATCH BY A PLAYER

Date	Player	Opponent	Pts.
06/02/2000	Thierry Teixeira	Georgia	30
23/03/2003	Gonçalo Malheiro	Spain	25
08/03/2003	Gonçalo Malheiro	Czech Republic	24

LEADING TRY SCORERS

Name	Tries
António Aguilar	14
Nuno Durão	14

MOST TRIES IN A MATCH BY A PLAYER

Date	Player	Opponent	Tries
21/03/2004	Nuno Garváo	Spain	3
10/06/2004	Gonçalo Malheiro	Barbarians	3
23/11/1996	Rohan Hoffman	Netherlands	3

LEADING CONVERSIONS SCORERS

Name	Cons
Joao Queimado	22
Gonçalo Malheiro	21
Nuno Mourao	16

MOST CONVERSIONS IN A MATCH BY A PLAYER

Date	Player	Opponent	Cons
23/11/1996	Nuno Maria Vilar Gomes	Netherlands	6

LEADING PENALTY SCORERS

Name	Pens
Joao Queimado	63
Gonçalo Malheiro	53
José Maria Vilar Gomes	28

MOST PENALTIES IN A MATCH BY A PLAYER

Date	Player	Opponent	Pens
06/02/2000	Thierry Teixeira	Georgia	9
23/03/2003	Gonçalo Malheiro	Spain	7
29/03/2003	Gonçalo Malheiro	Russia	6

LEADING DROP GOAL SCORERS

Name	DGs
Joao Queimado	12
Gonçalo Malheiro	2

MOST DROP GOALS IN A MATCH BY A PLAYER

Date	Player	Opponent	DGs
17/03/1985	Joao Queimado	Morocco	2

LEADING POINTS SCORERS

Name	Pts.
Joao Queimado	294
Gonçalo Malheiro	242
José Maria Vilar Gomes	134

MOST CAPPED PLAYERS

Name	Caps
Joaquim Ferreira	84
Luis Pissarra	72
Diogo Mateus	58

PORTUGAL INTERNATIONAL PLAYERS
UP TO 30TH SEPTEMBER 2008

Note: Years given for International Championship matches are for second half of season; eg 1972 means season 1971–72. Years for all other matches refer to the actual year of the match.

ED Acosta 2006 *Rus, Ur*, 2007 *R*, 2008 *Geo, Rus, R*
A Águas 1984 *H, Bel, De*, 1985 *Mor, Cze, Pol, Z*, 1986 *R, R*, 1987 *Z, Z, Tun, Bel*, 1988 *Ger*
D Aguiar 1970 *H, Mor, Sp*, 1981 *Swi, De, Swe*, 1982 *Mor, Sp*
R Aguiar 2005 *Ur*, 2006 *Ukr, CZR*, 2008 *Geo, CZR, Geo, Rus*
A Aguilar 1999 *H, Ur, Ur*, 2000 *Geo, Sp, SA23*, 2001 *R, H, Rus*, 2002 *R, Geo, Sp, H, Rus, Pol, Sp*, 2003 *Geo, Sp*, 2004 *Geo, R, CZR, Sp, Rus, Bb*, 2005 *Rus, R, Ch, Ur, Fj*, 2006 *Rus, Geo, R, Ukr, CZR, Rus, Ur, It, Rus, Geo, Geo*, 2007 *C, NZ, It, R, R*, 2008 *Geo, R, Sp*
E Albergaria 1935 *Sp*
JM Albergaria 1981 *Swi*
M Albuquerque 1987 *USS*, 1988 *Yug*
AV Almeida 1983 *Sp, H, Pol, Swe*, 1984 *Sp, H, Bel, De*, 1985 *Mor, Cze, Pol, Z*, 1986 *R, F, It, Tun, R*, 1987 *It, Bel*, 1988 *H, Ger, Yug*, 1989 *H, Bel, Yug, Ger, Cze, H*, 1990 *Bel, Tun, Sp*, 1991 *Nm*
J Almeida 1954 *Sp*
PM Almeida 1974 *Ger*
G Alpuim 1998 *US, And*, 2006 *CZR*
FP Álvares 1954 *Sp*
AF Amaral 1965 *Sp*, 1969 *Sp*
SF Amaral 1997 *Geo, Sp*, 1998 *Nm, Ger, US, CZR, Mor, Sp, And, S, Sp*, 1999 *H, Ur, Ur*, 2000 *Geo, Sp, R, Mor, H*
A Andrade 1970 *H, Mor*, 1972 *It*
AR Andrade 1994 *Bel, Ger, Mor, Tun, W, Sp*, 1995 *Mor*
LR Andrade 2002 *Sp*, 2003 *Rus*, 2004 *Geo, R, CZR, Sp, Rus, Bb, Ch, Ur, Ukr*, 2005 *Geo, CZR, Rus*, 2006 *Ukr, CZR*, 2007 *CZR*
T Antunes 1970 *Sp*
FX Araújo 1935 *Sp*, 1936 *Sp*
M Ascenção 1999 *Ur*
JC Augusto 1970 *Sp*, 1972 *It, It*
GB Ávila 1973 *It, Yug, Swi, Pol, Pol*
AM Avilez 1936 *Sp*
S Azevedo 1997 *Sp*, 1998 *Nm, Ger, US, CZR, Mor, Sp, And*
J Baptista 1998 *US, And*, 2002 *R*
M Baptista 1993 *It, Bel*, 1994 *Bel, Ger, Mor, Tun, W, Sp*
R Barata 1998 *Nm, Ger*
M Barbosa 1996 *Sp, H, Tun*, 1998 *S, Sp*, 1999 *H, Ur, Ur*, 2000 *Geo, Sp, R, Mor, H*, 2001 *H, Rus*
J Barceló 1936 *Sp*
R Bastos 1935 *Sp*
R Begonha 1966 *Sp, Bel*
FL Belo 1986 *R*, 1987 *It, F, Z*, 1988 *H, Ger, Yug*
J Belo 1954 *Sp*
JFL Belo 1985 *Mor, Cze, Pol*, 1986 *F, It, Tun, USS, R*, 1987 *It, F, Z, Z, Tun, USS*, 1988 *H, Ger, Yug*, 1989 *H, Bel, Yug, Ger, Cze, H*, 1990 *Sp*
R Benedito 2000 *SA23*, 2001 *Geo, Sp*
J Bento 1997 *Geo, Sp*, 1998 *Nm*
H Bergh 2003 *R, CZR, Sp, Rus*
JP Bessa 1969 *Sp, Mor*, 1972 *It, It*, 1974 *It*
A Borges 1966 *Sp, Bel*
F Borges 1989 *H*, 1991 *Mor, Nm*, 1992 *And, Mor, Tun*, 1993 *It, Tun, Swi*
O Borges 1979 *Swi*, 1981 *Swi, De, Swe*
R Borges 1997 *Geo, Sp*
F Braga 1995 *Mor, Sp*
A Branco 1968 *Sp, Bel, Mor, It*, 1970 *Sp*, 1974 *Ger*
E Branco 1935 *Sp*, 1936 *Sp*
E Branco 2000 *Mor, H*, 2001 *R*, 2002 *Geo, Sp, H, Rus*
MA Branco 1965 *Sp*, 1970 *H, Sp*
MdePC Branco 1965 *Sp*, 1966 *Sp, Bel*, 1967 *Sp, F, R*, 1968 *Sp, Bel, Mor, It*, 1969 *Sp, Mor*, 1970 *H, Mor*
GVB Bravo 1954 *Sp*
JS Brito 1973 *It, Yug, Swi, Pol, Pol*, 1974 *It, Ger*
L Briz 1973 *Yug, Pol, Pol*
C Bruxelas 1935 *Sp*
P Cabral 2006 *Ur*, 2007 *Sp, Rus, CZR, C, S, It, R*, 2008 *Geo, CZR, Geo, Rus, R, Sp*
P Cabrita 1966 *Sp, Bel*
L Caldas 1954 *Sp*
F Calheiros 1935 *Sp*
J Canha 1999 *Ur, Ur*
A Carapuço 1987 *It*
F Cardoso 1999 *H, Ur, Ur*
M Cardoso 2000 *Geo, Sp, R, Mor, H*, 2001 *R, Geo, Sp, H, Rus*
AM Carqueijeiro 1965 *Sp*
A Cartucho 1970 *Sp*
J Carvalho 1998 *Sp, Sp*, 1999 *H*, 2000 *Geo, Sp, R*
P Carvalho 2004 *Ch, Ur, Ukr*, 2005 *Geo, CZR, Rus, Fj*, 2006 *Ukr, CZR, Rus, Ur, It, Rus, Geo, Geo*, 2007 *Mor, Mor, Sp, Ur, Ur, CZR, C, S, NZ, R*
R Carvoeira 1990 *Mor, Nm*, 1991 *And, Nm*
C Castro 2000 *Sp, R, Mor, H, SA23*, 2001 *R, Sp, Rus*
PM Castro 1995 *Sp, CZR, Ger*, 1996 *It, Bel, R, Pol, Tun*, 1997 *Geo, Sp*, 1998 *Ger, CZR, Sp, And, S, Sp*, 2002 *Geo*, 2006 *Geo*
F Cather 2001 *Sp, H, Rus*
J Catulo 1993 *R*, 1996 *It, Bel, Pol*
V Cayola 1935 *Sp*
J Chança 1990 *Mor, Nm*, 1992 *Tun*
R Chança 1998 *Nm, Ger, US, CZR*
LM Chaves 1965 *Sp*, 1966 *Sp, Bel*, 1967 *It, F, R*, 1969 *Sp*, 1970 *Sp*
L Claro 1981 *Swi*
A Cláudio 1997 *Geo, Sp*, 1998 *Sp, And*
A Coelho 1935 *Sp*
B Conceicao 2006 *Rus, Geo, R*
P Consciência 1979 *Swi*
R Cordeiro 2002 *R, Geo, Sp, H, Rus, Pol, Sp*, 2003 *Geo, R, CZR, Sp, Rus*, 2004 *Geo, R, CZR, Sp, Rus, Bb, Ch, Ur, Ukr*, 2005 *Rus, R, Fj*, 2006 *Rus, Geo, R, CZR, Rus, Ur, It, Rus, Geo, Geo*, 2007 *Mor, Mor, Sp, Ur, CZR, S, NZ, It, R*
Correia 1990 *Mor, Nm, Bel, Tun*, 1993 *R, It, Swi, Sp*
E Correia 1998 *US, Mor*
H Correia 1935 *Sp*, 1936 *Sp*
J Correia 2003 *CZR, Sp*, 2004 *Bb, Ch, Ur, Ukr*, 2005 *Geo, CZR, Rus, R, Ch, Ur, Fj*, 2006 *Rus, R, Ukr, Rus, It, Rus, Geo, Geo*, 2007 *Mor, Mor, Sp, Ur, Ur, C, S, NZ, It, R, R*, 2008 *Geo, CZR, Geo, Rus, R, Sp*
J Correia 1999 *Ur*
AP Costa 1967 *Sp*, 1968 *Bel, It*, 1969 *Sp, Mor*, 1970 *H, Mor*
JP Costa 1996 *It, Bel, R, Pol*
LC Costa 1979 *Swi*, 1981 *Bel*, 1982 *Mor, Sp, Tun, Pol*
LP Costa 1969 *Sp, Mor*, 1970 *H, Mor*
MF Costa 1973 *Yug*, 1981 *Swi, De, Swe*, 1982 *Mor, Sp, H, Pol*, 1983 *Sp*, 1984 *Sp, H, Bel, De*
MMd Costa 1987 *Bel*
P Costa 2000 *R, H*

PORTUGAL

RB Costa 1969 *Sp, Mor*
T Costa 1998 *Nm*
V Couceiro 2004 *Sp*
D Coutinho 2000 *SA23*, 2001 *H, Rus*, 2002 *Sp, Pol, Sp*, 2004 *Bb*, 2005 *Geo, CZR, Ur, Fj*, 2006 *Rus, Geo, R, Ukr, CZR, Rus, Ur, It, Rus, Geo, Geo*, 2007 *Mor, Sp, Ur, Rus, CZR, C, S, NZ, R, R*
P Coutinho 1986 *USS*
C Cruz 1935 *Sp*, 1936 *Sp*
A Cunha 1990 *Nm, Tun, Sp*, 1991 *Nm*, 1992 *And, Mor, Tun*, 1993 *R, It, Tun, Bel, Swi, Sp*, 1994 *Mor, W, Sp*, 1995 *Mor, Sp, CZR, Ger*, 1996 *It, R, Pol, Sp, H, Tun*, 2000 *SA23*, 2001 *Geo, H*, 2002 *R, Geo, Sp, H, Rus, Pol, Sp*, 2003 *Geo, R, CZR, Sp, Rus*, 2004 *Geo, R, CZR, Sp, Rus, Bb, Ch, Ur, Ukr*, 2005 *Geo, CZR*
J Cunha 1969 *Mor*
S Cunha 1992 *And, Mor, Tun*, 1993 *R, It, Tun, Bel, Swi, Sp*, 1994 *Bel*
S Cunha 2004 *R, Ch, Ukr*, 2005 *Geo, CZR, Ch, Ur*, 2006 *Rus*, 2008 *Geo, CZR, Geo, Rus, Sp*
P Curvelo 1989 *Bel, Yug, Ger*
V Dias 1968 *Bel, Mor, It*
P Domingos 1994 *Bel, Ger, Mor, Tun, W, Sp*
A Dores 1979 *Swi*, 1981 *Swi, Bel, De*
M d'Orey 1996 *Sp, H, Tun*, 1997 *Geo, Sp*, 1998 *Nm, Ger, US, CZR, Mor, Sp, And, Sp*, 1999 *Ur*, 2002 *R, Geo, Sp, H, Rus, Pol, Sp*, 2003 *Geo, R, CZR, Sp, Rus*, 2004 *Geo, R, CZR, Sp, Rus, Bb, Ch, Ur, Ukr*, 2005 *Geo, CZR, Rus, R, Ch, Ur, Fj*, 2006 *Rus, Geo, R, Ukr, CZR, Ur, It, Rus, Geo, Geo*, 2007 *Mor, Mor, Ur, Ur, NZ*
R D'Orey Branco 2007 *Rus, CZR*
A Duarte 2008 *Geo, CZR, Geo, Rus, R*
B Duarte 2008 *Geo, CZR, Rus, Sp*
G Duarte 2006 *Geo*, 2007 *Mor, Sp, Rus, CZR*, 2008 *Geo, CZR, Geo, Rus*
J Duarte 1999 *Ur*
J Duarte 1936 *Sp*
AG Duque 1972 *It*, 1973 *It, Yug, Pol, Pol*, 1974 *It*, 1981 *De, Swe*, 1982 *Mor, Sp, Tun, Pol*
N Durão 1983 *Sp*, 1984 *H, Bel, De*, 1985 *Mor, Cze, Pol, Z*, 1986 *R, F, It, Tun, USS, R*, 1987 *It, F, Z, Z, Tun, USS, Bel*, 1988 *H, Ger, Yug*, 1989 *H, Bel, Yug, Ger, Cze, H*, 1990 *Sp*, 1991 *And, Tun, Mor*, 1992 *And, Mor, Tun*, 1994 *Bel, Ger*, 1995 *Mor, Sp, CZR, Ger*
R Durão 1986 *R, F, R*, 1987 *Z, Z, Tun, Bel*, 1988 *H, Ger, Yug*
V Durão 1990 *Mor, Nm, Bel, Tun*, 1991 *And, Mor, Nm*, 1992 *And, Mor, Tun*, 1995 *Mor, Sp, CZR, Ger*, 1996 *It, Bel, R, Pol, Sp, H, Tun*
P Eiró 1979 *Swi*, 1981 *Swi, Bel, De, Swe*, 1982 *Mor, Tun, H, Pol*
R Escarduça 1998 *And*
A Esteves 1995 *Mor, Sp*
A Esteves 2006 *Rus, It*, 2007 *Mor*, 2008 *Geo, CZR, Geo, Rus, R, Sp*
F Esteves 1995 *Ger*
O Fachada 1987 *It, Z, USS*
DL Faria 1979 *Swi*, 1981 *Bel*
G Faria 2001 *Geo*, 2002 *Pol, Sp*
J Faria 1967 *Sp, It*, 1968 *Sp, Bel, It*
LL Faria 1966 *Sp, Bel*, 1967 *Sp, It, F, R*, 1968 *Sp, Bel, Mor, It*
NL Faria 1968 *Sp, Bel, Mor, It*, 1970 *Sp*, 1972 *It, It*, 1973 *It, Yug, Swi, Pol, Pol*, 1974 *It, Ger*
PL Faria 1966 *Sp, Bel*, 1967 *Sp, It, F, R*, 1970 *H, Mor, Sp*, 1973 *It, Yug, Swi, Pol, Pol*
VL Faria 1981 *De, Swe*, 1982 *Mor, Sp, Tun, H*
A Fernandes 1973 *Swi*
AC Fernandes 1970 *H, Mor, Sp*, 1972 *It, It*, 1973 *Swi*, 1974 *Ger*
JC Fernandes 1972 *It, It*, 1974 *It*, 1979 *Swi*, 1981 *Swi, Bel, De, Swe*, 1982 *Mor, Sp, Tun, H, Pol*
PN Fernandes 1993 *R, Tun, Bel*, 1994 *Mor, Tun, W, Sp*, 1996 *Sp, H*
R Fernandes 1991 *Mor, Nm*
A Ferreira 2005 *Rus, R, Ur, Fj*
AB Ferreira 1982 *Sp, Tun, H, Pol*, 1983 *Sp, H, Pol*, 1984 *Sp, H, Bel, De*, 1985 *Mor, Cze, Pol, Z*, 1986 *R, F, It, Tun, USS*, 1987 *Z, Z, Tun, USS, Bel*, 1988 *H, Ger, Yug*, 1989 *H, Bel, Yug, Ger, Cze, H*
CD Ferreira 1979 *Swi*, 1981 *Swi, Bel*
CN Ferreira 1965 *Sp*, 1966 *Sp, Bel*, 1967 *Sp, It, F, R*, 1968 *Sp, Mor, It*, 1969 *Sp, Mor*, 1970 *H, Mor, Sp*, 1972 *It*, 1973 *It, Yug, Swi, Pol, Pol*
J Ferreira 1993 *R, It, Tun, Swi*, 1995 *Mor, Sp, CZR, Ger*, 1996 *It, Bel, R, Pol, Sp, H, Tun*, 1997 *Geo, Sp*, 1998 *Nm, Ger, US, CZR, Mor, Sp, And, S, Sp*, 1999 *H, Ur, Ur*, 2000 *Geo, Sp, R, Mor, H*, 2001 *R, Geo, Sp, H, Rus*, 2002 *H, Pol*, 2003 *Geo, R, CZR, Sp, Rus*, 2004 *Geo, R, CZR, Sp, Rus, Bb, Ch, Ur, Ukr*, 2005 *Geo, CZR, Rus, R, Ch, Ur, Fj*, 2006 *Rus, Geo, R, Ukr, CZR, Rus, Ur, It, Ru*
PB Ferreira *1983 H, Pol, Swe, 1984 Sp, Bel, De, 1985 Mor, Cze, Pol, Z, 1986 R, F, It, Tun, USS, R, 1987 Bel*
S Ferreira *1991 Mor, Nm, 1994 Bel, Ger, Mor, Tun, W, Sp, 1995 CZR, Ger, 1996 H, Tun, 1997 Geo, Sp, 1998 Nm, Ger, 2000 SA23*
D Fialho *2008 Geo, CZR*
DAA Figueiredo *2007 Ur, Rus, CZR, It, R*
P Fonseca *1996 Bel, 1998 Nm, 2000 SA23, 2001 R, Geo, H, Rus, 2002 R, Geo, Sp, H, Rus, Pol, Sp, 2003 Geo, R, CZR, Sp, Rus, 2004 CZR, Sp, Rus, Bb, 2005 Ch, Ur, Fj*
F Fontes *2003 Geo, R, CZR*
G Foro *2007 Rus, CZR, It, R, 2008 Geo, CZR, Geo, Rus*
F Fragateima *2007 CZR, 2008 Geo*
JS Franco *1974 Ger*
SM Franco *1983 Pol, Swe*
NCR Frazão *1974 Ger*
A Freitas *1992 Tun, 1993 R*
RM Gaio *1982 Pol, 1983 Sp, Swe*
E Galvão *1996 It, Bel*
D Gama *2006 Rus, Geo, R, 2007 Mor, Mor, Ur, Ur, Rus, CZR, It, R, 2008 Sp*
F Gameiro *1954 Sp*
FR Garcia *1983 H, Pol, Swe, 1984 H, Bel, De, 1985 Cze, Pol, Z, 1986 R, F, 1987 It, Z, USS*
M Garcia *1935 Sp*
N Garváo *2001 R, H, Rus, 2002 R, Geo, Sp, H, Rus, Pol, Sp, 2003 R, CZR, Sp, Rus, 2004 CZR, Sp, Bb, 2005 CZR*
JR Gaspar *1967 Sp, F, R*
V Gaspar *2008 Geo, CZR, Rus*
T Girão *2006 Geo, R, It, 2007 NZ, It, R, R, 2008 Geo, CZR, Geo, Rus, R, Sp*
F Goes *2000 SA23*
JMV Gomes *1989 Cze, H, 1990 Mor, Nm, Bel, Tun, Sp, 1991 And, Tun, Mor, Nm, 1992 And, Mor, Tun, 1993 R, Tun, Bel, Swi, 1994 Bel, Ger, Mor, Tun, W, Sp, 1995 Mor, Sp, CZR, Ger, 1996 It, Bel, Sp, 1998 S, 2000 SA23*
NMV Gomes *1996 It, Bel, R, Pol, H*
R Gomes *1998 S, Sp*
V Goncalves *2005 Ch*
G Gonçalves *1983 Sp, H, Pol, Swe*
G Gonçalves *1935 Sp*
P Gonçalves *2000 SA23, 2001 R, Geo, Sp, 2002 R, Geo, Sp, H, Rus, Pol, Sp, 2003 Geo, R, CZR, Sp*
F Grenho *2001 R, Geo, Rus, 2004 Geo, R, CZR, Ukr, 2005 Ch, Ur, Fj, 2006 Rus, Geo, R*
F Grenho *1979 Swi*
FN Guedes *1969 Sp, Mor, 1972 It, It*
JFN Guedes *1967 It, F, R, 1968 Sp, Bel, Mor, It, 1969 Mor, 1972 It*
R Heitor *2001 Geo, Sp, H, Rus, 2005 Ch*
J Herédia *1991 And, Tun, Mor, Nm, 1992 And, Mor, Tun, 1993 It, Tun, Bel, Swi, Sp, 1994 Bel*
PR Hoffman *1996 It, Pol, Sp, H, Tun, 1997 Geo, Sp, 1998 Nm, Ger, US, CZR, Sp, S, Sp, 1999 H, Ur, Ur, 2000 Geo, R, SA23, 2002 R, Geo, Sp, H, Rus, Pol, Sp*
A Jalles *1983 H, Pol, 1986 R, 1987 Z, Tun, 1988 Yug*
F Jesus *1968 Mor*
H Jónatas *1989 Cze, H*
J Jonet *1990 Mor, Nm, Bel, Tun, Sp, 1991 And, Tun, Mor, Nm, 1992 And, Mor, Tun, 1993 R, It, Swi, Sp, 1994 Bel, Ger, 1995 Mor, Sp, CZR, Ger*
V Jorge *2008 Sp*
L Kadosh *2008 Geo, CZR, Geo, Rus*
T King *1998 Sp, And, 2001 R, Geo, Sp, H, Rus*
L Lamas *1998 S, 2000 R, Mor, H, 2001 Geo, Sp*
J Laureano *1989 Bel, Yug, Ger, 1990 Mor, Nm, Bel, Sp*
P Leal *2005 CZR, R, Ch, Ur, Fj, 2006 Rus, R, Rus, Ur, It, Rus, Geo, Geo, 2007 Mor, Mor, Ur, Ur, Rus, CZR, C, S, NZ, R, R, 2008 R, Sp*
PR Leal *1973 Swi, Pol, Pol*

AL Leitão *1982 Sp, Tun, H, Pol, 1983 Sp, H, Pol, Swe, 1984 Sp, De*
O Leite *1970 Sp, 1972 It*
J Lencastre *1999 Ur*
P Lencastre *1967 Sp, It, F, R*
A Lima *1995 Mor, Sp, CZR, Ger, 1996 It, R, Sp, H, Tun, 1997 Sp*
JA Lima *2002 Pol, Sp, 2003 R, CZR, Sp, 2004 R*
MS Lima *1979 Swi, 1981 Bel, Swe, 1982 Tun*
F Lima *2000 SA23, 2001 R*
FR Lince *1954 Sp*
L Lino *1968 Bel, Mor, 1969 Sp, Mor*
AC Lopes *1987 It, Z*
JM Lopes *1954 Sp*
AdS Lourenço *2000 Geo, Sp, R, Mor, H, 2001 Geo, Sp, H, Rus*
F Lucena *1969 Sp, Mor, 1970 H, Mor*
L Luís *1986 F, It, 1987 It, F, Z, Z, USS, 1988 H, Ger, Yug, 1989 Bel, Yug, Ger, Cze, H, 1990 Mor, Nm, Bel, Tun, Sp, 1991 And, Tun, Mor, Nm, 1993 It, Tun, Bel, Swi, Sp*
S Luz *1987 Z*
E Macedo *1989 H, Bel, Cze, H, 1990 Mor, Nm, Bel, Tun, Sp, 1991 And, Tun, Nm, 1992 And, Mor, Tun, 1993 R, It, Tun, Bel, Swi, Sp, 1994 Mor, W, Sp*
H Macieira *1979 Swi, 1981 Swi, Bel, Swe, 1982 Mor, Tun*
F Magalhaes *2008 Geo, Geo, Rus*
JP Magalhães *1981 Bel, De, Swe*
VP Magalhães *1936 Sp*
MG Maia *1981 Bel, De, Swe*
E Maleitas *1979 Swi, 1983 Sp*
G Malheiro *1998 Mor, 1999 H, Ur, 2000 SA23, 2001 R, Geo, Sp, H, Rus, 2003 Geo, R, CZR, Sp, Rus, 2004 Geo, R, CZR, Sp, Rus, Bb, Ch, Ur, 2005 Geo, CZR, Rus, 2006 Ukr, CZR, Rus, Geo, Geo, 2007 Mor, Ur, Ur, Rus, NZ, R, R*
P Malo *1986 R, It, Tun, USS*
A Marques *1996 Bel, R*
JD Marques *1996 Pol, Sp, H, Tun*
MS Marques *1936 Sp*
P Marques *1998 Ger, US, CZR, Mor, Sp, And, S*
MB Martins *1954 Sp*
R Martins *1967 Sp, It, F, R, 1968 Sp, Bel, Mor, It, 1970 Sp, 1972 It, It, 1973 It, Yug, Swi, Pol, Pol, 1974 It, Ger, 1981 Swi, De, Swe*
D Mateus *2003 Geo, R, CZR, Sp, Rus, 2004 Geo, R, CZR, Rus, Bb, Ch, Ur, 2006 Rus, It, 2007 Mor, Ur, Rus, S, It, 2008 CZR, Geo, Rus, R, Sp*
D Mateus *2000 Geo, Sp, R, Mor, 2001 R, Geo, Sp, H, Rus, 2002 Pol, Sp, 2003 Geo, R, CZR, Sp, Rus, 2004 Geo, R, CZR, Sp, Rus, Bb, Ch, Ur, Ukr, 2005 Geo, CZR, Rus, R, Ch, Ur, Fj, 2006 Rus, Geo, R, Ukr, CZR, Rus, Ur, It, Rus, Geo, Geo, 2007 Mor, Mor, Sp, Ur, Rus, CZR, C, S, NZ, It, 2008 CZR, Geo, Rus, R, Sp*
M Mauricio *1990 Sp*
T Mayer *1965 Sp, 1966 Sp, Bel, 1967 It, F, R, 1970 H, Mor, 1972 It*
D Megre *1974 Ger, 1979 Swi, 1981 Swi, Bel, De, Swe, 1982 Mor, Sp, Tun, H, Pol, 1983 Sp, H, Pol, Swe, 1984 Sp, H, Bel, De, 1985 Mor, Cze, Pol, Z, 1986 R, F, It, Tun, USS, R, 1987 It, F, Z, Z, Tun, USS, Bel, 1989 H, Bel, Yug, Ger*
J Megre *1979 Swi*
A Meira *1936 Sp*
H Melo *2008 Geo*
JA Melo *1974 It*
M Melo *1998 Nm, US, S, 1999 H, Ur, Ur, 2000 Geo, Sp, R, 2001 R, H, Rus, 2002 R, H*
J Metelo *1968 Bel, Mor, It*
A Minhoto *1972 It, 1973 It, Yug, Swi, Pol*
F Mira *2007 Sp, R, 2008 Geo, CZR, Rus, R*
D Miranda *2008 Geo, Rus*
J Miranda *1965 Sp, 1966 Sp, Bel, 1967 Sp, It, F, R, 1968 Sp*
A Moita *1986 R, 1987 F, Z, 1989 Bel, Cze, H*
C Moita *1974 It, 1979 Swi, 1981 Swi, Bel, De, Swe, 1982 Mor, Sp, Tun, H, Pol, 1983 Sp, H, Pol, Swe, 1984 Sp, 1985 Cze, Z*
A Monteiro *1982 Sp*
B Monteiro *1965 Sp, 1966 Sp, Bel, 1967 Sp, It, F, R, 1968 Sp*
E Morais *1982 Sp, Tun, 1986 It, Tun, USS, 1987 It, F, Z*
L Morais *1984 Sp, H, Bel, De, 1986 F, It, R, 1987 F, Z, Tun, Bel, 1988 H, 1989 H, Bel, Yug, Ger, Cze, H*
N Morais *1985 Mor, Cze, Pol, Z, 1986 R, F, Tun, USS, 1987 It, Z, USS, 1988 Ger, Yug, 1995 Mor, Sp, CZR, Ger*
T Morais *1991 Tun, Mor, Nm, 1992 And, Mor, Tun, 1993 R, It, Tun, Bel, Swi, Sp, 1994 Mor, Tun, W, Sp, 1995 Mor, Sp, CZR, Ger*
A Morgado *1935 Sp*
B Mota *2000 SA23, 2004 Geo, R, Ukr, 2005 Rus, 2006 Geo*
JD Mota *1998 S, Sp, 1999 H, Ur, 2000 Sp, R, Mor, H, SA23, 2001 Sp, 2004 Ch, Ur, 2006 Geo, R, Ukr, CZR*
M Moura *1999 H, Ur, 2002 Sp, 2004 Ch, Ur, Ukr, 2005 Geo, CZR*
N Mourao *1993 R, It, Tun, Bel, Swi, Sp, 1994 Bel, Ger, Mor, Tun, W, Sp, 1995 CZR, Ger, 1996 It, Bel, R, Pol, Sp, H, Tun, 1997 Geo, Sp, 1998 Nm, Ger, US, CZR, Mor, Sp, And, S, Sp, 1999 H, Ur, Ur, 2000 Sp*
JM Muré *2007 C, S, It, R, R, 2008 Geo, Geo, Rus, R, Sp*
P Murinello *2003 Rus, 2004 Geo, R, CZR, Sp, Rus, Bb, Ch, Ur, Ukr, 2005 Geo, CZR, 2006 Ukr, CZR, Rus, It, Rus, Geo, Geo, 2007 Mor, Mor, Ur, Ur, C, S, NZ, It, R*
P Murinello *1993 R, It, Tun, Bel, Swi, Sp, 1994 Bel, Ger, Mor, Tun, W, Sp, 1995 Mor, Sp, CZR, Ger, 1996 It, Bel, R, Sp, H, Tun, 2000 Mor, H*
A Neto *1968 Sp, 1969 Sp, Mor, 1970 Sp, 1972 It, It, 1973 Yug, Swi, Pol, Pol, 1974 It, Ger*
G Neto *1997 Sp, 1998 US, Mor*
N Neto *1995 Mor*
M Neves *2002 R, H*
R Neves 2002 *R*
VP Neves *1986 R*
J Norton *1935 Sp*
AC Nunes *1954 Sp*
FP Nunes *2000 Geo, Sp, R, Mor, H, SA23, 2001 R, Sp, H, 2002 R, Geo, Sp, H, Rus, Pol, Sp, 2003 Geo, R, CZR, Sp, Rus, 2004 Ch, Ur, 2005 Ch*
M Nunes *1982 Tun, H, Pol*
R Nunes *1998 Nm, Ger, US, CZR, And, Sp, 1999 H, 2002 R, H*
LF Oliveira *1974 It, 1981 Swe, 1982 Mor, Sp, Tun, H, Pol, 1983 Sp, H, Pol, Swe*
M Paisana *1981 De, 1982 Mor, Sp, Tun, H, Pol*
JM Paixao *1974 It*
S Palha *2006 Geo, 2007 Rus, R, 2008 Geo*
CV Pardal *1965 Sp, 1967 It, 1969 Sp, Mor*
M Pardal *1989 Yug, Ger*
A Peças *1994 Ger, Mor, Tun, W, Sp*
C Pegado *1972 It*
D Penalva *2002 Sp, H, 2004 Sp, Ur, 2005 Rus, R, Ch, Ur, Fj, 2006 Rus, Geo, R, Ukr, CZR, Rus, Geo, 2007 Ur, Ur, Rus, C, S, NZ, It, R*
J Pereira *1965 Sp, 1966 Sp, Bel, 1967 Sp, R, 1970 H, Mor, Sp, 1974 Ger, 1981 De, 1982 Pol, 1983 Sp, H, Pol, Swe, 1984 Sp*
JC Pereira *1969 Mor, 1970 H, 1972 It*
JC Pereira *1984 H, Bel, De, 1986 R, USS, 1987 F, Z, Z, Tun, 1989 Cze, H, 1990 Mor, Nm, Bel, Tun*
MC Pereira *1965 Sp, 1966 Sp, 1967 Sp, R, 1968 Bel, Mor, It, 1969 Sp*
MM Pereira *2006 Ukr, CZR, Rus, It*
RC Pereira *1987 Bel, 1988 H, 1989 H, 1991 And, Tun, 1992 And, Mor, Tun, 1993 R, It, Tun, Bel, 1994 Bel, Ger, Mor, Tun, W, Sp, 1995 Mor, Sp*
VS Pereira *1973 It, Yug, Swi, Pol, Pol, 1974 Ger*
P Picão *1994 Ger, Mor, Tun, W, Sp*
PS Pimentel *1973 It, Yug, Swi, Pol, Pol*
A Pinto *1998 US, Mor, And, 1999 H, Ur, Ur*
AC Pinto *1970 Mor, 1972 It, It, 1973 It, Yug, Swi, Pol, Pol, 1974 It, Ger*
AF Pinto *1998 And, 2000 SA23, 2001 Sp, H*
BM Pinto *1979 Swi, 1981 Swi, Bel, De, Swe, 1982 Mor, Sp, Tun, H, Pol, 1983 Sp, H, Pol, Swe, 1984 Sp, H, 1985 Mor, Cze, Pol, Z, 1986 R, F, It, Tun, USS, R, 1987 It, F, Z, Z, Tun, USS, Bel, 1988 H, Ger, Yug, 1989 H, Bel, Yug, Ger, Cze, H*
CR Pinto *1972 It, It, 1973 It*
DC Pinto *2003 CZR, Rus, 2004 Sp, Bb, Ch, Ur, 2005 Rus, R, Ch, Ur, Fj, 2006 Geo, R, Ukr, CZR, Rus, Rus, Geo, Geo, 2007 Mor, Mor, Sp, Ur, Ur, Rus, CZR, C, S, NZ, It, R, 2008 CZR, Geo, Sp*
EA Pinto *1969 Mor, 1981 Swi, Bel, Swe, 1982 H*
J Pinto *2001 H, Rus, 2002 R, 2004 Sp, Bb, Ch, Ur, Ukr, 2005 Rus, R, Ch, Ur, Fj, 2006 Rus, Geo, R, Ukr, CZR, Rus, Ur, It, Rus, Geo, Geo, 2007 Mor, Sp, Ur, C, S, NZ, It, R, R, 2008 CZR, Sp*

JM Pinto *1982 Mor, Sp, H, Pol, 1983 H, Pol, Swe, 1984 Sp, H, Bel, De, 1985 Mor, Cze, Pol, Z, 1986 R, F, USS, R, 1987 Tun, USS, Bel, 1988 H, Ger, Yug, 1989 H, Bel, Yug, Ger, Cze, H*
F Pires *1982 Mor, H, Pol, 1983 Sp, H, Pol, Swe, 1984 Sp, H, Bel, De, 1985 Mor, Cze, Pol, Z, 1986 R, F, It, Tun, USS*
JC Pires *1990 Mor, Nm, Bel, Tun, 1991 And, Tun, Mor, Nm, 1993 R, Tun, Bel, Swi, Sp, 1994 Bel, Ger, Mor, Tun, W, Sp, 1996 Pol, 1997 Geo, Sp, 1998 Nm*
L Pissarra *1996 It, Bel, R, Pol, H, Tun, 1997 Geo, Sp, 1998 Nm, Ger, Sp, And, Sp, 1999 H, Ur, Ur, 2000 Geo, Sp, R, Mor, H, SA23, 2001 R, Geo, 2002 R, Geo, Sp, H, Rus, Pol, Sp, 2003 Geo, R, CZR, Sp, Rus, 2004 Geo, R, CZR, Sp, Rus, Bb, Ch, Ur, Ukr, 2005 Geo, CZR, Rus, Ur, Fj, 2006 Rus, Geo, R, Ukr, CZR, Rus, Rus, Geo, Geo, 2007 Mor, Mor, Sp, Ur, Ur, Rus, CZR, C, S, NZ, It, R* **M Portela** *1996 R, H, Tun, 1997 Geo, Sp, 1998 US, CZR, Mor, Sp, S, Sp, 1999 H, Ur, 2000 Geo, Sp, Mor, H, SA23, 2002 R, Geo, Sp, H, Rus, Pol, Sp, 2004 Sp, Rus, Bb, Ukr, 2005 Geo, CZR, Rus, R, Ch, Ur, Fj, 2006 Rus, Geo, R, Ukr, Rus, It, Rus, Geo, Geo, 2007 Mor, Mor, Sp, Ur, Ur, Rus, CZR, C, S, NZ, R*
A Quadrio *1966 Sp, Bel, 1967 It, F*
JF Queimado *1984 Sp, H, Bel, De, 1985 Mor, Cze, Pol, Z, 1986 F, It, Tun, USS, R, 1987 It, F, Z, Z, Tun, USS, Bel, 1989 H, Bel, Cze, H, 1990 Mor, Nm, Bel, Tun, Sp, 1991 And, Tun, Mor, Nm, 1992 And, Mor, Tun, 1993 R, It, Tun, Bel, Swi, Sp, 1994 Bel, Ger, Mor, Tun, W, Sp*
JA Rafachinho *1973 It, 1974 It, Ger*
JG Ramos *1967 Sp, 1968 Sp, Bel, Mor, It, 1969 Sp, Mor, 1970 H, Mor, Sp, 1972 It, It, 1973 It, Yug, Swi, Pol, Pol, 1974 It*
T Rankine *2000 Geo, Sp, R, Mor, H*
D Raws *1936 Sp*
CC Reis *1965 Sp, 1966 Sp, Bel, 1967 Sp, 1968 Sp*
CJ Reis *1984 H, Bel, 1985 Mor, Cze, Pol, Z, 1986 Tun, USS, R, 1987 Tun, USS, Bel, 1988 Yug, 1989 H, Bel, Yug, Ger*
LN Reis *1983 Sp, H, Pol, Swe, 1984 Sp, H, Bel, De, 1985 Mor*
P Reis *1981 Swi*
JC Ribeiro *1973 Yug, Pol*
MS Ribeiro *1998 Nm, Ger, US, CZR, Mor, Sp, And, S, Sp, 1999 H, Ur, Ur, 2000 Geo, Sp, R, H, SA23, 2001 R, Geo, Sp, 2008 Geo, Rus*
E Rocha *1973 Swi, Pol*
F Rocha *1998 Nm, Ger, US, CZR, Mor, S, 1999 H, Ur, Ur*
O Rocha *1954 Sp*
J Rocheta *1990 Mor, Nm, Bel, Tun, Sp, 1991 And, Tun, Nm, 1992 And, Mor, Tun, 1993 R, Tun, Bel, Swi, Sp*
JL Rodrigues *1982 Mor, 1984 Sp, H, Bel, De, 1985 Mor, Cze, Pol, Z, 1986 R, F, It, Tun, USS, R, 1987 It, F, Z, Z, Tun, USS, Bel, 1988 H, Ger, Yug, 1989 H, Bel, Yug, Ger, Cze, H, 1990 Mor, Nm, Tun, Sp, 1991 And, Tun, Mor, Nm, 1996 It, Bel*
P Rodrigues *1990 Nm, Bel, Sp, 1991 And, Tun, Mor, Nm, 1993 R, Swi*
M Rogério *1990 Bel, Tun, Sp, 1991 And, Tun, Mor, Nm, 1992 And, Mor, Tun, 1993 It, Tun, Bel, Sp, 1994 Bel, Ger, Mor, Tun, W, Sp, 1995 Mor, Sp, CZR, Ger, 1996 It, Bel, R, Pol, Sp, H, Tun, 1998 Ger, US, CZR, Mor, Sp, 2000 Mor*
JB Roque *1954 Sp*
LV Rosa *1954 Sp*
LF Roxo *1981 Bel, 1982 Mor, Sp*
JM Rozendo *1936 Sp*
N Sá *1998 Sp, 1999 Ur, Ur*
F Saldanha *1998 Mor, Sp, S, 1999 Ur, Ur, 2001 Geo*
M Salgado *1968 Sp, Bel, Mor, It, 1970 Mor*
JM Sampaio *1987 F, 1988 H, Ger*
F Santos *1936 Sp*
M Santos *1973 It, Yug, Swi, Pol, Pol, 1974 It*
P Santos *2004 Geo, R, CZR, 2005 CZR*
M Saraiva *1979 Swi*
A Sarmento *2004 R, Bb, 2007 R, 2008 Rus*
J Segurado *2005 Ch*
F Sequeira *1974 Ger*
JC Sequeira *2001 H, Rus, 2002 R, Geo, Sp, H, Pol, Sp, 2004 R, CZR, Sp, Rus, 2005 Geo*
L Sequeira *1997 Geo, Sp*
R Sequeira *1988 Ger*
A Silva *1935 Sp, 1936 Sp*
A Silva *1996 Sp, H, Tun, 1997 Geo, Sp, 1998 Nm, S*
A Silva *2007 Ur, Ur, Rus, NZ, It*
D Silva *1993 Tun*
JG Silva *1972 It, It*
JN Silva *1967 It, F, R, 1968 Sp, Bel, Mor, It*
M Silva *2000 R*
P Silva *1992 And, Mor, Tun, 1996 It, Bel, R, Pol, Sp, H, Tun, 1997 Geo, Sp, 1998 Nm, Ger, US, CZR, Mor, Sp, And, S, 1999 H, Ur, Ur, 2000 H, 2002 R, Geo, H, Pol, Sp, 2003 CZR, Sp*
V Silva *2000 Geo, Sp, R, Mor, H, 2001 R, Geo, Sp, H, Rus*
A Silvestre *1969 Sp, Mor, 1970 H, Mor, 1972 It, 1973 It, Swi, Pol, Pol, 1974 It*
AC Simões *1995 Ger, 1996 Bel, R, Tun, 2000 SA23, 2001 R*
C Soares *1987 Bel, 1988 H, Ger, Yug, 1989 H, Bel, Yug, Ger*
M Soares *1954 Sp*
JS Somoza *2006 Rus, Geo, Geo, 2007 Mor, Mor, Sp, Ur, Ur, Rus, CZR, C, S, 2008 Geo, CZR, Geo, R*
F Sousa *2000 Geo, Sp, 2001 R, Geo, Sp, H, Rus, 2002 R, Geo, Sp, H, Rus, 2003 Geo, R, CZR, Sp, Rus, 2004 Geo, R, CZR, Sp, Rus, Bb, Ukr, 2005 Geo, CZR, Rus, R, Ch, Ur, Fj, 2006 Ukr, CZR, Rus, Ur, It, Geo, Geo, 2007 CZR, C, S, It, R, R*
O Sousa *1986 R, F, It, Tun, USS, 1987 It*
V Sousa *1979 Swi, 1987 F, 1988 H*
RC Spachuck *2005 Geo, CZR, Rus, R, 2006 Rus, Geo, R, Ukr, CZR, Rus, It, Rus, Geo, Geo, 2007 Rus, CZR, C, S, NZ, It, R, R, 2008 R, Sp*
N Taful *2006 Ur, It*
AH Tavares *1970 H*
J Teixeira *1935 Sp*
T Teixeira *1998 Sp, 1999 H, Ur, 2000 Geo, Sp, R, Mor, H*
A Telles *1988 Yug*
LF Thomáz *1991 Mor, 1996 Pol*
NF Thomáz *1990 Mor, Nm, Bel, Tun, Sp, 1991 Tun, Mor, Nm, 1993 Swi, Sp*
J Tiago *1995 CZR, Ger*
M Tomé *2002 R, Geo, Sp, H, Rus, Pol, Sp, 2003 Geo, R, CZR, Sp, 2004 Ch, Ur, Ukr, 2005 Geo, CZR*
AN Trindade *1969 Sp, 1973 It, Swi*
G Uva *2004 Bb, Ukr, 2005 Geo, CZR, Rus, R, Ch, Ur, Fj, 2006 Rus, Geo, R, Ukr, CZR, Rus, Ur, It, Rus, Geo, Geo, 2007 Mor, Mor, Sp, Ur, Ur, Rus, C, S, NZ, It, R, R, 2008 CZR, R, Sp*
JS Uva *2000 SA23, 2001 R, Geo, Sp, 2003 Geo, R, CZR, Sp, Rus, 2004 Geo, R, CZR, Rus, Ch, Ur, Ukr, 2005 Rus, R, Ch, Ur, Fj, 2006 It, Rus, Geo, 2007 Mor, Mor, Sp, Ur, Ur, CZR, C, S, NZ, It, R, 2008 CZR, Geo, Sp*
VS Uva *2003 Geo, R, Sp, 2004 Geo, R, CZR, Sp, Rus, Bb, Ch, Ur, Ukr, 2005 Geo, CZR, Rus, R, Ch, Ur, Fj, 2006 Rus, Geo, R, Ukr, CZR, Rus, Ur, It, Rus, Geo, Geo, 2007 Mor, Mor, Sp, Ur, Ur, Rus, CZR, C, S, NZ, It, R, 2008 CZR, Rus, Sp*
AO Valente *1954 Sp*
G Vareiro *2002 R, Geo, Sp, Rus*
JP Varela *1997 Geo, Sp, 1998 Ger, US, CZR, Mor, Sp, And, S, 1999 Ur, Ur, 2000 H*
JM Vargas *2006 Rus, Ur*
JM Vasconcelos *1965 Sp, 1966 Bel, 1967 It, F, 1970 Mor*
CR Vaz *1981 Bel, 1987 F, Z, Tun, USS*
L Vaz *1935 Sp, 1936 Sp*
D Vicente *1965 Sp*
ÁM Vieira *1936 Sp*
P Vieira *1998 Nm, Sp, And, 1999 H, Ur, 2000 Sp, R, Mor, H, 2001 Geo, Sp, H, Rus, 2003 CZR, Sp, Rus, 2007 Mor, Mor, Sp*
R Vieira *1997 Geo, Sp*
JC Vilela *1973 Swi*

ROMANIA

ROMANIA'S 2007–08 RECORD

OPPONENTS	DATE	VENUE	RESULT
Russia	4 November	H	**Lost** 12–22
Portugal	1 December	A	**Won** 23–8
Georgia	9 February	A	**Lost** 7–22
Spain	23 February	A	**Won** 17–11
Portugal	8 March	H	**Won** 21–15
Russia	15 March	A	**Lost** 12–8
Czech Rep	22 March	H	**Won** 76–7
Uruguay	11 June	H	**Won** 10–6
Russia	15 June	H	**Won** 13–12
Emerging SA	20 June	H	**Lost** 13–25

ROMANIA TURNS THE PAGE

By Chris Thau

After a modest campaign in the 2007 Rugby World Cup, when ill-discipline and a reported dissent by several French-based senior players doomed the team efforts – who nevertheless came close to beating Italy – the Romanian Federation took some painful decisions aimed at restoring discipline and the long term prospects of the once proud rugby nation. First and foremost among these was to offer the national coaching job to New Zealander Ellis Meachen, a former Western Suburbs and Wellington hooker who was Tonga's assistant coach at the RWC 2007 and secondly to concentrate on the players based in Romania rather than the professionals playing overseas.

After two matches in the European Nations Cup, a defeat at the hands of Russia and a win against Portugal, under Romanian coaches Marin Mot and Alexandru Marin, Meachen joined the Bucharest team, the new-look national team in all but name, in January 2008, during their trip to the UK for the match against Worcester Warriors, after which he took the young Romanian outfit on a 10-day training camp in Neath, in Wales.

The players were vaguely familiar with his coaching exploits at Wellington, the Hurricanes and New Zealand age group levels, though it was his impact on the style and confidence of Tonga in the Rugby World Cup that was most vividly remembered.

At a short meeting at the camp in Neath following a disappointing match against the Warriors, it was said that Meachen informed the players, in his concise, no-nonsense style, that the holiday break was over and that the work was going to commence the following day.

The President of the Romanian Federation, George Straton, took time off from his business commitments to attend the arrival of Meachen and spent the first week of his assignment with the squad in Neath. "I am delighted with the intensity and attention to detail he brings to the team preparation and I am convinced that the Romanian squad will benefit. More significantly, Ellis will live in Bucharest at least 10 months a year and will oversee the entire coaching and teaching structure in Romania, from age-group level to the elite," Straton said.

"There are similarities between Tongan and Romanian rugby. Many players leave the country in search of employment," Meachen said. "Romania had about 10 locally-based players in their World Cup squad, while Tonga had seven. There are also similarities between the two nations regarding the standard of the players based locally, which is low compared to those playing overseas. Both are great rugby nations and are keen to progress, but the structure to help them progress must be set in place. The medium term objective is to qualify for the 2011 Rugby World Cup and to play there well enough to enable us to qualify directly for the 2015, which means finishing in the top three in our pool.

"But to be able to achieve this, we must have a format in place, starting with school level, where we need an expanded structure. There are eight years to RWC 2015, which means that some of those who will play are now 15–16 year olds in school. They must acquire the right individual skills and playing knowledge to be able to be successful.

"Regarding the national team, the players selected will need to have a desire to play for Romania. We are at the beginning of the process and I am sure there will be many other players that will compete for positions, even if they have never been selected before. The door is open, but there will be no automatic admission. I believe in trials, when the players, irrespective where they live and play, come back to Romania to stake their claim to a place in the team," Meachen said.

The decision to discard the former regulars had naturally impacted on the Romanian team performance, with The Oaks losing two high-profile matches to their East European adversaries, to Georgia 22–7 and to Russia 12–8 respectively, in the FIRA-AER European Nations Cup. Before the third IRB Nations Cup in June the Romanian Federation, in an attempt to expand the selection net far and wide, organised trials for the first time in living memory. The trials told Meachen the naked truth that in fact the cupboard was bare, with the domestic league seriously weakened by a continuous drain of players to France, Italy, Spain and the UK.

Significantly, it is not only the high-profile players leaving for lucrative contracts in the professional leagues in France, Italy and Spain. It is the ordinary club players, leaving Romania in their droves for employment in the West that has weakened the domestic structure.

The Romanian Federation has been aware of this phenomenon and has been investing heavily in the development programme, with particular emphasis on youth and juniors, in an attempt to reverse the balance, producing more players of quality to secure the demands of the domestic league, as the Federation President Straton – who has found in Meachen an enthusiastic partner – explained. "The key for the future of rugby in Romania lies out there in the regions. This is why we are investing heavily into the centres of excellence and have enlisted the help of several of Romania's former internationals Mihai Bucos, Laurentiu Constantin, Mircea Munteanu, Cornel Scarlat etc to help expand both the numbers and the quality of tuition," said Straton.

Painfully aware of the difficulties provincial rugby experiences in Romania, Straton has used the development blueprint of the Gura Humorului club, where he played in the 1970s, to develop similar structures elsewhere. Straton, a successful publisher applied his business acumen and attention to detail to rugby, making self-sufficiency a priority for the Federation and significantly the clubs.

"We have been trying to professionalise all structures in the game, evolving from a politically dependent state to self finance, and am pleased to say that have succeeded to become 100 per cent independent of state structures. The 2005 Sports Law, voted by the Parliament, has been vital in this respect, providing us with the framework for a structure able to operate in a market economy. We have been able to increase the income of the Federation by setting up lucrative partnerships with several high profile sponsors, including BDR Societe General, Orange, O'Neills, Stejar, Sofitel, the Town Hall of Sector 1 in Bucharest and the National Sports Agency to mention just a few. We needed money for facilities, good coaches and teachers, for Regional Academies and for the National Stadium Arcul de Triumf, our pride and joy. We are also negotiating with the national television station, TVR, the first comprehensive deal that would allow access of our domestic league on terrestrial TV, in addition to our international programme, which is crucial for the image of the game and sponsor satisfaction.

"In this respect the IRB Nations Cup has been a Godsend, and has helped us to project the game nationally on television, with the expected outcome in terms of numbers and enthusiasm. For this and all the investment from the governing body, that enable us to push forward this very ambitious programme, we are truly grateful to the IRB," he observed.

But all is very much a race against time, as the budding professional league in Romania has found out, and for the first time in history foreign club players and coaches appeared in Romania. Former Champion club Farul Constanta, the leading provincial club, employed four Georgian players, who became household names in the Romanian domestic league helping the club to reach the final of the Championship, which they narrowly lost to Dinamo Bucharest – who had employed South Africa's Chester Williams as Director of Rugby to help them reach the top. It paid off, with Williams guiding Dinamo to the league and cup double within a short while, although the Romanian pundits were unanimous in their view that two of Constanta's Georgian tyros, scrum-half Bidzina

Samkharadze and hooker Iuri Natriashvili were the best players in their position in Romanian rugby.

In their desire to go all the way and snatch pole position from the hands of the leading Bucharest clubs Steaua and Dinamo, Farul, helped by the local council, went further afield, and signed for the new season two New Zealanders Zane Winsdale and Ben Aoina and a Samoan Jeff Lapana Makapelu.

Unlike the Georgians, who are all international players, the new recruits become eligible for international selection in 2011, an aspect which has not escaped the eye of the canny New Zealander, who in a remarkable departure from tradition took all three of them on the development tour to New Zealand and South Pacific in the autumn.

Meachen is the first foreign coach to take permanent residence in Romania for the duration of his contract. The new Romanian Director of Rugby is supported by another full-time employee, former All Black world champion Steve Mcdowall, whose family have joined him Bucharest for the duration of his contract. "His experience in close quarter rugby, particularly in the 'engine room' will be of an enormous benefit to this programme," Meachen said. The other three members of this high-powered team are New Zealander Murray Roulston, the former Hurricanes and Highlanders backs coach, forwards coach Marin Mot, a former international hooker, and his backs counterpart, former international wing Alexandru Marin.

While the objective of the Romanian team in the previous Nations Cup tournament held in Bucharest was building up for the 2007 RWC finals in France, the 2008 event signaled the start of the preparations for the qualifying rounds for RWC 2011 – with 21 of the 26 players selected in their early 20s and only three playing abroad. Romania finished the tournament third with two wins out of three matches, having lost the title decider against Emerging South Africa 25–13. The fact that the six nation IRB competition returned to Bucharest for a second time, was a clear statement about the quality of the last year's event organised by the IRB and Romanian Rugby Federation. "We must give credit to Romania who have organised an outstanding tournament of genuine quality. The Nations Cup is not only great value for money, but also a positive event for the participants, Tier 2 and 3 Unions who experience the inner workings and the routines of a large tournament," said Mark Egan the IRB Head of Development and Performance.

After the IRB Nations Cup, an even a younger Romanian team, a development side in all but name, set off for a five-match tour of New Zealand, Fiji and Samoa, with the aim of both securing a sound foundation for the qualifying programme for RWC 2011 and a catalyst to further develop Romania's home grown talent. The youngest member of the 30-strong squad was 19-year old Dinamo Bucharest prop Constantin Dumitru, one of the nine uncapped players. Several players from the Under-20 team who played in the IRB Junior World Rugby Trophy in Chile are included. The only French based player is 21-year old Marius Sirbe, who although nominally with Narbonne club, has yet to play for their professional team.

"The tour of New Zealand and the Pacific will be invaluable for our RWC qualifying programme, which will kick off in February next year," Meachen said. "We will be squaring off against the Georgians, Russia, Spain and Portugal for a spot at the 2011 Rugby World Cup, which is not an easy task at all, so this tour will provide an excellent stepping stone for our players leading into the challenges that we face next season," Meachen said.

"On the other hand, we also need to inject pace and quality into the revival process the game has been experiencing lately in Romania. Romanian rugby shares, to a large extent, the fate of the Pacific rugby nations whose best players are lured abroad, effectively draining talent from our domestic structure. So basically, with many of Romania's leading players abroad, we intend to intensify our domestic development programme to strengthen our player base. This is why we have so many young players in the team, with only one player from France, and that one very much a newcomer at international level.

"We are still at the foot of the mountain, having taken a few steps towards the summit. However, we know where the top is and what is the standard required to be there. This is why we go Down Under. We also hope that this tour will build and strengthen the relations between Romania and the Pacific Unions, which is important for all involved, as really, we are aiming for the same thing, and this is the RWC in 2011."

ROMANIA INTERNATIONAL STATISTICS

MATCH RECORDS UP TO 30TH SEPTEMBER 2008

BIGGEST WINNING MARGIN

Date	Opponent	Result	Winning Margin
21/09/1976	Bulgaria	100–0	**100**
19/03/2005	Ukraine	97–0	**97**
13/04/1996	Portugal	92–0	**92**

MOST POINTS IN A MATCH

BY THE TEAM

Date	Opponent	Result	Points
21/09/1976	Bulgaria	100–0	**100**
19/03/2005	Ukraine	97–0	**97**
13/04/1996	Portugal	92–0	**92**

BY A PLAYER

Date	Name	Opponent	Points
05/10/2002	Ionut Tofan	Spain	**30**
13/04/1996	Virgil Popisteanu	Portugal	**27**
04/02/2001	Petre Mitu	Portugal	**27**

MOST TRIES IN A MATCH

BY THE TEAM

Date	Opponent	Result	Tries
17/11/1976	Morocco	89–0	**17**
21/10/1951	East Germany	64–26	**16**
19/03/2005	Ukraine	97–0	**15**

BY A PLAYER

Date	Name	Opponent	Tries
30/04/1972	Gheorghe Rascanu	Morocco	**5**
18/10/1986	Cornel Popescu	Portugal	**5**
13/04/1996	Ionel Rotaru	Portugal	**5**

MOST CONVERSIONS IN A MATCH

BY THE TEAM

Date	Opponent	Result	Cons
13/04/1996	Portugal	92–0	**12**
19/03/2005	Ukraine	97–0	**11**
04/10/1997	Belguim	83–13	**10**

BY A PLAYER

Date	Name	Opponent	Cons
13/04/1996	Virgil Popisteanu	Portugal	**12**
04/10/1997	Serban Guranescu	Belgium	**10**
19/03/2005	Dan Dumbrava	Ukraine	**8**

MOST PENALTIES IN A MATCH

BY THE TEAM

Date	Opponent	Result	Pens
14/05/1994	Italy	26–12	**6**
04/02/2001	Portugal	47–0	**6**

BY A PLAYER

Date	Name	Opponent	Pens
14/05/1994	Neculai Nichitean	Italy	**6**
04/02/2001	Petre Mitu	Portugal	**6**

MOST DROP GOALS IN A MATCH

BY THE TEAM

Date	Opponent	Result	DGs
29/10/1967	West Germany	27–5	**4**

BY A PLAYER

Date	Name	Opponent	DGs
29/10/1967	Valeriu Irimescu	West Germany	**3**
17/10/1976	Dumitru Alexandru	Poland	**3**

MOST CAPPED PLAYERS

Name	Caps
Adrian Lungu	77
Romeo Gontineac	75
Gabriel Brezoianu	71

LEADING PENALTY SCORERS

Name	Pens
Neculai Nichitean	54
Ionut Tofan	46
Petre Mitu	46

LEADING TRY SCORERS

Name	Tries
Petre Motrescu	33
Gabriel Brezoianu	28
Florica Murariu	26

LEADING DROP GOAL SCORERS

Name	DGs
Dumitru Alexandru	13
Neculai Nichitean	10
Valeriu Irimescu	10

LEADING CONVERSIONS SCORERS

Name	Cons
Ionut Tofan	51
Petre Mitu	49
Dan Dumbrava	38

LEADING POINTS SCORERS

Name	Points
Ionut Tofan	315
Petre Mitu	296
Neculai Nichitean	246

ROMANIA INTERNATIONAL PLAYERS

UP TO 30TH SEPTEMBER 2008

Note: Years given for International Championship matches are for second half of season; eg 1972 means season 1971–72. Years for all other matches refer to the actual year of the match.

A Achim 1974 *Pol*, 1976 *Pol*, *Mor*
M Adascalitei 2007 *Rus*
M Aldea 1979 *USS*, *W*, *Pol*, *F*, 1980 *It*, *USS*, *I*, *F*, 1981 *It*, *Sp*, *USS*, *S*, *NZ*, *F*, 1982 *WGe*, *It*, *USS*, *Z*, *Z*, *F*, 1983 *Mor*, *WGe*, *It*, *USS*, *Pol*, *W*, *USS*, *F*, 1984 *It*, *S*, *F*, 1985 *E*, *USS*
C Alexandrescu 1934 *It*
D Alexandru 1974 *Pol*, 1975 *Sp*, *JAB*, 1976 *Sp*, *USS*, *Bul*, *Pol*, *F*, *Mor*, 1977 *Sp*, *It*, *F*, *Pol*, *F*, 1978 *Cze*, *Sp*, 1979 *It*, *Sp*, *USS*, *W*, *F*, 1980 *It*, *I*, *Pol*, *F*, 1981 *Sp*, *USS*, *S*, *NZ*, *F*, 1982 *Z*, 1983 *It*, *USS*, *Pol*, *W*, 1984 *It*, *S*, *F*, *Sp*, 1985 *E*, 1987 *It*, *USS*, *Z*, *S*, *USS*, *F*, 1988 *USS*
N Anastasiade 1927 *Cze*, 1934 *It*
V Anastasiade 1939 *It*
I Andrei 2003 *W*, *I*, *Ar*, *Nm*, 2004 *CZR*, *Pt*, *Sp*, *Rus*, *Geo*, *It*, *W*, *J*, *CZR*, 2005 *Rus*, *US*, *S*, *Pt*, 2006 *CZR*, 2007 *Pt*, 2008 *Sp*, *Pt*, *Rus*
I Andriesi 1937 *It*, *H*, *Ger*, 1938 *F*, *Ger*, 1939 *It*, 1940 *It*
E Apjoc 1996 *Bel*, 2000 *It*, 2001 *Pt*
D Armasel 1924 *F*, *US*
A Atanasiu 1970 *It*, *F*, 1971 *It*, *Mor*, *F*, 1972 *Mor*, *Cze*, *WGe*, 1973 *Sp*, *Mor*, *Ar*, *Ar*, *WGe*, 1974 *Pol*
I Bacioiu 1976 *USS*, *Bul*, *Pol*, *F*, *Mor*
N Baciu 1964 *Cze*, *EGe*, 1967 *It*, *F*, 1968 *Cze*, *Cze*, *F*, 1969 *Pol*, *WGe*, *F*, 1970 *It*, 1971 *It*, *Mor*, *F*, 1972 *Mor*, *Cze*, *WGe*, 1973 *Ar*, *Ar*, 1974 *Cze*, *EGe*
B Balan 2003 *Pt*, *Sp*, *Geo*, 2004 *W*, 2005 *Rus*, *Ukr*, *J*, *US*, *S*, *Pt*, 2006 *Geo*, *Pt*, *Ukr*, *Rus*, *F*, *Geo*, *Sp*, *S*, 2007 *Sp*, *ESp*, *ItA*, *Nm*, *It*, *S*, *Pt*, *NZ*
D Balan 1983 *F*
PV Balan 1998 *H*, *Pol*, *Ukr*, *Ar*, *Geo*, *I*, 1999 *F*, *S*, *A*, *US*, *I*, 2000 *Mor*, *H*, *Pt*, *Sp*, *Geo*, *F*, *It*, 2001 *Pt*, *Sp*, *H*, *Rus*, *Geo*, *I*, *E*, 2002 *Pt*, *Sp*, *H*, *Rus*, *Geo*, *Sp*, *S*, 2003 *CZR*, *F*, *W*, *I*, *Nm*, 2004 *It*, *W*, *J*, *CZR*, 2005 *Geo*, *C*, *I*, 2006 *Geo*, *Pt*, *F*, *Geo*, *Sp*, *S*, 2007 *Geo*
L Balcan 1963 *Bul*, *EGe*, *Cze*
F Balmus 2000 *Mor*, *H*, *Pt*
S Bals 1927 *F*, *Ger*, *Cze*
G Baltaretu 1965 *WGe*, *F*
C Barascu 1957 *F*
M Baraulea 2004 *CZR*, *Pt*, *Geo*
A Barbu 1958 *WGe*, *It*, 1959 *EGe*, *Pol*, *Cze*, *EGe*, 1960 *F*
A Barbuliceanu 2008 *Rus*
S Bargaunas 1971 *It*, *Mor*, 1972 *F*, 1974 *Cze*, 1975 *It*
S Barsan 1934 *It*, 1936 *F*, *It*, 1937 *It*, *H*, *F*, *Ger*, 1938 *F*, *Ger*, 1939 *It*, 1940 *It*, 1942 *It*
RC Basalau 2007 *Pt*, 2008 *Geo*, *Pt*, *Rus*, *Ur*, *Rus*
E Beches 1979 *It*, *Sp*, *USS*, 1982 *WGe*, *It*, 1983 *Pol*
M Bejan 2001 *I*, *W*, 2002 *Pt*, 2003 *Geo*, *CZR*, 2004 *It*
C Beju 1936 *F*, *It*, *Ger*
G Bentia 1919 *US*, *F*, 1924 *F*, *US*
V Bezarau 1995 *Ar*, *F*, *It*
R Bezuscu 1985 *It*, 1987 *F*
G Bigiu 2007 *Pt*, 2008 *Geo*, *Sp*, *Pt*, *Ur*, *Rus*
M Blagescu 1952 *EGe*, *EGe*, 1953 *It*, 1955 *Cze*, 1957 *F*, *Cze*, *Bel*, *F*
G Blasek 1937 *It*, *H*, *F*, *Ger*, 1940 *It*, 1942 *It*

A Bogheanu 1980 *Mor*
D Boldor 1988 *It, Sp, US, USS, USS, W*, 1989 *It, E, Sp, Z*
A Boroi 1975 *Sp*
P Bors 1975 *JAB*, 1976 *Sp*, 1977 *It*, 1980 *It, USS, I, Pol, F*, 1981 *It, Sp, USS, S, NZ, F*, 1982 *WGe*, 1983 *Mor, WGe, It, USS*, 1984 *It*
D Bozian 1997 *Bel*, 1998 *H, Pol, Ukr*
V Brabateanu 1919 *US, F*
M Braga 1970 *It, F*
C Branescu 1994 *It, E*, 1997 *F*
I Bratulescu 1927 *Ger, Cze*
G Brezoianu 1996 *Bel*, 1997 *F*, 1998 *H, Pol, Ukr, Ar, Geo, I*, 1999 *F, S, A, US, I*, 2000 *H, Pt, Sp, Geo, F, It*, 2001 *Sp, Rus, Geo, I, W, E*, 2002 *Pt, Sp, H, Rus, Geo, I, It, Sp, W, S*, 2003 *Pt, Sp, Rus, Geo, CZR, F, W, I, A, Ar, Nm*, 2005 *Rus, Ukr, J, US, S, Pt, C, I*, 2006 *CZR, Pt, Ukr, Rus, F, Geo, Sp, S*, 2007 *Geo, Sp, CZR, ESp, ItA, Nm, It, S, NZ*
V Brici 1991 *NZ*, 1992 *USS, F, It*, 1993 *Tun, F, Sp, I*, 1994 *Sp, Ger, Rus, It, W, It, E*, 1995 *F, S, J, J, SA, A*, 1996 *Pt, F*, 1997 *F*
TE Brinza 1990 *It, USS*, 1991 *C*, 1992 *It, Ar*, 1993 *Pt, Tun, F, F, I*, 1994 *Sp, Ger, It, W, It, E*, 1995 *F, S, J, J, SA, A*, 1996 *Pt, F, Pol*, 1997 *F, W, Ar, F, It*, 1998 *Ukr*, 1999 *A, US, I*, 2000 *H, Geo*, 2002 *H*
I Bucan 1976 *Bul*, 1977 *Sp*, 1978 *Cze*, 1979 *F*, 1980 *It, USS, I, Pol, F*, 1981 *It, Sp, USS, S, NZ, F*, 1982 *WGe, It, USS, Z, Z, F*, 1983 *Mor, WGe, It, USS, Pol, W, USS, F*, 1984 *It, S, F, Sp*, 1985 *E, Tun, USS, USS, It*, 1986 *Pt, S, F, Pt*, 1987 *It, USS, Z, S, USS, F*
M Bucos 1972 *Mor, Cze, WGe*, 1973 *Sp*, 1975 *JAB, Pol, F*, 1976 *H, It, Sp, USS, Bul, Pol, F, Mor*, 1977 *Sp, It, F, Pol, It, F*, 1978 *Pol, F*, 1979 *W*, 1980 *It, Mor*
P Buda 1953 *It*, 1955 *Cze*, 1957 *F, Cze*
C Budica 1974 *Cze, EGe, Cze*
S Burcea 2006 *F*, 2007 *ESp, ItA, Nm, Rus, Pt*, 2008 *Geo, Ur, Rus*
M Burghelea 1974 *Cze, EGe, F*, 1975 *It*
S Burlescu 1936 *F, It, Ger*, 1938 *F, Ger*, 1939 *It*
M Butugan 2003 *Pt*
VN Calafeteanu 2004 *J*, 2005 *Ukr*, 2006 *CZR, Pt, Ukr, F, Sp, S*, 2007 *Geo, Sp, CZR, ESp, ItA, Nm, It, S, Pt, NZ*, 2008 *Geo, Sp*
A Caligari 1951 *EGe*, 1953 *It*
S Caliman 1958 *EGe*, 1960 *Pol, EGe, Cze*
P Calistrat 1940 *It*, 1942 *It*
Ion Camenita 1939 *It*
CF Caplescu 2007 *Sp, CZR, Rus, Pt*, 2008 *Ur*
C Capmare 1983 *Pol*, 1984 *It*
N Capusan 1960 *F*, 1961 *Pol, Cze, EGe, F*, 1962 *Cze, EGe, Pol*
R Capusan 1962 *It*, 1963 *Bul, EGe, Cze*
G Caracostea 1919 *US, F*
G Caragea 1980 *I, Pol, F*, 1981 *It, Sp, USS, S, NZ, F*, 1982 *WGe, It, USS, Z, Z, F*, 1983 *Mor, WGe, It, USS, Pol, W, F*, 1984 *F, Sp*, 1985 *E, Tun*, 1986 *S, F, Tun, Tun, Pt, F, I*, 1988 *It, Sp, US, USS*, 1989 *E*
C Carp 1989 *Z, Sa, USS*
D Carpo 2007 *ItA*, 2008 *Sp, Pt, Rus, Ur, Rus*
G Celea 1963 *EGe*
D Chiriac 1999 *S, A, I*, 2001 *H*
G Chiriac 1996 *Bel*, 2001 *Pt, Rus*, 2002 *Sp, H, Rus, Geo, I, Sp, W, S*, 2003 *Sp, Rus, Geo, F, W, I, A, Ar, Nm*
R Chiriac 1952 *EGe*, 1955 *Cze*, 1957 *F, Bel, F*, 1958 *Sp, WGe*, 1960 *F*, 1961 *Pol, EGe, Cze, EGe, F*, 1962 *Cze, EGe, Pol, It, F*, 1963 *Bul, EGe, Cze, F*, 1964 *Cze, EGe, WGe, F*
M Chiricencu 1980 *It, Pol*
S Chirila 1989 *Sp, S*, 1990 *F, H, Sp, It, USS*, 1991 *It*
V Chirita 1999 *S*
G Cilinca 1993 *Pt*
N Cioarec 1974 *Pol*, 1976 *It*, 1979 *Pol*
P Ciobanel 1961 *Pol, EGe, Cze, EGe, F*, 1962 *Cze, EGe, Pol, It, F*, 1963 *F*, 1964 *Cze, EGe, WGe, F*, 1965 *WGe, F*, 1966 *Cze, It, F*, 1967 *F*, 1968 *Cze, Cze, F*, 1969 *Pol, WGe, Cze, F*, 1970 *F*, 1971 *F*
I Ciobanu 1952 *EGe*
M Ciobanu 1949 *Cze*, 1951 *EGe*
R Cioca 1994 *Sp, Ger, Rus, It, It, E*, 1995 *S, J*, 1996 *Bel*
I Ciofu 2000 *It*, 2003 *Pt*
ML Ciolacu 1998 *Ukr, Ar, Geo, I*, 1999 *F*, 2001 *Sp, H, Rus, Geo, W, E*
S Ciorascu 1988 *US, USS, USS, F, W*, 1989 *It, E, Sp, Z, Sa, USS, S*, 1990 *It, F, H, Sp, USS*, 1991 *It, NZ, S, F, C, Fj*, 1992 *Sp, It, It, Ar*, 1994 *Ger, Rus, It, W*, 1995 *F, S, J, C, SA, A*, 1996 *F*, 1997 *F, It*, 1999 *F*
M Ciornei 1972 *WGe, F*, 1973 *Ar, Ar, WGe, F*, 1974 *Mor, Pol, EGe, F, Cze*, 1975 *It, Sp*
SE Ciuntu 2007 *NZ, Rus, Pt*, 2008 *Geo, Sp, Rus, Ur*
C Cocor 1940 *It*, 1949 *Cze*
M Codea 1998 *Ukr*, 2001 *E*
L Codoi 1980 *I, Pol*, 1984 *F*, 1985 *Tun, USS*
C Cojocariu 1990 *It, F, H, Sp, It, USS*, 1991 *It, NZ, F, S, F, C, Fj*, 1992 *Sp, It, USS, F, Ar*, 1993 *Pt, F, F, I*, 1994 *Sp, Ger, Rus, It, W, It, E*, 1995 *F, S, J, J, C, SA, A, Ar, F, It*, 1996 *F*
L Colceriu 1991 *S, Fj*, 1992 *Sp, It, It*, 1993 *I*, 1994 *Sp, Ger, Rus, It, W, It*, 1995 *F, J, J, C, SA, A*, 1997 *F, W, Bel, Ar, F, It*, 1998 *Pol, Ukr*
D Coliba 1987 *USS, F*
M Coltuneac 2002 *Sp, W, S*
T Coman 1984 *Sp*, 1986 *F, Tun, Tun, I*, 1988 *Sp, US, USS, USS*, 1989 *It*, 1992 *F*
C Constantin 2001 *Pt*, 2002 *Geo, W*
F Constantin 1972 *Mor, Cze, WGe*, 1973 *Ar, Ar, WGe*, 1980 *Mor*, 1982 *It*
I Constantin 1971 *Mor*, 1972 *WGe*, 1973 *Ar, Ar, WGe, F*, 1974 *Mor, Pol, Sp, F, Cze*, 1975 *It, Sp, JAB, Pol, F*, 1976 *H, It, Sp, USS, Bul, Pol*, 1977 *It, F*, 1978 *Pol, F*, 1979 *It, Sp, USS, W, Pol, F*, 1980 *It, USS, I, Pol, F*, 1981 *It, Sp, USS, S, NZ, F*, 1982 *WGe, It, USS, Z, Z*, 1983 *WGe, USS*, 1985 *It*
L Constantin 1983 *USS, F*, 1984 *It, S, F, Sp*, 1985 *E, It, Tun, USS, USS, It*, 1986 *Pt, S, F, Tun, Tun, Pt, F, I*, 1987 *It, USS, Z, F, S, USS, F*, 1991 *It, NZ, F*
LT Constantin 1985 *USS*
S Constantin 1980 *Mor*, 1982 *Z, Z*, 1983 *Pol, W, USS, F*, 1984 *S, F*, 1985 *USS*, 1986 *Pt, S, F, Tun*, 1987 *It, Z, S*
T Constantin 1992 *USS, F, It*, 1993 *Pt, F, Sp*, 1996 *Pt*, 1997 *It*, 1999 *F, US, I*, 2000 *Pt, Sp, Geo, F*, 2002 *Rus, Geo*
T Constantin 1985 *USS*
N Copil 1985 *USS, It*, 1986 *S*
D Coravu 1968 *F*
N Cordos 1958 *EGe*, 1961 *EGe*, 1963 *Bul, Cze*, 1964 *Cze, EGe*
V Cornel 1977 *F*, 1978 *Cze, Sp*
G Corneliu 1976 *USS, Bul*, 1977 *F*, 1979 *It*, 1981 *S*, 1982 *Z*
G Corneliu 1980 *Mor, USS*, 1982 *WGe, It, Z, Z*, 1986 *Tun, Pt, F*, 1993 *I*, 1994 *W*
M Corneliu 1979 *USS*
F Corodeanu 1997 *F, W*, 1998 *H, Pol, Ar, Geo*, 1999 *F, S, A, US, I*, 2000 *H, Sp, Geo, F, It*, 2001 *Pt, Sp, H, Rus, Geo, I, E*, 2002 *Pt, Sp, Rus, Geo, It, Sp, W, S*, 2003 *Sp*, 2005 *Geo, J, US, S, Pt, C, I*, 2006 *Geo, CZR, Pt, Geo, Sp, S*, 2007 *Geo, ESp, ItA, Nm, It, S, Pt, NZ*, 2008 *Ur, Rus*
Coste 2007 *Pt*, 2008 *Geo, Sp, Pt, Rus, Ur*
L Costea 1994 *E*, 1995 *S, J, J, Ar, F*, 1997 *F*
L Coter 1957 *F, Cze*, 1959 *EGe, Pol, Cze*, 1960 *F*
F Covaci 1936 *Ger*, 1937 *H, F, Ger*, 1940 *It*, 1942 *It*
C Cratunescu 1919 *US, F*
N Crissoveloni 1936 *F, It*, 1937 *H, F, Ger*, 1938 *F, Ger*
S Cristea 1973 *Mor*
C Cristoloveanu 1952 *EGe*
G Crivat 1938 *F, Ger*
V Csoma 1983 *WGe*
D Curea 2005 *Rus, Ukr, J, US, S, Pt*
V Daiciulescu 1966 *Cze, F*, 1967 *It, Pol*, 1968 *F*, 1969 *Pol*
A Damian 1934 *It*, 1936 *F, It, Ger*, 1937 *It*, 1938 *F, Ger*, 1939 *It*, 1949 *Cze*
G Daraban 1969 *Cze*, 1972 *Mor, Cze, WGe, F*, 1973 *Sp, Mor, Ar, Ar*, 1974 *Cze, EGe, F, Cze*, 1975 *It, Sp, JAB, Pol, F*, 1976 *H, It, Sp, USS, Bul, Pol, F, Mor*, 1977 *Sp*,

It, F, 1978 *Cze, Sp, Pol, F,* 1982 *F,* 1983 *Mor, WGe, It, USS, W*
CR Dascalu 2006 *Ukr, F, Geo, Sp, S,* 2007 *Sp, CZR, ESp, NZ, Rus, Pt,* 2008 *Geo, Rus, Ur, Rus*
V David 1984 *Sp,* 1986 *Pt, S, F, Tun,* 1987 *USS, Z, F,* 1992 *USS*
S Demci 1998 *Ar,* 2001 *H, Rus, Geo, I, W*
R Demian 1959 *EGe,* 1960 *F,* 1961 *Pol, EGe, Cze, EGe, F,* 1962 *Cze, Pol, It, F,* 1963 *Bul, EGe, Cze, F,* 1964 *WGe, F,* 1965 *WGe, F,* 1966 *Cze, It, F,* 1967 *It, Pt, Pol, WGe, F,* 1968 *Cze, F,* 1969 *Pol, WGe, F,* 1971 *It, Mor*
E Denischi 1949 *Cze,* 1952 *EGe, EGe*
I Diaconu 1942 *It*
C Diamandi-Telu 1938 *Ger,* 1939 *It*
D Dima 1999 *A, US, I,* 2000 *H, Pt, Geo, F, It,* 2001 *Sp, H, Rus, Geo, W, E,* 2002 *Pt, Sp, Rus, W, S,* 2004 *CZR, Pt, Sp, Rus, Geo*
TI Dimofte 2004 *It, W, CZR,* 2005 *C, I,* 2006 *Geo, CZR, Pt, Ukr, Rus, F, Geo, Sp, S,* 2007 *ESp, ItA, Nm, It, S, Pt, NZ, Rus, Pt,* 2008 *Geo, Sp, Pt, Rus, Ur, Rus*
C Dinescu 1934 *It,* 1936 *F, It, Ger,* 1937 *It, H, F, Ger,* 1938 *F, Ger,* 1940 *It,* 1942 *It*
C Dinu 1965 *WGe, F,* 1966 *Cze, It, F,* 1967 *It, Pt, Pol, WGe,* 1968 *F,* 1969 *Pol, WGe, Cze, F,* 1970 *It, F,* 1971 *Mor, F,* 1972 *Mor, Cze, WGe, F,* 1973 *Sp, Mor, Ar, Ar, WGe, F,* 1974 *Mor, Pol, Sp, Cze, F, Cze,* 1975 *It, Sp,* 1976 *H, It, Sp, Pol, F, Mor,* 1977 *Sp, It, F, Pol, It, F,* 1978 *Sp, Pol, F,* 1979 *Sp, USS, W, Pol,* 1980 *I, Pol, F,* 1981 *It, Sp, USS, NZ, F,* 1982 *F,* 1983 *Mor, WGe, It, USS*
F Dinu 2000 *Mor, H*
G Dinu 1975 *Pol,* 1979 *It, Sp,* 1983 *Pol, USS*
G Dinu 1990 *It, F, H, Sp, It, USS,* 1991 *It, S, F, C, Fj,* 1992 *Sp, It, USS, F, It,* 1993 *F*
F Dobre 2001 *E,* 2004 *W, CZR,* 2007 *Pt*
I Dobre 1951 *EGe,* 1952 *EGe,* 1953 *It,* 1955 *Cze,* 1957 *Cze, Bel, F,* 1958 *Sp*
I Doja 1986 *Tun, Pt, F, I,* 1988 *F, W,* 1989 *Sp, Z, Sa, S,* 1990 *It,* 1991 *It, NZ, F, C,* 1992 *Sp*
V Doja 1997 *Bel,* 1998 *Pol, Geo, I*
A Domocos 1989 *Z, Sa, USS*
I Dorutiu 1957 *Cze, Bel, F,* 1958 *Sp, WGe*
A Draghici 1919 *US*
C Dragnea 1995 *F,* 1996 *Pol,* 1997 *F, Bel, Ar, F, It,* 1998 *H, Pol,* 1999 *F,* 2000 *F*
I Dragnea 1985 *Tun*
S Dragnea 2002 *S*
M Dragomir 1996 *Bel,* 1997 *Bel,* 1998 *H, Pol, Ukr, Geo, I,* 2001 *I, W, E*
M Dragomir 2001 *H, Geo,* 2002 *I*
V Dragomir 1964 *Cze, EGe,* 1966 *It,* 1967 *Pol, WGe*
G Dragomirescu 1919 *F*
G Dragomirescu-Rahtopol 1963 *Bul, EGe, Cze, F,* 1964 *Cze, EGe, WGe, F,* 1965 *WGe, F,* 1966 *Cze,* 1967 *It, Pt, Pol, WGe, F,* 1968 *Cze, Cze, F,* 1969 *Pol, Cze, F,* 1970 *It, F,* 1971 *It, Mor,* 1972 *Mor, Cze, WGe, F,* 1973 *WGe, F*
N Dragos 1995 *Ar, It,* 1997 *F, Ar, F, It,* 1998 *H, Pol, Ukr, Ar, Geo, I,* 1999 *F, S,* 2000 *Sp, Geo, F*
CS Draguceanu 1994 *Sp, Ger, Rus, It, W, It, E,* 1995 *S, J, Ar, F, It,* 1996 *Bel,* 1997 *W, Bel, Ar, F, It,* 1998 *H, Pol, Ukr, Ar, Geo, I,* 1999 *S, A, US, I,* 2000 *Mor, H, Pt, Sp, Geo, F, It*
C Dragulescu 1969 *Cze,* 1970 *F,* 1971 *It,* 1972 *Cze*
G Drobota 1960 *Pol, Cze,* 1961 *EGe, EGe, F,* 1962 *Cze, EGe, Pol, F,* 1964 *Cze, EGe, F*
D Dumbrava 2002 *W,* 2003 *Sp, Rus, Geo, CZR, F, W, I, A, Nm,* 2004 *CZR, Pt, Sp, Rus, Geo, It, J, CZR,* 2005 *Rus, Geo, Ukr, J, US, S, Pt, C,* 2006 *Geo, Pt, Rus,* 2007 *Sp, CZR, Pt, Rus, Pt,* 2008 *Sp, Pt, Ur, Rus*
H Dumitras 1984 *It,* 1985 *E, It, USS,* 1986 *Pt, F, I,* 1987 *It, USS, Z, S, USS, F,* 1988 *It, Sp, US, USS, USS, F, W,* 1989 *It, E, Z, Sa, USS, S,* 1990 *It, F, H, Sp, USS,* 1991 *It, NZ, F, S, F, C, Fj,* 1992 *Sp, USS, F, Ar,* 1993 *Pt, Tun, F, Sp, F, I*
I Dumitras 2002 *H,* 2006 *Geo, CZR, Ukr, Rus, F,* 2007 *Geo, Sp, CZR, ESp, ItA, Nm, It, S, Pt, NZ*
E Dumitrescu 1953 *It,* 1958 *Sp, WGe*
G Dumitrescu 1988 *It, Sp, F, W,* 1989 *It, E, Sp, Z, Sa, USS, S,* 1990 *It, F, H, Sp, It, USS,* 1991 *It, NZ, F,* 1997 *It*
L Dumitrescu 1997 *Bel, Ar,* 2001 *W*
G Dumitriu 1937 *H, F, Ger*
G Dumitru 1973 *Sp, Mor, Ar, Ar, WGe, F,* 1974 *Mor, Sp, Cze, EGe, F,* 1975 *JAB, Pol, F,* 1976 *H, It, Sp,* 1977 *Sp, Pol, F,* 1978 *Cze, Sp, Pol, F,* 1979 *It, Sp, USS, W, Pol, F,* 1980 *It, Mor, USS, I, Pol, F,* 1981 *It, Sp, USS, S, NZ, F,* 1982 *WGe, It, USS, Z, Z, F,* 1983 *Mor, WGe, It, USS, Pol, USS, F,* 1984 *It, S, F,* 1985 *E, It, Tun, USS,* 1986 *F, I,* 1987 *USS, F, S, USS, F*
M Dumitru 1990 *F, H, Sp, It, USS,* 1991 *NZ, F, F, C,* 1992 *F,* 1993 *F, Sp, F*
M Dumitru 1998 *Ar,* 1999 *F,* 2000 *Mor, H, Pt, Sp, Geo, F,* 2002 *H,* 2003 *Sp*
M Dumitru 2002 *Pt, Sp, H, I*
S Dumitru 2004 *It,* 2005 *Rus, Ukr, US, S, Pt*
R Durbac 1968 *Cze,* 1969 *WGe, Cze,* 1970 *It, F,* 1971 *It, Mor, F,* 1972 *WGe, F,* 1973 *Ar, Ar, WGe, F,* 1974 *Mor, Pol, Sp, Cze, EGe, F, Cze,* 1975 *It, Sp, JAB, Pol, F*
A Duta 1973 *Ar*
R Eckert 1927 *F, Ger, Cze*
I Enache 1977 *It*
M Ezaru 2000 *Pt, Geo, F*
V Falcusanu 1974 *Sp, Cze*
G Fantaneanu 1934 *It,* 1936 *F, It, Ger,* 1937 *It, H, F, Ger*
C Fercu 2005 *C, I,* 2006 *Geo, CZR, Pt, Ukr, Rus, F, Geo, Sp,* 2007 *Geo, Sp, CZR, ESp, ItA, Nm, It, S, Pt,* 2008 *Geo, Sp, Pt, Rus, Ur, Rus*
C Florea 1937 *It, F, Ger*
G Florea 1981 *S, NZ, F,* 1982 *WGe, It, USS, Z, Z,* 1984 *Sp,* 1985 *USS,* 1986 *Pt, F*
S Florea 2000 *It,* 2001 *Sp, Geo, I, E,* 2002 *It, Sp, W,* 2003 *Sp, Rus, Geo, CZR, A, Ar, Nm,* 2007 *Sp, CZR, S, NZ*
I Florescu 1957 *F, Cze*
M Florescu 1995 *F*
P Florescu 1967 *It, Pt, Pol, WGe, F,* 1968 *Cze, Cze, F,* 1969 *Pol, WGe, Cze, F,* 1971 *Mor,* 1973 *Sp, Mor, Ar, Ar,* 1974 *Cze, EGe, F*
P Florian 1927 *F,* 1934 *It*
T Florian 1927 *F, Ger*
V Flutur 1994 *Ger,* 1995 *J, J, C, SA, A, Ar, F, It,* 1996 *Bel, Pol,* 1997 *F*
M Foca 1992 *It, USS, It, Ar,* 1993 *Pt, Tun, F*
C Fugigi 1992 *Ar*
C Fugigi 1964 *Cze,* 1969 *Cze,* 1972 *Mor, Cze, WGe, F,* 1973 *Sp, Ar, Ar, WGe, F,* 1974 *Mor, Sp, Cze, EGe,* 1975 *It, Sp, JAB*
R Fugigi 1995 *It,* 1996 *Pt, F, Pol,* 1998 *Ukr, Ar, I,* 1999 *S, I*
S Fuicu 1976 *H,* 1980 *USS, I, Pol, F,* 1981 *It, Sp, USS, S, NZ, F,* 1982 *Z, Z, F,* 1983 *Mor, WGe, It, USS, W,* 1984 *It*
N Fulina 1988 *F, W,* 1989 *It, E, Sp, Sa, USS,* 1990 *It, F, H, Sp, USS,* 1991 *NZ, C, Fj,* 1992 *It, It,* 1993 *Pt, F, Sp, F, I,* 1994 *Sp, Ger, Rus, It, W, It*
C Gal 2005 *I,* 2006 *Geo, CZR, Pt, S,* 2007 *Geo, CZR, ESp, ItA, Nm, It, S, NZ, Rus, Pt,* 2008 *Geo, Sp, Pt, Rus*
S Galan 1985 *It, It*
I Garlesteanu 1924 *F, US,* 1927 *F, Cze*
A Gealapu 1994 *It, E,* 1995 *F, S, J, J, C, SA, A, Ar, F, It,* 1996 *Pt, F, Pol*
C Gheara 2004 *CZR, Sp, Rus, Geo*
C Gheorghe 1992 *It,* 1993 *Tun, F, Sp,* 1994 *Sp, Ger, Rus, E*
D Gherasim 1959 *Cze*
V Ghiata 1951 *EGe*
S Ghica 1937 *H, F,* 1942 *It*
V Ghioc 2000 *It,* 2001 *Pt, Sp, Rus, Geo, I, W, E,* 2002 *Pt, Sp, H, W, S,* 2003 *CZR, Ar,* 2004 *It, W, CZR,* 2005 *Ukr, J, S,* 2008 *Pt*
N Ghiondea 1949 *Cze,* 1951 *EGe*
D Ghiuzelea 1951 *EGe,* 1952 *EGe, EGe,* 1953 *It,* 1955 *Cze,* 1957 *Cze*
A Girbu 1992 *Ar,* 1993 *Tun, Sp, F, I,* 1994 *Sp,* 1995 *Ar, F, It,* 1996 *Pt, F, Pol,* 1997 *F, Ar, F, It,* 1998 *H, Pol, Geo, I*

M Giucal 1985 *It, Tun, USS, It,* 1986 *Pt, F, Tun*
A Giugiuc 1963 *Bul, EGe, Cze,* 1964 *Cze, EGe,* 1966 *Cze*
V Giuglea 1986 *S, Tun*
I Glavan 1942 *It*
RS Gontineac 1995 *F, S, J, J, C, SA, A,* 1996 *Pt, F, Pol,* 1997 *F, W, Ar, F, It,* 1998 *H, Pol, Ukr, Ar, Geo, I,* 1999 *F, S, A, US, I,* 2000 *H, Sp, Geo, F,* 2001 *Rus, Geo,* 2002 *Pt, Sp, Rus, Geo, I, It, Sp, W, S,* 2003 *Pt, Sp, Geo, CZR, F, W, I, A, Ar, Nm,* 2004 *CZR, Pt, Rus, Geo, It, W, J, CZR,* 2005 *Geo, C,* 2006 *Geo, Pt, Ukr, Rus, F, Geo, Sp, S,* 2007 *Geo, Sp, It, S*
G Graur *1958 It, 1959 EGe, Pol, Cze, EGe, 1960 Pol, EGe, Cze, 1961 EGe, 1962 EGe, It*
E Grigore *1982 WGe, 1984 Sp, 1985 E, Tun, 1987 It, USS, Z, F, S*
V Grigorescu *1936 F, It, Ger, 1939 It*
M Guramare *1982 WGe, It, 1983 Mor, WGe, 1988 Sp*
A Guranescu *1991 S, F, 1992 USS, It, 1993 Pt, Tun, I, 1994 Ger, Rus, It, W, E, 1995 SA, A, Ar, F, It*
S Guranescu *1997 W, Bel, Ar, 2001 Sp, H, Rus, I*
A Hariton *1973 Mor, Ar, Ar, 1978 Cze, Sp*
T Hell *1958 EGe*
CN Hildan *1998 H, Pol, Geo, 1999 S*
L Hodorca *1984 It, 1985 Tun, 1986 Pt, S, F, Tun, Tun, I, 1987 It, Z, 1988 F*
M Holban *1980 Mor, 1982 F, 1985 It, USS, 1986 Pt, I*
J Hussar *1919 US*
D Iacob *1996 Bel, 2001 Pt, Sp, H, Geo, W*
ML Iacob *1997 W, Bel, Ar, F, It, 1999 S*
P Ianusevici *1974 Pol, Cze, EGe, Cze, 1975 It, 1976 USS, Bul, Pol, F, Mor, 1977 Sp, Pol, It, F, 1978 F*
I Iconomu *1919 US, F*
M Iconomu *1919 US, F*
N Ifrim *1937 F, Ger*
G Ignat *1986 Pt, S, F, Tun, 1988 It, Sp, US, USS, USS, F, W, 1989 It, E, Sp, S, 1990 It, F, H, Sp, 1991 It, NZ, 1992 Sp, It, USS, F*
V Ilca *1987 F*
I Ilie *1952 EGe, EGe, 1953 It, 1955 Cze, 1957 F, Cze, Bel, F, 1958 It, 1959 EGe*
M Iliescu *1961 EGe, 1963 Bul, EGe, Cze, F, 1965 WGe, F, 1967 WGe*
T Ioan *1937 H, F, Ger*
V Ioan *1927 Ger, Cze, 1937 It*
F Ion *1991 S, 1992 Sp, 1993 F*
G Ion *1984 Sp, 1986 F, I, 1988 USS, F, W, 1989 It, E, Sp, Sa, USS, S, 1990 It, F, H, Sp, It, USS, 1991 It, NZ, F, S, F, C, Fj, 1992 Sp, It, USS, F, Ar, 1993 Pt, F, Sp, F, 1994 Sp, It, W, It*
P Ion *2003 Ar, 2004 It, 2005 Rus, Ukr, J, US, S, 2006 Geo, CZR, Pt, Ukr, Rus, F, Geo, S, 2007 Geo, Sp, CZR, ESp, ItA, Pt, NZ, Rus, 2008 Geo, Sp, Rus, Ur, Rus*
V Ion *1980 Mor, USS, 1982 Z, Z, F, 1983 Mor, It, USS, W, USS, F, 1984 S, 1985 It, 1987 It, USS, Z, F, S*
A Ionescu *1958 EGe, It, 1959 EGe, Pol, Cze, 1960 Pol, EGe, Cze, 1961 Pol, Cze, EGe, F, 1962 EGe, It, F, 1963 F, 1964 Cze, EGe, F, 1965 WGe, 1966 Cze, It, F*
D Ionescu *1949 Cze, 1951 EGe, 1952 EGe, EGe, 1953 It, 1955 Cze, 1957 F, Cze, F, 1958 Sp, It*
G Ionescu *1949 Cze*
G Ionescu *1934 It, 1936 F, It, Ger, 1937 It, F, 1938 F, Ger, 1940 It, 1942 It*
M Ionescu *1972 Mor, 1976 USS, Bul, Pol, F, 1977 It, F, Pol, It, F, 1978 Cze, Sp, Pol, F, 1979 It, Sp, USS, W, Pol, F, 1980 I, 1981 NZ, 1983 USS*
R Ionescu *1968 Cze, Cze, 1971 F*
S Ionescu *1936 It, Ger, 1937 It*
V Ionescu *1992 It*
V Ionescu *1993 Tun, F, 1994 Rus, 1998 Ukr*
F Ionita *1974 Sp, 1978 Pol, F*
P Iordachescu *1957 F, Cze, Bel, F, 1958 Sp, WGe, EGe, It, 1959 EGe, Pol, Cze, EGe, 1960 Pol, EGe, Cze, 1961 EGe, 1963 F, 1964 Cze, EGe, WGe, 1965 WGe, F, 1966 Cze*
M Iordan *1980 Mor*
P Iordanescu *1949 Cze*
V Iorgulescu *1967 WGe, 1968 Cze, F, 1969 Pol, WGe, Cze, 1970 It, F, 1971 F, 1973 Ar, Ar*
V Irimescu *1960 F, 1961 Pol, Cze, EGe, F, 1962 Cze, EGe, Pol, It, F, 1963 F, 1964 F, 1965 WGe, F, 1966 Cze, It, F, 1967 It, Pt, Pol, WGe, F, 1968 Cze, Cze, F, 1969 Pol, WGe, Cze, F, 1970 It, F, 1971 F*
I Irimia *1936 F, It, Ger, 1937 It, H, Ger, 1938 F, Ger, 1939 It, 1940 It*
G Irisescu *1993 Sp*
A Iulian *2003 CZR*
I Ivanciuc *1991 Fj, 1994 E, 1995 J, C, SA, A*
I Jipescu *1927 F*
C Kramer *1955 Cze, 1958 Sp, WGe, It, 1960 Pol, EGe, Cze*
T Krantz *1940 It, 1942 It*
C Kurtzbauer *1939 It*
C Lapusneanu *1934 It*
MA Lazar *2008 Ur, Rus*
G Leonte *1984 S, F, 1985 E, It, USS, 1987 It, USS, Z, S, USS, F, 1988 It, Sp, US, USS, USS, F, W, 1989 It, E, Sp, Z, Sa, USS, S, 1990 It, F, H, Sp, It, 1991 It, NZ, F, S, F, C, 1992 USS, F, It, Ar, 1993 Tun, F, Sp, F, I, 1994 Sp, Ger, Rus, It, W, It, 1995 F, S, J, J, C, SA, A*
M Leuciuc *1987 F*
T Luca *1995 Ar, F, It, 1996 F*
V Lucaci *1996 Bel*
A Lungu *1980 It, USS, 1981 It, Sp, USS, S, NZ, F, 1982 WGe, It, USS, Z, Z, F, 1983 Mor, WGe, It, USS, Pol, W, USS, F, 1984 It, S, F, Sp, 1985 E, It, Tun, USS, USS, It, 1986 Pt, S, F, Tun, Tun, Pt, F, I, 1987 It, USS, Z, F, S, USS, F, 1988 It, Sp, US, USS, USS, F, W, 1989 It, E, Sp, Z, Sa, USS, S, 1990 It, F, It, 1991 It, NZ, F, S, F, C, Fj, 1992 Sp, It*
R Lungu *2002 Pt, H, It, Sp, W, 2003 Pt*
A Lupu *2006 S*
C Lupu *1998 Pol, I, 1999 F, 2000 Mor, It, 2001 Pt, H, Rus, W, 2002 H, Rus*
S Luric *1951 EGe, 1952 EGe, EGe, 1953 It, 1955 Cze*
V Luscal *1958 Sp, WGe, EGe*
F Macaneata *1983 USS*
M Macovei *2006 Ukr, Rus, 2007 Geo, Rus, Pt, 2008 Geo, Rus, Ur, Rus*
V Maftei *1995 Ar, F, It, 1996 Bel, 1997 W, F, 1998 Ar, 2001 Pt, Sp, H, Geo, I, 2002 Pt, Sp, Rus, Geo, I, It, Sp, S, 2003 Pt, Geo, CZR, F, W, I, A, Ar, Nm, 2004 Pt, Sp, Rus, Geo, W, J, CZR, 2005 Rus, Geo, Ukr, C, I, 2006 CZR*
G Malancu *1976 H, It, USS, Bul*
A Man *1988 US, USS, USS*
D Manoileanu *1949 Cze*
G Manole *1959 Pol, 1960 Pol, EGe, Cze*
A Manta *1996 Bel, 1997 F, 1998 Ar, Geo, I, 2000 F, 2001 Pt, Sp, Rus, Geo, 2002 Sp, H, Rus, I, It, Sp, 2003 Pt, Rus, 2005 C, I, 2006 Geo, CZR, Pt, Geo, 2007 It, S, NZ*
H Manu *1919 US, F, 1927 F, Ger*
N Marascu *1919 F, 1924 F, US, 1927 F, Cze*
A Marasescu *1927 F, Ger, 1936 It, Ger*
E Marculescu *1936 F, It, Ger, 1937 It, 1939 It, 1940 It*
A Marghescu *1980 Pol, 1981 It, 1983 W, USS, F, 1984 S, F, Sp, 1985 E*
I Marica *1972 WGe, F, 1973 Sp, Mor, WGe, F, 1974 Mor, Sp, Cze, EGe, F, Cze, 1975 It, Sp*
A Marin *1978 Cze, Sp, Pol, 1979 F, 1980 Pol, 1982 USS, 1983 Pol, 1984 Sp, 1985 USS, It, 1986 Pt, 1987 USS, Z*
N Marin *1991 Fj, 1992 Sp, It, 1993 F, I, 1995 Ar, F, It*
A Marinache *1949 Cze, 1951 EGe, 1952 EGe, EGe, 1955 Cze, 1957 F, Bel, F, 1960 F, 1961 Pol, EGe, Cze, EGe, F, 1962 Cze, Pol*
V Marinescu *1967 Pt, WGe, 1968 Cze, 1969 Cze, F*
F Marioara *1994 E, 1996 Pol, 1998 Geo, I*
A Mateescu *1959 EGe, Pol, Cze, EGe, 1960 Pol, EGe, Cze, 1962 EGe, Pol, 1963 Bul, EGe, Cze, 1964 Cze, EGe, 1965 WGe, F, 1966 F, 1970 It, F, 1973 Sp, WGe, F, 1974 Mor, Pol, Sp*
A Mateiescu *1934 It, 1936 F, Ger*
R Mavrodin *1998 Geo, I, 1999 F, A, US, I, 2000 H, Pt, Sp, Geo, F, It, 2002 Pt, Sp, H, I, It, Sp, W, 2003 I, A, Ar, Nm, Geo, F, It, 2002 Pt, Sp, H, I, It, Sp, W, 2003 I, A, Ar, Nm,*

G Mazilu *1958 Sp, WGe, 1959 EGe, Pol, Cze*
S Mehedinti *1951 EGe, 1953 It*
G Melinte *1958 EGe, It*
P Mergisescu *1960 Pol, EGe, Cze*
C Mersoiu *2000 Mor, Pt, 2001 I, 2002 S, 2003 Pt, Sp, Geo, CZR, F, W, 2004 CZR, Pt, Sp, Rus, It, W, J, CZR, 2005 Rus, Geo, Ukr, I, 2006 CZR, Pt, Geo, Sp, 2007 Geo, Sp, CZR, Rus, Pt, 2008 Geo, Sp, Pt, Rus, Ur, Rus*
A Miclescu *1971 Mor*
S Mihailescu *1919 F, 1924 F, US, 1927 F*
D Mihalache *1973 Mor*
M Mihalache *2007 Pt, 2008 Geo, Sp*
V Mihalascu *1967 Pol, WGe*
A Mitocaru *1992 Ar, 1993 Pt, Sp, F*
P Mitu *1996 Bel, Pol, 1997 W, Bel, Ar, It, 1998 H, Pol, Ukr, Ar, Geo, I, 1999 F, S, A, US, I, 2000 H, Pt, Sp, Geo, It, 2001 Pt, Sp, H, Rus, 2002 Pt, Sp, H, Rus, Geo, Sp, W, S, 2003 Geo, 2005 I, 2006 Geo*
M Miu *2003 Pt, Sp*
V Mladin *1955 Cze, 1957 Bel, F, 1958 Sp, WGe, It, 1959 EGe, 1960 F*
S Mocanu *1996 Bel, 1998 H, Pol, Ukr, 2000 Mor, Pt*
T Moldoveanu *1937 F, Ger, 1938 F, Ger, 1939 It, 1940 It*
F Morariu *1976 H, USS, Bul, Pol, F, Mor, 1977 Sp, It, F, Pol, It, F, 1978 Cze, Sp, Pol, F, 1979 It, Sp, USS, W, Pol, F, 1980 It, I, Pol, F, 1981 USS, NZ, 1982 USS, Z, Z, F, 1983 Mor, WGe, It, USS, Pol, W, F, 1984 It, S, F, Sp, 1985 E, It, Tun, USS, USS, It, 1986 Pt, S, F, Tun, 1987 It, USS, Z, S, USS, F, 1988 It, Sp, US, USS, USS, F, W, 1989 It, E, Sp, Z*
O Morariu *1984 Sp, 1985 Tun*
V Morariu *1952 EGe, EGe, 1953 It, 1955 Cze, 1957 F, Cze, Bel, F, 1959 EGe, 1960 F, 1961 Pol, Cze, EGe, F, 1962 Cze, EGe, Pol, It, F, 1963 F, 1964 WGe, F*
C Moscu *1934 It, 1937 It*
M Mot *1980 Mor, 1982 It, USS, Z, 1985 It, It, 1986 F, Tun, 1988 US, USS*
M Motoc *1988 US, 1989 S*
P Motrescu *1973 Mor, Ar, Ar, 1974 Mor, Pol, Sp, Cze, 1975 JAB, Pol, F, 1976 H, It, Sp, Bul, Pol, F, Mor, 1977 Sp, It, F, Pol, It, F, 1978 Cze, Sp, Pol, F, 1979 It, Sp, USS, W, Pol, 1980 It, Mor*
B Munteanu *2000 It*
IC Munteanu *1940 It, 1942 It*
M Munteanu *1973 WGe, F, 1974 Mor, Sp, Cze, EGe, F, Cze, 1975 It, Sp, JAB, Pol, F, 1976 H, It, Sp, Pol, Mor, 1978 Pol, F, 1979 It, Sp, W, Pol, 1980 It, I, Pol, F, 1981 It, Sp, USS, S, NZ, F, 1982 F, 1983 Mor, WGe, It, USS, Pol, W, USS, F, 1984 It, S, F, 1985 USS, 1986 S, Tun, Pt, F, 1988 It, Sp*
T Munteanu *2003 CZR, 2004 CZR*
D Musat *1974 Sp, Cze, EGe, Cze, 1975 It, JAB, Pol, F, 1976 Mor, 1980 Mor*
M Nache *1980 Mor*
M Nagel *1958 EGe, 1960 Pol, EGe, Cze*
R Nanu *1952 EGe, EGe, 1953 It, 1955 Cze, 1957 F, Bel, F*
V Nastase *1985 Tun, USS, 1986 Tun, Pt, F, I*
D Neaga *1988 It, Sp, USS, F, W, 1989 It, E, Sp, Z, Sa, USS, S, 1990 It, F, H, Sp, USS, 1991 It, F, S, F, C, Fj, 1993 Tun, F, Sp, I, 1994 Sp, Ger, Rus, It, W, It, E, 1995 F, S, J, J, C, 1996 Pt, F*
I Neagu *1972 Mor, Cze*
E Necula *1987 It, F*
P Nedelcovici *1924 F*
C Nedelcu *1964 Cze, EGe*
M Nedelcu *1993 Pt, Tun, F, 1994 Sp, It, 1995 Ar, F, It*
V Nedelcu *1996 Pol, 1997 F, W, Ar, F, 1998 H, Pol, Ukr, Ar, 2000 H, 2001 I, W, E, 2002 Rus, Geo*
I Negreci *1994 E, 1995 F, J, C, SA, A, Ar, F, It*
I Nemes *1924 F, US, 1927 Ger, Cze*
N Nere *2006 CZR, 2007 CZR, Rus, Pt, 2008 Sp, Pt*
G Nica *1964 Cze, EGe, WGe, 1966 It, F, 1967 Pol, F, 1969 Pol, WGe, Cze, F, 1970 It, F, 1971 It, Mor, F, 1972 Mor, Cze, WGe, F, 1973 Sp, Mor, Ar, Ar, WGe, F, 1974 Mor, Pol, Sp, Cze, EGe, F, Cze, 1975 It, Sp, JAB, Pol, F, 1976 H, It, Sp, USS, Bul, Pol, F, Mor, 1977 Sp, It, F, Pol, It, F, 1978 Pol, F*
N Nichitean *1990 It, Sp, It, USS, 1991 It, F, F, C, Fj, 1992 USS, It, Ar, 1993 Pt, Tun, F, Sp, 1994 Sp, Ger, Rus, It, W, It, 1995 F, S, J, J, C, 1997 F*
G Nicola *1927 F, Ger, Cze*
C Nicolae *2003 Pt, Rus, 2006 Sp, 2007 ItA, Nm, Pt, Rus*
M Nicolae *2003 I, A*
N Nicolau *1940 It*
M Nicolescu *1969 Pol, WGe, Cze, F, 1971 It, Mor, F, 1972 Mor, Cze, WGe, F, 1973 Sp, Mor, Ar, Ar, WGe, F, 1974 Mor, Cze, EGe, F, Cze, 1975 It, Sp, Pol, F*
P Niculescu *1958 It, 1959 EGe, Cze*
V Niculescu *1938 F, Ger*
F Nistor *1986 Tun*
V Nistor *1959 EGe, Pol, EGe*
M Oblomenco *1967 It, Pt, WGe, F*
G Olarasu *2000 Mor, H*
M Olarasu *2000 Mor*
V Onutu *1967 It, Pt, Pol, WGe, F, 1968 Cze, 1969 F, 1971 It, Mor*
N Oprea *2000 It, 2001 Pt, Sp, H, Rus, Geo, I, W, E*
F Opris *1986 F, Tun, Tun, Pt, F, I, 1987 F*
G Oprisor *2004 W, J, CZR, 2005 Rus, Ukr, J, US, S, Pt*
T Oroian *1988 F, W, 1989 It, E, Sp, Z, USS, 1990 Sp, It, 1993 Pt, Tun, F, Sp, I, 1994 Sp, Ger, Rus, It, W, It, E, 1995 F, S, J, J, C*
M Ortelecan *1972 Mor, Cze, WGe, F, 1974 Pol, 1976 It, Sp, USS, Bul, F, 1977 Sp, It, F, Pol, It, F, 1978 Cze, Sp, 1979 F, 1980 USS*
A Palosanu *1952 EGe, EGe, 1955 Cze, 1957 F, Cze*
E Pana *1937 F, Ger*
M Paraschiv *1975 Sp, JAB, Pol, F, 1976 H, It, Sp, USS, Bul, F, Mor, 1977 Sp, It, Pol, F, 1978 Cze, Sp, Pol, F, 1979 It, Sp, W, 1980 It, I, F, 1981 It, USS, S, NZ, F, 1982 WGe, It, USS, Z, Z, F, 1983 Mor, WGe, It, USS, Pol, W, USS, F, 1984 It, S, F, 1985 E, It, Tun, USS, USS, It, 1986 Pt, S, Tun, 1987 It, USS, Z, F, S, USS, F*
G Parcalabescu *1940 It, 1942 It, 1949 Cze, 1951 EGe, 1952 EGe, EGe, 1953 It, 1955 Cze, 1957 Cze, Bel, F, 1958 It, 1959 EGe, Pol, Cze, 1960 Pol, EGe, Cze*
G Pasache *2001 E*
V Pascu *1983 It, Pol, W, USS, F, 1984 It, 1985 USS, 1986 Pt, S, F, Tun, I, 1987 F, 1988 It*
C Patrichi *1993 Pt, Tun*
A Pavlovici *1972 Mor, Cze*
A Penciu *1955 Cze, 1957 F, Cze, Bel, F, 1958 Sp, WGe, EGe, It, 1959 EGe, Pol, Cze, EGe, 1960 F, 1961 Pol, EGe, Cze, EGe, F, 1962 Cze, EGe, Pol, It, F, 1963 Bul, Cze, F, 1964 WGe, F, 1965 WGe, F, 1966 It, F, 1967 F*
I Peter *1973 Sp, Mor*
AA Petrache *1998 H, Pol, 1999 F, S, A, US, I, 2000 Mor, H, Pt, Sp, Geo, F, 2001 W, E, 2002 Pt, Sp, H, Rus, I, It, Sp, W, S, 2003 Pt, Sp, Rus, 2004 It, W, J, CZR*
C Petre *2001 E, 2002 Pt, Sp, H, Rus, Geo, I, It, Sp, W, S, 2003 Pt, Rus, Geo, CZR, F, W, I, A, Ar, Nm, 2004 CZR, Pt, Sp, Rus, Geo, It, W, J, CZR, 2005 Rus, Geo, Ukr, J, US, S, Pt, C, I, 2006 Geo, CZR, Pt, Ukr, Rus, F, Geo, Sp, S, 2007 Geo, Sp, CZR, ESp, ItA, Nm, It, S, Pt, NZ, 2008 Sp, Rus*
A Petrichei *2002 I, S, 2003 Sp, Rus, Geo, CZR, F, W, I, Ar, Nm, 2004 Pt, Sp, Rus, Geo, 2007 ESp, Nm*
P Petrisor *1985 It, 1987 USS*
H Peuciulescu *1927 F*
M Picoiu *2001 Pt, H, 2002 Pt, Sp, H, Rus, I, It, Sp, W*
C Pinghert *1996 Bel*
I Pintea *1974 Pol, 1976 Pol, F, Mor, 1977 Sp, It, F, Pol, It, F, 1979 It, Sp, USS, W, Pol, F, 1980 It, USS*
D Piti *1987 USS, F, 1988 It, Sp, US, 1991 S*
A Plotschi *1985 It, Tun, 1987 S*
Plumea *1927 Ger*
S Podarescu *1979 Pol, F, 1980 USS, 1982 WGe, It, USS, F, 1983 Mor, WGe, USS, F, 1984 It, 1985 E, It*
C Podea *2001 Geo, I, 2002 I, It, Sp, W, 2003 Pt, Sp, Rus, F, A*
R Polizu *1919 US*
A Pop *1970 It, 1971 It, Mor, 1972 Mor, Cze, F, 1973 WGe, F, 1974 Mor, Pol, Sp, EGe, F, Cze, 1975 It, Sp, JAB, Pol, F*
D Popa *1994 Ger*

D Popa *1993 Tun, F, Sp*
I Popa *1934 It, 1936 F, It, Ger, 1937 H, F, 1938 F, Ger, 1939 It, 1940 It, 1942 It*
M Popa *1962 EGe*
N Popa *1952 EGe*
V Poparlan *2007 Nm, Pt, 2008 Geo, Sp, Pt, Ur, Rus*
A Popean *1999 S, 2001 Pt, H*
C Popescu *1986 Tun, Pt, F*
C Popescu *1997 Bel, 2003 CZR, F, W, I, A, Ar, Nm, 2004 CZR, Pt, Sp, Rus, Geo, J, CZR, 2005 Rus, S, Pt, C, 2006 CZR, Ukr, Rus, F, Geo, Sp, S, 2007 Geo, Sp, CZR, ESp, ItA, Nm, It, Pt*
I Popescu *2001 Pt, Sp, H, Rus, Geo*
I Popescu *1958 EGe*
C Popescu-Colibasi *1934 It*
V Popisteanu *1996 Pt, F, Pol*
F Popovici *1973 Sp, Mor*
N Postolache *1972 WGe, F, 1973 Sp, Mor, WGe, F, 1974 Mor, Pol, Sp, EGe, F, Cze, 1975 It, Sp, Pol, F, 1976 H, It*
C Preda *1961 Pol, Cze, 1962 EGe, F, 1963 Bul, EGe, Cze, F, 1964 Cze, EGe, WGe, F*
NF Racean *1988 USS, USS, F, W, 1989 It, E, Z, Sa, USS, 1990 H, Sp, It, USS, 1991 NZ, F, F, C, Fj, 1992 Sp, It, USS, F, It, Ar, 1993 Pt, Tun, F, Sp, 1994 Ger, Rus, It, W, 1995 F, S, J, J, C, SA, A*
M Radoi *1995 F, 1996 Pt, Pol, 1997 F, W, Bel, Ar, F, It, 1998 H, Pol, Ukr*
P Radoi *1980 Mor*
T Radu *1991 NZ*
C Raducanu *1985 It, 1987 It, USS, Z, F, S, 1989 It, E, Sp, Z*
A Radulescu *1980 USS, Pol, 1981 It, Sp, USS, S, F, 1982 WGe, It, USS, Z, Z, 1983 Pol, W, USS, F, 1984 It, S, F, Sp, 1985 E, USS, 1988 It, Sp, US, USS, USS, F, W, 1989 It, E, Sa, USS, 1990 It, F, H, Sp, It, USS*
T Radulescu *1958 Sp, WGe, 1959 EGe, Pol, Cze, EGe, 1963 Bul, EGe, Cze, 1964 F, 1965 WGe, F, 1966 Cze*
D Rascanu *1972 WGe, F*
G Rascanu *1966 It, F, 1967 It, Pt, Pol, WGe, F, 1968 Cze, Cze, F, 1969 Pol, WGe, Cze, F, 1970 It, F, 1971 It, Mor, F, 1972 Mor, Cze, WGe, F, 1974 Sp*
C Ratiu *2003 CZR, 2005 J, US, S, Pt, C, I, 2006 CZR, Pt, Ukr, Rus, F, Geo, Sp, S, 2007 Sp, CZR, ESp, It, S, Pt, NZ, Rus, Pt*
I Ratiu *1992 It*
S Rentea *2000 Mor*
I Roman *1976 Bul*
C Rosu *1993 I*
I Rotaru *1995 J, C, Ar, It, 1996 Pt, F, Pol, 1997 W, Bel, Ar, F*
L Rotaru *1999 F, A, I*
N Rus *2007 Rus*
V Rus *2007 Rus, Pt, 2008 Geo, Pt*
M Rusu *1959 EGe, 1960 F, 1961 Pol, Cze, 1962 Cze, EGe, Pol, It, F, 1963 Bul, EGe, Cze, F, 1964 WGe, F, 1965 WGe, F, 1966 Cze, It, F, 1967 It, Pt, Pol*
V Rusu *1960 Pol, EGe, Cze, 1961 EGe, F, 1962 Cze, EGe, Pol, It, F, 1964 Cze, EGe, WGe, F, 1965 WGe, 1966 It, F, 1967 WGe, 1968 Cze*
I Sadoveanu *1939 It, 1942 It*
AA Salageanu *1995 Ar, F, It, 1996 Pt, F, Pol, 1997 W, Bel, F*
V Samuil *2000 It, 2001 Pt, E, 2002 Pt, Sp, Geo*
C Sasu *1989 Z, 1991 It, NZ, F, S, F, C, Fj, 1993 I*
C Sauan *1999 S, A, US, I, 2000 It, 2002 Geo, I, It, Sp, 2003 Pt, Rus, Geo, CZR, F, W, I, A, Ar, Nm, 2004 CZR, Pt, Sp, Rus, Geo, It, W, J, CZR, 2005 Rus, Geo, Ukr, J, US, S, Pt, 2006 Rus, 2007 Geo*
G Sava *1989 Z, S, 1990 H, Sp, It, USS, 1991 It, F, S, F, C, 1992 Sp*
I Sava *1959 EGe, Pol, Cze, EGe, 1960 F, 1961 Pol, EGe, Cze, EGe, F, 1962 Cze, Pol, It, F*
C Scarlat *1976 H, Sp, 1977 F, 1978 Cze, Sp, 1979 It, Sp, USS, W, Pol, F, 1980 It, USS, 1982 USS*
R Schmettau *1919 US, F*
V Sebe *1960 Pol, EGe, Cze*
I Seceleanu *1992 It, USS, F, It, Ar, 1993 Pt, Tun, F, Sp, F*
S Seceleanu *1986 Pt, F, I, 1990 It*
E Septar *1996 Bel, Pol, 1997 W, 1998 Pol, Ukr, I, 1999 F, S, A, US, I, 2000 It*
B Serban *1989 Sa, USS, S, 1990 It, 1992 It, USS*
C Serban *1964 Cze, EGe, WGe, 1967 Pol, 1968 Cze, F, 1969 Pol, WGe, Cze, F, 1970 It, F, 1971 It, Mor, F, 1972 F, 1973 WGe, F, 1974 Mor*
M Serbu *1967 It*
E Sfetescu *1934 It, 1936 F, Ger, 1937 It*
E Sfetescu *1924 F, US, 1927 Cze*
G Sfetescu *1927 F, Ger*
M Sfetescu *1924 F, US, 1927 Ger, Cze*
N Sfetescu *1927 F, Ger, Cze*
G Simion *1919 US*
G Simion *1998 H*
I Simion *1976 H, It, Sp, 1979 Pol, F, 1980 F*
L Sirbu *1996 Pt, 2000 Mor, H, Pt, Geo, F, 2001 H, Rus, Geo, I, W, E, 2002 Pt, Sp, H, Rus, I, It, S, 2003 Pt, Sp, CZR, F, W, I, A, Ar, Nm, 2004 Pt, Sp, Rus, Geo, It, W, CZR, 2005 Rus, Geo, Ukr, J, US, S, Pt, C, 2006 Geo, Pt, Ukr, Rus, F, Geo, Sp, 2007 Geo, ItA, It, S, Pt, NZ*
M Slobozeanu *1936 F, 1937 H, F, Ger, 1938 F, Ger*
OS Slusariuc *1993 Tun, 1995 J, J, C, 1996 Pt, F, 1997 Bel, Ar, F, 1998 H, Ar, Geo, I, 1999 F, S, A*
S Soare *2001 I, W, 2002 Geo*
S Soare *1924 F, US*
M Socaciu *2000 It, 2001 I, W, E, 2002 It, W, S, 2003 Pt, Sp, Rus, Geo, CZR, F, W, I, A, Nm, 2004 CZR, Pt, Sp, Rus, Geo, It, W, J, CZR, 2005 Rus, Geo, Ukr, J, US, Pt, C, I, 2006 CZR*
S Socol *2001 Sp, H, Rus, Geo, 2002 Pt, It, Sp, W, 2003 Sp, Rus, Geo, F, W, I, A, Ar, Nm, 2004 CZR, Pt, Sp, Rus, Geo, 2005 Rus, Geo, Ukr, C, I, 2006 Geo, CZR, Pt, Ukr, Rus, F, Geo, Sp, S, 2007 Geo, Sp, CZR, It, S, Pt, NZ*
N Soculescu *1949 Cze, 1951 EGe, 1952 EGe, EGe, 1953 It, 1955 Cze*
N Soculescu *1927 Ger*
V Soculescu *1927 Cze*
GL Solomie *1992 Sp, F, It, Ar, 1993 Pt, Tun, F, Sp, F, I, 1994 Sp, Ger, W, It, E, 1995 F, S, J, J, C, SA, A, Ar, F, It, 1996 Pt, F, Pol, 1997 F, W, Bel, Ar, F, It, 1998 H, Pol, Ukr, Ar, Geo, I, 1999 S, A, US, I, 2000 Sp, F, It, 2001 Sp, H, Rus*
C Stan *1990 H, USS, 1991 It, F, S, F, C, Fj, 1992 Sp, It, It, Ar, 1996 Pt, Bel, F, Pol, 1997 F, W, Bel, 1998 Ar, Geo, 1999 F, S, A, US, I*
A Stanca *1996 Pt, Pol*
R Stanca *1997 F, 2003 Sp, Rus*
A Stanciu *1958 EGe, It*
G Stanciu *1958 EGe, It*
C Stanescu *1957 Bel, 1958 WGe, 1959 EGe, 1960 F, 1961 Pol, EGe, Cze, 1962 Cze, It, F, 1963 Bul, EGe, Cze, F, 1964 WGe, F, 1966 Cze, It*
C Stefan *1951 EGe, 1952 EGe*
E Stoian *1927 Cze*
E Stoica *1973 Ar, Ar, 1974 Cze, 1975 Sp, Pol, F, 1976 Sp, USS, Bul, F, Mor, 1977 Sp, It, F, Pol, It, F, 1978 Cze, Sp, Pol, F, 1979 It, Sp, USS, W, Pol, F, 1980 It, USS, I, Pol, F, 1981 It, Sp, USS, S, NZ, F, 1982 WGe, It, USS, Z, Z, F*
G Stoica *1963 Bul, Cze, 1964 WGe, 1966 It, F, 1967 Pt, F, 1968 Cze, Cze, F, 1969 Pol*
I Stroe *1986 Pt*
E Suciu *1976 Bul, Pol, 1977 It, F, It, 1979 USS, Pol, F, 1981 Sp*
M Suciu *1968 F, 1969 Pol, WGe, Cze, 1970 It, F, 1971 It, Mor, F, 1972 Mor, F*
O Sugar *1983 It, 1989 Z, Sa, USS, S, 1991 NZ, F*
K Suiogan *1996 Bel*
F Surugiu *2008 Ur, Rus*
D Talaba *1996 Bel, 1997 F, It*
C Tanase *1938 F, Ger, 1939 It, 1940 It*
A Tanasescu *1919 F, 1924 F, US*
N Tanoviceanu *1937 It, H, F, 1939 It*
I Tarabega *1934 It, 1936 It*
V Tata *1971 F, 1973 Ar, Ar*
CF Tatu *2003 Ar, 2004 CZR, Pt, Sp, Rus, Geo, It, W, 2005 Ukr, J*

I Tatucu *1973 Sp, Mor, 1974 Cze, F*
F Teasca *2008 Ur, Rus*
D Teleasa *1971 It, 1973 Sp, Ar, Ar*
D Tenescu *1951 EGe*
I Teodorescu *2001 I, W, E, 2002 Pt, Sp, S, 2003 Pt, Sp, Rus, W, I, A, Ar, Nm, 2004 CZR, Pt, Sp, Rus, Geo, W, J, CZR, 2005 Rus, Geo, Ukr, J, US, S, Pt, C, I, 2006 Geo, CZR, Pt, Ukr, F, Geo, S, 2007 ESp, ItA*
I Teodorescu *1958 Sp, WGe, EGe, It, 1960 Pol, EGe, Cze, 1963 Bul, EGe, Cze, 1965 WGe, F*
A Teofilovici *1957 F, Cze, Bel, F, 1958 Sp, WGe, 1959 EGe, 1960 F, 1961 Pol, EGe, Cze, EGe, F, 1962 Cze, Pol, It, F, 1963 Bul, EGe, Cze, F, 1964 WGe*
O Tepurica *1985 USS*
M Tibuleac *1957 Bel, F, 1959 Pol, Cze, 1966 Cze, 1967 It, Pt, Pol, WGe, 1968 Cze, Cze*
G Ticlean *1919 F*
M Tigora *2004 CZR*
A Tinca *1987 USS, F*
VM Tincu *2002 Pt, Sp, H, Rus, Geo, I, It, Sp, S, 2003 Pt, Sp, Rus, Geo, F, W, 2004 Sp, 2005 Geo, Ukr, C, I, 2006 Geo, CZR, F, S, 2007 Geo, Sp, CZR, ESp, ItA, Nm, It, S, Pt, NZ, 2008 Geo*
M Toader *1982 WGe, 1984 Sp, 1985 E, It, Tun, USS, 1986 S, F, Tun, Tun, Pt, F, I, 1987 It, USS, Z, F, S, USS, F, 1988 F, W, 1989 It, E, Sp, Sa, USS, S, 1990 It, F, It*
P Toderasc *2000 It, 2001 Pt, Rus, Geo, W, E, 2002 H, Rus, Geo, I, It, Sp, W, S, 2003 Sp, Rus, Geo, CZR, F, W, I, A, Ar, Nm, 2004 CZR, Pt, Sp, Rus, Geo, It, J, CZR, 2005 J, US, S, Pt, C, I, 2006 Geo, Pt, Ukr, Sp, 2007 Geo, ESp, ItA, Nm, It, S*
IR Tofan *1997 Bel, Ar, F, It, 1998 H, Ar, 1999 I, 2000 Mor, Sp, Geo, 2001 Pt, Sp, H, Geo, I, W, E, 2002 Pt, Sp, H, Rus, Geo, I, It, Sp, W, S, 2003 Pt, Sp, Rus, Geo, CZR, F, W, I, A, Ar, Nm, 2004 Sp, Geo, It, W, J, 2005 Rus, Geo, Ukr, J, US, I, 2006 Geo, CZR, Pt, Geo, Sp, S, 2007 Geo, ESp, ItA, Nm, S*
S Tofan *1985 USS, It, 1986 Tun, Pt, F, I, 1987 It, USS, Z, F, S, USS, F, 1988 It, Sp, US, USS, 1991 NZ, 1992 Ar, 1993 Pt, 1994 It, E*
O Tonita *2000 Mor, H, Pt, Sp, F, 2001 Pt, Sp, H, Rus, Geo, I, 2002 Sp, It, Sp, W, 2003 Rus, Geo, F, W, I, A, Ar, Nm, 2004 Sp, Rus, Geo, It, 2005 Rus, Pt, C, I, 2006 Geo, Pt, Geo, Sp, S, 2007 Sp, CZR, It, S, Pt, NZ*
Traian *1942 It*
N Tranca *1992 Sp*
B Tudor *2003 CZR, A*
F Tudor *1924 F, US*
M Tudor *1924 F, US*
AM Tudori *2003 F, W, I, A, Ar, Nm, 2004 Sp, Rus, Geo, W, J, CZR, 2005 Rus, Geo, Ukr, J, US, S, Pt, 2006 Geo, CZR, Ukr, Rus, F, 2007 Sp, CZR, ESp, ItA, Nm, It, S, Pt*
D Tudosa *1999 S, 2002 Geo, I, It, 2003 Pt, W*
T Tudose *1977 It, 1978 Cze, Sp, Pol, F, 1979 It, Sp, USS, 1980 USS*
V Tufa *1985 USS, 1986 Pt, S, 1990 It, 1991 F, 1995 F, S, J, J, SA, A, 1996 Pt, F, Pol*
D Tunaru *1985 It*
V Turlea *1974 Sp, 1975 JAB, Pol, F, 1977 Pol*
C Turut *1937 H, 1938 F*
I Tutuianu *1960 Pol, EGe, 1963 Bul, EGe, Cze, 1964 Cze, EGe, WGe, 1965 WGe, F, 1966 Cze, It, F, 1967 Pt, Pol, WGe, F, 1968 Cze, Cze, F, 1969 Pol, WGe, Cze, F, 1970 It, F, 1971 F*
G Tutunea *1992 Sp*
M Ungur *1996 Bel*
V Ungureanu *1979 It*
V Urdea *1979 F*
V Ursache *2004 It, W, CZR, 2005 S, C, 2006 Geo, Ukr, Rus, F, S, 2007 Geo, Sp, CZR, ESp, ItA, Nm, Pt, NZ, Rus, 2008 Rus, Rus*
R Vacioiu 1977 *It, F, It*
E Valeriu *1949 Cze, 1952 EGe*
M Vardala *1924 F, US*
N Vardela *1927 F, Ger*
G Varga *1976 It, USS, Bul, Pol, F, Mor, 1977 Sp, It, F, Pol, 1978 Sp*
N Varta *1958 EGe*
G Varzaru *1980 Mor, I, Pol, F, 1981 It, Sp, USS, F, 1983 Mor, WGe, It, USS, F, 1984 S, F, 1985 Tun, USS, 1986 F, 1988 It, Sp, US, USS, USS*
Z Vasluianu *1989 Sp, Z, Sa*
P Veluda *1967 It, Pt, Pol, WGe, F, 1968 Cze, Cze*
R Veluda *1949 Cze, 1952 EGe, 1967 Pol*
N Veres *1986 Tun, Pt, 1987 F, USS, F, 1988 It, Sp, USS*
M Vidrascu *1919 US, F*
P Vidrascu *1919 US, 1924 F, US, 1927 Cze*
M Vioreanu *1994 E, 1998 H, Pol, Ukr, Ar, Geo, I, 1999 F, S, A, US, I, 2000 Mor, Pt, Sp, Geo, F, 2001 Geo, 2002 Rus, Geo, I, It, Sp, 2003 Sp, Rus, F, I, A, Ar, Nm*
A Visan *1949 Cze*
D Vlad *2005 US, S, C, I, 2006 Rus, 2007 Sp, CZR, It, Rus, Pt, 2008 Sp*
G Vlad *1991 C, Fj, 1992 Sp, It, USS, F, It, Ar, 1993 Pt, F, I, 1994 Sp, Ger, Rus, It, W, It, E, 1995 F, C, SA, A, Ar, It, 1996 Pt, F, 1997 W, Ar, F, It, 1998 Ar*
V Vlad *1980 Mor*
FA Vlaicu *2006 Ukr, F, Geo, Sp, S, 2007 Geo, Sp, CZR, ESp, ItA, Nm, S, NZ, Pt, 2008 Geo, Pt, Rus, Ur*
C Vlasceanu *2000 Mor, Pt, Sp, Geo, F*
B Voicu *2003 CZR, 2004 CZR, Pt, Sp, Rus, It, J, 2005 J, Pt*
M Voicu *1979 Pol*
M Voicu *2002 Pt*
V Voicu *1951 EGe, 1952 EGe, EGe, 1953 It, 1955 Cze*
R Voinov *1985 It, 1986 Pt, S, F, Tun*
P Volvoreanu *1924 US*
G Vraca *1919 US, F*
M Vusec *1959 EGe, Pol, Cze, EGe, 1960 F, 1961 Pol, EGe, Cze, EGe, F, 1962 Cze, EGe, Pol, It, F, 1963 Bul, EGe, Cze, F, 1964 WGe, F, 1965 WGe, F, 1966 It, F, 1967 It, Pt, Pol, WGe, F, 1968 Cze, Cze, F, 1969 Pol, WGe, F*
RL Vusec *1998 Geo, I, 1999 F, S, A, US, I, 2000 Mor, H, Pt, Sp, F, 2002 H, Rus, I*
F Wirth *1934 It*
I Zafiescu *1979 W, Pol, F*
M Zafiescu *1980 Mor, 1986 I*
D Zamfir *1949 Cze*
B Zebega *2004 CZR, Pt, Rus, Geo, It, W, CZR, 2005 Rus, Ukr, US, S, 2006 Ukr, Sp, 2007 Rus, Pt, 2008 Geo, Pt, Rus, Ur*
D Zlatoianu *1958 Sp, WGe, EGe, It, 1959 EGe, 1960 Pol, EGe, Cze, 1961 EGe, EGe, F, 1964 Cze, EGe, 1966 Cze*

SAMOA

SAMOA'S 2008 RECORD

OPPONENTS	DATE	VENUE	RESULT
Fiji	7 June	A	**Lost** 17–34
Australia A	14 June	H	**Lost** 15–20
NZ Maori	21 June	A	**Lost** 6–17
Tonga	28 June	A	**Won** 20–15
Japan	5 July	H	**Won** 37–31
New Zealand	3 August	A	**Lost** 14–101

NEW START FOR MANU

By Frankie Deges

If, down the pipeline, Samoa's awful 101–14 loss against the All Blacks in New Plymouth brings the proud Pacific Islanders a place in a regular competition in New Zealand, as was suggested immediately after the game, then the loss will have meant something.

With New Zealand needing a friendly game to keep their machine well oiled before the end of the Tri-Nations, they turned to Samoa for opposition. This game was outside of the IRB approved Test window and with the huge number of superb Samoan players based overseas unable to leave their clubs, coach Tuala Lepale Nico Palamo was forced to select an untried XV. They paid the price.

Palamo said: "For the last two years we have been having a high-performance unit thanks to the IRB. Seventy per cent of these boys are in that high-performance unit. Four of them went with the Under-20 [team] to the IRB Junior World Championship this year."

"It is us who needs to do work, to look at our structure and the way we are developing our players back home."

This is a Test that should be looked at under that light – a one-off that should make people aware of the big differences that have to be bridged by Samoa, ranked 12th in the world.

Otherwise, Samoa had some success in 15s, some success in sevens and some success in the U20s. It seemed that they were unable to make that extra-step, but it all showed how close they could be to pushing into the top 10 in the IRB rankings.

Palamo started as national coach at the beginning of the year, replacing the great Michael Jones. He soon named two assistants in Paepaetele Stan To'omalatai (of RWC 1991 fame) and Fepulea'i Selefuti Patu. Their selection task began early, with a clean sheet and every player having to prove they deserved to wear the blue jersey.

The home-based players had ample opportunities during the IRB Pacific Rugby Cup, playing either for Savai'i Samoa or Upolu Samoa – both previous winners of this competition also involving two sides each from Tonga and Fiji.

A big trial was staged in the match in which Savai'i beat Upolu 14–9 in the IRB PRC. Despite this loss, Upolu Samoa secured a home final at Apia Park, yet could not control Tongan side Tautahi Gold, who took the Cup in a tense 11–3 win.

The coaches even held a trial that included overseas-based players needing to prove themselves against local talent. "Unlike previous years where the majority of overseas players would show up a week before a Manu Samoa game, now we don't want that because our team cannot wait for them," Palamo said at the time. He was true to his word and even someone like Semo Sititi, RWC 2007 captain and with more than 50 caps to his name, failed to make the initial training squad – he did, later, play a key role in the squad.

Despite the efforts put in place to ensure the best players would be up to the challenge, the IRB Pacific Nations Cup started on the wrong foot for Samoa. In Lautoka Park, home side Fiji beat them 34–17.

A week later, playing at home in Apia Park saw Manu Samoa perform better against a star-studded Australia A side. Despite their efforts, it was the Australians that celebrated a close 20–15 win. "We should have won, but handed Australia two easy tries," explained coach Palamo. "We are still developing our team to reach that certain stage where they can compete in test matches."

After two matches, Prime Minister Tuilaepa Lupesolaii Saiele Malielegaoi urged the team to move forward.

"At the moment we are ranked fifth, one place away from the last position," he told them in a farewell get-together, prior to travelling to New Zealand.

"None of the six countries in the tournament wants last place, and this can only be changed through your performance in your remaining games. So play well, and remember the support of your country behind you."

His strong encouragement words did not help them enough, as at the Waikato Stadium, Hamilton, eventual champions New Zealand Maori beat them 17–6, a match Manu Samoa never looked like winning.

Nuku'alofa was the next stop and two sides with no wins played one of the matches of the tournament – as happens when these two proud Pacific nations meet. It was eventually Manu Samoa that managed to take the much needed win back home. Fly-half Uale Mai, fresh from a superb Sevens season, saw the same kind of space as in the reduced version to break the pressure, right before half time, running around the scrumhalf to touch-down in the corner. The angled conversion of Gavin Williams – son of former All Black and Samoan coach Bryan – narrowed the gap to 7–9. With 12 minutes to go, winger David Lemi scored under the posts and Manu Samoa never looked back.

Playing at home in Apia, Japan was supposedly going to be cannon fodder for Manu Samoa, yet it needed a foot in touch before they could breathe easy. In the third minute of extra time, with the score at 37–31, a Japanese try was called back in the last move of the game.

This win took Samoa to third in the IRB Pacific Nations Cup 2008 standings by the smallest of margins – a single point differential from Fiji after both nations picked up 10 points from five matches.

At sevens, Samoa had a great season, finishing overall third in the IRB Sevens – 54 points behind winners New Zealand but only six points adrift from South Africa, the runners up. It seems it took Uale Mai's VII a couple of tournaments to get the motor started. They only picked-up six and four points respectively in Dubai and South Africa – they lost the plate final to Argentina by a single point in the UAE and the Plate semi-final against USA in South Africa. After that, with Mali showing the way, things changed.

In Wellington, Samoa were only stopped by the home team in the last move of the last game of the tournament. The return from the next three tournaments was exactly the same: in San Diego, Hong Kong and Adelaide, South Africa beat them in the semi-finals.

Their time to celebrate came at Twickenham, were in the Emirates Airline London Sevens they took the trophy.

It took three tries from blockbusting runner Lolo Lui for Samoa to beat Fiji 19–14 in the bruising final. It had controversy – Fiji scored with the last touch of the ball for a try that would have given them the lead after the easy conversion, but they were called back for a late tackle in the build-up to the interception that led to that try. Samoa celebrated and the Government contributed pay-cheques for each player.

They could not back it up a week later in Edinburgh where a semi-final exit at the hands of New Zealand was to be their last game for a couple of months.

Alafoti Fa'osiliva scored 175 points in the season, followed by Mikaele Pesamino with 157 and multiple try-scorer Lolo Lui.

Skipper Uale Mai, IRB Sevens Player of the Year two years ago, was again singled out as possible recipient of this honour. Nigel Starmer-Smith, the rugby sevens connoisseur, wrote of him: "Uale Mai continues to perform wonderfully well, having passed the grand old age of 30. Mai has wonderful rugby vision, a rugby brain made for Sevens. Fifty-four tournaments he's now played, surpassing Amasio Valence Raoma, 1002 points and also one of the two team captains who managed to beat New Zealand at one point in the season and lift a trophy, at Twickenham. He's so consistently good, the IRB Sevens Player of the Year two years ago and he's kept up that remarkable form. When Samoa are doing well he is the man who's making it all happen."

Having not reached the top eight at the previous RWC Sevens, Samoa hosted the Oceania Sevens over two days in July to decide which two nations – men and women – would travel to Dubai, for the RWC Sevens 2009. The Samoan men's team was by far the best, beating Tonga 52–0 in the final to book their ticket.

The girls, known as Manu Sinas, reached the semi-finals, when they were beaten 29–0 by Australia (with New Zealand, the two qualifiers). Regardless of not reaching the goal, the important aspect of the Manu Sinas was that there was a lot of work put into the preparation of a squad that included both local and New Zealand based players. Coached by Ramsey Tomokino, they were beaten by a more experienced Australian team. From the start of 2008 there was a concerted effort to re-launch development programmes for women.

Finishing seventh at the IRB Under-20 Junior World Championship in Wales was a fine reward for a team that had majority of home-based players. Prime Minister Malielegaoi was there to say farewell to them and in a moving speech told them, "Everyone is the same; the difference between winners and losers is the size of their heart."

En route to Wales they played New Zealand U20 in Auckland and lost 55–12. Many lessons were learnt and soon applied as Samoa beat Scotland 29–17 and USA 20–6 before losing to South Africa 16–11 in the three Pool B matches played at the Racecourse Ground, Wrexham.

They had few answers for Australia U20 in the 0–32 loss but recovered admirably to beat the Argentine Pumitas 30–10 to finish in seventh place. Captain Afa Aiono scored one of his side's five tries at Newport's Rodney Parade. About 60 per cent of the squad had been in the previous' years U19 World Championship where they had also beaten Argentina to claim the same position.

In an effort to raise funds and locate emerging talent, three major appointments of official overseas representatives were made. In New Zealand, the president of the Auckland Samoa Rugby Union, Aiolupo John Roach and former Manu Samoa legend, Papaliitele Peter Fatialofa, and in Australia, Nua Tavita Sio Lamositele, will work for the SRU.

In the 2009–2012 Strategic Investment programme announced by the IRB in the 2008–2011 period, Samoa will receive £2.2 million, which includes significant infrastructure investment.

SAMOA INTERNATIONAL RECORDS

MATCH RECORDS UP TO 30TH SEPTEMBER 2008

WINNING MARGIN

Date	Opponent	Result	Winning Margin
08/04/1990	Korea	74–7	**67**
10/06/2000	Japan	68–9	**59**
29/06/1997	Tonga	62–13	**49**

MOST POINTS IN A MATCH
BY A PLAYER

Date	Player	Opponent	Pts.
29/05/2004	Roger Warren	Tonga	**24**
03/10/1999	Silao Leaega	Japan	**23**
08/04/1990	Andy Aiolupo	Korea	**23**
08/07/2000	Toa Samania	Italy	**23**

MOST POINTS IN A MATCH
BY THE TEAM

Date	Opponent	Result	Pts.
08/04/1990	Korea	74–7	**74**
10/06/2000	Japan	68–9	**68**
29/06/1997	Tonga	62–13	**62**

MOST TRIES IN A MATCH
BY A PLAYER

Date	Player	Opponent	Tries
28/05/1991	Tupo Fa'amasino	Tonga	**4**
10/06/2000	Elvis Seveali'I	Japan	**4**
02/07/2005	Alesana Tuilagi	Tonga	**4**

MOST TRIES IN A MATCH
BY THE TEAM

Date	Opponent	Result	Tries
08/04/1990	Korea	74–7	**13**

MOST CONVERSIONS IN A MATCH
BY A PLAYER

Date	Player	Opponent	Cons
08/04/1990	Andy Aiolupo	Korea	**8**
10/06/2000	Tanner Vili	Japan	**6**
04/07/2001	Earl Va'a	Japan	**6**

MOST CONVERSIONS IN A MATCH
BY THE TEAM

Date	Opponent	Result	Cons
08/04/1990	Korea	74–7	**8**

MOST PENALTIES IN A MATCH
BY A PLAYER

Date	Player	Opponent	Pens
29/05/2004	Roger Warren	Tonga	**8**

MOST PENALTIES IN A MATCH
BY THE TEAM

Date	Opponent	Result	Pens
29/05/2004	Tonga	24–14	8

MOST DROP GOALS IN A MATCH
BY A PLAYER

1 on 9 Occasions

MOST DROP GOALS IN A MATCH
BY THE TEAM

1 on 9 Occasions

MOST CAPPED PLAYERS

Name	Caps
Brian Lima	**65**
To'o Vaega	**60**
Semo Sititi	**56**

LEADING PENALTY SCORERS

Name	Pens
Darren Kellett	**35**
Earl Va'a	**31**
Silao Leaega	**31**

LEADING TRY SCORERS

Name	Tries
Brian Lima	**31**
Afato So'oialo	**15**
To'o Vaega	**15**

LEADING DROP GOAL SCORERS

Name	DGs
Darren Kellett	**2**
Roger Warren	**2**
Steve Bachop	**2**

LEADING CONVERSIONS SCORERS

Name	Cons
Andy Aiolupo	**35**
Earl Va'a	**33**
Silao Leaega	**26**

LEADING POINTS SCORERS

Name	Pts.
Earl Va'a	**184**
Andy Aiolupo	**172**
Silao Leaega	**160**

SAMOA INTERNATIONAL PLAYERS (UP TO 30TH SEPTEMBER 2008)

Note: Years given for International Championship matches are for second half of season; eg 1972 means season 1971–72. Years for all other matches refer to the actual year of the match.

A'ati 1932 *Tg*
Agnew 1924 *Fj, Fj*
S Ah Fook 1947 *Tg*
F Ah Long 1955 *Fj*
Ah Mu 1932 *Tg*
T Aialupo 1986 *W*
F Aima'asu 1981 *Fj*, 1982 *Fj, Fj, Fj, Tg*, 1988 *Tg, Fj*
AA Aiolupo 1983 *Tg*, 1984 *Fj, Tg*, 1985 *Fj, Tg, Tg*, 1986 *Fj, Tg*, 1987 *Fj, Tg*, 1988 *Tg, Fj, I, W*, 1989 *Fj, WGe, Bel, R*, 1990 *Kor, Tg, J, Tg, Fj*, 1991 *W, A, Ar, S*, 1992 *Tg, Fj*, 1993 *Tg, Fj, NZ*, 1994 *Tg, W, A*
Aitofele 1924 *Fj, Fj*
P Alalatoa 1986 *W*
V Alalatoa 1988 *I, W*, 1989 *Fj*, 1991 *Tg, W, A, Ar, S*, 1992 *Tg, Fj*
R Ale 1997 *Tg, Fj*, 1999 *J, Ar, W, S*
A Alelupo 1994 *Fj*
T Aleni 1982 *Tg*, 1983 *Tg*, 1985 *Tg*, 1986 *W, Fj, Tg*, 1987 *Fj*
S Alesana 1979 *Tg, Fj*, 1980 *Tg*, 1981 *Fj, Fj*, 1982 *Fj, Tg*, 1983 *Tg, Fj*, 1984 *Fj, Tg*, 1985 *Fj, Tg*
T Allen 1924 *Fj, Fj*
T Aoese 1981 *Fj, Fj*, 1982 *Fj, Fj, Fj, Tg*, 1983 *Tg*
J Apelu 1985 *Tg*
F Asi 1975 *Tg*
F Asi 1963 *Fj, Fj, Tg*
SP Asi 1999 *S*, 2000 *Fj, J, Tg, C, It, US, W, S*, 2001 *Tg, Fj, NZ, Fj, Tg, Fj*
Atiga 1924 *Fj*
S Ati'ifale 1979 *Tg*, 1980 *Tg*, 1981 *Fj, Fj*
J Atoa 1975 *Tg*, 1981 *Fj*
SJ Bachop 1991 *Tg, Fj, W, A, Ar, S*, 1998 *Tg, Fj*, 1999 *J, C, F, NZ, US, Fj, J, Ar, W, S*
C Betham 1955 *Fj*
ML Birtwistle 1991 *Fj, W, A, Ar, S*, 1993 *Fj, NZ*, 1994 *Tg, W, Fj, A*, 1996 *I*
FE Bunce 1991 *W, A, Ar, S*
CH Capper 1924 *Fj*
J Cavanagh 1955 *Fj, Fj, Fj*
J Clarke 1997 *Tg*, 1998 *A*, 1999 *US, Fj, J*
A Collins 2005 *S, Ar*
A Cortz 2007 *Fj*
G Cowley 2005 *S, Ar*, 2006 *J, Tg*
T Cowley 2000 *J, C, It*
L Crichton 2006 *Fj, Tg*, 2007 *Fj, SA, J, Tg, SA, Tg, E, US*
O Crichton 1988 *Tg*
O Crichton 1955 *Fj, Fj, Fj*, 1957 *Tg, Tg*
T Curtis 2000 *Fj, J, Tg, C, It, US*
H Ekeroma 1972 *Tg, Tg*
G Elisara 2003 *I, Nm*
S Enari 1975 *Tg*
S Epati 1972 *Tg*
K Ese 1947 *Tg*
S Esera 1981 *Fj*
L Eves 1957 *Tg, Tg*
H Faafili 2008 *Fj, Tg, J*
T Faafou 2007 *Fj*
P Fa'alogo 1963 *Fj*
Fa'amaile 1947 *Tg*
T Fa'amasino 1988 *W*, 1989 *Bel, R*, 1990 *Kor, Tg, J, Tg, Fj*, 1991 *Tg, Fj, A*, 1995 *It, Ar, E, SA, Fj, Tg*, 1996 *NZ, Tg, Fj*
JS Faamatuainu 2005 *S, Ar*, 2008 *Fj, J*
S Fa'aofo 1990 *Tg*
Fa'asalele 1957 *Tg, Tg*
F Fa'asau 1963 *Fj, Tg*
M Fa'asavalu 2002 *SA*, 2003 *I, Nm, Ur, Geo, E, SA*
V Faasua 1987 *Fj*, 1988 *Tg, Fj, W*
S Fa'asua 2000 *W*
F Fa'asuaga 1947 *Tg*
L Fa'atau 2000 *Fj, Tg, C, US*, 2001 *I, It*, 2002 *Fj, Tg, Fj, Tg, SA*, 2003 *I, Ur, E, SA*, 2004 *Tg, S, Fj*, 2005 *A, Tg, Tg, Fj, S, E, Ar*, 2006 *J, Fj, Tg*, 2007 *Fj, SA, J, Tg, SA, US*
K Faiva'ai 1998 *Tg, Fj, A*, 1999 *J, C, Tg, NZ, US, Fj*
L Falaniko 1990 *Tg, Fj*, 1991 *Tg*, 1993 *Tg, Fj, NZ*, 1995 *SA, It, Ar, E, SA, Fj, Tg, S, E*, 1996 *NZ*, 1999 *US, Fj, W, S*
E Fale 2008 *Tg*
S Fale 1955 *Fj*
S Fanolua 1990 *Tg, Fj*, 1991 *Tg, Fj*
TL Fanolua 1996 *NZ, Fj*, 1997 *Tg*, 1998 *Tg, Fj, A*, 1999 *W, S*, 2000 *J, Tg, C, It, US*, 2001 *Tg, Fj, NZ, Fj, Tg, J, Fj*, 2002 *Fj*, 2003 *Nm, Ur, Geo, E*, 2005 *A, Tg, Fj, Fj*
R Fanuatanu 2003 *I, Geo*
M Faoagali 1999 *J, C*
A Faosilivia 2006 *J, Tg*, 2008 *Tg*
DS Farani 2005 *Tg, Fj, S, E, Ar*, 2006 *J, Fj, Tg*
M Fatialofa 1996 *Tg*
PM Fatialofa 1988 *I, W*, 1989 *Bel, R*, 1990 *Kor, Tg, J*, 1991 *Tg, Fj, W, A, Ar, S*, 1992 *Tg, Fj*, 1993 *Tg, Fj, NZ*, 1994 *Tg, W, Fj, A*, 1995 *SA, It, Ar, E, SA, Fj, Tg, S, E*, 1996 *NZ, Fj*
Fatu 1947 *Tg*
E Feagai 1963 *Fj, Tg*
S Feagai 1963 *Fj, Fj*
D Feaunati 2003 *Nm, Ur, Geo, E, SA*
I Fea'unati 1996 *I*, 1997 *Tg*, 1999 *Tg, NZ, Fj, Ar*, 2000 *Fj, J, Tg, C, It, US*, 2006 *Fj, Tg*
M Fepuleai 1957 *Tg*
V Fepuleai 1988 *W*, 1989 *Fj, WGe, R*
I Fesuiai'i 1985 *Fj, Tg*
JA Filemu 1995 *S, E*, 1996 *NZ, Tg, Fj, I*, 1997 *Fj*, 1999 *J, C, Tg, F, NZ*, 2000 *Fj, J, Tg, C, It, US*, 2001 *Tg, Fj, Tg, J*
F Fili 2003 *I, Nm*
F Filisoa 2005 *Tg*
T Fong 1983 *Tg, Fj*, 1984 *Fj, Tg*, 1986 *W, Fj, Tg*, 1987 *Fj, Tg*
S Fretton 1947 *Tg*
Fruean 1932 *Tg*
J Fruean 1972 *Tg*, 1975 *Tg*
S Fruean 1955 *Fj, Fj*
P Fuatai 1988 *Tg, Fj*, 1989 *Fj, WGe, R*
S Fuatai 1972 *Tg*
T Fuga 1999 *F, NZ, US*, 2000 *Fj, J, Tg, C, It, US*, 2007 *SA, Tg*
E Fuimaono-Sapolu 2005 *S, E, Ar*, 2006 *Fj, Tg*, 2007 *SA, E, US*, 2008 *Fj, Tg, J*
T Galuvao 1972 *Tg*
N George 2004 *Tg, Fj*
C Glendinning 1999 *J, C, Tg, F, NZ, US, Fj, J, W, S*, 2000 *Fj, J, Tg, C, It, US*, 2001 *Tg, Fj, NZ, Fj, Tg, Fj*
A Grey 1957 *Tg, Tg*
I Grey 1985 *Fj, Tg*
P Grey 1975 *Tg*, 1979 *Tg, Fj*, 1980 *Tg*
G Harder 1995 *SA, It, Ar, SA*
Hellesoe 1932 *Tg*
M Hewitt 1955 *Fj, Fj*
J Huch 1982 *Fj, Fj*, 1986 *Fj, Tg*
J Hunt 1957 *Tg, Tg*
A Ieremia 1992 *Tg, Fj*, 1993 *Tg, Fj, NZ*
I Imo 1924 *Fj*
T Imo 1955 *Fj, Fj, Fj*, 1957 *Tg, Tg*
A Ioane 1957 *Tg, Tg, Tg*
E Ioane 1990 *Tg, Fj*, 1991 *Tg, Fj, S*
T Iona 1975 *Tg*
T Iosua 2006 *J*
Iupati 1924 *Fj*
M Iupeli 1988 *Tg, Fj, I, W*, 1989 *Fj, WGe, R*, 1993 *Tg, NZ*, 1994 *Tg, W, Fj, A*, 1995 *SA, E*
S Iuta 1947 *Tg*
T Jensen 1987 *Tg*, 1989 *Bel*
CAI Johnston 2005 *A, Tg, Fj, S, E, Ar*, 2006 *Fj, Tg*, 2007 *SA, J, Tg, SA, Tg, E, US*, 2008 *Fj, J*
J Johnston 2008 *Tg, J*
MN Jones 1986 *W*
S Kalapu 1957 *Tg*
D Kaleopa 1990 *Kor, Tg, J*, 1991 *A*, 1992 *Fj*, 1993 *Tg, Fj*
S Kaleta 1994 *Tg, W*, 1995 *S, E*, 1996 *NZ*, 1997 *Tg, Fj*
T Kali 1975 *Tg*
L Kamu 1955 *Fj, Fj, Fj*
MG Keenan 1991 *W, A, Ar*, 1992 *Tg, Fj*, 1993 *NZ*, 1994 *Tg, W, Fj, A*
F Kelemete 1984 *Fj, Tg*, 1985 *Tg*, 1986 *W*
DK Kellet 1993 *Tg, Fj, NZ*, 1994 *Tg, W, Fj, A*, 1995 *It, Ar, Fj, Tg, S, E*
DA Kerslake 2005 *Tg, Fj, Tg, Fj*, 2006 *J, Tg*, 2007 *Fj, SA, J, Tg*
A Koko 1999 *J*
R Koko 1983 *Tg, Fj, Fj*, 1984 *Fj, Tg*, 1985 *Fj, Tg, Tg*, 1986 *W, Fj, Tg,*

1987 *Fj, Tg*, 1988 *Tg, Fj, I, W*, 1989 *WGe, R*, 1993 *Tg, NZ*, 1994 *Tg*
M Krause 1984 *Tg*, 1986 *W*
H Kruse 1963 *Fj, Fj, Tg*
JA Kuoi 1987 *Fj, Tg*, 1988 *I, W*, 1990 *Kor, Tg*
B Laban 1955 *Fj*, 1957 *Tg, Tg*
SL Lafaiali'I 2001 *Tg, Fj, NZ, Tg*, 2002 *Fj, Tg, Fj, Tg, SA*, 2003 *I, Nm, Ur, Geo, E, SA*, 2004 *Tg, S, Fj*, 2005 *A, S, E*, 2007 *Fj, J, Tg, Tg, US*
I Laga'aia 1975 *Tg*, 1979 *Tg, Fj*
F Lalomilo 2001 *I, It*
PR Lam 1991 *W, Ar, S*, 1994 *W, Fj, A*, 1995 *SA, Ar, E, SA, Fj, Tg, S, E*, 1996 *NZ, Tg, Fj, I*, 1997 *Tg, Fj*, 1998 *Tg, Fj, A*, 1999 *J, C, Tg, F, NZ, US, Fj, J, Ar, W, S*
F Lameta 1990 *Tg, Fj*
S Lameta 1982 *Fj*
G Latu 1994 *Tg, W, Fj, A*, 1995 *SA, Ar, E, SA, Fj, Tg*
E Lauina 2008 *Fj, Tg, J*
M Lautau 1985 *Fj*
S Leaega 1997 *Tg, Fj*, 1999 *J, J, Ar, W, S*, 2001 *Tg, Fj, NZ, Fj, Tg, Fj, I, It*, 2002 *Fj, SA*
K Lealamanua 2000 *Fj, J, Tg, C, It*, 2001 *NZ, Fj, Tg, J, Fj*, 2002 *Fj, Fj, Tg, SA*, 2003 *I, Nm, Ur, Geo, E, SA*, 2004 *Tg, S, Fj*, 2005 *S, E*, 2007 *SA, Tg, E, US*
GE Leaupepe 1995 *SA, Ar, E, Fj, Tg, S, E*, 1996 *NZ, Tg, Fj, I*, 1997 *Tg, Fj*, 1998 *Tg, A*, 1999 *J, C, Tg, F, NZ, US, Fj, J, Ar, W*, 2005 *A*
S Leaupepe 1979 *Tg, Fj*, 1980 *Tg*
P Leavai 1990 *J*
A Leavasa 1979 *Tg, Fj*, 1980 *Tg*
P Leavasa 1955 *Fj, Fj, Fj*, 1957 *Tg, Tg, Tg*
PL Leavasa 1993 *Tg, Fj*, 1995 *It, Ar, E, S, E*, 1996 *NZ, Tg, Fj, I*, 1997 *Tg, Fj*, 2002 *Tg, Fj, Tg, SA*
S Leavasa 1955 *Fj, Fj, Fj*, 1957 *Tg*
T Leiasamaivao 1993 *Tg, NZ*, 1994 *Tg, W, Fj*, 1995 *SA, It, Ar, E, SA, S, E*, 1996 *NZ, Tg, Fj, I*, 1997 *Tg, Fj*
N Leleimalefaga 2007 *Fj, US*
S Lemalu 2003 *Ur, Geo, E*, 2004 *Tg, S, Fj*, 2008 *Tg, J*
S Lemamea 1988 *I, W*, 1989 *Fj, WGe, Bel, R*, 1990 *J*, 1992 *Tg, Fj*, 1995 *E, SA, Fj, Tg*
D Lemi 2004 *Tg, S, Fj*, 2005 *Tg, Fj, Tg, Fj*, 2007 *Fj, SA, J, Tg, SA, Tg, E, US*, 2008 *Fj, Tg, J*
DA Leo 2005 *A, Tg, Fj, Tg, Fj, S, E, Ar*, 2006 *J, Fj, Tg*, 2007 *SA, J, Tg, SA, Tg, E*, 2008 *Tg, J*
M Leota 2000 *Fj, Tg, C*
P Leota 1990 Kor, Tg, J
T Leota 1997 *Tg, Fj*, 1998 *Tg, Fj, A*, 1999 *J, C, Tg, F, Fj, J, Ar, W, S*, 2000 *Fj, J*, 2001 *Tg, Fj, NZ, Fj, J, Fj*, 2002 *Fj, Tg, Fj, Tg, SA*, 2003 *I*, 2005 *A*
T Leupolu 2001 *I, It*, 2002 *Fj, Tg, Fj, Tg, SA*, 2003 *I, Nm, SA*, 2004 *Tg, S, Fj*, 2005 *Ar*
A Leu'u 1987 *Fj, Tg*, 1989 *WGe, R*, 1990 *Kor, J, Tg, Fj*, 1993 *Tg, Fj, NZ*, 1996 *I*
FH Levi 2007 *Fj, SA, J, Tg*, 2008 *Fj, J*
A Liaina 1963 *Fj, Fj, Tg*
S Liaina 1963 *Fj, Fj, Tg*
P Lilomaiava 1993 *NZ*
BP Lima 1991 *Tg, Fj, W, A, Ar, S*, 1992 *Tg, Fj*, 1993 *Fj, NZ*, 1994 *Tg, W, Fj, A*, 1995 *SA, It, Ar, E, SA, Fj, Tg, S, E*, 1996 *NZ, Tg, Fj*, 1997 *Fj*, 1998 *Tg, Fj, A*, 1999 *Tg, F, NZ, US, J, Ar, W, S*, 2000 *C, It, US*, 2001 *Fj, Tg, Fj, I, It*, 2002 *Fj, Tg*, 2003 *I, Nm, Ur, Geo, E, SA*, 2004 *Tg, S, Fj*, 2005 *A, Fj*, 2006 *J, Fj*, 2007 *Fj, Tg, SA, E*
F Lima 1981 *Fj*
M Lima 1982 *Fj, Fj*
M Lome 1957 *Tg, Tg, Tg*, 1963 *Fj*
M Luafalealo 1999 *J*, 2000 *It, US*, 2001 *Tg, Fj, NZ, Fj, J, Fj*
E Luaiufi 1987 *Fj, Tg*, 1988 *Tg, Fj*
Lui 1932 *Tg*
L Lui 2004 *Fj*, 2005 *Tg, Fj, Ar*, 2006 *J, Tg*, 2007 *Tg, Tg, E, US*
M Lupeli 1993 *Fj*
A Macdonald 1924 *Fj, Fj*, 1932 *Tg*
T Magele 1988 *Tg*
U Mai 2008 *Tg, J*
F Mailei 1963 *Fj, Tg*
F Malele 1979 *Tg, Fj*, 1980 *Tg*
J Maligi 2000 *W, S*
P Maligi 1982 *Fj, Tg*, 1983 *Tg, Fj*, 1984 *Fj, Tg*, 1985 *Fj, Tg, Tg*, 1986 *Fj, Tg*
L Malo 1979 *Fj*
J Mamea 2000 *W, S*
L Mano 1988 *Fj, I, W*
C Manu 2002 *Fj, Tg, Tg, SA*
S Mapusua 2006 *J, Fj, Tg*, 2007 *SA, J, Tg, Tg, E, US*
P Mareko 1979 *Fj*
K Mariner 2005 *Ar*
M Mata'afa 1947 *Tg*
P Matailina 1957 *Tg, Tg, Tg*
C Matauiau 1996 *Tg, Fj*, 1999 *Ar, W, S*, 2000 *It, W, S*
K Mavaega 1985 *Tg*
M McFadyen 1957 *Tg*
K McFall 1983 *Fj*
J Meafou 2007 *Tg, SA, E*
L Mealamu 2000 *W, S*
I Melei 1972 *Tg*
C Meredith 1932 *Tg*
J Meredith 2001 *I, It*, 2002 *Fj, Tg, Fj, Tg, SA*, 2003 *I, Nm, Ur, Geo, E, SA*, 2004 *Tg, S, Fj*, 2005 *A, Tg, Fj, Fj*
J Meredith 1963 *Fj, Fj, Tg*
O Meredith 1947 *Tg*
A Mika 2000 *S*
D Mika 1994 *W, A*
MAN Mika 1995 *SA, It, Ar, E, SA, S, E*, 1997 *Tg, Fj*, 1999 *Tg, F, NZ, J, Ar, W*
S Mika 2004 *Fj*, 2005 *A, Tg, Fj, Tg, Fj*
P Misa 2000 *W, S*
S Moala 2008 *Fj*
F Moamanu 1989 WGe
S Moamanu 1985 *Fj*, 1986 *Fj, Tg*
M Moke 1990 *Kor, Tg, J, Tg, Fj*
P Momoisea 1972 *Tg, Tg*
H Moors 1924 *Fj, Fj*
R Moors 1994 *Tg*
Mose 1932 *Tg*
S Motoi 1984 *Tg*
F Motusagu 2000 *Tg, It*, 2005 *A*
P Neenee 1987 *Fj, Tg*, 1991 *Tg, Fj*
O Nelson 1955 *Fj, Fj, Fj*, 1957 *Tg, Tg*
N Ngapaku 2000 *J, C, US*
F Nickel 1957 *Tg*
Nimmo 1957 *Tg*
T Nu'uali'itia 1994 *Tg, A*, 1995 *SA, It, Ar, E, SA*, 1996 *NZ*
A Olive 2008 *Tg*
FJP Palaamo 1998 *Tg, Fj, A*, 1999 *J, C, F, NZ, US, Fj*, 2007 *Fj, E*
S Pala'amo 1955 *Fj, Fj, Fj*, 1957 *Tg*
A Palamo 1979 *Tg, Fj*, 1980 *Tg*, 1981 *Fj, Fj*, 1982 *Fj, Fj, Fj, Tg*
LN Palamo 1979 *Tg, Fj*, 1981 *Fj, Fj*, 1982 *Fj, Fj, Fj, Tg*, 1984 *Fj, Tg*, 1985 *Tg*, 1986 *W, Fj, Tg*
T Palamo 1972 *Tg*
O Palepoi 1998 *Tg, Fj, A*, 1999 *J, F, NZ, US, Fj, J, Ar*, 2000 *J, C, It, US, W*, 2001 *Tg, Fj, NZ, Fj, Tg, J, Fj, I, It*, 2002 *Fj, Tg, Fj, Tg, SA*, 2003 *I, Nm, Ur, Geo, E, SA*, 2004 *Tg, S*, 2005 *A, Tg, Fj, Tg, Fj*
Panapa 1932 *Tg*
M Papali'I 1955 *Fj, Fj*
P Papali'I 1924 *Fj, Fj*
PJ Paramore 1991 *Tg, Fj, A*, 1992 *Fj*, 1994 *Tg*, 1995 *SA, It, Ar, SA, Fj, Tg*, 1996 *I*, 1997 *Tg, Fj*, 1998 *Tg, Fj, A*, 1999 *J, Ar, W*, 2001 *Tg, Fj, NZ, Fj, Tg, J, Fj*
J Parkinson 2005 *A, Tg*
T Pati 1997 *Tg*
M Patolo 1986 *W, Fj, Tg*
HV Patu 1995 *S, E*, 1996 *I*, 2000 *W, S*
O Patu 1980 *Tg*
T Patu 1979 *Tg, Fj*, 1980 *Tg*, 1981 *Fj, Fj*
P Paul 1955 *Fj, Fj, Fj*
P Paulo 1989 *Bel*, 1990 *Tg, Fj*
A Perelini 1991 *Tg, Fj, W, A, Ar, S*, 1992 *Tg, Fj*, 1993 *NZ*
S Perez 1963 *Fj, Fj, Tg*
N Petaia 1963 *Fj*
Petelo 1932 *Tg*
T Petelo 1985 *Fj*
P Petia 2003 *Nm*
O Pifeleti 1987 *Fj*
S Po Ching 1990 *Kor, Tg*, 1991 *Tg*
S Poching 2000 *W, S*, 2001 *Tg*
AJ Polu 2007 *SA, J, Tg, SA, Tg, E, US*
P Poulos 2003 *Ur, Geo, E, SA*
E Puleitu 1995 *SA, E*
S Punivalu 1981 *Fj, Fj*, 1982 *Fj, Fj, Fj*, 1983 *Tg, Fj*
JEP Purdie 2007 *Fj, SA, J, Tg, SA, Tg, E, US*
I Railey 1924 *Fj, Fj*
D Rasmussen 2003 *I, Ur, Geo, E, SA*, 2004 *Tg, S, Fj*
R Rasmussen 1997 *Tg*
B Reidy 1995 *SA, Fj, Tg*, 1996 *NZ, Tg, Fj, I*, 1998 *Fj, A*, 1999 *Tg, F, NZ, US, Fj, J, Ar, W, S*
K Roberts 1972 *Tg*
F Ropati 1982 *Fj, Fj, Fj*, 1984 *Fj, Tg*
R Ropati 2003 *SA*
W Ryan 1983 *Fj*, 1985 *Tg*
E Sa'aga 1924 *Fj, Fj*, 1932 *Tg*
PD Saena 1988 *Tg, Fj, I*, 1989 *Fj, Bel, R*, 1990 *Kor, Tg, J, Tg, Fj*, 1991 *Tg, Fj*, 1992 *Tg, Fj*, 1993 *Tg, Fj*
L Sagaga 1963 *Fj, Tg*
K Saifoloi 1979 *Tg, Fj*, 1980 *Tg*, 1982 *Fj, Fj*, 1984 *Fj, Tg*
P Saili 1957 *Tg, Tg, Tg*
M Salanoa 2005 *Tg, Fj*, 2006 *J, Fj, Tg*, 2007 *Fj, SA, J, Tg, Tg*
T Salesa 1979 *Tg, Fj*, 1980 *Tg*, 1981 *Fj, Fj*, 1982 *Fj, Fj, Fj, Tg*, 1983 *Tg, Fj, Fj*, 1984 *Fj, Tg*, 1985 *Fj, Tg, Tg*, 1986 *Fj, Tg*, 1987 *Fj, Tg*, 1988 *Tg, Fj, I*, 1989 *Fj, WGe, R*
Salima 2008 *Fj*
T Samania 1994 *W, Fj, A*, 1996 *NZ*, 2000 *Fj, J, C, It*, 2001 *Tg*
D Sanft 2006 *J*
Q Sanft 2000 *W, S*
L Sasi 1982 *Fj, Tg*, 1983 *Tg, Fj*, 1984 *Fj, Tg*, 1985 *Tg*, 1986 *W, Fj, Tg*, 1987 *Fj, Tg*, 1988 *Tg, Fj*
B Sasulu 2008 *Fj*
S Sauila 1989 *Bel*
L Savai'inaea 1957 *Tg, Tg*
J Schaafhausen 1947 *Tg*
W Schaafhausen 1947 *Tg*
P Schmidt 1989 *Fj, WGe*
P Schmidt 1980 *Tg*, 1985 *Tg*
R Schmidt 1979 *Tg*, 1980 *Tg*

D Schuster 1982 *Tg*, 1983 *Tg*, *Fj*, *Fj*
H Schuster 1989 *Fj*, 1990 *Kor*, *Tg*, *J*
J Schuster 1985 *Fj*, *Tg*, *Tg*
M Schuster 2000 *S*, 2004 *Tg*, *S*, *Fj*
NJ Schuster 1999 *Tg*, *F*, *US*
P Schuster 1975 *Tg*
MM Schwalger 2000 *W*, *S*, 2001 *It*, 2003 *Nm*, *Ur*, *Geo*, *E*, 2005 *S*, *E*, *Ar*, 2006 *J*, *Fj*, *Tg*, 2007 *Fj*, *SA*, *Tg*, *SA*, *Tg*, *E*, *US*, 2008 *Fj*
Sefo 1932 *Tg*
E Sefo 1984 *Fj*
T Sefo 1987 *Tg*, 1988 *I*
P Segi 2001 *Fj*, *NZ*, *Fj*, *Tg*, *J*, *I*, *It*, 2002 *Fj*, *Tg*, *Fj*, *Tg*
K Seinafo 1992 *Tg*
J Senio 2004 *Tg*, *S*, *Fj*, 2005 *Tg*, *Fj*, *Tg*, *Fj*, 2006 *J*, *Fj*, *Tg*
T Seumanutafa 1981 *Fj*
E Seveali'I 2000 *Fj*, *J*, *Tg*, *C*, 2001 *Tg*, *NZ*, *J*, *Fj*, *It*, 2002 *Fj*, *Tg*, *Fj*, *Tg*, *SA*, 2005 *E*, 2007 *SA*, *J*, *Tg*, *SA*, *Tg*, *US*
F Sililoto 1980 *Tg*, 1981 *Fj*, *Fj*, 1982 *Fj*, *Fj*, *Fj*
Simanu 1932 *Tg*
A Simanu 1975 *Tg*, 1981 *Fj*
Sinaumea 1924 *Fj*
F Sini 1995 *SA*, *Ar*, *E*, *SA*
K Sio 1988 *Tg*, *Fj*, *I*, *W*, 1989 *Fj*, *WGe*, *R*, 1990 *J*, *Tg*, *Fj*, 1992 *Tg*, *Fj*, 1993 *NZ*, 1994 *Tg*
T Sio 1990 *Tg*, 1992 *Fj*
P Sioa 1981 *Fj*, *Fj*
S Sititi 1999 *J*, *C*, *F*, *J*, *W*, *S*, 2000 *Fj*, *J*, *Tg*, *C*, *US*, 2001 *Tg*, *Fj*, *NZ*, *Fj*, *Tg*, *J*, *Fj*, *I*, *It*, 2002 *Fj*, *Tg*, *Fj*, *Tg*, *SA*, 2003 *I*, *Nm*, *Ur*, *Geo*, *E*, *SA*, 2004 *Tg*, *S*, *Fj*, 2005 *A*, *Fj*, *Tg*, *Fj*, *S*, *E*, *Ar*, 2006 *J*, *Fj*, *Tg*, 2007 *Fj*, *SA*, *J*, *Tg*, *SA*, *Tg*, *E*, *US*, 2008 *Fj*, *Tg*, *J*
F Siu 1975 *Tg*
P Siu 1963 *Fj*, *Fj*, *Tg*
S Skelton 1982 *Fj*
C Slade 2006 *J*, *Fj*, *Tg*, 2008 *Fj*, *Tg*
R Slade 1972 *Tg*
S Smith 1995 *S*, *E*, 1996 *Tg*, *Fj*, 1999 *C*, *Tg*, *F*, *NZ*
P Solia 1955 *Fj*, *Fj*
I Solipo 1981 *Fj*
F Solomona 1985 *Tg*
A So'oialo 1996 *I*, 1997 *Tg*, *Fj*, 1998 *Tg*, 1999 *Tg*, *F*, *NZ*, *US*, *Fj*, *J*, *Ar*, 2000 *Tg*, *It*, 2001 *Tg*, *Fj*, *NZ*, *Fj*, *Tg*, *J*, *I*
S So'oialo 1998 *Tg*, *Fj*, 1999 *NZ*, *US*, *Fj*, *J*, *Ar*, *W*, *S*, 2000 *W*, *S*, 2001 *Tg*, *Fj*, *NZ*, *Fj*, *J*, *Fj*, *I*, 2002 *Tg*, *Fj*, *Tg*, *SA*, 2003 *I*, *Nm*, *Ur*, *Geo*, *E*, *SA*, 2004 *Tg*, *S*, *Fj*, 2005 *E*, 2007 *Fj*, *SA*, *J*, *Tg*, *E*, *US*
F So'olefai 1999 *C*, *Tg*, 2000 *W*, *S*, 2001 *Tg*, *Fj*, *NZ*, *Fj*, *J*
V Stet 1963 *Fj*
A Stewart 2005 *A*, *Tg*
G Stowers 2001 *I*, 2008 *Fj*, *Tg*, *J*
R Stowers 2008 *Fj*
F Sua 1982 *Fj*, *Fj*, *Fj*, *Tg*, 1983 *Tg*, *Fj*, 1984 *Fj*, 1985 *Fj*, *Tg*, *Tg*, 1986 *Fj*, *Tg*, 1987 *Fj*
P Swepson 1957 *Tg*
S Ta'ala 1996 *Tg*, *Fj*, *I*, 1997 *Tg*, *Fj*, 1998 *Tg*, *Fj*, *A*, 1999 *J*, *C*, *Tg*, *US*, *Fj*, *J*, *Ar*, *W*, *S*, 2001 *J*
T Taega 1997 *Fj*
P Taele 2005 *Tg*, *Fj*, *E*, *Ar*, 2006 *J*, *Fj*, *Tg*
D Tafeamalii 2000 *W*, *S*
D Tafua 1981 *Fj*, *Fj*, 1982 *Fj*, *Fj*, *Fj*, *Tg*, 1983 *Tg*, *Fj*, 1985 *Fj*, *Tg*, *Tg*, 1986 *W*, *Fj*, *Tg*, 1987 *Tg*, 1989 *Fj*, *WGe*, *R*
L Tafunai 2004 *Tg*, *Fj*, 2005 *Tg*, *Fj*, *Tg*, *Fj*, *S*, *Ar*, 2008 *Tg*, *J*
TDL Tagaloa 1990 *Kor*, *Tg*, *J*, *Tg*, *Fj*, 1991 *W*, *A*, *Ar*, *S*
S Tagicakibau 2003 *Nm*, *Ur*, *Geo*, *E*, *SA*, 2004 *Tg*, *S*, *Fj*, 2005 *S*, *E*, *Ar*, 2007 *Tg*
Tagimanu 1924 *Fj*
I Taina 2005 *Tg*, *Fj*, *Tg*, *Fj*, *S*
F Taiomaivao 1989 *Bel*
F Talapusi 2005 *A*, *Fj*, *Tg*, *Fj*
F Talapusi 1979 *Tg*, *Fj*, 1980 *Tg*
Tamalua 1932 *Tg*
F Tanoa'i 1996 *Tg*, *Fj*
S Tanuko 1987 *Tg*
P Tapelu 2002 *SA*
V Tasi 1981 *Fj*, 1982 *Fj*, *Fj*, *Fj*, *Tg*, 1983 *Tg*, *Fj*, 1984 *Fj*, *Tg*
S Tatupu 1990 *Tg*, 1993 *Tg*, *Fj*, *NZ*, 1995 *It*, *Ar*, *E*, *SA*, *Fj*, *Tg*
N Tauafao 2005 *A*, *Tg*, *Fj*, *Tg*, *Fj*, *S*, *Ar*, 2007 *Fj*, 2008 *Fj*, *Tg*, *J*
I Tautau 1985 *Fj*, *Tg*, 1986 *W*
T Tavita 1984 *Fj*, *Tg*
H Tea 2008 *Tg*, *J*
I Tekori 2007 *SA*, *J*, *SA*, *Tg*, *E*, *US*
AT Telea 1995 *S*, *E*, 1996 *NZ*, *Tg*, *Fj*
E Telea 2008 *Fj*
S Telea 1989 *Bel*
A Teo 1947 *Tg*
F Teo 1955 *Fj*
V Teo 1957 *Tg*, *Tg*
KG Thompson 2007 *Fj*, *SA*, *Tg*, *SA*, *Tg*, *E*, *US*, 2008 *Tg*, *J*
H Thomson 1947 *Tg*
A Tiatia 2001 *Tg*, *Fj*, *NZ*, *Fj*, *Tg*, *J*, *Fj*
R Tiatia 1972 *Tg*
S Tilialo 1972 *Tg*
F Tipi 1998 *Fj*, *A*, 1999 *J*, *C*, *F*, *NZ*, *Fj*
F Toala 1998 *Fj*, 1999 *J*, *C*, *S*, 2000 *W*, *S*
L Toelupe 1979 *Fj*
P Toelupe 2008 *Fj*, *J*
T Tofaeono 1989 *Fj*, *Bel*
A Toleafoa 2000 *W*, *S*, 2002 *SA*
K Toleafoa 1955 *Fj*, *Fj*
PL Toleafoa 2006 *J*, *Fj*
K Tole'afoa 1998 *Tg*, *A*, 1999 *Ar*
F Toloa 1979 *Tg*, 1980 *Tg*
J Tomuli 2001 *I*, *It*, 2002 *Fj*, *Tg*, *Fj*, *Tg*, *SA*, 2003 *I*, *Nm*, *Ur*, *Geo*, *E*, *SA*, 2006 *J*
L Tone 1998 *Tg*, *Fj*, *A*, 1999 *J*, *C*, *Tg*, *F*, *NZ*, *US*, *J*, *Ar*, *W*, *S*, 2000 *Fj*, *J*, *Tg*, *C*, *It*, *US*, *S*, 2001 *NZ*, *Fj*, *Tg*, *J*, *Fj*
S Tone 2000 *W*
Toni 1924 *Fj*
J Tonunu 1993 *Tg*, *Fj*
OFJ Tonu'u 1992 *Tg*, 1993 *NZ*
F To'omalatai 1989 *Bel*
S To'omalatai 1985 *Fj*, *Tg*, 1986 *W*, *Fj*, *Tg*, 1988 *Tg*, *Fj*, *I*, *W*, 1989 *Fj*, *WGe*, *Bel*, *R*, 1990 *Kor*, *Tg*, *J*, *Tg*, *Fj*, 1991 *Tg*, *Fj*, *W*, *A*, *Ar*, *S*, 1992 *Tg*, *Fj*, 1993 *Fj*, 1994 *A*, 1995 *Fj*
Tualai 1924 *Fj*, *Fj*
I Tualaulelei 1963 *Fj*, *Fj*, *Tg*
F Tuatagaloa 1957 *Tg*
K Tuatagaloa 1963 *Fj*, *Fj*, *Tg*, 1972 *Tg*
V Tuatagaloa 1963 *Fj*, *Tg*
Tufele 1924 *Fj*
D Tuiavi'I 2003 *I*, *Nm*, *Ur*, *E*, *SA*
VL Tuigamala 1996 *Fj*, *I*, 1997 *Tg*, *Fj*, 1998 *Tg*, *Fj*, *A*, 1999 *F*, *NZ*, *US*, *Fj*, *J*, *Ar*, *W*, *S*, 2000 *Fj*, *J*, *Tg*, *US*, 2001 *J*, *Fj*, *I*, *It*
AF Tuilagi 2005 *Tg*, *Fj*, *Tg*, *Fj*, *S*, *Ar*, 2006 *J*, *Tg*, 2007 *Fj*, *SA*, *J*, 2008 *Tg*, *J*
AT Tuilagi 2002 *Fj*, *Tg*, *SA*, 2005 *A*, *Tg*, *Fj*, *Tg*, *Fj*, *S*, *E*, 2007 *SA*, *J*, *Tg*, *SA*, *Tg*, *E*, *US*
F Tuilagi 1992 *Tg*, 1994 *W*, *Fj*, *A*, 1995 *SA*, *SA*, *Fj*, 2000 *W*, *S*, 2001 *Fj*, *NZ*, *Tg*, 2002 *Fj*, *Tg*, *Fj*, *Tg*, *SA*
H Tuilagi 2002 *Fj*, *Tg*, *Fj*, *Tg*, 2007 *SA*, *E*, 2008 *J*
T Tuisaula 1947 *Tg*
R Tuivaiti 2004 *Fj*
A Tunupopo 1963 *Fj*
P Tupa'i 2005 *A*, *Tg*, *S*, *E*, *Ar*
S Tupuola 1982 *Fj*, *Fj*, *Fj*, *Tg*, 1983 *Tg*, *Fj*, 1985 *Tg*, 1986 *Fj*, *Tg*, 1987 *Fj*, *Tg*, 1988 *W*, 1989 *R*
P Tu'uau 1972 *Tg*, *Tg*, 1975 *Tg*
D Tyrrell 2000 *Fj*, *J*, *C*, 2001 *It*, 2002 *Fj*, *Tg*, *SA*, 2003 *I*, *Nm*, *Ur*, *Geo*, *E*, *SA*
S Uati 1988 *Tg*, *Fj*
T Ugapo 1988 *Tg*, *Fj*, *I*, *W*, 1989 *Fj*, *WGe*, *Bel*
U Ulia 2004 *Tg*, *S*, *Fj*, 2005 *Ar*, 2006 *J*, *Fj*, *Tg*, 2007 *Fj*, *Tg*, *Tg*, *US*
J Ulugia 1985 *Fj*, *Tg*
M Umaga 1995 *SA*, *It*, *Ar*, *E*, *SA*, 1998 *Tg*, *Fj*, *A*, 1999 *Tg*, *F*, *NZ*, *US*, *Fj*
A Utu'utu 1979 *Tg*, *Fj*
L Utu'utu 1975 *Tg*
E Va'a 1996 *I*, 1997 *Fj*, 1998 *A*, 1999 *Tg*, *NZ*, *Fj*, *J*, *W*, *S*, 2001 *Tg*, *Fj*, *NZ*, *Fj*, *Tg*, *J*, *Fj*, *I*, 2002 *Fj*, *Tg*, *Fj*, *Tg*, *SA*, 2003 *I*, *Nm*, *Ur*, *Geo*, *E*, *SA*
JH Va'a 2005 *A*, *Fj*, *Tg*, *Fj*, *S*, *E*, *Ar*, 2006 *Fj*, *Tg*, 2007 *SA*, *J*, *Tg*, *SA*
M Vaea 1991 *Tg*, *Fj*, *W*, *A*, *Ar*, *S*, 1992 *Fj*, 1995 *S*
K Vaega 1982 *Fj*, *Tg*, 1983 *Fj*
TM Vaega 1986 *W*, 1989 *WGe*, *Bel*, *R*, 1990 *Kor*, *Tg*, *J*, *Tg*, *Fj*, 1991 *Tg*, *Fj*, *W*, *A*, *Ar*, *S*, 1992 *Tg*, *Fj*, 1993 *Tg*, *Fj*, *NZ*, 1994 *Tg*, *W*, *Fj*, *A*, 1995 *SA*, *It*, *Ar*, *E*, *SA*, *Fj*, *Tg*, *S*, *E*, 1996 *NZ*, *Tg*, *Fj*, *I*, 1997 *Tg*, 1998 *Fj*, *A*, 1999 *J*, *C*, *F*, *NZ*, *Fj*, *J*, *Ar*, *W*, *S*, 2000 *Fj*, *J*, *Tg*, *C*, *It*, *US*, 2001 *Fj*, *Tg*, *J*, *Fj*, *I*
A Vaeluaga 2000 *W*, *S*, 2001 *Tg*, *Fj*, *Tg*, *J*, *Fj*, *I*, 2007 *SA*, *J*, *SA*, *E*, *US*
F Vagaia 1972 *Tg*
K Vai 1987 *Fj*, *Tg*, 1989 *Bel*
S Vaifale 1989 *R*, 1990 *Kor*, *Tg*, *J*, *Tg*, *Fj*, 1991 *Tg*, *Fj*, *W*, *Ar*, *S*, 1992 *Tg*, *Fj*, 1993 *NZ*, 1994 *Tg*, *W*, *Fj*, *A*, 1995 *SA*, *It*, *SA*, *Fj*, *S*, *E*, 1996 *NZ*, *Tg*, 1997 *Tg*, *Fj*
S Vaili 2001 *I*, *It*, 2002 *Fj*, *Tg*, *Fj*, *Tg*, 2003 *Geo*, 2004 *Tg*, *S*, *Fj*
L Vailoaloa 2005 *A*
S Vaisola Sefo 2007 *US*
T Veiru 2000 *W*, *S*
M Vili 1975 *Tg*
M Vili 1957 *Tg*
T Vili 1999 *C*, *Tg*, *US*, *Ar*, 2000 *Fj*, *J*, *Tg*, *C*, *It*, *US*, 2001 *Tg*, *Fj*, *J*, *Fj*, *I*, *It*, 2003 *Ur*, *Geo*, *E*, *SA*, 2004 *Tg*, *S*, *Fj*, 2005 *A*, *Tg*, *Fj*, *S*, *E*, 2006 *J*, *Fj*, *Tg*
K Viliamu 2001 *I*, *It*, 2002 *Fj*, *SA*, 2003 *I*, *Ur*, *Geo*, *E*, *SA*, 2004 *S*
T Viliamu 1947 *Tg*
Visesio 1932 *Tg*
FV Vitale 1994 *W*, *Fj*, *A*, 1995 *Fj*, *Tg*
F Vito 1972 *Tg*, 1975 *Tg*
M von Dincklage 2004 *S*
R Warren 2004 *Tg*, *S*, 2005 *Tg*, *Fj*, *Tg*, *Fj*, *S*, *Ar*, 2008 *Fj*, *Tg*, *J*
S Wendt 1955 *Fj*, *Fj*, *Fj*
DR Williams 1988 *I*, *W*, 1995 *SA*, *It*, *E*
G Williams 2007 *Fj*, *SA*, *SA*, *Tg*, 2008 *Tg*, *J*
H Williams 2001 *Tg*, *Tg*, *J*
P Young 1988 *I*, 1989 *Bel*

SCOTLAND

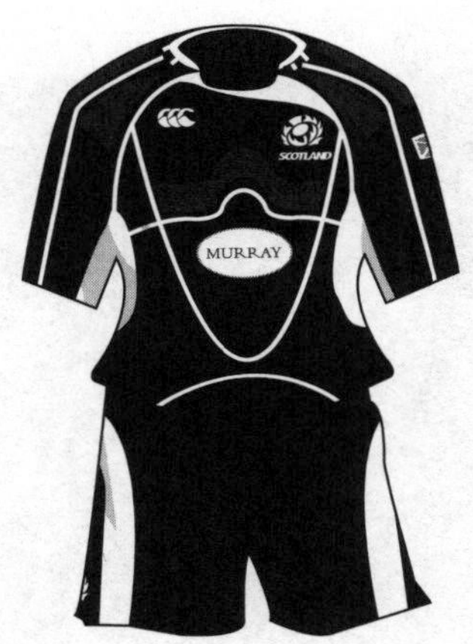

SCOTLAND'S 2008 TEST RECORD

OPPONENTS	DATE	VENUE	RESULT
France	3 February	H	**Lost** 6-27
Wales	9 February	A	**Lost** 15-30
Ireland	23 February	A	**Lost** 13-34
England	8 March	H	**Won** 15-9
Italy	15 March	A	**Lost** 20-23
Argentina	7 June	A	**Lost** 15-21
Argentina	14 June	A	**Won** 26-14

SCOTS SAVE FACE AGAINST PUMAS

By Iain Spragg

Dave Rogers/Getty Images

The win over England, and the capture of the Calcutta Cup, cheered Scottish hearts

Although the record books will testify that Scotland recorded just two wins in their seven Test outings for the first part of 2008, the statistics fail to tell the full story. Frank Hadden's side hardly set the world alight after a respectable World Cup campaign, there were two significant crumbs of comfort for the coach and his players to cling to.

An unexpected and undeniably ugly win over England at Murrayfield to claim the Calcutta Cup was the highlight of an otherwise disappointing Six Nations campaign, condemning Italy to the wooden spoon on points difference in the final reckoning. Victory over the auld enemy was certainly welcome but defeat to the Azzurri in Rome a week later told its own, demoralising story.

The summer excursion to Argentina for two Tests was equally mixed. The Pumas had been responsible for Scotland's World Cup exit in the quarter-finals but Hadden's troops were unable to exact revenge in the first game in Rosario, going down 21–15 in the Stadio Gigante de Arroyito.

That they were able to dust themselves off to win the second Test in Buenos Aires a week later was to their great credit but as Hadden and his players disbanded for their summer holidays, the sense that it had been another season in which Scotland had stagnated in terms of both performances and results was inescapable.

The season began in February at Murrayfield for the Six Nations opener against France. Les Bleus had a much-changed side after their World Cup heartbreak and a new coach in Marc Lièvremont and there was a cautiously optimistic atmosphere in Edinburgh as the two teams prepared to cross swords.

A drop goal from Dan Parks gave Hadden's side an early lead but it was as good as it got for the Scots as France cut loose and two tries from Vincent Clerc and a third from Julien Malzieu guided them to a comprehensive 27–6 victory.

"We're obviously bitterly disappointed that we've let down the fans who came here," Hadden admitted in the post-match post mortem. "We desperately wanted to win but we made the sort of elementary errors we made in the World Cup quarter-final. Some of our build-up work was good but when we got into their 22 we were like rabbits in front of headlights."

There was no respite six days later at the Millennium Stadium as Wales completed the second leg of what would become their Grand Slam. The clash was delicately poised at 17–15 to the home side on the hour but a try from Shane Williams broke Scotland's resistance and they were beaten 30–15. More ominously, it was the second game in succession the Scottish team had failed to cross the whitewash.

Even the most ardent Scottish fan expected little return from the side's visit to Croke Park to face the Irish and so it proved in Dublin as the home side produced a fine attacking display that tore Scotland apart.

Hadden shuffled his cards before the game, restoring Chris Paterson to fly-half at the expense of Parks in pursuit of a more potent threat going forward. Although they finally ended their try drought in the tournament courtesy of Simon Webster's second-half score, there was little else to comfort the coach as Ireland ran in five tries of their own in a 34–13 win.

Three defeats from three was hardly the ideal preparation for England's arrival in Edinburgh in early March but as so often in the past, adversity proved to be the catalyst they desperately needed and even though the English were buoyant after beating France in Paris a fortnight earlier, they had no answer to Scotland's ferocious commitment.

In truth, the savagely wet and windy conditions reduced the game to a lottery but it was Scotland who adapted better to the conditions and five Paterson penalties to three from Jonny Wilkinson were enough to secure a morale-boosting win.

"I felt we didn't have a great deal of luck in the first few rounds of the Championship, but I felt we had a little bit of luck against England," Hadden admitted after the game. "We knew it was going to be tough up front and it was a Herculean effort from our lighter pack to perform as they did, especially in the set-piece and also around the ruck area."

Scotland now had the chance to finish the Championship on a genuine high in their final game against Italy. Beating England was desperately welcome but victory in Rome against the winless Azzurri would provide more tangible evidence of a side taking significant steps forward.

The game began with Italy in the ascendancy and the forward dominance was rewarded with a penalty try awarded by Nigel Owens after he deemed the Scottish front row had collapsed a scrum but Hadden's team hit back with a well-worked try from Allister Hogg. Mike Blair added a second with a fine break and Scotland went in at half-time 17–10 to the good.

After the break, however, Scotland shot themselves in the foot when a long Parks pass was intercepted by Sergio Parisse, who sent Gonzalo Canale over. Parks and Andrea Marcato traded penalties in the final 10 minutes to leave the match level at 20–20 but just as it seemed the Scots would leave the Stadio Flaminio with a face-saving draw, Marcato landed a last-gasp drop goal to steal the game.

Scotland avoided the wooden spoon on points difference but the scenes of Italian jubilation at the final whistle, contrasted with the sight of dejected Scotland players trooping off the pitch, summed up how the respective camps view their Championship campaigns.

"We started the tournament badly but felt we progressed with every game up to the England match," Scotland flanker Alasdair Strokosch said. "We hoped to build on that here. It was a solid performance in the first half but we took our foot off the gas I think. We dropped our intensity. We'd had lots of bodies coming onto the ball and flying in but in the second half we didn't have too many options."

Hadden named three uncapped players – Ben Cairns, Moray Low and Thom Evans – in his squad for the summer tour of Argentina but was denied the services of his French-based players, including Simon Taylor, Nathan Hines and Chris Cusiter, and he was acutely aware his tenure as Scotland coach would come under increasing scrutiny if he returned home with two defeats.

The first Test in Rosario's Stadio Gigante de Arroyito was a predictably brutal affair as the Pumas attempted to bully the tourists into submission and the tactic was largely successful. Scotland's pack were on the back foot for much of the match and Argentina capitalised with tries from debutant Alvaro Tejeda and Gonzalo Tiesi. At one stage in the second-half Scotland led 15–10 but were unable to deliver the necessary coup de grace and went down 21–15.

It was their fifth defeat in six games and more worryingly, the fourth time in the sequence that they failed to score a try, relying exclusively on the boot of Paterson for their points. In his record-equalling 87th appearance for his country, Paterson landed five penalties to become Scotland all-time top points scorer ahead of Gavin Hastings but the Gloucester utility man was hardly in the mood to celebrate his achievement.

"I am proud to break the record but the result was a disappointment," Paterson said. "At 15–10 up, I felt we could push on for the win but Argentina are good at keeping the ball and they wore us down. I am disappointed we didn't score a try."

Hadden decided to make four personnel and six positional changes for the second Test and named a side with 10 Edinburgh players in the ranks for the clash in Buenos Aires. Scotland were up against it and the coach was in desperate need of a response from his team.

In the end, he got it. A week after allowing the Pumas to get on top early on, Scotland came out at Velez Sarsfield with real intent and commitment and they took the lead in the first-half with a try from hooker Ross Ford.

Argentina hit back in the second-half through Juan Fernandez Lobbe but a superb Scottish counter attack rounded off by centre Graeme Morrison re-established their advantage and 16 points from the ever-reliable boot of Paterson were enough to seal a famous 26-14 win.

"You could see the frustration from the players after coming so close last week and it was a very controlled performance," Hadden said. "I was getting fed up telling the press we had a good side here and the players were keen to prove it by delivering.

"We've had three weeks together which we never had during the Six Nations and that has given us the confidence and the belief to pull off this incredible achievement. I think we've set the tone for what's hopefully going to be a new era."

How accurate the coach's upbeat assessment of Scotland's future is, remains to be seen.

SCOTLAND INTERNATIONAL STATISTICS

MATCH RECORDS UP TO 30th SEPTEMBER 2008

MOST CONSECUTIVE TEST WINS

6 1925 *F,W,I,E*, 1926 *F,W*
6 1989 *Fj*, *R*, 1990 I,F,W,E

MOST CONSECUTIVE TESTS WITHOUT DEFEAT

Matches	Wins	Draws	Periods
9	6*	3	1885 to 1887
6	6	0	1925 to 1926
6	6	0	1989 to 1990
6	4	2	1877 to 1880
6	5	1	1983 to 1984

* includes an abandoned match

MOST POINTS IN A MATCH

BY THE TEAM

Pts.	Opponents	Venue	Year
100	Japan	Perth	2004
89	Ivory Coast	Rustenburg	1995
65	United States	San Francisco	2002
60	Zimbabwe	Wellington	1987
60	Romania	Hampden Park	1999
56	Portugal	Saint Etienne	2007
55	Romania	Dunedin	1987
53	United States	Murrayfield	2000
51	Zimbabwe	Murrayfield	1991
49	Argentina	Murrayfield	1990
49	Romania	Murrayfield	1995

BY A PLAYER

Pts.	Player	Opponents	Venue	Year
44	A G Hastings	Ivory Coast	Rustenburg	1995
40	C D Paterson	Japan	Perth	2004
33	G P J Townsend	United States	Murrayfield	2000
31	A G Hastings	Tonga	Pretoria	1995
27	A G Hastings	Romania	Dunedin	1987
26	K M Logan	Romania	Hampden Park	1999
24	B J Laney	Italy	Rome	2002
23	G Ross	Tonga	Murrayfield	2001
21	A G Hastings	England	Murrayfield	1986
21	A G Hastings	Romania	Bucharest	1986
21	C D Paterson	Wales	Murrayfield	2007

MOST TRIES IN A MATCH

BY THE TEAM

Tries	Opponents	Venue	Year
15	Japan	Perth	2004
13	Ivory Coast	Rustenburg	1995
12	Wales	Raeburn Place	1887
11	Zimbabwe	Wellington	1987
10	United States	San Francisco	2002
9	Romania	Dunedin	1987
9	Argentina	Murrayfield	1990

BY A PLAYER

Tries	Player	Opponents	Venue	Year
5	G C Lindsay	Wales	Raeburn Place	1887
4	W A Stewart	Ireland	Inverleith	1913
4	I S Smith	France	Inverleith	1925
4	I S Smith	Wales	Swansea	1925
4	A G Hastings	Ivory Coast	Rustenburg	1995

MOST CONVERSIONS IN A MATCH

BY THE TEAM

Cons	Opponents	Venue	Year
11	Japan	Perth	2004
9	Ivory Coast	Rustenburg	1995
8	Zimbabwe	Wellington	1987
8	Romania	Dunedin	1987
8	Portugal	Saint Etienne	2007

BY A PLAYER

Cons	Player	Opponents	Venue	Year
11	C D Paterson	Japan	Perth	2004
9	A G Hastings	Ivory Coast	Rustenburg	1995
8	A G Hastings	Zimbabwe	Wellington	1987
8	A G Hastings	Romania	Dunedin	1987

MOST PENALTIES IN A MATCH

BY THE TEAM

Penalties	Opponents	Venue	Year
8	Tonga	Pretoria	1995
7	Wales	Murrayfield	2007
6	France	Murrayfield	1986
6	Italy	Murrayfield	2005
6	Ireland	Murrayfield	2007
6	Italy	Saint Etienne	2007

BY A PLAYER

Pens	Player	Opponents	Venue	Year
8	A G Hastings	Tonga	Pretoria	1995
7	C D Paterson	Wales	Murrayfield	2007
6	A G Hastings	France	Murrayfield	1986
6	C D Paterson	Italy	Murrayfield	2005
6	C D Paterson	Ireland	Murrayfield	2007
6	C D Paterson	Italy	Saint Etienne	2007

MOST DROPPED GOALS IN A MATCH

BY THE TEAM

Drops	Opponents	Venue	Year
3	Ireland	Murrayfield	1973
2	on several	occasions	

BY A PLAYER

Drops	Player	Opponents	Venue	Year
2	R C MacKenzie	Ireland	Belfast	1877
2	N J Finlay	Ireland	Glasgow	1880
2	B M Simmers	Wales	Murrayfield	1965
2	D W Morgan	Ireland	Murrayfield	1973
2	B M Gossman	France	Parc des Princes	1983
2	J Y Rutherford	New Zealand	Murrayfield	1983
2	J Y Rutherford	Wales	Murrayfield	1985
2	J Y Rutherford	Ireland	Murrayfield	1987
2	C M Chalmers	England	Twickenham	1995

SCOTLAND

CAREER RECORDS

MOST CAPPED PLAYERS

Caps	Player	Career Span
88	C D Paterson	1999 to 2008
87	S Murray	1997 to 2007
82	G P J Townsend	1993 to 2003
75	G C Bulloch	1997 to 2005
71	S B Grimes	1997 to 2005
70	K M Logan	1992 to 2003
67	J P R White	2000 to 2008
65	S Hastings	1986 to 1997
61	A G Hastings	1986 to 1995
61	G W Weir	1990 to 2000
61	T J Smith	1997 to 2005
60	C M Chalmers	1989 to 1999
60	B W Redpath	1993 to 2003
60	S M Taylor	2000 to 2008
53	A R Henderson	2001 to 2008
53	N J Hines	2000 to 2008
52	J M Renwick	1972 to 1984
52	C T Deans	1978 to 1987
52	A G Stanger	1989 to 1998
52	A P Burnell	1989 to 1999
51	A R Irvine	1972 to 1982
51	G Armstrong	1988 to 1999

MOST TESTS AS CAPTAIN

25	D M B Sole	1989 to 1992
21	B W Redpath	1998 to 2003
20	A G Hastings	1993 to 1995
19	J McLauchlan	1973 to 1979
19	J P R White	2005 to 2008
16	R I Wainwright	1995 to 1998
15	M C Morrison	1899 to 1904
15	A R Smith	1957 to 1962
15	A R Irvine	1980 to 1982

MOST POINTS IN TESTS

Points	Player	Tests	Career
687	C D Paterson	88	1999 to 2008
667	A G Hastings	61	1986 to 1995
273	A R Irvine	51	1972 to 1982
220	K M Logan	70	1992 to 2003
210	P W Dods	23	1983 to 1991
166	C M Chalmers	60	1989 to 1999
164	G P J Townsend	82	1993 to 2003
141	B J Laney	20	2001 to 2004
123	D W Hodge	26	1997 to 2002
106	A G Stanger	52	1989 to 1998

MOST CONSECUTIVE TESTS

Tests	Player	Span
49	A B Carmichael	1967 to 1978
42	C D Paterson	2004 to 2008
40	H F McLeod	1954 to 1962
37	J M Bannerman	1921 to 1929
35	A G Stanger	1989 to 1994

MOST TRIES IN TESTS

Tries	Player	Tests	Career
24	I S Smith	32	1924 to 1933
24	A G Stanger	52	1989 to 1998
22	C D Paterson	88	1999 to 2008
17	A G Hastings	61	1986 to 1995
17	A V Tait	27	1987 to 1999
17	G P J Townsend	82	1993 to 2003
15	I Tukalo	37	1985 to 1992
13	K M Logan	70	1992 to 2003
12	A R Smith	33	1955 to 1962

MOST PENALTY GOALS IN TESTS

Penalties	Player	Tests	Career
140	A G Hastings	61	1986 to 1995
135	C D Paterson	88	1999 to 2008
61	A R Irvine	51	1972 to 1982
50	P W Dods	23	1983 to 1991
32	C M Chalmers	60	1989 to 1999
29	K M Logan	70	1992 to 2003
29	B J Laney	20	2001 to 2004
21	M Dods	8	1994 to 1996
21	R J S Shepherd	20	1995 to 1998

MOST CONVERSIONS IN TESTS

Cons	Player	Tests	Career
86	A G Hastings	61	1986 to 1995
83	C D Paterson	88	1999 to 2008
34	K M Logan	70	1992 to 2003
26	P W Dods	23	1983 to 1991
25	A R Irvine	51	1972 to 1982
19	D Drysdale	26	1923 to 1929
17	B J Laney	20	2001 to 2004
15	D W Hodge	26	1997 to 2002
14	F H Turner	15	1911 to 1914
14	R J S Shepherd	20	1995 to 1998

MOST DROPPED GOALS IN TESTS

Drops	Player	Tests	Career
12	J Y Rutherford	42	1979 to 1987
9	C M Chalmers	60	1989 to 1999
7	I R McGeechan	32	1972 to 1979
7	G P J Townsend	82	1993 to 2003
6	D W Morgan	21	1973 to 1978
5	H Waddell	15	1924 to 1930

Dave Rogers/Getty Images

Chris Paterson (right) is closing in on Gavin Hastings' record for penalties and conversions for Scotland.

INTERNATIONAL CHAMPIONSHIP RECORDS

RECORD	DETAIL	HOLDER	SET
Most points in season	120	in four matches	1999
Most tries in season	17	in four matches	1925
Highest Score	38	38-10 v Ireland	1997
Biggest win	28	31-3 v France	1912
	28	38-10 v Ireland	1997
Highest score conceded	51	16-51 v France	1998
Biggest defeat	40	3-43 v England	2001
Most appearances	43	G P J Townsend	1993 - 2003
	43	C D Paterson	2000 - 2008
Most points in matches	316	C D Paterson	2000 - 2008
Most points in season	65	C D Paterson	2007
Most points in match	24	B J Laney	v Italy, 2002
Most tries in matches	24	I S Smith	1924 - 1933
Most tries in season	8	I S Smith	1925
Most tries in match	5	G C Lindsay	v Wales, 1887
Most cons in matches	28	C D Paterson	2000 - 2008
Most cons in season	11	K M Logan	1999
Most cons in match	5	F H Turner	v France, 1912
	5	J W Allan	v England, 1931
	5	R J S Shepherd	v Ireland, 1997
Most pens in matches	77	A G Hastings	1986 - 1995
Most pens in season	16	C D Paterson	2007
Most pens in match	7	C D Paterson	v Wales, 2007
Most drops in matches	8	J Y Rutherford	1979 - 1987
	8	C M Chalmers	1989 - 1998
Most drops in season	3	J Y Rutherford	1987
Most drops in match	2	on several	occasions

MISCELLANEOUS RECORDS

RECORD	HOLDER	DETAIL
Longest Test Career	W C W Murdoch	1935 to 1948
Youngest Test Cap	N J Finlay	17 yrs 36 days in 1875*
Oldest Test Cap	J McLauchlan	37 yrs 210 days in 1979

* C Reid, also 17 yrs 36 days on debut in 1881, was a day *older* than Finlay, having lived through an extra leap-year day.

CAREER RECORDS OF SCOTLAND INTERNATIONAL PLAYERS (UP TO 30 SEPTEMBER 2008)

PLAYER	DEBUT	CAPS	T	C	P	D	PTS
BACKS							
M R L Blair	2002 v C	50	5	0	0	0	25
B J Cairns	2008 v Arg	2	0	0	0	0	0
C P Cusiter	2004 v W	39	3	0	0	0	15
S C J Danielli	2003 v It	16	5	0	0	0	25
R E Dewey	2006 v R	13	4	0	0	0	20
N J de Luca	2008 v F	4	0	0	0	0	0
M P di Rollo	2002 v US	21	2	0	0	1	13
T H Evans	2008 v Arg	1	0	0	0	0	0
P J Godman	2005 v R	9	1	5	1	0	18
A R Henderson	2001 v	53	8	0	0	0	40
R P Lamont	2005 v W	17	5	0	0	0	25
S F Lamont	2004 v Sm	35	7	0	0	0	35
R G.M.Lawson	2006 v A	12	0	0	0	0	0
G A Morrison	2004 v A	11	2	0	0	0	10
D A Parks	2004 v W	44	4	8	11	4	81
C D Paterson	1999 v Sp	88	22	83	135	2	687
H F G Southwell	2004 v Sm	42	8	0	0	0	40
N Walker	2002 v R	14	2	0	0	0	10
S L Webster	2003 v I	35	8	0	0	0	40
FORWARDS							
J A Barclay	2007 v NZ	4	0	0	0	0	0
J W Beattie	2006 v R	4	1	0	0	0	5
K D R Brown	2005 v R	26	3	0	0	0	15
D A Callam	2006 v R	11	1	0	0	0	5
A G Dickinson	2007 v NZ	5	0	0	0	0	0
R W Ford	2004 v A	22	2	0	0	0	10
D W H Hall	2003 v W	20	1	0	0	0	5
J L Hamilton	2006 v R	16	0	0	0	0	0
N J Hines	2000 v NZ	53	1	0	0	0	5
A Hogg	2004 v W	45	10	0	0	0	50
A F Jacobsen	2002 v C	31	0	0	0	0	0
A D Kellock	2004 v A	16	0	0	0	0	0
G Kerr	2003 v I	50	1	0	0	0	5

S Lawson	2005 v R	16	2	0	0	0	10
S J MacLeod	2004 v A	21	0	0	0	0	0
E A Murray	2005 v R	22	2	0	0	0	10
S Murray	1997 v A	87	3	0	0	0	15
M L Mustchin	2008 v Arg	2	0	0	0	0	0
R M Rennie	2008 v I	1	0	0	0	0	0
C J Smith	2002 v C	25	0	0	0	0	0
A K Strokosch	2006 v A	6	0	0	0	0	0
S M Taylor	2000 v US	60	6	0	0	0	30
F M A Thomson	2007 v I	8	0	0	0	0	0
J P R White	2000 v E	67	4	0	0	0	20

David Rogers/Getty Images

Jason White is set to go through the 70-cap barrier this season, a feat only achieved by six Scots.

SCOTLAND INTERNATIONAL PLAYERS

UP TO 30TH SEPTEMBER 2008

Note: Years given for International Championship matches are for second half of season; eg 1972 means season 1971-72. Years for all other matches refer to the actual year of the match. Entries in square brackets denote matches played in RWC Finals..

Abercrombie, C H (United Services) 1910 I, E, 1911 F, W, 1913 F, W
Abercrombie, J G (Edinburgh U) 1949 F, W, I, 1950 F, W, I, E
Agnew, W C C (Stewart's Coll FP) 1930 W, I
Ainslie, R (Edinburgh Inst FP) 1879 I, E, 1880 I, E, 1881 E, 1882 I, E
Ainslie, T (Edinburgh Inst FP) 1881 E, 1882 I, E, 1883 W, I, E, 1884 W, I, E, 1885 W, I 1,2
Aitchison, G R (Edinburgh Wands) 1883 I
Aitchison, T G (Gala) 1929 W, I, E
Aitken, A I (Edinburgh Inst FP) 1889 I
Aitken, G G (Oxford U) 1924 W, I, E, 1925 F, W, I, E, 1929 F
Aitken, J (Gala) 1977 E, I, F, 1981 F, W, E, I, NZ 1,2, R, A, 1982 E, I, F, W, 1983 F, W, E, NZ, 1984 W, E, I, F, R
Aitken, R (London Scottish) 1947 W
Allan, B (Glasgow Acads) 1881 I
Allan, J (Edinburgh Acads) 1990 NZ 1, 1991, W, I, R, [J, I, WS, E, NZ]
Allan, J L (Melrose) 1952 F, W, I, 1953 W
Allan, J L F (Cambridge U) 1957 I, E
Allan, J W (Melrose) 1927 F, 1928 I, 1929 F, W, I, E, 1930 F, E, 1931 F, W, I, E, 1932 SA, W, I, 1934 I, E
Allan, R C (Hutchesons' GSFP) 1969 I
Allardice, W D (Aberdeen GSFP) 1947 A, 1948 F, W, I, 1949 F, W, I, E
Allen, H W (Glasgow Acads) 1873 E
Anderson, A H (Glasgow Acads) 1894 I
Anderson, D G (London Scottish) 1889 I, 1890 W, I, E, 1891 W, E, 1892 W, E
Anderson, E (Stewart's Coll FP) 1947 I, E
Anderson, J W (W of Scotland) 1872 E
Anderson, T (Merchiston Castle School) 1882 I
Angus, A W (Watsonians) 1909 W, 1910 F, W, E, 1911 W, I, 1912 F, W, I, E, SA, 1913 F, W, 1914 E, 1920 F, W, I, E
Anton, P A (St Andrew's U) 1873 E
Armstrong, G (Jedforest, Newcastle) 1988 A, 1989 W, E, I, F, Fj, R, 1990 I, F, W, E, NZ 1,2, Arg, 1991 F, W, E, I, R, [J, I, WS, E, NZ], 1993 I, F, W, E, 1994 E, I, 1996 NZ, 1,2, A, 1997 W, SA (R), 1998 It, I, F, W, E, SA (R), 1999 W, E, I, F, Arg, R, [SA, U, Sm, NZ]
Arneil, R J (Edinburgh Acads, Leicester and Northampton) 1968 I, E, A, 1969 F, W, I, E, SA, 1970 F, W, I, E, A, 1971 F, W, I, E (2[1C]), 1972 F, W, E, NZ
Arthur, A (Glasgow Acads) 1875 E, 1876 E
Arthur, J W (Glasgow Acads) 1871 E, 1872 E
Asher, A G G (Oxford U) 1882 I, 1884 W, I, E, 1885 W, 1886 I, E
Auld, W (W of Scotland) 1889 W, 1890 W
Auldjo, L J (Abertay) 1878 E

Bain, D McL (Oxford U) 1911 E, 1912 F, W, E, SA, 1913 F, W, I, E, 1914 W, I
Baird, G R T (Kelso) 1981 A, 1982 E, I, F, W, A 1,2, 1983 I, F, W, E, NZ, 1984 W, E, I, F, A, 1985 I, W, E, 1986 F, W, E, I, R, 1987 E, 1988 I
Balfour, A (Watsonians) 1896 W, I, E, 1897 E
Balfour, L M (Edinburgh Acads) 1872 E
Bannerman, E M (Edinburgh Acads) 1872 E, 1873 E
Bannerman, J M (Glasgow HSFP) 1921 F, W, I, E, 1922 F, W, I, E, 1923 F, W, I, E, 1924 F, W, I, E, 1925 F, W, I, E, 1926 F, W, I, E, 1927 F, W, I, E, A, 1928 F, W, I, E, 1929 F, W, I, E
Barclay, J A (Glasgow Warriors) 2007 [NZ], 2008 F,W,Arg 2
Barnes, I A (Hawick) 1972 W, 1974 F (R), 1975 E (R), NZ, 1977 I, F, W
Barrie, R W (Hawick) 1936 E
Bearne, K R F (Cambridge U, London Scottish) 1960 F, W
Beattie, J A (Hawick) 1929 F, W, 1930 W, 1931 F, W, I, E, 1932 SA, W, I, E, 1933 W, E, I, 1934 I, E, 1935 W, I, E, NZ, 1936 W, I, E
Beattie, J R (Glasgow Acads) 1980 I, F, W, E, 1981 F, W, E, I, 1983 F, W, E, NZ, 1984 E (R), R, A, 1985 I, 1986 F, W, E, I, R, 1987 I, F, W, E
Beattie, J W (Glasgow Warriors) 2006 R,Pl, 2007 F, 2008 Arg 1
Beattie, R S (Newcastle, Bristol) 2000 NZ 1,2(R), Sm (R), 2003 E(R), It(R), I 2, [J(R), US,Fj]
Bedell-Sivright, D R (Cambridge U, Edinburgh U) 1900 W, 1901 W, I, E, 1902 W, I, E, 1903 W, I, 1904 W, I, E, 1905 NZ, 1906 W, I, E, SA, 1907 W, I, E, 1908 W, I
Bedell-Sivright, J V (Cambridge U) 1902 W
Begbie, T A (Edinburgh Wands) 1881 I, E
Bell, D L (Watsonians) 1975 I, F, W, E
Bell, J A (Clydesdale) 1901 W, I, E, 1902 W, I, E
Bell, L H I (Edinburgh Acads) 1900 E, 1904 W, I
Berkeley, W V (Oxford U) 1926 F, 1929 F, W, I
Berry, C W (Fettesian-Lorettonians) 1884 I, E, 1885 W, I 1, 1887 I, W, E, 1888 W, I
Bertram, D M (Watsonians) 1922 F, W, I, E, 1923 F, W, I, E, 1924 W, I, E
Beveridge, G (Glasgow) 2000 NZ 2(R), US (R), Sm (R), 2002 Fj(R), 2003 W 2, 2005 R(R)
Biggar, A G (London Scottish) 1969 SA, 1970 F, I, E, A, 1971 F, W, I, E (2[1C]), 1972 F, W
Biggar, M A (London Scottish) 1975 I, F, W, E, 1976 W, E, I, 1977 I, F, W, 1978 I, F, W, E, NZ, 1979 W, E, I, F, NZ, 1980 I, F, W, E
Birkett, G A (Harlequins, London Scottish) 1975 NZ
Bishop, J M (Glasgow Acads) 1893 I
Bisset, A A (RIE Coll) 1904 W
Black, A W (Edinburgh U) 1947 F, W, 1948 E, 1950 W, I, E
Black, W P (Glasgow HSFP) 1948 F, W, I, E, 1951 E
Blackadder, W F (W of Scotland) 1938 E
Blaikie, C F (Heriot's FP) 1963 I, E, 1966 E, 1968 A, 1969 F, W, I, E
Blair, M R L (Edinburgh) 2002 C, US, 2003 F(t+R), W 1(R), SA 2(R), It 2, I 2, [US], 2004 W(R),E(R),It(R),F(R),I(R),Sm(R),A1(R), 3(R),J(R),A4(R),SA(R),2005 I(t&R),It(R),W(R),E,R,Arg, Sm(R), NZ(R), 2006 F,W,E,I,It(R),SA 1,2,R,PI(R),A, 2007 I2,SA, [Pt,R, It,Arg], 2008 F,W,I,E,It,Arg 1,2
Blair, P C B (Cambridge U) 1912 SA, 1913 F, W, I, E
Bolton, W H (W of Scotland) 1876 E
Borthwick, J B (Stewart's Coll FP) 1938 W, I
Bos, F H ten (Oxford U, London Scottish) 1959 E, 1960 F, W, SA, 1961 F, SA, W, I, E, 1962 F, W, I, E, 1963 F, W, I, E
Boswell, J D (W of Scotland) 1889 W, I, 1890 W, I, E, 1891 W, I, E, 1892 W, I, E, 1893 I, E, 1894 I, E
Bowie, T C (Watsonians) 1913 I, E, 1914 I, E
Boyd, G M (Glasgow HSFP) 1926 E
Boyd, J L (United Services) 1912 E, SA
Boyle, A C W (London Scottish) 1963 F, W, I
Boyle, A H W (St Thomas's Hospital, London Scottish) 1966 A, 1967 F, NZ, 1968 F, W, I
Brash, J C (Cambridge U) 1961 E

Breakey, R W (Gosforth) 1978 E
Brewis, N T (Edinburgh Inst FP) 1876 E, 1878 E, 1879 I, E, 1880 I, E
Brewster, A K (Stewart's-Melville FP) 1977 E, 1980 I, F, 1986 E, I, R
Brotherstone, S J (Melrose, Brive, Newcastle) 1999 I (R), 2000 F, W, E, US, A, Sm, 2002 C (R)
Brown, A H (Heriot's FP) 1928 E, 1929 F, W
Brown, A R (Gala) 1971 E (2[1C]), 1972 F, W, E
Brown, C H C (Dunfermline) 1929 E
Brown, D I (Cambridge U) 1933 W, E, I
Brown, G L (W of Scotland) 1969 SA, 1970 F, W (R), I, E, A, 1971 F, W, I, E (2[1C]), 1972 F, W, E, NZ, 1973 E (R), P, 1974 W, E, I, F, 1975 I, F, W, E, A, 1976 F, W, E, I
Brown, J A (Glasgow Acads) 1908 W, I
Brown, J B (Glasgow Acads) 1879 I, E, 1880 I, E, 1881 I, E, 1882 I, E, 1883 W, I, E, 1884 W, I, E, 1885 I 1,2, 1886 W, I, E
Brown, K D R (Borders, Glasgow Warriors) 2005 R,Sm(R),NZ(R), 2006 SA 1(R),2(R),
R,PI,A, 2007 E,W,It,I1,2(R),SA,[Pt(R),R(R),NZ,It(R),Arg(R)], 2008 F(R),W,I,E(R),
It(R),Arg 1(R),2(R)
Brown, P C (W of Scotland, Gala) 1964 F, NZ, W, I, E, 1965 I, E, SA, 1966 A, 1969 I, E, 1970 W, E, 1971 F, W, I, E (2[1C]), 1972 F, W, E, NZ, 1973 F, W, I, E, P
Brown, T G (Heriot's FP) 1929 W
Brown, W D (Glasgow Acads) 1871 E, 1872 E, 1873 E, 1874 E, 1875 E
Brown, W S (Edinburgh Inst FP) 1880 I, E, 1882 I, E, 1883 W, E
Browning, A (Glasgow HSFP) 1920 I, 1922 F, W, I, 1923 W, I, E
Bruce, C R (Glasgow Acads) 1947 F, W, I, E, 1949 F, W, I, E
Bruce, N S (Blackheath, Army and London Scottish) 1958 F, A, I, E, 1959 F, W, I, E, 1960 F, W, I, E, SA, 1961 F, SA, W, I, E, 1962 F, W, I, E, 1963 F, W, I, E, 1964 F, NZ, W, I, E
Bruce, R M (Gordonians) 1947 A, 1948 F, W, I
Bruce-Lockhart, J H (London Scottish) 1913 W, 1920 E
Bruce-Lockhart, L (London Scottish) 1948 E, 1950 F, W, 1953 I, E
Bruce-Lockhart, R B (Cambridge U and London Scottish) 1937 I, 1939 I, E
Bryce, C C (Glasgow Acads) 1873 E, 1874 E
Bryce, R D H (W of Scotland) 1973 I (R)
Bryce, W E (Selkirk) 1922 W, I, E, 1923 F, W, I, E, 1924 F, W, I, E
Brydon, W R C (Heriot's FP) 1939 W
Buchanan, A (Royal HSFP) 1871 E
Buchanan, F G (Kelvinside Acads and Oxford U) 1910 F, 1911 F, W
Buchanan, J C R (Stewart's Coll FP) 1921 W, I, E, 1922 W, I, E, 1923 F, W, I, E, 1924 F, W, I, E, 1925 F, I
Buchanan-Smith, G A E (London Scottish, Heriot's FP) 1989 Fj (R), 1990 Arg
Bucher, A M (Edinburgh Acads) 1897 E
Budge, G M (Edinburgh Wands) 1950 F, W, I, E
Bullmore, H H (Edinburgh U) 1902 I
Bulloch, A J (Glasgow) 2000 US, A, Sm, 2001 F (t+R), E
Bulloch, G C (West of Scotland, Glasgow) 1997 SA, 1998 It, I, F, W, E, Fj, A 1, SA, 1999 W, E, It, I, F, Arg, [SA, U, Sm, NZ], 2000 It, I, W (R), NZ 1,2, A (R), Sm (R), 2001 F, W, E, It, I, Tg, Arg, NZ, 2002 E, It, I, F, W, C, US, R, SA, Fj, 2003 I 1, F, W 1, E, It 1, SA 1,2, It 2(R), W2, I 2, [US,F,Fj,A], 2004 W,E,It,F,I,Sm,A1,2,3,J,A4,SA, 2005 F,I,It,W,E
Burnell, A P (London Scottish, Montferrand) 1989 E, I, F, Fj, R, 1990 I, F, W, E, Arg, 1991 F, W, E, I, R, [J, Z, I, WS, E, NZ], 1992 E, I, F, W, 1993 I, F, W, E, NZ, 1994 W, E, I, F, Arg 1,2, SA, 1995 [Iv, Tg (R), F (R)], WS, 1998 E, SA, 1999 W, E, It, I, F, Arg, [Sp, Sm (R), NZ]
Burnet, P J (London Scottish and Edinburgh Acads) 1960 SA
Burnet, W (Hawick) 1912 E
Burnet, W A (W of Scotland) 1934 W, 1935 W, I, E, NZ, 1936 W, I, E
Burnett, J N (Heriot's FP) 1980 I, F, W, E
Burns, G G (Watsonians, Edinburgh) 1999 It (R), 2001 Tg (R), NZ (R), 2002 US (R)
Burrell, G (Gala) 1950 F, W, I, 1951 SA

Cairns, A G (Watsonians) 1903 W, I, E, 1904 W, I, E, 1905 W, I, E, 1906 W, I, E
Cairns, B J (Edinburgh) 2008 Arg 1,2
Calder, F (Stewart's-Melville FP) 1986 F, W, E, I, R, 1987 I, F, W, E, [F, Z, R, NZ], 1988 I, F, W, E, 1989 W, E, I, F, R, 1990 I, F, W, E, NZ 1,2, 1991 R, [J, I, WS, E, NZ]
Calder, J H (Stewart's-Melville FP) 1981 F, W, E, I, NZ 1,2, R, A, 1982 E, I, F, W, A 1,2, 1983 I, F, W, E, NZ, 1984 W, E, I, F, A, 1985 I, F, W
Callam, D A (Edinburgh) 2006 R(R),PI(R),A, 2007 E,W,It,I1,F(R),SA, [NZ], 2008 F
Callander, G J (Kelso) 1984 R, 1988 I, F, W, E, A
Cameron, A (Glasgow HSFP) 1948 W, 1950 I, E, 1951 F, W, I, E, SA, 1953 I, E, 1955 F, W, I, E, 1956 F, W, I
Cameron, A D (Hillhead HSFP) 1951 F, 1954 F, W
Cameron, A W C (Watsonians) 1887 W, 1893 W, 1894 I
Cameron, D (Glasgow HSFP) 1953 I, E, 1954 F, NZ, I, E
Cameron, N W (Glasgow U) 1952 E, 1953 F, W
Campbell, A J (Hawick) 1984 I, F, R, 1985 I, F, W, E, 1986 F, W, E, I, R, 1988 F, W, A
Campbell, G T (London Scottish) 1892 W, I, E, 1893 I, E, 1894 W, I, E, 1895 W, I, E, 1896 W, I, E, 1897 I, 1899 I, 1900 E
Campbell, H H (Cambridge U, London Scottish) 1947 I, E, 1948 I, E
Campbell, J A (W of Scotland) 1878 E, 1879 I, E, 1881 I, E
Campbell, J A (Cambridge U) 1900 I
Campbell, N M (London Scottish) 1956 F, W
Campbell, S J (Dundee HSFP) 1995 C, I, F, W, E, R, [Iv, NZ (R)], WS (t), 1996 I, F, W, E, 1997 A, SA, 1998 Fj (R), A 2(R)
Campbell-Lamerton, J R E (London Scottish) 1986 F, 1987 [Z, R(R)]
Campbell-Lamerton, M J (Halifax, Army, London Scottish) 1961 F, SA, W, I, 1962 F, W, I, E, 1963 F, W, I, E, 1964 I, E, 1965 F, W, I, E, SA, 1966 F, W, I, E
Carmichael, A B (W of Scotland) 1967 I, NZ, 1968 F, W, I, E, A, 1969 F, W, I, E, SA, 1970 F, W, I, E, A, 1971 F, W, I, E (2[1C]), 1972 F, W, E, NZ, 1973 F, W, I, E, P, 1974 W, E, I, F, 1975 I, F, W, E, NZ, A, 1976 F, W, E, I, 1977 E, I (R), F, W, 1978 I
Carmichael, J H (Watsonians) 1921 F, W, I
Carrick, J S (Glasgow Acads) 1876 E, 1877 E
Cassels, D Y (W of Scotland) 1880 E, 1881 I, 1882 I, E, 1883 W, I, E
Cathcart, C W (Edinburgh U) 1872 E, 1873 E, 1876 E
Cawkwell, G L (Oxford U) 1947 F
Chalmers, C M (Melrose) 1989 W, E, I, F, Fj, 1990 I, F, W, E, NZ 1,2, Arg, 1991 F, W, E, I, R, [J, Z (R), I, WS, E, NZ], 1992 E, I, F, W, A 1,2, 1993 I, F, W, E, NZ, 1994 W, SA, 1995 C, I, F, W, E, R, [Iv, Tg, F, NZ], WS, 1996 A, It, 1997 W, I, F, A (R), SA, 1998 It, I, F, W, E, 1999 Arg (R)
Chalmers, T (Glasgow Acads) 1871 E, 1872 E, 1873 E, 1874 E, 1875 E, 1876 E
Chambers, H F T (Edinburgh U) 1888 W, I, 1889 W, I
Charters, R G (Hawick) 1955 W, I, E
Chisholm, D H (Melrose) 1964 I, E, 1965 E, SA, 1966 F, I, E, A, 1967 F, W, NZ, 1968 F, W, I
Chisholm, R W T (Melrose) 1955 I, E, 1956 F, W, I, E, 1958 F, W, A, I, 1960 SA
Church, W C (Glasgow Acads) 1906 W
Clark, R L (Edinburgh Wands, Royal Navy) 1972 F, W, E, NZ, 1973 F, W, I, E, P
Clauss, P R A (Oxford U) 1891 W, I, E, 1892 W, E, 1895 I
Clay, A T (Edinburgh Acads) 1886 W, I, E, 1887 I, W, E, 1888 W
Clunies-Ross, A (St Andrew's U) 1871 E
Coltman, S (Hawick) 1948 I, 1949 F, W, I, E
Colville, A G (Merchistonians, Blackheath) 1871 E, 1872 E
Connell, G C (Trinity Acads and London Scottish) 1968 E, A, 1969 F, E, 1970 F
Cooper, M McG (Oxford U) 1936 W, I
Corcoran, I (Gala) 1992 A 1(R)
Cordial, I F (Edinburgh Wands) 1952 F, W, I, E
Cotter, J L (Hillhead HSFP) 1934 I, E
Cottington, G S (Kelso) 1934 I, E, 1935 W, I, 1936 E
Coughtrie, S (Edinburgh Acads) 1959 F, W, I, E, 1962 W, I, E, 1963 F, W, I, E
Couper, J H (W of Scotland) 1896 W, I, 1899 I
Coutts, F H (Melrose, Army) 1947 W, I, E
Coutts, I D F (Old Alleynians) 1951 F, 1952 E
Cowan, R C (Selkirk) 1961 F, 1962 F, W, I, E
Cowie, W L K (Edinburgh Wands) 1953 E

Cownie, W B (Watsonians) 1893 W, I, E, 1894 W, I, E, 1895 W, I, E
Crabbie, G E (Edinburgh Acads) 1904 W
Crabbie, J E (Edinburgh Acads, Oxford U) 1900 W, 1902 I, 1903 W, I, 1904 E, 1905 W
Craig, A (Orrell, Glasgow) 2002 C, US, R, SA, Fj, 2003 I 1, F(R), W 1(R), E, It 1, SA 1,2, W 2, I 2, [J,US,F], 2004 A3(R), 2005 F,I,It,W,E
Craig, J B (Heriot's FP) 1939 W
Craig, J M (West of Scotland, Glasgow) 1997 A, 2001 W (R), E (R), It
Cramb, R I (Harlequins) 1987 [R(R)], 1988 I, F, A
Cranston, A G (Hawick) 1976 W, E, I, 1977 E, W, 1978 F (R), W, E, NZ, 1981 NZ 1,2
Crawford, J A (Army, London Scottish) 1934 I
Crawford, W H (United Services, RN) 1938 W, I, E, 1939 W, E
Crichton-Miller, D (Gloucester) 1931 W, I, E
Crole, G B (Oxford U) 1920 F, W, I, E
Cronin, D F (Bath, London Scottish, Bourges, Wasps) 1988 I, F, W, E, A, 1989 W, E, I, F, Fj, R, 1990 I, F, W, E, NZ 1,2, 1991 F, W, E, I, R, [Z], 1992 A 2, 1993 I, F, W, E, NZ, 1995 C, I, F, [Tg, F, NZ], WS, 1996 NZ 1,2, A, It, 1997 F (R), 1998 I, F, W, E
Cross, M (Merchistonians) 1875 E, 1876 E, 1877 I, E, 1878 E, 1879 I, E, 1880 I, E
Cross, W (Merchistonians) 1871 E, 1872 E
Cumming, R S (Aberdeen U) 1921 F, W
Cunningham, G (Oxford U) 1908 W, I, 1909 W, E, 1910 F, I, E, 1911 E
Cunningham, R F (Gala) 1978 NZ, 1979 W, E
Currie, L R (Dunfermline) 1947 A, 1948 F, W, I, 1949 F, W, I, E
Cusiter, C P (Borders, Perpignan) 2004 W,E,It,F,I,Sm,A1 ,2,3,J,A4,SA,2005 F,I,It,W, Arg(R),Sm,NZ, 2006 F(R),W(R),E(R), I(R),It,R(R),PI, 2007 E,W,It,I1,F(R),I2(R), [R(R),NZ,It(R),Arg(R)], 2008 F(R),W(R),I(R)
Cuthbertson, W (Kilmarnock, Harlequins) 1980 I, 1981 W, E, I, NZ 1,2, R, A, 1982 E, I, F, W, A 1,2, 1983 I, F, W, NZ, 1984 W, E, A

Dalgleish, A (Gala) 1890 W, E, 1891 W, I, 1892 W, 1893 W, 1894 W, I
Dalgleish, K J (Edinburgh Wands, Cambridge U) 1951 I, E, 1953 F, W
Dall, A K (Edinburgh) 2003 W 2(R)
Dallas, J D (Watsonians) 1903 E
Danielli, S C J (Bath, Borders, Ulster) 2003 It 2, W 2, [J(R),US,Fj,A], 2004 W, E,It,F,I,2005 F,I, 2008 W(R),It,Arg 1
Davidson, J A (London Scottish, Edinburgh Wands) 1959 E, 1960 I, E
Davidson, J N G (Edinburgh U) 1952 F, W, I, E, 1953 F, W, 1954 F
Davidson, J P (RIE Coll) 1873 E, 1874 E
Davidson, R S (Royal HSFP) 1893 E
Davies, D S (Hawick) 1922 F, W, I, E, 1923 F, W, I, E, 1924 F, E, 1925 W, I, E, 1926 F, W, I, E, 1927 F, W, I
Dawson, J C (Glasgow Acads) 1947 A, 1948 F, W, 1949 F, W, I, 1950 F, W, I, E, 1951 F, W, I, E, SA, 1952 F, W, I, E, 1953 E
Deans, C T (Hawick) 1978 F, W, E, NZ, 1979 W, E, I, F, NZ, 1980 I, F, 1981 F, W, E, I, NZ 1,2, R, A, 1982 E, I, F, W, A 1,2, 1983 I, F, W, E, NZ, 1984 W, E, I, F, A, 1985 I, F, W, E, 1986 F, W, E, I, R, 1987 I, F, W, E, [F, Z, R, NZ]
Deans, D T (Hawick) 1968 E
Deas, D W (Heriot's FP) 1947 F, W
De Luca, N J (Edinburgh) 2008 F,W,I(t&R),Arg 2(R)
Dewey, R E (Edinburgh, Ulster) 2006 R, 2007 E(R),W,It,I1,F,I2,SA, [Pt,R,NZ(R),It,Arg]
Dick, L G (Loughborough Colls, Jordanhill, Swansea) 1972 W (R), E, 1974 W, E, I, F, 1975 I, F, W, E, NZ, A, 1976 F, 1977 E
Dick, R C S (Cambridge U, Guy's Hospital) 1934 W, I, E, 1935 W, I, E, NZ, 1936 W, I, E, 1937 W, 1938 W, I, E
Dickinson, A G (Gloucester) 2007 [NZ], 2008 E(R),It(R),Arg 1(R),2(t&R)
Dickson, G (Gala) 1978 NZ, 1979 W, E, I, F, NZ, 1980 W, 1981 F, 1982 W (R)
Dickson, M R (Edinburgh U) 1905 I
Dickson, W M (Blackheath, Oxford U) 1912 F, W, E, SA, 1913 F, W, I
Di Rollo, M P (Edinburgh) 2002 US (R), 2005 R,Arg,Sm,NZ, 2006 F,E,I,It,SA 1,2, R,PI,A, 2007 E,W,It,I1,F(R), [Pt,NZ]
Dobson, J (Glasgow Acads) 1911 E, 1912 F, W, I, E, SA
Dobson, J D (Glasgow Acads) 1910 I
Dobson, W G (Heriot's FP) 1922 W, I, E
Docherty, J T (Glasgow HSFP) 1955 F, W, 1956 E, 1958 F, W, A, I, E
Dods, F P (Edinburgh Acads) 1901 I
Dods, J H (Edinburgh Acads) 1895 W, I, E, 1896 W, I, E, 1897 I, E
Dods, M (Gala, Northampton) 1994 I (t), Arg 1,2, 1995 WS, 1996 I, F, W, E
Dods, P W (Gala) 1983 I, F, W, E, NZ, 1984 W, E, I, F, R, A, 1985 I, F, W, E, 1989 W, E, I, F, 1991 I (R), R, [Z, NZ (R)]
Donald, D G (Oxford U) 1914 W, I
Donald, R L H (Glasgow HSFP) 1921 W, I, E
Donaldson, W P (Oxford U, W of Scotland) 1893 I, 1894 I, 1895 E, 1896 I, E, 1899 I
Don-Wauchope, A R (Fettesian-Lorettonians) 1881 E, 1882 E, 1883 W, 1884 W, I, E, 1885 W, I 1,2, 1886 W, I, E, 1888 I
Don-Wauchope, P H (Fettesian-Lorettonians) 1885 I 1,2, 1886 W, 1887 I, W, E
Dorward, A F (Cambridge U, Gala) 1950 F, 1951 SA, 1952 W, I, E, 1953 F, W, E, 1955 F, 1956 I, E, 1957 F, W, I, E
Dorward, T F (Gala) 1938 W, I, E, 1939 I, E
Douglas, B A F (Borders) 2002 R, SA, Fj, 2003 I 1, F, W 1, E, It 1, SA 1,2, It 2, W 2, [J, US(t&R),F(R),Fj,A], 2004 W,E,It,F,I,Sm,A1,2,3,A4(R),SA(R),2005 F(R),I(R),It(R), W(R),E(R),R,Arg, NZ, 2006 F,W,E,I,It,SA 1,2(R)
Douglas, G (Jedforest) 1921 W
Douglas, J (Stewart's Coll FP) 1961 F, SA, W, I, E, 1962 F, W, I, E, 1963 F, W, I
Douty, P S (London Scottish) 1927 A, 1928 F, W
Drew, D (Glasgow Acads) 1871 E, 1876 E
Druitt, W A H (London Scottish) 1936 W, I, E
Drummond, A H (Kelvinside Acads) 1938 W, I
Drummond, C W (Melrose) 1947 F, W, I, E, 1948 F, I, E, 1950 F, W, I, E
Drybrough, A S (Edinburgh Wands, Merchistonians) 1902 I, 1903 I
Dryden, R H (Watsonians) 1937 E
Drysdale, D (Heriot's FP) 1923 F, W, I, E, 1924 F, W, I, E, 1925 F, W, I, E, 1926 F, W, I, E, 1927 F, W, I, E, A, 1928 F, W, I, E, 1929 F
Duff, P L (Glasgow Acads) 1936 W, I, 1938 W, I, E, 1939 W
Duffy, H (Jedforest) 1955 F
Duke, A (Royal HSFP) 1888 W, I, 1889 W, I, 1890 W, I
Dunbar, J P A (Leeds) 2005 F(R), It(R)
Duncan, A W (Edinburgh U) 1901 W, I, E, 1902 W, I, E
Duncan, D D (Oxford U) 1920 F, W, I, E
Duncan, M D F (W of Scotland) 1986 F, W, E, R, 1987 I, F, W, E, [F, Z, R, NZ], 1988 I, F, W, E, A, 1989 W
Duncan, M M (Fettesian-Lorettonians) 1888 W
Dunlop, J W (W of Scotland) 1875 E
Dunlop, Q (W of Scotland) 1971 E (2[1C])
Dykes, A S (Glasgow Acads) 1932 E
Dykes, J C (Glasgow Acads) 1922 F, E, 1924 I, 1925 F, W, I, 1926 F, W, I, E, 1927 F, W, I, E, A, 1928 F, I, 1929 F, W, I
Dykes, J M (Clydesdale, Glasgow HSFP) 1898 I, E, 1899 W, E, 1900 W, I, 1901 W, I, E, 1902 E

Edwards, D B (Heriot's FP) 1960 I, E, SA
Edwards, N G B (Harlequins, Northampton) 1992 E, I, F, W, A 1, 1994 W
Elgie, M K (London Scottish) 1954 NZ, I, E, W, 1955 F, W, I, E
Elliot, C (Langholm) 1958 E, 1959 F, 1960 F, 1963 E, 1964 F, NZ, W, I, E, 1965 F, W, I
Elliot, M (Hawick) 1895 W, 1896 E, 1897 I, E, 1898 I, E
Elliot, T (Gala) 1905 E
Elliot, T (Gala) 1955 W, I, E, 1956 F, W, I, E, 1957 F, W, I, E, 1958 W, A, I
Elliot, T G (Langholm) 1968 W, A, 1969 F, W, 1970 E
Elliot, W I D (Edinburgh Acads) 1947 F, W, E, A, 1948 F, W, I, E, 1949 F, W, I, E, 1950 F, W, I, E, 1951 F, W, I, E, SA, 1952 F, W, I, E, 1954 NZ, I, E, W
Ellis, D G (Currie) 1997 W, E, I, F
Emslie, W D (Royal HSFP) 1930 F, 1932 I
Eriksson, B R S (London Scottish) 1996 NZ 1, A, 1997 E
Evans, H L (Edinburgh U) 1885 I 1,2
Evans, T H (Glasgow Warriors) 2008 Arg 1
Ewart, E N (Glasgow Acads) 1879 E, 1880 I, E

Fahmy, E C (Abertillery) 1920 F, W, I, E
Fairley, I T (Kelso, Edinburgh) 1999 It, I (R), [Sp (R)]
Fasson, F H (London Scottish, Edinburgh Wands) 1900 W, 1901 W, I, 1902 W, E
Fell, A N (Edinburgh U) 1901 W, I, E, 1902 W, E, 1903 W, E
Ferguson, J H (Gala) 1928 W
Ferguson, W G (Royal HSFP) 1927 A, 1928 F, W, I, E
Fergusson, E A J (Oxford U) 1954 F, NZ, I, E, W
Finlay, A B (Edinburgh Acads) 1875 E
Finlay, J F (Edinburgh Acads) 1871 E, 1872 E, 1874 E, 1875 E
Finlay, N J (Edinburgh Acads) 1875 E, 1876 E, 1878 E, 1879 I, E, 1880 I, E, 1881 I, E
Finlay, R (Watsonians) 1948 E
Fisher, A T (Waterloo, Watsonians) 1947 I, E
Fisher, C D (Waterloo) 1975 NZ, A, 1976 W, E, I
Fisher, D (W of Scotland) 1893 I
Fisher, J P (Royal HSFP, London Scottish) 1963 E, 1964 F, NZ, W, I, E, 1965 F, W, I, E, SA, 1966 F, W, I, E, A, 1967 F, W, I, E, NZ, 1968 F, W, I, E
Fleming, C J N (Edinburgh Wands) 1896 I, E, 1897 I
Fleming, G R (Glasgow Acads) 1875 E, 1876 E
Fletcher, H N (Edinburgh U) 1904 E, 1905 W
Flett, A B (Edinburgh U) 1901 W, I, E, 1902 W, I
Forbes, J L (Watsonians) 1905 W, 1906 I, E
Ford, D St C (United Services, RN) 1930 I, E, 1931 E, 1932 W, I
Ford, J R (Gala) 1893 I
Ford, R W (Borders, Glasgow, Edinburgh) 2004 A3(R), 2006 W(R),E(R),PI(R),A(R), 2007 E(R),W(R),It(R),I1(R),F,I2,SA, [Pt(R),R,It,Arg], 2008 F,W,I,E,Arg 1,2
Forrest, J E (Glasgow Acads) 1932 SA, 1935 E, NZ
Forrest, J G S (Cambridge U) 1938 W, I, E
Forrest, W T (Hawick) 1903 W, I, E, 1904 W, I, E, 1905 W, I
Forsayth, H H (Oxford U) 1921 F, W, I, E, 1922 W, I, E
Forsyth, I W (Stewart's Coll FP) 1972 NZ, 1973 F, W, I, E, P
Forsyth, J (Edinburgh U) 1871 E
Foster, R A (Hawick) 1930 W, 1932 SA, I, E
Fox, J (Gala) 1952 F, W, I, E
Frame, J N M (Edinburgh U, Gala) 1967 NZ, 1968 F, W, I, E, 1969 W, I, E, SA, 1970 F, W, I, E, A, 1971 F, W, I, E (2[1C]), 1972 F, W, E, 1973 P (R)
France, C (Kelvinside Acads) 1903 I
Fraser, C F P (Glasgow U) 1888 W, 1889 W
Fraser, J W (Edinburgh Inst FP) 1881 E
Fraser, R (Cambridge U) 1911 F, W, I, E
French, J (Glasgow Acads) 1886 W, 1887 I, W, E
Frew, A (Edinburgh U) 1901 W, I, E
Frew, G M (Glasgow HSFP) 1906 SA, 1907 W, I, E, 1908 W, I, E, 1909 W, I, E, 1910 F, W, I, 1911 I, E
Friebe, J P (Glasgow HSFP) 1952 E
Fullarton, I A (Edinburgh) 2000 NZ 1(R),2, 2001 NZ (R), 2003 It 2(R), I 2(t), 2004 Sm(R), A1(R),2
Fulton, A K (Edinburgh U, Dollar Acads) 1952 F, 1954 F
Fyfe, K C (Cambridge U, Sale, London Scottish) 1933 W, E, 1934 E, 1935 W, I, E, NZ, 1936 W, E, 1939 I

Gallie, G H (Edinburgh Acads) 1939 W
Gallie, R A (Glasgow Acads) 1920 F, W, I, E, 1921 F, W, I, E
Gammell, W B B (Edinburgh Wands) 1977 I, F, W, 1978 W, E
Geddes, I C (London Scottish) 1906 SA, 1907 W, I, E, 1908 W, E
Geddes, K I (London Scottish) 1947 F, W, I, E
Gedge, H T S (Oxford U, London Scottish, Edinburgh Wands) 1894 W, I, E, 1896 E, 1899 W, E
Gedge, P M S (Edinburgh Wands) 1933 I
Gemmill, R (Glasgow HSFP) 1950 F, W, I, E, 1951 F, W, I
Gibson, W R (Royal HSFP) 1891 I, E, 1892 W, I, E, 1893 W, I, E, 1894 W, I, E, 1895 W, I, E
Gilbert-Smith, D S (London Scottish) 1952 E
Gilchrist, J (Glasgow Acads) 1925 F
Gill, A D (Gala) 1973 P, 1974 W, E, I, F
Gillespie, J I (Edinburgh Acads) 1899 E, 1900 W, E, 1901 W, I, E, 1902 W, I, 1904 I, E
Gillies, A C (Watsonians) 1924 W, I, E, 1925 F, W, E, 1926 F, W, 1927 F, W, I, E
Gilmour, H R (Heriot's FP) 1998 Fj
Gilray, C M (Oxford U, London Scottish) 1908 E, 1909 W, E, 1912 I
Glasgow, I C (Heriot's FP) 1997 F (R)
Glasgow, R J C (Dunfermline) 1962 F, W, I, E, 1963 I, E, 1964 I, E, 1965 W, I
Glen, W S (Edinburgh Wands) 1955 W
Gloag, L G (Cambridge U) 1949 F, W, I, E
Godman, P J (Edinburgh) 2005 R(R),Sm(R),NZ(R), 2006 R,PI(R),A(t&R), 2007 W,It, 2008 Arg 2
Goodfellow, J (Langholm) 1928 W, I, E
Goodhue, F W J (London Scottish) 1890 W, I, E, 1891 W, I, E, 1892 W, I, E
Gordon, R (Edinburgh Wands) 1951 W, 1952 F, W, I, E, 1953 W
Gordon, R E (Royal Artillery) 1913 F, W, I
Gordon, R J (London Scottish) 1982 A 1,2
Gore, A C (London Scottish) 1882 I
Gossman, B M (W of Scotland) 1980 W, 1983 F, W
Gossman, J S (W of Scotland) 1980 E (R)
Gowans, J J (Cambridge U, London Scottish) 1893 W, 1894 W, E, 1895 W, I, E, 1896 I, E
Gowland, G C (London Scottish) 1908 W, 1909 W, E, 1910 F, W, I, E
Gracie, A L (Harlequins) 1921 F, W, I, E, 1922 F, W, I, E, 1923 F, W, I, E, 1924 F
Graham, G (Newcastle) 1997 A (R), SA (R), 1998 I, F (R), W (R), 1999 F (R), Arg (R), R, [SA, U, Sm, NZ (R)], 2000 I (R), US, A, Sm, 2001 I (R), Tg (R), Arg (R), NZ (R), 2002 E (R), It (R), I (R), F (R), W (R)
Graham, I N (Edinburgh Acads) 1939 I, E
Graham, J (Kelso) 1926 I, E, 1927 F, W, I, E, A, 1928 F, W, I, E, 1930 I, E, 1932 SA, W
Graham, J H S (Edinburgh Acads) 1876 E, 1877 I, E, 1878 E, 1879 I, E, 1880 I, E, 1881 I, E
Grant, D (Hawick) 1965 F, E, SA, 1966 F, W, I, E, A, 1967 F, W, I, E, NZ, 1968 F
Grant, D M (East Midlands) 1911 W, I
Grant, M L (Harlequins) 1955 F, 1956 F, W, 1957 F
Grant, T O (Hawick) 1960 I, E, SA, 1964 F, NZ, W
Grant, W St C (Craigmount) 1873 E, 1874 E
Gray, C A (Nottingham) 1989 W, E, I, F, Fj, R, 1990 I, F, W, E, NZ 1,2, Arg, 1991 F, W, E, I, [J, I, WS, E, NZ]
Gray, D (W of Scotland) 1978 E, 1979 I, F, NZ, 1980 I, F, W, E, 1981 F
Gray, G L (Gala) 1935 NZ, 1937 W, I, E
Gray, S D (Borders) 2004 A3
Gray, T (Northampton, Heriot's FP) 1950 E, 1951 F, E
Greenlees, H D (Leicester) 1927 A, 1928 F, W, 1929 I, E, 1930 E
Greenlees, J R C (Cambridge U, Kelvinside Acads) 1900 I, 1902 W, I, E, 1903 W, I, E
Greenwood, J T (Dunfermline and Perthshire Acads) 1952 F, 1955 F, W, I, E, 1956 F, W, I, E, 1957 F, W, E, 1958 F, W, A, I, E, 1959 F, W, I
Greig, A (Glasgow HSFP) 1911 I
Greig, L L (Glasgow Acads, United Services) 1905 NZ, 1906 SA, 1907 W, 1908 W, I
Greig, R C (Glasgow Acads) 1893 W, 1897 I
Grieve, C F (Oxford U) 1935 W, 1936 E
Grieve, R M (Kelso) 1935 W, I, E, NZ, 1936 W, I, E
Grimes, S B (Watsonians, Newcastle) 1997 A (t+R), 1998 I (R), F (R), W (R), E (R), Fj, A 1, 2, 1999 W (R), E, It, I, F, Arg, R, [SA, U, Sm (R), NZ (R)], 2000 It, I, F (R), W, US, A, Sm (R), 2001 F (R), W (R), E (R), It, I (R), Tg, Arg, NZ, 2002 E, It, I, F (R), W (R), C, US, R, SA, Fj, 2003 I 1, F, W 1, E(R), It 1(R), W 2, I 2, [J,US,F,Fj,A], 2004 W,E,It,F, I,Sm,A1,J,A4,SA, 2005 F,I,It,W,E(R)
Gunn, A W (Royal HSFP) 1912 F, W, I, SA, 1913 F

Hall, A J A (Glasgow) 2002 US (R)
Hall, D W H (Edinburgh, Glasgow Warriors) 2003 W 2(R), 2005 R(R),Arg,Sm(R), NZ(R), 2006 F,E,I,It(R),SA 1(R),2,R,PI,A, 2007 E,W,It,I1,F(R), 2008 Arg 2(R)
Hamilton, A S (Headingley) 1914 W, 1920 F
Hamilton, C P (Newcastle) 2004 A2(R), 2005 R,Arg,Sm,NZ
Hamilton, H M (W of Scotland) 1874 E, 1875 E
Hamilton, J L (Leicester) 2006 R(R),A(R), 2007 E,W,It(R), I1(R),F(R),I2,SA, [R,NZ(R), It,Arg], 2008 F,W,I(R)
Hannah, R S M (W of Scotland) 1971 I
Harrower, P R (London Scottish) 1885 W
Hart, J G M (London Scottish) 1951 SA
Hart, T M (Glasgow U) 1930 W, I
Hart, W (Melrose) 1960 SA

Harvey, L (Greenock Wands) 1899 I
Hastie, A J (Melrose) 1961 W, I, E, 1964 I, E, 1965 E, SA, 1966 F, W, I, E, A, 1967 F, W, I, NZ, 1968 F, W
Hastie, I R (Kelso) 1955 F, 1958 F, E, 1959 F, W, I
Hastie, J D H (Melrose) 1938 W, I, E
Hastings, A G (Cambridge U, Watsonians, London Scottish) 1986 F, W, E, I, R, 1987 I, F, W, E, [F, Z, R, NZ], 1988 I, F, W, E, A, 1989 Fj, R, 1990 I, F, W, E, NZ 1,2, Arg, 1991 F, W, E, I, [J, I, WS, E, NZ], 1992 E, I, F, W, A 1, 1993 I, F, W, E, NZ, 1994 W, E, I, F, SA, 1995 C, I, F, W, E, R, [Iv, Tg, F, NZ]
Hastings, S (Watsonians) 1986 F, W, E, I, R, 1987 I, F, W, [R], 1988 I, F, W, A, 1989 W, E, I, F, Fj, R, 1990 I, F, W, E, NZ 1,2, Arg, 1991 F, W, E, I, [J, Z, I, WS, E, NZ], 1992 E, I, F, W, A 1,2, 1993 I, F, W, E, NZ, 1994 E, I, F, SA, 1995 W, E, R (R), [Tg, F, NZ], 1996 I, F, W, E, NZ 2, It, 1997 W, E (R)
Hay, B H (Boroughmuir) 1975 NZ, A, 1976 F, 1978 I, F, W, E, NZ, 1979 W, E, I, F, NZ, 1980 I, F, W, E, 1981 F, W, E, I, NZ 1,2
Hay, J A (Hawick) 1995 WS
Hay-Gordon, J R (Edinburgh Acads) 1875 E, 1877 I, E
Hegarty, C B (Hawick) 1978 I, F, W, E
Hegarty, J J (Hawick) 1951 F, 1953 F, W, I, E, 1955 F
Henderson, A R (Glasgow Warriors) 2001 I (R), Tg (R), NZ (R), 2002 It, I, US (R), 2003 SA 1,2, It 2, I 2, [US,F,Fj,A], 2004 W,E(t&R),It(R),F,I,Sm,A1,2,3,J,A4,SA, 2005 W(R),R, Arg, Sm,NZ, 2006 F,W,E,I,It,SA 1,2,PI,A, 2007 E,It(R),I1(R), F,I2,SA,[NZ, It(R),Arg(R)], 2008 F,W,I,It(R)
Henderson, B C (Edinburgh Wands) 1963 E, 1964 F, I, E, 1965 F, W, I, E, 1966 F, W, I, E
Henderson, F W (London Scottish) 1900 W, I
Henderson, I C (Edinburgh Acads) 1939 I, E, 1947 F, W, E, A, 1948 I, E
Henderson, J H (Oxford U, Richmond) 1953 F, W, I, E, 1954 F, NZ, I, E, W
Henderson, J M (Edinburgh Acads) 1933 W, E, I
Henderson, J Y M (Watsonians) 1911 E
Henderson, M M (Dunfermline) 1937 W, I, E
Henderson, N F (London Scottish) 1892 I
Henderson, R G (Newcastle Northern) 1924 I, E
Hendrie, K G P (Heriot's FP) 1924 F, W, I
Hendry, T L (Clydesdale) 1893 W, I, E, 1895 I
Henriksen, E H (Royal HSFP) 1953 I
Hepburn, D P (Woodford) 1947 A, 1948 F, W, I, E, 1949 F, W, I, E
Heron, G (Glasgow Acads) 1874 E, 1875 E
Hill, C C P (St Andrew's U) 1912 F, I
Hilton, D I W (Bath, Glasgow) 1995 C, I, F, W, E, R, [Tg, F, NZ], WS, 1996 I, F, W, E, NZ 1,2, A, It, 1997 W, A, SA, 1998 It, I (R), F, W, E, A 1,2, SA (R), 1999 W (R), E (R), It (R), I (R), F, R (R), [SA (R), U (R), Sp], 2000 It (R), F (R), W (R), 2002 SA(R)
Hines, N J (Edinburgh, Glasgow, Perpignan) 2000 NZ 2(R), 2002 C, US, R(R), SA(R), Fj(R), 2003 W 1(R), E, It 1, SA 1,2, It 2, W 2(R), I 2, [US,F(R),Fj,A], 2004 E(R),It(R), F(R),I(R),A3, J,A4,SA,2005 F(R),I(R),It(R),W(R),E, 2006 E(R),I,It,SA 1,2,R,PI, 2007 W(R),It,I1,F,I2,SA, [Pt,R,It,Arg], 2008 F,W,I,E,It
Hinshelwood, A J W (London Scottish) 1966 F, W, I, E, A, 1967 F, W, I, E, NZ, 1968 F, W, I, E, A, 1969 F, W, I, SA, 1970 F, W
Hinshelwood, B G (Worcester) 2002 C (R), R(R), SA(R), Fj, 2003 It 2, [J,US(R),Fj(R), A(R)], 2004 W,E,It,Sm,A1,2,J,A4,SA, 2005 It(R)
Hodge D W (Watsonians, Edinburgh) 1997 F (R), A, SA (t+R), 1998 A 2(R), SA, 1999 W, Arg, R, [Sp, Sm (R)], 2000 F (R), W, E, NZ 1,2, US (R), Sm (R), 2001 F (R), W, E, It, I (R), 2002 E, W (R), C, US
Hodgson, C G (London Scottish) 1968 I, E
Hogg, A (Edinburgh) 2004 W,E(R),It,F(R),I,Sm,A1,2,3,J,A4,SA, 2005 F,I,It,W,E,R,Arg, Sm,NZ, 2006 F,W,E,I,It,SA 1,2, 2007 E(R),W(R),It(R),I1(R),F,I2,SA(t&R), [Pt,R,It, Arg], 2008 W(R),I,E, It,Arg 1,2
Hogg, C D (Melrose) 1992 A 1,2, 1993 NZ (R), 1994 Arg 1,2
Hogg, C G (Boroughmuir) 1978 F (R), W (R)
Holmes, S D (London Scottish) 1998 It, I, F
Holms, W F (RIE Coll) 1886 W, E, 1887 I, E, 1889 W, I
Horsburgh, G B (London Scottish) 1937 W, I, E, 1938 W, I, E, 1939 W, I, E
Howie, D D (Kirkcaldy) 1912 F, W, I, E, SA, 1913 F, W
Howie, R A (Kirkcaldy) 1924 F, W, I, E, 1925 W, I, E
Hoyer-Millar, G C (Oxford U) 1953 I
Huggan, J L (London Scottish) 1914 E
Hume, J (Royal HSFP) 1912 F, 1920 F, 1921 F, W, I, E, 1922 F
Hume, J W G (Oxford U, Edinburgh Wands) 1928 I, 1930 F
Hunter, F (Edinburgh U) 1882 I
Hunter, I G (Selkirk) 1984 I (R), 1985 F (R), W, E
Hunter, J M (Cambridge U) 1947 F
Hunter, M D (Glasgow High) 1974 F
Hunter, W J (Hawick) 1964 F, NZ, W, 1967 F, W, I, E
Hutchison, W R (Glasgow HSFP) 1911 E
Hutton, A H M (Dunfermline) 1932 I
Hutton, J E (Harlequins) 1930 E, 1931 F

Inglis, H M (Edinburgh Acads) 1951 F, W, I, E, SA, 1952 W, I
Inglis, J M (Selkirk) 1952 E
Inglis, W M (Cambridge U, Royal Engineers) 1937 W, I, E, 1938 W, I, E
Innes, J R S (Aberdeen GSFP) 1939 W, I, E, 1947 A, 1948 F, W, I, E
Ireland, J C H (Glasgow HSFP) 1925 W, I, E, 1926 F, W, I, E, 1927 F, W, I, E
Irvine, A R (Heriot's FP) 1972 NZ, 1973 F, W, I, E, P, 1974 W, E, I, F, 1975 I, F, W, E, NZ, A, 1976 F, W, E, I, 1977 E, I, F, W, 1978 I, F, E, NZ, 1979 W, E, I, F, NZ, 1980 I, F, W, E, 1981 F, W, E, I, NZ 1,2, R, A, 1982 E, I, F, W, A 1,2
Irvine, D R (Edinburgh Acads) 1878 E, 1879 I, E
Irvine, R W (Edinburgh Acads) 1871 E, 1872 E, 1873 E, 1874 E, 1875 E, 1876 E, 1877 I, E, 1878 E, 1879 I, E, 1880 I, E
Irvine T W (Edinburgh Acads) 1885 I 1,2, 1886 W, I, E, 1887 I, W, E, 1888 W, I, 1889 I

Jackson, K L T (Oxford U) 1933 W, E, I, 1934 W
Jackson, T G H (Army) 1947 F, W, E, A, 1948 F, W, I, E, 1949 F, W, I, E
Jackson, W D (Hawick) 1964 I, 1965 E, SA, 1968 A, 1969 F, W, I, E
Jacobsen, A F (Edinburgh) 2002 C (R), US, 2003 I 2, 2004 It,F,I,A3,J,A4,SA, 2005 R, Arg(R),Sm, 2006 R(R),PI(R),A(R), 2007 E(R),W(R),It(t&R),I1(R), F(R),I2,SA(R), [Pt], 2008 F,W,I,E,It,Arg 1,2
Jamieson, J (W of Scotland) 1883 W, I, E, 1884 W, I, E, 1885 W, I 1,2
Jardine, I C (Stirling County) 1993 NZ, 1994 W, E (R), Arg 1,2, 1995 C, I, F, [Tg, F (t & R), NZ (R)], 1996 I, F, W, E, NZ 1,2, 1998 Fj
Jeffrey, J (Kelso) 1984 A, 1985 I, E, 1986 F, W, E, I, R, 1987 I, F, W, E, [F, Z, R], 1988 I, W, A, 1989 W, E, I, F, Fj, R, 1990 I, F, W, E, NZ 1,2, Arg, 1991 F, W, E, I, [J, I, WS, E, NZ]
Johnston, D I (Watsonians) 1979 NZ, 1980 I, F, W, E, 1981 R, A, 1982 E, I, F, W, A 1,2, 1983 I, F, W, NZ, 1984 W, E, I, F, R, 1986 F, W, E, I, R
Johnston, H H (Edinburgh Collegian FP) 1877 I, E
Johnston, J (Melrose) 1951 SA, 1952 F, W, I, E
Johnston, W C (Glasgow HSFP) 1922 F
Johnston, W G S (Cambridge U) 1935 W, I, 1937 W, I, E
Joiner, C A (Melrose, Leicester) 1994 Arg 1,2, 1995 C, I, F, W, E, R, [Iv, Tg, F, NZ], 1996 I, F, W, E, NZ 1, 1997 SA, 1998 It, I, A 2(R), 2000 NZ 1(R),2, US (R)
Jones, P M (Gloucester) 1992 W (R)
Junor, J E (Glasgow Acads) 1876 E, 1877 I, E, 1878 E, 1879 E, 1881 I

Keddie, R R (Watsonians) 1967 NZ
Keith, G J (Wasps) 1968 F, W
Keller, D H (London Scottish) 1949 F, W, I, E, 1950 F, W, I
Kellock, A D (Edinburgh, Glasgow Warriors) 2004 A3(t&R), 2005 R(R),Arg(R), Sm(R),NZ(R), 2006 F,W,E,It(R),SA 1(R),2,PI(R),A, 2007 E, 2008 Arg 1(t&R),2(R)
Kelly, R F (Watsonians) 1927 A, 1928 F, W, E
Kemp, J W Y (Glasgow HSFP) 1954 W, 1955 F, W, I, E, 1956 F, W, I, E, 1957 F, W, I, E, 1958 F, W, A, I, E, 1959 F, W, I, E, 1960 F, W, I, E, SA
Kennedy, A E (Watsonians) 1983 NZ, 1984 W, E, A
Kennedy, F (Stewart's Coll FP) 1920 F, W, I, E, 1921 E
Kennedy, N (W of Scotland) 1903 W, I, E
Ker, A B M (Kelso) 1988 W, E
Ker, H T (Glasgow Acads) 1887 I, W, E, 1888 I, 1889 W, 1890 I, E
Kerr, D S (Heriot's FP) 1923 F, W, 1924 F, 1926 I, E, 1927 W, I, E, 1928 I, E

Kerr, G (Leeds, Borders, Glasgow, Edinburgh) 2003 I 1(R), F(R), W 1(R), E(R), SA 1,2, W 2, [J(R),US,F], 2004 W(R),E(R),It(R),F(R),I(R),J,A4,SA, 2005 F,I,It,W,E,Arg,Sm(R), NZ, 2006 F,W,E,I,It,SA 1,2,R,PI,A, 2007 E,W,It,I1,F,SA, [Pt(R),R,NZ(R),It,Arg], 2008 F(R),W(R),I(R)

Kerr, G C (Old Dunelmians, Edinburgh Wands) 1898 I, E, 1899 I, W, E, 1900 W, I, E

Kerr, J M (Heriot's FP) 1935 NZ, 1936 I, E, 1937 W, I

Kerr, R C (Glasgow) 2002 C, US, 2003 W 2

Kerr, W (London Scottish) 1953 E

Kidston, D W (Glasgow Acads) 1883 W, E

Kidston, W H (W of Scotland) 1874 E

Kilgour, I J (RMC Sandhurst) 1921 F

King, J H F (Selkirk) 1953 F, W, E, 1954 E

Kininmonth, P W (Oxford U, Richmond) 1949 F, W, I, E, 1950 F, W, I, E, 1951 F, W, I, E, SA, 1952 F, W, I, 1954 F, NZ, I, E, W

Kinnear, R M (Heriot's FP) 1926 F, W, I

Knox, J (Kelvinside Acads) 1903 W, I, E

Kyle, W E (Hawick) 1902 W, I, E, 1903 W, I, E, 1904 W, I, E, 1905 W, I, E, NZ, 1906 W, I, E, 1908 E, 1909 W, I, E, 1910 W

Laidlaw, A S (Hawick) 1897 I

Laidlaw, F A L (Melrose) 1965 F, W, I, E, SA, 1966 F, W, I, E, A, 1967 F, W, I, E, NZ, 1968 F, W, I, A, 1969 F, W, I, E, SA, 1970 F, W, I, E, A, 1971 F, W, I

Laidlaw, R J (Jedforest) 1980 I, F, W, E, 1981 F, W, E, I, NZ 1,2, R, A, 1982 E, I, F, W, A 1,2, 1983 I, F, W, E, NZ, 1984 W, E, I, F, R, A, 1985 I, F, 1986 F, W, E, I, R, 1987 I, F, W, E, [F, R, NZ], 1988 I, F, W, E

Laing, A D (Royal HSFP) 1914 W, I, E, 1920 F, W, I, 1921 F

Lambie, I K (Watsonians) 1978 NZ (R), 1979 W, E, NZ

Lambie, L B (Glasgow HSFP) 1934 W, I, E, 1935 W, I, E, NZ

Lamond, G A W (Kelvinside Acads) 1899 W, E, 1905 E

Lamont, R P (Glasgow, Sale) 2005 W,E,R,Arg,Sm, 2007 E(R),I1(R),F(R),I2,SA, [Pt,R,It,Arg], 2008 F,I,E

Lamont, S F (Glasgow, Northampton) 2004 Sm,A1,2,3,J,A4,SA, 2005 F,I,It,W,E,R, Arg,Sm,NZ, 2006 F,W,E,I,It,SA1,R,PI,A, 2007 E,W,It,I1,F,I2, [Pt,R,It,Arg]

Laney, B J (Edinburgh) 2001 NZ, 2002 E, It, I, F, W, C, US, R, SA, Fj, 2003 I 1, F, SA 2(R), It 2(R), W 2, 2004 W,E,It,I(R)

Lang, D (Paisley) 1876 E, 1877 I

Langrish, R W (London Scottish) 1930 F, 1931 F, W, I

Lauder, W (Neath) 1969 I, E, SA, 1970 F, W, I, A, 1973 F, 1974 W, E, I, F, 1975 I, F, NZ, A, 1976 F, 1977 E

Laughland, I H P (London Scottish) 1959 F, 1960 F, W, I, E, 1961 SA, W, I, E, 1962 F, W, I, E, 1963 F, W, I, 1964 F, NZ, W, I, E, 1965 F, W, I, E, SA, 1966 F, W, I, E, 1967 E

Lawrie, J R (Melrose) 1922 F, W, I, E, 1923 F, W, I, E, 1924 W, I, E

Lawrie, K G (Gala) 1980 F (R), W, E

Lawson, A J M (Edinburgh Wands, London Scottish) 1972 F (R), E, 1973 F, 1974 W, E, 1976 E, I, 1977 E, 1978 NZ, 1979 W, E, I, F, NZ, 1980 W (R)

Lawson, R G M (Gloucester) 2006 A(R), 2007 E(R),W(R), It(R),I1(R),F,SA(R), [Pt(R), NZ(R)], 2008 E(R),Arg 1(R),2(R)

Lawson, S (Glasgow, Sale) 2005 R,Arg(R),Sm,NZ, 2006 F(R),W,I(R),It,SA 1,2(R),R(R), 2007 [Pt,R(R),NZ,Arg(R)], 2008 It(R)

Lawther, T H B (Old Millhillians) 1932 SA, W

Ledingham, G A (Aberdeen GSFP) 1913 F

Lee, D J (London Scottish, Edinburgh) 1998 I (R), F, W, E, Fj, A 1,2, SA, 2001 Arg, 2004 It(R),F,I(R)

Lees, J B (Gala) 1947 I, A, 1948 F, W, E

Leggatt, H T O (Watsonians) 1891 W, I, E, 1892 W, I, 1893 W, E, 1894 I, E

Lely, W G (Cambridge U, London Scottish) 1909 I

Leslie, D G (Dundee HSFP, W of Scotland, Gala) 1975 I, F, W, E, NZ, A, 1976 F, W, E, I, 1978 NZ, 1980 E, 1981 W, E, I, NZ 1,2, R, A, 1982 E, 1983 I, F, W, E, 1984 W, E, I, F, R, 1985 F, W, E

Leslie, J A (Glasgow, Northampton) 1998 SA, 1999 W, E, It, I, F, [SA], 2000 It, F, W, US, A, Sm, 2001 F, W, E, It, I, Tg, Arg, NZ, 2002 F, W

Leslie, M D (Glasgow, Edinburgh) 1998 SA (R), 1999 W, E, It, I, F, R, [SA, U, Sm, NZ], 2000 It, I, F, W, E, NZ 1,2, 2001 F, W, E, It, 2002 It (R), I (R), F, W, R, SA, Fj(R), 2003 I 1, F, SA 1(R), 2 (R), It 2(R), W 2, [J(R),US(R)]

Liddell, E H (Edinburgh U) 1922 F, W, I, 1923 F, W, I, E

Lind, H (Dunfermline) 1928 I, 1931 F, W, I, E, 1932 SA, W, E, 1933 W, E, I, 1934 W, I, E, 1935 I, 1936 E

Lindsay, A B (London Hospital) 1910 I, 1911 I

Lindsay, G C (London Scottish) 1884 W, 1885 I 1, 1887 W, E

Lindsay-Watson, R H (Hawick) 1909 I

Lineen, S R P (Boroughmuir) 1989 W, E, I, F, Fj, R, 1990 I, F, W, E, NZ 1,2, Arg, 1991 F, W, E, I, R, [J, Z, I, E, NZ], 1992 E, I, F, W, A 1,2

Little, A W (Hawick) 1905 W

Logan, K M (Stirling County, Wasps) 1992 A 2, 1993 E (R), NZ (t), 1994 W, E, I, F, Arg 1,2, SA, 1995 C, I, F, W, E, R, [Iv, Tg, F, NZ], WS, 1996 W (R), NZ 1,2, A, It, 1997 W, E, I, F, A, 1998 I, F, SA (R), 1999 W, E, It, I, F, Arg, R, [SA, U, Sm, NZ], 2000 It, I, F, Sm, 2001 F, W, E, It, 2002 I (R), F (R), W, 2003 I 1, F, W 1, E, It 1, SA 1,2, It 2, I 2, [J,US(R),F,Fj,A]

Logan, W R (Edinburgh U, Edinburgh Wands) 1931 E, 1932 SA, W, I, 1933 W, E, I, 1934 W, I, E, 1935 W, I, E, NZ, 1936 W, I, E, 1937 W, I, E

Longstaff, S L (Dundee HSFP, Glasgow) 1998 F (R), W, E, Fj, A 1,2 1999 It (R), I (R), Arg (R), R, [U (R), Sp], 2000 It, I, NZ 1

Lorraine, H D B (Oxford U) 1933 W, E, I

Loudoun-Shand, E G (Oxford U) 1913 E

Lowe, J D (Heriot's FP) 1934 W

Lumsden, I J M (Bath, Watsonians) 1947 F, W, A, 1949 F, W, I, E

Lyall, G G (Gala) 1947 A, 1948 F, W, I, E

Lyall, W J C (Edinburgh Acads) 1871 E

Mabon, J T (Jedforest) 1898 I, E, 1899 I, 1900 I

Macarthur, J P (Waterloo) 1932 E

MacCallum, J C (Watsonians) 1905 E, NZ, 1906 W, I, E, SA, 1907 W, I, E, 1908 W, I, E, 1909 W, I, E, 1910 F, W, I, E, 1911 F, I, E, 1912 F, W, I, E

McClung, T (Edinburgh Acads) 1956 I, E, 1957 W, I, E, 1959 F, W, I, 1960 W

McClure, G B (W of Scotland) 1873 E

McClure, J H (W of Scotland) 1872 E

McCowan, D (W of Scotland) 1880 I, E, 1881 I, E, 1882 I, E, 1883 I, E, 1884 I, E

McCowat, R H (Glasgow Acads) 1905 I

McCrae, I G (Gordonians) 1967 E, 1968 I, 1969 F (R), W, 1972 F, NZ

McCrow, J W S (Edinburgh Acads) 1921 I

Macdonald, A E D (Heriot's FP) 1993 NZ

McDonald, C (Jedforest) 1947 A

Macdonald, D C (Edinburgh U) 1953 F, W, 1958 I, E

Macdonald, D S M (Oxford U, London Scottish, W of Scotland) 1977 E, I, F, W, 1978 I, W, E

Macdonald, J D (London Scottish, Army) 1966 F, W, I, E, 1967 F, W, I, E

Macdonald, J M (Edinburgh Wands) 1911 W

Macdonald, J S (Edinburgh U) 1903 E, 1904 W, I, E, 1905 W

Macdonald, K R (Stewart's Coll FP) 1956 F, W, I, 1957 W, I, E

Macdonald, R (Edinburgh U) 1950 F, W, I, E

McDonald, W A (Glasgow U) 1889 W, 1892 I, E

Macdonald, W G (London Scottish) 1969 I (R)

MacDougall, B (Borders) 2006 W, SA2(R)

Macdougall, J B (Greenock Wands, Wakefield) 1913 F, 1914 I, 1921 F, I, E

McEwan, M C (Edinburgh Acads) 1886 E, 1887 I, W, E, 1888 W, I, 1889 W, I, 1890 W, I, E, 1891 W, I, E, 1892 E

MacEwan, N A (Gala, Highland) 1971 F, W, I, E (2[1C]), 1972 F, W, E, NZ, 1973 F, W, I, E, P, 1974 W, E, I, F, 1975 W, E

McEwan, W M C (Edinburgh Acads) 1894 W, E, 1895 W, E, 1896 W, I, E, 1897 I, E, 1898 I, E, 1899 I, W, E, 1900 W, E

MacEwen, R K G (Cambridge U, London Scottish) 1954 F, NZ, I, W, 1956 F, W, I, E, 1957 F, W, I, E, 1958 W

Macfadyen, D J H (Glasgow) 2002 C (R), US, 2004 Sm,A1,2,3,J,A4,SA, 2006 SA 1,2(R)

Macfarlan, D J (London Scottish) 1883 W, 1884 W, I, E, 1886 W, I, 1887 I, 1888 I

McFarlane, J L H (Edinburgh U) 1871 E, 1872 E, 1873 E

McGaughey, S K (Hawick) 1984 R

McGeechan, I R (Headingley) 1972 NZ, 1973 F, W, I, E, P, 1974 W, E, I, F, 1975 I, F, W, E, NZ, A, 1976 F, W, E, I, 1977 E, I, F, W, 1978 I, F, W, NZ, 1979 W, E, I, F

McGlashan, T P L (Royal HSFP) 1947 F, I, E, 1954 F, NZ, I, E, W

MacGregor, D G (Watsonians, Pontypridd) 1907 W, I, E

MacGregor, G (Cambridge U) 1890 W, I, E, 1891 W, I, E, 1893 W, I, E, 1894 W, I, E, 1896 E
MacGregor, I A A (Hillhead HSFP, Llanelli) 1955 I, E, 1956 F, W, I, E, 1957 F, W, I
MacGregor, J R (Edinburgh U) 1909 I
McGuinness, G M (W of Scotland) 1982 A 1,2, 1983 I, 1985 I, F, W, E
McHarg, A F (W of Scotland, London Scottish) 1968 I, E, A, 1969 F, W, I, E, 1971 F, W, I, E (2[1C]), 1972 F, E, NZ, 1973 F, W, I, E, P, 1974 W, E, I, F, 1975 I, F, W, E, NZ, A, 1976 F, W, E, I, 1977 E, I, F, W, 1978 I, F, W, NZ, 1979 W, E
McIlwham, G R (Glasgow Hawks, Glasgow, Bordeaux-Bègles) 1998 Fj, A 2(R), 2000 E (R), NZ 2(R), US (R), A (R), Sm (R), 2001 F (R), W (R), E (R), It (R), 2003 SA 2(R), It 2(R), W 2(R), I 2, [A(R)]
McIndoe, F (Glasgow Acads) 1886 W, I
MacIntyre, I (Edinburgh Wands) 1890 W, I, E, 1891 W, I, E
McIvor, D J (Edinburgh Acads) 1992 E, I, F, W, 1993 NZ, 1994 SA
Mackay, E B (Glasgow Acads) 1920 W, 1922 E
McKeating, E (Heriot's FP) 1957 F, W, 1961 SA, W, I, E
McKelvey, G (Watsonians) 1997 A
McKendrick, J G (W of Scotland) 1889 I
Mackenzie, A D G (Selkirk) 1984 A
Mackenzie, C J G (United Services) 1921 E
Mackenzie, D D (Edinburgh U) 1947 W, I, E, 1948 F, W, I
Mackenzie, D K A (Edinburgh Wands) 1939 I, E
Mackenzie, J M (Edinburgh U) 1905 NZ, 1909 W, I, E, 1910 W, I, E, 1911 W, I
McKenzie, K D (Stirling County) 1994 Arg 1,2, 1995 R, [Iv], 1996 I, F, W, E, NZ 1,2, A, It, 1998 A 1(R), 2
Mackenzie, R C (Glasgow Acads) 1877 I, E, 1881 I, E
Mackie, G Y (Highland) 1975 A, 1976 F, W, 1978 F
MacKinnon, A (London Scottish) 1898 I, E, 1899 I, W, E, 1900 E
Mackintosh, C E W C (London Scottish) 1924 F
Mackintosh, H S (Glasgow U, W of Scotland) 1929 F, W, I, E, 1930 F, W, I, E, 1931 F, W, I, E, 1932 SA, W, I, E
MacLachlan, L P (Oxford U, London Scottish) 1954 NZ, I, E, W
Maclagan, W E (Edinburgh Acads) 1878 E, 1879 I, E, 1880 I, E, 1881 I, E, 1882 I, E, 1883 W, I, E, 1884 W, I, E, 1885 W, I 1,2, 1887 I, W, E, 1888 W, I, 1890 W, I, E
McLaren, A (Durham County) 1931 F
McLaren, E (London Scottish, Royal HSFP) 1923 F, W, I, E, 1924 F
McLaren, J G (Bourgoin, Glasgow, Bordeaux-Bègles, Castres) 1999 Arg, R, [Sp, Sm], 2000 It (R), F, E, NZ 1, 2001 F, W, E (R), I, Tg, Arg, NZ, 2002 E, It, I, F, W, 2003 W 1, E, It 1, SA 1(R), It 2, I 2(R), [J,F(R),Fj(t&R),A(R)]
McLauchlan, J (Jordanhill) 1969 E, SA, 1970 F, W, 1971 F, W, I, E (2[1C]), 1972 F, W, E, NZ, 1973 F, W, I, E, P, 1974 W, E, I, F, 1975 I, F, W, E, NZ, A, 1976 F, W, E, I, 1977 W, 1978 I, F, W, E, NZ, 1979 W, E, I, F, NZ
McLean, D I (Royal HSFP) 1947 I, E
Maclennan, W D (Watsonians) 1947 F, I
MacLeod, D A (Glasgow U) 1886 I, E
MacLeod, G (Edinburgh Acads) 1878 E, 1882 I
McLeod, H F (Hawick) 1954 F, NZ, I, E, W, 1955 F, W, I, E, 1956 F, W, I, E, 1957 F, W, I, E, 1958 F, W, A, I, E, 1959 F, W, I, E, 1960 F, W, I, E, SA, 1961 F, SA, W, I, E, 1962 F, W, I, E
MacLeod, K G (Cambridge U) 1905 NZ, 1906 W, I, E, SA,1907 W, I, E, 1908 I, E
MacLeod, L M (Cambridge U) 1904 W, I, E, 1905 W, I, NZ
MacLeod, S J (Borders, Llanelli Scarlets) 2004 A3,J(t&R),A4(R) ,SA(R), 2006 F(R),
W(R),E,SA2(R), 2007 I2(R), [Pt(R),R(R),NZ,It(R),Arg(R)], 2008 F(R),W(R),I,E,It,Arg 1,2
Macleod, W M (Fettesian-Lorettonians, Edinburgh Wands) 1886 W, I
McMillan, K H D (Sale) 1953 F, W, I, E
MacMillan, R G (London Scottish) 1887 W, I, E, 1890 W, I, E, 1891 W, E, 1892 W, I, E, 1893 W, E, 1894 W, I, E, 1895 W, I, E, 1897 I, E
MacMyn, D J (Cambridge U, London Scottish) 1925 F, W, I, E, 1926 F, W, I, E, 1927 E, A, 1928 F
McNeil, A S B (Watsonians) 1935 I
McPartlin, J J (Harlequins, Oxford U) 1960 F, W, 1962 F, W, I, E
Macphail, J A R (Edinburgh Acads) 1949 E, 1951 SA
Macpherson, D G (London Hospital) 1910 I, E
Macpherson, G P S (Oxford U, Edinburgh Acads) 1922 F, W, I, E, 1924 W, E, 1925 F, W, E, 1927 F, W, I, E, 1928 F, W, E, 1929 I, E, 1930 F, W, I, E, 1931 W, E, 1932 SA, E
Macpherson, N C (Newport) 1920 W, I, E, 1921 F, E, 1923 I, E
McQueen, S B (Waterloo) 1923 F, W, I, E
Macrae, D J (St Andrew's U) 1937 W, I, E, 1938 W, I, E, 1939 W, I, E
Madsen, D F (Gosforth) 1974 W, E, I, F, 1975 I, F, W, E, 1976 F, 1977 E, I, F, W, 1978 I
Mair, N G R (Edinburgh U) 1951 F, W, I, E
Maitland, G (Edinburgh Inst FP) 1885 W, I 2
Maitland, R (Edinburgh Inst FP) 1881 E, 1882 I, E, 1884 W, 1885 W
Maitland, R P (Royal Artillery) 1872 E
Malcolm, A G (Glasgow U) 1888 I
Manson, J J (Dundee HSFP) 1995 E (R)
Marsh, J (Edinburgh Inst FP) 1889 W, I
Marshall, A (Edinburgh Acads) 1875 E
Marshall, G R (Selkirk) 1988 A (R), 1989 Fj, 1990 Arg, 1991 [Z]
Marshall, J C (London Scottish) 1954 F, NZ, I, E, W
Marshall, K W (Edinburgh Acads) 1934 W, I, E, 1935 W, I, E, 1936 W, 1937 E
Marshall, T R (Edinburgh Acads) 1871 E, 1872 E, 1873 E, 1874 E
Marshall, W (Edinburgh Acads) 1872 E
Martin, H (Edinburgh Acads, Oxford U) 1908 W, I, E, 1909 W, E
Masters, W H (Edinburgh Inst FP) 1879 I, 1880 I, E
Mather, C G (Edinburgh, Glasgow) 1999 R (R), [Sp, Sm (R)], 2000 F (t), 2003 [F,Fj,A], 2004 W,E,F
Maxwell, F T (Royal Engineers) 1872 E
Maxwell, G H H P (Edinburgh Acads, RAF, London Scottish) 1913 I, E, 1914 W, I, E, 1920 W, E, 1921 F, W, I, E, 1922 F, E
Maxwell, J M (Langholm) 1957 I
Mayer, M J M (Watsonians, Edinburgh) 1998 SA, 1999 [SA (R), U, Sp, Sm, NZ], 2000 It, I
Mein, J (Edinburgh Acads) 1871 E, 1872 E, 1873 E, 1874 E, 1875 E
Melville, C L (Army) 1937 W, I, E
Menzies, H F (W of Scotland) 1893 W, I, 1894 W, E
Metcalfe, G H (Glasgow Hawks, Glasgow) 1998 A 1,2, 1999 W, E, It, I, F, Arg, R, [SA, U, Sm, NZ], 2000 It, I, F, W, E, 2001 I, Tg, 2002 E, It, I, F, W (R), C, US, 2003 I 1, F, W 1, E, It 1, SA 1,2, W 2, I 2, [US,F,Fj,A]
Metcalfe, R (Northampton, Edinburgh) 2000 E, NZ 1,2, US (R), A (R), Sm, 2001 F, W, E
Methuen, A (London Scottish) 1889 W, I
Michie, E J S (Aberdeen U, Aberdeen GSFP) 1954 F, NZ, I, E, 1955 W, I, E, 1956 F, W, I, E, 1957 F, W, I, E
Millar, J N (W of Scotland) 1892 W, I, E, 1893 W, 1895 I, E
Millar, R K (London Scottish) 1924 I
Millican, J G (Edinburgh U) 1973 W, I, E
Milne, C J B (Fettesian-Lorettonians, W of Scotland) 1886 W, I, E
Milne, D F (Heriot's FP) 1991 [J(R)]
Milne, I G (Heriot's FP, Harlequins) 1979 I, F, NZ, 1980 I, F, 1981 NZ 1,2, R, A, 1982 E, I, F, W, A 1,2, 1983 I, F, W, E, NZ, 1984 W, E, I, F, A, 1985 F, W, E, 1986 F, W, E, I, R, 1987 I, F, W, E, [F, Z, NZ], 1988 A, 1989 W, 1990 NZ 1,2
Milne, K S (Heriot's FP) 1989 W, E, I, F, Fj, R, 1990 I, F, W, E, NZ 2, Arg, 1991 F, W (R), E, [Z], 1992 E, I, F, W, A 1, 1993 I, F, W, E, NZ, 1994 W, E, I, F, SA, 1995 C, I, F, W, E, [Tg, F, NZ]
Milne, W M (Glasgow Acads) 1904 I, E, 1905 W, I
Milroy, E (Watsonians) 1910 W, 1911 E, 1912 W, I, E, SA, 1913 F, W, I, E, 1914 I, E
Mitchell, G W E (Edinburgh Wands) 1967 NZ, 1968 F, W
Mitchell, J G (W of Scotland) 1885 W, I 1,2
Moffat, J S D (Edinburgh, Borders) 2002 R, SA, Fj(R), 2004 A3
Moir, C C (Northampton) 2000 W, E, NZ 1
Moncreiff, F J (Edinburgh Acads) 1871 E, 1872 E, 1873 E
Monteith, H G (Cambridge U, London Scottish) 1905 E, 1906 W, I, E, SA, 1907 W, I, 1908 E
Monypenny, D B (London Scottish) 1899 I, W, E
Moodie, A R (St Andrew's U) 1909 E, 1910 F, 1911 F
Moore, A (Edinburgh Acads) 1990 NZ 2, Arg, 1991 F, W, E
Morgan, D W (Stewart's-Melville FP) 1973 W, I, E, P, 1974 I, F, 1975 I, F, W, E, NZ, A, 1976 F, W, 1977 I, F, W, 1978 I, F, W, E

Morrison, G A (Glasgow Warriors) 2004 A1(R),2(R),3,J(R), A4(R),SA(R), 2008 W(R),
E,It,Arg 1,2
Morrison, I R (London Scottish) 1993 I, F, W, E, 1994 W, SA, 1995 C, I, F, W, E, R, [Tg, F, NZ]
Morrison, M C (Royal HSFP) 1896 W, I, E, 1897 I, E, 1898 I, E, 1899 I, W, E, 1900 W, E, 1901 W, I, E, 1902 W, I, E, 1903 W, I, 1904 W, I, E
Morrison, R H (Edinburgh U) 1886 W, I, E
Morrison, W H (Edinburgh Acads) 1900 W
Morton, D S (W of Scotland) 1887 I, W, E, 1888 W, I, 1889 W, I, 1890 I, E
Mowat, J G (Glasgow Acads) 1883 W, E
Mower, A L (Newcastle) 2001 Tg, Arg, NZ, 2002 It, 2003 I 1, F, W 1, E, It 1, SA 1,2, W 2, I 2
Muir, D E (Heriot's FP) 1950 F, W, I, E, 1952 W, I, E
Munnoch, N M (Watsonians) 1952 F, W, I
Munro, D S (Glasgow High Kelvinside) 1994 W, E, I, F, Arg 1,2, 1997 W (R)
Munro, P (Oxford U, London Scottish) 1905 W, I, E, NZ, 1906 W, I, E, SA, 1907 I, E, 1911 F, W, I
Munro, R (St Andrew's U) 1871 E
Munro, S (Ayr, W of Scotland) 1980 I, F, 1981 F, W, E, I, NZ 1,2, R, 1984 W
Munro, W H (Glasgow HSFP) 1947 I, E
Murdoch, W C W (Hillhead HSFP) 1935 E, NZ, 1936 W, I, 1939 E, 1948 F, W, I, E
Murray, C A (Hawick, Edinburgh) 1998 E (R), Fj, A 1,2, SA, 1999 W, E, It, I, F, Arg, [SA, U, Sp, Sm, NZ], 2000 NZ 2, US, A, Sm, 2001 F, W, E, It (R), Tg, Arg
Murray, E A (Glasgow, Northampton) 2005 R(R), 2006 R,PI,A, 2007 E,W,It,I1,F,I2,SA, [Pt,R,It,Arg], 2008 F,W,I,E,It,Arg 1,2
Murray, G M (Glasgow Acads) 1921 I, 1926 W
Murray, H M (Glasgow U) 1936 W, I
Murray, K T (Hawick) 1985 I, F, W
Murray, R O (Cambridge U) 1935 W, E
Murray, S (Bedford, Saracens, Edinburgh) 1997 A, SA, 1998 It, Fj, A 1,2, SA, 1999 W, E, It, I, F, Arg, R, [SA, U, Sm, NZ], 2000 It, I, F, W, E, NZ 1, US, A, Sm, 2001 F, W, E, It, I, Tg, Arg, NZ, 2002 E, It, I, F, W, R, SA, 2003 I 1, F, W 1, E, It 1, SA 1,2, It 2, W 2, [J,F,A(R)], 2004 W,E,It,F,I,Sm,A1,2, 2005 F,I,It,W,E,R,Arg,Sm,NZ, 2006 F,W,I,It,SA1, R,PI,A, 2007 E(t&R),W,It,I1,F,SA(R),[Pt,NZ]
Murray, W A K (London Scottish) 1920 F, I, 1921 F
Mustchin, M L (Edinburgh) 2008 Arg 1,2

Napier, H M (W of Scotland) 1877 I, E, 1878 E, 1879 I, E
Neill, J B (Edinburgh Acads) 1963 E, 1964 F, NZ, W, I, E, 1965 F
Neill, R M (Edinburgh Acads) 1901 E, 1902 I
Neilson, G T (W of Scotland) 1891 W, I, E, 1892 W, E, 1893 W, 1894 W, I, 1895 W, I, E, 1896 W, I, E
Neilson, J A (Glasgow Acads) 1878 E, 1879 E
Neilson, R T (W of Scotland) 1898 I, E, 1899 I, W, 1900 I, E
Neilson, T (W of Scotland) 1874 E
Neilson, W (Merchiston Castle School, Cambridge U, London Scottish) 1891 W, E, 1892 W, I, E, 1893 I, E, 1894 E, 1895 W, I, E, 1896 I, 1897 I, E
Neilson, W G (Merchistonians) 1894 E
Nelson, J B (Glasgow Acads) 1925 F, W, I, E, 1926 F, W, I, E, 1927 F, W, I, E, 1928 I, E, 1929 F, W, I, E, 1930 F, W, I, E, 1931 F, W, I
Nelson, T A (Oxford U) 1898 E
Nichol, J A (Royal HSFP) 1955 W, I, E
Nichol, S A (Selkirk) 1994 Arg 2(R)
Nicol, A D (Dundee HSFP, Bath, Glasgow) 1992 E, I, F, W, A 1,2, 1993 NZ, 1994 W, 1997 A, SA, 2000 I (R), F, W, E, NZ 1,2, 2001 F, W, E, I (R), Tg, Arg, NZ
Nimmo, C S (Watsonians) 1920 E

Ogilvy, C (Hawick) 1911 I, E, 1912 I
Oliver, G H (Hawick) 1987 [Z], 1990 NZ 2(R), 1991 [Z]
Oliver, G K (Gala) 1970 A
Orr, C E (W of Scotland) 1887 I, E, W, 1888 W, I, 1889 W, I, 1890 W, I, E, 1891 W, I, E, 1892 W, I, E
Orr, H J (London Scottish) 1903 W, I, E, 1904 W, I
Orr, J E (W of Scotland) 1889 I, 1890 W, I, E, 1891 W, I, E, 1892 W, I, E, 1893 I, E
Orr, J H (Edinburgh City Police) 1947 F, W
Osler, F L (Edinburgh U) 1911 F, W

Park, J (Royal HSFP) 1934 W
Parks, D A (Glasgow Warriors) 2004 W(R),E(R),F(R),I, Sm (t&R),A1,2,3,J,A4,SA, 2005 F,I,It, W,R,Arg,Sm,NZ, 2006 F,W,E,I,It(R),SA1,PI,A, 2007 E,I1,F,I2(R),SA(R), [Pt,R,NZ(R),It,Arg], 2008 F,W,I(R),E(R),It,Arg 1,2(R)
Paterson, C D (Edinburgh, Gloucester) 1999 [Sp], 2000 F, W, E, NZ 1,2, US, A, Sm, 2001 F, W, E, It, I, NZ, 2002 E, It, I, F, W, C, US, R, SA, Fj, 2003 I 1, F, W 1, E, It 1, SA 1,2, It 2(R), W 2(R), I 2, [J,US,F,Fj,A], 2004 W,E,It,F,I,Sm,A3,J, A4,SA,2005 F,I,It,W,E, R,Arg,Sm,NZ, 2006 F,W,E,I,It,SA 1,2,R(R),PI,A, 2007 E,W,It,I1,F,I2,SA,[Pt(R),R,NZ, It,Arg], 2008 F(R),W,I,E,It,Arg 1,2
Paterson, D S (Gala) 1969 SA, 1970 I, E, A, 1971 F, W, I, E (2[1C]), 1972 W
Paterson, G Q (Edinburgh Acads) 1876 E
Paterson, J R (Birkenhead Park) 1925 F, W, I, E, 1926 F, W, I, E, 1927 F, W, I, E, A, 1928 F, W, I, E, 1929 F, W, I, E
Patterson, D (Hawick) 1896 W
Patterson, D W (West Hartlepool) 1994 SA, 1995 [Tg]
Pattullo, G L (Panmure) 1920 F, W, I, E
Paxton, I A M (Selkirk) 1981 NZ 1,2, R, A, 1982 E, I, F, W, A 1,2, 1983 I, E, NZ, 1984 W, E, I, F, 1985 I (R), F, W, E, 1986 W, E, I, R, 1987 I, F, W, E, [F, Z, R, NZ], 1988 I, E, A
Paxton, R E (Kelso) 1982 I, A 2(R)
Pearson, J (Watsonians) 1909 I, E, 1910 F, W, I, E, 1911 F, 1912 F, W, SA, 1913 I, E
Pender, I M (London Scottish) 1914 E
Pender, N E K (Hawick) 1977 I, 1978 F, W, E
Penman, W M (RAF) 1939 I
Peterkin, W A (Edinburgh U) 1881 E, 1883 I, 1884 W, I, E, 1885 W, I 1,2
Peters, E W (Bath) 1995 C, I, F, W, E, R, [Tg, F, NZ], 1996 I, F, W, E, NZ 1,2, A, It, 1997 A, SA, 1998 W, E, Fj, A 1,2, SA, 1999 W, E, It, I
Petrie, A G (Royal HSFP) 1873 E, 1874 E, 1875 E, 1876 E, 1877 I, E, 1878 E, 1879 I, E, 1880 I, E
Petrie, J M (Glasgow) 2000 NZ 2, US, A, Sm, 2001 F, W, It (R), I (R), Tg, Arg, 2002 F (t), W (R), C, R(R), Fj, 2003 F(t+R), W 1(R), SA 1(R), 2 (R), It 2, W 2, I 2(R), [J,US, F(t&R),A(R)], 2004 It(R),I(R),Sm(R),A1(R),2(t&R),3(R),J,A4,SA(R), 2005 F,I,It,W,
E(R),R, 2006 F(R), W(R),I(R),SA 2
Philip, T K (Edinburgh) 2004 W,E,It,F,I
Philp, A (Edinburgh Inst FP) 1882 E
Pinder, S J (Glasgow) 2006 SA 1(R),2(R)
Pocock, E I (Edinburgh Wands) 1877 I, E
Pollock, J A (Gosforth) 1982 W, 1983 E, NZ, 1984 E (R), I, F, R, 1985 F
Polson, A H (Gala) 1930 E
Pountney, A C (Northhampton) 1998 SA, 1999 W (t+R), E (R), It (t+R), I (R), F, Arg, [SA, U, Sm, NZ], 2000 It, I, F, W, E, US,A, Sm, 2001 F, W, E, It, I, 2002 E, I, F, W, R, SA, Fj
Proudfoot, M C (Melrose, Glasgow) 1998 Fj, A 1,2, 2003 I 2(R)
Purdie, W (Jedforest) 1939 W, I, E
Purves, A B H L (London Scottish) 1906 W, I, E, SA, 1907 W, I, E, 1908 W, I, E
Purves, W D C L (London Scottish) 1912 F, W, I, SA, 1913 I, E

Rea, C W W (W of Scotland, Headingley) 1968 A, 1969 F, W, I, SA, 1970 F, W, I, A, 1971 F, W, E (2[1C])
Redpath, B W (Melrose, Narbonne, Sale) 1993 NZ (t), 1994 E (t), F, Arg 1,2, 1995 C, I, F, W, E, R, [Iv, F, NZ], WS, 1996 I, F, W, E. A (R), It, 1997 E, I, F, 1998 Fj, A 1,2, SA, 1999 R (R), [U (R), Sp], 2000 It, I, US, A, Sm, 2001 F (R), E (R), It, I, 2002 E, It, I, F, W, R, SA, Fj, 2003 I 1, F, W 1, E, It 1, SA 1,2, [J,US(R),F,Fj,A]
Reed, A I (Bath, Wasps) 1993 I, F, W, E, 1994 E, I, F, Arg 1,2, SA, 1996 It, 1997 W, E, I, F, 1999 It (R), F (R), [Sp]
Reid, C (Edinburgh Acads) 1881 I, E, 1882 I, E, 1883 W, I, E, 1884 W, I, E, 1885 W, I 1,2, 1886 W, I, E, 1887 I, W, E, 1888 W, I
Reid, J (Edinburgh Wands) 1874 E, 1875 E, 1876 E, 1877 I, E
Reid, J M (Edinburgh Acads) 1898 I, E, 1899 I
Reid, M F (Loretto) 1883 I, E
Reid, R E (Glasgow) 2001 Tg (R), Arg
Reid, S J (Boroughmuir, Leeds, Narbonne) 1995 WS, 1999 F, Arg, [Sp], 2000 It (t), F, W, E (t)

Reid-Kerr, J (Greenock Wand) 1909 E
Relph, W K L (Stewart's Coll FP) 1955 F, W, I, E
Rennie, R M (Edinburgh) 2008 I(R)
Renny-Tailyour, H W (Royal Engineers) 1872 E
Renwick, J M (Hawick) 1972 F, W, E, NZ, 1973 F, 1974 W, E, I, F, 1975 I, F, W, E, NZ, A, 1976 F, W, E (R), 1977 I, F, W, 1978 I, F, W, E, NZ, 1979 W, E, I, F, NZ, 1980 I, F, W, E, 1981 F, W, E, I, NZ 1,2, R, A, 1982 E, I, F, W, 1983 I, F, W, E, 1984 R
Renwick, W L (London Scottish) 1989 R
Renwick, W N (London Scottish, Edinburgh Wands) 1938 E, 1939 W
Richardson, J F (Edinburgh Acads) 1994 SA
Ritchie, G (Merchistonians) 1871 E
Ritchie, G F (Dundee HSFP) 1932 E
Ritchie, J M (Watsonians) 1933 W, E, I, 1934 W, I, E
Ritchie, W T (Cambridge U) 1905 I, E
Robb, G H (Glasgow U) 1881 I, 1885 W
Roberts, G (Watsonians) 1938 W, I, E, 1939 W, E
Robertson, A H (W of Scotland) 1871 E
Robertson, A W (Edinburgh Acads) 1897 E
Robertson, D (Edinburgh Acads) 1875 E
Robertson, D D (Cambridge U) 1893 W
Robertson, I (London Scottish, Watsonians) 1968 E, 1969 E, SA, 1970 F, W, I, E, A
Robertson, I P M (Watsonians) 1910 F
Robertson, J (Clydesdale) 1908 E
Robertson, K W (Melrose) 1978 NZ, 1979 W, E, I, F, NZ, 1980 W, E, 1981 F, W, E, I, R, A, 1982 E, I, F, A 1,2, 1983 I, F, W, E, 1984 E, I, F, R, A, 1985 I, F, W, E, 1986 I, 1987 F (R), W, E, [F, Z, NZ], 1988 E, A, 1989 E, I, F
Robertson, L (London Scottish United Services) 1908 E, 1911 W, 1912 W, I, E, SA, 1913 W, I, E
Robertson, M A (Gala) 1958 F
Robertson, R D (London Scottish) 1912 F
Robson, A (Hawick) 1954 F, 1955 F, W, I, E, 1956 F, W, I, E, 1957 F, W, I, E, 1958 W, A, I, E, 1959 F, W, I, E, 1960 F
Rodd, J A T (United Services, RN, London Scottish) 1958 F, W, A, I, E, 1960 F, W, 1962 F, 1964 F, NZ, W, 1965 F, W, I
Rogerson, J (Kelvinside Acads) 1894 W
Roland, E T (Edinburgh Acads) 1884 I, E
Rollo, D M D (Howe of Fife) 1959 E, 1960 F, W, I, E, SA, 1961 F, SA, W, I, E, 1962 F, W, E, 1963 F, W, I, E, 1964 F, NZ, W, I, E, 1965 F, W, I, E, SA, 1966 F, W, I, E, A, 1967 F, W, E, NZ, 1968 F, W, I
Rose, D M (Jedforest) 1951 F, W, I, E, SA, 1953 F, W
Ross, A (Kilmarnock) 1924 F, W
Ross, A (Royal HSFP) 1905 W, I, E, 1909 W, I
Ross, A R (Edinburgh U) 1911 W, 1914 W, I, E
Ross, E J (London Scottish) 1904 W
Ross, G (Edinburgh, Leeds) 2001 Tg, 2002 R, SA, Fj(R), 2003 I 1, W 1(R), SA 2(R), It 2, I 2, [J], 2004 Sm,A1(R), 2(R),J(R),SA(R),2005 It(R),W(R),E, 2006 F(R),W(R),E(R), I(R),It, SA 1(R),2
Ross, G T (Watsonians) 1954 NZ, I, E, W
Ross, I A (Hillhead HSFP) 1951 F, W, I, E
Ross, J (London Scottish) 1901 W, I, E, 1902 W, 1903 E
Ross, K I (Boroughmuir FP) 1961 SA, W, I, E, 1962 F, W, I, E, 1963 F, W, E
Ross, W A (Hillhead HSFP) 1937 W, E
Rottenburg, H (Cambridge U, London Scottish) 1899 W, E, 1900 W, I, E
Roughead, W N (Edinburgh Acads, London Scottish) 1927 A, 1928 F, W, I, E, 1930 I, E, 1931 F, W, I, E, 1932 W
Rowan, N A (Boroughmuir) 1980 W, E, 1981 F, W, E, I, 1984 R, 1985 I, 1987 [R], 1988 I, F, W, E
Rowand, R (Glasgow HSFP) 1930 F, W, 1932 E, 1933 W, E, I, 1934 W
Roxburgh, A J (Kelso) 1997 A, 1998 It, F (R), W, E, Fj, A 1(R),2(R)
Roy, A (Waterloo) 1938 W, I, E, 1939 W, I, E
Russell, R R (Saracens, London Irish) 1999 R, [U (R), Sp, Sm (R), NZ (R)], 2000 I (R), 2001 F (R), 2002 F (R), W (R), 2003 W 1(R), It 1(R), SA 1 (R), 2 (R), It 2, I 2(R), [J, F(R),Fj(t),A(R)] , 2004 W(R),E(R),F(R),I(R),J(R),A4(R),SA(R), 2005 It(R)
Russell, W L (Glasgow Acads) 1905 NZ, 1906 W, I, E
Rutherford, J Y (Selkirk) 1979 W, E, I, F, NZ, 1980 I, F, E, 1981 F, W, E, I, NZ 1,2, A, 1982 E, I, F, W, A 1,2, 1983 E, NZ, 1984 W, E, I, F, R, 1985 I, F, W, E, 1986 F, W, E, I, R, 1987 I, F, W, E, [F]
Sampson, R W F (London Scottish) 1939 W, 1947 W
Sanderson, G A (Royal HSFP) 1907 W, I, E, 1908 I
Sanderson, J L P (Edinburgh Acads) 1873 E
Schulze, D G (London Scottish) 1905 E, 1907 I, E, 1908 W, I, E, 1909 W, I, E, 1910 W, I, E, 1911 W
Scobie, R M (Royal Military Coll) 1914 W, I, E
Scotland, K J F (Heriot's FP, Cambridge U, Leicester) 1957 F, W, I, E, 1958 E, 1959 F, W, I, E, 1960 F, W, I, E, 1961 F, SA, W, I, E, 1962 F, W, I, E, 1963 F, W, I, E, 1965 F
Scott, D M (Langholm, Watsonians) 1950 I, E, 1951 W, I, E, SA, 1952 F, W, I, 1953 F
Scott, J M B (Edinburgh Acads) 1907 E, 1908 W, I, E, 1909 W, I, E, 1910 F, W, I, E, 1911 F, W, I, 1912 W, I, E, SA, 1913 W, I, E
Scott, J S (St Andrew's U) 1950 E
Scott, J W (Stewart's Coll FP) 1925 F, W, I, E, 1926 F, W, I, E, 1927 F, W, I, E, A, 1928 F, W, E, 1929 E, 1930 F
Scott, M (Dunfermline) 1992 A 2
Scott, R (Hawick) 1898 I, 1900 I, E
Scott, S (Edinburgh, Borders) 2000 NZ 2 (R), US (t+R), 2001 It (R), I (R), Tg (R), NZ (R), 2002 US (R), R(R), Fj(R), 2004 Sm(R), A1(R)
Scott, T (Langholm, Hawick) 1896 W, 1897 I, E, 1898 I, E, 1899 I, W, E, 1900 W, I, E
Scott, T M (Hawick) 1893 E, 1895 W, I, E, 1896 W, E, 1897 I, E, 1898 I, E, 1900 W, I
Scott, W P (W of Scotland) 1900 I, E, 1902 I, E, 1903 W, I, E, 1904 W, I, E, 1905 W, I, E, NZ, 1906 W, I, E, SA, 1907 W, I, E
Scoular, J G (Cambridge U) 1905 NZ, 1906 W, I, E, SA
Selby, J A R (Watsonians) 1920 W, I
Shackleton, J A P (London Scottish) 1959 E, 1963 F, W, 1964 NZ, W, 1965 I, SA
Sharp, A V (Bristol) 1994 E, I, F, Arg 1,2 SA
Sharp, G (Stewart's FP, Army) 1960 F, 1964 F, NZ, W
Shaw, G D (Sale) 1935 NZ, 1936 W, 1937 W, I, E, 1939 I
Shaw, I (Glasgow HSFP) 1937 I
Shaw, J N (Edinburgh Acads) 1921 W, I
Shaw, R W (Glasgow HSFP) 1934 W, I, E, 1935 W, I, E, NZ, 1936 W, I, E, 1937 W, I, E, 1938 W, I, E, 1939 W, I, E
Shedden, D (W of Scotland) 1972 NZ, 1973 F, W, I, E, P, 1976 W, E, I, 1977 I, F, W, 1978 I, F, W
Shepherd, R J S (Melrose) 1995 WS, 1996 I, F, W, E, NZ 1,2, A, It, 1997 W, E, I, F, SA, 1998 It, I, W (R), Fj (t), A 1,2
Shiel, A G (Melrose, Edinburgh) 1991 [I (R), WS], 1993 I, F, W, E, NZ, 1994 Arg 1,2, SA, 1995 R, [Iv, F, NZ], WS, 2000 I, NZ 1(R),2
Shillinglaw, R B (Gala, Army) 1960 I, E, SA, 1961 F, SA
Simmers, B M (Glasgow Acads) 1965 F, W, 1966 A, 1967 F, W, I, 1971 F (R)
Simmers, W M (Glasgow Acads) 1926 W, I, E, 1927 F, W, I, E, A, 1928 F, W, I, E, 1929 F, W, I, E, 1930 F, W, I, E, 1931 F, W, I, E, 1932 SA, W, I, E
Simpson, G L (Kirkcaldy, Glasgow) 1998 A 1,2, 1999 Arg (R), R, [SA, U, Sm, NZ], 2000 It, I, NZ 1(R), 2001 I, Tg (R), Arg (R), NZ
Simpson, J W (Royal HSFP) 1893 I, E, 1894 W, I, E, 1895 W, I, E, 1896 W, I, 1897 E, 1899 W, E
Simpson, R S (Glasgow Acads) 1923 I
Simson, E D (Edinburgh U, London Scottish) 1902 E, 1903 W, I, E, 1904 W, I, E, 1905 W, I, E, NZ, 1906 W, I, E, 1907 W, I, E
Simson, J T (Watsonians) 1905 NZ, 1909 W, I, E, 1910 F, W, 1911 I
Simson, R F (London Scottish) 1911 E
Sloan, A T (Edinburgh Acads) 1914 W, 1920 F, W, I, E, 1921 F, W, I, E
Sloan, D A (Edinburgh Acads, London Scottish) 1950 F, W, E, 1951 W, I, E, 1953 F
Sloan, T (Glasgow Acads, Oxford U) 1905 NZ, 1906 W, SA, 1907 W, E, 1908 W, 1909 I
Smeaton, P W (Edinburgh Acads) 1881 I, 1883 I, E
Smith, A R (Oxford U) 1895 W, I, E, 1896 W, I, 1897 I, E, 1898 I, E, 1900 I, E
Smith, A R (Cambridge U, Gosforth, Ebbw Vale, Edinburgh Wands) 1955 W, I, E, 1956 F, W, I, E, 1957 F, W, I, E, 1958 F, W, A, I, 1959 F, W, I, E, 1960 F, W, I, E, SA, 1961 F, SA, W, I, E, 1962 F, W, I, E
Smith, C J (Edinburgh) 2002 C, US (R), 2004 Sm(t&R),A1(R), 2(R),3(R),J(R), 2005 Arg(R),Sm,NZ(R), 2006 F(R),W(R),E(R),

I(R),It(R),SA 1(R),2,R(R), 2007 I2(R), [R(R), NZ,It(R),Arg(R)], 2008 E(R),It(R)
Smith, D W C (London Scottish) 1949 F, W, I, E, 1950 F, W, I, 1953 I
Smith, E R (Edinburgh Acads) 1879 I
Smith, G K (Kelso) 1957 I, E, 1958 F, W, A, 1959 F, W, I, E, 1960 F, W, I, E, 1961 F, SA, W, I, E
Smith, H O (Watsonians) 1895 W, 1896 W, I, E, 1898 I, E, 1899 W, I, E, 1900 E, 1902 E
Smith, I R (Gloucester, Moseley) 1992 E, I, W, A 1,2, 1994 E (R), I, F, Arg 1,2, 1995 [Iv], WS, 1996 I, F, W, E, NZ 1,2, A, It, 1997 E, I, F, A, SA
Smith, I S (Oxford U, Edinburgh U) 1924 W, I, E, 1925 F, W, I, E, 1926 F, W, I, E, 1927 F, I, E, 1929 F, W, I, E, 1930 F, W, I, 1931 F, W, I, E, 1932 SA, W, I, E, 1933 W, E, I
Smith I S G (London Scottish) 1969 SA, 1970 F, W, I, E, 1971 F, W, I
Smith, M A (London Scottish) 1970 W, I, E, A
Smith, R T (Kelso) 1929 F, W, I, E, 1930 F, W, I
Smith, S H (Glasgow Acads) 1877 I, 1878 E
Smith, T J (Gala) 1983 E, NZ, 1985 I, F
Smith T J (Watsonians, Dundee HSFP, Glasgow, Brive, Northampton) 1997 E, I, F, 1998 SA, 1999 W, E, It, I, Arg, R, [SA, U, Sm, NZ], 2000 It, I, F, W, E, NZ 1,2, US, A, Sm, 2001 F, W, E, It, I, Tg, Arg, NZ, 2002 E, It, I, F, W, R, SA, Fj, 2003 I 1, F, W 1, E, It 1,2, [J,US,F,Fj,A], 2004 W,E,Sm, A1,2,2005 F,I,It,W,E
Sole, D M B (Bath, Edinburgh Acads) 1986 F, W, 1987 I, F, W, E, [F, Z, R, NZ], 1988 I, F, W, E, A, 1989 W, E, I, F, Fj, R, 1990 I, F, W, E, NZ 1,2, Arg, 1991 F, W, E, I, R, [J, I, WS, E, NZ], 1992 E, I, F, W, A 1,2
Somerville, D (Edinburgh Inst FP) 1879 I, 1882 I, 1883 W, I, E, 1884 W
Southwell, H F G (Edinburgh) 2004 Sm(t&R),A1,2,3(R), J,A4,SA,2005 F,I,It,W,E,R(R),Arg(R),Sm(R),NZ, 2006 F,W,E,I,It, SA 1,2, 2006 R,PI(t&R),A(R), 2007 E,W,It,I1,
SA(R), [Pt(R),R(R),NZ,It(R),Arg(R)], 2008 F(R),W,I,E,It,Arg 2
Speirs, L M (Watsonians) 1906 SA, 1907 W, I, E, 1908 W, I, E, 1910 F, W, E
Spence, K M (Oxford U) 1953 I
Spencer, E (Clydesdale) 1898 I
Stagg, P K (Sale) 1965 F, W, E, SA, 1966 F, W, I, E, A, 1967 F, W, I, E, NZ, 1968 F, W, I, E, A, 1969 F, W, I (R), SA, 1970 F, W, I, E, A
Stanger, A G (Hawick) 1989 Fj, R, 1990 I, F, W, E, NZ 1,2, Arg, 1991 F, W, E, I, R, [J, Z, I, WS, E, NZ], 1992 E, I, F, W, A 1,2, 1993 I, F, W, E, NZ, 1994 W, E, I, F, SA, 1995 R, [Iv], 1996 NZ 2, A, It, 1997 W, E, I, F, A, SA, 1998 It, I (R), F, W, E
Stark, D A (Boroughmuir, Melrose, Glasgow Hawks) 1993 I, F, W, E, 1996 NZ 2(R), It (R), 1997 W (R), E, SA
Steel, J F (Glasgow) 2000 US, A, 2001 I, Tg, NZ
Steele, W C C (Langholm, Bedford, RAF, London Scottish) 1969 E, 1971 F, W, I, E (2[1C]), 1972 F, W, E, NZ, 1973 F, W, I, E, 1975 I, F, W, E, NZ (R), 1976 W, E, I, 1977 E
Stephen, A E (W of Scotland) 1885 W, 1886 I
Steven, P D (Heriot's FP) 1984 A, 1985 F, W, E
Steven, R (Edinburgh Wands) 1962 I
Stevenson, A K (Glasgow Acads) 1922 F, 1923 F, W, E
Stevenson, A M (Glasgow U) 1911 F
Stevenson, G D (Hawick) 1956 E, 1957 F, 1958 F, W, A, I, E, 1959 W, I, E, 1960 W, I, E, SA, 1961 F, SA, W, I, E, 1963 F, W, I, 1964 E, 1965 F
Stevenson, H J (Edinburgh Acads) 1888 W, I, 1889 W, I, 1890 W, I, E, 1891 W, I, E, 1892 W, I, E, 1893 I, E
Stevenson, L E (Edinburgh U) 1888 W
Stevenson, R C (London Scottish) 1897 I, E, 1898 E, 1899 I, W, E
Stevenson, R C (St Andrew's U) 1910 F, I, E, 1911 F, W, I
Stevenson, W H (Glasgow Acads) 1925 F
Stewart, A K (Edinburgh U) 1874 E, 1876 E
Stewart, A M (Edinburgh Acads) 1914 W
Stewart, B D (Edinburgh Acads, Edinburgh) 1996 NZ 2, A, 2000 NZ 1,2
Stewart, C A R (W of Scotland) 1880 I, E
Stewart, C E B (Kelso) 1960 W, 1961 F
Stewart, J (Glasgow HSFP) 1930 F
Stewart, J L (Edinburgh Acads) 1921 I
Stewart M J (Northampton) 1996 It, 1997 W, E, I, F, A, SA, 1998 It, I, F, W, Fj (R), 2000 It, I, F, W, E, NZ 1(R), 2001 F, W, E, It, I, Tg, Arg, NZ, 2002 E, It, I, F, W, C, US, R(R)
Stewart, M S (Stewart's Coll FP) 1932 SA, W, I, 1933 W, E, I, 1934 W, I, E
Stewart, W A (London Hospital) 1913 F, W, I, 1914 W
Steyn, S S L (Oxford U) 1911 E, 1912 I
Strachan, G M (Jordanhill) 1971 E (C) (R), 1973 W, I, E, P
Strokosch, A K (Edinburgh, Gloucester) 2006 A(R), 2008 I,E,It,Arg 1,2
Stronach, R S (Glasgow Acads) 1901 W, E, 1905 W, I, E
Stuart, C D (W of Scotland) 1909 I, 1910 F, W, I, E, 1911 I, E
Stuart, L M (Glasgow HSFP) 1923 F, W, I, E, 1924 F, 1928 E, 1930 I, E
Suddon, N (Hawick) 1965 W, I, E, SA, 1966 A, 1968 E, A, 1969 F, W, I, 1970 I, E, A
Sutherland, W R (Hawick) 1910 W, E, 1911 F, E, 1912 F, W, E, SA, 1913 F, W, I, E, 1914 W
Swan, J S (Army, London Scottish, Leicester) 1953 E, 1954 F, NZ, I, E, W, 1955 F, W, I, E, 1956 F, W, I, E, 1957 F, W, 1958 F
Swan, M W (Oxford U, London Scottish) 1958 F, W, A, I, E, 1959 F, W, I
Sweet, J B (Glasgow HSFP) 1913 E, 1914 I
Symington, A W (Cambridge U) 1914 W, E

Tait, A V (Kelso, Newcastle, Edinburgh) 1987 [F(R), Z, R, NZ], 1988 I, F, W, E, 1997 I, F, A, 1998 It, I, F, W, E, SA, 1999 W (R), E, It, I, F, Arg, R, [A, U, NZ]
Tait, J G (Edinburgh Acads) 1880 I, 1885 I 2
Tait, P W (Royal HSFP) 1935 E
Taylor, E G (Oxford U) 1927 W, A
Taylor, R C (Kelvinside-West) 1951 W, I, E, SA
Taylor, S M (Edinburgh, Stade FranÁais) 2000 US, A, 2001 E, It, I, NZ (R), 2002 E, It, I, F, W, C, US, R, SA, Fj, 2003 I 1, F, W 1, E, It 1, SA 1,2, It 2, I 2, [J,US,F,Fj,A], 2004 W,E,It,F,I, 2005 It,W,E,Arg,Sm,NZ, 2006 F,W,E,I,It,PI,A, 2007 E,W,It, I1,F,I2, [Pt,R, It,Arg], 2008 E,It
Telfer, C M (Hawick) 1968 A, 1969 F, W, I, E, 1972 F, W, E, 1973 W, I, E, P, 1974 W, E, I, 1975 A, 1976 F
Telfer, J W (Melrose) 1964 F, NZ, W, I, E, 1965 F, W, I, 1966 F, W, I, E, 1967 W, I, E, 1968 E, A, 1969 F, W, I, E, SA, 1970 F, W, I
Tennent, J M (W of Scotland) 1909 W, I, E, 1910 F, W, E
Thom, D A (London Scottish) 1934 W, 1935 W, I, E, NZ
Thom, G (Kirkcaldy) 1920 F, W, I, E
Thom, J R (Watsonians) 1933 W, E, I
Thomson, A E (United Services) 1921 F, W, E
Thomson, A M (St Andrew's U) 1949 I
Thomson, B E (Oxford U) 1953 F, W, I
Thomson, F M A (Glasgow Warriors) 2007 I2(t&R),SA(R), [NZ(R)], 2008 F(R),W(R), I(R),E(R),It
Thomson, I H M (Heriot's FP, Army) 1951 W, I, 1952 F, W, I, 1953 I, E
Thomson, J S (Glasgow Acads) 1871 E
Thomson, R H (London Scottish, PUC) 1960 I, E, SA, 1961 F, SA, W, I, E, 1963 F, W, I, E, 1964 F, NZ, W
Thomson, W H (W of Scotland) 1906 SA
Thomson, W J (W of Scotland) 1899 W, E, 1900 W
Timms, A B (Edinburgh U, Edinburgh Wands) 1896 W, 1900 W, I, 1901 W, I, E, 1902 W, E, 1903 W, E, 1904 I, E, 1905 I, E
Tod, H B (Gala) 1911 F
Tod, J (Watsonians) 1884 W, I, E, 1885 W, I 1,2, 1886 W, I, E
Todd, J K (Glasgow Acads) 1874 E, 1875 E
Tolmie, J M (Glasgow HSFP) 1922 E
Tomes, A J (Hawick) 1976 E, I, 1977 E, 1978 I, F, W, E, NZ, 1979 W, E, I, F, NZ, 1980 F, W, E, 1981 F, W, E, I, NZ 1,2, R, A, 1982 E, I, F, W, A 1,2, 1983 I, F, W, 1984 W, E, I, F, R, A, 1985 W, E, 1987 I, F, E (R), [F, Z, R, NZ]
Torrie, T J (Edinburgh Acads) 1877 E
Townsend, G P J (Gala, Northampton, Brive, Castres, Borders) 1993 E (R), 1994 W, E, I, F, Arg 1,2, 1995 C, I, F, W, E, WS, 1996 I, F, W, E, NZ 1,2, A, It, 1997 W, E, I, F, A, SA, 1998 It, I, F, W, E, Fj, A 1,2, SA (R), 1999 W, E, It, I, F, [SA, U, Sp (R), Sm, NZ], 2000 It, I, F, W, E, NZ 1,2, US, A, Sm, 2001 F, It, I, Arg, NZ, 2002 E, It, I, F, W, R(R), SA(R), Fj, 2003 I 1(R), F, W 1, E, It 1, SA 1,2, W 2, [J(R),US,F,Fj,A]
Tukalo, I (Selkirk) 1985 I, 1987 I, F, W, E, [F, Z, R, NZ], 1988 F, W, E, A, 1989 W, E, I, F, Fj, 1990 I, F, W, E, NZ 1, 1991 I, R, [J, Z, I, WS, E, NZ], 1992 E, I, F, W, A 1,2
Turk, A S (Langholm) 1971 E (R)

Turnbull, D J (Hawick) 1987 [NZ], 1988 F, E, 1990 E (R), 1991 F, W, E, I, R, [Z], 1993 I, F, W, E, 1994 W
Turnbull, F O (Kelso) 1951 F, SA
Turnbull, G O (W of Scotland) 1896 I, E, 1897 I, E, 1904 W
Turnbull, P (Edinburgh Acads) 1901 W, I, E, 1902 W, I, E
Turner, F H (Oxford U, Liverpool) 1911 F, W, I, E, 1912 F, W, I, E, SA, 1913 F, W, I, E, 1914 I, E
Turner, J W C (Gala) 1966 W, A, 1967 F, W, I, E, NZ, 1968 F, W, I, E, A, 1969 F, 1970 E, A, 1971 F, W, I, E (2[1C])

Usher, C M (United Services, Edinburgh Wands) 1912 E, 1913 F, W, I, E, 1914 E, 1920 F, W, I, E, 1921 W, E, 1922 F, W, I, E
Utterson, K N (Borders) 2003 F, W 1, E(R)

Valentine, A R (RNAS, Anthorn) 1953 F, W, I
Valentine, D D (Hawick) 1947 I, E
Veitch, J P (Royal HSFP) 1882 E, 1883 I, 1884 W, I, E, 1885 I 1,2, 1886 E
Villar, C (Edinburgh Wands) 1876 E, 1877 I, E

Waddell, G H (London Scottish, Cambridge U) 1957 E, 1958 F, W, A, I, E, 1959 F, W, I, E, 1960 I, E, SA, 1961 F, 1962 F, W, I, E
Waddell, H (Glasgow Acads) 1924 F, W, I, E, 1925 I, E, 1926 F, W, I, E, 1927 F, W, I, E, 1930 W
Wade, A L (London Scottish) 1908 E
Wainwright, R I (Edinburgh Acads, West Hartlepool, Watsonians, Army, Dundee HSFP) 1992 I (R), F, A 1,2, 1993 NZ, 1994 W, E, 1995 C, I, F, W, E, R, [Iv, Tg, F, NZ], WS, 1996 I, F, W, E, NZ 1,2, 1997 W, E, I, F, SA, 1998 It, I, F, W, E, Fj, A 1,2
Walker, A (W of Scotland) 1881 I, 1882 E, 1883 W, I, E
Walker, A W (Cambridge U, Birkenhead Park) 1931 F, W, I, E, 1932 I
Walker, J G (W of Scotland) 1882 E, 1883 W
Walker, M (Oxford U) 1952 F
Walker, N (Borders, Ospreys) 2002 R, SA, Fj, 2007 W(R),It(R),F,I2(R),SA, [R(R),NZ], 2008 F,W,I,E
Wallace, A C (Oxford U) 1923 F, 1924 F, W, E, 1925 F, W, I, E, 1926 F
Wallace, W M (Cambridge U) 1913 E, 1914 W, I, E
Wallace, M I (Glasgow High Kelvinside) 1996 A, It, 1997 W
Walls, W A (Glasgow Acads) 1882 E, 1883 W, I, E, 1884 W, I, E, 1886 W, I, E
Walter, M W (London Scottish) 1906 I, E, SA, 1907 W, I, 1908 W, I, 1910 I
Walton, P (Northampton, Newcastle) 1994 E, I, F, Arg 1,2, 1995 [Iv], 1997 W, E, I, F, SA (R), 1998 I, F, SA, 1999 W, E, It, I, F (R), Arg, R, [SA (R), U (R), Sp]
Warren, J R (Glasgow Acads) 1914 I
Warren, R C (Glasgow Acads) 1922 W, I, 1930 W, I, E
Waters, F H (Cambridge U, London Scottish) 1930 F, W, I, E, 1932 SA, W, I
Waters, J A (Selkirk) 1933 W, E, I, 1934 W, I, E, 1935 W, I, E, NZ, 1936 W, I, E, 1937 W, I, E
Waters, J B (Cambridge U) 1904 I, E
Watherston, J G (Edinburgh Wands) 1934 I, E
Watherston, W R A (London Scottish) 1963 F, W, I
Watson, D H (Glasgow Acads) 1876 E, 1877 I, E
Watson, W S (Boroughmuir) 1974 W, E, I, F, 1975 NZ, 1977 I, F, W, 1979 I, F
Watt, A G J (Glasgow High Kelvinside) 1991 [Z], 1993 I, NZ, 1994 Arg 2(t & R)
Watt, A G M (Edinburgh Acads) 1947 F, W, I, A, 1948 F, W
Weatherstone, T G (Stewart's Coll FP) 1952 E, 1953 I, E, 1954 F, NZ, I, E, W, 1955 F, 1958 W, A, I, E, 1959 W, I, E
Webster, S L (Edinburgh) 2003 I 2(R), 2004 W(R),E,It,F,I, Sm,A1,2, 2005 It,NZ(R), 2006 F(R), W(R), E(R), I(R),It(R),SA 1(R),2,R,PI,A, 2007 W(R),I2,SA, [Pt,R,NZ,It, Arg], 2008 F,I,E,It,Arg 1(R),2
Weir, G W (Melrose, Newcastle) 1990 Arg, 1991 R, [J, Z, I, WS, E, NZ], 1992 E, I, F, W, A 1,2, 1993 I, F, W, E, NZ, 1994 W (R), E, I, F, SA, 1995 F (R), W, E, R, [Iv, Tg, F, NZ], WS, 1996 I, F, W, E, NZ 1,2, A, It (R), 1997 W, E, I, F, 1998 It, I, F, W, E, SA, 1999 W, Arg (R), R (R), [SA (R), Sp, Sm, NZ], 2000 It (R), I (R), F
Welsh, R (Watsonians) 1895 W, I, E, 1896 W
Welsh, R B (Hawick) 1967 I, E
Welsh, W B (Hawick) 1927 A, 1928 F, W, I, 1929 I, E, 1930 F, W, I, E, 1931 F, W, I, E, 1932 SA, W, I, E, 1933 W, E, I
Welsh, W H (Edinburgh U) 1900 I, E, 1901 W, I, E, 1902 W, I, E
Wemyss, A (Gala, Edinburgh Wands) 1914 W, I, 1920 F, E, 1922 F, W, I
West, L (Edinburgh U, West Hartlepool) 1903 W, I, E, 1905 I, E, NZ, 1906 W, I, E
Weston, V G (Kelvinside Acads) 1936 I, E
White, D B (Gala, London Scottish) 1982 F, W, A 1,2, 1987 W, E, [F, R, NZ], 1988 I, F, W, E, A, 1989 W, E, I, F, Fj, R, 1990 I, F, W, E, NZ 1,2, 1991 F, W, E, I, R, [J, Z, I, WS, E, NZ], 1992 E, I, F, W
White, D M (Kelvinside Acads) 1963 F, W, I, E
White, J P R (Glasgow, Sale) 2000 E, NZ 1,2, US (R), A (R), Sm, 2001 F (R), I, Tg, Arg, NZ, 2002 E, It, I, F, W, C, US, SA(R), Fj, 2003 F(R), W 1, E, It 1, SA 1,2, It 2, [J, US(R),F,Fj(R),A], 2004 W(R),E,It,F,I,Sm,A1,2,J(R),A4(R),SA, 2005 F,I,E,Arg,Sm,NZ, 2006 F,W,E,I,It,SA 1,2,R, 2007 I2,SA, [Pt,R,It,Arg], 2008 F,W,E(R),It(R)
White, T B (Edinburgh Acads) 1888 W, I, 1889 W
Whittington, T P (Merchistonians) 1873 E
Whitworth, R J E (London Scottish) 1936 I
Whyte, D J (Edinburgh Wands) 1965 W, I, E, SA, 1966 F, W, I, E, A, 1967 F, W, I, E
Will, J G (Cambridge U) 1912 F, W, I, E, 1914 W, I, E
Wilson, A W (Dunfermline) 1931 F, I, E
Wilson, A W (Glasgow) 2005 R(R)
Wilson, G A (Oxford U) 1949 F, W, E
Wilson, G R (Royal HSFP) 1886 E, 1890 W, I, E, 1891 I
Wilson, J H (Watsonians) 1953 I
Wilson, J S (St Andrew's U) 1931 F, W, I, E, 1932 E
Wilson, J S (United Services, London Scottish) 1908 I, 1909 W
Wilson, R (London Scottish) 1976 E, I, 1977 E, I, F, 1978 I, F, 1981 R, 1983 I
Wilson, R L (Gala) 1951 F, W, I, E, SA, 1953 F, W, E
Wilson, R W (W of Scotland) 1873 E, 1874 E
Wilson, S (Oxford U, London Scottish) 1964 F, NZ, W, I, E, 1965 W, I, E, SA, 1966 F, W, I, A, 1967 F, W, I, E, NZ, 1968 F, W, I, E
Wood, A (Royal HSFP) 1873 E, 1874 E, 1875 E
Wood, G (Gala) 1931 W, I, 1932 W, I, E
Woodburn, J C (Kelvinside Acads) 1892 I
Woodrow, A N (Glasgow Acads) 1887 I, W, E
Wotherspoon, W (W of Scotland) 1891 I, 1892 I, 1893 W, E, 1894 W, I, E
Wright, F A (Edinburgh Acads) 1932 E
Wright, H B (Watsonians) 1894 W
Wright, K M (London Scottish) 1929 F, W, I, E
Wright, P H (Boroughmuir) 1992 A 1,2, 1993 F, W, E, 1994 W, 1995 C, I, F, W, E, R, [Iv, Tg, F, NZ], 1996 W, E, NZ 1
Wright, R W J (Edinburgh Wands) 1973 F
Wright, S T H (Stewart's Coll FP) 1949 E
Wright, T (Hawick) 1947 A
Wyllie, D S (Stewart's-Melville FP) 1984 A, 1985 W (R), E, 1987 I, F, [F, Z, R, NZ], 1989 R, 1991 R, [J (R), Z], 1993 NZ (R), 1994 W (R), E, I, F

Young, A H (Edinburgh Acads) 1874 E
Young, E T (Glasgow Acads) 1914 E
Young, R G (Watsonians) 1970 W
Young, T E B (Durham) 1911 F
Young, W B (Cambridge U, London Scottish) 1937 W, I, E, 1938 W, I, E, 1939 W, I, E, 1948 E

SCOTLAND DOMESTIC RUGBY
BACK FROM THE BRINK

Boroughmuir proved the dominant force north of the border as they walked away with the Scottish Hydro Electric Premiership, claiming the title by 21 clear points from a distant, second-placed Watsonians.

It was the Edinburgh side's first league triumph since 2003 – and only the third in the club's history – and if the title race the previous season had produced a titanic tussle between Currie and Ayr to be crowned champions, the 2007–08 incarnation of the competition resembled a regal procession as Boroughmuir swept all before them to make a mockery of their reputation as the division's great underachievers.

The previous campaign had seen the side languishing in midtable mediocrity but 12 months later they finally found the steel to compliment their undisputed flair and a 28–19 victory over Ayr at Millbrae in mid January confirmed Eammon John's side as champions.

The champagne could have been opened a week earlier had Boroughmuir's fixture with GHA not been postponed but seven days later they ensured the trophy was heading back to Meggetland for the first time in five years.

"To actually get over the finishing line, I'm just delighted for the players," John said as the celebrations finally began. "Sometimes your last steps are your hardest steps. Ayr hadn't lost since our home meeting with them and so I knew that they would throw the kitchen sink at us, and they certainly did. When we've got the ball we are able to do things with it. We didn't play as well as we might have liked or as well as at other times in the season, but what we did show here was the character that has got us through this season. The players have worked hard off the field and it's been a long time coming in relation to the club's facilities. Our facilities are first-class now in Scottish club rugby and, thankfully, we have a team now that is worthy of that."

Muir's triumphant campaign began in September with the visit of Melrose to Meggetland and although they eventually emerged 23–19 winners, it was a performance that barely hinted at the superb run of results they were to embark on.

Tries from captain Rory Couper and flanker Angus Martyn helped the home side establish a 15–9 lead at half-time and when Couper crossed for his second score after the break, Boroughmuir appeared home and dry. Indiscipline however nearly cost them and yellow cards for Martyn and lock Fergus Pringle allowed Melrose to stage a comeback and by the final whistle, Muir were clinging on.

A week later the team travelled to Glasgow to face the Hawks at Old Anniesland and they were again severely tested despite the home side gifting the visitors two early tries to Malcolm Clapperton and Tom Bury. Glasgow enjoyed the lions' share of possession and clawed their way back into contention and with the game heading into second-half injury time, they trailed 24–17.

The stage was set for one last moment of drama and when prop Gavin Mories bundled his way over the line, the Hawks had the chance to snatch a share of the spoils but were denied when fly-half Ruaridh Jackson failed with the conversion.

The two close encounters seemed to have a galvanising effect on Muir and they were barely troubled in their next two outings, despatching Dundee HSFP 44–10 before recording a 52–13 mauling of Stirling County at Bridgehaugh, a morale-boosting result which proved to be ideal preparation ahead of their top of the table clash with local rivals Watsonians at Meggetland.

Muir were uncharacteristically sluggish in the opening exchanges but when Watsonians captain Will Rowley was shown a first-half yellow card for persistent infringement at the breakdown, Muir rediscovered their spark from the resulting penalty, taking a quick tap and working space for Elgan O'Donnell for their first try. O'Donnell himself converted and despite a second-half Watsonians rally further scores from Couper, Stephen Ruddick and Freddie Lait eased the side to a 29–20 victory that yielded a bonus point and confirmed Boroughmuir as the team to beat.

"We had to win the game twice," Eammon John conceded. "From 15–3 up we let them back into it, but we came good in the end to get the bonus point."

Boroughmuir were now firmly in their stride and while Watsonians, Melrose and Currie all performed fitfully at best, John's side were irresistible and between October and early December they strung together a run of nine wins that was to break the back of the chasing pack.

The sequence finally came to an end against Watsonians at New Myreside. A 10th minute try from Dougie Brown gave the home side an early lead and a second score on the hour mark from Steve Lawrie sealed a 17–9 win. It was however to prove a temporary setback rather than major stumble for the champions elect.

The defeat was soon forgotten when Muir put Heriots to the sword the following week and a tense 17–16 win over Hawick at Mansfield Park in their next fixture left the Edinburgh outfit needing just one victory to secure the title.

The opportunity to confirm their triumph came against Ayr at Millbrae but if Muir were hoping for a routine victory, they were to be disappointed. Early scores from Euan Matheson and Cam Wars helped the visitors establish a 14–3 advantage but second-half tries from back rows Glen Tippet and Jeff Wilson sparked an Ayr revival and with just 10 minutes left, Muir held a precarious 21–19 lead. Nerves were frayed but a late try from Malcolm Clapperton, converted by Elgan O'Donnell, finally put the match to bed and the Boroughmuir party could begin.

"It seemed like an eternity in injury-time, but we still wouldn't allow them to cross the line and I was pleased with that," John said after the all-important victory. "It's important to show that when our backs were to the wall we can still deal with it. You don't lose your composure and I think we've shown that really good balance this year.

Boroughmuir captain Rory Couper added: "It's been a long time coming since it's a few years since we last won the trophy but today is the culmination of a special season for us. We've only lost one game yet we were behind in some six matches and I suppose if there's any ingredient to what we've achieved it's that we've been prepared to work hard for each other right throughout all our games."

There was however to be no league and cup double for Muir, who were knocked out of the National Cup by Melrose in the sixth round of the competition and it was Craig Chalmers' side who battled through to the final to face Heriots.

Over 6,000 fans were at Murrayfield for the game but expectations of 80 minutes of cut and thrust were quickly dispelled as Melrose ran riot in the first-half with four superb tries that effectively ended the game as a genuine contest.

Melrose opened the scoring after just five minutes with a try from full-back Jordan Macey. David Whiteford, Callum Anderson and Wayne Mitchell added the second, third and fourth tries respectively and with Scott Wight converting each score, Melrose found themselves with an improbable but imposing 28–0 lead at half-time.

A Wight penalty soon after the break made it 31–0 but suddenly Heriots seemed to rouse themselves and on 55 minutes the Edinburgh side finally made a breakthrough when Cameron Goodall crossed. Innes Brown, Oliver Brown and James Thompson all added tries and although the scores earned Heriots a degree of respectability, it was too little too late and Melrose claimed their first piece of silverware for 11 years with a 31–24 victory.

Whether Melrose's triumph is consigned to history as the final outing for the National Cup remains to be seen amid speculation that the Scottish

Rugby Union were considering shelving the competition to accommodate a radical overhaul of domestic season.

"We do need change I think to help the club game but not at the expense of the cup," Chalmers argued after the final. "This was great to win as a player in 1997 and feels just as good now as a coach, maybe even better.

"We could play the league championships through to January or whenever, and then the clubs split into regional leagues – the Border League, Glasgow League, Edinburgh League and Caledonia League. They would be great for clubs, cutting down on travel costs, getting back the great rivalries each area has and then the top clubs, maybe the top two in each league, meet for the knock-out stages of the cup.

"That could run through the lower leagues as well to keep the shield, bowl and plate and, crucially, this great day out at the end of the season. That's a possible way forward, but whatever clubs support it would be ridiculous to take the Scottish Cup away from the game."

SCOTTISH HYDRO ELECTRIC PREMIERSHIP 2007–08

1 September: **Edinburgh Academicals** 10 **Heriots** 10, **GHA** 9 **Stirling County** 36, **Boroughmuir** 23 **Melrose** 19, **Ayr** 22 **Dundee HSFP** 23, **Hawick** 25 **Watsonians** 16, **Currie** 51 **Glasgow Hawks** 26. 8 September: **Heriots** 36 **Hawick** 29, **Stirling County** 18 **Ayr** 18, **Glasgow Hawks** 22 **Boroughmuir** 24, **Watsonians** 40 **GHA** 15, **Melrose** 40 **Edinburgh Academicals** 6, **Dundee HSFP** 6 **Currie** 16. 15 September: **Boroughmuir** 44 **Dundee HSFP** 10, **Edinburgh Academicals** 12 **Hawick** 13, **Ayr** 20 **Watsonians** 27, **Melrose** 32 **Glasgow Hawks** 25, **Currie** 28 **Stirling County** 22, **GHA** 31 **Heriots** 27. 22 September: **Glasgow Hawks** 27 **Edinburgh Academicals** 7, **Stirling County** 13 **Boroughmuir** 52, **Hawick** 37 **GHA** 30,**Watsonians** 27 **Currie** 16 **Dundee HSFP** 13 **Melrose** 46, **Heriots** 17 **Ayr** 27. 29 September: **Glasgow Hawks** 19 **Dundee HSFP** 20, **Boroughmuir** 29 **Watsonians** 20, **Ayr** 18 **Hawick** 17, **Melrose** 33 **Stirling County** 16 **Edinburgh Academicals** 16 **GHA** 12, **Currie** 27 **Heriots** 32. 6 October: **Stirling County** 19 **Glasgow Hawks** 20, **Hawick** 31 **Currie** 27 **Dundee HSFP** 19 **Edinburgh Academicals** 20 **Watsonians** 16 **Melrose** 24, **GHA** 16 **Ayr** 16 **Heriots** 17 **Boroughmuir** 35. 13 October: **Glasgow Hawks** 31 **Watsonians** 41, **Edinburgh Academicals** 20 **Ayr** 21, **Boroughmuir** 40 **Hawick** 20, **Dundee HSFP** 32 **Stirling County** 25, **Melrose** 41 **Heriots** 27, **Currie** 33 **GHS** 25. 20 October: **Ayr** 17 **Currie** 3, **Hawick** 30 **Melrose** 22 **Watsonians** 23 **Dundee HSFP** 20, **GHA** 18 **Boroughmuir** 24, **Stirling County** 23 **Edinburgh Academicals** 21, **Heriots** 20 **Glasgow Hawks** 5. 27 October: **Boroughmuir** 32 **Ayr** 15, **Dundee HSFP** 23 **Heriots** 26, **Edinburgh Academicals** 26 **Currie** 27, **Melrose** 33 **GHA** 17, **Stirling County** 19 **Watsonians** 20, **Glasgow Hawks** 24 **Hawick** 10. 3 November: **Ayr** 11 **Melrose** 10, **GHA** 10 **Glasgow Hawks** 16, **Heriots** 37 **Stirling County** 16, **Watsonians** 38 **Edinburgh Academicals** 22 **Hawick** 25 **Dundee HSFP** 12, **Currie** 10 **Boroughmuir** 39. 10 November: **Watsonians** 16 **Heriots** 33, **Dundee HSFP** 12 **GHA** 29, **Melrose** 28 **Currie** 30, **Edinburgh Academicals** 12 **Boroughmuir** 14, **Glasgow Hawks** 10 **Ayr** 13 **Stirling County** 49 **Hawick** 6. 17 November, 2007 **GHA** 17 **Watsonians** 27, **Edinburgh Academicals** 16 **Melrose** 8, **Hawick** 22 **Heriots** 31, **Currie** 20 **Dundee HSFP** 7, **Boroughmuir** 20 **Glasgow**

Hawks 18, **Ayr** 20 **Stirling County** 17. 24 November: **Glasgow Hawks** 15 **Melrose** 9, **Heriots** 25 **GHA** 0, **Dundee HSFP** 30 **Boroughmuir** 33, **Watsonians** 10 **Ayr** 13 **Stirling County** 6 **Currie** 6, **Hawick** 20 **Edinburgh Academicals** 12. 1 December: **Melrose** 17 **Dundee HSFP** 13, **Edinburgh Academicals** 18 **Glasgow Hawks** 15, **GHA** 38 **Hawick** 17 **Ayr** 24 **Heriots** 17, **Currie** 22 **Watsonians** 10 **Boroughmuir** 61 **Stirling County** 3. 8 December: **Stirling County** 12 **Melrose** 6, GHA 17 **Edinburgh Academicals** 15, **Heriots** 10 **Currie** 26, **Dundee HSFP** 16 **Glasgow Hawks** 17, **Watsonians** 17 **Boroughmuir** 9, **Hawick** 8 **Ayr** 19. 15 December: **Edinburgh Academicals** 30 **Dundee HSFP** 6, **Melrose** 12 **Watsonians** 20, **Currie** 49 **Hawick** 3, **Ayr** 6 **GHA** 6, **Boroughmuir** 49 **Heriots** 22, **Glasgow Hawks** 27 Stirling County 27. 5 January: **Heriots** 16 **Melrose** 15, **GHA** 8 **Currie** 5, **Hawick** 16 **Boroughmuir** 17, **Stirling County** 18 **Dundee HSFP** 6, **Watsonians** 32 **Glasgow Hawks** 17, **Ayr** 10 **Edinburgh Academicals** 10. 19 January: **GHA** 16 **Melrose** 16, **Heriots** 15 **Dundee HSFP** 7, **Currie** 16 **Edinburgh Academicals** 23, **Hawick** 19 **Glasgow Hawks** 3, **Ayr** 19 **Boroughmuir** 28, **Watsonians** 29 **Stirling County** 24. 26 January: **Melrose** 38 **Ayr** 7, **Edinburgh Academicals** 6 **Watsonians** 31, **Dundee HSFP** 21 **Hawick** 22, **Boroughmuir** 27 **Currie** 6, **Glasgow Hawks** 26 **GHA** 7. 2 February: **Melrose** 19 **Hawick** 13. 9 March: **Boroughmuir** 26 **GHA** 19. 15 March: **Edinburgh Academicals** 21 **Stirling County** 26. 22 March: **Currie** 17 **Melrose** 22, **Hawick** 29 **Stirling County** 17, **Boroughmuir** 18 **Edinburgh Academicals** 14, **Ayr** 14 **Glasgow Hawks** 5, **Heriots** 22 **Watsonians** 31, **GHA** 29 **Dundee HSFP** 3. 29 March: **Dundee HSFP** 17 **Ayr** 17, **Watsonians** 55 **Hawick** 6, **Glasgow Hawks** 16 **Currie** 22, **Heriots** 18 **Edinburgh Academicals** 34, **Stirling County** 6 **GHA** 0, **Melrose** 22 **Boroughmuir** 15. 5 April: **Glasgow Hawks** 25 **Heriots** 26. 19 April: **Currie** 25 **Ayr** 12. 24 April: **Stirling County** 64 **Heriots** 14. 26 April: **Dundee HSFP** 29 **Watsonians** 33,

FINAL TABLE

	P	W	D	L	F	A	Pts
Boroughmuir	22	20	0	2	659	362	96
Watsonians	22	16	0	6	579	431	75
Melrose	22	12	1	9	512	374	64
Currie	22	12	1	9	482	423	63
Ayr	22	11	5	6	359	374	58
Heriots	22	11	1	10	498	557	57
Stirling	22	8	3	11	476	495	49
Hawick	22	10	0	12	418	567	47
Glasgow	22	7	1	14	409	457	45
Edinburgh	22	7	2	13	371	429	41
GHA	22	6	3	13	369	462	39
Dundee	22	3	1	18	345	546	25

HYDRO ELECTRIC NATIONAL CUP 2007–08 RESULTS

QUARTER-FINALS

5 April, 2008

Haddington 10 **Jedforest** 11

Watsonians 29 **Biggar** 10

Hawick 17 **Melrose** 34

10 April, 2008

Ayr 13 **Heriots** 17

SEMI-FINALS

19 April, 2008

Watsonians 10 **Melrose** 23

Heriots 47 **Jedforest** 14

FINAL

3 May, 2008, Murrayfield, Edinburgh

MELROSE 31 (4G, 1PG) HERIOTS 24 (2G, 2T)

MELROSE: J Macey; C Anderson, J Murray (*captain*), G Stewart, D Whiteford; S Wight, S McCormick; A Gillie, W Mitchell, R Higgins, G Dodds, A Clark, S Johnson, W Wallace, R Miller *Substitutions:* N Beavon for Higgins (31 mins); G Innes for Mitchell (47 mins)

SCORERS *Tries:* Macey, Whiteford, Anderson, Mitchell *Conversions:* Wight (4) Penalty *Goals:* Wight

HERIOTS: C Goudie; M Teague (*captain*), J Thompson, R Mill, C Goodall ; M Strang, G Wilson; B McNeil, N Meikle, W Blacklock, P Eccles, G Noonan, T McVie, C Fusaro, C Simmonds *Substitutions:* I Brown for Blacklock (34 mins); S Mustard for Meikle (55 mins); J Parker for Fusaro (55 mins); O Brown for Strang (60 mins); R Gray for Eccles (60 mins); J Alston for Goodall (65 mins); G Anderson for Noonan (70 mins)

SCORERS *Tries:* Goodall, I Brown, O Brown, Thompson Conversions: Wilson (2)

REFEREE J Steele (Dumfries)

SOUTH AFRICA

SOUTH AFRICA'S 2007–08 TEST RECORD

OPPONENTS	DATE	VENUE	RESULT
Wales	24 Nov	A	**Won** 34–12
Wales	7 June	H	**Won** 43–17
Wales	14 June	H	**Won** 37–21
Italy	21 June	H	**Won** 26–0
New Zealand	5 July	A	**Lost** 8–19
New Zealand	12 July	A	**Won** 30–28
Australia	19 July	A	**Lost** 9–16
Argentina	9 Aug	H	**Won** 63–9
New Zealand	16 Aug	H	**Lost** 0–19
Australia	23 Aug	H	**Lost** 15–27
Australia	30 Aug	H	**Won** 53–8

BACK DOWN TO EARTH

By Iain Spragg

Ross Land/Getty Images

South Africa showed their Rugby World Cup form against New Zealand, winning 30–28

If 2007 was the year in which South Africa re-asserted themselves as a major power in the world game with their victory over England in the World Cup final in Paris, lifting the Webb Ellis Cup for a second time since their post-Apartheid rehabilitation, then 2008 was the year in which the euphoric Springboks were forced to face a less palatable reality.

Admittedly, a respectable record of seven victories in 11 post-Paris outings does not immediately suggest South Africa fell into disarray after their exertions in the Stade de France in October but last place in the Tri-Nations, with a mere two wins from six, told its own story. The Springboks had ruled the roost at the Rugby World Cup but found building on their triumph an altogether harder proposition.

There was, of course, a new coach to bed in. Jake White's reign came to an end after steering his newly-crowned world champions to a 34–12 victory over Wales in a one-off Test at the Millennium Stadium in November and the SARU busied itself in a search for his successor. Bulls coach Heyneke Meyer, White's backline assistant Allister Coetzee and Chester Williams, the iconic wing from South Africa's 1995 World Cup triumph, were all considered for the position but the SARU were to prove bolder and finally named Peter de Villiers, who became the first black man to coach the Springboks.

The appointment of the former Under-19 and Under-21 coach in January was certainly a cause of debate. SARU president Oregan Hoskins publicly conceded the decision had not been based solely on rugby issues – an honest admission of South African rugby's post-apartheid responsibilities – but de Villiers was eager to forget the politics and focus on the future.

"The fact that I am the first black coach must end now," he insisted as he fielded the inevitable questions about why he had been offered the job. "I know I can do the job and I'll go out there and use the structures that are already in place. I intend to build on those foundations that our previous coach laid. We are in a very privileged position that we are a winning side.

"It is very important that I don't let down the people who trust me, the people who put their faith in the whole process. I think I have the right people around me to help to do the right stuff.

"Rugby is a collective thing and the players are our most important assets. If we as coaches can work together in the interests of the players, that will be the best thing to do. Players out there must understand they will all stand an equal chance. If they are good enough, talented enough and work hard enough they will be part of the squad."

The first challenge de Villiers faced was a two-Test summer series against the Welsh, the recently-installed Grand Slam winners.

The battle between the kings of the northern and southern hemisphere, however, failed to produce anything approaching an epic encounter and once full back Conrad Jantjes went over for the first of his side's four tries in Bloemfontein on the half hour mark, the first Test was over as a contest. Jean de Villiers, Pierre Spies and Percy Montgomery added further scores, while Butch James slotted all four conversions and five penalties, as South Africa cantered to a 43–17 win that gave de Villiers a dream start to his tenure.

The second Test in Pretoria a week later was a tighter affair. Tries from Jean de Villiers and Ricky Januarie gave the Springboks an early advantage but Wales came storming back with scores from Shane Williams and Gareth Cooper and with just quarter of an hour remaining, the tourists trailed by two points. It was time for South Africa to live up to their status as world champions and they duly obliged with a second score from Jean de Villiers and a try from replacement hooker Bismarck du Plessis in the final minute to emerge 37–21 winners.

It was now time for de Villiers and his troops to focus on the Tri-Nations and the sterner challenges of the All Blacks and the Wallabies ahead. They warmed up for the tournament with a 26–0 win over Italy at a rain-soaked Newlands before flying to New Zealand for back-to-back Tests against the Kiwis.

The first match in Wellington was typically windy with points at a premium and after 80 minutes the two sides had mustered just one try apiece – from Jerome Kaino and Bryan Habana respectively – but it was 14 points from the boot of Dan Carter that proved the difference and New Zealand emerged 18–9 winners to extend the All Blacks' record sequence of home victories to 30 matches.

Seven days later the two sides crossed swords again in Dunedin but Kiwi hopes of extending their winning run were shattered by the Springboks, who led 17–15 at half-time courtesy of a JP Pietersen try and a Butch James drop goal but seemed to have been denied their first victory in New Zealand in a decade by Carter's boot, only to snatch a 30–28 win courtesy of a stunning solo try from Januarie six minutes from time.

"I have got nothing to prove," said de Villiers after the game when asked if the result justified his appointment. "If I believe in myself, if I believe in my players, if I believe in my God I don't need people around me," he said. "Everybody has got an opinion and we respect their opinions but it doesn't mean we agree with their opinion. I think if we can stand up as we did today as a group, people will change their own opinions."

South Africa crossed the Tasman Sea to face Australia the following week in Perth but were unable to build on their Dunedin success as fatigue and a spirited Wallabies display took their inevitable toll. A Francois Steyn penalty opened the scoring for the visitors but tries from Lote Tuqiri and Stirling Mortlock eased the home side into the lead and Australia held on for a hard-fought if not exactly fluent 16–9 win.

With a month-long Tri-Nations hiatus, the Springboks maintained their match sharpness with a comprehensive 63–9 win over Argentina at Ellis Park and were back in competitive action in mid-August with a clash with the All Blacks, the first of three home games to conclude their campaign.

The Cape Town clash was Percy Montgomery's 100th appearance for South Africa but there was to be no fairytale result for the evergreen full back as New Zealand scored three tries to none to exact revenge for the Dunedin reverse and run out 19–0 winners.

"There's a lot of things that the players didn't do today," de Villiers conceded. "We made simple mistakes and they are a very disappointed lot out there now. We were happy for Percy and the guys were feeling for him. It's not a characteristic of my team to make so many mistakes on one day."

Back-to-back Tests against Australia completed the South African season and produced wildly contrasting results – and emotions – for the home side. The first game in Durban witnessed a lacklustre display from the Springboks and they were outscored three tries to one in a 27–15 defeat, which handed Australia their first win in South Africa in eight years and ended any lingering hopes de Villiers' side had of winning the Tri-Nations.

The second match in Johannesburg was spectacularly different, however, as South Africa steeled themselves for one last push to produce a scintillating display, score eight tries and record a thumping 53–8 triumph. Wing Jongi Nokwe became the first player in history to score four tries in a Tri-Nations game and the Springboks had ended their campaign on a resounding high.

The result left the Wallabies and the All Blacks to battle it out for the Tri-Nations crown in the final match of the competition and South Africa to reflect on just two wins in six Tri-Nations fixtures.

"This performance is what I expect from the team, but we're only about 60 per cent to 70 per cent of where we want to be," de Villiers said after his side's face-saving victory. "It wasn't an opportunity to show up their critics, but an opportunity for the players to showcase their talents. There has been plenty of criticism, but it shows that the process is now beginning to work."

SOUTH AFRICA INTERNATIONAL STATISTICS

MATCH RECORDS UP TO 30TH SEPTEMBER 2008

MOST CONSECUTIVE TEST WINS

17 1997 *A*2,*It*, *F* 1,2, *E*,*S*, 1998 *I* 1,2,*W* 1,*E* 1, *A* 1,*NZ* 1,2, *A* 2, *W* 2, *S*, *I* 3

15 1994 *Arg* 1,2, *S*, *W* 1995 *WS*, *A*, *R*, *C*, *WS*, *F*, *NZ*, *W*, *It*, *E*, 1996 *Fj*

MOST CONSECUTIVE TESTS WITHOUT DEFEAT

Matches	Wins	Draws	Period
17	17	0	1997 to 1998
16	15	1	1994 to 1996
15	12	3	1960 to 1963

MOST POINTS IN A MATCH

BY THE TEAM

Pts.	Opponent	Venue	Year
134	Uruguay	E London	2005
105	Namibia	Cape Town	2007
101	Italy	Durban	1999
96	Wales	Pretoria	1998
74	Tonga	Cape Town	1997
74	Italy	Port Elizabeth	1999
72	Uruguay	Perth	2003
68	Scotland	Murrayfield	1997
64	USA	Montpellier	2007
63	Argentina	Johannesburg	2008
62	Italy	Bologna	1997
61	Australia	Pretoria	1997

BY A PLAYER

Pts.	Player	Opponent	Venue	Year
35	P C Montgomery	Namibia	Cape Town	2007
34	J H de Beer	England	Paris	1999
31	P C Montgomery	Wales	Pretoria	1998
30	T Chavhanga	Uruguay	E London	2005
29	G S du Toit	Italy	Port Elizabeth	1999
29	P C Montgomery	Samoa	Paris	2007
28	G K Johnson	W Samoa	Johannesburg	1995
26	J H de Beer	Australia	Pretoria	1997
26	P C Montgomery	Scotland	Murrayfield	1997
25	J T Stransky	Australia	Bloemfontein	1996
25	C S Terblanche	Italy	Durban	1999

MOST TRIES IN A MATCH

BY THE TEAM

Tries	Opponent	Venue	Year
21	Uruguay	E London	2005
15	Wales	Pretoria	1998
15	Italy	Durban	1999
15	Namibia	Cape Town	2007
12	Tonga	Cape Town	1997
12	Uruguay	Perth	2003
11	Italy	Port Elizabeth	1999
10	Ireland	Dublin	1912
10	Scotland	Murrayfield	1997

BY A PLAYER

Tries	Player	Opponent	Venue	Year
6	T Chavhanga	Uruguay	E London	2005
5	C S Terblanche	Italy	Durban	1999
4	C M Williams	W Samoa	Johannesburg	1995
4	P W G Rossouw	France	Parc des Princes	1997
4	C S Terblanche	Ireland	Bloemfontein	1998
4	B G Habana	Samoa	Paris	2007
4	J L Nokwe	Australia	Johannesburg	2008

MOST CONVERSIONS IN A MATCH

BY THE TEAM

Cons	Opponent	Venue	Year
13	Italy	Durban	1999
13	Uruguay	E London	2005
12	Namibia	Cape Town	2007
9	Scotland	Murrayfield	1997
9	Wales	Pretoria	1998
9	Argentina	Johannesburg	2008
8	Italy	Port Elizabeth	1999
8	USA	Montpellier	2007
7	Scotland	Murrayfield	1951
7	Tonga	Cape Town	1997
7	Italy	Bologna	1997
7	France	Parc des Princes	1997
7	Italy	Genoa	2001
7	Samoa	Pretoria	2002
7	Samoa	Brisbane	2003
7	England	Bloemfontein	2007

BY A PLAYER

Cons	Player	Opponent	Venue	Year
12	P C Montgomery	Namibia	Cape Town	2007
9	P C Montgomery	Wales	Pretoria	1998
9	A D James	Argentina	Johannesburg	2008
8	P C Montgomery	Scotland	Murrayfield	1997
8	G S du Toit	Italy	Port Elizabeth	1999
8	G S du Toit	Italy	Durban	1999
7	A O Geffin	Scotland	Murrayfield	1951
7	J M F Lubbe	Tonga	Cape Town	1997
7	H W Honiball	Italy	Bologna	1997
7	H W Honiball	France	Parc des Princes	1997
7	A S Pretorius	Samoa	Pretoria	2002
7	J N B van der Westhuyzen	Uruguay	E London	2005
7	P C Montgomery	England	Bloemfontein	2007

MOST PENALTIES IN A MATCH

BY THE TEAM

Pens	Opponent	Venue	Year
8	Scotland	Port Elizabeth	2006
7	France	Pretoria	1975
7	France	Cape Town	2006
6	Australia	Bloemfontein	1996
6	Australia	Twickenham	1999
6	England	Pretoria	2000
6	Australia	Durban	2000
6	France	Johannesburg	2001
6	Scotland	Johannesburg	2003

BY A PLAYER

Pens	Player	Opponent	Venue	Year
7	P C Montgomery	Scotland	Port Elizabeth	2006
7	P C Montgomery	France	Cape Town	2006
6	G R Bosch	France	Pretoria	1975
6	J T Stransky	Australia	Bloemfontein	1996
6	J H de Beer	Australia	Twickenham	1999
6	A J J van Straaten	England	Pretoria	2000
6	A J J van Straaten	Australia	Durban	2000
6	P C Montgomery	France	Johannesburg	2001
6	L J Koen	Scotland	Johannesburg	2003

MOST DROPPED GOALS IN A MATCH

BY THE TEAM

Drops	Opponent	Venue	Year
5	England	Paris	1999
4	England	Twickenham	2006
3	S America	Durban	1980
3	Ireland	Durban	1981
3	Scotland	Murrayfield	2004

BY A PLAYER

Drops	Player	Opponent	Venue	Year
5	J H de Beer	England	Paris	1999
4	A S Pretorius	England	Twickenham	2006
3	H E Botha	S America	Durban	1980
3	H E Botha	Ireland	Durban	1981
3	J N B van der Westhuyzen	Scotland	Murrayfield	2004
2	B L Osler	N Zealand	Durban	1928
2	H E Botha	NZ Cavaliers	Cape Town	1986
2	J T Stransky	N Zealand	Johannesburg	1995
2	J H de Beer	N Zealand	Johannesburg	1997
2	P C Montgomery	N Zealand	Cardiff	1999
2	F P L Steyn	Australia	Cape Town	2007

CAREER RECORDS

MOST CAPPED PLAYERS

Caps	Player	Career Span
102	P C Montgomery	1997 to 2008
89	J H van der Westhuizen	1993 to 2003
80	J P du Randt	1994 to 2007
78	J W Smit	2000 to 2008
77	M G Andrews	1994 to 2001
77	V Matfield	2001 to 2008
66	A G Venter	1996 to 2001
64	B J Paulse	1999 to 2007
56	C J van der Linde	2002 to 2008
54	A-H le Roux	1994 to 2002
52	J P Botha	2002 to 2008
52	J H Smith	2003 to 2008
51	P A van den Berg	1999 to 2007
51	J C van Niekerk	2001 to 2008
47	J T Small	1992 to 1997
46	S W P Burger	2003 to 2008
43	J de Villiers	2002 to 2008
43	J Dalton	1994 to 2002
43	P W G Rossouw	1997 to 2003
43	B G Habana	2004 to 2008
42	G H Teichmann	1995 to 1999
42	R B Skinstad	1997 to 2007
42	P F du Preez	2004 to 2008
39	D W Barry	2000 to 2006
39	C P J Krige	1999 to 2003
39	J Fourie	2003 to 2008
38	F C H du Preez	1961 to 1971
38	J H Ellis	1965 to 1976
38	K Otto	1995 to 2000
38	A H Snyman	1996 to 2006

MOST CONSECUTIVE TESTS

Tests	Player	Span
46	J W Smit	2003 to 2007
39	G H Teichmann	1996 to 1999
26	A H Snyman	1996 to 1998
26	A N Vos	1999 to 2001
25	S H Nomis	1967 to 1972
25	A G Venter	1997 to 1999
25	A-H le Roux	1998 to 1999

MOST TESTS AS CAPTAIN

Tests	Captain	Span
52	J W Smit	2003 to 2008
36	G H Teichmann	1996 to 1999
29	J F Pienaar	1993 to 1996
22	D J de Villiers	1965 to 1970
18	C P J Krigé	1999 to 2003
16	A N Vos	1999 to 2001
15	M du Plessis	1975 to 1980
12	R B Skinstad	2001 to 2007
11	J F K Marais	1971 to 1974

MOST POINTS IN TESTS

Pts	Player	Tests	Career
893	P C Montgomery	102	1997 to 2008
312	H E Botha	28	1980 to 1992
240	J T Stransky	22	1993 to 1996
221	A J J van Straaten	21	1999 to 2001
190	J H van der Westhuizen	89	1993 to 2003
181	J H de Beer	13	1997 to 1999
171	A S Pretorius	31	2002 to 2007
156	H W Honiball	35	1993 to 1999
155	B G Habana	43	2004 to 2008
146	A D James	35	2001 to 2008
145	L J Koen	15	2000 to 2003
135*	B J Paulse	64	1999 to 2007
130	P J Visagie	25	1967 to 1971

* includes a penalty try

MOST TRIES IN TESTS

Tries	Player	Tests	Career
38	J H van der Westhuizen	89	1993 to 2003
31	B G Habana	43	2004 to 2008
27*	B J Paulse	64	1999 to 2007
25	P C Montgomery	94	1997 to 2008
22	J Fourie	39	2003 to 2008
21	P W G Rossouw	43	1997 to 2003
20	J T Small	47	1992 to 1997
19	D M Gerber	24	1980 to 1992
19	C S Terblanche	37	1998 to 2003
16	J de Villiers	43	2002 to 2008
14	C M Williams	27	1993 to 2000

* includes a penalty try

MOST CONVERSIONS IN TESTS

Cons	Player	Tests	Career
153	P C Montgomery	102	1997 to 2008
50	H E Botha	28	1980 to 1992
38	H W Honiball	35	1993 to 1999
33	J H de Beer	13	1997 to 1999
31	A S Pretorius	31	2002 to 2007
30	J T Stransky	22	1993 to 1996
25	G S du Toit	14	1998 to 2006
25	A D James	35	2001 to 2008
23	A J J van Straaten	21	1999 to 2001
23	L J Koen	15	2000 to 2003
20	P J Visagie	25	1967 to 1971

MOST PENALTY GOALS IN TESTS

Pens	Player	Tests	Career
148	P C Montgomery	102	1997 to 2008
55	A J J van Straaten	21	1999 to 2001
50	H E Botha	28	1980 to 1992
47	J T Stransky	22	1993 to 1996
31	L J Koen	15	2000 to 2003
27	J H de Beer	13	1997 to 1999
26	A D James	35	2001 to 2008
25	H W Honiball	35	1993 to 1999
25	A S Pretorius	31	2002 to 2007
23	G R Bosch	9	1974 to 1976
19	P J Visagie	25	1967 to 1971

MOST DROPPED GOALS IN TESTS

Drops	Player	Tests	Career
18	H E Botha	28	1980 to 1992
8	J H de Beer	13	1997 to 1999
8	A S Pretorius	31	2002 to 2007
6	P C Montgomery	102	1997 to 2008
5	J D Brewis	10	1949 to 1953
5	P J Visagie	25	1967 to 1971
4	B L Osler	17	1924 to 1933

TRI-NATIONS RECORDS

RECORD	DETAIL		SET
Most points in season	148	in four matches	1997
Most tries in season	18	in four matches	1997
Highest Score	61	61–22 v Australia (h)	1997
Biggest win	45	53–8 v Australia (h)	2008
Highest score conceded	55	35–55 v N Zealand (a)	1997
Biggest defeat	49	0–49 v Australia (a)	2006
Most points in matches	210	P C Montgomery	1997 to 2008
Most points in season	64	J H de Beer	1997
Most points in match	26	J H de Beer	v Australia (h),1997
Most tries in matches	7	B J Paulse	1999 to 2007
Most tries in season	4	J L Nokwe	2008
Most tries in match	4	J L Nokwe	v Australia (h) 2008
Most cons in matches	26	P C Montgomery	1997 to 2008
Most cons in season	12	J H de Beer	1997
Most cons in match	6	J H de Beer	v Australia (h),1997
Most pens in matches	43	P C Montgomery	1997 to 2008
Most pens in season	13	A J J van Straaten	2000
	13	A J J van Straaten	2001
Most pens in match	6	J T Stransky	v Australia (h),1996
	6	A J J van Straaten	v Australia (h),2000

MISCELLANEOUS RECORDS

RECORD	HOLDER	DETAIL
Longest Test Career	J P du Randt	1994–2007
Youngest Test Cap	A J Hartley	18 yrs 18 days in 1891
Oldest Test Cap	J N Ackermann	37 yrs 34 days in 2007

CAREER RECORDS OF SOUTH AFRICA INTERNATIONAL PLAYERS (UP TO 30 SEPTEMBER 2008)

PLAYER	DEBUT	CAPS	T	C	P	D	PTS
BACKS							
G Bobo	2003 v S	6	0	0	0	0	0
T Chavhanga	2005 v U	4	6	0	0	0	30
M Claassens	2004 v W	8	0	0	0	0	0
J H Conradie	2002 v W	18	2	0	0	1	13
J de Villiers	2002 v F	43	16	0	0	0	80
P F du Preez	2004 v I	42	10	0	0	0	50
B A Fortuin	2006 v I	2	0	0	0	0	0
J Fourie	2003 v U	39	22	0	0	0	110
P J Grant	2007 v A	5	0	0	0	0	0
B G Habana	2004 v E	43	31	0	0	0	155
D J Hougaard	2003 v U	8	2	13	10	1	69
A A Jacobs	2001 v It	18	5	0	0	0	25
A D James	2001 v F	35	3	25	26	1	146
C A Jantjes	2001 v It	21	4	1	0	0	22
E R Januarie	2005 v U	31	5	0	0	0	25
P C Montgomery	1997 v BI	102	25	153	148	6	893
W M Murray	2007 v Sm	3	0	0	0	0	0
A Z Ndungane	2006 v A	11	1	0	0	0	5
O M Ndungane	2008 v It	3	1	0	0	0	5
J L Nokwe	2008 v Arg	3	5	0	0	0	25
W Olivier	2006 v S	21	0	0	0	0	0
R Pienaar	2006 v NZ	24	4	0	1	0	23
J-P R Pietersen	2006 v A	21	10	0	0	0	50
A S Pretorius	2002 v W	31	2	31	25	8	171
J C Pretorius	2006 v I	2	0	0	0	0	0
F P L Steyn	2006 v I	24	5	4	7	3	63
A K Willemse	2003 v S	19	4	0	0	0	20
FORWARDS							
E P Andrews	2004 v I	23	0	0	0	0	0
A Bekker	2008 v W	10	1	0	0	0	5
B J Botha	2006 v NZ	17	0	0	0	0	0

G van G Botha	2005 v A	12	0	0	0	0	0
J P Botha	2002 v F	52	7	0	0	0	35
S B Brits	2008 v It	3	0	0	0	0	0
G J J Britz	2004 v I	13	0	0	0	0	0
S W P Burger	2003 v Gg	46	10	0	0	0	50
B W du Plessis	2007 v A	19	5	0	0	0	25
J N du Plessis	2007 v A	6	0	0	0	0	0
R Kankowski	2007 v W	4	1	0	0	0	5
V Matfield	2001 v It	77	5	0	0	0	25
T Mtawarira	2008 v W	7	1	0	0	0	5
B V Mujati	2008 v W	9	0	0	0	0	0
G J Muller	2006 v S	22	0	0	0	0	0
M C Ralepelle	2006 v NZ	2	0	0	0	0	0
D J Rossouw	2003 v U	34	6	0	0	0	30
J W Smit	2000 v C	78	4	0	0	0	20
J H Smith	2003 v S	52	10	0	0	0	50
P J Spies	2006 v A	16	4	0	0	0	20
G G Steenkamp	2004 v S	18	1	0	0	0	5
J A Strauss	2008 v A	5	0	0	0	0	0
P A van den Berg	1999 v It	51	4	0	0	0	20
C J van der Linde	2002 v S	56	4	0	0	0	20
H S van der Merwe	2007 v W	1	0	0	0	0	0
J L van Heerden	2003 v S	14	1	0	0	0	5
J C van Niekerk	2001 v NZ	51	10	0	0	0	50
P J Wannenburg	2002 v F	20	3	0	0	0	15
L A Watson	2007 v Sm	10	0	0	0	0	0

SOUTH AFRICA INTERNATIONAL PLAYERS

UP TO 30TH SEPTEMBER 2008

Note: Years given for International Championship matches are for second half of season; eg 1972 means season 1971-72. Years for all other matches refer to the actual year of the match. Entries in square brackets denote matches played in RWC Finals.

Ackermann, D S P (WP) 1955 BI 2,3,4, 1956 A 1,2, NZ 1,3, 1958 F 2
Ackermann, J N (NT, BB, N) 1996 Fj, A 1, NZ 1, A 2, 2001 F 2(R), It 1, NZ 1(R), A 1, 2006 I, E1,2, 2007 Sm, A2
Aitken, A D (WP) 1997 F 2(R), E, 1998 I 2(R), W 1(R), NZ 1,2(R), A 2(R)
Albertyn, P K (SWD) 1924 BI 1,2,3,4
Alexander, F A (GW) 1891 BI 1,2
Allan, J (N) 1993 A 1(R), Arg 1,2(R), 1994 E 1,2, NZ 1,2,3, 1996 Fj, A 1, NZ 1, A 2, NZ 2
Allen, P B (EP) 1960 S
Allport, P H (WP) 1910 BI 2,3
Anderson, J W (WP) 1903 BI 3
Anderson, J H (WP) 1896 BI 1,3,4
Andrew, J B (Tvl) 1896 BI 2
Andrews, E P (WP) 2004 I1,2,W1(t&R),PI,NZ1,A1,NZ2,A2,W2,I3,E, 2005 F1,A2,NZ2(t),Arg(R),F3(R), 2006 S1,2,F,A1(R),NZ1(t), 2007 A2(R),NZ2(R)
Andrews, K S (WP) 1992 E, 1993 F 1,2, A 1(R), 2,3, Arg 1(R), 2, 1994 NZ 3
Andrews, M G (N) 1994 E 2, NZ 1,2,3, Arg 1,2, S, W, 1995 WS, [A, WS, F, NZ], W, It, E, 1996 Fj, A 1, NZ 1, A 2, NZ 2,3,4,5, Arg 1,2, F 1,2, W, 1997 Tg (R), BI 1,2, NZ 1, A 1, NZ 2, A 2, It, F 1,2, E, S, 1998 I 1,2, W 1, E 1, A 1, NZ 1,2, A 2, W 2, S, I 3, E 2, 1999 NZ 1,2(R), A 2(R), [S, U, E, A 3, NZ 3], 2000 A 2, NZ 2, A 3, Arg, I, W, E 3, 2001 F 1,2, It 1, NZ 1, A 1,2, NZ 2, F 3, E
Antelme, J G M (Tvl) 1960 NZ 1,2,3,4, 1961 F
Apsey, J T (WP) 1933 A 4,5, 1938 BI 2
Ashley, S (WP) 1903 BI 2
Aston, F T D (Tvl) 1896 BI 1,2,3,4
Atherton, S (N) 1993 Arg 1,2, 1994 E 1,2, NZ 1,2,3, 1996 NZ 2
Aucamp, J (WT) 1924 BI 1,2

Baard, A P (WP) 1960 I
Babrow, L (WP) 1937 A 1,2, NZ 1,2,3
Badenhorst, C (OFS) 1994 Arg 2, 1995 WS (R)
Bands, R E (BB) 2003 S 1,2, Arg (R), A 1, NZ 1, A 2, NZ 2, [U,E,Sm(R),NZ(R)]
Barnard, A S (EP) 1984 S Am 1,2, 1986 Cv 1,2
Barnard, J H (Tvl) 1965 S, A 1,2, NZ 3,4
Barnard, R W (Tvl) 1970 NZ 2(R)
Barnard, W H M (NT) 1949 NZ 4, 1951 W
Barry, D W (WP) 2000 C, E 1,2, A 1(R), NZ 1, A 2, 2001 F 1,2, US (R), 2002 W 2, Arg, Sm, NZ 1, A 1, NZ 2, A 2, 2003 A 1, NZ 1, A 2, [U,E,Sm,NZ], 2004 PI,NZ1,A1,NZ2,A2,W2,I3,E,Arg(t), 2005 F1,2,A1,NZ2,W(R),F3(R), 2006 F
Barry, J (WP) 1903 BI 1,2,3
Bartmann, W J (Tvl, N) 1986 Cv 1,2,3,4, 1992 NZ, A, F, 1,2
Bastard, W E (N) 1937 A 1, NZ 1,2,3, 1938 BI 1,3
Bates, A J (WT) 1969 E, 1970 NZ 1,2, 1972 E
Bayvel, P C R (Tvl) 1974 BI 2,4, F 1,2, 1975 F 1,2, 1976 NZ 1,2,3,4
Beck, J J (WP) 1981 NZ 2(R), 3(R), US
Bedford, T P (N) 1963 A 1,2,3,4, 1964 W, F, 1965 I, A 1,2, 1968 BI 1,2,3,4, F 1,2, 1969 A 1,2,3,4, S, E, 1970 I, W, 1971 F 1,2
Bekker, A (WP) 2008 W1,2(R),It(R),NZ1(R),2(t&R), A1(t&R),Arg(R),NZ3,A2,3
Bekker, H J (WP) 1981 NZ 1,3
Bekker, H P J (NT) 1952 E, F, 1953 A 1,2,3,4, 1955 BI 2,3,4, 1956 A 1,2, NZ 1,2,3,4
Bekker, M J (NT) 1960 S
Bekker, R P (NT) 1953 A 3,4
Bekker, S (NT) 1997 A 2(t)
Bennett, R G (Border) 1997 Tg (R), BI 1(R), 3, NZ 1, A 1, NZ 2
Bergh, W F (SWD) 1931 W, I, 1932 E, S, 1933 A 1,2,3,4,5, 1937 A 1,2, NZ 1,2,3, 1938 BI 1,2,3
Bestbier, A (OFS) 1974 F 2(R)
Bester, J J N (WP) 1924 BI 2,4
Bester, J L A (WP) 1938 BI 2,3
Beswick, A M (Bor) 1896 BI 2,3,4
Bezuidenhout, C E (NT) 1962 BI 2,3,4
Bezuidenhout, C J (MP) 2003 NZ 2(R), [E,Sm,NZ]
Bezuidenhout, N S E (NT) 1972 E, 1974 BI 2,3,4, F 1,2, 1975 F 1,2, 1977 Wld
Bierman, J N (Tvl) 1931 I
Bisset, W M (WP) 1891 BI 1,3
Blair, R (WP) 1977 Wld
Bobo, G (GL, WP) 2003 S 2(R), Arg, A 1(R), NZ 2, 2004 S(R), 2008 It
Boome, C S (WP) 1999 It 1,2, W, NZ 1(R), A 1, NZ 2, A 2, 2000 C, E 1,2, 2003 S 1(R),2(R), Arg (R), A 1(R), NZ 1(R), A 2, NZ 2(R), [U(R),Gg,NZ(R)]
Bosch, G R (Tvl) 1974 BI 2, F 1,2, 1975 F 1,2, 1976 NZ 1,2,3,4
Bosman, H M (FS) 2005 W,F3, 2006 A1(R)
Bosman, N J S (Tvl) 1924 BI 2,3,4
Botha, B J (N) 2006 NZ2(R),3,A3, I(R),E1,2, 2007 E1,Sm, A1,NZ1,Nm(R),S(t&R), [Sm(R),E1,Tg(R),US], 2008 W2
Botha, D S (NT) 1981 NZ 1
Botha, G van G (BB) 2005 A3(R), F3(R), 2007 E1(R),2(R),Sm(R),A1(R),NZ1,A2,NZ2(R),Nm,S, [Tg]
Botha, H E (NT) 1980 S Am 1,2, BI 1,2,3,4, S Am 3,4, F, 1981 I 1,2, NZ 1,2,3, US, 1982 S Am 1,2, 1986 Cv 1,2,3,4, 1989 Wld 1,2, 1992 NZ, A, F 1,2, E
Botha, J A (Tvl) 1903 BI 3
Botha, J P (BB) 2002 F, 2003 S 1,2, A 1, NZ 1, A 2(R), [U,E,Gg,Sm,NZ], 2004 I1,PI,NZ1,A1, NZ2,A2,W2,I3,E,S,Arg, 2005 A1,2,3, NZ1,A4,NZ2,Arg,W,F3, 2007 E1,2,A1,NZ1,Nm,S, [Sm,E1,Tg,US(R),Fj,Arg,E2],W, 2008 W1,2,It,NZ1,2,A1,Arg
Botha, J P F (NT) 1962 BI 2,3,4
Botha, P H (Tvl) 1965 A 1,2
Boyes, H C (GW) 1891 BI 1,2
Brand, G H (WP) 1928 NZ 2,3, 1931 W, I, 1932 E, S, 1933 A 1,2,3,4,5, 1937 A 1,2, NZ 2,3, 1938 BI 1
Bredenkamp, M J (GW) 1896 BI 1,3
Breedt, J C (Tvl) 1986 Cv 1,2,3,4, 1989 Wld 1,2, 1992 NZ, A

Brewis, J D (NT) 1949 NZ 1,2,3,4, 1951 S, I, W, 1952 E, F, 1953 A 1
Briers, T P D (WP) 1955 BI 1,2,3,4, 1956 NZ 2,3,4
Brink D J (WP) 1906 S, W, E
Brink, R (WP) 1995 [R, C]
Brits, S B (WP) 2008 It(R),NZ2(R),A1
Britz, G J J (FS, WP) 2004 I1(R),2(R),W1(R),PI,A1,NZ2,A2(R),I3(t),S(t&R),Arg(R), 2005 U, 2006 E2(R), 2007 NZ2(R)
Britz, W K (N) 2002 W 1
Brooks, D (Bor) 1906 S
Brosnihan, W (GL, N) 1997 A 2, 2000 NZ 1(t+R), A 2(t+R), NZ 2(R), A 3(R), E 3(R)
Brown, C B (WP) 1903 BI 1,2,3
Brynard, G S (WP) 1965 A 1, NZ 1,2,3,4, 1968 BI 3,4
Buchler, J U (Tvl) 1951 S, I, W, 1952 E, F, 1953 A 1,2,3,4, 1956 A 2
Burdett, A F (WP) 1906 S, I
Burger, J M (WP) 1989 Wld 1,2
Burger, M B (NT) 1980 BI 2(R), S Am 3, 1981 US (R)
Burger, S W P (WP) 1984 E 1,2, 1986 Cv 1,2,3,4
Burger, S W P (WP) 2003 [Gg(R),Sm(R),NZ(R)], 2004 I1,2,W1,PI,NZ1,A1,NZ2,A2,W2,I3,E, 2005 F1,2,A1,2(R),3(R),NZ1,A4,NZ2,Arg(R),W,F3, 2006 S1,2, 2007 E1,2,A1,NZ1,Nm,S, [Sm,US,Fj,Arg,E2],W, 2008 It(R),NZ1,2,A1,NZ3,A2,3
Burger, W A G (Bor) 1906 S, I, W, 1910 BI 2

Carelse, G (EP) 1964 W, F, 1965 I, S, 1967 F 1,2,3, 1968 F 1,2, 1969 A 1,2,3,4, S
Carlson, R A (WP) 1972 E
Carolin, H W (WP) 1903 BI 3, 1906 S, I
Carstens, P D (N) 2002 S, E, 2006 E1(t&R),2(R), 2007 E1,2(t&R),Sm(R)
Castens, H H (WP) 1891 BI 1
Chavhanga, T (WP) 2005 U, 2007 NZ2(R), 2008 W1,2
Chignell, T W (WP) 1891 BI 3
Cilliers, G D (OFS) 1963 A 1,3,4
Cilliers, N V (WP) 1996 NZ 3(t)
Claassen, J T (WT) 1955 BI 1,2,3,4, 1956 A 1,2, NZ 1,2,3,4, 1958 F 1,2, 1960 S, NZ 1,2,3, W, I, 1961 E, S, F, I, A 1,2, 1962 BI 1,2,3,4
Claassen, W (N) 1981 I 1,2, NZ 2,3, US, 1982 S Am 1,2
Claassens, M (FS) 2004 W2(R),S(R),Arg(R), 2005 Arg(R),W,F3, 2007 A2(R),NZ2(R)
Clark, W H G (Tvl) 1933 A 3
Clarkson, W A (N) 1921 NZ 1,2, 1924 BI 1
Cloete, H A (WP) 1896 BI 4
Cockrell, C H (WP) 1969 S, 1970 I, W
Cockrell, R J (WP) 1974 F 1,2, 1975 F 1,2, 1976 NZ 1,2, 1977 Wld, 1981 NZ 1,2(R), 3, US
Coetzee, D (BB) 2002 Sm, 2003 S 1,2, Arg, A 1, NZ 1, A 2, NZ 2, [U,E,Sm(R),NZ(R)], 2004 S(R),Arg(R), 2006 A1(R)
Coetzee, J H H (WP) 1974 BI 1, 1975 F 2(R), 1976 NZ 1,2,3,4
Conradie, J H (WP) 2002 W 1,2, Arg (R), Sm, NZ 1, A 1, NZ 2(R), A 2(R), S, E, 2004 W1(R),PI,NZ2,A2, 2005 Arg, 2008 W1,2(R),NZ1(R)
Cope, D K (Tvl) 1896 BI 2
Cotty, W (GW) 1896 BI 3
Crampton, G (GW) 1903 BI 2
Craven, D H (WP) 1931 W, I, 1932 S, 1933 A 1,2,3,4,5, 1937 A 1,2, NZ 1,2,3, 1938 BI 1,2,3,
Cronjé, G (BB) 2003 NZ 2, 2004 I2(R),W1(R)
Cronjé, J (BB, GL) 2004 I1,2,W1,PI,NZ1,A1,NZ2(R),A2(t&R),S(t&R),Arg, 2005 U,F1,2,A1,3,NZ1(R),2(t),Arg,W,F3, 2006 S2(R),F(R),A1(t&R),NZ1,A2,NZ2,A3(R), I(R),E1, 2007 A2(R),NZ2,Nm
Cronje, P A (Tvl) 1971 F 1,2, A 1,2,3, 1974 BI 3,4
Crosby, J H (Tvl) 1896 BI 2
Crosby, N J (Tvl) 1910 BI 1,3
Currie, C (GW) 1903 BI 2

D'Alton, G (WP) 1933 A 1
Dalton, J (Tvl, GL, Falcons) 1994 Arg 1(R), 1995 [A, C], W, It, E, 1996 NZ 4(R),5, Arg 1,2, F 1,2, W, 1997 Tg (R), BI 3, NZ 2, A 2, It, F 1,2, E, S, 1998 I 1,2, W 1, E 1, A 1, NZ 1,2, A 2, W 2, S, I 3, E 2, 2002 W 1,2, Arg, NZ 1, A 1, NZ 2, A 2, F, E
Daneel, G M (WP) 1928 NZ 1,2,3,4, 1931 W, I, 1932 E, S
Daneel, H J (WP) 1906 S, I, W, E
Davidson, C D (N) 2002 W 2(R), Arg, 2003 Arg, NZ 1(R), A 2
Davids, Q (WP) 2002 W 2, Arg (R), Sm (R), 2003 Arg, 2004 I1(R),2,W1,PI(t&R),NZ1(R)
Davison, P M (EP) 1910 BI 1
De Beer, J H (OFS) 1997 BI 3, NZ 1, A 1, NZ 2, A 2, F 2(R), S, 1999 A 2, [S, Sp, U, E, A 3]
De Bruyn, J (OFS) 1974 BI 3
De Jongh, H P K (WP) 1928 NZ 3
De Klerk, I J (Tvl) 1969 E, 1970 I, W
De Klerk, K B H (Tvl) 1974 BI 1,2,3(R), 1975 F 1,2, 1976 NZ 2(R), 3,4, 1980 S Am 1,2, BI 2, 1981 I 1,2
De Kock, A N (GW) 1891 BI 2
De Kock, D (Falcons) 2001 It 2(R), US
De Kock, J S (WP) 1921 NZ 3, 1924 BI 3
De Kock, N A (WP) 2001 It 1, 2002 Sm (R), NZ 1(R),2, A 2, F, 2003 [U(R),Gg,Sm(R),NZ(R)]
Delport, G M (GL, Worcester) 2000 C (R), E 1(t+R), A 1, NZ 1, A 2, NZ 2, A 3, Arg, I, W, 2001 F 2, It 1, 2003 A 1, NZ 2, [U,E,Sm,NZ]
Delport, W H (EP) 1951 S, I, W, 1952 E, F, 1953 A 1,2,3,4
De Melker, S C (GW) 1903 BI 2, 1906 E
Devenish, C E (GW) 1896 BI 2
Devenish, G St L (Tvl) 1896 BI 2
Devenish, G E (Tvl) 1891 BI 1
De Villiers, D I (Tvl) 1910 BI 1,2,3
De Villiers, D J (WP, Bol) 1962 BI 2,3, 1965 I, NZ 1,3,4, 1967 F 1,2,3,4, 1968 BI 1,2,3,4, F 1,2, 1969 A 1,4, E, 1970 I, W, NZ 1,2,3,4
De Villiers, H A (WP) 1906 S, W, E
De Villiers, H O (WP) 1967 F 1,2,3,4, 1968 F 1,2, 1969 A 1,2,3,4, S, E, 1970 I, W
De Villiers, J (WP) 2002 F, 2004 PI,NZ1,A1,NZ2,A2,W2(R),E, 2005 U,F1,2,A1,2,3,NZ1,A4,NZ2,Arg,W,F3, 2006 S1,NZ2,3,A3,I,E1,2, 2007 E1,2,A1,NZ1,Nm, [Sm], 2008 W1,2,It,NZ1,2,A1,Arg,NZ3,A2,3
De Villiers, P du P (WP) 1928 NZ 1,3,4, 1932 E, 1933 A 4, 1937 A 1,2, NZ 1
Devine, D (Tvl) 1924 BI 3, 1928 NZ 2
De Vos, D J J (WP) 1965 S, 1969 A 3, S
De Waal, A N (WP) 1967 F 1,2,3,4
De Waal, P J (WP) 1896 BI 4
De Wet, A E (WP) 1969 A 3,4, E
De Wet, P J (WP) 1938 BI 1,2,3
Dinkelmann, E E (NT) 1951 S, I, 1952 E, F, 1953 A 1,2
Dirksen, C W (NT) 1963 A 4, 1964 W, 1965 I, S, 1967 F 1,2,3,4, 1968 BI 1,2
Dlulane, V T (MP) 2004 W2(R)
Dobbin, F J (GW) 1903 BI 1,2, 1906 S, W, E, 1910 BI 1, 1912 S, I, W
Dobie, J A R (Tvl) 1928 NZ 2
Dormehl, P J (WP) 1896 BI 3,4
Douglass, F W (EP) 1896 BI 1
Drotské, A E (OFS) 1993 Arg 2, 1995 [WS (R)], 1996 A 1(R), 1997 Tg, BI 1,2,3(R), NZ 1, A 1, NZ 2(R), 1998 I 2(R), W 1(R), I 3(R), 1999 It 1,2, W, NZ 1, A 1, NZ 2, A 2, [S, Sp (R), U, E, A 3, NZ 3]
Dryburgh, R G (WP) 1955 BI 2,3,4, 1956 A 2, NZ 1,4, 1960 NZ 1,2
Duff, B R (WP) 1891 BI 1,2,3
Duffy, B A (Bor) 1928 NZ 1
Du Plessis, B W (N) 2007 A2(t&R),NZ2,Nm(R),S(R),[Sm(R),E1(R),US(R),Arg(R),E2(t)],W(R), 2008 W1(R),2(R),It,NZ1(R),2,Arg,NZ3,A2,3
Du Plessis, C J (WP) 1982 S Am 1,2, 1984 E 1,2, S Am 1,2, 1986 Cv 1,2,3,4, 1989 Wld 1,2
Du Plessis, D C (NT) 1977 Wld, 1980 S Am 2
Du Plessis, F (Tvl) 1949 NZ 1,2,3

Du Plessis, J N (FS) 2007 A2,NZ2, [Fj,Arg(t&R)],W, 2008 A3(R)
Du Plessis, M (WP) 1971 A 1,2,3, 1974 BI 1,2, F 1,2, 1975 F 1,2, 1976 NZ 1,2,3,4, 1977 Wld, 1980 S Am 1,2, BI 1,2,3,4, S Am 4, F
Du Plessis, M J (WP) 1984 S Am 1,2, 1986 Cv 1,2,3,4, 1989 Wld 1,2
Du Plessis, N J (WT) 1921 NZ 2,3, 1924 BI 1,2,3
Du Plessis, P G (NT) 1972 E
Du Plessis, T D (NT) 1980 S Am 1,2
Du Plessis, W (WP) 1980 S Am 1,2, BI 1,2,3,4, S Am 3,4, F, 1981 NZ 1,2,3, 1982 S Am 1,2
Du Plooy, A J J (EP) 1955 BI 1
Du Preez, F C H (NT) 1961 E, S, A 1,2, 1962 BI 1,2,3,4, 1963 A 1, 1964 W, F, 1965 A 1,2, NZ 1,2,3,4, 1967 F 4, 1968 BI 1,2,3,4, F 1,2, 1969 A 1,2, S, 1970 I, W, NZ 1,2,3,4, 1971 F 1,2, A 1,2,3
Du Preez, G J D (GL) 2002 Sm (R), A 1(R)
Du Preez, J G H (WP) 1956 NZ 1
Du Preez, P F (BB) 2004 I1,2,W1,PI(R),NZ1,A1,NZ2(R),A2(R),W2,I3,E,S,Arg, 2005 U(R),F1,2(R),A1(R),2(R),3,NZ1(R),A4(R), 2006 S1,2,F,A1(R),NZ1,A2,NZ2,3,A3, 2007 Nm,S, [Sm,E1,US,Fj,Arg,E2], 2008 Arg(R),NZ3,A2,3
Du Preez, R J (N) 1992 NZ, A, 1993 F 1,2, A 1,2,3
Du Rand, J A (R, NT) 1949 NZ 2,3, 1951 S, I, W, 1952 E, F, 1953 A 1,2,3,4, 1955 BI 1,2,3,4, 1956 A 1,2, NZ 1,2,3,4
Du Randt, J P (OFS, FS) 1994 Arg 1,2, S, W, 1995 WS, [A, WS, F, NZ], 1996 Fj, A 1, NZ 1, A 2, NZ 2,3,4, 1997 Tg, BI 1,2,3, NZ 1, A 1, NZ 2, A 2, It, F 1,2, E, S, 1999 NZ 1, A 1, NZ 2, A 2, [S, Sp (R), U, E, A 3, NZ 3], 2004 I1,2,W1,PI,NZ1,A1, NZ2,A2,W2,I3,E,S(R),Arg(R), 2005 U(R),F1, A1,NZ1,A4,NZ2,Arg,W(R),F3, 2006 S1,2,F, A1,NZ1,A2,NZ2,3,A3, 2007 Sm,NZ1,Nm,S, [Sm,E1,US,Fj,Arg,E2]
Du Toit, A F (WP) 1928 NZ 3,4
Du Toit, B A (Tvl) 1938 BI 1,2,3
Du Toit, G S (GW, WP) 1998 I 1, 1999 It 1,2, W (R), NZ 1,2, 2004 I1,W1(R),A1(R),S(R),Arg, 2006 S1(R),2(R),F(R)
Du Toit, P A (NT) 1949 NZ 2,3,4, 1951 S, I, W, 1952 E, F
Du Toit, P G (WP) 1981 NZ 1, 1982 S Am 1,2, 1984 E 1,2
Du Toit, P S (WP) 1958 F 1,2, 1960 NZ 1,2,3,4, W, I, 1961 E, S, F, I, A 1,2
Duvenhage, F P (GW) 1949 NZ 1,3

Edwards, P (NT) 1980 S Am 1,2
Ellis, J H (SWA) 1965 NZ 1,2,3,4, 1967 F 1,2,3,4, 1968 BI 1,2,3,4, F 1,2, 1969 A 1,2,3,4, S, 1970 I, W, NZ 1,2,3,4, 1971 F 1,2, A 1,2,3, 1972 E, 1974 BI 1,2,3,4, F 1,2, 1976 NZ 1
Ellis, M C (Tvl) 1921 NZ 2,3, 1924 BI 1,2,3,4
Els, W W (OFS) 1997 A 2(R)
Engelbrecht, J P (WP) 1960 S, W, I, 1961 E, S, F, A 1,2, 1962 BI 2,3,4, 1963 A 2,3, 1964 W, F, 1965 I, S, A 1,2, NZ 1,2,3,4, 1967 F 1,2,3,4, 1968 BI 1,2, F 1,2, 1969 A 1,2
Erasmus, F S (NT, EP) 1986 Cv 3,4, 1989 Wld 2
Erasmus, J C (OFS, GL) 1997 BI 3, A 2, It, F 1,2, S, 1998 I 1,2, W 1, E 1, A 1, NZ 2, A 2, S, W 2, I 3, E 2, 1999 It 1,2, W, A 1, NZ 2, A 2, [S, U, E, A 3, NZ 3], 2000 C, E 1, A 1, NZ 1,2, A 3, 2001 F 1,2
Esterhuizen, G (GL) 2000 NZ 1(R),2, A 3, Arg, I, W (R), E 3(t)
Etlinger, T E (WP) 1896 BI 4

Ferreira, C (OFS) 1986 Cv 1,2
Ferreira, P S (WP) 1984 S Am 1,2
Ferris, H H (Tvl) 1903 BI 3
Fleck R F (WP) 1999 It 1,2, NZ 1(R), A 1, NZ 2(R), A 2, [S, U, E, A 3, NZ 3], 2000 C, E 1,2, A 1, NZ 1, A 2, NZ 2, A 3, Arg, I, W, E 3, 2001 F 1(R),2, It 1, NZ 1, A 1,2, 2002 S, E
Floors, L (FS) 2006 E2
Forbes, H H (Tvl) 1896 BI 2
Fortuin, B A (FS) 2006 I, 2007 A2
Fourie, C (EP) 1974 F 1,2, 1975 F 1,2
Fourie, J (GL) 2003 [U,Gg,Sm(R),NZ(R)], 2004 I2,E(R),S,Arg, 2005 U(R),F2(R),A1(R),2,3,NZ1,A4,NZ2,Arg,W,F3, 2006 S1,A1,NZ1,A2,NZ2,3,A3, 2007 Sm(R),A1,NZ1,Nm,S, [Sm,E1,US,Fj,Arg,E2],W, 2008 Arg(R)
Fourie, T T (SET) 1974 BI 3
Fourie, W L (SWA) 1958 F 1,2
Francis, J A J (Tvl) 1912 S, I, W, 1913 E, F
Frederickson, C A (Tvl) 1974 BI 2, 1980 S Am 1,2
Frew, A (Tvl) 1903 BI 1
Froneman, D C (OFS) 1977 Wld
Froneman, I L (Bor) 1933 A 1
Fuls, H T (Tvl, EP) 1992 NZ (R), 1993 F 1,2, A 1,2,3, Arg 1,2
Fry, S P (WP) 1951 S, I, W, 1952 E, F, 1953 A 1,2,3,4, 1955 BI 1,2,3,4
Fynn, E E (N) 2001 F 1, It 1(R)
Fyvie, W (N) 1996 NZ 4(t & R), 5(R), Arg 2(R)

Gage, J H (OFS) 1933 A 1
Gainsford, J L (WP) 1960 S, NZ 1,2,3,4, W, I, 1961 E, S, F, A 1,2, 1962 BI 1,2,3,4, 1963 A 1,2,3,4, 1964 W, F, 1965 I, S, A 1,2, NZ 1,2,3,4, 1967 F 1,2,3
Garvey, A C (N) 1996 Arg 1,2, F 1,2, W, 1997 Tg, BI 1,2,3(R), A 1(t), It, F 1,2, E, S, 1998 I 1,2, W 1, E1, A 1, NZ 1,2 A 2, W 2, S, I 3, E 2, 1999 [Sp]
Geel, P J (OFS) 1949 NZ 3
Geere, V (Tvl) 1933 A 1,2,3,4,5
Geffin, A O (Tvl) 1949 NZ 1,2,3,4, 1951 S, I, W
Geldenhuys, A (EP) 1992 NZ, A, F 1,2
Geldenhuys, S B (NT) 1981 NZ 2,3, US, 1982 S Am 1,2, 1989 Wld 1,2
Gentles, T A (WP) 1955 BI 1,2,4, 1956 NZ 2,3, 1958 F 2
Geraghty, E M (Bor) 1949 NZ 4
Gerber, D M (EP, WP) 1980 S Am 3,4, F, 1981 I 1,2, NZ 1,2,3, US, 1982 S Am 1,2, 1984 E 1,2, S Am 1,2, 1986 Cv 1,2,3,4, 1992 NZ, A, F 1,2, E
Gerber, H J (WP) 2003 S 1,2
Gerber, M C (EP) 1958 F 1,2, 1960 S
Gericke, F W (Tvl) 1960 S
Germishuys, J S (OFS, Tvl) 1974 BI 2, 1976 NZ 1,2,3,4, 1977 Wld, 1980 S Am 1,2, BI 1,2,3,4, S Am 3,4, F, 1981 I 1,2, NZ 2,3, US
Gibbs, B (GW) 1903 BI 2
Goosen, C P (OFS) 1965 NZ 2
Gorton, H C (Tvl) 1896 BI 1
Gould, R L (N) 1968 BI 1,2,3,4
Grant, P J (WP) 2007 A2(R),NZ2(R), 2008 W1(t&R),It(R),A1(R)
Gray, B G (WP) 1931 W, 1932 E, S, 1933 A 5
Greeff, W W (WP) 2002 Arg (R), Sm, NZ 1, A 1, NZ 2, A 2, F, S, E, 2003 [U,Gg]
Greenwood, C M (WP) 1961 I
Greyling, P J F (OFS) 1967 F 1,2,3,4, 1968 BI 1, F 1,2, 1969 A 1,2,3,4, S, E, 1970 I, W, NZ 1,2,3,4, 1971 F 1,2, A 1,2,3, 1972 E
Grobler, C J (OFS) 1974 BI 4, 1975 F 1,2
Guthrie, F H (WP) 1891 BI 1,3, 1896 BI 1

Habana, B G (GL, BB) 2004 E(R),S,Arg, 2005 U,F1,2,A1,2,3,NZ1,A4,NZ2,Arg,W,F3, 2006 S2,F,A1,NZ1,A2,NZ2,3, I, E1,2, 2007 E1,2, S, [Sm,E1,Tg(R),US,Fj,Arg,E2], W, 2008 W1,2,It,NZ1,2,A1,NZ3
Hahn, C H L (Tvl) 1910 BI 1,2,3
Hall, D B (GL) 2001 F 1,2, NZ 1, A 1,2, NZ 2, It 2, E, US, 2002 Sm, NZ 1,2, A 2
Halstead, T M (N) 2001 F 3, It 2, E, US (R), 2003 S 1,2
Hamilton, F (EP) 1891 BI 1
Harris, T A (Tvl) 1937 NZ 2,3, 1938 BI 1,2,3
Hartley, A J (WP) 1891 BI 3

Hattingh, H (NT) 1992 A (R), F 2(R), E, 1994 Arg 1,2
Hattingh, L B (OFS) 1933 A 2
Heatlie, B H (WP) 1891 BI 2,3, 1896 BI 1,4, 1903 BI 1,3
Hendricks, M (Bol) 1998 I 2(R), W 1(R)
Hendriks, P (Tvl) 1992 NZ, A, 1994 S, W, 1995 [A, R, C], 1996 A 1, NZ 1, A 2, NZ 2,3,4,5
Hepburn, T B (WP) 1896 BI 4
Heunis, J W (NT) 1981 NZ 3(R), US, 1982 S Am 1,2, 1984 E 1,2, S Am 1,2, 1986 Cv 1,2,3,4, 1989 Wld 1,2
Hill, R A (R) 1960 W, I, 1961 I, A 1,2, 1962 BI 4, 1963 A 3
Hills, W G (NT) 1992 F 1,2, E, 1993 F 1,2, A 1
Hirsch, J G (EP) 1906 I, 1910 BI 1
Hobson, T E C (WP) 1903 BI 3
Hoffman, R S (Bol) 1953 A 3
Holton, D N (EP) 1960 S
Honiball, H W (N) 1993 A 3(R), Arg 2, 1995 WS (R), 1996 Fj, A 1, NZ 5, Arg 1,2, F 1,2, W, 1997 Tg, BI 1,2,3(R), NZ 1(R), A 1(R), NZ 2, A 2, It, F 1,2, E, 1998 W 1(R), E 1, A 1, NZ 1,2, A 2, W 2, S, I 3, E 2, 1999 [A 3(R), NZ 3]
Hopwood, D J (WP) 1960 S, NZ 3,4, W, 1961 E, S, F, I, A 1,2, 1962 BI 1,2,3,4, 1963 A 1,2,4, 1964 W, F, 1965 S, NZ 3,4
Hougaard, D J (BB) 2003 [U(R),E(R),Gg,Sm,NZ], 2007 Sm,A2,NZ2
Howe, B F (Bor) 1956 NZ 1,4
Howe-Browne, N R F G (WP) 1910 BI 1,2,3
Hugo, D P (WP) 1989 Wld 1,2
Human, D C F (WP) 2002 W 1,2, Arg (R), Sm (R)
Hurter, M H (NT) 1995 [R, C], W, 1996 Fj, A 1, NZ 1,2,3,4,5, 1997 NZ 1,2, A 2

Immelman, J H (WP) 1913 F

Jackson, D C (WP) 1906 I, W, E
Jackson, J S (WP) 1903 BI 2
Jacobs, A A (Falcons, N) 2001 It 2(R), US, 2002 W 1(R), Arg, Sm (R), NZ 1(t+R), A 1(R), F, S, E (R), 2008 W1,2,NZ1,2,Arg,NZ3,A2,3
James, A D (N, Bath) 2001 F 1,2, NZ 1, A 1,2, NZ 2, 2002 F (R), S, E, 2006 NZ1,A2,NZ2,3(R),E1, 2007 E1,2,A1,NZ1,Nm,S, [Sm,E1,US,Fj,Arg,E2], 2008 W1,2,NZ1,2,A1,Arg,NZ3,A2,3
Jansen, E (OFS) 1981 NZ 1
Jansen, J S (OFS) 1970 NZ 1,2,3,4, 1971 F 1,2, A 1,2,3, 1972 E
Jantjes, C A (GL, WP) 2001 It 1, A 1,2, NZ 2, F 3, It 2, E, US, 2005 Arg,W, 2007 W(R), 2008 W1,2,It,NZ1,2(R),A1,Arg,NZ3(R),A2,3
Januarie, E R (GL, WP) 2005 U,F2,A1,2,3(R), NZ1,A4,NZ2, 2006 S1(R),2(R),F(R),A1, I,E1,2, 2007 E1,2,Sm,Nm(R), [Sm(R),Tg], W, 2008 W2,It,NZ1,2,A1,Arg,NZ3(R),A2(R),3(R)
Jennings, C B (Bor) 1937 NZ 1
Johnson, G K (Tvl) 1993 Arg 2, 1994 NZ 3, Arg 1, 1995 WS, [R, C, WS]
Johnstone, P G A (WP) 1951 S, I, W, 1952 E, F, 1956 A 1, NZ 1,2,4
Jones, C H (Tvl) 1903 BI 1,2
Jones, P S T (WP) 1896 BI 1,3,4
Jordaan, N (BB) 2002 E (R)
Jordaan, R P (NT) 1949 NZ 1,2,3,4
Joubert, A J (OFS, N) 1989 Wld 1(R), 1993 A 3, Arg 1, 1994 E 1,2, NZ 1,2(R), 3, Arg 2, S, W, 1995 [A, C, WS, F, NZ], W, It, E, 1996 Fj, A 1, NZ 1,3,4,5, Arg 1,2, F 1,2, W, 1997 Tg, BI 1,2, A 2
Joubert, M C (Bol, WP) 2001 NZ 1, 2002 W 1,2, Arg (R), Sm, NZ 1, A1, NZ 2, A 2, F (R), 2003 S 2, Arg, A 1, 2004 I1,2,W1,PI,NZ1,A1,NZ2,A2,W2,I3,E,S,Arg, 2005 U,F1,2,A1
Joubert, S J (WP) 1906 I, W, E
Julies, W (Bol, SWD, GL) 1999 [Sp], 2004 I1,2,W1,S,Arg, 2005 A2(R),3(t), 2006 F(R), 2007 Sm, [Tg]

Kahts, W J H (NT) 1980 BI 1,2,3, S Am 3,4, F, 1981 I 1,2, NZ 2, 1982 S Am 1,2
Kaminer, J (Tvl) 1958 F 2
Kankowski, R (N) 2007 W, 2008 W2(R),It,A1(R)
Kayser, D J (EP, N) 1999 It 2(R), A 1(R), NZ 2, A 2, [S, Sp (R), U, E, A 3], 2001 It 1(R), NZ 1(R), A 2(R), NZ 2(R)
Kebble, G R (N) 1993 Arg 1,2, 1994 NZ 1(R), 2
Kelly, E W (GW) 1896 BI 3
Kempson, R B (N, WP, Ulster) 1998 I 2(R), W 1, E 1, A 1, NZ 1,2 A 2, W 2, S, I 3, E 2, 1999 It 1,2, W, 2000 C, E 1,2, A 1, NZ 1, A 2,3, Arg, I, W, E 3, 2001 F 1,2(R), NZ 1, A 1,2, NZ 2, 2003 S 1(R),2(R), Arg, A 1(R), NZ 1(R), A 2
Kenyon, B J (Bor) 1949 NZ 4
Kipling, H G (GW) 1931 W, I, 1932 E, S, 1933 A 1,2,3,4,5
Kirkpatrick, A I (GW) 1953 A 2, 1956 NZ 2, 1958 F 1, 1960 S, NZ 1,2,3,4, W, I, 1961 E, S, F
Knight, A S (Tvl) 1912 S, I, W, 1913 E, F
Knoetze, F (WP) 1989 Wld 1,2
Koch, A C (Bol) 1949 NZ 2,3,4, 1951 S, I, W, 1952 E, F, 1953 A 1,2,4, 1955 BI 1,2,3,4, 1956 A 1, NZ 2,3, 1958 F 1,2, 1960 NZ 1,2
Koch, H V (WP) 1949 NZ 1,2,3,4
Koen, L J (GL, BB) 2000 A 1, 2001 It 2, E, US, 2003 S 1,2, Arg, A 1, NZ 1, A 2, NZ 2, [U,E,Sm(R),NZ(R)]
Kotze, G J M (WP) 1967 F 1,2,3,4
Krantz, E F W (OFS) 1976 NZ 1, 1981 I 1,
Krige, C P J (WP) 1999 It 2, W, NZ 1, 2000 C (R), E 1(R),2, A 1(R), NZ 1, A 2, NZ 2, A 3, Arg, I, W, E 3, 2001 F 1,2, It 1(R), A 1(t+R), It 2(R), E (R), 2002 W 2, Arg, Sm, NZ 1, A 1, NZ 2, A 2, F, S, E, 2003 Arg, A 1, NZ 1, A 2, NZ 2, [E,Sm,NZ]
Krige, J D (WP) 1903 BI 1,3, 1906 S, I, W
Kritzinger, J L (Tvl) 1974 BI 3,4, F 1,2, 1975 F 1,2, 1976 NZ 4
Kroon, C M (EP) 1955 BI 1
Kruger, P E (Tvl) 1986 Cv 3,4
Kruger, R J (NT, BB) 1993 Arg 1,2, 1994 S, W, 1995 WS, [A, R, WS, F, NZ], W, It, E, 1996 Fj, A 1, NZ 1, A 2, NZ 2,3,4,5, Arg 1,2, F 1,2, W, 1997 Tg, BI 1,2, NZ 1, A 1, NZ 2, 1999 NZ 2, A 2(R), [Sp, NZ 3(R)]
Kruger, T L (Tvl) 1921 NZ 1,2, 1924 BI 1,2,3,4, 1928 NZ 1,2
Kuhn, S P (Tvl) 1960 NZ 3,4, W, I, 1961 E, S, F, I, A 1,2, 1962 BI 1,2,3,4, 1963 A 1,2,3, 1965 I, S

Labuschagne, J J (GL) 2000 NZ 1(R), 2002 W 1,2, Arg, NZ 1, A 1, NZ 2, A2, F, S, E
La Grange, J B (WP) 1924 BI 3,4
Larard, A (Tvl) 1896 BI 2,4
Lategan, M T (WP) 1949 NZ 1,2,3,4, 1951 S, I, W, 1952 E, F, 1953 A 1,2
Laubscher, T G (WP) 1994 Arg 1,2, S, W, 1995 It, E
Lawless, M J (WP) 1964 F, 1969 E (R), 1970 I, W
Ledger, S H (GW) 1912 S, I, 1913 E, F
Leonard, A (WP, SWD) 1999 A 1, [Sp]
Le Roux, A H (OFS, N) 1994 E 1, 1998 I 1,2, W 1(R), E 1(R), A 1(R), NZ 1(R),2(R), A 2(R), W 2(R), S (R), I 3(R), E 2(t+R), 1999 It 1(R),2(R), W (R), NZ 1(R), A 1(R), NZ 2(R), A 2(R), [S(R), Sp, U (R), E (R), A 3(R), NZ 3(R)], 2000 E 1(t+R),2(R), A 1(R),2(R), NZ 2, A 3(R), Arg (R), I (t), W (R), E 3(R), 2001 F 1(R),2, It 1, NZ 1(R), A 1(R),2(R), NZ 2(R), F 3, It 2, E, US (R), 2002 W 1(R),2(R), Arg, NZ 1(R), A 1(R), NZ 2(R), A 2(R)
Le Roux, H P (Tvl) 1993 F 1,2, 1994 E 1,2, NZ 1,2,3, Arg 2, S, W, 1995 WS [A, R, C (R), WS, F, NZ], W, It, E, 1996 Fj, NZ 2, Arg 1,2, F 1,2, W
Le Roux, J H S (Tvl) 1994 E 2, NZ 1,2
Le Roux, M (OFS) 1980 BI 1,2,3,4, S Am 3,4, F, 1981 I 1
Le Roux, P A (WP) 1906 I, W, E
Little, E M (GW) 1891 BI 1,3
Lobberts, H (BB) 2006 E1(R), 2007 NZ2(R)
Lochner, G P (WP) 1955 BI 3, 1956 A 1,2, NZ 1,2,3,4, 1958 F 1,2

SOUTH AFRICA

Lochner, G P (EP) 1937 NZ 3, 1938 BI 1,2
Lockyear, R J (GW) 1960 NZ 1,2,3,4, 1960 I, 1961 F
Lombard, A C (EP) 1910 BI 2
Lombard, F (FS) 2002 S, E
Lötter, D (Tvl) 1993 F 2, A 1,2
Lotz, J W (Tvl) 1937 A 1,2, NZ 1,2,3, 1938 BI 1,2,3
Loubscher, R I P (EP, N) 2002 W 1, 2003 S 1, [U(R),Gg]
Loubser, J A (WP) 1903 BI 3, 1906 S, I, W, E, 1910 BI 1,3
Lourens, M J (NT) 1968 BI 2,3,4
Louw, F H (WP) 2002 W 2(R), Arg, Sm
Louw, J S (Tvl) 1891 BI 1,2,3
Louw, M J (Tvl) 1971 A 2,3
Louw, M M (WP) 1928 NZ 3,4, 1931 W, I, 1932 E, S, 1933 A 1,2,3,4,5, 1937 A 1,2, NZ 2,3, 1938 BI 1,2,3
Louw, R J (WP) 1980 S Am 1,2, BI 1,2,3,4 S Am 3,4, F, 1981 I 1,2, NZ 1,3, 1982 S Am 1,2, 1984 E 1,2, S Am 1,2
Louw, S C (WP) 1933 A 1,2,3,4,5, 1937 A 1, NZ 1,2,3, 1938 BI 1,2,3
Lubbe, E (GW) 1997 Tg, BI 1
Luyt, F P (WP) 1910 BI 1,2,3, 1912 S, I, W, 1913 E
Luyt, J D (EP) 1912 S, W, 1913 E, F
Luyt, R R (W P) 1910 BI 2,3, 1912 S, I, W, 1913 E, F
Lyons, D J (EP) 1896 BI 1
Lyster, P J (N) 1933 A 2,5, 1937 NZ 1

McCallum, I D (WP) 1970 NZ 1,2,3,4, 1971 F 1,2, A 1,2,3, 1974 BI 1,2
McCallum, R J (WP) 1974 BI 1
McCulloch, J D (GW) 1913 E, F
MacDonald, A W (R) 1965 A 1, NZ 1,2,3,4
Macdonald, D A (WP) 1974 BI 2
Macdonald, I (Tvl) 1992 NZ, A, 1993 F 1, A 3, 1994 E 2, 1995 WS (R)
McDonald, J A J (WP) 1931 W, I, 1932 E, S
McEwan, W M C (Tvl) 1903 BI 1,3
McHardy, E E (OFS) 1912 S, I, W, 1913 E, F
McKendrick, J A (WP) 1891 BI 3
Malan, A S (Tvl) 1960 NZ 1,2,3,4, W, I, 1961 E, S, F, 1962 BI 1, 1963 A 1,2,3, 1964 W, 1965 I, S
Malan, A W (NT) 1989 Wld 1,2, 1992 NZ, A, F 1,2, E
Malan, E (NT) 1980 BI 3(R), 4
Malan, G F (WP) 1958 F 2, 1960 NZ 1,3,4, 1961 E, S, F, 1962 BI 1,2,3, 1963 A 1,2,4, 1964 W, 1965 A 1,2, NZ 1,2
Malan, P (Tvl) 1949 NZ 4
Mallett, N V H (WP) 1984 S Am 1,2
Malotana, K (Bor) 1999 [Sp]
Mans, W J (WP) 1965 I, S
Marais, C F (WP) 1999 It 1(R),2(R), 2000 C, E 1,2, A 1, NZ 1, A 2, NZ 2, A 3, Arg (R), W (R)
Marais, F P (Bol) 1949 NZ 1,2, 1951 S, 1953 A 1,2
Marais, J F K (WP) 1963 A 3, 1964 W, F, 1965 I, S, A 2, 1968 BI, 1,2,3,4, F 1,2, 1969 A 1,2,3,4, S, E, 1970 I, W, NZ 1,2,3,4, 1971 F 1,2, A 1,2,3, 1974 BI 1,2,3,4, F 1,2
Maré, D S (Tvl) 1906 S
Marsberg, A F W (GW) 1906 S, W, E
Marsberg, P A (GW) 1910 BI 1
Martheze, W C (GW) 1903 BI 2, 1906 I, W
Martin, H J (Tvl) 1937 A 2
Matfield, V (BB) 2001 It 1(R), NZ 1, A 2, NZ 2, F 3, It 2, E, US, 2002 W 1, Sm, NZ 1, A 1, NZ 2(R), 2003 S 1,2, Arg, A 1, NZ 1, A 2, NZ 2, [U,E,Sm,NZ], 2004 I1,2,W1,NZ2,A2,W2,I3,E,S,Arg, 2005 F1,2,A1, 2,3,NZ1,A4,NZ2,Arg,W,F3, 2006 S1,2,F,A1, NZ1,A2,NZ2,3,A3, 2007 E1,2,A1,NZ1,Nm,S, [Sm,E1,Tg(R),US,Fj,Arg,E2], 2008 W1(R),2,It,NZ1,2,A1,Arg,NZ3,A2,3
Mellet, T B (GW) 1896 BI 2
Mellish, F W (WP) 1921 NZ 1,3, 1924 BI 1,2,3,4
Mentz, H (N) 2004 I1,W1(R)
Merry, J (EP) 1891 BI 1
Metcalf, H D (Bor) 1903 BI 2
Meyer, C du P (WP) 1921 NZ 1,2,3
Meyer, P J (GW) 1896 BI 1
Meyer, W (OFS, GL) 1997 S (R), 1999 It 2, NZ 1(R), A 1(R), 2000 C (R), E 1, NZ 1(R),2(R), Arg, I, W, E 3, 2001 F 1(R),2, It 1, F 3(R), It 2, E, US (t+R), 2002 W 1,2, Arg, NZ 1,2, A 2, F
Michau, J M (Tvl) 1921 NZ 1
Michau, J P (WP) 1921 NZ 1,2,3
Millar, W A (WP) 1906 E, 1910 BI 2,3, 1912 I, W, 1913 F
Mills, W J (WP) 1910 BI 2
Moll, T (Tvl) 1910 BI 2
Montini, P E (WP) 1956 A 1,2
Montgomery, P C (WP, Newport, N, Perpignan) 1997 BI 2,3, NZ 1, A 1, NZ 2, A 2, F 1,2, E, S, 1998 I 1,2, W 1, E 1, A 1, NZ 1,2, A 2, W 2, S, I 3, E 2, 1999 It 1,2, W, NZ 1, A 1, NZ 2, A 2, [S, U, E, A 3, NZ 3], 2000 C, E 1,2, A 1, NZ 1, A 2(R), Arg, I, W, E 3, 2001 F 1, 2(t), It 1, NZ 1, F 3(R), It 2(R), 2004 I2,W1,PI,NZ1,A1,NZ2,A2,W2,I3,E,S, 2005 U,F1,2,A1,2,3,NZ1,A4,NZ2,Arg,W,F3, 2006 S1,2,F,A1,NZ1,A2,NZ2, 2007 E1,2,Sm(R), A1,NZ1,Nm,S, [Sm,E1,Tg(R),US,Fj,Arg,E2], 2008 W1(R),2(R),NZ1(R),2,Arg(R),NZ3,A2(R),3(R)
Moolman, L C (NT) 1977 Wld, 1980 S Am 1,2, BI 1,2,3,4, S Am 3,4, F, 1981 I 1,2, NZ 1,2,3, US, 1982 S Am 1,2, 1984 S Am 1,2, 1986 Cv 1,2,3,4
Mordt, R H (Z-R, NT) 1980 S Am 1,2, BI 1,2,3,4, S Am 3,4, F, 1981 I 2, NZ 1,2,3, US, 1982 S Am 1,2, 1984 S Am 1,2
Morkel, D A (Tvl) 1903 BI 1
Morkel, D F T (Tvl) 1906 I, E, 1910 BI 1,3, 1912 S, I, W, 1913 E, F
Morkel, H J (WP) 1921 NZ 1
Morkel, H W (WP) 1921 NZ 1,2
Morkel, J A (WP) 1921 NZ 2,3
Morkel, J W H (WP) 1912 S, I, W, 1913 E, F
Morkel, P G (WP) 1912 S, I, W, 1913 E, F, 1921 NZ 1,2,3
Morkel, P K (WP) 1928 NZ 4
Morkel, W H (WP) 1910 BI 3, 1912 S, I, W, 1913 E, F, 1921 NZ 1,2,3
Morkel, W S (Tvl) 1906 S, I, W, E
Moss, C (N) 1949 NZ 1,2,3,4
Mostert, P J (WP) 1921 NZ 1,2,3, 1924 BI 1,2,4, 1928 NZ 1,2,3,4, 1931 W, I, 1932 E, S
Mtawarira, T (N) 2008 W2,It,A1(R),Arg,NZ3,A2,3
Muir, D J (WP) 1997 It, F 1,2, E, S
Mujati, B V (WP) 2008 W1,It(R),NZ1(R),2(t),A1(R), Arg(R),NZ3(R),A2(R),3
Mulder, J C (Tvl, GL) 1994 NZ 2,3, S, W, 1995 WS, [A, WS, F, NZ], W, It, E, 1996 Fj, A 1, NZ 1, A 2, NZ 2,5, Arg 1,2, F 1,2, W, 1997 Tg, BI 1, 1999 It 1(R),2, W, NZ 1, 2000 C(R), A 1, E 3, 2001 F 1, It 1
Muller, G H (WP) 1969 A 3,4, S, 1970 W, NZ 1,2,3,4, 1971 F 1,2, 1972 E, 1974 BI 1,3,4
Muller, G J (N) 2006 S1(R),NZ1(R),A2,NZ2,3,A3, I(R),E1,2, 2007 E1(R),2(R),Sm(R),A1(R),NZ1(R), A2,NZ2,Nm(R), [Sm(R),E1(R),Fj(t&R),Arg(t&R)],W
Muller, G P (GL) 2003 A 2, NZ 2, [E,Gg(R),Sm,NZ]
Muller, H L (OFS) 1986 Cv 4(R), 1989 Wld 1(R)
Muller, H S V (Tvl) 1949 NZ 1,2,3,4, 1951 S, I, W, 1952 E, F, 1953 A 1,2,3,4
Muller, L J J (N) 1992 NZ, A
Muller, P G (N) 1992 NZ, A, F 1,2, E, 1993 F 1,2, A 1,2,3, Arg 1,2, 1994 E 1,2, NZ 1, S, W, 1998 I 1,2, W 1, E 1, A 1, NZ 1,2, A 2, 1999 It 1, W, NZ 1, A 1, [Sp, E, A 3, NZ 3]
Murray, W M (N) 2007 Sm,A2,NZ2
Myburgh, F R (EP) 1896 BI 1
Myburgh, J L (NT) 1962 BI 1, 1963 A 4, 1964 W, F, 1968 BI 1,2,3, F 1,2, 1969 A 1,2,3,4, E, 1970 I, W, NZ 3,4
Myburgh, W H (WT) 1924 BI 1

Naude, J P (WP) 1963 A 4, 1965 A 1,2, NZ 1,3,4, 1967 F 1,2,3,4, 1968 BI 1,2,3,4

Ndungane, A Z (BB) 2006 A1,2,NZ2,3,A3, E1,2, 2007 E2,Nm(R), [US],W(R)
Ndungane, O M (N) 2008 It,NZ1,A3
Neethling, J B (WP) 1967 F 1,2,3,4, 1968 BI 4, 1969 S, 1970 NZ 1,2
Nel, J A (Tvl) 1960 NZ 1,2, 1963 A 1,2, 1965 A 2, NZ 1,2,3,4, 1970 NZ 3,4
Nel, J J (WP) 1956 A 1,2, NZ 1,2,3,4, 1958 F 1,2
Nel, P A R O (Tvl) 1903 BI 1,2,3
Nel, P J (N) 1928 NZ 1,2,3,4, 1931 W, I, 1932 E, S, 1933 A 1,3,4,5, 1937 A 1,2, NZ 2,3
Nimb, C F (WP) 1961 I
Nokwe, J L (FS) 2008 Arg,A2,3
Nomis, S H (Tvl) 1967 F 4, 1968 BI 1,2,3,4, F 1,2, 1969 A 1,2,3,4, S, E, 1970 I, W, NZ 1,2,3,4, 1971 F 1,2, A 1,2,3, 1972 E
Nykamp, J L (Tvl) 1933 A 2

Ochse, J K (WP) 1951 I, W, 1952 E, F, 1953 A 1,2,4
Oelofse, J S A (Tvl) 1953 A 1,2,3,4
Oliver, J F (Tvl) 1928 NZ 3,4
Olivier, E (WP) 1967 F 1,2,3,4, 1968 BI 1,2,3,4, F 1,2, 1969 A 1,2,3,4, S, E
Olivier, J (NT) 1992 F 1,2, E, 1993 F 1,2 A 1,2,3, Arg 1, 1995 W, It (R), E, 1996 Arg 1,2, F 1,2, W
Olivier, W (BB) 2006 S1(R),2,F,A1,NZ1,A2,NZ2(R),3,A3, I(R), E1,2, 2007 E1,2,NZ1(R),A2,NZ2, [E1(R),Tg, Arg(R)],W(R)
Olver, E (EP) 1896 BI 1
Oosthuizen, J J (WP) 1974 BI 1, F 1,2, 1975 F 1,2, 1976 NZ 1,2,3,4
Oosthuizen, O W (NT, Tvl) 1981 I 1(R), 2, NZ 2,3, US, 1982 S Am 1,2, 1984 E 1,2
Osler, B L (WP) 1924 BI 1,2,3,4, 1928 NZ 1,2,3,4, 1931 W, I, 1932 E, S, 1933 A 1,2,3,4,5
Osler, S G (WP) 1928 NZ 1
Otto, K (NT, BB) 1995 [R, C (R), WS (R)], 1997 BI 3, NZ 1, A 1, NZ 2, It, F 1,2, E, S, 1998 I 1,2, W 1, E 1, A 1, NZ 1,2, A 2, W 2, S, I 3, E 2, 1999 It 1, W, NZ 1, A 1, [S (R), Sp, U, E, A 3, NZ 3], 2000 C, E 1,2, A 1
Oxlee, K (N) 1960 NZ 1,2,3,4, W, I, 1961 S, A 1,2, 1962 BI 1,2,3,4, 1963 A 1,2,4, 1964 W, 1965 NZ 1,2

Pagel, G L (WP) 1995 [A (R), R, C, NZ (R)], 1996 NZ 5(R)
Parker, W H (EP) 1965 A 1,2
Partridge, J E C (Tvl) 1903 BI 1
Paulse, B J (WP) 1999 It 1,2, NZ 1, A 1,2(R), [S (R), Sp, NZ 3], 2000 C, E 1,2, A 1, NZ 1, A 2, NZ 2, A 3, Arg, W, E 3, 2001 F 1,2, It 1, NZ 1, A 1,2, NZ 2, F 3, It 2, E, 2002 W 1,2, Arg, Sm (R), A 1, NZ 2, A 2, F, S, E, 2003 [Gg], 2004 I1,2,W1,PI,NZ1,A1,NZ2, A2,W2,I3,E, 2005 A2,3,NZ1,A4,F3, 2006 S1,2,A1(R),NZ1,3(R),A3(R), 2007 A2,NZ2
Payn, C (N) 1924 BI 1,2
Pelser, H J M (Tvl) 1958 F 1, 1960 NZ 1,2,3,4, W, I, 1961 F, I, A 1,2
Pfaff, B D (WP) 1956 A 1
Pickard, J A J (WP) 1953 A 3,4, 1956 NZ 2, 1958 F 2
Pienaar, J F (Tvl) 1993 F 1,2, A 1,2,3, Arg 1,2, 1994 E 1,2, NZ 2,3, Arg 1,2, S, W, 1995 WS, [A, C, WS, F, NZ], W, It, E, 1996 Fj, A 1, NZ 1, A 2, NZ 2
Pienaar, R (N) 2006 NZ2(R),3(R),A3(R), I(t), E1(R), 2007 E1(R),2(R),Sm(R),A1,NZ1,A2,NZ2,Nm(R),S(R), [E1(t&R),Tg,US(R),Arg(R)],W, 2008 W1(R),It(R),NZ2(R), A1(R),3(R)
Pienaar, Z M J (OFS) 1980 S Am 2(R), BI 1,2,3,4, S Am 3,4, F, 1981 I 1,2, NZ 1,2,3
Pietersen, J-P R (N) 2006 A3, 2007 Sm,A1,NZ1,A2,NZ2,Nm,S, [Sm,E1,Tg,US(R),Fj, Arg,E2],W, 2008 NZ2,A1,Arg,NZ3,A2
Pitzer, G (NT) 1967 F 1,2,3,4, 1968 BI 1,2,3,4, F 1,2, 1969 A 3,4
Pope, C F (WP) 1974 BI 1,2,3,4, 1975 F 1,2, 1976 NZ 2,3,4
Potgieter, H J (OFS) 1928 NZ 1,2
Potgieter, H L (OFS) 1977 Wld
Powell, A W (GW) 1896 BI 3
Powell, J M (GW) 1891 BI 2, 1896 BI 3, 1903 BI 1,2
Prentis, R B (Tvl) 1980 S Am 1,2, BI 1,2,3,4, S Am 3,4, F, 1981 I 1,2
Pretorius, A S (GL) 2002 W 1,2, Arg, Sm, NZ 1, A 1, NZ 2, F, S (R), E, 2003 NZ 1(R), A 1, 2005 A2,3,NZ1,A4,NZ2,Arg, 2006 NZ2(R),3,A3, I, E1(t&R),2, 2007 S(R), [Sm(R),E1(R),Tg,US(R), Arg(R)],W
Pretorius, J C (GL) 2006 I, 2007 NZ2
Pretorius, N F (Tvl) 1928 NZ 1,2,3,4
Prinsloo, J (Tvl) 1958 F 1,2
Prinsloo, J (NT) 1963 A 3
Prinsloo, J P (Tvl) 1928 NZ 1
Putter, D J (WT) 1963 A 1,2,4

Raaff, J W E (GW) 1903 BI 1,2, 1906 S, W, E, 1910 BI 1
Ralepelle, M C (BB) 2006 NZ2(R), E2(R)
Ras, W J de Wet (OFS) 1976 NZ 1(R), 1980 S Am 2(R)
Rautenbach, S J (WP) 2002 W 1(R),2(t+R), Arg (R), Sm, NZ 1(R), A 1, NZ 2(R), A 2(R), 2003 [U(R),Gg,Sm,NZ], 2004 W1,NZ1(R)
Reece-Edwards, H (N) 1992 F 1,2, 1993 A 2
Reid, A (WP) 1903 BI 3
Reid, B C (Bor) 1933 A 4
Reinach, J (OFS) 1986 Cv 1,2,3,4
Rens, I J (Tvl) 1953 A 3,4
Retief, D F (NT) 1955 BI 1,2,4, 1956 A 1,2, NZ 1,2,3,4
Reyneke, H J (WP) 1910 BI 3
Richards, A R (WP) 1891 BI 1,2,3
Richter, A (NT) 1992 F 1,2, E, 1994 E 2, NZ 1,2,3, 1995 [R, C, WS (R)]
Riley, N M (ET) 1963 A 3
Riordan, C A (Tvl) 1910 BI 1,2
Robertson, I W (R) 1974 F 1,2, 1976 NZ 1,2,4
Rodgers, P H (NT, Tvl) 1989 Wld 1,2, 1992 NZ, F 1,2
Rogers, C D (Tvl) 1984 E 1,2, S Am 1,2
Roos, G D (WP) 1910 BI 2,3
Roos, P J (WP) 1903 BI 3, 1906 I, W, E
Rosenberg, W (Tvl) 1955 BI 2,3,4, 1956 NZ 3, 1958 F 1
Rossouw, C L C (Tvl, N) 1995 WS, [R, WS, F, NZ], 1999 NZ 2(R), A 2(t), [Sp, NZ 3(R)]
Rossouw, D H (WP) 1953 A 3, 4
Rossouw, D J (BB) 2003 [U,Gg,Sm(R),NZ], 2004 E(R),S,Arg, 2005 U,F1,2,A1,W(R),F3(R), 2006 S1,2,F,A1,I,E1,2, 2007 E1,Sm,A1(R),NZ1,S, [Sm,E1,Tg,Fj,Arg,E2], 2008 W1(t&R),NZ3(R),A3(R)
Rossouw, P W G (WP) 1997 BI 2,3, NZ 1, A 1, NZ 2(R), A 2(R), It, F 1,2, E, S, 1998 I 1,2, W 1, E 1, A 1, NZ 1,2, A 2, W 2, S, I 3, E 2, 1999 It 1, W, NZ 1, A 1(R), NZ 2, A 2, [S, U, E, A 3], 2000 C, E 1,2, A 2, Arg (R), I, W, 2001 F 3, US, 2003 Arg
Rousseau, W P (WP) 1928 NZ 3,4
Roux, F du T (WP) 1960 W, 1961 A 1,2, 1962 BI 1,2,3,4, 1963 A 2, 1965 A 1,2, NZ 1,2,3,4, 1968 BI 3,4, F 1,2 1969 A 1,2,3,4, 1970 I, NZ 1,2,3,4
Roux, J P (Tvl) 1994 E 2, NZ 1,2,3, Arg 1, 1995 [R, C, F (R)], 1996 A 1(R), NZ 1, A 2, NZ 3
Roux, O A (NT) 1969 S, E, 1970 I, W, 1972 E, 1974 BI 3,4
Roux, W G (BB) 2002 F (R), S, E
Russell, R B (MP, N) 2002 W 1(R),2, Arg, A 1(R), NZ 2(R), A 2, F, E (R), 2003 Arg (R), A 1(R), NZ 1, A 2(R), 2004 I2(t&R),W1,NZ1(R),W2(R),Arg(R), 2005 U(R),F2(R),A1(t),Arg(R),W(R), 2006 F

Samuels, T A (GW) 1896 BI 2,3,4
Santon, D (Bol) 2003 A 1(R), NZ 1(R), A 2(t), [Gg(R)]
Sauermann, J T (Tvl) 1971 F 1,2, A 1, 1972 E, 1974 BI 1
Schlebusch, J J J (OFS) 1974 BI 3,4, 1975 F 2
Schmidt, L U (NT) 1958 F 2, 1962 BI 2
Schmidt, U L (NT, Tvl) 1986 Cv 1,2,3,4, 1989 Wld 1,2, 1992 NZ, A, 1993 F 1,2, A 1,2,3, 1994 Arg 1,2, S, W

Schoeman, J (WP) 1963 A 3,4, 1965 I, S, A 1, NZ 1,2
Scholtz, C P (WP, Tvl) 1994 Arg 1, 1995 [R, C, WS]
Scholtz, H (FS) 2002 A 1(R), NZ 2(R), A 2(R), 2003 [U(R),Gg]
Scholtz, H H (WP) 1921 NZ 1,2
Schutte, P J W (Tvl) 1994 S, W
Scott, P A (Tvl) 1896 BI 1,2,3,4
Sendin, W D (GW) 1921 NZ 2
Sephaka, L D (GL) 2001 US, 2002 Sm, NZ 1, A 1, NZ 2, A 2, F, 2003 S 1,2, A 1, NZ 1, A 2(t+R), NZ 2, [U,E(t&R),Gg], 2005 F2,A1,2(R),W, 2006 S1(R),NZ3(t&R),A3(R), I
Serfontein, D J (WP) 1980 BI 1,2,3,4, S Am 3,4, F, 1981 I 1,2, NZ 1,2,3, US, 1982 S Am 1,2, 1984 E 1,2, S Am 1,2
Shand, R (GW) 1891 BI 2,3
Sheriff, A R (Tvl) 1938 BI 1,2,3
Shimange, M H (FS, WP) 2004 W1(R),NZ2(R), A2(R),W2(R), 2005 U(R),A1(R),2(R),Arg(R), 2006 S1(R)
Shum, E H (Tvl) 1913 E
Sinclair, D J (Tvl) 1955 BI 1,2,3,4
Sinclair, J H (Tvl) 1903 BI 1
Skene, A L (WP) 1958 F 2
Skinstad, R B (WP, GL, N) 1997 E (t), 1998 W 1(R), E 1(t), NZ 1(R),2(R), A 2(R), W 2(R), S, I 3, E 2, 1999 [S, Sp (R), U, E, A 3], 2001 F 1(R),2(R), It 1, NZ 1, A 1,2, NZ 2, F 3, It 2, E, 2002 W 1,2, Arg, Sm, NZ 1, A 1, NZ 2, A 2, 2003 Arg (R), 2007 E2(t&R),Sm,NZ1,A2, [E1(R),Tg,US(R),Arg(R)]
Slater, J T (EP) 1924 BI 3,4, 1928 NZ 1
Smal, G P (WP) 1986 Cv 1,2,3,4, 1989 Wld 1,2
Small, J T (Tvl, N, WP) 1992 NZ, A, F 1,2, E, 1993 F 1,2, A 1,2,3, Arg 1,2, 1994 E 1,2, NZ 1,2,3(t), Arg 1, 1995 WS, [A, R, F, NZ], W, It, E (R), 1996 Fj, A 1, NZ 1, A 2, NZ 2, Arg 1,2, F 1,2, W, 1997 Tg, BI 1, NZ 1(R), A 1(R), NZ 2, A 2, It, F 1,2, E, S
Smit, F C (WP) 1992 E
Smit, J W (N, Clermont-Auvergne) 2000 C (t), A 1(R), NZ 1(t+R), A 2(R), NZ 2(R), A 3(R), Arg, I, W, E 3, 2001 F 1,2, It 1, NZ 1(R), A 1(R),2(R), NZ 2(R), F 3(R), It 2, E, US (R), [U(R),E(t&R),Gg,Sm,NZ], 2004 I1,2,W1,PI,NZ1,A1,NZ2,A2,W2,I3,E,S,Arg, 2005 U,F1,2,A1,2,3,NZ1,A4,NZ2,Arg,W,F3, 2006 S1,2,F,A1,NZ1,A2,NZ2,3,A3, I, E1,2, 2007 E1,2,Sm,A1, [Sm,E1,Tg(R),US,Fj,Arg,E2],W, 2008 W1,2,NZ1
Smith, C M (OFS) 1963 A 3,4, 1964 W, F, 1965 A 1,2, NZ 2
Smith, C W (GW) 1891 BI 2, 1896 BI 2,3
Smith, D (GW) 1891 BI 2
Smith D J (Z-R) 1980 BI 1,2,3,4
Smith, G A C (EP) 1938 BI 3
Smith, J H (FS) 2003 S 1(R),2(R), A 1, NZ 1, A 2, NZ 2, [U,E,Sm,NZ], 2004 W2, 2005 U(R),F2(R), A2,3,NZ1,A4,NZ2,Arg,W,F3, 2006 S1,2,F,A1,NZ1,A2, I, E2, 2007 E1,2,A1,Nm,S, [Sm,E1,Tg(t&R), US,Fj,Arg,E2],W, 2008 W1,2,It,NZ1,2,A1, Arg,NZ3,A2,3
Smith, P F (GW) 1997 S (R), 1998 I 1(t),2, W 1, NZ 1(R),2(R), A 2(R), W 2, 1999 NZ 2
Smollan, F C (Tvl) 1933 A 3,4,5
Snedden, R C D (GW) 1891 BI 2
Snyman, A H (NT, BB, N) 1996 NZ 3,4, Arg 2(R), W (R), 1997 Tg, BI 1,2,3, NZ 1, A 1, NZ 2, A 2, It, F 1,2, E, S, 1998 I 1,2, W 1, E 1, A 1, NZ 1,2, A 2, W 2, S, I 3, E 2, 1999 NZ 2, 2001 NZ 2, F 3, US, 2002 W 1, 2003 S 1, NZ 1, 2006 S1,2
Snyman, D S L (WP) 1972 E, 1974 BI 1,2(R), F 1,2, 1975 F 1,2, 1976 NZ 2,3, 1977 Wld
Snyman, J C P (OFS) 1974 BI 2,3,4
Sonnekus, G H H (OFS) 1974 BI 3, 1984 E 1,2
Sowerby, R S (N) 2002 Sm (R)
Spies, J J (NT) 1970 NZ 1,2,3,4
Spies, P J (BB) 2006 A1,NZ2,3,A3, I, E1, 2007 E1(R),2,A1, 2008 W1,2,A1,Arg,NZ3,A2,3
Stander, J C J (OFS) 1974 BI 4(R), 1976 NZ 1,2,3,4
Stapelberg, W P (NT) 1974 F 1,2
Starke, J J (WP) 1956 NZ 4
Starke, K T (WP) 1924 BI 1,2,3,4
Steenekamp, J G A (Tvl) 1958 F 1
Steenkamp, G G (FS, BB) 2004 S,Arg, 2005 U,F2(R),A2,3,NZ1(R),A4(R), 2007 E1(R),2,A1,[Tg,Fj(R)], 2008 W1,2(R),NZ1,2,A1
Stegmann, A C (WP) 1906 S, I
Stegmann, J A (Tvl) 1912 S, I, W, 1913 E, F
Stewart, C (WP) 1998 S, I 3, E 2
Stewart, D A (WP) 1960 S, 1961 E, S, F, I, 1963 A 1,3,4, 1964 W, F, 1965 I
Steyn, F P L (N) 2006 I,E1,2, 2007 E1(R),2(R), Sm,A1(R),NZ1(R),S, [Sm(R),E1,Tg(R),US,Fj,Arg,E2],W, 2008 W2(R),It,NZ1(R),2(R),A1,NZ3(R),A2(R)
Stofberg, M T S (OFS, NT, WP) 1976 NZ 2,3, 1977 Wld, 1980 S Am 1,2, BI 1,2,3,4, S Am 3,4, F, 1981 I 1,2, NZ 1,2, US, 1982 S Am 1,2, 1984 E 1,2
Strachan, L C (Tvl) 1932 E, S, 1937 A 1,2, NZ 1,2,3, 1938 BI 1,2,3
Stransky, J T (N, WP) 1993 A 1,2,3, Arg 1, 1994 Arg 1,2, 1995 WS, [A, R (t), C, F, NZ], W, It, E, 1996 Fj (R), NZ 1, A 2, NZ 2,3,4,5(R)
Straeuli, R A W (Tvl) 1994 NZ 1, Arg 1,2, S, W, 1995 WS, [A, WS, NZ (R)], E (R)
Strauss, C P (WP) 1992 F 1,2, E, 1993 F 1,2, A 1,2,3, Arg 1,2, 1994 E 1, NZ 1,2, Arg 1,2
Strauss, J A (WP) 1984 S Am 1,2
Strauss, J A (FS) 2008 A1(R),Arg(R),NZ3(R),A2(R),3(R)
Strauss, J H P (Tvl) 1976 NZ 3,4, 1980 S Am 1
Strauss, S S F (GW) 1921 NZ 3
Strydom, C F (OFS) 1955 BI 3, 1956 A 1,2, NZ 1,4, 1958 F 1,
Strydom, J J (Tvl, GL) 1993 F 2, A 1,2,3, Arg 1,2, 1994 E 1, 1995 [A, C, F, NZ], 1996 A 2(R), NZ 2(R), 3,4, W (R), 1997 Tg, BI 1,2,3, A 2
Strydom, L J (NT) 1949 NZ 1,2
Styger, J J (OFS) 1992 NZ (R), A, F 1,2, E, 1993 F 2(R), A 3(R)
Suter, M R (N) 1965 I, S
Swanepoel, W (OFS, GL) 1997 BI 3(R), A 2(R), F 1(R), 2, E, S, 1998 I 2(R), W 1(R), E 2(R), 1999 It 1,2(R), W, A 1, [Sp, NZ 3(t)], 2000 A 1, NZ 1, A 2, NZ 2, A 3
Swart, J (WP) 1996 Fj, NZ 1(R), A 2, NZ 2,3,4,5, 1997 BI 3(R), It, S (R)
Swart, J J N (SWA) 1955 BI 1
Swart, I S (Tvl) 1993 A 1,2,3, Arg 1, 1994 E 1,2, NZ 1,3, Arg 2(R), 1995 WS, [A, WS, F, NZ], W, 1996 A 2

Taberer, W S (GW) 1896 BI 2
Taylor, O B (N) 1962 BI 1
Terblanche, C S (Bol, N) 1998 I 1,2, W 1, E 1, A 1, NZ 1,2, A 2, W 2, S, I 3, E 2, 1999 It 1(R),2, W, A 1, NZ 2(R), [Sp, E (R), A 3(R), NZ 3], 2000 E 3, 2002 W 1,2, Arg, Sm, NZ 1, A 1,2(R), 2003 S 1,2, Arg, A 1, NZ 1, A 2, NZ 2, [Gg]
Teichmann, G H (N) 1995 W, 1996 Fj, A 1, NZ 1, A 2, NZ 2,3,4,5, Arg 1,2, F 1,2, W, 1997 Tg, BI 1,2,3, NZ 1, A 1, NZ 2, A 2, It, F 1,2 E, S, 1998 I 1,2, W 1, E 1, A 1, NZ 1,2, A 2, W 2, S, I 3, E 2, 1999 It 1, W, NZ 1
Theron, D F (GW) 1996 A 2(R), NZ 2(R), 5, Arg 1,2, F 1,2, W, 1997 BI 2(R), 3, NZ 1(R), A 1, NZ 2(R)
Theunissen, D J (GW) 1896 BI 3
Thompson, G (WP) 1912 S, I, W
Tindall, J C (WP) 1924 BI 1, 1928 NZ 1,2,3,4
Tobias, E G (SARF, Bol) 1981 I 1,2, 1984 E 1,2, S Am 1,2
Tod, N S (N) 1928 NZ 2
Townsend, W H (N) 1921 NZ 1
Trenery, W E (GW) 1891 BI 2
Tromp, H (NT) 1996 NZ3,4, Arg 2(R), F 1(R)
Truter, D R (WP) 1924 BI 2,4
Truter, J T (N) 1963 A 1, 1964 F, 1965 A 2
Turner, F G (EP) 1933 A 1,2,3, 1937 A 1,2, NZ 1,2,3, 1938 BI 1,2,3
Twigge, R J (NT) 1960 S

Tyibilika, S (N) 2004 S,Arg, 2005 U,A2,Arg, 2006 NZ1,A2,NZ2

Ulyate, C A (Tvl) 1955 BI 1,2,3,4, 1956 NZ 1,2,3
Uys, P de W (NT) 1960 W, 1961 E, S, I, A 1,2, 1962 BI 1,4, 1963 A 1,2, 1969 A 1(R), 2
Uys, P J (Pumas) 2002 S

Van Aswegen, H J (WP) 1981 NZ 1, 1982 S Am 2(R)
Van Biljon, L (N) 2001 It 1(R), NZ 1, A 1,2, NZ 2, F 3, It 2(R), E (R), US, 2002 F (R), S, E (R), 2003 NZ 2(R)
Van Broekhuizen, H D (WP) 1896 BI 4
Van Buuren, M C (Tvl) 1891 BI 1
Van de Vyver, D F (WP) 1937 A 2
Van den Berg, D S (N) 1975 F 1,2, 1976 NZ 1,2
Van den Berg, M A (WP) 1937 A 1, NZ 1,2,3
Van den Berg, P A (WP, GW, N) 1999 It 1(R),2, NZ 2, A 2, [S, U (t+R), E (R), A 3(R), NZ 3(R)], 2000 E 1(R), A 1, NZ 1, A 2, NZ 2(R), A 3(t+R), Arg, I, W, E 3, 2001 F 1(R),2, A 2(R), NZ 2(R), US, 2004 NZ1, 2005 U,F1,2,A1(R),2(R),3(R),4(R),Arg(R),F3(R), 2006 S2(R),A1(R),NZ1,A2(R),NZ2(R),A3(R), I, E1(R),2(R), 2007 Sm,A2(R),NZ2,Nm(t&R),S(R), [Tg,US],W(R)
Van den Bergh, E (EP) 1994 Arg 2(t & R)
Van der Linde, A (WP) 1995 It, E, 1996 Arg 1(R), 2(R), F 1(R), W (R), 2001 F 3(R)
Van der Linde, C J (FS) 2002 S (R), E(R), 2004 I1(R),2(R),PI(R),A1(R),NZ2(t&R),A2(R),W2(R),I3(R),E(t&R),S,Arg, 2005 U,F1(R),2,A1(R),3,NZ1,A4,NZ2,Arg, W,F3, 2006 S2(R),F(R),A1,NZ1,A2,NZ2, I, E1,2, 2007 E1(R),2,A1(R),NZ1(R),A2,NZ2,Nm,S, [Sm,E1(R),Tg,US(R),Arg,E2],W, 2008 W1(t&R),It,NZ1,2,A1,Arg,NZ3,A2
Van der Merwe, A J (Bol) 1955 BI 2,3,4, 1956 A 1,2, NZ 1,2,3,4, 1958 F 1, 1960 S, NZ 2
Van der Merwe, A V (WP) 1931 W
Van der Merwe, B S (NT) 1949 NZ 1
Van der Merwe, H S (NT) 1960 NZ 4, 1963 A 2,3,4, 1964 F
Van der Merwe, H S (GL) 2007 W(t+R)
Van der Merwe, J P (WP) 1970 W
Van der Merwe, P R (SWD, WT, GW) 1981 NZ 2,3, US, 1986 Cv 1,2, 1989 Wld 1
Vanderplank, B E (N) 1924 BI 3,4
Van der Schyff, J H (GW) 1949 NZ 1,2,3,4, 1955 BI 1
Van der Watt, A E (WP) 1969 S (R), E, 1970 I
Van der Westhuizen, J C (WP) 1928 NZ 2,3,4, 1931 I
Van der Westhuizen, J H (WP) 1931 I, 1932 E, S
Van der Westhuizen, J H (NT, BB) 1993 Arg 1,2, 1994 E 1,2(R), Arg 2, S, W, 1995 WS, [A, C (R), WS, F, NZ], W, It, E, 1996 Fj, A 1,2(R), NZ 2,3(R), 4,5, Arg 1,2, F 1,2, W, 1997 Tg, BI 1,2,3, NZ 1, A 1, NZ 2, A 2, It, F 1, 1998 I 1,2, W 1, E 1, A 1, NZ 1,2, A 2, W 2, S, I 3, E 2, 1999 NZ 2, A 2, [S, Sp (R), U, E, A 3, NZ 3], 2000 C, E 1,2, A 1(R), NZ 1(R), A 2(R), Arg, I, W, E 3, 2001 F 1,2, It 1(R), NZ 1, A 1,2, NZ 2, F 3, It 2, E, US (R), 2003 S 1,2, A 1, NZ 1, A 2(R), NZ 2, [U,E,Sm,NZ]
Van der Westhuyzen, J N B (MP, BB) 2000 NZ 2(R), 2001 It 1(R), 2003 S 1(R),2, Arg, A 1, 2003 [E,Sm,NZ], 2004 I1,2,W1,PI,NZ1,A1,NZ2,A2,W2, I3,E,S,Arg, 2005 U,F1,2,A1,4(R),NZ2(R), 2006 S1,2,F,A1
Van Druten, N J V (Tvl) 1924 BI 1,2,3,4, 1928 NZ 1,2,3,4
Van Heerden, A J (Tvl) 1921 NZ 1,3
Van Heerden, F J (WP) 1994 E 1,2(R), NZ 3, 1995 It, E, 1996 NZ 5(R), Arg 1(R),2(R), 1997 Tg, BI 2(t+R),3(R), NZ 1(R),2(R), 1999 [Sp]
Van Heerden, J L (NT, Tvl) 1974 BI 3,4, F 1,2, 1975 F 1,2, 1976 NZ 1,2,3,4, 1977 Wld, 1980 BI 1,3,4, S Am 3,4, F
Van Heerden, J L (BB) 2003 S 1,2, A 1, NZ 1, A 2(t), 2007 A2,NZ2,S(R), [Sm(R),E1,Tg,US,Fj(R),E2(R)]
Van Jaarsveld, C J (Tvl) 1949 NZ 1
Van Jaarsveldt, D C (R) 1960 S
Van Niekerk, J A (WP) 1928 NZ 4
Van Niekerk, J C (GL, WP) 2001 NZ 1(R), A 1(R), NZ 2(t+R), F 3(R), It2, US, 2002 W 1(R),2(R), Arg (R), Sm, NZ 1, A 1, NZ 2, A 2, F, S, E, 2003 A 2, NZ 2, [U,E,Gg,Sm], 2004 NZ1(R),A1(t),NZ2,A2,W2,I3,E,S, Arg(R), 2005 U(R),F2(R),A1(R),2,3,NZ1,A4,NZ2, 2006 S1,2,F,A1,NZ1(R),A2(R), 2008 It(R),NZ1,2,Arg(R),A2(R)
Van Reenen, G L (WP) 1937 A 2, NZ 1
Van Renen, C G (WP) 1891 BI 3, 1896 BI 1,4
Van Renen, W (WP) 1903 BI 1,3
Van Rensburg, J T J (Tvl) 1992 NZ, A, E, 1993 F 1,2, A 1, 1994 NZ 2
Van Rooyen, G W (Tvl) 1921 NZ 2,3
Van Ryneveld, R C B (WP) 1910 BI 2,3
Van Schalkwyk, D (NT) 1996 Fj (R), NZ 3,4,5, 1997 BI 2,3, NZ 1, A 1
Van Schoor, R A M (R) 1949 NZ 2,3,4, 1951 S, I, W, 1952 E, F, 1953 A 1,2,3,4
Van Straaten, A J J (WP) 1999 It 2(R), W, NZ 1(R), A 1, 2000 C, E 1,2, NZ 1, A 2, NZ 2, A 3, Arg (R), I (R), W, E 3, 2001 A 1,2, NZ 2, F 3, It 2, E
Van Vollenhoven, K T (NT) 1955 BI 1,2,3,4, 1956 A 1,2, NZ 3
Van Vuuren, T F (EP) 1912 S, I, W, 1913 E, F
Van Wyk, C J (Tvl) 1951 S, I, W, 1952 E, F, 1953 A 1,2,3,4, 1955 BI 1
Van Wyk, J F B (NT) 1970 NZ 1,2,3,4, 1971 F 1,2, A 1,2,3, 1972 E, 1974 BI 1,3,4, 1976 NZ 3,4
Van Wyk, S P (WP) 1928 NZ 1,2
Van Zyl, B P (WP) 1961 I
Van Zyl, C G P (OFS) 1965 NZ 1,2,3,4
Van Zyl, D J (WP) 2000 E 3(R)
Van Zyl, G H (WP) 1958 F 1, 1960 S, NZ 1,2,3,4, W, I, 1961 E, S, F, I, A 1,2, 1962 BI 1,3,4
Van Zyl, H J (Tvl) 1960 NZ 1,2,3,4, I, 1961 E, S, I, A 1,2
Van Zyl, P J (Bol) 1961 I
Veldsman, P E (WP) 1977 Wld
Venter, A G (OFS) 1996 NZ 3,4,5, Arg 1,2, F 1,2, W, 1997 Tg, BI 1,2,3, NZ 1, A 1, NZ 2, It, F 1,2, E, S, 1998 I 1,2, W 1, E 1, A 1, NZ 1,2, A 2, W 2, S (R), I 3(R), E 2(R), 1999 It 1,2(R), W (R), NZ 1, A 1, NZ 2, A 2, [S, U, E, A 3, NZ 3], 2000 C, E 1,2, A 1, NZ 1, A 2, NZ 2, A 3, Arg, I, W, E 3, 2001 F 1, It 1, NZ 1, A 1,2, NZ 2, F 3(R), It 2(R), E (t+R), US (R)
Venter, A J (N) 2000 W (R), E 3(R), 2001 F 3, It 2, E, US, 2002 W 1,2, Arg, NZ 1(R),2, A 2, F, S (R), E, 2003 Arg, 2004 PI,NZ1,A1,NZ2(R),A2,I3,E, 2006 NZ3,A3
Venter, B (OFS) 1994 E 1,2, NZ 1,2,3, Arg 1,2, 1995 [R, C, WS (R), NZ (R)], 1996 A 1, NZ 1, A 2, 1999 A 2, [S, U]
Venter, F D (Tvl) 1931 W, 1932 S, 1933 A 3
Versfeld, C (WP) 1891 BI 3
Versfeld, M (WP) 1891 BI 1,2,3
Vigne, J T (Tvl) 1891 BI 1,2,3
Viljoen, J F (GW) 1971 F 1,2, A 1,2,3, 1972 E
Viljoen, J T (N) 1971 A 1,2,3
Villet, J V (WP) 1984 E 1,2
Visagie, I J (WP) 1999 It 1, W, NZ 1, A 1, NZ 2, A 2, [S, U, E, A 3, NZ 3], 2000 C, E 2, A 1, NZ 1, A 2, NZ 2, A 3, 2001 NZ 1, A 1,2, NZ 2, F 3, It 2(R), E (t+R), US, 2003 S 1(R),2(R), Arg
Visagie, P J (GW) 1967 F 1,2,3,4, 1968 BI 1,2,3,4, F 1,2, 1969 A 1,2,3,4, S, E, 1970 NZ 1,2,3,4, 1971 F 1,2, A 1,2,3
Visagie, R G (OFS, N) 1984 E 1,2, S Am 1,2, 1993 F 1
Visser, J de V (WP) 1981 NZ 2, US
Visser, M (WP) 1995 WS (R)
Visser, P J (Tvl) 1933 A 2
Viviers, S S (OFS) 1956 A 1,2, NZ 2,3,4
Vogel, M L (OFS) 1974 BI 2(R)
Von Hoesslin, D J B (GW) 1999 It 1(R),2, W (R), NZ 1, A 1(R)
Vos, A N (GL) 1999 It 1(t+R),2, NZ 1(R),2(R), A 2, [S (R), Sp, E (R), A 3(R), NZ 3], 2000 C, E 1,2, A 1, NZ

1, A 2, NZ 2, A 3, Arg, I, W, E 3, 2001 F 1,2, It 1, NZ 1, A 1,2, NZ 2, F 3, It 2, E, US

Wagenaar, C (NT) 1977 Wld
Wahl, J J (WP) 1949 NZ 1
Walker, A P (N) 1921 NZ 1,3, 1924 BI 1,2,3,4
Walker, H N (OFS) 1953 A 3, 1956 A 2, NZ 1,4
Walker, H W (Tvl) 1910 BI 1,2,3
Walton, D C (N) 1964 F, 1965 I, S, NZ 3,4, 1969 A 1,2, E
Wannenburg, P J (BB) 2002 F (R), E, 2003 S 1,2, Arg, A 1(t+R), NZ 1(R), 2004 I1,2,W1,PI(R), 2006 S1(R),F,NZ2(R),3,A3, 2007 Sm(R),NZ1(R),A2,NZ2
Waring, F W (WP) 1931 I, 1932 E, 1933 A 1,2,3,4,5
Watson, L A (WP) 2007 Sm, 2008 W1,2,It,NZ1(R),2(R),Arg,NZ3(R),A2(R),3(t&R)
Wegner, N (WP) 1993 F 2, A 1,2,3
Wentzel, M van Z (Pumas) 2002 F (R), S
Wessels, J J (WP) 1896 BI 1,2,3
Whipp, P J M (WP) 1974 BI 1,2, 1975 F 1, 1976 NZ 1,3,4, 1980 S Am 1,2
White, J (Bor) 1931 W, 1933 A 1,2,3,4,5, 1937 A 1,2, NZ 1,2
Wiese, J J (Tvl) 1993 F 1, 1995 WS, [R, C, WS, F, NZ], W, It, E, 1996 NZ 3(R), 4(R), 5, Arg 1,2, F 1,2, W
Willemse, A K (GL) 2003 S 1,2, NZ 1, A 2, NZ 2, [U,E,Sm,NZ], 2004 W2,I3, 2007 E1,2(R), Sm,A1,NZ1,Nm,S(R), [Tg]
Williams, A E (GW) 1910 BI 1
Williams, A P (WP) 1984 E 1,2
Williams, C M (WP, GL) 1993 Arg 2, 1994 E 1,2, NZ 1,2,3, Arg 1,2, S, W, 1995 WS, [WS, F, NZ], It, E, 1998 A 1(t), NZ 1(t), 2000 C (R), E 1(t),2(R), A 1(R), NZ 2, A 3, Arg, I, W (R)
Williams, D O (WP) 1937 A 1,2, NZ 1,2,3, 1938 BI 1,2,3
Williams, J G (NT) 1971 F 1,2, A 1,2,3, 1972 E, 1974 BI 1,2,4, F 1,2, 1976 NZ 1,2
Wilson, L G (WP) 1960 NZ 3,4, W, I, 1961 E, F, I, A 1,2, 1962 BI 1,2,3,4, 1963 A 1,2,3,4, 1964 W, F, 1965 I, S, A 1,2, NZ 1,2,3,4
Wolmarans, B J (OFS) 1977 Wld
Wright, G D (EP, Tvl) 1986 Cv 3,4, 1989 Wld 1,2, 1992 F 1,2, E
Wyness, M R K (WP) 1962 BI 1,2,3,4, 1963 A 2

Zeller, W C (N) 1921 NZ 2,3
Zimerman, M (WP) 1931 W, I, 1932 E, S

TONGA

TONGA'S 2008 RECORD

OPPONENTS	DATE	VENUE	RESULT
New Zealand Maori	7 June	A	**Lost** 9–20
Japan	15 June	A	**Lost** 13–35
Australia A	22 June	A	**Lost** 7–90
Samoa	28 June	H	**Lost** 15–20
Fiji	5 July	H	**Won** 27–16

ISLANDS UPS AND DOWNS

By Frankie Deges

Tonga's season consisted of a blend of highs and lows but overall was a satisfactory follow-up to a previous year that had finished with a very good showing in Rugby World Cup 2007.

On the one hand, a Tongan team won the 2008 IRB Pacific Rugby Cup, which involves two provincial sides each from Tonga, Samoa and Fiji; on the other, the proud 'Ikale Tahi only managed one win in five games in the 2008 IRB Pacific Nations Cup and finished last.

The Tonga Rugby Union continued its work to maintain the International Rugby Board's High Performance initiatives. "The goal is to assist our players to a higher level of competition and in this respect, the IRB assistance is important," said Tonga RU CEO Siosaia Fonua.

During 2008, the IRB announced that within the £48 million Strategic Investment Programme, Tonga was one of the 22 countries targeted over the next four years. The 20 per cent increase in funding from the previous 2006–2008 cycle was a well-received. Tonga is maintained at mid-level funding of £1.05 million.

The domestic season opened with the 2008 IRB Pacific Rugby Cup, which had two teams selected from within Tonga – Tautahi Gold and Tauuta Reds. This tournament is a key element of the IRB's global strategic investment programme aimed at providing an athlete development opportunity for over 180 players in the three island countries. They are exposed and tested in a high intensity international representative competition that bridges the gap between domestic and international competition. In 2007, in the second season of the IRB Pacific Rugby Cup, 15 Tongan players graduated from this tournament to the full national team.

After five rounds and 15 games, it seemed that the Samoan domination would continue; Upolu Samoa, with four wins in five games, playing host to Tautahi Gold, with three wins, in a capacity-filled Apia.

Upolu Samoa might have entered the final with a false sense of confidence; but the Tongan team showed their intentions early on in a game that had all those qualities that make Pacific rugby such a joy. Full-back Sitaleki Lu'au was the best performer on the day – he scored a try in the sixth minute and added a 45-metre penalty.

The team's campaign was dedicated to 15-year-old Tae Kim, who was at the time battling heart problems. She was visited at her bedside by the team upon returning from Samoa. Tae was inspirational for the team but sadly passed away in August.

The other Tongan team, Tauuta Reds (finalists in 2007) finished in fourth place.

Next came the Pacific Nations Cup, a tough fixture list for Tonga, having to play their opening three matches on the road: first in Albany against the New Zealand Maori, in Sendai versus Japan and in Sydney against Australia A, on consecutive weekends. The Test window would finish with consecutive home ties against Manu Samoa and Fiji. Understandably, the best performances came in Nuku'alofa. The home environment helped and by then a handful of key players had been released by their European clubs.

When it came to Sevens, Tonga finished 11th in the 2007–08 IRB Sevens World Series. In Wellington, they reached the Cup semi-finals after first day wins against USA and Argentina followed by a superb quarter-final win against South Africa 14–10. They only narrowly failed to make it to the final, losing in the semi against Samoa by three points, 21–24.

They also qualified for the Rugby World Cup Sevens and reached the Plate semis in Hong Kong and the Cup quarters in Adelaide.

Tonga finished 13th of 16 teams in the new IRB Junior World Championship held in Wales. With a superb sense of continuity, this team was made up mostly of players in the island, the core of which had played for Tonga U18 and U19 in the two previous years. In 2007, Tonga U19 had finished fifth in the B Division and had not been invited to play in the IRB U21 World Championship.

The final match of the tournament, which secured 13th place, was a celebrated 28–20 win against neighbours Fiji.

To celebrate the Coronation of His Majesty King George Tupou V on August 1, the first in Tonga since 1967 when the late King Taufa'ahau Tupou IV ascended to the throne, a number of sports tournaments were held in the Tongan capital, Nuku'alofa, from July 15 to August 2.

Rugby was central to the celebrations as it all opened with an Under-19 tournament, with six teams from Tongatapu, Niua, 'Eua, Ha'apai, Vava'u and a Tongan team from New Zealand. The King George V Cup was won by the Tongatapu team, which defeated Niua 14–11 in the final.

The highlight was a game in which a Tongan XV beat a World XV 60–24. This was organised by international Epi Taione, and attended by the new King, who arrived at the Teufaiva Stadium in his chauffeured London cab to greet invited international guests. Amongst them were former Wallaby hooker Jeremy Paul, former England Sevens captain Ben Gollings, Colin Charvis from Wales, Samoan Semo Sititi and former All Black Josh Kronfeld.

The Tonga XV had former All Blacks Va'aiga Tuigamala and Michael Jones as coaches, and defeated the World XV team 60–24, running in 10 tries to the delight of the more than 2,000 spectators. Each half saw seven tries. The World XV was coached by former Wallaby Daniel Herbert and skippered by former Welsh captain Charvis.

TONGA INTERNATIONAL STATISTICS

MATCH RECORDS UP TO 30TH SEPTEMBER 2008

WINNING MARGIN

Date	Opponent	Result	Winning Margin
21/03/2003	Korea	119–0	**119**
08/07/2006	Cook Islands	90–0	**90**
01/01/1979	Solomon Islands	92–3	**89**
10/02/2007	Korea	83–3	**80**
15/03/2003	Korea	75–0	**75**

MOST POINTS IN A MATCH
BY THE TEAM

Date	Opponent	Result	Pts.
21/03/2003	Korea	119–0	**119**
01/01/1979	Solomon Islands	92–3	**92**
08/07/2006	Cook Islands	90–0	**90**
06/12/2002	Papua New Guinea	84–12	**84**
10/02/2007	Korea	83–3	**83**

MOST TRIES IN A MATCH
BY THE TEAM

Date	Opponent	Result	Tries
21/03/2003	Korea	119–0	**17**
08/07/2006	Cook Islands	90–0	**14**
10/02/2007	Korea	83–3	**13**
24/06/2006	Cook Islands	77–10	**13**
15/03/2003	Korea	75–0	**12**

MOST CONVERSIONS IN A MATCH
BY THE TEAM

Date	Opponent	Result	Cons
21/03/2003	Korea	119–0	**17**
08/07/2006	Cook Islands	90–0	**10**
10/02/2007	Korea	83–3	**9**
05/07/1997	Cook Islands	68–12	**9**
06/12/2002	Papua New Guinea	84–12	**9**

MOST PENALTIES IN A MATCH
BY THE TEAM

Date	Opponent	Result	Pens
10/11/2001	Scotland	20–43	**5**
28/06/2008	Samoa	15–20	**5**
	5 Matches		**4**

MOST DROP GOALS IN A MATCH
BY THE TEAM

Date	Opponent	Result	DGS
	8 Matches		**1**

MOST POINTS IN A MATCH
BY A PLAYER

Date	Player	Opponent	Pts.
21/03/2003	Pierre Hola	Korea	**39**
10/02/2007	Fangatapu Apikotoa	Korea	**28**
04/05/1999	Sateki Tu'ipulotu	Korea	**27**
21/03/2003	Benhur Kivalu	Korea	**25**
06/12/2002	Pierre Hola	Papua New Guinea	**24**

MOST TRIES IN A MATCH
BY A PLAYER

Date	Player	Opponent	Tries
21/03/2003	Benhur Kivalu	Korea	**5**
24/06/2006	Viliami Hakalo	Cook Islands	**3**
08/07/2006	Tevita Vaikona	Cook Islands	**3**
05/07/1997	Siua Taumalolo	Cook Islands	**3**
28/03/1999	Siua Taumalolo	Georgia	**3**
04/05/1999	Jonny Koloi	Korea	**3**

MOST CONVERSIONS IN A MATCH

BY A PLAYER

Date	Player	Opponent	Cons
21/03/2003	Pierre Hola	Korea	17
08/07/2006	Fangatapu Apikotoa	Cook Islands	9
10/02/2007	Fangatapu Apikotoa	Korea	9
06/12/2002	Pierre Hola	Papua New Guinea	9
05/07/1997	Kusitafu Tonga	Cook Islands	9

MOST PENALTIES IN A MATCH

BY A PLAYER

Date	Player	Opponent	Pens
25/05/2001	Kusitafu Tonga	Fiji	4
10/11/2001	Sateki Tu'ipulotu	Scotland	4
19/02/1995	Sateki Tu'ipulotu	Japan	4
23/07/2005	Fangatapu Apikotoa	Samoa	4
16/09/2007	Pierre Hola	Samoa	4

MOST DROP GOALS IN A MATCH

BY A PLAYER

Date	Player	Opponent	DGS
	8 Matches		1

MOST CAPPED PLAYERS

Name	Caps
'Elisi Vunipola	41
Benhur Kivalu	38
Manu Vunipola	34
Pierre Hola	34
Fe'ao Vunipola	32

LEADING TRY SCORERS

Name	Tries
Siua Taumalolo	12
Fepikou Tatafu	11
Benhur Kivalu	10
Fakahau Valu	9
Pierre Hola	9

LEADING CONVERSIONS SCORERS

Name	Cons
Pierre Hola	62
Sateki Tu'ipulotu	33
Fangatapu 'Apikotoa	30
Kusitafu Tonga	25
Valita Ma'ake	10

LEADING PENALTY SCORERS

Name	Pens
Pierre Hola	32
Sateki Tu'ipulotu	32
Siua Taumalolo	12
Tomasi Lovo	12
Kusitafu Tonga	9
Valita Ma'ake	9

LEADING DROP GOAL SCORERS

Name	DGs
Pierre Hola	3
Sateki Tu'ipulotu	1
Sione Tu'ipulotu	1
Tomasi Lovo	1
Valeli	1
Inoke Afeaki	1

LEADING POINTS SCORERS

Name	Pts.
Pierre Hola	274
Sateki Tu'ipulotu	190
Siua Taumalolo	108
Fangatapu 'Apikotoa	99
Kusitafu Tonga	82

TONGA INTERNATIONAL PLAYERS
UP TO 30TH SEPTEMBER 2008

Note: Years given for International Championship matches are for second half of season; eg 1972 means season 1971–72. Years for all other matches refer to the actual year of the match. Entries in square brackets denote matches played in RWC Finals.

I Afeaki 1995 *F*, *S*, *Iv*, 1997 *Fj*, 2001 *S*, *W*, 2002 *J*, *Fj*, *Sa*, *Fj*, 2003 *Kor*, *Kor*, *I*, *Fj*, *Fj*, *It*, *C*, 2004 *Sa*, *Fj*, 2005 *It*, 2007 *Sa*, *SA*, *E*
P Afeaki 1983 *Fj*, *Sa*
S Afeaki 2002 *Fj*, *Fj*, *PNG*, *PNG*, 2003 *Kor*, *Kor*, *I*, *Fj*, *It*, *W*, *NZ*
V Afeaki 1997 *Sa*, 2002 *Sa*, *Fj*
J Afu 2008 *J*, *Sa*, *Fj*
A Afu Fungavaka 1982 *Sa*, 1984 *Fj*, *Fj*, 1985 *Fj*, 1986 *W*, *Fj*, *Fj*, 1987 *C*, *W*, *I*, *Sa*, *Fj*
M Ahekeheke 1986 *Fj*
S 'Aho 1974 *S*, *W*
Ahoafi 2007 *AuA*, *Sa*
P Ahofono 1990 *Sa*
K Ahota'e'iloa 1999 *Sa*, *F*, *Fj*, 2000 *C*, *Fj*, *J*
P 'Ake 1926 *Fj*
A Alatini 2001 *S*, 2002 *J*, *Fj*, 2003 *I*, *Fj*
M Alatini 1969 *M*, 1972 *Fj*, *Fj*, 1973 *M*, *A*, *A*, *Fj*, 1974 *S*, *W*, *C*, 1975 *M*, 1977 *Fj*
PF Alatini 1995 *Sa*
S Alatini 1994 *Sa*, *Fj*, 1998 *Sa*, *Fj*, 2000 *NZ*, *US*
S Alatini 1977 *Fj*, 1979 *NC*, *M*, *E*
T Alatini 1932 *Fj*
V 'Alipate 1967 *Fj*, 1968 *Fj*, *Fj*, *Fj*, 1969 *M*
A Amone 1987 *W*, *I*, *Sa*, *Fj*
T Anitoni 1995 *J*, *Sa*, *Fj*, 1996 *Sa*, *Fj*
V Anitoni 1990 *Sa*
F Apikotoa 2004 *Sa*, *Fj*, 2005 *Fj*, *Sa*, *Fj*, *Sa*, *It*, *F*, 2006 *Coo*, *Coo*, 2007 *Kor*, *AuA*, *J*, *JAB*, 2008 *J*, *Sa*, *Fj*
T Apitani 1947 *Fj*, *Fj*
S Asi 1987 *C*
T Asi 1996 *Sa*
H 'Asi 2000 *C*
S Ata 1928 *Fj*
S Atiola 1987 *Sa*, *Fj*, 1988 *Fj*, 1989 *Fj*, *Fj*, 1990 *Fj*, *J*
K Bakewa 2002 *PNG*, *PNG*, 2003 *Fj*
O Beba 1932 *Fj*, *Fj*, *Fj*
O Blake 1983 *M*, *M*, 1987 *Sa*, *Fj*, 1988 *Sa*, *Fj*, *Fj*
T Bloomfield 1973 *M*, *A*, *A*, *Fj*, 1986 *W*
D Briggs 1997 *W*
J Buloka 1932 *Fj*, *Fj*
D Edwards 1998 *A*, 1999 *Geo*, *Geo*, *Kor*, *US*, *Sa*, *F*, *Fj*, *C*, *NZ*, *It*, *E*
T Ete'aki 1984 *Fj*, 1986 *W*, *Fj*, *Fj*, 1987 *C*, *W*, *I*, 1990 *Fj*, *J*, *Sa*, *Kor*, *Sa*, 1991 *Sa*
U Fa'a 1994 *Sa*, *W*, 1995 *J*, 1998 *Sa*, *A*, *Fj*
L Fa'aoso 2004 *Sa*, *Fj*, 2005 *Fj*, *Sa*, *Fj*, *Sa*, 2007 *US*, *E*
P Fa'apoi 1963 *Fj*
V Fa'aumu 1986 *Fj*, *Fj*
T Fainga'anuku 1999 *NZ*, *It*, *E*, 2000 *C*, *Fj*, *J*, *NZ*, 2001 *Fj*, *Sa*, *Fj*, *Sa*
S Faka 'osi'folau 1997 *Z*, *Nm*, *SA*, *Fj*, *Sa*, *Coo*, *W*, 1998 *A*, *Fj*, 1999 *Geo*, *Kor*, *Fj*, 2001 *Sa*
P Fakalelu 2005 *It*, 2006 *Coo*, *Coo*
J Fakalolo 1926 *Fj*
P Fakana 1963 *Fj*, *Fj*
F Fakaongo 1993 *S*, *Fj*, 1995 *Iv*, *Sa*, *Fj*, 2000 *Fj*, *J*, *NZ*, *Sa*, 2001 *S*, *W*, 2002 *J*, *Fj*, *Sa*
V Fakatou 1998 *Sa*, *A*, *Fj*, 1999 *Kor*, *NZ*
V Fakatulolo 1975 *M*
P Fakaua 1988 *Sa*
S Fakaua 2005 *Sa*
P Faka'ua 1967 *Fj*, *Fj*, *Fj*, 1968 *Fj*, *Fj*, *Fj*, 1969 *M*, *M*, 1972 *Fj*
N Fakauho 1977 *Fj*, *Fj*
FP Faletau 1999 *Geo*, *Kor*, *Kor*, *J*, *US*, *Sa*, *F*, *Fj*, *C*
K Faletau 1988 *Sa*, *Fj*, 1989 *Fj*, *Fj*, 1990 *Sa*, 1991 *Fj*, 1992 *Fj*, 1997 *Nm*, *SA*, *Fj*, *Sa*, *Coo*, *W*, 1999 *Sa*, *F*, *Fj*, *C*
M Fanga'uta 1982 *Fj*
F Faotusa 1990 *Sa*
IT Fatani 1992 *Fj*, 1993 *Sa*, *S*, *Fj*, *A*, *Fj*, 1997 *Fj*, *Coo*, 1999 *Geo*, *Kor*, *Kor*, *J*, *US*, *Sa*, *F*, *Fj*, *C*, *NZ*, *It*, *E*, 2000 *C*, *Fj*, *J*, *NZ*, *Sa*, *US*
S Fe'ao 1995 *F*, *S*
SL Fekau 1983 *M*, *M*
K Feke 1988 *Fj*, *Fj*, 1989 *Fj*, 1990 *Fj*, *Sa*
M Felise 1987 *W*, *I*
I Fenukitau 1993 *Sa*, *S*, *Fj*, *A*, *Fj*, 1994 *Sa*, *Fj*, 1995 *J*, *J*, *F*, *S*, 2002 *J*, *Fj*, *Sa*, 2003 *It*, *W*, *NZ*, *C*
Fetu'ulele 1967 *Fj*
K Fielea 1987 *C*, *W*, *I*, *Sa*, *Fj*, 1990 *J*, *Sa*, *Kor*, *Sa*, 1991 *Sa*
P Fifita 1983 *Fj*
P Fifita 2003 *C*
S Fifita 1974 *S*, *W*, *C*, 1975 *M*
T Fifita 2001 *Fj*, *Fj*, 2003 *Fj*, 2006 *J*, 2008 *J*
T Fifita 1984 *Fj*, *Fj*, 1986 *W*, *Fj*, *Fj*, 1987 *C*, *W*, *I*, 1991 *Sa*, *Fj*, *Fj*
V Fifita 2005 *F*
V Fifita 1982 *Fj*
F Filikitonga 1990 *Fj*, *Sa*
L Fililava 1960 *M*
M Filimoehala 1968 *Fj*, 1974 *W*, *C*, 1975 *M*, *M*
OAML Filipine 2000 *C*, 2006 *J*, *Fj*, *Coo*, *Sa*, 2007 *US*, *SA*, 2008 *J*
M Filise 1986 *Fj*, *Fj*
T Filise 2001 *Fj*, *Fj*, *S*, *W*, 2002 *Sa*, *Fj*, 2004 *Sa*, *Fj*, 2005 *Fj*, *Sa*, *Fj*, *Sa*, 2007 *Fj*, *Sa*, *E*
S Filo 2004 *Sa*, *Fj*
I Finau 1987 *Sa*, *Fj*, 1990 *Fj*, *J*, *Sa*
M Finau 1979 *NC*, *M*, *E*, *Sa*, 1980 *Sa*, 1984 *Fj*
M Finau 2007 *AuA*, 2008 *J*
S Finau 1926 *Fj*
S Finau 1989 *Fj*, *Fj*, 1990 *Fj*, *J*, *Sa*, *Kor*, *Sa*
S Finau 1998 *Sa*, 1999 *Geo*, *Sa*, *F*, *Fj*, *C*, *E*, 2001 *Fj*, *Fj*, *S*, 2005 *It*, *F*
T Finau 1967 *Fj*
V Finau 1987 Sa, Fj
I Fine 2007 *Kor*, *AuA*, *JAB*, *Sa*
K Fine 1987 *C*, *W*, *I*, 1988 *Fj*
J Finisi 1932 *Fj*, *Fj*, *Fj*
S Finisi 1928 *Fj*
P Fisi'iahi 1992 *Sa*
K Fisilau 1999 *J*, *US*, 2000 *C*, 2005 *Fj*, *Sa*, *It*
K Fokofuka 1995 *Sa*
K Folea 1991 *Fj*
S Foliaki 1973 *A*, *A*, 1977 *Fj*
Fololisi 1991 *Fj*
V Fono 2005 *Sa*, *Fj*, *It*, *F*
H Fonua 1973 *M*, *A*, *A*, *Fj*, 1974 *S*, *W*, *C*
S Fonua 1928 *Fj*
SO Fonua 2002 *Sa*, *Sa*, 2003 *It*, *W*, *NZ*, *C*, 2007 *Kor*, *AuA*, *J*, *JAB*, *Fj*, *Sa*

T Fonua 2007 *Kor*
K Fotu 1990 *Fj, Sa, Kor, Sa*
L Fotu 1991 *Sa*, 1992 *Fj*, 1993 *S, Fj*
R Fotu 1979 *M*, 1983 *Fj, Sa*
S Fotu 1968 *Fj, Fj, Fj*, 1969 *M, M*
S Fotu 1947 *Fj*
TK Fotu 1987 *C*, 1988 *Sa*, 1989 *Fj*, 1990 *J*
P Fua'ava 1985 *Fj*
T Fuataimi 1928 *Fj*, 1932 *Fj, Fj, Fj*
F Fuka Kitekei'aho 1987 *C, W, I*
F Fukofuka 1926 *Fj*, 1928 *Fj*
T Fukofuka 1993 *Fj*, 1995 *J, J, F, S, Iv, Fj*
A Fungavaka 1982 *Fj*
L Fusimalohi 1987 *Fj*, 1988 *Fj*, 1990 *J, Sa*
W Gibbons 2002 *PNG*, 2003 *Fj*
F Hafoka 1932 *Fj, Fj, Fj*
I Hafoka 1932 *Fj, Fj, Fj*
K Hafoka 1967 *Fj, Fj*, 1968 *Fj, Fj, Fj*
M Hafoka 1977 *Fj, Fj*, 1979 *M*, 1980 *Sa*
S Hafoka 1997 *W*
T Hafoka 1987 *Fj*
Hakalo 2006 *J, Coo, Sa*
S Hala 1999 *Geo, Geo, Kor*, 2002 *J, Fj, Sa, Sa, Fj*, 2003 *Kor, Kor*
M Halafatu 1989 *Fj*
T Halafihi 1982 *Sa, Fj*, 1983 *Sa*, 1985 *Fj*
A Halangahu 2007 *Kor*
C Halangi 2002 *Fj*
T Halasika 1988 *Fj*
C Hala'ufia 2000 *C*, 2001 *Fj, Sa, Fj, Sa, W*, 2002 *Sa*, 2004 *Sa, Fj*, 2005 *Fj, Fj, Sa, It, F*, 2006 *J, Fj, Coo, Sa, Coo*, 2007 *JAB, Fj*
S Hala'ufia 1977 *Fj*, 1979 *NC, M, E, Sa*, 1981 *Fj*
L Halavatau 1982 *Sa, Fj*
T Haumono 1926 *Fj*, 1928 *Fj*, 1932 *Fj, Fj, Fj*
D Havea 2000 *NZ, US*
S Havea 2004 *Sa, Fj*, 2005 *Fj, Sa, Fj, Sa, It, F*, 2006 *J, Fj, Coo, Sa*, 2007 *Kor, JAB, Fj, Sa, US, SA*, 2008 *J, Sa, Fj*
AP Havili 2000 *C, Fj, J, Sa, US*, 2001 *Fj, Sa, Fj*, 2007 *AuA, J, JAB, US, SA, E*
M Havili 1987 *Sa*, 1988 *Fj*
P Havili 1981 *Fj, Fj*
KP Hehea 2006 *J, Fj, JAB, Coo, Sa, Coo*, 2007 *US, Sa, SA, E*, 2008 *Sa, Fj*
SE Hehepoto 1972 *Fj*, 1973 *M, A, A, Fj*
M Hekeheke 1986 *Fj*
Helehele 1985 *Fj*
T Helu 1967 *Fj, Fj*
O Hiko 1979 *E*
RP Hola 1998 *Sa, A, Fj*, 2001 *W*, 2002 *J, Fj, Sa, Sa, Fj, PNG, PNG*, 2003 *Kor, Kor, I, Fj, It, W, NZ, C*, 2005 *Fj*, 2006 *J, Fj, JAB, Coo, Sa, Coo*, 2007 *Sa, US, Sa, SA, E*, 2008 *J, Sa, Fj*
S Hola 1979 *Fj*
L Hopoate 1986 *W*
V Hosea 1967 *Fj, Fj*
F Hufanga 1973 *M*
S Hufanga 2003 *Fj, W, NZ, C*, 2004 *Sa, Fj*, 2005 *It, F*, 2006 *J, Fj, JAB*, 2007 *Fj, US, Sa, SA, E*, 2008 *Sa*
F Ika 1988 *Sa, Fj, Fj*, 1989 *Fj, Fj*
S Ika 2008 *J*
M Ilolahia 1947 *Fj*
Inoke 1947 *Fj*
K 'Inoke 1967 *Fj, Fj, Fj*, 1968 *Fj, Fj, Fj*, 1969 *M, M*, 1972 *Fj*, 1973 *A*, 1975 *M*
K 'Iongi 1967 *Fj, Fj, Fj*, 1968 *Fj, Fj, Fj*, 1969 *M, M*, 1972 *Fj*, 1973 *M, A, Fj*
T 'Isitolo 1995 *Iv, Sa, Fj*
M Kafatolu 2002 *J, Fj, Sa*
T Kaho 1973 *A*
J Kaihau 1932 *Fj, Fj*
P Kaihau 1975 *M*, 1977 *Fj, Fj, Fj*
M Kaihea 1999 *Geo, Kor, Kor, J, Sa, F*
L Kaiqa 1928 *Fj*
'A Kaitu'u 2000 *C*
J Kalaivalu 1996 *Sa*
SM Kalamafoni 2007 *Kor, AuA, J, JAB, Fj, Sa*
N Kalaniuvalu 1963 *Fj*
R Kapeli 1992 *Sa, Fj*, 1993 *Fj, A*
S Kapeli 2005 *Sa*
T Kapeli 1982 Sa
L Katoa 1996 *Sa, Fj*, 1997 *Nm, Fj, Sa*
P Katoa 1977 *Fj, Fj, Fj*, 1979 *NC, M, E, Sa, Fj*, 1981 *Fj, Fj*
T Kaufana 1947 *Fj*
T Kaufusi 2007 *Kor, AuA, J, JAB, Fj, Sa*
L Kauhalaniua 1984 *Fj*
E Kauhenga 2002 *Sa, Fj*, 2003 *Fj*, 2006 *J*, 2007 *SA*, 2008 *J*
S Kava 1967 *Fj*
T Kavapalu 1967 *Fj*, 1968 *Fj, Fj, Fj*, 1969 *M, M*, 1972 *Fj*, 1973 *M, A, Fj*, 1974 *W*, 1975 *M, M*
A Kefu 1926 *Fj*
F Kefu 1972 *Fj, Fj*, 1973 *A*, 1974 *W, C*, 1975 *M*
M Kefu 1959 *Fj*, 1960 *M*, 1963 *Fj, Fj*
E Kelemeni 1967 *Fj, Fj, Fj*
K Kioa 1959 *Fj*, 1960 *M*
P Kiole 1977 *Fj, Fj, Fj*, 1979 *M, E, Fj*, 1980 *Sa*
S Kiole 2005 *Fj, Fj, Sa*, 2007 *AuA, J, JAB, Fj, Sa*, 2008 *Fj*
T kitekei'aho 1979 *Fj*
BH Kivalu 1998 *Sa, A*, 1999 *Geo, Geo, Kor, Sa, F, Fj, C, NZ, It, E*, 2000 *C, Fj, J, NZ, Sa, US*, 2002 *J, Sa, Sa, Fj, PNG, PNG*, 2003 *Kor, Kor, Fj, Fj, It, W, NZ, C*, 2004 *Sa, Fj*, 2005 *Fj, Sa, Fj, Sa*
T Kolo 1993 *A*, 1995 *Sa, Fj*
C Koloi 1999 *US*
S Koloi 1998 *Sa, Fj*, 1999 *Geo, Geo, Kor, Kor, J, C, NZ, It, E*, 2000 *NZ, Sa, US*, 2001 *Sa*
E Koloto 1986 *W*
F Lagilagi 1991 *Fj*
Jione Laiseni 1932 *Fj, Fj*
E Langi 2003 *NZ*
F Langi 1990 *Fj, J*
P Langi 1986 *W, Fj*
F Lani 1986 *Fj*
T Latailakepa 1992 *Sa, Fj*, 1993 *Sa*
K Latu 1987 *Fj*
O Latu 2006 *J, Fj, JAB, Coo, Sa, Coo*, 2007 *Kor, AuA, J, JAB, Fj, Sa, US, Sa, SA, E*, 2008 *J, Sa, Fj*
P Latu 1994 *W*, 1995 *J, J, F, S, Iv, Sa, Fj*
S Latu 1984 *Fj, Fj*
S Latu 1972 *Fj*, 1973 *M, A, A, Fj*, 1974 *S, W, C*, 1975 *M, M*
S Latu 1992 *Fj*, 1993 *Fj, A*
U Latu 1997 *W*, 1998 *Sa*, 2002 *PNG, PNG*, 2003 *Kor, Kor, I, It, W, NZ, C*
U Latufeku 1959 *Fj*, 1960 *M*, 1963 *Fj*, 1968 *Fj, Fj, Fj*
P Latukefu 1995 *J, J, S, Iv, Sa, Fj*, 1998 *A, Fj*
T Latukefu 1967 *Fj, Fj, Fj*, 1968 *Fj, Fj, Fj*
M Latunipulu 1926 *Fj*
F Latusela 2003 *Kor, Kor*
F Lauei 1985 *Fj*
H Lavaka 1996 *Sa*, 1997 *SA, Fj, Sa, Coo, W*, 2003 *I, Fj, Fj, It, W, NZ, C*
K Lavaka 1996 *Fj*
M Lavaka 1993 *S, Fj, A, Fj*
S Lavaka 2008 *J*
T Lavaki 1990 *J, Kor*, 1993 *S*
F Lavemai 1984 *Fj, Fj*, 1985 *Fj*, 1986 *W*
M Lavulo 1979 *E*
T Lea'aetoa 2002 *PNG, PNG*, 2003 *Kor, Kor, I, It, W, NZ, C*, 2005 *It, F*, 2006 *J, Fj, JAB, Coo, Sa, Coo*, 2008 *J, Sa, Fj*
J Leba 1932 *Fj, Fj, Fj*
G Leger 2001 *S, W*, 2002 *J, Fj, Sa, Sa, Fj*, 2003 *Kor, Kor, I, Fj, It, NZ, C*
T Leger 1967 *Fj, Fj*
T Leha 1983 *M, M*
S Leilani 1981 *Fj*, 1983 *Fj, Sa*
FVMH Lemoto 2007 *Fj*
A Liava'a 1979 *E*, 1981 *Fj, Fj, Fj*, 1983 *Fj, Sa, M, M*, 1984 *Fj, Fj*, 1985 *Fj*, 1987 *C, W, I*
S Liava'a 1979 *M, E*, 1981 *Fj*
V Likio 1947 *Fj, Fj*
L Lile 2002 *Fj*, 2003 *Fj*
VF Lilo 2007 *Kor, J, JAB, US, Sa, SA, E*, 2008 *J, Sa, Fj*
J Lino 1926 *Fj*
S Lisala 2005 *Sa, Fj*

S Lo'amanu 1926 *Fj*, 1928 *Fj*
L Lokotui 2001 *W*
S Lolo 1993 *Sa*
T Lolo'ahea 1987 *Sa*, 1990 *J*, *Sa*, *Kor*, *Sa*, 1991 *Sa*, *Fj*, *Fj*
L Lolohea 2007 *JAB*
P Lolohea 1983 *M*, *M*
K Lomu 1979 *Fj*
W Lose 1995 *F*, *S*, *Iv*
L Loto'ahea 1994 *Sa*
T Loto'ahea 1987 *Fj*, 1988 *Fj*, *Fj*, 1989 *Fj*, *Fj*, 1993 *S*, *Fj*, 1994 *W*, *Fj*
T Lovo 1982 *Sa*, 1986 *W*, *Fj*, *Fj*, 1987 *Sa*, 1988 *Fj*, 1989 *Fj*, *Fj*, 1990 *Sa*
S Lu'au 2007 *AuA*
I Lupina 1969 *M*, 1972 *Fj*
T Lutua 1990 *Kor*, 1992 *Fj*, 1994 *Sa*, *W*, *Fj*, 1995 *J*, *J*, *Iv*
V Lutua 1981 *Fj*, *Fj*, 1987 *W*, *I*, 1988 *Fj*, *Fj*
A Lutui 1999 *Geo*, *J*, *Sa*, *F*, 2001 *Fj*, *Fj*, *S*, *W*, 2004 *Sa*, *Fj*, 2005 *Fj*, *Sa*, *Fj*, *Sa*, 2006 *Fj*, *JAB*, 2007 *AuA*, *J*, *JAB*, *Fj*, *Sa*, *US*, *Sa*, *SA*, *E*
F Ma'afa 1981 *Fj*, *Fj*
F Ma'afu 1985 *Fj*, 1986 *Fj*, *Fj*, 1988 *Sa*, *Fj*, *Fj*
P Ma'afu 1979 *M*, *E*, *Sa*, *Fj*, 1980 *Sa*, 1981 *Fj*, *Fj*, 1983 *M*, *M*
P Ma'afu 1959 *Fj*, 1960 *M*, 1963 *Fj*
T Ma'afu 1983 *M*, *M*
V Ma'ake 1973 *M*, *A*, *A*, *Fj*, 1974 *S*, *W*, *C*, 1975 *M*, *M*, 1977 *Fj*, *Fj*, *Fj*, 1979 *NC*, *M*, *E*, *Sa*, *Fj*, 1980 *Sa*
V Ma'asi 1997 *W*, 2000 *C*, *J*, *Sa*, *US*, 2001 *Fj*, *Fj*, *Sa*, *S*, *W*, 2002 *J*, *Fj*, *Sa*, *Sa*, 2003 *I*, *Fj*, *Fj*, *It*, *W*, *NZ*, *C*, 2005 *Fj*, *Sa*, *It*, *F*, 2008 *J*, *Sa*, *Fj*
S Mafana 1959 *Fj*, 1960 *M*, 1963 *Fj*, *Fj*
A Mafi 1995 *Iv*
F Mafi 1993 *A*, *Fj*, 1994 *Sa*, *W*, *Fj*, 1995 *J*, *J*, *F*, 1996 *Sa*, *Fj*, 1998 *Sa*, *A*, 1999 *Geo*, *Geo*, *Kor*, *J*, *US*, *NZ*, *It*, *E*
S Mafi 1969 *M*, *M*, 1972 *Fj*, *Fj*, *Fj*, 1973 *M*, *A*, *A*, *Fj*, 1974 *S*, *W*, *C*, 1975 *M*, *M*
S Mafi 1988 *Fj*, 1989 *Fj*, 1990 *Fj*, *Kor*, 1993 *Sa*
S Mafile'o 1995 *Iv*, *Sa*, *Fj*, 1997 *Z*, *Nm*, *SA*, 2002 *J*, 2003 *Kor*, *Kor*, *I*, *Fj*
R Mahe 2005 *Sa*, *It*, *F*, 2006 *Fj*, *JAB*, *Coo*, *Coo*, 2007 *Kor*
S Mahe 1981 *Fj*, *Fj*
F Mahoni 1993 *Sa*, *A*, *Fj*, 1995 *J*, *J*, *F*, *Sa*, *Fj*, 1996 *Sa*, *Fj*, 1999 *Geo*, *J*
F Mailangi 1968 *Fj*, *Fj*, *Fj*, 1969 *M*
L Mailangi 1959 *Fj*, 1960 *M*, 1963 *Fj*, *Fj*
P Mailefihi 1979 *E*, 1982 *Fj*
A Mailei 2002 *J*, *Fj*, *Sa*, *Sa*, *Fj*, *PNG*, *PNG*, 2003 *Kor*, *Kor*
A Ma'ilei 2005 *Fj*, *Sa*, *F*
T Mak 1988 *Fj*
A Maka 2005 *F*
F Maka 2007 *US*, *Sa*, *SA*, *E*
L Maka 1997 *Z*, 1999 *Geo*, *J*, *US*, *F*, *NZ*, *It*, *E*, 2000 *C*, *Fj*, *J*, *NZ*, *US*, 2002 *J*, *Sa*, *Fj*, 2003 *Kor*, *Kor*
P Maka 1985 *Fj*
T Maka 1979 *NC*, *Sa*, 1981 *Fj*, *Fj*
V Maka 1983 *Fj*, *Sa*, 1984 *Fj*, *Fj*
H Makahoi 1974 *C*, 1975 *M*, *M*, 1977 *Fj*, *Fj*, *Fj*, 1979 *Sa*, *Fj*, 1980 *Sa*
S Makalo 1975 *M*
M Makasini 2005 *Fj*, *Sa*, *Fj*, *Sa*
T Makisi 1983 *M*, *M*, 1989 *Fj*, *Fj*
Malu 1947 *Fj*
M Malu 1979 *NC*, *Sa*
L Manako 2000 *NZ*, *Sa*
T Manako 1995 *J*, *J*
T Manako 2000 *J*
C Manu 1987 *Sa*, *Fj*, 1989 *Fj*, *Fj*
E Manu 1996 *Sa*, *Fj*, 1999 *Kor*, *J*, *US*
F Manukia 1993 *A*, *Fj*, 1994 *Sa*, *W*, *Fj*, 1995 *J*, *J*
M Manukia 1993 *Sa*, *S*, *Fj*, *A*, *Fj*, 1994 *Fj*
T Mapa 1967 *Fj*, *Fj*
P Mapakaitolo 1977 *Fj*, *Fj*
S Martens 1998 *A*, *Fj*, 1999 *Geo*, *Geo*, *Kor*, *Kor*, *J*, *US*, *Sa*, *F*, *Fj*, *C*, *NZ*, *It*, *E*, 2001 *S*, *W*, 2002 *Fj*, *Sa*, *Sa*, *Fj*, 2003 *Kor*, *Kor*, *It*, *W*, *NZ*, *C*
S Masi 1989 *Fj*
F Masila 1990 *J*, 1991 *Fj*, 1993 *Sa*, *S*, *A*, *Fj*, 1994 *W*, 1995 *F*, *Fj*, 1998 *Sa*, *A*
Masili 1991 *Fj*
S Masima 2005 *Fj*
T Matakaiongo 1997 *W*
S Matangi 2000 *J*, *Sa*, 2001 *Fj*, *Sa*, 2002 *Fj*, *PNG*, 2004 *Sa*, *Fj*
S Matapule 1973 *M*, 1975 *M*
SH Mata'u 2007 *AuA*, 2008 *J*
K Ma'u 1983 *Fj*, *Sa*, *M*, 1984 *Fj*, *Fj*
T Ma'u 1947 *Fj*, *Fj*
V Ma'u 1947 *Fj*
O Misa 2004 *Sa*, *Fj*
S Misa 1926 *Fj*
S Moa 1928 *Fj*
U Moa 1998 *A*, *Fj*, 1999 *Geo*
V Moa 1993 *Sa*, *S*, 1998 *Sa*
F Moala 1982 *Sa*, *Fj*, 1983 *Fj*, *Sa*, *M*, *M*, 1984 *Fj*, *Fj*, 1985 *Fj*
F Moala 1982 *Sa*, 1983 *Sa*, 1985 *Fj*
F Moala 1963 *Fj*, *Fj*, 1968 *Fj*, *Fj*, *Fj*
K Moala 1959 *Fj*, 1960 *M*, 1963 *Fj*, 1967 *Fj*, *Fj*
M Moala 1986 *W*, *Fj*, *Fj*
M Moala 2004 *Sa*, *Fj*
P Moala 1981 *Fj*, *Fj*, *Fj*
P Moala 1982 *Sa*, 1986 *W*, *Fj*, *Fj*, 1987 *Sa*, *Fj*
T Moala 1972 *Fj*
V Moala'eua 1977 *Fj*, *Fj*, *Fj*, 1979 *NC*, *M*, *Sa*, *Fj*, 1981 *Fj*
Mofuike 1986 *Fj*
S Mohi 1986 *W*, *Fj*, *Fj*, 1987 *C*, *W*, *I*
S Moimoi 2001 *W*
S Moli 1992 *Fj*
F Molitika 2000 *C*, *J*, 2001 *Fj*, *Sa*, *S*, 2005 *It*, *F*
MK Molitika 1997 *Nm*, *SA*, *Fj*, *Sa*, *Coo*, *W*, 2000 *NZ*, *Sa*, *US*, 2001 *S*, 2005 *It*, 2006 *Fj*, *JAB*, *Coo*, *Sa*, 2007 *E*
S Moto'apuaka 1980 *Sa*, 1987 *C*
K Motu'apuaka 1972 *Fj*
S Motu'apuaka 1969 *M*, *M*, 1972 *Fj*
S Motu'apuka 1979 *Fj*
S Motuliki 1967 *Fj*
Mounga 1947 *Fj*
F Muller 1967 *Fj*, 1968 *Fj*, *Fj*, *Fj*, 1969 *M*, *M*, 1972 *Fj*, *Fj*
T Na'aniumotu 2006 *J*, *JAB*, *Coo*, *Sa*, *Coo*
F Naitoko 2005 *Sa*
S Nau 2000 *C*, *Fj*, *J*, 2001 *Fj*, 2003 *Fj*, 2005 *It*, *F*, 2006 *JAB*, *Coo*, *Sa*
N Naufahu 2001 *Fj*, *Sa*, *Fj*, *W*, 2002 *J*, *Sa*, *Sa*, *Fj*, *PNG*, *PNG*, 2003 *Kor*, *Kor*, *I*, *W*, *C*
S Nauvai 1960 *M*
T Ngaluafe 1974 *S*, *W*, *C*, 1975 *M*, *M*
J Ngauamo 2003 *Kor*, *I*, *Fj*, *It*, *C*, 2005 *It*
MM Ngauamo 2002 *PNG*, *PNG*, 2003 *Kor*, *I*, *Fj*, *It*, *W*, *NZ*, *C*, 2005 *F*, 2006 *Fj*, *JAB*, 2008 *Sa*, *Fj*
S Ngauamo 1997 *Coo*, 1998 *A*
T Nisa 1991 *Fj*, 1992 *Fj*
U Niuila 1990 *Sa*
S Nuku 1981 *Fj*, *Fj*, *Fj*, 1984 *Fj*, *Fj*
L Ofa 1983 *Fj*, *Sa*, *M*, *M*, 1984 *Fj*
I Omani 1928 *Fj*, 1932 *Fj*, *Fj*, *Fj*
M 'Otai 1995 *J*, *J*, *F*, *S*, *Iv*
M 'Ota'ota 2000 *C*, 2005 *Fj*, *Sa*, *Fj*
H Paea 2007 *Kor*
L Pahulu 1973 *A*, *Fj*, 1974 *S*
V Pahulu 1967 *Fj*, *Fj*, *Fj*, 1968 *Fj*, *Fj*, *Fj*, 1969 *M*, *M*, 1973 *M*
U Palavi 1960 *M*, 1963 *Fj*, *Fj*
J Pale 2001 *S*, *W*, 2002 *J*, *Fj*, *Sa*, *Sa*, *Fj*, 2003 *Fj*
M Pale 1998 *A*, 1999 *Geo*, 2002 *J*, *Fj*, 2006 *J*, *Coo*, *Sa*
S Palenapa 1990 *Fj*, *J*, *Sa*, *Kor*, *Sa*, 1996 *Sa*, *Fj*
D Palu 2002 *PNG*, *PNG*, 2003 *Kor*, *Kor*, *I*, *Fj*, *C*, 2006 *J*, *JAB*, *Coo*, 2007 *AuA*, *J*, *JAB*
P Palu 1979 *NC*, 1981 *Fj*
T Palu 2008 *J*
H Pau'u 1983 *Fj*, *Sa*
T Pau'u 1992 *Fj*
J Payne 2002 *PNG*, *PNG*, 2003 *Kor*, *Kor*, *I*, *Fj*, *It*, *W*, *NZ*, *C*
D Penisini 1997 *Nm*, *Coo*, 1999 *Geo*, *Kor*, *C*
'O Pepa 1928 *Fj*
H Petelo 1982 *Fj*
H Pierra 2005 *Sa*

O Pifeleti 1983 *Fj, Sa, M, M*, 1984 *Fj, Fj*, 1985 *Fj*, 1989 *Fj, Fj*, 1990 *Sa*, 1991 *Sa, Fj, Fj*
H Pohiva 1997 *W*, 1998 *Sa, Fj*
THN Pole 2007 *Kor, AuA, J, JAB, Fj, Sa, US, Sa, E*, 2008 *Sa, Fj*
S Pone 2008 *Sa, Fj*
S Pongi 1990 *Sa*
E Poteki 2007 *Kor*
V Poteki 2007 *Kor*
S Pouanga 1947 *Fj, Fj*
E Pou'uhila 1988 *Fj*
K Pulu 2002 *Fj, PNG, PNG*, 2003 *Kor, Kor, I, Fj, It, W, NZ*, 2005 *Fj, Sa, Fj, Sa*, 2006 *J*, 2007 *US, Sa, SA, E*, 2008 *Fj*
M Pulumu 1979 *NC, Sa, Fj*, 1980 *Sa*, 1981 *Fj, Fj*
T Pulumufila 1974 *S, W, C*
H Saafi 2000 *NZ*
T Samiu 1947 *Fj*
Sanilaita 1981 *Fj*
A Saulala 1991 *Fj*
C Schaumkel 1992 *Sa, Fj*, 1997 *SA, Fj*
S Selupe 1963 *Fj, Fj*, 1967 *Fj, Fj*, 1969 *M, M*, 1972 *Fj*, 1973 *M, A, Fj*
S Selupe 1967 *Fj*, 1969 *M*, 1972 *Fj*
S Selupe 1928 *Fj*
T Siale 1997 *Nm, Sa*
M Sifa 1947 *Fj*
S Sika 1968 *Fj, Fj, Fj*, 1969 *M, M*
A Sikalu 2007 *AuA, J*
T Sime 1963 *Fj*
T Sitanilei 1932 *Fj*
J Sitoa 1998 *A*
T Soaiti 1932 *Fj, Fj, Fj*
T Soane 1982 *Sa, Fj*, 1983 *Fj, Sa*, 1984 *Fj, Fj*, 1985 *Fj*
L Stanley 1985 *Fj*
L Susimalofi 1989 *Fj*
L Tafa 2007 *J*
S Tahaafe 1987 *C*
P Taholo 1983 *M*
S Tai 1997 *W*, 1998 *A*
U Tai 1969 *M*, 1972 *Fj*
E Taione 1999 *It, E*, 2000 *Fj, J*, 2001 *S, W*, 2005 *F*, 2006 *JAB, Sa*, 2007 *Fj, Sa, US, Sa, SA, E*, 2008 *Sa, Fj*
K Take 1989 *Fj*
E Talakai 1993 *Sa, S, Fj, Fj*, 1995 *S, Iv, Sa, Fj*
P Tanginoa 1995 *Fj*, 1997 *W*, 1998 *Sa, A*, 1999 *Geo*
T Tanginoa 2007 *AuA, J*
F Taniela 1982 *Fj*
I Tapueluelu 1990 *Fj, J, Sa, Sa*, 1993 *Sa, S*, 1999 *Kor, Kor, J, US, NZ, It, E*
F Tatafu 1996 *Fj*, 1997 *Z, Nm, Fj, Sa, Coo, W*, 1999 *Geo, Kor, Kor, J, Sa, Fj, C, NZ, E*, 2002 *J, Fj, Sa, PNG, PNG*
S Tatafu 1967 *Fj*
T Tatafu 1963 *Fj*
V Tau 1999 *US*
A Taufa 1993 *A*, 1995 *J, J, F, S*
E Taufa 2007 *Sa*, 2008 *J, Sa, Fj*
I Taufa 1972 *Fj*
S Taufa 2005 *Fj, Sa, Fj, Sa*
S Taufa 1984 *Fj*
T Taufa 1990 *Fj*
T Taufahema 1998 *Sa, A, Fj*, 1999 *Sa, F, NZ, It*, 2000 *C, Fj, J, NZ, Sa*, 2001 *Fj, Sa, Fj, S, W*
M Taufateau 1983 *M, M*, 1984 *Fj*, 1987 *Fj*
V Taufatofua 1926 *Fj*
A Ta'ufo'ou 1997 *Nm, SA, Fj, Sa, Coo*
E Ta'ufo'ou 2000 *C, Fj, J, NZ, Sa, US*
N Taufo'ou 1996 *Sa, Fj*, 1997 *Nm, SA, Fj, Sa, Coo, W*, 1998 *Sa, A, Fj*, 1999 *Geo, Kor, F, Fj, NZ, It, E*, 2000 *NZ, Sa, US*
E Taukafa 2002 *PNG, PNG*, 2003 *Kor, Kor, Fj, Fj, It, W, NZ, C*, 2005 *Fj, Sa, It, F*, 2006 *J, Fj, Coo, Sa, Coo*, 2007 *US, Sa, SA, E*, 2008 *Sa, Fj*
S Taukapo 2005 *Sa*
P Taukolo 1982 *Sa, Fj*
S Taumalolo 1996 *Sa, Fj*, 1997 *Z, Nm, SA, Coo, W*, 1999 *Geo, Geo, Sa, F, Fj, C, NZ*, 2000 *NZ, Sa, US*, 2001 *Fj, Sa, S, W*, 2006 *J*, 2007 *JAB, Fj, Sa*
P Taumiuvao 1986 *Fj*
N Taumoefolau 1979 *NC, E, Sa, Fj*
P Taumoepeau 1928 *Fj*
T Taumoepeau 1988 *Fj*
T Taumoepeau 1999 *Geo, Kor, Kor, J, US, NZ, E*, 2000 *Fj, J, NZ, Sa, US*, 2001 *Fj, Sa, Sa, S, W*, 2002 *J, Fj, Sa*, 2006 *J, Fj, JAB, Coo, Sa, Coo*, 2007 *AuA, J, Fj, Sa*
V Taumoepeau 1994 *Sa, W*, 1995 *Sa, Fj*
P Taumoua 2007 *J*
S Taupeaafe 1994 *W, Fj*, 1998 *Sa, A, Fj*, 1999 *Kor, J, NZ, It, E*, 2000 *NZ, US*, 2001 *Fj, Sa*
F Tautau'a 2007 *Kor*
S Tavo 1959 *Fj*, 1960 *M*, 1963 *Fj, Fj*, 1967 *Fj, Fj, Fj*, 1968 *Fj, Fj, Fj*, 1969 *M, M*
M Te Pou 1998 *A, Fj*, 1999 *Geo, Geo, Kor, Kor, J, US, F, NZ, It*, 2001 *S, W*
Telanisi 1967 *Fj*
S Telefoni 2008 *J, Sa, Fj*
Teri 1991 *Fj*
Teutau 1991 *Fj*
S Timani 2008 *J*
D Tiueti 1997 *Fj, Sa, W*, 1999 *Geo, Geo, Kor, Sa, F, Fj, C, NZ, It, E*, 2000 *C, Fj, J, NZ, Sa, US*, 2001 *S, W*
T Tofua 1926 *Fj*
T Toga 1968 *Fj*
T Tohi 1997 *Nm, SA*
T Toke 2007 *Kor, J, JAB, Fj, Sa, US, Sa*
V Toloke 1995 *J, Sa, Fj*, 1996 *Sa, Fj*, 1999 *Geo, Geo, Kor, Kor, US, NZ, E*, 2000 *NZ, Sa, US*, 2002 *J, Sa*
M Toma 1988 *Sa, Fj*, 1991 *Sa, Fj, Fj*
G Tonga 1997 *Z, W*
K Tonga 1996 *Fj*, 1997 *Nm, SA, Fj, Sa, Coo*, 1999 *Geo, Geo, Kor*, 2001 *Fj, Sa*
K Tonga 2003 *Fj, C*, 2004 *Sa, Fj*, 2005 *Fj, Fj*
K Tonga 1947 *Fj, Fj*
M Tonga 1947 *Fj, Fj*
M Tonga 2001 *Fj, Sa, Fj, Sa*, 2003 *Kor, Kor*
P Tonga 1973 *A*
S Tonga 2005 *Sa, Fj, Sa*
T Tonga 1990 *Sa*
S Tonga Simiki 1926 *Fj*
H Tonga'uiha 2005 *Fj, Sa, Sa*, 2006 *J, Fj, JAB, Coo, Sa, Coo*, 2007 *Kor, AuA, J, JAB, Fj, Sa, E*, 2008 *J, Sa, Fj*
SL Tonga'uiha 2005 *It, F*, 2007 *JAB, US, Sa, SA, E*
'O Topeni 2000 *J*
J Tuamoheloa 2003 *Fj*
S Tuamoheloa 2003 *Fj, C*, 2005 *Fj*
T Tuavao 1986 *Fj*
N Tufui 1990 *Fj, J, Sa, Sa*, 1992 *Fj*, 1994 *Fj*, 1995 *S, Iv*
S Tufui 1926 *Fj*, 1928 *Fj*, 1932 *Fj, Fj, Fj*
TH Tu'ifua 2003 *Fj, It, W, NZ*, 2006 *J, Fj, JAB, Coo, Sa*, 2007 *Fj, Sa, US, Sa, SA, E*
S Tu'ihalamaka 1999 *Kor, Kor, J, US*, 2001 *Sa, Fj*
P Tui'halamaka 1972 *Fj*, 1973 *M, A, A, Fj*, 1974 *S, C*, 1975 *M, M*, 1977 *Fj, Fj*, 1979 *NC*, 1981 *Fj, Fj*, 1987 *C*
Tu'ikolovatu 1983 *Fj*
T Tu'ineua 1992 *Fj*, 1993 *Sa, S, Fj, A, Fj*
E Tu'ipolotu 1926 *Fj*
S Tu'ipolotu 1981 *Fj*
S Tu'ipolotu 1947 *Fj, Fj*
K Tuipulotu 1994 *Fj*, 1997 *Fj, Sa, Coo*
K Tu'ipulotu 1994 *W*, 1997 *SA, Fj, Coo, W*, 1999 *Kor, Kor, J, US, Fj, It, E*, 2000 *Fj, J*, 2001 *Fj*
M Tu'ipulotu 1977 *Fj, Fj, Fj*
P Tu'ipulotu 1979 *Sa*, 1980 *Sa*
S Tu'ipulotu 1993 *Fj*, 1994 *Sa, W, Fj*, 1995 *J, J, F, S, Iv*, 1999 *Kor, F, Fj, C, It, E*, 2001 *S*, 2003 *Fj, Fj, It, NZ*
SM Tu'ipulotu 1997 *W*, 1998 *Sa, A*, 1999 *Sa, F, NZ, E*, 2000 *C, NZ, Sa, US*, 2001 *Fj, Fj, Sa*, 2005 *Fj, Sa, It, F*, 2006 *J, Fj, JAB, Coo, Sa*, 2007 *US, Sa, SA, E*, 2008 *J, Sa*
V Tu'ipulotu 1977 *Fj, Fj, Fj*, 1979 *M, E, Fj*
J Tu'itavake 1932 *Fj*
L Tu'itavake 1959 *Fj*, 1960 *M*, 1963 *Fj, Fj*
P Tu'itavake 1995 *Fj*
I Tuivai 1993 *Sa*
K Tuivailala 1987 *Sa*, 1988 *Sa, Fj, Fj*, 1989 *Fj, Fj*, 1990 *Fj, J, Sa, Kor*, 1991 *Fj*
K Tuivailala 1988 *Fj*

M Tuku'aho 1979 *NC, Sa,* 1980 *Sa,* 1982 *Sa*
M Tuku'aho 1979 *Fj*
T Tulia 2003 *Kor, Kor, I, Fj,* 2004 *Sa, Fj,* 2005 *Fj, Sa*
A Tulikaki 1993 *S*
S Tulikifanga 1997 *SA, Fj, Sa, Coo*
F Tupi 1973 *A, A, Fj,* 1974 *S, W,* 1975 *M, M*
H Tupou 1982 *Sa, Fj,* 1983 *M, M,* 1984 *Fj, Fj,* 1987 *C, W, I*
IM Tupou 2006 *Coo, Coo,* 2007 *Kor, AuA, J, JAB, US, Sa, SA,* 2008 *J*
J Tupou 1994 *Fj*
M Tupou 2005 *Fj, Fj, Sa*
P Tupou 1984 *Fj,* 1986 *W*
S Tupou 1975 *M*
M Tu'ungafasi 1986 *W,* 1987 *W, I*
M Tuungafufi 1986 *Fj*
T Tu'utu Kakato 1987 *C, W, I,* 1990 *Sa, Kor,* 1991 *Sa, Fj,* 1992 *Fj*
A Uasi 1993 *S,* 1994 *Sa, Fj*
L Uhatafe 1987 *Sa, Fj*
V Uhi 1997 *Z, Nm, SA, Fj, Sa, Coo*
S Ula 1959 *Fj,* 1960 *M,* 1963 *Fj, Fj*
L Ulufonua 2002 *PNG,* 2003 *Kor, Kor, Fj*
S Vaea 1928 *Fj*
S Vaea 1974 *S, W, C,* 1975 *M,* 1977 *Fj, Fj*
L Vaeno 1986 *Fj*
S Vaeno 1991 *Sa*
S Va'enuku 2003 *Fj, It, W, NZ,* 2004 *Sa, Fj,* 2005 *Sa, Fj, Sa, It,* 2007 *AuA, Sa*
T Va'enuku 1991 *Sa, Fj,* 1992 *Sa, Fj,* 1993 *S, Fj, A, Fj,* 1994 *Sa, W, Fj,* 1995 *F, S, Iv*
U Va'enuku 1995 *F, S, Iv*
L Va'eono 1987 *W*
L Vaeuo 1985 *Fj*
S Vaha'akolo 1990 *J, Kor*
S Vahafolau 2007 *J, Fj, Sa,* 2008 *Sa, Fj*
N Vahe 1977 *Fj*
S Vai 1981 *Fj, Fj,* 1988 *Sa*
A Vaihu 1975 *M*
T Vaikona 2006 *J, Fj, JAB, Coo*
T Vaioletti 2005 *F*
L Vaipulu 1987 *C*
JW Vaka 2004 *Sa, Fj,* 2005 *Sa,* 2007 *US, Sa, SA, E*
P Vakamalolo 1993 *Sa*
I Vaka'uta 1959 *Fj,* 1963 *Fj, Fj*
V Vaka'uta 1959 *Fj,* 1960 *M*
V Vake 1932 *Fj*
VL Vaki 2001 *Fj, Sa, Fj, Sa, S, W,* 2002 *J, Fj, Sa, Sa, Fj,* 2003 *Fj, Fj, It, W, NZ, C,* 2005 *Fj, Sa, It, F,* 2006 *JAB, Coo, Sa, Coo,* 2007 *US, Sa, SA, E,* 2008 *Fj*
Valeli 1947 *Fj*
F Valu 1973 *M, A, A, Fj,* 1974 *S, W, C,* 1975 *M, M,* 1977 *Fj, Fj, Fj,* 1979 *NC, M, E, Sa, Fj,* 1980 *Sa,* 1981 *Fj,* 1983 *Fj, Sa, M, M,* 1987 *C, W, I*
V Vanisi 1969 *M, M*
L Vano 1986 *Fj*
A Vasi 1993 *Fj*
I Vave 1973 *A, A, Fj,* 1974 *S, C*
T Vave 1993 *A*
M Vea 1992 *Fj*
S Veehala 1987 *Sa, Fj,* 1988 *Fj, Fj,* 1989 *Fj,* 1990 *J, Kor,* 1991 *Sa, Fj, Fj*
J Vikilani 1932 *Fj, Fj*
T Vikilani 1992 *Fj,* 1994 *Sa, W*
T Viliame 1979 *M*
O Vitelefi 1986 *W*
F Vuna 1977 *Fj, Fj, Fj,* 1979 *NC, M, Sa,* 1981 *Fj*
V Vuni 1932 *Fj, Fj, Fj*
A Vunipola 1982 *Fj*
E Vunipola 1990 *Fj, Kor,* 1993 *Sa, S, Fj, A, Fj,* 1994 *Sa, W,* 1995 *J, J, F, S, Iv,* 1996 *Sa, Fj,* 1997 *Z,* 1999 *Geo, Geo, Kor, Kor, J, F, Fj, NZ, It, E,* 2000 *C, Fj, J, NZ, Sa, US,* 2001 *Fj, Sa, Fj, Sa, S,* 2004 *Sa, Fj,* 2005 *F*
F Vunipola 1988 *Fj,* 1991 *Sa, Fj, Fj,* 1994 *Sa, W, Fj,* 1995 *J, J, F, S, Iv, Sa, Fj,* 1996 *Sa, Fj,* 1997 *SA, Fj, Coo,* 1998 *Sa, Fj,* 1999 *Geo, Kor, Kor, Fj, C, NZ, E,* 2000 *NZ, Sa, US,* 2001 *Sa*
K Vunipola 1982 *Sa, Fj,* 1983 *Fj, Sa, M, M*
M Vunipola 1987 *W, Sa,* 1988 *Sa, Fj, Fj,* 1989 *Fj, Fj,* 1990 *Kor,* 1991 *Fj, Fj,* 1992 *Sa,* 1993 *Sa, S, Fj, A, Fj,* 1994 *Sa, W,* 1995 *J, J, F, S, Sa, Fj,* 1996 *Sa, Fj,* 1997 *Nm, SA, Coo,* 1999 *Geo, Kor, Kor, US, Fj*
S Vunipola 1977 *Fj,* 1981 *Fj,* 1982 *Sa*
V Vunipola 1982 *Fj*
VS Vunipola 2004 *Sa, Fj,* 2005 *It*
S Vunipoli 1960 *M,* 1963 *Fj*
B Woolley 1998 *Sa, Fj,* 1999 *Geo, Geo, Kor, J, US, Sa, C, It*

USA

USA'S 2008 RECORD

OPPONENTS	DATE	VENUE	RESULT
England Saxons	7 June	N	**Lost** 10–64
Ireland A	11 June	N	**Lost** 9–46
Canada	21 June	H	**Lost** 10–26
Clermont-Auvergne	9 Aug	H	**Lost** 14–37
Munster	23 Aug	H	**Lost** 22–46

URGENCY AND PATIENCE FOR USA

By Alex Goff

Two USA teams left France and the World Cup in 2007, the team that failed to win a game, and the team that was lauded for how well it pushed England and scored the try of the year.

Such an identity crisis isn't new for the American programme, which has at times showed signs of emerging as a real player in world rugby, despite operating on a shoestring. It was, then, a fresh start for Director of Rugby Nigel Melville as the Eagles embarked on their 2008 campaign.

The question on everybody's mind was who would be head coach? Melville, pushing the Eagles forward on and off the field with new strong commercial deals, wanted experience and cast his net wide. While there was interest from within the USA, he ultimately opted for a coach with a proven track record and in came the sometimes outspoken, but forward thinking Scott Johnson in early 2008. Johnson passed up bigger paydays to coach the Eagles, but said it was what he wanted.

"World rugby is better off if North America is strong, and a lot of people, including me, have talked about the USA's potential. I thought it was time to put my money where my mouth was," Johnson said.

Immediately rumors began to fly that Johnson would back out of the deal to coach the HSBC New South Wales Waratahs. Anyone who thought he would renege didn't know him very well, said Melville, and Johnson laughed off the Waratahs offer and arrived in the USA in time for the Churchill Cup.

For the USA players Johnson's arrival was a breath of fresh air. Not everyone had seen eye-to-eye with previous coach Peter Thorburn, who could veer toward the crotchety, and many responded to Johnson's approach.

"So far so good," said star center Paul Emerick after his first few days working with Johnson. "No doubt there will be growing pains for both the team and Scott."

The coach's first move was the take the captaincy away from the one player he knew well, Mike Hercus, and give it to flanker Todd Clever.

Clever's first game ended early as he was carted off against the England Saxons with a knock to the head. The Eagles kept it close for a while before the Saxons exploded in the second half to win 64–10. That would become the ongoing story for the USA, as they pushed all their opponents in the opening 40 minutes only to see the score run away from them in the second half.

"We're clearly not fit enough to play this game," growled Johnson after the Eagles blew a 10–0 lead to Canada and lost 26–10 in the Churchill Cup Bowl Final.

With his overseas pros going back to their clubs and the Eagles off until August, attention moved to the future. Melville, also CEO of USA Rugby, put on his trainers and took the All American team, the best university players, to wet and windy Wellington for a tour where they recorded a competitive 1–2.

A USA 'A' team took on England Counties, losing twice but playing competitively. In the IRB-funded North American 4, two US teams, the Hawks and the Falcons, took on Canada East and Canada West.

The American teams went with youth, with players like 17-year-old Hanno Dirsken and 20-year-olds Zach Pangelinan, Shawn Pittman and Scott Lavalla. The Falcons ultimately lost to Canada West 16–11 in the final in Glendale, Colo, while Canada East and the Hawks tied for third, but perhaps the best part of the contest was the emergence of those young players.

Johnson thought so, and shocked many with a very young line-up for two August matches against European professional teams ASM Clermont-Auvergne and Munster. Waiting for American players to reach international standard by playing in their domestic club game wasn't going to do the job, said Johnson.

"We haven't won doing it the old way, so why keep doing it?" he said. "We could stay with many 29–30-year-olds, but the fact is that those 29–30-year-olds didn't do it on the world stage.

"In our previous games we weren't fit enough and one way to get that right is to inject energy into the group. Young, athletic players inject energy, experience can be an excuse to do less."

But it won't be just about getting young players on the field. Plenty more has to change, and a lot of the responsibility for that change falls on the desk of Melville, Director of Rugby and CEO. It is Melville who has landed sponsorship deals for USA Rugby and who has preached over-delivering on deals to get sponsors to come back. And it is Melville who has put the people in place to change the USA's elite-player pathway.

What he can't do is warp time and space. The USA will still be almost four million square miles, and getting a national team in assembly on a regular basis will never be easy, or cheap.

He is looking at a series of challenges on all fronts – the need to lower the age where athletes play rugby, the need to fast-track athletes now, the need to bring crossover athletes to the game, and the need to schedule more meaningful test matches for the Eagles along the way.

The USA Sevens team is a huge part of this plan as well. Coach Al Caravelli made some hard choices when he came on as coach in 2006, he continues to shake up the selection process with some surprising choices.

The 2008 season saw the USA earn IRB Sevens Series points for the first time since 2003, and discounting an 0–5 opener at Dubai, they won more than they lost. That performance earned the Eagles an invitation to be a core team playing in all eight IRB Series as well as the Sevens World Cup.

"Our first priority is to do well at the Sevens World Cup," said Melville, highly mindful that a good showing by the USA might sway American votes on the Olympics.

It's been so much about the future that urgency gets left behind, and that's what both Caravelli and Johnson tried to change when they met with USA Rugby's Board of Directors in August. All the biggest plans in the world won't work if they don't get money, and soon.

The pay-offs are going to be a long way down the road, but the investment needs to be now.

USA Rugby's club championships might be noteworthy as much for where they were won as to who won them. Certainly New York Athletic Club's dramatic sudden death overtime victory over Belmont Shore in the Super League final was one to savor (and for once the final was on television), but the venue was the thing.

Two years ago the City of Glendale, Colorado, surrounded on all four sides by the larger city of Denver, decided to set itself apart by adopting a sport: rugby. They hired a Director of Rugby and invested millions in a rugby-specific stadium. That ended up being Infinity Park. Director of Rugby Mark Bullock took his Glendale Raptors to the national Division I final in their second year in existence, where they lost to Life University by a point 15–14.

Glendale also quickly became the showcase venue for American rugby. All four club championships, the collegiate all-star championships, and the North America 4 final were all held in Glendale.

And that new stadium looked very nice as Luke Milton's penalty goal sailed over it and though the posts to give NYAC the 31–28 victory over Belmont Shore. For Shore it was their sixth straight Super League final, and perhaps their toughest road. Coach Jonnie Cox balanced injuries and player moves all season to somehow get his team to the title game. Meanwhile NYAC coach Mike Tolkin made his biggest move at the beginning of the season. Scrumhalf Mike Petri, who had helped Belmont Shore to the 2007 title, was back in his native New York and that meant incumbent scrum-half Christian Mayo moved to fly-half. The two worked well together behind a cohesive set of forwards and a gritty game plan.

Milton's goalkicking didn't hurt either. In the final NYAC raced out to a lead that looked big enough to hold, but Shore scored twice in the waning minutes to tie the game at 25–25 at full time. Both teams traded penalties in the overtime – Milton's with no time left – and that set the stage for a final next-score-wins surge, led by Petri, and Milton's heroics.

"I don't feel bad about losing, this was a great game," said Belmont Shore's massive No. 8 Henry Bloomfield. "We played as hard as we could and it was in a great venue."

USA INTERNATIONAL STATISTICS

MATCH RECORDS UP TO 30TH SEPTEMBER 2008

WINNING MARGIN

Date	Opponent	Result	Winning Margin
01/07/2006	Barbados	91–0	**91**
06/07/1996	Japan	74–5	**69**
07/11/1989	Uruguay	60–3	**57**
12/03/1994	Bermuda	60–3	**57**
08/04/1998	Portugal	61–5	**56**

MOST POINTS IN A MATCH
BY THE TEAM

Date	Opponent	Result	Pts.
01/07/2006	Barbados	91–0	**91**
06/07/1996	Japan	74–5	**74**
17/05/2003	Japan	69–27	**69**
12/04/2003	Spain	62–13	**62**
08/04/1998	Portugal	61–5	**61**

MOST TRIES IN A MATCH
BY THE TEAM

Date	Opponent	Result	Tries
01/07/2006	Barbados	91–0	**13**
17/05/2003	Japan	69–27	**11**
07/11/1989	Uruguay	60–3	**11**
06/07/1996	Japan	74–5	**11**

MOST CONVERSIONS IN A MATCH
BY THE TEAM

Date	Opponent	Result	Cons
01/07/2006	Barbados	91–0	**13**
07/11/1989	Uruguay	60–3	**8**
06/07/1996	Japan	74–5	**8**
17/05/2003	Japan	69–27	**7**
12/03/1994	Bermuda	60–3	**6**
27/04/2003	Spain	58–13	**6**

MOST PENALTIES IN A MATCH
BY THE TEAM

Date	Opponent	Result	Pens
18/09/1996	Canada	18–23	**6**
21/09/1996	Uruguay	27–13	**5**
20/10/2003	Scotland	15–39	**5**
22/05/1999	Fiji	25–14	**5**
09/06/1984	Canada	21–13	**5**
02/10/1993	Australia	22–26	**5**

MOST DROP GOALS IN A MATCH
BY THE TEAM

Date	Player	Opponent	DGS
	14 Matches		**1**

MOST POINTS IN A MATCH
BY A PLAYER

Date	Player	Opponent	Pts.
07/11/1989	Chris O'Brien	Uruguay	**26**
31/05/2004	Mike Hercus	Russia	**26**
01/07/2006	Mike Hercus	Barbados	**26**
12/03/1994	Chris O'Brien	Bermuda	**25**
06/07/1996	Matt Alexander	Japan	**24**

MOST TRIES IN A MATCH
BY A PLAYER

Date	Player	Opponent	Tries
06/07/1996	Vaea Anitoni	Japan	**4**
07/06/1997	Brian Hightower	Japan	**4**
08/04/1998	Vaea Anitoni	Portugal	**4**
	6 Players		**3**

MOST CONVERSIONS IN A MATCH

BY A PLAYER

Date	Player	Opponent	Cons
01/07/2006	Mike Hercus	Barbados	13
06/07/1996	Matt Alexander	Japan	8
07/11/1989	Chris O'Brien	Uruguay	7
17/05/2003	Mike Hercus	Japan	7
12/03/1994	Chris O'Brien	Bermuda	6
27/04/2003	Mike Hercus	Spain	6

MOST PENALTIES IN A MATCH

BY A PLAYER

Date	Player	Opponent	Pens
18/09/1996	Matt Alexander	Canada	6
21/09/1996	Matt Alexander	Uruguay	5
20/10/2003	Mike Hercus	Scotland	5
22/05/1999	Kevin Dalzell	Fiji	5
09/06/1984	Ray Nelson	Canada	5
02/10/1993	Chris O'Brien	Australia	5

MOST DROP GOALS IN A MATCH

BY THE TEAM

Date	Player	Opponent	DGS
	14 Players		1

MOST CAPPED PLAYERS

Name	Caps
Luke Gross	62
Dave Hodges	53
Alec Parker	50
Mike MacDonald	48
Kort Schubert	47

LEADING TRY SCORERS

Name	Tries
Vaea Anitoni	26
Philip Eloff	10
Riaan van Zyl	10
Mike Hercus	9
5 Players	8

LEADING CONVERSIONS SCORERS

Name	Cons
Mike Hercus	76
Matt Alexander	45
Chris O'Brien	24
Grant Wells	14
Mark Williams	13

LEADING PENALTY SCORERS

Name	Pens
Mike Hercus	60
Matt Alexander	55
Mark Williams	35
Chris O'Brien	22
Grant Wells	22

LEADING DROP GOAL SCORERS

Name	DGs
Mike Hercus	3
Matt Alexander	2
Dave Horton	2
Grant Wells	2

LEADING POINTS SCORERS

Name	Pts.
Mike Hercus	386
Matt Alexander	286
Chris O'Brien	144
Mark Williams	143
Vaea Anitoni	130

USA INTERNATIONAL PLAYERS
UP TO 30TH SEPTEMBER 2008

Note: Years given for International Championship matches are for second half of season; eg. 1972 means season 1971–72. Years for all other matches refer to the actual year of the match. Entries in square brackets denote matches played in RWC Finals.

M Alexander 1995 *C*, 1996 *I*, *C*, *HK*, *J*, *HK*, *J*, *Ar*, *C*, *Ur*, 1997 *W*, *C*, *HK*, *J*, *J*, *HK*, *C*, *W*, *W*, 1998 *Pt*, *Sp*, *J*, *HK*, *C*
S Allen 1996 *J*, 1997 *HK*, *J*, *J*, *C*, *W*, *W*
T Altemeier 1978 *C*
D Anderson 2002 *S*
B Andrews 1978 *C*, 1979 *C*
VN Anitoni 1992 *C*, 1994 *C*, *Ar*, *Ar*, *I*, 1995 *C*, 1996 *I*, *C*, *C*, *HK*, *J*, *HK*, *J*, *Ar*, *C*, *Ur*, 1997 *W*, *C*, *J*, *HK*, *C*, *W*, *W*, 1998 *Pt*, *Sp*, *J*, *HK*, *C*, *C*, *J*, *HK*, *Fj*, *Ar*, *C*, *Ur*, 1999 *Tg*, *Fj*, *J*, *C*, *Sa*, *E*, *I*, *R*, *A*, 2000 *Fj*, *Sa*
S Auerbach 1976 *A*
M Aylor 2006 *IrA*, *M*, *C*, *Bar*, *Ur*, *Ur*, 2007 *S*, *C*, *Sa*, *SA*
A Bachelet 1993 *C*, *A*, 1994 *Ber*, *C*, *Ar*, *Ar*, *I*, 1995 *C*, 1996 *I*, *C*, *C*, *HK*, *J*, *HK*, *J*, *Ar*, *C*, 1997 *W*, *C*, *HK*, *J*, *J*, *HK*, *C*, *W*, *W*, 1998 *Pt*, *Sp*, *J*, *HK*, *C*, *C*, *J*
R Bailey 1979 *C*, 1980 *NZ*, 1981 *C*, *SA*, 1982 *C*, 1983 *C*, *A*, 1987 *Tun*, *C*, *J*, *E*
B Barnard 2006 *IrA*, *M*, *Bar*, *C*
I Basauri 2007 *S*, *E*, *Tg*
D Bateman 1982 *C*, *E*, 1983 *A*, 1985 *J*, *C*
P Bell 2006 *IrA*, *M*, *C*, *Bar*, *C*, *Ur*, *Ur*
W Bernhard 1987 *Tun*
TW Billups 1993 *C*, *A*, 1994 *Ber*, *C*, *Ar*, *Ar*, *I*, 1995 *C*, 1996 *I*, *C*, *C*, *HK*, *HK*, *J*, *Ar*, *C*, *Ur*, 1997 *W*, *C*, *HK*, *HK*, *W*, *W*, 1998 *Pt*, *Sp*, *J*, *HK*, *C*, *C*, *J*, *HK*, *Fj*, *Ar*, *C*, *Ur*, 1999 *Tg*, *Fj*, *J*, *C*, *Sa*, *E*, *I*, *R*, *A*
A Blom 1998 *Sp*, *J*, *HK*, *C*, *C*, *HK*, *Fj*, *Ar*, *Ur*, 1999 *Sa*, 2000 *J*, *C*, *I*
H Bloomfield 2007 *E*, *Tg*, *SA*, 2008 *C*
R Bordley 1976 *A*, *F*, 1977 *C*, *E*, 1978 *C*
S Bracken 1994 *Ar*, 1995 *C*
G Brackett 1976 *A*, *F*, 1977 *E*
N Brendel 1983 *A*, 1984 *C*, 1985 *J*, *C*, 1987 *Tun*, *E*
D Briley 1979 *C*, 1980 *W*, *C*, *NZ*
J Buchholz 2001 *C*, 2002 *S*, 2003 *Sp*, *E*, *Ar*, *Fj*, *J*, *F*, 2004 *C*
B Burdette 2006 *Ur*, *Ur*, 2007 *E*, *S*, *C*, *E*, *Tg*, *Sa*, *SA*
J Burke 2000 *C*, *I*
JR Burke 1990 *C*, *J*, 1991 *J*, *J*, *S*, *C*, *F*, *NZ*, 1992 *C*
J Burkhardt 1983 *C*, 1985 *C*
E Burlingham 1980 *NZ*, 1981 *C*, *SA*, 1982 *C*, *E*, 1983 *C*, *A*, 1984 *C*, 1985 *C*, 1986 *J*, 1987 *Tun*, *C*, *J*, *E*
C Campbell 1993 *C*, *A*, 1994 *Ber*, *C*, *Ar*
D Care 1998 *Pt*, *J*, *C*
M Carlson 1987 *W*, *C*
M Caulder 1984 *C*, 1985 *C*, 1989 *C*
R Causey 1977 *C*, 1981 *C*, *SA*, 1982 *C*, *E*, 1984 *C*, 1986 *J*, 1987 *E*
W Chai 1993 *C*
D Chipman 1976 *A*, 1978 *C*
JE Clark 1979 *C*, 1980 *C*
J Clarkson 1986 *J*, 1987 *Tun*, *C*, *J*, *E*
J Clayton 1999 *C*, *R*, *A*, 2000 *J*, *C*, *I*, *Fj*, *Tg*, *Sa*, *S*, *W*
T Clever 2003 *Ar*, 2005 *C*, *R*, *W*, *ArA*, *C*, 2006 *IrA*, *M*, *C*, *Bar*, *C*, *Ur*, *Ur*, 2007 *E*, *S*, *C*, *E*, *Tg*, *Sa*, *SA*, 2008 *C*
R Cooke 1979 *C*, 1980 *W*, *C*, *NZ*, 1981 *C*, *SA*
B Corcoran 1989 *Ur*, *Ar*, 1990 *Ar*
J Coulson 1999 *A*
M Crick 2007 *E*, *S*, *C*, 2008 *C*
R Crivellone 1983 *C*, 1986 *C*, 1987 *C*
K Cross 2003 *Sp*, *Sp*, *J*, *C*, *E*, *E*, *Ar*, *C*, *Fj*, *S*, 2004 *C*, *Rus*
C Culpepper 1977 *E*, 1978 *C*
C Curtis 1997 *C*, *HK*, *J*, 1999 *Sa*, 2001 *Ar*
B Daily 1989 *Ur*, *Ar*, 1990 *Ar*, *C*, *A*, *J*, 1991 *J*, *J*, *S*, *F*, *F*, *It*
K Dalzell 1996 *Ur*, 1998 *Sp*, *C*, *HK*, *C*, *Ur*, 1999 *Tg*, *Fj*, *J*, *C*, *Sa*, *E*, *I*, *R*, *A*, 2000 *J*, *C*, *I*, *Fj*, *Tg*, *Sa*, *S*, *W*, 2001 *C*, *E*, *SA*, 2002 *S*, *C*, *C*, *Ch*, *Ur*, 2003 *Sp*, *Sp*, *J*, *C*, *E*, *C*, *Ur*, *Fj*, *S*, *J*, *F*
G De Bartolo 2008 *C*
MG de Jong 1990 *C*, 1991 *J*, *J*, *S*, *C*, *F*, *F*, *It*, *E*
M Deaton 1983 *A*, 1984 *C*, 1985 *J*
M Delai 1996 *I*, *HK*, *J*, 1997 *HK*, 1998 *HK*, 2000 *J*, *C*, *I*, *Fj*, *Tg*, *Sa*, *S*, *W*, 2001 *C*, *Ar*, *Ur*
D Dickson 1986 *J*, 1987 *A*
C Doherty 1987 *W*
D Dorsey 2001 *SA*, 2002 *S*, *C*, *C*, *Ch*, *Ur*, *Ch*, *Ur*, 2003 *Sp*, *Sp*, *J*, *C*, *E*, *Ar*, *C*, *Ur*, *Fj*, *S*, *J*, *F*, 2004 *C*, *Rus*, *C*, *F*
G Downes 1992 *HK*
B Doyle 2008 *C*
R Duncanson 1977 *E*
P Eloff 2000 *J*, *C*, *I*, *Fj*, *Tg*, *Sa*, *S*, *W*, 2001 *C*, *Ar*, *Ur*, *E*, *SA*, 2002 *S*, *C*, *Ch*, *Ur*, 2003 *Sp*, *Sp*, *J*, *C*, *E*, *C*, *Ur*, *Fj*, *S*, *J*, *F*, 2006 *Bar*, *C*, *Ur*, *Ur*, 2007 *Tg*, *Sa*, *SA*
P Emerick 2003 *Sp*, *E*, *Ar*, *C*, *Ur*, *Fj*, *S*, *J*, 2004 *C*, *F*, *I*, *It*, 2005 *C*, *R*, *W*, *ArA*, *C*, 2006 *C*, *Bar*, *C*, *Ur*, *Ur*, 2007 *S*, *C*, *E*, 2008 *C*
C Erskine 2006 *C*, *Ur*, *Ur*, 2007 *E*, *Tg*, *Sa*, *SA*
V Esikia 2006 *IrA*, *M*, *Bar*, *C*, *Ur*, *Ur*, 2007 *E*, *E*, *Tg*, *Sa*, *SA*
J Everett 1984 *C*, 1985 *J*, 1986 *J*, *C*, 1987 *Tun*, *J*, *E*
W Everett 1985 *J*, 1986 *J*, *C*
M Fabling 1995 *C*
M Fanucchi 1979 *C*, 1980 *W*
R Farley 1989 *I*, *Ur*, *Ar*, 1990 *Ar*, *C*, *A*, *J*, 1991 *J*, *J*, *S*, *C*, *F*, *F*, *It*, *E*, 1992 *C*
P Farner 1999 *Tg*, *Fj*, *J*, *C*, 2000 *J*, *C*, *I*, *Fj*, *Tg*, *Sa*, *S*, *W*, 2002 *C*, *C*, *Ch*, *Ur*, *Ch*, *Ur*
D Fee 2002 *C*, *C*, *Ch*, *Ur*, *Ch*, *Ur*, 2003 *Sp*, *Sp*, *J*, *C*, *E*, *C*, *Ur*, *Fj*, *S*, *J*, *F*, 2004 *C*, *Rus*, *C*, *F*, *I*, *It*, 2005 *C*, *R*, *W*, *ArA*, *C*
O Fifita 2000 *Fj*, *Tg*, *Sa*, *S*, *W*, 2001 *C*, *Ar*, *Ur*, *E*, *SA*, 2002 *C*, *C*, 2003 *Sp*, *E*, *E*, *Ar*, *S*
S Finkel 1981 *C*, 1983 *C*, *A*, 1986 *C*, 1987 *A*, *E*
AW Flay 1990 *J*, 1991 *J*, *J*, *S*, *F*, *It*, *E*
R Flynn 2000 *C*, *I*, *Fj*, *Tg*, *Sa*, *W*, 2001 *C*, *Ar*
J Fowler 1980 *W*, *C*, *NZ*, 1981 *C*, *SA*, 1982 *C*, *E*
W Fraumann 1976 *F*, 1977 *E*
A Freeman 1995 *C*, 1996 *I*
M French 2005 *W*, *ArA*, 2006 *IrA*, *M*, *Ur*, *Ur*, 2007 *E*, *C*
B Furrow 1998 *C*, *C*, *J*, *HK*
M Gale 1992 *C*
B Geraghty 1993 *C*
J Gillam 2000 *Tg*
D Gillies 1998 *Ar*, 1999 *Tg*
D Gonzalez 1990 *A*, 1993 *C*
G Goodman 1992 *C*
J Gouws 2003 *E*, *E*, *Ar*, *C*, *Ur*, *S*, *F*, 2004 *I*, *It*
J Grant 1981 *SA*
R Grant 2000 *Tg*
S Gray 1976 *F*, 1977 *E*, 1979 *C*, 1980 *W*, *NZ*, 1981 *SA*
R Green 1994 *I*, 1995 *C*, 1996 *I*, *C*, *C*, *HK*, *J*, *HK*, *J*, 1998 *Fj*, *Ar*
M Griffin 2003 *Sp*, *J*, *E*, 2004 *Rus*, *C*, *F*, 2005 *C*, *R*

J Grobler 1996 *Ar, C, Ur,* 1997 *C, J, J,* 1998 *J, Fj, C, Ur,* 1999 *Fj, J, C, Sa, E, I, R, A,* 2000 *J, C, I, Tg, Sa, S, W,* 2001 *C, Ar, Ur, E, SA,* 2002 *C, Ch, Ur*
L Gross 1996 *I, C, C, HK, J, HK, J, C, Ur,* 1997 *C, HK, J, J, HK, C, W, W,* 1998 *Pt, Sp, J, HK, C, C, J, HK, Fj, Ar, C, Ur,* 1999 *Tg, Fj, J, C, Sa, E, I, R, A,* 2000 *Fj, Tg, Sa, S, W,* 2001 *C, Ar, E, SA,* 2002 *S, C,* 2003 *Sp, Sp, J, C, E, E, Ar, C, Ur, Fj, S, J, F*
D Guest 1976 *F,* 1977 *C*
I Gunn 1982 *E*
M Halliday 1977 *E,* 1978 *C,* 1980 *W, C,* 1982 *C, E*
C Hansen 2005 *C,* 2006 *IrA, M, C*
J Hanson 1977 *C, E,* 1980 *W, C,* 1981 *C,* 1983 *C, A*
J Hartman 2005 *C, ArA*
J Hartman 1983 *A,* 1984 *C*
W Hayward 1991 *J, C*
GM Hein 1987 *Tun, C, J, A, E, W, C,* 1988 *R, USS,* 1989 *I, C, Ur, Ar,* 1990 *Ar, A,* 1991 *J, F, F, It, NZ, E,* 1992 *HK,* 1993 *C, A,* 1994 *Ber*
R Helu 1981 *C, SA,* 1982 *C, E,* 1983 *C, A,* 1985 *J, C,* 1987 *Tun, C, J, A*
B Henderson 1977 *C*
M Hercus 2002 *S, C, C, Ch, Ur, Ch, Ur,* 2003 *Sp, Sp, J, C, Ur, Fj, S, J, F,* 2004 *C, Rus, C, F, I, It,* 2005 *C, R, W, ArA, C,* 2006 *Bar, C, Ur, Ur,* 2007 *E, Tg, Sa, SA,* 2008 *C*
SJ Hiatt 1993 *A,* 1998 *Ar, C*
KG Higgins 1985 *J, C,* 1986 *J, C,* 1987 *Tun, C, J, A, E, W, C,* 1988 *C, R, USS,* 1989 *I, C, Ur, Ar,* 1990 *Ar, A, J,* 1991 *J, J, S, C, F, It, E*
B Hightower 1997 *W, J, HK, C, W, W,* 1998 *Fj, C, Ur,* 1999 *Tg, Fj, J, C, Sa, I, R, A*
D Hobson 1991 J
M Hobson 2005 *R*
D Hodges 1996 *Ur,* 1997 *W, W,* 1998 *Pt, Sp, J, HK, C, J, HK, Fj, Ar, C, Ur,* 1999 *Tg, Fj, J, C, Sa, E, I, R, A,* 2000 *J, C, I, Fj, Tg, Sa, S, W,* 2001 *C, Ar, Ur, E, SA,* 2002 *S, C, C, Ch, Ur, Ch, Ur,* 2003 *Sp, J, C, E, Fj, S, J, F,* 2004 *C, F*
C Hodgson 2002 *S, C, Ch, Ch,* 2003 *Sp, Sp, J, C, E, C,* 2004 *C, Rus*
J Hollings 1979 *C,* 1980 *NZ*
J Holtzman 1995 *C,* 1997 *HK, J,* 1998 *Ar*
J Hopkins 1996 *HK*
D Horton 1986 *C,* 1987 *A, C*
B Horwath 1984 *C,* 1985 *J, C,* 1986 *C,* 1987 *A, W,* 1990 *J*
B Hough 1991 *C,* 1992 *HK,* 1994 *Ar*
B Howard 1998 *HK, Fj, Ar,* 1999 *Sa*
C Howard 1980 *NZ*
J Hullinger 2006 *IrA, C, Bar, Ur, Ur*
M Inns 1985 *J, C,* 1986 *C*
R Isaac 1989 *C, Ar*
D Jablonski 1977 *C,* 1978 *C,* 1979 *C,* 1980 *W*
DW James 1990 *C, A,* 1993 *C, A,* 1994 *Ber, C, Ar, Ar, I*
WL Jefferson 1985 *J, C,* 1986 *C,* 1987 *W, C,* 1989 *I*
J Jellaco 1982 *C, E*
D Jenkinson 1984 *C,* 1985 *C,* 1986 *J*
PW Johnson 1987 *C, A, W, C,* 1988 *C, R, USS,* 1989 *I, C, Ar,* 1990 *A,* 1991 *F, F, NZ,* 1992 *HK, C*
S Jones 2005 *ArA,* 2006 *Ur*
G Judge 1991 *C,* 1992 *HK*
M Kane 2000 *J, I, Fj,* 2004 *C, F,* 2005 *ArA, C*
J Kelleher 1978 *C,* 1979 *C*
T Kelleher 2000 *C, I,* 2001 *C, Ar, Ur*
J Keller 1992 *HK, C*
J Kelly 2006 *M, C, Bar*
S Kelso 1977 *C, E,* 1978 *C*
D Kennedy 1997 *HK,* 1998 *Pt, Sp, J, HK*
J Keyter 2000 *W,* 2001 *SA,* 2002 *S, C, C, Ch, Ur, Ch, Ur,* 2003 *C, E, Ar, C, Ur, S, F*
F Khasigian 1976 *A*
K Khasigian 1998 *Ar,* 1999 *J, E, I, R, A,* 2000 *J, C, I, Fj, Sa, S, W,* 2001 *C, Ar, Ur, E, SA,* 2002 *S, C, C, Ch, Ur, Ch, Ur,* 2003 *Sp, Sp, J, C, E, Ar, C, Ur, Fj, S, J, F*
K Kjar 2001 *Ar, SA,* 2002 *S, C, C, Ch, Ur, Ch,* 2003 *E, E, Ar, S, J,* 2005 *ArA, C,* 2006 *C,* 2007 *E, S, C*
T Klein 1976 *A,* 1977 *C,* 1978 *C*
S Klerck 2003 *Ar, Ur, J,* 2004 *C, Rus, C, I, It*
T Kluempers 1996 *J,* 2000 *W,* 2001 *C, Ar, Ur*
Knutson 1988 *USS*
CD Labounty 1998 *C, J*
A Lakomskis 2002 *Ch, Ur,* 2004 *I, It*
G Lambert 1981 *C, SA,* 1982 *C, E,* 1984 *C,* 1985 *C,* 1987 *Tun, C, J, A, E,* 1988 *C, R, USS,* 1989 *C, Ur, Ar,* 1990 *Ar*
S Laporta 1989 *Ur, Ar*
M Laulaupeaalu 2008 *C*
S Lawrence 2006 *C, Bar, C, Ur, Ur*
R Le Clerc 1998 *C, Ur*
W LeClerc 1996 *HK, J,* 1997 *W, J, HK, C,* 1998 *C,* 1999 *Tg, Fj, J, C, Sa*
R Lehner 1995 *C,* 1996 *C, C, HK, J, HK, J, Ar, C,* 1997 *W, C, J, J, HK, C, W, W,* 1998 *Pt, Sp, J, HK, C, C, Ar, Ur,* 1999 *Tg, Fj, J, Sa, E, I, R,* 2000 *J, C, I, Fj, Tg, Sa*
O Lentz 2006 *IrA, M, Bar,* 2007 *E, Tg, Sa, SA*
J Lett 2008 *C*
WN Leversee 1988 *R,* 1989 *I, Ur,* 1990 *Ar, C, A, J,* 1991 *J, J, S, F, It,* 1994 *Ar, I,* 1996 *Ar*
R Lewis 1990 *C,* 1991 *S*
M L'Huillier 1999 *E, A*
R Liddington 2003 *Ar, C, S,* 2004 *Rus, C*
J Lik 2005 *C, R, ArA*
S Lipman 1988 *C, R, USS,* 1990 *C, J,* 1991 *F, It, NZ, E*
C Lippert 1989 *C, Ur, Ar,* 1990 *Ar, C, A, J,* 1991 *J, S, C, F, F, It, NZ,* 1993 *A,* 1994 *Ber, C, Ar, Ar, I,* 1996 *HK, J, Ar, C, Ur,* 1997 *C, HK, J, J, HK, W, W,* 1998 *J, HK, C, C, J, HK*
M Liscovitz 1977 *C, E,* 1978 *C*
R Lockerem 1996 *C, Ur*
J Lombard 1977 *C, E,* 1979 *C*
C Long 2003 *Sp*
J Lopez 1978 *C*
I Loveseth 1983 *A*
RA Lumkong 1994 *Ber, C, Ar, Ar, I,* 1996 *C, C, HK, J, HK, J, Ar, C, Ur,* 1997 *W,* 1998 *Pt, Sp, J, HK, C, C, J, HK, Fj, C, Ur,* 1999 *E, R, A*
D Lyle 1994 *I,* 1995 *C,* 1996 *I, C, C, HK, J, HK, J,* 1997 *W, C, HK, J, J, HK, C, W, W,* 1999 *Tg, Fj, J, C, Sa, E, I, R,* 2000 *S, W,* 2001 *C, Ar, E, SA,* 2002 *Ch, Ur,* 2003 *Sp, Sp, J, C, E, C, Ur, Fj, S, J, F*
M MacDonald 2000 *Fj,* 2001 *C, Ar, Ur, E, SA,* 2002 *S, C, C, Ch, Ur, Ch, Ur,* 2003 *Sp, Sp, J, C, E, E, C, Ur, Fj, S, J, F,* 2004 *C, Rus, F, I, It,* 2005 *C, R, W, ArA, C,* 2006 *IrA, C, Bar, C, Ur, Ur,* 2007 *S, C, E, Tg, Sa, SA,* 2008 *C*
A Magleby 2000 *W,* 2001 *Ar, Ur, E*
V Malifa 2007 *E, S, C, E, SA,* 2008 *C*
P Malloy 1995 *C*
L Manga 1986 *J,* 1989 *Ar,* 1991 *J, C, NZ, E,* 1992 *HK, C*
M Mangan 2005 *C, R, W, ArA, C,* 2006 *IrA, M, C, Bar, C, Ur,* 2007 *E, S, C, E, Tg, SA*
J McBride 1998 *Pt, Sp, C, Fj, Ar, C, Ur,* 2000 *J, C, I, Tg, Sa*
T McCormack 1989 *Ur, Ar,* 1990 *Ar, C*
G McDonald 1989 *I,* 1996 *I, C*
A McGarry 2002 *S, Ch*
M McLeod 1997 *J, HK, C*
T Meek 2006 *IrA, M, C, Bar*
H Mexted 2006 *Bar, Ur, Ur,* 2007 *E, S, C, E, Sa*
J Meyersieck 1982 *C,* 1983 *C, A,* 1985 *J,* 1986 *C*
J Mickel 1986 *C*
K Miles 1982 *C, E*
C Miller 2002 *Ch, Ur*
M Moeakiola 2007 *E, Tg, Sa, SA,* 2008 *C*
B Monroe 1985 *C*
A Montgomery 1986 *C,* 1987 *W, C,* 1988 *C,* 1989 *I, C*
B Morrison 1979 *C,* 1980 *W*
C Morrow 1997 *W, C, HK, C, W, W,* 1998 *Pt, C, C,* 1999 *Tg, C, E*
T Moser 1980 *W*
N Mottram 1990 *Ar, J,* 1991 *J, S, C, F, NZ, E,* 1992 *C*
F Mounga 1998 *C, J, HK, Fj, C, Ur,* 1999 *Sa, E, I, R, A,* 2003 *Sp, J,* 2004 *F, I, It,* 2005 *R,* 2007 *E, C, Sa*
D Murphy 1976 *F*
J Naivalu 2000 *Sa, S, W,* 2001 *C, Ur, E,* 2004 *C, Rus, C, F*
J Naqica 2001 *E, SA,* 2002 *S, C, C, Ch, Ur,* 2003 *Ar*
J Nash 2006 *M, C*
RB Nelson 1983 *C, A,* 1984 *C,* 1985 *C,* 1986 *J,* 1987 *C, J, A, E,* 1988 *R, USS,* 1989 *I, Ur, Ar,* 1990 *Ar, C, A, J,* 1991 *J, S, C, F, F, It, E*

T Ngwenya 2007 *E, Tg, Sa, SA*, 2008 *C*
C Nicolau 2002 *C*, 2003 *J, C, E*
S Niebauer 1976 *A*, 1979 *C*, 1980 *W, C, NZ*, 1981 *C, SA*, 1982 *C, E*
D Niu 1999 *Tg, Fj, J, C, E, I, R, A*
CP O'Brien 1988 *C, R, USS*, 1989 *I, C, Ur, Ar*, 1990 *Ar, A, J*, 1991 *S, C, F, F, NZ, E*, 1992 *HK*, 1993 *C, A*, 1994 *Ber*
T O'Brien 1980 *NZ*, 1983 *C, A*
M O'Donnell 1976 *F*
C Okezie 1979 *C*, 1980 *C, NZ*, 1981 *C*, 1982 *C, E*
M Ording 1976 *A, F*, 1977 *E*, 1978 *C*
M Ormsby 1983 *C*
A Osborne 2007 *C*
C Osentowski 2004 *It*, 2005 *C, R, W*, 2006 *IrA, M, C, Bar, C, Ur, Ur*, 2007 *E, S, C, E, Tg, Sa, SA*
K Oxman 1976 *A*
S Paga 1998 *C, C*, 1999 *C, Sa, E, I, R, A*, 2002 *Ch, Ur, Ch, Ur*, 2003 *J*, 2004 *C, Rus, F*
T Palamo 2007 *SA*
M Palefau 2005 *C, R, W, ArA, C*, 2006 *IrA, M, C*, 2007 *E, S*
AF Paoli 1982 *E*, 1983 *C*, 1985 *J*, 1986 *J, C*, 1987 *C, J, A, W, C*, 1988 *C, R, USS*, 1989 *I, C, Ur, Ar*, 1991 *J, F, It*
A Parker 1996 *HK, J, HK, J, Ar, C, Ur*, 1997 *W*, 1998 *Pt, Sp, J, HK, C, C, J, HK, Fj*, 1999 *Fj, C, Sa, E, I, R, A*, 2002 *Ch, Ur, Ch, Ur*, 2003 *Sp, Sp, C, E, C, Ur, Fj, S, F*, 2004 *C, Rus, C, I, It*, 2005 *W*, 2006 *C, Ur, Ur*, 2007 *E, Tg, Sa, SA*
D Parks 1980 *C*
E Parthmore 1977 *E*
D Payne 2007 *S, SA*
J Peter 1987 *W, C*
T Petersen 1993 *C*
M Petri 2007 *SA*, 2008 *C*
A Petruzzella 2004 *C, F, I*, 2005 *W, ArA, C*, 2006 *IrA, M, Bar*
MD Pidcock 1991 *C, NZ, E*
M Purcell 1980 *W*, 1981 *C, SA*, 1982 *C, E*, 1983 *C, A*, 1984 *C*, 1986 *J, C*, 1987 *Tun, C, J, E*
J Pye 2005 *ArA, C*
P Quinn 2007 *E*
RR Randell 1993 *A*, 1994 *Ber, C, Ar, I*, 1995 *C*, 1996 *I, HK, J, Ar, C*, 1997 *C*
J Raven 1998 *C, J*
E Reed 1999 *A*, 2001 *Ur, E, SA*, 2002 *S, C, C*
AM Ridnell 1987 *A*, 1988 *C, R, USS*, 1991 *J, S, C, F, F, It, NZ, E*, 1992 *HK*, 1993 *C*
J Rissone 1996 *I, C, C, HK, Ur*
R Rosser 2006 *Ur, Ur*
D Rowe 2005 *R, W*
A Russell 2006 *C, Ur*
A Ryland 2005 *C, R, W, C*
R Samaniego 1992 *HK*
L Sanft 1996 *J*
J Santos 1995 *C*, 1996 *C, C, HK*
A Satchwell 2002 *S*, 2003 *Ur*
A Saulala 1997 *C, HK, C, W, W*, 1998 *Pt, Sp, HK, C, J, HK*, 1999 *Tg, Fj, J, C, Sa, E, A*, 2000 *Fj, Tg*
M Saunders 1987 *Tun, C, J, A, E, W, C*, 1988 *C, R, USS*, 1989 *I, C*
MH Sawicki 1990 *Ar, J*, 1991 *J, F, NZ*
MA Scharrenberg 1993 *A*, 1994 *Ber, C, Ar, Ar*, 1995 *C*, 1996 *I, J, HK, J, Ar, C, Ur*, 1997 *W, C, HK, J, J, HK, C, W, W*, 1998 *Pt, Sp, J, HK, C, C, Ar, C, Ur*, 1999 *Tg, Fj, J, C, Sa, I, R, A*
J Scheitlin 1979 *C*
CJ Schlereth 1993 *C*, 1994 *I*, 1998 *J*
G Schneeweis 1976 *A*, 1977 *E*
B Schoener 2006 *IrA, M, C*
E Schram 1993 *A*, 1994 *Ber, C, Ar, Ar*, 1996 *J, Ar*
J Schraml 1991 *C*, *1992 HK*, 1993 *C*
K Schubert 2000 *J, C, I, Fj, Tg, Sa*, 2001 *C, Ar, Ur, E, SA*, 2002 *S, C, C, Ch, Ur, Ch, Ur*, 2003 *Sp, Sp, J, C, E, Ar, C, Ur, Fj, S, J, F*, 2004 *C, Rus, C, F, I, It*, 2005 *C, R, W, ArA, C*, 2006 *IrA, M, C, Bar, C*, 2008 *C*
RE Schurfeld 1992 *HK, C*, 1993 *A*, 1994 *Ber, C*
T Scott 1976 *F*
T Selfridge 1976 *A, F*, 1977 *C*, 1980 *W, C*
D Shanagher 1980 *NZ*, 1981 *C, SA*, 1982 *C, E*, 1984 *C*, 1985 *J*, 1986 *J*, 1987 *W*
R Shaw 2008 *C*
P Sheehy 1991 *NZ, E*, 1992 *HK, C*
M Sherlock 1977 *C*
M Sherman 2003 *E, Ar, F*, 2004 *Rus*, 2005 *C, W, ArA*
W Shiflet 1983 *C, A*, 1985 *J*, 1987 *A*
K Shuman 1997 *HK, J, J, W*, 1998 *J, HK, C, C, J, Ar*, 1999 *Tg, Fj, J, E, I, R, A*, 2000 *J, C, I, Fj, Tg, Sa, S, W*, 2001 *Ar, Ur, E, SA*
M Siano 1989 *I, C, Ur, Ar*
MK Sika 1993 *C, A*, 1994 *Ber, C, Ar, Ar, I*, 1996 *C, C, J, HK, J, Ar, C, Ur*, 1997 *J, W*
S Sika 2003 *Fj, J, F*, 2004 *C, F, I, It*, 2005 *W, C*, 2006 *IrA, M*, 2007 *S, C, E, Tg, Sa, SA*, 2008 *C*
C Slaby 2008 *C*
M Smith 1988 *C*
T Smith 1980 *C*, 1981 *C, SA*, 1982 *E*
B Smoot 1992 *C*
M Stanaway 1997 *C, HK, J, C*, 1998 *HK*
L Stanfill 2005 *C*, 2006 *C*, 2007 *E, S, C, E, Tg, Sa, SA*
D Steinbauer 1992 *C*, 1993 *C*
J Stencel 2006 *C*
D Stephenson 1976 *A, F*, 1977 *C*
I Stevens 1998 *C*
P Still 2000 *S, W*, 2001 *C, Ar, Ur, E, SA*
W Stone 1976 *F*
D Straehley 1983 *C*, 1984 *C*
G Sucher 1998 *C, J, HK, Fj, C, Ur*, 1999 *Tg, Fj, J, C, Sa, E, I, R, A*
B Surgener 2001 *SA*, 2002 *C, Ur*, 2003 *Sp, E, E*, 2004 *C, F, I, It*, 2005 *W*
E Swanson 1976 *A*
C Sweeney 1976 *A, F*, 1977 *C, E*
M Swiderski 1976 *A*
B Swords 1980 *W, C, NZ*
KR Swords 1985 *J, C*, 1986 *C*, 1987 *Tun, C, J, A, W, C*, 1988 *C, R, USS*, 1989 *I, C, Ur, Ar*, 1990 *Ar, C, A, J*, 1991 *J, J, S, C, F, F, It, NZ, E*, 1992 *C*, 1993 *C, A*, 1994 *Ber, C, Ar, Ar*
TK Takau 1994 *Ar, Ar, I*, 1996 *C, C, HK, J, HK*, 1997 *C, HK, J, HK, W, W*, 1998 *Sp, HK, C, C, J, HK, Ur*, 1999 *E, I, R, A*
R Tardits 1993 *A*, 1994 *Ber, C, Ar, Ar, I*, 1995 *C*, 1996 *I, C, C, J, Ar*, 1997 *W, C*, 1998 *Sp, HK, Fj*, 1999 *Tg, Fj, J, C, Sa, I, R*
J Tarpoff 2002 *S, C, C, Ch*, 2003 *Sp, Sp, C, E, E*, 2006 *IrA, M, C, Bar*
M Timoteo 2000 *Tg*, 2001 *C, Ar, Ur, SA*, 2002 *S, C, C, Ch, Ur, Ch*, 2003 *Sp, Sp, J, E, Ar, C, F*, 2004 *C, Rus, C, F, I, It*, 2005 *C, R*, 2006 *IrA, M, C, Bar*
A Tuilevuka 2006 *IrA, M, C*
A Tuipulotu 2004 *C, Rus, C, I, It*, 2005 *C, R, W*, 2006 *C, Bar, C, Ur, Ur*, 2007 *E, S, C, Tg, Sa*
CE Tunnacliffe 1991 *F, NZ, E*, 1992 *HK*
Vaka 1987 *C*
M van der Molen 1992 *C*
R van Zyl 2003 *Sp, Sp, J, C, E, C, Ur, Fj, S, J, F*, 2004 *C, F*
J Vandergeissen 2008 *C*
F Viljoen 2004 *Rus, C, F, I, It*, 2005 *C, R, W, ArA, C*, 2006 *IrA, M, C, Ur, Ur*, 2007 *E, S, C*
T Vinick 1986 *C*, 1987 *A, E*
J Vitale 2006 *C, Ur*, 2007 *E*
BG Vizard 1986 *J, C*, 1987 *Tun, C, J, A, E, W, C*, 1988 *C, R, USS*, 1989 *I, C*, 1990 *C, A*, 1991 *J, J, S, C, F, It*
C Vogl 1996 *C, C*, 1997 *W, C, HK, J, J, HK, C*, 1998 *HK, Fj, Ar*
J Waasdorp 2003 *J, E, Ar, Ur, J, F*, 2004 *C, Rus, C, F, I, It*, 2005 *C, ArA, C*
D Wack 1976 *F*, 1977 *C*, 1978 *C*, 1980 *C*
B Waite 1976 *F*
J Walker 1996 *I, C, HK, J, Ar, C, Ur*, 1997 *W, J, HK, C, W, W*, 1998 *Sp, J, HK, C, C, J, HK, Ar, C, Ur*, 1999 *Tg, J*
L Walton 1980 *C, NZ*, 1981 *C, SA*
A Ward 1980 *NZ*, 1983 *C*
B Warhurst 1983 *C, A*, 1984 *C*, 1985 *J, C*, 1986 *J*, 1987 *Tun, C, J*
M Waterman 1992 *C*
G Wells 2000 *J, C, I, Fj, Tg, Sa, S, W*, 2001 *C, Ar, Ur, E*

T Whelan 1982 *E*, 1987 *C*, 1988 *C*, *R*, *USS*
EA Whitaker 1990 *J*, 1991 *F*, *F*, *It*, *NZ*
B Wiedemer 2007 *E*, 2008 *C*
L Wilfley 2000 *I*, *Tg*, *W*, 2001 *Ar*, *Ur*, *SA*, 2002 *S*, *C*, *C*, *Ch*, *Ur*, *Ch*, *Ur*, 2003 *Sp*, *Sp*, *J*, *C*, *E*, *E*, *S*
JP Wilkerson 1991 *E*, 1993 *A*, 1994 *C*, 1996 *C*, *Ur*, 1997 *W*, *C*, *HK*, *J*, *J*, *C*, *W*, *W*, 1998 *Pt*, *Sp*, *J*, *HK*
B Williams 1988 *C*, *R*, *USS*, 1989 *C*, 1992 *C*
C Williams 1990 *C*, *A*, *J*, 1991 *J*, *S*, *C*
D Williams 2004 *C*, *Rus*, *C*, *F*, *I*, *It*, 2005 *ArA*, 2006 *Ur*, *Ur*, 2007 *E*, *C*
MA Williams 1987 *W*, *C*, 1988 *C*, *R*, *USS*, 1989 *I*, *Ur*, *Ar*, 1990 *Ar*, *C*, *A*, 1991 *J*, *J*, *F*, *F*, *It*, *NZ*, *E*, 1992 *HK*, 1994 *C*, *Ar*, *Ar*, *I*, 1996 *I*, *C*, *C*, *HK*, 1997 *W*, 1998 *Fj*, *Ar*, *Ur*, 1999 *Tg*, *J*, *C*, *Sa*, *E*, *I*
G Wilson 1978 *C*, 1980 *W*, *C*, 1981 *C*, *SA*
M Wyatt 2003 *Ar*, *C*, *Ur*, *J*, *F*, 2004 *C*, *Rus*, *C*, *F*, *I*, *It*, 2005 *W*, *ArA*, *C*, 2006 *C*
C Wyles 2007 *E*, *S*, *C*, *E*, *Tg*, *Sa*, *SA*, 2008 *C*
D Younger 2000 *J*, *C*, *I*, *Fj*
S Yungling 1997 *HK*, *W*
R Zenker 1987 *W*, *C*

WALES

WALES' 2007–08 TEST RECORD

OPPONENTS	DATE	VENUE	RESULT
South Africa	24 November	H	**Lost** 12–34
England	2 February	A	**Won** 26–19
Scotland	9 February	A	**Won** 30–15
Italy	23 February	H	**Won** 47–8
Ireland	8 March	A	**Won** 16–12
France	15 March	H	**Won** 29–12
South Africa	7 June	A	**Lost** 17–43
South Africa	14 June	A	**Lost** 21–37

GATLAND MASTERMINDS RECOVERY

By Iain Spragg

Stu Forster / Getty Images

Warren Gatland (left) and Shaun Edwards made an instant impact as Wales coaches, delivering the Grand Slam in their first season

When Wales trudged dejectedly off the pitch at the Stade de la Beaujoire on 29 September 2007, defeated by Fiji and unceremoniously dumped out of the World Cup, the Principality went into collective mourning. Six months later, having conquered France at the Millennium Stadium to complete a famous Grand Slam, the country was finally in the mood to party.

The rehabilitation of the team from World Cup failures to the kings of the northern hemisphere was as dramatic as it was unexpected and their performances in the Championship were full of the self-belief and flair that had been so conspicuous by its absence in France.

There were, predictably, casualties on the way. The WRU moved swiftly to remove Gareth Jenkins as head coach after the World Cup debacle and in November turned to former Ireland and Wasps coach Warren Gatland to rekindle the team's fortunes, hoping the experienced

Stu Forster / Getty Images

Ryan Jones (centre) had a sensational first season as Wales captain

Kiwi would be able to rebuild and revive the side. Even the WRU, however, could surely not have anticipated how quickly Gatland would make his mark.

"Wales is the sleeping giant of world rugby," Gatland said in November when his appointment was confirmed. "I want to achieve potential. I want to base success on strong foundations and I will be working closely with the regional coaches to achieve my aims.

"My priorities are clearly defined with the short-term goal to ensure we put the right things in place to face England in the Six Nations and in the long term I will be working to develop a team for the next World Cup."

The road to recovery began in November with the visit of world champions South Africa to Cardiff for a one-off Test. Gatland did not officially take up the reins until December so Nigel Davies, the WRU's head of rugby development, was installed as caretaker coach for the Springboks clash but Welsh fans hoping to see their side prove their World Cup hangover was a distant memory were left disappointed.

Wales battled manfully for the first 20 minutes of the contest in the Millennium Stadium but once flanker Juan Smith galloped over, there was only going to be one winner. Two more tries from Jaque Fourie before the half hour mark emphasised South Africa's superiority and although the home side crossed through Colin Charvis and Morgan Stoddart either side of the break, the Springboks strolled to a convincing 34–12 triumph.

Julian Finney / Getty Images

Shane Williams was back to his best for Wales in 2008

"They were very clinical and that is what being world champions is all about," Davies said as he prepared to hand over to Gatland. "The difference was we didn't finish enough of our line breaks off and South Africa did. This is the first step in a new era of Welsh rugby and we have a lot to look forward to."

One of Gatland's first decisions was to appoint Wasps' Shaun Edwards as his defence coach and Wales readied themselves for the Six Nations and difficult opener against England at Twickenham, a ground where they had not experienced victory for 20 years.

Initially it seemed Gatland's side did not have a prayer of ending the drought. A first-minute Jonny Wilkinson penalty set the tone for the first-half and a Toby Flood try underlined England's dominance and at the break the home side were sitting on a comfortable, seemingly match-winning 16–6 lead.

Gatland's half-time team talk was nothing if not effective, however, and Wales emerged for the second-half looking like a different side. Wilkinson and James Hook traded penalties but England began to falter and Wales pounced on the home side's indecision, scoring two tries in the space of three minutes late on from Lee Byrne and Mike Phillips to complete a memorable comeback and secure a famous 26–19 victory.

"I was disappointed with the first half but we regrouped at half-time and hung in there," Gatland said modestly after the final whistle. "As the game went on I think we got stronger and the guys got a bit of self belief and confidence. It ended up being a great result for us. We've got a lot of work to do but hopefully we'll get better as this competition goes on."

He was not wrong. Scotland came to Cardiff for the next game and although it was a tight game for the first-half, the momentum created by victory at Twickenham carried the home side through against a stubborn but limited Scotland side and a spectacular brace from Shane Williams steered the team to a 30–15 win. The Championship was only two games old but the words Grand Slam were already being whispered throughout the Principality.

Wales were arguably at their most potent against Italy in the Millennium Stadium in their third game of the campaign and ran in five tries, including two for Byrne, to register a record 47–8 triumph over the Azzurri.

Victory kept the Welsh on course for the Grand Slam but they would have to go to Dublin and beat the Irish at Croke Park to keep the dream alive. Wales had not won in the Irish capital since 2000 and with the Triple Crown tantalisingly close, it was a major test of the side's progress under Gatland.

The match was fierce but lacked fluidity. Ireland went in at half-time 6–3 up courtesy of two Ronan O'Gara penalties to one from Stephen Jones but the pivotal score went to the visitors after the break when Shane Williams raced over for a record-equalling 40th Test try for his country. Jones converted and although O'Gara's boot dragged Ireland to within a point, a late penalty from Hook saw Wales home 16–12.

"Occasions like this demand big performances from big players and I think there were 15 big performances out there," said skipper Ryan Jones after landing the Triple Crown. "There are very few opportunities in your career to win silverware and we've come here and delivered. We've got one more week and we could be celebrating again."

Only France now stood between Wales and the Grand Slam and the first-half in Cardiff was predictably cagey with the home side shading the battle of the kickers 9–6. The second-half followed the same pattern until Shane Williams produced another moment of magic for a breakaway try – his sixth of the tournament – and suddenly the crowd sensed victory. Wales kept Les Bleus at arms' length and then delivered the coup de grace with a Martyn Williams try three minutes from time to complete a famous 29–12 victory. Wales had won the Grand Slam and the World Cup was now nothing but a distant memory.

"A lot of those players have had it pretty tough for the last six or 12 months," Gatland said as the celebrations began. "When they get the reward, they deserve the recognition. To have only conceded two tries in this competition makes this Grand Slam thoroughly deserved.

"We've won the Grand Slam but you don't want to stop there. You've got to test yourself against the best teams in the world and South Africa are the number one side in the world at the moment."

The summer tour to face the Springboks was certainly a tough prospect. Wales had never beaten South Africa in their own back yard and the last time they ventured to the Rainbow Nation in 2004, they were mauled 53–18 by the Boks in Pretoria.

The first Test in Bloemfontein was certainly a chastening experience as Gatland tasted defeat as Wales coach for the time. The Springboks simply outmuscled the tourists and there were few positives for the coach to cling to as Wales were hammered 43–17.

"We were well beaten and there are no excuses for the performance," Gatland conceded. "We were physically dominated by a better side and I'm a little embarrassed by that display. Some people were a bit like startled rabbits in the headlights. I don't like losing too much so I'm hurting."

It was clear the players felt their coach's pain and Wales were far more competitive in the second Test in Pretoria but there ultimately was no stopping the World Cup winners. In truth, the final 37–21 scoreline flattered the Springboks and first-half tries from Gareth Cooper and Shane Williams gave Wales genuine hope of a result until South Africa's power told in the second-half and took the game away from the visitors. It was a disappointing but far from disastrous end to the season and Gatland was quick to put the tour and the two results into context.

"Playing against teams like South Africa is a good litmus test, it's a new level for us," Gatland said as he reflected on his first six months in charge. "If we had been playing another Six Nations team today, we would have won comfortably. We need to start winning against the southern hemisphere nations, first at home and then away. "We need to look at England, who tried to play southern hemisphere opposition as much as possible. First they began beating them at Twickenham, which got their confidence up, then they started winning away from home and then they went on to win the World Cup."

WALES INTERNATIONAL STATISTICS

MATCH RECORDS UP TO 30TH SEPTEMBER 2008

MOST CONSECUTIVE TEST WINS

11 1907 I, 1908 E,S,F,I,A, 1909 E,S,F,I, 1910 F
10 1999 F1,It,E,Arg 1,2,SA,C,F2,Arg 3,J
8 1970 F, 1971 E,S,I,F, 1972 E,S,F
8 2004 J, 2005 E,It,F,S,I,US,C

MOST CONSECUTIVE TESTS WITHOUT DEFEAT

Matches	Wins	Draws	Periods
11	11	0	1907 to 1910
10	10	0	1999 to 1999
8	8	0	1970 to 1972
8	8	0	2004 to 2005

MOST POINTS IN A MATCH

BY THE TEAM

Pts.	Opponent	Venue	Year
102	Portugal	Lisbon	1994
98	Japan	Cardiff	2004
81	Romania	Cardiff	2001
77	U S A	Hartford	2005
72	Japan	Cardiff	2007
70	Romania	Wrexham	1997
66	Romania	Cardiff	2004
64	Japan	Cardiff	1999
64	Japan	Osaka	2001
61	Canada	Cardiff	2006
60	Italy	Treviso	1999
60	Canada	Toronto	2005
58	Fiji	Cardiff	2002
57	Japan	Bloemfontein	1995
55	Japan	Cardiff	1993

BY A PLAYER

Pts.	Player	Opponent	Venue	Year
30	N R Jenkins	Italy	Treviso	1999
29	N R Jenkins	France	Cardiff	1999
28	N R Jenkins	Canada	Cardiff	1999
28	N R Jenkins	France	Paris	2001
28	G L Henson	Japan	Cardiff	2004
27	N R Jenkins	Italy	Cardiff	2000
27	C Sweeney	U S A	Hartford	2005
26	S M Jones	Romania	Cardiff	2001
24	N R Jenkins	Canada	Cardiff	1993
24	N R Jenkins	Italy	Cardiff	1994
24	G L Henson	Romania	Wrexham	2003
23	A C Thomas	Romania	Wrexham	1997
23	N R Jenkins	Argentina	Llanelli	1998
23	N R Jenkins	Scotland	Murrayfield	2001
22	N R Jenkins	Portugal	Lisbon	1994
22	N R Jenkins	Japan	Bloemfontein	1995
22	N R Jenkins	England	Wembley	1999
22	S M Jones	Canada	Cardiff	2002
22	J Hook	England	Cardiff	2007

MOST TRIES IN A MATCH

BY THE TEAM

Tries	Opponent	Venue	Year
16	Portugal	Lisbon	1994
14	Japan	Cardiff	2004
11	France	Paris	1909
11	Romania	Wrexham	1997
11	Romania	Cardiff	2001
11	U S A	Hartford	2005
11	Japan	Cardiff	2007
10	France	Swansea	1910
10	Japan	Osaka	2001
10	Romania	Cardiff	2004
9	France	Cardiff	1908
9	Japan	Cardiff	1993
9	Japan	Cardiff	1999
9	Japan	Tokyo	2001
9	Canada	Toronto	2005
9	Canada	Cardiff	2006

BY A PLAYER

Tries	Player	Opponent	Venue	Year
4	W Llewellyn	England	Swansea	1899
4	R A Gibbs	France	Cardiff	1908
4	M C R Richards	England	Cardiff	1969
4	I C Evans	Canada	Invercargill	1987
4	N Walker	Portugal	Lisbon	1994
4	G Thomas	Italy	Treviso	1999
4	S M Williams	Japan	Osaka	2001
4	T G L Shanklin	Romania	Cardiff	2004
4	C L Charvis	Japan	Cardiff	2004

MOST CONVERSIONS IN A MATCH

BY THE TEAM

Cons	Opponent	Venue	Year
14	Japan	Cardiff	2004
11	Portugal	Lisbon	1994
11	U S A	Hartford	2005
10	Romania	Cardiff	2001
8	France	Swansea	1910
8	Japan	Cardiff	1999
8	Romania	Cardiff	2004
8	Canada	Cardiff	2006
7	France	Paris	1909
7	Japan	Osaka	2001
7	Japan	Cardiff	2007

BY A PLAYER

Cons	Player	Opponent	Venue	Year
14	G L Henson	Japan	Cardiff	2004
11	N R Jenkins	Portugal	Lisbon	1994
11	C Sweeney	U S A	Hartford	2005
10	S M Jones	Romania	Cardiff	2001
8	J Bancroft	France	Swansea	1910
8	N R Jenkins	Japan	Cardiff	1999
8	J Hook	Canada	Cardiff	2006
7	S M Jones	Japan	Osaka	2001
7	S M Jones	Romania	Cardiff	2004
6	J Bancroft	France	Paris	1909
6	G L Henson	Romania	Wrexham	2003
6	C Sweeney	Canada	Toronto	2005

MOST PENALTIES IN A MATCH

BY THE TEAM

Pens	Opponent	Venue	Year
9	France	Cardiff	1999
8	Canada	Cardiff	1993
7	Italy	Cardiff	1994
7	Canada	Cardiff	1999
7	Italy	Cardiff	2000
6	France	Cardiff	1982
6	Tonga	Nuku'alofa	1994
6	England	Wembley	1999
6	Canada	Cardiff	2002

BY A PLAYER

Pens	Player	Opponent	Venue	Year
9	N R Jenkins	France	Cardiff	1999
8	N R Jenkins	Canada	Cardiff	1993
7	N R Jenkins	Italy	Cardiff	1994
7	N R Jenkins	Canada	Cardiff	1999
7	N R Jenkins	Italy	Cardiff	2000
6	G Evans	France	Cardiff	1982
6	N R Jenkins	Tonga	Nuku'alofa	1994
6	N R Jenkins	England	Wembley	1999
6	S M Jones	Canada	Cardiff	2002

MOST DROP GOALS IN A MATCH

BY THE TEAM

Drops	Opponent	Venue	Year
3	Scotland	Murrayfield	2001
2	Scotland	Swansea	1912
2	Scotland	Cardiff	1914
2	England	Swansea	1920
2	Scotland	Swansea	1921
2	France	Paris	1930
2	England	Cardiff	1971
2	France	Cardiff	1978
2	England	Twickenham	1984
2	Ireland	Wellington	1987
2	Scotland	Cardiff	1988
2	France	Paris	2001

BY A PLAYER

Drops	Player	Opponent	Venue	Year
3	N R Jenkins	Scotland	Murrayfield	2001
2	J Shea	England	Swansea	1920
2	A Jenkins	Scotland	Swansea	1921
2	B John	England	Cardiff	1971
2	M Dacey	England	Twickenham	1984
2	J Davies	Ireland	Wellington	1987
2	J Davies	Scotland	Cardiff	1988
2	N R Jenkins	France	Paris	2001

CAREER RECORDS

MOST CAPPED PLAYERS

Caps	Player	Career Span
100	Gareth Thomas	1995 to 2007
94	C L Charvis	1996 to 2007
92	G O Llewellyn	1989 to 2004
87	N R Jenkins	1991 to 2002
81	M E Williams	1996 to 2008
72	I C Evans	1987 to 1998
72	S M Jones	1998 to 2008
61	D J Peel	2001 to 2008
60	G D Jenkins	2002 to 2008
59	R Howley	1996 to 2002
58	G R Jenkins	1991 to 2000
58	S M Williams	2000 to 2008
55	J P R Williams	1969 to 1981
54	R N Jones	1986 to 1995
54	T G L Shanklin	2001 to 2008
53	G O Edwards	1967 to 1978
53	I S Gibbs	1991 to 2001
52	L S Quinnell	1993 to 2002
52	I M Gough	1998 to 2008
52	D J Jones	2001 to 2008
51	D Young	1987 to 2001
49	A R Jones	2003 to 2008
48	D R James	1996 to 2007
48	K A Morgan	1997 to 2007
46	T G R Davies	1966 to 1978
46	P T Davies	1985 to 1995
46	J Thomas	2003 to 2008

MOST CONSECUTIVE TESTS

Tests	Player	Career span
53	G O Edwards	1967 to 1978
43	K J Jones	1947 to 1956
39	G Price	1975 to 1983
38	T M Davies	1969 to 1976
33	W J Bancroft	1890 to 1901

MOST TESTS AS CAPTAIN

Tests	Player	Career span
28	I C Evans	1991 to 1995
22	R Howley	1998 to 1999
22	C L Charvis	2002 to 2004
21	Gareth Thomas	2003 to 2007
19	J M Humphreys	1995 to 2003
18	A J Gould	1889 to 1897
14	D C T Rowlands	1963 to 1965
14	W J Trew	1907 to 1913

MOST DROP GOALS IN TESTS

Drops	Player	Tests	Career
13	J Davies	32	1985 to 1997
10	N R Jenkins	87	1991 to 2002
8	B John	25	1966 to 1972
7	W G Davies	21	1978 to 1985

MOST TRIES IN TESTS

Tries	Player	Tests	Career
43	S M Williams	58	2000 to 2008
40	Gareth Thomas	100	1995 to 2007
33	I C Evans	72	1987 to 1998
22	C L Charvis	94	1996 to 2007
20	G O Edwards	53	1967 to 1978
20	T G R Davies	46	1966 to 1978
18	G R Williams	44	2000 to 2005
18	T G L Shanklin	54	2001 to 2008
17	R A Gibbs	16	1906 to 1911
17	J L Williams	17	1906 to 1911
17	K J Jones	44	1947 to 1957

MOST CONVERSIONS IN TESTS

Cons	Player	Tests	Career
130	N R Jenkins	87	1991 to 2002
115	S M Jones	72	1998 to 2008
43	P H Thorburn	37	1985 to 1991
38	J Bancroft	18	1909 to 1914
32	J Hook	27	2006 to 2008
30	A C Thomas	23	1996 to 2000
29	G L Henson	28	2001 to 2008
25	C Sweeney	35	2003 to 2007
20	W J Bancroft	33	1890 to 1901
20	I R Harris	25	2001 to 2004

MOST PENALTY GOALS IN TESTS

Penalties	Player	Tests	Career
235	N R Jenkins	87	1991 to 2002
120	S M Jones	72	1998 to 2008
70	P H Thorburn	37	1985 to 1991
36	P Bennett	29	1969 to 1978
35	S P Fenwick	30	1975 to 1981
32	A C Thomas	23	1996 to 2000
28	J Hook	27	2006 to 2008
22	G Evans	10	1981 to 1983

MOST POINTS IN TESTS

Points	Player	Tests	Career
1049	N R Jenkins	87	1991 to 2002
629	S M Jones	72	1998 to 2008
304	P H Thorburn	37	1985 to 1991
215	S M Williams	58	2000 to 2008
211	A C Thomas	23	1996 to 2000
200	Gareth Thomas	100	1995 to 2007
184	J Hook	27	2006 to 2008
166	P Bennett	29	1969 to 1978
157	I C Evans	72	1987 to 1998

INTERNATIONAL CHAMPIONSHIP RECORDS

RECORD	DETAIL		SET
Most points in season	151	in five matches	2005
Most tries in season	21	in four matches	1910
Highest Score	49	49-14 v France	1910
Biggest win	39	47-8 v Italy	2008
Highest score conceded	60	26-60 v England	1998
Biggest defeat	51	0-51 v France	1998
Most appearances	45	G O Edwards	1967 - 1978
Most points in matches	406	N R Jenkins	1991 - 2001
Most points in season	74	N R Jenkins	2001
Most points in match	28	N R Jenkins	v France, 2001
Most tries in matches	18	G O Edwards	1967 - 1978
Most tries in season	6	M C R Richards	1969
	6	S M Williams	2008
Most tries in match	4	W Llewellyn	v England, 1899
	4	M C R Richards	v England, 1969
Most cons in matches	57	S M Jones	2000 – 2008
Most cons in season	12	S M Jones	2005
Most cons in match	8	J Bancroft	v France, 1910
Most pens in matches	93	N R Jenkins	1991 – 2001
Most pens in season	16	P H Thorburn	1986
	16	N R Jenkins	1999
Most pens in match	7	N R Jenkins	v Italy, 2000
Most drops in matches	8	J Davies	1985 – 1997
Most drops in season	5	N R Jenkins	2001
Most drops in match	3	N R Jenkins	v Scotland, 2001

MISCELLANEOUS RECORDS

RECORD	HOLDER	DETAIL
Longest Test Career	G O Llewellyn	1989 to 2004
Youngest Test Cap	N Biggs	18 yrs 49 days in 1888
Oldest Test Cap	T H Vile	38 yrs 152 days in 1921

CAREER RECORDS OF WALES INTERNATIONAL PLAYERS (UP TO 30 SEPTEMBER 2008)

PLAYER BACKS	DEBUT	CAPS	T	C	P	D	PTS
A Bishop	2008 v SA	1	0	0	0	0	0
A Brew	2007 v I	3	0	0	0	0	0
L M Byrne	2005 v NZ	19	5	0	0	0	25
G J Cooper	2001 v F	37	8	0	0	0	40
C D Czekaj	2005 v C	6	1	0	0	0	5
Gavin Evans	2006 v PI	1	0	0	0	0	0
W Fury	2008 v SA	2	0	0	0	0	0
G L Henson	2001 v J	28	3	29	18	1	130
J Hook	2006 v Arg	27	6	32	28	2	184
D R James	1996 v A	48	15	0	0	0	75
T James	2007 v E	3	0	0	0	0	0
M A Jones	2001 v E	41	12	0	0	0	60
S M Jones	1998 v SA	72	6	115	120	3	629
H N Luscombe	2003 v S	16	2	0	0	0	10
K A Morgan	1997 v US	48	12	0	0	0	60
S T Parker	2002 v R	31	6	0	0	0	30
D J Peel	2001 v J	61	5	0	0	0	25
M Phillips	2003 v R	33	4	0	0	0	20
J Roberts	2008 v S	3	1	0	0	0	5
J P Robinson	2001 v J	23	7	0	0	0	35
T G L Shanklin	2001 v J	54	18	0	0	0	90
M Stoddart	2007 v SA	2	1	0	0	0	5
C Sweeney	2003 v It	35	4	25	5	1	88
A Williams	2003 v R	5	0	0	0	0	0
S M Williams	2000 v F	58	43	0	0	0	215
FORWARDS							
H Bennett	2003 v I	18	0	0	0	0	0
L C Charteris	2004 v SA	7	0	0	0	0	0
C L Charvis	1996 v A	94	22	0	0	0	110
B J Cockbain	2003 v R	24	1	0	0	0	5
Mefin Davies	2002 v SA	38	2	0	0	0	10
G L Delve	2006 v S	9	1	0	0	0	5
Ian Evans	2006 v Arg	14	1	0	0	0	5
I M Gough	1998 v SA	52	1	0	0	0	5
R Hibbard	2006 v Arg	6	0	0	0	0	0

C L Horsman	2005 v NZ	14	1	0	0	0	5
W James	2007 v E	4	0	0	0	0	0
G D Jenkins	2002 v R	60	3	0	0	0	15
A R Jones	2003 v E	49	1	0	0	0	5
A-W Jones	2006 v Arg	23	3	0	0	0	15
Ceri Jones	2007 v A	2	0	0	0	0	0
D A R Jones	2002 v Fj	31	2	0	0	0	10
D J Jones	2001 v A	52	0	0	0	0	0
D L Jones	2000 v Sm	5	0	0	0	0	0
R P Jones	2004 v SA	23	2*	0	0	0	10
S Morgan	2007 v A	1	0	0	0	0	0
M J Owen	2002 v SA	41	2	0	0	0	10
A J Popham	2003 v A	33	4	0	0	0	20
M Rees	2005 v US	22	2	0	0	0	10
R A Sidoli	2002 v SA	42	2	0	0	0	10
R Sowden-Taylor	2005 v It	5	0	0	0	0	0
G V Thomas	2001 v J	22	4	0	0	0	20
J Thomas	2003 v A	46	7	0	0	0	35
Rhys Thomas	2006 v Arg	5	0	0	0	0	0
T R Thomas	2005 v US	27	1	0	0	0	5
M E Williams	1996 v Bb	81	14	0	0	1	73

* Ryan Jones's figures include a penalty try awarded against Canada in 2006

WALES INTERNATIONAL PLAYERS
UP TO 30TH SEPTEMBER 2008

Note: Years given for International Championship matches are for second half of season; eg 1972 means season 1971-72. Years for all other matches refer to the actual year of the match. Entries in square brackets denote matches played in RWC Finals.

Ackerman, R A (Newport, London Welsh) 1980 NZ, 1981 E, S, A, 1982 I, F, E, S, 1983 S, I, F, R, 1984 S, I, F, E, A, 1985 S, I, F, E, Fj
Alexander, E P (Llandovery Coll, Cambridge U) 1885 S, 1886 E, S, 1887 E, I
Alexander, W H (Llwynypia) 1898 I, E, 1899 E, S, I, 1901 S, I
Allen, A G (Newbridge) 1990 F, E, I
Allen, C P (Oxford U, Beaumaris) 1884 E, S
Andrews, F (Pontypool) 1912 SA, 1913 E, S, I
Andrews, F G (Swansea) 1884 E, S
Andrews, G E (Newport) 1926 E, S, 1927 E, F, I
Anthony, C T (Swansea, Newport, Gwent Dragons) 1997 US 1(R),2(R), C (R), Tg (R), 1998 SA 2, Arg, 1999 S, I (R), 2001 J 1,2, I (R), 2002 I, F, It, E, S, 2003 R (R)
Anthony, L (Neath) 1948 E, S, F
Appleyard, R C (Swansea) 1997 C, R, Tg, NZ, 1998 It, E (R), S, I, F
Arnold, P (Swansea) 1990 Nm 1, 2, Bb, 1991 E, S, I, F 1, A, [Arg, A], 1993 F (R), Z 2, 1994 Sp, Fj, 1995 SA, 1996 Bb (R)
Arnold, W R (Swansea) 1903 S
Arthur, C S (Cardiff) 1888 I, M, 1891 E
Arthur, T (Neath) 1927 S, F, I, 1929 E, S, F, I, 1930 E, S, I, F, 1931 E, S, F, I, SA, 1933 E, S
Ashton, C (Aberavon) 1959 E, S, I, 1960 E, S, I, 1962 I
Attewell, S L (Newport) 1921 E, S, F

Back, M J (Bridgend) 1995 F (R), E (R), S, I
Badger, O (Llanelli) 1895 E, S, I, 1896 E
Baker, A (Neath) 1921 I, 1923 E, S, F, I
Baker, A M (Newport) 1909 S, F, 1910 S
Bancroft, J (Swansea) 1909 E, S, F, I, 1910 F, E, S, I, 1911 E, F, I, 1912 E, S, I, 1913 I, 1914 E, S, F
Bancroft, W J (Swansea) 1890 S, E, I, 1891 E, S, I, 1892 E, S, I, 1893 E, S, I, 1894 E, S, I, 1895 E, S, I, 1896 E, S, I, 1897 E, 1898 I, E, 1899 E, S, I, 1900 E, S, I, 1901 E, S, I
Barlow, T M (Cardiff) 1884 I
Barrell, R J (Cardiff) 1929 S, F, I, 1933 I
Bartlett, J D (Llanelli) 1927 S, 1928 E, S
Bassett, A (Cardiff) 1934 I, 1935 E, S, I, 1938 E, S
Bassett, J A (Penarth) 1929 E, S, F, I, 1930 E, S, I, 1931 E, S, F, I, SA, 1932 E, S, I
Bateman, A G (Neath, Richmond, Northampton) 1990 S, I, Nm 1,2, 1996 SA, 1997 US, S, F, E, R, NZ, 1998 It, E, S, I, 1999 S, Arg 1,2, SA, C, [J, A (R)], 2000 It, E, S, I, Sm, US, SA, 2001 E (R), It (t), R, I, Art (R), Tg
Bater, J (Ospreys) 2003 R (R)
Bayliss, G (Pontypool) 1933 S
Bebb, D I E (Carmarthen TC, Swansea) 1959 E, S, I, F, 1960 E, S, I, F, SA, 1961 E, S, I, F, 1962 E, S, F, I, 1963 E, F, NZ, 1964 E, S, F, SA, 1965 E, S, I, F, 1966 F, A, 1967 S, I, F, E
Beckingham, G (Cardiff) 1953 E, S, 1958 F
Bennett, A M (Cardiff) 1995 [NZ] SA, Fj
Bennett, H (Ospreys) 2003 I 2(R), S 2(R), [C(R),Tg(R)], 2004 S(R),F(R),Arg 1(R),2,
SA1(R), 2006 Arg 2,PI(R), 2007 E2, [J(R)],SA, 2008 E,S,It(R),F
Bennett, I (Aberavon) 1937 I
Bennett, P (Cardiff Harlequins) 1891 E, S, 1892 S, I
Bennett, P (Llanelli) 1969 F (R), 1970 SA, S, F, 1972 S (R), NZ, 1973 E, S, I, F, A, 1974 S, I, F, E, 1975 S (R), I, 1976 E, S, I, F, 1977 I, F, E, S, 1978 E, S, I, F
Bergiers, R T E (Cardiff Coll of Ed, Llanelli) 1972 E, S, F, NZ, 1973 E, S, I, F, A, 1974 E, 1975 I
Bevan, G W (Llanelli) 1947 E
Bevan, J A (Cambridge U) 1881 E
Bevan, J C (Cardiff, Cardiff Coll of Ed) 1971 E, S, I, F, 1972 E, S, F, NZ, 1973 E, S
Bevan, J D (Aberavon) 1975 F, E, S, A
Bevan, S (Swansea) 1904 I
Beynon, B (Swansea) 1920 E, S
Beynon, G E (Swansea) 1925 F, I
Bidgood, R A (Newport) 1992 S, 1993 Z 1,2, Nm, J (R)
Biggs, N W (Cardiff) 1888 M, 1889 I, 1892 I, 1893 E, S, I, 1894 E, I
Biggs, S H (Cardiff) 1895 E, S, 1896 S, 1897 E, 1898 I, E, 1899 S, I, 1900 I
Birch, J (Neath) 1911 S, F
Birt, F W (Newport) 1911 E, S, 1912 E, S, I, SA, 1913 E
Bishop, A (Ospreys) 2008 SA2(R)
Bishop, D J (Pontypool) 1984 A
Bishop, E H (Swansea) 1889 S
Blackmore, J H (Abertillery) 1909 E
Blackmore, S W (Cardiff) 1987 I, [Tg (R), C, A]
Blake, J (Cardiff) 1899 E, S, I, 1900 E, S, I, 1901 E, S, I
Blakemore, R E (Newport) 1947 E
Bland, A F (Cardiff) 1887 E, S, I, 1888 S, I, M, 1890 S, E, I
Blyth, L (Swansea) 1951 SA, 1952 E, S
Blyth, W R (Swansea) 1974 E, 1975 S (R), 1980 F, E, S, I
Boobyer, N (Llanelli) 1993 Z 1(R),2, Nm, 1994 Fj, Tg, 1998 F, 1999 It (R)
Boon, R W (Cardiff) 1930 S, F, 1931 E, S, F, I, SA, 1932 E, S, I, 1933 E, I
Booth, J (Pontymister) 1898 I
Boots, J G (Newport) 1898 I, E, 1899 I, 1900 E, S, I, 1901 E, S, I, 1902 E, S, I, 1903 E, S, I, 1904 E
Boucher, A W (Newport) 1892 E, S, I, 1893 E, S, I, 1894 E, 1895 E, S, I, 1896 E, I, 1897 E
Bowcott, H M (Cardiff, Cambridge U) 1929 S, F, I, 1930 E, 1931 E, S, 1933 E, I
Bowdler, F A (Cross Keys) 1927 A, 1928 E, S, I, F, 1929 E, S, F, I, 1930 E, 1931 SA, 1932 E, S, I, 1933 I
Bowen, B (S Wales Police, Swansea) 1983 R, 1984 S, I, F, E, 1985 Fj, 1986 E, S, I, F, Fj, Tg, WS, 1987 [C, E, NZ], US, 1988 E, S, I, F, WS, 1989 S, I
Bowen, C A (Llanelli) 1896 E, S, I, 1897 E
Bowen, D H (Llanelli) 1883 E, 1886 E, S, 1887 E
Bowen, G E (Swansea) 1887 S, I, 1888 S, I
Bowen, W (Swansea) 1921 S, F, 1922 E, S, I, F
Bowen, Wm A (Swansea) 1886 E, S, 1887 E, S, I, 1888 M, 1889 S, I, 1890 S, E, I, 1891 E, S
Brace, D O (Llanelli, Oxford U) 1956 E, S, I, F, 1957 E, 1960 S, I, F, 1961 I
Braddock, K J (Newbridge) 1966 A, 1967 S, I
Bradshaw, K (Bridgend) 1964 E, S, I, F, SA, 1966 E, S, I, F
Brew, A (Newport Gwent Dragons, Ospreys) 2007 I(R),A2,E2
Brew, N R (Gwent Dragons) 2003 R
Brewer, T J (Newport) 1950 E, 1955 E, S
Brice, A B (Aberavon) 1899 E, S, I, 1900 E, S, I, 1901 E, S, I, 1902 E, S, I, 1903 E, S, I, 1904 E, S, I

Bridges, C J (Neath) 1990 Nm 1,2, Bb, 1991 E (R), I, F 1, A
Bridie, R H (Newport) 1882 I
Britton, G R (Newport) 1961 S
Broster, B G J (Saracens) 2005 US(R),C
Broughton, A S (Treorchy) 1927 A, 1929 S
Brown, A (Newport) 1921 I
Brown, J (Cardiff) 1925 I
Brown, J A (Cardiff) 1907 E, S, I, 1908 E, S, F, 1909 E
Brown, M (Pontypool) 1983 R, 1986 E, S, Fj (R), Tg, WS
Bryant, D J (Bridgend) 1988 NZ 1,2, WS, R, 1989 S, I, F, E
Bryant, J (Celtic Warriors) 2003 R (R)
Buchanan, D A (Llanelli) 1987 [Tg, E, NZ, A], 1988 I
Buckett, I M (Swansea) 1994 Tg, 1997 US 2, C
Budgett, N J (Ebbw Vale, Bridgend) 2000 S, I, Sm (R), US, SA, 2001 J 1(R),2, 2002 I, F, It, E, S
Burcher, D H (Newport) 1977 I, F, E, S
Burgess, R C (Ebbw Vale) 1977 I, F, E, S, 1981 I, F, 1982 F, E, S
Burnett, R (Newport) 1953 E
Burns, J (Cardiff) 1927 F, I
Bush, P F (Cardiff) 1905 NZ, 1906 E, SA, 1907 I, 1908 E, S, 1910 S, I
Butler, E T (Pontypool) 1980 F, E, S, I, NZ (R), 1982 S, 1983 E, S, I, F, R, 1984 S, I, F, E, A
Byrne, L M (Llanelli Scarlets, Ospreys) 2005 NZ(R),Fj,SA, 2006 E(t&R),S(t&R),I,It,F,Arg 1,2, Pl, 2007 F1,A1,E2, 2008 E,S,It,I,F

Cale, W R (Newbridge, Pontypool) 1949 E, S, I, 1950 E, S, I, F
Cardey, M D (Llanelli) 2000 S
Carter, A J (Newport) 1991 E, S
Cattell, A (Llanelli) 1883 E, S
Challinor, C (Neath) 1939 E
Charteris, L C (Newport Gwent Dragons) 2004 SA2(R),R, 2005 US,C,NZ(R),Fj, 2007 SA(R)
Charvis, C L (Swansea, Tarbes, Newcastle, Newport Gwent Dragons) 1996 A 3(R), SA, 1997 US, S, I, F, 1998 It (R), E, S, I, F, Z (R), SA 1,2, Arg, 1999 S, I, F 1, It, E, Arg 1, SA, F 2, [Arg 3, A], 2000 F, It (R), E, S, I, Sm, US, SA, 2001 E, S, F, It, R, I, Arg, Tg, A, 2002 E (R), S, SA 1,2, R, Fj, C, NZ, 2003 It, E 1(R), S 1(R), I 1, F,A, NZ, E 2, S 2, [C,Tg,It,NZ,E], 2004 S,F,E,It,Arg 1,2,SA1,2,R,NZ,J, 2005 US,C,NZ,SA,A, 2006 E,S,I,It, 2007 A1,2,E2,Arg(R),F2(R), [C(t&R),A,J,Fj],SA
Clapp, T J S (Newport) 1882 I, 1883 E, S, 1884 E, S, I, 1885 E, S, 1886 S, 1887 E, S, I, 1888 S, I
Clare, J (Cardiff) 1883 E
Clark, S S (Neath) 1882 I, 1887 I
Cleaver, W B (Cardiff) 1947 E, S, F, I, A, 1948 E, S, F, I, 1949 I, 1950 E, S, I, F
Clegg, B G (Swansea) 1979 F
Clement, A (Swansea) 1987 US (R), 1988 E, NZ 1, WS (R), R, 1989 NZ, 1990 S (R), I (R), Nm 1,2, 1991 S (R), A (R), F 2, [WS, A], 1992 I, F, E, S, 1993 I (R), F, J, C, 1994 S, I, F, Sp, C (R), Tg, WS, It, SA, 1995 F, E, [J, NZ, I]
Clement, W H (Llanelli) 1937 E, S, I, 1938 E, S, I
Cobner, T J (Pontypool) 1974 S, I, F, E, 1975 F, E, S, I, A, 1976 E, S, 1977 F, E, S, 1978 E, S, I, F, A 1
Cockbain, B J (Celtic Warriors, Ospreys) 2003 R, [C,It,NZ,E], 2004 S,I,F,E,Arg 1,2,SA2,NZ, 2005 E,It,F,S,I,US,C(R),NZ,Fj, 2007 F1(t&R),A1
Coldrick, A P (Newport) 1911 E, S, I, 1912 E, S, F
Coleman, E O (Newport) 1949 E, S, I
Coles, F C (Pontypool) 1960 S, I, F
Collins, J E (Aberavon) 1958 A, E, S, F, 1959 E, S, I, F, 1960 E, 1961 F
Collins, R G (S Wales Police, Cardiff, Pontypridd) 1987 E (R), I, [I, E, NZ], US, 1988 E, S, I, F, R, 1990 E, S, I, 1991 A, F 2, [WS], 1994 C, Fj, Tg, WS, R, It, SA, 1995 F, E, S, I
Collins, T J (Mountain Ash) 1923 I
Conway-Rees, J (Llanelli) 1892 S, 1893 E, 1894 E
Cook, T (Cardiff) 1949 S, I
Cooper, G J (Bath, Celtic Warriors, Newport Gwent Dragons, Gloucester) 2001 F, J 1,2, 2003 E 1, S 1, I 1, F(R), A, NZ, E 2, [C,Tg,It(t&R),NZ,E], 2004 S,I,F,E,It,R(R),NZ(R),J, 2005 E(R), It(R),F(R),NZ(R),Fj,SA,A, 2006 E(R),Pl(R), 2007 A1(R),E2, [J(R)], 2008 SA1,2
Cooper, V L (Llanelli) 2002 C, 2003 I 2(R), S 2
Cope, W (Cardiff, Blackheath) 1896 S
Copsey, A H (Llanelli) 1992 I, F, E, S, A, 1993 E, S, I, J, C, 1994 E (R), Pt, Sp (R), Fj, Tg, WS (R)
Cornish, F H (Cardiff) 1897 E, 1898 I, E, 1899 I
Cornish, R A (Cardiff) 1923 E, S, 1924 E, 1925 E, S, F, 1926 E, S, I, F
Coslett, T K (Aberavon) 1962 E, S, F
Cowey, B T V (Welch Regt, Newport) 1934 E, S, I, 1935 E
Cresswell, B R (Newport) 1960 E, S, I, F
Cummins, W (Treorchy) 1922 E, S, I, F
Cunningham, L J (Aberavon) 1960 E, S, I, F, 1962 E, S, F, I, 1963 NZ, 1964 E, S, I, F, SA
Czekaj, C D (Cardiff Blues) 2005 C, 2006 Arg 1(R), 2007 I,S,A1,22007 I,S,A1,2

Dacey, M (Swansea) 1983 E, S, I, F, R, 1984 S, I, F, E, A, 1986 Fj, Tg, WS, 1987 F (R), [Tg]
Daniel, D J (Llanelli) 1891 S, 1894 E, S, I, 1898 I, E, 1899 E, I
Daniel, L T D (Newport) 1970 S
Daniels, P C T (Cardiff) 1981 A, 1982 I
Darbishire, G (Bangor) 1881 E
Dauncey, F H (Newport) 1896 E, S, I
Davey, C (Swansea) 1930 F, 1931 E, S, F, I, SA, 1932 E, S, I, 1933 E, S, 1934 E, S, I, 1935 E, S, I, NZ, 1936 S, 1937 E, I, 1938 E, I
David, R J (Cardiff) 1907 I
David, T P (Llanelli, Pontypridd) 1973 F, A, 1976 I, F
Davidge, G D (Newport) 1959 F, 1960 S, I, F, SA, 1961 E, S, I, 1962 F
Davies, A (Cambridge U, Neath, Cardiff) 1990 Bb (R), 1991 A, 1993 Z 1,2, J, C, 1994 Fj, 1995 [J, I]
Davies, A C (London Welsh) 1889 I
Davies, A E (Llanelli) 1984 A
Davies, B (Llanelli) 1895 E, 1896 E
Davies, B (Llanelli Scarlets) 2006 I(R)
Davies, C (Cardiff) 1947 S, F, I, A, 1948 E, S, F, I, 1949 F, 1950 E, S, I, F, 1951 E, S, I
Davies, C (Llanelli) 1988 WS, 1989 S, I (R), F
Davies, C A H (Llanelli, Cardiff) 1957 I, 1958 A, E, S, I, 1960 SA, 1961 E
Davies, C H (Swansea, Llanelli) 1939 S, I, 1947 E, S, F, I
Davies, C L (Cardiff) 1956 E, S, I
Davies, C R (Bedford, RAF) 1934 E
Davies, D B (Llanelli) 1907 E
Davies, D B (Llanelli) 1962 I, 1963 E, S
Davies, D E G (Cardiff) 1912 E, F
Davies, D G (Cardiff) 1923 E, S
Davies, D H (Neath) 1904 S
Davies, D H (Bridgend) 1921 I, 1925 I
Davies, D H (Aberavon) 1924 E
Davies, D I (Swansea) 1939 E
Davies, D J (Neath) 1962 I
Davies, D M (Somerset Police) 1950 E, S, I, F, 1951 E, S, I, F, SA, 1952 E, S, I, F, 1953 I, F, NZ, 1954 E
Davies, E (Maesteg) 1919 NZA
Davies, E G (Cardiff) 1928 F, 1929 E, 1930 S
Davies, E P (Aberavon) 1947 A, 1948 I
Davies, G (Swansea) 1900 E, S, I, 1901 E, S, I, 1905 E, S, I
Davies, G (Cambridge U, Pontypridd) 1947 S, A, 1948 E, S, F, I, 1949 E, S, F, 1951 E, S
Davies, H (Swansea) 1898 I, E, 1901 S, I
Davies, H (Bridgend) 1984 S, I, F, E
Davies, H G (Llanelli) 1921 F, I, 1925 F
Davies, H J (Neath) 1912 E, S
Davies, H J (Newport) 1924 S
Davies, H J (Cambridge U, Aberavon) 1959 E, S
Davies, H S (Treherbert) 1923 I
Davies, I T (Llanelli) 1914 S, F, I
Davies, J (Neath, Llanelli, Cardiff) 1985 E, Fj, 1986 E, S, I, F, Fj, Tg, WS, 1987 F, E, S, I, [I, Tg (R), C, E, NZ, A], 1988 E, S, I, F, NZ 1,2, WS, R, 1996 A 3, 1997 US (t), S (R), F (R), E
Davies, Rev J A (Swansea) 1913 S, F, I, 1914 E, S, F, I
Davies, J D (Neath, Richmond) 1991 I, F 1, 1993 F (R), Z 2, J, C, 1994 S, I, F, E, Pt, Sp, C, WS, R, It, SA, 1995 F, E, [J, NZ, I] SA, 1996 It, E, S, I, F 1, A 1, Bb, F 2, It, 1998 Z, SA 1
Davies, J H (Aberavon) 1923 I
Davies, L (Swansea) 1939 S, I
Davies, L (Bridgend) 1966 E, S, I
Davies, L B (Neath, Cardiff, Llanelli) 1996 It, E, S, I, F 1, A 1, Bb, F 2, It (R), 1997 US 1,2, C, R, Tg, NZ (R), 1998 E (R), I, F, 1999 C, 2001 I, 2003 It

Davies, L M (Llanelli) 1954 F, S, 1955 I
Davies, M (Swansea) 1981 A, 1982 I, 1985 Fj
Davies, Mefin (Pontypridd, Celtic Warriors, Gloucester) 2002 SA 2(R), R, Fj, 2003 It, S 1(R), I 1(R), F, A(R), NZ(R), I 2, R, [Tg,NZ(R), E(R)], 2004 S,F,It(R),Arg 1,2(R),SA1,2(R),R,NZ,J, 2005 E,It,F,S,I, C(R),NZ,SA(R),A(t), 2006 S(R),I(R),It(R),F(R), 2007 A2
Davies, M J (Blackheath) 1939 S, I
Davies, N G (London Welsh) 1955 E
Davies, N G (Llanelli) 1988 NZ 2, WS, 1989 S, I, 1993 F, 1994 S, I, E, Pt, Sp, C, Fj, Tg (R), WS, R, It, 1995 E, S, I, Fj, 1996 E, S, I, F 1, A 1,2, Bb, F 2, 1997 E
Davies, P T (Llanelli) 1985 E, Fj, 1986 E, S, I, F, Fj, Tg, WS, 1987 F, E, I, [Tg, C, NZ], 1988 WS, R, 1989 S, I, F, E, NZ, 1990 F, E, S, 1991 I, F 1, A, F 2, [WS, Arg, A], 1993 F, Z 1, Nm, 1994 S, I, F, E, C, Fj (R), WS, R, It, 1995 F, I
Davies, R H (Oxford U, London Welsh) 1957 S, I, F, 1958 A, 1962 E, S
Davies, S (Swansea) 1992 I, F, E, S, A, 1993 E, S, I, Z 1(R),2, Nm, J, 1995 F, [J, I], 1998 I (R), F
Davies, T G R (Cardiff, London Welsh) 1966 A, 1967 S, I, F, E, 1968 E, S, 1969 S, I, F, NZ 1,2, A, 1971 E, S, I, F, 1972 E, S, F, NZ, 1973 E, S, I, F, A, 1974 S, F, E, 1975 F, E, S, I, 1976 E, S, I, F, 1977 I, F, E, S, 1978 E, S, I, A 1,2
Davies, T J (Devonport Services, Swansea, Llanelli) 1953 E, S, I, F, 1957 E, S, I, F, 1958 A, E, S, F, 1959 E, S, I, F, 1960 E, SA, 1961 E, S, F
Davies, T M (London Welsh, Swansea) 1969 S, I, F, E, NZ 1,2, A, 1970 SA, S, E, I, F, 1971 E, S, I, F, 1972 E, S, F, NZ, 1973 E, S, I, F, A, 1974 S, I, F, E, 1975 F, E, S, I, A, 1976 E, S, I, F
Davies, W (Cardiff) 1896 S
Davies, W (Swansea) 1931 SA, 1932 E, S, I
Davies, W A (Aberavon) 1912 S, I
Davies, W G (Cardiff) 1978 A 1,2, NZ, 1979 S, I, F, E, 1980 F, E, S, NZ, 1981 E, S, A, 1982 I, F, E, S, 1985 S, I, F
Davies, W T H (Swansea) 1936 I, 1937 E, I, 1939 E, S, I
Davis, C E (Newbridge) 1978 A 2, 1981 E, S
Davis, M (Newport) 1991 A
Davis, W E N (Cardiff) 1939 E, S, I
Dawes, S J (London Welsh) 1964 I, F, SA, 1965 E, S, I, F, 1966 A, 1968 I, F, 1969 E, NZ 2, A, 1970 SA, S, E, I, F, 1971 E, S, I, F
Day, H C (Newport) 1930 S, I, F, 1931 E, S
Day, H T (Newport) 1892 I, 1893 E, S, 1894 S, I
Day, T B (Swansea) 1931 E, S, F, I, SA, 1932 E, S, I, 1934 S, I, 1935 E, S, I
Deacon, J T (Swansea) 1891 I, 1892 E, S, I
Delahay, W J (Bridgend) 1922 E, S, I, F, 1923 E, S, F, I, 1924 NZ, 1925 E, S, F, I, 1926 E, S, I, F, 1927 S
Delaney, L (Llanelli) 1989 I, F, E, 1990 E, 1991 F 2, [WS, Arg, A], 1992 I, F, E
Delve, G L (Bath, Gloucester) 2006 S(R),I(R),Arg 1(R),2(R), 2008 S(R),It(R),I(R),SA1(R),2
Devereux, D B (Neath) 1958 A, E, S
Devereux, J A (S Glamorgan Inst, Bridgend) 1986 E, S, I, F, Fj, Tg, WS, 1987 F, E, S, I, [I, C, E, NZ, A], 1988 NZ 1,2, R, 1989 S, I
Diplock, R S (Bridgend) 1988 R
Dobson, G A (Cardiff) 1900 S
Dobson, T (Cardiff) 1898 I, E, 1899 E, S
Donovan, A J (Swansea) 1978 A 2, 1981 I (R), A, 1982 E, S
Donovan, R E (S Wales Police) 1983 F (R)
Douglas, M H J (Llanelli) 1984 S, I, F
Douglas, W M (Cardiff) 1886 E, S, 1887 E, S
Dowell, W H (Newport) 1907 E, S, I, 1908 E, S, F, I
Durston, A P R (Bridgend) 2001 J 1,2
Dyke, J C M (Penarth) 1906 SA
Dyke, L M (Penarth, Cardiff) 1910 I, 1911 S, F, I

Edmunds, D A (Neath) 1990 I (R), Bb
Edwards, A B (London Welsh, Army) 1955 E, S
Edwards, B O (Newport) 1951 I
Edwards, D (Glynneath) 1921 E
Edwards, G O (Cardiff, Cardiff Coll of Ed) 1967 F, E, NZ, 1968 E, S, I, F, 1969 S, I, F, E, NZ 1,2, A, 1970 SA, S, E, I, F, 1971 E, S, I, F, 1972 E, S, F, NZ, 1973 E, S, I, F, A, 1974 S, I, F, E, 1975 F, E, S, I, A, 1976 E, S, I, F, 1977 I, F, E, S, 1978 E, S, I, F
Eidman, I H (Cardiff) 1983 S, R, 1984 I, F, E, A, 1985 S, I, Fj, 1986 E, S, I, F
Elliott, J (Cardiff) 1894 I, 1898 I, E
Elsey, W J (Cardiff) 1895 E
Emyr, Arthur (Swansea) 1989 E, NZ, 1990 F, E, S, I, Nm 1,2, 1991 F 1,2, [WS, Arg, A]
Evans, A (Pontypool) 1924 E, I, F
Evans, B (Llanelli) 1933 E, S, 1936 E, S, I, 1937 E
Evans, B R (Swansea, Cardiff Blues) 1998 SA 2(R), 1999 F 1, It, E, Arg 1,2, C, [J (R), Sm (R), A (R)], 2000 Sm, US, 2001 J 1(R), 2002 SA 1,2, R(R), Fj, C, NZ, 2003 It, E 1, S 1, I 2, R, 2004 F(R),E(t),It(R)
Evans, B S (Llanelli) 1920 E, 1922 E, S, I, F
Evans, C (Pontypool) 1960 E
Evans, D (Penygraig) 1896 S, I, 1897 E, 1898 E
Evans, D B (Swansea) 1926 E
Evans, D B (Swansea) 1933 S
Evans, D D (Cheshire, Cardiff U) 1934 E
Evans, D P (Llanelli) 1960 SA
Evans, D W (Cardiff) 1889 S, I, 1890 E, I, 1891 E
Evans, D W (Oxford U, Cardiff, Treorchy) 1989 F, E, NZ, 1990 F, E, S, I, Bb, 1991 A (R), F 2(R), [A (R)], 1995 [J (R)]
Evans, E (Llanelli) 1937 E, 1939 S, I
Evans, F (Llanelli) 1921 S
Evans, G (Cardiff) 1947 E, S, F, I, A, 1948 E, S, F, I, 1949 E, S, I
Evans, G (Maesteg) 1981 S (R), I, F, A, 1982 I, F, E, S, 1983 F, R
Evans, G D (Llanelli Scarlets) 2006 PI(R)
Evans, G L (Newport) 1977 F (R), 1978 F, A 2(R)
Evans, G R (Cardiff) 1889 S
Evans, G R (Llanelli) 1998 SA 1, 2003 I 2, S 2, [NZ]
Evans, H I (Swansea) 1922 E, S, I, F
Evans, Ian (Ospreys) 2006 Arg 1,2,A,C,NZ, 2007 [J(R),Fj],SA, 2008 E(R),S,It,F(R),SA1(R),2(R)
Evans, I (London Welsh) 1934 S, I
Evans, I C (Llanelli, Bath) 1987 F, E, S, I, [I, C, E, NZ, A], 1988 E, S, I, F, NZ 1,2, 1989 I, F, E, 1991 E, S, I, F 1, A, F 2, [WS, Arg, A], 1992 I, F, E, S, A, 1993 E, S, I, F, J, C, 1994 S, I, E, Pt, Sp, C, Fj, Tg, WS, R, 1995 E, S, I, [J, NZ, I], SA, Fj, 1996 It, E, S, I, F 1, A 1,2, Bb, F 2, A 3, SA, 1997 US, S, I, F, 1998 It
Evans, I L (Llanelli) 1991 F 2(R)
Evans, J (Llanelli) 1896 S, I, 1897 E
Evans, J D (Cardiff) 1958 I, F
Evans, J E (Llanelli) 1924 S
Evans, J H (Pontypool) 1907 E, S, I
Evans, J R (Newport) 1934 E
Evans, J W (Blaina) 1904 E
Evans, O J (Cardiff) 1887 E, S, 1888 S, I
Evans, P D (Llanelli) 1951 E, F
Evans, R (Bridgend) 1963 S, I, F
Evans, R L (Llanelli) 1993 E, S, I, F, 1994 S, I, F, E, Pt, Sp, C, Fj, WS, R, It, SA, 1995 F, [NZ, I (R)]
Evans, R T (Newport) 1947 F, I, 1950 E, S, I, F, 1951 E, S, I, F
Evans, S (Swansea, Neath) 1985 F, E, 1986 Fj, Tg, WS, 1987 F, E, [I, Tg]
Evans, T D (Swansea) 1924 I
Evans, T G (London Welsh) 1970 SA, S, E, I, 1972 E, S, F
Evans, T H (Llanelli) 1906 I, 1907 E, S, I, 1908 I, A, 1909 E, S, F, I, 1910 F, E, S, I, 1911 E, S, F, I
Evans, T P (Swansea) 1975 F, E, S, I, A, 1976 E, S, I, F, 1977 I
Evans, T W (Llanelli) 1958 A
Evans, V (Neath) 1954 I, F, S
Evans, W F (Rhymney) 1882 I, 1883 S
Evans, W G (Brynmawr) 1911 I
Evans, W H (Llwynypia) 1914 E, S, F, I
Evans, W J (Pontypool) 1947 S
Evans, W R (Bridgend) 1958 A, E, S, I, F, 1960 SA, 1961 E, S, I, F, 1962 E, S, I
Everson, W A (Newport) 1926 S

Faulkner, A G (Pontypool) 1975 F, E, S, I, A, 1976 E, S, I, F, 1978 E, S, I, F, A 1,2, NZ, 1979 S, I, F
Faull, J (Swansea) 1957 I, F, 1958 A, E, S, I, F, 1959 E, S, I, 1960 E, F
Fauvel, T J (Aberavon) 1988 NZ 1(R)
Fear, A G (Newport) 1934 S, I, 1935 S, I
Fender, N H (Cardiff) 1930 I, F, 1931 E, S, F, I
Fenwick, S P (Bridgend) 1975 F, E, S, A, 1976 E, S, I, F, 1977 I, F, E, S, 1978 E, S, I, F, A 1,2, NZ, 1979 S, I, F, E, 1980 F, E, S, I, NZ, 1981 E, S
Finch, E (Llanelli) 1924 F, NZ, 1925 F, I, 1926 F, 1927 A, 1928 I

Finlayson, A A J (Cardiff) 1974 I, F, E
Fitzgerald, D (Cardiff) 1894 S, I
Ford, F J V (Welch Regt, Newport) 1939 E
Ford, I R (Newport) 1959 E, S
Ford, S P (Cardiff) 1990 I, Nm 1,2, Bb, 1991 E, S, I, A
Forster, J A (Newport Gwent Dragons) 2004 Arg 1
Forward, A (Pontypool, Mon Police) 1951 S, SA, 1952 E, S, I, F
Fowler, I J (Llanelli) 1919 NZA
Francis, D G (Llanelli) 1919 NZA, 1924 S
Francis, P W (Maesteg) 1987 S
Funnell, J S (Ebbw Vale) 1998 Z (R), SA 1
Fury, W (London Irish) 2008 SA1(R),2(R)

Gabe, R T (Cardiff, Llanelli) 1901 I, 1902 E, S, I, 1903 E, S, I, 1904 E, S, I, 1905 E, S, I, NZ, 1906 E, I, SA, 1907 E, S, I, 1908 E, S, F, I
Gale, N R (Swansea, Llanelli) 1960 I, 1963 E, S, I, NZ, 1964 E, S, I, F, SA, 1965 E, S, I, F, 1966 E, S, I, F, A, 1967 E, NZ, 1968 E, 1969 NZ 1(R),2, A
Gallacher, I S (Llanelli) 1970 F
Garrett, R M (Penarth) 1888 M, 1889 S, 1890 S, E, I, 1891 S, I, 1892 E
Geen, W P (Oxford U, Newport) 1912 SA, 1913 E, I
George, E E (Pontypridd, Cardiff) 1895 S, I, 1896 E
George, G M (Newport) 1991 E, S
Gething, G I (Neath) 1913 F
Gibbs, A (Newbridge) 1995 I, SA, 1996 A 2, 1997 US 1,2, C
Gibbs, I S (Neath, Swansea) 1991 E, S, I, F 1, A, F 2, [WS, Arg, A], 1992 I, F, E, S, A, 1993 E, S, I, F, J, C, 1996 It, A 3, SA, 1997 US, S, I, F, Tg, NZ, 1998 It, E, S, SA 2, Arg, 1999 S, I, F 1, It, E, C, F 2, [Arg 3, J, Sm, A], 2000 I, Sm, US, SA, 2001 E, S, F, It
Gibbs, R A (Cardiff) 1906 S, I, 1907 E, S, 1908 E, S, F, I, 1910 F, E, S, I, 1911 E, S, F, I
Giles, R (Aberavon) 1983 R, 1985 Fj (R), 1987 [C]
Girling, B E (Cardiff) 1881 E
Goldsworthy, S J (Swansea) 1884 I, 1885 E, S
Gore, J H (Blaina) 1924 I, F, NZ, 1925 E
Gore, W (Newbridge) 1947 S, F, I
Gough, I M (Newport, Pontypridd, Newport Gwent Dragons, Ospreys) 1998 SA 1, 1999 S, 2000 F, It (R), E (R), S, I, Sm, US, SA, 2001 E, S, F, It, Tg, A, 2002 I (R), F (R), It, S, 2003 R, 2005 It(R),US(R),SA,A, 2006 E,S,I,It,F,Arg 1,2,A,C,NZ, 2007 I,S(R),F1,It,E1,Arg,F2, [C,A,Fj(R)], 2008 E,S,It,I,F,SA1,2
Gould, A J (Newport) 1885 E, S, 1886 E, S, 1887 E, S, I, 1888 S, 1889 I, 1890 S, E, I, 1892 E, S, I, 1893 E, S, I, 1894 E, S, 1895 E, S, I, 1896 E, S, I, 1897 E
Gould, G H (Newport) 1892 I, 1893 S, I
Gould, R (Newport) 1882 I, 1883 E, S, 1884 E, S, I, 1885 E, S, 1886 E, 1887 E, S
Graham, T C (Newport) 1890 I, 1891 S, I, 1892 E, S, 1893 E, S, I, 1894 E, S, 1895 E, S
Gravell, R W R (Llanelli) 1975 F, E, S, I, A, 1976 E, S, I, F, 1978 E, S, I, F, A 1,2, NZ, 1979 S, I, 1981 I, F, 1982 F, E, S
Gray, A J (London Welsh) 1968 E, S
Greenslade, D (Newport) 1962 S
Greville, H G (Llanelli) 1947 A
Griffin, Dr J (Edinburgh U) 1883 S
Griffiths, C R (Llanelli) 1979 E (R)
Griffiths, D (Llanelli) 1888 M, 1889 I
Griffiths, G (Llanelli) 1889 I
Griffiths, G M (Cardiff) 1953 E, S, I, F, NZ, 1954 I, F, S, 1955 I, F, 1957 E, S
Griffiths, J (Swansea) 2000 Sm (R)
Griffiths, J L (Llanelli) 1988 NZ 2, 1989 S
Griffiths, M (Bridgend, Cardiff, Pontypridd) 1988 WS, R, 1989 S, I, F, E, NZ, 1990 F, E, Nm 1,2, Bb, 1991 I, F 1,2, [WS, Arg, A], 1992 I, F, E, S, A, 1993 Z 1,2, Nm, J, C, 1995 F (R), E, S, I, [J, I], 1998 SA 1
Griffiths, V M (Newport) 1924 S, I, F
Gronow, B (Bridgend) 1910 F, E, S, I
Gwilliam, J A (Cambridge U, Newport) 1947 A, 1948 I, 1949 E, S, I, F, 1950 E, S, I, F, 1951 E, S, I, SA, 1952 E, S, I, F, 1953 E, I, F, NZ, 1954 E
Gwynn, D (Swansea) 1883 E, 1887 S, 1890 E, I, 1891 E, S
Gwynn, W H (Swansea) 1884 E, S, I, 1885 E, S

Hadley, A M (Cardiff) 1983 R, 1984 S, I, F, E, 1985 F, E, Fj, 1986 E, S, I, F, Fj, Tg, 1987 S (R), I, [I, Tg, C, E, NZ, A], US, 1988 E, S, I, F
Hall, I (Aberavon) 1967 NZ, 1970 SA, S, E, 1971 S, 1974 S, I, F
Hall, M R (Cambridge U, Bridgend, Cardiff) 1988 NZ 1(R),2, WS, R, 1989 S, I, F, E, NZ, 1990 F, E, S, 1991 A, F 2, [WS, Arg, A], 1992 I, F, E, S, A, 1993 E, S, I, 1994 S, I, F, E, Pt, Sp, C, Tg, R, It, SA, 1995 F, S, I, [J, NZ, I]
Hall, W H (Bridgend) 1988 WS
Hancock, F E (Cardiff) 1884 I, 1885 E, S, 1886 S
Hannan, J (Newport) 1888 M, 1889 S, I, 1890 S, E, I, 1891 E, 1892 E, S, I, 1893 E, S, I, 1894 E, S, I, 1895 E, S, I
Harding, A F (London Welsh) 1902 E, S, I, 1903 E, S, I, 1904 E, S, I, 1905 E, S, I, NZ, 1906 E, S, I, SA, 1907 I, 1908 E, S
Harding, C T (Newport) 1888 M, 1889 S, I
Harding, G F (Newport) 1881 E, 1882 I, 1883 E, S
Harding, R (Swansea, Cambridge U) 1923 E, S, F, I, 1924 I, F, NZ, 1925 F, I, 1926 E, I, F, 1927 E, S, F, I, 1928 E
Harris, C A (Aberavon) 1927 A
Harris, D J E (Pontypridd, Cardiff) 1959 I, F, 1960 S, I, F, SA, 1961 E, S
Harris, I R (Cardiff) 2001 Arg, Tg, A, 2002 I, It (R), E, S (R), Fj(R), C(R), NZ(R), 2003 It, E 1(R), S 1(R), I 1(R), F, I 2, S 2, [C,Tg,It,E], 2004 S,I,F,It
Hathway, G F (Newport) 1924 I, F
Havard, Rev W T (Llanelli) 1919 NZA
Hawkins, F J (Pontypridd) 1912 I, F
Hayward, B I (Ebbw Vale) 1998 Z (R), SA 1
Hayward, D J (Newbridge) 1949 E, F, 1950 E, S, I, F, 1951 E, S, I, F, SA, 1952 E, S, I, F
Hayward, D J (Cardiff) 1963 E, NZ, 1964 S, I, F, SA
Hayward, G (Swansea) 1908 S, F, I, A, 1909 E
Hellings, D (Llwynypia) 1897 E, 1898 I, E, 1899 S, I, 1900 E, I, 1901 E, S
Henson, G L (Swansea, Ospreys) 2001 J 1(R), R, 2003 NZ(R), R, 2004 Arg 1,2,SA1,2,R,NZ,J, 2005 E,It,F,S,I, 2006 I(R),F(R),A,NZ(R), 2007 A1(t&R),2(R),SA, 2008 E,S,It,I,F
Herrer·, R C (Cross Keys) 1925 S, F, I, 1926 E, S, I, F, 1927 E
Hiams, H (Swansea) 1912 I, F
Hibbard, R (Ospreys) 2006 Arg 1(R),2(R), 2007 A1(R),2(R), 2008 SA1(R),2
Hickman, A (Neath) 1930 E, 1933 S
Hiddlestone, D D (Neath) 1922 E, S, I, F, 1924 NZ
Hill, A F (Cardiff) 1885 S, 1886 E, S, 1888 S, I, M, 1889 S, 1890 S, I, 1893 E, S, I, 1894 E, S, I
Hill, S D (Cardiff) 1993 Z 1,2, Nm, 1994 I (R), F, SA, 1995 F, SA, 1996 A 2, F 2(R), It, 1997 E
Hinam, S (Cardiff) 1925 I, 1926 E, S, I, F
Hinton, J T (Cardiff) 1884 I
Hirst, G L (Newport) 1912 S, 1913 S, 1914 E, S, F, I
Hodder, W (Pontypool) 1921 E, S, F
Hodges, J J (Newport) 1899 E, S, I, 1900 E, S, I, 1901 E, S, 1902 E, S, I, 1903 E, S, I, 1904 E, S, 1905 E, S, I, NZ, 1906 E, S, I
Hodgson, G T R (Neath) 1962 I, 1963 E, S, I, F, NZ, 1964 E, S, I, F, SA, 1966 S, I, F, 1967 I
Hollingdale, B G (Swansea) 1912 SA, 1913 E
Hollingdale, T H (Neath) 1927 A, 1928 E, S, I, F, 1930 E
Holmes, T D (Cardiff) 1978 A 2, NZ, 1979 S, I, F, E, 1980 F, E, S, I, NZ, 1981 A, 1982 I, F, E, 1983 E, S, I, F, 1984 E, 1985 S, I, F, E, Fj
Hook, J (Ospreys) 2006 Arg 1(R),2,A(R),PI, C,NZ(R), 2007 I,S,F1,It,E1,A1,2,Arg,F2,[C,A(R),J,Fj],SA, 2008 E,S,It(R),I(R), F,SA1(R),2
Hopkin, W H (Newport) 1937 S
Hopkins, K (Cardiff, Swansea) 1985 E, 1987 F, E, S, [Tg, C (R)], US
Hopkins, P L (Swansea) 1908 A, 1909 E, I, 1910 E
Hopkins, R (Maesteg) 1970 E (R)
Hopkins, T (Swansea) 1926 E, S, I, F
Hopkins, W J (Aberavon) 1925 E, S
Horsman, C L (Worcester) 2005 NZ(R),Fj,SA,A, 2006 PI, 2007 I,F1,It,E1,A2(R),E2,F2, [J,Fj]
Howarth, S P (Sale, Newport) 1998 SA 2, Arg, 1999 S, I, F 1, It, E, Arg 1,2, SA, C, F 2, [Arg 3, J, Sm, A], 2000 F, It, E
Howells, B (Llanelli) 1934 E

Howells, W G (Llanelli) 1957 E, S, I, F
Howells, W H (Swansea) 1888 S, I
Howley, R (Bridgend, Cardiff) 1996 E, S, I, F 1, A 1,2, Bb, F 2, It, A 3, SA, 1997 US, S, I, F, E, Tg (R), NZ, 1998 It, E, S, I, F, Z, SA 2, Arg, 1999 S, I, F 1, It, E, Arg 1,2, SA, C, F 2, [Arg 3, J, Sm, A], 2000 F, It, E, Sm, US, SA, 2001 E, S, F, R, I, Arg, Tg, A, 2002 I, F, It, E, S
Hughes, D (Newbridge) 1967 NZ, 1969 NZ 2, 1970 SA, S, E, I
Hughes, G (Penarth) 1934 E, S, I
Hughes, H (Cardiff) 1887 S, 1889 S
Hughes, K (Cambridge U, London Welsh) 1970 I, 1973 A, 1974 S
Hullin, W G (Cardiff) 1967 S
Humphreys, J M (Cardiff, Bath) 1995 [NZ, I], SA, Fj, 1996 It, E, S, I, F 1, A 1,2, Bb, It, A 3, SA, 1997 S, I, F, E, Tg (R), NZ (R), 1998 It (R), E (R), S (R), I (R), F (R), SA 2, Arg, 1999 S, Arg 2(R), SA (R), C, [J (R)], 2003 E 1, I 1
Hurrell, R J (Newport) 1959 F
Hutchinson, F O (Neath) 1894 I, 1896 S, I
Huxtable, R (Swansea) 1920 F, I
Huzzey, H V P (Cardiff) 1898 I, E, 1899 E, S, I
Hybart, A J (Cardiff) 1887 E

Ingledew, H M (Cardiff) 1890 I, 1891 E, S
Isaacs, I (Cardiff) 1933 E, S

Jackson, T H (Swansea) 1895 E
James, C R (Llanelli) 1958 A, F
James, D (Swansea) 1891 I, 1892 S, I, 1899 E
James, D M (Cardiff) 1947 A, 1948 E, S, F, I
James, D R (Treorchy) 1931 F, I
James, D R (Bridgend, Pontypridd, Llanelli Scarlets) 1996 A 2(R), It, A 3, SA, 1997 I, Tg (R), 1998 F (R), Z, SA 1,2, Arg, 1999 S, I, F 1, It, E, Arg 1,2, SA, F 2, [Arg 3, Sm, A], 2000 F, It (R), I (R), Sm (R), US, SA, 2001 E, S, F, It, R, I, 2002 I, F, It, E, S (R), NZ(R), 2005 SA,A, 2006 I,F, 2007 E2,Arg, [J]
James, E (Swansea) 1890 S, 1891 I, 1892 S, I, 1899 E
James, J B (Bridgend) 1968 E
James, P (Ospreys) 2003 R
James, T (Cardiff Blues) 2007 E2(R),SA(R), 2008 SA2(R)
James, T O (Aberavon) 1935 I, 1937 S
James, W (Gloucester) 2007 E2,Arg(R),F2(R), [J]
James, W J (Aberavon) 1983 E, S, I, F, R, 1984 S, 1985 S, I, F, E, Fj, 1986 E, S, I, F, Fj, Tg, WS, 1987 E, S, I
James, W P (Aberavon) 1925 E, S
Jarman, H (Newport) 1910 E, S, I, 1911 E
Jarrett, K S (Newport) 1967 E, 1968 E, S, 1969 S, I, F, E, NZ 1,2, A
Jarvis, L (Cardiff) 1997 R (R)
Jeffery, J J (Cardiff Coll of Ed, Newport) 1967 NZ
Jenkin, A M (Swansea) 1895 I, 1896 E
Jenkins, A E (Llanelli) 1920 E, S, F, I, 1921 S, F, 1922 F, 1923 E, S, F, I, 1924 NZ, 1928 S, I
Jenkins, D M (Treorchy) 1926 E, S, I, F
Jenkins, D R (Swansea) 1927 A, 1929 E
Jenkins, E (Newport) 1910 S, I
Jenkins, E M (Aberavon) 1927 S, F, I, A, 1928 E, S, I, F, 1929 F, 1930 E, S, I, F, 1931 E, S, F, I, SA, 1932 E, S, I
Jenkins, G D (Pontypridd, Celtic Warriors, Cardiff Blues) 2002 R, NZ(R), 2003 E 1(R), S 1(R), I 1, F, A, NZ, I 2(R), E 2, [C,Tg,It(R),NZ(R),E(R)], 2004 S(R),I(R),F,E,It,Arg 1(R),2(R),SA1, 2(R),R,NZ,J, 2005 E,It,F,S,I, 2006 E(R),S(R),I(R),It(R),F(R), A,C,NZ(R), 2007 I,S(R),F1,It,E1,2(R), Arg(R),F2(R), [C,A,J(R),Fj], SA, 2008 E(R),S(R),It,I,F,SA1,2
Jenkins, G R (Pontypool, Swansea) 1991 F 2, [WS (R), Arg, A], 1992 I, F, E, S, A, 1993 C, 1994 S, I, F, E, Pt, Sp, C, Tg, WS, R, It, SA, 1995 F, E, S, I, [J], SA (R), Fj (t), 1996 E (R), 1997 US, US 1, C, 1998 S, I, F, Z, SA 1(R), 1999 I (R), F 1, It, E, Arg 1,2, SA, F 2, [Arg 3, J, Sm, A], 2000 F, It, E, S, I, Sm, US, SA
Jenkins, J C (London Welsh) 1906 SA
Jenkins, J L (Aberavon) 1923 S, F
Jenkins, L H (Mon TC, Newport) 1954 I, 1956 E, S, I, F
Jenkins, N R (Pontypridd, Cardiff) 1991 E, S, I, F 1, 1992 I, F, E, S, 1993 E, S, I, F, Z 1,2, Nm, J, C, 1994 S, I, F, E, Pt, Sp, C, Tg, WS, R, It, SA, 1995 F, E, S, I, [J, NZ, I], SA, Fj, 1996 F 1, A 1,2, Bb, F 2, It, A 3(R), SA, 1997 S, I, F, E, Tg, NZ, 1998 It, E, S, I, F, SA 2, Arg, 1999 S, I, F 1, It, E, Arg 1,2, SA, C, F 2, [Arg 3, J, Sm, A], 2000 F, It, E, I (R), Sm (R), US (R), SA, 2001 E, S, F, It, 2002 SA 1(R),2(R), R
Jenkins, V G J (Oxford U, Bridgend, London Welsh) 1933 E, I, 1934 S, I, 1935 E, S, NZ, 1936 E, S, I, 1937 E, 1938 E, S, 1939 E
Jenkins, W J (Cardiff) 1912 I, F, 1913 S, I
John, B (Llanelli, Cardiff) 1966 A, 1967 S, NZ, 1968 E, S, I, F, 1969 S, I, F, E, NZ 1,2, A, 1970 SA, S, E, I, 1971 E, S, I, F, 1972 E, S, F
John, D A (Llanelli) 1925 I, 1928 E, S, I
John, D E (Llanelli) 1923 F, I, 1928 E, S, I
John, E R (Neath) 1950 E, S, I, F, 1951 E, S, I, F, SA, 1952 E, S, I, F, 1953 E, S, I, F, NZ, 1954 E
John G (St Luke's Coll, Exeter) 1954 E, F
John, J H (Swansea) 1926 E, S, I, F, 1927 E, S, F, I
John, P (Pontypridd) 1994 Tg, 1996 Bb (t), 1997 US (R), US 1,2, C, R, Tg, 1998 Z (R), SA 1
John, S C (Llanelli, Cardiff) 1995 S, I, 1997 E (R), Tg, NZ (R), 2000 F (R), It (R), E (R), Sm (R), SA (R), 2001 E (R), S (R), Tg (R), A, 2002 I, F, It (R), S (R)
Johnson, T A W (Cardiff) 1921 E, F, I, 1923 E, S, F, 1924 E, S, NZ, 1925 E, S, F
Johnson, W D (Swansea) 1953 E
Jones , A E (SEE Emyr)
Jones, A H (Cardiff) 1933 E, S
Jones, A M (Llanelli Scarlets) 2006 E(t&R),S(R)
Jones, A R (Ospreys) 2003 E 2(R), S 2, [C(R),Tg(R),It,NZ,E], 2004 S,I,Arg 1,2,SA1,2,R,NZ,J(t&R), 2005 E,It,F,S,I,US,NZ, Fj(R),SA(t&R),A(R), 2006 E,S,I,It,F,Arg 1,2, A,PI(R),C,NZ, 2007 S,It(R),E1(R),A1,Arg, [C,A], 2008 E,S,I,F,SA1
Jones, A W (Mountain Ash) 1905 I
Jones, A-W (Ospreys) 2006 Arg 1,2,PI,C(R),NZ(R), 2007 I,S,F1,It,E1,2,Arg,F2, [C,A,J,Fj],SA, 2008 E,I,F,SA1,2
Jones, B J (Newport) 1960 I, F
Jones, B L (Devonport Services, Llanelli) 1950 E, S, I, F, 1951 E, S, SA, 1952 E, I, F
Jones, C (Harlequins) 2007 A1(R),2
Jones, C W (Cambridge U, Cardiff) 1934 E, S, I, 1935 E, S, I, NZ, 1936 E, S, I, 1938 E, S, I
Jones, C W (Bridgend) 1920 E, S, F
Jones, D (Aberavon) 1897 E
Jones, D (Treherbert) 1902 E, S, I, 1903 E, S, I, 1905 E, S, I, NZ, 1906 E, S, SA
Jones, D (Neath) 1927 A
Jones, D (Cardiff) 1994 SA, 1995 F, E, S, [J, NZ, I], SA, Fj, 1996 It, E, S, I, F 1, A 1,2, Bb, It, A 3
Jones, D A R (Llanelli Scarlets) 2002 Fj, C, NZ, 2003 It(R), E 1, S 1, I 1, F, NZ, E 2, [C,Tg,It,NZ(R),E], 2004 S,I,F,E,It,Arg 2,SA1,2,R,NZ,J, 2005 E,Fj, 2006 F(R), 2008 SA1,2(R)
Jones, D C J (Swansea) 1947 E, F, I, 1949 E, S, I, F
Jones, D J (Neath, Ospreys) 2001 A (R), 2002 I (R), F (R), 2003 I 2, S 2,[C,It], 2004 S,E,It,Arg1,2,SA1(R),2,R(R),NZ(t&R),J, 2005 US,C,NZ,SA,A, 2006 E,S,I,It,F,Arg 1,2, A(R),PI,C(R),NZ, 2007 I(R),S,F1(R),It(R),E1(R),Arg,F2, [C(R),A(R),J,Fj(R)],SA(R), 2008 E,S,It(R),I(R),F(t&R),SA1(R),2(R)
Jones, D K (Llanelli, Cardiff) 1962 E, S, F, I, 1963 E, F, NZ, 1964 E, S, SA, 1966 E, S, I, F
Jones, D L (Newport) 1926 E, S, I, F, 1927 E
Jones, D L (Ebbw Vale, Celtic Warriors, Cardiff Blues) 2000 Sm, 2003 R (R), 2004 SA1, 2008 S(R),It(R)
Jones, D P (Pontypool) 1907 I
Jones, E H (Swansea, Neath) 1930 I, F
Jones, E L (Llanelli) 1930 F, 1933 E, S, I, 1935 E
Jones, E L (Llanelli) 1939 S
Jones, G (Ebbw Vale) 1963 S, I, F
Jones, G (Llanelli) 1988 NZ 2, 1989 F, E, NZ, 1990 F
Jones, G G (Cardiff) 1930 S, 1933 I
Jones, G H (Bridgend) 1995 SA
Jones, H (Penygraig) 1902 S, I
Jones, H (Neath) 1904 I
Jones, H J (Neath) 1929 E, S
Jones, I C (London Welsh) 1968 I
Jones, I E (Llanelli) 1924 E, S, 1927 S, F, I, A, 1928 E, S, I, F, 1929 E, S, F, I, 1930 E, S
Jones, J (Aberavon) 1901 E
Jones, J (Bedwellty) (Abertillery) 1914 E, S, F, I
Jones, J (Swansea) 1924 F

Jones, J (Aberavon) 1919 NZA, 1920 E, S, 1921 S, F, I
Jones, J A (Cardiff) 1883 S
Jones, J P (Tuan) (Pontypool) 1913 S
Jones, J P (Jack) (Pontypool) 1908 A, 1909 E, S, F, I, 1910 F, E, 1912 E, F, 1913 F, I, 1920 F, I, 1921 E
Jones, K D (Cardiff) 1960 SA, 1961 E, S, I, 1962 E, F, 1963 E, S, I, NZ
Jones, K J (Newport) 1947 E, S, F, I, A, 1948 E, S, F, I, 1949 E, S, I, F, 1950 E, S, I, F, 1951 E, S, I, F, SA, 1952 E, S, I, F, 1953 E, S, I, F, NZ, 1954 E, I, F, S, 1955 E, S, I, F, 1956 E, S, I, F, 1957 S
Jones, K P (Ebbw Vale) 1996 Bb, F 2, It, A 3, 1997 I (R), E, 1998 S, I, F (R), SA 1
Jones, K W J (Oxford U, London Welsh) 1934 E
Jones, Matthew (Ospreys) 2005 C(R)
Jones, M A (Neath, Ebbw Vale) 1987 S, 1988 NZ 2(R), 1989 S, I, F, E, NZ, 1990 F, E, S, I, Nm 1,2, Bb, 1998 Z
Jones, M A (Llanelli Scarlets) 2001 E (R), S, J 1, 2002 R, Fj, C, NZ, 2003 It, I 1, A, NZ, E 2, [C,Tg,It,E], 2006 E,S,I,It,Arg 1,2,PI,C,NZ, 2007 S,F1,It,E1,Arg,F2, [C,A,Fj], SA, 2008 E,It,I,F,SA1,2
Jones, P E R (Newport) 1921 S
Jones, P L (Newport) 1912 SA, 1913 E, S, F, 1914 E, S, F, I
Jones, R (Llwynypia) 1901 I
Jones, R (Northampton) 1926 E, S, F
Jones, R (London Welsh) 1929 E
Jones, R B (Cambridge U) 1933 E, S
Jones, R E (Coventry) 1967 F, E, 1968 S, I, F
Jones, R G (Llanelli, Cardiff) 1996 It, E, S, I, F 1, A 1, 1997 US (R), S (R), US 1,2, R, Tg, NZ
Jones, R H (Swansea) 1901 I, 1902 E, 1904 E, S, I, 1905 E, 1908 F, I, A, 1909 E, S, F, I, 1910 F, E
Jones, R L (Llanelli) 1993 Z 1,2, Nm, J, C
Jones, R N (Swansea) 1986 E, S, I, F, Fj, Tg, WS, 1987 F, E, S, I, [I, Tg, E, NZ, A], US, 1988 E, S, I, F, NZ 1, WS, R, 1989 I, F, E, NZ, 1990 F, E, S, I, 1991 E, S, F 2, [WS, Arg, A], 1992 I, F, E, S, A, 1993 E, S, I, 1994 I (R), Pt, 1995 F, E, S, I, [NZ, I]
Jones, R P (Ospreys) 2004 SA2,NZ(R),J, 2005 E(R),F,S,I,US, 2006 A,C,NZ, 2007 I,S,
F1,It,E1, 2008 E,S,It,I,F,SA1,2
Jones, S (Neath, Newport Gwent Dragons) 2001 J 1(R), 2004 SA2,R(R),NZ(R),J(R)
Jones, S M (Llanelli Scarlets, Clermont Auvergne) 1998 SA 1(R), 1999 C (R), [J (R)], 2000 It (R), S, I, 2001 E, F (R), J 1,2, R, I, Arg, Tg, A, 2002 I, F, It, S, SA 1,2, R(R), Fj, C, NZ, 2003 S 1, I 1, F, A, NZ, E 2, [Tg,It(R),NZ,E], 2004 S,I,F,E,It,SA2,R,NZ, 2005 E,It,F,S,I,NZ,SA,A, 2006 E,S,I,It,F,A,NZ, 2007 I,S,F1,It, [C(R),A,J,Fj], 2008 S(R),It,I,F(R),SA1,2
Jones, S T (Pontypool) 1983 S, I, F, R, 1984 S, 1988 E, S, F, NZ 1,2
Jones, T (Newport) 1922 E, S, I, F, 1924 E, S
Jones, T B (Newport) 1882 I, 1883 E, S, 1884 S, 1885 E, S
Jones, T I (Llanelli) 1927 A, 1928 E, S, I, F
Jones, W (Cardiff) 1898 I, E
Jones, W D (Llanelli) 1948 E
Jones, W H (Llanelli) 1934 S, I
Jones, W I (Llanelli, Cambridge U) 1925 E, S, F, I
Jones, W J (Llanelli) 1924 I
Jones, W K (Cardiff) 1967 NZ, 1968 E, S, I, F
Jones, W R (Swansea) 1927 A, 1928 F
Jones-Davies, T E (London Welsh) 1930 E, I, 1931 E, S
Jones-Hughes, J (Newport) 1999 [Arg 3(R), J], 2000 F
Jordan, H M (Newport) 1885 E, S, 1889 S
Joseph, W (Swansea) 1902 E, S, I, 1903 E, S, I, 1904 E, S, 1905 E, S, I, NZ, 1906 E, S, I, SA
Jowett, W F (Swansea) 1903 E
Judd, S (Cardiff) 1953 E, S, I, F, NZ, 1954 E, F, S, 1955 E, S
Judson, T H (Llanelli) 1883 E, S
Kedzlie, Q D (Cardiff) 1888 S, I
Keen, L (Aberavon) 1980 F, E, S, I
Knight, P (Pontypridd) 1990 Nm 1,2, Bb (R), 1991 E, S
Knill, F M D (Cardiff) 1976 F (R)

Lamerton, A E H (Llanelli) 1993 F, Z 1,2, Nm, J
Lane, S M (Cardiff) 1978 A 1(R),2, 1979 I (R), 1980 S, I
Lang, J (Llanelli) 1931 F, I, 1934 S, I, 1935 E, S, I, NZ, 1936 E, S, I, 1937 E
Law, V J (Newport) 1939 I
Lawrence, S D (Bridgend) 1925 S, I, 1926 S, I, F, 1927 E
Legge, W S G (Newport) 1937 I, 1938 I
Leleu, J (London Welsh, Swansea) 1959 E, S, 1960 F, SA
Lemon, A W (Neath) 1929 I, 1930 S, I, F, 1931 E, S, F, I, SA, 1932 E, S, I, 1933 I
Lewis, A J L (Ebbw Vale) 1970 F, 1971 E, I, F, 1972 E, S, F, 1973 E, S, I, F
Lewis, A L P (Cardiff) 1996 It, E, S, I, A 2(t), 1998 It, E, S, I, F, SA 2, Arg, 1999 F 1(R), E (R), Arg 1(R),2(R), SA (R), C (R), [J (R), Sm (R), A (R)], 2000 Sm (R), US (R), SA (R), 2001 F (R), J 1,2, 2002 R(R)
Lewis, B R (Swansea, Cambridge U) 1912 I, 1913 I
Lewis, C P (Llandovery) 1882 I, 1883 E, S, 1884 E, S
Lewis, D H (Cardiff) 1886 E, S
Lewis, E J (Llandovery) 1881 E
Lewis, E W (Llanelli, Cardiff) 1991 I, F 1, A, F 2, [WS, Arg, A], 1992 I, F, S, A, 1993 E, S, I, F, Z 1,2, Nm, J, C, 1994 S, I, F, E, Pt, Sp, Fj, WS, R, It, SA, 1995 E, S, I, [J, I], 1996 It, E, S, I, F 1
Lewis, G (Pontypridd, Swansea) 1998 SA 1(R), 1999 It (R), Arg 2, C, [J], 2000 F (R), It, S, I, Sm, US (t+R), 2001 F (R), J 1,2, R, I
Lewis, G W (Richmond) 1960 E, S
Lewis, H (Swansea) 1913 S, F, I, 1914 E
Lewis, J G (Llanelli) 1887 I
Lewis, J M C (Cardiff, Cambridge U) 1912 E, 1913 S, F, I, 1914 E, S, F, I, 1921 I, 1923 E, S
Lewis, J R (S Glam Inst, Cardiff) 1981 E, S, I, F, 1982 F, E, S
Lewis, M (Treorchy) 1913 F
Lewis, P I (Llanelli) 1984 A, 1985 S, I, F, E, 1986 E, S, I
Lewis, R A (Abertillery) 1966 E, S, I, F, A, 1967 I
Lewis, T W (Cardiff) 1926 E, 1927 E, S
Lewis, W (Llanelli) 1925 F
Lewis, W H (London Welsh, Cambridge U) 1926 I, 1927 E, F, I, A, 1928 F
Llewellyn, D S (Ebbw Vale, Newport) 1998 SA 1(R), 1999 F 1(R), It (R), [J (R)]
Llewellyn, G D (Neath) 1990 Nm 1,2, Bb, 1991 E, S, I, F 1, A, F 2
Llewellyn, G O (Neath, Harlequins, Ospreys, Narbonne) 1989 NZ, 1990 E, S, I, 1991 E, S, A (R), 1992 I, F, E, S, A, 1993 E, S, I, F, Z 1,2, Nm, J, C, 1994 S, I, F, E, Pt, Sp, C, Tg, WS, R, It, SA, 1995 F, E, S, I, [J, NZ, I], 1996 It, E, S, I, F 1, A 1,2, Bb, F 2, It, A 3, SA, 1997 US, S, I, F, E, US 1,2, NZ, 1998 It, E, 1999 C (R), [Sm], 2002 E (R), SA 1,2, R(R), Fj, C, NZ, 2003 E 1(R), S 1(R), I 1, F, A, NZ, I 2, S 2(R), [C,Tg,It,E(R)], 2004 S,F(R),E(R),It,Arg 1,2,SA1,R,NZ
Llewellyn, P D (Swansea) 1973 I, F, A, 1974 S, E
Llewellyn, W (Llwynypia) 1899 E, S, I, 1900 E, S, I, 1901 E, S, I, 1902 E, S, I, 1903 I, 1904 E, S, I, 1905 E, S, I, NZ
Llewelyn, D B (Newport, Llanelli) 1970 SA, S, E, I, F, 1971 E, S, I, F, 1972 E, S, F, NZ
Lloyd, A (Bath) 2001 J 1
Lloyd, D J (Bridgend) 1966 E, S, I, F, A, 1967 S, I, F, E, 1968 S, I, F, 1969 S, I, F, E, NZ 1, A, 1970 F, 1972 E, S, F, 1973 E, S
Lloyd, D P M (Llanelli) 1890 S, E, 1891 E, I
Lloyd, E (Llanelli) 1895 S
Lloyd, G L (Newport) 1896 I, 1899 S, I, 1900 E, S, 1901 E, S, 1902 S, I, 1903 E, S, I
Lloyd, R (Pontypool) 1913 S, F, I, 1914 E, S, F, I
Lloyd, T (Maesteg) 1953 I, F
Lloyd, T J (Neath) 1909 F, 1913 F, I, 1914 E, S, F, I
Loader, C D (Swansea) 1995 SA, Fj, 1996 F 1, A 1,2, Bb, F 2, It, A 3, SA, 1997 US, S, I, F, E, US 1, R, Tg, NZ
Lockwood, T W (Newport) 1887 E, S, I
Long, E C (Swansea) 1936 E, S, I, 1937 E, S, 1939 S, I
Luscombe, H N (Newport Gwent Dragons, Harlequins) 2003 S 2(R), 2004 Arg 1,2,SA1,2,R,J, 2005 E,It,S(t&R), 2006 E,S,I,It,F, 2007 I
Lyne, H S (Newport) 1883 S, 1884 E, S, I, 1885 E

McBryde, R C (Swansea, Llanelli, Neath, Llanelli Scarlets) 1994 Fj, SA (t), 1997 US 2, 2000 I (R), 2001 E, S, F, It, R, I, Arg, Tg, A, 2002 I, F, It, E, S (R), SA 1,2, C, NZ, 2003 A, NZ, E 2, S 2, [C,It,NZ,E], 2004 I,E,It, 2005 It(R),F(R),S(R),I(R)
McCall, B E W (Welch Regt, Newport) 1936 E, S, I

McCarley, A (Neath) 1938 E, S, I
McCutcheon, W M (Swansea) 1891 S, 1892 E, S, 1893 E, S, I, 1894 E
McIntosh, D L M (Pontypridd) 1996 SA, 1997 E (R)
Madden, M (Llanelli) 2002 SA 1(R), R, Fj(R), 2003 I 1(R), F(R)
Maddock, H T (London Welsh) 1906 E, S, I, 1907 E, S, 1910 F
Maddocks, K (Neath) 1957 E
Main, D R (London Welsh) 1959 E, S, I, F
Mainwaring, H J (Swansea) 1961 F
Mainwaring, W T (Aberavon) 1967 S, I, F, E, NZ, 1968 E
Major, W C (Maesteg) 1949 F, 1950 S
Male, B O (Cardiff) 1921 F, 1923 S, 1924 S, I, 1927 E, S, F, I, 1928 S, I, F
Manfield, L (Mountain Ash, Cardiff) 1939 S, I, 1947 A, 1948 E, S, F, I
Mann, B B (Cardiff) 1881 E
Mantle, J T (Loughborough Colls, Newport) 1964 E, SA
Margrave, F L (Llanelli) 1884 E, S
Marinos, A W N (Newport, Gwent Dragons)) 2002 I (R), F, It, E, S, SA 1,2, 2003 R
Marsden-Jones, D (Cardiff) 1921 E, 1924 NZ
Martin, A J (Aberavon) 1973 A, 1974 S, I, 1975 F, E, S, I, A, 1976 E, S, I, F, 1977 I, F, E, S, 1978 E, S, I, F, A 1,2, NZ, 1979 S, I, F, E, 1980 F, E, S, I, NZ, 1981 I, F
Martin, W J (Newport) 1912 I, F, 1919 NZA
Mason, J E (Pontypridd) 1988 NZ 2(R)
Mathews, Rev A A (Lampeter) 1886 S
Mathias, R (Llanelli) 1970 F
Matthews, C M (Bridgend) 1939 I
Matthews, J (Cardiff), 1947 E, A, 1948 E, S, F, 1949 E, S, I, F, 1950 E, S, I, F, 1951 E, S, I, F
May, P S (Llanelli) 1988 E, S, I, F, NZ 1,2, 1991 [WS]
Meek, N N (Pontypool) 1993 E, S, I
Meredith, A (Devonport Services) 1949 E, S, I
Meredith, B V (St Luke's Coll, London Welsh, Newport) 1954 I, F, S, 1955 E, S, I, F, 1956 E, S, I, F, 1957 E, S, I, F, 1958 A, E, S, I, 1959 E, S, I, F, 1960 E, S, F, SA, 1961 E, S, I, 1962 E, S, F, I
Meredith, C C (Neath) 1953 S, NZ, 1954 E, I, F, S, 1955 E, S, I, F, 1956 E, I, 1957 E, S
Meredith, J (Swansea) 1888 S, I, 1890 S, E
Merry, J A (Pill Harriers) 1912 I, F
Michael, G M (Swansea) 1923 E, S, F
Michaelson, R C B (Aberavon, Cambridge U) 1963 E
Millar, W H (Mountain Ash) 1896 I, 1900 E, S, I, 1901 E, S, I
Mills, F M (Swansea, Cardiff) 1892 E, S, I, 1893 E, S, I, 1894 E, S, I, 1895 E, S, I, 1896 E
Moon, R H StJ B (Llanelli) 1993 F, Z 1,2, Nm, J, C, 1994 S, I, F, E, Sp, C, Fj, WS, R, It, SA, 1995 E (R), 2000 S, I, Sm (R), US (R), 2001 E (R), S (R)
Moore, A P (Cardiff) 1995 [J], SA, Fj, 1996 It
Moore, A P (Swansea) 1995 SA (R), Fj, 1998 S, I, F, Z, SA 1, 1999 C, 2000 S, I, US (R), 2001 E (R), S, F, It, J 1,2, R, I, Arg, Tg, A, 2002 F, It, E, S
Moore, S J (Swansea, Moseley) 1997 C, R, Tg
Moore, W J (Bridgend) 1933 I
Morgan, C H (Llanelli) 1957 I, F
Morgan, C I (Cardiff) 1951 I, F, SA, 1952 E, S, I, 1953 S, I, F, NZ, 1954 E, I, S, 1955 E, S, I, F, 1956 E, S, I, F, 1957 E, S, I, F, 1958 E, S, I, F
Morgan, C S (Cardiff Blues) 2002 I, F, It, E, S, SA 1,2, R(R), 2003 F, 2005 US
Morgan, D (Swansea) 1885 S, 1886 E, S, 1887 E, S, I, 1889 I
Morgan, D (Llanelli) 1895 I, 1896 E
Morgan, D E (Llanelli) 1920 I, 1921 E, S, F
Morgan, D R R (Llanelli) 1962 E, S, F, I, 1963 E, S, I, F, NZ
Morgan, E (Swansea) 1914 E, S, F, I
Morgan, E (London Welsh) 1902 E, S, I, 1903 I, 1904 E, S, I, 1905 E, S, I, NZ, 1906 E, S, I, SA, 1908 F
Morgan, F L (Llanelli) 1938 E, S, I, 1939 E
Morgan, G R (Newport) 1984 S
Morgan, H J (Abertillery) 1958 E, S, I, F, 1959 I, F, 1960 E, 1961 E, S, I, F, 1962 E, S, F, I, 1963 S, I, F, 1965 E, S, I, F, 1966 E, S, I, F, A
Morgan, H P (Newport) 1956 E, S, I, F
Morgan, J L (Llanelli) 1912 SA, 1913 E
Morgan, K A (Pontypridd, Swansea, Newport Gwent Dragons) 1997 US 1,2, C, R, NZ, 1998 S, I, F, 2001 J 1,2, R, I, Arg, Tg, A, 2002 I, F, It, E, S, SA 1,2, 2003 E 1, S 1, [C,It], 2004 J(R), 2005 E(R),It(R),F,S,I,US,C,NZ,Fj, 2006 A,PI, NZ, 2007 I,S,It,E1,Arg,F2, [C,A(R),J]
Morgan, M E (Swansea) 1938 E, S, I, 1939 E
Morgan, N H (Newport) 1960 S, I, F
Morgan, P E J (Aberavon) 1961 E, S, F
Morgan, P J (Llanelli) 1980 S (R), I, NZ (R), 1981 I
Morgan, S (Cardiff Blues) 2007 A2(R)
Morgan, T (Llanelli) 1889 I
Morgan, W G (Cambridge U) 1927 F, I, 1929 E, S, F, I, 1930 I, F
Morgan, W I (Swansea) 1908 A, 1909 E, S, F, I, 1910 F, E, S, I, 1911 E, F, I, 1912 S
Morgan, W L (Cardiff) 1910 S
Moriarty, R D (Swansea) 1981 A, 1982 I, F, E, S, 1983 E, 1984 S, I, F, E, 1985 S, I, F, 1986 Fj, Tg, WS, 1987 [I, Tg, C (R), E, NZ, A]
Moriarty, W P (Swansea) 1986 I, F, Fj, Tg, WS, 1987 F, E, S, I, [I, Tg, C, E, NZ, A], US, 1988 E, S, I, F, NZ 1
Morley, J C (Newport) 1929 E, S, F, I, 1930 E, I, 1931 E, S, F, I, SA, 1932 E, S, I
Morris, D R (Neath, Swansea, Leicester) 1998 Z, SA 1(R),2(R), 1999 S, I, It (R), 2000 US, SA, 2001 E, S, F, It, Arg, Tg, A, 2004 Arg 1(R),2(R),SA1(R)
Morris, G L (Swansea) 1882 I, 1883 E, S, 1884 E, S
Morris, H T (Cardiff) 1951 F, 1955 I, F
Morris, J I T (Swansea) 1924 E, S
Morris, M S (S Wales Police, Neath) 1985 S, I, F, 1990 I, Nm 1,2, Bb, 1991 I, F 1, [WS (R)], 1992 E
Morris, R R (Swansea, Bristol) 1933 S, 1937 S
Morris, S (Cross Keys) 1920 E, S, F, I, 1922 E, S, I, F, 1923 E, S, F, I, 1924 E, S, F, NZ, 1925 E, S, F
Morris, W (Llanelli) 1896 S, I, 1897 E
Morris, W D (Neath) 1967 F, E, 1968 E, S, I, F, 1969 S, I, F, E, NZ 1,2, A, 1970 SA, S, E, I, F, 1971 E, S, I, F, 1972 E, S, F, NZ, 1973 E, S, I, A, 1974 S, I, F, E
Morris, W G H (Abertillery) 1919 NZA, 1920 F, 1921 I
Morris, W J (Newport) 1965 S, 1966 F
Morris, W J B (Pontypool) 1963 S, I
Moseley, K (Pontypool, Newport) 1988 NZ 2, R, 1989 S, I, 1990 F, 1991 F 2, [WS, Arg, A]
Murphy, C D (Cross Keys) 1935 E, S, I
Mustoe, L (Cardiff) 1995 Fj, 1996 A 1(R),2, 1997 US 1,2, C, R (R), 1998 E (R), I (R), F (R)

Nash, D (Ebbw Vale) 1960 SA, 1961 E, S, I, F, 1962 F
Newman, C H (Newport) 1881 E, 1882 I, 1883 E, S, 1884 E, S, 1885 E, S, 1886 E, 1887 E
Nicholas, D L (Llanelli) 1981 E, S, I, F
Nicholas, T J (Cardiff) 1919 NZA
Nicholl, C B (Cambridge U, Llanelli) 1891 I, 1892 E, S, I, 1893 E, S, I, 1894 E, S, 1895 E, S, I, 1896 E, S, I
Nicholl, D W (Llanelli) 1894 I
Nicholls, E G (Cardiff) 1896 S, I, 1897 E, 1898 I, E, 1899 E, S, I, 1900 S, I, 1901 E, S, I, 1902 E, S, I, 1903 I, 1904 E, 1905 I, NZ, 1906 E, S, I, SA
Nicholls, F E (Cardiff Harlequins) 1892 I
Nicholls, H C W (Cardiff) 1958 I
Nicholls, S H (Cardiff) 1888 M, 1889 S, I, 1891 S
Norris, C H (Cardiff) 1963 F, 1966 F
Norster, R L (Cardiff) 1982 S, 1983 E, S, I, F, 1984 S, I, F, E, A, 1985 S, I, F, E, Fj, 1986 Fj, Tg, WS, 1987 F, E, S, I, [I, C, E], US, 1988 E, S, I, F, NZ 1, WS, 1989 F, E
Norton, W B (Cardiff) 1882 I, 1883 E, S, 1884 E, S, I

Oakley, R L (Gwent Dragons) 2003 I 2, S 2(R)
O'Connor, A (Aberavon) 1960 SA, 1961 E, S, 1962 F, I
O'Connor, R (Aberavon) 1957 E
O'Neil, W (Cardiff) 1904 S, I, 1905 E, S, I, 1907 E, I, 1908 E, S, F, I
O'Shea, J P (Cardiff) 1967 S, I, 1968 S, I, F
Oliver, G (Pontypool) 1920 E, S, F, I
Osborne, W T (Mountain Ash) 1902 E, S, I, 1903 E, S, I
Ould, W J (Cardiff) 1924 E, S
Owen, A D (Swansea) 1924 E
Owen, G D (Newport) 1955 I, F, 1956 E, S, I, F
Owen, M J (Pontypridd, Newport Gwent Dragons) 2002 SA 1,2, R, C(R), NZ(R), 2003 It, I 2, S 2, 2004 S(R),I(R),F,E,It,Arg 1,2,SA2,R,NZ,J, 2005 E,It,F,S,I,NZ,Fj,SA,A, 2006 E,S,I,It,F,

PI, 2007 A1(R),2,E2, [C(R),A(R),J(R),Fj(R)]
Owen, R M (Swansea) 1901 I, 1902 E, S, I, 1903 E, S, I, 1904 E, S, I, 1905 E, S, I, NZ, 1906 E, S, I, SA, 1907 E, S, 1908 F, I, A, 1909 E, S, F, I, 1910 F, E, 1911 E, S, F, I, 1912 E, S

Packer, H (Newport) 1891 E, 1895 S, I, 1896 E, S, I, 1897 E
Palmer, F C (Swansea) 1922 E, S, I
Parfitt, F C (Newport) 1893 E, S, I, 1894 E, S, I, 1895 S, 1896 S, I
Parfitt, S A (Swansea) 1990 Nm 1(R), Bb
Parker, D S (Swansea) 1924 I, F, NZ, 1925 E, S, F, I, 1929 F, I, 1930 E
Parker, E T (Swansea) 1919 NZA, 1920 E, S, I, 1921 E, S, F, I, 1922 E, S, I, F, 1923 E, S, F
Parker, S T (Pontypridd, Celtic Warriors, Newport Gwent Dragons, Ospreys) 2002 R, Fj, C, NZ, 2003 E 2, [C,It,NZ], 2004 S,I,Arg 1,2,SA1,2,NZ, 2005 Fj,SA,A, 2006 PI,C,NZ, 2007 A1,2,F2(t&R), [C,A],SA, 2008 E,S(R),It(R),SA1
Parker, W J (Swansea) 1899 E, S
Parks, R D (Pontypridd, Celtic Warriors) 2002 SA 1(R), Fj(R), 2003 I 2, S 2
Parsons, G (Newport) 1947 E
Pascoe, D (Bridgend) 1923 F, I
Pask, A E I (Abertillery) 1961 F, 1962 E, S, F, I, 1963 E, S, I, F, NZ, 1964 E, S, I, F, SA, 1965 E, S, I, F, 1966 E, S, I, F, A, 1967 S, I
Payne, G W (Army, Pontypridd) 1960 E, S, I
Payne, H (Swansea) 1935 NZ
Peacock, H (Newport) 1929 S, F, I, 1930 S, I, F
Peake, E (Chepstow) 1881 E
Pearce, P G (Bridgend) 1981 I, F, 1982 I (R)
Pearson, T W (Cardiff, Newport) 1891 E, I, 1892 E, S, 1894 S, I, 1895 E, S, I, 1897 E, 1898 I, E, 1903 E
Peel, D J (Llanelli Scarlets) 2001 J 2(R), R (R), Tg (R), 2002 I (R), It (R), E (R), S (R), SA 1,2, R, Fj, C, NZ, 2003 It, S 1(R), I 1(R), F, NZ(R), I 2, S 2, [C(R),Tg(R),It,NZ(R),E(R)], 2004 S(R),I(R), F(R),E(R),It(R),Arg 1,2,SA1,2,R,NZ, 2005 E,It,F,S,I, 2006 E,S,I,It,A,C,NZ, 2007 I,S,F1,It,E1,Arg,F2, [C,A,Fj],SA, 2008 S(R),It
Pegge, E V (Neath) 1891 E
Perego, M A (Llanelli) 1990 S, 1993 F, Z 1, Nm (R), 1994 S, I, F, E, Sp
Perkins, S J (Pontypool) 1983 S, I, F, R, 1984 S, I, F, E, A, 1985 S, I, F, E, Fj, 1986 E, S, I, F
Perrett, F L (Neath) 1912 SA, 1913 E, S, F, I
Perrins, V C (Newport) 1970 SA, S
Perry, W J (Neath) 1911 E
Phillips, A J (Cardiff) 1979 E, 1980 F, E, S, I, NZ, 1981 E, S, I, F, A, 1982 I, F, E, S, 1987 [C, E, A]
Phillips, B (Aberavon) 1925 E, S, F, I, 1926 E
Phillips, D H (Swansea) 1952 F
Phillips, H P (Newport) 1892 E, 1893 E, S, I, 1894 E, S
Phillips, H T (Newport) 1927 E, S, F, I, A, 1928 E, S, I, F
Phillips, K H (Neath) 1987 F, [I, Tg, NZ], US, 1988 E, NZ 1, 1989 NZ, 1990 F, E, S, I, Nm 1,2, Bb, 1991 E, S, I, F 1, A
Phillips, L A (Newport) 1900 E, S, I, 1901 S
Phillips, M (Llanelli Scarlets, Cardiff Blues, Ospreys) 2003 R, 2004 Arg 1(R),2(R),J(R), 2005 US,C,NZ,Fj(R),SA(R), 2006 S(R),It(R),F,Arg 1,2,PI,C(R),NZ(R), 2007 I(R),F1(R),E1(R),A1, 2,F2(R), [C(R),A(R),J,Fj(R)],SA(R), 2008 E,S,It(R),I,F
Phillips, R D (Neath) 1987 US, 1988 E, S, I, F, NZ 1,2, WS, 1989 S, I
Phillips, W D (Cardiff) 1881 E, 1882 I, 1884 E, S, I
Pickering, D F (Llanelli) 1983 E, S, I, F, R, 1984 S, I, F, E, A, 1985 S, I, F, E, Fj, 1986 E, S, I, F, Fj, 1987 F, E, S
Plummer, R C S (Newport) 1912 S, I, F, SA, 1913 E
Pook, T R (Newport) 1895 S
Popham, A J (Leeds, Llanelli Scarlets) 2003 A (R), I 2, R, S 2, [Tg,NZ], 2004 I(R),It(R),SA1,J(R), 2005 C,Fj(R), 2006 E(R), It(R),F,Arg 1,2,PI,NZ(R), 2007 I,S,F1,It,E1,2(R),Arg,F2, [C,A(t), J,Fj],SA(R), 2008 E(R)
Powell, G (Ebbw Vale) 1957 I, F
Powell, J (Cardiff) 1923 I
Powell, J A (Cardiff) 1906 I
Powell, R D (Cardiff) 2002 SA 1(R),2(R), C(R)
Powell, R W (Newport) 1888 S, I
Powell, W C (London Welsh) 1926 S, I, F, 1927 E, F, I, 1928 S, I, F, 1929 E, S, F, I, 1930 S, I, F, 1931 E, S, F, I, SA, 1932 E, S, I, 1935 E, S, I
Powell, W J (Cardiff) 1920 E, S, F, I
Price, B (Newport) 1961 I, F, 1962 E, S, 1963 E, S, F, NZ, 1964 E, S, I, F, SA, 1965 E, S, I, F, 1966 E, S, I, F, A, 1967 S, I, F, E, 1969 S, I, F, NZ 1,2, A
Price, G (Pontypool) 1975 F, E, S, I, A, 1976 E, S, I, F, 1977 I, F, E, S, 1978 E, S, I, F, A 1,2, NZ, 1979 S, I, F, E, 1980 F, E, S, I, NZ, 1981 E, S, I, F, A, 1982 I, F, E, S, 1983 E, I, F
Price, M J (Pontypool, RAF) 1959 E, S, I, F, 1960 E, S, I, F, 1962 E
Price, R E (Weston-s-Mare) 1939 S, I
Price, T G (Llanelli) 1965 E, S, I, F, 1966 E, A, 1967 S, F
Priday, A J (Cardiff) 1958 I, 1961 I
Pritchard, C C (Newport, Pontypool) 1904 S, I, 1905 NZ, 1906 E, S
Pritchard, C C (Pontypool) 1928 E, S, I, F, 1929 E, S, F, I
Pritchard, C M (Newport) 1904 I, 1905 E, S, NZ, 1906 E, S, I, SA, 1907 E, S, I, 1908 E, 1910 F, E
Proctor, W T (Llanelli) 1992 A, 1993 E, S, Z 1,2, Nm, C, 1994 I, C, Fj, WS, R, It, SA, 1995 S, I, [NZ], Fj, 1996 It, E, S, I, A 1,2, Bb, F 2, It, A 3, 1997 E(R), US 1,2, C, R, 1998 E (R), S, I, F, Z, 2001 A
Prosser, D R (Neath) 1934 S, I
Prosser, F J (Cardiff) 1921 I
Prosser, G (Pontypridd) 1995 [NZ]
Prosser, I G (Neath) 1934 E, S, I, 1935 NZ
Prosser, T R (Pontypool) 1956 S, F, 1957 E, S, I, F, 1958 A, E, S, I, F, 1959 E, S, I, F, 1960 E, S, I, F, SA, 1961 I, F
Prothero, G J (Bridgend) 1964 S, I, F, 1965 E, S, I, F, 1966 E, S, I, F
Pryce-Jenkins, T J (London Welsh) 1888 S, I
Pugh, C H (Maesteg) 1924 E, S, I, F, NZ, 1925 E, S
Pugh, J D (Neath) 1987 US, 1988 S (R), 1990 S
Pugh, P (Neath) 1989 NZ
Pugh, R (Ospreys) 2005 US(R)
Pugsley, J (Cardiff) 1910 E, S, I, 1911 E, S, F, I
Pullman, J J (Neath) 1910 F
Purdon, F T (Newport) 1881 E, 1882 I, 1883 E, S

Quinnell, D L (Llanelli) 1972 F (R), NZ, 1973 E, S, A, 1974 S, F, 1975 E (R), 1977 I (R), F, E, S, 1978 E, S, I, F, A 1, NZ, 1979 S, I, F, E, 1980 NZ
Quinnell, J C (Llanelli, Richmond, Cardiff) 1995 Fj, 1996 A 3(R), 1997 US (R), S (R), I (R), E (R), 1998 SA 2, Arg, 1999 I, F 1, It, E, Arg 1,2, SA, C, F 2, [Arg 3, J, A], 2000 It, E, 2001 S (R), F (R), It (R), J 1,2, R (R), I (R), Arg, 2002 I, F
Quinnell, L S (Llanelli, Richmond) 1993 C, 1994 S, I, F, E, Pt, Sp, C, WS, 1997 US, S, I, F, E, 1998 It, E, S (R), Z, SA 2, Arg, 1999 S, I, F 1, It, E, Arg 1,2, SA, C, F 2, [Arg 3, Sm, A], 2000 F, It, E, Sm, US, SA, 2001 E, S, F, It, Arg, Tg, A, 2002 I, F, It, E, R, C(R)

Radford, W J (Newport) 1923 I
Ralph, A R (Newport) 1931 F, I, SA, 1932 E, S, I
Ramsay, S (Treorchy) 1896 E, 1904 E
Randall, R J (Aberavon) 1924 I, F
Raybould, W H (London Welsh, Cambridge U, Newport) 1967 S, I, F, E, NZ, 1968 I, F, 1970 SA, E, I, F (R)
Rayer, M A (Cardiff) 1991 [WS (R), Arg, A (R)], 1992 E (R), A, 1993 E, S, I, Z 1, Nm, J (R), 1994 S (R), I (R), F, E, Pt, C, Fj, WS, R, It
Rees, A (Maesteg) 1919 NZA
Rees, A (Maesteg) 1962 E, S, F
Rees, A M (London Welsh) 1934 E, 1935 E, S, I, NZ, 1936 E, S, I, 1937 E, S, I, 1938 E, S
Rees, B I (London Welsh) 1967 S, I, F
Rees, C F W (London Welsh) 1974 I, 1975 A, 1978 NZ, 1981 F, A, 1982 I, F, E, S, 1983 E, S, I, F
Rees, D (Swansea) 1900 E, 1903 E, S, 1905 E, S
Rees, D (Swansea) 1968 S, I, F
Rees, E B (Swansea) 1919 NZA
Rees, H E (Neath) 1979 S, I, F, E, 1980 F, E, S, I, NZ, 1983 E, S, I, F
Rees, H T (Cardiff) 1937 S, I, 1938 E, S, I
Rees, J (Swansea) 1920 E, S, F, I, 1921 E, S, I, 1922 E, 1923 E, F, I, 1924 E
Rees, J I (Swansea) 1934 E, S, I, 1935 S, NZ, 1936 E, S, I, 1937 E, S, I, 1938 E, S, I

Rees, L M (Cardiff) 1933 I
Rees, M (Llanelli Scarlets) 2005 US, 2006 Arg 1,A,C,NZ(R), 2007 I(R),S(t&R),F1,It,E1,A1,Arg,F2, [C,A,Fj], 2008 E(R),S(R),It, I,F(R),SA1
Rees, P (Llanelli) 1947 F, I
Rees, P M (Newport) 1961 E, S, I, 1964 I
Rees, R (Swansea) 1998 Z
Rees, T A (Llandovery) 1881 E
Rees, T E (London Welsh) 1926 I, F, 1927 A, 1928 E
Rees, T J (Newport) 1935 S, I, NZ, 1936 E, S, I, 1937 E, S
Rees-Jones, G R (Oxford U, London Welsh) 1934 E, S, 1935 I, NZ, 1936 E
Reeves, F C (Cross Keys) 1920 F, I, 1921 E
Reynolds, A D (Swansea) 1990 Nm 1,2(R), 1992 A (R)
Rhapps, J (Penygraig) 1897 E
Rice-Evans, W (Swansea) 1890 S, 1891 E, S
Richards, D S (Swansea) 1979 F, E, 1980 F, E, S, I, NZ, 1981 E, S, I, F, 1982 I, F, 1983 E, S, I, R (R)
Richards, E G (Cardiff) 1927 S
Richards, E I (Cardiff) 1925 E, S, F
Richards, E S (Swansea) 1885 E, 1887 S
Richards, H D (Neath) 1986 Tg (R), 1987 [Tg, E (R), NZ]
Richards, K H L (Bridgend) 1960 SA, 1961 E, S, I, F
Richards, M C R (Cardiff) 1968 I, F, 1969 S, I, F, E, NZ 1,2, A
Richards, R (Aberavon) 1913 S, F, I
Richards, R C (Cross Keys) 1956 F
Richards, T B (Swansea)1960 F
Richards, T L (Maesteg) 1923 I
Richards, W C (Pontypool) 1922 E, S, I, F, 1924 I
Richardson, S J (Aberavon) 1978 A 2(R), 1979 E
Rickards, A R (Cardiff) 1924 F
Ring, J (Aberavon) 1921 E
Ring, M G (Cardiff, Pontypool) 1983 E, 1984 A, 1985 S, I, F, 1987 I, [I, Tg, A], US, 1988 E, S, I, F, NZ 1,2, 1989 NZ, 1990 F, E, S, I, Nm 1,2, Bb, 1991 E, S, I, F 1,2, [WS, Arg, A]
Ringer, J (Bridgend) 2001 J 1(R),2(R)
Ringer, P (Ebbw Vale, Llanelli) 1978 NZ, 1979 S, I, F, E, 1980 F, E, NZ
Roberts, C R (Neath) 1958 I, F
Roberts, D E A (London Welsh) 1930 E
Roberts, E (Llanelli) 1886 E, 1887 I
Roberts, E J (Llanelli) 1888 S, I, 1889 I
Roberts, G J (Cardiff) 1985 F (R), E, 1987 [I, Tg, C, E, A]
Roberts, H M (Cardiff) 1960 SA, 1961 E, S, I, F, 1962 S, F, 1963 I
Roberts, J (Cardiff) 1927 E, S, F, I, A, 1928 E, S, I, F, 1929 E, S, F, I
Roberts, J (Cardiff Blues) 2008 S,SA1,2
Roberts, M G (London Welsh) 1971 E, S, I, F, 1973 I, F, 1975 S, 1979 E
Roberts, T (Newport, Risca) 1921 S, F, I, 1922 E, S, I, F, 1923 E, S
Roberts, W (Cardiff) 1929 E
Robins, J D (Birkenhead Park) 1950 E, S, I, F, 1951 E, S, I, F, 1953 E, I, F
Robins, R J (Pontypridd) 1953 S, 1954 F, S, 1955 E, S, I, F, 1956 E, F, 1957 E, S, I, F
Robinson, I R (Cardiff) 1974 F, E
Robinson, J P (Cardiff Blues) 2001 J 1(R),2(R), Arg (R), Tg (R), A, 2002 I, Fj(R), C, NZ, 2003 A, NZ, I 2, S 2, 2006 Arg 1,2, 2007 I,S,F1(R),A1,2,Arg(t&R),F2,[J]
Robinson, M F D (Swansea) 1999 S, I, F 1, Arg 1
Robinson, N J (Cardiff Blues) 2003 I 2, R, 2004 Arg 1(R),2,SA1, 2005 US,C,NZ(R),Fj, 2006 S(R),Arg 1,2
Rocyn-Jones, D N (Cambridge U) 1925 I
Roderick, W B (Llanelli) 1884 I
Rogers, P J D (London Irish, Newport, Cardiff) 1999 F 1, It, E, Arg 1,2, SA, C, F 2, [Arg 3, J, Sm, A], 2000 F, It, E, S, I, SA
Rosser, M A (Penarth) 1924 S, F
Rowland, E M (Lampeter) 1885 E
Rowlands, C F (Aberavon) 1926 I
Rowlands, D C T (Pontypool) 1963 E, S, I, F, NZ, 1964 E, S, I, F, SA, 1965 E, S, I, F
Rowlands, G (RAF, Cardiff) 1953 NZ, 1954 E, F, 1956 F
Rowlands, K A (Cardiff) 1962 F, I, 1963 I, 1965 I, F
Rowles, G A (Penarth) 1892 E
Rowley, M (Pontypridd) 1996 SA, 1997 US, S, I, F, R
Roy, W S (Cardiff) 1995 [J (R)]
Russell, S (London Welsh) 1987 US

Samuel, D (Swansea) 1891 I, 1893 I
Samuel, J (Swansea) 1891 I
Samuel, T F (Mountain Ash) 1922 S, I, F
Scourfield, T B (Torquay Athletic) 1930 F
Scrine, F G (Swansea) 1899 E, S, 1901 I
Selley, T J (Llanelli Scarlets) 2005 US(R)
Shanklin, J L (London Welsh) 1970 F, 1972 NZ, 1973 I, F
Shanklin, T G L (Saracens, Cardiff Blues) 2001 J 2, 2002 F, It, SA 1(R),2(R),R, Fj, 2003 It, E 1, S 1, I 1, F(t+R), A, NZ, S 2, [Tg,NZ], 2004 I(R),F(R),E,It(R),Arg 1(R),2, SA1,2(R),R, NZ,J, 2005 E,It,F,S,I, 2006 A,C,NZ, 2007 S(R),F1,It,E1,2,Arg, [C,A,J(R),Fj], SA, 2008 E(R),S,It,I,F,SA1,2
Shaw, G (Neath) 1972 NZ, 1973 E, S, I, F, A, 1974 S, I, F, E, 1977 I, F
Shaw, T W (Newbridge) 1983 R
Shea, J (Newport) 1919 NZA, 1920 E, S, 1921 E
Shell, R C (Aberavon) 1973 A (R)
Sidoli, R A (Pontypridd, Celtic Warriors, Cardiff Blues) 2002 SA 1(R),2(R),R, Fj, NZ, 2003 It, E 1, S 1, I 1, F, A, NZ, E 2, [C(R),Tg, It(R),NZ,E], 2004 I,It(R), 2005 E,It,F,S,I,C,NZ, Fj(R),SA,A, 2006 E,S,I,It,F,PI,C(R), 2007 I(t&R),S,A1,2,E2
Simpson, H J (Cardiff) 1884 E, S, I
Sinkinson, B D (Neath) 1999 F 1, It, E, Arg 1,2, SA, F 2, [Arg 3, J, Sm, A], 2000 F, It, E, 2001 R (R), I, Arg (R), Tg, A, 2002 It (R)
Skrimshire, R T (Newport) 1899 E, S, I
Skym, A (Llanelli) 1928 E, S, I, F, 1930 E, S, I, F, 1931 E, S, F, I, SA, 1932 E, S, I, 1933 E, S, I, 1935 E
Smith, J S (Cardiff) 1884 E, I, 1885 E
Smith, R (Ebbw Vale) 2000 F (R)
Sowden-Taylor, R (Cardiff Blues) 2005 It(R),C(R),NZ(R), 2007 A2(R),SA
Sparks, B A (Neath) 1954 I, 1955 E, F, 1956 E, S, I, 1957 S
Spiller, W (Cardiff) 1910 S, I, 1911 E, S, F, I, 1912 E, F, SA, 1913 E
Squire, J (Newport, Pontypool) 1977 I, F, 1978 E, S, I, F, A 1, NZ, 1979 S, I, F, E, 1980 F, E, S, I, NZ, 1981 E, S, I, F, A, 1982 I, F, E, 1983 E, S, I, F
Stadden, W J (Cardiff) 1884 I, 1886 E, S, 1887 I, 1888 S, M, 1890 S, E
Stephens, C (Bridgend) 1998 E (R), 2001 J 2(R)
Stephens, C J (Llanelli) 1992 I, F, E, A
Stephens, G (Neath) 1912 E, S, I, F, SA, 1913 E, S, F, I, 1919 NZA
Stephens, I (Bridgend) 1981 E, S, I, F, A, 1982 I, F, E, S, 1984 I, F, E, A
Stephens, Rev J G (Llanelli) 1922 E, S, I, F
Stephens, J R G (Neath) 1947 E, S, F, I, 1948 I, 1949 S, I, F, 1951 F, SA, 1952 E, S, I, F, 1953 E, S, I, F, NZ, 1954 E, I, 1955 E, S, I, F, 1956 S, I, F, 1957 E, S, I, F
Stock, A (Newport) 1924 F, NZ, 1926 E, S
Stoddart, M (Llanelli Scarlets) 2007 SA, 2008 SA1(R)
Stone, P (Llanelli) 1949 F
Strand-Jones, J (Llanelli) 1902 E, S, I, 1903 E, S
Sullivan, A C (Cardiff) 2001 Arg, Tg
Summers, R H B (Haverfordwest) 1881 E
Sutton, S (Pontypool, S Wales Police) 1982 F, E, 1987 F, E, S, I, [C, NZ (R), A]
Sweeney, C (Pontypridd, Celtic Warriors, Newport Gwent Dragons) 2003 It(R), E 1, NZ(R), I 2, S 2, [C,It,NZ(t&R),E(t)], 2004 I(R),F(R),E(R),It(R),Arg 1,SA1(R),2(R),R(R),J, 2005 It(R),F(t), S(R),US,C,NZ,Fj(R),SA(t&R),A(R), 2006 PI,C(R), 2007 S(t),A2(R),E2,F2(R), [J(R)],SA(R)
Sweet-Escott, R B (Cardiff) 1891 S, 1894 I, 1895 I

Tamplin, W E (Cardiff) 1947 S, F, I, A, 1948 E, S, F
Tanner, H (Swansea, Cardiff) 1935 NZ, 1936 E, S, I, 1937 E, S, I, 1938 E, S, I, 1939 E, S, I, 1947 E, S, F, I, 1948 E, S, F, I, 1949 E, S, I, F
Tarr, D J (Swansea, Royal Navy) 1935 NZ
Taylor, A R (Cross Keys) 1937 I, 1938 I, 1939 E
Taylor, C G (Ruabon) 1884 E, S, I, 1885 E, S, 1886 E, S, 1887 E, I
Taylor, H T (Cardiff) 1994 Pt, C, Fj, Tg, WS (R), R, It, SA, 1995 E, S, [J, NZ, I], SA, Fj, 1996 It, E, S, I, F 1, A 1,2, It, A 3

Taylor, J (London Welsh) 1967 S, I, F, E, NZ, 1968 I, F, 1969 S, I, F, E, NZ 1, A, 1970 F, 1971 E, S, I, F, 1972 E, S, F, NZ, 1973 E, S, I, F
Taylor, M (Pontypool, Swansea, Llanelli Scarlets, Sale) 1994 SA, 1995 F, E, SA (R), 1998 Z, SA 1,2, Arg, 1999 I, F 1, It, E, Arg 1,2, SA, F 2, [Arg 3, J, Sm, A], 2000 F, It, E, S, Sm, US, 2001 E, S, F, It, 2002 S, SA 1,2, 2003 E 1, S 1, I 1, F, A, NZ, E 2, [C(R),Tg,NZ,E], 2004 F,E,It,R(R), 2005 I,US,C,NZ
Thomas, A C (Bristol, Swansea) 1996 It, E, S, I, F 2(R), SA, 1997 US, S, I, F, US 1,2, C, R, NZ (t), 1998 It, E, S (R), Z, SA 1, 2000 Sm, US, SA (R)
Thomas, A R F (Newport) 1963 NZ, 1964 E
Thomas, A G (Swansea, Cardiff) 1952 E, S, I, F, 1953 S, I, F, 1954 E, I, F, 1955 S, I, F
Thomas, B (Neath, Cambridge U) 1963 E, S, I, F, NZ, 1964 E, S, I, F, SA, 1965 E, 1966 E, S, I, 1967 NZ, 1969 S, I, F, E, NZ 1,2
Thomas, B M G (St Bart's Hospital) 1919 NZA, 1921 S, F, I, 1923 F, 1924 E
Thomas, C J (Newport) 1888 I, M, 1889 S, I, 1890 S, E, I, 1891 E, I
Thomas, C R (Bridgend) 1925 E, S
Thomas, D J (Swansea) 1904 E, 1908 A, 1910 E, S, I, 1911 E, S, F, I, 1912 E
Thomas, D J (Swansea) 1930 S, I, 1932 E, S, I, 1933 E, S, 1934 E, 1935 E, S, I
Thomas, D L (Neath) 1937 E
Thomas, D L (Aberavon) 1961 I
Thomas, E (Newport) 1904 S, I, 1909 S, F, I, 1910 F
Thomas, E J R (Mountain Ash) 1906 SA, 1908 F, I, 1909 S
Thomas, G (Newport) 1888 M, 1890 I, 1891 S
Thomas, G (Bridgend, Cardiff, Celtic Warriors, Toulouse, Cardiff Blues) 1995 [J, NZ, I], SA, Fj, 1996 F 1, A 1,2, Bb, F 2, It, A 3, 1997 US, S, I, F, E, US 1,2, C, R, Tg, NZ, 1998 It, E, S, I, F, SA 2, Arg, 1999 F 1(R), It, E, Arg 2, SA, F 2, [Arg 3, J (R), Sm, A], 2000 F, It, E, S, I, US (R), SA, 2001 E, F, It, J 1,2, R, Arg, Tg, A, 2002 E, R, Fj, C, NZ, 2003 It, E 1, S 1, I 1, F, I 2, E 2, [C,It,NZ(R),E], 2004 S,I,F,E,It,SA2,R,NZ, 2005 E,It,F,NZ,SA,A, 2006 E,S,A,C, 2007 It(t&R),E1,A1,2,E2,Arg,F2, [C(R),A,Fj]
Thomas, G V (Bath, Ospreys, Llanelli Scarlets) 2001 J 1,2, R, I (R), Arg, Tg (R), A (R), 2002 S (R), SA 2(R),R(R), 2003 It(R), E 1, S 1, F, E 2(R), R, 2006 Arg 1,2,PI, 2007 I(t&R),A1,2
Thomas, H M (Llanelli) 1912 F
Thomas, H W (Swansea) 1912 SA, 1913 E
Thomas, H W (Neath) 1936 E, S, I, 1937 E, S, I
Thomas, I (Bryncethin) 1924 E
Thomas, I D (Ebbw Vale, Llanelli Scarlets) 2000 Sm, US (R), SA (R), 2001 J 1,2, R, I, Arg (R), Tg, 2002 It, E, S, SA 1,2, Fj, C, NZ, 2003 It, E 1, S 1, I 1, F, A, NZ, E 2, [Tg,NZ,E], 2004 I,F, 2007 A1,2,E2
Thomas, J (Swansea, Ospreys) 2003 A, NZ(R), E 2(R), R, [It(R),NZ,E], 2004 S(t&R),I, F,E,Arg 2(R),SA1(R),R(t&R),J, 2005 E(R),It,F(R),S(R),US,C,NZ, 2006 It(R),F(R),A, PI(R),C,NZ, 2007 S(R),F1(R),It(R),E1(R),A1,2,Arg,F2, [C,A], SA, 2008 E,S,It,I,F,SA1,2
Thomas, J D (Llanelli) 1954 I
Thomas, L C (Cardiff) 1885 E, S
Thomas, M C (Newport, Devonport Services) 1949 F, 1950 E, S, I, F, 1951 E, S, I, F, SA, 1952 E, S, I, F, 1953 E, 1956 E, S, I, F, 1957 E, S, 1958 E, S, I, F, 1959 I, F
Thomas, N (Bath) 1996 SA (R), 1997 US 1(R),2, C (R), R, Tg, NZ, 1998 Z, SA 1
Thomas, R (Swansea) 1900 E, S, I, 1901 E
Thomas, R (Pontypool) 1909 F, I, 1911 S, F, 1912 E, S, SA, 1913 E
Thomas, Rhys (Newport Gwent Dragons) 2006 Arg 2(R), 2007 E2(R),SA, 2008 It,SA2
Thomas, R C C (Swansea) 1949 F, 1952 I, F, 1953 S, I, F, NZ, 1954 E, I, F, S, 1955 S, I, 1956 E, S, I, 1957 E, 1958 A, E, S, I, F, 1959 E, S, I, F
Thomas, R L (London Welsh) 1889 S, I, 1890 I, 1891 E, S, I, 1892 E
Thomas, S (Llanelli) 1890 S, E, 1891 I
Thomas, S G (Llanelli) 1923 E, S, F, I
Thomas, T R (Cardiff Blues) 2005 US(R),C,NZ(R),Fj,SA,A, 2006E,S,I,It,F,PI,C(R),NZ, 2007 I,S,F1(R),It(R),E1(R),2(R), F2(R), [C(R),A(R),J,Fj(R)],SA(R), 2008 SA2(R)
Thomas, W D (Llanelli) 1966 A, 1968 S, I, F, 1969 E, NZ 2, A, 1970 SA, S, E, I, F, 1971 E, S, I, F, 1972 E, S, F, NZ, 1973 E, S, I, F, 1974 E
Thomas, W G (Llanelli, Waterloo, Swansea) 1927 E, S, F, I, 1929 E, 1931 E, S, SA, 1932 E, S, I, 1933 E, S, I
Thomas, W H (Llandovery Coll, Cambridge U) 1885 S, 1886 E, S, 1887 E, S, 1888 S, I, 1890 E, I, 1891 S, I
Thomas, W J (Cardiff) 1961 F, 1963 F
Thomas, W J L (Llanelli, Cardiff) 1995 SA, Fj, 1996 It, E, S, I, F 1, 1996 Bb (R), 1997 US
Thomas, W L (Newport) 1894 S, 1895 E, I
Thomas, W T (Abertillery) 1930 E
Thompson, J F (Cross Keys) 1923 E
Thorburn, P H (Neath) 1985 F, E, Fj, 1986 E, S, I, F, 1987 F, [I, Tg, C, E, NZ, A], US, 1988 S, I, F, WS, R (R), 1989 S, I, F, E, NZ, 1990 F, E, S, I, Nm 1,2, Bb, 1991 E, S, I, F 1, A
Titley, M H (Bridgend, Swansea) 1983 R, 1984 S, I, F, E, A, 1985 S, I, Fj, 1986 F, Fj, Tg, WS, 1990 F, E
Towers, W H (Swansea) 1887 I, 1888 M
Travers, G (Pill Harriers, Newport) 1903 E, S, I, 1905 E, S, I, NZ, 1906 E, S, I, SA, 1907 E, S, I, 1908 E, S, F, I, A, 1909 E, S, I, 1911 S, F, I
Travers, W H (Newport) 1937 S, I, 1938 E, S, I, 1939 E, S, I, 1949 E, S, I, F
Treharne, E (Pontypridd) 1881 E, 1883 E
Trew, W J (Swansea) 1900 E, S, I, 1901 E, S, 1903 S, 1905 S, 1906 S, 1907 E, S, 1908 E, S, F, I, A, 1909 E, S, F, I, 1910 F, E, S, 1911 E, S, F, I, 1912 S, 1913 S, F
Trott, R F (Cardiff) 1948 E, S, F, I, 1949 E, S, I, F
Truman, W H (Llanelli) 1934 E, 1935 E
Trump, L C (Newport) 1912 E, S, I, F
Turnbull, B R (Cardiff) 1925 I, 1927 E, S, 1928 E, F, 1930 S
Turnbull, M J L (Cardiff) 1933 E, I
Turner, P (Newbridge) 1989 I (R), F, E

Uzzell, H (Newport) 1912 E, S, I, F, 1913 S, F, I, 1914 E, S, F, I, 1920 E, S, F, I
Uzzell, J R (Newport) 1963 NZ, 1965 E, S, I, F

Vickery, W E (Aberavon) 1938 E, S, I, 1939 E
Vile, T H (Newport) 1908 E, S, 1910 I, 1912 I, F, SA, 1913 E, 1921 S
Vincent, H C (Bangor) 1882 I
Voyle, M J (Newport, Llanelli, Cardiff) 1996 A 1(t), F 2, 1997 E, US 1,2, C, Tg, NZ, 1998 It, E, S, I, F, Arg (R), 1999 S (R), I (t), It (R), SA (R), F 2(R), [J, A (R)], 2000 F (R)

Wakeford, J D M (S Wales Police) 1988 WS, R
Waldron, R G (Neath) 1965 E, S, I, F
Walker, N (Cardiff) 1993 I, F, J, 1994 S, F, E, Pt, Sp, 1995 F, E, 1997 US 1,2, C, R (R), Tg, NZ, 1998 E
Waller, P D (Newport) 1908 A, 1909 E, S, F, I, 1910 F
Walne, N J (Richmond, Cardiff) 1999 It (R), E (R), C
Walters, N (Llanelli) 1902 E
Wanbon, R (Aberavon) 1968 E
Ward, W S (Cross Keys) 1934 S, I
Warlow, D J (Llanelli) 1962 I
Waters, D R (Newport) 1986 E, S, I, F
Waters, K (Newbridge) 1991 [WS]
Watkins, D (Newport) 1963 E, S, I, F, NZ, 1964 E, S, I, F, SA, 1965 E, S, I, F, 1966 E, S, I, F, 1967 I, F, E
Watkins, E (Neath) 1924 E, S, I, F
Watkins, E (Blaina) 1926 S, I, F
Watkins, E V (Cardiff) 1935 NZ, 1937 S, I, 1938 E, S, I, 1939 E, S
Watkins, H V (Llanelli) 1904 S, I, 1905 E, S, I, 1906 E
Watkins, I J (Ebbw Vale) 1988 E (R), S, I, F, NZ 2, R, 1989 S, I, F, E
Watkins, L (Oxford U, Llandaff) 1881 E
Watkins, M J (Newport) 1984 I, F, E, A
Watkins, M J (Llanelli Scarlets) 2003 It(R), E 1(R), S 1(R), I 1(R), R, S 2, 2005 US(R),C(R),Fj,SA(R),A, 2006 E,S,I,It,F,Arg 1,2(R)
Watkins, S J (Newport, Cardiff) 1964 S, I, F, 1965 E, S, I, F, 1966 E, S, I, F, A, 1967 S, I, F, E, NZ, 1968 E, S, 1969 S, I, F, E, NZ 1, 1970 E, I
Watkins, W R (Newport) 1959 F
Watts, D (Maesteg) 1914 E, S, F, I
Watts, J (Llanelli) 1907 E, S, I, 1908 E, S, F, I, A, 1909 S, F, I

Watts, W H (Newport) 1892 E, S, I, 1893 E, S, I, 1894 E, S, I, 1895 E, I, 1896 E
Watts, W J (Llanelli) 1914 E
Weatherley, D J (Swansea) 1998 Z
Weaver, D S (Swansea) 1964 E
Webb, A (Jim) (Abertillery) 1907 S, 1908 E, S, F, I, A, 1909 E, S, F, I, 1910 F, E, S, I, 1911 E, S, F, I, 1912 E, S
Webb, J (Newport) 1888 M, 1889 S
Webbe, G M C (Bridgend) 1986 Tg (R), WS, 1987 F, E, S, [Tg], US, 1988 F (R), NZ 1, R
Webster, R E (Swansea) 1987 [A], 1990 Bb, 1991 [Arg, A], 1992 I, F, E, S, A, 1993 E, S, I, F
Wells, G T (Cardiff) 1955 E, S, 1957 I, F, 1958 A, E, S
Westacott, D (Cardiff) 1906 I
Wetter, J J (Newport) 1914 S, F, I, 1920 E, S, F, I, 1921 E, 1924 I, NZ
Wetter, W H (Newport) 1912 SA, 1913 E
Wheel, G A D (Swansea) 1974 I, E (R), 1975 F, E, I, A, 1976 E, S, I, F, 1977 I, E, S, 1978 E, S, I, F, A 1,2, NZ, 1979 S, I, 1980 F, E, S, I, 1981 E, S, I, F, A, 1982 I
Wheeler, P J (Aberavon) 1967 NZ, 1968 E
Whitefoot, J (Cardiff) 1984 A (R), 1985 S, I, F, E, Fj, 1986 E, S, I, F, Fj, Tg, WS, 1987 F, E, S, I, [I, C]
Whitfield, J J (Newport) 1919 NZA, 1920 E, S, F, I, 1921 E, 1922 E, S, I, F, 1924 S, I
Whitson, G K (Newport) 1956 F, 1960 S, I
Wilkins, G (Bridgend) 1994 Tg
Williams, A (Ospreys, Bath) 2003 R (R), 2005 v US(R),C(R), 2006 Arg 2(R), 2007 A2(R)
Williams, B (Llanelli) 1920 S, F, I
Williams, B H (Neath, Richmond, Bristol) 1996 F 2, 1997 R, Tg, NZ, 1998 It, E, Z (R), SA 1, Arg (R), 1999 S (R), I, It (R), 2000 F (R), It (R), E (t+R), 2001 R (R), I (R), Tg (R), A (R), 2002 I (R), F (R), It (R), E (R), S
Williams, B L (Cardiff) 1947 E, S, F, I, A, 1948 E, S, F, I, 1949 E, S, I, 1951 I, SA, 1952 S, 1953 E, S, I, F, NZ, 1954 S, 1955 E
Williams, B R (Neath) 1990 S, I, Bb, 1991 E, S
Williams, C (Llanelli) 1924 NZ, 1925 E
Williams, C (Aberavon, Swansea) 1977 E, S, 1980 F, E, S, I, NZ, 1983 E
Williams, C D (Cardiff, Neath) 1955 F, 1956 F
Williams, D (Ebbw Vale) 1963 E, S, I, F, 1964 E, S, I, F, SA, 1965 E, S, I, F, 1966 E, S, I, A, 1967 F, E, NZ, 1968 E, 1969 S, I, F, E, NZ 1,2, A, 1970 SA, S, E, I, 1971 E, S, I, F
Williams, D (Llanelli) 1998 SA 1(R)
Williams, D A (Bridgend, Swansea) 1990 Nm 2(R), 1995 Fj (R)
Williams, D B (Newport, Swansea) 1978 A 1, 1981 E, S
Williams, E (Neath) 1924 NZ, 1925 F
Williams, E (Aberavon) 1925 E, S
Williams, F L (Cardiff) 1929 S, F, I, 1930 E, S, I, F, 1931 F, I, SA, 1932 E, S, I, 1933 I
Williams, G (London Welsh) 1950 I, F, 1951 E, S, I, F, SA, 1952 E, S, I, F, 1953 NZ, 1954 E
Williams, G (Bridgend) 1981 I, F, 1982 E (R), S
Williams, G J (Bridgend, Cardiff) 2003 It(R), E 1(R), S 1, F(R), E 2(R)
Williams, G M (Aberavon) 1936 E, S, I
Williams, G P (Bridgend) 1980 NZ, 1981 E, S, A, 1982 I
Williams, G R (Cardiff Blues) 2000 I, Sm, US, SA, 2001 S, F, It, R (R), I (R), Arg, Tg (R), A (R), 2002 F (R), It (R), E (R), S, SA 1,2, R, Fj, C, NZ, 2003 It, E 1, S 1, I 1, F, A, NZ, E 2, [Tg,It(R)], 2004 S,I,F,E,It,Arg1,R,J, 2005 F(R),S,US,C
Williams, H R (Llanelli) 1954 S, 1957 F, 1958 A
Williams, J F (London Welsh) 1905 I, NZ, 1906 S, SA
Williams, J J (Llanelli) 1973 F (R), A, 1974 S, I, F, E, 1975 F, E, S, I, A, 1976 E, S, I, F, 1977 I, F, E, S, 1978 E, S, I, F, A 1,2, NZ, 1979 S, I, F, E
Williams, J L (Cardiff) 1906 SA, 1907 E, S, I, 1908 E, S, I, A, 1909 E, S, F, I, 1910 I, 1911 E, S, F, I
Williams, J L (Blaina) 1920 E, S, F, I, 1921 S, F, I
Williams, J P R (London Welsh, Bridgend) 1969 S, I, F, E, NZ 1,2, A, 1970 SA, S, E, I, F, 1971 E, S, I, F, 1972 E, S, F, NZ, 1973 E, S, I, F, A, 1974 S, I, F, 1975 F, E, S, I, A, 1976 E, S, I, F, 1977 I, F, E, S, 1978 E, S, I, F, A 1,2, NZ, 1979 S, I, F, E, 1980 NZ, 1981 E, S
Williams, L H (Cardiff) 1957 S, I, F, 1958 E, S, I, F, 1959 E, S, I, 1961 F, 1962 E, S
Williams, M E (Pontypridd, Cardiff Blues) 1996 Bb, F 2, It (t), 1998 It, E, Z, SA 2, Arg, 1999 S, I, C, J, [Sm], 2000 E (R), 2001 E, S, F, It, 2002 I, F, It, E, S, SA 1,2, Fj, C, NZ, 2003 It, E 1, S 1, I 1, F, A, NZ, E 2, [C,Tg(R),It,E(R)], 2004 S,I, F(t&R),E(R),It, SA2(t&R),R(R),NZ(R),J(R), 2005 E,It,F,S,I,Fj, SA,A, 2006 E,S,I,It,F,A,C,NZ, 2007 I,S,F1,It,E1,Arg,F2, [C,A, J,Fj], 2008 E,S,It,I,F
Williams, M T (Newport) 1923 F
Williams, O (Llanelli) 1947 E, S, A, 1948 E, S, F, I
Williams, O L (Bridgend) 1990 Nm 2
Williams, R D G (Newport) 1881 E
Williams, R F (Cardiff) 1912 SA, 1913 E, S, 1914 I
Williams, R H (Llanelli) 1954 I, F, S, 1955 S, I, F, 1956 E, S, I, 1957 E, S, I, F, 1958 A, E, S, I, F, 1959 E, S, I, F, 1960 E
Williams, S (Llanelli) 1947 E, S, F, I, 1948 S, F
Williams, S A (Aberavon) 1939 E, S, I
Williams, S M (Neath, Cardiff, Northampton) 1994 Tg, 1996 E (t), A 1,2, Bb, F 2, It, A 3, SA, 1997 US, S, I, F, E, US 1,2(R), C, R (R), Tg (R), NZ (t+R), 2002 SA 1,2, R, Fj(R), 2003 It, E 1, S 1, F(R)
Williams, S M (Neath, Ospreys) 2000 F (R), It, E, S, I, Sm, SA (R), 2001 J 1,2, I, 2003 R, [NZ,E], 2004 S,I,F,E,It,Arg 1,2,SA1,2,NZ,J, 2005 E,It,F,S,I,NZ,Fj,SA,A, 2006 E,S,It,F, Arg 1,2,A,PI(R),C,NZ, 2007 F1,It,E1,F2, [C,A,J,Fj], 2008 E,S,It,I,F,SA1,2
Williams, T (Pontypridd) 1882 I
Williams, T (Swansea) 1888 S, I
Williams, T (Swansea) 1912 I, 1913 F, 1914 E, S, F, I
Williams, T (Swansea) 1921 F
Williams, T G (Cross Keys) 1935 S, I, NZ, 1936 E, S, I, 1937 S, I
Williams, W A (Crumlin) 1927 E, S, F, I
Williams, W A (Newport) 1952 I, F, 1953 E
Williams, W E O (Cardiff) 1887 S, I, 1889 S, 1890 S, E
Williams, W H (Pontymister) 1900 E, S, I, 1901 E
Williams, W L T (Llanelli, Cardiff) 1947 E, S, F, I, A, 1948 I, 1949 E
Williams, W O G (Swansea, Devonport Services) 1951 F, SA, 1952 E, S, I, F, 1953 E, S, I, F, NZ, 1954 E, I, F, S, 1955 E, S, I, F, 1956 E, S, I
Williams, W P J (Neath) 1974 I, F
Williams-Jones, H (S Wales Police, Llanelli) 1989 S (R), 1990 F (R), I, 1991 A, 1992 S, A, 1993 E, S, I, F, Z 1, Nm, 1994 Fj, Tg, WS (R), It (t), 1995 E (R)
Willis, W R (Cardiff) 1950 E, S, I, F, 1951 E, S, I, F, SA, 1952 E, S, 1953 S, NZ, 1954 E, I, F, S, 1955 E, S, I, F
Wiltshire, M L (Aberavon) 1967 NZ, 1968 E, S, F
Windsor, R W (Pontypool) 1973 A, 1974 S, I, F, E, 1975 F, E, S, I, A, 1976 E, S, I, F, 1977 I, F, E, S, 1978 E, S, I, F, A 1,2, NZ, 1979 S, I, F
Winfield, H B (Cardiff) 1903 I, 1904 E, S, I, 1905 NZ, 1906 E, S, I, 1907 S, I, 1908 E, S, F, I, A
Winmill, S (Cross Keys) 1921 E, S, F, I
Wintle, M E (Llanelli) 1996 It
Wintle, R V (London Welsh) 1988 WS (R)
Wooller, W (Sale, Cambridge U, Cardiff) 1933 E, S, I, 1935 E, S, I, NZ, 1936 E, S, I, 1937 E, S, I, 1938 S, I, 1939 E, S, I
Wyatt, C P (Llanelli) 1998 Z (R), SA 1(R),2, Arg, 1999 S, I, F 1, It, E, Arg 1,2, SA, C (R), F 2, [Arg 3, J (R), Sm, A], 2000 F, It, E, US, SA, 2001 E, R, I, Arg (R), Tg (R), A (R), 2002 I, It (R), E, S (R), 2003 A(R), NZ(t+R), E 2, [Tg(R),NZ(R)]
Wyatt, G (Pontypridd, Celtic Warriors) 1997 Tg, 2003 R (R)
Wyatt, M A (Swansea) 1983 E, S, I, F, 1984 A, 1985 S, I, 1987 E, S, I

Yapp, J (Cardiff Blues) 2005 E(R),It(R),F(R),S(R),I(R),C(R),Fj, 2006 Arg 1(R)
Young, D (Swansea, Cardiff) 1987 [E, NZ], US, 1988 E, S, I, F, NZ 1,2, WS, R, 1989 S, NZ, 1990 F, 1996 A 3, SA, 1997 US, S, I, F, E, R, NZ, 1998 It, E, S, I, F, 1999 I, E (R), Arg 1(R),2(R), SA, C (R), F 2, [Arg 3, J, Sm, A], 2000 F, It, E, S, I, 2001 E, S, F, It, R, I, Arg
Young, G A (Cardiff) 1886 E, S
Young, J (Harrogate, RAF, London Welsh) 1968 S, I, F, 1969 S, I, F, E, NZ 1, 1970 E, I, F, 1971 E, S, I, F, 1972 E, S, F, NZ, 1973 E, S, I, F
Young, P (Gwent Dragons) 2003 R (R)

ALL BLACKS AT THE DOUBLE

Neath became the first side in the semi-professional era in the Principality to complete the league and cup double to underline their recent, unrivalled superiority in the club game in Wales and in the process finally exorcised the ghosts of previous failures to land the domestic clean sweep.

The Welsh All Blacks wrapped up their fourth successive Principality Premiership title in April after 23 of their scheduled 26 league outings and were confirmed as Minolta Konica Cup champions in May after a 28–22 triumph over Pontypridd at the Millennium Stadium.

The club's Premiership triumph was their sixth since the introduction of the league format in 1990. Inaugural winners of the title 18 years ago, Neath were also crowned champions in 1996 and 2006 but on both occasions were denied the double after they were beaten by Pontypridd in the cup final.

However it proved to be third time lucky in 2008 as the All Blacks once again met their old foes in Cardiff and although Ponty had the psychological advantage having already recorded home and away league wins over their West Glamorgan rivals, it was Neath who held their nerve in a titanic struggle in the capital to emerge 28–22 winners.

The league season began at the start of September and it was clear from the outset that Neath were eager to pick up where they had left off from the previous campaign and four successive victories in their opening fixtures against Bridgend, Llanelli, Glamorgan Wanderers and Maesteg, in which the All Blacks averaged over 27 points per game, sent out an unequivocal message that the champions meant business once again.

The run came to an abrupt and surprising end in October when Ebbw Vale were the visitors to the Gnoll. Neath were widely expected to dispatch the Steelmen with the minimum of fuss but two tries from James Lewis inspired the visitors and Ebbw Vale pulled off a shock 24–17 win which, coupled with Cardiff's narrow victory over Bridgend at the Brewery Field, saw the All Blacks surrender top spot in the table.

It was to be a fleeting setback. Cardiff lost their next two games to

Glamorgan Wanderers and Ebbw Vale while Neath recorded three successive victories and normal service was partially resumed.

The month of November however was to severely test the All Blacks' title credentials. An unspectacular 19–12 win over Cross Keys was routine enough but they were ambushed 15–10 by Pontypridd at Sardis Road the following week courtesy of Gavin Dacey's second-half try and a late penalty from Neil Burnett for the home side and when Cardiff came away from the Gnoll with a 20–13 win seven days later, there were real questions hanging over the champions' ability to defend their title.

The double blow may have fostered serious self doubt in a lesser side but Neath now set about proving their mettle. A month's hiatus from league action allowed the club to regroup and when they took to the field again for a Boxing Day clash with Aberavon, they were back to their dominant best and ran out 43–12 winners.

It was to be the catalyst for a nine-match unbeaten run. Llanelli held the All Blacks to an 18–18 draw at the Gnoll in early January but seven wins, including an 80–0 massacre of Llandovery, put Neath firmly back into the driving seat. Aberavon sprung a surprise at the Athletic Ground in March when wing Richard Carter scored after just 40 seconds to inspire his side to a 29–22 win but the All Blacks were still honing in on the title. Victory at Bedwas put them within touching distance of the silverware and when Newport were dispatched 23–10 at the Gnoll in mid April, they were all but there.

Three days later the party could begin after Ebbw Vale's convincing 48–20 defeat of Aberavon at Eugene Cross Park – a result which confirmed Neath as the Premiership champions for a fourth successive season and for the sixth time in the club's history.

In truth, the champions took their foot off the pedal in their remaining three league games, losing to both Cardiff and Pontypridd but Rowland Phillips' focus was now firmly on the Konica Minolta Cup final clash with Pontypridd in Cardiff.

The match began with Ponty in the ascendency and they opened the scoring after 10 minutes with a Gareth McCarthy penalty but Neath's pack slowly began to impose themselves and tries from scrum-half Martin Roberts and skipper and number eight Lee Beach saw the All Blacks ease into the lead.

Trailing 14–3 at half-time, Pontypridd found themselves on the back foot once again after the restart and they looked dead and buried when full-back Gareth King touched down for Neath's third try of the afternoon.

To their credit, Ponty refused to lie down and were given renewed hope when wing Matthew Nuthall was shown a yellow card on 66 minutes for killing the ball. Pontypridd kicked to touch and from the resulting lineout, they were awarded a penalty try after Neath were adjudged to have collapsed the maul.

The All Blacks' lead had been cut to a mere four points but any fears the league champions had of snatching defeat from the jaws of victory were quickly allayed. From the restart, Ponty tamely surrendered possession, King made good ground and then sent flanker James Merriman crashing over for what was effectively the winning score. Substitute Tom Riley scored Ponty's third try with the final move of the match to give the final score a greater degree of respectability but Neath had done the hard work and the fabled double was safely in the bag.

The final also proved a perfect send-off for former Wales fly-half Arwel Thomas, who was playing his 100th and final game for the All Blacks. The number 10 had already announced he would be taking up a coaching role with the club and 14 years after pulling on the famous black jersey for the first time, Thomas was delighted to end his playing career on a historic high.

Neath ended the sesson is mourning with the death of scrum-half Gareth Jones, who died age of 28, in June, as a result of injuries suffered while playing in a match on April 20.

Jones was hurt at a ruck in a Welsh Premier Division game against Cardiff at the Arms Park and had received intensive care treatment at the University Hospital of Wales since the incident.

Neath backs coach Gruff Rees said: "Gareth was a wonderfully loyal and honest person. He was a real character, and the heartbeat and energy of any side he played for.

"He was a positive free spirit, who had so many close friends in the club and elsewhere."

PRINCIPALITY PREMIERSHIP 2007–08 RESULTS

1 September, 2007: **Aberavon** 13 **Llanelli** 26, **Bedwas** 12 **Pontypridd** 21, **Cross Keys** 21 **Cardiff** 35, **Ebbw Vale** 25 **Swansea** 26, **Neath** 42 **Bridgend** 6, **Newport** 3 **Llandovery** 6, **Wanderers** 41 **Maesteg** 28. 8 September, 2007: **Bedwas** 54 **Llandovery** 25, **Bridgend** 15 **Newport** 27, **Cardiff** 25 **Aberavon** 23, **Llanelli** 10 **Neath** 17, **Maesteg** 13 **Ebbw Vale** 13, **Pontypridd** 33 **Swansea** 20, **Wanderers** 20 **Cross Keys** 21. 22 September, 2007: **Cross Keys** 25 **Bedwas** 26, **Ebbw Vale** 28 **Bridgend** 13, **Llandovery** 27 **Pontypridd** 35, **Llanelli** 53 **Maesteg** 19, **Neath** 27 **Wanderers** 15, **Newport** 20 **Aberavon** 24, **Swansea** 34 **Cardiff**

34. 29 September, 2007: **Aberavon** 17 **Ebbw Vale** 22, **Bedwas** 19 **Wanderers** 25, **Llandovery** 10 **Cardiff** 26, **Llanelli** 34 **Bridgend** 13, **Maesteg** 16 **Neath** 23, **Pontypridd** 6 **Cross Keys** 22, **Swansea** 22 **Newport** 26. 13 October, 2007: **Aberavon** 23 **Pontypridd** 12, **Bedwas** 19 **Swansea** 6, **Bridgend** 15 **Cardiff** 18, **Cross Keys** 37 **Llandovery** 10, **Neath** 17 **Ebbw Vale** 24, **Newport** 20 **Maesteg** 0, **Wanderers** 15 **Llanelli** 15. 20 October, 2007: **Bridgend** 16 **Aberavon** 19, **Cardiff** 12 **Wanderers** 18, **Cross Keys** 18 **Llanelli** 23, **Ebbw Vale** 15 **Bedwas** 12, **Llandovery** 6 **Neath** 41, **Pontypridd** 19 **Newport** 3, **Swansea** 29 **Maesteg** 13. 27 October, 2007: **Aberavon** 19 **Swansea** 18, **Bridgend** 33 **Llandovery** 14, **Ebbw Vale** 12 **Cardiff** 9, **Llanelli** 13 **Pontypridd** 13, **Maesteg** 10 **Cross Keys** 10, **Neath** 34, **Bedwas** 13, **Wanderers** 20 **Newport** 16. 3 November, 2007: **Aberavon** 15 **Wanderers** 18, **Bedwas** 30 **Llanelli** 15, **Cardiff** 21 **Newport** 16 **Llandovery** 35 **Maesteg** 17, **Neath** 19 **Cross Keys** 12, **Pontypridd** 12 **Ebbw Vale** 16, **Swansea** 23 **Bridgend** 16. 10 November, 2007: **Bedwas** 27 **Maesteg** 28, **Cross Keys** 23 **Bridgend** 17, **Llandovery** 15 **Aberavon** 20 **Llanelli** 37 **Cardiff** 13, **Newport** 11 **Ebbw Vale** 12, **Pontypridd** 15 **Neath** 10, **Swansea** 9 **Wanderers** 26. 17 November, 2007: **Aberavon** 30 **Cross Keys** 6, **Bridgend** 27 **Bedwas** 27, **Maesteg** 9 **Pontypridd** 41, **Neath** 13 **Cardiff** 20, **Swansea** 30 **Llandovery** 9, **Wanderers** 16 **Ebbw Vale** 8. 23 November, 2007: **Newport** 33 **Llanelli** 19. 1 December, 2007: **Cardiff** 28 **Maesteg** 5, **Cross Keys** 18 **Swansea** 7, **Ebbw Vale** 16 **Llanelli** 0. 22 December, 2007: **Cardiff** 29 **Bedwas** 8, **Newport** 19 **Cross Keys** 14, **Wanderers** 16 **Pontypridd** 20, **Llanelli** 19 **Swansea** 19. 26 December, 2007: **Ebbw Vale** 31 **Llandovery** 13, **Maesteg** 3 **Bridgend** 8, **Neath** 43 **Aberavon** 12. 29 December, 2007: **Aberavon** 25 **Maesteg** 21, **Bedwas** 21 **Newport** 8, **Bridgend** 12 **Wanderers** 7, **Cross Keys** 11 **Ebbw Vale** 10, **Llandovery** 3 **Llanelli** 28, **Swansea** 14 **Neath** 27, **Pontypridd** 10 **Cardiff** 23. 5 January, 2008: **Aberavon** 42 **Cardiff** 14, **Cross Keys** 13 **Wanderers** 8, **Ebbw Vale** 28 **Maesteg** 13, **Llandovery** 7 **Bedwas** 25, **Neath** 18 **Llanelli** 18, **Newport** 16 **Bridgend** 12, **Swansea** 10 **Pontypridd** 8. 12 January, 2008: **Aberavon** 27 **Newport** 15, **Bedwas** 14 **Cross Keys** 18, **Bridgend** 32 **Ebbw Vale** 18, **Maesteg** 17 **Llanelli** 13, **Pontypridd** 29 **Llandovery** 7, **Wanderers** 22 **Neath** 35. 13 January, 2008: **Cardiff** 5 **Swansea** 14. 19 January, 2008: **Bridgend** 9 **Llanelli** 7, **Cardiff** 15 **Llandovery** 0, **Cross Keys** 0 **Pontypridd** 13, **Neath** 17 **Maesteg** 6, **Newport** 15 **Swansea** 18, **Wanderers** 14 **Bedwas** 0. 30 January, 2008: **Cardiff** 23 **Cross Keys** 19. 8 February, 2008 **Cardiff** 12 **Bridgend** 10, **Ebbw Vale** 12 **Neath** 22, **Llandovery** 19 **Cross Keys** 5, **Llanelli** 9 **Wanderers** 3, **Maesteg** 27 **Newport** 39, **Pontypridd** 23 **Aberavon** 10, **Swansea** 10 **Bedwas** 3. 22 February, 2008: **Bridgend** 16 **Neath** 23. 1 March, 2008: **Aberavon** 33 **Bridgend** 3, **Bedwas** 23 **Ebbw Vale** 20, **Llanelli** 32 **Cross Keys** 26, **Maesteg** 15 **Swansea** 30, **Neath** 80 **Llandovery** 0 **Newport** 36 **Pontypridd** 31, **Wanderers** 3 **Cardiff** 26. 5 March, 2008: **Newport** 16 **Neath** 28. 7 March, 2008: **Pontypridd** 9 **Bedwas** 6. 14 March, 2008: **Bridgend** 10 **Swansea** 25, **Cross Keys** 9 **Neath** 21, **Ebbw Vale** 13 **Pontypridd** 6, **Llanelli** 12 **Bedwas** 13, **Maesteg** 20 **Llandovery** 10, **Wanderers** 10 **Aberavon** 14. 22 March, 2008: **Bedwas** 27 **Cardiff** 11, **Bridgend** 21 **Maesteg** 18, **Cross Keys** 10 **Newport** 14, **Llandovery** 31 **Ebbw Vale** 22, **Pontypridd** 23 **Wanderers** 13. 24 March, 2008: **Aberavon** 29 **Neath** 22, **Swansea** 25 **Llanelli** 24. 25 March, 2008: **Ebbw Vale** 16 **Newport** 12. 29 March, 2008: **Bedwas** 6 **Neath** 17, **Cardiff** 21 **Ebbw Vale** 0, **Cross Keys** 23 **Maesteg** 10, **Llandovery** 10 **Bridgend** 3, **Newport** 16 **Wanderers** 8, **Swansea** 27 **Aberavon** 17. 5 April, 2008: **Cardiff** 38 **Llanelli** 20, **Maesteg** 8 **Bedwas** 30. 8 April, 2008: **Aberavon** 42 **Llandovery** 26, **Newport** 24 **Cardiff** 11. 9 April, 2008: **Pontypridd** 33 **Llanelli** 29, **Wanderers** 6 **Swansea** 13. 12 April, 2008: **Aberavon** 33 **Bedwas** 27, **Bridgend** 20 **Pontypridd** 0, **Llanelli** 13 **Ebbw Vale** 28, **Maesteg** 20 **Cardiff** 24, **Wanderers** 32 **Llandovery** 12, **Neath** 23 **Newport** 10, **Swansea** 23 **Cross Keys** 19. 15 April, 2008: **Ebbw Vale** 48 **Aberavon** 20. 16 April, 2008: **Pontypridd** 31 **Bridgend** 10. 19 April, 2008: **Bedwas** 14 **Bridgend** 17, **Cross Keys** 31 **Aberavon** 14, **Ebbw Vale** 13 **Wanderers** 13, **Llandovery** 15 **Swansea** 26, **Llanelli** 10 **Newport** 17, **Pontypridd** 31 **Maesteg** 26. 20 April, 2008: **Cardiff** 24 **Neath** 22. 26 April, 2008: **Ebbw Vale** 29 **Cross Keys** 12, **Llanelli** 20 **Llandovery** 12, **Newport** 9 **Bedwas** 12. 29 April, 2008: **Bridgend** 23 **Cross Keys** 7. 30 April, 2008: **Llanelli** 28 **Aberavon** 7, **Llandovery** 26 **Wanderers** 10. 2 May, 2008: **Neath** 10 **Pontypridd** 23. **Swansea** 42 **Ebbw Vale** 20. 3 May, 2008: **Bedwas** 31 **Aberavon** 31, **Llandovery** 36 **Newport** 0, **Maesteg** 29 **Wanderers** 24. 6 May, 2008: **Cardiff** 27 **Pontypridd** 26, **Neath** 46 **Swansea** 27. 7 May, 2008: **Maesteg** 24 **Aberavon** 32, **Wanderers** 36 Bridgend 20.

FINAL TABLE 2007–08

	P	W	D	L	For	A	Pts
Neath	26	19	1	6	697	381	93
Cardiff	26	18	1	7	544	449	80
Pontypridd	26	16	1	9	523	411	77
Swansea	26	16	2	8	547	487	76
Ebbw Vale	26	15	2	9	494	430	74
Aberavon	26	15	1	10	591	571	72
Newport	26	12	0	14	441	462	60
Bedwas	26	11	2	13	499	474	60
Llanelli	26	10	4	12	527	468	60
Glam Wdrs	26	10	2	14	439	451	55
Cross Keys	26	10	1	15	430	475	51
Bridgend	26	9	1	16	397	503	47
Llandovery	26	7	0	19	384	691	33
Maesteg	26	4	2	20	415	675	26

LEAGUE ONE EAST

Winners: Pontypool

LEAGUE ONE WEST

Winners: Tonmawr

LEAGUE TWO EAST

Winners: Ystrad Rhondda

LEAGUE TWO WEST

Winners: Felinfoel

LEAGUE THREE EAST

Winners: Brynmawr

LEAGUE THREE SOUTH EAST

Winners: Bedlinog

LEAGUE THREE SOUTH WEST

Winners: BP Llandarcy

LEAGUE THREE WEST

Winners: Ammanford

LEAGUE FOUR EAST

Winners: Gwernyfed

LEAGUE FOUR SOUTH EAST

Winners: Llandaff North

LEAGUE FOUR SOUTH WEST

Winners: Glynneath

LEAGUE FOUR WEST

Winners: Morriston

LEAGUE FOUR NORTH

Winners: Caernarfon

LEAGUE FIVE EAST

Winners: Crumlin

LEAGUE FIVE SOUTH EAST

Winners: Porth Harlequins

LEAGUE FIVE SOUTH CENTRAL

Winners: Aberavon Green Stars

LEAGUE FIVE SOUTH WEST

Winners: Betws

LEAGUE FIVE WEST

Winners: Burry Port

LEAGUE FIVE NORTH

Winners: Pwllheli

LEAGUE SIX EAST

Winners: Hartridge

LEAGUE SIX CENTRAL

Winners: Bryncethin

LEAGUE SIX WEST

Winners: Penlan

KONICA MINOLTA CUP 2007–08 RESULTS

QUARTER-FINALS

25 April, 2008	
Aberavon 32 **Ebbw Vale** 22	**Glam Wdrs** 29 **Newport** 12
Cross Keys 28 **Neath** 44	**Pontypridd** 41 **Bridgend** 11

SEMI-FINALS

26 April, 2008
Aberavon 10 **Pontypridd** 33
27 April, 2008
Glam Wdrs 37 **Neath** 49

FINAL

17 May, Millennium Stadium, Cardiff

NEATH 28 (4G) PONTYPRIDD 22 (2G, 1PG, 1T)

NEATH: G King; K James, S Thomas, J Spratt, M Nuthall; A Thomas, M Roberts; M Jones, A Littehales, R Davies, E Evans, M Morgan, G Gravell, J Merriman, L Beach (captain)

Substitutes: J Richards; C Mitchell; N Downs; S Martin; A Llewellyn; G James; H Thomas

SCORERS Tries: Roberts, Beach, King, Merriman Conversions: A Thomas (4)

PONTYPRIDD: L Price; C Clayton, G Dacey, A Thomas, O Williams; G McCarthy, A Jenkins; I Poley, D Goodfield, S Hobbs, R Savage, C Dicomidis, G Lewis, R Shellard, N Strong (captain)

Substitutes: T Riley; M Hutchings; G Holloway; R Harford; R Williams; L Evans; W O'Connor

SCORERS Tries: Penalty try, L Evans, Riley Conversions: McCarthy (2) Penalty Goal: McCarthy

YELLOW CARD Nuthall (66 mins)

REFEREE N Ballard (Cardiff)

COMBINED TEAMS

Alex Livesey/Getty Images

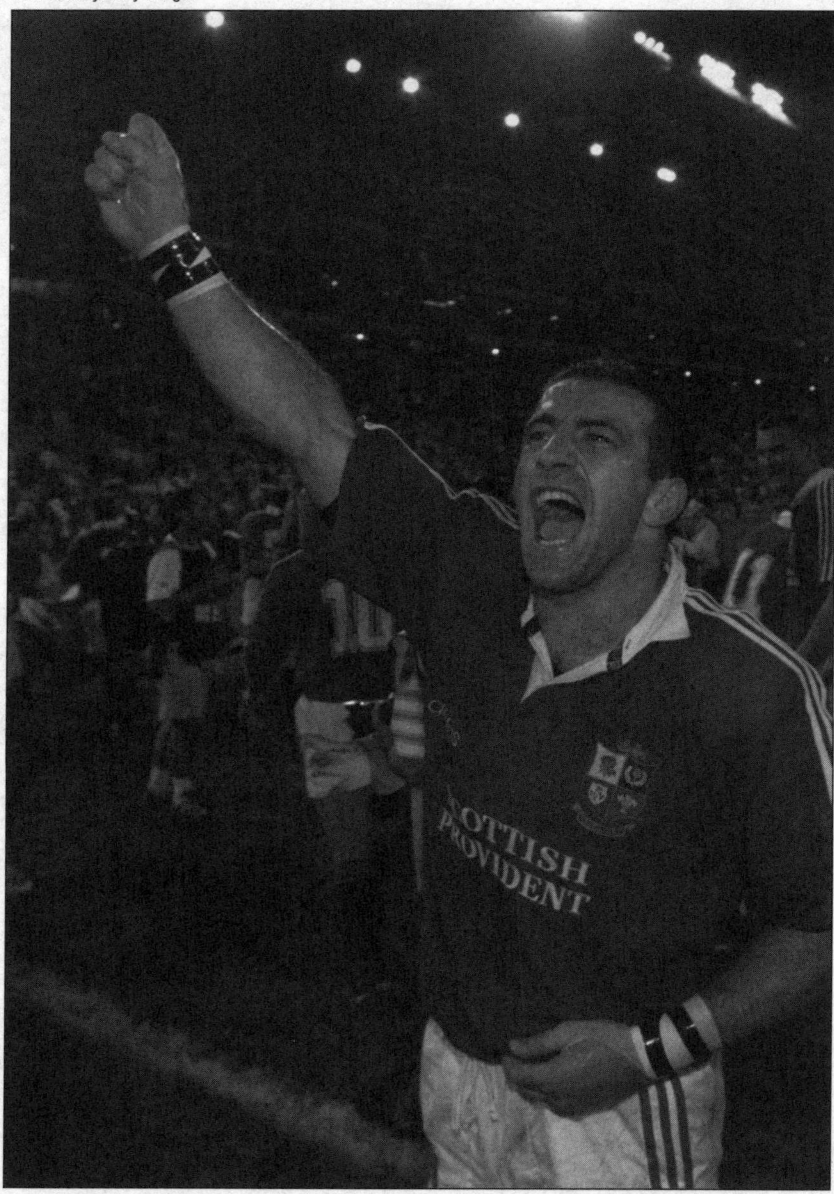

The last time the Lions won a Test series, it was in South Africa in 1997, John Bentley (above) celebrating the victory.

THOSE FAMOUS MEN IN RED

By John Griffiths

The 13th British/Irish Lions party to tour South Africa will be chosen at the end of the 2009 Six Nations. They will follow in the paths of more than 250 of the finest players that the Home Unions have produced during the past 117 years and have a long and distinguished tradition to uphold.

The first tourists to South Africa set out in 1891, three years after a British rugby party had visited Australia and New Zealand. The 1891 visitors were the first, however, to carry the full blessing of the RFU and they were the first to play Test matches overseas.

The team was selected by invitation and comprised mainly Oxbridge men of means, several of whom had gained international honours. The manager was Edwin Ash who, as a former secretary of the RFU and prominent member of the Richmond club, possessed credentials for leadership that were beyond question – a sharp contrast to the suspected professional veil that had cloaked their intrepid entrepreneurial predecessors in New Zealand in 1888.

South African rugby at the time was in its infancy and the touring side captained by veteran Scottish threequarter Bill Maclagen finished with an immaculate record of 19 wins in 19 matches including a 3–0 series victory in the Tests. Moreover, the side conceded only one score on the entire visit.

Even so reports gave an indication of what future tourists would be up against in South Africa. Hard grounds, marked changes in altitude and big, powerful forwards were all noted by Maclagen's team. Even

David Rogers/Getty Images

The Lions could be followed by as many as 30,000 fans in 2009.

so, in 1891 the superior combination and accurate passing of the tourists were too effective for the hosts to contain.

The pattern for relaxation enjoyed by every subsequent touring team was established on this visit. The tourists were regaled at countless receptions, shooting parties and social occasions. Indeed, writing more than forty years later Paul Clauss, the Scottish threequarter, vividly recalled the visit as "all champagne and travel".

There was a missionary element to the expedition as there was five years later when, bolstered by several members of Ireland's Championship-winning pack, the tourists were again unbeaten in the Test series. Ireland hadn't supplied anyone for the original visit, but the names of Louis Magee, Tom Crean and Larry Bulger were among the first writ large in emerald green on the ledger of famous Irish Lions in South Africa.

By 1903 South African rugby was thriving. The 1891 tourists had presented a Cup donated by Sir Donald Currie, the British chairman of the flourishing line that had shipped the team to the Cape. The hosts adopted the trophy as their main domestic rugby prize and the interest the so-called "Currie Cup" competition engendered accelerated the improvement in playing standards.

If the 1891 South Africans were their missionaries' pupils, by 1903 they had become peers, winning the Test series 1–0 with the first two Tests drawn. And since 1910, when the first fully representative British/Irish tour party selected by the Four Home Unions committee visited, the Springboks have invariably proved to be masters.

The 1910, 1924 and 1938 Lions visits were bedevilled by injuries. Less intensive itineraries were demanded but never somehow materialised. Overcrowded match schedules, the effects of heavy tackling on bone-hard grounds and tiresome train journeys took their toll on the players.

All three tour parties to South Africa between 1910 and 1938 found themselves having to dragoon forwards into deputising in unfamiliar positions behind the scrum and, under such circumstances, it was little surprise that the Springboks took each of the three series' with ease.

In 1955, however, a magical tour that captured the imagination of the sporting public back in Britain and Ireland heralded the modern Lions era. It was the first Lions visit to the Republic since the war, the party was the first to fly to its destination and it was the first tour to be covered by members of the British media.

The Lions were led by Irish lock Robin Thompson, but benefited from a strong Welsh influence in the scrum and at fly-half, and had the teenaged Tony O'Reilly on the wing to score the tries.

A fit, mobile Lions pack held the Springboks in check for the first time since 1891. An all-Welsh front-row packed down before a then world record crowd of 95,000 in the first Test at Ellis Park, Johannesburg and, bolstered by giants Rhys Williams, Jim Greenwood and the hard-working English flanker Reg Higgins won plenty of good ball for their exciting backs.

Welsh fly-half Cliff Morgan flourished at the end of Dickie Jeeps's

David Rogers/Getty Images

The Lions will be coached by Ian McGeechan on the Lions tour, the Scot returning to the helm for the first time since 1997.

quick service and set alight an exciting threequarter line that had England's Jeff Butterfield and Phil Davies at its core with Ireland's Cecil Pedlow and O'Reilly on the wings.

The Lions won a breathtaking Test 23–22, the South African full-back missing a conversion with the last act of the game. From the press box, Viv Jenkins (*Sunday Times*) and Bryn Thomas (Cardiff *Western Mail*) rattled out thrilling reports for readers in the Home Unions to absorb.

Their colourful descriptions of the tour's progress created an unprecedented level of interest in rugby in Britain and Ireland. The tourists' departure had barely been announced in the press. By the mid-point of the tour, several newspapers had sent special correspondents out to cover the Lions' progress, and after the tourists had drawn the series 2–2 the team returned in a blaze of glory to heroes' welcomes.

Scotland's Arthur Smith and Ireland's Tom Kiernan led Lions sides that were plagued by injuries during the sixties and each returned with a disappointing Test record of one draw and three defeats in their respective 1962 and 1968 series' with the Springboks. But for the next visit in 1974 the Lions were to enjoy their finest hour of the modern era.

A side led by Willie-John McBride went unbeaten through a 22-match itinerary. They won the Test rubber 3–0 and the only blot on their copybook was a drawn fourth Test in Johannesburg. Numerous scoring records were set by the side and for the first time in the 20th century South Africa were defeated at home in a full-scale series.

The Lions owed their victory to forward mastery and astute back play and the success was a marvellous tribute to McBride. He was making his fifth and last Lions tour – his third to South Africa – and this final triumph was an appropriate reward for his immense contribution to the Lions cause over a 12-year span.

Bill Beaumont, fresh from leading England to a Grand Slam, took the 1980 Lions to South Africa. They were to pass into history as the unluckiest side ever to tour the high veldt. They were popular and well-led by Beaumont and manager Syd Millar, but lost so many key players to injury that eight replacements had to be called during the tour.

They lost the series 3–1, salvaging respect by showing what they might have been capable of with a splendid fightback to win the final Test and thus maintain the record that no Lions team in South Africa has yet suffered the humiliation of a series whitewash.

The apartheid era meant that there was no Lions tour for 17 years until the class of 1997 captained by Martin Johnson and coached by the Scottish wizard Ian McGeechan returned triumphant with a 2–1 series win. McGeechan was an integral part of the brilliant 1974 side out there and will be there again in the summer to plot what the massed

David Rogers/Getty Images

The last time the Lions were in South Africa, in 1997, current England coach Martin Johnson (above with Scott Gibbs, left) was captaining the side.

ranks of British/Irish followers who are lined up for the trip hope will be another Lions triumph.

He will have as his manager Gerald Davies of Wales, a Lion in South Africa in 1968 and star of the 1971 Lions in New Zealand. Davies and McGeechan know that the visit will not be "all champagne and travel"; nor will they concede only one score on tour like their illustrious predecessors of 1891.

They are hard-nosed, experienced rugby realists who have an important job to do. But they are also steeped in the Lions tradition and will do everything in their powers to ensure that everyone with an interest in this tour will enjoy the experience. Roll on May 2009.

Dave Rogers/Getty Images

The world champion Springboks will be waiting for the Lions in May, June and July, just like they did in 1997.

THE 2009 LIONS TOUR

The British and Irish Lions have announced their schedule for the 2009 tour of South Africa. The tour will include three Tests against the reigning world champions, the first on June 20.

British and Irish Lions Chairman Andy Irvine said: "We are looking forward to touring such a wonderful country and playing the World Champions on their own turf, The tour itself promises to be full of challenges in a country where rugby is a real passion but I am confident that the 2009 Lions will acquit themselves well. Lions tours are unique events and as such extremely popular. We are expecting tens of thousands of Lions fans to travel to South Africa in 2009 and are certain that every one of them will come back with amazing memories."

SARU Managing Director Jonathan Stones added: "The Lions tour will be a massive sporting event on a par with Rugby World Cup and is expected to be a huge success.

"We are putting in place an exciting programme and look forward to hosting this unique team.

"It is anticipated that South Africa will reap significant economic benefits from this tour."

Since 1891 the Lions have won 16 Tests against the Springboks and lost 21, while seven Tests have been drawn.

Sat May 30
Highveld XV, Royal Bafokeng
Wed June 3
Golden Lions, Ellis Park, Johannesburg
Sat June 6
Cheetahs, Vodacom Park, Bloemfontein
Wed June 10
Sharks, ABSA Park, Durban
Sat June 13
Western Province, Newlands, Cape Town
Tues or Weds June 16 or 17
Coastal XV
Sat June 20
First Test, ABSA Park, Durban
Tues June 23
Emerging Springboks, Newlands, Cape Town
Sat June 27
Second Test, Loftus Versfeld, Pretoria
Sat July 4
Third Test, Ellis Park, Johannesburg

BRITISH & IRISH LIONS INTERNATIONAL STATISTICS

UP TO 30TH SEPTEMBER 2008

MATCH RECORDS

MOST CONSECUTIVE TEST WINS

6	1891	*SA* 1,2,3,	1896 *SA* 1,2,3
3	1899	*A* 2,3,4	
3	1904	*A* 1,2,3	
3	1950	*A* 1,2,	1955 *SA* 1
3	1974	*SA* 1,2,3	

MOST CONSECUTIVE TESTS WITHOUT DEFEAT

Matches	Wins	Draws	Periods
6	6	0	1891 to 1896
6	4	2	1971 to 1974

MOST POINTS IN A MATCH

BY THE TEAM

Pts.	Opponent	Venue	Year
31	Australia	Brisbane	1966
29	Australia	Brisbane	2001
28	S Africa	Pretoria	1974
26	S Africa	Port Elizabeth	1974
25	S Africa	Cape Town	1997
25	Argentina	Cardiff	2005
24	Australia	Sydney	1950
24	Australia	Sydney	1959

BY A PLAYER

Pts.	Player	Opponent	Venue	Year
20	J P Wilkinson	Argentina	Cardiff	2005
18	A J P Ward	S Africa	Cape Town	1980
18	A G Hastings	N Zealand	Christchurch	1993
18	J P Wilkinson	Australia	Sydney	2001
17	T J Kiernan	S Africa	Pretoria	1968
16	B L Jones	Australia	Brisbane	1950

MOST TRIES IN A MATCH

BY THE TEAM

Tries	Opponent	Venue	Year
5	Australia	Sydney	1950
5	S Africa	Johannesburg	1955
5	Australia	Sydney	1959
5	Australia	Brisbane	1966
5	S Africa	Pretoria	1974

BY A PLAYER

Tries	Player	Opponent	Venue	Year
2	A M Bucher	Australia	Sydney	1899
2	W Llewellyn	Australia	Sydney	1904
2	C D Aarvold	N Zealand	Christchurch	1930
2	J E Nelson	Australia	Sydney	1950
2	M J Price	Australia	Sydney	1959
2	M J Price	N Zealand	Dunedin	1959
2	D K Jones	Australia	Brisbane	1966
2	T G R Davies	N Zealand	Christchurch	1971
2	J J Williams	S Africa	Pretoria	1974
2	J J Williams	S Africa	Port Elizabeth	1974

MOST CONVERSIONS IN A MATCH

BY THE TEAM

Cons	Opponent	Venue	Year
5	Australia	Brisbane	1966
4	S Africa	Johannesburg	1955
3	Australia	Sydney	1950
3	Australia	Sydney	1959
3	Australia	Brisbane	2001

BY A PLAYER

Cons	Player	Opponent	Venue	Year
5	S Wilson	Australia	Brisbane	1966
4	A Cameron	S Africa	Johannesburg	1955
3	J P Wilkinson	Australia	Brisbane	2001

Dave Rogers/Getty Images

Jonny Wilkinson is leading scorer in Tests for the Lions.

MOST PENALTIES IN A MATCH

BY THE TEAM

Pens	Opponent	Venue	Year
6	N Zealand	Christchurch	1993
6	Argentina	Cardiff	2005
5	S Africa	Pretoria	1968
5	S Africa	Cape Town	1980
5	Australia	Sydney	1989
5	S Africa	Cape Town	1997
5	S Africa	Durban	1997

BY A PLAYER

Pens	Player	Opponent	Venue	Year
6	A G Hastings	N Zealand	Christchurch	1993
6	J P Wilkinson	Argentina	Cardiff	2005
5	T J Kiernan	S Africa	Pretoria	1968
5	A J P Ward	S Africa	Cape Town	1980
5	A G Hastings	Australia	Sydney	1989
5	N R Jenkins	S Africa	Cape Town	1997
5	N R Jenkins	S Africa	Durban	1997

MOST DROPPED GOALS IN A MATCH

BY THE TEAM

Pens	Opponent	Venue	Year
2	S Africa	Port Elizabeth	1974

BY A PLAYER

Pens	Player	Opponent	Venue	Year
2	P Bennett	S Africa	Port Elizabeth	1974

CAREER RECORDS

MOST CAPPED PLAYERS

Caps	Player	Career Span
17	W J McBride	1962 to 1974
13	R E G Jeeps	1955 to 1962
12	C M H Gibson	1966 to 1971
12	G Price	1977 to 1983
10	A J F O'Reilly	1955 to 1959
10	R H Williams	1955 to 1959
10	G O Edwards	1968 to 1974

MOST CONSECUTIVE TESTS

Tests	Player	Span
15	W J McBride	1966 to 1974
12	C M H Gibson	1966 to 1971
12	G Price	1977 to 1983

MOST TESTS AS CAPTAIN

Tests	Captain	Span
6	A R Dawson	1959
6	M O Johnson	1997 to 2001

MOST POINTS IN TESTS

Points	Player	Tests	Career
67	J P Wilkinson	6	2001 to 2005
66	A G Hastings	6	1989 to 1993
44	P Bennett	8	1974 to 1977
41	N R Jenkins	4	1997 to 2001
35	T J Kiernan	5	1962 to 1968
30	S Wilson	5	1966
30	B John	5	1968 to 1971

MOST TRIES IN TESTS

Tries	Player	Tests	Career
6	A J F O'Reilly	10	1955 to 1959
5	J J Williams	7	1974 to 1977
4	W Llewellyn	4	1904
4	M J Price	5	1959

MOST CONVERSIONS IN TESTS

Cons	Player	Tests	Career
7	J P Wilkinson	6	2001 to 2005
6	S Wilson	5	1966
4	J F Byrne	4	1896
4	C Y Adamson	4	1899
4	B L Jones	3	1950
4	A Cameron	2	1955

Getty Images

Willie John McBride is a Lions legend, playing in a record 17 Tests for the side.

MOST PENALTY GOALS IN TESTS

Penalties	Player	Tests	Career
20	A G Hastings	6	1989 to 1993
16	J P Wilkinson	6	2001 to 2005
13	N R Jenkins	4	1997 to 2001
11	T J Kiernan	5	1962 to 1968
10	P Bennett	8	1974 to 1977
7	S O Campbell	7	1980 to 1983

MOST DROPPED GOALS IN TESTS

Drops	Player	Tests	Career
2	P F Bush	4	1904
2	D Watkins	6	1966
2	B John	5	1968 to 1971
2	P Bennett	8	1974 to 1977
2	C R Andrew	5	1989 to 1993

SERIES RECORDS

RECORD	HOLDER	DETAIL
Most team points		79 in S Africa 1974
Most team tries		10 in S Africa 1955 & 1974
Most points by player	N R Jenkins	41 in S Africa 1997
Most tries by player	W Llewellyn	4 in Australia 1904
	J J Williams	4 in S Africa 1974

MAJOR TOUR RECORDS

RECORD	DETAIL	YEAR	PLACE
Most team points	842	1959	Australia, NZ & Canada
Most team tries	165	1959	Australia, NZ & Canada
Highest score & biggest win	116–10	2001	v W Australia President's XV
Most individual points	188 by B John	1971	Australia & N Zealand
Most individual tries	22 by A J F O'Reilly	1959	Australia, NZ & Canada
Most points in match	37 by A G B Old	1974 v SW Districts	Mossel Bay, S Africa
Most tries in match	6 by D J Duckham	1971 v W Coast/Buller	Greymouth, N Zealand
	6 by J J Williams	1974 v SW Districts	Mossel Bay, S Africa

MISCELLANEOUS RECORDS

RECORD	HOLDER	DETAIL
Longest Test Career	W J McBride	13 seasons, 1962–1974
Youngest Test Cap	A J F O'Reilly	19 yrs 91 days in 1955
Oldest Test Cap	N A Back	36 yrs 160 days in 2005

BRITISH & IRISH LIONS INTERNATIONAL PLAYERS

UP TO 30TH SEPTEMBER 2008

From 1891 onwards.
* Indicates that the player was uncapped at the time of his first Lions Test but was subsequently capped by his country.

Aarvold, C D (Cambridge U, Blackheath and England) 1930 NZ 1,2,3,4, A
Ackerman, R A (London Welsh and Wales) 1983 NZ 1,4 (R)
Ackford, P J (Harlequins and England) 1989 A 1,2,3
Adamson, C Y (Durham City) 1899 A 1,2,3,4
Alexander, R (NIFC and Ireland) 1938 SA 1,2,3
Andrew, C R (Wasps and England) 1989 A 2,3, 1993 NZ 1,2,3
Arneil, R J (Edinburgh Acads and Scotland) 1968 SA 1,2,3,4
Archer, H A (Guy's H and *England) 1908 NZ 1,2,3
Ashcroft, A (Waterloo and England) 1959 A 1, NZ 2
Aston, R L (Cambridge U and England) 1891 SA 1,2,3
Ayre-Smith, A (Guy's H) 1899 A 1,2,3,4

Back, N A (Leicester and England) 1997 SA 2(R),3, 2001 A 2,3, 2005 NZ 1
Bainbridge, S J (Gosforth and England) 1983 NZ 3,4
Baird, G R T (Kelso and Scotland) 1983 NZ 1,2,3,4
Baker, A M (Newport and Wales) 1910 SA 3
Baker, D G S (Old Merchant Taylors' and England) 1955 SA 3,4
Balshaw, I R (Bath and England) 2001 A 1(R),2(R),3(R)
Bassett, J A (Penarth and Wales) 1930 NZ 1,2,3,4, A
Bateman, A G (Richmond and Wales) 1997 SA 3(R)
Bayfield, M C (Northampton and England) 1993 NZ 1,2,3
Beamish, G R (Leicester, RAF and Ireland) 1930 NZ 1,2,3,4,A
Beattie, J R (Glasgow Acads and Scotland) 1983 NZ 2(R)
Beaumont, W B (Fylde and England) 1977 NZ 2,3,4, 1980 SA 1,2,3,4
Bebb, D I E (Swansea and Wales) 1962 SA 2,3, 1966 A 1,2, NZ 1,2,3,4
Bedell-Sivright, D R (Cambridge U and Scotland) 1904 A 1
Bell, S P (Cambridge U) 1896 SA 2,3,4
Belson, F C (Bath) 1899 A 1
Bennett, P (Llanelli and Wales) 1974 SA 1,2,3,4, 1977 NZ 1,2,3,4
Bentley, J (Newcastle and England) 1997 SA 2,3
Bevan, J C (Cardiff Coll of Ed, Cardiff and Wales) 1971 NZ 1
Bevan, T S (Swansea and Wales) 1904 A 1,2,3, NZ
Black, A W (Edinburgh U and Scotland) 1950 NZ 1,2
Black, B H (Oxford U, Blackheath and England) 1930 NZ 1,2,3,4, A
Blakiston, A F (Northampton and England) 1924 SA 1,2,3,4
Bowcott, H M (Cambridge U, Cardiff and Wales) 1930 NZ 1,2,3,4, A
Boyd, C A (Dublin U and *Ireland) 1896 SA 1
Boyle, C V (Dublin U and Ireland) 1938 SA 2,3
Brand, T N (NIFC and *Ireland) 1924 SA 1,2
Bresnihan, F P K (UC Dublin and Ireland) 1968 SA 1,2,4
Bromet, E (Cambridge U) 1891 SA 2,3
Bromet, W E (Oxford U and England) 1891 SA 1,2,3
Brophy, N H (UC Dublin and Ireland) 1962 SA 1,4
Brown, G L (W of Scotland and Scotland) 1971 NZ 3,4, 1974 SA 1,2,3, 1977 NZ 2,3,4
Bucher, A M (Edinburgh Acads and Scotland) 1899 A 1,3,4
Budge, G M (Edinburgh Wands and Scotland) 1950 NZ 4
Bulger, L Q (Lansdowne and Ireland) 1896 SA 1,2,3,4
Bulloch, G C (Glasgow and Scotland) 2001 A l(t), 2005 NZ 3(R)
Burcher, D H (Newport and Wales) 1977 NZ 3
Burnell, A P (London Scottish and Scotland) 1993 NZ 1
Bush, P F (Cardiff and *Wales) 1904 A 1,2,3, NZ
Butterfield, J (Northampton and England) 1955 SA 1,2,3,4
Byrne, J F (Moseley and England) 1896 SA 1,2,3,4
Byrne, J S (Leinster and Ireland) 2005 Arg, NZ 1,2(R),3

Calder, F (Stewart's-Melville FP and Scotland) 1989 A 1,2,3
Calder, J H (Stewart's-Melville FP and Scotland) 1983 NZ 3
Cameron, A (Glasgow HSFP and Scotland) 1955 SA 1,2
Campbell, S O (Old Belvedere and Ireland) 1980 SA 2(R),3,4, 1983 NZ 1,2,3,4
Campbell-Lamerton, M J (Halifax, Army and Scotland) 1962 SA 1,2,3,4, 1966 A 1,2, NZ 1,3
Carey, W J (Oxford U) 1896 SA 1,2,3,4
Carleton, J (Orrell and England) 1980 SA 1,2,4, 1983 NZ 2,3,4
Carling, W D C (Harlequins and England) 1993 NZ 1
Catt, M J (Bath and England) 1997 SA 3
Cave, W T C (Cambridge U and *England) 1903 SA 1,2,3
Chalmers, C M (Melrose and Scotland) 1989 A 1
Chapman, F E (Westoe, W Hartlepool and *England) 1908 NZ 3
Charvis, C L (Swansea and Wales) 2001 A 1(R),3(R)
Clarke, B B (Bath and England) 1993 NZ 1,2,3
Clauss, P R A (Oxford U and Scotland) 1891 SA 1,2,3
Cleaver, W B (Cardiff and Wales) 1950 NZ 1,2,3
Clifford, T (Young Munster and Ireland) 1950 NZ 1,2,3, A 1,2
Clinch, A D (Dublin U and Ireland) 1896 SA 1,2,3,4
Cobner, T J (Pontypool and Wales) 1977 NZ 1,2,3
Colclough, M J (Angoulême and England) 1980 SA 1,2,3,4, 1983 NZ 1,2,3,4
Collett, G F (Cheltenham) 1903 SA 1,2,3
Connell, G C (Trinity Acads and Scotland) 1968 SA 4
Cookson, G (Manchester) 1899 A 1,2,3,4
Cooper, G J (Newport Gwent Dragons and Wales) 2005 Arg
Corry, M E (Leicester and England) 2001 A 1,2(t+R),3, 2005 Arg, NZ 1,2(R),3(R)
Cotton, F E (Loughborough Colls, Coventry and England) 1974 SA 1,2,3,4, 1977 NZ 2,3,4
Coulman, M J (Moseley and England) 1968 SA 3
Cove-Smith, R (Old Merchant Taylors' and England) 1924 SA 1,2,3,4
Cowan, R C (Selkirk and Scotland) 1962 SA 4
Crean, T J (Wanderers and Ireland) 1896 SA 1,2,3,4
Cromey, G E (Queen's U, Belfast and Ireland) 1938 SA 3
Crowther, S N (Lennox) 1904 A 1,2,3, NZ
Cueto, M J (Sale and England) 2005 NZ 3
Cunningham, W A (Lansdowne and Ireland) 1924 SA 3
Cusiter, C P (Borders and Scotland) 2005 Arg (R)

Dallaglio, L B N (Wasps and England) 1997 SA 1,2,3
Dancer, G T (Bedford) 1938 SA 1,2,3
D'Arcy, G (Leinster and Ireland) 2005 Arg
Davey, J (Redruth and England) 1908 NZ 1
Davidson, I G (NIFC and Ireland) 1903 SA 1
Davidson, J W (London Irish and Ireland) 1997 SA 1,2,3
Davies, C (Cardiff and Wales) 1950 NZ 4
Davies, D M (Somerset Police and Wales) 1950 NZ 3,4, A 1
Davies, D S (Hawick and Scotland) 1924 SA 1,2,3,4
Davies, H J (Newport and Wales) 1924 SA 2
Davies, T G R (Cardiff, London Welsh and Wales) 1968 SA 3, 1971 NZ 1,2,3,4

Davies, T J (Llanelli and Wales) 1959 NZ 2,4
Davies, T M (London Welsh, Swansea and Wales) 1971 NZ 1,2,3,4, 1974 SA 1,2,3,4
Davies, W G (Cardiff and Wales) 1980 SA 2
Davies, W P C (Harlequins and England) 1955 SA 1,2,3
Dawes, S J (London Welsh and Wales) 1971 NZ 1,2,3,4
Dawson, A R (Wanderers and Ireland) 1959 A 1,2, NZ 1,2,3,4
Dawson, M J S (Northampton, Wasps and England) 1997 SA 1,2,3, 2001 A 2(R),3, 2005 NZ 1(R),3(R)
Dibble, R (Bridgwater Albion and England) 1908 NZ 1,2,3
Dixon, P J (Harlequins and England) 1971 NZ 1,2,4
Dobson, D D (Oxford U and England) 1904 A 1,2,3, NZ
Dodge, P W (Leicester and England) 1980 SA 3,4
Dooley, W A (Preston Grasshoppers and England) 1989 A 2,3
Doran, G P (Lansdowne and Ireland) 1899 A 1,2
Down, P J (Bristol and *England) 1908 NZ 1,2,3
Doyle, M G (Blackrock Coll and Ireland) 1968 SA 1
Drysdale, D (Heriot's FP and Scotland) 1924 SA 1,2,3,4
Duckham, D J (Coventry and England) 1971 NZ 2,3,4
Duggan, W P (Blackrock Coll and Ireland) 1977 NZ 1,2.3,4
Duff, P L (Glasgow Acads and Scotland) 1938 SA 2,3

Easterby, S H (Llanelli Scarlets and Ireland) 2005 NZ 2,3
Edwards, G O (Cardiff and Wales) 1968 SA 1,2, 1971 NZ 1,2,3,4, 1974 SA 1,2,3,4
Edwards, R W (Malone and Ireland) 1904 A 2,3, NZ
Evans, G (Maesteg and Wales) 1983 NZ 3,4
Evans, G L (Newport and Wales) 1977 NZ 2,3,4
Evans, I C (Llanelli and Wales) 1989 A 1,2,3, 1993 NZ 1,2 3, 1997 SA 1
Evans, R T (Newport and Wales) 1950 NZ 1,2,3,4, A 1,2
Evans, T P (Swansea and Wales) 1977 NZ 1
Evans, W R (Cardiff and Wales) 1959 A 2, NZ 1,2,3
Evers, G V (Moseley) 1899 A 2,3,4

Farrell, J L (Bective Rangers and Ireland) 1930 NZ 1,2,3,4,A
Faull, J (Swansea and Wales) 1959 A 1, NZ 1,3,4
Fenwick, S P (Bridgend and Wales) 1977 NZ 1,2,3,4
Fitzgerald, C F (St Mary's Coll and Ireland) 1983 NZ 1,2,3,4
Foster, A R (Queen's U, Belfast and Ireland) 1910 SA 1,2
Francombe, J S (Manchester) 1899 A 1

Gabe, R T (Cardiff and Wales) 1904 A 1,2,3, NZ
Gibbs, I S (Swansea and Wales) 1993 NZ 2,3, 1997 SA 1,2 3
Gibbs, R A (Cardiff and Wales) 1908 NZ 1,2
Gibson, C M H (Cambridge U, NIFC and Ireland) 1966 NZ 1,2,3,4, 1968 SA 1(R),2,3,4, 1971 NZ 1,2,3,4
Gibson, G R (Northern and England) 1899 A 1,2,3,4
Gibson, T A (Cambridge U and *England) 1903 SA 1,2,3
Giles, J L (Coventry and England) 1938 SA 1,3
Gillespie, J I (Edinburgh Acads and Scotland) 1903 SA 1,2,3
Gould, J H (Old Leysians) 1891 SA 1,2
Gravell, R W R (Llanelli and Wales) 1980 SA 1(R),2,3,4
Graves, C R A (Wanderers and Ireland) 1938 SA 1,3
Gray, H G S (Scottish Trials) 1899 A 1,2
Greenwood, J T (Dunfermline and Scotland) 1955 SA 1,2,3,4
Greenwood, W J H (Harlequins and England) 2005 NZ 1(R),3
Greig, L L (US and *Scotland) 1903 SA 1,2,3
Grewcock, D J (Bath and England) 2001 A 1,2,3, 2005 Arg, NZ 1(R)
Grieve, C F (Oxford U and Scotland) 1938 SA 2,3
Griffiths, G M (Cardiff and Wales) 1955 SA 2,3,4
Griffiths, V M (Newport and Wales) 1924 SA 3,4
Guscott, J C (Bath and England) 1989 A 2,3, 1993 NZ 1,2,3, 1997 SA 1,2,3

Hall, M R (Bridgend and Wales) 1989 A 1
Hammond, J (Cambridge U, Blackheath) 1891 SA 1,2,3, 1896 SA 2,4
Hancock, P F (Blackheath and England) 1891 SA 1,2,3, 1896 SA 1,2,3,4
Hancock, P S (Richmond and *England) 1903 SA 1,2,3
Handford, F G (Manchester and England) 1910 SA 1,2,3
Harding, A F (London Welsh and Wales) 1904 A 1,2,3, NZ, 1908 NZ 1,2,3
Harding, W R (Cambridge U, Swansea and Wales) 1924 SA 2,3,4
Harris, S W (Blackheath and England) 1924 SA 3,4
Harrison, E M (Guy's H) 1903 SA 1
Hastings, A G (London Scottish, Watsonians and Scotland) 1989 A 1,2,3, 1993 NZ 1,2,3
Hastings, S (Watsonians and Scotland) 1989 A 2,3
Hay, B H (Boroughmuir and Scotland) 1980 SA 2,3,4
Hayes, J J (Munster and Ireland) 2005 Arg
Hayward, D J (Newbridge and Wales) 1950 NZ 1,2,3
Healey, A S (Leicester and England) 1997 SA 2(R),3(R)
Henderson, N J (Queen's U, Belfast, NIFC and Ireland) 1950 NZ3
Henderson, R A J (Wasps and Ireland) 2001 A 1,2,3
Henderson, R G (Northern and Scotland) 1924 SA 3,4
Hendrie, K G P (Heriot's FP and Scotland) 1924 SA 2
Henson, G L (Neath-Swansea Ospreys and Wales) 2005 NZ 2
Hewitt, D (Queen's U, Belfast, Instonians and Ireland) 1959 A 1,2, NZ 1,3,4, 1962 SA 4
Hickie, D A (Leinster and Ireland) 2005 Arg
Higgins, R (Liverpool and England) 1955 SA 1
Hill, R A (Saracens and England) 1997 SA 1,2, 2001 A 1,2, 2005 NZ 1
Hind, G R (Guy's H and *England) 1908 NZ 2,3
Hinshelwood, A J W (London Scottish and Scotland) 1966 NZ 2,4, 1968 SA 2
Hodgson, J McD (Northern and *England) 1930 NZ 1,3
Holmes, T D (Cardiff and Wales) 1983 NZ 1
Hopkins, R (Maesteg and Wales) 1971 NZ 1(R)
Horgan, S P (Leinster and Ireland) 2005 Arg (R),NZ 1(R),2(R),3(R)
Horrocks-Taylor, J P (Leicester and England) 1959 NZ 3
Horton, A L (Blackheath and England) 1968 SA 2,3,4
Howard, W G (Old Birkonians) 1938 SA 1
Howie, R A (Kirkcaldy and Scotland) 1924 SA 1,2,3,4
Howley, R (Cardiff and Wales) 2001 A 1,2
Hulme, F C (Birkenhead Park and England) 1904 A 1

Irvine, A R (Heriot's FP and Scotland) 1974 SA 3,4, 1977 NZ 1,2,3,4, 1980 SA 2,3,4
Irwin, D G (Instonians and Ireland) 1983 NZ 1,2,4
Isherwood, G A M (Old Alleynians, Sale) 1910 SA 1,2,3

Jackett, E J (Falmouth, Leicester and England) 1908 NZ 1,2,3
Jackson, F S (Leicester) 1908 NZ 1
Jackson, P B (Coventry and England) 1959 A 1,2, NZ 1,3,4
James, D R (Llanelli and Wales) 2001 A 1,2,3
Jarman, H (Newport and Wales) 1910 SA 1,2,3
Jarman, J W (Bristol and *England) 1899 A 1,2,3,4
Jeeps, R E G (Northampton and *England) 1955 SA 1,2,3,4, 1959 A 1,2, NZ 1,2,3, 1962 SA 1,2,3,4
Jenkins, G D (Cardiff Blues and Wales) 2005 NZ 1,2,3
Jenkins, N R (Pontypridd, Cardiff and Wales) 1997 SA 1,2,3, 2001 A 2(R)
Jenkins, V G J (Oxford U, London Welsh and Wales) 1938 SA 1
John, B (Cardiff and Wales) 1968 SA 1, 1971 NZ 1,2,3,4
John, E R (Neath and Wales) 1950 NZ 1,2,3,4, A 1,2
Johnson, M O (Leicester and England) 1993 NZ 2,3, 1997 SA 1,2,3, 2001 A 1,2,3
Johnston, R (Wanderers and Ireland) 1896 SA 1,2,3
Jones, B L (Devonport Services, Llanelli and Wales) 1950 NZ 4, A 1,2
Jones, D K (Llanelli, Cardiff and Wales) 1962 SA 1,2,3, 1966 A 1,2, NZ 1
Jones, E L (Llanelli and *Wales) 1938 SA 1,3
Jones, I E (Llanelli and Wales) 1930 NZ 1,2,3,4, A
Jones, J P "Jack" (Newport and Wales) 1908 NZ 1,2,3, 1910 SA 1,2,3
Jones J P "Tuan" (Guy's H and *Wales) 1908 NZ 2,3
Jones K D (Cardiff and Wales) 1962 SA 1,2,3,4
Jones K J (Newport and Wales) 1950 NZ 1,2,4
Jones R N (Swansea and Wales) 1989 A 1,2,3
Jones, R P (Neath-Swansea Ospreys) 2005 NZ 1(R),2,3
Jones, S M (Clermont Auvergne and Wales) 2005 NZ 1,2(R),3
Jones S T (Pontypool and Wales) 1983 NZ 2,3,4

Judkins, W (Coventry) 1899 A 2,3,4

Kay, B J (Leicester and England) 2005 Arg (R),NZ 1
Keane, M I (Lansdowne and Ireland) 1977 NZ 1
Kennedy, K W (CIYMS, London Irish and Ireland) 1966 A 1,2, NZ 1,4
Kiernan, M J (Dolphin and Ireland) 1983 NZ 2,3,4
Kiernan, T J (Cork Const and Ireland) 1962 SA 3, 1968 SA 1,2,3,4
Kininmonth, P W (Oxford U, Richmond and Scotland) 1950 NZ 1,2,4
Kinnear, R M (Heriot's FP and *Scotland) 1924 SA1,2,3,4
Kyle, J W (Queen's U, Belfast, NIFC and Ireland) 1950 NZ 1,2,3,4, A 1,2
Kyrke, G V (Marlborough N) 1908 NZ 1

Laidlaw, F A L (Melrose and Scotland) 1966 NZ 2,3
Laidlaw, R J (Jedforest and Scotland) 1983 NZ 1(R),2,3,4
Lamont, R A (Instonians and Ireland) 1966 NZ 1,2,3,4
Lane, M F (UC Cork and Ireland) 1950 NZ 4, A 2
Larter, P J (Northampton, RAF and England) 1968 SA 2
Laxon, H (Cambridge U) 1908 NZ 1
Leonard, J (Harlequins and England) 1993 NZ 2,3, 1997 SA 1(R), 2001 A 1(R),2(R)
Lewis, R A (Abertillery and Wales) 1966 NZ 2,3,4
Lewsey, O J (Wasps and England) 2005 NZ 1,2,3
Llewellyn, W (Llwynypia, Newport and Wales) 1904 A 1,2,3, NZ
Lynch, J F (St Mary's Coll and Ireland) 1971 NZ 1,2,3,4

McBride, W J (Ballymena and Ireland) 1962 SA 3,4, 1966 NZ 2,3,4, 1968 SA 1,2,3,4, 1971 NZ 1,2,3,4, 1974 SA 1,2,3,4
Macdonald, R (Edinburgh U and Scotland) 1950 NZ 1, A 2
McEvedy, P F (Guy's H) 1904 A 2,3, NZ, 1908 NZ 2,3
McFadyean, C W (Moseley and England) 1966 NZ 1,2,3,4
McGeechan, I R (Headingley and Scotland) 1974 SA 1,2,3,4, 1977 NZ 1,2,3(R),4
McGown, T M W (NIFC and Ireland) 1899 A 1,2,3,4
McKay, J W (Queen's U, Belfast and Ireland) 1950 NZ 1,2,3,4, A 1,2
McKibbin, H R (Queen's U, Belfast and Ireland) 1938 SA 1,2,3
Mackie, O G (Wakefield Trinity and *England) 1896 SA 1,2,3,4
Maclagan, W E (London Scottish and Scotland) 1891 SA 1,2,3
McLauchlan, J (Jordanhill and Scotland) 1971 NZ 1,2,3,4, 1974 SA 1,2,3,4
McLeod, H F (Hawick and Scotland) 1959 A 1,2, NZ 1,2,3,4
McLoughlin, R J (Gosforth, Blackrock Coll and Ireland) 1966 A 1,2, NZ,4
Macmillan, R G (London Scottish and Scotland) 1891 SA 1,2,3
MacNeill, H P (Oxford U and Ireland) 1983 NZ 1,2,4 (R)
Macpherson, N C (Newport and Scotland) 1924 SA 1,2,3,4
Macrae, D J (St Andrew's U and Scotland) 1938 SA 1
McVicker, J (Collegians and Ireland) 1924 SA 1,3,4
Magee, A M (Bective R and Ireland) 1896 SA 1,2,3,4
Magee, J M (Bective R) 1896 SA 2,4
Marques, R W D (Harlequins and England) 1959 A 2, NZ 2
Marsden-Jones, D (London Welsh and Wales) 1924 SA 1,2
Marshall, H (Blackheath and *England) 1891 SA 2,3
Martin, A J (Aberavon and Wales) 1977 NZ 1
Martelli, E (Dublin U) 1899 A 1
Martindale, S A (Kendal and England) 1930 A
Massey, B F (Hull and ER) 1904 A 3
Matthews, J (Cardiff and Wales) 1950 NZ 1,2,3,4, A 1,2
Maxwell, R B (Birkenhead Park) 1924 SA 1
Mayfield, W E (Cambridge U) 1891 SA 2,3
Mayne, R B (Queen's U, Belfast and Ireland) 1938 SA 1,2,3
Meares, A W D (Dublin U and *Ireland) 1896 SA 3,4
Meredith, B V (Newport and Wales) 1955 SA 1,2,3,4, 1962 SA 1,2,3,4
Meredith, C C (Neath and Wales) 1955 SA 1,2,3,4
Millar, S (Ballymena and Ireland) 1959 A 1,2, NZ 2, 1962 SA 1,2,3,4, 1968 SA 1,2
Miller, E R P (Leicester and England) 1997 SA 2(R)
Milliken, R A (Bangor and Ireland) 1974 SA 1,2,3,4
Milne, K S (Heriot's FP and Scotland) 1993 NZ 1
Mitchell, W G (Richmond and England) 1891 SA 1,2,3
Moody, L W (Leicester and England) 2005 Arg, NZ 2,3
Moore, B C (Nottingham, Harlequins and England) 1989 A 1,2,3, 1993 NZ 2,3
Morgan, C I (Cardiff and Wales) 1955 SA 1,2,3,4
Morgan, D W (Stewart's-Melville FP and Scotland) 1977 NZ 3(R),4
Morgan, E (London Welsh, Guy's H and Wales) 1904 A 1,2,3, NZ
Morgan, E (Swansea and *Wales) 1908 NZ 2,3
Morgan, G J (Clontarf and Ireland) 1938 SA 3
Morgan, H J (Abertillery and Wales) 1959 NZ.3,4, 1962 SA 2,3
Morgan, M E (Swansea and Wales) 1938 SA 1,2
Morgan, W L (Cardiff and *Wales) 1908 NZ 2,3
Morley, J C (Newport and Wales) 1930 NZ 1,2,3
Morris, C D (Orrell and England) 1993 NZ 1,2,3
Morris, D R (Swansea and Wales) 2001 A 3(R)
Morrison, M C (Royal HSFP and Scotland) 1903 SA 1,2,3
Mortimer, W (Marlborough N and *England) 1896 SA 1,2,3,4
Mulcahy, W A (UC Dublin and Ireland) 1959 A 1, NZ 4, 1962 SA 1,2,3,4
Mullen, K D (Old Belvedere and Ireland) 1950 NZ 1,2, A 2
Mulligan, A A (Wanderers, London Irish and Ireland) 1959 NZ 4
Mullin, B J (London Irish and Ireland) 1989 A 1
Mullineux, M (Blackheath) 1896 SA 1, 1899 A 1
Mullins, R C (Oxford U) 1896 SA 1,3
Murphy, G E A (Leicester and Ireland) 2005 Arg, NZ 3
Murphy, N A A (Cork Const and Ireland) 1959 A 2, NZ 1,2,4, 1966 A 1,2, NZ 2,3
Murray, P F (Wanderers and Ireland) 1930 NZ 1,2,4, A

Neale, M E (Bristol, Blackheath and *England) 1910 SA 1,2,3
Neary, A (Broughton Park and England) 1977 NZ 4
Neill, R M (Edinburgh Acads and Scotland) 1903 SA 2,3
Nelson, J E (Malone and Ireland) 1950 NZ 3,4, A 1,2
Nicholls, E G (Cardiff and Wales) 1899 A 1,2,3,4
Nicholson, B E (Harlequins and England) 1938 SA 2
Nicholson, E T (Birkenhead Park and *England) 1899 A 3,4
Norris, C H (Cardiff and Wales) 1966 NZ 1,2,3
Norster, R L (Cardiff and Wales) 1983 NZ 1,2, 1989 A 1
Novis, A L (Blackheath and England) 1930 NZ 2,4, A

O'Brien, A B (Guy's H) 1904 A 1,2,3, NZ
O'Callaghan, D P (Munster and Ireland) 2005 Arg, NZ 2,3
O'Connell, P J (Munster and Ireland) 2005 NZ 1,2,3
O'Donnell, R C (St Mary's Coll and Ireland) 1980 SA I
O'Driscoll, B G (Blackrock Coll, Leinster and Ireland) 2001 A 1,2,3, 2005 NZ 1
O'Driscoll, J B (London Irish and Ireland) 1980 SA 1,2,3,4, 1983 NZ 2,4
O'Gara, R J R (Munster and Ireland) 2005 NZ 3(R)
O'Neill, H O'H (Queen's U, Belfast and Ireland) 1930 NZ 1,2,3,4, A
O'Reilly, A J F (Old Belvedere and Ireland) 1955 SA 1,2,3,4, 1959 A 1,2, NZ 1,2,3,4
Oldham, W L (Coventry and England) 1908 NZ 1
Orr, P A (Old Wesley and Ireland) 1977 NZ 1
O'Shea, J P (Cardiff and Wales) 1968 SA 1
Owen, M J (Newport Gwent Dragons and Wales) 2005 Arg

Parker, D S (Swansea and Wales) 1930 NZ 1,2,3,4, A
Pask, A E I (Abertillery and Wales) 1962 SA 1,2,3, 1966 A 1,2, NZ 1,3,4
Patterson, C S (Instonians and Ireland) 1980 SA 1,2,3
Patterson, W M (Sale and *England) 1959 NZ 2
Paxton, I A M (Selkirk and Scotland) 1983 NZ 1,2,3,4
Pedlow, A C (CIYMS and Ireland) 1955 SA 1,4
Peel, D J (Llanelli Scarlets and Wales) 2005 NZ 1,2,3
Perry, M B (Bath and England) 2001 A 1,2,3
Pillman, C H (Blackheath and England) 1910 SA 2,3
Piper, O J S (Cork Const and Ireland) 1910 SA 1
Poole, H (Cardiff) 1930 NZ 3
Popplewell, N J (Greystones and Ireland) 1993 NZ 1,2,3
Preece, I (Coventry and England) 1950 NZ 1

Prentice, F D (Leicester and England) 1930 NZ 2, A
Price, B (Newport and Wales) 1966 A 1,2, NZ 1,4
Price, G (Pontypool and Wales) 1977 NZ 1,2,3,4, 1980 SA 1,2,3,4, 1983 NZ 1,2,3,4
Price, M J (Pontypool and Wales) 1959 A 1,2, NZ 1,2,3
Prosser, T R (Pontypool and Wales) 1959 NZ,4
Pullin, J V (Bristol and England) 1968 SA 2,3,4, 1971 NZ 1,2,3,4

Quinnell, D L (Llanelli and *Wales) 1971 NZ. 3, 1977 NZ 2,3, 1980 SA 1,2
Quinnell, L S (Llanelli and Wales) 2001 A 1,2,3

Ralston, C W (Richmond and England) 1974 SA 4
Reed, A I (Bath and Scotland) 1993 NZ 1
Rees, H E (Neath and *Wales) 1977 NZ 4
Reeve, J S R (Harlequins and England) 1930 NZ 1,3,4, A
Regan, M P (Bristol and England) 1997 SA 3
Reid, T E (Garryowen and Ireland) 1955 SA 2,3
Renwick, J M (Hawick and Scotland) 1980 SA 1
Rew, H (Blackheath, Army and England) 1930 NZ 1,2,3,4
Reynolds, F J (Old Cranleighans and England) 1938 SA 1,2
Richards, D (Leicester and England) 1989 A 1,2,3, 1993 NZ 1,2,3
Richards, D S (Swansea and Wales) 1980 SA 1
Richards, M C R (Cardiff and Wales) 1968 SA 1,3,4
Richards, T J (Bristol and Australia) 1910 SA 1,2
Rimmer, G (Waterloo and England) 1950 NZ 3
Ringland, T M (Ballymena and Ireland) 1983 NZ 1
Risman, A B W (Loughborough Colls and England) 1959 A 1,2, NZ 1,4
Ritson, J A S (Northern and *England) 1908 NZ 1
Robbie, J C (Greystones and Ireland) 1980 SA 4
Robins, J D (Birkenhead Park and Wales) 1950 NZ 1,2,3, A 1,2
Robins, R J (Pontypridd and Wales) 1955 SA 1,2,3,4
Robinson, J T (Sale and England) 2001 A 1,2,3, 2005 NZ 1,2
Rodber, T A K (Northampton and England) 1997 SA 1,2
Rogers, D P (Bedford and England) 1962 SA 1,4
Rogers, R J (Bath) 1904 NZ
Rotherham, A (Cambridge U and *England) 1891 SA 1,3
Rowlands, K A (Cardiff and Wales) 1962 SA 1,2,4
Rowntree, G C (Leicester and England) 2005 Arg, NZ 2(t+R),3(R)
Rutherford, D (Gloucester and England) 1966 A 1
Rutherford, J Y (Selkirk and Scotland) 1983 NZ 3

Saunders, S M (Guy's H) 1904 A 1,2
Savage, K F (Northampton and England) 1968 SA 1,2,3,4
Scotland, K J F (Cambridge U, Heriot's FP and Scotland) 1959 A 1,2, NZ 1,3,4
Scott, W P (West of Scotland and Scotland) 1903 SA 1,2,3
Sealy, J (Dublin U and *Ireland) 1896 SA 1,2,3,4
Sharp, R A W (Oxford U, Redruth and England) 1962 SA 3,4
Simpson, C (Cambridge U) 1891 SA 1
Skrimshire, R T (Newport and Wales) 1903 SA 1,2,3
Slattery, J F (Blackrock Coll and Ireland) 1974 SA 1,2,3,4
Slemen, M A C (Liverpool and England) 1980 SA 1
Smith, A R (Edinburgh Wands, London Scottish and Scotland) 1962 SA 1,2,3
Smith, D F (Richmond and England) 1910 SA 1,2,3
Smith, D W C (London Scottish and Scotland) 1950 A 1
Smith, G K (Kelso and Scotland) 1959 A 1,2, NZ 1,3
Smith, I S (Oxford U, London Scottish and Scotland) 1924 SA 1,2
Smith, O J (Leicester and England) 2005 Arg
Smith, T J (Watsonians, Northampton and Scotland) 1997 SA 1,2,3, 2001 A 1,2,3
Smith, T W (Leicester) 1908 NZ 2,3
Smyth, R S (Dublin U and Ireland) 1903 SA 1,2,3
Smyth, T (Malone, Newport and Ireland) 1910 SA 2,3
Sole, D M B (Edinburgh Acads and Scotland) 1989 A 1,2,3
Spong, R S (Old Millhillians and England) 1930 NZ 1,2,3,4, A
Spoors, J A (Bristol) 1910 SA 1,2,3
Squire, J (Newport, Pontypool and Wales) 1977 NZ 4, 1980 SA 1,2,3,4, 1983 NZ 1
Squires, P J (Harrogate and England) 1977 NZ 1
Stagg, P K (Oxford U, Sale and Scotland) 1968 SA 1,3,4
Stanger-Leathes, C F (Northern and *England) 1904 A 1
Steele, W C C (Bedford, RAF and Scotland) 1974 SA 1,2
Stephens, I (Bridgend and Wales) 1983 NZ 1
Stephens, J R G (Neath and Wales) 1950 A 1,2
Stevenson, R C (St Andrew's U and Scotland) 1910 SA 1,2,3
Stimpson, T R G (Newcastle and England) 1997 SA 3(R)
Stout, F M (Gloucester and England) 1899 A 1,2,3,4, 1903 SA 1,2,3
Surtees, A A (Cambridge U) 1891 SA 1,2,3
Swannell, B I (Northampton and *Australia) 1899 A 2,3,4, 1904 A 1,2,3, NZ

Tait, A V (Newcastle and Scotland) 1997 SA 1,2
Tanner, H (Swansea and Wales) 1938 SA 2
Taylor, A R (Cross Keys and Wales) 1938 SA 1,2
Taylor, J (London Welsh and Wales) 1971 NZ 1,2,3,4
Taylor, R B (Northampton and England) 1968 SA 1,2,3,4
Teague, M C (Gloucester, Moseley and England) 1989 A 2,3, 1993 NZ 2(t)
Tedford, A (Malone and Ireland) 1903 SA 1,2,3
Telfer, J W (Melrose and Scotland) 1966 A 1,2, NZ 1,2,4, 1968 SA 2,3,4
Thomas, G (Toulouse and Wales) 2005 NZ 1,2,3
Thomas, M C (Devonport Services, Newport and Wales) 1950 NZ 2,3, A 1, 1959 NZ 1
Thomas, R C C (Swansea and Wales) 1955 SA 3,4
Thomas, W D (Llanelli and *Wales) 1966 NZ 2,3, 1968 SA 3(R),4, 1971 NZ 1,2,4 (R)
Thompson, C E K (Lancashire) 1899 A 2,3,4
Thompson, R (Cambridge U) 1891 SA 1,2,3
Thompson, R H (Instonians, London Irish and Ireland) 1955 SA 1,2,4
Thompson, S G (Northampton and England) 2005 Arg (R), NZ 1(R),2
Timms, A B (Edinburgh U and Scotland) 1899 A 2,3,4
Todd, A F (Blackheath and *England) 1896 SA 1,2,3,4
Townsend, G P J (Northampton and Scotland) 1997 SA 1,2
Trail, D H (Guy's H) 1904 A 1,2,3, NZ
Travers, W H (Newport and Wales) 1938 SA 2,3
Tucker, C C (Shannon and Ireland) 1980 SA 3,4
Turner, J W C (Gala and Scotland) 1968 SA 1,2,3,4

Underwood, R (RAF, Leicester and England) 1989 A 1,2,3, 1993 NZ 1,2,3
Underwood, T (Newcastle and England) 1997 SA 3
Unwin, E J (Rosslyn Park, Army and England) 1938 SA 1,2
Uttley, R M (Gosforth and England) 1974 SA 1,2,3,4

Vassall, H H (Blackheath and England) 1908 NZ 1,2,3
Vickery, P J (Gloucester and England) 2001 A 1,2,3
Vile, T H (Newport and *Wales) 1904 A 2,3, NZ
Voyce, A T (Gloucester and England) 1924 SA 3,4

Waddell, G H (Cambridge U, London Scottish and Scotland) 1962 SA 1,2
Waddell, H (Glasgow Acads and Scotland) 1924 SA 1,2,4
Wainwright, R I (Watsonians and Scotland) 1997 SA 3
Walker, E F (Lennox) 1903 SA 2,3
Walker, S (Instonians and Ireland) 1938 SA 1,2,3
Wallace, Jos (Wanderers and Ireland) 1903 SA 1,2,3
Wallace, P S (Saracens and Ireland) 1997 SA 1,2,3
Wallace, W (Percy Park) 1924 SA 1
Waller, P D (Newport and Wales) 1910 SA 1,2,3
Ward, A J P (Garryowen and Ireland) 1980 SA 1
Waters, J A (Selkirk and Scotland) 1938 SA 3
Watkins, D (Newport and Wales) 1966 A 1,2, NZ 1,2,3,4
Watkins, S J (Newport and Wales) 1966 A 1,2, NZ 3
Webb, J (Abertillery and Wales) 1910 SA 1,2,3
Welsh, W B (Hawick and Scotland) 1930 NZ 4
Weston, M P (Richmond, Durham City and England) 1962 SA 1,2,3,4, 1966 A 1,2
Wheeler, P J (Leicester and England) 1977 NZ 2,3,4, 1980 SA 1,2,3,4
White, D B (London Scottish and Scotland) 1989 A 1
White, J M (Leicester and England) 2005 Arg (R),NZ 1,2,3

Whitley, H (Northern and *England) 1924 SA 1,3,4
Whittaker, T S (Lancashire) 1891 SA 1,2,3
Wilkinson, J P (Newcastle and England) 2001 A 1,2,3, 2005 Arg, NZ 1,2
Willcox, J G (Oxford U, Harlequins and England) 1962 SA 1,2,4
Williams, B L (Cardiff and Wales) 1950 NZ 2,3,4, A 1,2
Williams, C (Swansea and Wales) 1980 SA 1,2,3,4
Williams, D (Ebbw Vale and Wales) 1966 A 1,2, NZ 1,2,4
Williams, D B (Cardiff and *Wales) 1977 NZ 1,2,3
Williams, J F (London Welsh and Wales) 1908 NZ 3
Williams, J J (Llanelli and Wales) 1974 SA 1,2,3,4, 1977 NZ 1,2,3
Williams, J L (Cardiff and Wales) 1908 NZ 1,2
Williams, J P R (London Welsh and Wales) 1971 NZ 1,2,3,4, 1974 SA 1,2,3,4
Williams, M E (Cardiff Blues and Wales) 2005 NZ 3(R)
Williams, R H (Llanelli and Wales) 1955 SA 1,2,3,4, 1959 A 1,2, NZ 1,2,3,4
Williams, S H (Newport and *England) 1910 SA 1,2,3
Williams, S M (Neath-Swansea Ospreys and Wales) 2005 Arg, NZ 2
Williams, W O G (Swansea and Wales) 1955 SA 1,2,3,4
Willis, W R (Cardiff and Wales) 1950 NZ 4, A 1,2
Wilson, S (London Scottish and Scotland) 1966 A 2, NZ 1,2,3,4
Windsor, R W (Pontypool and Wales) 1974 SA 1,2,3,4, 1977 NZ 1
Winterbottom, P J (Headingley, Harlequins and England) 1983 NZ 1,2,3,4, 1993 NZ, 1,2,3
Wood, B G M (Garryowen and Ireland) 1959 NZ 1,3
Wood, K B (Leicester) 1910 SA 1,3
Wood, K G M (Harlequins and Ireland) 1997 SA 1,2, 2001 A 1,2,3
Woodward, C R (Leicester and England) 1980 SA 2,3
Wotherspoon, W (Cambridge U and Scotland) 1891 SA 1

Young, A T (Cambridge U, Blackheath and England) 1924 SA 2
Young, D (Cardiff and Wales) 1989 A 1,2,3
Young, J (Harrogate, RAF and Wales) 1968 SA 1
Young, J R C (Oxford U, Harlequins and England) 1959 NZ 2
Young, R M (Queen's U, Belfast, Collegians and Ireland) 1966 A 1,2, NZ 1, 1968 SA 3

Anton Want/Getty Images

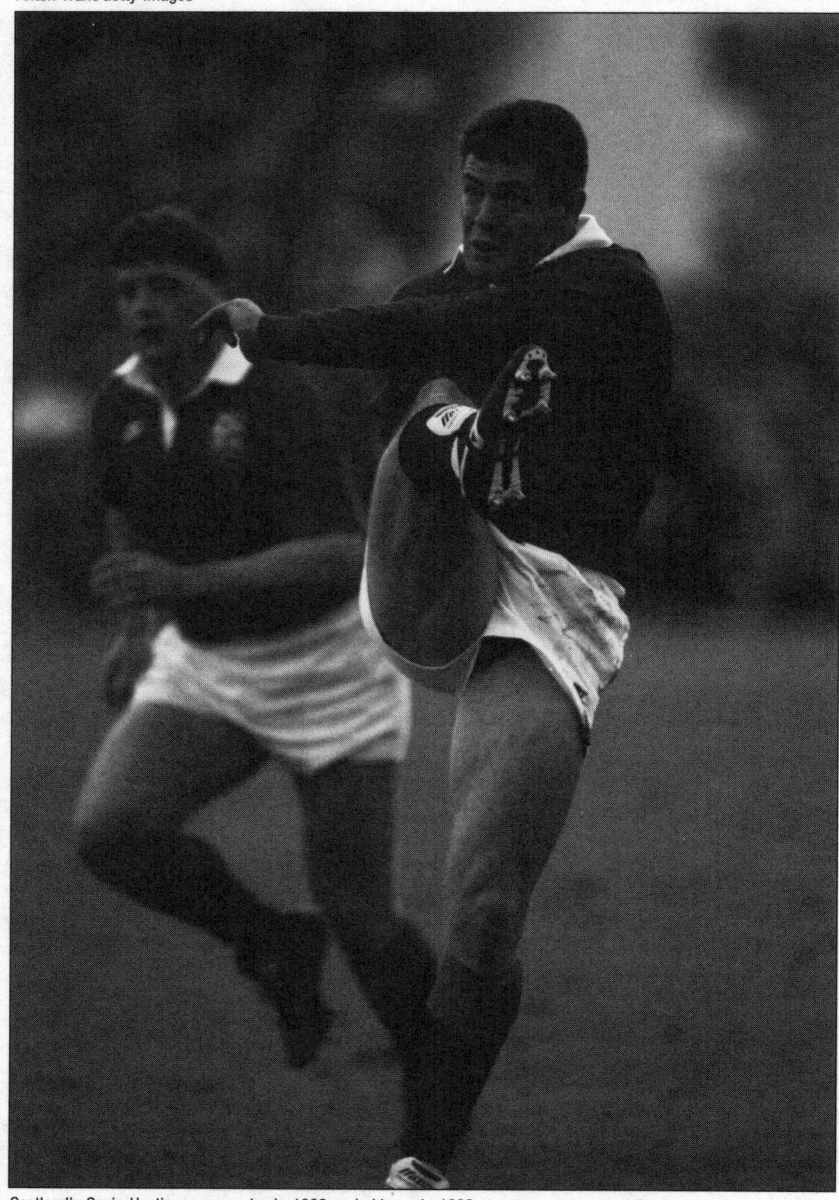

Scotland's Gavin Hastings was a star in 1989 and skipper in 1993.

THE COMBINED TEAMS
FROM STRENGTH TO STRENGTH

Getty Images

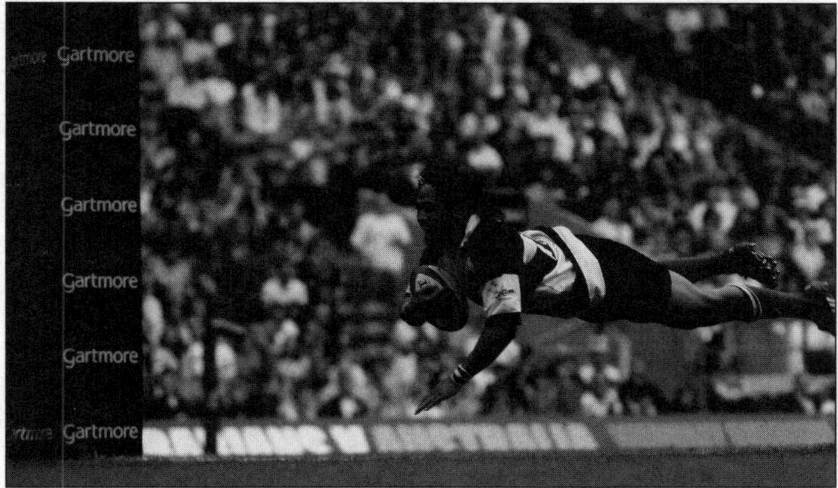

The Barbarians graced Twickenham in 2008, Seilila Mapusua scoring (above) in the 17–14 loss to England.

When William Percy Carpmael sat down for dinner with some 'high-spirited team-mates' at the Leuchters Restaurant in Bradford in 1890 and suggested the formation of a cosmopolitan touring team to be known as the Barbarians, even he surely could not have envisaged how popular or enduring his simple idea would be.

A few short months later, the Barbarians were on the road for their inaugural tour, playing Hartlepool Rovers and Bradford and although frost put pay to Carpmael's plans to tackle Swinton, the trip was a resounding success.

Over a century later, the Baa-Baas continue to preserve the spirit of a game much changed by professionalism, within the higher echelons at least, since Carpmael's day. And judging by the side's results in 2007–08, the competitive but always amicable fires still burn brightly for those fortunate to pull on the famous black and hooped white shirt.

The season began, just after the World Cup, in mid-November with a clash against the Combined Services in Plymouth in a Remembrance Day match that produced a thrilling contest and a dramatic climax. Leading 24–20 courtesy of tries from Esher's Matt Moore and Spain's Diego Zarzosa, the Baa-Baas were overhauled at the death by a spectacular score from England Sevens international Isoa Damudamu and the Services claimed a 27–24 triumph.

The following month South Africa were the opponents in a high-profile clash at Twickenham. The Springboks had been crowned world champions two months earlier but captained by the ever pugnacious Mark Regan, the Barbarians tore into South Africa and scores from Australian duo Matt Giteau and Ricky Elsom, and another by evergreen Wales flanker Martyn Williams, were more than enough to give the side a famous 22–5 victory.

"We came together this week and had just four days of preparation," said Baa-Baas' wing Jason Robinson. "That just shows the commitment and the quality of the players we had out there. A lot of people have been saying why are we having this fixture but everybody that saw it witnessed an outstanding game. In the first-half there were some great tries and in the second-half to defend like that and to keep them out was fantastic."

The slightly less imposing surroundings of the Goldington Road Ground was the venue for the team's next outing in March against Bedford – the 81st Mobbs Memorial Match – but a much-changed side picked up where it had left off at Twickenham to record a 34–19 win. A month later and coached by Scotland legend John Jeffrey, Edinburgh Academicals were dispatched 43–0 at Raeburn Place in a game to help celebrate the club's 150th season.

In May, the Barbarians broke new ground when they played a Belgium XV. It was the first time the side had ventured to the country but hot on the heels of recent tours to Germany, Portugal, Russia, Georgia, Tunisia and Spain to increase the profile of the international game, the club were eager to add Belgium to the list and the side marked the occasion with an entertaining 84–10 victory in the Heysel Stadium in Brussels.

The final two games of another action-packed season were all-international affairs with a clash with Ireland at Gloucester's Kingsholm followed by a return to Twickenham to face England.

The Ireland game was a classic illustration of organisation overcoming flair and although the Baa-Baas scored two fluid tries from All Black Craig Newby and South African Pedrie Wannenburg, the Irish were too powerful and ran out 39–14 winners.

It was a similar if altogether tighter story against England, who were fine-tuning their preparations for their two-Test tour of New Zealand. In truth, the game was not the free-flowing spectacle to which Baa-Baa followers have become accustomed but an interception try from Samoan man-of-the-match Seilala Mapusua and a second from Wales veteran Gareth Thomas ensured a close encounter that England eventually edged 17–14.

For the world-famous travelling HSBC Penguins, 2008 represented the club's 49th year of service since Sidcup RFC club members, the late Tony Mason and Alan Wright, sat down and decided to form their own travelling club with a mission statement to foster the development and fraternity of the game worldwide.

Players from 30 countries as diverse as Israel and Fiji, Mexico and Sierra Leone have donned the club colours over the years and teams from some 57 different nations have lined-up against the Penguins since then and 2008 was the club's usual mixture of fun, frolics and some rugby thrown in for good measure.

Their year kicked-off with a clash with Oxford University in late February at Iffley Road and the fixture produced a thrilling encounter that saw the lead change no less than eight times.

The first 40 minutes saw six tries scored with a brace from wing Ronalko Dailly and a third from centre Bryan Milne giving the Penguins a slender two-point lead at half-time. A fourth score from flanker Sam Viggers seemed to have handed the visitors victory but Oxford hit back with a late penalty from Tim Catling to wrap up a hugely entertaining 25–24 win – their first victory over the Penguins since 2002.

The following month the students of Cambridge University were the Penguins opposition at Grange Road and conjured up another feast of running rugby. This time, however, it was the Penguins who emerged 36–25 victors.

Two weeks later the Penguins were back in action on Easter Saturday, returning to their spiritual home of Sidcup to help the club celebrate its 125th anniversary with 12 internationals on show and there was ample action for the assembled crowd who witnessed a deluge of tries and a 48–24 win for the visitors.

It was passports at the ready a few days later as the Penguins headed east for a second appearance at the prestigious Hong Kong 10s tournament.

The team kicked off with a crushing 83–0 demolition of the Marauders and followed up with wins over Cardiff University and the Borneo Eagles to book their place in the Cup quarter-finals. Day Two saw the Penguins dispatch the Hong Kong Barbarians in the last eight and then beat the

Aliens 14–5 in the semi-finals to set-up a showpiece clash with New Zealand Metro, a repeat of the 2007 final. Metro had triumphed 24–0 a year earlier and it was the same again in 2008 as the Kiwis ran out 38–0 winners.

The Penguins were back in the UK in May to face Bedford Athletic as part of the clubs centenary celebrations and their season finished in June in Italy at the Roma Sevens, where the side cruised through the group stages but were finally beaten 26–21 by the White Hart Marauders in the quarter-finals.

Elsewhere, the New Zealand Maori side continued to represent indigenous Kiwis with great pride and distinction in 2007–08, bouncing back from disappointment in the Churchill Cup in the summer of 2007 to claim the IRB's Pacific Nations Cup at the first attempt 12 months later.

Narrowly beaten by the England Saxons in the final of the Churchill Cup at Twickenham in June, the Maori side were handed the chance to put the defeat behind them in the Pacific Nations Cup, replacing the Junior All Blacks as New Zealand's representative in the competition.

They began the tournament with a hard-fought 20–9 win over Tonga in Albany and were similarly pushed when they met Fiji in Lautoka, relying on lock Jason Eaton's second-half try to set up a 11–7 win. Samoa were despatched 17–6 in Hamilton a week later before Japan were put to the sword 65–22 in Napier.

The win set-up a winner-takes-all game with Australia A in Sydney in July and the showcase game did not disappoint. The second-string Wallabies appeared to be heading to the title with an 18–14 lead deep into the second-half only for Thomas Waldrom to score a dramatic try which substitute Piri Weepu converted to give the Maori a 21–18 lead. A last-gasp penalty attempt from Australia full-back Mark Gerrard missed the target and the New Zealanders were champions.

"We had some experienced guys to get us through but we didn't make it easy for ourselves, we were really scrambling at the end," admitted Maori head coach Donny Stevenson. "We thought if we could put some phases together the opportunities would come, but we lost the ball at critical times. I was concerned at some of the decision making."

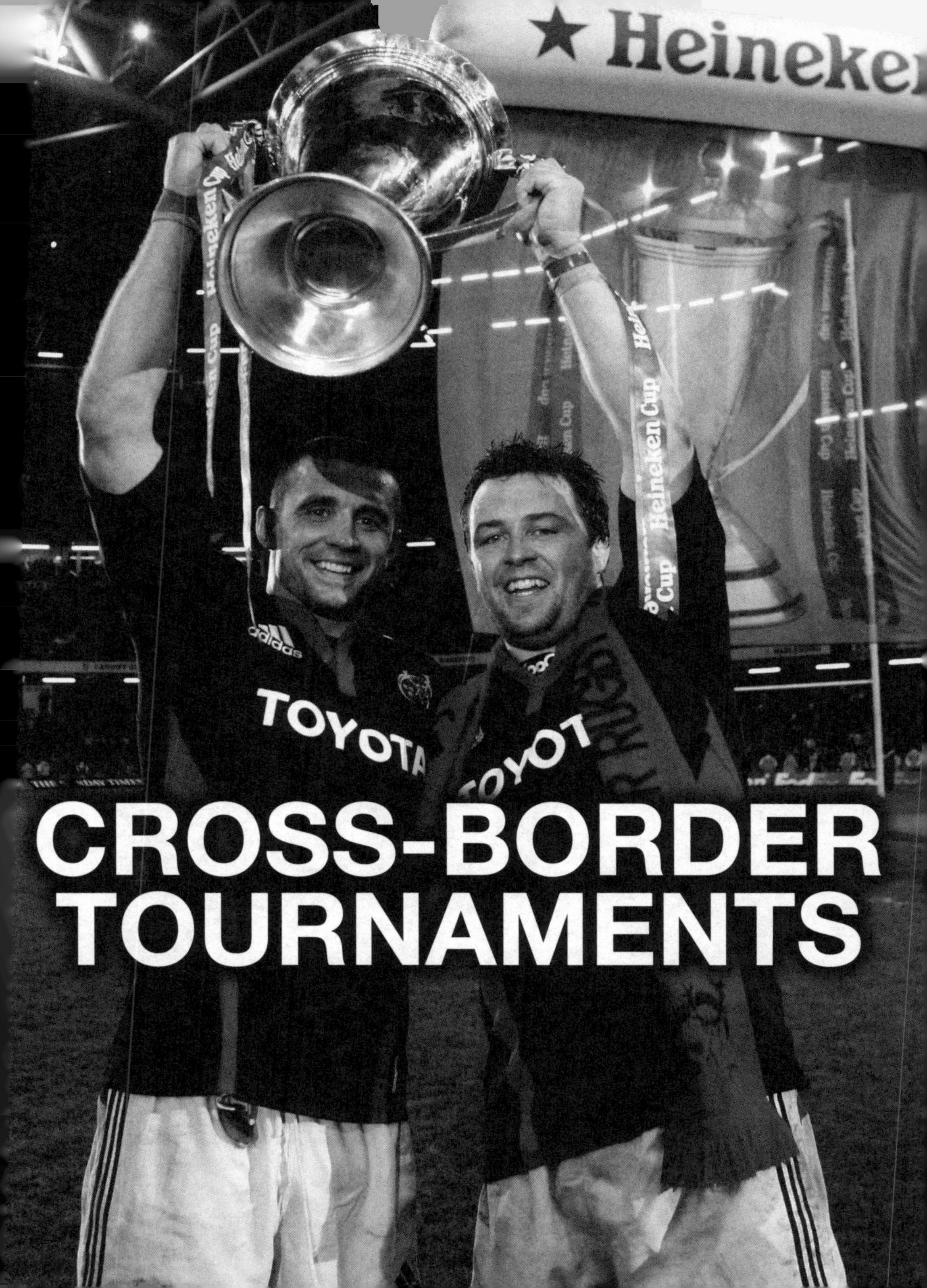

CROSS-BORDER TOURNAMENTS

Dave Rogers/Getty Images

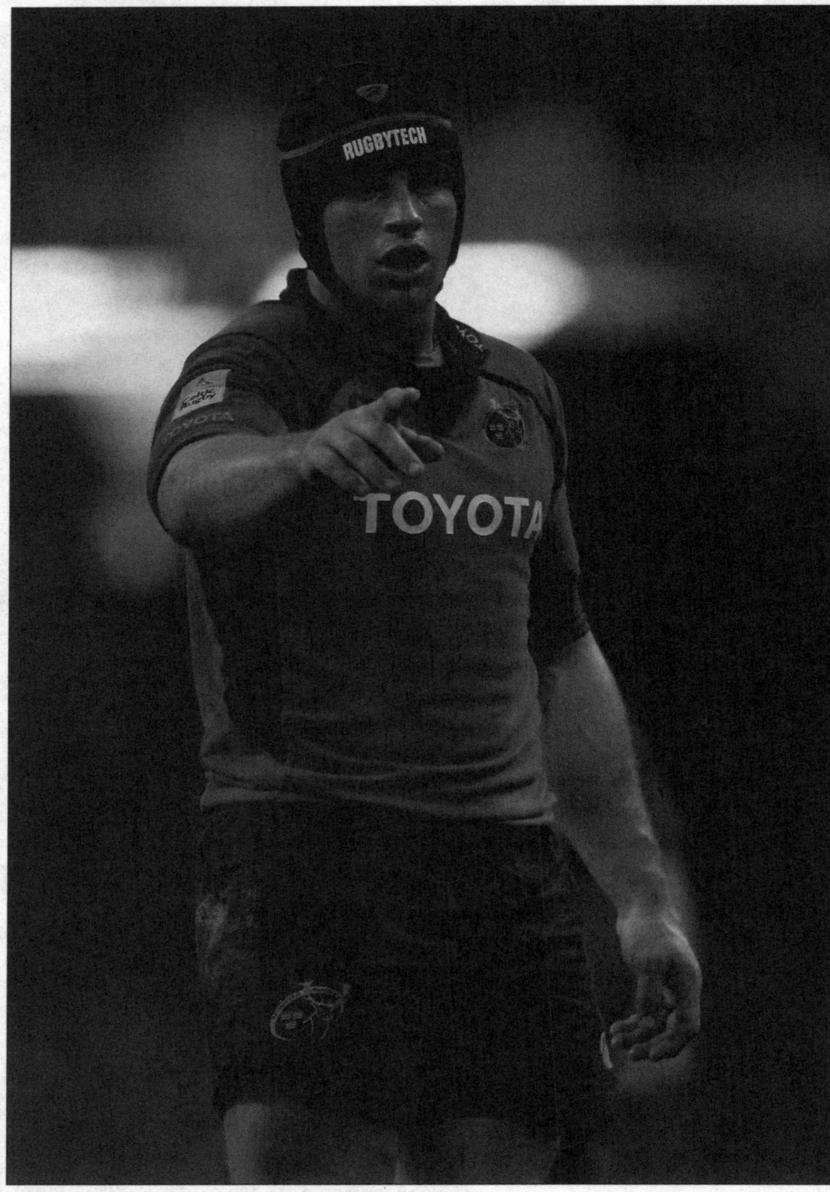

Denis Leamy scored Munster's only try in the Heineken Cup final.

RED ARMY TRIUMPH IN CARDIFF

By Iain Spragg

Shaun Botterill / Getty Images

Donncha O'Callaghan, Paul O'Connell and Alan Quinlan are rightly ecstatic after helping Munster win the cup

Munster confirmed their membership of European rugby's elite with a bruising 16–13 victory over Toulouse in the Heineken Cup final at the Millennium Stadium to give the Red Army their second European triumph in the space of three years and further erase the painful memories of the province's past failures.

The Irishmen finally lifted their first Heineken Cup in 2006 after beating Biarritz. That victory proved a cathartic experience after the agony of losing in the final in both 2000 and 2002 and they underlined their transformation from the competition's nearly men to genuine heavyweights as they downed the three-times champions Toulouse in Cardiff.

The result was also a perfect final chapter for departing coach Declan Kidney. The architect of Munster's 2006 triumph, the Toulouse game was his final match in charge before succeeding Eddie O'Sullivan as Ireland coach and his players ensured he bid farewell to the province in the best possible way.

"It was an emotional dressing room – it was a special place to be," Kidney admitted after the final whistle. "To win this trophy once is special, but twice is a dream. You have good days and some tough days, but not many teams finish on top against Toulouse."

In truth, the final was a war of attrition between the two protagonists rather than a free-flowing spectacle but Munster were untroubled by the lack of cohesion as they made it a third Irish success in the competition.

"It was a war up front but we took the game by the scruff of the neck," admitted Munster captain Paul O'Connell. "We worked our socks off. There have not been many happy days for a lot of us since our 2006 win. We had a tough European campaign last year and those of us in the Ireland team had a tough World Cup. People have shown bottle and courage to achieve this."

For Toulouse, the titanic clash in Cardiff was their fifth appearance in the final but the champions in 1996, 2003 and 2005, as well as runners-up to Wasps in 2004, were unable to find an answer to the heroic efforts of the Munster pack.

"It was Munster's capacity to keep the ball and stop us playing that enabled them to win," conceded Toulouse skipper Fabien Pelous. "We played well and were right in it to the end but we didn't finish our chances and turn our play into points."

The 13th season of Heineken Cup action began in September with 24 clubs hoping to be crowned the kings of Europe.

In Pool One, London Irish and Perpignan proved head and shoulders above the Dragons and Treviso and both sides qualified with ease for the quarter-finals with five wins and one solitary reverse respectively.

Pool Two followed exactly the same pattern with Gloucester and the Ospreys far too strong for the challenge of either Bourgoin or Ulster and both teams made it to the knockout stages.

Pool Three was a tighter affair but Cardiff emerged as the group winners while Stade Francais, twice runners-up in the tournament, finished second but missed out on a place in the last eight.

Saracens were the only qualifiers in Pool Four with five victories from their six games while Toulouse emerged as Pool Six winners ahead of Leicester, who failed to make the cut.

Getty Images

Saracens made their first semi-final but fell to Munster

That left Pool Five, the proverbial 'Group of Death', with Munster, Clermont, the defending champions Wasps and Llanelli all hoping to reach the quarter-finals. It was a fiercely-contested group and the outcome was only decided by the final round of games. Wasps only needed a draw against Munster at Thomond Park to guarantee their progress but were beaten 19–3 and did not secure the all-important losing bonus point, while Clermont thumped the Scarlets 41–0 to steal second place. It was not however enough to earn the French side one of the best runners-up places and Munster alone qualified from the group.

The first quarter-final was an Anglo-French encounter as London Irish faced Perpignan at the Madejski Stadium and the only try of the match from Declan Danaher and five penalties from Peter Hewat were enough to earn the Exiles a 20–9 victory and a place in the last four for the first time.

"There's a lot of belief in this side," said Irish coach Brian Smith, who was appointed England Attack Coach in July. "We deserve to be in a Heineken Cup semi-final and we'll know in three weeks time if we deserve to go on from there."

Munster travelled to Kingsholm to play Gloucester in the next game but the Cherry and Whites' hopes of progressing were hit when Chris Paterson uncharacteristically missed three early penalty chances and the visitors capitalised on their hosts' profligacy. Ian Dowling and Doug Howlett both crossed either side of the break and Munster emerged 16–3 winners.

A day later Saracens entertained the Ospreys at Vicarage Road and although the Welshmen were hot favourites it was Saracens who gained revenge for their 30–3 mauling in the EDF Energy Cup semi-final a month earlier with a 19–10 victory.

"There's been a lot of things said by the pundits and the press about whether we should have been in the quarter-finals or not," Saracens director of rugby Alan Gaffney said after his team secured their first appearance in the semis. "Today I think our guys answered the critics, went out there and performed."

The last quarter-final saw Cardiff make the journey to France to face Toulouse but the Blues made a disastrous start in the Stade Municipal, gifting Maxime Medard a first minute try and there was no way back for Dai Young's side. Toulouse scored three more tries and ran out comfortable 41–17 victors.

The first semi-final at Twickenham in late April was between London Irish and Toulouse. The French club were denied the services of Vincent Clerc, Clément Poitrenaud, Florian Fritz, Maleli Kunavore and Jean-Baptiste Poux through injury but their greater European pedigree was much in evidence as they kept the Exiles at arm's length throughout the game and tries from Manu Ahotaeiloa and William Servat steered them to 21–15 win and a place in the final.

"There was a lot of skill on show in our semi-final," Toulouse's All Black scrum-half Byron Kelleher said. "The spirit of rugby was there with both teams looking to create chances. If anyone back home thinks northern hemisphere rugby is boring, I can tell them it's not."

A day later, Munster and Saracens crossed swords at the Ricoh Arena in Coventry but hopes of Gaffney's side carrying the English torch through to the final were dashed by a typically abrasive Munster performance.

The Irish side led 15–7 at half-time thanks to tries from fly-half Ronan O'Gara and flanker Alan Quinlan but Saracens fought back after the break with three penalties from fly-half Glen Jackson and not for the first time Munster were indebted to the boot of O'Gara, whose second penalty of the game wrapped up a tense 18–16 victory.

"They brought extra passion and emotion into the game with it being Alan Gaffney's last European game and Richard Hill's last shot at silverware," O'Connell said after the match. "They were prepared to do anything and everything they could to win the game, which is a great credit to them. They were outstanding and we had to dig deep."

The final against Toulouse in Cardiff was to be just as tight, as Munster found themselves on the back foot in the early exchanges. Scrum-half Jean-Baptiste Elissalde drew first blood for the Frenchman after nine minutes with a well-taken drop goal and Kidney's side were not on the scoreboard until the 33rd minute when Denis Leamy capitalised on a disintegrating Toulouse scrum to score the first try of the game. The conversion from O'Gara and a penalty three minutes later followed but Elissalde replied with his first penalty and at half-time, Munster had a 10–6 lead.

There was little to choose between the two sides after the restart but the game took a dramatic turn on 51 minutes when Pelous was shown a yellow card for kicking Quinlan and O'Gara slotted the resulting penalty.

Munster were hoping to make their numerical supremacy count but it was Toulouse who reacted the more positively to the absence of Pelous and just three minutes after their captain was sin binned, they scored their only try with a moment of brilliance from full-back Cédric Heymans setting up Yves Donguy. Elissalde added the conversion and the score was 13–13.

The nerves were getting to both sides by now and the signs were one score could settle the outcome. It was O'Gara who was to supply it with a 65th minute penalty and although Munster had to weather the inevitable Toulouse storm in the final 10 minutes, they clung on for a famous victory.

"Toulouse had us on the rack for the first 15 minutes and we had to hold on to avoid conceding more scores," admitted Munster's man-of-the-match Quinlan. "The amount of work which has gone into this has been immense and I count myself lucky to be a part of this team. We had great support from people who believed in us."

Toulouse coach Guy Noves agreed his side's best chance of victory came in the early phase of the match. "We put them under a lot of pressure for the first 25 minutes or so," he said. "We were there in terms of physicality. We know Munster are a team of great quality but I felt a turning point was the yellow card for Fabien Pelous."

HEINEKEN CUP 2007–08 RESULTS

ROUND ONE

9 September, 2007

Ulster 14 **Gloucester** 32

Perpignan 23 **Dragons** 19

10 September, 2007

Leinster 22 **Leicester** 9

Edinburgh 15 **Toulouse** 19

Viadana 11 **Biarritz** 19

Wasps 24 **Munster** 23

Stade Francais 37 **Harlequins** 17

Ospreys 22 **Bourgoin** 15

London Irish 42 **Treviso** 9

11 September, 2007

Cardiff 34 **Bristol** 18

Clermont Auvergne 48 **Llanelli** 21

Saracens 33 **Glasgow** 31

ROUND TWO

16 September, 2007

Glasgow 41 **Viadana** 31

Bourgoin 24 **Ulster** 17

Gloucester 26 **Ospreys** 18

17 September, 2007

Dragons 17 **London Irish** 45

Harlequins 13 **Cardiff** 13

Treviso 17 **Perpignan** 29

Biarritz 22 **Saracens** 21

Leicester 39 **Edinburgh** 0

Llanelli 17 **Wasps** 33

18 September, 2007

Munster 36 **Clermont Auvergne** 13

Toulouse 33 **Leinster** 6

Bristol 17 **Stade Francais** 0

ROUND THREE

7 December, 2007

Leinster 28 **Edinburgh** 14

Bourgoin 7 **Gloucester** 31

Ospreys 48 **Ulster** 17

8 December, 2007

Treviso 33 **Dragons** 35

Saracens 71 **Viadana** 7

Clermont Auvergne 37 **Wasps** 27

Leicester 14 **Toulouse** 9

Harlequins 3 **Bristol** 17

Llanelli 16 **Munster** 29

9 December, 2007

Glasgow 9 **Biarritz** 6

Stade Francais 12 **Cardiff** 6

London Irish 24 **Perpignan** 16

ROUND FOUR

14 December, 2007

Ulster 8 **Ospreys** 16

Biarritz 21 **Glasgow** 14

15 December, 2007

Cardiff 31 **Stade Francais** 21

Edinburgh 29 **Leinster** 10

Dragons 22 **Treviso** 24

Perpignan 23 **London Irish** 6

Viadana 26 **Saracens** 34

Wasps 25 **Clermont Auvergne** 24

Gloucester 51 **Bourgoin** 27

16 December, 2007

Munster 22 **Llanelli** 13

Toulouse 22 **Leicester** 11

Bristol 20 **Harlequins** 7

ROUND FIVE

11 January, 2008

Ulster 25 **Bourgoin** 24

Stade Francais 19 **Bristol** 11

Cardiff 23 **Harlequins** 12

12 January, 2008

Leinster 20 **Toulouse** 13

Saracens 45 **Biarritz** 16

London Irish 41 **Dragons** 24

Ospreys 32 **Gloucester** 15

Viadana 15 **Glasgow** 18

Perpignan 55 **Treviso** 13

Edinburgh 17 **Leicester** 12

13 January, 2008

Wasps 40 **Llanelli** 7

Clermont Auvergne 26 **Munster** 19

ROUND SIX

18 January, 2008	
Glasgow 17 **Saracens** 21	**Biarritz** 25 **Viadana** 16
19 January, 2008	
Dragons 0 **Perpignan** 25	**Toulouse** 34 **Edinburgh** 10
Treviso 11 **London Irish** 24	**Llanelli** 0 **Clermont Auvergne** 41
Leicester 25 **Leinster** 9	**Munster** 19 **Wasps** 3
20 January, 2008	
Gloucester 29 **Ulster** 21	**Bristol** 0 **Cardiff** 17
Bourgoin 21 **Ospreys** 28	**Harlequins** 10 **Stade Francais** 31

GROUP TABLES

POOL ONE

	P	W	D	L	F	A	Pts
London Irish	6	5	0	1	182	100	24
Perpignan	6	5	0	1	171	79	22
Dragons	6	1	0	5	117	19	18
Treviso	6	1	0	5	107	207	5

POOL FOUR

	P	W	D	L	F	A	Pts
Saracens	6	5	o	1	225	119	24
Biarritz	6	4	0	2	109	116	18
Glasgow	6	3	0	3	130	127	16
Viadana	6	0	0	6	106	208	3

POOL TWO

	P	W	D	L	F	A	Pts
Gloucester	6	5	0	1	184	119	24
Ospreys	6	5	0	1	164	102	21
Bourgoin	6	1	0	5	118	174	8
Ulster	6	1	0	5	102	173	5

POOL FIVE

	P	W	D	L	F	A	Pts
Munster	6	4	0	2	148	95	19
Clermont	6	4	0	2	189	128	19
Wasps	6	4	0	2	152	127	18
Llanelli	6	0	0	6	74	213	0

POOL THREE

	P	W	D	L	F	A	Pts
Cardiff	6	4	1	1	124	76	20
Stade Francais	6	4	0	1	120	92	18
Bristol	6	3	0	3	83	80	12
Harlequins	6	0	1	5	62	14	12

POOL SIX

	P	W	D	L	F	A	Pts
Toulouse	6	4	0	2	130	76	20
Leicester	6	3	0	3	110	79	14
Leinster	6	3	0	3	95	123	12
Edinburgh	6	2	0	4	85	142	9

QUARTER-FINALS

5 April, 2008	
London Irish 20 **Perpignan** 9	**Gloucester** 3 **Munster** 16
6 April, 2008	
Saracens 19 **Ospreys** 10	**Toulouse** 41 **Cardiff** 17

SEMI-FINALS

26 April, Twickenham, London

LONDON IRISH 15 (1G, 1PG, 1T) TOULOUSE 21 (1G, 3PG, 1T)

London Irish: P Hewat; T Ojo, P Richards, S Mapusua, S Tagicakibau; S Geraghty, P Hodgson; D Murphy, D Paice, F Rautenbach, N Kennedy, R Casey (*captain*), D Danaher, S Armitage, P Murphy *Substitutions:* T Lea'aetoa for D Murphy (40 mins); J M Leguizamon for P Murphy (55 mins)

SCORERS *Tries:* Ojo, Tagicakibau Conversion: Hewat Penalty Goal: Hewat

Toulouse: C Heymans; M Médard, M Ahotaeiloa, Y Jauzion, Y Donguy; J-B Elissalde, B Kelleher; D Human, W Servat, S Perugini, F Pelous (*captain*), P Albacete, J Bouilhou, Y Nyanga, S Sowerby *Substitutions:* T Dusautoir for Nyanga (60 mins); R Millo-Chluski for Pelous (71 mins); O Hasan for Perugini (71 mins); Nyanga for Ahotaeiloa (74 mins); G Lamboley for Bouilhou (77 mins); A Vernet Basualdo for Servat (80 mins)

SCORERS *Tries:* Ahotaeiloa, Servat Conversion: Elissalde Penalty Goals: Elissalde (3)

REFEREE A Lewis (Ireland)

27 April, Ricoh Arena, Coventry

SARACENS 16 (1G, 3PG)
MUNSTER 18 (1G, 2PG, 1T)

Saracens: R Haughton; F Leonelli, K Sorrell, A Powell, K Ratuvou; G Jackson, N de Kock (*captain*); N Lloyd, M Cairns, C Visagie, H Vyvyan, K Chesney, P Gustard, R Hill, B Skirving *Substitutions:* T Ryder for Skirving (33 mins); C Johnston for Visagie (47 mins); Visagie for Gustard (temp 63–66 mins); M Rauluni for de Kock (77 mins)

SCORERS *Try:* Ratuvou Conversion: Jackson Penalty Goals: Jackson (3)

Munster: D Hurley; D Howlett, R Tipoki, L Mafi, I Dowling; R O'Gara, T O'Leary; M Horan, J Flannery, J Hayes, D O'Callaghan, P O'Connell (*captain*), A Quinlan, D Wallace, D Leamy *Substitutions:* D Ryan for O'Callaghan (75 mins)

SCORERS *Tries:* O'Gara, Quinlan Conversion: O'Gara Penalty Goals: O'Gara (2)

YELLOW CARDS Tipoki (58 mins) Lloyd (60 mins) Johnston (62 mins) Referee N Owens (Wales)

FINAL

24 May, Millennium Stadium, Cardiff

MUNSTER 16 (1G, 3PG)
TOULOUSE 13 (1G, 1PG, 1DG)

Munster: D Hurley; D Howlett, L Maki, R Tipoki, I Dowling; R O'Gara, T O'Leary; M Horan, J Flannery, J Hayes, D O'Callaghan, P O'Connell (*captain*), A Quinlan, D Wallace, D Leamy *Substitutions:* M O'Driscoll for O'Connell (temp 58 to 61 mins); T Buckley for Horan (temp 64 to 74 mins)

SCORERS *Try:* Leamy Conversion: O'Gara Penalty Goals: O'Gara (3)

Toulouse: C Heymans; M Medard, M Kunavore, Y Jauzion, Y Donguy; J-B Elissalde, B Kelleher; D Human, W Servat, S Perugini, F Pelous (*captain*), P Albacete, J Boiulhou, T Dusautoir, S Sowerby *Substitutions:* Y Nyanga for Dusautoir (38 mins); J B Poux for Perugini (56 mins); R Millo-Chlusky for Albacete (62 mins); G Lamboley for J Bouilhou (62 mins); M Ahotaeiloa for Y Donguy (73 mins)

SCORERS *Try:* Donguy Conversion: Ellisalde Penalty Goal: Ellisalde Drop Goal: Ellisalde

YELLOW CARD Pelous (51 mins)

REFEREE N Owens (Wales)

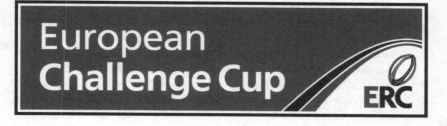

European Challenge Cup
ERC

LONG WAIT OVER FOR BATH

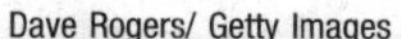
Dave Rogers/ Getty Images

Bath's ten-year wait for a trophy is over, and Matt Stevens (centre) is delighted.

Bath finally shrugged off the malaise that had hung over The Recreation Ground for a decade by beating Worcester in the final of the European Challenge Cup and securing the club's first silverware since they famously beat Brive in the Heineken Cup final in 1998.

The game's professional era has not been kind to the former undisputed kings of England but the fallen West Country giants rediscovered their winning knack against the Warriors, at Kingsholm, with a triumph that owed much to departing captain Steve Borthwick, who was playing his last game for the club before joining Saracens next season.

Just a week after the bitter disappointment of losing to Wasps in the Guinness Premiership play-off semi-final, Bath picked themselves up for one last push and first-half tries from flanker Jonny Faamatuainu and full-back Nick Abendanon provided the platform for a 24-16 victory.

It was a case of third time lucky for Bath after losing the 2003 Challenge Cup final to Wasps and the 2007 showpiece match to Clermont Auvergne and was the seventh English success in the 12-year history of the European rugby's second tier competition.

"I'm just so happy for the guys who have worked so hard for so many years, and for these fans," an emotional Borthwick said after the final whistle. "It's been an honour for me to play with them. It's a great team effort. I'm looking forward to what's ahead of me, but for the next couple of days I will enjoy the time I've had with these boys."

For Bath coach Steve Meehan, victory at Kingsholm was the opportunity to lay ghosts to rest and finally end the persistent talk of the club's decade-long trophy drought.

"I'm delighted," he said. "It takes all those questions of never having won anything for 10 years out of the equation now. We were very disappointed to lose the Premiership semi-final against Wasps but to come out and prove a point was fantastic.

"I think over the course of the whole game we made some errors and put ourselves under pressure. I'm pleased the boys didn't go into their shells, they kept going. Hopefully we can build on this for next season."

The group phases began in November and the initial exchanges highlighted the strength of the tournament's Guinness Premiership contingent.

Bath were drawn in Pool One with Auch, Albi and Parma. Meehan's side travelled to Auch for their opener and tries from Butch James and Andrew Beattie at the Stade Patrice Brocas steered the visitors to a 28-6 win. They were rarely troubled in their remaining five group games and qualified for the quarter-finals with an unbeaten record.

Pool Two was a similarly regal procession for Worcester, who started their campaign with an 18-8 win over Bucharest at the Arcul de Triumf stadium and never looked back, reaching the last eight with six wins from six.

In contrast, Newcastle did not have things all their own way in Pool Three despite topping the table with five wins. The Falcons opened up with an eye-catching 71-10 demolition of El Salvador in Spain but narrowly lost to Connacht at The Sports Ground in December, tarnishing their unbeaten record. Brive also qualified for the quarter-finals after finishing second to Newcastle and securing one of the three best runners-up places.

Pool Four was another tale of English dominance as Sale battled with Montpellier for top spot and eventually emerged victorious. The Sharks rattled through their first five fixtures, despatching Montpellier at Edgeley Park before beating Padova and Bayonne home and away but were denied a perfect six when they travelled to the Stade Yves Du-Manoir for the return fixture with Montpellier but could only secure a hard-fought 14-14 draw, a result which also saw the Frenchmen reach the knockout stages as runners-up.

The only group in which the English were not in the ascendancy was Pool Five, where Castres restored a degree of Gallic pride with top spot ahead of Leeds and the quarter-final line-up was finalised with five Premiership sides and three Top 14 teams in contention.

The first quarter-final saw Sale, champions in both 2002 and 2005, entertain Brive at Edgeley Park in early April but any hopes the Frenchmen had of throwing off their indifferent Top 14 form were dashed by a dynamic Sharks display and the deadly accuracy of Luke McAlister's boot and the home side cantered to a 49-24 win.

Bath were in equally emphatic form against Leeds at The Rec the following day and a hat-trick from wing Matt Banahan and seven conversions from Olly Barkley comprehensively crushed the visitors and Meehan's side emerged 57-5 winners.

The third quarter-final pitted Worcester against Montpellier at the Sixways Stadium but it was once again the English side who enjoyed the spoils after a brace from Kiwi wing Rico Gear inspired the Warriors to a 36-26 triumph.

The semi-final line-up was completed after Newcastle's clash with Castres at Kingston Park and the Falcons ensured the last four of the tournament would be an all-English affair with a 40-13 victory.

The first semi-final saw Worcester tackle Newcastle and although the Falcons took an early lead at the Sixways with a Tom May drop goal, it was the Warriors who stamped their authority on the first-half proceedings with tries from Marcel Garvey and Sam Tuitupou. It proved to be the game's decisive period and a second try from Tuitupou after the break ensured there was no way back for Newcastle and Worcester were 31-16 winners.

"We're delighted to make the final," said Warriors director of rugby Mike Ruddock. "Our defence held tight and was fantastic and we took our opportunities in the first half.

"It was a big effort from the boys, they have come a long way this season and we are very proud of them. There was real pride, passion and commitment. They really were Warriors tonight."

The second semi-final between Bath and Sale at the Rec followed a similar pattern to the first, with the visitors snatching an early lead with a drop goal from Charlie Hodgson but it was the only time the Sharks were to enjoy the lead in the match. Scrum-half Michael Claassens helped himself to the first try of the game after charging down a ponderous Hodgson clearance after just four minutes and Michael Lipman, Danny Grewcock, Andy Higgins and Banahan all crossed as Bath powered their way to a 36-14 victory.

"We've proved that we have the attacking prowess to finish games off," said Bath prop Matt Stevens. "And we've also got the defence to shut them out.

"In the last four weeks we've improved in every match and we're reaching our peak at the right time of the season in all competitions. We're really happy to get through to the final and now we've got the chance of picking up silverware."

Both sides had a month to prepare for the final, although Bath went into the game with a psychological edge having beaten the Warriors home and away in the Premiership and they drew first blood at Kingsholm when Barkley who, like Borthwick, was playing his last game for the club having signed for Gloucester for next season, landed a 15th minute penalty.

Worcester were back on terms eight minutes later when Shane Drahm was on target with a penalty but the game was about to enter into a pivotal period in which Bath struck twice and effectively quelled the Warriors challenge.

The first Bath try came on 31 minutes, a result of incisive and clinical attack, which saw Butch James work space for Faamatuainu and the Samoan flanker crashed over. Four minutes later they crossed again after good work from Barkley and Joe Maddock set up Abendanon and although Drahm added a second penalty a minute before the break, Bath held a 15-6 lead at half-time.

Drahm and Barkley traded penalties after the restart but Bath crucially extended their advantage with a Barkley drop goal and a James penalty. Full-back Thinus Delport scored a 79th minute try for the Warriors but with the clock against them and the deficit still eight points, it proved to be no more than a consolation score. Bath were the champions and their 10 barren years were finally consigned to history.

"Over the course of 80 minutes we were the better team," Meehan said after the final whistle. "This has to be the start of something and we have to get better. You can't stand still but we have now proved we can win grand finals. We knew we had to play a tighter game because of the conditions but with the pack we have got, I didn't see any problems."

The result was a bitter pill to swallow for Worcester. Defeat handed the Premiership's final Heineken Cup place for 2008-09 to Harlequins and left the club still waiting for its first major trophy, 137 years after its formation.

"Bath were more streetwise and played the conditions better," Ruddock conceded. "I think they have learnt from their losing finals just what it takes to nail down a win on these big occasions.

We fell a little bit short today but Bath had done their homework and we have to be proud of our achievement in getting to this European Challenge Cup final."

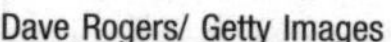

Dave Rogers/ Getty Images

Five of the eight quarter-finalists, including Worcester, were English sides.

EUROPEAN CHALLENGE CUP 2007–08 RESULTS

ROUND ONE	
8 November, 2007	
Sale 49 **Montpellier** 6	
9 November, 2007	
Montauban 65 **Parma** 6	**Bayonne** 37 **Padova** 20
Brive 15 **Connacht** 6	**Leeds** 35 **Castres** 18
10 November, 2007	
Bucharest 8 **Worcester** 18	**Overmach** 23 **Albi** 28
El Salvador 10 **Newcastle** 71	**Auch** 6 **Bath** 28
Calvisano 54 **Dax** 19	
ROUND TWO	
15 November, 2007	
Newcastle 25 **Brive** 19	
16 November, 2007	
Connacht 75 **El Salvador** 8	**Dax** 20 **Leeds** 23
17 November, 2007	
Bath 28 **Overmach** 0	**Parma** 23 **Bucharest** 23
Padova 14 **Sale** 53	**Worcester** 41 **Montauban** 18
Castres 61 **Calvisano** 28	**Albi** 30 **Auch** 31
Montpellier 18 **Bayonne** 12	
ROUND THREE	
7 December, 2007	
Connacht 16 **Newcastle** 13	**Albi** 18 **Bath** 26
8 December, 2007	
Bucharest 19 **Montauban** 17	**Parma** 25 **Auch** 20
Padova 13 **Montpellier** 19	**Worcester** 50 **Parma** 0
Castres 25 **Dax** 15	**Bayonne** 12 **Sale** 51
9 December, 2007	
Brive 71 **El Salvador** 0	**Leeds** 45 **Calvisano** 5
ROUND FOUR	
13 December, 2007	
Sale 32 **Bayonne** 10	
14 December, 2007	
Montauban 34 **Bucharest** 6	**Montpellier** 31 **Padova** 3
15 December, 2007	
Bath 59 **Albi** 15	**Parma** 16 **Worcester** 66
Auch 24 **Parma** 20	**Dax** 15 **Castres** 16

16 December, 2007	
El Salvador 8 **Brive** 40	**Calvisano** 27 **Leeds** 26
Newcastle 39 **Connacht** 0	
ROUND FIVE	
11 January, 2008	
Montauban 7 **Worcester** 24	**Brive** 12 **Newcastle** 19
Sale 45 **Padova** 6	**Leeds** 25 **Dax** 18
12 January, 2008	
Calvisano 9 **Castres** 27	**Parma** 13 **Bath** 31
Auch 15 **Albi** 13	**Bayonne** 24 **Montpellier** 26
13 January, 2008	
El Salvador 0 **Connacht** 60	**Bucharest** 21 **Parma** 20
ROUND SIX	
17 January, 2008	
Castres 13 **Leeds** 3	
18 January, 2008	
Connacht 15 **Brive** 22	**Dax** 22 **Calvisano** 0
19 January, 2008	
Bath 31 **Auch** 13	**Parma** 17 **Montauban** 34
Padova 17 **Bayonne** 5	**Worcester** 46 **Bucharest** 0
Albi 26 **Parma** 23	**Montpellier** 14 **Sale** 14
20 January, 2008	
Newcastle 97 **El Salvador** 0	

GROUP TABLES

POOL ONE

	P	W	D	L	F	A	PTS
Bath	6	6	0	0	203	65	28
Auch	6	3	0	3	109	147	14
Albi	6	2	0	4	130	177	11
Parma	6	1	0	5	104	157	7

POOL TWO

	P	W	D	L	F	A	PTS
Worcester	6	6	0	0	245	49	29
Montauban	6	3	0	3	175	113	16
Bucharest	6	2	1	3	77	158	10
Parma	6	0	1	5	82	259	3

POOL THREE

	P	W	D	L	F	A	PTS
Newcastle	6	5	0	1	264	57	24
Brive	6	4	0	2	179	73	20
Connacht	6	3	0	3	172	97	15
El Salvador	6	0	0	6	26	414	0

POOL FOUR

	P	W	D	L	F	A	PTS
Sale	6	5	1	0	244	62	27
Montpellier	6	4	1	1	115	115	19
Bayonne	6	1	0	5	100	165	8
Padova	6	1	0	5	73	190	5

POOL FIVE

	P	W	D	L	F	A	PTS
Castres	6	5	0	1	160	105	21
Leeds	6	4	0	2	157	101	19
Calvisano	6	2	0	4	123	200	9
Dax	6	1	0	5	109	143	7

QUARTER-FINALS

4 April, 2008	
Sale 49 **Brive** 24	
5 April, 2008	
Bath 57 **Leeds** 5	**Worcester** 36 **Montpellier** 26
Newcastle 40 **Castres** 13	

SEMI-FINALS

25 April, Sixways Stadium, Worcester

WORCESTER 31 (4G, 1PG)
NEWCASTLE 16 (1G, 2PG, 1DG)

WORCESTER: T Delport ; M Garvey, D Rasmussen, S Tuitupou, M Benjamin; S Drahm, M Powell; T Windo, A Lutui, T Taumoepeau, G Rawlinson, C Gillies, D Hickey, P Sanderson (captain), K Horstmann Substitutions: M Mullan for Windo (51 mins); T Wood for Hickey (60 mins); R Gear for Delport (70 mins); J Arr for Powell (70 mins); W Bowley for Gillies (70 mins)

SCORERS Tries: Garvey, Tuitupou (2) Wood Conversions: Drahm (4) Penalty Goal: Drahm

NEWCASTLE: M Tait; T May, J Noon, T Flood, J Rudd; J Wilkinson, J Grindal; M Ward, M Thompson, C Hayman, A Perry, M Sorensen, A Buist, B Wilson, P Dowson (captain) Substitutions: T Visser for Noon (31 mins); J Golding for Ward (44 mins); G Parling for Perry (44 mins); A Long for Thompson (55 mins); L Dickson for Grindal (67 mins); E Williamson for Sorensen (77 mins)

SCORERS Try: Wilson Conversion: Wilkinso; Penalty Goals: Wilkinson (2) Drop Goal: May

YELLOW CARD Rawlinson (59 mins)

REFEREE P Allan (Scotland)

26 April, Recreation Ground, Bath

BATH 36 (4G, 1PG, 1T)
SALE 14 (2PG, 1DG, 1T)

BATH: N Abendanon; A Higgins, A Crockett, O Barkley, M Banahan; B James, M Claassens; D Barnes, L Mears, M Stevens, S Borthwick (captain), D Grewcock, J Faamatuainu, M Lipman, C Goodman Substitutions: I Feaunati for Goodman (51 mins); T Cheeseman for Crockett (67 mins); P Dixon for Mears (67 mins); D Bell for Stevens (67 mins); P Short for Grewcock (67 mins); S Berne for Abendanon (76 mins); M Baxter for Claassens (76 mins)

SCORERS Tries: Claassens, Lipman, Grewcock, Higgins, Banahan Conversions: Barkley (4) Penalty Goal: Barkley

SALE: B Foden; C Mayor, C Bell, L McAlister, O Ripol; C Hodgson, R Wigglesworth; A Sheridan, S Bruno, S Turner, I Fernandez Lobbe (captain), D Schofield, S Cox, C Jones, JM Fernandez-Lobbe Substitutions: J Laharrague for Bell (18 mins); L Faure for Sheridan (43 mins); W Cliff for Ripol (46 mins); M Hills for Lobbe (48 mins); E Roberts for Turner (51 mins); N Briggs for Bruno (55 mins); B Cockbain for Hodgson (67 mins)

SCORERS Try: Mayor Penalty Goals: McAlister, Hodgson Drop Goal: Hodgson

REFEREE C Berdos (France)

FINAL

25 May, Kingsholm, Gloucester

BATH 24 (1G, 3PG, 1T, 1DG)
WORCESTER 16 (1G, 3PG)

BATH: N Abendanon; J Maddock, A Crockett, O Barkley, M Banahan; A James, M Claassens; D Flatman, L Mears, M Stevens, D Grewcock, S Borthwick (captain), J Fa'amatuainu, M Lipman, D Browne

SUBSTITUTIONS: D Bell for Flatman (64 mins); P Short for Lipman (72 mins); S Berne for Barkley (76 mins); P Dixon for Mears (76 mins); I Fea'unati for Browne (76 mins); T Cheeseman for Abendanon (80 mins); N Walshe for Claassens (80 mins)

SCORERS Tries: Faamatuainu, Abendanon Conversion: Barkley Penalty Goals: Barkley (2), James Drop Goal: Barkley

WORCESTER: T Delport; M Garvey, D Rasmussen, S Tuitupou, M Benjamin; S Drahm, M Powell; A Windo, A Lutui, T Taumoepeau, G Rawlinson, C Gillies, D Hickey, P Sanderson (captain), K Horstmann Substitutions: N Talei for Hickey (52 mins); M Mullan for Windo (55 mins); C Horsman for Taumoepeau (60 mins); R Powell for M Powell (69 mins); R Gear for Rasmussen (72 mins); W Bowley for Gillies (72 mins); J Carlisle for Drahm (80 mins)

SCORERS Try: Delport Conversion: Carlisle Penalty Goals: Drahm (3)

REFEREE C Berdos (France)

OSPREYS SOAR TO CUP WIN

Dave Rogers / Getty Images

Ryan Jones wins again, at Twickenham

A domestic campaign lasts nine months but a mere 80 minutes can define it and so it proved for the star-studded Ospreys, who salvaged the wreckage of their season with a convincing 23–6 victory over Leicester in the final of the EDF Energy Cup at Twickenham.

In the process, the Welsh region exacted revenge on the Tigers for their 41–35 mauling in the final a year earlier and became the first side from the Principality to claim the trophy in the three-year history of the cross border competition.

The sighs of relief from the Ospreys bench and beleaguered coach Lyn Jones at the final whistle were almost audible. Just a week before the Twickenham clash, the team had been unceremoniously dumped out of the Heineken Cup quarter-finals at Saracens and with the defence of their Magners League title in tatters; victory for Jones' expensively-assembled side was vital. They did not disappoint.

Twelve months earlier the Ospreys had been on the receiving end of an avalanche of first-half points against Leicester but a year on, it was an altogether different story.

The Tigers edged into a precarious six-point lead courtesy of the boot of Andy Goode but after that it was one-way traffic. Fly-half James Hook pulled the strings with a maturity that belied his 22 years, man of the match Marty Holah was outstanding in the pack and scores either side of half-time from Andy Bishop and Alun Wyn Jones ensured it was the Ospreys who were flying high at full-time.

"That was a very important turning point for us," conceded Jones after the game. "We've crossed that line of getting a win in a big game. We've learnt a lot from Leicester, in the last final and in our Heineken Cup clashes with them.

"The Saracens defeat was a kick in the pants, we were devastated. But there was a very positive attitude from everyone today. Coming here, I knew we were going to win and it was a comprehensive performance from one to 15. This was our day. We're absolutely delighted but now we have to build on this success."

For Leicester, defeat was a bitter pill to swallow after their failure to reach the knockout stages of the Heineken Cup and their stuttering Guinness Premiership campaign.

"We were second best by quite some way," admitted skipper Martin Corry. "You've got to give credit to the Ospreys defence. We just couldn't get into our game, get the foundation and win the sort of ball we thrive on."

The tournament began in late October with the group stages and it was soon apparent that the Ospreys would be the team to beat. A 47–16 demolition of Worcester at Sixways in their opening game signalled their intent and Jones's side were equally ruthless in their second outing, running in seven tries against London Irish in a 51–16 romp at the Liberty Stadium. Harlequins however provided a sterner test when the two sides met at the Stoop in December. At one point in the first-half, the visitors were reduced to 12 men as referee Huw Watkins brandished three yellow cards to Ospreys players in quick succession but a try, conversion and four penalties from Gavin Henson steered his side to 19–8 win and a place in the semi-finals.

In contrast, the other three groups were headed by English sides. In Group A, it was Wasps who eventually prospered although their progress through to the knockout stages was far from serene. They began their campaign against the Dragons at Rodney Parade but points were at a premium and they emerged with an unlikely 3–3 draw after Danny Cipriani and Ceri Sweeney traded solitary penalties.

The next game saw Gloucester visit Adams Park but with 15 minutes remaining and facing a 26–8 deficit, Wasps looked dead and buried. Their rally in the final quarter of an hour was as spectacular as it was unexpected and when Tom Voyce was bundled over the line with just 20 seconds of normal time left, the Londoners had somehow secured a 29–26 victory. An altogether less dramatic 24–6 win over Newcastle followed and Wasps were through.

Leicester claimed the honours in Group B ahead of Cardiff despite going down 20–14 in their opener against Bath at The Rec. The Tigers bounced back with a 42–20 thumping of the Blues at Welford Road and victory over Sale in their last game ensured they kept alive their hopes of a successful defence of the trophy.

In Group D, Saracens narrowly edged out Llanelli courtesy of an extra bonus point. High-scoring wins over Leeds and Bristol laid the foundations for the Premiership side and although the Scarlets triumphed 36–32 in the clash of the group's two teams at Stradey Park, Saracens collected two crucial bonus points in defeat and it was Alan Gaffney's team that made the last four.

The first of the semi-finals in March saw Leicester tackle Wasps at the Millennium Stadium in a battle of the English heavyweights and a repeat of the 2007 Heineken Cup final, claimed by the Londoners.

The Tigers felt they had a point to prove and this time it was the Midlanders who tasted victory after a superb all-round performance from fly-half Andy Goode, eclipsing the contribution of much-vaunted opposite number and England rival Cipriani.

Goode – who moved to Brive in July – scored one of Leicester's four tries, as well as two penalties and four conversions in the 34–24 win, for a haul of 19 points and the Man of the Match award and although Cipriani helped himself to two tries, it was the Tigers' number 10 who emerged with the plaudits.

"Andy is a very good player. His consistency lets him down at times but when he is on form, he is as good as any guy in the country," said forwards coach Richard Cockerill.

The Ospreys were next up in Cardiff against Saracens but any thoughts the Premiership outfit had of making it an all English final were dashed by a scintillating second-half display from the Welshman. The Ospreys led by just eight points at the interval but scores from Shane Williams, his second of the match, Henson and Filo Tiatia guided them to a comprehensive 30–3 victory and the chance to avenge their final defeat to the Tigers.

"We're a more effective side now than we were 12 months ago," said Jones as he looked ahead to his side's rematch with Leicester. "A team needs to go through experiences in order to improve."

The final at Twickenham certainly bore out his theory. Even without the rejuvenated Henson in their ranks after the Wales centre was ruled out with an ankle injury, the Ospreys looked a completely different side to that which had been swamped by the same opposition a year earlier and although Leicester took an initial six-point lead, a first Welsh triumph in the competition rarely looked in doubt.

The Ospreys were on the board after 25 minutes when Bishop – Henson's late replacement – crashed through some timid tackling and seven minutes after the break another scything break from Hook and a perfectly-timed pass to Wyn Jones brought their second try. A third penalty from the superb Hook ended the day's scoring and the Ospreys were on the way to the podium at Twickenham to collect the EDF Energy Cup.

"You are going to get thunderbolts in a season and we took a kick in the pants last week [against Saracens in the Heineken Cup] but we came here today knowing exactly what we had to do," Jones said as the Ospreys' celebrations began.

"As a coaching staff we were very apprehensive going to Saracens last week but this week we were quite confident what would happen. When you are playing at the highest level all the time you are always going to have a dip."

For Ospreys skipper Ryan Jones it was second opportunity to get his hands on some silverware after leading Wales to the Grand Slam and he was quick to pay tribute to the contribution of the side's travelling support.

"I'm a proud man at the moment, proud to be captain of the Ospreys and proud to be able to lift the EDF Energy Cup in front of such magnificent support.

"We could hear them right the way through the match, they were like our 16th man, lifting us at times when it was getting a bit tough out there but it wasn't until after the final whistle, when we doing a lap of honour that we could really appreciate how many of them were there.

"That was when it really hit home, and I'd like to thank them on behalf of all the squad for getting behind us so vocally once again."

GROUP STANDINGS

POOL A

	P	W	D	L	F	A	BP	Pts
Wasps	3	2	1	0	56	35	1	11
Gloucester	3	1	1	1	57	58	2	8
Newcastle	3	1	1	1	53	66	1	7
Dragons	3	0	1	2	38	45	3	5

POOL C

	P	W	D	L	F	A	BP	Pts
Ospreys	3	3	0	0	117	40	2	14
London Irish	3	1	0	2	72	88	2	6
Worcester	3	1	0	2	66	117	1	5
Harlequins	3	1	0	2	40	50	1	5

POOL B

	P	W	D	L	F	A	BP	Pts
Leicester	3	2	0	1	88	48	3	11
Cardiff	3	2	0	1	66	63	1	9
Sale	3	1	0	2	48	74	0	4
Bath	3	1	0	2	36	53	0	4

POOL D

	P	W	D	L	F	A	BP	Pts
Saracens	3	2	0	1	123	79	4	12
Llanelli	3	2	0	1	106	69	3	11
Bristol	3	1	1	1	46	69	0	6
Leeds	3	0	1	2	60	11	81	3

SEMI-FINALS

22 March, Millennium Stadium, Cardiff

LEICESTER 34 (4G, 2PG) WASPS 24 (2G, 2T)

LEICESTER: J Murphy; T Varndell, S Rabeni, D Hipkiss, A Tuilagi; A Goode, H Ellis; B Stankovich, G Chuter, M Castrogiovanni, L Deacon, B Kay, T Croft, B Herring, M Corry (*captain*) *Substitutions:* J White for Castrogiovanni (temp 10–21 mins); M Ayerza for Stankovich (44 mins); J Crane for Herring (49 mins); B Kayser for Chuter (72 mins); White for Castrogiovanni (72 mins); S Vesty for Goode (77 mins)

SCORERS *Tries:* Goode, Rabeni, Hipkiss, Castrogiovanni Conversions: Goode (4) *Penalty Goals:* Goode (2)

WASPS: J Lewsey; P Sackey, F Waters, R Flutey, D Doherty; D Cipriani, E Reddan; T Payne, R Ibanez, P Vickery, G Skivington, T Palmer, J Hart, J Haskell, L Dallaglio (*captain*) *Substitutions:* D Walder for Doherty (57 mins); D Leo for Hart (61 mins); D Waldouck for Waters (66 mins); M McMillan for Reddan (72 mins); J Ward for Ibanez (72 mins); T French for Vickery (73 mins); R Birkett for Palmer (73 mins)

SCORERS *Tries:* Sackey (2), Cipriani (2) *Conversions:* Cipriani, Walder

REFEREE N Owens (Wales)

22 March, Millennium Stadium, Cardiff

OSPREYS 30 (2G, 2PG, 2T) SARACENS 3 (PG)

OSPREYS: L Byrne; J Vaughton, S Parker, G Henson, S Williams; J Hook, M Phillips; P James, R Hibbard, A Jones, A-W Jones, I Evans, J Thomas, M Holah, R Jones (*captain*) *Substitutions:* H Bennett for Hibbard (temp 12–23 mins); J Marshall for Byrne (temp 43–49 mins); D Jones for James (60 mins); F Tiatia for Thomas (60 mins); Bennett for Hibbard (60 mins); Marshall for Phillips (69 mins); James for A Jones (71 mins); A Bishop for Henson (72 mins); C Bateman for Evans (72 mins); D Biggar for Hook (77 mins)

SCORERS *Tries:* Williams (2), Henson, Tiatia *Conversions:* Hook (2) *Penalty Goals:* Hook (2)

SARACENS: B Russell; R Haughton, F Leonelli, A Farrell, D Scarbrough; G Jackson, N de Kock (*captain*); N Lloyd, F Ongaro, C Visagie, C Jack, H Vyvyan, K Chesney, D Barrell, B Skirving *Substitutions:* M Rauluni for de Kock (40 mins); T Ryder for Jack (43 mins); A Kyriacou for Ongaro (60 mins); P Gustard for Chesney (60 mins); K Sorrell for Leonelli (68 mins); K Yates for Lloyd (71 mins)

SCORERS *Penalty Goal:* Jackson

REFEREE W Barnes (London)

FINAL

2 April, Twickenham, London

OSPREYS 23 (2G, 3PG) LEICESTER 6 (PG, DG)

OSPREYS: L Byrne; J Vaughton, S Parker, A Bishop, S Williams; J Hook, J Marshall; P James, R Hibbard, Adam Jones, Alun-Wyn Jones, I Evans, Ryan Jones (captain), M Holah, F Tiatia *Substitutions:* H Bennett for Hibbard (68 mins); J Thomas for Tiatia (72 mins); Gough for Evans (72 mins); D Jones for James (temp 74–81 mins); J Spratt for Bishop (81 mins); A Brew for Vaughton (82 mins); G Owen for Hook (82 mins)

SCORERS *Tries:* Bishop, A-W Jones Conversions: Hook (2) Penalty Goals: Hook (3)

LEICESTER: J Murphy; O Smith, D Hipkiss, A Mauger, A Tuilagi; A Goode, H Ellis; B Stankovich, G Chuter, M Castrogiovanni, L Deacon, B Kay, M Corry (*captain*), B Herring, J Crane *Substitutions:* J White for Stankovich (51 mins); T Croft for Herring (57 mins) Stankovich for Castrogiovanni (76 mins); B Kayser for Stankovitch (78 mins); T Varndell for Tuilagi (82 mins)

SCORERS *Penalty Goal:* Goode *Drop Goal:* Goode

REFEREE A Rolland (Ireland)

DEANS DEPARTS IN STYLE

By Iain Spragg

Cameron Spencer/Getty Images

We've done it! The Crusaders are champions once again.

The all-conquering Crusaders regained the Super 14 title, beating the New South Wales Waratahs 20–12 in a brutal final in Christchurch and in the process gave departing coach Robbie Deans a fitting farewell after eight years in charge of the Canterbury-based franchise.

Appearing in their ninth final, the Crusaders were heavily indebted to the prolific boot of All Black fly-half Dan Carter, who landed four

Matt King/Getty Images

The Waratahs had a great season, leading the Aussie charge.

penalties and a drop goal to see off the spirited Waratahs and end Deans' hugely successful reign in triumph.

The final in the AMI Stadium was Deans' final match in charge before heading across the Tasman Sea to become head coach of the Wallabies and his team were clearly determined to send him off with his fifth title.

"I consider myself incredibly lucky to have been part of this organisation," Deans said after lifting the trophy again. "None of us are here forever, people come and go. The critical thing is that it carries on. I've got no doubt that it will and I look forward to coming back and being entertained by these blokes.

"It is never easy saying goodbye. This is especially so, when the time comes to close the door on a team and organization that has been such a massive part of one's life, as the Crusaders have been for me.

"While there have been some enjoyable moments, and the outcomes of the various games and championships will stand for all time in the history books, it is the growth of the individuals – both as rugby players, and as people, that I will remember most. "On a personal note, it was always my desire, when the time came to depart, to leave with a solid base in place that ensured the Crusaders continued to grow and strengthen in the future."

The 2008 Super 14 was not only notable for the Crusaders' record-extending seventh title – it was also the year in which the competition trialled the contentious Experimental Law Variations. Designed to increase the amount of time the ball is in play and the speed of the game, the ELVs saw many penalty offences downgraded to free-kicks and allowed teams to legally collapse mauls.

The statistics for the tournament appeared to vindicate the innovation. The 2008 Super 14 saw 497 tries scored in total compared to 440 the previous year and a mere 297 penalties were kicked, significantly fewer than the 409 that were put to the boot in 2007.

The new laws, however, won critics and advocates in seemingly equal measure. Deans was unequivocally in favour of the ELVs while Springboks and Bulls scrum-half Fourie du Preez was far from convinced.

"The game has become less and less discernible from what was there before," Deans argued. "This is good because there is scope for teams to be attacking and positive."

In contrast, du Preez was not a fan. "In putting the ELVs into effect they wanted to get more attacking rugby," he said. "But if you look at the amount of free-kicks and penalties in a game and it's slowing down the ruck situation. Rugby is a lot more negative than positive at the moment."

The introduction of the ELVs and the third Super 14 season began in February with South Africa's Sharks setting the early pace and the Durban-based franchise certainly began their campaign in emphatic style. Starting the season against the Force in mid February, Dick Muir's side kicked off with a 17–10 victory. The win proved the catalyst for an eight-match unbeaten sequence and had they not been held 13–13 by the Hurricanes at the Westpac Stadium in early April, the South Africans would have enjoyed a 100 per cent start to their campaign.

The Crusaders, however, were clearly determined not to allow the Sharks to dominate and also went unbeaten in their opening eight fixtures, comprehensively outplaying the defending champions the Bulls in week two in a 54–19 win and edging past domestic rivals Hurricanes in week seven.

Both franchises were to suffer their first reverses in week nine. The Sharks were surprisingly beaten 27–21 by the Brumbies at the Canberra

Stadium while the Crusaders found themselves on the wrong end of an 18–5 scoreline against the Chiefs in Waikato.

The results proved a temporary setback for the Crusaders, who bounced back with three wins in succession to ensure home advantage in the semi-finals but the Sharks visibly faltered after defeat, losing to both the Waratahs and the Crusaders to limp home in third.

The Sharks misfortune allowed the Waratahs to seal second place and a home tie in the last four while the Hurricanes were embroiled in a fierce battle with the Stormers and the Blues for fourth spot, eventually clinching a place in the semi-finals ahead of the South Africans courtesy of their superior points difference.

The first semi-final was an all Kiwi affair as the Crusaders tackled the Hurricanes in Christchurch and although it was the visitors who drew first blood as early as the second minute with a try from winger Zac Guildford, who charged down a Carter clearance, the hosts dominated proceedings throughout and when Leon MacDonald crossed two minutes before the break, there was no way back for the Hurricanes.

Cameron Spencer/Getty Images

The Sharks led the way for the South African sides, finishing third in the table.

A second score from MacDonald and a third from Keiran Read in the second-half put the Crusaders firmly in the driving seat and Carter made amends for his earlier faux pas with four penalties and three conversions to steer his side to a 33–22 win.

"We went in at half-time and had spent a lot of energy," captain Richie McCaw said after the match. "But they had defended a fair bit so we had to punish them early in the second half. We had a huge amount of territory in their 22 and we had to make it pay in the end. When you've got the ball and you're breathing pretty hard you hope the defending team's breathing harder."

The second semi-final later the same day pitted the Waratahs against the Sharks in Sydney. There has been little to choose between the two sides during the round robin stage of the competition but it was the Australians who had the greater hunger in the knockout phase to emerge 28–13 victors.

The superb Waratah forwards laid the foundations and the backs who supplied the cutting edge and four tries from wing Lote Tuqiri, centre Rob Horne, fly-half Kurtley Beale and scrum-half Luke Burgess were enough to dismiss the Sharks' lacklustre challenge.

"Defence has been a big part of our game this year and we stood up again tonight," said Waratahs captain Phil Waugh. "We're off to Christchurch next week, we'll freshen up and it's a big week. Our execution could have been a lot better but it's a very pleasing result."

The final was a repeat of the 2005 showpiece game in which the Crusaders edged the Waratahs 35–25 and the rematch was to prove equally tight, tense and titanic as the battle between New Zealand and Australia's finest unfolded in the AMI Stadium.

Carter scored the first points of the game with a second-minute penalty but the early exchanges suggested the Waratahs could finally land their first ever Super 14 title and they scored the contest's first try with their first attack when Lachlan Turner was first to Beale's inviting cross field kick.

The visitors extended their lead with a thrilling counter-attack after an intercept in his own half by Waugh and it was Turner again who was on hand to supply the finishing touch, collecting his own chip to score under the posts and establish a 12–3 advantage for the Australians.

The Crusaders rallied with a second Carter penalty and moments before the break they manufactured a try after good work from Brad Thorn, making his final appearance for the side, and McCaw to put number eight Mose Tuiali'i over in the corner. Carter missed the difficult conversion and it was 12–11 to the Waratahs at half-time.

The second period was a bone-crunching tussle between the two protagonists and it was the home side who took control with a third Carter penalty after a high tackle by Waratahs lock Dean Mumm on Tim Bateman.

The Crusaders now held a slender 14–12 advantage and thought they had scored their second try of the game on 55 minutes when prop Wyatt Crockett crashed over only for the referee to pull the play back after Thorn was spotted punching Dan Vickerman. Thorn saw yellow and the Waratahs had 10 minutes in which to claw their way back into the match.

It was now or never for the Australians but the Crusaders' 14-men held firm and when Carter landed a 70th minute drop goal, the writing was on the wall. The Kiwi number 10 added his fourth penalty minutes later and the Crusaders had given Deans his fairytale farewell.

"There was a lot of emotion out there and I guess there will be more tonight," McCaw said as his team prepared to celebrate and bid farewell to their coach. "Towards the end of the round robin, our defence was letting us down. So last week in the semi-final we took a step up and tonight the hits that were going in were just outstanding.

"We felt like we were on top. We played a lot of the rugby. We knew that if we could keep our composure at the start of the second half the points would come, and we kept our composure and got what we needed."

SUPER 14 2008 RESULTS

15 February: **Crusaders** 34 **Brumbies** 3, **Reds** 22 **Highlanders** 16, **Sharks** 17 **Force** 10. 16 February: **Blues** 32 **Chiefs** 14, **Waratahs** 20 **Hurricanes** 3, **Stormers** 9 **Bulls** 16, **Cheetahs** 22 **Lions** 23. 22 February: **Hurricanes** 23 **Reds** 18, **Cheetahs** 15 **Force** 16, **Bulls** 19 **Crusaders** 54. 23 February: **Chiefs** 20 **Waratahs** 17, **Brumbies** 22 **Highlanders** 20, **Sharks** 12 **Stormers** 10, **Lions** 10 **Blues** 55. 29 February: **Hurricanes** 39 **Chiefs** 19, **Lions** 16 **Force** 18, **Stormers** 0 **Crusaders** 22. 1 March: **Highlanders** 12 **Waratahs** 15, **Brumbies** 43 **Reds** 11, **Cheetahs** 26 **Blues** 50, **Bulls** 15 **Sharks** 29. 7 March: **Highlanders** 6 **Hurricanes** 10, **Waratahs** 24 **Brumbies** 17, **Bulls** 31 **Lions** 17. 8 March: **Chiefs** 22 **Cheetahs** 20, **Reds** 16 **Stormers** 34, **Blues** 17 **Sharks** 22. 9 March: **Force** 24 **Crusaders** 29. 14 March: **Chiefs** 26 **Stormers** 35, **Brumbies** 15 **Hurricanes** 33. 15 March: **Blues** 17 **Force** 27, **Crusaders** 55 **Cheetahs** 7, **Reds** 40 **Bulls** 8, **Lions** 8 **Sharks** 16. 21 March: **Crusaders** 34 **Waratahs** 7, **Brumbies** 29 **Cheetahs** 23. 22 March: **Highlanders** 28 **Force** 36, **Blues** 17 **Stormers** 14, **Chiefs** 43 **Bulls** 27, **Lions** 24 **Reds** 24. 28 March: **Hurricanes** 13 **Crusaders** 20 **Waratahs** 23 **Cheetahs** 19, **Force** 16 **Stormers** 32. 29 March: **Chiefs** 39 **Highlanders** 24, **Blues** 23 **Bulls** 21, **Sharks** 22 **Reds** 10. 4 April: **Highlanders** 29 **Lions** 20, **Brumbies** 28 **Chiefs** 42, **Force** 15 **Bulls**14. 5 April: **Hurricanes** 13 **Sharks** 13, **Waratahs** 37 **Blues** 16, **Cheetahs** 29 **Reds** 14. 11 April: **Highlanders** 17 **Sharks** 19. 12 April: **Crusaders** 31 **Lions** 6 **Blues** 11 **Brumbies** 16, **Force** 12 **Waratahs** 17, **Stormers** 34 **Cheetahs** 22, **Bulls** 22 **Hurricanes** 50. 18 April: **Chiefs** 18 **Crusaders** 5, **Reds** 29 **Force** 12. 19 April: **Waratahs** 26 **Lions** 3, **Brumbies** 27 **Sharks** 21, **Bulls** 47 **Highlanders** 17, **Stormers** 20 **Hurricanes** 12. 25 April: **Crusaders** 26 **Blues** 22, **Brumbies** 28 **Lions** 21. 26 April: **Chiefs** 32 **Reds** 20, **Waratahs** 25 **Sharks** 10, **Cheetahs** 10 **Hurricanes** 38, **Stormers** 26 **Highlanders** 16. 2 May: **Crusaders** 18 **Sharks** 10, **Reds** 22 **Blues** 35, **Cheetahs** 28 **Highlanders** 31. 3 May: **Hurricanes** 38 **Lions** 12, **Force** 22 **Chiefs** 21, **Bulls** 16 **Waratahs** 13, **Stormers** 20 **Brumbies** 10. 9 May: **Hurricanes** 21 **Force** 10, **Bulls** 28 **Brumbies** 17. 10 May: **Highlanders** 15 **Blues** 40, **Reds** 21 **Crusaders** 27, **Sharks** 33 **Cheetahs** 14, **Lions** 33 **Chiefs** 27, **Stormers** 13 **Waratahs** 13. 16 May: **Hurricanes** 17 **Blues** 19, **Force** 29 **Brumbies** 22. 17 May: **Crusaders** 14 **Highlanders** 26, **Reds** 11 **Waratahs** 18, **Lions** 13 **Stormers** 22, **Cheetahs** 20 **Bulls** 60, **Sharks** 47 **Chiefs** 25

FINAL TABLE

	P	W	D	L	F	A	Pts
Crusaders	13	11	0	2	369	176	52
Waratahs	13	9	1	3	255	186	43
Sharks	13	9	1	3	271	209	42
Hurricanes	13	8	1	4	308	204	41
Stormers	13	8	1	4	269	211	41
Blues	13	8	0	5	354	267	40
Chiefs	13	7	0	6	346	349	33
Force	13	7	0	6	247	278	33
Brumbies	13	6	0	7	277	317	30
Bulls	13	6	0	7	324	347	28
Highlanders	13	3	0	10	257	338	19
Reds	13	3	1	9	258	323	18
Cheetahs	13	1	0	12	255	426	13
Lions	13	2	1	10	206	365	12

SEMI-FINALS

24 May, AMI Stadium, Christchurch

CRUSADERS 33 (3G, 4PG)
HURRICANES 22 (2G, 1PG, 1T)

CRUSADERS: L MacDonald; K Poki, C Laulala, T Bateman, S Hamilton; D Carter, A Ellis; W Crockett, C Flynn, G Somerville, B Thorn, A Williams, K Read, R McCaw (captain), M Tuiali'i

SUBSTITUTES: T Paulo, B Franks, R Thorne, N Manu, K Fotuali'i, S Brett, S Maitland

SCORERS *Tries*: MacDonald (2), Read *Conversions*: Carter (3) *Penalty Goals*: Carter (4)

HURRICANES: C Jane; H Gear, C Smith, M Nonu, Z Guildford; W Ripia, P Weepu; J Schwalger, A Hore, T Fairbrother, J Thrush, J Eaton, J Collins, C Masoe, R So'oialo (captain)

SUBSTITUTES: H Elliot, N Tialata, C Clarke, S Waldrom, A Mathewson, J Gopperth, T Ellison

SCORERS *Tries*: Guildford, Thrush, Tialata *Conversions*: Gopperth, Collins *Penalty Goal*: Weepu

REFEREE S Dickinson (Australia)

24 May, Sydney Football Stadium, Sydney

WARATAHS 28 (1G, 1PG, 3T, 1DG)
SHARKS 13 (1G, 1PG, 1DG)

WARATAHS: S Norton-Knight; L Turner, R Horne, T Carter, L Tuqiri; K Beale, L Burgess; B Robinson, A Freier, A Baxter, D Mumm, D Vickerman, R Elsom, P Waugh (captain), W Palu

SUBSTITUTES: A Manning, M Dunning, W Caldwell, B Robinson, B Sheehan, M Carraro, T Tahu

SCORERS *Tries*: Tuqiri, Horne, Beale, Burgess *Conversion*: Beale *Penalty Goal*: Beale Drop Goal: Beale

SHARKS: S Terblanche; O Ndungane, A Jacobs, F Steyn, JP Pietersen; R Pienaar, R Kockott; T Mtawarira, B du Plessis, J du Plessis, S Sykes, J Muller (captain), J Botes, AJ Venter, R Kankowski

SUBSTITUTES: C Burden, D Carstens, A van den Berg, J Deysel, E Taione, B Barritt, W Murray

SCORERS *Try*: Burden *Conversion*: Kockott *Penalty Goal*: Pienaar *Drop Goal*: Pienaar

REFEREE B Lawrence (New Zealand)

FINAL

31 May, AMI Stadium, Christchurch

CRUSADERS 20 (4PG, 1T, 1DG)
NSW WARATAHS 12 (1G, 1T)

CRUSADERS: L MacDonald; K Poki, C Laulala, T Bateman, S Hamilton; D Carter, A Ellis; W Crockett, T Paulo, G Somerville, B Thorn, A Williams, K Read, R McCaw (captain), M Tuiali'i

SUBSTITUTES: S Fualau, B Franks, R Thorne, N Manu, K Fotuali'i, S Brett, S Maitland

SCORERS *Try*: Tuiali'i *Penalty Goals*: Carter (4) *Drop Goal*: Carter

YELLOW CARD: Thorne (55 mins)

WARATAHS: S Norton-Knight; L Turner, R Horne, T Carter, L Tuqiri; K Beale, L Burgess; B Robinson, T Polota-Nau, A Baxter, D Mumm, D Vickerman, R Elsom, P Waugh (captain), W Palu

SUBSTITUTES: A Freier, M Dunning, W Caldwell, B Robinson, B Sheehan, M Carraro, T Tahu

SCORERS *Tries*. Turner (2) *Conversion*: Beale

REFEREE M Lawrence (South Africa)

THIRD TIME LUCKY FOR LEINSTER

INPHO

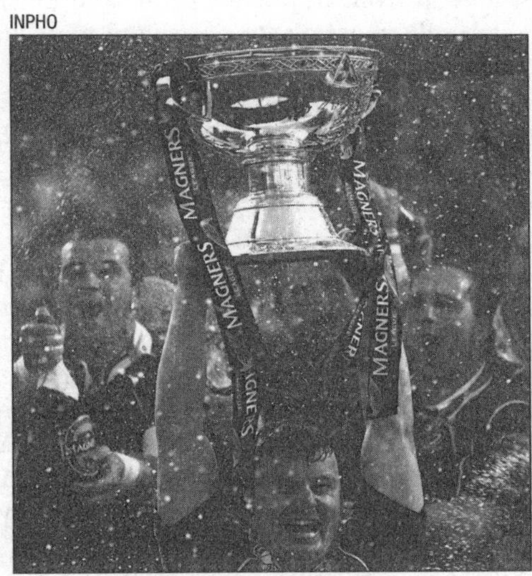

Leinster celebrate their second Magners League

Leinster erased the bitter and painful memories of two dramatic near misses to claim the Magners League trophy and, coupled with Munster's Heineken Cup triumph, gave Irish rugby a timely fillip in the wake of the national team's hugely disappointing Six Nations campaign.

Michael Cheika's side secured the title with a game to spare with a comprehensive 41–8 victory over the Dragons at the RDS in early May and in the process ensured Leinster were finally popping the champagne corks rather than drowning their sorrows at the end of another season of cross border hostilities.

Leinster had been dramatically denied the title in 2006 when David Humphreys' 78th minute drop goal on the final day of the season saw Ulster beat the Ospreys at the death to be crowned champions and were also in contention as the 2007 campaign reached its climax, only to lose to the Blues in Cardiff in their last game, and see the Ospreys clinch the title.

But the Irish province made no mistake in 2008 and made certain of their triumph with a six-try romp against the Dragons that rendered their final game – a potentially nerve-jangling return fixture against the Dragons in Wales – meaningless.

"This is the culmination of three hard years," said Cheika after his side's success. "This title is very important for us. We've worked very hard to have success and that's what every sportsman wants.

"To win the league in front of our own fans and in that manner was really great. We were able to get plenty of ball out wide but our forwards laid the groundwork once again. There was always a danger that if we gave them a sniff they, having no pressure on them, could cause us problems. But we took control of the game very early on and we dominated thereafter."

Victory against the Dragons also proved to be a fitting finale for South African prop Ollie Le Roux and Ireland flanker Keith Gleeson, who were both playing their last games for the province. Le Roux marked his swansong with two first-half tries while Gleeson, who made his debut for Leinster in 2001, was named the man of the match.

"In one year Ollie has made such a significant impact on Leinster," Cheika said. "He's a brilliant player and he's still in demand. The Stormers want him to go back and play Super 14 for the remainder of the season.

"And what can you say about Keith? He's the consummate professional. He was unbelievable at the breakdown. He stayed on his feet the whole game and every time the ball dropped on the ground he was on top of it. I think he went out playing his best football. He played brilliantly tonight, both of them did. The reception that they got from the fans pretty much said it all."

The seventh season of the Celtic cross border competition rolled into action in late August with defending champions Ospreys widely expected to mount another strong challenge for the title but the star-studded Welsh region made a disastrous start to their campaign.

Beaten 17–15 in their opening game against Cardiff at the Arms Park, Lyn Jones' side then surrendered their 15-month unbeaten home record in all competitions against Llanelli. Over 10,000 fans packed into the Liberty Stadium for the game but a controversial Adam Eustace try helped the Scarlets to a 14–9 triumph and the Ospreys were on the ropes.

Worse was to follow in their next fixture against Ulster at Ravenhill. A fiercely contested clash, the game was decided at the death when Niall O'Connor landed a late, late penalty to give the Irish province a precarious 17–16 lead. Ospreys' fly-half Shaun Connor then had a last-gasp chance to snatch victory, but his penalty attempt sailed wide and the Welshmen were beaten again.

Leinster however were faring little better. Successive wins over Edinburgh and Cardiff appeared to have given Cheika's side momentum but they were beaten by Llanelli and Glasgow and then held to a 16–16 draw at Ulster, a sequence of results which seemed to leave their title aspirations looking distinctly unrealistic.

It was left to Cardiff to make the early running and the Blues began their challenge with victory over the Ospreys and then hammered the Dragons 40–13 at Rodney Parade thanks in large part to a brace from centre Tal Selley. It was a result that confirmed that Cardiff, the runners-up in 2007, would once again be serious title contenders.

"We would have settled for that coming down here," said Blues coach Dai Young after despatching the Dragons. "It was a great performance. We've still got things to work on but I've got a big smile on my face. We didn't play silly and I thought we were competitive around the park."

They followed up with a 32–16 win over Glasgow and although they suffered a 30–19 reverse at home to Leinster, they bounced back with wins over Munster at Musgrave Park and Connacht in Cardiff to maintain their push.

The emphasis was now on Leinster to respond to the Blues and the Irishmen did so in style after their three-match run without a victory, embarking on a 10-match winning run that was to ultimately secure them the title.

The run began in early November with a 29–9 success over Connacht. The Ospreys were their next victims before they travelled to Munster, looking for their first win at Musgrave Park in 22 years. The two sides were locked at 3–3 after an hour of hostilities but Shane Horgan grabbed the only try of the match for the visitors on 66 minutes and Leinster emerged 10–3 winners, finally ending their Musgrave Park hoodoo and going top of the Magners League table.

The win tangibly bolstered Leinster's self belief and seven more successive victories followed. The most significant came in February when Cardiff were the visitors to the RDS and with the Blues looking to recover from back-to-back defeats to the Ospreys and Edinburgh, it was to prove a crucial clash.

It was Cardiff who were the quickest out of the blocks with tries from blindside forward Maama Molitika and fly-half Nick MacLeod inside the opening 12 minutes but Leinster rallied and a Michael Berne score and three Felipe Contepomi penalties left the game was delicately poised.

Either side could have claimed victory in the dying minutes but it was the Irish side who came up with the goods when it mattered, full-back Luke Fitzgerald collecting his own chip on 75 minutes for the decisive score. Leinster were 24–17 winners and now six points clear at the top of the table.

Their superb run finally came to an end in April when the team faced Edinburgh at Murrayfield. A bonus point victory in the Scottish capital would have seen Leinster confirmed as champions but Edinburgh, who were in pursuit of their highest ever Magners League finish, had other ideas and with the 80 minutes almost over, the home side led 15-13. There was however time for one last moment of drama as Leinster were awarded a stoppage time penalty but Contepomi's kick hit the post. Leinster's celebrations would have to wait until May.

The visit of the Dragons to the RDS in their penultimate game of the campaign could have been a tense, nervous affair with the big prize so tantalisingly close but le Roux dispelled any lingering doubts with a fourth-minute try after a quick tap penalty and Leinster were up and running.

Five minutes later le Roux crashed over again to the cheers of the delirious RDS crowd and further tries from Horgan, Shane Jennings, Chris Whitaker and Cameron Jowitt ensured the game was played out in a carnival atmosphere. The Irishmen eventually emerged convincing 41–8 winners and Leinster were crowned champions for the first time since they won the inaugural cross border competition in 2002.

"We've been close in the last few years but no cigar so we'll go in and smoke a few cigars in the dressing-room now," said Leinster skipper Brian O'Driscoll after finally getting his hands on the trophy. "This title is a stepping-stone hopefully. Now we want to go out and chase the big one in Europe."

The captain's views were echoed by young fly-half Jonathan Sexton, who enhanced his chances of a full Ireland cap with a series of assured performances throughout the tournament.

"We're all delighted to have won the title but we're determined to use this success as a stepping stone to go on and really challenge for the Heineken Cup," he said.

"It was great to beat Munster home and away, beating Ulster at home on St Stephens Day was a good feeling, but I suppose the one constant source throughout the campaign was in playing in front of big crowds at the RDS.

"It was just incredible. Hopefully the supporters and the fan base will continue to be a major part of our success for many years to come."

MAGNERS LEAGUE RESULTS 2007–08

31 August: **Cardiff** 17 **Ospreys** 15. 1 September: **Llanelli** 23 **Dragons** 30. 7 September: **Dragons** 13 **Cardiff** 40. 11 September: **Ospreys** 9 **Llanelli** 14. 21 September: **Connacht** 22 **Dragons** 7, Cardiff 32 **Glasgow** 16, **Ulster** 17 **Ospreys** 16. 22 September: **Leinster** 23 **Edinburgh** 8, **Munster** 26 **Llanelli** 16. 28 September: **Dragons** 16 **Munster** 26, **Llanelli** 34 **Connacht** 11, **Cardiff** 19 **Leinster** 30, **Edinburgh** 24 **Ulster** 10. 30 September: **Ospreys** 37 **Glasgow** 23. 5 October: **Leinster** 23 **Llanelli** 52, **Edinburgh** 13 **Ospreys** 13, **Glasgow** 16 **Connacht** 15, **Munster** 17 **Cardiff** 19. 6 October: **Dragons** 31 **Ulster** 11.12 October: **Llanelli** 32 **Ulster** 8 **Cardiff** 30 **Connacht** 16, **Edinburgh** 13 **Dragons** 19, **Glasgow** 21 **Leinster** 17. 14 October: **Ospreys** 16 **Munster** 3. 26 October: **Connacht** 14 **Edinburgh** 14, **Glasgow** 11 **Munster** 11, **Ulster** 16 **Leinster** 16. 2 November: **Glasgow** 25 **Ulster** 6, **Leinster** 29 **Connacht** 9. 3 November: **Munster** 19 **Edinburgh** 16, 23 November: **Ospreys** 19 **Leinster** 26, **Connacht** 13 **Ulster** 30, **Glasgow** 17 **Cardiff** 5. 24 November: **Munster** 45 **Dragons** 19, 25 November: **Edinburgh** 27 **Llanelli** 17. 30 November: **Connacht** 10 **Glasgow** 6, **Munster** 3 **Leinster** 10, **Ulster** 14 **Edinburgh** 20. 26 December: **Cardiff** 11 **Dragons** 6, **Leinster** 29 **Ulster** 0. 27 December: **Munster** 17 **Connacht** 0, **Llanelli** 17 **Ospreys** 12. 28 December: **Edinburgh** 35 **Glasgow** 31. 31 December: Ospreys 22 **Cardiff** 3. 1 January: **Dragons** 15 **Llanelli** 13. 4 January: **Connacht** 20 **Llanelli** 18, **Cardiff** 10 **Edinburgh** 11, **Glasgow** 16 **Dragons** 18. 5 January: **Leinster** 26 **Ospreys** 15. 15 February: **Llanelli** 30 **Glasgow** 7, **Edinburgh** 7 **Munster** 11, **Ulster** 38 **Dragons** 13. 16 February: **Ospreys** 37 **Connacht** 7, **Leinster** 24 **Cardiff** 17. 29 February: **Dragons** 10 **Edinburgh** 10, **Connacht** 10 **Leinster** 16, **Glasgow** 9 **Ospreys** 6, **Ulster** 20 **Llanelli** 8. 1 March: **Cardiff** 25 **Munster** 22. 21 March: **Llanelli** 35 **Cardiff** 17, **Edinburgh** 38 **Connacht** 8 **Leinster** 34 **Glasgow** 18. 22 March: **Munster** 42 **Ulster** 6. 28 March, 2008: **Ospreys** 32 **Ulster** 7, **Connacht** 5 **Munster** 16, **Edinburgh** 0 **Cardiff** 20. 29 March: **Llanelli** 10 **Leinster** 24. 30 March: **Dragons** 14 **Glasgow** 20. 11 April: **Ulster** 18 **Connacht** 6, **Cardiff** 35 **Llanelli** 26, **Glasgow** 23 **Edinburgh** 14. 12 April: **Leinster** 21 **Munster** 12. 18 April: **Dragons** 11 **Connacht** 13, **Edinburgh** 15 **Leinster** 13, **Glasgow** 25 **Llanelli** 23. 19 April: **Cardiff** 30 **Ulster** 17, **Munster** 9 **Ospreys** 8. 25 April: **Ospreys** 16 **Dragons** 3. 30 April: **Ulster** 19 **Munster** 9. 2 May: **Connacht** 11 **Cardiff** 39, **Ospreys** 18 **Edinburgh** 19. 3 May: **Llanelli** 23 **Munster** 24, **Ulster** 24 **Glasgow** 35, **Leinster** 41 **Dragons** 8. 6 May: **Dragons** 18 **Ospreys** 10. 9 May: **Connacht** 24 **Ospreys** 20, **Dragons** 31 **Leinster** 26, **Ulster** 17 **Cardiff** 26. 10 May: **Munster** 18 **Glasgow** 21, **Llanelli** 12 **Edinburgh** 29

FINAL TABLE

	P	W	D	L	F	A	Pts
	P	W	D	L	F	A	PTS
Leinster	18	13	1	4	428	283	61
Cardiff	18	12	0	6	395	315	56
Munster	18	10	1	7	330	258	48
Edinburgh	18	9	3	6	313	285	48
Glasgow	18	10	1	7	340	349	46
Llanelli	18	7	0	11	403	362	39
Ospreys	18	6	1	11	321	255	37
Dragons	18	7	1	10	282	394	34
Ulster	18	6	1	11	278	407	29
Connacht	18	5	1	12	214	396	24

PREVIOUS WINNERS

Celtic League Winners

2001/02: **Leinster**
2002/03: **Munster**
2003/04: **Llanelli Scarlets**
2004/05: **Neath Swansea Ospreys**
2005/06: **Ulster**

Magners League Winners

2006/07: **Ospreys**
2007/08: **Leinster**

Dave Rogers/Getty Images

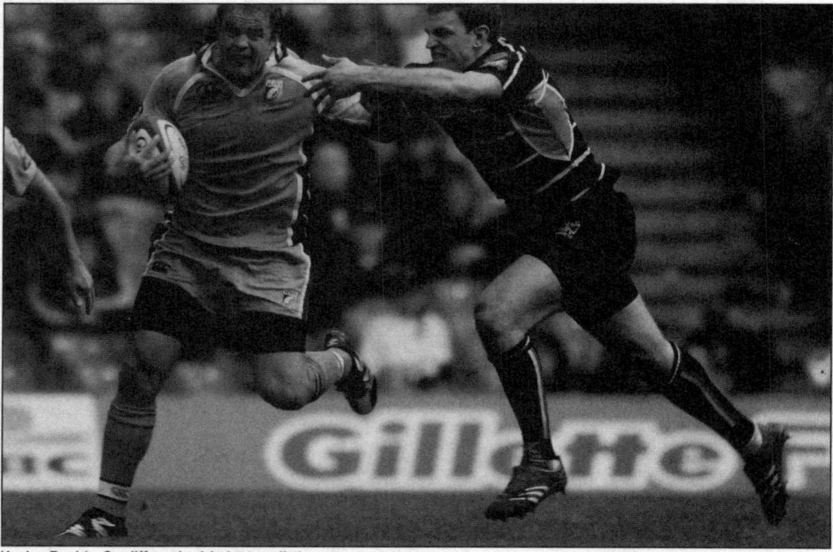

Xavier Rush's Cardiff pushed Leinster all the way.

MAORI BRING IT HOME

By Dominic Rumbles

Brendon Thorne/Getty Images

The Maori take the title at the first time of asking.

The 2008 IRB Pacific Nations Cup was a fascinating tournament that had much to offer in terms of excitement and drama, not least a superb final round of matches, which kept everyone guessing until the last.

Few could deny that New Zealand Maori deserved their maiden Pacific title as they played some exceptional rugby at times and had the big game experience to perform when it mattered. The fact that they snatched the title away from Australia A in dramatic fashion in the final minutes of a gripping winner-takes-all match in Sydney was impressive and indicative of a team that simply refused to admit defeat.

Heading into the game at the Sydney Football Stadium it was the Australia A side containing eight players capped by the Wallabies that held the advantage, owing to a superior points differential amassed during the five-week campaign. Yet the Maori, winners of two Churchill Cup titles, stunned a large home crowd two minutes from time as Thomas Waldrom crossed for the try that handed his side a shock 21–18 lead.

Yet there was still more drama to come in a gripping final as Australia A had the opportunity to clinch a draw with the final act of the match. Knowing that the draw would claim his side the coveted title owing to a superior points differential, Mark Gerrard lined up a crucial penalty attempt from 45 metres. However, the international winger's attempt fell just short of the crossbar and with it slipped Australia A's chances and so the Maori were crowned champions for the first time.

Five weeks previously there was little sense of the drama that was to unfold as the tournament exploded into action. Much of the pre-tournament hype surrounded the Pacific Island nations and whether they would be able to replicate their incredible performances of the previous year's Rugby World Cup, while it was unclear how strong the Maori, who had replaced double winners the Junior All Blacks, and Australia A would be in comparison to the Test teams.

Any lingering questions were answered in emphatic style on the opening weekend. Australia A highlighted their title credentials with an emphatic 42–21 victory against an out of sorts Japan in Fukuoka. The Australians ran in six tries, including a brace for Brumbies lock Peter Kimlin. It was an ominous start. The Maori, meanwhile, were slow to get their campaign underway and were made to work extremely hard as they battled past Tonga 20–9 in a bruising encounter in North Harbour.

The weekend's other big match saw Fiji and Samoa go head to head in a bruising encounter at Churchill Park in Lautoka. The hosts had been indifferent in their three PNC campaigns to date, but produced a resounding performance, bristling with pace and power to outclass their Pacific Island rivals 34–17. The Rugby World Cup 2007 quarter-finalists had raced into a 26–0 lead midway through the half before the Samoans finally hit back with three consolation tries. Fiji had announced that they were serious title contenders.

In round two all eyes were on the mouth-watering encounter in Lautoka between Fiji and the Maori and whether Fiji could record a first PNC victory against a Tier 1 A side. The match did not disappoint. In torrential conditions, Fiji were a matter of minutes from recording a historic victory courtesy of Sireli Naqelevuki's first half try. The Maori, though, were not done and they staged a late rally with All Black second row Jason Eaton crossing to snatch victory. It was a bitter blow for the

Fijians, who never really recovered for the remainder of their campaign.

If Fiji's performance had demonstrated how the Pacific Islands had bridged the gap, then Samoa's brave performance against the eventual tournament winners, Australia A in Apia underlined the advances made. In front of a capacity 15,500 at Apia Park, the Samoans staged a remarkable second half fightback, coming from 20–8 down to almost steal the game at the death.

Yet the most impressive performance of round two was claimed by Japan. Under the weather in their opening match, John Kirwan's side showed great mental resolve to brush aside Tonga 35–13 in a highly entertaining affair in Sendai. It was a performance made all the more impressive by Japan's attacking approach to the game. Tonga were not a poor outfit on the day and they struggled not only to come to terms with the pace that their hosts applied to the game, but perhaps more significantly, the physicality of a Japanese pack that competed valiantly against Australia A the previous week. Japan, fresh from their Asia 5 Nations success, were back in the hunt.

In round three it was a case of so close, yet so far for the luckless Samoans who, for the third week running were defeated despite performing well. This time it was New Zealand Maori who claimed their scalp, but the New Zealanders were made to fight every inch of the way in Waikato as Samoa prevented the home side from scoring in the second half in a 17–6 defeat.

For Tonga, the round three fixture against table-topping Australia A was one not to remember for several reasons. Not only were the Tongans woeful at the Sydney Oval, crashing to a record 90–7 defeat, but the Islanders were missing a number of key players and, without a win, were effectively out of the running for the title. Fiji, though, were back in the frame and came back from a 9–3 half time deficit to defeat rapidly improving 24–12 in Tokyo, denying their hosts a second successive victory.

By round four it was evident that the tournament was developing in a two horse race, but there were signs aplenty that each of the other four participating teams would be more than capable of throwing a sizeable spanner in the works. Yet despite the optimism it was a difficult weekend for the Pacific Island teams. Japan were crushed 65–22 in Napier, maintaining the Maori's one hundred per cent record, while Australia A confirmed a winner-takes-all grand finale the following weekend by making light work of Fijian resistance in a 50–12 thrashing of Fiji. Test hopeful Lachie Turner was the star of the show, capping a fine performance with a brace of tries.

The final round had two specific areas of interest; who would win the overall title in the winner-takes-all finale in Sydney and who would claim the pride of being the best placed Pacific Island nation? Watched by King Taufa'ahu Tupou V, the Tongans finally claimed their debut victory of the 2008 PNC campaign, scoring four tries to defeat Fiji 27–16 and retain their immaculate record over their Island neighbours in the competition. However the bonus point was not enough to lift Tonga off the foot of the table as Japan produced a late rally to secure a bonus point against Samoa in Apia. The 37–31 victory was also enough for Samoa to finish third overall and secure the 'best of the rest' mantle, despite a below par showing in the competition.

For the Maori though it was a successful campaign and the victory once again enhanced New Zealand's dominance of the international scene, coupled with the IRB Junior World Championship and IRB Sevens World Series titles. Yet despite their crown, the 2008 PNC campaign will be remembered as a classic and one where the Pacific Island sides continued to close the gap on the Tier 1 A teams.

FINAL TABLE

Team	P	W	D	L	PF	PA	BP	PTS
NZ Maori	5	5	0	0	134	62	1	21
Australia A	5	4	0	1	220	77	4	20
Samoa	5	2	0	3	95	117	2	10
Fiji	5	2	0	3	94	117	2	10
Japan	5	1	0	4	121	181	3	7
Tonga	5	1	0	4	71	181	2	6

Results		
07-06-2008	**Fiji** 34, **Samoa** 17	Churchill Park, **Lautoka**
08-06-2008	**Japan** 21 v **Australia A** 42	Hakata No Mori, **Fukuoka**
08-06-2008	**New Zealand Maori** 20, **Tonga** 9	North Harbour, **Albany**
14-06-2008	**Samoa** 15, **Australia A** 20	Apia Park, **Samoa**
14-06-2008	**Fiji** 7, **New Zealand Maori** 11	Churchill Park, **Lautoka**
15-06-2008	**Japan** 35, **Tonga** 13	Sendai Yurtec Stadium, **Sendai**
21-06-2008	**New Zealand Maori** 17, **Samoa** 6	Waikato Stadium, **Hamilton**
22-06-2008	**Japan** 12, **Fiji** 24	National Olympic Stadium, **Tokyo**
22-06-2008	**Australia A** 90, **Tonga** 7	North Sydney Oval, **Sydney**
28-06-2008	**Tonga** 15, **Samoa** 20	Teufaiva Stadium, **Nuku'alofa**
28-06-2008	**New Zealand Maori** 65, **Japan** 22	McLean Park, **Napier**
29-06-2008	**Australia A** 50, **Fiji** 13	Ballymore, **Brisbane**
05-07-2008	**Tonga** 27, **Fiji** 16	Teufaiva Stadium, **Nuku'alofa**
05-07-2008	**Samoa** 37, **Japan** 31	Apia Park, **Samoa**
06-07-2008	**Australia A** 18, **New Zealand Maori** 21	Sydney Football Stadium, **Sydney**

TAUTAHI BREAK NEW GROUND

By Dominic Rumbles

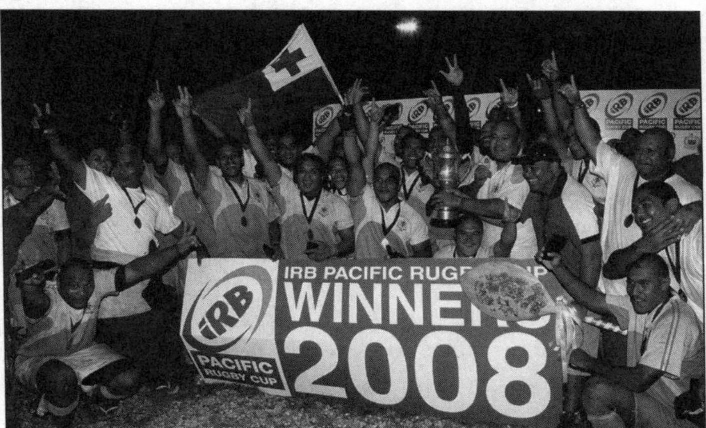

The Tongans celebrate their victory in the final

Tautahi Gold became the first Tongan side to lift the IRB Pacific Rugby Cup title with an 11–3 defeat of defending champions Upolu Samoa in the grand final, ending Samoan dominance of the competition over the previous two years.

The final, played in front of a near-capacity crowd at Apia Park, was played in true Pacific style. Ruthless in the forwards, physical at the breakdown and tight throughout, something that followers of the Pacific Rugby Cup have become accustomed to. It was also a match that completed an impressive turnaround for Tautahi Gold.

Bottom of the standings a year ago, Tautahi Gold turned the tables on the defending champions, avenging their 26–10 loss at the same venue only seven days earlier in the final round robin matches with Tonga captain Nili Latu catching the eye.

"This was a big win for us and for Tongan Rugby," said the veteran flanker, Latu, one of the best players at the 2007 Rugby World Cup. "We came here as underdogs, but we played well and I am thankful to all the team and management that we were able to deliver a historic victory."

In the final, Sitaleki Lu'au, the leading try-scorer in the competition, got Tautahi off to the perfect start, scoring the opening try, while 'Apikotoa's drop goal handed the visitors a shock 8–3 advantage at the interval.

Defending champions Upolu fought back in the second half, but were frustrated by a determined Tautahi defence that refused to buckle. Yet despite their hard work, the Samoans could not find the breakthrough and it was Lu'au who put the game beyond doubt for Tauhai, landing a penalty midway through the half to seal a memorable victory.

Tautahi's success in the final capped what had been a memorable tournament for the three participating nations and the event organisers, the International Rugby Board.

The improved performance of Fiji and Tonga and to and lesser extent, Samoa, at the Rugby World Cup 2007 had proven the competition's value as a key player development tool for rugby within the Pacific Islands, while also injecting fresh enthusiasm for provincial representative rugby in the Oceania region.

The result was a memorable 2008 competition, fiercely competitive throughout and well attended across each of the five rounds. Tautahi's early competition form did little to suggest that less they would lift the silverware as they lost to Fiji Warriors 21–19 in the opening round as both Upolu Samoa and 2006 champions Savai'i Samoa got off to characteristically good starts with victories over Tau'uta Reds and Fiji Barbarians respectively. Interestingly, the largest margin of victory across the three matches was just eight points.

The action was no less competitive in round two. Upolu Samoa outlined their championship credentials with a comprehensive 22–5 victory over Fiji Barbarians, catapulting them to the top of the standings, while Savai'i maintained their winning start, holding on for a 20–18 victory over Fiji Barbarians at Prince Edward Park. Tautahi, boosted by the return of inspirational captain Nili Latu, defeated Tau'uta Reds 21–11, scoring two tries in the all-Tongan affair in Nuku'alofa to consign the Reds to a second consecutive defeat.

With Latu at the helm, Tautahi continued to make improvements and struck a hammer blow by defeating pre-competition favourites Savai'i Samoa 27–17 on home soil. Full-back Setaleki Lu'au scoring twice as the Tongans earned a maiden bonus point. Meanwhile, Uplou Samoa, containing Samoa Sevens star Uale Mai, made it three victories in a row, held their nerve to defeat Fiji Warriors 13–8 at Apia Park in a match that changed hands three times.

For the Fijians the defeat was another glum result in a campaign that garnered just two victories – a poor return for the Rugby World Cup 2007 quarter-finalists – though the Barbarians did lift spirits with a nail-biting 25–24 victory against 2007 finalists Tau'uta Reds.

As round four neared, speculation surrounded whether Upolu would romp through to the final. Clear at the top of the standings, victory against local rivals Savai'i would all but seal passage to the luxury of a home final. Yet, Savai'i had different ideas and threw a sizeable spanner in the works by winning the crunch match in Apia 14–9 and in doing so opening the door for Tautahi Gold, who were steadily improving.

Playing the day before, the Tongans recorded an impressive 20–0 victory over an outclassed Fiji Barbarians to raise hopes of qualifying for the final, but would have to do it the hard way by playing Upolu on Samoan soil in the final round of matches. Meanwhile, their chances were also given a boost by Tau'uta Reds' second-successive victory, a 14–13 defeat of finalist hopefuls Savai'i.

The final round was full of permutations. Victory for Upolu would guarantee the Samoans a place in the final for the second successive year. Their final round opponents Tautahi Gold would have to win or hope that countrymen Tau'uta Reds could record a famous victory against 2006 champions, Savai'i. It was to be the Gold's weekend, just. Despite losing 26–10 to Upolu in a match where they did not get out of second gear, the match was effectively a dead rubber with nothing but a psychological marker at stake as the night before Tau'uta delivered the shock victory that booked Tautahi's place in the final in the same venue against the same opposition a week later.

Having watched his team flattened in the dress rehearsal, Tautahi coach Liueli Lafoe Fusimalohi called for a performance of "pride, power and passion" as the Gold looked to avenge the defeat. He was not to be disappointed as his side produced an astute defencive performance to ensure Tongan hands clasped the IRB Pacific Rugby Cup trophy for the first time in the competition's history.

IRB Pacific Rugby Cup Final – 24 May, Apia Park, Apia

Upola Samoa 3 (1PG)
Tautahi Gold 11 (1T, 1PG, 1DG)

UPOLU SAMOA: P Toelupe; D Lemi, G Salima, S Moala, M Salesa; R Warren, N Tauafao; E Telea, M Salanoa (*captain*), T Moala, T Fitiao, R Petaia, O Pipili, A Cordtz, F Levi.

Penalty: Roger Warren

TAUTAHI GOLD: S Lu'au; V Pauga, S Heimule Pangai, K Tupou, S Pone, F 'Apikotoa (*captain*), S Havea; M Finau, F Moala, S Maama, P Pifeleti, T Tu'akoi, L Uafi, N Latu, A Taka.

Try: Sitaleki Lu'ua

Penalty: Sitaleki Lu'ua

Drop goal: Fangatapu 'Apikotoa

FINAL TABLE

	P	W	D	L	F	A	PD	BP	Pts
Upolu Samoa	5	4	0	1	90	49	41	1	17
Tautahi Golds	5	3	0	2	97	75	22	2	14
Savaii Samoa	5	3	0	2	79	81	-2	1	13
Tau'uta Reds	5	2	0	3	84	95	-11	2	10
Fiji Barbarians	5	2	0	3	72	88	-16	2	10
Fiji Warriors	5	1	0	4	70	104	-34	3	7

THREE IN A ROW

By Karen Bond

IRB

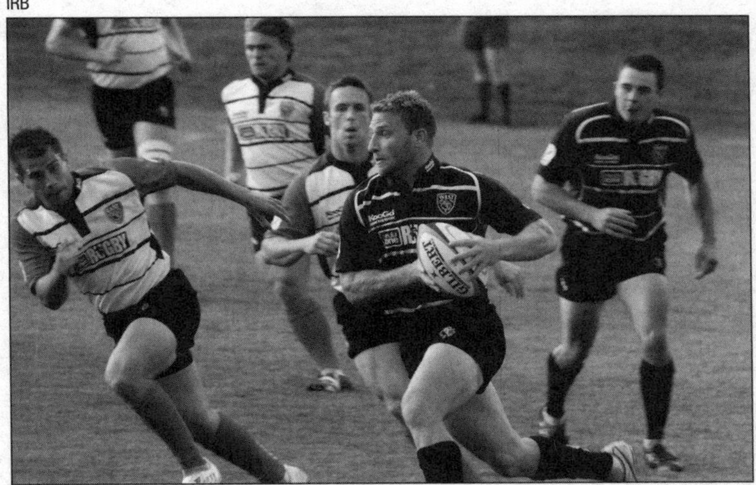

Canada West on the way to another try

Canada West remain the only side to lift the IRB North America 4 trophy in the cross-border competition's three-year history after once again beating the USA Falcons in the final, this time by the smallest margin yet, 16–11 at the Glendale Infinity Park in Glendale, Colorado. This was the third time the two representative sides had met in the final, West triumphing 31–20 in 2006 and then 43–11 last year.

The fact that the final was a closer run affair would have surprised some, given West had convincingly beaten their rivals 55–3 only a fortnight earlier in the round robin stages, scoring eight tries and dominating every aspect of the match.

The heavy loss, though, gave the Falcons extra motivation with captain

Rikus Pretorius admitting they were "licking their chops and excited to get another shot at them", to set the record straight.

With temperatures touching 35 degrees, it was the defending champions who edged into an early lead with two penalties from outside-half Matt Evans in the first 10 minutes. The Falcons, though, were determined not to leak tries like they had in their previous meeting and seemed content to try to stop West playing the expansive game they favour, thereby frustrating their opponents.

The Falcons made the most of two kickable penalties to level the scores with their talented outside-half Zachary Pangelinan slotting both between the uprights, although it was Canada West who went in leading 9–6 at half-time thanks to another Evans penalty. The outside-half missed a chance to extend that lead with a long range effort in the 48th minute and then had a drop goal attempt charged down just before West worked the ball wide for No 8 Tom McKeen to score the first try.

With West now leading 16–7 the pressure was on the Falcons, but it wasn't until the 77th minute that they found a way through when replacement Volney Rouse touched down after a side-step and slick offload from Pangelinan. The conversion was crucially wide, meaning a penalty they were awarded two minutes later was not a kickable option, they had to keep the ball in hand. West defended with all their worth and when the ball was turned over Evans booted it into touch to seal the 'three-peat'.

There was to be no Canadian double on American soil though as Canada East saw yet another victory slip through their fingers in the dying stages, this time a 79th minute try from No 8 Pat Quinn snatching a 17–17 draw for USA Hawks in the third place play-off. This try meant that East ended the 2008 competition without a win to their name, the first time that has happened in the North America 4's short history.

The opening quarter of the match had passed by scoreless before the Hawks, who recorded their only 2008 win by defeating East 32–5 in the round robin stages, established a 10–0 advantage after 32 minutes, only to see their opponents hit back to lead 14–10 at the interval with tries from Aaron Carpenter and Tyler Wish. That advantage was increased to seven points with Steven Piatek's penalty just before the hour, but there was to be one final twist to East's dismay.

The IRB North America 4 continues to play a significant role in the ongoing player and competition development programmes for both Rugby Canada and USA Rugby, a fact highlighted by the number of players who went on to represent both unions at last year's Rugby World Cup in France and also the handful of players who graduated from representing their countries at the IRB Junior World Championship 2008 to get a taste of this competition.

Canada West outside-half Evans was one prime example of this progression, just as their No 10 last year had been in Nathan Hirayama who went from the IRB Under-19 World Championship to RWC 2007 via the NA4 in the space of six months. Struan Robertson sat on the bench, while the Falcons had Shawn Pittman in the front row and USA Under 20 captain Scott Lavalla among their replacements.

They weren't alone with Canada East fielding another pair of Under-20 players in Tony Wodzicki and Keegan Selby on the bench in the third place play-off, while the Hawks gave 17-year-old Hanno Dirksen his first North America 4 start after he impressed as a replacement in their 30–12 semi-final defeat by the Falcons a few days earlier.

A number of players who represented Canada and USA on the IRB Sevens World Series also took to the field throughout the competition, which kicked off in May with the all-Canadian affair that went right down to the wire, Pat Riordan's injury-time try breaking the deadlock and giving West a 20–15 victory over East at Fletcher's Fields, Markham.

The competition resumed nearly two months later in mid July after Canada and USA's participation in the Barclays Churchill Cup with the all-American encounter, another match full of twists and turns before four second half tries saw the Falcons triumph 39–24 at Mount Hood Community College in Portland, Oregon.

Next stop was Shawnigan Lake in British Columbia for the first double header of 2008 and contrasting results with Canada West signalling their intention to retain their title with a clinical 48–0 defeat of USA Hawks, scoring eight tries in the process. The Falcons found life harder against East, having to recover from 15–3 down at half time to triumph 26–22 and leave the Canadians with only a losing bonus point as consolation for the second match running.

There was little more for East to smile about four days later when they were beaten 32–5 by the Hawks in the battle of the winless sides, meaning they propped up the standings and would face the top-ranked side after the round robin stage in the semi-finals a week later in Glendale. That turned out to be the defending champions after West ended the Falcons' unbeaten run in emphatic style with captain Adam Kleeberger and Brock Nicholson both scoring two of their side's eight tries.

East were hungry to avenge their injury-time loss by West in round one, but while they scored the opening try, it was the defending champions who again came from behind in the final 10 minutes to seal a 30–24 victory with Nick Blevins' try. The Falcons had an easier passage as, inspired by Pangelinan, they ran in four tries to triumph 30–12 and earn the chance to make it third time lucky – or not as it turned out – against Canada West in the final.

FINAL STANDINGS

Team	P	W	D	L	PF	PA	BP	PTS
Canada West	3	3	0	0	123	18	2	14
USA Falcons	3	2	0	1	68	101	1	9
USA Hawks	3	1	0	2	56	92	1	5
Canada East	3	0	0	3	42	78	2	2

ROUND ONE

Canada East 15–20 **Canada West**, **USA Falcons** 39–24 **USA Hawks**, **Canada West** 48–0 **USA Hawks**, **Canada East** 22–26 **USA Falcons**, **Canada East** 5–32 **USA Hawks**, **Canada West** 55–3 **USA Falcons**.

SEMI-FINALS

Canada West 30–24 **Canada East** and **USA Falcons** 30–12 **USA Hawks**.

THIRD PLACE PLAY-OFF

Canada East 17–17 **USA Hawks**

2 August 2008 – Glendale Infinity Park, Glendale, Colorado

Canada West 16 (1G, 3P)
USA Falcons 11 (1T, 2P)

CANADA WEST: P Mack; S Duke, B Keys, B Grant, B Nicholson; S Dalziel, T McKeen; H Buydens, P Riordan, E Christensen, N Miles, J Oudyk, N Meechan, A Kleeberger (*capt*), T McKeen.

REPLACEMENTS: Ryan Hamilton, Rogan Verboven, Struan Robertson, Nanyak Dala, Jason Marshall, Robin MacDowell, Nick Blevins.

SCORERS: *Try*: Tom McKeen, *Conversion*: Matt Evans, *Penalties*: Matt Evans (3)

USA FALCONS: J Naqica; J Pye, A Tuilevuka, G Golding, J Gillenwater; Z Pangelina, R Shaw; M Moeakiola, J Brown, S Pittman, L Stanfill, B Wiedemer, D La Prevotte, R Pretorius (*capt*), M Hawkins.

REPLACEMENTS: Saimone Laulaupeaalu, Mark Kernen, Samual Manoa, Scott Lavalla, Mose Timoteo, Volney Rouse, Tyson Meek.

SCORERS: *Try*: Volney Rouse. *Penalties*: Zachary Pangelinan (2)

REFEREE: Dave Smortchevsky

JAPAN STAY ON TOP

By Karen Bond

IRBKAZUHIRO NOGI / AFP

Japan lift the new trophy after the win over Hong Kong

There were no surprises when it came to the inaugural HSBC Asian Five Nations champions with Japan lifting the distinctive trophy after sweeping aside the competition, claiming four bonus point victories over Korea, Arabian Gulf, Kazakhstan and Hong Kong, scoring 49 tries in the process.

Japan, the only Asian side to play on the Rugby World Cup stage, were simply too strong for their opponents, the superior skills and fitness of John Kirwan's side ensuring that even matches which had been close at one stage had turned into convincing margins of victory by the final whistle.

However Kirwan was not interested in simply confirming Japan's status as Asia's number one side. His philosophy that the tournament was the perfect tool to develop the next generation of players was precisely the reason the Asian Five Nations, with its four tiers of competition involving all 25 Member Unions in the region, was introduced.

Kirwan's intentions were clear from his squad selection with a third of the 30 players uncapped, a further eight boasted caps in single figures with RWC 2007 captain Takuro Miuchi the most experienced with 40 caps, not to mention being one of only four players aged 30 or over.

"It is very important that we win it, but is very important that we also have a good mix," Kirwan admitted at the time. "It is really a chance also to blood some younger players. We are really excited because this year is an important year for us from a transition point of view. We want to be able to back up our performance in the World Cup, but to do that we have to keep one eye on the next World Cup so the Asian competition is great for us. We can play a mixture of old and new."

This blend of experience and exciting young talent headed to the Korean city of Incheon on the opening weekend of the Top Five competition – as the top tier of the Asian Five Nations is known – in late April. The tournament, which received funding in the form of a £250,000 grant from the International Rugby Board, was played as a round robin over five consecutive weekends.

Korea had lost their last encounter with Japan 82–0, but this side were far more tenacious and, despite being outscored seven tries to two, kept the final score to a respectable 39–17. Japan had established a 29–0 lead by half-time with Go Aruga, James Arlidge, Hirotoki Onozawa, Bryce Robins and Hiroki Yoshida all touching down, so when another try followed soon after the break a runaway victory seemed likely.

However Korea were rewarded for their determination with two tries either side of another Japanese score, the final try of the match coming from an interception in their own 22 that ultimately saw Kim Sung Yoo cross to the delight of the crowd. Kirwan wasn't pleased with the overall performance of his side, but Japan still ended the opening round on top of the standings, after Hong Kong triumphed 20–12 over Arabian Gulf in the United Arab Emirates.

Kazakhstan, one of the most improving nations in Asia, entered the fray in round two with a 23–17 defeat by Hong Kong, although they did salvage a losing bonus point thanks to replacement hooker Ivan Ossikovskiy's late try. However for Kazakhstan coach Valeriy Popov, the opportunity to play against Asia's elite nations can only be beneficial for rugby's development in the country.

"The quality of our game leaves much to be desired. We felt we were like students and this was a learning experience for us," Popov admitted afterwards. "This is the first time we have participated in this kind of tournament. Playing against strong Asian teams such as Hong Kong, Japan and Korea will help to raise the status of Kazakhstan and motivate us to play better."

Hong Kong remained unbeaten ahead of their third round bye, but it was Japan who strengthened their title credentials with an emphatic 114–6 defeat of Arabian Gulf in Osaka. Kirwan had asked his players to play for the full 80 minutes, which they duly did with Onozawa claiming a hat-trick among the 18 tries Japan scored.

Next stop for Japan was the Kazakhstan capital Almaty and, despite playing at 900 metres above sea level, they emerged 82–6 winners with nine players scoring tries. In the round's other match, Korea's superior fitness told with three late tries sealing a 43–20 victory over Arabian Gulf in Doha, Qatar.

Japan's final match was at home in Niigata against the only other unbeaten side Hong Kong. Sixteen minutes passed with no score as Hong Kong made life difficult for Japan, but by the final whistle the champions had been crowned following a 75–29 victory. Japan had scored 11 tries, but lapses in concentration had enabled Rowan Varty to score a hat-trick for Hong Kong.

The title may have been decided, but there was still plenty at stake in the final round with Hong Kong battling Korea for second place and Kazakhstan facing Arabian Gulf with the loser relegated to Division I next year and replaced by either China, Chinese Taipei, Singapore or Sri Lanka who contest that competition in November.

That turned out to be Arabian Gulf, who suffered a 56–27 defeat by a Kazakhstan side inspired by full back Maxim Lifontov and the 31-point haul which saw him finish as the tournament's leading point scorer. Korea, meanwhile, scored 24 unanswered points in the opening 13 minutes to lay the foundations for a 50–24 defeat of Hong Kong.

The Asian Five Nations, though, was about more than just the elite nations going head to head with each other – the desire to expand and develop the game across the region was also a key element behind its introduction, with promotion and relegation between the divisions. The fact that the Division I and II competitions in 2008 also kick off the region's qualifying process for Rugby World Cup 2011 was another incentive, one Thailand seized by winning Division II with a 30–7 defeat of Malaysia in Bangkok in June, earning promotion to Division I for 2009.

There are also four regional tournaments below this level, two of them already completed with the Philippines triumphing in Guam by beating the hosts 20–8 and Brunei 101–0 in July. Indonesia then tasted

Test success on home soil for the first time, beating Laos 23–11 and Cambodia 55–3 to win the tournament. The two other regional tournaments take place in September with Qatar hosting Macau and Mongolia, while Iran and Uzbekistan travel to Kyrgyzstan.

FINAL STANDINGS

Team	P	W	D	L	PF	PA	BP	PTS
Japan	4	4	0	0	310	58	4	24
Korea	4	3	0	1	150	104	3	18
Hong Kong	4	2	0	2	96	154	1	11
Kazakhstan	4	1	0	3	100	172	2	7
Arabian Gulf	4	0	0	4	65	233	1	1

RESULTS

TOP FIVE

Korea 17–39 **Japan, Arabian Gulf** 12–20 **Hong Kong, Hong Kong** 23–17 **Kazakhstan, Japan** 114–6 **Arabian Gulf, Arabian Gulf** 20–43 **Korea, Kazakhstan** 6–82 **Japan, Korea** 40–21 **Kazakhstan, Japan** 75–29 **Hong Kong, Kazakhstan** 56–27 **Arabian Gulf, Hong Kong** 24–50 **Korea**

DIVISION II

Final: **Thailand** 30–7 **Malaysia.** *Third Place Play-off:* **India** 92–0 **Pakistan.** *Grouped matches:* **Malaysia** 30–5 **Pakistan, Thailand** 30–22 **India**

REGIONAL TOURNAMENTS

GUAM: Guam 74–0 **Brunei, Brunei** 0–101 **Philippines, Guam** 8–20 **Philippines**

INDONESIA: Cambodia 0–33 **Laos, Indonesia** 23–11 **Laos, Indonesia** 55–3 **Cambodia**

BOKS KEEP THEIR TITLE

By Dominic Rumbles

IRB

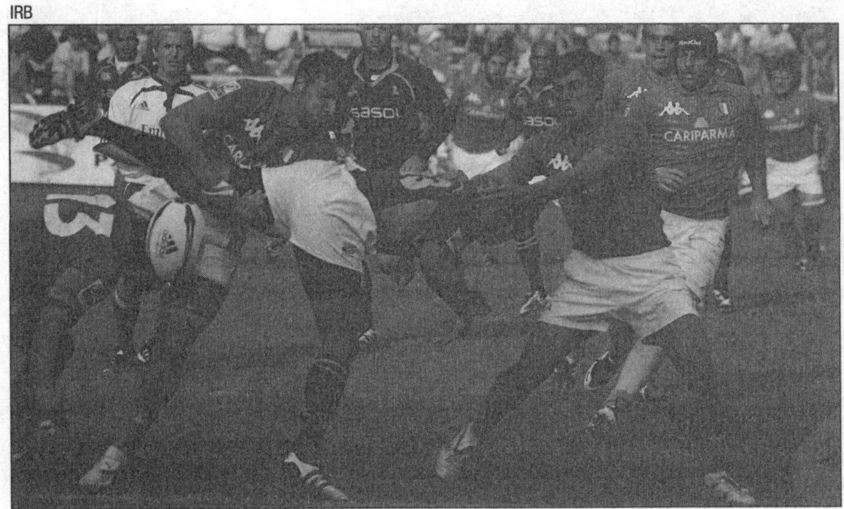

Italy A clash with the eventual winners, Emerging South Africa.

A **second-successive triumph** for Emerging South Africa, a genuine competitiveness throughout with drama and excitement in equal measure – the 2008 IRB Nations Cup was a tournament that refused to become predictable, even if the final standings suggested otherwise.

After South Africa's Test hopefuls romped through the 2007 tournament, few would have bet against another title for the side now coached by Chester Williams. Yet, despite emerging from the 2008 tournament undefeated, Emerging South Africa did not have it all their own

Phil Walter / Getty Images

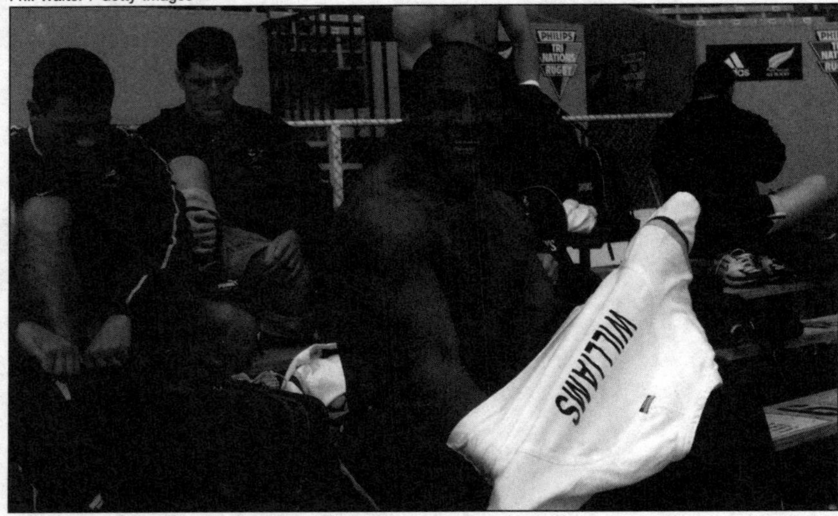

The victorious South Africa coach, Chester Williams

way as the performances of a resurgent Romania and combative Georgia suggested that the gap is slowly being closed between the Tier One 'superpowers' and emerging rugby nations.

Bucharest opened with welcome arms a second staging of the six-nation international tournament, which in 2008 saw Russia and Uruguay take the places of Argentina A and Namibia to join Emerging South Africa, Italy A, Georgia and Romania in the title race.

Hopes were also high in the Romanian capital that their own team could fair better than fourth place in 2007 and as a result a large crowd was in attendance at the Stadionul National Arcul de Triumf for each of the three match days.

The opening matches set the tone for the rest of the tournament, which kicked off in searing heat with the encounter between Italy A and Russia. The Italians, containing a sprinkling of internationals including experienced wing Marko Stanojevic, were many neutrals' favourites to challenge the South Africans and duly mastered the oppressive conditions and an exciting Russia team to score five tries in a 38–15 triumph to get their campaign off to a winning start.

Next was the turn of the defending champions, who were up against Georgia and looking for their fourth straight win in the Nations Cup. On paper it should have been close affair as Emerging South Africa, bristling with Super 14 talent, took on a young Georgian outfit containing a sprinkling of those who had impressed at RWC 2007 in France. Georgia, though, are a rising force on the world stage and are continually proving to be a tough nut to crack as proved the case with Howard Noble's breakaway try early in the second half the vital score in 11–3 victory.

Georgia, inspired by a powerful display from their pack, would have felt aggrieved at not causing an upset as twice they hit the uprights with penalty attempts in a second half that they had the better of on balance. Despite the defeat, the Lelos had certainly put down a marker of their intent to challenge for the title.

The earlier drama had whetted the huge crowd's appetite ahead of Romania's clash against the tournament's new boys Uruguay. The hosts were determined to make a winning start and did just that as Marin Mot's side eased their way into the tournament with a 10–6 victory. It was far from impressive as errors reigned, but there were signs of what was to come later in the tournament with some superb passages of play.

Day two was no less dramatic. A four-day hiatus had passed, wounds were licked and all six teams returned to the Arcul de Triumf determined to up the stakes. Georgia and Uruguay opened proceedings and entertained another large crowd with a match of high drama as the European side recorded their first victory of the 2008 tournament, squeezing past Uruguay 20–18. In what was only the third ever fixture between the two nations, Los Teros could have sneaked the victory themselves had Matias Arocena slotted over a penalty with the last kick of the game.

The margin of victory in the second match of the afternoon was even less. Italy A, looking to maintain their excellent start to the tournament, put in a powerful performance against Emerging South Africa, but fell short by a point as the defending champions edged past them 20–19. The champions had led 10–0 at the interval, but Italy A came back strongly and replacement hooker Franco Sbaraglini's late try set up a nervous finish.

Romania then made it three narrow victories in a row on day two, squeezing past European Nations Cup rivals Russia 13–12 to maintain their own title ambitions. In a tense affair before a partisan Bucharest crowd, the odds were stacked against the Russians. However, they produced a much improved performance, one bristling with passion and attacking flair and as a result the scores were locked 6–6 at the interval.

Russia took the lead early in the second half as outside-half Alexander Yanyushkin landed two penalties, but it was a converted try 12 minutes from time scored by Florin Teasca that proved to be the eventual difference between two good sides at the final whistle.

The result sparked mass celebrations within the capital. Romania, after fairing indifferently on home soil in 2007, would now face Emerging South Africa in their final match – a winner takes all affair with the defending champions the only other unbeaten side in the tournament.

It was a celebration of hope that Emerging South Africa could be defeated as Romania's Director of Rugby Ellis Meachen was quick to point out at the time.

"I know how good the Emerging Springboks are, with very pacy backs and they are keen to defend the title they won last year. This win against Russia has given us a bit of confidence. We have a young team that's starting to play well under pressure and I hope they will show that against the South Africans," said Meachen.

The final matchday was to be dramatic. Three teams had a mathematical chance of lifting the title with Italy A still in the frame, but requiring a bonus point win over Georgia and for Romania also to draw with Emerging South Africa to achieve an unlikely, but possible crowning as champions.

Russia and Uruguay, though, got the action under way and the match appeared to be going the way of the improving Russians, until a dramatic final sequence of events that saw victory snatched from their grasp.

Trailing 19–9 with just five minutes to go, all seemed to be lost for Uruguay, but they regrouped for one last assault and, following enormous pressure from their forwards, hit back courtesy of a converted penalty try.

With time up on the clock, the advantage was still 19–16 in Russia's favour, but again the Uruguayans came back and snatched a dramatic 23–19 victory when No 8 Ignacio Conti crashed over for another converted try. The defeat left the Russians stunned, but afterwards even they would acknowledge their part in a truly wonderful match.

Compared to this opening match, Italy A's encounter with Georgia was a tame affair, but the result was no less significant. With an outside chance of lifting the title, the Italians were confident heading into the match, but in the upset of the tournament they were put to the sword by a Georgian side that totally outclassed them, scoring three tries on the way to a 25–3 victory and ultimately second place in the final standings.

Sensing another upset on the cards, the large Romanian crowd were hopeful of their team's chances against an under par Emerging South Africa when the teams emerged for the final match of the tournament and one which would determine the destination of the silverware.

The early signs were good. Propelled into an early 3–0 lead courtesy of the boot of Dan Dumbrava, the Romanians were enjoying the better of the crucial forward exchanges. Yet, showing their ability to perform when under great pressure, the Emerging Springboks weathered the storm, both metaphorically and literally, as the heavens opened in Bucharest, and edged into a 10–6 lead at the break thanks to full-back Bjorn Basson's try.

Romania fought back after the break, but the South Africans stretched their advantage to 20–6 through the boot of their captain Morgan Newman and a try by Noble. Second row Florin Corodeanu gave the home side hope with a try, but it was a case of too little too late for the hosts as Emerging South Africa made certain of victory when Jody Jenneker crossed for their third try to secure a second successive IRB Nations Cup title.

IRB NATIONS CUP 2008 FINAL TOURNAMENT STANDINGS

	P	W	L	D	PF	PA	BP	PTS
Emerging SA	3	3	0	0	56	35	0	12
Georgia	3	2	0	1	48	32	0	8
Romania	3	2	0	1	36	43	0	8
Italy A	3	1	0	2	60	60	2	6
Uruguay	3	1	0	2	47	49	2	6
Russia	3	0	0	3	46	74	2	2

RESULTS

11/06/2008	Italy A	38–15	Russia	Bucharest
11/06/2008	Emerging South Africa	11–3	Georgia	Bucharest
11/06/2008	Uruguay	6–10	Romania	Bucharest
15/06/2008	Georgia	20–18	Uruguay	Bucharest
15/06/2008	Italy A	19–20	Emerging South Africa	Bucharest
15/06/2008	Russia	12–13	Romania	Bucharest
20/06/2008	Russia	19–23	Uruguay	Bucharest
20/06/2008	Italy A	3–25	Georgia	Bucharest
20/06/2008	Emerging South Africa	25–13	Romania	Bucharest

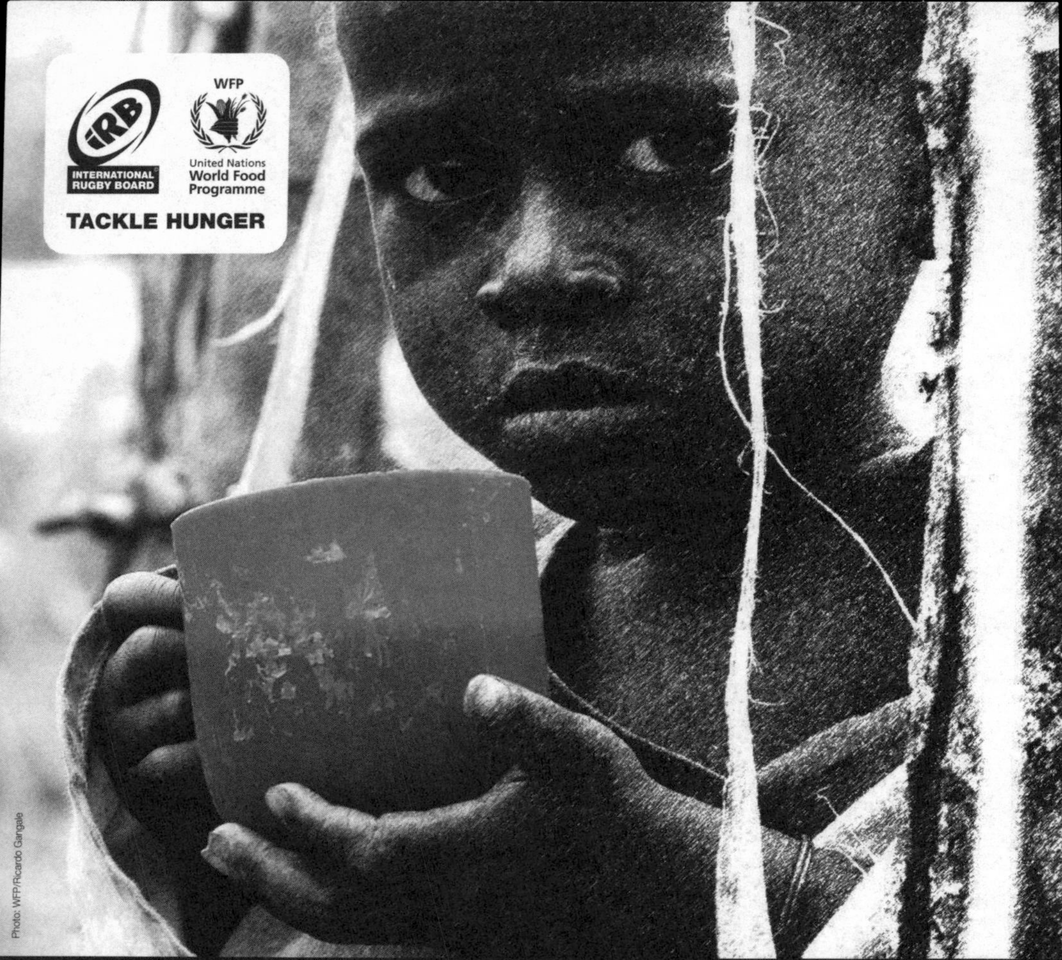

MAJOR RUGBY TOURS 2007-08

By Chris Rhys

SOUTH AFRICA TO WALES 2007

24 November 2007, Millennium Stadium, Cardiff
Wales 12 (1G 1T) South Africa 34 (3G 1PG 2T)

WALES: M Stoddart (Scarlets); MA Jones (Scarlets), ST Parker (Ospreys), GL Henson (Ospreys), TGL Shanklin (Blues); J Hook (Ospreys), D Peel (Scarlets); GD Jenkins (Blues, captain), H Bennett (Ospreys), R Thomas (Dragons); I Evans (Ospreys), A-W Jones (Ospreys); CL Charvis (Dragons), J Thomas (Ospreys), R Sowden-Taylor (Blues)

SUBSTITUTIONS: M Phillips (Ospreys), LC Charteris (Dragons) & TR Thomas (Blues) for Peel, I Evans, & Bennett (53 mins), AJ Popham (Scarlets) for Charvis (61 mins), T James (Blues) & DJ Jones (Ospreys) for Stoddart & R Thomas (68 mins), C Sweeney (Dragons) for Hook (71 mins),

SCORERS: Tries: Charvis, Stoddart Conversion: Hook

SOUTH AFRICA: R Pienaar (Sharks); J-P R Pietersen (Sharks), J Fourie (Lions), FPL Steyn (Sharks), BG Habana (Bulls); A Pretorius (Lions), ER Januarie (Lions); CJ Van der Linde (Cheetahs), JW Smit (CA Clermont-Auvergne, France)(capt), J du Plessis (Sharks); JP Botha (Bulls), J Muller (Sharks); SWP Burger (Stormers), R Kankowski (Sharks), JH Smith (Cheetahs)

SUBSTITUTIONS: A van den Berg (Sharks) for JP Botha (40 mins), W Olivier (Bulls) for Pretorius (59 mins), H van der Merwe (Lions) for J du Plessis (64 mins), OM Ndungane (Bulls) & BW du Plessis (Sharks) for Pietersen & Van der Linde (75 mins), H Lobberts (Bulls) & CA Jantjies (Stormers) for Kankowski & Januarie (78 mins),

SCORERS: *Tries*: Fourie (2), Smith, Pietersen, Kankowski *Conversions*: Steyn (3) *Penalty goals*: Steyn

REFEREE: C White (England)

IRELAND TO NEW ZEALAND & AUSTRALIA 2008

Tour party

FULL BACKS: GT Dempsey (Leinster), RDJ Kearney (Leinster)

THREEQUARTERS: TJ Bowe (Ulster), SP Horgan (Leinster), I Dowling (Munster), GW Duffy (Connacht), L Fitzgerald (Leinster), GEA Murphy (Leicester Tigers), BG O'Driscoll (Leinster)(captain)

HALF BACKS: RJR O'Gara (Munster), PW Wallace (Ulster) IJ Boss (Ulster), EG Reddan (London Wasps), PA Stringer (Munster)

FORWARDS: R Best (Ulster), JP Flannery (Munster), BJ Jackman (Leinster), JJ Hayes (Munster), MJ Horan (Munster) T Buckley (Munster), BG Young (Ulster), DP O'Callaghan (Munster), PJ O'Connell (Munster), MR O'Driscoll (Munster), ME O'Kelly (Leinster), AN Quinlan (Munster), *S Ferris (Ulster), JPR Heaslip (Leinster), S Jennings (Leinster), DP Leamy (Munster), DP Wallace (Munster)

* Replacement on tour

MANAGER J Miles **ACTING HEAD COACH** MT Bradley **ASSISTANT COACHES** N O'Donovan, G Steadman **CAPTAIN**: BG ODriscoll

Match 1, 7 June, Westpac Stadium, Wellington
New Zealand 21 (1G 3PG 1T) Ireland11 (2PG 1T)

NEW ZEALAND: JM Muliaina (Chiefs): AT Tuitavake (Blues), CG Smith (Hurricanes), MA Nonu (Hurricanes), SW Sivivatu (Chiefs); DW Carter (Crusaders), AM Ellis (Crusaders); NS Tialata (Hurricanes), AK Hore (Hurricanes), IF Afoa (Blues), BC Thorn (Crusaders), AJ Williams (Crusaders), R So'oialo (Hurricanes), J Kaino (Blues), RH McCaw (Crusaders)(capt)
SUBSTITUTIONS: JE Schwalger (Hurricanes) for Afoa (33 mins), LR MacDonald (Crusaders) for Tuitavake (50 mins), KF Mealamu (Blues) for Hore (55 mins), AJ Thomson (Highlanders) for So'oialo (temp 43-48 mins & for Kaino 75 mins)
SCORERS: *Tries*: Sivivatu, Nonu *Conversion*: Carter *Penalty goals*: Carter (3)
IRELAND: Kearney; S Horgan, B O'Driscoll (capt), P Wallace, Bowe; O'Gara, Reddan; Horan, Flannery, Hayes, O'Connell, O'Callaghan, Leamy, Heaslip, D Wallace
SUBSTITUTIONS: R Best for Flannery (51 mins), Buckley for Horan (63 mins), Jennings & Stringer for Heaslip & Reddan (71 mins), Murphy for Kearney (75 mins)
SCORERS: *Try*: P Wallace *Penalty goals*: O'Gara (2)
REFEREE: C White (England)

Match 2, 14 June, Telstra Stadium, Melbourne
Australia 18 (1G 2PG 1T) Ireland 12 (1G 1T)

AUSTRALIA: CB Shepherd (Western Force): PJ Hynes (Queensland Reds), SA Mortlock (ACT Brumbies)(capt), BS Barnes (Queensland Reds), LD Tuqiri (NSW Waratahs); MJ Giteau (Western Force), L Burgess (NSW Waratahs); BA Robinson (NSW Waratahs), ST Moore (Queensland Reds), MJ Dunning (NSW); JE Horwill (Queensland Reds), NC Sharpe (Western Force); RD Elsom (NSW Waratahs), WL Palu (NSW Waratahs), GB Smith (ACT Brumbies)
SUBSTITUTIONS: DW Mumm (NSW Waratahs) for Sharpe (temp 45-55 mins) & for Elsom (70 mins), AKE Baxter (NSW Waratahs) for Dunning (58 mins), AL Freier (NSW Waratahs) & PR Waugh (NSW Waratahs) for Moore & Palu (73 mins), SJ Cordingley (ACT Brumbies) for Burgess (76 mins)
SCORERS: *Tries*: Barnes, Horwill *Conversion*: Giteau *Penalty goals*: Giteau (2)
Ireland: Kearney; S Horgan, B O'Driscoll (capt), P Wallace, Bowe; O'Gara, Stringer; Horan, R Best, Hayes, O'Connell, O'Callaghan, Leamy, Heaslip, Jennings
SUBSTITUTIONS: Ferris for Jennings (25 mins), Reddan & Flannery for Stringer & R Best (50 mins), Buckley for Hayes (53 mins), Murphy for Horgan (59 mins), Dempsey for O'Driscoll (70 mins), Hayes for Horan (73 mins)
SCORERS: *Tries*: Leamy, B O'Driscoll *Conversion*: O'Gara
REFEREE: C Berdos (France)

WALES TO SOUTH AFRICA 2008

Tour party

FULL BACKS: J Roberts (Blues), M Stoddart (Scarlets)
THREEQUARTERS: T James (Blues), MA Jones (Scarlets), SM Williams (Ospreys), A Bishop (Ospreys), ST Parker (Ospreys), TGL Shanklin (Blues)
HALF BACKS: J Hook (Ospreys), SM Jones (Scarlets), GJ Cooper (Gloucester Rugby), W Fury (London irish)

Getty Images

New Zealand kicked off their 2008 campaign with a hard-fought win over Ireland in treacherous conditions.

FORWARDS: R Hibbard (Ospreys), M Rees (Scarlets), *TR Thomas (Blues), GD Jenkins (Blues), DJ Jones (Ospreys), AR Jones (Ospreys), R Thomas (Dragons),
* LC Charteris (Dragons), I Evans (Ospreys), IM Gough (Ospreys), A-W Jones (Ospreys), J Thomas (Ospreys), GL Delve (Gloucester Rugby), DR Jones (Scarlets), RP Jones (Ospreys)

* Replacement on tour

MANAGER AJ Phillips **HEAD COACH** WD Gatland **ASSISTANT COACHES** S Edwards, R Howley, RC McBryde, NR Jenkins **CAPTAIN** RP Jones

Match 1, 7 June, Vodacom Park, Bloemfontein
South Africa 43 (4G 5PG) Wales 17 (2G 1PG)

SOUTH AFRICA: CA Jantjies (Stormers); T Chavanga (Stormers), AA Jacobs (Sharks), J de Villiers (Stormers), BG Habana (Bulls); AD James (Bath Rugby, England), JHJ Conradie (Stormers); GG Steenkamp (Bulls), JW Smit (CA Clermont Auvergne, France)(capt), BV Mujati (Stormers), JP Botha (Sharks), A Bekker (Stormers), JH Smith (Cheetahs), PJ Spies (Bulls), LA Watson (Stormers)

SUBSTITUTIONS: CJ van der Linde (Cheetahs) for Steenkamp (temp 24-32 mins) & Mujati (45 mins), PJ Grant (Stormers) for Jacobs (temp 32-45 mins) & James (72 mins), V Matfield (RC Toulon, France, & Bulls) for Bekker (45 mins), R Pienaar (Sharks) & BW du Plessis (Sharks) for Conradie & Smit (57 mins), DJ Rossouw (Bulls) for Botha (temp 58-64 mins) & Smith (74 mins), PC Montgomery (USA Perpignan, France) for Jacobs (61 mins)

SCORERS: *Tries*: Jantjies, De Villiers, Spies, Montgomery *Conversions*: James (4) *Penalty goals*: James (5)

WALES: Roberts; MA Jones, Shanklin, Parker, SM Williams; SM Jones, Cooper; Jenkins, Rees, AR Jones, Gough, A-W Jones, J Thomas, RP Jones (capt), D Jones

SUBSTITUTIONS: Stoddart, Hook, Hibbard & DJ Jones for Roberts, SM Jones, Rees & AR Jones (55 mins), Delve for DR Jones (57 mins), Fury for Cooper (62 mins), Evans for Gough (67 mins)

SCORERS: *Tries*: Roberts, SM Williams *Conversions*: SM Jones, Hook *Penalty goal*: SM Jones

REFEREE: D Pearson (England)

Match 2, 14 June, Loftus Versveld, Pretoria
South Africa 37 (4G 3PG) Wales 21 (1G 3PG 1T)

SOUTH AFRICA: CA Jantjies (Stormers); T Chavanga (Stormers), AA Jacobs (Sharks), J de Villiers (Stormers), BG Habana (Bulls); AD James (Bath Rugby, England), ER Januarie (Stormers); T Mtawarira (Sharks), JW Smit (CA Clermont Auvergne, France)(capt), BJ Botha (Sharks), JP Botha (Sharks), V Matfield (Bulls), JH Smith (Cheetahs), PJ Spies (Bulls), LA Watson (Stormers),

SUBSTITUTIONS: FPL Steyn (Sharks), BW du Plessis (Sharks) & R Kankowski (Sharks) for Jacobs, Smit & Spies (59 mins), GG Steenkamp (Bulls) for Mtawarira (60 mins), PC Montgomery (USA Perpignan, France) and A Bekker (Stormers) for Chavanga & BJ Botha (64 mins), JHJ Conradie (Stormers) for Januarie (77 mins)

SCORERS: *Tries*: De Villiers (2), Januarie, BW du Plessis *Conversions*: James (4) *Penalty goals*: James (3)

WALES: Hook; MA Jones, Shanklin, Roberts, SM Williams; SM Jones, Cooper; Jenkins, Hibbard, R Thomas; Gough, A-W Jones; RP Jones (capt), Delve, J Thomas

SUBSTITUTIONS: DR Jones for Delve (22 mins), I Evans & Bishop for RP Jones & Shanklin (69 mins), DJ Jones for R Thomas (71 mins), TR Thomas for Hibbard (72 mins), Fury for Cooper (76 mins), James for MA Jones (78 mins)

SCORERS: *Tries*: Cooper, SM Williams *Conversion*: SM Jones *Penalty goals*: SM Jones (3)

REFEREE: LE Bray (New Zealand)

Getty Images

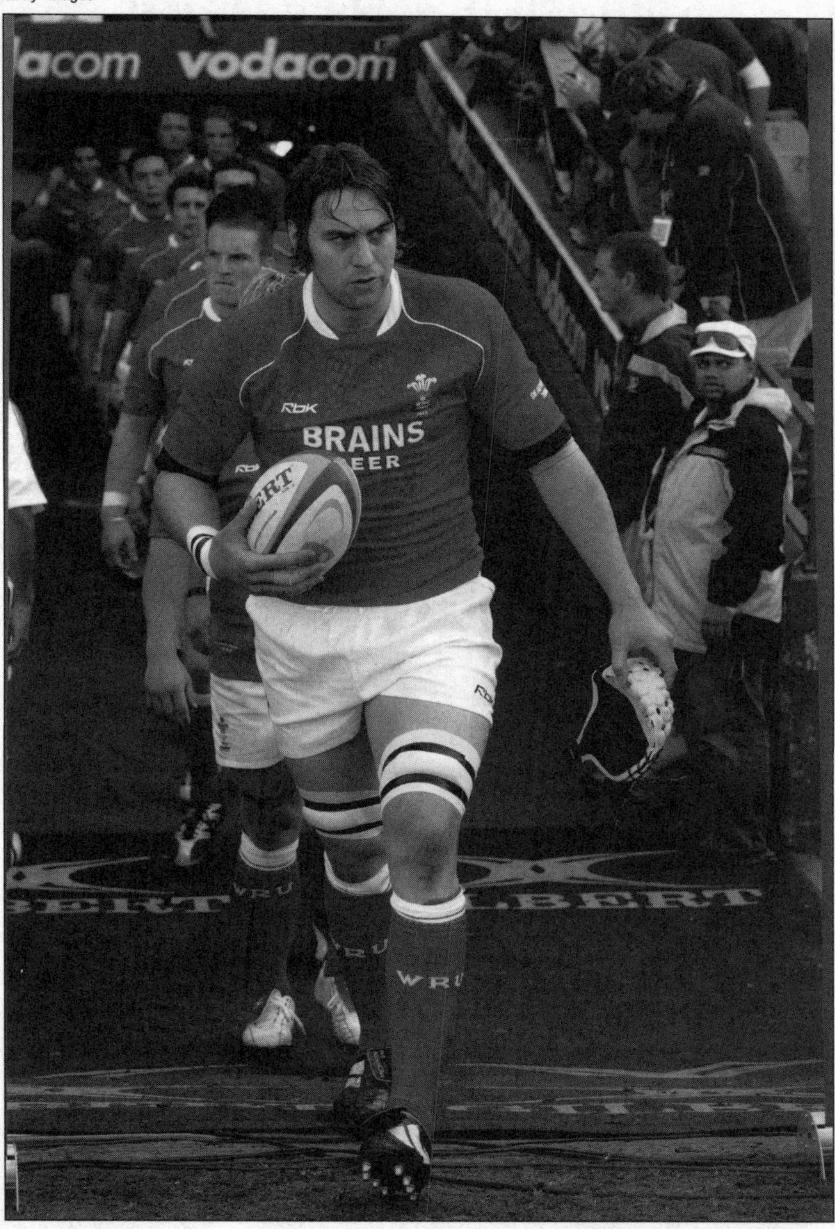

Wales roared back in their second Test against South Africa, but failed to clinch their first win on Springbok soil

SCOTLAND TO ARGENTINA 2008

Tour party

FULL BACKS: CD Paterson (Edinburgh Rugby), HFG Southwell (Edinburgh Rugby)

THREEQUARTERS: SCJ Danielli (Ulster Rugby), TH Evans (Glasgow Warriors), MB Evans (Glasgow Warriors), BJ Cairns (Edinburgh Rugby), GA Morrison (Glasgow Warriors), AR Henderson (Glasgow Warriors), N de Luca (Edinburgh Rugby), SL Webster (Edinburgh Rugby)

HALFBACKS: DA Parks (Glasgow Warriors), PJ Godman (Edinburgh Rugby), RGM Lawson (Gloucester Rugby), MRL Blair (Edinburgh Rugby)

FORWARDS: RW Ford (Edinburgh Rugby), DWH Hall (Glasgow Warriors), AF Jacobsen (Edinburgh Rugby), A Dickinson (Gloucester Rugby), EA Murray (Northampton Saints), GDS Cross (Edinburgh Rugby), SJ MacLeod (Llanelli Scarlets), AD Kellock (Glasgow Warriors), CP Hamilton (Edinburgh Rugby), DA Callam (Edinburgh Rugby), JW Beattie (Glasgow Warriors), JA Barclay (Glasgow Warriors), KDR Brown (Glasgow Warriors), A Hogg (Edinburgh Rugby), AK Strokosch (Gloucester Rugby), ML Mustchin (Edinburgh Rugby)

MANAGER G Richardson **HEAD COACH** F Hadden **COACHES** SRP Lineen, RA Robinson ASSISTANT **COACHES** AV Tait, DW Hodge, M Bitcon, A Smith **CAPTAIN** MRL Blair

Match 1, 7 June, Gigante de Arroyito Stadium, Rosario
Argentina 21 (1G 3PG 1T) Scotland 15 (5PG)

ARGENTINA: BH Stortoni (Glasgow Warriors, Scotland); J-M Nunez Piossek (Huirapuca), GP Tiesi (NEC Harlequins, England), F Contepomi (Leinster, Ireland)(capt), T de Vedia (London Irish, England); FJ Todeschini (RC Montpellier-Herault, France), N Vergallo (Jockey Club, Rosario); M Ayerza (Leicester Tigers, England), A Tejeda (Overmach Parma, Italy), SN Gonzalez Bononrino (Capitolina, Italy), CI Fernandez-Lobbe (Northampton Saints, England), E Lozada (RC Toulon, France), M Durand (Champagnat), J-M Leguizamon (London Irish, England), JM Fernandez-Lobbe (Sale Sharks, England)

SUBSTITUTIONS: P Gambarini (CA San Isidro) & JF Gomez (Los Matreros & Leinster, Ireland) for Tejeda & Bonorino (67 mins), A Campos (Pueyrredon) for Durand (74 mins)

SCORERS: *Tries*: Tejeda, Tiesi *Conversion*: Todeschini *Penalty goals*: Todeschini (3)

SCOTLAND: Paterson; Danielli, Cairns, Morrison, TH Evans; Parks, Blair (capt); Jacobsen, Ford, E Murray; Mustchin, MacLeod; Strokosch, Beattie, Hogg

SUBSTITUTIONS: Brown for Beattie (57 mins), Dickinson for Jacobsen (67 mins), Kellock for MacLeod (temp 67-71 mins) & for Mustchin (71 mins), Webster for TH Evans (71 mins), Lawson for Blair (76 mins)

SCORERS: *Penalty goals*: Paterson (5)

REFEREE: DA Lewis (Ireland)

Match 2, 14 June, Velez Sarsfield Stadium, Buenos Aires
Argentina 14 (2G) Scotland 26 (2G 4PG)

ARGENTINA: BH Stortoni (Glasgow Warriors, Scotland); L Borges (Treviso, Italy), GP Tiesi (NEC Harlequins, England), F Contepomi (Leinster, Ireland)(capt), H Agulla (US Dax, France); FJ Todeschini (RC Montpellier-Herault, France), N Vergallo (Jockey Club, Rosario); M Ayerza (Leicester Tigers, England), A Tejeda (Overmach Parma, Italy), SN Gonzalez Bonorino (Capitolina, Italy), CI Fernandez-Lobbe (Northampton Saints, England), E Lozada (RC Toulon, France), M Durand (Champagnat), J-M Leguizamon (London Irish, England), JM Fernandez-Lobbe (Sale Sharks, England)

SUBSTITUTIONS: FM Aramburu (USA Perpignan, France) for Tiesi (13 mins), JF Gomez (Los Matreros & Leinster, Ireland) for Bonorino (45 mins), J Stuart (CA San Isidro) & A Galindo (AS Beziers, France) for Lozada & Durand (58 mins), F Serra Miras (San Isidro Club) for Aramburu (77 mins)

SCORERS: *Tries*: CI Fernandez-Lobbe, Agulla *Conversions*: Todeschini (2)

SCOTLAND: Southwell; Webster, Cairns, Morrison, Paterson; Godman, Blair (capt); Jacobsen, Ford, E Murray; Mustchin, MacLeod; Strokosch, Hogg, Barclay

SUBSTITUTIONS: Dickinson for Barclay (temp 58-65 mins & for Jacobsen 65 mins), Kellock for MacLeod (61 mins), Brown for Hogg (67 mins), Parks for Godman (70 mins), Hall for Ford (71 mins), Lawson & De Luca for Blair & Morrison (74 mins)

SCORERS: *Tries*: Ford, Morrison *Conversions*: Paterson (2), *Penalty goals*: Paterson (4)

REFEREE: AC Rolland (Ireland)

ENGLAND TO NEW ZEALAND 2008

Tour party

FULL BACKS: M Brown (NEC Harlequins),

THREEQUARTERS: T Ojo (London Irish), D Strettle (NEC Harlequins), TW Varndell (Leicester Tigers), T Flood (Newcastle Falcons), JD Noon (Newcastle Falcons), M Tait (Newcastle Falcons), MJ Tindall (Gloucester Rugby), D Waldouck (London Wasps)

HALFBACKS: OJ Barkley (Bath Rugby), CC Hodgson (Sale Sharks), D Care (NEC Harlequins), PC Richards (London Irish), REP Wigglesworth (Sale Sharks)

FORWARDS: D Hartley (Northampton Saints), LA Mears (Bath Rugby), D Paice (London Irish), J Hobson (Bristol Rugby), TAN Payne (London Wasps), AJ Sheridan (Sale Sharks), MJH Stevens (Bath Rugby), *D Wilson (Newcastle Falcons), SW Borthwick (Bath Rugby), BJ Kay (Leicester Tigers), N Kennedy (London Irish), T Palmer (London Wasps),T Croft (Leicester Tigers), N Easter (NEC Harlequins), J Haskell (London Wasps), MR Lipman (Bath Rugby), L Narraway (Gloucester Rugby), T Rees (London Wasps), JPR Worsley (London Wasps)

* Replacement on tour

MANAGER A Ward **TEAM MANAGER** CR Andrew **ASSISTANT COACHES** M Ford, J Wells, G Rowntree, JEB Callard **CAPTAIN** SW Borthwick

Match 1, 14 June, Eden Park, Auckland
New Zealand 37 (4G 3PG) England 20 (2G 2PG)

NEW ZEALAND: JM Muliaina (Chiefs): AT Tuitavake (Blues), CG Smith (Hurricanes), MA Nonu (Hurricanes), SW Sivivatu (Chiefs); DW Carter (Crusaders), AM Ellis (Crusaders); NS Tialata (Hurricanes), AK Hore (Hurricanes), GM Somerville (Crusaders); BC Thorn (Crusaders), AJ Williams (Crusaders); R So'oialo (Hurricanes), J Kaino (Blues), RH McCaw (Crusaders)(capt)

SUSBSTITUTIONS: KF Mealamu (Blues) for Hore (temp 7-9 mins & 48 mins), ST Lauaki (Chiefs) for Kaino (48 mins), AF Boric (Blues) & LR MacDonald (Crusaders) for Thorn & Muliaina (52 mins), QJ Cowan (Highlanders) for Ellis (60 mins), SR Donald (Chiefs) for Carter (69 mins)

SCORERS: *Tries*: Smith, Carter, Muliaina, Sivivatu *Conversions*: Carter (4) *Penalty goals*: Carter (3)

ENGLAND: Brown; Ojo, Tindall, Barkley, Strettle; Hodgson, Wigglesworth; Sheridan, Mears, Stevens; Palmer, Borthwick (capt); Haskell, Narraway, Rees

SUBSTITUTIONS: Payne for Sheridan (temp 32-42 mins & 62 mins), Noon for Hodgson (49 mins), Kay for Palmer (53 mins), Worsley & Care for Haskell & Wigglesworth (62 mins), Paice for Mears (76 mins)

SCORERS: *Tries*: Ojo (2) *Conversions*: Barkley (2) *Penalty goals*: Barkley (2)

REFEREE: N Owens (Wales)

Match 2, 21 June, AMI Stadium, Lancaster Park, Christchurch
New Zealand 44 (5G 3PG) England 12 (1G 1T)

NEW ZEALAND: LR MacDonald (Crusaders); SW Sivivatu (Chiefs), RD Kahui (Chiefs), MA Nonu (Hurricanes), RN Wulf (Blues); DW Carter (Crusaders), AM Ellis (Crusaders); NS Tialata (Hurricanes), AK Hore (Hurricanes), GM Somerville (Crusaders); BC Thorn (Crusaders), AJ Williams (Crusaders); AJ Thomson (Highlanders), R So'oialo (Hurricanes), RH McCaw (Crusaders)(capt)

SUBSTITUTIONS: AF Boric (Blues) for Williams (15 mins), ST Lauaki (Chiefs) for McCaw (27 mins), KF Mealamu (Blues) for Hore (temp 34-37 mins & 50 mins), TD Woodcock for Tialata (46 mins), QJ Cowan (Highlanders) for Ellis (67 mins), JM Muliaina (Chiefs) for Kahui (temp 72-74 mins), SR Donald (Chiefs) for Carter (74 mins), JM Muliaina (Chiefs) for Kahui (temp 71-75 mins)

SCORERS: *Tries*: Kahui, Carter, Nonu, Lauaki, Cowan *Conversions*: Carter (4), Donald *Penalty goals*: Carter (3)

ENGLAND: Tait; Ojo, Tindall, Noon, Varndell; Flood, Care; Payne, Mears, Stevens; Palmer, Borthwick (capt); Haskell, Narraway, Rees

SUBSTITUTIONS: Barkley for Flood (29 mins), Worsley for Rees (55 mins), Croft for Narraway (57 mins), Kay for Palmer (68 mins), Hobson & Richards for Stevens & Tait (72 mins), Paice for Mears (75 mins)

SCORERS: *Tries*: Care, Varndell *Conversion*: Barkley

REFEREE: JI Kaplan (South Africa)

ITALY TO SOUTH AFRICA & ARGENTINA 2008

Tour party

FULL BACK: A Marcato (Treviso)

THREEQUARTERS: LM Nitoglia (Calvisano), M Pratichetti (Calvisano), K Robertson (Viadana), G Garcia (Calvisano), E Patrizio (Padova), R Pavan (Overmach Parma), *Mirco Bergamasco (Stade Francais, France)

HALFBACKS: A Masi (Biarritz Olympique, France), S Picone (Treviso), L McLean (Calvisano), P Canavosio (Castres Olympique, France)

FORWARDS: L Ghiraldini (Calvisano), F Ongaro (Saracens, England), A Moreno (Leicester Tigers, England), C Nieto (Gloucester Rugby), M Rizzo (Padova), I Rouyet (Viadana), C-A del Fava (Ulster Rugby, Ireland), S Dellape (Biarritz Olympique, France), T Reato (Rovigo), J Erasmus (Viadana), R Barbieri (Treviso), J Sole (Viadana), A Zanni (Calvisano), * S Parisse (Stade Franacis, France), * Mauro Bergamasco (Stade Francais, France)

* Argentina section only

MANAGER C Checchinato **HEAD COACH** NVH Mallett **ASSISTANT COACHES** J-P Cariat, C Orlandi, A Troncon **CAPTAINS** L Ghiraldini & S Parisse

Match 1, 21 June, Newlands, Cape Town
South Africa 26 (3G 1T) Italy 0

SOUTH AFRICA: CA Jantjies (Stormers); OM Ndungane (Sharks), G Bobo (Stormers), J de Villiers (Stormers), BG Habana (Bulls); FPL Steyn (Sharks), ER Januarie (Stormers); T Mtawarira (Sharks), BW du Plessis (Sharks), CJ van der Linde (Cheetahs), JP Botha (Sharks), V Matfield (Bulls)(capt), JH Smith (Cheetahs) R Kankowski (Sharks), LA Watson (Stormers),

SUBSTITUTIONS: JC van Niekerk (Lions) for Kankowski (36 mins), PJ Grant (Stormers) & SWP Burger (Stormers) for Jantjies & Watson (55 mins), A Bekker (Stormers) & BV Mujati (Stormers) for JP Botha & Van der Linde (64 mins), R Pienaar (Sharks) & SB Brits (Stormers) for Januarie & BW du Plessis (65 mins), Van der Linde for Mtawarira (77 mins)

SCORERS: *Tries*: BW du Plessis (2), Steyn, Mtawarira *Conversions*: Steyn (3)
ITALY: Marcato; Robertson, Masi, Garcia, Pratichetti; McLean, Picone; Rizzo, Ghiraldini (capt), Nieto; Dellape, Del Fava; Zanni, Sole, Barbieri
SUBSTITUTIONS: Patrizio for Masi (34 mins), Rouyet for Rizzo (48 mins), Ongaro for Ghiraldini (55 mins), Canavosio for Picone (62 mins), Reato & Pavan for Dellape & Marcato (67 mins), Erasmus for Garcia (72 mins)
REFEREE: G Clancy (Ireland)

Match 2, 28 June, Estadio Olimpico, Cordoba
Argentina 12 (4PG) Italy 13 (1G 2PG)

ARGENTINA: BH Stortoni (Glasgow Warriors, Scotland); L Borges (Treviso, Italy), MT Bosch (Biarritz Olympique, France), M Avramovic (RC Montauban, France), H Agulla (US Dax, France); JM Hernandez (Stade Francais, France), N Vergallo (Jockey Club, Roario); R Roncero (Stade Francais, France)(capt), A Tejeda (Overmach Parma, Italy), JF Gomez (Los Matreros & Leinster, Ireland), M Carizza (Biarritz Olympique, France), E Lozada (RC Toulon, France), M Durand (Champagnat), J-M Leguizamon (London Irish, England), A Galindo (AS Beziers, France)
SUBSTITUTIONS: H Senillosa (Hindu) for Hernandez (18 mins), AP Ledesma (Stade Francais, France) for Gomez (46 mins), A Campos (Pueyrredon) for Leguizamon (57 mins), J Stuart (CA San Isidro) for Carizza (75 mins)
SCORERS: *Penalty goals*: Hernandez (2), Bosch (2)
ITALY: Marcato; Robertson, Mi Bergamasco, Garcia, Pratichetti; McLean, Picone; Rouyet, Ongaro, Nieto; Dellape, Del Fava; Sole, Parisse (capt), Ma Bergamasco
SUBSTITUTIONS: Zanni for Sole (57 mins), Reato for Dellape (64 mins), Canavosio & Moreno for Picone & Rouyet (66 mins), Ghiraldini for Ongaro (71 mins)
SCORERS: *Try*: Ghiraldini Conversion: Marcato *Penalty goals*: Marcato (2)
REFEREE: M Goddard (Australia)

FRANCE TO AUSTRALIA 2008

Tour party

FULL BACKS: P Elhorga (AS Bayonne), B Thiery (Biarritz Olympique)
THREEQUARTERS: T Lacroix (SC Albi), M Mermoz (Stade Toulousain), D Traille (Birarritz Olympique), D Janin (CS Bourgoin-Jallieu), A Palisson (CA Brive Correze), J-B Peyras (AS Bayonne)
HALF BACKS: S Tillous-Bordes (Castres Olympique), D Yachvili (Biarritz Olympique), B Boyet (CS Bourgoin-Jallieu), F Trinh-Duc (RC Montpellier-Herault)
FORWARDS: S Bruno (Sale Sharks, England), B Kayser (Leicester Tigers, England), R Boyoud (US Dax), P Correia (SC Albi), L Faure (Sale Sharks, England) B Lecouls (Biarritz Olympique), S Chabal (Sale Sharks, England), D Couzinet (Biarritz Olympique), L Nallet (Castres Olympique), Y Caballero (US Montauban), Matthieu Lievremont (US Dax), F Ouedraogo (RC Montpellier-Herault), I Harinordoquy (Biarritz Olympique), L Picamoles (RC Montpellier-Herault)

MANAGER J Maso HEAD **COACH:** Marc Lievremont **ASSISTANT COACHES** E Ntamack, D Retiere, D Ellis, G Quesada **CAPTAIN** L Nallet

Match 1, 28 June, ANZ Stadium, Sydney
Australia 34 (4G 2PG) France 13 (1G 2PG)

AUSTRALIA: CB Shepherd (Western Force): PJ Hynes (Queensland Reds), SA Mortlock (ACT Brumbies)(capt), BS Barnes (Queensland Reds), LD Tuqiri (NSW Waratahs); MJ Giteau (Western Force), L Burgess (NSW Waratahs); BA Robinson (NSW Waratahs), ST Moore (Queensland Reds), AKE Baxter (NSW Waratahs); JE Horwill (Queensland Reds), NC Sharpe (Western Force); RD Elsom (NSW Waratahs), WL Palu (NSW Waratahs), GB Smith (ACT Brumbies)

SUBSTITUTIONS: AP Ashley-Cooper (ACT Brumbies) for Tuqiri (29 mins), PR Waugh (NSW Waratahs) for Palu (41 mins), RP Cross (Western Force) for Barnes (57 mins), B Alexander (ACT Brumbies) for Robinson (60 mins), DW Mumm (NSW Waratahs) for Smith (64 mins), AL Freier (NSW Waratahs) for Moore (70 mins), SJ Cordingley (ACT Brumbies) for Burgess (71 mins)

SCORERS: *Tries*: Giteau, Sharpe, Elsom, Mortlock *Conversions*: Giteau (4) *Penalty goals:* Giteau (2)

FRANCE: Elhorga; Palisson, Traille, Trinh-Duc, Thiery; Boyet, Yachvili; Lecouls, Bruno, Faure; Chabal, Nallet (capt), Ouedraogo, Picamoles, Harinordoquy

SUBSTITUTIONS: Janin for Elhorga (23 mins), Boyoud for Favre (46 mins), Kayser for Bruno (50 mins), Lacroix for Boyet (57 mins), Matthieu Lievremont for Picamoles (58 mins), Tillous-Bordes for Yachvili (60 mins), Couzinet for Nallet (70 mins), Boyet for Thiery (75–79 mins)

SCORERS: *Try*: Palisson *Conversion*: Trinh-Duc *Penalty goals*: Yachvili (2)

REFEREE: M Jonker (South Africa)

Match 2, 5 July, Suncorp Stadium, Brisbane
Australia 40 (4G 4PG) France 10 (1G 1PG)

AUSTRALIA: AP Ashley-Cooper (A CT Brumbies): PJ Hynes (Queensland Reds), SA Mortlock (ACT Brumbies)(capt), BS Barnes (Queensland Reds), LD Turner (NSW Waratahs); MJ Giteau (Western Force), L Burgess (NSW Waratahs); BA Robinson (NSW Waratahs), ST Moore (Queensland Reds), AKE Baxter (NSW Waratahs); JE Horwill (Queensland Reds), DW Mumm (NSW Waratahs); RD Elsom (NSW Waratahs), SA Hoiles (ACT Brumbies), PR Waugh (NSW Waratahs)

SUBSTITUTIONS: SJ Cordingley (ACT Brumbies) for Burgess (temp 24-34 mins & 74 mins), HJ McMeniman (Queensland Reds) for Horwill (39 mins), GB Smith (ACT Brumbies) for Hoiles (51 mins), RP Cross (Western Force) for Barnes (53 mins), B Alexander (ACT Brumbies) for Robinson (71 mins), CB Shepherd (Western Force) for Mortlock (72 mins), AL Freier (NSW Waratahs) for Moore (74 mins)

SCORERS: *Tries*: Cross 2, Hynes, Horwill *Conversions*: Giteau (4) *Penalty goals*: Giteau (4)

FRANCE: Thiery; Palisson, Mermoz, Lacroix, Janin; Trinh-Duc, Tillous-Borde; Correia, Bruno, Boyoud; Chabal, Nallet (capt); Matthieu Lievrement, Harinordoquy Ouedraogo

SUBSTITUTIONS: Picamoles for Harinordoquy (temp 24-34 mins) & for Ouedraogo (57 mins). Boyet for Mermoz (40 mins), Lecouls for Correia (51 mins), Peyras for Lacroix (53 mins), Kayser for Bruno (61 mins), Caballero for Chabal (67 mins), Yachvili for Tillous-Borde (76 mins)

SCORERS: *Try:* Trinh-Duc *Conversion*: Yachvili *Penalty goal*: Trinh-Duc

REFEREE: PG Honiss (New Zealand)

REFEREES' SIGNALS

PENALTY KICK
Shoulders parallel with the touchline. Arm angled up, pointing towards non-offending team.

FREE KICK
Shoulders parallel with touchline. Arm bent square at elbow, upper arm pointing towards non-offending team.

TRY AND PENALTY TRY
Referee's back to dead ball line. Arm raised vertically.

ADVANTAGE
Arm outstretched, waist high, towards non-offending team, for a period of approximately five seconds.

SCRUM AWARDED
Shoulders parallel with touchline. Arm horizontal, pointing towards team to throw in the ball.

FORMING A SCRUM
Elbows bent, hands above head, fingers touching.

THROW FORWARD/FORWARD PASS
Hands gesture as if passing an imaginary ball forward.

KNOCK ON
Arm out-stretched with open hand above head, and moves backwards and forwards.

NOT RELEASING BALL IMMEDIATELY IN THE TACKLE
Both hands are close to the chest as if holding an imaginary ball.

TACKLER NOT RELEASING TACKLED PLAYER
Arms brought together as if grasping a player and then opening as if releasing a player.

TACKLER OR TACKLED PLAYER NOT ROLLING AWAY
A circular movement with the finger and arm moving away from the body.

ENTERING TACKLE FROM THE WRONG DIRECTION
Arm held horizontal then sweep of the arm in a semi-circle.

INTENTIONALLY FALLING OVER ON A PLAYER
Curved arm makes gesture to imitate action of falling player. Signal is made in direction in which offending player fell.

DIVING TO GROUND NEAR TACKLE Straight arm gesture, pointing downwards to imitate diving action.

UNPLAYABLE BALL IN RUCK OR TACKLE
Award of scrum to team moving forward at time of stoppage. Shoulders parallel with the touchline, arm horizontal pointing towards the team to throw in the ball, then pointing the arm and hand towards the other team's goal line whilst moving it backwards and forwards.

UNPLAYABLE BALL IN MAUL
Arm out to award scrummage to side not in possession at maul commencement. Other arm out as if signalling advantage and then swing it across body with hand ending on opposite shoulder..

JOINING A RUCK OR A MAUL IN FRONT OF THE BACK FOOT AND FROM THE SIDE
The hand and arms are held horizontally. Moving sideways.

INTENTIONALLY COLLAPSING RUCK OR MAUL
Both arms at shoulder height as if bound around opponent. Upper body is lowered and twisted as if pulling down opponent who is on top.

PROP PULLING DOWN OPPONENT
Clenched fist and arm bent. Gesture imitates pulling opponent down.

PROP PULLING OPPONENT ON
Clenched fist and arm straight at shoulder height. Gesture imitates pulling opponent on.

WHEELING SCRUM MORE THAN 90 DEGREES
Rotating index finger above the head.

FOOT UP BY FRONT ROW PLAYER
Foot raised, foot touched.

THROW IN AT SCRUM NOT STRAIGHT
Hands at knee level imitating throw not straight.

FAILURE TO BIND FULLY
One arm out-stretched as if binding. Other hand moves up and down arm to indicate the extent of a full bind.

HANDLING BALL IN RUCK OR SCRUM
Hand at ground level, making sweeping action, as if handling the ball.

THROW IN AT LINEOUT NOT STRAIGHT
Shoulders parallel with touchline. Hand above head indicates the path of the ball, not straight.

CLOSING GAP IN LINEOUT
Both hands at eye level, pointing up, palms inward. Hands meet in squeezing action.

BARGING IN LINEOUT
Arm horizontal, elbow pointing out. Arm and shoulder move outwards as if barging opponent.

LEANING ON PLAYER IN LINEOUT
Arm horizontal, bent at elbow, palm down. Downward gesture.

PUSHING OPPONENT IN LINEOUT
Both hands at shoulder level, with palms outward, making pushing gesture.

EARLY LIFTING AND LIFTING IN LINEOUT
Both fists clenched in front, at waist level, making lifting gesture.

OFFSIDE AT LINEOUT
Hand and arm move horizontally across chest, towards offence.

OBSTRUCTION IN GENERAL PLAY
Arms crossed in front of chest at right angles to each other, like open scissors.

OFFSIDE AT SCRUM, RUCK OR MAUL
Shoulders parallel with touchline. Arm hanging straight down, swings in arc along offside line.

OFFSIDE CHOICE: PENALTY KICK OR SCRUM
One arm is for penalty kick. Other arm points to place where scrum may be taken instead of a kick.

OFFSIDE UNDER 10-METRE LAW OR NOT 10 METRES AT PENALTY AND FREE KICKS
Both hands held open above head.

HIGH TACKLE (FOUL PLAY)
Hand moves horizontally in front of neck.

STAMPING (FOUL PLAY: ILLEGAL USE OF BOOT)
Stamping action or similar gesture to indicate the offence..

PUNCHING (FOUL PLAY)
Clenches fist punches open palm.

DISSENT (DISPUTING REFEREE'S DECISION)
Outstretched arm with hand opening and closing to imitate talking.

AWARD OF DROP-OUT ON 22-METRE LINE
Arm points to centre of 22-metre line.

BALL HELD UP IN IN-GOAL
Space between hands indicates that the ball was not grounded.

PHYSIOTHERAPIST NEEDED
One arm raised indicates physiotherapist is needed for injured player.

TIMEKEEPER TO STOP AND START WATCH
Arm held up in the air and whistle blown when watch should be stopped or started

INTERNATIONAL REFEREES

DISMISSALS IN MAJOR INTERNATIONAL MATCHES

Up to 30 September 2008 in major international matches. These cover all matches for which the eight senior members of the International Board have awarded caps, and also all matches played in Rugby World Cup final stages.

A E Freethy	sent off	C J Brownlie (NZ)	E v NZ	1925
K D Kelleher	sent off	C E Meads (NZ)	S v NZ	1967
R T Burnett	sent off	M A Burton (E)	A v E	1975
W M Cooney	sent off	J Sovau (Fj)	A v Fj	1976
N R Sanson	sent off	G A D Wheel (W)	W v I	1977
N R Sanson	sent off	W P Duggan (I)	W v I	1977
D I H Burnett	sent off	P Ringer (W)	E v W	1980
C Norling	sent off	J-P Garuet (F)	F v I	1984
K V J Fitzgerald	sent off	H D Richards (W)	NZ v W	*1987
F A Howard	sent off	D Codey (A)	A v W	*1987
K V J Fitzgerald	sent off	M Taga (Fj)	Fj v E	1988
O E Doyle	sent off	A Lorieux (F)	Arg v F	1988
B W Stirling	sent off	T Vonolagi (Fj)	E v Fj	1989
B W Stirling	sent off	N Nadruku (Fj)	E v Fj	1989
F A Howard	sent off	K Moseley (W)	W v F	1990
F A Howard	sent off	A Carminati (F)	S v F	1990
F A Howard	sent off	A Stoop (Nm)	Nm v W	1990
A J Spreadbury	sent off	A Benazzi (F)	A v F	1990
C Norling	sent off	P Gallart (F)	A v F	1990
C J Hawke	sent off	F E Mendez (Arg)	E v Arg	1990
E F Morrison	sent off	C Cojocariu (R)	R v F	1991
J M Fleming	sent off	P L Sporleder (Arg)	WS v Arg	*1991
J M Fleming	sent off	M G Keenan (WS)	WS v Arg	*1991
S R Hilditch	sent off	G Lascubé (F)	F v E	1992
S R Hilditch	sent off	V Moscato (F)	F v E	1992
D J Bishop	sent off	O Roumat (Wld)	NZ v Wld	1992
E F Morrison	sent off	J T Small (SA)	A v SA	1993
I Rogers	sent off	M E Cardinal (C)	C v F	1994
I Rogers	sent off	P Sella (F)	C v F	1994
D Mené	sent off	J D Davies (W)	W v E	1995
S Lander	sent off	F Mahoni (Tg)	F v Tg	*1995
D T M McHugh	sent off	J Dalton (SA)	SA v C	*1995
D T M McHugh	sent off	R G A Snow (C)	SA v C	*1995
D T M McHugh	sent off	G L Rees (C)	SA v C	*1995
J Dumé	sent off	G R Jenkins (W)	SA v W	1995
W J Erickson	sent off	V B Cavubati (Fj)	NZ v Fj	1997
W D Bevan	sent off	A G Venter (SA)	NZ v SA	1997

C Giacomel	sent off	R Travaglini (Arg)	F v Arg	1997
W J Erickson	sent off	D J Grewcock (E)	NZ v E	1998
S R Walsh	sent off	J Sitoa (Tg)	A v Tg	1998
R G Davies	sent off	M Giovanelli (It)	S v It	1999
C Thomas	sent off	T Leota (Sm)	Sm v F	1999
C Thomas	sent off	G Leaupepe (Sm)	Sm v F	1999
S Dickinson	sent off	J-J Crenca (F)	NZ v F	1999
E F Morrison	sent off	M Vunibaka (Fj)	Fj v C	*1999
A Cole	sent off	D R Baugh (C)	C v Nm	*1999
W J Erickson	sent off	N Ta'ufo'ou (Tg)	E v Tg	*1999
P Marshall	sent off	B D Venter (SA)	SA v U	*1999
P C Deluca	sent off	W Cristofoletto (It)	F v It	2000
J I Kaplan	sent off	A Troncon (It)	It v I	2001
R Dickson	sent off	G Leger (Tg)	W v Tg	2001
P C Deluca	sent off	N J Hines (S)	US v S	2002
P D O'Brien	sent off	M C Joubert (SA)	SA v A	2002
P D O'Brien	sent off	J J Labuschagne (SA)	E v SA	2002
S R Walsh	sent off	V Ma'asi (Tg)	Tg v I	2003
N Williams	sent off	S D Shaw (E)	NZ v E	2004
S J Dickinson	sent off	P C Montgomery (SA)	W v SA	2005
S M Lawrence	sent off	L W Moody (E)	E v Sm	2005
S M Lawrence	sent off	A Tuilagi (Sm)	E v Sm	2005
S R Walsh	sent off	S Murray (S)	W v S	2006
S M Lawrence	sent off	A Tuilagi (Sm)	E v Sm	2005
S R Walsh	sent off	S Murray (S)	W v S	2006
J I Kaplan	sent off	H T-Pole (Tg)	Sm v Tg	*2007
A C Rolland	sent off	J Nieuwenhuis (Nm)	F v Nm	*2007

* Matches in World Cup final stages

OBITUARIES

By Adam Hathaway

The Rugby World lost some of its favourite sons in the 2007–08 season. Here we pay tribute to some of those who touched our hearts, and made a big impact on our great game. The obituaries will perform an important part of future IRB World Rugby Yearbooks so if you would like to report a death for inclusion in the Yearbook email paul_morgan@ipcmedia.com.

RAY GRAVELL, who died on 31 October 2007, aged 56, was a hugely popular figure in the world of rugby whose funeral was attended by more than 10,000 people and was broadcast on two television channels. A tough, hard-running centre for Llanelli, Wales and the British Lions, Gravell won 23 caps for his country and helped the Scarlets beat the All Blacks in 1972. After retiring from the game he became president of Llanelli RFC and the Llanelli Scarlets, while also forging a career as a rugby broadcaster for S4C and the BBC. He also became a big screen and television actor but it was rugby which always remained the focus of his life away from his wife Mari and their two daughters.

JACK ELLIS, was England's oldest surviving rugby union international until his death on 27 November 2007, aged 95. A classics teacher who taught at Fettes College, Rossall and Scarborough Boys' High School, he was born on October 28, 1912 in Rothwell near Leeds. He played club rugby for Wakefield, playing five times for Yorkshire in 1938 and representing England the following year. He made his only appearance in the last England international before the outbreak of World War II, playing at scrum half in the 9–6 victory over Scotland at Murrayfield on March 18, 1939 and also played five games for the Barbarians.

ROY PROSSER, who died from a heart attack on 13 August 2008 aged 66, was one of the great characters in Australian rugby. Prosser played 25 Tests for the Wallabies as a prop between 1967 and 1972 and went on to coach Western Districts where he unearthed future Australian full-back Roger Gould and assisted in the development of Stan Pilecki. Prosser made his Test debut in Australia's 23–11 win over England at Twickenham in 1967 when his team mates included Ken Catchpole, Peter Johnson, Phil Hawthorne and Jim Lenehan. He made his last international appearance against Fiji in Suva in 1972 when the tourists scraped home 21–19.

PIERRE DURANT, who died of a suspected heart attack on 15 February 2008 aged 31, was a prop for London Irish, Saracens, London Welsh, Eastern Province, Free State Cheetahs, Catania and South Africa under-21. Durant played for London Irish for three seasons between 2002 and 2005, making 31 appearances in the front row, and went on to join London Welsh in the summer of 2006.

GARETH JONES, who died on 16 June 2008 aged 28 from a neck injury suffered when playing, was a scrum-half for Neath. The father of two sustained the injury playing for Neath against Cardiff in April and passed away two months later at The University Hospital in Cardiff. Jones, who previously played for Glyncoch, Beddau and Pontypridd, made his debut for Neath against Newport in 2006 and worked as a decorator. He won a league title with the Welsh All Blacks and was also a Konica Minolta Cup winner with Pontypridd. Neath head coach Rowland Phillips said: "Gareth always had a twinkle in his eye. He was a breath of fresh air – someone who approached everything with a smile. He was also a fantastic rugby player."

GORDON MACKAY, who died on 24 July 2008 aged 39 from a heart attack, was rated as one of the best players never to win full Scotland international honours. The back row forward, who played for Scotland under-21s and Scottish Schools, was educated at Glasgow Academy and began his playing career with Glasgow Academicals. Following a short time with Stirling County in the mid-nineties he returned to Anniesland and played for Glasgow Hawks, winning the national second division title and the Scottish Cup in the club's inaugural season of 1997–98. In all, he played 17 matches for the Glasgow pro-team during the first three seasons of professional rugby in Scotland while he also had a spell playing in Lyon in France serious injury ended his playing career. He took a coaching post at Glasgow, steering the club away from relegation in his first season. Off the field he had a coffee bar in the West End of Glasgow and was involved with property development.

MIKE TITCOMB, who died on 2 May 2008 aged 75, became the youngest international referee – at 32 – when he took charge of Wales' match against Scotland in 1966. He refereed a further nine internationals, five England trials, three Barbarian fixtures and 26 county matches, including three finals. He also became the only Englishman to referee England in what was recognised as a full international against a President's XV in the RFU centenary year of the 1971/1972 season. From Bristol, Titcomb was a teacher, a lecturer at Bristol University and after that became Head of Physical Education at Bristol Polytechnic. As one of the polytechnic rugby committee members he became one of the founder members of the England

Students' organisation, then made up of Colleges, Polytechnics and Universities. He was a member of the England Students committee until he fell ill five years before his death. The RFU's Elite Referee Development Manger Ed Morrison said: "He was also an outstanding man, full of character and personality and he brought that to the field every time he refereed a match. He spent 10 years on the international panel and became the first international referee to come from the Bristol Referee's Society."

DONALD SLOAN, who died in March 2008 aged 81, was a Scottish international centre who won seven caps between 1950 and 1953, scoring two tries in the 13–11 win over England at Murrayfield in his debut season. On 3 February 1951 he received the news in the morning that he had qualified as a chartered accountant, then, that afternoon, he played in a young Scottish side that triumphed 19–0 against a Welsh team containing 11 British Lions. Sloan followed his father Allen into the national team. Allen, a stand-off, won nine caps between 1914 and 1921. It was the first instance of a father and son from Edinburgh Academicals both winning Scotland caps. In addition to representing Edinburgh Accies, Donald Sloan also played for London Scottish, of whom he was made captain in 1956, and was a Barbarian in 1949 and 1950. He was also a gifted sevens player, and with fellow internationalist Doug Elliot alongside, helped Edinburgh Accies to a memorable success at the 1949 Melrose Sevens.

JIM JOSEPH, who died from lung cancer on 21 September 2008 aged 70, was a legend of Marlborough rugby and the father of All Black flanker Jamie. Joseph played 142 matches for Marlborough Red Devils, mostly as a tight-head prop between 1963 and 1977, was a Maori All Black and only just missed out on selection for the All Blacks. Former Marlborough captain Ramon Sutherland said: "I'd rate him as good a tight-head prop as there was around at the time. I never saw him bettered by anyone and I always packed on him. He was a great team man too. He was right up there. Good enough to be an All Black. We never got beaten in scrummaging when he was around." Joseph started his playing career as a winger before finding his natural home in the front row and went on to coach Redwood and Marlborough.

ROBBIE LYE, who died on 19 April 2008 aged 62, was a stalwart of Bath Rugby Club playing more than 450 games for the first team and was club captain during the 1980–81 season. He also played for Somerset, Walcot, Avonvale and coached at Keynsham. Lye, a father of three, died of a heart attack and it is a measure of the esteem he was held in at Bath that former players such as Steve Ojomoh, John Hall, Matt Perry and David Hilton turned out in a memorial match for him in August to raise money for local charities.

THE DIRECTORY

MEMBER UNIONS OF THE INTERNATIONAL RUGBY BOARD

ANDORRA Federació Andorrana de Rugby
www.far.ad

ARABIAN GULF Arabian Gulf Rugby Football Union
www.agrfu.com

ARGENTINA Union Argentina de Rugby
www.uar.com.ar

AUSTRALIA Australian Rugby Union
www.rugby.com.au

AUSTRIA Osterreichischer Rugby Verband
www.rugby-austria.at

BAHAMAS Bahamas Rugby Football Union
www.rugbybahamas.com

BARBADOS Barbados Rugby Football Union
www.rugbybarbados.com

BELGIUM Fédération Belge de Rugby
www.rugby.be

BERMUDA Bermuda Rugby Union
www.bermudarfu.com

BOSNIA & HERZEGOVINA Ragbi Savez Republike Bosne

BOTSWANA Botswana Rugby Union

BRAZIL Associação Brasileira de Rugby
www.brasilrugby.com.br

BULGARIA Bulgarian Rugby Federation
www.bfrbg.org

CAMEROON Fédération Camerounaise de Rugby

CANADA Rugby Canada
www.rugbycanada.ca

CAYMAN Cayman Rugby Football Union
www.caymanrugby.com

CHILE Federación de Rugby de Chile
www.feruchi.cl

CHINA Chinese Rugby Football Association

CHINESE TAIPEI Chinese Taipei Rugby Football Union

COLOMBIA Union Colombiana de Rugby

COOK ISLANDS Cook Islands Rugby Union
www.rugby.co.ck

CROATIA Hrvatski Ragbi Savez
www.rugby.hr

CZECH REPUBLIC Ceska Rugbyova Unie
www.rugbyunion.cz

DENMARK Dansk Rugby Union
www.rugby.dk

ENGLAND The Rugby Football Union
www.rfu.com

FIJI Fiji Rugby Union
www.fijirugby.com

FINLAND Suomen Rugbyliitto
www.rugby.fi

FRANCE Fédération Française de Rugby
www.ffr.fr

GEORGIA Georgian Rugby Union
www.rugby.ge

GERMANY Deutscher Rugby Verband
www.rugby.de

GUAM Guam Rugby Football Union
www.rugbyonguam.com

GUYANA Guyana Rugby Football Union

HONG KONG Hong Kong Rugby Football Union
www.hkrugby.com

HUNGARY Magyar Rögbi Szövetség

INDIA Indian Rugby Football Union
www.indianrugby.com

IRELAND Irish Rugby Football Union
www.irishrugby.ie

ISRAEL Israel Rugby Union
www.rugby.org.il

ITALY Federazione Italiana Rugby
www.federugby.it

IVORY COAST Fédération Ivoirienne de Rugby

JAMAICA Jamaica Rugby Football Union
www.jamaicarugby.com

JAPAN Japan Rugby Football Union
www.rugby-japan.jp

KAZAKHSTAN Kazakhstan Rugby Football Federation

KENYA Kenya Rugby Football Union
www.kenyarfu.com

KOREA Korea Rugby Union
rugby.sports.or.kr

LATVIA Latvia Rugby Federation
www.rugby.lv

LITHUANIA Fédération Lithuanienne de Rugby
www.litrugby.lt

LUXEMBOURG Fédération Luxembourgeoise de Rugby
www.rugby.lu

MADAGASCAR Fédération Malagasy de Rugby

MALAYSIA Malaysian Rugby Union
www.mru.org.my

MALTA Malta Rugby Football Union
www.maltarugby.com

MEXICO Federación Mexicana de Rugby
www.mexrugby.com

MOLDOVA Federatia de Rugby din Moldovei

MONACO Fédération Monégasque de Rugby
www.monaco-rugby.com

MOROCCO Fédération Royale Marocaine de
www.frmr.ma

NAMIBIA Namibia Rugby Union

NETHERLANDS Nederlands Rugby Bond
www.rugby.nl

NEW ZEALAND New Zealand Rugby Union
www.allblacks.com

NIGERIA Nigeria Rugby Football Association

NIUE ISLANDS Niue Rugby Football Union

NORWAY Norges Rugby Forbund
www.rugby.no

PAPUA NEW GUINEA Papua New Guinea Rugby Football Union

PARAGUAY Union de Rugby del Paraguay
http://www.urp.org.py

PERU Union Peruana de Rugby
www.rugbyperu.org

POLAND Polski Zwiazek Rugby
www.pzrugby.pl

PORTUGAL Federação Portuguesa de Rugby
www.fpr.pt

ROMANIA Federatia Romana de Rugbi
www.rugby.ro

RUSSIA Rugby Union Of Russia
www.rugby.ru

SAMOA Samoa Rugby Football Union
www.samoarugbyunion.ws

SCOTLAND Scottish Rugby Union
www.scottishrugby.org

SENEGAL Fédération Sénégalaise de Rugby
www.senegal-rugby.com

SERBIA Rugby Union of Serbia

SINGAPORE Singapore Rugby Union
www.rugby@sru.org.sg

SLOVENIA Rugby Zveza Slovenie

SOLOMON ISLANDS Solomon Islands R.U. Federation

SOUTH AFRICA South Africa Rugby Union
www.sarugby.co.za

SPAIN Federación Española de Rugby
www.ferugby.com

SRI LANKA Sri Lanka Rugby Football Union
www.srilankanrugby.com

ST. LUCIA St. Lucia Rugby Football Union (Status pending)

ST. VINCENT & THE GRENADINES St. Vincent & The Grenadines Rugby Union Football

SWAZILAND Swaziland Rugby Football Union
www.swazilandrugby.com

SWEDEN Svenska Rugby Forbundet
www.rugby.se

SWITZERLAND Fédération Suisse de Rugby
www.rugby.ch

TAHITI Fédération Tahitienne de Rugby de Polynésie Française
www.tahitirugbyunion.com

THAILAND Thai Rugby Union
www.thairugbyunion.com

TONGA Tonga Rugby Football Union

TRINIDAD & TOBAGO Trinidad and Tobago Rugby Football Union
www.ttrfu.com

TUNISIA Fédération Tunisienne de Rugby

UGANDA Uganda Rugby Football Union
www.urfu.org

UKRAINE National Rugby Federation Of Ukraine
www.rugby.org.ua

URUGUAY Union de Rugby del Uruguay
www.uru.org.uy

USA USA Rugby
www.usarugby.org

VANUATU Vanuatu Rugby Football Union

VENEZUELA Federación Venezolana de Rugby Amateur
www.fvrugby.com

WALES Welsh Rugby Union
www.wru.co.uk

ZAMBIA Zambia Rugby Football Union

ZIMBABWE Zimbabwe Rugby Union
www.zimbabwerugby.com